HEARTS OF THE CITY

HEARTS OF THE CITY

THE SELECTED WRITINGS OF

HERBERT MUSCHAMP

ALFRED A. KNOPF · NEW YORK

2009

THIS IS A BORZOI BOOK
PUBLISHED BY ALFRED A. KNOPF

Library of Congress Cataloging-in-Publication Data
Muschamp, Herbert.
[Essays. Selections]
Hearts of the city : the selected writings of Herbert Muschamp /
by Herbert Muschamp. — 1st ed.
p.   cm.
ISBN 978-0375-40406-1
1. Architecture, Modern—20th century.   2. Architecture, Modern—21st century.
I. Title.
NA680.M872 2009
724'.6—dc22   2009021219

Manufactured in the United States of America
First Edition

CONTENTS

Acknowledgments   xi

Introduction by Nicolai Ouroussoff   xiii

THE NEW REPUBLIC, 1987–1992

The Temple of Marketing   3
Corbu Saved from Drowning   7
The Breached Wall   15
The Perils of Public Art   22
The Leaning Tower of Theory   28
The Lie of the Land   34
How Buildings Remember   40
The Winds of Windsorism   51
When the Cathedral Turned Black   61
American Gothic   71
The Wrong Prescription   83
East/West Side Story   88
Crowds and Power   94

ARTFORUM, 1995, 1999

Critical Reflections   103
Moral of the Stories   108

THE NEW YORK TIMES, 1992–2007

One Building That Knows What It's About   115
For All the Star Power, a Mixed Performance   117
Steel and Backbone in Hard Times   119
Barcelona Breaks the Record for Inspired Urbanism   121
For Times Square, a Reprieve and Hope of a Livelier Day   124
The Thrill of Outer Space for Earthbound Lives   127
In Philadelphia, a Showcase of Abandoned Hopes   130

Reduced to Luxury   133
The *Niña*, the *Pinta*, and the Fate of the "White City"   136
Art and Science Politely Disagree on an Architectural
    Jewel's Fate   138
For Staten Island, A Ferry Terminal Rooted in the Past   141
Gehry's Disney Hall: A Matterhorn for Music   144
St. John the Divine: It Can't Go On. It Goes On.   147
Thinking About Tomorrow, and How to Build It   150
The Tale of a Chimney That Turned into an Oasis   154
Some Unfinished Business on St.-Germain   156
Roadside Attractions to Reckon With   159
Modernism and Morality in the South Bronx   162
New Public Housing, French Vintage 1922   166
Shaping a Monument to Memory   170
This Time, Eisenman Goes Conventional   176
To the Beach: A Baedeker for Baskers; Long Beach Island   179
The Unconventional as a Convention   180
"Things Generally Wrong in the Universe"   182
In This Dream Station Future and Past Collide   185
Miami Virtue: Arquitectonica's Low-Rent Housing   190
Viñoly's Vision for Tokyo, and for the Identity of Japan   192
More Is Less at a Free-Form Jamboree in Chicago   195
A Nervous Prism of a Building for Manhattan   198
What Makes a Building Shrivel Up and Die?   200
The Gehry House: A Brash Landmark Grows Up   202
A Man Who Lives in Two Glass Houses   207
Fear, Hope, and the Changing of the Guard   213
Frank Gehry Lifts Creativity Out of the Box   217
The Homeless and the New Cold War   219
Rude Awakening; Quake Jars Assumptions: A Critic's View   223
Architecture as Social Action, and Vice Versa   226
An Appraisal; Columbus Circle's Changing Face:
    More than Geometry   229
Back to the Future   232
Queens West: Why Not Something Great?   235
In Paris, a Building That Melts Away Like Ice   239
Frank Gehry's American (Center) in Paris   242
"Boss" Design: A Los Angeles Sketchbook   244
Radical Moderation, Right Out of the '60s   247
If You Squint, This Is Not a Faulty Tower   252
In California, an Art Center Grown from Fragments   256
Visions of Community with Roots in the '60s   258

A Show Brings on a Severe Case of Period Envy   262
Rem Koolhaas's New York State of Mind   264
Stay of Execution for a Dazzling Airline Terminal   269
Sighting Beauty on the Far Side of Fear   271
The Moment When the World Seemed New   274
An Architect with a Knack for Synthesis   276
An Emporium for Art Rises in the West   279
Playful, Even Goofy, but What Else? It's Disney   282
What of Cities If the Blueprint Is Republican?   285
Art, Setting, and the Architecture of the Heart   288
A Declaration of the '60s, Before the Doubts   292
Preserving the Shrines of an Age, Not the Spirit   295
A Flare for Fantasy: *Miami Vice* Meets Forty-second Street   298
Where the Readers Are Inside the Books   302
Broadway's Real Hits Are Its Antique Theaters   306
A "Monster" of a Masterpiece in Connecticut   310
Among the Fountains with Tadao Ando: Concrete Dreams in the Sun
    King's Court   313
Remodeling New York for the Bourgeoisie   317
In a Bygone Day, This Was the Look of the Future   322
Getting Goofy on the Santa Ana Freeway   325
Chelsea Dawning: Reawakened and Resplendent   327
Buildings Born of Dreams and Demons   331
The Prisoner of Beauty   336
A City Poised on Glitter and Ashes   341
In the Public Interest   346
The Short, Scorned Life of an Aesthetic Heresy: Designed in Defiance
    of Modernist Tenets, 2 Columbus Circle Awaits Its Fate   348
Nostalgia Tripping in Times Square   351
In Japan, Art and a Museum Breathe as One   354
A Primal Phantasmagoria Not Just for Gamblers   357
Where a Room Is a Calling Card   361
Architecture of Light and Remembrance   364
Darling: Having a Surreal Time. Are You Here, Too?   372
A Crystal Palace of Culture and Commerce   376
Worthy of a World Capital   380
Rethinking the Meaning of the Modern   384
Form Follows Function into Ideal Circles   387
Making a Rush-Hour Battleground High Art   390
A Chance for an Architect to Let His Imagination Run Free   393
A Flower Reopens in the Bronx   397
Architects' Visions of How the Modern May One Day Appear   401

A Palace for a New Magic Kingdom, Forty-second Street   404
Make the Modern Modern? How Very Rash!   409
The Designs of a Genius Redesigning Himself   414
For the Body, a Curvy Home That Calls to the Soul   417
Searching for Yourself in Versace's Mirror   420
In Form and Function, It's a Tale of Two Terminals   422
The Miracle in Bilbao   424
It's Dark. It's Scary. It's Your Garage.   435
A Midas of the Gold (Yes, I Do Mean Gold) Cudgel   437
A Mountaintop Temple Where Art's Future Worships Its Past   439
Leading Lights, Whose Destiny Was to Be Dimmed   445
Aalto, a Modernist Ahead of His Time   448
A Return to the Glamour of Flying: Kennedy's New Terminal Offers
    Style and Comfort for Jaded Travelers   452
Of Sculpture and the Past Revivified   455
Looking at the Lawn, and Below the Surface   458
Choosing Prose over Poetry to Span a Bay   463
Restoration Liberates Grand Vistas, and Ideas   466
An Islamic Reminder of the Sacred in Design   469
Living Boldly on the Event Horizon   477
The Village as a Satirist's Milieu and Muse   481
Blueprint: The Shock of the Familiar   487
A Twelve-Block Glimmer of Hope for New York   492
The Premiere of a Koolhaas Fantasy   497
The New Berlin—Building on the Rubble of History: Once Again, a
    City Rewards the Walker   500
Culture's Power Houses: The Museum Becomes an Engine of
    Urban Redesign   511
New Zoning Leaves Room for Skyline of the Future   516
If the Cityscape Is Only a Dream   519
An Appreciation: Style and Symbolism Meet in Design
    for Penn Station   522
A Stunning Pier Hotel Design Stands Out Amid a Flawed Plan   526
A Humble Manhole Cover Conveys the Global Grid   530
A Tower That Flaunts Its Contradictions   531
Art Deco Authenticity   535
Trump, His Gilded Taste, and Me   539
Crystal Corridor in the City of Glass   550
The Passages of Paris and of Benjamin's Mind   556
Exploring Space and Time, Here and Now   563
It's Something New Under the Stars (and Looking Up)   567
Tray Chic   572

Our Anxieties to the Lions   574
Reaching for Power over Streets and Sky   579
Fusing Beauty and Terror, Reverence and Desecration   588
How Modern Design Remains Faithful to Its Context   591
Tibor Kalman: Seeing, Disbelieving   595
Public Space or Private, a Compulsion to Fill It   600
The Air-conditioned Reverie of a Fundamentalist   603
Interior City: Hotel as the New Cosmopolis   608
Where Ego Sashays in Style   612
A Rare Opportunity for Real Architecture Where It's Needed   618
A Rational Vision That Lets You Know Who's Boss   628
Lincoln Center's Next Big Production: Itself   632
Defining Beauty in Swanky American Terms   641
Imaginative Leaps into the Real World   644
A Message from a Poet of Public and Private Memory   648
Camelot's Once and Future Glamour   652
Postcards from the Old World Gone Global   656
Austro Turf   665
Forget the Shoes, Prada's New Store Stocks Ideas   669
With Viewing Platforms, a Dignified Approach to Ground Zero   673
Leaping from One Void into Others   677
The Deadly Importance of Making Distinctions   683
A Courtyard at the Heart of the Story   685
A Lesson Abroad: Get Comfortable with Continuity   689
When Art Puts Down a Bet in a House of Games   692
A Gift of Vienna That Skips the *Schlag*   696
A Handsome Hunk of a Glass Tower   700
Lessons of a Humanist Who Can Disturb the Peace   703
Peace Lobby   706
A Latin Jolt to the Skyline   710
Castles in the Air Adorn Cities on Paper   715
Fashion's High Priestess of Gnosticism   719
The Memorial Would Live in the Architecture   722
A Heritage Rediscovered, Then Remade   726
From Olympus, Divine Dresses   728
The Way We Live Now: 5-18-03; Who Gets It ?   733
Zaha Hadid's Urban Mothership   735
Blond Ambition on Red Brick   741
A Building with a Song in Its Heart   746
A Moon Palace for the Hollywood Dream   749
Design Guidelines for Ground Zero Point More to
    Space City, U.S.A.   752

Lunch Box for Art: A New Museum   755
A Building's Bold Spirit, Clad in Marble and Controversy   758
Uncertain Future for the Past's Treasures   761
PATH Station Becomes a Procession of Flight   767
Glamorous Glass Gives 10 Columbus Circle a Look of
    Crystallized Noir   769
For Lower Manhattan, Tower Offers a Residential Stairway
    to the Sky   772
Planet Prada   774
The Library That Puts on Fishnets and Hits the Disco   777
For the Classy and the Climbers, the High Priest of Art Deco   782
Peep Show   785
Eden Rocks   786
The Secret History of 2 Columbus Circle   789
The Grassi Is Greener   821
Schadenfreude.com   825
Freudian Slipcovers   827
The Heir Bag   830

FRAGMENTS FROM **HEARTS OF THE CITY, 2006**

A Dozen Years   835
Metroscope   842
Atomic Secrets   847

Index   853

ACKNOWLEDGMENTS

This book would not have been possible without the help of many people. We want to thank Leon Wieseltier and Linda Gerth at *The New Republic*, Knight Landesman at *Artforum*, and, at *The New York Times*, Joe Lelyveld, Bill Keller, Jill Abramson, Sam Sifton, and Alex Ward for so generously making available Herbert Muschamp's many pieces that we have used in this collection. All the pieces collected here appear as they were edited by Leon Wieseltier, Ingrid Sischy, Nora Kerr, Ariel Kaminer, and Myra Forsberg. We would like to thank John Rockwell and Julie Iovine and particularly Randy Bourscheidt, Lisa Dennison, Mirella Haggiag, and Amanda Burden, who were not only great friends to Herbert but also have offered advice and ideas, suggested material for this project, and been supportive from the start. And finally we owe a debt of gratitude to Michael Stout, Herbert's great friend and executor, who has counseled us, opened files, and overseen this project all along.

INTRODUCTION

NICOLAI OUROUSSOFF

Herbert Muschamp's death from lung cancer in 2007, at the age of fifty-nine, not only silenced one of the most unique voices in American criticism but also signaled the close of one of the most tumultuous periods in the recent history of architecture.

When Muschamp first began writing as a critic in the early 1980s, Postmodernism was only beginning to loosen its suffocating grip on the profession. The great talents of his generation were still mostly involved with theoretical work, unknown to the average American. By the time of Muschamp's death, these architects were part of the mainstream, building luxurious residential towers, museums, and corporate headquarters around the world. The rebels had become the establishment.

This collection, which includes columns written for *The New Republic*, *The New York Times*, and *Artforum*, as well as excerpts from an unpublished book, reflects the extremes of that era, from its creative exuberance to its self-indulgent excesses. It reveals a mind at war with easy formulas and intellectual complacency. And if some of the columns seem less concerned with buildings than with the debates that surround them, it is because Muschamp's aim was to provoke, and by doing so to open us up to new ideas.

As a critic, his greatest contribution may have been his liberal use of the subjective voice. He did not write with the cool detached eye of the omnipotent observer but as an active participant, someone who wanted, with his whole heart, to fall in love with the work he was writing about. He often placed himself at the center of a story—as a refugee from suburbia, a gay man in the cosmopolitan city, and a survivor of an AIDS-ravaged New York. And if this was maddening to some, it also enabled him to forge a powerful emotional bond with his audience.

The basic message was this: we are all subjective beings, "individualistic, competitive, rootless, hungry, exhibitionistic, freakish," as he once put it. Architecture—or at least the architecture that mattered—was as adept at expressing this inner turmoil as it was at defining the values we share as a society.

His devotion to the cosmopolitan city was forged in the suburbs. He was born in 1947 to an upper-middle-class family in suburban Philadelphia—

the kind of community, as he writes in *Hearts of the City*, his unfinished book, "where inhibition was mistaken for character." The suburbs were a place of constant anxiety and trauma, where a young gay Jewish boy was under constant assault from "the disapproving gaze of WASP couples."

Cities meant freedom. In the 1950s, he began taking weekend train trips to New York, where he eventually fell in with Andy Warhol's Factory crowd. He drifted from school to school, enrolling first at the University of Pennsylvania and then at Parsons School of Design in Manhattan. After a brief stint at London's Architectural Association, he returned to Parsons, where he taught criticism in the late 1980s.

When Muschamp emerged onto the architectural scene, first as a writer for *Artforum* and then as a critic for *The New Republic*, American architecture was divided into two opposing poles: the sterile functionalism of late Modernism and a Postmodernist movement rooted in more traditional models. Muschamp had no desire to return to the "tight, responsible world of the stern-faced modern fathers."

But Postmodernism, too, seemed like a dead end. If he was appreciative of the aesthetic freedom won by architects like Robert Venturi and Aldo Rossi in the 1960s, he scorned the movement's turn to a false Classicism that seemed to deny that the modern world existed at all. That this was a misreading of history was disturbing enough. What was unforgivable was that these architects had squandered the aesthetic freedom they had won only a decade before.

"By the mid-eighties," he wrote many years later, "the movement had deteriorated into a career strategy for reactionaries, opportunists, and their deeply uncultivated patrons."

Muschamp felt a close kinship with those designers who came of age during the student uprisings of 1968, architects like Koolhaas, Hadid, Wolf Prix, Thom Mayne, Frank Israel, and Eric Owen Moss. Unlike their Modernist fathers, these architects did not seek to smooth over differences; their desire was to expose the conflicts that existed at the core of society and that gave the city its vibrancy and meaning. Their aim was to make room for the dark subconscious forces that the Modernists often suppressed.

Muschamp saw projects like Jean Nouvel's Cartier Foundation in Paris as part of a Surrealist tradition that blurred the border "between waking reality and the dream state." The warped ramps of Koolhaas's unbuilt design for the Jussieux Library in Paris were not only "a psychological provocation" but "a form of social therapy" as well.

It was Frank Gehry's work, however, that brought out Muschamp's most rapturous writing. Muschamp sometimes referred to Gehry as a father figure, and he saw him as the standard bearer of an American, democratic architecture. Like Frank Lloyd Wright, Gehry sought to create forms that reflected a culture unfettered by binding, worn-out traditions. But if Wright's vision of America celebrated the spirit of individual freedom embodied in the nation's endless landscapes, Gehry spoke for a generation that had found itself trapped once again, this time in the monotonous conformity of suburban California. The intentionally crude, fragmented forms of his early houses—cobbled together out of chain link, plywood, and galvanized metal—expressed not just the hidden tensions that threatened to break down the traditional nuclear family but also a desire to regain lost freedom.

This dream reached its fullest expression in Gehry's design for the Guggenheim Museum in Bilbao, Spain, which Muschamp summed up in a review that for many came to define his unchecked exuberance.

"After my first visit to the building," he wrote, "I went back to the hotel to write notes. It was early evening and starting to rain. I took a break to look out the window and saw a woman standing alone outside a bar across the street. She was wearing a long, white dress with matching white pumps, and she carried a pearlescent handbag. Was her date late? Had she been stood up?

"When I looked back a bit later, she was gone. And I asked myself, *Why can't a building capture a moment like that?* Then I realized the reason I had that thought was that I'd just come from such a building. And that the building I'd just come from was the reincarnation of Marilyn Monroe."

He went on: "What twins the actress and the building in my memory is that both of them stand for an American style of freedom. That style is voluptuous, emotional, intuitive, and exhibitionist. It is mobile, fluid, material, mercurial, fearless, radiant, and as fragile as a newborn child. It can't resist doing a dance with all the voices that say 'No.' It wants to take up a lot of space. And when the impulse strikes it likes to let its dress fly up in the air."

Such audacious writing was unusual anywhere, but it was particularly startling in a daily newspaper. Its power stemmed from Muschamp's ability to weave together seemingly unconnected threads—Marilyn, the postindustrial city, the writer's own exhibitionism—until they began to make intuitive sense. The boundary between private and public life gets blurry. Architecture becomes something deeply personal again.

In the following years, Muschamp witnessed Gehry's triumphant retrospective at the Guggenheim Museum in New York, as well as the first buildings by Koolhaas and Hadid built in the United States. The architects that he had once championed as rebellious outsiders became major forces on the world cultural scene. Those he saw as the enemies of serious architecture—bottom-line developers, supporters of a formulaic retro-historicism—increasingly seemed relegated to the sidelines.

The euphoria didn't last. His last years as the *Times's* architecture critic were partly spent lambasting the convoluted reconstruction efforts at Ground Zero, where the worst American values—jingoism, crass commercialism, political posturing—triumphed over the cosmopolitan ideals that he had championed his entire career. And if he continued to write inspired stories, including columns for the *Times's T Magazine*, the excitement he had felt for new architectural breakthroughs seemed harder to sustain.

Toward the end of his life, as the excesses of the Bush years began to infect the profession, Muschamp embarked on a process of self-reinvention. He fantasized about editing the *Times's* Travel section. He focused on his book. Lying in his hospital bed, he sketched out ideas for shows he hoped to curate if he recovered. He was through with criticism, he told me. Organizing an exhibition seemed a more active way to challenge our cultural assumptions.

A month later he was dead. A rich chapter in architectural history would also soon come to a close, and the stories he wrote now seem like a vision from a more lavish—and forgiving—era.

THE NEW REPUBLIC
1987–1992

THE TEMPLE OF MARKETING

Helmut Jahn's new United Airlines Terminal at Chicago's O'Hare International Airport is a terminal in more ways than one. United has christened its gleaming half-billion-dollar facility the Terminal for Tomorrow. But what Jahn has given us is an architectural echo of yesterday, a deliberate evocation of the soaring iron and glass pavilions of the great Victorian railway stations. From the vantage point of the world's busiest airport, one fin de siècle looks back with longing at another, recasting our lapsed faith in technological progress as a nostalgic dream. It's time for the twentieth century to fasten its seat belts as Tomorrow descends for a final approach.

Management has not yet installed the royal palm trees shown in Jahn's scale models, but you don't need the palms to make out the ghost of Joseph Paxton, the Victorian greenhouse designer whose 1851 Crystal Palace first elevated prefabricated metal and glass construction to the scale of civic architecture. Like the Palace, Jahn's terminal and its companion "satellite" building are axial structures (each 1,500 feet long to Paxton's 1,800), metal-framed, glass-paneled, capped with soaring barrel vaults, drenched throughout with natural light. And, like Paxton, Jahn has stocked his greenhouse with the fruits of Industry ("The luggage laser scans 480 bags a minute") and Empire (an "international cuisine" of teriyaki, enchiladas, and couscous replaces the standard shrink-wrapped sandwich).

Yet Jahn's high-tech update of nineteenth-century engineering is a far cry from such explicitly historicist buildings as John Burgee and Philip Johnson's headquarters for AT&T in New York or Robert A. M. Stern's cheap editions of Gilded Age opulence. Jahn has issued no polemical statement against the functionalist aesthetic of Modernism, nor renounced the ideal of social progress that aesthetic once expressed. His oxymoronic treatment of the future-as-past reflects a more complex state of perplexity. His problem is how modernity can be visually represented at a time when the correlation between the aesthetic and the ideal has collapsed.

The railway pavilion to which Jahn's design pays tribute is one of the most symbolically loaded images in architectural history. Modern architecture began, in effect, with the twentieth century's retrospective view that the iron and glass shed covering the tracks and platforms at the station's rear, a purely utilitarian structure, possessed an expressive power far greater than the ornamented masonry capital-A Architecture of the station's facade. To the early Modernists, this split between the station's front and rear epitomized the crisis they sought to resolve: the Victorian architect's stubborn clinging to the authority of history and tradition, his inability to conceive of architecture as other than an eclectic reworking of the historical styles blinded him to the potential of new structural materials and methods to express the legitimate authority of the industrial age.

The equation between industrial technology and social progress long preceded its architectural articulation by the Bauhaus masters. In the eighteenth century, theorists such as Turgot and Condorcet idealized industry as a system governed by rational methods and therefore as a paradigm for social organization, a vehicle of scientific application destined to deliver society from the despotic rule of church and state into the realm of reason. By the end of the nineteenth century, the architectural vocabulary to communicate this sociological message had been in place for some time. All the Modern architect had to do was reveal it: strip away "the styles" from the front of the station and allow the building's structure to announce its own expressive power. By then, of course, industrial production had progressed far beyond the Enlightenment's utopian paradigm for organizing the future; its managers had already displaced the traditional figureheads as administrators of social authority. For the architect to give this authority visual expression was to allow society to recognize the truth of its own life through the medium of its buildings.

But this solution to the crisis of nineteenth-century architecture was acceptable only so long as technology retained the progressive connotation the Enlightenment had accorded it. The crisis of contemporary architecture is that this connotation has been untenable for some time. "Architecture or Revolution," Le Corbusier sang out in 1923 to promote his machines for living; "Revolution can be avoided." But before a half century had passed, the Modern style had become the official face of the imperial corporation, an authority governed not by reason but by greed, wielding power as despotically as any king or pope. The proliferation of the Modern "glass box" in the 1960s and '70s helped to provoke a rupture with the very faith in technological progress that the buildings had been designed to reinforce.

The airport is a stage on which the breakdown of this faith is reenacted repeatedly in the glare of TV cameras. In the Modern vision of Tomorrow depicted by such architects as Le Corbusier, Ivan Leonidov, Frank Lloyd Wright, and Buckminster Fuller, airplanes, airships, and airborne housing figured as sacred images; they were totems of technology's power to free us from the weight of earthbound tradition and dogma. At Kennedy Airport's Terminal City, with individual buildings by star second-generation Modernists such as I. M. Pei; Eero Saarinen; and Skidmore, Owings, and Merrill, air travel provided the pretext to conceive a theme park on the theme of progress, a magnificent showcase of our technological capacity to defy gravity, to shrink the globe, to provide each of us with a ticket to the blue skies of upward mobility. The world to which that ticket actually admits us, however, is a dystopia of chaos, discomfort, and fear, a full-scale demonstration of technology's power to afflict us with loss of time, temper, life, limb, sanity, and Samsonite, the migraine world of the near miss and the terrorist attack.

The course of Helmut Jahn's development as an architect recapitulates the breakdown of the Modern faith. Like the Victorian railway station, Jahn's work is split into two apparently contradictory parts, though arranged in a sequence that reverses the logic of the Modern breakthrough. In 1966, while still a student, Jahn emigrated from Germany to Chicago on account of his admiration for Mies van der Rohe, then at the peak of his prestige as the father of the modern office tower. Jahn's earliest buildings proclaimed his fealty to the great master of structural expression, and earned him a privileged place in the "Second Chicago School" that had sprung up around Mies during his tenure as director of architecture at the Illinois Institute of Technology.

But by the late 1970s, Jahn had already begun to turn the example of the master on its head. Instead of devoting himself to the gradual refinement of a limited vocabulary of structural form, Jahn swiftly transformed himself into the prototype of the "designer architect," a brilliant packager valued by real estate developers for his talent to endow each commission with a unique, spectacular profile. Throughout the 1980s, with projects as stylistically diverse as Television City, Bank of the Southwest Tower, and the State of Illinois Center, Jahn has dedicated his career to disproving the Miesian dictum that "it is not necessary nor possible to invent a new kind of architecture every Monday morning."

To judge from Jahn's development sketches, which are included in the monograph on his work published last year by Rizzoli, he finds it both possible and necessary to design a series of often radically different alternatives for each commission he receives. It is this gift for formal invention, coupled with the sartorial flair that landed him on the cover of *GQ* a few seasons back, that has brought Jahn the considerable celebrity he enjoys outside the architectural profession. Many architects less favored by the media are inclined to disparage Jahn as an architect whose flashy, one-of-a-kind creations are designed less to serve the needs of their users than to feed the media's insatiable appetite for novelty: What will Helmut design next?

Jahn is hardly the only architect, hardly even the only erstwhile

Miesian, to abandon the strictures of canonical Modernism. Architects have been laboring now for two decades in the void left by the erosion of the industrial paradigm. What distinguishes Jahn from the postmodern historicists, and also from such committed Modernists as Norman Foster and Richard Meier, is that his work has moved progressively toward the embodiment of a new paradigm.

What Jahn understands better than any architect of his generation is that the cultural authority of industrial production has been supplanted by the authority of marketing. His work represents a recognition that this development holds aesthetic as well as socioeconomic implications. "You have to accept the fact," Jahn says,

> that when people hire you to do new and different things, you can't go around defending one kind of thing and develop a philosophy around it. If I had a philosophy, all the buildings would be the same. The only way to succeed in this area is to satisfy people who want something fresh and flamboyant for marketing.

This may not exactly qualify as a philosophy, but it is certainly a prevailing cultural attitude. The enthusiasm with which Jahn embraces this attitude not only stands behind his professional success, it also lends even his flimsiest works a horrifying fascination.

The fascination of the new terminal at O'Hare lies in how successfully it simulates an architecture that did arise from profound philosophical conviction. This time out Jahn has literally buried his customary flamboyance. Only in the underground concourse connecting the main building to the "satellite" terminal does the trademark flash fully erupt, in a style one might call Perpendicular Disco: rainbow neon pulsating to piped-in "space music," mock fan-vaulting in translucent plastic. Above ground, Jahn plays it straight in a sleek monochrome display of structural muscle. It's a very handsome display. United's employees are said to hate the new terminal (largely because they resent its cost), but passengers have reason to be grateful for the abundant natural light, the no-wait "flow through" ticket counters, the efficient organization of passenger circulation.

What is significant about the terminal, however, is not how effectively it mimics the rational principles of Modern design but how thoroughly it subverts them. Modernists acclaimed the old railway terminals because, unlike the historical romance embodied in the facade, the shed spoke honestly of the cold facts of the industrial age. Jahn, by contrast, has selected this image precisely because it is fiction. "We wanted it to have a certain romance, a certain feeling of fantasy that you associate with travel." To impart a feeling like that to those who are actually traveling does indeed require fantasy in quite a heavy dose. What Jahn has accomplished toward that end is an architectural equivalent of a TV spot for the Friendly Skies. As we step onto the people mover and glide down the concourse, lifting our eyes to gaze at the postcard-perfect clouds through the glazed barrel vault, we can forget about hijackings, microwaved sirloin tips, and holes in the ozone layer.

The paradox is that Jahn's architectural fictions give us a factual representation of values in the postindustrial age of the service economy. In this sense, at least, Jahn is a true heir of the Mies who once defined architecture as "the will of an epoch translated into space." When Jahn insists that we "have to accept the fact" of marketing, we hear an echo of Mies defending the technological paradigm in 1930: "The new era is a fact: it exists, irrespective of our 'yes' or 'no.'" In 1987 the culture of consumer marketing is also a fact, however justifiably we may protest its promiscuous blurring of image and substance.

But must we say "yes" to marketing? Must we surrender technology's heroic march of progress to marketing's dog-eat-dog pursuit of novelty? It does seem like an enormous letdown. Still, before we get too indignant, it is worth remembering that we've heard this kind of grumbling once before: not everyone thought technology was something to build temples to either. True, probably nobody outside the advertising industry would equate marketing with social progress. But perhaps one of Modernism's most important lessons is that it doesn't pay to place too much faith in the zeitgeist.

October 26, 1987

CORBU SAVED FROM DROWNING

Charles-Édouard Jeanneret (1887–1965) loved to make up catchy names. In 1915, when the Swiss-born architect conceived his first recognizably Modern design, a system for concrete mass-produced housing, he was not content to let the design speak for itself. No, the plan had to be labeled the Domino system and announced to the world as though it were a new line of standardized office equipment or industrial hardware. In 1920 he called a residential design the Citrohan House, a verbal play on the car manufacturer Citroën; the allusion underscored Jeanneret's belief that the Modern house should be a "machine for living." In time, such bursts of copyrighting flair as *pilotis* (stilts designed to elevate a building above ground level), *brise-soleil* (fixed concrete louvers mounted on exterior walls), and Modulor (a system of architectural proportions) further invested Jeanneret's formal vocabulary with the snappy allure of the patented scientific invention. But the most memorable name of all was applied to the most outstanding invention of Jeanneret's brilliant career: Le Corbusier, *lui-même*.

In 1920, when Jeanneret first used the name Le Corbusier to sign articles in his newly founded art journal *l'Esprit Nouveau*, he had lived in Paris for three years, practiced architecture for fifteen, and produced a respectable body of built work, respectable not only in quantity but also in style. With their walls and corbels of rough stone, their steeply pitched roofs, their pine-paneled interiors, and ornamental systems based on the flora of his native Jura, such early buildings as the Fallet House (1906) and the Stotzer and Jacquenet houses (both 1908) were lavish tributes to the ideal of regional tradition.

But it was all far too respectable for Le Corbusier's taste: none of these works appears in the volumes of his misnamed *Oeuvre complète*. Le Corbusier suppressed his own early history, just as his aesthetic of industrial technology suppressed the history of architecture itself. The creation of Le Corbusier (an aggrandized version of the family name Lecorbesier) was the autobiographical counterpart of his mission to create architecture anew by cleansing it of formal references to the past.

He was a machine for inventing Modern architecture. None of the characteristic elements of that invention (the unadorned surface, the formal deployment of new materials and methods of construction, the replacement of mass by volume, the generation of exterior form from interior function) originated with Le Corbusier himself. His invention was, rather, the vision in which these individual elements were brought to a climactic synthesis. A NEW EPOCH HAS BEGUN, headlined the first issue of *l'Esprit Nouveau*. Le Corbusier's first task was to exhort the public to recognize that modern times demanded modern spaces, and his second was to persuade that public that he could personally satisfy the demand.

Le Corbusier's designs for private houses in the 1920s, culminating in the 1929 Villa Savoye, soon came to epitomize the formal values of the International Style. His urban plans, beginning with the 1922 Contemporary City for Three Million, imbued those values with a sense of social mission, a vision that inspired architects throughout the world to recast architecture on the scale of global planning. In later years, after he had transformed the cool precision of the industrial aesthetic into a more poetic mode of personal expression, buildings such as the Church of Ronchamp (1950–53), the monastery of la Tourette (1957–60), and the capital buildings of Chandigarh (1957–65) enlarged and extended his role as spiritual mentor to young architects well into the 1960s.

A single year is too short a time to commemorate an achievement of such magnitude. And yet, like the Mies van der Rohe centennial a few years ago, last year's Le Corbusier anniversary fell somewhat flat. Yes, ambitious exhibitions were mounted in London and Paris; impressive new publications joined reprinted editions of Le Corbusier's own books in the display windows of fancy bookstores; learned scholars assembled in well-attended panels; reporters from the design press were duly dispatched to the offices of young architects to dig up (or make up) evidence of a Corbusian revival. But all of this ostensibly festive commotion seemed to be weighted down by an oppressive air of duty. If our museums, our schools, our publishers had neglected to light the candles for Corbu, we would all quite properly accuse them of falling down on the job.

Shame on us, then, for blowing out the candles with our yawns. Yet it is not difficult to fathom reasons for the apathy. For one thing, Le Corbusier has not been away long enough to allow us either to miss him or to redis-cover him. His death in 1965 did not remove him from our consciousness; if anything, it expanded his influence as Modernism's *éminence blanche*, the Architect of the Century from whose ghostly embrace only the turn of another century could release us. And it is the ghost that has worn us out: we're still suffering battle fatigue from the unwon and fundamentally unwinnable war between Modern and Postmodern architects, a Twenty Years' War (and some are still counting) in which the name Le Corbusier arose again and again as a banner to be saluted or knocked down.

It would be a pleasure to lavish praise on Le Corbusier if we could do so without lending encouragement to those who invoke the Great Mod-ern Masters merely to beat down or belittle the work of a younger gener-ation. And it would be a challenge to attempt a more critical approach if we could avoid the risk of rehashing all the stale Postmodern polemics against the sins of the Modern movement. But alas, it is too late for more revisionism, too early to revise substantially the revision. It seems like only yesterday that the beloved Corbu was transformed into an object of scorn, only yesterday that he was to be reviled as the stalking Godzilla of the postwar city, as a crypto-totalitarian whose megalomaniacal vision of the modern metropolis aroused a generation of architects to commit monu-mental acts of urbicide. It was not until the mid-1970s, for example, that Michael Graves, the most gifted architect associated with the Postmodern movement, expunged the Corbusian influence from his own work and began castigating his absentee mentor as a twentieth-century Hun.

And now we're supposed to sing many happy returns? The wishful thought behind the new crop of books and exhibitions seems to be that at last the time has come to bury all our differences over the Corbusian legacy and that the best way to accomplish this is to let loose with an ava-lanche of scholarship. Never mind that honoring Le Corbusier with a shower of scholarly tomes is like honoring Lenin with a showcase of

Fabergé eggs. If what we want is an objective assessment of Le Corbusier, History is where we are supposed to find it. But what history cannot settle, what in fact these anniversary tributes to the Modern Masters only magnify, is the disruption that the historical perspective of Modernism has itself brought about.

Here lies the great irony of architecture at the present moment. We are widely supposed to have entered a period in which architects are engaged in the worthy task of healing the great rupture caused by the Modern Movement's break with the past. What, the Postmodernists asked, was Modernism's great defect? It was the belief in the tabula rasa, the determination to sweep away the accumulated debris of history and make a fresh start. The evidence to support this assessment of Modernism's failure lay all around us: in the piles of limestone to which the wrecker's ball had reduced great landmarks, in the systematic destruction of the traditional city street by the set-back Modern tower, in the funereal cortege of scaleless monoliths that had turned lively downtown districts into bleak zones of visual monotony and psychological deprivation. Even dedicated Modernists were willing to concede that the Modern architect's attempt to remake the city without regard for its historic fabric had not fallen short of catastrophe.

If the catastrophe could be attributed to the Modern ban on history, then the solution was very simple: rescind the ban. Retrieve the great books of architecture that Le Corbusier had thrown out the window and restore them to a place of honor beside the drafting table. Let architects cover miles of tracing paper with copies of classical columns. Give them free passes for rides on the carousel slide show of forms by Palladio, by Bulfinch, by McKim, Mead, & White. Connect the Postmodern with the "Pre-Modern," as Charles Jencks advised, and let ornament grow over architecture, like ivy over a battered wall, to cover the scars left by the Modern rupture with history's grand procession.

But there was one little problem with this solution. To reopen the history books was to explode the idea that Modernism represented a genuine rupture with the grand tradition in the first place. The books tell a different story: how the tabula rasa descended honorably from the Enlightenment's program to liberate the mind from the weight of tradition; how the Modern emphasis on function and elementary geometric form traced its lineage to the efforts of progressive architects in eighteenth-century France to reveal the intrinsic qualities of architecture by peeling away layers of historical and literary reference; how the Modern iconography that was derived from mechanical technology rendered in built form the nineteenth-century Realist conviction that art should be "of its time." Far from being a perversity practiced by aesthetic degenerates in Weimar

Germany, then, Modernism had developed organically from the sturdiest roots in Western culture.

If history showed the legitimate descent of Modernism from artistic movements that preceded it, what were the Postmodernists fussing about? Where was the historical rupture? And if there was no rupture to repair, what is it that the Postmodernists have been offering us? Granted that the break with history was a myth fostered by Modernists themselves; but wasn't the purpose of "retrieving" history to break the spell of Modernism's myths?

What Postmodernists have been offering, of course, is a rupture of their own—indeed, a renewal of the very idea of "rupture" as an animating force in art. They have offered us the spectacle of their own development as artists, tracing again that curve on the spiral along which the rules and conventions of the preceding generation must be tossed out the window. If the Modern canon has proscribed ornament, then naturally ornament must be brought back by the cartload. If structure has been upheld as the only legitimate authority for form, then naturally structure must now be covered up with forms unrelated to structure. If Le Corbusier has been the hero, he must now be the villain. And so on. What we have been seeing, in other words, is not history but self-creation; not a solemn return to "the classical tradition" but the persistence of the Romantic tradition of rebellious self-assertion.

The Postmodern "rupture" would provide little cause for objection had the flowering of its ideology into built form not coincided with a moment in which the use of "history" to mask the imperatives of self-creation has led to such glaringly objectionable consequences in our national life. But we have seen, in the pageantry of the Reagan years, how easily the mask can become a substitute for the self; how readily the myth of a more secure, more meaningful, more coherent past is invoked as an escape from the need to think about the present; how "history" is the costume that inertia wears when it wants to look respectable. And we have seen, in these same seven years, how flatteringly Postmodernism has camouflaged the mental vacuum of young urban professionalism; how the "classical tradition" has been called forth to validate regressive notions of social privilege; how all these spotlit Corinthian columns, real and simulated marbles, broken pediments, and assorted country squire paraphernalia have been assembled to lend the illusion of weight and substance to transient, cupidinous lives.

The result has been a cityscape as oppressively cluttered as the Modern panorama was overwhelmingly bare. And even before Black Monday sent its burst of cold air blowing through the grand cafés, the clutter had begun to look like a visual correlative of the Reagan prosperity, opulence adrift on debt. All these comforting images from the past had been financed by mortgaging the future. For a while, it was such a pretty show that it didn't seem to matter much that no one was running it, that we had been looking at nothing but a collage of memories projected into places where minds are supposed to be at work. Only as the collage grew denser did it become increasingly apparent that "history" was being exploited as an elaborate strategy for avoiding the message history was actually trying to tell us: that if we didn't wake up soon, we were likely to find our future behind us.

The meretriciousness of the Postmodern collage should remind us of the Modernist reason for resisting the authority of history in the first place. Their argument was not with the past; it was with the willingness of their contemporaries to surrender authority for the present to the past. They had seen the nineteenth century's parade of architectural period costumes lead to self-loathing, to a heightened fear of the industrial age and its social upheavals; and they concluded that history could not offer a refuge from the turmoil, nor even a fixed set of references to help navigate a passage through it. It is time, they announced, to clear the ground and make a place for ourselves in the world to which history brought us.

But the Modernist tabula rasa cannot define the place in which we find ourselves now. Its erasure of the past is now itself the past. To clear the ground today is simply to repeat yesterday's news about how the ground drops from beneath our feet each time we think we've fixed things in place. (Postmodernism restates the same message in period costume; its "revival" of history suggests that history is accessible to contemporary architects only in the self-erasing form of novelty.) The stark tower arising from the bare plaza makes a fitting monument to the birthplace of the modern world—but we've traveled quite a distance since birth. Another vocabulary is needed to mark the place to which our absorption of the Modern erasure has propelled us.

A small book on Le Corbusier's work that appeared some years before the current jubilee—Philippe Boudon's *Lived-in Architecture: Le Corbusier's Pessac Revisited*—offered a glimpse of what such a vocabulary might look like. In the late '60s Boudon returned for a fresh look at the community of fifty-one residential houses built by Le Corbusier in 1926 in a small town outside Bordeaux. His book's primary focus, as its title suggested, was not the designs of Le Corbusier but rather the alterations to those designs carried out over a period of forty-odd years by the residents themselves, in Pessac and in an earlier Le Corbusier housing project in the nearby town of Lège.

The alterations were extensive. At Pessac, new walls filled in the empty volumes between the stilts at ground level, shattering the unifying rhythm of solid and void; strip windows, divided into halves or otherwise reduced in size, now sported cozy shutters; cornices, moldings, fake stonework, garden statuary, and ornamental fencing obliterated the project's crisp geometric lines and virtually every feature that would identify these buildings as the products of Le Corbusier's vision. At Lège, the alterations included pitched roofs set atop the buildings' distinctive rooftop terraces.

Boudon's book aroused quite a stir; it was widely misinterpreted as an attack on Le Corbusier and his vision of the Modern city. For anyone looking for a particularly graphic way to discredit the blank-slate approach to urban design, Boudon's photographs alone provided a compelling brief. Here, it seemed, was the definitive case study of Modernism's failure, irrefutable evidence of Le Corbusier's callous indifference to human needs and wants. At a time when the social consciousness of the 1960s had inspired "advocacy" architects to open offices in the storefronts of slum neighborhoods, the residents of Pessac were hailed at a distance as model citizens: they had refused to be victimized by the rigid blank cells to which Le Corbusier had condemned them and, by extension, all of us whose built world bore his imprint.

Ada Louise Huxtable, writing some years later about a trip she made to Pessac, took issue with the idea that the changes wrought by the residents disproved the validity of Le Corbusier's design. (She also took the trouble to point out that this had not been Boudon's conclusion either.) Expecting the worst, Huxtable instead found herself asking, "If this is so bad, how can it be this good? . . . The scale and relationship of the houses to one another and to the gardens are excellent; the shapes and proportions of the buildings are still strong and good. . . . This is a very pleasant place to be." And Huxtable left no doubt that this favorable impression must be credited entirely to Le Corbusier:

> It is also clear that Pessac is a survivor precisely because of its architecture. Its strong identity absorbs almost anything time and residents can inflict. . . . Pessac continues to give something to the eye and the spirit that only buildings shaped by a superior eye and spirit can. This still holds true, even with all the changes made by the residents.

But to some observers, the claim that Le Corbusier had been right in the first place was as much beside the point as the accusation that he had been wrong. Boudon's pictures of the transformed Pessac transcended the debate over historical revisionism, and pointed instead to the possibility of a new vision altogether. Le Corbusier's "lived-in architecture" was an allegory of the lived-in Modern world. It was not Corbu who had absorbed the residents. Quite the contrary. In the exchange over time between architect and residents, the buildings of Pessac had incorporated the Modern erasure of history as part of their history—and then gone on to erase the erasure in the act of making history of their own. The history captured by Boudon's camera was not an authority; it was a process. It was the record of a building's becoming, not (as Huxtable treated it) an aesthetic yardstick to which the present must be submitted for a correct measurement of its worth.

The open question raised by Boudon's pictures was not, then, whether or not Le Corbusier's vision had failed. It was whether the potential for the new vision suggested by those pictures could be consciously embodied in a work of architecture as successfully as it was in the ad hoc exchange between architect and residents. And we did not have to wait long for the affirmative answer. In 1978 the California architect Frank Gehry took "a dumb little house with charm" (Dutch gambrel roof, pink asbestos shingle siding) and subjected it to a similar process of transformation: gutting much of the building's interior, slicing away sections of exterior wall, surrounding and replacing parts of the old house with new walls and screens of corrugated metal, chain-link fence, and glass paneling.

Gehry's Santa Monica house reversed the transformation of Pessac: an object of bland suburban domesticity had been rendered an aggressively eye-catching work of contemporary art. Still, Gehry's emphasis on the building process speaks similarly of our received ideas of history. His house challenged the conventional view of history as the source of stability, continuity, and psychological comfort. The true history of this house, Gehry made clear, was a saga of physical and cultural disruption. For those living atop the San Andreas Fault—or, for that matter, in a neighborhood undergoing gentrification, a city trying to meet its municipal payroll by encouraging rampant real estate development, or anywhere at all in a country where "housing starts" are considered essential to economic stability—the tabula rasa is not an intellectual concept but the imminent prospect of daily life. And where conventional architecture seeks to conceal this fact from view, Gehry's surgical operations compelled his "dumb little house" to reveal its complex hidden history, expressing at the same time Gehry's own story as an architect inspired by vernacular forms.

It happens that an exhibition devoted to the work of Frank Gehry has been crisscrossing the country at the time of the Le Corbusier centennial. I suggest that a visit to the Gehry show is the best way to celebrate the ideal of the "New Spirit" that Le Corbusier brought to architecture nearly seventy years ago. To juxtapose the work of these two architects is to see how past and present can animate each other. Le Corbusier shows us where Gehry, where a good deal of architecture today, is coming from; and Gehry compels us to recognize that what remains of greatest value in

Le Corbusier's work is his unfailing sense of responsibility to the present. At different times, using different means, both architects have given us the same message: history is the story of how we got to the place where history cannot help us, the place where invention must take over or else history stops.

January 18, 1988

THE BREACHED WALL

About a year ago, Paul Byard, a vice president of the Architectural League in New York, published an op-ed piece in *The New York Times* decrying the withering away of social idealism in the architectural profession. "These are disquieting times for architects in New York," Byard began on a note of understatement:

> The curious, conflicted historicism of much of our new work, our confused search for validation in publicity and chic, our exceptional readiness to promote and decorate projects that by ordinary standards should not be built at all—these are signs of a pervasive trouble. They are symptoms of an unconcealable lack of principle and purpose that is close to embarrassing.

Close to? Come on, now: architects have been struggling with a serious image problem for some time. They may not occupy the Satan roles in which we have cast their clients—the Trumps, the Helmsleys, and other real estate developers who have turned New York into our leading fairground for championship rich-bashing. But in a way the architect's image is even worse. As Byard suggested, architects have been coming across as Satan's decorators, hired flunkies retained to outfit this hell with a bit of dash. And the truth is that what may be most embarrassing by today's standards is not the architects' lack of principle; it is their lack of whatever black magic it takes to transmute unprincipled behavior into *The Art of the Deal.*

Byard's article went on to sketch a depressing saga of the rise and fall of the ideal of building for socially constructive purposes. The 1980s, in his view, have marked the end of a "50-year cycle in the history of building in America and in New York":

> From at least the early 1930s to the present decade, the building process was inspired in significant part by evolving visions of large-

scale physical change undertaken for powerful reasons that were felt to be moral. Developers and architects, led by government's injection of both resources and a commitment to higher goals into the development process, combined their individual interests in projects intended to bring about significant human and environmental reforms . . . housing for the poor, housing for middle-income families, schools, parks, parkways, pools, and a host of other reformist buildings.

What brought down the curtain on this Golden Age? It was, Byard wrote, "the municipal fiscal crisis of the 1970s, [which] seemed to justify the sale of city land to make money and to encourage the inflation of the value of that land by inflating its zoning size." Ever since the city's fiscal recovery a few years later, architects—members of "a profession that is ethical at its core"—have been floundering around "without demand for our vision or our solutions," reduced to creating "demoralizing 'decotecture' for the fashion pages."

In a season as festively lit as this one has been by well-stoked bonfires of the vanities, architects can be proud that a Savonarola from their own ranks was kindling his flame some months before Black Monday set off the general conflagration. Yet I confess that my initial reaction to Byard's sermon was of a piece with the cynicism he was trying to diagnose. Without a real Howard Roark to set out sticks of dynamite, where, I wondered, was all this professional soul-searching going to lead, except maybe to business as usual with a slightly clearer conscience? After all, nobody has been forcing architects to create these designer tax shelters. As Frank Lloyd Wright once reminded a group of students, the architect unhappy with client demands can always Just Say No.

I didn't doubt Byard's sincerity, but I was skeptical about the power of his argument to affect the status quo, particularly since his view of the problem rested on a dubious historical premise. Yes, fifty years ago New York did lead the way in the use of architecture for socially progressive ends. And yes, at about the same time American architects embraced the Modern movement's idealistic program of architecture and urban design. But these two developments do not belong to a single history; they arose from separate visions, each unfolding according to its own internal logic. The first vision was predominantly social, a vision in which "reformist buildings" were among a range of means employed toward the end of New Deal social reform. The second was a predominantly architectural vision, in which architectural reform was less a means than an end in itself.

. . .

These two developments did not, of course, unfold in total isolation from each other; the glowing record of civic building recalled by Byard was to some extent an outcome of the interaction between them. But the reasons for the decline of socially progressive architecture do not lie in the history of socially progressive politics. These reasons long predate the fiscal crisis of the 1970s. Their roots extend back to the 1930s, the decade when Modern architecture made its first appearance on American soil. This was a pivotal moment in Modernism's history, a time when Modern forms began to be drained of their social content and rendered into elements of style. In the International Style exhibition organized by Philip Johnson and Henry-Russell Hitchcock at the Museum of Modern Art in 1932, the curators were at pains to conceal the socialist ideology informing much of the work on display. Their goal, after all, was to promote what they were calling the most important style of architecture to emerge since the Middle Ages. Their strategy was to establish architecture as high art, on a level with the cathedrals, not to scare away potential patrons with intimations of Karl Marx and Rosa Luxemburg.

Byard's fifty-year cycle of idealistic building was thus, at the same time, a period of mounting disillusionment with the capacity of Modern architecture to embody progressive social ideals. Long before Tom Wolfe began ridiculing American CEOs for permitting their architects to replace the opulent corporate image of the past with the stripped-down look of "workers' housing," critics were challenging the moral authority of an aesthetic that lent itself far more congenially to the travertine treatment on Park Avenue than to the regulation issue of subsidizing housing. The most influential of these challenges was mounted by Jane Jacobs in 1960, in *The Death and Life of Great American Cities*. To Jacobs, the Modern "reformist building" signified not the social idealism of architects but rather their overbearing arrogance. "Like a great, visible ego," Jacobs wrote, "an imitation Le Corbusier shouts, 'Look what I have made!' "

In the two decades that followed Jacobs's blast, architects were increasingly unwilling to suspend their disbelief in Modernism's commitment to social change. But what were the alternatives? In his "critical history" of Modern architecture, Kenneth Frampton observed that one of the most notable developments since the 1960s was that "many of [the profession's] more intelligent members have abandoned traditional practice, either to resort to direct social action or to indulge in the projection of architecture as a form of art." Thus, on the one hand, "advocacy" architects such as

Robert Goodman opened up storefront offices to help communities prevent large-scale "reformist buildings" from reforming their neighborhoods out of existence. And architects like Michael Graves, on the other hand, began investigating issues of form and meaning as a way of freeing architecture from a moribund "vision" whose essential features had been worked out in the 1920s. In both cases, architects were pursuing paths they took to be culturally progressive. Their reasons for relinquishing the Modern vision were scarcely less moral than the reasons that had once persuaded architects to embrace it.

The abandonment of traditional practice by the profession's emerging talents did not result, of course, in the collapse of traditional practice. Its effect, predictably, was to deliver that practice into the hands of lesser, or at least less progressively minded, talents, and into the hands of clients oblivious to the news that talented architects weren't designing buildings anymore. And for all its emphasis on renewed morality, the position Byard took in his article was itself symptomatic of this state of default. Why mourn the morality of an architecture that followed the initiative of government? If it is possible to speak of Modern architecture as a moral vision, it is because Modern architects claimed for themselves the responsibility to initiate reform.

As it turned out, happily, this was not Byard's final word. Last June, in cooperation with the city's Department of Housing Preservation and Development, the Architectural League sent out a call for architects to come up with innovative designs for low-cost housing. Each architect was asked to develop plans for one of ten model sites, tiny neighborhood lots typical of thousands of city-owned properties that are considered too small to sustain economically feasible development. Project guidelines encouraged targeting proposals to specific "use groups," such as the elderly, the homeless, the handicapped. Seventy teams of architects, mostly designers in their thirties, responded to the invitation. Their work went on public view last fall in an exhibition called Vacant Lots. Some of the teams, meanwhile, have been meeting with government officials, social welfare agencies, and private developers in an effort to get their projects built.

Vacant Lots was a heartening antidote, if not to the recent wave of overbuilding, then at least to the cynicism and despair it has engendered. While the stated purpose of the show was to reinvigorate housing, its real subject was the reinvigoration of idealism. What form can idealism take for architects who remain as deeply skeptical of utopianism as they are embarrassed by venality? Small, local forms, this show proposed, forms that envision progress not as the complete overhaul of the physical world but on the scale of daily life, the "Jacobsian" scale on which it is pointless to speak of idealism if you are the sort of person who resents making contact with the neighbors.

At the heart of the show was a paradox: architects were asked to design practical solutions for real sites, as though a contractor were waiting to translate their drawings into buildings. To go along with this premise, however, was to produce architectural fiction; there were, after all, no cement mixers waiting to move onto the sites, no bulldozers, no city officials standing by with contracts and work permits. Many of the architects simply ignored the paradox and produced painstakingly practical, bare-bones designs, fully costed out, in strict conformity with zoning regulations, devoid of any stylistic flourishes that might scare off a city bureaucrat. Others took the position that, given the odds of roughly seven proposals per site and no philanthropist waiting in the wings, it was more "realistic" to assume that these projects would never get off the drawing board. For these architects, the drawing itself became the medium to communicate a message on the exhibition's theme.

In some of these projects, Frampton's polarity between "art" architecture and social action collapsed into a form of agitprop poster architecture. Yann Andre Leroy's project, for example, flattened the "building" (its forms inspired by those of early Soviet Constructivists) into a backdrop for a graphically depicted scene of urban brutality: a group of New York City cops, looming like storm troopers, surround the body of a fallen victim—of racial attack? mugging? overdose? hypothermia? The drawing's polemic force lay in its inversion of the classic "artist's rendering" of new civic projects, in which cheerful citizens are depicted radiant with the joy that the building has brought into their lives. Leroy's drawing is a warning against raising utopian expectations.

But it was Gustavo Bonevardi and Lee Ledbetter's project for housing homeless people with AIDS, one of the "practical" designs, that offered a good case study in the problems and the opportunities generated by the show as a whole. The architects conceived the building as the prototype for a projected network of facilities to be built at various sites throughout the city, a system that would allow people with AIDS to continue to live in or near their own neighborhoods, instead of dispatching them to a hospital. Each of these residences would house up to twelve people, in private rooms, with balconies overlooking a rear garden. Common rooms and offices for nursing staff would face the street; the front part of the building containing these rooms could be modified in size, proportion, and materials to adopt the neighborhood's existing architectural context.

Rational, modular, crisply Modern, the design looked at first glance as unprepossessing as the graphics on generic supermarket packaging. It was the title of the project that delivered the initial jolt—the kind of jolt you instinctively ward off with humor. Homeless people with AIDS? Wasn't that taking the idea of special "use groups" to the point of comic overkill, like *Vampire Lesbians of Sodom*? But the problem is no laughing matter; in fact, just around the corner from the theater where *Vampire Lesbians* is regaling audiences for its "3rd Laff Year," a man sat sprawled on the sidewalk for two days last winter, a hand-lettered sign between his knees introducing him to passersby as a HOMELESS PWA. City officials estimate that there are four hundred homeless PWAs in New York: people who can no longer work and pay rent, people who've been thrown out by their partners, people without families to go home to.

Though the problem is real and the solution practical, Bonevardi and Ledbetter's design was perhaps no more "realistic" than the impractically visionary projects in the Vacant Lots show. Given the glacial speed with which city projects come into being, it may be more realistic to hope that researchers will develop effective treatments for AIDS years before this building would open its doors. Additional delays would no doubt arise from the kind of community resistance encountered by private physicians who treat AIDS outpatients. Moreover, the city already provides rent stipends and home care services for PWAs, and these services, rather than architecture, may be the most effective way to address the problem the architects set for themselves.

But there is more than one way to be practical. Suppose you are an architect. If you live in New York, there's a good chance that you know more than one person who is sick with AIDS or has already died. You also know that AIDS is not only a disease but a cultural crisis, a crisis of faith in our power and will to solve problems and even to recognize them. So what are you going to do about it? You can perform the acts of any conscientious citizen: write your congressman, make out a check. That may be enough, but what if it isn't? Your work is what defines the shape of the place you occupy in the cultural scheme of things. It is that place you want to dedicate to the resolution of this crisis.

There was a hush in the room when Bonevardi, Ledbetter, and their consultants got up to present their work at an evening forum sponsored by the League last November. Perhaps it was because the PA system was bad that night; but there may also have been a collective recognition that this presentation marked an important moment in architecture. Two architects, acting on their own initiative, had stood up and asserted the obligation of their art to address a critical area of their lives. The considerable work devoted to this project—the consultation with planners, psychologists, doctors, social workers, hospice specialists, the hours at the drawing board—had all gone into the articulation of this demand. The demand by itself could not resolve the crisis it addressed: it could not, on paper, house one person with AIDS, much less cure him. But neither was this a private fantasy with no power to affect the world of practical reality. It dealt concretely with an aspect of the suffering to which people with AIDS are subject.

Those whose lives have been affected by this disease live in a separate world, a world that is collapsing, while the world outside, the world now called euphemistically "the general population," a world to which one belonged only yesterday, goes about its business. To inhabit this separate world, to live behind this wall, is to witness one's suffering converted into issues, one's hope for survival into the material that furnishes the others with their posters, their news, their columns, their opinion polls. The strength of Bonevardi and Ledbetter's design lay in symbolically breaking through this thickening wall of stigma, reminding us, as Poe did, of the moral doom invited by those who imagine themselves protected by such walls. The architects offered their response on a practical, not a metaphorical, level; yet the breached wall can stand as a metaphor for what the Vacant Lots show achieved. The architects of all the projects were saying that they too are trapped by the walls of privilege they have been designing, walled up alive by their own projections of Top Dog values.

This is scarcely the first time architects have been caught in this trap. Architecture has traditionally been the art of making privilege visible, which is why angry mobs attack palaces: the Bourbons', the Romanovs', Marcos's, Trump's. Attacking walls is one of the most potent symbolic forms we use to renegotiate the social contract. The difference today is that Modernism was thought to have delivered architects from the contract that once firmly bound them to the privileged client; the Modern contract made architects responsible for initiating visions from which the forms of buildings would ultimately arise.

"Go away! We don't want your yuppie high-rise!" To judge from the graffiti scrawled on the construction fences surrounding new building sites, the vacant lot in the city is itself a symbol, in many neighborhoods, of a community's determination to control its own destiny. The Vacant Lots show was the architecture community's version of those angry painted messages. Many architects, it turns out, don't want their own high-rises either. They're fed up with hanging balconies off a forty-story box and calling it a dream come true. They are tired of seeing "quality architecture" billed as a luxury amenity, up there with twenty-four-hour concierge service and the rooftop health club. Well, we may say, isn't that a shame. We don't want your yuppie mea culpas. We don't want idealism to be just another appetizing item on the grazing menu at the grand café. How is the architecture community's collective frustration going to house a single person? The answer is that it won't. But without recognizing and voicing that frustration there is little hope that architects can resume responsibility for breathing life into ideals.

April 11, 1988

THE PERILS OF PUBLIC ART

This past May some three thousand members of the American Institute of Architects gathered in New York City for a three-day conference devoted, at least in title, to the theme of Art in Architecture. Actually, this was the usual boilerplate affair, with workshops on structural technologies, lighting systems, and client relations, interspersed with guided tours, addresses from local dignitaries, and nights out on the town to see *Phantom* and *Les Miz*. Still, that the AIA chose this particular theme was significant. But what did it signify?

On the bottom line, the line on which professional groups tend to congregate, "Art in Architecture" meant "Paintings and Sculptures in Buildings"—a more or less literal allusion to the emergence of the art museum as the glamour project of the 1980s. And, like the boom in museum building, the allusion also no doubt reflected the inflation of contemporary art as the supreme status commodity among architecture's client class—and the parallel tendency among many architects today to represent themselves to the public as artists, not just boring old businessmen or would-be social engineers. Art in Architecture connoted art as architecture's inner essence, the secret heart of a profession traditionally governed by more practical concerns.

What all these connotations add up to is an amplification of the idea that a new harmony has recently grown up between the fields of art and architecture, an epochal development that deserves to be heralded as a new Renaissance. Instead of functioning as architecture's unmanageable Other, its rambunctious id, its visual or conceptual foil (the Henry Moore sculpture plopped down on the plaza outside the glass slab tower), art has finally reunited with architecture in a spirit of blissful reconciliation.

The most conspicuous issue of this happy union is public art. Today sculptors are eagerly collaborating with architects to produce lobby and street furniture of museum quality. Painters are mounting ladders to create murals in high-rises all over town. Whole waterfronts are being

reclaimed from urban blight by inspired partnerships between city planners and site-specific artists. Such projects were the major focus of Architectural Art: Affirming the Design Relationship, an exhibition organized
by the American Craft Museum to coincide with the AIA's conference.

Quite a few worthwhile projects were on display in Architectural Art,
but at the service of a lamentable idea; for, like the Feel-Good Era in
national politics, the new harmony between art and architecture paints a
picture that conceals more than it tells. At the Equitable Center in Manhattan (street furniture by Scott Burton, mural by Roy Lichtenstein,
changing exhibitions by the Whitney Museum of American Art) the
alliance between art and architecture was from its inception a business
partnership, a corporate merger designed to persuade prospective tenants
to pay premium rents outside the high-rent district. More recently, when
the city sued developers of another high-rise for exceeding the height
allowed by local zoning, the developers turned to Art (in this case, a suite
of dance studios) in a successful campaign to weaken the city's resolve to
enforce its own laws. In such cases, Art in Architecture begins to look
something like Jonah inside the whale; it becomes little more than a particularly flavorful chunk at the feast of urban development.

Yet it is not quite fair to blame architects for this kind of deception.
Not the architect, or the artist, or even the developer is responsible for
art's usefulness as a means of bestowing prestige on commercial enterprises. Moreover, to limit criticism, as some writers do, to the economic
underpinnings of public art projects, as though this constituted a radical
exposé, is itself a kind of deception, since it can blind us to other reasons
why artists and architects have been gravitating toward each other in
recent years. If the relationship between art and architecture has changed,
it is in large part due to a change in the cultural mythologies that have
shaped the contours of these two fields and defined the boundaries
between them.

According to these myths, architects are responsible for articulating
the normative structure of a society, while the artist speaks for the individual mind. The artist's job is to give access to a subjective realm, to carve
out a unique place in the world of competing, individual selves. The architect's highest calling, on the other hand, is to identify visual and spatial
codes that transcend the subjective perceptions of our separate selves.
Together, art and architecture form an antithetical relationship, the classic
opposition of individual to society.

But this division of cultural labor has been challenged by developments
that have been taking place in art and architecture for some time. We
value the city today not for its architectural embodiment of normative values but, on the contrary, for its capacity to hold before our eyes differences

in the ways societies and social groups have structured individual units of urban space that, together, make up a complex urban whole. Since 1966, when Robert Venturi published *Complexity and Contradiction in Architecture*, many architects have followed Venturi's preference "for messy vitality over obvious unity."

On the other side, ever since Andy Warhol named his studio the Factory, artists have been working to dismantle the hierarchy of autonomy, originality, alienation, individual genius, and other myths of Romantic and Modern art. And it is artists, not architects, who have most nearly approximated the architectural ideal of establishing a flexible framework for social cohesion within the unstable urban world. Art districts like SoHo and the East Village are social magnets for this reason, despite our misgivings about conformity in the art world, our nostalgic laments for the days when artists felt comfortable only in alienation from the crowd.

Of course, the mythologies built up around such ideas as genius and norm, and the opposition between them, are not easily shed. As Norbert Elias observed, the roots of the individual/society antithesis lie "at the foundation of philosophical theories of perception and knowledge." The old Romantic myths remain deeply embedded in today's art world, its economic structure, and the public expectations that support it. What artist is willing to forswear the opportunity of being called a genius? What collector wants to eliminate the chance of having one of them to dinner? Nor are the vast majority of the architects who convened in New York in May poised to abandon their traditional mission to formalize collective social values; to do so would be to break the social contract from which their authority as a profession still derives. The public is not clamoring for architects to fill up cities with monuments to their idiosyncratic visions, and Prince Charles is hardly the only outspoken advocate for community design. Artists and architects who do question the validity of these ideologies thus find themselves staring at each other from opposite sides of a cultural impasse, mutually dependent on the wall that divides them even as they attempt to undermine its foundations.

Ten years or so ago, the appeal of public art was that it seemed to offer a way out of this impasse. The way led to a fallow field but not a new one; the boosterish rhetoric that has come to surround public art is similar in tone to that which launched the City Beautiful movement a century ago. Then, as now, collaborations between architects, sculptors, and landscape designers were hailed as evidence of an American Renaissance, symbols of urban America's cultural coming of age. Beyond the similarity of rhetoric, however, there is a fundamental difference between the two movements. City Beautiful artists viewed the public as a uniform mass with a common

cultural heritage and shared civic values. Public artists today tend to operate with little clear sense of what "the public" is or what its values are, and
with even less confidence in their right to prescribe what those values
ought to be.

The key, problematic word in "public art" is not *art* but *public*. Just as
twentieth-century art has frequently addressed the question What is art?
so public art has asked, What is the public? What is a public at a time
when we are uncomfortably conscious of the differences that divide us
into subcultures, when we have grown to mistrust those forces (media
homogenization, psychotherapeutic authority, consumer marketing,
including the marketing of art and culture) that would flatten the differences into a spurious unity or, worse, a genuine unity? It is through questions, rather than through aesthetic ideas, that public art has most deeply
engaged us.

Sometimes the engagement is deliberate. In *Running Fence* by Christo
(who pioneered in this field), the function of the physical art object—
a nylon ribbon looping over the hills of Northern California—was to disclose the social process involved in its making. How do you raise money to
construct a project on the scale of public works with no apparent social
utility? How do you get permission to build it? How do you turn community resistance into public support?

Maya Lin's Vietnam Veterans' Memorial, in Washington, D.C., com-
memorates two tragedies, one of fate, one of folly: the loss of those killed
in the war, and the enlargement of that loss by the government's determination to foist a spurious national unity ("American will") on a divided
nation and a changing world. Lin's abstract form declines to turn the public into an abstraction. The dead are represented by their own names. The
public is represented as itself, reflected in the black granite: veterans, war
resisters, relatives, tourists, whoever shows up on a given day to pay
witness.

Richard Serra's *Tilted Arc*, placed in the courtyard of Federal Plaza in
Lower Manhattan, prompted the office workers who daily trudged
through the plaza to petition for the sculpture's removal. Hearings held to
debate the issue in 1985 amounted to a bankruptcy proceeding against the
antithesis between individual and society on which the artist based his
case. Serra presented himself as a virtual Noble Savage, complete with
blue-collar background, as if this somehow certified his authority to represent "the people." What many of the (mostly white-collar) workers
resented was not Serra's aesthetics but his manipulative social psychology:
provoking "the public" into rejecting him, then losing his temper when it
did so.

Yet it is possible to be grateful to Serra for providing relief from the bland, predictable pieties of the growing public art industry. There is now a well-entrenched network of artists who work exclusively in this field, good government types who champion it, and art critics at considerable pains to distinguish public art from public relations. As the same familiar faces turn up repeatedly at conferences on public art and juries that award commissions, it is easy to arrive at the opinion that this field has been drastically overcultivated and should be returned to its fallow state for at least another century.

But one project worth watching in the months ahead is notable because its four collaborators do not carry the customary public art credentials, though they are gifted luminaries in their own fields: Henry Smith-Miller and Laurie Hawkinson (architects), Barbara Kruger (artist), and Nicholas Quinnell (landscape architect). Last January this team entered a national competition to create a new park on 164 acres of rolling, partly wooded landscape on the outskirts of Raleigh, North Carolina. Their winning entry, entitled Imperfect Utopia, was singled out because it promised to introduce critical thinking in place of the usual platitudes.

As it happens, the site in its present state offers a field day for post-structuralist excavations. One side is bordered by a suburban housing development of the 1960s, the proverbial little houses made of ticky-tacky whose mass production flattened Frank Lloyd Wright's suburban dream into a caricature of individual sovereignty. On the other side is a prison, or as we now say, a correctional facility, an architectural machine for processing individuals who have failed to curtail their sovereignty within socially approved boundaries. Horses graze on the site, but as wards of the nearby state agricultural school these poignant reminders of Arcadia are as much a part of industrial life as the cars speeding down the highway that abuts their pasture. And at the center of this suburban vista squats the North Carolina Museum of Art, a Modern clunk designed in 1976 by the office of Edward Durell Stone.

With its blank, fortresslike walls, its green *cordon sanitaire* of clipped golf course grass, the museum building embodies the idea of art as something isolated, set apart from its surroundings and from the history that produced it. This conception—the idea that Civilization must be protected from civilization—is not shared by the museum's present administration. They have commissioned the new park to reconfigure physically and conceptually the museum's relationship to its urbanized context. Imperfect Utopia is public art about a public art museum. It asks, What is the place of an art institution at a time when the walls between high and low art have become, at most, a set of movable partitions? How can such an institution physically embody the rapid shifts of context in which we are now willing to recognize art's pleasant and unpleasant eruptions: a carving on a rock, a saxophonist on the subway platform, an environmental artist moving tons of earth around in a remote corner of the desert?

What the design team is proposing in response to these questions is closer in concept to a set of city zoning ordinances than a traditional architect's master plan. Instead of envisioning permanent structures, what the team calls The Document will set forth guidelines for programming the site for a variety of changing cultural and horticultural uses. Visual artists, performers, architects, curators, and others who want to use the site will occupy the role of "developers"; the museum administration, guided by The Document, will function as a kind of planning board.

This is not the sort of park that preservationists will feel obliged to protect from the onslaughts of crass concessionaries. Landscaping and signs (designed by Kruger) are being developed not, in the Olmsted manner, to simulate a primordial landscape that culture has spoiled, but to show, through a geography of the site's past and present uses (agricultural, scientific, economic, aesthetic), that nature, too, has a social history. The title "Imperfect Utopia" alludes to the experience of the sixteenth-century English explorers of this territory who soon discovered the difference between idealized European views of the New Virginia and the harsh realities of taking up residence in that "natural paradise" (including the reality of their population being decimated by members of the culture whose home it already was). Cars will park in a grove of trees; the horses will not be banned.

This may well be the sort of project that offends those still hoping to preserve the sanctity of the museum from outside onslaughts. It is an open question whether the new poststructuralist dispensation will produce something worth replacing the old borders between nature, culture, art, and life. As far as the designers of this project are concerned, the question should remain open indefinitely: "to have no end in sight" is one of the objectives set forth in their proposal. Even so, it is possible to see that somewhere down the line the park could turn into an aesthetic Hooverville, with busloads of craftspeople covering the lawns with handmade belts and "You Gotta Have Art" T-shirts. It's one thing when Kruger violates the pseudosanctity of the commercial art gallery with slogans like "I shop therefore I am" that call attention to art's traffic with commerce. But does the museum stand to benefit from a similar critique? What museum doesn't already boast one or more gift shops and a flock of peddlers and street performers gathered about the gates? I think we're justified in asking whether it's a gain to know that a festival atmosphere has been programmed by planners acquainted with Foucault and Baudrillard—though I also think that the museum has shown vision in inviting this quartet to sprout a few ideas on the instability of art's position in a built-up world.

August 8 and 15, 1988

THE LEANING TOWER OF THEORY

1988 has been a very good year for 1968. From cover stories in *Time* and *Life* to features in *Artforum* and *Artscribe*, the media have declared the year's enduring importance, and their interpretations of its meaning for us have been more or less the same. The system survived in 1968. It absorbed the shocks, it withstood the attacks on its integrity. If you live at the *Artforum* end of the world, this message is stated with a twinge of regret; over at *Time*, it is cause for relief.

Deconstructivist Architecture is the Museum of Modern Art's inadvertent tribute to 1968. In its presentation of the work of seven contemporary architects, in the way it leads the viewer to experience this work, the show is an exceedingly handsome display of the architectural system's ability to absorb concerted attacks on its integrity. Here "the system" consists of Philip Johnson, the Museum of Modern Art, and the doctrine of formalism that these two venerable institutions have been propounding for more than fifty years. The "attackers," who here appear in the unexpected public role of collaborators, are Frank Gehry, Peter Eisenman, Coop Himmelb(l)au, Daniel Libeskind, Bernard Tschumi, Rem Koolhaas, and Zaha Hadid.

The show is presented in three small galleries, of which the first is devoted to examples of Russian Constructivist architecture, borrowed from the museum's own collection, and presented here as formal antecedents for the contemporary work that follows. Exposed trusses, skewed and tilted planes, twisted structural frames, projecting beams and columns: this vocabulary proposed the building not as a product but as a process, analogous to the building of a new society. In the years just after the revolution, Constructivist projects articulated not simply a building's structure, but also the eruption of a new order into the world of tradition that the revolution had set out to overthrow.

The new work selected for this show has been chosen on the basis of its formal resemblance to these projects. Covering a ten-year span, the ten projects on view range in scale from Gehry's home in Santa Monica, remodeled initially in 1978, to Tschumi's Parc de la Villette, now nearing completion in Paris. The show includes projects that display a conscious intention to recall Constructivist forms (Hadid's design for a private club in Hong Kong), those that utilize Constructivist elements as part of a larger composition (Koolhaas's 1982 apartment building and observation tower for Rotterdam), along with work that, like the Gehry house, provokes an unintended echo of the Russian avant-garde.

MoMA's coverage of contemporary architecture has been desultory in recent decades. The late Arthur Drexler, longtime director of the museum's department of architecture and design, made no secret of his animosity toward the Postmodern movement. This new work explodes into the sacred precincts of Good Design with the force of pent-up energy. There is not a dud in the bunch. Yet this is a show that, for better or worse, is different than the sum of its distinguished parts. And, decidedly for the worse, it is a show whose rationale, indeed whose purpose, is to suppress all evidence of that difference in the name of form.

A wall plaque at the entrance to the show reminds us that architecture is a "conservative institution," one that traditionally seeks "to sustain the central cultural values of stability, harmony, and security, of comfort, order, and unity." No news here; architecture wasn't called the gentleman's art for nothing. The news is that the work we are about to see represents a historic break with this conservative tradition. These projects "mark the emergence of a new sensibility in architecture. They radically displace traditional ideas about the nature of the architectural object." A bit inflated, but never mind: the majority of the projects on view at the Modern are indeed among the most challenging of our time, worth almost any amount of hoopla, especially after the museum's long silence. More's the pity, then, that what is truly challenging about this work has been neutralized by as conservative a brand of architectural thinking as you are likely to find outside Colonial Williamsburg.

There's an innate conservatism operating in the very idea of such a show. Obviously, it is pointless to assemble a diverse group of visual objects into a coherent collection without undertaking to isolate the visual characteristics they share. But to formulate normative criteria for projects that are designed to resist normative values runs the risk of undermining the ideas that brought them into being in the first place. The organizers should have recognized this risk and attempted to counteract it. Instead they have taken every opportunity to augment it. For example, they did not have to enlist Philip Johnson, the premier power broker in the architectural profession, to serve as curator, and thus mock the idea that this work radically challenges established values. Nor did they have to devote one-third of the exhibition to the authority of historical precedent, and thus risk obliterating the difference between these architects and the Postmodern historicists whose work they bitterly oppose. Perhaps the show's organizers feel that all this pandering to the status quo is irrelevant to the show's success or failure, since they claim that what is radical about this work resides not in its context, but in the autonomous realm of architectural form; but that claim is the most reactionary part of the whole spectacle.

Here is a summary of the thesis propounded by Mark Wigley, the show's associate curator and the author of the catalog essay that introduces this new work to MoMA's audience. Architects have "always" sought to create an architecture of "pure form based on the inviolate integrity of simple geometric figures." It is through the use of these pure forms that architects have sustained the "central cultural values" of order, stability, unity, and so on. For a brief period in the early twentieth century, this conservative tradition of cultural stability was shattered by the skewed geometric compositions of the Russian Constructivists. Ultimately, the Russian avant-garde shrank back from pushing their assault on pure form into fully realized buildings. But their attack left a wound that was covered up, but not healed, by the Modern movement's return to formal purity. In the past ten years, the architects in this show have uncovered this wound and exposed the impurity and the instability repressed beneath the sleek, taut skin of the canonical modern building. The aim of these architects is not, like the Postmodernists, to overthrow Modernism but rather "to infect" the Modern tradition, to "contaminate" it from within the center of orthodox practice.

What's this thing Wigley has about impurity? The impure seems to hold for him the kind of fetishist value that purity often holds in other extremist ideologies of culture, race, and religion, and I find it just as creepy. His thinking is saturated throughout with a rapturous disregard for the world and its present conditions, and even for the meaning of the work he claims to interpret. It is true that Modern architects have often projected into the world designs of geometric purity. But the origins of this tradition are not lost to us in the mists of eternal time. It was a project of French eighteenth-century architects to use geometric forms to get free representation, and they used these forms not to affirm traditional order but to challenge it. That is why their work came to be known as revolutionary classicism. Their impulse did not arise from within "the center" of architectural practice. It migrated to architecture from the tracts of Enlightenment philosophers whose ideal of reason, opposed to the status quo, architects then sought to embody.

Nor do the ideas with which Wigley promotes the doctrine of impure form arise from the center of architectural practice (or, for that matter, from Russia during the teens). They have drifted into his impressionable mind from poststructural philosophy as it developed in Paris following the student uprisings of 1968: buzzwords like strategy, agent, intervention, subversion, undermine, disrupt, extremity, enigma; *prêt-à-penser* modes like the ecstasy over instability and the collapse of meaning; the intoxicating idea that distinctions need not be made between wishes and achievements, between assertions and facts; the stimulating thought that a misreading of history is a creative act.

I am not one of those who think that poststructuralism is phony or worthless. But the sad thing about poststructuralism, as the painter Izhar Patkin remarked to me recently, is that what could have been a valuable tool for analysis ended up instead as just another means of production, a mechanism for grinding out dissertations, pictures, art criticisms, careers. We're supposed to admire this production because of its theory's rigor, but a good deal of the writing turned out by the theory machine since the deaths of Barthes and Foucault is what I call "wigor"—rigor with a rubbery kind of wiggle. Wigor is to intellectual discipline what Barbara Walters is to journalism: an aura of penetrating inquiry wrapped around a fawning over stars.

In the shifting twilight zone of wigorous thinking, it is easy to slip into amnesia and forget that the forms of the seventeenth-century Baroque (read: irregular, misshapen, imperfect) were used to construct the most authoritarian, centralized architecture the West has ever known. And it is easy to persuade yourself that an imperfect shape is somehow something other than pure form. But where are the impure forms? A circle with a bite taken out of it is no less a figure of pure form than a perfect circle. Wigley writes that these buildings derive their power from the tension between pure and impure form.

It happens that much of the work in this show does build on tension between visual form and other kinds of information. To name but a few of these sources (they are not just speculations on my part): Frank Gehry has absorbed information from the architectural "cuttings" of Gordon Matta-Clark, the fragmented sociology of Southern California tract housing, and the personal narratives of his clients. Peter Eisenman has drawn from a succession of theorists, including Chomsky and Derrida, and from contemporary American sculptors, including Sol LeWitt and Richard Serra. Bernard Tschumi is drawn not only to "the enigma" but also to detection, as in Hollywood thrillers and the stories of Poe. Daniel Libeskind's work reflects his acute interest in the phenomenology of Husserl, and in Husserl's analysis of the origins of geometry in land surveying. Even Zaha

Hadid's work, which is the most strictly formal in the show, derives not internally from the center of architecture but externally from history: from a period of architecture from which she is separated by a century, half a continent, and one or two belief systems.

All of this information has been withheld, however, both in the exhibition and in its theory-drunk catalog. And what has been lost in the process is not just the individual histories of these architects and their projects but, more important, the message that they collectively propose. In his 1981 book, *Between Zero and Infinity*, Libeskind stated the message clearly. He stands opposed to the conception of "architecture as autonomous and self-referential discipline, inventing its own tradition through mute monuments." Instead, he proposes to follow an approach that "seeks to explore the deeper order rooted not only in visible forms, but in the invisible and hidden sources which nourish culture itself, in its thought, art, literature, song, and movement." The idea is not that buildings should be little essays on philosophy or movies, or frozen string quartets. It is that a building embodies a crossroads of the channels of information that the architect drew upon to arrive at its form. Like the grid of streets that define its physical location, the building stands at an intersection of ideas that neither begin nor end with its visual form. Meet me at Hollywood and Quine.

In his model for City Edge, an office and residential project for Berlin that resembles a mammoth, squared-off obelisk in the process of being raised to an upright position, Libeskind tried to convey this approach with a collaged surface made of fragments of printed text. But in MoMA's neutral, white gallery space, bereft even of identifying labels, the effect is a bit silly, like a present of scotch that you'd wrapped up in newsprint because you ran out of proper gift wrap.

Of course, the man in the street would not have labels to consult either. What's the point of all this information if it is not available to the innocent eye? Part of the answer is that, for Libeskind, there is no innocent eye. To a pedestrian walking in the Tiergarten, City Edge might well look like a bunch of old newspapers flying in the wind, and in time perhaps it could become known and cherished as the Flying Newspaper Building, just as Gaudí's Casa Milà became popularly known in Barcelona as la Pedrera, the Quarry, because it resembles a pile of stones. Libeskind's approach accommodates this. He works consciously with the fact that a building's design is only one chapter of its history, that another chapter begins when it goes up and begins to acquire a mutable symbolism from the projections of observers. City Edge is about that process of contextual weaving— about making architecture open to ideas.

. . .

I think it's all right, probably even for Peter Eisenman, to look at Eisenman's Biocenter for Frankfurt University and say: What a wild, crazy building. But we don't need a museum catalog to tell us, in so many wigorous words, that "this is a wild, crazy building." To understand why the facility's research pavilions appear to be piling up on one another like a demolition derby, it would be useful to know of Eisenman's unwillingness, in the nuclear age, to transmit intact the Enlightenment rule of reason, of which both research science and canonical modernism are cultural heirs; his reluctance to create a rational architecture to house a compulsive activity with potentially mad effects; and his quirky desire to insinuate his private psychoanalytic history into his public persona. We may not agree with Eisenman that science has lost credibility, that meanings and values have lost their moorings, or that architecture is the appropriate means to correct the path of reason gone bananas, but at least we should see that this is not depleted post-Enlightenment formalism, that the madness behind the madness was Eisenman's.

You can make any object look autonomous if you cut away the connective tissue that links it to other ideas. This has been standard operating procedure at the Museum of Modern Art for years. Take an object, drain away its meaning, and hold up this empty husk as though you'd delivered its precious essence. What that leaves us with, in the case of this show, is a collection of exotic-looking figurines, and the strong impression that what has emerged here is not the stifled subversiveness of Constructivism but the English Baroque tradition of adorning pleasure parks with sham pagodas.

Yet this work is not about pagodas, enigmas, and empty containers. It is about reclaiming the critical function that the use of geometric form once connoted. In substituting geometry for historically derived forms, French architects wanted to drain away meanings that supported the hierarchical authority of architecture's traditional patrons. And many architects today, including most of those represented here, have been trying to flush the values of formalism out of forms for *precisely* the same reason: these values are no longer neutral, they are the style of the corporate world. They are the values that permitted Philip Johnson, in his International Style show in 1932, to gut the social aims of Modern architecture, and promote its forms as a new standard of elite taste.

It isn't a crime to make beautiful forms without complex ideas behind them. I don't see much theoretical intensity in Zaha Hadid's work, but her visual intelligence is acute. Hadid's elegant, idiosyncratic graphic style has already made her the Michael Graves of the '80s, an architect exercising wide influence through drawings alone. Students at architecture schools everywhere are adept at making simulated Zahas. And Hadid will not remain a paper architect for long; of the younger architects represented in this show, she seems likely to make the swiftest advance into the world of corporate architecture.

But why insist that her work is subversive? At Bleecker Bob's around the corner, T-shirts emblazoned with early Soviet agitprop designs have been a hot item for several years. Those bold black and red Cyrillic letters look great twisting down the block to the beat of ghetto blasters, and Hadid could make a terrific tower to rise above them. When I say that she has more in common with those kids than with Tatlin, I mean it as a compliment. Why must Johnson and Wigley deny that what we're looking at is a style? Why not just come out and say: It's a style! It's fabu! Because that would really sully the purity of this formalist game, that's why.

Anyone familiar with the wiles of wigor has met the logic that it is good to do a bad show, because of all the attention it will provoke; and the view that it's OK to package work as formalist even if you know better, because who goes to a museum for anything but packaging anyhow, aren't we smart to be working within the system, and what does criticism matter, so long as they spell the names right. Cynicism? Hey, man, we're into a whole new episteme.

August 29, 1988

THE LIE OF THE LAND

Soon, when the vines begin to spread their leaves over walls and columns, softening the raw look of freshly poured concrete, San Antonio's new Lucille Halsell Conservatory will grow into the design its architect envisioned. Even as it looks now, however, Emilio Ambasz's first major building is recognizably a milestone in contemporary architecture. With Postmodern historicism collapsing back into history, and deconstructivism fitfully subsiding beneath the featherweight of its theories, many architects today—including some linked to these two movements—have begun looking to landscape to refresh their vision. Ambasz's dramatically landscaped building rises like an early settlement on this new conceptual terrain.

In appearance, the conservatory is more settlement than building: a complex of variously shaped enclosures half-sunk into the Texas soil like some hybrid village of the Stone Age and the Space Age. At a distance, the conservatory complex presents a sparkling, crystalline skyline of aluminum and glass pyramids and truncated cones, but to enter this deceptively Modern space the visitor plunges through an opening in a rough stone wall into the bowels of the earth primeval. No other exterior walls define this as "a building." Instead, the land has been bulldozed into a three-acre earthen container whose edges blend seamlessly with the surrounding landscape of San Antonio's thirty-three-acre Botanical Gardens. What lies beyond that wall is an essay on the relationship of nature to civilization, and on the power of architecture to define that relationship.

The first space a visitor walks into is a cylindrical outdoor room occupied by a single tree (at present a California fan palm), eloquent with symbolic significance in its solitude and its circular surroundings; this is the tree on which the idea of "shelter" first was hung, the first post, the tree commemorated in the leafy capitals of Egyptian and Greek columns. The room cues us that in this conservatory we are not just going to see plants, we will be touring a metaphysical reflection on how we see plants, on how the ways in which we perceive the environment constitute an initial form of our power to transform the surface of the earth.

From this opening statement, the conservatory's grand circuit progresses along an arcade surrounding an open trapezoidal courtyard, an arrangement adapted from traditional architecture of the Southwest. The courtyard is bordered by five enclosed rooms (lit by the metal and glass skylights that compose the "skyline" you see from outside), each with a different climate to support a variety of flora ranging from tall desert cacti to rare tropical ferns. The rooms themselves also range considerably in design—from the fern room's artificial grotto, complete with waterfall, fog machine, and imitation rock walls of molded fiberglass, to a soaring glass palm house that terminates the conservatory's formal axis with a cathedral-like reach toward the sky. In the center of the courtyard, a free-form pool reflects the sky amid clusters of aquatic flowers. Soil, light, water: the elements of natural creation are brought together in symbolic amorphousness at the heart of this finely tuned, man-made structure.

Like the building, the career of forty-four-year-old Emilio Ambasz has taken time to grow. *Creation Is a Patient Search*, the title of a book by Le Corbusier, could also summarize the calm deliberation with which Ambasz has followed his singular path in the era of Postmodern glitz. Forty-four may not be so advanced an age for an architect to build his first major work, but Ambasz has been a prominent figure in the architectural community for nearly two decades. As curator of design at the Museum of Modern Art in the early 1970s, Ambasz organized exhibitions that stressed the possibilities for continuing evolution within the Modern tradition. His show on Italian design in 1972, and the one on Luis Barragán in 1974, showed how sumptuous Modern design could be if it would only forget about the brain and concentrate on the body; if it were willing to be playful, to be sensuous, to relax in the sun for a while and exchange its bleak white pallor for a tan and some tropical colors.

Since 1976, when he left the museum to start his own firm, Ambasz has achieved success as an industrial designer of objects ranging from manual shavers to diesel engines. But his reputation in the architectural community is based largely on a series of unbuilt projects notable for the introduction of landscape as an architectural (perhaps, more strictly, an anti-architectural) element: private houses carved into the earth, a flotilla of museum galleries floating on a lagoon, an urban plaza sunk beneath an eye-level canopy of the tops of trees. Ambasz has written that his use of landscape reflects the need "for finding ways of gracefully relating and juxtaposing the artificial to the natural," a search for "the roots of a genuinely balanced architecture as a form of man-made nature."

It was the strength of these unrealized projects that led the San Antonio administrators to call upon Ambasz three years ago for a proposal for the new conservatory. The choice was, as they say, inspired; it's exciting to see an architect make the transition from theory to practice. And yet the irony is that the very particulars that made Ambasz an excellent choice for this project turn out to be disadvantages in clarifying what his architecture is about. For one thing, since a conservatory, unlike a museum or a research facility, is inherently about nature, Ambasz's use of nature here loses much of its polemical thrust. We know from his writing that for Ambasz the use of earth walls signifies the "elimination of architecture," but in the context of a botanical garden, such a reading becomes absurd: even half-buried, his conservatory has introduced into this natural setting the most assertively "architectural" presence for miles around.

Moreover, the traditional landscaping of the surrounding gardens makes one acutely conscious that Ambasz's rooms lack the enveloping lushness that the word *conservatory* traditionally conjures up. When you enter the classic greenhouse, your feet crunch on gravel, you inhale the mossy scent of damp earth, you push aside a palm frond and step onto a path that invites exploration. That sense of invitation is missing here. In most of the rooms, you enter onto a wide concrete apron that runs the full length of the space. And because the planting beds are set on raised tiers, you can see the entire scheme laid out before you when you walk inside; there's no incentive of surprise to lure you on. Even in the fern room, with its tropical mists, the path is fully visible from the entrance; the image of lushness does not blossom into the space it occupies. When the conservatory's concrete surfaces are covered with vines, the impression will be lusher, but the surfaces will still be flat.

Ambasz may have thought that to bury the entire complex beneath the earth would provide an abundant sense of natural enclosure, but in fact, though the image of excavated earth reads strongly when you are on the hillside looking down into the courtyard, from within the complex itself you don't have that much awareness of the bermed earth outside. You could be inside almost any building on a normal grade level. These effects may not be miscalculations. Ambasz did not set out to create Adventure-land, or the kind of fairy-tale winter garden that has become the cliché of corporate lobbies and hotel atriums across the country. I doubt it was his intention that we should feel buried. Still, I suspect that, as an architect long accustomed to working on the scale of models and drawings, he may have overestimated our ability to retain a design concept in memory as we progress through different kinds of space.

What is bound to be a more serious problem for some observers, however, is that, for all its focus on nature, this building is maddeningly indifferent to the environmental crisis inevitably evoked by that very focus. That is the central paradox raised by Ambasz's work as a whole. Ambasz didn't mastermind the greenhouse effect, didn't organize a conspiracy to fill last summer's newspapers with headlines on quarantined beaches, ozone holes, depleted rain forests, and Third World outrage over American plans to dump our garbage on foreign soil. But, with his first new building now completed and a major retrospective of his entire work due this February at the Museum of Modern Art, his timing could not have been better. For it isn't only battle fatigue over the "Style Wars" that has driven architects to start looking at land—and at Ambasz, an architect who's been patiently tilling the land for some years. It is also the growing awareness that they can no longer afford to look at the earth as a roll of tracing paper that can be thrown into the wastebasket when we goof up.

The San Antonio conservatory will do little, however, to establish Ambasz as the answer to the Sierra Club's prayers. Yes, the earth walls will save energy costs. Take, for instance, the Alpine Window, the first display you come to after that initial solitary tree. A look-in environment about the size of a refrigerator, filled with northern flora, this display appears to be the kind of self-contained ecosystem that can sustain itself indefinitely without human intervention. But look again. If the plants look shockingly healthy, it is because management has taken to replacing peaked-looking specimens with more spritely greens; evidently visitors didn't cotton to the look of edelweiss in its dormant phase. And the window isn't just the size of a refrigerator, it *is* a refrigerator, a mammoth crisper box supported by "backstage" air-cooling equipment the size of six Frigidaires. So what we're seeing in this shrine to nature is the botanical equivalent of those

Miami hotels where the air-conditioning is maintained at arctic levels to allow guests to promenade in their minks.

The remainder of the conservatory isn't artificial to this degree, but throughout the complex there is the constant hum of circulated air, the click and whir of computer-driven mechanisms that adjust the windows, the sense of nature sanitized, deodorized, pressed under glass. It is disconcerting, in the second-largest of the rooms, to see that plants are in pots set into the ground, rather like a florist shop. Just as Le Corbusier's houses were handcrafted to look like machine products, so Ambasz's conservatory begins to look like a sophisticated high-tech product engineered in the image of nature.

Of course, to criticize these elements is to take issue with the fundamental premise of a conservatory. Conservatories are artificial environments designed to protect plants that could not survive local climates. This is not a terrarium; we're not being misled. More to the point, Ambasz has never represented himself as an environmentalist. Indeed, you can infer from his writings that he is temperamentally alien to the strident polemic of environmentalism. Though he accepts the formal inventiveness of Modernism, he rejects its utopian belief that forms of individual buildings should be justified by their power to evoke a perfected future.

Ambasz believes that the architect's task is fundamentally one of image making, of inventing local responses to conditions in the present. This raises the question whether present conditions are not now so extreme that it is irresponsible for architects to concern themselves with images, whether strident polemic isn't just what's called for. To state the problem in more general terms, a building like Ambasz's compels us to ask whether the environmental crisis has circumscribed the architect's freedom to speak in the language of metaphor. Many people are genuinely outraged to hear architects going on about art while the world goes to hell in a handbasket. They see architecture as something wholly concerned with the material world—the "real" world of "real" buildings that address "real" problems, not only environmental pollution but also housing, crime, and other issues of urban life. They reject the idea that architects can also function on the level of symbol customarily accorded artists and writers.

Many architects themselves, including those who do claim the right to work with image and metaphor, are not unreceptive to these criticisms. The opportunity to work on the level of material reality, after all, is what drew many of them to architecture in the first place, instead of to painting or writing. Moreover, architects were as nervous as anyone else last summer. They like a beach vacation as much as the next person. And they know that they bear a greater responsibility than the next person for the garbage on the beach. They may not be the biggest villains in the environ-mental crisis (they're not manufacturing fluorocarbons or dumping radio-isotopes at sea), but their products are among its most conspicuous targets. And they know that they are members of an organized profession that has shown a conspicuous reluctance to accept its share of responsibility.

At the same time, no one is more aware than architects of the gap between what society expects of them and the tools it has placed in their command. They know that their ability to reform the material world is limited not only by the inertia of their own traditions but also by the way the material world itself operates. Architects are rarely called upon to ini-tiate projects; at most, they are hired to package them with a look, a style. They work at metaphor in part because of material powerlessness, and also because they have learned from their own history that this level affords them the greatest potential to influence the built world. To this extent, the metaphoric realm is the architect's real world.

Or, to put it another way, for many architects, architecture is a tool for organizing the interior landscape as well as the exterior landscape. That is the fundamental difference between Ambasz and a building contractor or a manufacturer of solar panels. Ambasz's site is not only the landscape of Texas; he is also building in a landscape that is furnished—he might say cluttered—with tradition, with the history of visual culture, with obsolete distinctions between the natural and the cultural, the material and the ideal, with our fears of environmental catastrophe and our yearning for Arcadia, with our inconsistent determination to live as planetary tourists even as we cry out for roots.

Arcadia, for Ambasz, is an idea to be explored visually, spatially, criti-cally. It is not an authority to be worshipped. He has no desire to substi-tute nature for technology, not least because that would repeat the Modern fallacy of polarizing the two. Nor has he the inclination to repeat the '60s countercultural self-deception of "living on the earth" with a little help from food stamps. He suggests rather that civilization depends as much on the vitality of the interior landscape as it does on the health of the earth.

I read Ambasz's complex of earth, metal, stone, and glass as an attempt to join these two landscapes, as an act of communion between the material and the ideal, between the conceptual world in which architects visualize aspirations and the physical world in which, with luck and effort, their val-ues attain form. For Ambasz, as for Emerson, architecture is transparently a "mixed art, whose end is sometimes beauty and sometimes use." And one of its uses, as I think Ambasz's building beautifully demonstrates, is to stir us to reconsider the mixture's proper proportions.

December 19, 1988

HOW BUILDINGS REMEMBER

"Did you see the gas vans?" Claude Lanzmann asks Mrs. Michelsohn, an old German woman, in his film *Shoah*. Mrs. Michelsohn lived in Chelmno, fifty yards from the spot where Jews were loaded onto the vans at the first Nazi extermination center. "No," she answers at first, with a look of annoyance. Then her face registers the recognition that Lanzmann and his movie cameras will not be deflected. "Yes," she acknowledges, she saw the vans, "from the outside. They shuttled back and forth. I never looked inside; I didn't see Jews in them. I only saw things from the outside."

She would rather talk of other things, things she saw from the inside: how primitive the living conditions were in Chelmno during the war; how there were no toilets, only privies; how her "pioneering spirit" sustained her. She never saw inside the vans, this pioneer, but she knew what went on there. From the outside, she heard the screams. "Horrifying screams. Screams of terror! Because they knew what was happening to them."

Lanzmann asks, "Do you know how many Jews were exterminated there?"

"Four something. Four hundred thousand, forty thousand."

"Four hundred thousand."

"Four hundred thousand, yes. I knew it had a four in it. Sad, sad, sad!"

It's chilling to watch the mechanisms of denial still at work forty years later, to listen to a person speak of her experience with a mind still divided between what she saw and what she knew. For those with a knowledge of Modern architecture, there's an added shock of recognition in this woman's words. Asked to recall a catastrophic event in history, she inadvertently exposes the nerve of an issue that aroused a generation of architects to revolutionize their art.

When we walk down the street of any large city in the world today and gaze up at the tall glass office towers that are still a virtual emblem of Modern architecture, we are looking at an architecture that began in a movement to erase the barriers between what we know and what we see. We are looking at a style of building designed to reveal the truth of the modern world to those who lived in it, a movement to dismantle the sham historical facades that screened the facts of industrial culture behind the elaborate pageantry of the nineteenth-century styles.

It was German architecture that first framed the formal program in which this ambition was attempted. In the years between the wars, the members of the German Glass Chain championed the use of glass not just for its aesthetic properties but, even more significantly, for its potential as a tool for adjusting social psychology to the facts of modern life. Like Freud, Modern architects sought to improve mental hygiene by eliminating illusions. Masonry buildings connoted concealment, darkness, complacency, and disease, withdrawal from the real world. The substitution of transparent glass walls for opaque materials of brick and stone would wrench the world from its desire for coziness, for a retreat from reality into a fictitious past.

The glass towers in today's cities show how imperfectly this ambition was realized. We long ago learned to read these buildings as symbols of fantasy, privilege, and corporate power; and often, as with projects such as the Renaissance Center in Detroit, they are symbols of an escapism from urban reality scarcely less fantastic than the nineteenth century's retreat into period costume.

But the utopian aspirations of the Modern glass tower were subverted long before the corporate headquarters began their rigid march up Park Avenue. The Columbus Haus, a Berlin skyscraper designed by Erich Mendelsohn in 1929, was among the first buildings to translate the Modern dream into built form. Completed in 1932, the building was named by its developers after Columbus to emphasize that the building was a harbinger of the modernity associated with the New World. The Nazis had other plans. In February 1933, a month after Hitler became chancellor, the SS leased the new building's top six floors. Pleased with the open floor plan and the functional efficiency (service elevators were concealed at the rear of the building), the SS designed the space for use as a place to detain and interrogate political prisoners. By the following month, this glass flower of Weimar culture had become, in effect, a high-rise concentration camp. In 1919, Paul Scheerbart, the leading theorist of glass architecture, had written that "a person who daily sets his eyes on the splendors of glass cannot do wicked deeds." But for three years, until the space proved too small, the SS operated its torture chamber in complete secrecy behind Mendelsohn's crisp glass facade.

What is most disturbing about Columbus Haus, however, is not the stark contrast between the idealism embodied by the building and the brutality exercised by its tenants. It is, rather, the ideological echoes between the Modern and the Nazi programs of social reform: the violent wrenching of society from old habits to construct a new social order; the flattening of privacy and individual difference beneath structures emphasizing mass, scale, and standardization. Above all, perhaps, they shared a mania for purity, for rooting out and purging elements unconducive to the new dispensation. "Hurray for the transparent, the clear! Hurray for purity!" wrote Bruno Taut in 1919. "Death to everything stuffy!"

Too much can be made of the parallels between the Moderns and the Nazis. The two movements envisioned different ends and proposed different means to reach them. Taut's call for death was directed at ideas, not at human beings; to him, the vision of "everlasting architecture" called forth a "kingdom without force," not a thousand-year Reich built on genocide. Modern architects were the victims of Hitler, rarely his willing collaborators. Mendelsohn, a Jew, left Germany the day after Hitler attained power, and he never returned.

Still, to look back at a building like Columbus Haus is to risk a loss of faith in the privileged status that surrounds artistic ideas, the status that declares one form of purity to be symbolic and another form of purity to be all too real. It is to see that the difference between artistic ideology and political propaganda does not preclude disturbing overlaps between them; that architecture is not just the making of places where historical events transpire but an activity bound up tightly in form and meaning with those events.

If we think of glass in connection with the Holocaust, the image most likely to arise is the shattered glass of smashed shopwindows sparkling in German streets. Like Columbus Prison, the memory of Crystal Night also mocks the belief that exposing the darker recesses of life can (in Scheerbart's words) "raise our culture to a higher level." For here was an event that did not take place behind opaque walls. Here was an eruption of brutality whose visibility to the entire world did nothing to weaken the world's determination to deny the evidence of its senses.

Now, fifty years after Crystal Night, we have a flourishing type of architecture nurtured by the belief that visibility can defeat denial. Holocaust museums are not only monuments to an event in history. They are also offerings to an idea about history, to the idea of Santayana, inscribed on the wall at the exit of the museum at Dachau, that those who will not learn from it are condemned to repeat it. Holocaust museums are shrines to the therapeutic properties of memory, as cure and as prevention. They embody the hope that making the past a visible part of the present will help to keep it in the past, to prevent it from reaching out of its burial ground to clutch the future.

Holocaust museums also affirm a belief in the power of architecture to make ideas visible. Books, paintings, sculptures, films, television shows, photographs, and even musical compositions have kept the Holocaust before the eyes of the world. But Holocaust museums are grounded in the belief that buildings can establish that visibility on a permanent basis, as though their size, their placement in the context of daily life, and their capacity to house as well as to depict events give them a claim to reality— and to its meaning—beyond that exercised by other works of art.

These claims—to permanence, to reality, to objective truth—account for some of the discomfort aroused in some people's minds by Holocaust museums. There are many who do not question the importance of learning from history—people whose shelves groan beneath the weight of books on the Holocaust; who are profoundly moved by a film like *Shoah* or by Anselm Kiefer's paintings—who are quicker to see the problems than the benefits of a building dedicated to recalling the nightmare. They complain that Holocaust museums have become a kind of industry that exists to produce replicas almost as mechanically as fast-food franchises; that they seem to serve the social ambitions of rich Jews more faithfully than the cause of historical understanding; that they undermine the impartiality of history by linking the Holocaust to the politics of Israel (even that they undermine political support for Israel by providing a sop); that they present to the world a view of Jewish culture dominated by the theme of victimization.

Underlying these objections is the assumption that architecture must be held to a higher standard of morality because it is a less personal form of art than music, painting, even a miniseries. The implication is that a building about the Holocaust is the reflection not of individual desires but of history's impartial judgment that such a building deserves a prominent place in the fabric of public life. As such, what may be most unsettling about a Holocaust museum is the proximity of this conventional view of architecture to the fascist conception of art: that it is the business of art to represent a collective view of the world.

On the one hand, there is a lot of rhetoric framed with the intention of placing Holocaust museums above criticism. On the other hand, a lot of rhetoric is aimed at persuading us that the Holocaust should be placed above the reach of art. And both these ideas, that the Holocaust museum must be above criticism and that the Holocaust is above art, reflect a third idea, that the Holocaust is more a matter of religion than of history, not the religion of Judaism but the religion of itself. Of course, the Holocaust has filled a theological void; for a secular culture, unable to turn to religion for an authoritative standard of absolute good, history has provided us with as close as we are likely to come to a standard of absolute evil. In this sense, at least, the Holocaust museum cannot escape the sanctity of the temple.

Yet I think it is possible to be skeptical and still conclude that this moment in our history offers us no greater opportunity in architecture than a building that bears witness to the Holocaust—to the specific atrocities committed at the death camps; to the general themes of inhumanity, of recognizing it, of acting on that recognition. Yes, the Holocaust may have become a business bound up with social, political, and economic agendas. No, such a building will not prevent cruelty from occurring again in the world, even in the building's own shadow (we should already be prepared for the midnight visits of swastika-happy vandals). But all this does not mean that the ideal of preventing inhumanity should not be physically, architecturally embodied.

To visit the Mall in Washington, for a thirtysomething critic, is not a simple matter. It means recalling the Official Script read and duly absorbed from the marble on the fifth-grade school trip circa 1960; the antithetical eruption just a few years later, when the temples came to look like a cruel hoax organized by J. Edgar Hoover; and then the recognition that one's anger was a step toward engagement with the meaning of these monuments, toward accepting the responsibility for action, for realizing the changes on which liberal culture depends.

Part of what makes Maya Lin's Vietnam Memorial so moving is that it re-creates a public occasion out of this personal experience. It is moving in itself to discover that a monument can genuinely move you. The message is not simply that thousands of young Americans did not give their lives in vain (whatever the lesson we draw from their sacrifice); it is also that stones are not erected in vain, that they can claim a value greatly surpassing the cost and effort it takes to build them. This discovery can transform the way we see the other monuments. We may trudge from the Vietnam Memorial over to the Lincoln Memorial, look up, and feel that even though we remain unreceptive to a race of marble giants, we are willing to accept the message coded in their inhuman scale. We, too, can have ideas bigger than our individual concerns, and make individual contributions to implement them. On the Mall, in short, one may learn to be receptive to symbolic language.

Last February I went to look at the plot of earth where the Holocaust Museum is now under construction. It was a cold, cloudy day with snow in the air. The earth was gouged into deep brown furrows. Since I'd seen Kiefer's paintings not long before, I found it easy to imagine a Holocaust memorial that would be nothing more than what I saw that day: a chilly field of roughly plowed dirt, a site of burial and disinterment, of bodies, of history, of truth.

The Mall puts you in the state of mind to see *everything* symbolically. I was struck by a large sign at the site announcing that the general contractor for the Holocaust Museum is named Gassman. (A friend remarked that the guy must have come in with a very low bid.) And it seemed similarly insensitive to symbolism that a monument to counteract anti-Semitism should be wedged between the Bureau of Printing and Engraving and the Bureau of Accounting. For a moment I felt I'd stumbled into the Mall's secret ghetto, into a marble equivalent of the old medieval quarter of moneylenders.

Some, including survivors of the Holocaust, have argued that a Holocaust Museum has no legitimate place in this symbolic center of American life. It's hard to believe that they've ever been to the Washington Mall. Out-of-placeness is the essence of the place. The Mall is packed with artifacts of foreign experience—museums of African and Asian art, masterpieces of the Italian Renaissance—elements that remind us, more eloquently than Greek and Roman forms, that ours is a culture of aliens. But more than that, the Mall is an epic abstraction, where nothing is rooted in anything like a central cultural experience. Indeed, its neoclassical vocabulary was devised in eighteenth-century Europe precisely to transcend nationalism, and to articulate the ideal of universal laws—the rational categories of history, science, art, government, and justice—that underlie differences of time and place. The Mall is where rationalism welcomes pluralism, because finally pluralism is the most rational way to live.

The United States Holocaust Memorial Museum will be a five-story building, clad on three sides with buff-colored limestone, on the fourth flanked by tower-like shapes of red brick. The museum will contain 225,000 square feet of floor space (roughly two and a half times the size of the Whitney Museum in New York). The museum's permanent exhibition will occupy about a quarter of this space. Divided into three segments and spread out over as many floors, the exhibition will trace the repression of the Jews (1933–39), the implementation of the Final Solution (1939–45), and finally the struggle in the decades since to make meaning of the Holocaust. The top floor of the building will house library facilities, study rooms, and administrative offices. Two auditoriums and meeting and conference rooms will be located on a concourse level belowground.

In addition to these programmatic spaces, the museum will contain two large ceremonial halls whose primary function will be to arouse reflections on the Holocaust through the medium of architecture itself. The Hall of Witness, an atrium-like space, extends nearly the full length of the building and rises five stories to a skylight roof. It serves as a circulation spine for access to various parts of the building. Attached to the building's west side, but projecting forward from it into a forecourt overlooking the Tidal Basin, is a monumentally scaled Hall of Remembrance, a place for contemplation following the viewing of the exhibition. The forecourt commands a stirring prospect of "symbolic Washington," with views of the Lincoln and Jefferson monuments, as well as the Tidal Basin. Other vantage points within the building offer glimpses of the Washington Monument and the White House.

Woven into the city's symbolic fabric by these views, the building is also stitched into its physical context by the use of materials (limestone and brick) and proportions that echo the buildings immediately adjacent. Any new building on the Mall must satisfy, of course, the conservative taste of the Washington Commission of Fine Arts, and from the outside, at least, this building fits the governing neoclassical ethos of order, harmony, and reason. Within this package of deference to local and national myth, however, lies a message of skepticism about the power of these values to determine human affairs.

James Ingo Freed, the architect selected to design the United States Holocaust Museum, is well acquainted with the Rule of Reason and its architectural representation. He began his career as an associate of Mies van der Rohe, the architect whose pared-down steel and glass towers epitomized the "New Objectivity" with which German architects in the 1920s moved away from the Romantic sensibility of Expressionist architecture toward a rational, pragmatic approach. He was a student at the Illinois Institute of Technology, the Chicago academy where Mies relocated after leaving Germany in 1938; and in the 1970s, Freed was dean of IIT's School of Architecture.

Since 1956 Freed has been associated with I. M. Pei, an architect whose work has epitomized the corporate acceptance of a once-radical style of design. The projects Freed has designed for Pei—Kips Bay Plaza apartments, the Jacob Javits Convention Center, 499 Park Avenue—are late-Modern classics that achieve visual interest through the minimal manipulation of expressed structure and geometric form. (To some critics, Freed is glibly known as Mr. Space Frame.) Unlike many architects of his generation, he has never accepted the erosion of the Modern movement as a historical inevitability.

Freed also has a strong personal connection to the Holocaust. Born in Germany, he was a young child at the time of Crystal Night. His family left Germany abruptly, but several relatives who were unable to leave perished in the camps. (One reason Freed has continued to embrace Modernism may be that he has something personal at stake in regarding the Modern movement as the struggle of enlightened values against the forces of unreason.)

When Freed was asked to design the building, he recognized that there were two different approaches an architect could follow. The first was to design the building as a more or less neutral container, in effect a shed that could house dinosaur skeletons or abstract expressionist canvases as easily as photographs of Treblinka. The second approach was to make the container one with the contained: to make architecture express the experience to which the building is dedicated.

I. M. Pei is a firm that specializes in giving the grand treatment to the first approach. Had this been a typical Pei project, Freed might merely have joined structural acrobatics to powerful abstract geometric forms and left another team of designers to install the building's content. But this is not a typical project. It is a building in which the symbolic meanings of forms take precedence over architectural abstractions; in which the sleek unity of the architectural package has been fragmented and exploded; in which allusions to architectural history verge on a Postmodern sensibility.

How does a building represent a catastrophe? What forms do you use to create an American building for an event that occurred far away? How does an architect schooled in the International Style deal with another nation's frenzy of nationalism? For a site like the Mall, whose neoclassical forms are typically read as nationalistic symbols? At a time when the International Style has also lost its original meaning? Having chosen the second approach, to make the container one with the contained, Freed faced the challenge of devising a vocabulary capable of realizing it.

Obviously, the American continent offered Freed no source of explicit formal reference to the Holocaust itself. There are no concentration camp buildings in Washington to preserve; no piles of the effects of victims, no vandalized tombstones to mount up into a monument; no explicitly religious symbolism congruent with national belief; no view that can be framed through a window of streets where shopwindows were shattered and citizens herded into trucks. What Freed could draw upon, rather, was the tradition of the Mall itself: the architectural vocabulary of the State, and its sometimes troubling relationship with the architecture of modernity, from the Enlightenment to now.

What Freed has done is to collide two kinds of vocabulary in this work. The first, most evident on the building's exterior, is drawn from the architecture of the "Empire of Reason" that shapes official Washington, from the roots of Enlightenment to the glazed space frame of the twentieth century. Freed's use of this vocabulary is most evident in the elevations at either end of the building, facing the two streets from which visitors will enter. The main entrance to the building is marked by a freestanding screen, classically proportioned, capped by a cornice. At the opposite end, the severe geometry of the Hall of Remembrance recalls the "radical classicism" with which eighteenth-century architects sought to translate enlightened values into physical structure. The elevation behind this pavilion is of conventional Modern design: a prismatic tent of glass capping a masonry wall, a wall that could have been lifted intact from the science lab of any state university campus built in the last quarter century.

But Freed has not used this vocabulary of the res publica uncritically. He understands that the story his building tells is about the use of official masks of high ideals to veil inner horrors. He is aware that the entrance facade to the building recalls the historicism of Postmodernism. While this satisfies the requirements of the art commission, Freed also intends it as a criticism of Postmodernism's complacent fetishizing of classical manners to cover up our inner life. He has separated the classically symmetrical entrance from the building because he wants it to be just that: a screen, a facade with no true relationship to what is going on inside.

And it is inside that the second of Freed's formal vocabularies comes into full play. This vocabulary is also drawn from the history of architecture, but it is an unwritten history, unwritten at least in the history of architecture: the history of the ghettos and the death camps. Freed acquainted himself with this history on a trip to Europe. Finding himself creatively blocked while working on the design, he visited camp sites and later did research in photography archives. He studied the characteristic forms of the ghettos: the street plans, the wooden bridges that led from one quarter of the ghetto over a public thoroughfare to another quarter. He looked, then, at the architecture of death: the metal gates, sometimes elaborately designed, with inscriptions like WORK MAKES YOU FREE; the shape of the oven doors; the metal bands placed around the ovens whose walls were at risk of explosion from uninterrupted use; the forms of the windows, with their shutters often closed; and, looming always, the watchtowers, symbols of control, and of its loss.

The Hall of Witness, a 6,000-square-foot space, is a work that synthesizes Freed's journey of discovery, incorporating abstracted versions of camp and ghetto architecture, communicating on a large spatial scale his own emotional fracture. It is a remarkable composition, almost an anticomposition, made of parts that do not fit or are about to come apart at the seams. Floors drop away before meeting walls, leaving long open trenches that must be crossed by short bridges, their entrances guarded by thin metal gates. Strips of glass block are set into the floor to create the sense of fracture, of the loss of solid ground.

At the far wall, toward which visitors walk to reach the exhibition halls, panels of marble are shattered with an enormous fissure, a symbol of the breakdown in a civilization but a breakdown also in an architect's capacity to convey what he has seen and felt. The walls of the room are brick, punctuated with false windows concealed by closed shutters and crossed by wide metal bands, as if to contain some invisible horror expanding within. Spanning the full length of the hall is no mere Modern space frame but a series of roof trusses, their metal forms twisted as if under pressure from walls closing in. Visible through the trusses, looming over the entire space, are four square brick blocks that recall watchtowers.

These two formal vocabularies derive from a common source: they are the two faces of the State. And when we leave the building and take a second look from the outside, we see that these faces are not cleanly separated from each other but wrap around each other, poke through each other, dissolve into one another, as though the official body of the State were slowly revolving to face us with a gun. We see that the brick that seems designed to harmonize so happily with the Bureau of Accounting is in fact derived from the barracks at Auschwitz. The roofline that recalls Louis Kahn's Richards Medical Building at the University of Pennsylvania could be the source of machine fire directed against escaping internees. The commissioners who sent Freed back to the drawing board with the complaint that the Hall of Remembrance looked too much like a gun turret weren't your usual philistines; they were picking up on the way the building's mood alters our perception of its parts, from benign or idealistic to sinister and violent. (In viewing an earlier version of the entrance facade, some observers were struck by the resemblance of the cornice to the brim of an SS officer's hat.)

The Hall of Remembrance has six sides. It is hexagonal because when Freed was approached to undertake the design, he was asked whether he had any objection to including a six-sided enclosure as a feature of the project. He answered that he did not. He understood the request as a reference to the 6 million Jews who lost their lives under the Nazi regime; we might also infer a reference to the Star of David. The six sides do not touch but stand slightly separated from one another, like six tablets, or six tombstones. The Hall of Remembrance, in other words, is not quite the empty void suggested by its abstract geometric forms. It is an example of architectural rhetoric, in which the building has been enlisted to subvert gently the museum's official mandate to erect a "nonsectarian" memorial. Probably few visitors to the Holocaust Museum will even bother to count the sides, much less equate a hexagon with a statistic. A more explicit reference to the Jewishness of the Holocaust would risk offending those eager to exploit the irony of an excluded subculture excluding others.

Still, as I contemplate what it might feel like to sit inside this space for contemplation, I find myself grateful to the museum and to the architect for resisting the blanket assimilation called for by the official mandate, for insisting on the "Jewishness" of this catastrophe. Not only because Jews were overwhelmingly Hitler's victims but because it is Jewish survivors who have created a place for the Holocaust in contemporary consciousness by making so conspicuous a symbol as this building. To sit inside this hexagonal pavilion is to be reminded that it is through its meaning as a Jewish experience that the Holocaust has been recovered as something unresolved in the experience of others.

What Freed's two vocabularies also have in common is that both are architecture. Freed visited the camps not only as a refugee from the Nazis but also as a member of a profession that has identified itself with ethics as well as economics. And what struck him was that the ghettos and the death camps and all the parts of which they were made had been *designed*. Albert Speer was not the only architect designing for Hitler. The machinery of death, too, had an architecture. And it, even more than Speer's, was an architecture of reason, an architecture of order carried to madness, a rectilinear environment constructed to house and to destroy bodies. Indeed, it was the strict order of industrial architecture that appealed to the pioneer Modernist. In the Hall of Witness, Freed is bearing witness not only to "others." He is taking note of the role architecture has played in causing and concealing the events of others. He is forcing the official architecture to confront the hidden.

The fragmentation of the building's forms, and in particular the warping of the roof trusses, has led some observers to see an affinity between this building and some of the work exhibited in last year's Deconstructivist Architecture show at the Museum of Modern Art. But Freed's thinking is miles away from the positions of that movement. He does not accept the Frankfurt school view that the Holocaust was a consequence of the Enlightenment, not a deviation from it. At the pinnacle of his building, he has placed study rooms for scholars inside the forms derived from the watchtowers of the camps. The ultimate inside-out, it is the affirmation of a liberal's belief in the power of learning to dispel likeness.

As the record of an artist's search for meaning, Freed's building affirms the Enlightenment belief in having the courage to use your own understanding (in Kant's famous formulation of "the motto of the Enlightenment"). The hexagonal shape of Freed's design reminds us of the extent to which the controversies over the meaning of the Holocaust—indeed, over the right of the artist to seek that meaning in visual images—lie in the erosion of religious systems that once served to interpret experience, and to sanction all the forms of visual representation. The search for meaning is now truly a search, not a surrender to those eager to impose meaning from outside: the state, the church, the historian, the architecture critic. And for Kant, the search was vital to resist that imposition: "Those guardians who have kindly taken supervision upon themselves see to it that the over-whelming majority of mankind should consider the step to maturity not only as hard, but as extremely dangerous." That was the problem faced by the schoolteacher's wife in *Shoah*. She had allowed her inside to be formed from the outside, by the ideology that encouraged her and her husband to mistake a poisonous myth for reality.

It isn't only totalitarian governments that generate such myths. I'm curious to know what the National Air and Space Museum (an earlier Pei building, in the firm's deluxe box mode) will look like to the schoolchild who has just been exposed to an exhibition on Auschwitz. Just down the Mall, the Holocaust Museum will be illustrating the consequences of accepting a symbolic language of propaganda as reality. We will see what went on behind the veils of national identity, chosen destiny, collective spirit. At Air and Space, meanwhile, the project of nationalism, including the evidence of a possible holocaust to come, proceeds, and it is shrouded in the veils of progress and internationalism. The *Spirit of St. Louis* has not been placed here to disturb us with the hints of a possible link between Lindbergh's heroic high spirits and his attraction to fascism. The missiles have not been raised up on their retroburners to teach of Operation Paperclip, the postwar U.S. recruitment of Nazi scientists.

Freed knows that, unlike Air and Space, his building is part of a wave of "anti-monuments," of which Maya Lin's was the first and the Holocaust Museum is by no means the last. These works may look alien next to neo-classicism's stately colonnades, but they remind us that the Mall's marble columns grew, like modern democracy and modern architecture, from the soil of the critical tradition. Far from violating the spirit of the Mall's architecture, these structures uncover its roots.

August 28, 1989

THE WINDS OF WINDSORISM

Tudor, Regency, Georgian, Victorian, Edwardian: as every suburban real estate agent knows, some of the most attractive styles in the history of architecture and design took their names from British monarchs. Until a few years ago, however, probably no one imagined that there were still more floats to come in this stately parade of royally sanctioned decorative art. I doubt very much, for instance, that the current monarch either hoped or wished her name linked to the Festival of Britain style, a prissy modernoid mode named after the 1951 event held two years before her coronation, much less to the style called Brutalism that captivated architects a few years later.

But then, in 1984, rounding the bend of the peculiar time warp in modern history known as Postmodernism, the heir to the throne loped into view, cupped hand waving, media horns blowing, cameras running as he stirred the stagnant air of contemporary Britain with a stream of sophomoric insults aimed at proposed architectural projects. Monstrous carbuncle. Giant glass stump. Old 1930s wireless. Frankenstein's monster. Last year this killer wit fleshed out his views to the length of a seventy-five-minute BBC documentary, *A Vision of Britain;* and now there's a book of the same title, based on the broadcast. Sumptuously illustrated with watercolors by the prince, paintings by Turner and Canaletto, and dozens of color photos of buildings he dislikes and those he favors, its endpapers and chapter headings adorned with his personal crest, the book sets forth the tenets of a new Power Look. Windsorism, anyone?

The selling point of the book is that it marks the first publication of Charles's fully developed Ten Principles—"a set of sensible and widely-agreed rules, saying what people can and what they cannot do." But some may find the book more useful as a textbook study in the use of language to prop up the privileges and the self-esteem of a declining nation's pooped-out ruling class. Anyone who's spent time on the sceptered isle will recognize with a shudder the mixture of heavy cream laced with bile that Charles pours out in his prose: the false modesty ("I humbly acknowledge my lack of academic credentials"), the scribble, scribble, eh, Mr. Gibbon? contempt for achievement (the twentieth century has produced no great architects, only "great architects"), the ostrich stance toward the present ("Many architects and developers believe that architecture should reflect the spirit of the age—whatever that might be!"), and the utterly charming loopiness ("Have you noticed how unfinished so many new housing developments seem nowadays without chimneys?").

There's nothing specifically English about the most egregious of Charles's rhetorical devices. It is the "silent majority" tactic cherished by demagogues everywhere. There would be more substance to Charles's "personal view of architecture," as his subtitle describes it, if he didn't feel the need to prop himself up with populist crutches on every other page. But in a way that's the real subject of this book: not architecture but the contract between a Postmodern prince and his subjects. He wants us to know that "99 percent [of the letters he received after his BBC broadcast] agreed with my feelings," that "although I'll be criticized for my ideas [by 'porcupine-like professionals and cantankerous critics'] I'm sure there is general agreement" among the good folks. No doubt Charles does feel deeply for Madge Atkins, the resident of a Modern high-rise building that has developed such serious structural problems that water pours in through the cracks and the window frames keep falling out. But, like silent majoritarians everywhere, Charles exploits the plight of the poor Madges of the world to hide the cracks in his own privileged position. It's Madge's job to wrap the populist veneer over a sagging structure of privilege.

As for the Ten Principles themselves, they are intellectually closer to Hints from Heloise than to Ruskin's Seven Lamps, but they are reasonable enough. Buildings, Charles advises, should enhance the landscape (The Place); their size, and the proportions of their constituent elements, should match their cultural and functional significance (Hierarchy); they should respect the proportions of the human form and that of the existing physical context (Scale); their exteriors should also relate visually to their surroundings (Harmony); they should provide a sense of shelter from the world (Enclosure); utilize the physical resources of the region (Materials); offer pleasure to the eye (Decoration); incorporate paintings and sculptures (Art); remain undisturbed by visual distractions (Signs and Lights); reflect the needs and desires of the public (Community).

These are all useful things to keep in mind when we're looking at architecture. The problem is not with the Principles but rather with the thesis they have been constructed to support. These ideas, Charles believes, are "a simple extension of the rules and patterns that have guided architects and builders for centuries"—until, that is, the postwar period, when suddenly Things Went Wrong. Suddenly, in the 1950s and 1960s, architects abandoned the time-honored lessons of the forefathers and set out across the land on an orgy of destruction, tearing down beloved landmarks, herding the populace into bleak boxes, trampling on all the values the English have held dear since the dawn of time. Suddenly there was *Modernism:* concrete bunkers on the Thames to house, of all things, the performing arts; blocks of functionalist council flats scarring the countryside, spoiling the view.

There's only one solution: send the architects back to school for a classical education. Let them relearn "the true and ancient *art* of architecture." Let them reclaim the heritage of the traditional styles. And Charles makes quite clear that the matter of style takes precedence over even the best of his Principles, the advocacy of community involvement. "I feel if architects are not thoroughly versed in an architectural tradition, Gothic or Classical, no amount of community consultation can produce really good buildings."

Charles gets a lot of mileage, in this book and in the press, by presenting himself as a fearless interloper, willing to endure the scorn of architects for venturing onto their territory without the proper credentials. But the problem is not that Charles is not qualified to speak about architecture. The problem is that he presents himself as an advocate of history and he knows next to nothing about it.

"There's nothing wrong in learning from the past," Charles pouts. There certainly isn't. One day he ought to give it a whirl. Modern architecture was not born the day before yesterday. At a modest estimate, its history is two hundred years long. It begins in late-eighteenth-century France with a show of initiative by architects seeking to reform the environment in accordance with ideas that evolved, over the years, to embrace aims not dissimilar to Charles's Principles: to enhance the lives of those previously disfranchised by the restriction of "architecture" to socially powerful institutions; to find a common language for building that can be understood without access to privileged information; to integrate architecture with painting, sculpture, nature, and open space; to construct cities based on reason, harmony, proportion, and the hierarchical relationships of social institutions. Unfortunately, being born the embodiment of tradition has not endowed Charles with either a knowledge of history or a capacity to interpret it.

If Charles is so intent on recovering national heritage, let him ponder the extent to which the Modern program was framed by British architects, designers, and critics, many of whom had passed into history long before the dreaded 1950s rolled around: by John Ruskin, who brought to architectural criticism a sense of morality and a voice for the working class; William Morris, who encoded these messages in household furnishings; Joseph Paxton, whose Crystal Palace of 1851 (under the patronage of Prince Albert) gave the public its first look at the architectural potential of modern materials and construction methods; Lewis Cubitt, whose design for King's Cross train station demonstrated that modern functions such as mechanized transportation need not hide behind historical facades to be dignified; William Lethaby, who in 1893 called on his fellow architects to devise "a symbolism real and comprehensible by the vast majority of spectators"; Charles Rennie Mackintosh, the Scotsman who turned this idea into built form; Ebenezer Howard, inventor of the "Garden City"; Nikolaus Pevsner, the adopted Englishman whose classic histories of the Modern movement clearly (if somewhat overgenerously) established the importance of the English contribution to the formation of the Modern canon; and, closer to our time, Peter and Alison Smithson, who, in the 1960s, modified the canon to create an urban vocabulary for Britain's postwar welfare state.

Which is hardly to say that the Modern movement, as codified in the years after 1923, was primarily an English invention. If we're going to talk about orgies of destruction, let's not forget that the movement's internationalism, which Charles finds so deplorable, had its roots in a very big Thing Gone Wrong called World War I. Modern architects not only sought to rebuild a continent ravaged by that war; they were also determined to build across national differences in the hope of preventing a repeat of the catastrophe into which Europe's ruling classes had plunged a civilization.

Nor does the British contribution to twentieth-century design die out with the waning, in the 1960s, of the International Style. For the past twenty years, the Architectural Association in London has rivaled and perhaps even surpassed the Bauhaus as a training ground for young architects. It has spawned a generation of some of the most gifted practitioners now entering the building phase of their careers: Zaha Hadid, Bernard Tschumi, Rem Koolhaas, Peter Wilson, Nigel Coates, to name a few. Coates, an architect scarcely less outspoken than Charles in his contempt for the British architectural establishment, has sought particularly to adapt urbanism to the social issues of Thatcher's Britain. In a series of radical, visionary projects such as the 1986 Gamma City, Coates and his "NATO" group have tapped the driving street smarts that have energized British fashion, music, and commercial design.

A history of two centuries may seem a flash in the pan compared with the 2,500-year-old legacy Charles claims to represent. The truth is that the Modern tradition is no less venerable than the heritage he proposes to restore. Builders have indeed been active in the British isles since prehistoric times, but the tradition Charles holds up for us to emulate—the idea that the "styles" of Gothic and Classical should be recovered from the past—is a product only of the Victorian age. Historicism is a little older than Ralph Lauren's Polo look, but not much. The White House had been standing for half a century before they held a competition to design the Houses of Parliament—which during the Victorian period served the similar purpose of masking the stresses of an anxious age behind symbols of stability and order. Like the innocent tourist who mistakes Gothic Revival buildings for medieval monuments, Charles seems unaware that his view of the "true, ancient art" is a nineteenth-century fiction.

Charles is right to object when his critics accuse him of wanting to create a Disneyland. Compared with the global scale of Victoria's historical re-creations, Disney's theme parks are, well, Mickey Mouse. But, like Disney, nineteenth-century historicism could embody progressive ideas as well as nostalgia for a fictional past. When Victorian narrative painters employed Gothic motifs—depicting Queen Victoria, for instance, as a figure from Arthurian legend—the glorification of monarchy was often incidental; the real subject was Britain's heroic resistance to feudal oppression. These paintings proclaimed that the true tradition of England is social progress. The Greek Revival, similarly, sought an affinity between modern democracy and its ancient antecedent to prop up democracy's advance. And despite the vigor with which the War of the Styles was waged, the two architectural vocabularies could even be combined—as in the Houses of Parliament, for which a classical plan, denoting democracy, was clothed in Gothic ornament, denoting the British development of representative government.

But it was one thing to evoke the medieval world in narrative painting and another to consign the British population to an antiquarian architect's faithful reconstruction of the medieval world. Often these reconstructions appealed less to progressive instincts than to a craving for traditional authority to step in and clean up the mess that progress had made. This was the case with Pugin's *Contrasts*, a book whose 1841 edition used graphic images to juxtapose the harmony of medieval times and the chaos of the industrial city. (Charles's book forces a similarly odious comparison by setting a photograph of modern London atop a painting by Canaletto.)

Every fan of *Upstairs, Downstairs* (itself, of course, a historical recreation) knows how the desire to smooth over the bumps of modern life with the illusion of harmony and grace served to perpetuate social privilege. Virginia Woolf, writing at the height of the Edwardian age, satirized in *Mrs. Dalloway* the "grand deception practiced by hostesses in Mayfair from one-thirty to two, when, with a wave of the hand, the traffic [of aproned, white-capped maids] ceases, and there arises instead this profound illusion in the first place about the food—how it is not paid for; and then that the table spreads itself voluntarily with glass and silver." Windsorism is less a style than a bid to revive this kind of "grand deception." For all his appeal to populism, Charles's vision denies the connection between the architecture he values and the submerged social structure that kept it running smoothly. He wants to extend the Edwardian hostess's sleight of hand from the dining room to the street of every town and village in Great Britain.

The point of Modernism was, in fact, to make such connections visible, to exhibit as physical structure a social framework in which value was derived from work. That is partly why Modern buildings took their cues from factories: not from some perverse inhuman whim but to embody what Charles terms *hierarchy*. Architects hoped to impress upon our consciousness that work was the basis of wealth, the connecting fiber of society. Perhaps it's not surprising that this meaning has escaped the author of a book whose dust jacket declares that "all royalties will be donated to the Prince of Wales' Charities." When he looks out at the London skyline, he must see nothing but lèse-majesté: all these ugly, boring boxes that blot out his view of St. Paul's. He is unable to see, or to accept, the idealism of an architecture that elevated workers from the squalor that Canaletto found so picturesque to the eminence enjoyed by the princes of church and state. He's not alone in this blindness; it is a mark of our unexamined elitism when we look out at this cityscape and feel disgust instead of at least a measure of pride.

Modern architecture is not above criticism, and architects themselves are not above offering it. Many modern buildings are eyesores. Worse, the functional vocabulary long since ceased to convey the social message it held half a century ago. In the past twenty-five years, architects as diverse in their sensibilities as Aldo Rossi, Robert Venturi, and James Stirling have adopted our relationship to the past as an architectural subject; they recognize that at the end of the twentieth century our view of the past—and the future—differs from the view that prevailed at the century's beginning. But Charles refuses to accept these changes, because he hates the idea that architecture can change. "Don't be confused by post-modernism," he warns his readers, "and all the other 'isms' that clever architecture critics and commentators conjure up in order to lull us into a false sense of security!" Never mind that false security is what his life is made of. Charles doesn't want history, he wants an escape from history. He's like someone—he *is* someone—who has grown up in the midst of an elaborate stage set, and he's furious that there's a tear in the backdrop, that you can see the pulleys, that the stagehands have walked off the job.

And his vision of beauty is uglier than Pugin's, because it blots out issues of race as well as class. When Charles recalls the English to their heritage, he speaks, whether he knows it or not, for all who resent the invasion of former colonials. This time around, the white man's burden isn't religion, it's classicism. Charles has nice things to say about contemporary Islamic architects who use traditional forms, but he uses this praise as an analogy to drive his countrymen back to their Gothic and Classical roots. Since he doesn't believe in "the spirit of an age," he has no idea that at this moment the issue of cultural difference is critical. He can't see that to describe classicism as a language "universally understood" is to cast out the cultures that won't share that language. But then, to many Englishmen, India and China are still just something you choose before adding cream or sugar.

Charles is careful to exempt developers from his attacks. If he went after the building trades, or anyone else with real economic clout, there would be no more riding around in open carriages. Instead, he believes it was "the architectural establishment, or a powerful group within it, which made the running in the '50s and '60s. It was they who set the cultural agenda. . . . It was the 'great architects' of this period who convinced everyone that the world would be safe in their hands." Charles is not far wrong in these accusations. Yet I suspect he hates architects not because they are powerful, but because, like himself, they lack political power. Like princes, architects deal in symbols. And it can't be easy to be a cultural symbol for a culture in whose creativity you play no part; a culture that, for two hundred years, has run counter to the belief that birth should confer privileges—and moreover one that, until the twentieth century, rarely thought twice about enlisting architecture to provide a symbolic representation of royal power. At one time, after all, cities were simply extensions of royal households.

It's understandable that Charles should want to do something more useful than cut ribbons and produce an heir; that, I assume, is why he has embarked with painful sincerity on this career of architecture critic. But all the opinion polls in the world can't change the fact that, except by accident of birth, and by grace of the media's appetite for mediocrity in all forms and especially in high places, he would not be in the position to occupy our attention with his poor ideas. Is Charles a joke, then, not worth taking seriously? Not unless you think that architecture is a joke. They're laughing a lot these days in England, where this idiotic crusade has caused architects to lose work and creativity to lose stature.

And yet Charles has opened up a set of questions that can be useful in helping us to recall Modern architecture's aims and the sources of its discontent. How do you judge whether a building is good or bad? Who are the clients for public buildings, and what is the public's stake in privately owned buildings that help to define a cityscape?

The issue of evaluation also arose in the nineteenth century, as architects found themselves buffeted by the competing claims of industrialization, middle-class prosperity, historical tradition, political reform, and Romantic rebellion. In his brilliant book *Victorian Architecture in England*, John Summerson writes that Victorian architecture confronts us with a "huge distortion of social and artistic relationships." Ordinarily, Summerson notes, "we are accustomed to begin evaluating the contents of a period of architecture on the assumption that in relation to the society which built it, it was right. Where the Victorians are concerned it would be much safer to begin, at least, on the assumption that it was wrong." This is not simply the retroactive appraisal of a Modern ideologue. As the book documents, "Early and mid-Victorian architecture was, in its own time and in the eye of its best-informed critics, horribly unsuccessful."

The problem was not merely the dichotomy between architecture and engineering, or the conflict between the nineteenth century's desire for an architecture "of its time" and its belief that it could locate one through a synthesis of the historical styles, or the lack of historical precedent for the new building types and social configurations produced by the nineteenth century. Victorian architecture was "wrong" in large part because there was no one to say that it was right. Historical forms—"pre-approved," as they say on today's credit card applications—simply filled up the vacuum left when architecture, like government, was no longer subject to the claims of a central authority. To go back to the Victorian world for anything more than a superficial whiff of the picturesque, then, is to find not a reliable model for guidance, but a muddle of confusion, anxiety, failure, and doubt. Those great hulks of masonry that look so solid, so confident, turn out to be quivering masses of jelly.

Even Victorian painters came to recognize the failure of the historicist enterprise. "But what did I know about Arabella Stewart and James I," confessed G. A. Storey in 1899, after a lifetime of painting them, "except what Miss Lucy Aiken had told me in her two volumes, and what I could pick up from prints of the period? I got up my accessories just as a stage manager would do for a new piece, borrowed costumes. . . ." For Storey, the revelation came with a hard look at a painting by Velázquez, in which faces, costumes, and attitudes belonged "so completely to [their] own day, even as the hand that wrought it, that I felt I had a true page of history before me, and not a theatrical makeup of a scene dimly realized in the pages of some book written many years after the event."

The consensus achieved by the Modern movement in the years after 1923 did not resolve the crisis of evaluation. It proposed that evaluation would have to start from scratch. The Modern tabula rasa cleared a metaphorical space to visualize what a public space might look like. If Modern architects rejected the past, it was partly because the past only clouded the vision of this new entity. All those charming squares, handsome piazzas, stately boulevards merely contained the public; they offered no guidance in how best to represent it. The Modern consensus proposed that in a democratic culture responsibility for architecture should begin with architects. Anyone can become one, even a prince.

This responsibility did not exempt architects from criticism. Quite the contrary, it removed the protection of tradition that Victorian architects had tried to hide behind. The postwar decades, which Charles describes as the origin of the Modern architect's assault on society, in fact brought forth an escalating series of criticisms of architecture, from outside and inside the profession, which made it clear that architects had no more right than monarchs to impose their will on others; that the architect's social contract was provisional and subject to a constant renegotiation of its terms. Housing, land use, building density, transportation, and historical preservation were all inscribed on the slate in these decades as the focus of critical debate to "set the agenda" for architecture and urban design.

Of these, preservation has probably been the most problematic aesthetically, because it continued to raise the question of architectural evaluation. Why should this building rather than that building be declared a landmark? What makes it so great? Preservationists have been no better equipped than the Victorians to set forth rules. In place of aesthetics, they have offered anthropology, the claim that a particular building is "representative of its time." Even so, the most astute critics of these years—Summerson, Mumford, Huxtable—found it not only possible but necessary to advance the cause of Modern architecture *and* to breathe life into the preservation movement. The two goals were complementary ways of staking the public's claim to public space.

The point is that for well over a century the history of architecture has been inseparable from the history of criticism. A good deal of twentieth-century architecture is about criticism: how architects, often drawn to architecture to exercise their critical faculties through the medium of buildings, reset the agenda of competing cultural pressures. The contemporary city is the physical record of renegotiations of the architect's social contract—between economic, political, aesthetic, and social criteria—and these renegotiations have been carried out in public ever since the Enlightenment began to expand the definition of architecture from sacred and state monuments to embrace the community at large.

The lesson that many of today's most gifted architects have drawn from the past is not success but failure: that to operate in this expanded field is to build things people won't like. The fragmented forms of Postmodernism and deconstruction, the Venturian theory that buildings should accommodate, not oppose, their surroundings—all arise from the awareness that architecture unfolds in an arena where criticism reigns. Of course architects can be arrogant. The profession, like all professions, can easily sink into complacent habits of thought. (Even by 1941, Summerson stated that the functionalist canon was old hat.) The combination of stagnant architectural ideas and hyperactive real estate development can be lethal. These tendencies all require sustained criticism—from professionals as well as laypeople—to keep architecture alive. And it also takes criticism to make a place for work that may not be popularly pleasing, to point out that to exalt popularity as a criterion is to condemn architecture to the level occupied in literature by Charles's in-law, Barbara Cartland. Whether innovation is inevitably elitist, whether the borders of creativity should be more tightly circumscribed in architecture than they are, say, in fiction, are questions that neither a popular vote nor history can finally settle. It is up to criticism to keep them open.

To the extent that Charles's campaign prods complacency within the profession, that he reminds us unwittingly that the staid architecture of the Victorian era was in fact the swirl of controversy from which Modernism arose, that he reminds us also of the honor of the architect's failures, he is nurturing one of the hardiest roots of Modern architecture itself. To the quite considerable extent that he mistakes the nineteenth century's confusion as the embodiment of classic and timeless values, however, he is merely delivering a vital tradition into the hands of a dead one.

December 11, 1989

WHEN THE CATHEDRAL TURNED BLACK

The CBS Building turns twenty-five this year. That's five years short of the thirty that must pass before a building can be designated a New York City landmark, but Black Rock is already a landmark in my book. Eero Saarinen's only skyscraper, CBS is the last great building built in New York. I know that's a sweeping statement. Let me sweep it by you one more time. *Not one great building has gone up in this city for twenty-five years.* Not since many of us who live and work here got to town. Not since nearly a third of the population was born.

Now for a little serious backpedaling. There's been a lot to compensate for the lack of first-rate architecture in New York since 1965: the growth of architectural preservation from scattershot protests to a major force in urban planning: the use of "contextual" design to heal the gashes inflicted on the urban fabric by Modern planning concepts; the substitution of neighborhood renovation for urban renewal; the empowerment of community boards to influence design decisions. Because of these developments in urbanism (even allowing for the real estate free-for-all of the Koch years), we can count the past quarter century as a period of progress toward discovering how democracies should build.

To unpack the significance of CBS, a building eloquently mute, aggressively withdrawn, is to go some distance toward understanding this development—why New York architecture has lapsed behind urbanism in the years since Black Rock arose. It is also to see why covering up the failures of Modern design cannot suffice to bring architecture up to date. For that, we also need to reexamine our disenchantment with Modernism's successes.

Like the black slab from outer space in *2001*, another 1960s classic, Black Rock materialized from an alignment of forces; not Earth, Moon, Sun, and Jupiter but New York, Modernism, industry, and media. It climaxed a decade's streak of brilliant buildings shaped by the first three of these forces, a run that included Lever House, the Seagram Building, the Guggenheim Museum, and the Pepsi-Cola Building. These buildings joined Modern promise to Manhattan confidence. They buttressed an arc of faith in the city's destiny to lead the postwar world toward the good modern life.

Though the vocabulary of most of these buildings derived from Europe, they spoke in New York accents. Weimar Germany may have been the laboratory for Modern architecture, but Manhattan had long been its spiritual home: in European eyes, an eruption of raw industrial energy calling out to be tamed by the enlightened modern hand. This was the city that in 1925 gave Fritz Lang his glimpse of *Metropolis*, that inspired Le Corbusier a decade later, in his book *When the Cathedrals Were White*, to extol New York's skyscrapers as equivalent in aspiration to the spires of medieval Europe. "Compared with the Old World," Le Corbusier wrote, New York "has established, after twenty years, the Jacob's ladder of modern times." And it was here, after the war, that the United Nations set up the world's last, best hope, in the city's first major complex of Modern buildings, following Le Corbusier's plans.

The UN buildings gave the new style the prestige of a global authority. But to climb Jacob's ladder of Modernism, architects first had to scale the corporate ladder of industry. The 1932 International Style exhibition at the Museum of Modern Art had been organized by Philip Johnson and Henry-Russell Hitchcock expressly to persuade captains of industry to adopt the aesthetic. Later, the museum mounted its Good Design shows to change the look of industrial products. For that matter, the Museum of Modern Art was itself the creature of corporate culture; so was the UN's physical plant. Both owed their existence to Rockefeller largesse, their crisp Modern looks to the family's choice of architects.

It is often thought that the corporate hold on Modernism was an American, capitalist perversion of European socialist ideals. Yet it had long been the European view that industry would take the lead in ushering in a progressive social order. That is one reason why Modern forms were based on industrial models. Le Corbusier's 1922 Citrohan house, an early version of the "machine for living," was a conscious play on the name Citroën, a deliberate play for industrial patronage. Modernism had always been an architecture of the workplace. The great New York towers of the 1950s and 1960s were an homage to the capital of the culture of work.

At the time of its appearance, not every observer was willing to admit Black Rock to the roster of great Modern buildings. Much of the criticism focused on the building's unrelieved verticality. "I wanted a building that would stand firmly on the ground and would grow straight up," Saarinen said. He achieved this by placing structural columns on the outside of the building and running them the full height of its thirty-eight stories. Gone was the traditional, tripartite division of base, shaft, and top. Gone was the transfer of the building load to widely spaced, two- or three-story-high columns at the ground floor, typically used in other Modern buildings to make a transition from the scale of the street to that of the tower. Gone was the entrance canopy, or the low, horizontal slab used to balance (as at Lever House) the tower's vertical thrust. To many, the result was a building devoid of scale, an impression magnified nearly to the point of physical menace by the dark tinted windows, the surface of charcoal granite.

I never shared that impression. The notion that entrance canopies and wider column spacing introduce "human scale" has always struck me as truer in theory than in space. To my eye, these features exaggerate the scale of the tower by raising it above eye level. At CBS, by contrast, the tower reaches down as well as up. It lets you touch the very columns that scrape the sky. The effect is to magnify the scale of the body at the building's base. (Fashion photographers, who instantly adopted the building as a favorite location, recognized that it sets off the body beautifully.) Saarinen introduced human scale *horizontally* into this vertical composition. The width of the columns (each five feet, alternating with five foot openings for windows) is body-scaled: it was determined by the minimum-size opening for revolving doors. The sunken court and the five easy steps one descends to reach it also set the tower firmly within physical reach.

The most dramatic demonstration of the building's sensitivity to human scale is the extent to which the viewer controls the building's actual appearance. It's an effect that has delighted me for twenty-five years: the apparent opening and closing of the V-shaped columns as you walk past them, transforming the exterior (at the viewer's own pace) from a sheer cliff of solid granite to a lustrous setting—like jeweler's velvet—for the dark sparkle of reflections in the windows and of office lights glinting behind them.

But the main problem people had with CBS was not scale. They were reluctant to concede that Saarinen had designed a truly Modern building. Modern buildings, for instance, did not have load-bearing walls. They had glass curtain walls that allowed, in theory, the interpenetration of interior and exterior space. And Modern typefaces did not have serifs, like the distinctive graphics that Lou Dorfsman designed for use throughout the building and on CBS stationery. Sure, it was elegant, but it wasn't Helvetica. And some of those big, black, butch columns—weren't they (swift kick) *hollow* at the core?

More to the point, many critics were unwilling to admit that Saarinen was a genuinely Modern architect. To true believers in the canon, Saarinen was something of a traitor. Like his contemporary Johnson, Saarinen began his career with buildings that strictly toed the standard Miesian line. But in later work, such as the TWA terminal at JFK and the Ingalls Hockey Rink at Yale, Saarinen abandoned the canonical vocabulary and adopted instead a personal expressionism that treated each building as an opportunity to create a unique, distinctive form.

To his detractors, it was obvious that Saarinen had sold out, as though the packaging ethos of the Styling Center he designed for General Motors in 1956 had taken over his mind. "Through them runs the insistent American instinct for simplistic and, in this case, spectacular solutions," wrote Vincent Scully of Saarinen's late buildings; they "give the impression of having been designed in the form of models for dramatic unveiling at board meetings and of having never been detailed beyond that point." The TWA terminal was a particularly flagrant violation of the Modern rule that form should express structure. Designed to look as though its enormous cantilevered "wings" exploited the structural properties of concrete, concrete was in fact barely more than a veneer covering the vast amount of steel support required to hold the roof in place. Similarly, at the Yale rink a central concrete supporting arch, evidently held aloft by its own internal tension, in fact needed to be stabilized by cables anchored to the ground on either side of the building.

Saarinen *was* Modern if you were willing to extend the word to include the phase of Expressionism that immediately preceded the formation of the Bauhaus canon in the mid-1920s. But that is precisely what the keepers of the canon refused to do. Canonical Modernism, though framed by architects many of whom had themselves been Expressionists, was a reaction against Expressionism; and once they had embraced the ideal of building for a machine age, canonical Modernists did not even want to be reminded that Expressionism had ever happened. By the mid-1960s it had been a buried episode in Modern architecture for three decades, referred to as a curiosity—if at all. (Pevsner dismisses this "riotous style" in a paragraph of *Pioneers of Modern Design*.)

Saarinen's architecture not only reverted to a condemned style, it also refuted the standard rationale for the condemnation: that Expressionism's poetic forms stood little chance of realization in the tough world of real building. As Scully acknowledged, "Saarinen's buildings are the most popular packages of their time and a revealing image of it." And yet, if you were willing to accept the bearing wall and the serifed letters (and Le Corbusier himself had employed both), the fact is that Saarinen produced for CBS a building that could pass the strongest Modern muster. Structurally as well as visually innovative, it was the first reinforced concrete office tower in New York. Modern, too, was the emphasis on standardization, or, as a glowing feature in *Life* magazine proclaimed, the building's "Total Design." The five-foot rhythm of column and window was extended throughout the building's interior. Laid out by CBS's president Frank Stanton, the offices offered configurations of a basic five-foot module, a tatami-mat proportion that recalled the early Modern fascination with the Japanese vernacular.

Even the building's striking visual impact was rooted in Modern ideology. The sheer rise from street to sky harked back to the ideas of an acknowledged Modern hero, Louis Sullivan, the Chicago-based "father of the skyscraper." CBS went beyond Sullivan's own pioneering towers toward fulfilling his prescription that the skyscraper "must be every inch a proud and soaring thing, rising in sheer exultation that from bottom to top it is a unit without a single dissenting line." And the system of structural columns provided an elegant solution to that obsessive Modern problem, "turning the corner." At the corners of CBS, the walls bring two columns into abutment without breaking the ten-foot rhythm, forming a single column of double size, its axis rotated forty-five degrees to the plane of the wall. The turn is almost automatic.

Here, the simplistic package had been refined into a simple statement—simpler, even, than the Seagram Building, with its "facade" of nonstructural T-beams, its bracing at the rear concealed behind a glass curtain wall. And the spectacular was transmuted into the spectacularly understated: a charcoal business suit beside which Lever House looked like a loud checked jacket.

Today it seems like splitting hairs to question whether CBS was or was not a Modern building. Not so in 1965, for a lot was invested in the importance of that distinction: the collective ego of a generation that had inherited the belief that it was the architect's destiny to remake the entire modern world. That belief depended on consensus: we could not have a generation of architects each remaking the world to a different design. That had been the Expressionist folly. To deviate from the canon was to undermine the consensus, hence to weaken the validity of the claim.

But the problem raised by CBS went deeper, precisely because the building was so respectably Modern. For what did it mean if an image-maker created a Modern building? It meant that the distinction between the package and the canon had worn thin. It meant that perhaps the canon was just another package. It meant that maybe architects had been fooling themselves in thinking that by adhering to the canon they, not the CEOs, were setting the terms of corporate culture. Perhaps corporate America had been calling the shots all along.

And indeed, by the time CBS opened, the influence of Modernism was already on the wane. Saarinen died in 1961 (leaving his associates John Dinkeloo and Kevin Roche to complete work on CBS and other projects). In 1962 the jackhammers began hacking away at Penn Station, rousing into being the preservation movement and its challenge to the Modern movement's contempt for the past. In 1963 the Pan Am Building, designed by a team of architects that included Bauhaus founder Walter Gropius, became the conspicuous focus of public anger over its destruction of the vista down Park Avenue.

These events were not in themselves sufficiently powerful to halt Modern architecture in its tracks—until the 1970s who but a few cranks like the classicist Henry Hope Reed had any conception of an alternative?— but they did contribute to a change in public perception. They weakened the contract that had equated Modernism with enlightened progress and revealed instead an alliance with the darker, more destructive forces of modern life. By 1966 it was possible to interpret Marcel Breuer's fortress-like Whitney Museum as a reflection of growing defensiveness in the profession itself. "Beware of boiling oil!" cracked the entry on the Whitney in the *AIA Guide to New York City*. But such martial impressions were not a joke to those who felt oppressed by Modern architecture's aggression, or to Modernists who began to sense that the days of their movement, so newly victorious, might soon be numbered.

The pivotal New York building in this shift of opinion was the Ford Foundation Building, built in 1967 and designed by Saarinen's successors, Kevin Roche, John Dinkeloo, and Associates. The building was a great critical success. Its indoor garden was an instant hit: a welcome note of bucolic delight after the somber urbanity of CBS. But some found the garden as troubling to contemplate as it was spectacular to behold. The garden was visually arresting, but it was programmatically as inhospitable as the stark granite walls the building turned to the street. The public could enter but not use this space; guards stood by to make sure no one loitered, sat down, pulled out a sandwich.

And at that moment the contradiction between image and program conformed too closely to the ruses of corporate culture of which Americans were becoming less tolerant. By 1967, of course, the 1960s had become The Sixties. "Total Design" had come to look suspiciously like totalitarian design. Who *were* these people to tell secretaries they couldn't keep family pictures on their desks? That the Ford Foundation was headed by McGeorge Bundy, an architect of the Vietnam War, only confirmed the feeling that this building typified the smugness of the military-industrial complex, serene in its garden, indifferent to the world. Scully gave voice to this response in 1969, when he wrote that all of this firm's buildings shared "a quality at once cruelly inhuman and trivial, as if they had been designed by the Joint Chiefs of Staff." For Scully, this "paramilitary dandyism [was] especially disturbing at the present moment in American history."

Ada Louise Huxtable, a passionate admirer of the Ford Foundation Building, tried to brush off this criticism. To attack the building on the basis of the foundation's politics was to commit what she termed the "socio-aesthetic fallacy." "Monumentally and urbanistically," Huxtable wrote, "the structure works well." But the problem was that, monumentally and urbanistically, the architecture confirmed what people detested about the politics. You could admire the architecture, the way you could admire the sleek design of a military helicopter. But to persist at this late date in the belief that Good Design redeemed all was to expose a problem far more serious than the restricted garden: the extent to which the aesthetics and the sociology of Modernism had diverged.

Socio-aesthetic fallacy indeed! As if social ideology were not a foundation on which the legitimacy of Modern forms was based. To dismiss this connection as a "fallacy" was to confess how weak the foundation had become. The true fallacy was a failure to recognize that without its supporting ideology the Modern aesthetic would soon collapse like a house of cards.

What was lost was more than a style. It was the consensus that had made it possible to believe that this style was leading us toward a better world. From this point, the social agenda of Modernism was embodied in resistance to Modernism, the ideals of its consensus in a resistance to consensus. Soon Robert Venturi's *Complexity and Contradiction in Architecture*, published in 1966 by the Museum of Modern Art, would propagate a theoretical framework for dismantling Modern form, substituting the ideal of diversity for the unity of the International Style. Soon the Art and Architecture Building at Yale, Paul Rudolph's 1966 tribute to Corbusian principles, would be set ablaze by students who saw it as a symbol of the growing gap between Modern pieties and the increasing social complexities of urban life.

All that was still in the future when Black Rock opened its doors. New York in 1965 stood at the summit of the good modern life. In many ways it was still the 1950s, only slicker, more prosperous, more cosmopolitan, without the sentimental suburban nationalism of the immediate postwar years. The modernity of that moment was remarkably layered. It was the peak of the Jet Set years, but you could still drive along the West Side Highway and review the great transatlantic liners—the *Queens*, the *France*, the *United States*—all symbols of an earlier generation's idea of the modern. The Rockettes were still kicking, even if the kick in the whole idea of "Radio City" was gloriously out of line with the times. The first discos had arrived, though veneered with the supper-club élan of the word *discotheque*. Good Design furniture still served its ambivalent role as a symbol of social progress and a sign of elite good taste. The crisp International Style look of The Four Seasons coexisted with the French swag of Le Pavillon, itself a remnant of an earlier embodiment of the modern, the 1939 World's Fair.

In 1965 New York again hosted a World's Fair, though the effect of this one was not to reinforce the appeal of "the modern" but rather to call it into question. Conceived to celebrate the city's preeminence, the 1964–65 fair turned out to be a shapeless mess. Part of the problem was redundancy; the city hardly needed to trump up an international tribute to its cultural prestige, and no one needed to go to Queens to find out why. But the failure was also due to a breakdown in the ideology that had spawned World's Fairs, and shaped Modern architecture as well.

From their origin in London in 1851, World's Fairs were showcases for industrialization and the social progress it fostered. At the 1851 fair, Paxton's Crystal Palace gave the public its first exposure to what would become the Modern machine aesthetic. By 1964, however, the industrial ethos had lost the strength to serve as an organizing principle. The car manufacturers were back, trying to put us through the same old Futurama paces that had worked in 1939. But who wanted to dream of cars and highways when to get to the fairgrounds they'd have to reckon with the Long Island Expressway? People didn't need more wonder appliances. They wanted to consume images, and in this the fair delivered handsomely: Michelangelo's *Pietà*, the world's largest Cheddar cheese, Disney robots, Les Poupées de Paris, and a full-scale replica of a Flemish village circa 1800.

Another late Saarinen project grasped the message lying beneath the chaos: the fair's IBM Pavilion, conceived in collaboration with Charles Eames. Saarinen and Eames had agreed that the pavilion should be "unarchitectural," that visitors should "remember the experience and not the architecture." The experience was images, few of them of IBM products. Seated on moving bleachers, visitors ascended ninety feet into an egg-shaped theater of molded plastic called the Information Machine. There they were bombarded by a thirty-minute mix of animated, still, and live-action images, projected onto twenty-two screens of different shapes and sizes. Though the pavilion was located on the Pool of Industry, it looked beyond modern mechanics toward the shores of consumer imagery and the media that dispensed it.

To go from the IBM pavilion to Black Rock is to go from twenty-two screens to the millions controlled by CBS—and into the mind of the visionary behind the power conferred by that control. William Paley did not just step into a position of media power. He built television from nothing. In his memoir, *As It Happened,* Paley also recounts the building of a self: the childhood education in style from reading *Vogue* and *Harper's Bazaar*; the career change from manufacturing (the family cigar business) to media (radio ads for a stogie called La Palina); the first marriage to the former wife of a Hearst; the country estate purchased from a Pulitzer.

By the time Paley built Black Rock, it was no longer just speculation that the power of electronic media would far surpass that of print. Kennedy's administration had established the media's power to influence events; and Johnson's career (supported by a fortune built on the awarding of a CBS radio affiliation in 1938) dramatized the media's power to create them. As Johnson came to understand, particularly after the Tet offensive, presidential power had become a shadow of media power. Who needed the Joint Chiefs if you had Walter Cronkite and *I Love Lucy*? And politics was only part of the story. In 1964 Marshall McLuhan's *Understanding Media* probed the ways television had begun to alter our perception of space and redraw the borders between public and private life.

The CBS Building is an exercise in the poetics of media power as a supreme but unauthorized institution. Like the IBM Pavilion, it makes a presence of absence, though one unredeemed here by a media show. When you're heading up Sixth Avenue, the building is concealed by its neighbors until you've reached it; and if it's night, and you're in a taxi, the building is invisible even when you're gliding past it. You stare out the window into what looks like empty space—prime-time blackout. The tinted windows, the peekaboo columns deepen the impression of restraint so powerful it speaks of far greater power held within.

These effects were carefully planned. Paley spent months hunting down the perfect site from which this nearly invisible architecture could be "seen" to its best advantage. After Saarinen's death, when he and Stanton became virtual collaborators in the design, Paley ordered full-scale mock-ups of the columns, set them up in the country, and adjusted their proportions. Stanton (known to his colleagues as Mr. Image) combined a training in psychology and a passion for design in overseeing every detail of this cathedral of electronic faith. What the building said was that media power came from the masking of power. The media's mastery of events was emphasized by concealment: it was better to be the puppeteer than the puppet.

Paley's traditionally decorated office suite—it was, along with the boardroom, the only part of the building exempt from Stanton's Total Design—was another form of concealment. Antique-filled, memento-lined, the office propelled the chairman imaginatively back to a time when media power had not usurped political power. It spoke instead of patrician power, of a mellowed tradition of public service. It aligned CBS with the image of privileged disinterest, symbolically distancing it from money-grubbing, from the pursuit of power for its own sake. In this office, the chairman functioned as his own puppet, pulling the strings of an insouciant aristocrat named William S. Paley.

This style of tightly controlled discretion is light-years away from the media age of million-dollar anchors, news reenactments, and movie-star politicians. And Black Rock stands at some distance from buildings by Philip Johnson and Helmut Jahn (another reformed Miesian). Far from being shunned, like Saarinen, for adopting an aesthetic of packaging, imagery, and novelty, these architects found themselves in the 1980s at the center of the profession precisely because they had mastered the art of architecture on those terms. Urged on by corporate clients and a fawning press toward heights of whimsy beyond the Expressionists' wildest dreams, Postmodern architects completed the transition from machines to media as the source of an ethos. Their buildings grab us as though they had only thirty seconds of our time.

So perhaps it is fitting that Paley has commissioned Johnson to design what each, evidently, regards as his swan song, the Museum of Broadcasting now under construction just down the block from CBS. A better idea might be to convert Black Rock itself into a museum; at least that would ensure its upkeep. For since 1986, when Laurence Tisch assumed control of CBS, the building has been allowed to deteriorate. Once crisp interiors have yellowed; a reduced maintenance staff, though movingly devoted to this building as the physical embodiment of Paley's vision, lacks sufficient resources to preserve its luster. A feeling of loss pervades the building, as though a center of power had become its own tombstone. Office space is rented out to tenants; there are rumors that the building will be put up for sale, like the other assets Tisch sold off to pay for the fight against Ted Turner's takeover attempt.

Still, even though the media empire it once housed is history, Saarinen's building remains a powerful monument to Paley and the cultural forces he deployed. Paley is that exquisite modern figure, the great man who is also the impersonation of a great man. Saarinen's building is the architectural equivalent: a great Modern building disguised as a great Modern building. It is at once a monument of Modern architecture and a stunning black void where Modernism's towers of light had lately beckoned. To look at it today is to behold a dark cloud passing over the radiant Modern sun. And, when the cloud moves away, there is a big picture tube in place of the sun, regaling a captive public with cheap jokes to a lot of canned applause.

April 23, 1990

AMERICAN GOTHIC

After an hour in Italy, I wish I'd become an architect. After a week, I begin to think it's not too late. When I get home, I'll take some stones, pile them up, cover them with stucco, paint my wall a nice earth color, let it age, plant a vine to spill over the top, have a fountain bubbling nearby, and invite everyone over for an *aperitivo*. The spell of those old stones can hold me clear across the Atlantic. Then I hit Kennedy, and the futility starts to set in; soon I'm slouched in the back of a broken-down cab, gazing from the expressway over spec housing, gutted factories, commercial strips, and, mostly, other cars. *Arrivederci*, architecture.

That's the moment when I grasp the architecture of Robert Venturi and Denise Scott Brown. The blissful revelation that real buildings can be prettier than postcards, and the rude awakening from the illusion that their effects can be duplicated anywhere with ease: Venturi and Scott Brown's buildings embody those states of mind simultaneously. Their buildings start out as shrines to the glories of Western tradition that made Italy every young architect's spiritual home. Then the forms are filtered through a sharp, unsentimental awareness that people came to this country to get away from the conditions that made those glories possible. Then they push beyond that deflating idea to see what can be made from the conditions we've created. No place for architecture? Let's have architecture anyway.

Finally, this past May, Venturi was awarded the Pritzker Architecture Prize. If the Pritzker were as distinguished an award as it's cracked up to be, it would be a scandal that Venturi had to wait in line behind such lesser talents as Philip Johnson and I. M. Pei, and that the prize was not made jointly to Scott Brown, his partner for twenty-five years. (John Rauch, a partner largely responsible for the business end of things, left the firm in 1988.) But the timing of the award is useful. This is the 25th anniversary of the publication of Venturi's *Complexity and Contradiction in Architecture*, the "gentle manifesto" that set the Postmodern movement in motion. And it is good to be reminded, now that this movement has run out of the hype that passed for steam, that these begetters of Postmodernism neither coined the term nor shared the values, at once mincing and crude, that the term came to denote.

Though Venturi was the pivotal figure in nullifying the Modern movement's declaration of independence from history, he was careful not to repeat the error by declaring his independence from a movement as historically rooted as Modernism itself. Modern forms dominate his influential early work. I grew up around the corner from the Philadelphia home that Venturi designed for his mother in 1962, a building often cited as the birthplace of Postmodernism's revival of tradition. Could have fooled us. With its angular profile, flat surfaces, and quirky windows, the house stood aesthetically on the Modern—that is, the wrong—side of the tracks from the Norman, Georgian, and Tudor mansions where the rest of the neighborhood was living out its upscale fantasy version of William Penn's Greene Countrie Towne. Today, after the Postmodern deluge of cornices, porticoes, and Corinthian columns, it's hard to see why Guild House, Venturi's 1963 home for the elderly, once had Modernists in an uproar. The building's unorthodox details, such as the small cuts at the roofline that reveal the front elevation to be a facade, or the fat round column at the entrance, only subtly contradict the initial impression that Guild House is an ordinary dumb Modern block of brick.

More important, Venturi's use of unmodern forms did not so much contradict as resuscitate Modern ideals. His use of sign language from suburban America extended to our own backyard the aesthetic affinity that Modern architects such as Gropius and Le Corbusier once felt for the craft works of exotic and primitive cultures. In drawing on this vernacular, Venturi continued the honorable Modern aim of pushing the gentlemanly art of architecture further along in a democratic direction.

Still, however gentle his intentions, Venturi knew how to jolt. He and Scott Brown bid good-bye to Good Design and headed for Las Vegas. They called their buildings "bill-ding-boards," and they spoke of the need to "accommodate" public taste instead of trying to reform it. Tossing aside Modernism's moral stake in "honestly" expressed architectural structure, they spoke of buildings as "decorated sheds," and proceeded to decorate exterior walls with stars, stripes, checks, words, and floral patterns lifted from grandma's sofa.

These flamboyant polemics soon got Venturi and Scott Brown pigeonholed as purveyors of architectural kitsch, a reputation they have been at some pains to counter over the years. Venturi has written that "I would like to make it plain that I consider myself an architect who adheres to the Classical tradition of Western architecture." He is right to insist that his buildings are more than pop cartoons. But why use the term *Classical* to describe an architecture so profoundly at odds with the ideal of order that the term has come to connote? Of course, Venturi and Scott Brown are sympathetic to the traditional association of Classicism with Jeffersonian democracy, even (or especially) in its knock-off version as a Colonial motif for diners and motels. They are populist humanists. Also, Venturi has long found inspiration in sixteenth-century Mannerism, a period when architects pushed the grammar of the Classical orders past orderly bounds. Yet, as John Shearman has observed, Mannerist architecture owes as much to Gothic as to Classical sources. And it has always struck me that the most telling precedent for Venturi and Scott Brown's ideas is the Victorian rage for Venetian Gothic kindled by that arch anticlassicist, John Ruskin.

Venturi's conception of complexity and contradiction is often taken as an expression of the disorderliness of modern life. (Rudolf Arnheim, for instance, dismissed *Complexity and Contradiction* as little more than a symptom of modern pathology.) But for Ruskin it was precisely through order that modernity showed its ugly face. In his own ungentle manifesto, *The Stones of Venice*, Ruskin begins his attack on Classicism ("this pestilent art of the Renaissance") by denying that architecture has anything to do with order. "I would not impeach love of order," Ruskin wrote; "it is one of the most useful elements of the English mind; it helps us in our commerce and in all purely practical matters; and it is in many cases one of the foundation stones of morality. Only do not let us suppose that the love of order is love of art."

For Ruskin, Gothic architecture is not primarily a matter of soaring heights, arched windows, and slender columns that admit light and allow a more open ground plan. Nor does he view Gothic buildings as examples of structural rationalism, as Viollet-le-Duc viewed them. On the contrary, for Ruskin "The Nature of Gothic" lies in such qualities as Savageness, Disturbed Imagination, Generosity, and Love of Change. He delights in the rich variations of Venetian tracery, startling juxtapositions of pattern, encrusted marble surfaces, composite styles. He applauds the architects of the Doge's Palace for not caring whether the large windows on the Molo facade are horizontally aligned: "A modern architect, terrified at the idea of violating external symmetry, would have . . . placed the larger windows at the same level with the other two. . . . But the old Venetian . . . suffered the external appearance to take care of itself. . . . And I believe the whole pile rather gains than loses in effect by the variation thus obtained in the spaces of wall above and below the windows."

A century later Venturi showed the same disregard for symmetry in allowing the internal program to affect the size and placement of the windows on the facade of his mother's house.

For Ruskin, the Doge's Palace was "the central building of the world," because of its fusion of Byzantine, Gothic, and Classical elements. For me, the Lewis Thomas Laboratory, one of four buildings Venturi and Scott Brown have designed for Princeton University, is the central building in their oeuvre to date, because of the ducal scale on which it pulls together the trio of sources that typically figure in their work: historical allusion (in this case, William Butterfield's Victorian Gothic Revival churches), vernacular forms (New England textile mills), and cues from contemporary art (Robert Kushner's Pattern and Decoration painting from the late 1970s).

Thomas Lab, completed in 1986, is the ultimate decorated shed. It is a giant, 140,000-square-foot rectangular box wrapped up in visual candy: four kinds of check and diaper patterns, executed in polychrome brick and cast stone ornamental brick bands, divide the building's three laboratory floors; rows of square-paned windows, set off by warm stone, weave a tartan of solid and void in acceptably Modern fashion. Bold red checks cover the massive mechanical services floor above the labs; the imposing scale of this floor recalls the top-heavy upper stories of the Doge's Palace, a resemblance that is heightened by the large air-intake ducts that puncture the lab's main facade.

The collage of patterns does not quite bring the building down to human scale; I doubt that Venturi wanted it to. Like a grade school glimpsed for the first time through a young child's fearful eyes, Thomas Lab is Gothic in more than its decorative details. While no cries are heard from tortured prisoners, the ominous, blind sockets of the air ducts hint at potentially ghastly results from the experiments in genetic engineering that are carried out behind the walls. But these whiffs of the sinister are more than dispelled by the building's rosy palette, and by such comic details as the truncated ogee arch at the entrance. Lopped off just beneath the crown as if by careless retrofitting, the portal ushers the visitor into a stately home lately converted into a reformatory for the criminally tasteful.

Thomas Lab was a collaboration between Venturi's firm and Payette Associates, a firm with previous experience in the design of laboratory buildings. Venturi's contribution was primarily decorative; the rationale for his forms is visual and associational rather than structural and programmatic. This is a problem only if you think that structure should dictate form. It would not have been a problem for Ruskin, long reviled by Modernists for his proclamation that "ornament is the principal part of architecture." And it was Venturi's idea of architecture as a decorated shed that marked the decisive break with the Modern canon.

That canon was largely based on one elementary idea: the desire to eliminate the nineteenth-century schism between architecture and engineering. To "create architecture out of building," in Neal Levine's phrase, instead of regarding architecture as separate from or opposed to methods of construction: this was the great Modern task. But for second-generation Modernists, the task no longer called for major invention; there was little to do but play out variations on the theme. Venturi's book got architecture out of that bind by asking, Why should the outside look like the inside? They are not the same thing. Buildings do more than stand up; they occupy vision as well as ground. Forms don't have to follow functions; they can also perform functions of their own.

The message was liberating but not anarchic. It arose organically from the Modern premise. Venturi and Scott Brown, too, have made architecture out of building; but for them building is not synonymous with engineering. It refers rather to those forms that have been denied a place in architecture's hierarchical scheme of things: resort hotels, storefront churches, restaurant chains, highway attractions. The function of their forms is to collapse this hierarchy, often into a single image. Thus, an early unbuilt project for the National Football Hall of Fame affixed an electronic billboard to a Romanesque chapel. The notorious gold "antenna" designed for the roof of Guild House served as a piece of abstract sculpture and as a sign of television's importance to the building's elderly residents. The freestanding pillars in the forecourt of Gordon Wu Hall, their first commission for Princeton, are at once a pair of spheres atop rectangular solids, a jolly cartoon version of a picturesque suburban gatepost, and a double echo of the Altar of Fortune designed by Goethe for his Weimar Garden (so blessed a campus must have two altars of fortune).

The layering of associational meanings, the precedence of vision over structure, the playful ordering of forms: these are the ingredients of an American Picturesque, an architecture that seeks to make of the built-up American landscape what eighteenth-century designers brought to English gardens. And it restores to the picturesque its lapsed philosophical dimension as an aesthetic quality "between the Beautiful and the Sublime." For Venturi and Scott Brown, the power of the sublime does not lie with God or Nature, it resides in the Market, with its awesome, leveling assault on the life of the mind. In its buildings, conventions of beauty—of abstract geometric forms, of old-world charm—are repeatedly thwarted by glaring commercial interruptions. Soon after Thomas Lab opened, the joke went around that the building's bold checked pattern was a quote from a bag of Ralston pet food: laboratory animals are, after all, the building's only full-time residents. In fact, the firm had employed a similar pattern several years before in its addition to the Oberlin College art museum. But though the pattern may derive from such lofty sources as Butterfield (William Butterfield, the English Gothic Revivalist), the scale of its application evokes commercial billboard graphics. (Don't be a paleface; the Oberlin addition rebukes its tasteful Classical neighbor.)

The market is not only a destructive power. It can also be a force for freedom—from dogma, from complacency, from the socially fragmenting pressures of privilege. Wu Hall is clad with bright orange brick. It's not a pretty brick; compared with the patina of the surrounding quadrangles, it looks commercial, more warehouse than college dining hall. One look and you think, Why didn't they use *old* brick? It would have cost the same and it would have made a better fit. Another look and you recognize that it's not meant to make a better fit. The building is a meditation on the cost of fitting in too well in a privileged enclave ringed by a protective industrial corridor. We can summon up the magic of old-world stones well enough, but it takes more than money. It takes a willingness to shut our eyes to where the money comes from, as graduates who hope to live in places this lovely will discover soon enough. Before the ivy begins to creep over our minds, Venturi and Scott Brown break in with a word from our sponsors.

Clearly the Princeton buildings bear little resemblance to what many Modern architects considered "social" architecture: the design of affordable housing, the provision of open space, the planning of entire cities according to rational, humane principles. The social significance of Wu Hall is wholly symbolic. But in fact architecture has been almost wholly consigned to the symbolic level by the increasing privatization of urban life in recent decades. As Scott Brown writes in her new book, *Urban Concepts* (Academy Editions/St. Martin's Press), "Planning is like a haunted house since we have had Nixon and Reagan." Largely reduced to the role of rubber-stampers for private development initiatives, today's departments of city planning bear little resemblance to the politically empowered agencies that inspired gifted architects of Scott Brown's generation with the ideal of public service.

Urban Concepts presents a selection of the firm's urban design schemes for Miami, Memphis, Princeton, Minneapolis, and other American cities, along with Scott Brown's penetrating analysis of the factors that were reckoned with in each case. What are the social stakes? Who are the constituents for design? What are the limits of architectural solutions? "Who decides what is pro bono publico?"

The book is a polemic as well as a portfolio. Scott Brown presents it to illustrate the point that the work of her firm has always been strongly rooted in contemporary social concerns. It is not just formal maneuvers. With or without public support for planning, Scott Brown believes that individual buildings can aspire to the social dimension of a plan for regional development. Indeed, she feels that the division between architecture and planning is bad for both professions. For Scott Brown there is a "sociological imagination" as well as a visual one, and architects and planners must embrace both. She objects that Venturi

> was not considered an "urban designer" at Penn, because he dealt mainly with individual buildings. I found this outlook ridiculous and still do. Whether a building or building complex is "urban design" or not seems to me to lie not in its size or its connectedness to other buildings, but in the way it is approached. A suburban home can be a piece of urban design, even a teaspoon can be urbane, and a downtown multistory development can look as if it were designed to rise from a green field.

Scott Brown also has a personal ax to grind: a trained architect as well as a planner, she wants to remind us that she is a full collaborator with Venturi in all of the firm's projects.

Hennepin Avenue Entertainment Centrum, an unrealized 1981 redevelopment plan for a major street in downtown Minneapolis, is a good example of Scott Brown's methods for bringing architectural cohesion to a diverse cityscape without sacrificing its diversity. By the time the firm was hired, this former boulevard of legitimate theaters and movie palaces had fallen on hard times, a casualty of the suburban malls. Proliferating peep shows, bars, adult book stores, and run-down hotels had made the street a target for civic cleanup. The risk was that the street's rich architectural mix, including several historic theaters, would be razed to allow the spread of office towers from the adjacent central business district. "The pressure will be to exchange the red silk petticoat image of Hennepin Avenue for a gray flannel one," Scott Brown's report cautioned. "Although a gray flannel image may be suitable to, and a valid requirement of, new office and hotel complexes on Hennepin Avenue, this image on the Avenue as a whole would not benefit the city at large." The plan sought to revive the street's former glory as a regional Rialto and encourage new development consistent with that aim.

Obviously, as Scott Brown saw it, the market was not the villain here. The market created the buildings and the uses that she wanted to protect, and would be instrumental in reviving them. Her plan sought to preserve, through design control, an environment that once existed without it. In this, it resembles the approach of the nineteenth-century Viennese planner Camillo Sitte, who also sought by deliberate artistic means to hold on to a vanishing culture threatened with extinction. Indeed, if Ruskin is the pertinent antecedent for Venturi and Scott Brown's buildings, Sitte is the philosophical precursor of their urban projects.

For Sitte, too, order was the bane of Modern life. "Modern systems! Yes! To conceive everything systematically, and never to deviate a hair's breadth from the formula once it's established, until all genius is tortured to death, all joyful sense of life suffocated, that is the mark of our time." Sitte's mission was to protect the irregularities of the older, artisan city from further encroachment by the civil engineer's grids. The off-center placement of civic statues, the nonaxial organization of town squares and the streets leading into them: by such archaic devices Sitte hoped that new urban development could proceed according to what he considered the "artistic principles" of the medieval city.

Scott Brown also employs analysis and prescription to create effects that initially developed without their aid. But her effects hold a different message. Sitte sought an ideal of cultural unity. An ardent Wagnerian, he wanted architects to create an urban *Gesamtkunstwerk* designed to steep citizens in awareness of a common cultural heritage. For Sitte, the focus of urban design was the town square. In this social space, streets and people would converge, submerging individual differences in the common pool of community. Scott Brown's aim, by contrast, is to strengthen the ideal of pluralism against creeping homogeneity. For her, the urban focus is the street, a line that cuts across urban differences—skyscrapers, department stores, skid rows, peep shows, Chinese restaurants, parks adorned with the statues of forgotten generals—the entire range of what she calls "taste cultures."

Squares are closed, streets are open, and subject to every force of change. The Hennepin Avenue proposal involved the study of existing buildings and their uses, transportation systems, and growth patterns for the central business district and the metropolitan region. Its recommendations included traffic routes, designs for bus stops, plazas, and skywalks, and the development of design guidelines for future construction. But the main goal of the plan was to give the street a strong visual "entertainment" image. "Sparkle trees," lofty metal branches festooned with reflecting discs, were designed to line the street at curbside and create "a framework within which the variety will appear complex and not ugly." With the delicacy of Gothic tracery, the trees formed the bones of a honky-tonk chapel for which the street's bright lights and neon signs would provide the stained glass.

. . .

The key to this work is that it emphasized perception over construction. Seedy the street may have become, but, as Scott Brown pointed out, Hennepin Avenue "is certainly not dead. . . . It has a definite character and one that has great potential." The design proposed to develop the potential by helping people to recognize the character, to see beauty and vitality where they might otherwise see only squalor and decay. This approach is miles away from the standard Postmodern practice of cribbing from European forms. Instead of plopping down an imported temple, the plan sought to raise a temple from the materials at hand. We may not have the means to create a Ste. Chapelle, it said, but the reds and the blues of our neons have their own radiance. We need not romanticize the anonymous craftsmen of the Middle Ages, when our sign-makers, display artists, even peep-show operators can do wonders with windows.

Like all of the urban schemes presented here, this one shows the mark of one of Venturi's best-known dictums: "Main Street is almost all right." This idea broke so radically from the Modern prescription to bulldoze cities into blank slates for "total design" that it is easy to miss the curiously Modern thinking behind it. Subtle changes in street lighting, signs, curb lines: What could be closer to the Miesian aesthetic of "almost nothing"? What could be more "less is more" than Scott Brown's belief that pluralism is best accommodated by minimal means? And the underlying idea behind this design—that economic forces should not be spurned but rather channeled toward humane ends—was the central principle on which the Bauhaus was founded.

Scott Brown was not the first to focus attention on the small scale. In the early '60s Jane Jacobs dealt the death blow to the large-scale urban development that Modern architects favored. And Scott Brown's concepts are vulnerable to the same criticism that Lewis Mumford hurled at "Mother Jacobs' home remedies for urban cancer." It's all very well to delight in the colorful threads of the urban fabric. The danger is that enchantment with the small scale can resign us to our failure to deal effectively with large-scale issues of housing, transportation, economic growth, and their impact on the environment. Who cares whether Main Street is almost all right when our urban policies are almost all wrong?

A more serious objection to Scott Brown's approach is that pluralism may be as pernicious a myth as Sitte's Germanic monoculture. It is fine to value diversity, but the risk then arises of creating an image of diversity beneath which the consolidation of economic power and social uniformity can continue as before. True, Scott Brown's approach will not produce the scorched earth policy practiced by Modern architects. The risk with her approach, however, is that it could act like a neutron bomb, preserving the varied texture of cities while encouraging the further displacement of the subcultures responsible for creating the variety in the first place. Or what if those cultures don't want to provide our local color? In the years since Jacobs wrote so lyrically about mom-and-pop candy stores, many of us have found ourselves thinking we would rather watch cities subside into natural ruins than see them turned into theme parks. What's to prevent our appetite for "taste cultures" from turning the city into an endless yuppie smorgasbord of cultural tastes that somehow all taste the same?

Scott Brown is hardly unaware of these problems ("yuppie" is a dirtier word in her lexicon than it is in mine). The great strength of her book, in fact, is that it gives us a framework in which to examine them. What are the alternatives to the "theme park" city? Would we prefer cities to continue along their present course as theme parks of the apocalypse? Should we retreat to the theme parks of social atomization furnished by the suburbs? *Urban Concepts* does not settle these questions. What it offers instead is a guide to the process of eliciting preferences. As such, the book's most valuable service may be to bring back to the table the awkward topic of taste.

Do we care? Is this a major urban issue? The bridges are crumbling, senior citizens are sleeping in the subways, and our thoughts should turn to *taste*? Yes, because architecture is a social art, but it is not sociology. It is a partner of social policy, but it is not a substitute for it. Buildings cannot create ideal societies, but if they are to embody social ideals then the issue of taste cannot be avoided, because taste is where art and sociology meet. "Tell me what you like," as Ruskin bluntly put it, "and I will tell you what you are." The question that Venturi and Scott Brown have consistently asked is how architecture, as a social art, can tell us what we are as a society.

Classicism has enjoyed an honored claim as a style for modern democracy because in theory it is a style of orders and laws, and therefore ideal for a civilization that places the rule of law over the rule of men. This was an Enlightenment proposition: the geometric abstraction of late-eighteenth-century Neoclassicism proclaimed an affinity with the impersonal laws of nature, and with the "natural" order of human society that philosophers expected to uncover. Two shifts in architecture mark this idea: in style, from Baroque to Neoclassicism, and in building type, from churches and palaces to public and institutional buildings.

The Classical laws are "above taste," as the law of gravity is above opinion. But it was to subjective taste that the architects of the Enlightenment had to appeal, for with the eclipse of palaces and churches and the authority they exerted, taste became the basis of the social contract on which architectural forms acquire moral significance. In theory, proper cultivation will ensure that taste will concur on correct forms. The role of the academies is to apply the theory. Under academic tutelage, the taste of individuals will converge, like the radial avenues leading toward the Neo-classical public buildings that occupy the center of Ledoux's ideal town of Chaux. The pattern repeated itself in the 1920s, when the Modern move-ment coalesced around the New Objectivity of Hannes Meyer, Mart Stam, Walter Gropius, and Mies van der Rohe. Once again the associative value of scientific truth was invoked to elevate form above taste, and soon the academy, this time the Museum of Modern Art, again undertook pub-lic instruction.

But what if you weren't convinced? Ruskin's problem with Classicism was not the Modern objection that ancient forms are wrong for modern uses; he objected that the analogy of architecture with science was simply false. "Our architects gravely inform us that, as there are four rules of arithmetic, there are five orders of architecture; we, in our simplicity, think this sounds consistent, and believe them." For Scott Brown, it came as no surprise when MoMA mounted a show of Beaux Arts architecture in 1975. Though MoMA had once opposed the Beaux Arts and everything it stood for, the museum had long been "a pompier of the Modern move-ment." Its sudden interest in Classicism, Scott Brown found, served only to subvert the renewal of interest in history and allow "a continuation of [Modern] purism in a new guise."

To recognize the academicism of these movements, however, is not to grant that the academy is invariably wrong, stupid, or an elitist conspiracy foisted on a grumbling public. There is a "taste culture" of architecture itself, a tradition sustained by the impulse to rise above subjective taste through normative order. That impulse is not ignoble, nor is it as divorced from public desires as Ruskin and Scott Brown seem to think. Ruskin erred in presuming to speak for everyone when he wrote that "we take no pleasure in [a Classical building] resembling that which we take in a new book or a new picture." For one thing, writing and painting can be as for-mulaic as any architectural system; for another, the art of creating a system can be as inventive as the act of breaking one. Precisely because life is messy, it can be very compelling to imagine a life of order, simplicity, and purity, and a great pleasure indeed to look at works by Balanchine, Agnes Martin, Mies van der Rohe, and Buckminster Fuller that give form to that ideal.

Whether or not the Classical vocabulary employed in the Chicago

World's Fair of 1893 was appropriate for a democracy in the industrial age, the White City's vision of urban unity proved immensely popular. For years now we've had it drummed into our heads that the public hates Modern architecture. The truth is, many Modern buildings captured the public's imagination with enormous success. People really did gather in the street outside Manufacturers Hanover Trust to gawk at the steel safe gleaming behind the glass curtain wall. It was Hollywood art directors, not a bunch of highbrows, who recognized the powerful mass appeal of the UN Secretariat Building and the Seagram Building. No doubt many people liked these buildings for the "wrong" reasons—because they were novel, or glamorous—but so what? In satisfying our taste for novelty and glamour, these buildings gave bold expression to "who we are." It is only when Modern buildings ceased to satisfy this taste, when Lever House was no longer the announcer with the news but merely one pane in an endless wall of glass, that alarm bells went off.

Today many architects feel that their profession is in crisis because there is no academy authorizing a dominant visual vocabulary or a concerted social purpose. Instead, we have good work as varied as that by Frank Gehry, Charles Moore, and Richard Meier, each aligned with a different aesthetic, none enjoying a legitimate claim to represent the only or the best way to design. The "taste culture" of architecture, in other words, is in disarray, despite the heroic efforts of Postmodernists, Neomodernists, and Deconstructionists and their apologists to coax the divergent waters of the mainstream back into that tired old riverbed so that it will flow obediently toward them. If it would go too far to credit (or to blame) Venturi and Scott Brown for architecture's current fragmentation, it is at least the case that their inclusive approach, with its implicit rejection of the historicist notion of One Epoch, One Style, anticipated this condition, and remains a viable approach to understanding and even feeling grateful for it.

Taste does not converge on formulas for art and architecture the way experimentation converges on a law of physics. Taste converges on differences: the new tower on the block, the old eyesore left standing, the alternations between order and violation, stasis and change, like and dislike. That is why Ruskin, a supreme moralist, insisted that architects "should be not only correct, but entertaining." That is why, for Venturi and Scott Brown, the city street has been a guiding metaphor, why Thomas Lab plants a billboard in the ivy. The street does not rise above taste, it slices through taste. It tells us who we are by showing us what others like. What is democratic about Venturi and Scott Brown's architecture is not that it is designed by referendum, or even that it tries to be popular, but that, in challenging the normative impulse of architectural "taste culture," it shows how the aims of art and the aims of self-government coincide. Each renews its authority not by its power to enforce laws but through our power to affect them.

August 12, 1991

THE WRONG PRESCRIPTION

Earth, Air, Water, Fire: no American building welcomes the visitor to a more elemental realm than Louis Kahn's Salk Institute for Biological Studies in La Jolla, California. I have no idea whether Kahn intended an explicit analogy between Jonas Salk's advanced research and the four elements of ancient science. But Kahn seems never to have undertaken any project without trying to imagine himself back at the origin of things. Nowhere did he exercise that imagination more persuasively than in these two laboratory buildings and the courtyard that joins them atop the La Jolla cliffs. The sea, the sun, the sky, and the cliffs are as elemental to Kahn's architecture as the concrete, the travertine, the wood, and the glass that he assembled on the site.

In January the Salk Institute (designed and built between 1959 and 1965) received the Twenty-five Year Award from the American Institute of Architects. No building is more deserving. Still, I suspect that many who have visited the Salk would agree that in this instance a quarter-century salute seems almost an impertinence. We're talking pyramids here: a monument that asks to be judged by the measure of centuries, and looks almost as though it's been around that long. That impression is heightened by the building's contrast with the fast-lane culture that provides the prelude to a visit. Particularly if you're exhilarated by a spin down Route 405, you will want to pause a moment in the Institute's parking lot, which is really an open-air decompression chamber for recovering the use of your feet. This is architecture you don't pass at highway speeds.

You approach the buildings through a grove of eucalyptus trees, a permeable wall, the choir screen before a sanctuary. For it is indeed ecclesiastical architecture. Built with money from the March of Dimes, dedicated to the ongoing battle against disease, the Salk is a modern descendent of the Old World's plague churches. Like the Salute in Venice or Palladio's great Redontore, Kahn's masterwork is a votive church to science.

Today the grove looks somewhat scrappy, which only accentuates the plot's earthiness as a foil for the vision veiled by the trees: first, sky; then, as you walk through the grove, the rooflines of the two laboratory build-

ings that rise up ahead on either side. The roof lines look saw-toothed, an
effect of the angled windows of the study towers attached to the labs, and
as you move closer the rooflines slice through the sky like two serrated
blades, carving it into a solid block of space that descends to fill the central
court.

You enter this void—the sanctuary itself—through a second screen, again
of trees, but this time of clipped, regularly spaced orange trees, a green
hinge between the grove and the symmetric geometry of Kahn's buildings.
Straight ahead is the Pacific and, often, hang gliders spreading rainbow
wings. Upward reflections sculpt the space into form: the glaring rectangular solid of light, bounced upward from the court's travertine paving
stones, is set off by a larger arc of radiance rising from the water. As the
afternoon progresses, the void becomes nearly material as it fills up with
the sunlight's increasingly dense gold.

The light—captured with stunning fidelity by Grant Mudford's photographs in an essential new book, *Louis I. Kahn: In the Realm of Architecture*
by David B. Brownlee and David G. DeLong (Rizzoli)—is more awesome
even than the light of Venice, because the surroundings offer so little distraction: no ogee windows, mosaics, arched bridges, or Harry's Bar.
Instead, there are the proportions of the laboratories, the thickness of
their concrete walls, and a mottled bloom on the surface of the concrete
that picks up the light and gives the walls a mirage-like shimmer. A narrow
canal of water runs down the center of the court, a perspective line that
draws the water from the horizon to your feet.

Kahn initially planned to line the sides of the canal with cypress trees,
perhaps an allusion to Hadrian's Villa, which, along with the monastery of
San Francisco at Assisi, provided him with historical points of departure.
It was Luis Barragán, Mexico's great Modernist architect, who suggested
that the court remain bare. He argued that a view of the ocean horizon
would create sufficient closure to unify the complex. But unity suggests a
classical composure that is elusive here. The effect is closer to the uncanny
classicism of de Chirico: a stage too stark for repose. From time to time,
figures cross the court, but they don't linger. Wearing long white lab
coats, they resemble not people but props, mechanical swans in some Brutalist ballet.

The uncanniness thickens as you proceed along the canal, past the
angled surfaces of the study towers, concrete cliffs that "open" as you pass
to reveal windows handsomely framed with weathered teak. Never was
openness so transparently shut. The views from inside are spectacular, but
from without the windows gape along a ghost town Main Street.
Cypresses, hell; the place cries out for tumbleweed.

The labs themselves dramatize Kahn's distinction between "served" and "servant" spaces, between enclosures for people and for building mechanics. Each six-story lab building (two of the floors are below grade) is a triple sandwich: lab floors alternate with three "interstitial spaces" filled with conduits, compressors, tubes that siphon off waste. This arrangement allows the labs to be quickly refitted to accommodate the researchers' changing needs. And what a grand gesture to build luxury suites for plumbing! Threading my way one afternoon through the labs' vaporous innards, I remembered "stinks," colloquial for the natural sciences, Auden recalls in "The Greeks and Us," an essay on British middle-class education. Stinks were the Modern Side, history and mathematics the more socially acceptable Classical Side. At the Salk, a classicist places himself at the service of stinks—here classicism exchanges its high literary gloss for the hard crust of fossils—and in that subservience ennobles both.

Go in the middle or late afternoon, but go quickly, for the integrity of Kahn's work is now in jeopardy. A year ago Salk unveiled plans for a new building that would seriously compromise the power of Kahn's work. What he envisions are two rectangular buildings (containing meeting rooms, administrative offices, and additional lab space) set end to end, perpendicular to the axis of Kahn's labs, on a portion of the grove. (The size of the portion varies with different versions of the design.) A cylindrical structure between the two wings would serve as a reception area. Groundbreaking for the revision, originally scheduled for early last year, has been postponed; perhaps the best way to celebrate the Salk's Twenty-five Year Award would be to cancel the unfortunate scheme altogether.

The addition's most conspicuous impact would be to obstruct the dynamic unfolding of space that visitors activate by passing through the grove. Besides eliminating the gradual unveiling of the labs and the space that they carve, the new addition would impose a strict axial approach on them by channeling visitors through the reception kiosk. A parallel could be drawn between the pathways through the grove and the narrow medieval streets that once intensified the experience of entering St. Peter's Square. Like the bombastic Via della Conciliazione, the addition would weaken the power of the open space it seeks to enhance. Salk has described the grove as a drainage ditch. Alas, it would drain away more than water.

Another problem, less-easily described, concerns not only formal matters but also Salk's philosophical ambitions. What he originally envisioned for the Institute was far grander than a lab. He and Kahn first discussed the project in 1959, the year that C. P. Snow delivered his widely publicized lecture on the "two cultures." Salk saw the Institute as a place where people of the sciences and people of the humanities could meet and bridge the gulf between them. In a famous remark, Salk charged Kahn with designing a place in which he would feel comfortable receiving Picasso. He hoped that the Institute could find formulas for healing culture as well as bodies.

Though the two labs were designed for science, their binary configuration may owe something to this idea. Or perhaps the idea and the formal arrangement both sprang from something deeper in Salk's way of thinking. In any case, the power of the central court arises from the absence of formal hierarchy between the two separate-but-equal labs. At the focal point, where you would expect to see a monumental form (think, for instance, of the Capitol on the Mall, or the Rotunda at the University of Virginia), there are hang gliders hovering in space. While the addition would not shatter the symmetry, it would reduce the tension between the two vertical slabs. Instead of maintaining a separation between them, and demonstrating the spatial eloquence of which separation is capable, the two halves of the binary system would, in effect, merge.

The proposed addition falls short in other ways, too. Nothing could contrast more sharply with the functional clarity of Kahn's labs than this confused programmatic jumble of meeting rooms, labs, offices, and areas for public reception, all wrapped up together in vaguely Kahnesque walls. It grates to contemplate such a structure raised in close proximity to Kahn's masterful integration of program and form. Worse, the addition would weaken the Institute's integral relationship to the land that it occupies. The eucalyptus grove does not scream something; it says something. It says that we are leaving an urban world and entering a natural domain, a place where buildings and land are joined on an intermediary plane between the microbe and the cosmos. As Harriet Pettison, a landscape architect who worked with Kahn, points out, the proposed addition is an urban building; its design is oblivious to the Institute's coastal terrain. To place it between the parking lot and the court would shatter the logical sequence of walking from the place of cars onto primal ground.

This is not a simple case of protecting a landmark building from the bad guys. Salk's stature as a humanitarian hero for a generation of American families is not architecturally irrelevant. The primary function of a plague church, after all, was to ward off disease or to offer thanksgiving for deliverance from it. So long as we place our faith in science, we have a stake in Salk's right to run his own show. And the building would not exist had Salk not selected Kahn to design it, nor would it have attained its present form had he not developed an extraordinary rapport with Kahn while they worked on the design. As Kahn acknowledged, it was Salk who urged that a single open court would be stronger than the two courts the architect proposed in an earlier scheme. In the basement of the north lab, you can still see the patchwork wall where the two worked together to perfect the concrete's extraordinary finish.

Moreover, much as we may want to freeze the building in its present state of grace, the fact remains that the Salk is an unfinished work; what we see today is one-third of the complex that Kahn designed. A meetinghouse for the Institute's fellows was to be located on a promontory overlooking the water to the north; Kahn also designed a housing complex for a corresponding site to the south. These two parts were conceived to face each other across the ravine that cuts a triangle into the bluffs, with the lab buildings rising at its apex. Kahn's master plan, in other words, employed the kind of hierarchical organization that is now fortuitously absent. As it stands, only the hang gliders are in a position to appreciate what Kahn evidently intended: the Salk's true facade faces the sea. Spectacular though the existing entrance may be, in fact we come in through the back door.

Perhaps that is why Salk does not quite grasp why people are upset by his proposal. My impression, after a conversation with Salk some months before plans for the addition were made public, is that this may be literally a case of lost perspective: the man has been at the heart of the building for so long that he may no longer perceive what visitors from the outside journey to see. Clearly Salk reveres Kahn, and takes great pride in their collaboration. He believes that he has done well by Kahn in hiring John MacAllister, an architect who worked on the original buildings, to design the proposed addition. And although MacAllister's design is an architectural muddle, Salk could make the case that it would allow him to *un*muddle Kahn's work by removing from the south the lab offices that were placed there pending completion of the master plan.

Salk is well aware of the explosion of outrage that prevented a proposed addition to Kahn's Kimbell Art Museum in Fort Worth. He emphasized to me that his addition, unlike the Kimbell's, would not come into physical contact with Kahn's forms. Of course, since the Salk's principal form is unbounded space, that claim has little meaning. To support his plan, Salk has in hand two drawings from Kahn's office that locate a reception building on the site he has chosen. But Pettison, who prepared one of these drawings, maintains that this was a tentative sketch, done at Salk's request, and that Kahn himself opposed it.

So why not complete the master plan that Kahn designed? Salk has apparently not ruled out the possibility of building Kahn's meetinghouse at some point in the future, but, unlike the new addition, the plans for the meetinghouse do not provide space for new labs. There's also an economic incentive to build on the grove site, since it would enable the new facility to tap into the underground plant that services the existing labs.

Fortunately, Salk is willing to listen to critics of his proposal. Following a round of protest letters from a number of prominent American architects, he has met privately with several of them to discuss their objections. He has already modified his original proposal, shifting the site of the new buildings about thirty feet to the east, which would preserve a portion of the grove. He has also indicated that he is open to other suggestions. The best of these so far has been volunteered by Kahn's former associate Anne Griswold Tyng. Tyng suggests breaking apart the two halves of the addition, rotating them 90 degrees (so that they would lie parallel with Kahn's labs), and shifting them out to the north and south edges of the parking lot. An underground connection between the two parts could provide space for additional facilities. Tyng's proposal does not pretend to be architecture; its advantage is that it would have only peripheral impact on Kahn's building.

But some who have spoken with Salk believe that he *wants* to interpose a barrier between the Institute and the world. He may feel, in fact, that he is performing an act of architectural preservation, by putting up what amounts to a dike between Kahn's buildings and the wave of development that in recent years has swept this part of San Diego. I would speculate, too, that Salk would like to resolve the tension of the architecture's binary configuration. A set of conceptual diagrams prepared by his architects uses shaded and bisected circles to develop what resembles a Jungian motif of "dualities and unity." Perhaps Salk believes that his building can symbolically fuse the dualisms that his Institute set out to bridge. But to attempt such an occult philosophical reconciliation with this design would be a tragic error. And it would be redundant, besides. Jonas Salk already bridged the "two cultures" twenty-five years ago, when he collaborated with Louis Kahn on one of the century's supreme works of art. Now it's up to him alone to guard the bridge.

February 10, 1992

EAST/WEST SIDE STORY

A Review of Noguchi East and West *by Dore Ashton*

Many artists today believe that SoHo is as important as Silicon Valley in the shaping of global culture, and so their work explores the power of images to define cultural relationships. Dore Ashton has written an engaging full-length portrait of an artist who explored cultural relationships to define himself. Isamu Noguchi was a one-man foreign exchange program, a human bridge between multiculturalism and an earlier cosmopolitan ideal. Born in Los Angeles in 1904 to a Japanese father and an American mother, shuttled between Japan and the United States as a child, Noguchi faced his Other every time he looked in the mirror.

He used art to reduce the anxieties of that confrontation, in work that fused the abstract forms and enigmatic content of modern art and Eastern religion. Over time, inspired by the global outlook of his friend Buckminster Fuller, Noguchi nourished his vision with an ever-expanding range of sources. Temples, totem poles, stupas, piazzas, and burial mounds were absorbed into the conceptual clay from which he hoped to fashion his elusive image of "the world in a single sculpture." And his reach for synthesis sets him apart from many artists today, who strain to articulate cultural differences.

It aligned him, however, with artists of an earlier generation who believed that abstract art expressed universal values. Noguchi's sculptures, discernibly inflected by Brancusi and Zen, affirmed the mission of modern art to cross cultural borders. Similarly, his settings of classical legends choreographed by Martha Graham and George Balanchine encouraged belief in the universality of Western myths. Moreover, the Buddhist concepts that Noguchi often applied to the carving and the placement of his stones gave weight to the idea that we could see in abstract forms not just materials but also patterns and the traces of a spiritual essence.

Ashton traces the uphill struggle that Noguchi faced in achieving his deceptively serene fusion of East and West. Neither a detached Zen master nor a blithe American tourist, Noguchi paid a price to make something universal from his dual cultural heritage: he felt universally displaced. In Japan his pale eyes marked him as a *gaijin*, an "outside person"; and even his father never let him forget that he did not belong. In the United States he endured (not without protest) the wave of anti-Japanese prejudice that followed Pearl Harbor.

Noguchi faced similar obstacles in making his work understood. Reviews of his early shows in New York were marked by racial epithets both veiled ("wily") and not so veiled ("Once an Oriental, always an Oriental"). Even many years later, after he had achieved renown, Noguchi's work was often discounted or dismissed. Thus Rosalind Krauss, in an essay in 1979 on "Sculpture in the Expanded Field," managed to write Noguchi out of the history of the very fields that he had been cultivating years before the advent of Robert Smithson, Robert Morris, and Mary Miss: earthworks, site-specific sculpture, public art that aspires to architectural scale.

Noguchi's reception in Japan was even more complex. As an international figure, a man who had lived with the legends in Paris, Noguchi enjoyed high esteem among Japanese artists. At the same time, his eagerness to master traditional forms, such as terra-cotta pottery, alienated those who felt that modernity demanded a break with the past. His effort to make himself at home in "old Japan" is the most fascinating part of Ashton's story; from a New York perspective, it reads like the account of a bigamist's other life. On a visit in 1931, Noguchi resisted his father's efforts to introduce him to contemporary Japanese artists, later saying, "I wanted, on the contrary, the Orient." Actually, what he wanted was more a kind of Orientalism: a state of aesthetic bliss furnished with old stone lanterns, tea houses, cherry blossoms, poems to the moon. In 1951 Noguchi created for himself a kind of theme park of Old Japan on a farm in Kamakuru, complete with a bride, Yoshiko Yamaguchi, formerly known as Shirley in her days as a Hollywood actress.

Life with Noguchi was evidently not all that different from playing in a costume production. He donned traditional robes and insisted that Yamaguchi wear them also, along with straw sandals that pinched her feet. "When she complained, he said that uncomfortable or not, he wanted her to wear them because they were beautiful." But soon Noguchi packed away the robes and took off for Paris, and then for New York, as if propelled by an irony: greater harmony of being awaited him in the disruptive West than in a Zen garden. Even his role as a gentleman of Old Japan owed more to Western self-invention than to Eastern tradition.

Ashton shows that Noguchi was also displaced in time. He does not fit comfortably in the art movements that unfolded during his lifetime. *Biomorphic*, the term often used to shoehorn him into the New York school, applies only to Noguchi's sculpture of the 1940s, before his mature work emerged. That maturity took a long time to develop, and the development took place in public. While still in his early twenties, Noguchi made a name for himself as a sculptor of portrait busts. The book includes a photograph of one of them, the sculptor posed beside it. If there is art here, it is all in the pose.

An apprenticeship with Brancusi in Paris in 1927 introduced Noguchi to modern sculpture's cutting edge. It also introduced him to apprenticeship as a way of life. Soon after his sojourn in the French capital, Noguchi went to live in Kyoto, where he learned from Jinmatsu Uno, a master potter, to apply celadon glaze. It was the first of many associations that Noguchi formed with Japan's traditional craftsmen to enlarge his technique and his outlook. Yet Japan could not provide a stage sufficiently large for Noguchi to show off his enlarged ambitions. Back in New York after his fling with pots, Noguchi turned briefly to Social Realism. *Death*, a metal sculpture of 1935, depicts a lynched black man.

Ashton's account of those restless movements suggests that East and West were Noguchi's geographical analogues for the familiar poles of a modern artist's dilemma: how to create art that reflects its time but transcends it. Japan stood for timelessness, the West stood for change. But the West also offered posterity, a form of timelessness that Noguchi could not renounce. Unable to resolve the dilemma in favor of any one place, he resolved it in motion, routinely, dividing his last two decades between his New York studio and a retreat on the island of Sikoku.

The work of these years, an abundant outpouring of large pieces in marble, granite, and basalt, is a testament to equilibrium attained. As if bearing traces of time and weather, their surfaces are chipped, pitted, gouged, square-cut, rounded off, rubbed smooth as lacquer; and the effects are knowingly juxtaposed, as though the elements have embraced the middle way. In those pieces Noguchi has finally excavated his art from beneath the weight of his influences. Where Michelangelo sought to liberate a sculpture from a stone, Noguchi freed stone from his desire to make a "sculpture."

Ashton does not recount this story in facile multicultural terms. She writes of racism, not of "Eurocentrism"; of art, not of "privileged discourses." Nor is she one to speculate on resemblances between Noguchi's globalism and, say, Conrad Hilton's. She assumes the reader will share her belief that art is of a different order than Coca-Cola. Ashton's conventional art historical approach has its advantages: she makes a good case that Noguchi deserves to stand with the luminaries already chronicled in her book *The New York School*. Still, to treat Noguchi in the familiar terms of art history is to risk missing what was most pioneering about his work: the extent to which he aimed to dissolve the boundaries of art itself.

For Noguchi's is not just an East-West story. It is also a High-Low story. Noguchi's efforts to transcend the differences between New York and Kyoto were paralleled by his attempts to erase the line between fine and applied art. These two ambitions were linked, and the connection did not begin with Noguchi. Since the Arts and Crafts movement, Western designers had looked to Japan as the model of a culture in which aesthetic values were integrated with social ones. Frank Lloyd Wright's Organic Architecture owed much to this model, which also influenced the Bauhaus ideal of the building as an artistic synthesis. "For the first time in my life, I felt myself with the majority," observed Walter Gropius after a visit to Japan in 1954. There, as in the Bauhaus, no clear line divided objects of everyday use from those of aesthetic contemplation.

Noguchi fit into this Modern agenda with the ease of a built-in modern table. And he exploited the fit to advance an agenda of his own. His theater decors, his Akari lamps, and his boomerang tables were not just a sculptor's sidelines. They were means for dispersing sculptural values beyond sculpture into space. This ambition found its full expression in

Noguchi's last decades, when he received commissions for such magnificent public spaces as the Billy Rose Sculpture Garden in Jerusalem, Detroit's Hart Plaza, and *California Scenario* in Costa Mesa. Noguchi had long regarded landscape as a more congenial medium than sculpture for his cross-disciplinary ideas. In 1933 he conceived the massive *Monument to the Plough*, a low, three-sided pyramid of earth, each base stretching a mile in length. *Play Mountain*, an urban version of this rural scheme, was designed to occupy an entire New York City block.

But these projects, though huge in scale, remained sculpted objects. In the late 1940s Noguchi grasped the need to push his vision further, into the space that objects occupy. In 1949, with a grant from the Bollingen Foundation, he traveled through Europe, India, and Southeast Asia to study sacred sites where sculpture, architecture, and landscape achieved a "communal, emotional, and mystic" synthesis. This journey shifted the focus of his ambitions not only from sculpture to space but from art to "culture . . . the integration of art and life." The chance to realize these "compositions in topological space" finally came in the 1950s. Invited by Marcel Breuer to design a small garden for UNESCO's Paris headquarters, Noguchi quickly expanded the scope of the project into an environment that embraced Breuer's architecture within a varied terrain of stone, water, maple and bamboo, stark and dappled light.

Not all of Noguchi's collaborations with architects were so fortunate. His work with Gordon Bunshaft of Skidmore, Owings & Merrill is significant chiefly for exposing that Noguchi's fit with Modern architecture could be too comfortable for his own good. These projects began as well-intended efforts to compensate for the brutish impact of Modern buildings at street scale. By 1960 it had become painfully apparent even to Modern architects that the effect of their buildings was far from the "towers in a park" fantasy of which they had dreamed. Instead of generously opening up new vistas of open space, Modern buildings declared a sensory void. Bunshaft invited Noguchi to augment the gift of space with the gift of art, a form of civic generosity that passersby would find harder to overlook. Alas, in their collaborations on buildings for two New York banks, the art became the urban equivalent of the toaster bestowed on customers for opening an account.

The Chase Manhattan Headquarters (1960) was a violent urban disruption; street traffic in lower Manhattan was permanently rerouted to make room for this stolid block of aluminum and glass. Yet here was Noguchi, down on hands and knees in a sunken plaza at the building's base, fitting together stones he'd traveled through Japan to collect, as though a little oasis of tranquility could suffice to tame this architectural King Kong. Noguchi's 1973 sculpture for Bunshaft's Marine Midland

Bank Headquarters, a block away from Chase on lower Broadway, evokes a good deal more urban drama: the upended vermilion cube shoots into the air like a spurt of blood, squeezed from the urban tissue where Bunshaft's shiny black boot comes thudding down. The cube's hollow cylindrical core takes aim at the building like the gun barrel of a disgruntled client, or an anti-modernist run amok. Yet in the end the piece stands as an abstract sculpture, a classic example of "plop art," and its contrapuntal relationship to the building undermines Noguchi's intention. Instead of dispersing sculpture into the environment, the cube gathers Art into its finite shape. The result makes a poor contrast with Bunshaft's 1954 design for the Fifth Avenue branch of Manufacturers Hanover Trust, where the bank's gleaming steel vault, framed by its glass curtain wall as an object of contemplation, erases the distinction between fine art and applied art.

Ashton provides a superb account of the ideas behind these projects and the complexities of building them. She does not reckon, however, with the extent to which the building compromised the ideas. This is not a minor omission in a book that offers to revise our estimation of Noguchi from the perspective of the present. These outdoor works not only pioneered the field of "public art"; they also anticipated the crisis that has emerged with the corporate annexation of that field. Like Noguchi, artists such as Mary Miss, Scott Burton, and Ned Smythe started out with idealistic convictions, determined to free their work from the traditional boundaries of sculpture and the commercial grip of the galleries. But many found themselves, at the end of the 1980s, hostage to a far more hazardous form of commerce, providing window dressing for the "public-private" development partnerships that have been systematically short-changing the public on the quality of urban life.

Nothing throws their predicament into sharper relief than Noguchi's own major work of the 1980s. It was a civic gift without compromise. The Isamu Noguchi Garden Museum is one of the few real gems that New York has added in recent years to its tarnished cultural diadem. The place is a shrine to touch; only Garbo in that scene in *Queen Christina* has displayed a more voluptuous talent for intimacy with the inanimate. Is it strange that an artist who stepped over art's borders should sum up his legacy by stepping back behind the walls of a museum? Not in a world that has seen those borders nearly buried beneath an avalanche of pop culture.

Noguchi's aim was to integrate art, not to abandon it. His museum breathes with that ideal, an effect due partly to its location. Set in Long Island City's industrial landscape, the museum presents his work in the context of making objects, not just looking at them. Inside, we see models of the projects through which Noguchi exerted art's pressure outward. Above all, this permanent retrospective links Noguchi's sculpture to the contours of his life. So does Ashton's book. She persuades us that Noguchi had more than art in mind when he invited us to "call it sculpture when it moves you so."

June 15, 1992

CROWDS AND POWER

Making the Mummies Dance: Inside the Metropolitan Museum of Art *by Thomas Hoving*

Thomas Hoving's *Making the Mummies Dance* is essential reading for students and survivors of that dancing mummy of a decade, the 1960s. In his book *Popism*, Andy Warhol gave us "the Warhol '60s." *Making the Mummies Dance* presents the Hoving '60s. The two books would make a peerless boxed set. Both are compulsively readable firsthand testimonials to the spirit and the power of pop.

By 1967, when Hoving became director of the Metropolitan Museum of Art, Pop Art was over, but the pop sensibility was rampant. Its ruling principle was transposition. Instead of a place for everything, it demanded that everything be jerked out of place. The street went both ways: while the beer can, the soup can, and the Popsicle went from the supermarket to the art gallery, the art object was trucked out to the curb. In 1967 the City of New York began a program of what would later be called public art. In the waiting room at Grand Central Station, a mammoth sculpture by Chryssa flashed blue neon behind dark glass. Tony Rosenthal's *Alamo* went up at Astor Place, and the Seagram Building Plaza was host to Barnett Newman's *Broken Obelisk*.

The program included some fine works, but their impact was collective and urban. Each was a sign of some force that was displacing art from its usual habitat. Context was the important thing: not the object, but the space around it. This, too, was a transposition, a shift of emphasis from figure to ground. Art was now as much a matter of moving furniture as making things. If a place was not a traditional site for art, then you put art in it. If it was an art place, then you put something else there, or you took the art down, as Warhol did in 1966 for the opening of his show at Philadelphia's Institute for Contemporary Art.

The strategy of transposition required two poles, a north and a south, or, as they would later be called, a Hi and a Lo, and if the supermarket lay, metaphorically, at the low end of the axis, the Metropolitan Museum of Art surely dominated the high. No other cultural institution could boast such monumental staircases or such high flights of prestige. In the palatial iconography of its architecture, it was already a virtual pop icon, the Marilyn Monroe of art history, tempting and aloof. All it needed was someone who knew how to make it a star.

Hoving, a scholar in medieval art with a doctorate in art history from Princeton, knew a lot about context. As commissioner of what was then called the Department of Parks, Recreation and Cultural Affairs, Hoving's domain spanned the spheres of nature and culture, and he became famous for events that collapsed the difference between them. "Hoving's Happenings," a sanitized, populist version of Alan Kaprow's downtown events of the early 1960s, had music lovers hanging from the trees.

Hoving grasped that the aesthetic of displacement held a social message, welcome to some, threatening to others. Pop-Tarts and superstars were expelling a regime of good taste and good breeding. Plastic and neon were supplanting mahogany and silver. Downtown discos were drowning out uptown balls. If the effect was not quite a social leveling, it was at least a new order of privilege, and New York's uptown mummies didn't want to feel left out of the dance. Hoving knew how to make the improper introductions. He was a gifted mismatchmaker, even in the construction of his own media persona: the hip patrician, the scholar with flair.

Hoving's book puts that persona on display with all the dubious sensationalism of his blockbuster shows. It's a scrapbook of gossip and press clips, a transcribed Accoustiguide tour to the backstage intrigues behind the objects hanging on the walls. Unfortunately, Hoving has only fleeting insight into the larger significance of his own tenure, but he demonstrates his intuitive grasp of the moment on which he set his seal.

Logically, Hoving made his zeitgeist debut at the Met with a pop painting, James Rosenquist's *F-111*, a billboard-sized painted collage of billboard-like images. The show introduced the museum's newly created department of contemporary art and announced its lifting of the ban on showing work by living artists. Logically, too, Hoving chose to present the work alongside a small group of history paintings from the museum's collection. "The art press gazed open-mouthed at the epic-sized *F-111*, the David, the Poussin and the Leutze and got very upset." Hoving was banking on that reaction. For this was not a show about a painting that depicted spaghetti, a jet plane, and a girl under a hair dryer. It was a display of context, in which spaghetti, plane, and hair dryer collided with Socrates, George Washington, and the Sabine Women.

If the *F-111* show was a pop chapel, the notorious Harlem on My Mind show of 1969 was a zeitgeist cathedral. Not a display of art, this was a curatorial *gesamtkunstwerk* of photomurals, music, and public relations.

But this time the PR backfired. Black artists were enraged that the show included no paintings. A scandal erupted over a catalog essay by a black high-school senior who wrote that black anti-Semitism "makes us feel more completely American in sharing a national prejudice." Paintings in the Met's collection were slashed. The city threatened to withdraw funding.

Again, the show obeyed the pop logic of transposition: it introduced images of the underclass into the citadel of the overclass. But the maneuver failed. What the transposition brought to mind was not Harlem but limousine jaunts to the Cotton Club in the 1920s; it was actually a regression from those days, since the show offered an aestheticized substitute for a journey that really might have opened eyes and minds to less palatable images. While pop could effectively rearrange the symbols of the affluent society, it reduced more complex social realities to surface events.

Ultimately, Hoving's mission of displacement could not be satisfied by the mere presentation of objects within the museum's walls. Inevitably, it led to the recasting of the walls themselves. Of all the controversies aroused during his tenure, none surpassed the fracas over the museum's plans to expand into Central Park. Turf is turf, parkland is scarce, and those who opposed the expansion were right in principle, even if the expansion was not a great threat. (The adoption of a "voluntary" paid admissions policy was, I think, a more serious breach of contract between the museum and the public.)

But this supreme version of Hoving's Happenings was more than an enlargement. It was a reformation. The master plan sought to provide not just room but coherence, to impose a master narrative on the museum's holdings. In Hoving's account, this idea originated with Kevin Roche, the master plan's architect. "The most distressing aspect of the Metropolitan," Roche told Hoving at their first meeting, "is that there's an appalling lack of continuity. A visitor can go from Egyptian art to Japanese armor without any indication that a civilization—and thousands of years—has changed. The Met is actually a bleeding mess; it's more an open storeroom than a series of public galleries. I would concentrate on solving that *lack of continuity*."

The aim of the master plan, in other words, was not just architectural; it was pedagogical. The plan would set forth a coherent view of the museum's holdings. It would clarify the hierarchy from which viewers could derive meanings and values. As Hoving recounts, Roche felt that he had to interrogate the museum before he could redesign it. "How many civilizations?" Roche wanted to know, "how many works of art? what were the finest and most important ones? were they the curatorially important ones? were they the 'emotional' ones?"

But the attempt to create a coherent view produced some strange results. For one thing, it put the museum itself into the picture. So long as the Met was content to be an "open storeroom" in the royal manner—a palace of treasures opened up for the edification of modern democracy—it sufficed to regard the museum as a neutral container. But as soon as it tried to bring the container's contents into a coherent relationship, it had to ask what they were doing there in the first place. That question brought the museum to confront its own image inside the frame.

That image is highly unstable. Museums are at once the champions of art—they stand for the historical elevation of merit over inherited privilege—and the enemies of art: they stand for the institutional authority that modern art has historically opposed. *F-111* represented only the most recent in a series of movements that challenged that authority. To make "continuity" from the Western art of modern times—realism, impressionism, cubism, dada, surrealism, abstract expressionism—was to assemble a parade of movements that emerged in the same epoch as the museum itself and challenged its authority to create such an assembly in the first place.

It is not quite fair, in other words, to accuse Hoving of a failure to protect the sanctity of the museum from corrosive pressures. Those pressures had been building up for some time from within the museum itself, from the art that was hanging on the walls before Hoving was born. In choosing to clarify the continuity of its holdings, the museum cast itself in the image of a citadel with an identity crisis: an institution whose function is to present a series of assaults on itself, mounted with increasing frequency until finally it is the museum that is carrying out the assault from within. In the end, the museum began to take on the role of the protagonist in some absurdist, first-person fiction who gradually comes to realize that he is narrating the story of his own liquidation.

In the Met's "liquidation," the collection of objects gave way to the collection of crowds. Hoving grasped that to acquire a crowd was, in a way, to acquire an artwork: a piece of Pop Art as significant as a roomful of Warhols. Or, rather, a room without Warhols. In *Popism*, Warhol famously describes how, when the paintings were removed for the opening of his first museum show in Philadelphia, the artist and his entourage were revealed as "the art incarnate." At Hoving's Met, the crowd of museum-goers became the art incarnate. They populated a picture of modern democracy, an image of people caught in the process of figuring out the delicate chemistry between populism and elitism, appreciating how each represents some essential ingredient in an unstable democratic mix.

That mix was not, of course, to everyone's taste. Many believe that in focusing on the crowds, Hoving betrayed the art. And even those who feel that he did well by art may be tempted to think that the hordes stampeding through the Met have been allowed to go too far, that their unruly presence must now be balanced by restoring a more scholarly approach to the art. Actually, what is needed now is a more scholarly approach to the crowds. What has long been missing at the Met is the means to convert the crowd into an audience.

The ingredients are there. Here, under one roof, lies a vast assembly of objects from almost every world culture. And here, on the doorstep, is an equally vast polyglot metropolis. No institution was ever better poised to foster understanding of today's emerging global culture. Hoving seems to have sensed this. In his efforts to revive the Met's role as an educational institution, he evidently understood that the city had as much to teach the museum as the museum had to teach the city. But he was not up to the task of forging a new curriculum. He brought the museum and the city into closer contact, without using their interaction to power the city and the museum toward a higher level of cultural understanding.

For that matter, Hoving had only limited comprehension of his own cultural transactions. It is fascinating to read his accounts of the trips he took—to Egypt, to Russia—to assemble the objects for his blockbuster shows. But it is also frustrating, because Hoving gives no sign of understanding that the expeditions served a more important function than to gather shiny things for crowds to gawk at: the shows, and Hoving's travels, were in themselves structural elements in the engineering of a global network. They were accelerated, jet-age versions of cultural diffusion. He treated these shows as connoisseurship. In fact, they were ethnology.

So, in a sense, was Pop Art. Though he was pop in his showmanship, Hoving missed pop's most important cultural implications. Pop Art didn't just feed more objects into the category of art. It placed the category itself on view. Its chief value was not formal, it was taxonomic. It asked viewers to reflect on the criteria by which some objects are assigned to the category of art, while others are dispatched to design, commerce, science, politics, ethnography, or religion. It created a chance to revive the contract between viewers and those who formulate the criteria and do the dispatching.

Hoving did not renegotiate the traditional terms of that contract. He regrets that he didn't push through his plan to tear down the Met's grand staircase. He does not regret having let stand the hierarchy of connoisseurship and art history embodied in its steps. He was content to entice the crowds up the stairs in order to consume culture. But he shrank back from the recognition that the museum and its audience together possessed the power, and in fact the obligation, to produce culture. He did not press his curators to meet the forces that his own vision of the museum had set in motion.

How many civilizations? Which are the most important works of art? Roche asked the right questions, but there was no need to create a master plan that imposed a coherent set of answers to them. Instead Hoving could have created a forum in which such questions could be pursued publicly, and in depth. Instead of imposing an ideal of coherence upon the museum's holdings, Hoving might have undertaken to explore how the museum, the city, and the world became heirs to such a dangerously incoherent cultural heritage.

The Met could yet become such a forum. Its collections provide it with unparalleled opportunities not just to examine objects within the familiar contexts of geography, time, and personality but to set them into such relatively unfamiliar contexts as travel, war, and trade. How many contacts were there between civilizations? What was the nature of those contacts? What is art's map? What are its trade routes? What do landscapes, idols, chalices, and suits of armor show about the migration, coexistence, struggle, appropriation, and mutual enrichment of ideas in a global arena? What is at stake for the city in the global stories that its leading cultural institution chooses to tell? Or fails to hear?

Such questions of reception and diffusion now lie well within art's compass. A large and growing body of scholarship is being brought to bear on them (some recent examples appear in *Exhibiting Cultures* and *Museums and Communities*, two anthologies published by Smithsonian Institution Press), and the enlistment of these ideas could open new pathways through the Met's collections. The choice is not between scholarly rigor and populist pandemonium; it is between embracing or refusing new forms of rigor that have the potential to engage audiences in something more constructive than crowd control, fashionable openings, admissions statistics, and shopping. The task now is not to undo Hoving's excesses but to use them as fuel to achieve the transposition that Hoving only half completed: from the Metropolitan Museum of Art to a museum of metropolitan art.

April 12, 1993

ARTFORUM

1995, 1999

CRITICAL REFLECTIONS

Writing an introduction to an essay by an architecture critic who has written, to this point, rather kindly of my work, and who at some point will inevitably have a reason to do otherwise, presents a rather precarious position.

The world we live in is a place where a lot of buildings are made, but very few eke out the merits to be called "architecture." When they do, it is the job of the architecture critic to tell people, from some intelligent vantage or viewpoint, what they are looking at. The critic presents a context for the work, and a passion for both its successes and its failures, and does so with an understanding befitting a trusted partner.

Herbert Muschamp shoulders that responsibility and then some. He became *The New York Times* architecture critic a couple of years ago, following in the footsteps of two formidable giants in the field: Ada Louise Huxtable, who still has a powerful presence in the architectural community, and Paul Goldberger, who has taken a more diverse journalistic path (including architecture) since appointing Muschamp to his former position. Herbert hit the deck running. From the beginning, he established a style different from his predecessors', and one distinctly his own: as a writer, he's willing to allow some of his own agony and angst in the preparation of his arguments to show through. This and the level of seriousness and commitment he brings to his work are comforting to me as a reader and as a maker of architecture, for they reveal a creative process like what I go through in creating buildings.

Herbert is a perceptive and articulate observer of the art of architecture, and he has a passionate sense of the social and urban concerns that inform the field at its best. Not given to superficial or trivial discussion, he does not pander to the winds of style and fashion but probes deeply into architecture's relationship to cultural, economic, and political conditions while at the same time reveling in the medium's sensual power. His brilliance in articulating the complex web of factors and aspirations that inform architectural work makes his columns accessible and interesting to a large audience; they have become a significant agent in refocusing the perception of the built environment in the national cultural debate.

—Frank Gehry

I am grateful for this homecoming to *Artforum*, which is the magazine that gave me my first chance to practice journalism. That was in 1984, when Ingrid Sischy, then *Artforum*'s editor, started the monthly columns section and invited me to contribute a column on architecture. Ingrid could be tough. I called her "my trainer," partly because her editing sessions could leave me sore, but also because she taught me a lot. The first time we met to discuss the column, for example, Ingrid shocked me by asking, "Don't you think writing books is a kind of death wish?"

Well! I'd written two books by that time, and was proud of them. But it was like Ingrid to use a shock tactic to get a message across, and this time the message was: Journalism moves at the speed of life. So it's a very unjournalistic thing that I'm about to do: look backward over the past three years and trace a few arcs along the learning curve that began in June 1992, when I took the job of architecture critic at *The New York Times*.

Writing for the *Times* is a kid's outsized fantasy of what he might do when he grows up. I mean, the reality of it is outsized and fantastic. It's the *Times*. And it occupies this immense Gothic château in the city's heart. The atmosphere, the tradition, the power of the institution—all these can bring out the scared twelve-year-old in anyone. But for a writer, that château can also be an enchanted palace.

It's a place dedicated to storytelling. *Have you filed your story yet? When are you filing your story? That was a great story yesterday. Do you have a moment to go over your story?* I used to write essays. Now I write stories. That's probably the best way to sum up the way my writing has changed since I began at the *Times*. Essays have the deliberation, detachment, and polish of a literary form. They have some aspiration to permanence; you can imagine them collected between hard covers, sitting on a shelf. Stories—newspaper stories—are more informal, more gut-driven. They're more oral than literary. (I usually talk them aloud as I write them.) Stories exist in the moment; yesterday's story is old news.

It's scary to write on gut. What if you don't have a gut to go on? The fear is not just that there's too little time to revise and polish, it's that perhaps there's been nothing there *but* polish all these years. Maybe when all that gloss is taken away, your hollowness will be unmistakably revealed. Since the *Times* is widely and closely read, this fear can become acute. The first time I did a cover story for the Sunday Arts and Leisure section, I was appalled when I walked past the newsstand on Saturday night and saw a stack of papers with my story facing out. It was like seeing a wanted poster with my face on it. I felt guilty—of half-baked thoughts, faulty logic, clunky language, the hubris of supposing I had anything to say that belonged on a front page.

But I didn't have time to dwell on it. I had another story to get out. And eventually I learned that this is one of the advantages of writing for a daily: the stories are nearly as ephemeral as the thoughts that pass through your head when you're walking down the street. Whether it's a good story or a bad one, it's gone in twenty-four hours. Or, looked at another way, it's a brief episode in one long continuous story. When you're trying to do justice to an important subject but you only have 1,100 or 1,200 words, what you're mostly conscious of is the stuff you have to leave out. And that stuff can get the ball rolling for a future column.

The *Times* was the first newspaper in the world to hire a full-time architecture critic. Only three people, including me, have held the job. The Architecture View column on Sunday remains the only critical coverage of the field offered with consistent frequency to a general readership. The job, in other words, is sacred, and it can be inhibiting to inhabit something sacred. One fears soiling it, fears thinking of it too much as an "it," an existing model to which, swayed by the eminence of the institution, one feels obliged to tailor one's ideas.

If that was ever the case with my *Times* columns, though, I had no one to blame but myself. Again and again, when I was interviewed for the job, editors had said the same thing: Don't censor yourself. We hire people because they have fresh voices; some of them freeze up when they get here. It was Max Frankel, then the paper's executive editor, who most helped me to overcome this inhibition. At one point before I was hired, I asked Max if I could occasionally write for other publications. Max agreed, then added, "But if you have something to say, and you don't say it here, you're crazy."

This was the best thing he could have said. Up to that point, I'd been allowing myself to fear that the job wasn't really about whether or not I had anything to say, it was about trying to figure out what an institution like the *Times* "ought" to say. By his assumption that what I would say in the column was what *I* had to say, though, Max was telling me to be myself.

Having something to say is more than a matter of content. It's also a matter of voice. Content itself is partly a matter of voice; people are often quicker to pick up on an idea when it is implicit in diction than when it is explicitly spelled out. Experimenting with voice is one of this job's greatest pleasures. A voice is really voices, a gathering of dictions and attitudes that coexist, not always harmoniously, like multiple personalities, or perhaps temperaments or humors. I have names for some of mine: Wanda (sanguine), Mona (choleric), Theresa (phlegmatic), and Droopsy (melancholic).

What may have been missing from my stories in the first couple of years, though, was the benignly driven voice of Eros, at once selfish and self-effacing. Perhaps the superego took the upper hand. I don't think my early stories lacked passion, mood, sensuousness, a sense of play; what they lacked was the charge that flows from the primitive desire to make something beautiful for someone you love. Unromantic though it may seem, I half suspect that I had to cook up a romance to move my writing forward. Too many readers were writing in to praise my writing's "ethical core." Not that I wanted my work to lack a moral dimension, but I wanted its core to be emotional.

Though my subject is architecture, and my columns are often reviews of individual buildings, my larger framework is the city, and my bond to the city is sentimental. Sybil Moholy-Nagy called the city "the matrix of man." I think of it as the great mother substitute. An ancient idea: think of Rome and its great seal, the she-wolf suckling the twins. For me, more prosaically, the first city was downtown Philadelphia, which I began to explore as a suburban boy of twelve, tapping into the city's power to nurture a child's sense of possibility. I started writing, in part, to give that sense some palpable form, to bring the city into my life before I was old enough actually to live there.

When George Balanchine said that "everything a man does he does for his ideal woman," he was talking about the fascination of the unattainable—it's the subject of many of his ballets—and I think that the city I write about is ideal and unattainable in a similar way. When I was younger, I wrote about the city because it wasn't mine, and perhaps my real subject wasn't so much the city as it was my yearning for it, or for the sense of completion or fulfillment that it represented. Maybe that is still my subject, only now the city is as much mine as it is ever going to be, and the yearning can be that much harder to sustain. But the city seen through the eyes of a lover is unattainable, in the sense that the beloved is ultimately unattainable. Even when you are with the person, you can never fully inhabit their outlook, though that outlook may be what drew you to them.

Still, that outlook can stimulate you to bring out what's good about your own view. It can heighten your perception and increase your sense of drama or beauty or urgency or empathy. Then you can make a picture of that heightened view of things—in my case, using words. Needless to say, this doesn't preclude the use of analytic tools. Balanchine was precisely analytic in his understanding of musical scores and dancers' bodies. This gave his ballets their rigor. But Balanchine placed his mastery of music and physique at the service of the elusive object of his desire. And this gave his ballets their beauty.

My impulse to treat architecture emotionally may come from personal experience, but it corresponds to what has been going on in architecture itself. I'm not injecting something foreign; I'm looking for the words to describe ideas that have been floating around architecture for some time, particularly since the decline of the Modern movement. Emotional content is not a new theme in architecture, but for much of this century it was downplayed. The Modern movement crystallized around the concept of the New Objectivity. Postmodernism opened the door to a richer emotional content, especially the retrieval of memory, but then cloaked it beneath the dubious authority of historical style. Postmodernism made classicism respectable again, but who wants a respectable classicism? Why not an indecent classicism, like that described by Eleanor Clark in her chapter on fountains in *Rome and a Villa*? "You walk close to your dreams," Clark writes. "Sometimes it seems that these pulsing [Roman] crowds . . . will in another minute all be naked, or will have fish tails or horses' behinds like the characters of the fountains." Isn't that the real reason architects used to go to Rome?

If I have an agenda, it is to peek beneath the mantles of authority with which architecture needlessly cloaks itself, and reveal the fish tails and horses' behinds. It's not that I want buildings to look ridiculous (usually it's the cloaks that are ridiculous); I want them to step up to their civic duty and take a more profound role in the life of the mind. These days, if people think at all of American cities in terms of passion, what often comes to mind are images of street crime and sex shops. Architecture, by contrast, comes across as the great inhibitor, the force that will stamp out red-light districts and keep violence at bay.

Typically, people turn to fiction or movies for more complex insights into connections between urban forms and human emotions. I'm thinking, for instance, of how, in *Another Country*, James Baldwin contrasts the imagery of New York and Paris in describing the different range of emotional possibilities peculiar to each city. Or how Bret Easton Ellis has traced a mode of passive aggression—a certain upper-middle-class anomie—that has become commonplace since Los Angeles loomed large in the national imagination. I want to write columns that illuminate similar relationships among people, places, and things.

This is a traditional, even conservative agenda. Love as education, the city as a syllabus in the training of the senses: these are ancient Western ideas, hallmarks of classical thought. Recently I've been meditating on something Janet Flanner wrote in a letter to her companion, the Italian editor Natalia Denesi Murray, in response to a love letter (not published) that Murray wrote to Flanner in 1958. "Always since I have known you I have said that the Italian civilization was maintained through the centuries not only by the art of their landscapes and of their artists' works, but by the perfecting of their knowledge of the education of passion, and how it has preserved and informed your race, since before the time of Christians back into the classic spirit of body and heart, in your land."

May 1995

MORAL OF THE STORIES

Sidewalk Critic, Lewis Mumford's Writings on New York, *edited by Robert Wojtowicz.*

I used to think of myself as the love child of Lewis Mumford and Diana Vreeland. Meaning, architecture critics need a moralistic streak (Mumford's was a mile wide), but we should also know how to wrap and tie it into a fetching bow from time to time. If the ethical dimension of architecture is giving you a headache, Why Don't You . . . wear a headache band?

Everyone of my generation grew up with their heads glued to two previous paperback collections of Mumford's *New Yorker* Skyline columns from the 1940s and '50s, *The Highway and the City* and *From the Ground Up*. This new volume of *New Yorker* columns from the '30s is a useful thing to have. Unlike the earlier collections, it shows that Mumford wasn't limited to major pronouncements on big civic projects. He also had a fine sense of style. Some of the freshest pieces in the book deal with ephemeral designs, like the interior of a new Longchamps restaurant ("vermilion walls are kind to girls' complexions") or the facade of Helena Rubenstein's Fifth Avenue salon ("it is one of the few places on the Avenue that might effectively use a nude figure sculpture or a well-composed abstraction of cosmetic bottles to suggest in austere fashion the holy Corinthian rites that are practiced within").

Shades of Jungle Red. There are also nice short takes on shoe stores and cheap but refined eateries like Schrafft's, the Horn & Hardart Automat, and the Little Whitehouse chain of lunchrooms. Mumford's deftly rendered sketches beautifully evoke New York before World War II and the mass suburban exodus in the decades that followed, when style helped ease the pain of the Depression for rich and poor alike.

Mumford's Skyline columns of the time are emblematic of the city's rise to cultural preeminence in the period between the two world wars. In those years, European architects were mobilizing themselves into the Modern movement, but New York was eclipsing the European city as the fountainhead of twentieth-century energy. Mumford was the most vigorous writer on architecture since Ruskin, and these pieces are an extraordinary record of that era. Like Ruskin, he can appear wildly off in his critical judgments, but we don't hold it against him. As Pauline Kael observed, "We read critics for the insights. The judgments we can usually make for ourselves."

Of Mumford's journalism from the '30s, I'd read only excerpts from articles he'd written for *The New Republic,* and these didn't whet my appetite for more. There was a Depression on, and many intellectuals who'd lived through the rollicking '20s, like Mumford and Edmund Wilson, veered toward the radical Left. In *The New Republic,* Mumford attacks individualism as the great American evil. We can't afford individualism anymore. Individualism must be stamped out. In hindsight, you begin to have more sympathy for figures like Philip Johnson and Charles Lindbergh, who careened toward the radical Right. Both extremes seem achingly naïve and idealistic. Both understood that the economic crisis was a cultural crisis and believed that the only way to resolve it was to attain solidarity of one sort or another. If equality could be achieved only at the expense of freedom, too bad for freedom.

Mumford's *New Yorker* pieces take a much softer line, but his political outlook still influenced his architectural judgments. If he'd had the power, he would have whisked away what we now call SoHo, i.e., the Cast Iron District, formerly known as Hell's Hundred Acres, because it was notorious for sweatshops where nonunion workers toiled in squalid surroundings that often burst into flames. Nor could he stand Rockefeller Center. He viewed it as the ultimate expression of the capitalist jungle that had overtaken American society. In fact, Mumford did not like skyscrapers, period. To him, they represented corporate greed.

Mumford's failure to appreciate tall buildings somewhat cramps his style. Perhaps his column should have been called The Anti-Skyline. In the '20s, New York came into its own as a global capital and this was symbolized by the convergence of vertical and horizontal forces. The latter were represented by the great transatlantic liners that, as late as the early '70s, one could see along Manhattan's Hudson River piers: beautiful British, French, Dutch, Italian, Swedish, and German steamships, each of them like a city, suckling at the breast of the mother metropolis. This heart-lifting spectacle was a visual reminder of the country's roots in westward emigration, and also a sign that the Old World now paid homage to the New.

The skyscraper boom of the '20s, meanwhile, had accelerated New York's powerful sense of vertical thrust, with new towers like those for Standard Oil, Paramount, and American Radiator, their skyward push captured in the charcoal renderings of Hugh Ferriss. Inertia kept the boom going into the early years following the stock market crash, with the City Services, Empire State, and Chrysler Buildings, and that "series of bad guesses, blind stabs, and grandiose inanities," Rockefeller Center.

Mumford has nothing against the Rockefellers personally. He praises the Rockefeller Apartments on West Fifty-fourth Street. He likes the modesty of their drab brick facades, the interior layouts, especially the convex bays provided as dining alcoves, and the sympathetic scale in relation to the street. He is grateful to the new Museum of Modern Art for not looking like a temple or a palace and for enclosing a luxury of space behind a spartan front. He writes rapturously about the Cloisters, another cultural showpiece funded by the Rockefellers, though he cannot resist adding that perhaps this museum of medieval art has a hidden capitalist agenda. "Maybe this is an experimental model to help us face more cheerfully the Dark Ages," i.e., the economic collapse precipitated, as Mumford saw it, by industrial tycoons like Rockefeller.

Mumford wants the city to be rational. This is a function of his essential humanism. He wants a livable city, and for this people need adequate light, air, open space, ease of access, and a sense of community. This calls for rational planning. Mumford's ideal locale is Sunnyside Gardens, Queens, where he lived for a time, because it places these things within affordable range. He is an early champion of the Regional Plan Association, because he recognizes the critical relationship of suburbs and city, a dysfunctional link that will become even more problematic with the emergence of mass suburbanization in the years after World War II.

Today, Mumford is useful mainly as an antidote, as a corrective to Nietzschean attitudes that we all tend to get so excited about. He was still writing when these anti-rationalist ideas began to surface in the early '60s. He took vicious exception to Jane Jacobs's 1961 *Death and Life of Great American Cities*, which he described as "Mother Jacobs' Home Remedies for Urban Cancer." Jacobs, an editor for *Architectural Forum*, lived in Greenwich Village and led the crusade against Robert Moses in his attempt to run a highway through Lower Manhattan. Her book was an attack on city planning as then practiced. She celebrated diversity, attacked the uniformity of planning, and lit into Ebenezer Howard, father of the British Garden Cities movement and a hero of Mumford's.

In 1966, Robert Venturi's *Complexity and Contradiction in Architecture* continued the turn against planning with remarks like "Main Street is almost all right." In the following decade, Rem Koolhaas's *Delirious New York* extolled what he called "the culture of congestion," an urban condition that Mumford would have considered simply pathological. Nor would he have looked favorably on Diana Agrest's depiction of the city as the "subconscious of architecture," the messy, unruly grab bag of memories, desires, and traumas lurking beneath the ordered surfaces envisioned by design.

Today, some of us who write about architecture find ourselves in the position of latter-day (or reborn) Surrealists. This is partly because of the work we're seeing. Buildings by Koolhaas, Frank Gehry, Jean Nouvel, and others operate most fully in a relationship of intersubjectivity with the viewer. Also, at this moment in history, psychology offers an interpretive language critics and general readers are likely to share, even if it hasn't been applied extensively to architecture in the past.

But the use of this language is also an acknowledgment that many of the forces shaping the city require a specialized knowledge we're unlikely to master: global finance; political agendas; complex zoning codes; federal, state, and municipal land-use policies. Mumford writes of such things with impressive omniscience. Perhaps they were simpler in his day. Perhaps he was better informed. Perhaps he faked it much of the time. Whatever, Mumford is a reminder of the need to constantly update the Rolodex with sources of specialized information that an individual critic may never grasp.

Mumford's literary persona is itself worthy of psychological study. He shows what happens when the conscience is made to do the work of the libido. There's a voluptuous pleasure in his assaults on projects like Rockefeller Center and the 1939 New York World's Fair. He seduces readers into thinking we're in his company. We're all much smarter, more sensible—better people, really—than all these millionaires and politicians. And when the whip comes down, you can sense Mumford's reveling in his power to administer real stings. This isn't some Helmut Newton simulation; Mumford only gets off on the genuine Ouch. We get off on watching it and, in the process, get to regard ourselves as superior cultural beings.

Unlike previous collections of his essays, *Sidewalk Critic* shows that Mumford had more in common with Walter Benjamin, Siegfried Kracauer, Franz Hessel, and other Weimar writers on the Berlin street scene than we tend to remember. Many of his early pieces are *feuilletoniste* in style. They comment on casual moments in the cityscape as well as larger social issues. Death and exile came to Berlin's flaneurs in the '30s. This collection demonstrates that Mumford continued his version of the walk much longer.

April 1999

THE NEW YORK TIMES

1992–2007

ONE BUILDING THAT KNOWS WHAT IT'S ABOUT

Henry James wrote eloquently about New York, but he missed the point of its architecture. On a 1904 visit, the novelist railed against the city's first skyscrapers; it pained him to see "those monsters of the mere market" towering over the spire of Trinity Church. Why didn't he recognize that the skyscraper, too, elevates spirit over matter? A prolific writer, James was no stranger to the work ethic. Skyscrapers are the work aesthetic, monuments to work as the moral victory of energy over inertia.

The new twenty-three-story office building at 101 Avenue of the Americas, designed by Bruce Fowle of the New York firm Fox & Fowle, doesn't stretch the art of architecture to giddy new heights. But it is a finely wrought homage to a heroic age in the history of the New York workplace. Designed as a headquarters for Local 32B-32J, the union of building services employees, 101 Avenue of the Americas is notable for the remarkable context to which it pays its respects.

The building is at the corner of Watts Street in Lower Manhattan. This is the district where the printing industry once flourished in the enormous industrial buildings that still line Hudson and Varick Streets near the Hudson River between Greenwich Village and TriBeCa. Compared to nearby SoHo, this district, which is called Hudson Square, remains relatively unexplored, even by the intrepid *AIA Guide to New York City*.

A gold mine for industrial archeologists, this part of town is also instructive for students of modern architecture. Modernism, in theory, was rooted in an industrial aesthetic. But what a contrast these authentically blue-collar buildings present to their white-collar descendants, like that bleak stretch of office towers along the same avenue sixty blocks uptown. Festooned with turrets, pilasters, loggias, crenellations, and polychrome reliefs, the old printing plants go to exotic lengths to compensate for their hulking scale. It's that improbable effort, and the public-mindedness it expresses, that gives this district its character.

At 101 Avenue of the Americas, it is as though a modern monolith has slipped downtown to learn a civics lesson from its industrial ancestors. The new skyscraper does not try to pass itself off as a period piece. Save for an Art Deco panel on the cooling tower at the building's summit and a scattering of cast-stone medallions across its surface of brick and pale green glass, it is devoid of the applied ornament that lifts industrial lofts above the utilitarian.

The twist here is that Mr. Fowle strips industrial architecture down to its structural skeleton—the masonry grid filled in with large factory windows—and fashions the bones into a rich ornamental system. Two grids of brick are woven across the building's surface. The main grid, of warm brown brick, corresponds to the building's concrete frame structure; a secondary grid of light gray marks individual floors and wraps across a gently curved section of the main facade. Window mullions in black repeat the tartan in a finer pattern.

But maintaining context is not just a matter of matching surface patterns. The bigger challenge is to weave coherent patterns in urban space. That's not a small task for a site that is the urban equivalent of a six-car pileup. Two incongruent downtown street grids collide here. Canal Street and Avenue of the Americas race through like hit-and-run drivers. The adjacent entrance to the Holland Tunnel is an asphalt snarl.

Mr. Fowle maneuvers this spatial intersection with the stern grace of a traffic cop at rush hour. He flanks the central twenty-three-story tower with two six-story wings, which project out toward the side streets, preserving the scale of residential buildings nearby. One wing is pulled forward and slightly angled to frame an entrance plaza. From the central shaft he extracts a vertical panel and tilts it into alignment with Sullivan Street to the north. Besides modulating the visual impact of the building's bulk, this asymmetric sculptural massing shifts the building's east-west axis toward the south, as if to conduct the flow of space from the avenue up the plaza steps through an entrance colonnade. In effect, the building becomes a gateway to the Hudson Square district.

This is the second Fox & Fowle building in this part of town. Their 1987 headquarters for Saatchi & Saatchi, the advertising firm, is a stylish refrain of the 1931 Starrett-Lehigh Building, a landmark factory in Chelsea. The invasion of the media moguls (Della Femina McNamee occupies renovated loft quarters across the street) is a reminder that the significance of Hudson Square is as much historical as architectural: these palaces of the printing press occupy a middle ground between the machine age and the age of information.

Fox & Fowle's buildings are products of the latter era; their forms speak not of mechanical functions but of visual codes. Neither building is a factory; their use of an industrial vocabulary is as much a matter of Postmodern style as of modern structural expression. In a way, they are architecture's answer to the Gap, a fusion of utility and fashion. It is a dress code suited to a postindustrial world, where the line betweeen blue and white collars has blurred. As translated into architecture, it's a code worthy of the city that gave working its class.

January 12, 1992

FOR ALL THE STAR POWER, A MIXED PERFORMANCE

A friend once joked that Woody Allen exploits New York architecture the way other movie directors exploit women. Mr. Allen bathes the city's sky-scrapers with mood lighting and music, and the effect is as intoxicating as a dry Manhattan served straight up. Alas, many architects also treat build-ings like starlets. They fail to grasp that an urban building has more important things to do than stand there and look dreamy. It must also shoulder the serious job of organizing urban space.

Like Woody Allen, the New York architect Frank Williams delights in the romance of the city's skyline. Mr. Williams's design for Trump Palace, a new luxury residential complex on Third Avenue at Sixty-eighth Street, is a soaring tribute to Irwin Chanin, a supreme stylist of Manhattan's Art Deco architecture. And it provides a golden opportunity to compare Chanin's work with architecture today.

Chanin, a builder of Broadway theaters before he undertook tall build-ings, understood the fact that architecture is a performing art. Chanin's two twin-towered apartment buildings on Central Park West, the Majes-tic (1930) and the Century (1932), are the ultimate in urban sophistica-tion. The Chanin Building (1928), an office structure at Forty-second Street and Lexington Avenue designed by Sloane and Robertson, epito-mized Chanin's vision of modern architecture as a theatrical setting for a dynamic society.

Mr. Williams took a risk by invoking Irwin Chanin; he is asking to be judged by the high standards Chanin set. The risk has produced mixed results: a building that possesses star power but lacks a significant urban role.

On the positive side, Trump Palace's central tower, rising fifty-four stories from a base of low-rise shops and town houses, is a skillful compo-sition of brick and glass. Shallow setbacks and the organization of win-dows and balconies into neat horizontal and vertical bands compress the tower's mass into crystalline contours. Corner windows, borrowed from the Century and the Majestic, adorn the edges of the tower like faceted gems. Trump Palace is marred by tacky Art Deco trim at street level, and its pink brick walls, glamorous from a distance, look cheap up close. Provided you indulge these defects with a bit of soft focus, however, Mr. Williams has created a distinctive object: a rose-colored prism rising into the clouds.

But Chanin's greatness didn't depend solely on his talent for thrusting glamour into the sky. It also arose from his ability to connect buildings to the city on ground level. From the ornate lobby of the Chanin Building, for example, a handsome staircase descends to the subway station at Grand Central, linking the building's elevators to the terminal's railway network. Originally the Chanin Building was a terminal itself. Motor-coaches serving the outer boroughs pulled into the building and swiveled around on a turntable, depositing passengers onto one platform, receiving them from another. Foot traffic is still well served by the shopping arcade that slices through the lobby floor, providing a superb transition from the public space outdoors to the private offices upstairs.

These public amenities were not grudging concessions. They were integral to the Chanin Building's drama. The building tells a story of New York as the legendary beacon for immigrants. *City of Opportunity* is the title of the allegorical panels, sculpted by Rene Chambellan, that adorn the Chanin's lobby. The series, a blend of abstract and figurative design, depicts such values as Courage, Vision, and Success. In other words, the illuminated crown at the Chanin's summit doesn't just glorify Success. It lights the pathways leading to it: trains, buses, actions of mind and hand.

Trump Palace, by contrast, is long on Success and short on any Vision of the public role urban buildings ought to play. Although a roadway also cuts through the Palace, it is designed for private cars. The apartments above have many fine details—the eight-foot-high doorways are truly grand—but they are private dwellings.

Of course, the Chanin Building is an office tower, Trump Palace a res-idential one. Too bad, then, that Mr. Williams didn't pay more attention to the lessons Chanin taught in his residential work. The Century and the Majestic are distinguished by their strongly defined street walls, their adaptation of the two-towered building type already prominent on Cen-tral Park West, and the adept matching of their masses to adjacent build-ings. These qualities led Diana Agrest, author of *A Romance with the City*, a monograph on Chanin, to rank his apartment buildings among "the few examples of truly urban contextual architecture for New York."

Trump Palace makes little effort to fit into its surroundings. It wants to stick out on the skyline like a prima donna. So does the Chanin Building, but for good reasons. Chanin gave it a high public profile because it per-formed an important public role. Obviously, Mr. Williams is not to blame that Grand Central Terminal isn't across the street, that cars have undermined public transit, that civic-mindedness is out of fashion. But he has not taxed himself greatly to make the best of his circumstances. The building shows no sign that he has addressed one of the major questions facing urban architects: How can buildings help to pierce the thickening wall between private amenity and public void?

Trump Palace's one concession to the public is a small plaza fronting on East Sixty-eighth Street. It's a pleasant space; yet, like the low-rise town houses at the tower's base, the plaza was a zoning requirement, imposed by forces outside the architect's control. It shows no initiative, much less vision, on his part. One feature at Trump Palace does display vision, but in a very restricted sense. It is the large glass window set into the wall that separates the outdoor plaza from the building's lobby. The window lets people look inside, but they can't pass to the other side. If the window were an allegorical panel, its title would be *Exclusion*. It says: Look, but don't mingle. Keep your distance. Only disconnect.

The truth is that Trump Palace is less an homage to the '20s and '30s than it is a hangover from the '80s. That is its true period style. And the staggering views from the apartments bring that period deliriously back to life. Gazing out their windows, a visitor comes face-to-face with the soaring designer skyscrapers of those gilded years, each tower trying to upstage the others like sumptuously costumed guests at a charity ball. Trump Palace holds its head up proudly in their motley midst. But now buildings will have to work harder to earn their crowns.

July 12, 1992

STEEL AND BACKBONE IN HARD TIMES

Leave it to the Municipal Art Society to mount a tasteful political protest. Last week, when the Democrats were in town, the members of this century-old organization of civic do-gooders didn't surround Madison Square Garden with bullhorns or scrawled posters. Instead they occupied the decorous Urban Center Galleries and opened a dignified rally of a show. Its theme is New York's tradition of great public works; its purpose is to stimulate ideas for reviving that tradition.

Steel, Stone, and Backbone, which runs through September 19, is a protest against recessionary thinking. It's a strike against the idea that in hard economic times people should lower their expectations about what kind of city they want to live in. In fact, the point of the show is to offer historical proof to the contrary. When the going gets tough, the tough get ambitious about architecture. Much of the New York that is most admired—its water and transportation systems, housing, cultural institutions—emerged from periods of economic crisis.

The show, put together by Laura Rosen, an archivist with the Triborough Bridge and Tunnel Authority, offers a look at six of these periods and the public works they produced. Many viewers will already be familiar with one of them: the Great Depression and its astounding record in projects for housing, recreation, and transportation. With segments devoted to such projects as LaGuardia Airport, Orchard Beach in the Bronx, and the Queens-Midtown Tunnel (with a video presentation on the "sandhogs" who built it), the 1930s takes up most of the exhibition space.

But the real news of the show is that the building boom of the '30s wasn't the exception. It was the rule. Such booms have frequently coincided with financial busts, or as they were termed in the nineteenth century, "panics." The Panic of 1837 saw the building of the Croton Water System, including the monumental Egyptian Revival reservoir that used to stand on the current site of the New York Public Library. After the panics of 1873 and 1893, work began on the Metropolitan Museum of Art, the American Museum of Natural History, and the New York Zoological Society, later known as the Bronx Zoo. What a panic.

Steel, Stone, and Backbone deals more with economics, politics, and labor than with architectural aesthetics. Still, the works on view convey the power of buildings to create strong images of public service. When government officials are holding fire sales on urban properties, it's instructive to review the monuments left by periods when serving the public was a noble end that called for noble forms. The design of the Orchard Beach bathhouse, for example, equals the Rainbow Room in Art Deco elegance.

These examples of urban bootstrapping are inspiring, but it would be helpful to have something more than inspiration. What is the key to these success stories? Does history offer a pattern we can follow today?

Sorry. There is no key. The motives behind these works are as varied as the projects themselves. Disastrous fires and a cholera epidemic prompted the building of the Croton Water System. Social ambition—the oblige of would-be noblesse—spurred wealthy collectors to erect the Metropolitan Museum to "educate and better the lot of the working classes." And the record of the '30s would be a good deal skimpier if it hadn't been for Robert Moses's rabid lust for power. Since history doesn't hand us a key, however, the implicit message of this show is that we will have to invent one for ourselves. And perhaps invention is the key we're looking for.

This political speech of a show has visual as well as polemic appeal. Among the curiosities on view are two panels prepared by Calvert Vaux and Frederick Law Olmsted for the 1857 competition to design Central

Park. Combining cartography, photography, and painting, each panel features a map of the park site and "before" and "after" images showing how Olmsted and Vaux proposed to transform different portions of the landscape. These forward-looking mixed-media works (photography was a recent invention) should jolt us out of the habit of equating Olmsted with the sweetly picturesque. If he were alive today, this pioneering artist would be dazzling us with holograms.

Ms. Rosen offers some smart image mixes of her own. Pictures of the Bronx Zoo, for instance, are set beside William Holbrook Beard's 1879 painting of vicious bears and bulls rampaging on Wall Street. The juxtaposition brings to mind the financial predators of a more recent day who have done time behind bars.

Steel, Stone, and Backbone goes soft at the end, with strained attempts to declare the present a time of maintaining the "basic infrastructure" of a "mature cityscape." It would be great indeed if the kind of energy that went into building these projects could be applied to maintaining them. But clearly the Municipal Art Society has its sights set on bigger things than rust-proofing. And there's an ulterior motive here as well: a bid by the society to refurbish its public image. Just as the Democrats are seeking more mainstream appeal, the Municipal Art Society wants to cast off its image of upscale gentility. That's why, instead of potted palms, they've adorned the galleries with such tough-guy paraphernalia as hard hats and rubber pylons.

Actually, this organization outgrew its tea-party image long ago. In recent years it has shown its well-developed political muscle in major projects all over town. Sometimes it flexes its biceps publicly, as when it brought suit to halt a development proposal for Columbus Circle. More often its members have worked behind the scenes, political equivalents of the sandhogs toiling beneath the East River. Steel, Stone, and Backbone is one of several events that will honor the society's centennial. What better way to ward off recessionary blues than to toast the vigor of this venerable group?

July 24, 1992

BARCELONA BREAKS THE RECORD FOR INSPIRED URBANISM

Even in the heat of a Spanish summer, a visitor entering the Barcelona Pavilion may feel a chill run down the spine. The reason is partly the stunning beauty of Ludwig Mies van der Rohe's building, partly the uncompromising coolness of its design. But mainly, it's the shock of seeing a ghost.

The original version of this modern milestone vanished years ago. Designed for Barcelona's 1929 World's Fair, the German Pavilion was never meant to last. But its taut geometric forms, rendered in marble, steel, glass, and water, lived on in photographs, and several generations of architects have called the building home. The precise, asymmetric balance of sumptuous materials and simple forms introduced a new ideal of beauty. It proclaimed that the twentieth century could produce its own distinctive style.

The reconstruction of the pavilion in the mid-1980s was also a manifesto, not of a style this time but of a city. It declared Barcelona's resolve to revive its lapsed creative spirit after the stifling Franco era. And the city has translated that resolve into action with spectacular results: dozens of new parks and public spaces, restored landmarks, and first-rate new buildings, including the sports stadiums and apartment complexes designed especially for the Olympic Games. For the past week, sports fans have had the chance to discover what architects and city planners have been cheering about for several years. Barcelona has broken all records for inspired urbanism in our time.

The people of Barcelona regard architecture and design as major political issues. That fact was dramatized during the city's mayoral elections a year ago. Each of the candidates had an architectural adviser, and these architects received prominent press coverage during the campaign. The election was in part a referendum on urban form. And the reelection of the incumbent, Pasqual Maragall, was a vote of appreciation for his architect, Oriol Bohigas. Barcelona today is the result of the vision Mr. Bohigas implemented during his tenure as director of the city's Department of Architecture and Design.

The key to the Bohigas approach lies in its balance between urban scope and architectural scale. The renewal of Barcelona has avoided the deadly monotony of much modern planning by playing down all-embracing master plans in favor of what architects call interventions— individual projects that respond to specific places. But it has spawned enough projects to ensure the critical mass required for citywide change. While retaining overall control over the choice of projects, sites, and architects, Mr. Bohigas allowed his designers wide latitude to pursue visions of their own.

Of course, such an experimental approach does not guarantee success. More important, it throws open to question the standards by which success is measured. A case in point is La Plaça dels Països Catalans, a city square adjacent to Barcelona's main railway station, a fifteen-minute walk from the pavilion. Completed in 1983, the plaza was the first of the city's major new public spaces, and it remains controversial. Calls are still heard for its demolition.

It's not an easy space to love. Surrounded on all sides by modern architecture at its most abysmal, awash in a sea of cars, the site is as flat and scaleless as a parking lot, which in fact it was. And the plaza's architects, Albert Viaplana and Helio Piñon, have done little to alleviate its harshness. "At first we were desolate," wrote the architects after inspecting this urban wasteland. Then they resolved to make desolation the project's theme: to coax some kind of poetic order from this tangled mess of steel, asphalt, concrete, and exhaust fumes. They wanted, in short, to create a Barcelona Pavilion for today—to find beauty in the wrenching conditions modernity itself has unleashed.

The plaza resembles a pavilion, actually, though its parts are fragmented and dispersed over the site; and, like the Mies van der Rohe building, the plaza is a highly abstract composition, architectural in scale but sculptural in spirit. Its most conspicuous feature is an enormous metal canopy, held aloft by spindly columns. Sants Station is a major entry into the city, although like Penn Station in New York it scarcely rises to the occasion. The canopy contributes the monumental scale appropriate to a ceremonial urban gateway, but it makes no concession to the Beaux Arts grandeur typical of railway architecture—or, indeed, to any conventional idea of grace. And it is flanked by "amenities" devoid of charm: fountains that bring to mind rows of stylized dripping faucets; tables and seating suitable for a postapocalyptic picnic; a covered walkway that offers no protection from sun and rain; nighttime lighting so bright it could foil prison escapes.

"Arrogant," I wrote in my notebook after a first visit to the plaza. "Unfeeling, in your face, misses the *generosity* Barcelona's renewal is all about." My reaction was strong, and it lingered. The next day I was still sorting it out. So I went back, and in the course of several visits changed my mind. No, the plaza is not generous, not charming, does not invite the visitor to sit down and stay awhile. But it invites the mind to linger, and the visitor to return. Like the Barcelona Pavilion, it has the power to affect not only the way we build but the way we see.

Is it possible that one day people will find the plaza as beautiful as the pavilion? Let's hope things won't get that bad. But if the plaza is not the pavilion's architectural equal, neither is it a failure on its own terms. The two works have different aims and effects. The Barcelona Pavilion attains a perfection so balanced and self-contained that it makes the surroundings look ghastly. The plaza achieves the opposite effect. It confers an admittedly bleak poetry upon its context by opening itself up to the cityscape and consenting to speak in its harsh tongue.

The grit of industrial cities is a familiar ingredient in movies, paintings, photographs, and other art forms. Barcelona has made a place for architects to experiment with similar effects. That meant taking a risk that the results wouldn't be popular, or even good. But it's by taking such risks that Barcelona has captured the gold.

August 2, 1992

FOR TIMES SQUARE, A REPRIEVE AND HOPE OF A LIVELIER DAY

Times Square Center, the cluster of blockbuster skyscrapers by Philip Johnson and John Burgee that would have been the centerpiece of the $2.5 billion Times Square redevelopment project, was the apotheosis of architecture as entertainment for the starstruck. The project's apparent collapse turns a symbolic page on an era when architecture became the all-too-willing servant of high-powered public relations. And it creates an opportunity to write a new and more buoyant chapter in the life of this troubled district.

The vast towers of Times Square Center, which once threatened to turn Broadway and Forty-second Street into an office canyon with looming walls of dreary postmodern pastiche, were the grotesque, paradoxical climax of what had once seemed a highly desirable end: not just fixing up Times Square but also using one of the favorite preoccupations of the 1980s—architecture—to do it.

Jumbos and Whoppers

The eminence of Mr. Burgee and Mr. Johnson was used to market the fiction that buildings of any size, in any place, could be nothing less than sheer genius when architects of stature were hired to style them. (So, too, with Kohn Pedersen Fox, the firm that designed the enormous merchandise mart that was to have filled two blockfronts at the project's west end, also now on indefinite hold.)

In fact, the architecture of Times Square Center was abysmal, a Victorian fantasy of mansard-roofed behemoths locked in a grim quadrille at the "Crossroads of the World." The architects refined it through the

1980s, then went back to the drawing board entirely in 1989, but the last version—a stodgy imitation of the jazzy style pioneered by the Miami firm Arquitectonica—only confirmed what an impoverished conception of architecture had been operating here all along. The "new" design by Mr. Burgee and Mr. Johnson simply applied a new veneer to the same set of jumbo parcels. Here was evidence, if more were needed, that for all its appeals to history and tradition, postmodernism was often no more than modern formalism in period dress.

But the chief fault did not lie with the architects, or with their developer, Park Tower Realty. It lay with the city and state agencies that supported them. The plan to redevelop Times Square and Forty-second Street had started out with a reasonable set of design guidelines. Instead of enforcing these regulations, however, state officials allowed the architects to toss them out the window, on the ground that only development of this scale could prevent Times Square from continuing its shabby decline.

This was an architectural variation on the Big Lie, a whopper whose outrageousness made it all the harder to deny. To oppose the project was to risk being branded antidevelopment, as if architecture would now be available only in two equally unappetizing varieties: new Super Jumbo Size and leftover Sleazy Fire Trap.

Actually, private development in Times Square boomed in the 1980s, with support from city zoning regulations but without any boost from the very project that was promoted as essential to the area's rebuilding. Indeed, almost the only undeveloped sites in the area today are the ones that were vacated and boarded up to make room for this project.

Architecture became famous in the 1980s, and who wanted to complain about that? Wasn't it a good thing that the public was covering its coffee tables with lavish books on Italian villas, flocking to exhibitions of architectural drawings, shuffling dutifully into lecture halls?

Surely architects saw little cause to complain. Many of them rode the wave of '80s affluence with surpassing aplomb, and their new celebrity status certainly seemed to bode well for the vitality of their art. Real estate developers were quick to get the message, and what was wrong with that? For years the pressure had been on developers to care about something more than the bottom line. In the '80s many of them met and even surpassed this expectation. But few had counted on the power of public relations to turn the public's interest in architecture into a license for laissez-faire.

Developers quickly learned the trick that snazzy design by star designers could help win support for dubious projects. When a well-known architect was hired to design a blockbuster development, criticizing it was nearly tantamount to attacking artistic freedom. Publicity agents mounted elaborate campaigns highlighting the "world-class" design, the stylish covers of their press kits packed with fact sheets, design statements, glossy pictures, political testimonials, and architects' biographies.

Beliefs of True Believers

But what people opposed at Times Square was not development. It was loss of reason on the part of those who could present such projects and seriously expect to be applauded for them. Indeed, what makes this Times Square story so disturbing is that the powers behind it were not cynical. They gave every indication of sincere belief that their plan was wholly admirable. They were creating art, or something like it, so why complain that the buildings were too big? How can a city have too much art?

The paradox is that even in its current state of dilapidation Times Square has more to teach architects about art than nearly any other site in America. It remains rich in the kind of visual and cultural collisions few artists can pull off in style. A "Beverly Hills" polo player, four stories tall, prepares to strike his mallet against the top of a police station lodged in a trailer concealed behind warped plywood painted with classical columns. A Japanese whisky bottle lights up to wish Tony Bennett a happy birthday. Here is a public space defined by private enterprise, a permanent festival to celebrate Broadway's unruly rupture of Manhattan's straight-arrow grid.

Looking should be the top priority for Times Square now. The place is in trouble, socially and economically, and the demise of Times Square Center is bound to provoke a new round of suggestions about how this historic place should be saved. But perhaps the most constructive approach would be simply to stop, look, and listen to Times Square's own ideas about what it wants to be.

An Aspiring Id

And what it mostly wants to be is a version of the Freudian id. It's the great maw of pleasure, desire, and fear, opening itself wide for our entertainment like hell's mouth in a medieval morality play. We'd feel cheated if we didn't see streams of exotic, devilish creatures come skipping out of those jaws in search of cheap thrills and tawdry glamour, and we'd be equally disappointed if we couldn't also depend on the morality brigade to come scampering right after, like the Save-a-Soul Mission in *Guys and Dolls*, wielding nightsticks, Bibles, and urgent referrals to social service agencies, prodding the little devils to clean up their acts.

Architecture does not fit naturally into this context, for the reality is that Times Square is truly more Damon Runyon than Philip Johnson. (Is it an accident that the biggest hit on Broadway in this year of the demise of the Times Square redevelopment project is *Guys and Dolls?*) Architects are more comfortable taking the superego role, the great cleaner-uppers, the traffic cops of urban space. Though zoning regulations adopted in 1986 call upon architects to emulate Times Square's dazzle, few of the new buildings manage to look lively. They leave it up to neon signs to inject the required pizazz. Take away the signs and you're left with spectacles like 1585 Broadway, a square chaperone dressed in starchy gray, peering down sternly at the indecorous doings in the street below.

Only one of the new buildings walks a perfect line between the sober and the gaudy: 2 Times Square, originally conceived as an office tower, and converted in mid-design into the Ramada Renaissance Hotel. Mayers & Schiff, the building's architects, helped devise the current Times Square zoning. Instead of pasting their signs onto the facade, they've turned the signs into the facade. They're attached directly to the building's structure, its concrete columns exposed through notches cut through the skin of dark gray brick and glass. This taut fusion of architectural rigor and Madison Avenue seduction is the most advanced piece of design to go up in Times Square since the TKTS booth was created (also by Mayers & Schiff) nineteen years ago.

With the office towers of Times Square Center gone for now, if not for good, the focus has shifted to the plan for which the center was supposed to have provided financing: the restoration and programming of Forty-second Street's theaters. To succeed now, this plan will need the strongest possible support from the public and private sectors. It deserves that support overwhelmingly, not just because this tarnished boulevard is home to so many architectural gems but also because the plan has its priorities in order. The play's the thing on Broadway—and the movie, the dance troupe, the stand-up comic—and the best thing architecture can do to stage its own revival is to remember who's the star.

August 6, 1992

THE THRILL OF OUTER SPACE FOR EARTHBOUND LIVES

An anniversary is upon us, and attention must be paid. It has been twenty-five years since the opening of Atlanta's Hyatt Regency Hotel, the first of the atrium-style extravaganzas created by the architect and developer John Portman. Is it possibly redundant to celebrate this milestone? After all, the Portman atrium has been a nonstop celebration for the past quarter century. A festive mix of fountains, flapping banners, and lightbulb-studded elevators rising to the skies like effervescent bubbles, the Portman atrium is architecture at happy hour. It's a building that's gone out of town to a convention, determined to have a blast.

Still, a toast is in order for a concept that set out to give pleasure and in fact did so. Architects work with space, and few architects of this century have created such drama out of three dimensions. Twenty-three stories tall, set off by balconies carpeted a rich red, the Atlanta atrium presented space as the ultimate luxury. Here the empty void became a commodity as precious as the marble and gold that adorned the grand hotels of the Edwardian age.

Portman's is not a subtle space. With its elevators hurtling into the firmament like space capsules, the enclosed court is less Apollo than Apollo Space Program. It injects into earthbound lives the thrill of America's first ventures into outer space. Portman was our leading scientist of inner space. Psychologically as well as physically introverted, his voids maintained a constant emotional pitch with their suave blend of pleasure and terror, cocktails and vertigo.

In his later hotels, like the Bonaventure in Los Angeles and the Peachtree Center Plaza in Atlanta, the rocket imagery was even more explicit. Towering round cylinders encased in mirrored glass, these buildings evoked silos from which missiles might momentarily erupt. But where were these spaceships headed? For buildings, outer space is the city, and in this realm Portman's space mission sadly fizzled. Indeed, his introverted architecture remains a conspicuous symbol of what went wrong with cities over the past quarter century: the accelerating retreat from the public realm into enclaves of private luxury.

The most glaring example appeared in 1977, with Portman's design for the Renaissance Center in Detroit. Though $357 million was poured into the project in the hope of stirring the revival of this economically depressed city, the complex of office buildings, retail shops, and a hotel sat isolated from the urban context within a gleaming fortress. Suburban shoppers could drive into the Renaissance without setting foot downtown.

Portman's Marriott Marquis Hotel, in Times Square, also imposes a barrier between the atrium and the city outside. With a lobby lodged eight stories above street level, as though guests should ideally arrive by helicopter, the hotel affronts the street with gloomy overhangs and a mid-block driveway. The effect is to turn the sidewalk into a subterranean parking garage.

But the exclusionary thrust of the design is secondary to an eager inclusiveness that coerces people to eat, drink, shop, and sleep within the hotel walls. Tourists encounter the city only visually here, through windows of the revolving rooftop cocktail lounge, where machinery, rather than visitors' feet, dictates the view. Throughout the hotel, design issues a protective order that makes the city outside a forbidding presence, mercifully kept at bay.

In 1976, with the city planner Jonathan Barnett, Portman coauthored a manifesto, "The Architect as Developer." It is clear from the text that he believed his concept contributed something valuable to urban life. He writes perceptively of the failure of modern city planning, of the architect's responsibility to reengage the public. But a Portman atrium is not, of course, a public space. It is a tightly controlled private environment outfitted with the trappings of public space: openness, fountains, trees, bustling crowds. At the Marriott Marquis, there's even a town clock. But this visual dissembling is exploitive, if not sinister, especially considering that Portman received concessions from the public sector in the hope that the hotel would help revive Times Square.

The fact remains, however, that John Portman made a genuine effort to imagine some form of public life at a time when the very concept was in crisis. For by the mid-1960s, America's older industrial cities had witnessed the collapse of two overarching ideas that had governed their design: the historicism of the nineteenth-century City Beautiful movement and the rationalism of the Modern movement. And the era's most influential minds were opposed to new master-plan approaches. In 1961, Jane Jacobs had argued persuasively that diversity, not unified order, was what made cities live. A decade later, as Portman's second atrium hotel arose at O'Hare Airport in Chicago, Richard Sennett championed "the social uses of disorder."

Given this climate, it is not surprising that architecture turned inward, or that, when federal support for urban renewal began to wane in the 1970s, projects by private entrepreneurs like Portman and James Rouse were hailed as the answer to the urban crisis. And to an extent the optimism was well founded. Projects like Portman's took a step in the right direction—toward the city. In doing so, they confronted the problem underlying the urban crisis: the old American tradition of build and move on; leave your messes behind you; there will always be a new place to start over.

By the 1960s there was no new place to start over, except, perhaps, the moon. On Earth, as the urbanist Charles Abrams aptly phrased it, the city was the frontier, and so it remains. Portman made little effort to adapt to frontier life. His atriums shifted the controlled order of the suburban mall to disordered downtown locations. At best, they marked a transition between the old industrial city and some postindustrial metropolis that will not emerge until architects, planners, and developers have realized more integrated approaches to urban design. But if Portman did not bring this new city into being, he created glorious space capsules for the voyage to it. So it's Happy Birthday, Dear Atrium—but hold the happy returns.

September 20, 1992

IN PHILADELPHIA, A SHOWCASE OF ABANDONED HOPES

It was the largest building in America, and reputedly the most expensive. Its bold, original design influenced architecture internationally. Tocqueville came from France to study it; Dickens declared it (along with Niagara Falls) one of the two sights he hoped to see on his 1842 American tour. Today the Eastern State Penitentiary is something of an embarrassment, an abandoned ruin overgrown with weeds. But this gloomy landmark is still worthy of wide public attention. Few buildings shed a more penetrating light on modern democracy and its discontents.

Located just a few blocks from the Philadelphia Museum of Art, Eastern State is also a museum, a showcase of lost hopes. Empty since the last prisoners departed in 1970, the prison's stone-walled cells are haunting tableaux of a failed experiment in utopian social planning. Designed in 1821 by the Philadelphia architect John Haviland, Eastern State was born from the fusion of Quaker social conscience with the Enlightenment's faith in reason. Its innovative form arose from humanitarian concern for the treatment of prisoners and from philosophical speculation about the cause and cure of crime.

Few visitors today, however, will find this place either humane or reasonable. For it was here, in the city of the Liberty Bell, that the concept of solitary confinement was put to its first major test. This was the dubious achievement of the place known around the world as "the Prison at Philadelphia."

Today a preservation task force, financed by the Pew Charitable Trusts, is studying ways to reuse Eastern State and educate the public about its history. In the mid-1980s the prison, now owned by the city of Philadelphia, was the target of several redevelopment proposals, including plans for luxury housing and an urban shopping mall. All the proposals called for substantial demolition of Haviland's architecture, however, and in

1988, in response to a petition from the task force, Mayor W. Wilson Goode turned them all down pending further study.

But the popularity of Alcatraz notwithstanding, prisons make awkward landmarks. Compared to, say, a courthouse, a prison lacks the luster of civic pride. The classical form of a courthouse extols a supreme democratic virtue: the law and its impartiality, the consent of the governed to the rules that make their liberty possible. A prison speaks of the loss of freedom. Its message is not the law but the consequences of transgressing it: guilt, disgrace, the stigma of the outlaw state.

These qualities are not easily rendered into architecture, though Piranesi, memorably, transformed Baroque court design into "imaginary prisons" of nightmarish power. Still, for a young democratic nation, dedicated to reforming society and its institutions, the prison was an irresistible challenge. What could be more idealistic than to reform a brutal institution into an enlightened system for reforming individuals?

Viewed from outside, Eastern State resembles a Gothic fortress. Square in plan, the crenellated granite walls enclose a ten-acre site. A stone tower marks the entrance; from the corners, turrets rise. The design turns the form of a medieval city inside out. No hordes clamored to enter Eastern State, though the forbidding walls were designed to deter people from acts that might land them there. The massive ramparts also gave reassurance that those confined within would remain outside the city of the law-abiding.

But it is inside the walls that the prison's experimental plan unfolded. Traditionally, prisons were squalid places where people were thrown together in common rooms, often regardless of sex, age, or the severity of their offenses. They were places of disorder and social neglect. By contrast, "penitentiaries" like Eastern State were places of discipline. They were built on the theory that criminals are psychological slobs, people who failed to acquire discipline early in life. Within the penitentiary's controlled environment, criminals would reform themselves through penance—hence the name. The Pennsylvania Plan, as solitary (or "separate") confinement was called, took the theory a step further. Criminals would acquire discipline more readily if they were isolated from other undisciplined souls.

Philadelphia's prison officials considered several options before choosing Haviland's plan. They deliberated over a panopticon, a circular building with an observation tower in the middle, similar to one Benjamin Latrobe had designed for Richmond Prison in 1795. Though an observation tower rises from the center of Haviland's building, this is not the true panopticon form conceived by the British political economist Jeremy Bentham. Instead of forming a circle, Eastern State's seven cellblocks—

containing 250 cells altogether—radiate from the central observation tower like spokes. (Four additional blocks and other outbuildings were added later.) This plan allowed surveillance of the open yards but, unlike a panopticon, did not permit guards to look into the cells.

Instead of "the eye of power," to use Michel Foucault's term for the technique of constant prisoner surveillance, Eastern State relied on the power of the invisible. On arriving at the prison, prisoners were hooded before being led to their cells, to prevent them from seeing where they were going. Each cell measured eight by twelve feet and was equipped with a flush toilet and running water. A walled yard outside the cell permitted solitary exercise. An 1831 report explained: "No prisoner is seen by another, after he enters the wall. When the years of his confinement have passed, his old associates in crime will be scattered over the earth, or in the grave . . . and the prisoner can go forth into a new and industrious life, where his previous deeds are unknown."

It sounds a bit like heaven, and indeed the roots of the Pennsylvania Plan lay in monastic architecture and in the solitary life of Carthusian monks. Inmates at Eastern State were provided with Bibles and expected to work at weaving and other crafts. They received regular visits from members of the Philadelphia Prison Society, the Quaker organization that had championed the creation of Eastern State. It is as if, by emulating a monastic structure, the prison could convert a criminal calling into a religious one, sinners into saints. "The Pennsylvania System is a Divine System," hailed one contemporary advocate.

But to Dickens, who visited the prison 150 years ago, the system was infernal, precisely because of its reliance on the unseen. Prisoners were invisible to the world as well as to one another, and their punishment left no visible scars. Society did not have to witness the consequences of confining people here. Dickens thought public flogging preferable to this "slow and daily tampering with the mysteries of the brain."

But the governing concept of reform hinged on that tampering: on the prison's capacity to turn the private recesses of the mind into a matter of public interest. What stands out most vividly in Dickens's account of his visit (in his *American Notes*) is the eagerness of prison officials to secure the prisoners' assent to the system that held them. One inspector asks a prisoner, Are you resigned now? Are you a better man? A female prisoner is asked, Are you happy here?

Such questioning was critical to the experiment's success. By a circular logic, only the prisoners could say if the system worked. Only they could provide the evidence that, yes, they had reformed. They had acquired discipline. They had mended their ways.

If Dickens paused to visit Independence Hall and the Liberty Bell, he did not record it. From Philadelphia he traveled south to Washington, where he spent several days attending Congressional sessions at the Capitol, "a fine building of the Corinthian order, placed upon a noble and commanding eminence."

There's a logic to Dickens's itinerary that is conceptual as well as geographic, for Latrobe's 1811 design is the complement of Haviland's: both buildings are concerned with the process of self-government. Gleaming, proud, the Capitol lifts its dome high over the landscape, the public symbol of the Republic's collective mind. From the Capitol, government power radiates outward into the city along the avenues of L'Enfant's Baroque plan. Inside the building, Latrobe's interiors (inspired, in part, by Piranesi) lay out the structure of reason within which the contentious process of self-government will unfold.

At Eastern State, the Capitol's dark twin, abusers of liberty were compelled to bring themselves back into line. The sphere of this building is the private, psychological life of we the people. Instead of radiating outward, the building presses in. It expresses its power in physical confinement, in the constant pressure it applied to the cells and their inhabitants, to the inner lives of individuals where democratic authority resides.

October 4, 1992

REDUCED TO LUXURY

Simplify, eliminate, pare down: these are impulses of taste, but they are also dictates of democracy, marking the renewal of a tradition that has animated architects and designers for more than two centuries. Neoclassicism, Arts and Crafts, Art Nouveau, and the Modern movement each added a distinguished chapter to the history of this tradition. Its overarching aims: to align the aristocratic art of architecture with modern democratic ideals; to replace the opulence of the past with a display of sheer visual intelligence, and to establish simplicity of effect as the aesthetic equivalent of individual merit.

Two centuries ago, these ideals attained sufficient power to penetrate to the heart of the old aristocratic order. Though we may laugh at historical accounts of Marie Antoinette dressing up to play dairymaid with the ladies of her court, the queen's diversion, in fact, was a sympathetic response to the Enlightenment ideas that would ultimately bring down the ancien régime. The queen's dairy at the Château de Rambouillet, a neoclassical work of 1785 distinguished by a primitive stone grotto, was a royal rehearsal of the simple life. In America, Thomas Jefferson adopted classicism as the architectural vocabulary of democracy, not only because of its association with ancient Greece but also because its simple geometric forms proclaimed an order ruled by laws, not men.

The Arts and Crafts movement updated these aspirations for the mid-nineteenth century, producing something more important than such handsome artifacts as Morris fabrics and Stickley furniture. It also promoted the idea that the middle-class home had as much claim to the status of "architecture" as a château. In fact, according to Arts and Crafts theory, the home held a more legitimate claim. It represented the renegotiated social contract, the decentralized power of modern democracy. Whereas architecture once meant the publicly imposing, the word could now be applied to the modest and private. In their designs for Red House in 1859, Philip Webb and William Morris built upon the tradition of Gothic revival to establish a dignified vernacular for middle-class life.

Art Nouveau furthered these democratic aims by harnessing the power of the machine age. Though we may now regard the style's tendril-like forms as the essence of romantic nostalgia, in its own time Art Nouveau was a forward-looking style that tried to come to grips with the realities of industrial production. While Arts and Crafts was steeped in medievalism, Art Nouveau broke with past styles to forge new forms appropriate to the industrial city. Hector Guimard's landmark Metro stations in Paris brought the highest artistic standards into the realm of subway riders: the modern labyrinth of iron, steam, and speed. The Tiffany lampshades that now command such staggeringly high prices were designed to put art within the reach of average people. If one could not afford a garden, or even an Impressionist landscape, one could nonetheless enjoy an illuminated bough of wisteria blossoms tumbling in profusion over the table.

In the 1920s, architects developed a vocabulary designed to suggest that buildings themselves could be industrially produced without undue aesthetic sacrifice. Indeed, in the eyes of the modernists, architecture stood only to gain from the application of machine technology, for the machine pared away material excess, lifting buildings into the ethereal realm of formal abstraction. At the Weissenhof housing exhibition, held in Stuttgart, Germany, in 1927, designs by Mies van der Rohe, Le Corbusier, and Walter Gropius displayed the elemental luxuries afforded by this reduction: light, generously cascading into the interior through the use of plate-glass windows; space, made possible by steel and concrete framing and the elimination of interior walls; and convenience, made possible by streamlined forms that in theory, at least, possessed the efficiency of steamship cabins.

No architect in history made a stronger contribution to this democratization of architecture than Frank Lloyd Wright. With his roots in the Arts and Crafts tradition, Wright expanded the aims of that movement to the scale of the world's most democratic nation. For Wright, the essential luxury was space, both architectural and geographic. With such innovations as the open floor plan and corner windows, he created a spatial flow that related the individual building to America's vast dimensions. In the postwar years, with Wright's introduction of the carport as an architectural feature, his houses expressed the freedom of the open road. Himself a passionate devotee of automobiles (the spiral of New York's Guggenheim Museum derived from his 1925 design for a car ramp), Wright championed suburban living as a liberation from older cities and their traditional rankings of social class.

Today Wright's vision of a mobile America is carried on by architects like Neil Denari, who is based in Los Angeles and whose most recent project, a mobile home, is inspired by the freeway culture of Southern California. The project's theme is spatial expansion. When parked at its (presumably temporary) destination, Denari's caravan can open up to double its size. But its real meaning lies in its power to consume distance. Where the palace expressed a monarch's power by occupying large amounts of land, Denari's design speaks of the power to conquer space by traveling through it.

But it's possible that this archetypal dream of an America moving on down the highway is nearing the end of the road. We're becoming increasingly conscious of the drawbacks of eating up land and eating up the fuel required to move across it. While few would like to surrender the freedom symbolized by private cars and suburban subdivisions, pressures for more compact urban settlements are likely to increase. The future of democratic design may well lie with apartment buildings of medium scale, shoehorned into the built-up landscape. A 1987 design for low-cost housing by the architects Tod Williams and Billie Tsien, for example, envisions silo-like structures poised over the surrounding roofline. The meaning of this design resides not only in the quality of the architecture but in its strong connection to the urban context. It reminds us that, for all their problems, cities remain rich in their social and cultural diversity.

October 11, 1992

THE *Niña*, THE *Pinta*, AND THE
FATE OF THE "WHITE CITY"

Columbia, enthroned on her "Barge of State," sails into the grand lagoon, with Father Time at the helm and Victory at the prow. Eight plaster maidens, representing Arts and Industries, work the oars. From the rim of the lagoon a white city arises, its gleaming arcades and pavilions designed by America's leading architects. Fountains gush. Fireworks explode nightly.

Now, that's the way to celebrate Columbus. Or so it seemed to the builders of the World's Columbian Exposition, held in Chicago nearly a century ago. Unlike the makers of this year's dud Hollywood epics, the architects of the Chicago World's Fair knew how to throw a party. Allegory. Spectacle. Classical architecture, an entire city of it, went up in Jackson Park in 1893 to commemorate the discovery of the New World. And for a generation thereafter, Chicago's fabled "White City" was an ideal to which every American city aspired. From the fair emerged the nationwide City Beautiful movement, a progenitor of modern city planning and the force behind such New York landmarks as Grand Central Terminal and the Public Library.

The fair's legacy endures. It is evident not just in such banal manifestations as theme parks and festival marketplaces but in the shift of the urban economic base from manufacturing to information. People came to the World's Fair not to live, work, or shop but to acquire information—to gain a global perspective on art, science, history, and commerce. A century later, the "world cities" of the global marketplace have come to resemble the White City as places geared primarily to the exchange of ideas.

For Henry Adams, the fair was "the first expression of American thought as a unity." The fair's unified architectural composition of classical facades, spray-painted a uniform white, conferred a semblance of consistency on nineteenth-century America's cultural hodgepodge. But the unity evoked by the fair's architecture was more than an abstract cultural ideal. In 1893, the Civil War was still a potent memory. An allegorical statue of the Republic, the most prominent sculpture at the fair, was reflected in the lagoon's placid surface; it symbolized a reunified nation.

Above all, the White City expressed the unification of American commerce. As Lewis Mumford observed in the 1920s, the fair's "imperial facade" marked a historical shift in American enterprise: from small, entrepreneurial businesses to large financial trusts; from local industries to national monopolies and the unified rail systems that connected their far-flung operations; from manufacturing to finance.

The World's Fair launched the consolidated empire of the robber barons onto a world stage. Its message was commercial warfare. Thus the California Pavilion featured a colossal statue of a knight on horseback made entirely of prunes. As the fair's guidebook made clear, the statue "metaphorically impressed the fact that the prunes of that state are being introduced victoriously into all lands, to the discomfiture of the products of other countries." The White City, in short, was a full dress rehearsal for the American Century. It announced to the nations gathered around the lagoon: Thanks very much for the *Niña,* the *Pinta,* the *Santa Maria,* not to mention the *Mayflower* and General Lafayette, too. Now it's the New World's turn to frame a new world order.

We got our American Century. So where's our Beautiful City? How come, instead of fountains and fireworks, the world's richest nation ended up with glass boxes along Sixth Avenue and burnt-out storefronts in South Central Los Angeles?

Today the monuments of the City Beautiful movement loom like haunting reminders of a vision that failed to materialize. For every fixed-up Bryant Park, a dozen neglected Beaux Arts beauties languish. Spray-painted with graffiti, or with white paint to cover the discordant scrawl, their facades speak not of unity but of fragmentation. They lie scattered about a city increasingly polarized into privileged enclaves and settlements that recall Beirut. Nothing could contrast more sharply with the harmonious vision that arose in Jackson Park.

And yet, for all its visual chaos and social segregation, today's splintered city recalls the White City in one critical respect. It, too, marks a historic shift in commercial enterprise. Manuel Castells, a professor of planning at the University of California at Berkeley, has analyzed this development in depth. His book *The Informational City* traces the decline of manufacturing jobs and their traditional social supports; economic globalization and the new information technologies on which it depends; the mismatch between the city's new immigrant populations and the skills required to succeed in the new service industries. These factors have combined to produce a "dual city" that differs in kind from the industrial city's division between rich and poor.

This city is indeed a New World. It has its intrepid explorers: scholars like Castells, and the economist Saskia Sassen, who have pioneered the study of this new urban terrain. Photographers, filmmakers, metropolitan news reporters, and songwriters are also feeding glimpses of the new city into the cultural mainstream.

Architects have had a harder time getting a handle on things. Buildings are identified more closely with the social segregation of cities than with strategies that might overcome it. Designs for corporate towers, luxury housing, museums, and other high-end institutions reinforce the view that architecture chiefly serves the elite.

The view is not entirely a distortion. After two centuries of modern democracy, architecture is still a "white city." Even a recession does not drive buildings down in price that far. But the problem lies only partly with the way buildings are designed and paid for. It is also rooted in the way architecture is perceived, taught, and written about. There is no shortage of "downscale" buildings. Courthouses, clinics, schools, subways: if building forms such as these seldom conform to our conception of art, the fault lies with the conception, not just the forms.

Information thus has an important role to play in mending the fractured "informational city." A change in the perception of architecture cannot, by itself, heal a divided city. But it could lead us to discover what lies beyond.

November 8, 1992

ART AND SCIENCE POLITELY DISAGREE
ON AN ARCHITECTURAL JEWEL'S FATE

A ground-breaking was held on Thursday on a plot of land that many architects hold sacred: a grove of sixty-seven eucalyptus trees in La Jolla, California. What's so special about this place? By itself, the grove is nothing much to look at: just some dirt and trees and the pathways through the empty space around them. But walking through this porous barrier prepares the senses to be stunned by what lies beyond.

The Salk Institute for Biological Studies, designed by Louis I. Kahn between 1959 and 1965, has probably inspired more effusive praise—and even more awestruck silence—than any American building of this century. Kahn's two laboratory buildings, of poured concrete fitted with panels of weathered teak, are as ruggedly handsome as the coastal terrain from which they rise. The courtyard between them, a radiant void overlooking the ocean, sculpts form out of light and space.

But for the last two years, this serene site has been a zone of contention. The Salk Institute, which needs more space for offices and other facilities, is planning to build a new addition in the eucalyptus grove: four hundred feet long, set perpendicular to Kahn's labs, it would ruin the most sublime landscape ever created by an American architect.

A group of about 135 architects, critics, and scholars gathered at the Urban Center in New York two weeks ago to meet with Jonas Salk, the Institute's founding director. At the meeting, which was sponsored by the Architectural League, Dr. Salk presented a slightly modified version of the plan, by the San Francisco firm Anshen & Allen, and listened as members of the audience voiced their opposition to it. The speakers included the architect's widow, Esther Kahn; the historians Vincent Scully and Kenneth Frampton; and the architects Anne Tyng, Bart Voorsanger, Susana Torre, and Carles Enrique Vallhonrat.

The dynamics of this meeting were complex. Architects seldom criticize one another's work publicly. To do so goes against a deeply ingrained professional code, and it can expose them to nasty speculation about their motives. Aren't they really trying to get the job for themselves?

Moreover, this is not the first time that architects have spoken out against a proposed addition to a Kahn building. In 1989 a plan to expand the Kimbell Art Museum in Fort Worth also aroused strong opposition. Though the plan was subsequently abandoned, those who opposed it were subjected to bitter accusations of "East Coast elitism." No one could relish the prospect of repeating that ordeal.

And Jonas Salk, it goes without saying, is not the typical custodian of a landmark building. This landmark would not exist without him. San Diego donated the building's spectacular site because of the eminence of Dr. Salk. The March of Dimes put up money to build it on condition that the Institute bear his name. Dr. Salk hired Louis Kahn to design it and worked with him closely on the design.

Finally, there is a matter of priorities. The Salk Institute is a living organization that requires adequate, up-to-date research facilities. In the larger scheme of things, which is more important: the preservation of a landmark or a possible cure for AIDS? Ideally, there would be no need to choose between architecture and science, for Kahn's buildings beautifully fuse the two. But given the Institute's need for growth and the absence of Louis Kahn to accommodate it, practical matters must be balanced with aesthetic considerations.

Not surprisingly, the meeting in New York was a strange blend of awkwardness and goodwill, reason and passion. Dr. Salk spoke movingly of his joy in working with Louis Kahn. Those in the audience spoke, with similar emotion, of the building's importance to American architecture and to their lives. Taking Dr. Salk at his word that he was receptive to their suggestions, those who opposed his plan did so without rancor. Clearly, people were torn between admiration for a man responsible for this building and anger over a plan that would diminish it.

But the benign mood could only smooth over a conflict that remained unresolved at the meeting's conclusion. To those in the audience, the eucalyptus grove is integral to Kahn's vision. To Dr. Salk, the "so-called grove" is little more than a drainage ditch that, if anything, would be enhanced by his new building.

Why the difference in perception? Possibly, different angles of vision. For those who work there, the Salk is a place of test tubes and telephones, offices and corridors, books and papers. It is an interior. For its architectural pilgrims, the Salk is above all a great outdoors: the magnificent landscape to which the buildings give shape.

The architects Robert Venturi and Denise Scott Brown, who were unable to attend the Architectural League's meeting, later sent an eloquent written tribute to the visual and symbolic power of this outdoor mecca: "Its common space poised between a vast continent—symbolized by the bosk of trees—and a vast ocean—defined by an infinite horizon—is perceptually, physically and poignantly American. In framing the sea and the land in its composition, it marks the end of the Western frontier and the beginning of a new frontier."

Dr. Salk is not blind to the risks of tampering with a masterpiece. From the start he hoped to avoid the kind of outcry that exploded over the Kimbell by hiring architects who had worked with Kahn and by setting his addition apart from the existing buildings. He responded to criticism of the initial plan by increasing the separation. In the most recent version, a central entrance kiosk that joined the addition's two wings has been removed, allowing approaching visitors a narrow glimpse of sky.

But these modifications, far from resolving the problem, reinforce the impression that Dr. Salk has failed to grasp it. It is by no means clear that the Institute has exhausted the possibility for alternative schemes. At the Architectural League meeting, Dr. Salk offered no plausible explanation why the addition could not be situated elsewhere on the twenty-seven-acre site. He dismissed without comment a proposal by Kahn's associate, Anne Tyng, that would use the grove site but minimize the addition's impact on it.

It is disturbing that Dr. Salk failed to inform the League's audience that a ground-breaking had already been scheduled. Asked to confirm a report about the event as the meeting was breaking up, he insisted that it was merely a ceremonial occasion that did not preclude the possibility of further revisions.

It cannot be pleasant to be hounded by a posse of architectural busybodies. With building permits in hand, Dr. Salk is not legally obliged to heed their objections. Nonetheless, he should recognize that he is now enmeshed in a cultural conflict of interest. As Kahn's patron, he has gained an honored place in architectural history. As a custodian of Kahn's work, he is responsible for protecting that work from harm. Dr. Salk has yet to understand that the two roles are not one and the same. His immense stature as a patron cannot shield him from criticism of his custodial shortcomings.

At the meeting he observed that it is natural for things to evolve. It is indeed natural for the Salk Institute to evolve, but only Louis Kahn could make his work evolve, and that is no longer a possibility. The objective now should be to protect the integrity of Kahn's architecture even as the Institute grows in ways Kahn himself did not foresee. Fortunately, plans, too, can evolve, as Dr. Salk's experience with Kahn so beautifully demonstrates. Some further evolution is needed for the Institute's plans to be worthy of that experience.

November 16, 1992

FOR STATEN ISLAND, A FERRY TERMINAL ROOTED IN THE PAST

It's about time. That's one way to read the big clock that adorns the winning entry, announced this month, in the competition to design a new Manhattan terminal for the Staten Island ferry. No, our Swatch-infested city doesn't need another clock. But a building by Robert Venturi and Denise Scott Brown is long overdue.

These Philadelphia architects have been on the verge of building in New York many times over the years: a housing project for Brighton Beach; a juicy Big Apple for Times Square; neighborhood parks for Westway. And their influence has long been felt here. Buildings as diverse as the AT&T headquarters and the new Stuyvesant High School look as they do because of the path Mr. Venturi blazed out of the International Style with his 1966 book, *Complexity and Contradiction in Architecture*. Now New York will have a Venturi, Scott Brown original. And the architects (in association with Anderson/Schwartz Architects of Manhattan) have outdone themselves to make this the Venturiest, Scott Browniest building ever.

The terminal, which is scheduled to be completed by 1998, is a hybrid of the two types into which Mr. Venturi once breezily divided all buildings: the Decorated Shed (a container enlivened by ornament) and the Duck (the landmark of unique shape). With its landmark clock affixed to a barrel-vaulted nave, the terminal is a shed that quacks. And tells time, too.

In form and spirit, the design harks back to the Football Hall of Fame, an unbuilt work of Mr. Venturi's from 1967. In that project (for which Mr. Venturi coined the term *bill-ding-board*), a 100-foot-tall electric sign was clamped to the side of a barrel-vaulted structure whose cathedral scale alluded to our worshipful attitude toward sports heroes. For the terminal, the billboard has been transformed into a clock 125 feet in diameter, over-looking the harbor. The nave houses a waiting room with a 125-foot ceiling, though the allusion here is to Grand Central and the old Penn Station, temples to civic amenity. One wall of the waiting room features a Sony JumboTron television sign that could be programmed to display, among other things, live-action pictures of ferries pulling into the terminal.

These hyperscale features somewhat overshadow the design's more refined elements: circulation, lighting, the interplay of expansive indoor space and snug exterior arcades. As in much of their recent work, the architects use windows brilliantly to animate large expanses of wall; the tartan weave of the terminal's windows may be its most impressive feature.

To match the green-tinted glass, the terminal's walls are clad with green metal panels. On the south wall, the panels are painted with a full-scale rendering of a Beaux Arts facade echoing that of the Battery Maritime Building next door. (The existing ferry terminal, a resolutely undecorated shed, wore the same facade until it was renovated in 1954.)

The clock has stirred up a commotion. Some Staten Island residents, including Borough President Guy V. Molinari, object to its scale and playfulness. Since Mr. Venturi and Ms. Scott Brown pride themselves on their ability to appeal to a broad range of tastes, this clock bashing must give them pause. Still, they are sophisticated enough to know that public outcry is often the necessary precondition to public embrace. And, with the likelihood that changes in the design will be negotiated, we can probably look forward to 1993 as the year of the incredible shrinking clock.

Of course, the real problem with the design isn't the size of the clock. It's that the whole building has lost track of the time. Ferry travelers will have no trouble figuring out the hour. But what about the year? What is a transit hub for the year 2000 doing wearing a Beaux Arts ball gown? Why must a new civic symbol flirt with the old, even in jest?

Actually, the design's deference to the past could have been predicted from the way the competition was pitched by its sponsors, the city's Economic Development Corporation. The booklet the agency prepared for the six finalists is an illuminating document. It starts off with a period photograph of Lower Manhattan. It recounts the history of the site and of the city's ferry service, with passing nods to Giovanni da Verrazano, Cornelius Vanderbilt, and Edna St. Vincent Millay. It explicitly advises the architects to "acknowledge sympathetically" the landmark Battery Maritime Building.

But this program of instructions has nothing whatever to say about the transportation needs of New York in the approaching century; about projected changes in the kinds of jobs New Yorkers will be commuting to; about the impact of those changes on commuting patterns; about the power of a transportation system to shape that impact toward urbanistically desirable ends. In calling for architects to create a civic symbol, the program sets forth a notion of civic identity rooted in the past.

Given this retro slant, it is not surprising that the designs by the six finalists ran heavily toward nostalgia. The question that then confronted the jurors was: Which nostalgia would be best? Mr. Venturi and Ms. Scott Brown, at least, know how to deflect nostalgia with humor. Their use of tradition is almost progressive. They know how to play with Beaux Arts scale, symmetry, hierarchy; how to substitute food stands and electric signs for allegorical statues and academic murals; how to make monuments laugh at themselves. No one grasps more fully the irony of a city that tries to hold on to the past even as time visibly dissolves it.

Alas, it will take more than irony to rebuild the city's infrastructure. It will take clear, straightforward thinking about how urbanism and engineering can be brought into coherent relationship. Architecture is a medium in which that coherence might be formally expressed. But the expression won't mean much if the thinking remains backward. The context of a transportation building, for example, is much more than the building next door. It is a network of steel, space, and power that continues to shape a metropolitan region. The civic symbols of our time will be clearly rooted in that context.

In short, the Venturi, Scott Brown design is the right building for the wrong program. The architects have done more than accommodate the brief set before them. With their JumboTron wit, they've transcended it. They deserve to catch this ferry. It's their sponsors who are missing the boat.

November 22, 1992

GEHRY'S DISNEY HALL:
A MATTERHORN FOR MUSIC

Walt Disney is a trademark. Walt Disney is an empire. But Walt Disney is also the name of a popular American artist whose subject was enchantment. A pumpkin grows into a coach. A kiss breaks the spell. Trick photography makes the bud blossom. Disney's enchantment was America's. His images of wonder were metaphors for a nation that, in his time, was as blessed as any magic kingdom. Then, like American moral authority, the Disney magic waned. The padded Mickeys, the bloated theme parks, the denatured wholesomeness came to seem like desperate overcompensations for curdled American innocence.

Last week, ground was broken in downtown Los Angeles for a building that will recast that lost enchantment in a bold, contemporary form. Walt Disney Concert Hall, designed by the Los Angeles architect Frank Gehry, is by no means innocent of worldly ambitions. The $80 million, 2,400-seat hall, the future home of the Los Angeles Philharmonic, doesn't shrink from civic booster scale. Like the Museum of Contemporary Art, its neighbor on Bunker Hill, Disney Hall is expected to help revitalize the city's downtown district and lift its cultural profile. Fortunately, Gehry has resolved not to be crushed by the burden of such exemplary goals. For once, an architectural imagination soars to the level of the highest civic hopes.

Frank Gehry has often looked to artists for inspiration, so it is not surprising that his design takes more from Disney than a name. (Disney Hall, which is not affiliated with the Disney Corporation, is a beneficiary of a $50 million donation from Lillian Disney, the artist's widow.) Yet the design offers no nostalgic escape into the realms of Tinker Bell or the Seven Dwarfs, or a Main Street that never was. Nor does it rely on smoke, lasers, hidden machines, or the theme park's cordon sanitaire. Gehry's fiercely idealistic design creates a place of wonder in the city's hard, contentious core. It turns the pumpkin of family entertainment into the coach of art.

Like *Fantasia*, Disney Hall is an epic of music visualization, though what Gehry has set out to visualize is both more and less concrete than a musical score. Acoustics and empathy are the two forces driving the design. The building's acoustical structure is straightforward. The ideal concert hall, say experts, is a shoe box lined with wood and plaster. But, as those who've felt the panic of premature burial at Avery Fisher Hall can attest, it takes more than measurably good vibrations to make concertgoing a joy. Gehry and his project designer, Michael Maltzen, have worked closely with the noted acoustician Minoru Nagata on the design, and they've adopted the basic shoe-box shape. But this is a box fit for Cinderella's slippers.

The walls of the box slope outward, shaping the auditorium into a trapezoid. It resembles the hull of a primitive ship, an effect heightened by the convex slope of the seating that surrounds the orchestra on three sides. Gehry has described the hall as a "ceremonial barge for music," and ship shapes play subtly throughout the house. The ceiling, sculptured in gentle scallops, resembles billowing sails but also a theater curtain's festive swags. A bank of organ pipes rises at the "prow," though in their jumbled profusion the pipes could also be a Baroque altarpiece remodeled by Duchamp.

The ship image, though intuitively arrived at, is not an arbitrary symbol. It holds meanings in tune with the Romantic spirit of the symphonic repertory: adventure, discovery, and, ultimately, survival—the idea that art is not a pastime but a necessity of life. For Gehry, creativity is not a Romantic abstraction but an imperative of his time and place. In his most important public work to date, he has fashioned a symbol of social harmony for a city that has come to stand for the dissonance of contemporary life.

It has been said, and not unfairly, that Frank Gehry is the poet of this troubled condition, that the fragmented forms of his buildings speak of the breakup and dispersal of the traditional urban center. It is a paradox, then, that he has been called upon to design a project intended to symbolize the rejuvenation of downtown Los Angeles. But, in fact, fragmentation is just as much the rule downtown as further out along the freeways. The fragments are more concentrated, and they sprawl not only horizontally but in the jagged verticals of the skyline.

Gehry has responded to this context by enlarging to civic scale the layering techniques he employed when remodeling his own Santa Monica home in 1978. There he wrapped an existing suburban house with screens of glass, chain-link fence, and corrugated metal. At Disney Hall, the auditorium is clad with stainless steel panels, then partly wrapped with walls of French limestone. Or, rather, unwrapped, for the effect is like a gift from which the paper has been torn by an impatient birthday boy.

The "wrappers" peel away from the auditorium in curves subtle and pronounced. Some rise vertically to a height just above the hall's roofline. Others form curving horizontal strips at the building's base. Glass walls bulge forth from breaks between the wrappers, or rise above them in towering crystalline cages of Coney Island contour.

The main hall is not the only gift within this elaborate presentation. Like Mother Ginger, Gehry has tucked an array of surprises into the areas between the wrappers and the auditorium: lobbies, terraces, foyers, a café and gift shop, a "pre-concert" room for smaller musical events, a founders' room, and two areas Gehry calls "the baggages." Free-form containers, slung off the sides of the auditorium like saddlebags, they provide space for stairways, elevators, and restrooms.

You can, if you like, read the fragmentation of these forms as an expression of social breakdown. Actually, what the design breaks down is the hierarchical order that large civic buildings traditionally express. The asymmetrical wrappings, the fissures that open up between them, the hall's off-center axis and its thrusting diagonal lines break up the building's imposing mass without recourse to classical scaling. Instead of proceeding toward a monumental entrance framed by a symmetrical facade, people will enter through movable glass panels that further erode the barrier between inside and out. More than simply providing access, the design promotes accessibility.

In the past, Gehry has relied on ostentatiously humble materials to convey a populist ideal. Humility, perhaps, is not the first thing French limestone will bring to mind. But the stainless steel segments that push through the wrappers will reveal a blue collar beneath the formal dress. And Gehry hopes to line the interior of the hall with Douglas fir. With the right lighting, this staple of weekend carpentry takes on a candle glow.

The cumulative impression of these complex forms is less building than landscape: a Matterhorn for music where thousands can gather to take the ride. Mrs. Disney requested that a garden adjoin the hall, and Gehry has laid out a sumptuous one. But he has also turned the entire city block that the site occupies into an urban park. Its cascading stairways, planted terraces, and plazas are as ample as the foyers and staircases of the old Paris Opera, with the added advantage that they are set outside. You won't need a ticket to enjoy them. Nor will you have to quit the outdoors entirely to attend a concert. Skylights will admit natural light into the hall during the day.

What is most democratic about the design is the mutability of the images its forms give rise to. Gehry has not included fish, the creature that has occupied a place in his work analogous to the mouse in Disney's. Yet his grappling with those slippery shapes is discernible in the mercurial images that slither through Disney Hall's wavy contours. A ship. A cello. An unfolding flower. Hands thrust upward in delighted surprise. These images never crystallize. They surface and submerge like "the thing that dashes through the water," as Virginia Woolf once termed elusive insight.

The building is generous both in inviting such images and in refraining from making them explicit. It does not restrict the capacity of individual viewers to quarry their own figures and abstract images as they move through the building's serpentine spaces. That empathic approach is the essence of this building. It achieves unity by provoking multiple perspectives, and inviting them to coexist in one place. The place will be the sum of the perceptions it invokes. That is why, when people climb the steps to Disney Hall, it is not a magic kingdom they'll be entering. It is a magic democracy.

December 13, 1992

ST. JOHN THE DIVINE:
IT CAN'T GO ON. IT GOES ON.

A week from today, New York's greatest postmodern skyscraper celebrates its 100th birthday. And the building is barely two-thirds complete. An absurdity? An anachronism? No more so than the building itself: the glorious Cathedral Church of St. John the Divine.

Manhattan's twentieth-century French Gothic cathedral, the Colossus of Morningside Heights, is indeed absurd. Yet the century that has given us Camus, Genet, and Steve Martin is one that has found in absurdity a redeeming spiritual grace. In this sense, at least, St. John's stained-glass windows reflect our age as accurately as the glass curtain wall of an office tower designed by Mies van der Rohe. To paraphrase Beckett, the cathedral can't go on. It goes on. It has been going on since December 27, 1892, when the cornerstone was laid. There have been interruptions. Now and then the cathedral has halted construction to reexamine its motives or rethink its design. These ruminations have contributed to the impression that "St. John the Unfinished" is the existential cathedral, a building at once alienated and engaged. The opposite of Hamlet in modern dress, St. John's is the anxious modern hero in period costume.

Actually, to call St. John's postmodern is not the anachronism it may seem. Ralph Adams Cram, the architect responsible for most of the cathedral we see today, did not use the word *postmodern*. Even so, he longed for modernity to go away and believed that his buildings could hasten its disappearance. He knew that it was anachronistic to build in the style of thirteenth-century French cathedrals. He wanted the anachronism to be noticed. He designed his buildings as criticisms of modern life and its erosion of spiritual values.

Anti-modernist perhaps better conveys the substance of Cram's thought. That is the term used by Jackson Lears in *No Place of Grace*, his superb 1981 book on turn-of-the-century American culture. Lears locates Cram among a group of American thinkers who were alarmed by the rise of modern consumer culture. Like Henry Adams, Cram was obsessed with the collapse of moral authority in industrial civilization. Like Adams, Cram found in medieval buildings an ideal cultural unity of matter and spirit.

Unlike Adams (who dedicated his book on Chartres cathedral to Cram), Cram did not confine his medievalism to writing. He believed he could build a more spiritual world, and on the basis of that belief he developed a hugely successful architectural practice, with projects that included St. Thomas's on Fifth Avenue and chapels at Princeton, West Point, and St. George's School in Newport, Rhode Island. Cram's crowning success arrived in 1911, when he was commissioned to recast the original scheme for St. John's, a Romanesque design by Heins and LaFarge.

Cram's decision to remodel St. John's as a thirteenth-century French cathedral was not a matter of style but of belief. Like John Ruskin, Cram insisted that aesthetics and morality were inseparable, a theory his own work tends to disprove. Cram's buildings could be beautiful but his ideas were often repellent. His intolerance for his times led him to revile democracy, and in later life he entertained fascist sympathies. He envisioned Americans withdrawing into "walled cities," Williamsburg-like recreations of medieval life governed by static feudal hierarchies.

Both Cram and his buildings embodied anti-modernism's peculiar mix of idealism and denial, sincerity, and hypocrisy. Though Cram railed against modern industry, the success of his practice was due to the wealth that industry generated. His churches allowed their patrons to play a similarly ambivalent role, building impressive tributes to the spirit as they went about their business of modernizing America at an accelerating pace.

In some respects, Cram's holy mission mirrored that of the Bauhaus. Though that high temple of modernism rejected period styles for the forms of modern technology, it did so with the aim of raising those forms to a higher spiritual plane. A woodcut of a "crystal cathedral" adorned the 1919 Bauhaus manifesto. The school's studios, organized like medieval workshops, were to lay the foundations for a cultural fusion of matter and spirit. In this sense, the Bauhaus, too, was anti-modern. Like Cram, it sought to regain a place for the spirit in a secularized society.

The significant difference, of course, is that the Bauhaus sought to regain that place without the benefit of traditional religious practice. For Cram, architecture was chiefly a means to attract people back into the fold. The function of his buildings was to reestablish religious sacrament at the center of culture. For the Bauhaus, architecture itself was a form of sacrament, a ritual for a culture that had irrevocably lost the authority of religious orthodoxy. The function of Bauhaus training was to reveal spiritual values within the everyday material world: the dignity of work, the preciousness of ordinary materials, the beauty of simple forms. Rather than retreat behind walls inscribed with signs of Gothic piety, the Bauhaus resolved to reform modernity by mastering its tools.

Heresy though it may be to say so, the Bauhaus ideal has found a home at St. John's in recent years. Cathedral Stoneworks, one of the cathedral's most vibrant programs, was established in 1979 to train Harlem youth in the arts of cutting and carving stone. The program came on the heels of St. John's decision to resume building after a period largely devoted to social activism. As conceived by the Very Reverend James Parks Morton, dean of the cathedral, the program combines architecture with social service.

The stoneworks has considerably outgrown its quaint beginnings. Under the supervision of David Teitelbaum (an advocate for architectural preservation and a former real estate developer), it has shrugged off its Tiny Tim–ish aura of earnest fragility and become the sort of robust enterprise even a Scrooge could love. With a staff of sixty, the institute now commands the support of technology more advanced than anything the Bauhaus ever dreamed of, including computers, lasers, and digital cameras.

No longer restricted to producing stonework for the cathedral itself, the stoneyard has received commissions for projects throughout the city and beyond. They have included repairing sculptures, carvings, and stone facades at Rockefeller Center, Grand Central Terminal, the Woolworth Building, and the Waldorf-Astoria Hotel. The stoneworks has also taken on commissions for new buildings, like Kevin Roche's recent addition to the Jewish Museum and Pei Cobb Freed & Partners' Federal Triangle Building in Washington. To supply the stone, it has even acquired its own quarry in Alabama.

What would Cram make of these worldly transactions? Would he rage against collaborating with the secular world? Would he hold his tongue because the revenues from these projects are helping to pay for the completion of his design? Or would he recognize that there is a spiritual dimension to the cathedral's undertaking to work outside its own "walled town"? For it is irresistible, particularly at this season, to believe that in ministering to the architectural needs of others, St. John's is conferring a kind of grace on itself as well.

December 20, 1992

THINKING ABOUT TOMORROW, AND
HOW TO BUILD IT

And now the baby boomers get to build a public realm. That is the opportunity set before us by the new administration, alluring or horrifying as the prospect may be. How will that prospect materialize? What is the role of architecture in creating a space for change?

Even a mandate for change has a past. The shape of things to come in the next four years will be partly colored by the history of Bill Clinton's generation and the ideals of community it has formed. The yearning for a public realm figures strongly in the mythology of the baby boomers. They came of age, legendarily, at Woodstock, a gathering of strangers brought together chiefly by the chance to be together. The music was almost a pretext. The main event was an experiment in tribalism: an instant, three-day city built on a farm's muddy fields.

Antiwar demonstrations, like the one Mr. Clinton joined in London in 1969, offered a similar sense of occasion. These gatherings were about something more than opposition to America's involvement in Vietnam. They were also protests against isolationism at home: against the divisive culture of the car and the suburb and their failure to supply the social cohesion advertised by the traditionalist forms of suburban buildings. For the children of the postwar mass-produced suburbs, it became a rite of passage to rebel against their parents' version of the American dream.

Utopia, '60s style, was a place that could prosper without material props. So perhaps it is not surprising that the rebellion had little impact on the architecture of cities. Despite a trickle of countermigration from the suburbs to the inner cities, and the renovation of older buildings and neighborhoods that followed, urban decentralization has not been reversed. Nor have Americans given up their claim to a life of social and physical mobility, despite the fundamental contradiction between that life and the desire for stable community roots.

Mr. Clinton's generation has looked to the media to provide the social cohesion once supplied by public spaces. Streets, squares, and parks have been displaced, though not eliminated, by telephones, television sets, and computers. Yet, as Robert Reich, Mr. Clinton's labor secretary designate, has observed, the impact of this communications technology on cities has by no means been beneficial. It has further fragmented the environment into islands of privilege surrounded by the decaying remains of the old industrial cities and the poor populations that can no longer count on the older industries that once offered blue-collar jobs.

What the government needs to address is not the vibrant information industry, an announced priority for the incoming administration, but rather those large chunks of the environment that cannot be digitized or transferred to silicon chips. Housing, transportation, and the kind of public space not reducible to airwaves: these traditional segments of the urban spine have fallen into varying degrees of decomposition. It is in these areas that the country's new management could have a major impact.

The word *infrastructure* has already taken root as a guiding concept of Mr. Clinton's vision. It is a vague term, and that is part of its appeal. For many, it evokes images of the massive public works projects undertaken in the 1930s: dams, bridges, and tunnels that shook the rust off the aging nineteenth-century cities and propelled the United States to the peak of industrial prosperity. It's a word that has taken on a lot of ideological baggage. During the presidential campaign, it served the political purpose of reminding Americans that the rust was back—and persuading them that they needed a new team to deal with it. Let's stop the kidding around and get down to basics, this word said. The foundations are rotten. It's time to face bedrock reality after, in the words of the political columnist Sidney Blumenthal, "our long national daydream." Yet so far the word *infrastructure* is itself largely a symbol, a metaphor capable of generating some pretty fancy daydreams of its own.

Recently, the word has gained currency among the generation of architects now coming of age. This is partly a matter of aesthetics, partly a question of generational change. For architects looking for a way to distinguish themselves from the postmodern generation that preceded them, the sinewy industrial vocabulary of public works holds great appeal. Work by such architects as Renzo Piano (currently the subject of a show at the Urban Center in New York) and Santiago Calatrava (whose work will be featured at the Museum of Modern Art in March) has attracted increasing admiration for the visual lyricism it brings to structural engineering.

But for many young architects the appeal of infrastructure is that it offers a chance to shift their profession from aesthetics toward social service. Now at the age when architects traditionally graduate from a painfully prolonged apprenticeship to a mature practice, they are looking for something more substantial than the applied decoration into which postmodernism often degenerated. In New York, architects in their forties look back with something like nostalgia to the years when Mayor John Lindsay attracted architects to public service by conferring a Kennedy-esque glamour on urban planning.

For these architects, the aesthetic power of public works is less important than their power to shape landscapes and mold cities—to create
community, in short. As witnesses to privatization and its fragmenting
effects, they regard infrastructure as a means to link buildings, neighborhoods, and regions that have become disconnected. Above all, perhaps,
they see it as a way to link themselves and their art to a sense of common
purpose and to an ethical ideal. To them, infrastructure has become the
code word for a rebuilt public realm.

There is considerable irony in these lofty expectations. The American
highway system, after all, is infrastructure—the most ambitious example
of it. This system has caused more problems than it has solved and, moreover, has provided the getaway route to avoid dealing with them. Roadways that once promised to relieve urban congestion ended up depleting
urban vitality. It remains to be seen how Henry Cisneros, Mr. Clinton's
secretary of housing and urban development designate, will deal with this
problem. San Antonio, where Mr. Cisneros served as mayor, is a case
study in urban escapism. A ring highway, encrusted with malls, does not
serve the city but drains it. A downtown Riverwalk, chockablock with
tourist restaurants, festooned with twinkle lights, offers scant compensation for the ghost town that visitors encounter when they step outside this
two-dimensional fairy tale of urban revival.

Still, Mr. Cisneros didn't invent this flawed approach. He was mayor in
the '80s, when federal leadership insisted that the function of the public
realm was, in effect, to dissolve the public realm. Amenities had to pay
their way or die. So perhaps the urgent task at hand is to expose this
Orwellian view of "public life" as the seductive self-deception it has been
all along. For a public realm is, very simply, a place that can exist even
though someone isn't directly profiting from it. Its bottom line is that it is
not governed by the bottom line.

The climate has already been altered by the thawing of the Cold War.
So long as the United States was performing the role of flag bearer for the
free enterprise system, turning the public realm over to private interests
served a strategic purpose. But the election was, among other things, a referendum on whether or not that strategy should continue now that the
Cold War is over. For the screens of the American electronic town hall
showed something terribly out of whack. We had shipped the public realm
abroad and allowed it to crumble at home. We helped other distressed
nations rebuild themselves while the homeless were piling up on our
doorsteps.

Of all the public works that have been allowed to languish in recent
years, housing now deserves the highest priority. But the virtue of infra-

structure is its flexibility. It can be expanded to embrace, and join together, many elements of the built environment, including housing, transportation, and public space. That expansion is already under way, thanks to federal legislation passed in October 1991. The Intermodal Surface Transportation Efficiency Act (informally known as ISTEA and pronounced "ice tea"), a bill brokered in large part by Senator Daniel Patrick Moynihan, has already begun to enlarge the prospects for architects who want to engage in public building. The bill, which sets up a six-year program budgeted at $151 billion, significantly increases funds available for mass transit systems. But of potentially greater importance is the support it provides for "enhancement activities" that can be hooked on to transportation systems. These could include the restoration of older neighborhoods affected by a new road; the renovation of historic train stations for nontransportation uses; and the creation of new public spaces adjacent to subway, bus, or ferry lines.

Although the enhancements program is scheduled to receive a modest $3.4 billion over the next six years, amendments to the ISTEA bill could increase the appropriation and widen the range of uses. It is encouraging that Robert Peck, an official of the American Institute of Architects who helped frame the legislation, has been an adviser to the Clinton transition team. Input like his could shape an approach to urban development that would integrate building programs normally carried out by separate government fiefdoms. Construction of new schools, housing, health care facilities, and transit systems could go forward as inseparable components of urban infrastructure.

So the pendulum swings again. And if the time is indeed ripe for change, perhaps it is also time to remember something critical about pendulums. They move but they go nowhere. They're all *tick* and *tock*. And those who think that architecture should forswear aesthetics may as well abandon their hopes for change. Art is where change materializes.

The problem with architecture in recent years has not been an overemphasis on art but an extreme disconnection between aesthetics and sociology. Politicians are not the only people trapped by gridlock. Architects, too, have been caught in a stalemate between conflicting visions of public life. Architects, however, don't need the permission of governments to initiate change. It is possible, even in a cynical time, to articulate ideals. Big public works are only one alternative to big corporate skyscrapers, and a new transportation system is only one way to stitch together the urban fabric. A drawing, a city mural, even a department-store window display can also spark new visions of community. Architecture does not shape physical reality only. It also shapes consciousness. It operates in the realm of image and metaphor as well as that of matter. And to close the door on either realm is to trample the grass roots of architectural creativity.

Mr. Clinton has been working overtime in the metaphor factory. The morning jogs to McDonald's, the strolls along inner-city streets, the measuring of White House walls for bookshelves—such actions, while symbolic, are not without substance. They are changing the context in which political actions will unfold.

Architecture is embarking on a similar process. A change is taking place in the context in which buildings will be viewed. The prospect now is not that every building will, for instance, house the homeless, but that buildings will not have to be judged against a backdrop of indifference to the homeless. They will arise in a culture that has at last acknowledged the need to correct policies that allow homelessness to persist. Instead of withdrawing into forlorn remembrances of a civic culture that once existed, architects may now have the chance to piece together a metropolis for today.

January 10, 1993

THE TALE OF A CHIMNEY THAT TURNED INTO AN OASIS

Think of parks and it's natural to visualize vegetation: lawns, groves, and flower beds organized in space. But the light that nurtures trees and grass is also part of nature, as artists from Turner to James Turrell have shown. And in a city of tall buildings, a piece of sky is as precious as a patch of green. For New Yorkers, the Hudson River waterfront is an unplanned park of light. Even without one blade of grass, a single bench, or a cast-iron lamppost, the city's scrappy strip of shoreline is a ribbon park where people come to soak up the incandescent air of light reflected over water.

Manhattan's newest park is a neat little bow stitched into this tattered ribbon. New Yorkers are familiar with look-in parks, those fenced-in plots of green that people can peer into but not enter. Morton Street Park is a look-out park, a place for gazing at the sky. It is also a vantage point for peering into the future. The park's designers, Stan Eckstut of Ehrenkrantz & Eckstut and Lee Weintraub of Weintraub & di Domenico, offer a preview of the ways civic amenities can be integrated into urban infrastructure.

This is a Cinderella story, about a chimney that turned into an oasis. It began six years ago when the Port Authority of New York and New Jersey announced plans to build two ventilation towers at the head of Morton Street pier in Greenwich Village. The vents were needed to provide emergency air and an exit route from the PATH trains beneath the Hudson River. Needed or not, it was NIMBY time in the West Village. Residents were understandably up in arms about a plan that threatened to blight the neighborhood's main recreational asset. The proposal to build the vents, coupled with the pier's general dilapidation, was like a one-two punch of bureaucratic indifference. It was bad enough to lose physical access to the water; now the vents seemed likely to cut off visual access as well.

The Port Authority, responding to community antagonism, invited three architectural teams to submit proposals that would at least make these potential eyesores less painful to behold. But what set the winning plan apart was not the strength of its design. It was that the architects strongly urged the Authority to reconsider the program. Instead of merely devising designs to make the shafts more palatable, Mr. Eckstut and Mr. Weintraub proposed that the vents provide the occasion to create a new public space.

Obviously, there wasn't room to build a Riverside Park, or even a Bryant Park, on this tiny, 17,000-square-foot site. But the designers were looking beyond this site. Mr. Eckstut, an architect known for thinking urbanistically, was the codesigner, with Alexander Cooper, of the 1979 master plan for Battery Park City. He recognized that the Morton Street vents could be enlarged to create the first segment in the waterfront esplanade that will one day extend from Battery Park City to Riverside Park. He and Mr. Weintraub have treated the project as a design laboratory for testing ways to create a linear park that is likely to develop piecemeal over the next decade. Their goal was not simply to repeat the design of the Battery Park City esplanade like an endless loop but to show how the esplanade might be enhanced along its length with a series of diversely designed public spaces.

At Morton Street, the design was driven by the need to integrate the vent towers into a park setting. Greenhouses provided the inspiration for the metal and glass grids at the top of the forty-foot-high shafts. Garden pergolas are evoked by granite colonnades that support cube-shaped lighting fixtures. The towers are clad in panels of warm granite, set in patterns that alternate smooth with rusticated stone.

Bayberry trees and grasses are the park's horticultural features. These are set in low planters whose asymmetrical design reflects the context of this urban edge: straight-sided where the park meets the street, wavy where it faces water. The cruciform columns, also of granite, rise to about one-third the height of the vents. These scaling devices not only reduce the visual impact of the towers; they also make them appear essential to the design. They provide a visual anchor and a sense of protection for what would otherwise be a somewhat forlorn stretch of windswept pavement.

Though the park's forms are derived from traditional garden architecture, no attempt has been made to reproduce these structures literally, or to create a period look. The design manifests a clear sense of the difference between drawing on history for inspiration and retreating to it out of fear. Visitors to the park will know that they are in New York in 1993, not at the Palm House in Kew. The park's lighting, in particular, sends a strong message of contemporaneity. As a designer of the Battery Park City esplanade, Mr. Eckstut was largely responsible for the revival of old-fashioned lampposts that in the years since has become something of an urban contagion. Mr. Eckstut has apparently come to feel that there are better ways to light up a path to the future than sleepwalking down memory lane.

The objective here, however, is not to deny tradition but on the contrary to reinvigorate New York's magnificent heritage of great public works. Clearly, Mr. Eckstut has been looking at the massive ventilation systems that service the city's tunnels, at the anchorages and bridge approaches that create strong architectural statements about the power of engineering to link the city together and drive it forward. Morton Street Park is not on a scale with those monuments physically, and it could also be bolder in its design. But it emulates admirably the breadth of their urban vision.

Beyond that, this project provides a good model for architects and public agencies that are seeking to forge a new pact for civic action. Two designers with a strong sense of public service gained the support of a government agency with the flexibility and the money to back their ideas. The result is a salutary formula for contemporary urbanism: grassroots ideas and political clout. An engineering project opposed by the public was transformed into a place where the public comes first. The enlightenment of the undertaking is nearly as radiant as the view from the site.

January 31, 1993

SOME UNFINISHED BUSINESS ON ST.-GERMAIN

At a lecture in New York last fall, the Dutch architect Rem Koolhaas began by wondering aloud why his generation has taken so long to make its mark upon the city. Koolhaas, forty-seven, is part of the postwar European generation that came of age with the "events of May," the student upheavals that rocked Paris and other cities in 1968. For Koolhaas, '68 remains a touchstone—not for sentimental reasons, or not mainly—but because the protests revealed attitudes that, for better or worse, remain in force.

To paraphrase his musings: if architects of this generation feel "marginalized," that is because they chose to occupy the margins, because they staked their identity to a stance of opposition they have yet to outgrow. No one is stopping them from crossing over their self-imposed barricades, nor is the city still the stern father's stone face.

Koolhaas had a point, but does it apply to him? Unlike many of his contemporaries, he has never shrunk back from the urban center, as the name of his firm—Office for Metropolitan Architecture, or OMA— suggests. Yet that firm retains a countercultural spirit. Based in Rotterdam, OMA is, in effect, an office of city planning without a city to plan, the self-appointed bureaucracy of some imaginary city that has replaced its bureaucrats with dreamers. Images of New York and Atlanta float through Koolhaas's built and theoretical projects like wish fulfillments for a New World. But the work remains philosophically attuned to Paris and to the role students have traditionally played throughout the city's cultural history.

Now it looks as if Koolhaas will get to add a chapter to that history. In December he won a competition to design a new library building for the Jussieu Campus of the University of Paris, a pivotal site in the May uprising a quarter-century ago. For this architect it is a dream of a job, a chance to explore his generation's social mythology at its historic root. And Koolhaas's design is dream architecture: a building where space flows out of confining compartments into a high-rise full of free associations.

The location is at once a dream and a nightmare. The Jussieu Campus is on the Left Bank, where the Boulevard St.-Germain meets the Seine, not far from Notre Dame. But the campus itself is infernal. Designed in the early 1960s by Edouard Albert, it is mostly housed in one immense building, a square metal labyrinth that seems to go on forever. Within the steel walls, modular units are laid out like a checkerboard, each module enclosing an abyss of a courtyard. Outside, a strip of emptiness tries to pass for public space. Only the faceless figures that populate architectural renderings would feel at home here.

The building was unfinished at the time of the 1968 riots, when construction was suspended. The government hoped to ward off future unrest by shifting resources—and thereby students—from Parisian schools to suburban campuses. That left Albert's building with a ragged, saw-toothed corner, which is where the new building will rise. Containing two separate libraries and facilities for student recreation, the project will mark the campus's symbolic completion.

Koolhaas's "completion" is also an inversion: transparent, vertical, and fluid where Albert is opaque, horizontal, and stiff. Seven concrete floor slabs, with twenty-three feet between them, define the main levels of a square, glass-clad tower. Instead of stacking up the floors in the usual horizontal layers, Koolhaas has made large, irregular cuts in each slab, removing a third of their floor area. Wide ramps, inserted into the cuts, slope at different angles and meet at intermediary levels between the floors. The result is the most spectacular use of the spiral form since Frank Lloyd Wright's Guggenheim Museum.

Entering the building at the third-floor level (through connectors to Albert's building), students can descend to a library of scientific books or mount the ramps to one devoted to the humanities. But this wide-open space will encourage a porous relationship between its components. Reading rooms, stacks, classrooms, offices, and audiovisual centers will occupy both sloping and level floors. Some slopes will form natural amphitheaters; others will be landscaped, like indoor parks. Cafés and sports areas will supplement a scheme conceived to resemble the mix of an urban street. In effect, Koolhaas has scooped up the barren public space outside Albert's building, folded it this way and that to create a continuous vertical landscape, built up the landscape to keep it constantly active, and wrapped the whole thing up in a transparent skin. University life will become visibly part of the city.

While the warping of the floor planes may seem idiosyncratic, it is not without precedent in twentieth-century architecture. Those slopes will be familiar terrain to anybody who has climbed the steps of the Metropolitan Opera House or has seen pictures of the Helicline at the 1939 New York World's Fair. Wallace K. Harrison, who designed these monuments, has been a major influence on Koolhaas, and so has Mies van der Rohe. His somewhat quixotic goal has been to forge a synthesis between these two irreconcilable figures. It is Mies that we see reflected in the library's unadorned skin of glass, in the regular rhythm of its exposed concrete columns. An interplay between the disciplined and the polymorphous is the library's underlying formal idea.

While it may seem logical to identify the structural system with science, the free-form floors with the humanities, in fact Koolhaas designs against that logic. Like the philosopher of science Gaston Bachelard, he wants to pierce the wall between these disciplines. For Bachelard, a Sorbonne professor whose influence on architecture has grown since his death in 1962, the poet and the scientist were creative beings allied against the excessive claims of reason. For Koolhaas, structure may be essential to architecture but need not dictate its form. Here the structural grid supports an experiment to show that form can depart from regularity yet deepen its obligation to function.

As such, the design converts to constructive form the explosive forces that erupted here twenty-five years ago. As James Miller observes in his biography of Michel Foucault, the student protest was more potent for being apparently aimless. It was focused beyond concrete political demands toward "the very order of things in the modern world generally."

Regularized, homogenized, rigid—that order remains on permanent display in Albert's building, though Koolhaas is mature enough to recognize the idealism it once represented. Paired with it, his building will be at once a gesture of reconciliation and a permanent act of rupture. Functionally flexible, formally indeterminate, the library is designed to show that architecture can do more than contain the mind's adventures. It can also lead minds out of containment by embarking on adventures of its own. Naturally, the students who use this building may find Koolhaas's dizzying adventure as intolerable as he found Albert's.

February 14, 1993

ROADSIDE ATTRACTIONS TO RECKON WITH

Architects who hope that infrastructure holds the magic key to rebuilding American cities need to reckon with a sobering truth: throughout this century, infrastructure—highways, communications, even mass transit—has been the major force responsible for dismantling American cities. And they will also have to reckon with Frank Lloyd Wright, the greatest "infra structural" architect America has produced.

Wright didn't build highways. He made images. His residential architecture beckoned to city dwellers with the promise of a bold adventure in living that could be theirs if they would leave the city behind. For Wright, the city was "the triumph of the herd instinct," "the great mouth," "the Moloch that knows no god but More." His houses offered the hearty independence of life on the prairie, but with all the modern conveniences. As the century unfolded, increasing numbers of Americans responded to his call. In the postwar years, Wright lent cultural prestige to those who abandoned the city for the suburbs.

Yet Wright believed that his vision was urban. Though most of his practice was devoted to building private houses, he understood perfectly that architecture cannot exist without a public realm. In the 1930s he began a series of drawings to show what his realm looked like. Broadacre City, as he called his plan, focused less on houses than on the connective tissue between them. Highways, cars, gas stations, air travel, even broadcast media figured in his grand continental design for a decentralized urban America.

As the historian Grant Hildebrand writes in *The Wright Space*, a fine study of Wright's residential architecture, Wright's houses were a synthesis of "prospect" and "refuge." Broadacre City showed the prospect, while the houses of Wright's later years linked buildings to it. With simplified, open exteriors, and prominently placed carports, the houses came to resemble extensions of the highway, pinwheeling in space. More than private dwellings, they were fragments of a dispersed, redefined public domain.

What's needed now is designs that reweave the pattern of prospect and refuge to fit a transformed urban condition. For the country has traveled some distance down the highway in the years since Broadacre City. Today Wright's barbs about herds and mouths would stick more firmly to the suburban panorama he helped bring about. The city is the contemporary frontier, the horizon for poor immigrants from other countries and rich ones from the suburbs.

It will take more than infrastructure to develop this frontier. It will take policies that link infrastructure to housing. Wright's drawings for Broadacre City anticipated Government policies that linked the federal highway system to suburban development. What architects can provide now is images that will reverse the traffic—designs for housing that electrify the urban prospect. Just as Wright's images enticed people away from the city, images now can graphically reinforce the urban center as the superstructure of all infrastructures—airports, subways, buses, highways, trains, and, most of all, the street.

In the most recent wave of building, architects have behaved as though they agreed with Wright that the city's best days were behind it. At Battery Park City, to cite one highly influential example, designs were modeled on prewar apartment buildings in the belief that such images of stability would make people feel more comfortable in a city where stability is in notoriously short supply. Art Deco resurfaced in the 1980s as a favored style, a motif that revealed a desire to turn the city into a theme park of its more glamorous past.

These buildings offered superficial images of refuge, but when it came to providing prospect, they couldn't quite bring themselves to face the world. This is understandable, given the extent to which today's prospect is one of constant menace, a constant barrage of assaults on mind and body.

Yet, as Mr. Hildebrand points out, Wright's powerful images of refuge were all the more impressive because they were closely bound to prospects of danger. At Fallingwater, to name an extreme example, Wright deliberately perched a country house where it would appear to be continuously on the verge of becoming Fallinghouse. Rejecting his client's preference for a site downstream from the waterfall that graced his property, Wright planted the house directly atop the falls. And his design dramatized the precarious balance, with its thrusting cantilevers and features that brought the prospect into the house itself: expanses of glass, boulders that erupt into the living room floor, even the constant sound of water. Here, as Mr. Hildebrand remarks, "we are invited to savor danger from a haven of safety."

Elaborating, Mr. Hildebrand quotes Jay Appleton, the landscape historian from whom he adopted his theory of prospect and refuge. "If we were to be interested only in those features of our environment which are suggestive of safety, coziness and comfort, and not at all concerned with those which suggest danger, what sort of recipe for survival would that be? Seeking the assurance that we can handle danger by actually experiencing it is therefore a source of pleasure."

In the city, the hazards are social and cultural as well as natural. But the most powerful images for new urban housing may well arise from the architect's willingness to face these hazards. Muggings, riots, drugs, and homelessness are pernicious evils that drive people away from cities. But these hazards are also signs of urban life. Cities don't just consume culture. They produce it. They offer more than magnetic malls where people surrender to fantasies devised by market researchers. They provide a stage where new chapters in cultural history are now being written.

It's time architects elbowed their way onto that stage, along with the musicians, writers, artists, and filmmakers who have been up there for years. Instead of making buildings that apologize for the way the city is, they should give form to those elements of contemporary mythology that strengthen the city's magnetic force: openness to change, resistance to norms, exposure to difference, the maintenance of poise amid conflict, tension and imbalance. These are, of course, the same democratic virtues to which Wright's often startling vocabulary gave such eloquent voice. It would be heartening to see architecture that is not afraid to startle.

February 28, 1993

MODERNISM AND MORALITY IN THE SOUTH BRONX

Come 1998, a gleaming new police academy building will streak through the center of the South Bronx like a marathon runner dashing toward the ribbon. The academy's architects have designed a modern athletic thoroughbred of a building. With a sleek, translucent facade of steel and glass, curving as it rounds the bend at East 153rd Street just off the Grand Concourse, the design looks every inch a champion, and indeed it is one. Last December, the design won a competition for the most important new public building to go forward during the Dinkins administration.

A lot is riding on this project. With a budget of $230 million, the Police Academy is an important civic symbol, a sign that even in hard times, New York can build major public works. Now housed in crowded quarters on East Twentieth Street in Manhattan, the Academy will be relocated to the South Bronx in an effort to erase the borough's image as a metaphor for urban decline. Not least, at a time when law and order promises to become a major issue in the approaching mayoral campaign, this project offers a conspicuous show of support for the city's law enforcement officers. It also offers an opportunity of overpowering importance: a chance to rethink the critical place of law enforcement in American cities today. This is what lifts the project out of the realm of local news and into a national spotlight.

For some the building represents a change in course for architecture. Earlier last year, the city's competition to design the Whitehall Ferry Terminal was won by a Postmodern entry by Venturi, Scott Brown & Associates, with Frederic Schwartz. By contrast, the Police Academy competition (in which Venturi, Scott Brown was also an entrant) was won by an aggressively modernist design by Ellerbe Becket and Michael Fieldman & Partners. Some interpret this contrast as a sign of a modernist revival.

More likely, the contrast signifies a crisis of faith in the supremacy of architectural aesthetics. Underlying the crisis is the belief that architecture ought to do more than it has done in recent years to ameliorate social conditions. But how? How far can buildings make up for society's shortcomings? The Police Academy is a case study in the dysfunctional relationship between aesthetic means and social ends. It illustrates the fallacy in thinking that modernist images can revive modernism's utopian mission.

Government officials and architects are not the only ones now reckoning with the place of law enforcement in the cities. As a result of the Rodney King beating and its politically charged aftermath, Americans have never been more aware of the tensions between the public and the police. The King trials will not resolve those tensions, because the beating did not create them. They will persist so long as society expects the police to compensate for its own failure to reframe the social contract. If police behavior is sometimes warped, the public's expectations of law enforcement are also warped. Police are supposed to maintain civil order within a society that has retreated from the moral order once embedded in the public realm.

As those who have followed the trials have witnessed, law enforcement is more than a profession. It is a culture. And a police academy is where that culture is transmitted. Here cadets are trained not just in firearms, arrest procedures, and other technical skills but also in the codes of a fellowship: its bonds of solidarity, ideals of heroism and sacrifice, the unstable mix of service and distrust that binds the police to the public, or fails to.

The city's decision to organize a design competition—in effect, to honor architecture along with the men and women in blue—gave due recognition to the importance of this project. And the Ellerbe Becket–Fieldman scheme was visually the strongest of the seven finalists. In model form, it is a beautiful piece of architectural sculpture, at once muscular and lyrical, formally assertive but not visually overbearing, its airy translucence a deliberate attempt to avoid a fortress-like impression. With its taut, horizontally stretched skin of steel and glass, the design recalls the work of Erich Mendelsohn, the pioneer modernist who imbued static forms with the quality of dynamic motion.

In this, as in much of his recent work, Peter Pran, Ellerbe Becket's principal designer, is also heavily indebted to Zaha Hadid and to the Russian modernists who have long inspired her. It is delicious to contemplate that in five years' time the capital city of capitalism will be policed by officers trained inside a building that harks back to the Soviet avant-garde.

The shape of the building, and the configuration of the outdoor campus it partly frames, make the best of an awkward site, an irregularly shaped eight-and-a-half-acre parcel that is bordered on the south by an elevated roadway and on the east by commuter rail tracks. Two buildings are enfolded within the Academy's broad horizontal sweep. Administration offices are housed in the curved, eight-story tower at the western end, while classrooms are in the wing that stretches four hundred feet to the northeast. A library, an auditorium, and other public spaces are set at the juncture of the two wings.

The design's elegance derives partly from its tiny footprint. By stacking the functions vertically, the architects were able to shape a block that is linear, not block-like. At its western edge, the facade rises to a sharp, glittering peak and pulls partly away from the building envelope, as if it were doing stretching exercises before a morning run.

Outdoor athletic areas, in fact, take up the greater share of the campus. Set within the building's curving frame are a running track, basketball courts, and two muster decks, platforms where cadets assemble each morning. One of the decks, protected by a sweeping metal canopy, is designed for use in foul weather. On sunny days, the southeastern orientation will take advantage of the maximum solar exposure.

Although the Police Academy will not open its doors for another five years, it has already begun to play an educational role. The design has become a focus for discussions on the contributions the Academy could make to the South Bronx. A group of pro bono architects and planners called Bronx Center has provided the catalyst for these discussions. Initiated by Borough President Fernando Ferrer of the Bronx, and chaired by Richard A. Kahan, a former president of the New York State Urban Development Corporation, the group has come up with some excellent ideas. They include creating new housing, so recruits can live in the neighborhood while they study there, and hiring local construction firms to benefit the community economically as well as architecturally.

Their most exciting proposal is to create a high school that would focus on criminal justice studies, a kind of High School of the Performing Arts for the commishes of tomorrow. Mr. Kahan envisions a place where recruits would serve as student mentors, helping to bridge the frightening gap between police and public. Naturally, it would have made more sense to hold these discussions before the design competition. Fortunately, the Police Department and the Board of Education have been receptive to the Bronx Center proposals, even though they would reorganize the Police Academy's public spaces and, quite likely, change the building's design.

There's something else at stake in this building, at least for Mr. Pran: nothing less than the very soul of his profession. In a preface to a recent monograph of his work, he depicts contemporary architecture as a Manichaean struggle between the forces of light and darkness. "The main opposition today," he writes, "is between the new authentic modern architecture and the regressive post-modern (unhistoric) historicism." Evidently seeing himself as architecture's answer to 911, Mr. Pran supplies a list of other architects who he thinks fall into line on the correct side of the struggle. It reads like a roll call on his personal muster deck, a line-'em-up inspection of the good guys willing to fight the undesirable Postmodern elements that have ruined the old modern neighborhood.

Mr. Pran's buildings may well be progressive, but his thinking is out of

date. The Postmodern bandwagon passed by some time ago. The movement's most ardent promoters, such as Charles Jencks and Philip Johnson,
were among the first to leap off it. And few architects today are eager to
crank up another bandwagon. For them, and for much of the public also,
phrases like "the new modernism" have the same hollow, promotional
ring that turned Postmodernism into such a nightmare.

Still, Mr. Pran's anxieties about the state of architecture are widely
shared. Many architects today would like to regain the moral authority of
the modern movement. They yearn for the solidarity of purpose that once
united architects in the cause of building a better world. But what are the
means by which those goals can be achieved today?

For Mr. Pran, the means is architectural form. He thinks that "the
tremendous heritage of early modern architecture" can be revived by
evoking its formal vocabulary. But the Police Academy tells a different
story. What edges this project into the utopian dimension of early modernism is the potential of the building program to reduce the tensions
between the public and police. While the architects partly developed this
potential, the Bronx Center has pushed the hardest to make it happen.
And any number of formal vocabularies could be used to accommodate
their goals.

Mr. Pran writes that "architecture is about giving people the opportunity to live better lives." That is a fine piece of rhetoric, and so is the
Police Academy design. But the moral value of this building depends on
how far it can be pushed out of the realm of high-flown rhetoric and into
the turbulent South Bronx. This marathon champion of a building could
easily be an alien presence, streaking through the neighborhood without
looking around.

It is understandable that architects now have such an inflated idea of
the moral power of forms. Forms are virtually all they have to work with.
In a way, architects are in a position precisely analogous to that of the
police. They are expected to provide order and cohesion in an environment that has become fragmented. They are asked to create symbols of a
public realm that scarcely exists unless volunteers are willing to provide it.

It is tempting, in fact, to interpret the Police Academy's thin, warped
facade as an emblem of this condition. The warp mirrors our warped
expectations. The facade is handsome. But it can no more restore modernism's moral order than a fluted column can restore a world of classical
harmony.

If this is a time of change for architecture, it need not be the time for
architects to lock-step into another dreary stylistic movement, or to promote themselves by trashing the work of the preceding era. Thus it is

regrettable that Mr. Pran singles out for attack the "anti-modern" work of Robert Venturi and Denise Scott Brown. Mr. Venturi and Ms. Scott Brown did indeed open up paths that some of their followers took in retrogressive directions. But there is nothing anti-modern about their work. In fact, it is hyper-modern. It recognizes that the glass tower and the golden arches are both products of modernity. Painfully aware of the wholesale discrediting of the past that occurred in the heyday of the Modern movement, Mr. Venturi and Ms. Scott Brown have no desire to repeat it by throwing out the glass tower.

Nothing could be more "unhistoric" than to fantasize that Postmodernism did not happen, or to deny that its best examples shared the creative ideals that Mr. Pran rightly advocates. It is also blatantly unhistorical to equate modernism solely with the pioneering work of Walter Gropius, Le Corbusier, and Mies van der Rohe. If architects want to ground their work more fully in modern history, they must remember what came after the pioneers: the exhausted state of modernism in the 1960s, when Mr. Venturi and Ms. Scott Brown developed their ideas.

By then, modern invention had been reduced to dogma and modern morality to a club for keeping people in line. Modern architects had become creatures of corporate culture but fancied themselves artistic iconoclasts. Does anyone really want to live through that again?

Though different in style, the Police Academy raises precisely the same dilemma that surfaced with the ferry terminal project for Staten Island last year. Admiration for the design must be tempered by the fear that "world-class" architecture has become an acceptable way to camouflage poverty-class planning. With the ferry terminal, the city's welcome support for architecture had to be measured against a transportation system that is coming apart at the seams.

With the Police Academy, the dilemma is even more acute. The design's strengths must be weighed against the ravaged condition of schools, housing, and entire inner-city neighborhoods where law and order has become a desperate substitute for public life.

March 28, 1993

NEW PUBLIC HOUSING, FRENCH VINTAGE 1922

Young architects are supposed to make a splash. It's a letdown when their first building doesn't herald a new voice. But Jean Dubus, forty-one, and Jean Pierre Lott, thirty-one, have done something truly original. Their first work, an apartment building in Paris, reverberates with the shock of the old.

They've dusted off an unbuilt 1922 design for public housing by Le Corbusier, one of the most influential voices in twentieth-century architecture, and brought it startlingly to life. What makes their debut even more stunning is that, after seventy years, the design still looks fresh. Not a dim echo, it's the bold refrain of an idea whose time has come again.

This building should be of special interest to Americans, in part because Le Corbusier was a prophet more honored in the United States than in France. Twenty-five years ago, before the federal government had withdrawn its support for subsidized housing, Le Corbusier was the major influence on the design of public housing in the United States. That influence was not altogether benign.

Le Corbusier's proposals to rebuild cities as complexes of tall "towers in a park" was alluring in theory. But in practice it was a bomb dropped on traditional urban form. While the concept produced some successes, like New York University's housing complex at Bleecker Street and LaGuardia Place, designed in 1966 by I. M. Pei & Partners, more often it resulted in bleak public housing projects that disfigured many American cities and became warehouses for the poor.

It's time to take another look. Social housing is on its way back in the United States. In his confirmation hearings, Henry G. Cisneros, Secretary of Housing and Urban Development, pledged that his agency would resume housing construction. Architects are calling once again for socially responsible work. Architecture schools, like those at the Massachusetts Institute of Technology and Parsons School of Design, are devoting conferences to public housing issues.

Those issues are not limited to design. Public housing depends on public policy. But design has a role to play, and so does architectural history. Mr. Dubus and Mr. Lott have looked to the tradition of social housing as an inspiration for the present. They've taken a flawed design and made it work.

I came upon this remarkable building at the end of a long day spent trekking through government-sponsored housing projects. The day was long because looking at social housing can bring on a tiring mix of emotions. Envy for a city that recognizes the importance of providing housing for the middle class. Admiration for the high quality of the designs, which are usually chosen in juried competitions. And, not least, a heavy dose of guilt for wishing one were elsewhere, for any tourist with only a few days to spend in Paris would gladly trade in the city's entire stock of social housing for an afternoon at the Louvre.

Sure, it's great to see all the terrific things young architects are doing with windows these days. But it's only twenty minutes to closing time at Ste.-Chappelle. Taxi!

"Patience," advised my guide, a young French architect named Jean Mas. "There's one more building I'd like to show you."

We zipped down to south Paris, to a neighborhood not far from the site where the horrible new Grande Bibliothèque, now under construction, is poking a quartet of towers into the sky. We pulled into a side street off Porte d'Italie and screeched to a halt beside the architectural apparition that arose before us. "See?" Mr. Mas asked. "It looks familiar?"

Mais oui. To the student of modern architecture, Le Corbusier's Immeubles Villas is as familiar as the Eiffel Tower. Designed in 1922, this was Le Corbusier's most ambitious project to date. With it, he applied the principles of modern architecture to the task of city planning, enlarging to urban scale his concept of the house as a "machine for living." First sketched out on the back of a restaurant menu, the design was exhibited later that year at the Salon d'Automne, where the public got its first look at Le Corbusier's ambition to transform his adopted city of Paris into a machine-age utopia.

The concept was simple. Duplex maisonettes, each with its own outdoor garden, were arranged in rows of twenty-four, then stacked atop one another in long blocks five double stories tall. In one version of the plan, the blocks were arranged in quadrangles around a central garden. The private "hanging gardens," which alternated with two-story living rooms enclosed by large glass walls, faced on to this public space. On the rear side of the block, open corridors (Le Corbusier called them "streets in the air") provided access to the units. City traffic was routed underground. Laundry and meal services would be provided, as in a grand hotel. The Immeubles Villas project preceded by a few years Le Corbusier's radical proposal to rebuild Paris as a city of "towers in a park," and was actually quite traditional in scale and organization. Inspired by the architect's visit to a Carthusian monastery outside Florence, this "park inside a square" resembled a stripped-down version of the Palais Royale.

Mr. Dubus and Mr. Lott's explicit homage to a dead modernist is not quite the polemical act it may seem. It was the French housing authority's idea to call on architects to submit designs in the spirit of Le Corbusier, for a competition held in 1987, the centennial of the architect's birth. But Mr. Dubus and Mr. Lott were delighted to get into the spirit. Like many young architects today, they believe that the paths opened up by the pioneer modernists have not reached a dead end. Nor, like some of their American counterparts, do they believe that it is desirable or even possible to detach modern forms from progressive social goals. The notion that one can have modernism without utopianism would strike them as absurd, indeed unnecessary, since they are fortunate to live in a nation that has not allowed privatization to dissolve the public realm.

Their building is not a shelter for the homeless. Like most social housing in central Paris, the project is designed for lower-middle-class families. A mix of government subsidies—for land acquisition, construction costs, and rent supports—enables the housing authority to rent the units for about 30 percent below market value. Eligibility is based on income and family size. Of the building's ninety-five apartments, eleven are reserved for artists, who also receive subsidies.

Completed a year ago and now fully occupied, the Immeubles Villas is an homage but not a copy. Mr. Dubus and Mr. Lott have modified Le Corbusier's design and, in fact, substantially improved it. Their block is only a quarter of the quadrangle Le Corbusier envisioned. There are no hotel services, and in place of sunken roadways there is an underground garage for about three hundred cars. These alterations help to integrate the building comfortably into the existing context of streets and small local shops. It does not stand alone like a walled compound.

Mr. Dubus and Mr. Lott have also modified the internal organization of the apartments and the garden facade on which that organization is expressed. Instead of alternating stiffly between an open terrace and an enclosed living room, the design doubles the rhythm. The living rooms are joined in pairs horizontally within glazed vertical shafts, while the gardens are carried (again in pairs) on concrete bridges that stretch between the shafts. This arrangement leaves room for a wide, open well behind the terraces, through which air and natural light flow into the building's interior.

But the most radical change from the original is the building's circulation. Instead of arranging the "streets in the air" along the exterior rear wall, the architects have run them straight through the building's heart. But they have not fully enclosed them. One side, planted with greenery, opens onto the airwell and the terraces. And instead of placing these corridors even with the terraces, the architects have set them on a level halfway between them. This organization creates a spectacularly rich spatial and social composition. The apartments are entered through a small vestibule that leads to a bedroom in the rear. Depending on the layout, a Le Corbusier–style spiral staircase either ascends or descends from the vestibule to a main floor with more than double the floor area.

The master bedroom and bath are here, next to a small sitting area that can be used as an extra bedroom. A kitchen and dining area occupy the central core of the apartment, and in half of the apartments these are placed on a balcony overlooking the living room with its atelier-style window. A door leads off from the living room to the terrace. The openness of these interiors is a striking contrast to the warren of mazes common in American housing projects.

The prospect outside the "villas" is even more extraordinary. Walking along the streets in the air, one passes through a rhythmic sequence of enclosing walls and open air, gazing past the private terraces toward a public garden below. The result is a masterful weaving of form and sociology, supremely urban in its clear articulation of private, semiprivate, and public space. It is thrilling to reflect on the difference such a design can make in the lives of families and communities.

Heavy balcony railings mar the fluid space inside the apartments, and the stairs would have benefited from having open risers. Traditional furniture looks surprisingly at home inside these classically white modern rooms. In several living rooms, the airy delicacy of old-fashioned lace curtains makes the perfect foil for the broad expanse of glass.

In the building's public areas, the palette of white and gray is relieved with patches of dusty green and rose. At dusk, in a gem of a detail, the corridors are suffused with mellow light from small halogen lamps set into the floor. Then the entire building takes on the glow of a dream rekindled.

April 8, 1993

SHAPING A MONUMENT TO MEMORY

In 1986, when he announced the appointment of the architect who would design the United States Holocaust Memorial Museum here, Elie Wiesel said: "The Holocaust in its enormity defies language and art, and yet both must be used to tell the tale, the tale that must be told.

"In James Freed," continued Mr. Wiesel, then head of the council that would build the museum, "we have found an architect who can master this unique challenge."

Now, as the Holocaust Memorial Museum approaches its opening later this month, it is blazingly clear that Mr. Wiesel's trust in its architect was well placed. James Ingo Freed, of Pei Cobb Freed & Partners, has designed a work of such enormous power that it, too, defies language. Even those who have studied the published drawings of Mr. Freed's design may find themselves unprepared for the shattering impact of the finished work.

The $90 million public project, financed by private donations, combines the functions of an architectural memorial to the Holocaust and a museum devoted to its history. And while the building cannot be compared to the harrowing exhibitions it contains, it provides far more than a neutral background for the tale that must be told. The building invites interpretation but confounds analysis. Its monumental forms appear to be shaped not by architecture but by history. It is not a building about the past. It is about the historical present. It compels us to see that events that transpired half a century ago have not lost their grip on the world.

In a century of shifting, elastic morality, the Holocaust stands out as something very close to firm. For a civilization that cannot agree on a standard of absolute good, Auschwitz asserts itself as an absolute evil. Perversely, it offers the foundation of a moral universe. It is an ethical baseline, humanity's nadir.

There is no substitute for a visit to the camps. No book, no film can convey the intensity of standing where unspeakable events took place. Several years ago, just as the Holocaust Memorial was going into construction, I took the Munich S-Bahn to Dachau—not a death camp, like Auschwitz, although many thousands died at Dachau and guards for most of the death camps were trained there. Dread seeped into the present well before my arrival at the camp, when the conductor announced that the next stop would be Dachau. The S-Bahn is a suburban commuter train. I tried to imagine how it would feel to be riding home to Westchester, and hearing the conductor's voice say, instead of White Plains, "Dachau, next stop, Dachau." My fellow commuters didn't even rustle their newspapers.

But some may have been looking over the tops of them. For the commuters must be used to sharing the ride with foreigners who have come to inspect their shame. Or so it seemed to me when I got off the train and looked around for directions to the camp. There's no way to ask gracefully, "Which way to the concentration camp?" But an elderly woman on the platform sized me up. "Bus!" she said, and she pointed, smiling. "Bus!"

You enter the camp in a state of heightened empathy, only to find that this is a place from which design has banished all emotion. The military precision is unrelieved. All but one of the barracks are gone, but their rectangular foundations remain, marching in platoon formation across a gravel field. The bunks within the reconstructed barracks are also precisely rectangular, and the regularity of design helps to explain how people could bear to work here. The camp was a machine whose wheels turned one ratchet at a time. When an inmate neglected to give his blanket the precise military tuck, a rule book specified the discipline to be imposed. When the infraction was repeated, the machine would revolve another notch. No one had to make a decision, much less a moral judgment.

Dachau's gas chamber was never used. People were killed by gunshot, from illness or medical abominations, or were shipped elsewhere to be gassed. The small size of the gas chamber comes as a surprise. There is nothing to see besides four walls, a floor, a ceiling, and the door that leads outside. It is when you cross the threshold of that door that you grasp the reason for visiting Dachau. You walk out into daylight, but part of you does not leave. The doorway divides you. The part that is free to walk through the door feels disembodied, a weightless ghost. You feel light-headed, as though you have broken the law, as indeed you have. Your passage through that door has violated the design. The room was not meant to be exited alive.

This is a privileged moment. Not because we are free to walk out of the gas chamber but because we are not. Because part of us remains behind, wondering how, since no one deserved to die here, we deserve to leave. A moral universe could arise from the imperative to answer the self we left behind.

A place is a form of knowledge. James Freed's design arises from that pivotal idea. Mr. Freed began by immersing himself in the architecture of the Final Solution. He visited death camps, studied archival photographs, and drew on memories of his childhood in Nazi Germany. Some images stood out unforgettably. The observation towers that reminded people of the state's power to control their movements. The wooden footbridges that crossed over the streets of Warsaw, connecting blocks of the ghetto. The brick walls of the ovens and the steel bands that were placed around them when the ovens threatened to explode from overuse.

Wrapped around these designs for death were designs for denial. The heroic neoclassical buildings of Hitler's architect, Albert Speer. The camp gates whose inscription perpetrated the cruel hoax that WORK WILL SET YOU FREE. The regimented visual order with which the Nazis cloaked a lawless regime.

In his museum, which opens on April 26, Mr. Freed has not literally reproduced these forms. Rather, he has absorbed them, tracing their contours as if he could distill their meaning in a ritual of recollection. The result is an architectural vocabulary that is partly symbolic, partly abstract. Images of confinement, observation, atrocity, and denial surface and recede within the building's hard industrial forms: expanses of brick wall bolted with steel, floating glass bridges engraved with the names of devastated cities, lead pyramids clustered into sentry-box rooflines. A memorial in form as well as function, the museum is a place quarried from the memory of other places.

While Mr. Freed avoids literal representation, his design re-creates with excruciating fidelity the psychic split that a visit to the camp induces. The sensation begins even before you enter the building. Located just off the Washington Mall on a site overlooking the Tidal Basin, the building is clad with facades of limestone and brick. These materials are contextually correct choices; they match the government buildings that flank the memorial on either side. But if the aim of contextualism is to knit buildings together, then Mr. Freed has mounted an assault on context. The combination of the two materials has produced not an integrated composition but a disintegrated one, a building that often appears to be coming apart at the seams.

Approaching from the main entrance, visitors walk toward a monumental portico, a turret-shaped bulge of limestone that provides a frame for three tall rectangular arches. The stone, the scale, the symmetry speak the official language of the Washington Mall, but what does this facade say? The arches do not welcome. They gape. Four large square holes, set just above the arches, are fitted with stone grids that contradict the concept of opening. These openings are closings. They are windows that warn: Don't look.

Once beyond the arches, we find that we're still outside the building. The limestone bulge is a screen, a mask of state, but no less intimidating for being merely a mask. Two sets of doors thrust out into the roofless enclosure, as if extruded by pent-up pressure within. Instead of issuing an invitation to enter, the building exerts a repulsive force.

Through the doors, through a lobby, visitors are deposited onto a raised steel platform made of crude industrial plate, like the loading dock at the rear of a factory. It is an insult to the feet, an unwelcome mat for the mind, the eye's threshold into the Hall of Witness, the building's most dramatic space. This is the atrium from hell, a room purged of every pleasure that large indoor spaces often provide. The side walls are of brick, clamped with wedge-shaped brackets of steel. Even those who do not recognize the allusion to steel bracing around the ovens will respond to the intensity of pressure. The pressure's source is enigmatic. It is oppression in its extreme, most crushing form, and also the unsettling power of truth. But there is nothing enigmatic about the message. Witnessing is not just looking. It is an exertion of will. To witness is to be "antisocial," to leave polite facades in tatters.

The floor stops short of the wall on the right, creating a crevice that is crossed by short bridges and guarded by metal gates. Overhead, the skylight is set in a massive frame of steel. The frame's trusses are dramatically warped, as if buckling in compression. The skylight recalls the sheds of train stations, while the forced perspective of a monumental staircase, narrowing as it ascends at the far end of the hall, resembles receding railroad tracks. The eye is drawn up the staircase, but the feet may not be keen to follow. We remember the fate that awaited passengers on Hitler's trains.

To the left of the staircase, another flight leads downward, punctuated in its path by a steel slab, sculptured by Richard Serra. Beyond, a wall of black granite is cracked into splinters, while a band of glass block, illuminated from below, streaks across the floor in a diagonal gash. These fissures are empathic devices. Their disruption of the surface is paradoxically reassuring. If we feel shattered here, we are meant to.

But ambiguity of meaning is Mr. Freed's most powerful empathic tool. The fissure that bisects the floor is at once a sign of social calamity and an axis of hope, for it points toward the Lincoln Memorial and the idea that government can liberate as well as oppress.

From the Hall of Witness, visitors ascend by stair or elevator to the permanent collection that unfolds over three floors. Designed by Ralph Applebaum Associates, the exhibition includes hundreds of artifacts, oral histories, documentary films, and photographs to guide viewers through the three stages in Hitler's war against the Jews: isolation, deportation, and extermination. Here the architecture of the Holocaust is presented literally: the defaced wooden doorway of a Polish synagogue, the casting of a brick wall and stone paving blocks from the Warsaw Ghetto, a wooden boxcar, a barracks. One moves from harrowing abstraction to the harrowing particular.

While the permanent exhibition will be the destination for most visitors to the memorial, the building also contains a research library and archive, temporary exhibition galleries, classrooms, offices, and two auditoriums for lectures, films, and other events. Mr. Freed faced a formidable challenge in designing these areas. To make them functionally viable, he had to lessen the intensity of the design somewhat. But to dilute it too much would destroy the integrity of the building.

Mr. Freed has met this challenge with masterly poise. We never quite leave the Hall of Witness behind. We gain glimpses of it from balconies overlooking the hall, from the glass bridges that pass above the skylight. But the referential elements thin out, becoming more abstract, more minimalist, more recognizably akin, perhaps, to other work by Pei Cobb Freed. The rounded arch form recurs in doorways throughout, and not necessarily to remind us of ovens. The red brick Victorian building next door bears rows of windows similarly shaped.

The Hall of Remembrance, designed as a place where visitors can reflect after seeing the permanent exhibition, stands at the far end of abstraction. Housed in a six-sided, partly free-standing structure attached to the main building, the hall occupies a plaza facing Raoul Wallenberg Place. The site commands a magnificent prospect of monumental Washington, with views of the Washington Monument and the Jefferson and Lincoln memorials. Limestone clad, classically proportioned, the Hall of Remembrance takes its place among these dignified neighbors without a trace of irony. Unlike the main facade, which evokes the oppressiveness of the state, the Hall of Remembrance idealizes American democracy as the repository of Enlightenment values. Yet even here, in this largely neutral, abstract space, symbolic meanings surface. Six sides for 6 million, for 6 points of a star.

Does the Holocaust Museum cross the line into kitsch? That was the delicate question that arose when Mr. Freed's design was first made public. Mr. Freed is a modern architect, known for buildings, like the Jacob K. Javits Center in New York, that rigorously exploit the abstract qualities of structure. The highly expressive, symbolic vocabulary of the Holocaust Museum has no precedent in his work. But it veers perilously close to the rage for simulation that has loomed large on the architectural landscape in recent years. In an era that regards the old-fashioned fantasy resort of Seaside, Florida, as an example of urbanism, it was natural to fear that Mr. Freed's embrace of symbolism might produce a Holocaust theme park.

Actually, the design gains in strength from Mr. Freed's willingness to risk the ersatz. The departure from his usual approach seems an act of courage. And his powerful use of references rebukes those architects who have reduced symbolic form to genteel imitations of period styles. Implicitly, he asks, You want the past? You want European traditions? Here: Take another look.

This building is not easy to look at, and it is even harder to assess. Because its theme is so important, there is a risk of overestimating the importance of its architecture. Would we find the design so overwhelming if it served a less urgent moral cause? There is no answer to that question. And it is a testament to the building's strength that it makes the question seem absurd. Mr. Freed defies us to separate aesthetics from morality, art from politics, form from content. His fusion of these distinct spheres is somewhat archaic. It harks back to an ideal of moral beauty that prevailed before ethics and aesthetics went their separate ways.

In fact, despite the cracks and fissures that run rampant through it, this building is a work of synthesis. It compels us to reconnect the pieces of a fragmented culture. The force with which James Freed reunites them will reverberate through the art of building for years to come.

April 11, 1993

THIS TIME, EISENMAN GOES CONVENTIONAL

For once, you don't need advanced training in French philosophy to decipher a building by Peter Eisenman. To understand it is not necessarily to
love it. Still, as the work of an architect who has labored long, and with
notable success, to pitch his ideas beyond mortal understanding, the
viewer-friendly Greater Columbus Convention Center comes as a pleasant surprise. Visitors familiar with Eisenman's past enigmas—staircases
stuck to the ceiling or leading to a blank wall—may find themselves
bowled over by waves of gratitude. Fortunately, legibility isn't all this
building has going for it. It brings a brash, poetic order to a chaotic urban
landscape, shaping a middle ground between a city and the forces that
threaten it. Plus, it's got snazzy looks.

Ten years ago, opacity was Eisenman's pure delight. His exercises in
abstract form did not just ignore the usual conventions of function, context, and meaning. They deliberately thwarted those conventions. Their
function was to have no function; their meaning was to be meaningless;
they arose within the context of no context. Eisenman has not abandoned
his fascination with abstract forms. The Convention Center is a formally
exuberant building. What he has abandoned, at least for now, is the adolescent idea that conventions are the enemy of architecture. He's discovered that conventions can be played with.

The $94 million Convention Center, which opened in March, is
Eisenman's first civic commission and his largest built work to date. It
rises on the edge of downtown Columbus: not a dead city but one that
doesn't put on a wholly convincing show of life, either. From a distance,
the skyline is a rising graph of prosperity. Up close, that robust image only
intensifies the forlorn impression created by depopulated streets and stale
urban-renewal clichés. Modern and postmodern office towers, equally
desolate at dusk. Skywalks. Public art. In place of a center city, something
called City Center—a transplanted suburban shopping mall that sucks
into its climate-controlled atriums all the upscale shops that might enliven
the streets outside.

A spaghetti tangle of elevated freeway lanes brushes against the edge of
downtown, uncoiling as it stretches out across a flat industrial landscape of
solid old brick factory buildings, flimsy aluminum-sided sheds, water towers, and gas tanks. The highway is a hemorrhage, an engineered gash

draining life from the city as the physical center of culture. But the highway is also the spine of a decentralized city that we ignore at our peril.

Convention centers are hybrid buildings, born of the collision between city and highway. At once a civic amenity and a monument to mobility, a center provides its host city with steady income. But it also turns the host into a parasite, a concrete sponge feeding off the asphalt and plastic of highways and airports and the transient culture they serve. Eisenman's design gives form to this hybrid condition.

The landmark Union Station once stood here, a traditional portal to the center city. Eisenman has replaced the portal with an intersection. One side of the 580,000-square-foot building (half the size of New York City's Javits Center) faces the city, another slips into the spaghetti. In its colossal horizontal spread, the building aspires to highway scale, but the architect's task is to contain the spread within the scale of a civic building. Eisenman's perverse solution is to create a building that looks like a highway.

The building has no conventional front or back. Like a racetrack, it has a start and a finish. It appears to start in reverse: ten "lanes" rise up, in barrel vaults, from loading bays that abut a highway overpass. Sheathed in aluminum in gleaming metallic colors—gold, silver, copper—the curving strips snake across the thirteen-acre roof before screeching to a halt at High Street, on the downtown edge. Merchandise enters through the freeway side, conventioneers from High Street, and the design declines to declare either one the main facade. If any side has priority, it is the roof, visible from passing cars, airplanes and nearby convention hotels. Eisenman calls this spectacular roofscape the building's fifth facade.

For all his immersion in theory, Eisenman is a visually generous architect, and the Convention Center's High Street entrance is a riotously ornate set piece. The three-block-long facade is broken up into eleven segments, clad alternately in masonry and glass that match the proportions of the sturdy brick industrial buildings across the street. Window mullions in the glazed blocks reiterate the architect's familiar motif of tilted and overlapping grids, while the brick segments are studded with cast-stone panels. Dummy versions of factory windows, the panels also resemble sugar cubes, and the entire High Street facade has a jolly confectionary look, oddly akin to the clunky swank of old Art Deco hotels. Add a row of palm trees, and we could almost be sauntering along a stretch of South Beach. It even looks as if a hurricane has passed by.

The concourse just inside the High Street entrance is the only place where Eisenman lets go with space. Paralleling the street facade, the concourse cuts a diverting zigzag that breaks up its enormous length, while skylights, overhead footbridges, and suspended ceilings create the illusion of soaring height. Here, Dr. Caligari meets Morris Lapidus in an Expressionist shock corridor, sugarcoated with mellow colors: pastel, penny-candy versions of the roof's metallic tones.

Nothing much can be done to minimize the overwhelming impact of the 216,000-square-foot exhibit hall; exhibitors need unobstructed space to install their booths. But Eisenman has exploited the scale to create an atmosphere. With its Necco Wafer walls and oversized concession stands, stretching seemingly to the horizon beneath the ceiling's billowing metal waves, the hall is a seaside pavilion from the 1930s, seen through the eyes of a child.

Though the building offers an abundance of enjoyable visual candy, it also provides an on-ramp to the theoretical high road its architect has been traveling for thirty years. The contorted grids, for example, are Eisenman's symbolic critique of Cartesian rationality. Applying that critique to a crisis of urbanism, Eisenman seems to be saying that the highway and the city are not in opposition, for they spring from the same worldview. The downtown grid and the highway spaghetti are both engineered articulations of the modern mind. Both detach culture from nature; either can be swept away when a new, improved machine dream—virtual reality, for example—swings into view.

Eisenman's perennial play with dualisms is also evident in his metallic palette. The gold and silver symbolize commerce, yet Eisenman may also want to call forth the ancient association of precious metals with religious art. His fusion of sacred and profane aligns the convention center with the Woolworth Building in New York, designed by Cass Gilbert in 1913. Gilbert's veneer of Gothic ornament linked his "Cathedral of Commerce" to a transcendent realm of the spirit. Eisenman seeks redemption from the realm of high academic discourse. Dinner with Derrida is his idea of heaven.

This is Eisenman's second major building for Columbus. His first, the Wexner Center for the Arts, which opened in 1989, attempted a similar urban maneuver; it was designed to act as a pivot between the city street grid and the University of Ohio's campus. But his intention there was hard to grasp, in part because it was unnecessary. There is nothing undesirable about the contrast between a campus and a city. The clash between the highway and the city, however, has long been urban planning's most critical challenge.

Does this building really face that challenge? Or is "controversial architecture" just one more booster gimmick, like skywalks and atriums? Clearly, the center's promoters are banking that Eisenman's quirky reputation will give their facility a competitive edge. "The atypical look is a marketing point," says Claire S. Hazucha, executive director of the government authority behind the project, and no one has even accused Peter Eisenman of lacking promotional flair. His design should do what a tourist attraction is supposed to do: attract tourists. And tourism has become the main industry on which many old centers now rely.

This is, of course, a work of symbolism. Its infrastructural imagery is no substitute for comprehensive urban planning. And Eisenman's critique of rationalism is howlingly out of place here. Cities need more reason, not less. In fact, the best thing about this building is that it is startlingly clear-eyed about the contemporary urban prospect and architecture's limited capacity to address it. It neither promises a future machine Utopia that architecture cannot deliver, nor drips with nostalgia for a civic past that it is powerless to revive. The building changes the way we see the landscape because it acknowledges, in a big way, that the landscape has changed. It's a keeled-over, liquefied Woolworth Building for a dispersed, melted-down metropolis: a nonelectronic town hall for a nation where all roads lead to Home Shopping.

May 2, 1993

TO THE BEACH:
A Baedeker for Baskers; Long Beach Island

You can lead a child to water but you can't make him swim in it. Or sail on it. Or even look at it. When I was young, my parents had a summerhouse on Long Beach Island, on the Jersey Shore between Seaside Heights and Atlantic City. The house was right on the dunes and had a terrific view of the ocean. The only thing that spoiled the view was me.

I was a spoiled suburban child who failed to see the point of driving two hours just to exchange a view of green lawns for one of green water swilling around outside the window. I spent my summers hunting for bits of a city I hadn't discovered yet. Dropped off for a sailing lesson, I would loiter a while at the door of the yacht club, then dash to the miniature golf course next door. Learning to ride a bike was a pleasure because I could pedal away from the beach and find some stray bits of city thrown up on the island like jetsam. The shop that sold amber jewelry. The Chinese gift store, a miniature Chinatown, with lanterns, chopsticks, and the clam-shells that you plunged into water, releasing paper flowers. I had a particular passion for the exterminator Jeep that tore about the streets at night, releasing great Tiepolo clouds of poison.

One summer I had a change of heart about the beach. A film called *Land of the Pharaohs* came to play at the movie theater in nearby Toms River. Faulkner was credited with the screenplay. Joan Collins played a pharaoh's wife. The movie told the story of the architects and masons who were building a great pyramid, and the pyramid was the movie's star. In the climactic scene, slaves with amputated tongues shatter rows of clay pipes, releasing the sand inside them and activating a hydraulic system. As the sand spills out on the floor, giant stone blocks descend, sealing the pyramid's corridors, trapping the pharaoh's beautiful, treacherous wife. Pharaoh thinks you can take it with you, and one of the things he takes is Joan. "I'm too young to die!" she screams, as the blocks settle into place with unspeakable finality.

So you could do something with sand beside lie on it, pack it into metal pails, or track it into the house and make everyone angry because you forgot to hose your feet. Sand could look like fate. You could use it to make a magic building with walls that moved. Slaves would have their tongues cut off to protect your secret. Joan Collins would die. Faulkner would write the screenplay. For the rest of the summer, I tried to duplicate the trick, using driftwood and dried dune grass to control the sand. A dead sand shark played Joan Collins. My parents began to worry about the influence of movies. And I've since wished many times that you could go (summer) home again. My favorite beach is the one that tried to become a pyramid.

May 28, 1993

THE UNCONVENTIONAL AS A CONVENTION

The small, wedge-shaped gallery at Storefront for Art and Architecture, which can resemble a nightmare torture chamber with sadistically contracting walls, is a poignant metaphor for the perennially pinched economic circumstances of this "alternative" downtown space. If the walls contracted one more inch, Storefront would be out on the street, and architecture would move another step closer to homelessness in the imperial city of real estate. No other New York gallery or museum has provided new architectural ideas with such stalwart shelter.

But the '90s have challenged the identity of alternative galleries. With the loosening of Postmodernism's grip on the mainstream, and the weakening of the economy that supported it, the question arises: Alternative to what? No one movement dominates architecture today. Theoretical "paper architecture," which once offered an alternative to conventional practice, has itself become a convention. Everything is an alternative on architecture's fragmented terrain.

Discontinuous Spaces, a small show of recent work by the New York firm Smith-Miller & Hawkinson, tries to reckon with this changed configuration. Henry Smith-Miller and Laurie Hawkinson, the firm's principals, are not conventional commercial architects, but neither are they space cadets who think that to build is to compromise their artistic standards. Though the projects on view here—a mix of commercial and residential designs and two large public works projects—are designed to be built, they are conceptually sharp.

So is the show's installation. Working with the artist Silvia Kolbowski, Smith-Miller & Hawkinson has transformed Storefront's funky space into a pint-sized parody of a gallery at the Museum of Modern Art. Sloping plywood platforms straighten out the triangular floor into a more respectable rectangle. Bright overhead lighting, dazzling white walls, a gray painted floor, and crisp modern graphics complete the clinical simulation, while the crumbling tin ceiling injects a hint of grunge. It's a downtown dream of uptown glory.

This kind of conceptual transposition is typical of Smith-Miller & Hawkinson's work. Many of their projects are intended to break down the barriers between dualisms like "uptown" and "downtown" by combining the visual forms that represent them. At times their work can seem like wordplay rather than design, especially in their collaborations with Barbara Kruger, a master of verbal visuals. They also want to erode architecture's conventional boundaries, as in two of the projects represented here: large outdoor "art parks" for two American cities.

Working with Ms. Kruger and with the landscape architect Nicholas Quennell, Smith-Miller & Hawkinson seems to view architecture as a mediator between nature and culture. The Textualized Landscape, shown here in models, is part of the team's master plan for a 160-acre park, now in construction, surrounding the North Carolina Museum of Art in Raleigh. The words *picture this* are spelled out in jumbo (85-foot-tall) capital letters, variously executed in boulders, gravel, plantings, concrete, and jets of sprayed mist. The picture we're asked to imagine could be a movie, shown on a giant outdoor screen (the plan provides seating for 2,500 people), or it could be a vision of nature projected on the mind's inner screen. Landscape is land transformed by the eye into a visual image.

Unoccupied Territory, the team's entry in a 1989 competition to design a cultural park for Los Angeles, rethinks the idea of the urban park in a decentralized city. The concept here is recentralization; instead of following the competition's instructions to disperse built elements over the sixty-acre site, this plan concentrates them in one corner. In the remaining acres, new landscaped areas are juxtaposed with terrain carved naturally by floods. It's Capability Brown in La-La Land: a postmodern, desert version of an artificially natural English garden.

Like the proverbial beauty who sports fake eyeglasses, Smith-Miller & Hawkinson seems to fear that people won't respect their minds. The team often accompanies its projects with elaborate texts, packed with more ideas than mere forms can easily convey. The most striking object in the show is a section from a metal canopy the firm designed to hang over the ticket counter at the new USAir Terminal at LaGuardia. The wing-shaped form, designed in collaboration with Guy Nordenson of Ove Arup & Partners, floats within an airy skein of cables and glass panels. Whether or not travelers will grasp all the ideas behind it, this ethereal object nonetheless conveys a primal connection between flying and aspiration. It says, "Look up!"

Ascent is also a theme in a current project for the New Jersey Institute of Architecture in Newark. Asked to design a staircase in the open space between two existing campus buildings, Smith-Miller & Hawkinson has turned a simple circulation route into a place where people will want to linger. Made of steel and concrete, the stair will rise five stories in a gentle slope; broad steps at the top will provide informal seating. At once glamorous and severe, this is a theatrical design, like something Ziegfeld might have commissioned from Piranesi.

May 28, 1993

"THINGS GENERALLY WRONG IN THE UNIVERSE"

A bomb explodes, a building quakes, a cloud hangs over the horizon. Though the smoke soon disperses, public attention lingers, as if the explosion at the World Trade Center had released an important piece of information that could be discerned by tuning into the rippling waves of its aftershock. The message the public is straining to hear is not reported on the evening news. It is not a matter of whodunit, howdunit, whydunit. Even after the authorities have identified suspects, interpreted motives, and recommended strategies to prevent a repeat occurrence, something intangible remains: a mood, an atmosphere that persists like background radiation.

Chaos. Turbulence on a global scale. A feeling Virginia Woolf once described in her diary as "things generally wrong in the universe." That is part of the message that came pulsing out of the World Trade Center's blasted subbasements earlier this year. And it's a message that buildings have been transmitting quite a lot lately. Dubrovnik. Sarajevo. South Central Los Angeles. Waco.

These images of exploding buildings provoke ambivalent reactions. We respond to them with feelings of horror, anger, or fear. We identify them as problems for which there must be solutions. Suspected terrorists must be deported. Cease-fires must be negotiated. Relief should be expedited. Metal detectors and surveillance cameras should be monitored with greater vigilence. Send in the National Guard.

Yet there's a sense in which these disasters are not problems. They are solutions. They provide a quick, dramatic answer to a question of agonizing complexity. What is the new world order? What is the glue that holds things together now that the global framework of the Cold War has been dismantled?

Buildings mark boundaries. Individually, or in groups, they divide space into ordered regions—islands of homogeneity floating in a heterogeneous sea. The end of the Cold War has subjected such boundaries to intensified pressure. For four decades, global tensions were focused on one principal boundary: the border between East and West and the difference in world outlook it stood for. The collapse of that border has not eliminated the tension. It has only removed the focus, allowing the pressure to be dispersed elsewhere. Though Checkpoint Charlie is a thing of the past, there are now countless boundaries requiring Checkpoint Charlies. Religious cults. Ethnic enclaves. Corporate parks. Even the single-family suburban house. But who is the enemy they are checking for?

The collapse of the Berlin Wall ended an era, but it also began one. It started a process of global reordering that feels more like an unraveling. When we peer out from whatever bubble of security we occupy—a job, a walled condominium compound, the Psychic Friends Network—it is hard to discern any connective tissue between the bubbles.

Chaos is a substitute for the connective tissue. It is not the most comforting kind of order we could imagine. Still, there is comfort in the perception that we are all in this chaos together. Though the world has become fragmented, we are all fragmented equally. A community of chaos is still a community, of a kind.

Exploding buildings are this community's landmarks—its inverted arches of triumph, its sinister Taj Mahals. They provide images of a collective experience that is otherwise elusive. Traditionally, we look to buildings to provide symbols of social cohesion. Exploding buildings now perform an equivalent symbolic role. People may build in different styles, but explosions are universal. Though each may have a different cause, they become linked in our perceptions to some fearful grand design. They focus public attention. They fill up TV screens. The World Trade Center bombing spawned a new style of disaster T-shirt.

While images of exploding buildings easily lend themselves to millennial forebodings, they should also remind us that throughout history architecture has been as much a military as a civil art. Today we deplore the fragmentation of cities into fortress enclaves. But enclave making has always been fundamental to urban form. "A city without walls is not a city," J. F. Sobry wrote in 1776. Not long ago, Paris and Vienna were still encircled by military fortifications, and in the modern city, pleasure and the picturesque remained fused with strategic defense. In Paris, Baron Haussmann draped a facade of theaters, cafés, and shops over boulevards laid out for the benefit of troops who might be called upon to quell civil disturbances. Today it's the informational highway that seeks to keep the peace, with its data banks and video monitors, its surveillance cameras greeting us at every doorway.

Perhaps it will take chaos theory to make sense of the complex evolving order of the post–Cold War world: its turbulence, its convoluted borders, its interacting global systems. But anyone who walks down the streets of an American inner city can get a pretty good idea of the new world order. The mix of uses and populations, the porous borders surrounding neighborhoods, the interdependency of skills and services: the city is the most accessible model we have for understanding the shape of the world after the collapse of global bipolarity.

For more than a century, in fact, our most influential urban theorists have been theorists of chaos: thinkers who have looked for order and meaning beneath the apparent chaos of urban development. Camillo Sitte, the nineteenth-century Austrian who helped found modern town planning, based his theories on the discovery that the picturesque irregularities of the medieval city were not just the result of chance but of an emerging social order. More recently, the American urbanist Kevin Lynch advocated individual perception as the basis of centralized planning. Thirty years ago, Jane Jacobs shook up the field of city planning by arguing passionately against the imposition of superficial visual order upon complex urban diversity.

"To see complex systems of functional order as order, and not chaos, takes understanding," Ms. Jacobs wrote in *The Death and Life of Great American Cities:* "The leaves dropping from the trees in the autumn, the interior of an airplane engine, the entrails of a dissected rabbit, the city desk of a newspaper, all appear to be chaos if they are seen without comprehension. Once they are understood as systems of order, they actually look different."

These urban theorists have not been advocating anarchy. On the contrary, each of them sought to identify urban forms appropriate to modern democracy and to define the role of government in the shaping of those forms. Jean Gardner, an environmentalist who teaches at the Parsons

School of Design, observes that what we often perceive as disorder is simply a sign of social inclusiveness: people are participating. Sitte valued the irregular design of medieval city squares because they represented the social rise of the craft guilds. Ms. Jacobs extolled the New York City street as a self-policing entity, secured by "eyes on the street"—people drawn by the linkage of heterogeneous uses.

The end of the Cold War years has renewed the urgency of these ideas, for cities were among the casualties of those years. Private enterprise became synonymous with public good; the public sphere abdicated its responsibility to steer private interest toward the public good. But inner cities are now the laboratories for change. They are microcosms of a new world order—places where the conflict between heterogeneity and homogeneity is being staged in the glare of television.

The chaos that erupted last year in South Central Los Angeles was caused in large part by the lack of integration between the homogenized culture of corporations and developers and the culture of minority neighborhoods. And now it is widely reported that efforts to "rebuild L.A." have failed. But what did people expect to happen in a year's time? For that matter, what do they expect now? Do inner-city neighborhoods want to be remade in the image of corporate culture? Must success always look like a Marriott Hotel? A Kmart? A cluster of glass high-rises? Or are we prepared to acknowledge that, for integration to occur, the corporate culture must also be remade?

Not readily. It is easier to imagine blowing things sky-high than to give up homogenized order as a measure of urban success. It is easier to talk about the breakup of the former Soviet Union than to reintegrate our own fragmented society, particularly since reintegration requires the breakup of our own Cold War apparatus. Heterogeneity, by definition, presupposes the foreign, the unknown, and it is easier to visualize fear of the unknown—the terrorist explosion, the decline of the West, the vision of "things generally wrong in the universe"—than to overcome that fear. Breaking up is hard to do. Rethinking how to build is harder.

May 30, 1993

IN THIS DREAM STATION FUTURE
AND PAST COLLIDE

Already it is a landmark: that soaring arch of white steel, rising above granite walls of classical Beaux Arts grandeur. Depicted in architect's renderings with sunlight streaming through its sparkling glass skin, the arch brings out the primal emotions aroused by the sight of a rainbow after a storm. It may be years before this vision materializes. The $315 million needed to build it is not yet in hand. But Amtrak's proposal to resurrect Pennsylvania Station from a pit beneath Madison Square Garden and enshrine it within the landmark general post office building across the street has aroused more anticipation than any civic project in years.

No wonder, for this project pushes some of the hottest buttons in architecture and urbanism today. Public space. Infrastructure. Mass transit. Regional planning. But the hottest button of all is one that touches off a painful memory: the destruction of the original Pennsylvania Station station thirty years ago. The razing of this station, McKim, Mead & White's 1910 masterpiece of Beaux Arts design, was one of the greatest traumas New York City ever suffered. Public reaction was profound, and in some ways beneficial. Historical preservation was transformed from a genteel pastime to a nationwide movement with political clout. Architects began to admit that the Modern movement was turning out to be less than a boon for cities. Above all, New Yorkers began to assert a proprietary interest in the city as their collective cultural heritage.

Still, New York has never completely recovered from the station's loss. How could it? Each day more than 500,000 commuters—38 percent of Amtrak's total national ridership—descend to the abyss Penn Station fell into. Even those with no memory of the old station can recognize the present one as a symbol of urban decline. Though the loss of the old Penn Station shocked the city to its senses, the idea persists that the shock may have come too late to save it.

With Amtrak's proposal, then, we're not dealing solely with the pragmatic world of glass and granite, tracks and timetables. We enter the realm of symbols and memories and the emotions they evoke. Do cities get a second chance? That is the fearsome question this project raises, and, of course, no building can turn back the clock. A new Penn Station won't bring the *Normandie* back to the harbor or the Lunts back to Broadway. It won't roll back the car and the highway, the forces chiefly responsible for undermining the old station and the old New York. But it could bring some important reconstructive forces into sharper focus.

Designed by the architectural firm Hellmuth, Obata & Kassabaum, the proposed station is a tribute to the fact that grassroots movements can triumph. The preservation movement did not flicker and die. It has become integral to the way cities do business. That is why the James A. Farley Building (as the soon-to-be-vacated post office is called) is still around today, and why it could one day have a public use worthy of its scale. Designed in 1918 by William Kendell of McKim, Mead & White, the Farley Building would not only receive Amtrak's passengers in style. It would also send the immensely cheering message that civic will can be exerted to effect, and not always in the wrong direction.

The steel parabolic vault in the station's great hall (at 120 feet, it matches the height of the concourse at Grand Central Terminal) also sounds a note of victory. It is an arch raised to commemorate the triumph of mass transit over those who seem to think there's something un-American about it.

The modernity of the arch is apt. While the McKim, Mead & White building harks back to the past, the real promise of the proposed station is that it looks ahead toward the use of the mass transit as a tool for reshaping the metropolitan region. Amtrak's intercity riders are only a small fraction of the travelers who use Penn Station. The great majority are local commuters on New Jersey Transit and the Long Island Rail Road. Many of them also regularly use the station's connecting subway lines. The opportunity now exists to make Penn Station a true regional hub, functionally and architecturally. The goal is not just to create a more comfortable environment but to attract more riders to mass transit and thereby increase public support for it.

The plan only partly realizes this opportunity. The Regional Plan Association, which strongly endorses the new station, is calling for a more ambitious program that would join the region's seven rail systems in a network. Coupled with other regional strategies to make commuting more attractive—like Skidmore, Owings & Merrill's community development guidelines for areas served by New Jersey Transit—the new Penn Station could become a means of redefining the relationship between the city center and the metropolitan region.

But those who hope that the new station will help New York regain its civic soul must reckon with a crucial difference between this project and the original station: the amount of space, and the degree of visibility, that the plan dedicates to retail shopping. In the post office building, roughly equal space would be set aside for retail and for circulation and waiting areas. The Great Hall itself would be ringed with two tiers of restaurants and shops, and the steel vault would be hung with giant electronic advertising panels facing into the waiting area.

This picture contrasts sharply with the vintage photographs of the original Penn Station and with the idea the station embodied. When people use words like *majestic* and *civic splendor* to describe the old station, they're not just talking about high ceilings and classical columns. They're evoking an ideal of public amenity: the idea that even in the citadel of private enterprise, some places will not be governed by the bottom line.

The original Penn Station was a monument to that ideal. To build it, Charles McKim talked the railroad out of its plan to build an enormous hotel in the air space over the station. As Lewis Mumford later observed, the lack of advertising in the station was "a point the European traveler often remarked on with surprise, as a pleasing contradiction in the land of the almighty dollar." Penn Station's glory, in other words, wasn't just what was there. It was what wasn't there.

But the glory had dimmed some years before the station was razed. In the mid-1950s, a modernization program equipped the station with shops, booths, television monitors, even cars on revolving drums. Mumford, predictably horrified, described the results as "a vast electronic jukebox," adding, "A West Forty-second Street garishness and tawdriness characterize the whole reconstruction."

What would Mumford make of the proposed station's advertising panels? The tiers of shops? "One entered the city like a God," the architectural historian Vincent Scully famously wrote of the original station. "One scuttles in now like a rat." Is the idea now that one should come browsing in like a shopper?

But before we mount Mumford's high horse and go charging along Thirty-third Street to denounce commercial defilement, it's worth recalling that the proposed station began as a shopping expedition. Three years ago, Amtrak asked a group of private developers to submit proposals to upgrade Penn Station's retail operations. The plan to expand the station into the post office building across Eighth Avenue grew out of discussions with Penn Station Associates, the winning developer, which saw the chance to create something of urban as well as commercial value. The realistic choice, in other words, was not between a new Penn Station with retail shopping or one without it. The choice was between shopping with or without a new Penn Station.

In a sense, the developers and architects guided Amtrak toward McKim's ideal. If the result differs, that is largely because the railroad's fortunes have changed. In McKim's day, trains made a profit. Today they are operated by the government, with shaky political support. Until the government is prepared to back all the nice talk about rebuilding the nation's infrastructure, Amtrak must turn to the private sector for support.

To grant this, however, is not to say that retail uses should have unlimited license. Indeed, the issue is not primarily how many stores there ought to be in train stations. It is how the partnership between the public and private sectors should be configured in the creation of public works. At a time when public works are once again on the table, this issue is paramount. Indeed, it is just as important today as architectural preservation was thirty years ago.

As with all public-private developments, the question with Amtrak's proposal is, Where do you draw the line? The station's planners compare their project to other recently renovated monumental stations: Union Station in Washington and Thirtieth Street Station in Philadelphia. But they are radically different models. In Philadelphia the station has been beautifully restored without an increase in retail uses; it is still a station. Union Station, by contrast, is now a spectacularly beautiful shopping mall where travelers are apt to feel like second-class citizens. While the station's architecture has been preserved, its character has been lost.

The planned Penn Station would fall somewhere between these two models. The architects have conceived the steel vault as a visual screen that would partly veil the shops around the perimeter of the hall and put the visual focus on transportation. That is one reason they have brought the base of the arch straight down to the floor. This conspicuous display of engineering is designed to be the visual equivalent of "All aboard!" In the same spirit, the developers pledge to limit retail to what they call "non-committed" shopping: purchases of less than $100.

These provisions are important, not only because they draw a line that is reasonable, given how the plan originated, but also because they reflect the recognition that there is such a line to draw. It's that recognition that has been so appallingly absent in recent years. Supporters of projects like Union Station often cite increased numbers of visitors as evidence of their success, but that measure does not take into account the qualities of place that have been obliterated in the process. How do you measure the submersion of a place like South Street Seaport beneath waves of merchandise?

More to the point, how do you retrieve the idea of a station from waves of disbelief in the future of trains? How can a building restore to civic dignity the sensations of arriving in a great city or decompressing from its tensions? It's easy to accommodate shoppers. But how can architecture honor those who share what Walter Benjamin called "the passion for waiting"?

Shops and signs can enhance these sensations. But there is a difference between citizens and consumers, and one of the major functions of public space is to keep that distinction clear. Market forces helped to destroy the old Penn Station, and now they have created the opportunity to build a new one.

It is up to the public sector to keep those pressures in check. If the line can be held here, the result will be more than a stunning new terminal. It will be a signal that public works are headed down the right track.

June 20, 1993

MIAMI VIRTUE:
ARQUITECTONICA'S LOW-RENT HOUSING

Bernardo Fort-Brescia tried to steer me away from Edison Terrace, a new apartment complex in Liberty City designed by his firm, Arquitectonica. He would be out of town that weekend, and hadn't I heard about the German woman? Pulled from her car and run over by thugs?

Yet the danger of visiting Edison Terrace added to the building's allure. Isn't Miami supposed to be the dark metropolis of sin and insurrection, the city where death lurks behind pastel facades? And isn't Arquitectonica the firm that helped to give the once dowdy city a racy new image? Alas, these thrilling stereotypes have had their day. Miami never had a monopoly on urban violence, and it has been five years since the last episode of *Miami Vice*, the series that brought Arquitectonica instant notoriety with those glamorous shots of the Atlantis condominium complex and its fabulous "sky patio." Fringed with palms, bubbling with Jacuzzi effervescence, the patio became an architectural logo for a city basking in a lurid aura of opulent dissolution.

Edison Terrace is Miami Virtue. A low-income housing project, the first of two low-rental apartment buildings that Arquitectonica has designed for Liberty City, the building gives this poor, predominantly black community the kind of visual lift that these architects brought to the rich side of town with their residential high rises on Brickell Avenue. Architecture has been described as frozen music. Arquitectonica makes something closer to frozen margarita: a tangy architectural cocktail with the power to inspire deliriously upbeat thoughts about the world. Architecture with a splash of tonic. Even the firm's name sounds like something you'd serve with a wedge of lime.

Not everyone is intoxicated by Arquitectonica's blend of tropical fizz. Andrés Duany and Elizabeth Plater-Zyberk, fellow Floridian architects best known for the "neotraditional" resort town of Seaside, have accused Arquitectonica of creating buildings that look good from moving cars. I can't dispute the accusation, at least in regard to Edison Terrace, since the young architect from Mr. Fort-Brescia's office who escorted me to the building was reluctant to let me out of his Rabbit convertible. We cruised around the building, but I saw its interior (two- and three-bedroom apartments, each with private balcony) only in floor plans. I guess you could call this a case of drive-by criticism.

Still, if you are located less than a block from I-95, it's not a vice to look great from a passing car. Though Edison Terrace is only six stories tall, its brightly painted stucco facade pops out like a billboard: if you lived here, you'd not only be home by now, you'd be smart. Simple shapes and clearly defined proportions make up the building's rhythmic, graphic effects. The facade, crisply punctured with square windows, is broken into three segments that are hinged at the edges by tiers of balconies. Stained a throbbing red, the balconies project slightly forward in shallow horizontal chevrons. Slim bays, painted a neutral green, anchor the block at both ends; they tie the building to the landscaped parking areas around it and set off its bright colors. An adjacent recreation building, also of green stucco, sports a snappy blue canopy supported by slim red columns.

Though slightly overscaled for this neighborhood of one- and two-story buildings, Edison Terrace is not an imposing tower disconnected from its surroundings. In fact, its height creates a welcome visual connection between the lower buildings of Liberty City and the highway overpass that runs through it and the neighboring Overtown, a name that suggests only too vividly a place reduced to a passing blur. Now the eyes will want to linger in this landscape, even if fear freezes an outsider's foot to the gas pedal.

Edison Terrace, whose project architect is Daniel Sabowsky, is not public housing but a private development, created under the enlightened auspices of the Tacolcy Economic Development Corporation, a nonprofit, community-based organization. Financing from several public agencies, notably the Dade County Special Housing Program, has made it possible to keep rents about 25 percent below market rates. It's the sixty low-rent apartments, not the bright package Arquitectonica has wrapped them in, that make Edison Terrace a community asset. Design is no substitute for public housing policies.

But Arquitectonica's formal vocabulary is well suited to the social dimension of this project. Its forms pulse with the energy that can result from the clash of cultures. The firm's work, like its name, asserts a Latin heritage. The rhythmic, angled geometry of its buildings, the bold, primary colors that excite abstract forms into sensual images, draw on the strain of European modernism that took root in Central and South America in the 1930s.

Some orthodox modernists looked askance at this exotic variation of the Bauhaus's hard, Germanic truth. Nikolaus Pevsner, the architectural historian, believed that Le Corbusier had been infected by fantastic irrationalism on his 1936 visit to Brazil. Today it's the element of fantasy that makes Latin modernism so invigorating. It shows how an internationalist ethos can be translated into a vibrant regional identity.

Arquitectonica has woven into these historical strands a thread that is even more international than the International Style: the athletic, casual style of contemporary popular culture. Mr. Fort-Brescia and his partner, Laurinda Spear, were the first architects of the baby boom generation to put up large-scale buildings. They took pop style for granted as the classical order of the twentieth-century city. Going beyond the conventionally bleak ideal of "workers' housing" promoted by the modern movement, Arquitectonica dipped into the image pool of the Coca-Cola red ribbon and Levi 501s, white sports cars and the city's nighttime visual jazz. It's as democratic a style as anyone has yet imagined, and it is exhilarating precisely because it demonstrates that American style is not meant to be an elite proposition. Mass is not without class.

Arquitectonica's work is uneven; it doesn't always hit the note of popular sophistication. But at Edison Terrace the architects are working in the form that made their Brickell Avenue buildings such bracing additions to the skyline. The project does not just bring a bit of Brickell Avenue to Liberty City. Rather, it shows that an architectural language can speak across social distances. Different economic circumstances need not wrench people into totally different cities. The eye can be quicker than a highway at connecting points in urban space.

July 11, 1993

VIÑOLY'S VISION FOR TOKYO, AND FOR THE IDENTITY OF JAPAN

Those who have forgiven the Japanese for buying a big chunk of Rockefeller Center may find it more difficult to excuse them for snapping up Rafael Viñoly to design the Tokyo International Forum, a colossal performing arts and convention center now going up in the heart of the Japanese capital. Rockefeller Center, after all, isn't leaving New York. But why must we travel to Japan to see major public buildings as fine as the one Mr. Viñoly has designed for Tokyo? This prodigiously gifted architect lives right here.

At least we get to see the models. Mr. Viñoly's plans for the Tokyo International Forum are on view now in the architecture and design galleries at the Museum of Modern Art, as part of the museum's continuing series of shows devoted to important public works. This is the first show in the series to feature a single project by one firm, and the honor is richly deserved. The $1 billion project, which will be completed in 1996, is one of the largest under construction in the world today. It is also among the most sublime. Mr. Viñoly's design goes far toward dispelling disillusionment with the bloated scale of recent civic projects. And it revives faith in architecture as an instrument of intellectual clarity.

The Tokyo International Forum isn't just an architecture story. Like the Pompidou Center in Paris, this building exploits civic scale and prominence to set a national cultural agenda. The French critic Roland Barthes described Tokyo as a city with an "empty center," a modern metropolis that revolves around the ancient, opaque, and politically impotent Imperial Palace. The forum, situated two blocks from the palace gardens, will be the antithesis to this venerable void. Lucid, accessible, deftly knit into the urban fabric, the forum will provide a public stage to dramatize Japan's leading role in world affairs. More important, it will inject an outward-looking, cosmopolitan ideal into the center of today's Japan. The innocuous word *international* carries a charged meaning here: although Japan has long been subject to foreign influences, it is widely perceived as a closed society. The forum is designed to counter that xenophobic image.

Mr. Viñoly has translated this symbolic goal into an appropriately symbolic form. His design is a monument to the idea of openness. The clarity of the forum's planning, its sparkling glass surfaces and exposed structural engineering, its generous public spaces, and its links to mass transit will add up to a celebration of public access. Here, light and transparency become metaphors for a reconfigured cultural ideal.

There is nothing overtly Japanese about the design. But Western architects since Frank Lloyd Wright have found inspiration in the Japanese vernacular of spare, light, spatially sonorous forms. Mr. Viñoly, born in Uruguay in 1944 and educated in Argentina, has described architecture as an "art of dealing with heaviness." For him, creating shelter is less a matter of containing space than of escaping inertia. It is this idea, rather than a facile infatuation with industrial technology, that explains the prominence Mr. Viñoly gives to structure and the lyricism he extracts from it. Like trained bodies in motion, his soaring, structurally athletic enclosures convey the thrill of triumph over gravity.

(Fortunately, New Yorkers will have the opportunity to savor that thrill, though on a much smaller scale, when Mr. Viñoly's gymnasium for Lehman College, his most important New York project to date, opens in Riverdale, the Bronx, in September.)

What is discernibly Japanese is the forum's program, which combines four theaters for performing arts with spaces for major trade shows. This union of commercial and cultural uses would be anomalous in the West; we prefer to segregate Mammon from the muses. But it is consistent with a culture where art is traditionally fused with life. That tradition may be one of Japan's strategic advantages in today's international marketplace, where, increasingly, economic exchange is cultural exchange. Straddling the porous line between art and industry, the Tokyo Forum will reflect a global economy in which creative talent has displaced the primacy of raw materials and consumer goods.

The forum's seven-acre, trapezoidal site also straddles a physical line: a border between a grid of densely built-up commercial blocks in Tokyo's central business district and the curve of a rail viaduct that cuts through it. The forum's plan takes its cue from these two urban geometries. The four theaters, one of which will be the largest in Tokyo, are aligned along the site's eastern edge, attached to a slim slab building that faces the downtown grid.

Modular in form but variable in scale, the theaters diminish in size as the site narrows toward its apex. They look across an open plaza toward the Glass Hall, the forum's most spectacular component. With curving contours derived from the rail viaduct's adjacent arc, this ship-shaped atrium rises 190 feet to a crystalline roof of metal and glass, designed in collaboration with the structural engineer Kunio Watanabe. If Tiffany made skyscrapers, the result might look something like this exquisite marquise.

Unfolding as a sequence of landscaped, triangular terraces, the plaza forms a pedestrian boulevard between the commuter rail stations that lie at opposite ends of the complex. Rows of zelkova trees will turn the plaza into a garden (this reverses the arrangement at the Imperial Palace, where gardens occupy the perimeter). The trees are to be ornamental, but their airy, spreading canopies will express a structural principle. Throughout the building, Mr. Vinoly translates vertical thrust into horizontal expression. He resists gravity not by erecting tall spires but by lifting the urban horizon.

A gigantic, illuminated walk-through model is the centerpiece of the Modern's show, which was organized by Terence Riley and Anne Dixon of the museum's architecture and design department. Split down the central axis of the plaza, the model lets viewers play at being benign Godzillas. A separate model of the Glass Hall's giant steel truss, suspended from the ceiling, highlights its resemblance to an ancient Egyptian solar bark. A selection of Mr. Viñoly's energetic charcoal drawings shows him exploring the texture of light.

Sociologically or aesthetically, openness doesn't come easily. Large expanses of glass are unusual for earthquake-prone Tokyo. Sophisticated mechanics will protect the glass from seismic shocks, but Mr. Viñoly understands that terror is integral to the sublime. Like a moviemaker, he skillfully manipulates fear.

I suspect, too, that he regards the Glass Hall as a metaphor for modern architecture. For Mr. Viñoly's classically modern approach has also withstood shocks. It has survived public disfavor, critical disillusionment, even its own calamitous hubris.

Some may find the design excessively retrospective, an evocation of yesterday's vision of things to come. Well, those things did come, but seldom with the grace Mr. Viñoly promises to confer upon the vision. He has not launched a new style. He seeks to enlarge the expressive potential and the urban dimension of a vernacular that originated a century and a half ago with Joseph Paxton's Crystal Palace in London, designed for the first World's Fair. Appearing now, at the end of a century that has seen movements rise and fall with accelerating futility, the design's evolutionary stance is refreshing. Not all radiance has perished in this brutal century: that is the elevating message that the Tokyo Forum could pass on to the next.

July 16, 1993

MORE IS LESS AT A FREE-FORM JAMBOREE IN CHICAGO

If you know Mies van der Rohe only from the Seagram Building, you may feel let down at first by 860-880 Lake Shore Drive. There's no bronze. There's no bronze-tinted glass. There's no Four Seasons, with its bronzed and burnished clientele. At 860-880, the glass is clear; the structural skeletons of the two apartment towers are painted black. No sleek curtain wall smooths over their jutting bones. And unlike Seagram's rows of neatly calibrated window shades, the windows at 860–880 are dressed with heavy curtains, randomly bunched against the sun.

It may take a while, in other words, to register that Miesian refinement did not depend on sumptuous materials or polished perfection. It required clarity of purpose, three thousand years of geometry, and a good eye. Number 860-880 has the rawness of invention. This is Mies fresh out of the box or, more accurately, fresh into it. Built in 1949–51, these two Chicago towers are the first examples of the steel-and-glass high-rises that conquered the world. If they look fresh today that is partly because to see these buildings now we have to take them out of a box ourselves: the framework of misperceptions that helped the generation after Mies pack him off to history.

Number 860-880, for example, is endlessly complex, acutely sensitive to context. As the architect James Ingo Freed has observed, the pair of towers is one building, not two. "It closes and opens and shapes itself as you move around it," he said, "yet it always addresses the lake and it always holds the street." You don't envy the residents their view of the lake, because the building's columns and canopies frame such magnificent vistas from the street. Instead of forming a wall against the water like its Gold Coast neighbors, 860-880 takes the lake in. In effect, Lake Michigan becomes an infinitely extended version of the pool in Mies's 1929 Barcelona Pavilion. Water and city flow together here; space becomes something to swim in. A building that appears to disclose all its secrets at first glance turns out to reveal itself only gradually, as you move around it. That is its spellbinding paradox.

For better or worse, the generation after Mies had to break his spell. To see how violently it was shattered, it's worth a visit to the Art Institute of Chicago's exhibition Chicago Architecture and Design: 1923–1993 (through August 29). The show, a sequel to a survey of the period 1872–1922, was organized by John Zukowsky, a curator at the museum, and designed by a team of young architects under the supervision of Stanley Tigerman. Mr. Tigerman is an architect who has worked zestfully in many formal genres, and his festive, eclectic sensibility sets the show's tone. Graphics march across the floor, sound effects blare from loudspeakers. Airplanes roar. Lights blink. Drawings and photographs clutter the wire-mesh partitions. It is the city as carnival, something for everyone, a riot of style.

Subtitled Reconfiguration of an American Metropolis, the exhibition actually seems to document the disintegration of one. While the earlier show focused on the heroic figures of Daniel Burnham, Louis Sullivan, and Frank Lloyd Wright, this one takes a stance against heroic figures and master plans. It begins with a survey of "urban fragments," partly realized versions of Chicago's grand master plans, then plunges us into a potpourri of McDonald's burger stands, suburban ranch houses, postmodern skyscrapers, even a fantastic kitchen sink. As the catalog makes clear, a good deal of thought and scholarship went into the show, and the installation organizes the material into thematic areas. None of this rigor, however, pollutes the prevailing atmosphere of a free-form jamboree.

A show opposed to the idea of heroes and masters has a hard time reckoning with Mies. How can a display of antiheroism accommodate an architect as great as any who ever practiced in this town? If 1923–93 is an era of messy urban vitality, then, far from expressing the zeitgeist, Mies was radically out of step with it. Though the catalog devotes a chapter to his work, the show itself submerges him beneath its studiously indiscriminate mix. In Mr. Tigerman's 1978 photomontage *Titanic*, included here,

Mies's iconic Crown Hall is shown slipping beneath the waves. And yet the show left me thinking that I'd stepped aboard a ship of fools.

In an essay in this month's *Atlantic*, the dance critic Mindy Aloff asked, "How does a person bred on the glamour of complexity retool to appreciate simplicity?" The Art Institute's show supplies one answer: there's nothing like an overdose of complexity to revive simplicity's allure. Faced with this elaborate tribute to the spirit of anything goes, one's impulse is to rush back to the Miesian ideal of "almost nothing." Less may not be more, but at least it gives you room to breathe. Is this impulse just nostalgia for a simpler order of things? Partly. It's a yearning for a time when people believed that there was such a thing as a historical mainstream and that it must flow, in our time, toward one style of building. And it's a yearning for the vanished consensus that architects ought to be in the business of creating believable norms.

Yet Mies did not only create norms. He also broke them. And, once, he inadvertently hit on one reason why younger architects had to smash his. Surrounded in later life by apostates, Mies cried out in exasperation: "What went wrong? We showed them how to do it." What went wrong is that people want to show as well as to be shown. They want to be more than the faceless figures in someone else's rendering, particularly when the rendering has become the official portrait of the corporate society. Others have stories to tell.

Isn't that the democratic way? And wasn't it Mies's way too? Mies polished up his version of the Zeitgeist so persuasively that it's easy to forget that he had more than a craftsman's eye for detail. He had an eye for the big picture. He saw, and made others see, a vision the world had not seen before. And even in its debased form, his vision remained singular. In a city of glass towers, each tower stands alone.

Today, faced with the Art Institute's portrait of diversity unbound, we may be tempted to ask, What went wrong? Pluralism was such a good idea. How did it end up such a mess? Why did the collapse of consensus erode clarity of purpose? Surely that collapse is itself a condition architects could be clear about. At the Art Institute show, we see diversity affirmed but not rendered into form. We see urban fragments but scant evidence of buildings that crystallize the fragments into art. If we are no longer enchanted by norms, then it is time to see some spellbinding abnorms.

Perhaps that is why, on leaving the Art Institute, I found myself thinking not only of Chicago but of Los Angeles, not only of Mies but of Frank Gehry, Thom Mayne, Eric Owen Moss, Frank Israel, and other California architects who have drawn the shattered idea of consensus up into themselves and made a new vision out of the pieces.

July 18, 1993

A NERVOUS PRISM OF A BUILDING
FOR MANHATTAN

Raimund Abraham's design for the Manhattan headquarters of the Austrian Cultural Institute, which went on view yesterday at the Museum of Modern Art, promises a welcome answer to a perennially awkward question. What do you tell people from out of town who ask you to point them toward New York's important new buildings?

In recent years, this city has invested its architectural energies in some very worthy causes, such as preservation of the past and sensitivity to urban context. But for an international city, New York is sadly lacking in contemporary world-class buildings. And the lack is especially glaring considering how many world-class talents live here. Where are the buildings that can compare in formal intelligence to Peter Eisenman's Columbus Convention Center, Richard Meier's Paris headquarters for Canal Plus, or Williams and Tsien's New College at the University of Virginia? By late 1995, when the Austrian Cultural Institute is scheduled for completion, the answer will be: 11 East Fifty-second Street.

The Austrian Cultural Institute, a small, nervous prism of a building designed by one of New York's most distinguished teachers of architecture, will give this town a long-overdue shot in the skyline. Beyond that, the building will help fulfill the Institute's mission to revise the American view of Austrian culture. With its facade of sharp-edged glass sliding down like a blade, the building seems designed to shear away the popular image of Austria as a place of prancing white stallions, cherubic choirboys, and pastries slathered with clouds of heavenly whipped cream. In its sharply angled glass surfaces, we will see reflections not only of the sky over New York but also of the darker, edgier Vienna of Freud and the pioneering modernist architect Adolf Loos.

This building slices on the diagonal. Its street facade, rising twenty stories, is composed of three large overlapping segments of glass, their bottom edges beveled at 45-degree angles. For once a curtain wall is as much curtain as wall, since the edges project beyond the building envelope, uncontained by conventional frames. Abraham's articulation of the glass surface is polemical as well as elegant, for it stands in pointed contrast to the postmodern idea that architecture can be legitimately confined to the treatment of the building skin. Here, Abraham suggests, you could peel away the skin and still find architecture underneath: the glazed surface is at once a distinct architectural element and an integral part of a rigorously unified whole.

To the classical tripartite division of the skyscraper into base, shaft, and capital, Abraham has added a three-part vertical division, which he calls the mask, core, and vertebrae. The glass skin, clipped to a wedge-shaped metal shaft, forms the building's mask. With a slope that conforms precisely to the envelope prescribed by zoning regulations, the skin is punctured by forms determined by the spaces within. A box shape, projecting forward from the seventh story, houses the director's office, while inside the narrow wedge just underneath it a stair descends to the public areas below. A slim metal fin, rising above the box, helps stabilize the glass and provides support for window-cleaning equipment.

The central core, of reinforced concrete, provides the building's structure and encloses most of its interior space. Offices, galleries, meeting rooms, and a small auditorium will occupy the lower eleven floors, while the upper stories will contain apartments. A metal utility stair, required by fire regulations, zips up the rear of the building in a squared-off zigzag. It does indeed resemble vertebrae, though Abraham also likens it to Brancusi's *Endless Column*. The form starts out following function, then floats freely above it.

There hasn't been a building like this in Manhattan for more than twenty-five years. You would have to go back to the decade preceding 1967—the years that produced the Seagram Building, the Guggenheim and Whitney museums, the CBS Building and the Ford Foundation—to find functionality and structure raised to such bold expressionistic effect. But you don't have to look back quite that far to see why these principles fell from favor. Just look at the slope-sided skyscraper Gordon Bunshaft built at 9 West Fifty-seventh Street in 1974. Like Abraham's, this building took its cue by molding structural expression to the zoning envelope. And its hideousness went far toward discrediting rational design. If this was honest architecture, as the Modern movement had defined it, then perhaps it was time buildings learned how to tell pretty lies.

Presented at the Museum of Modern Art (through October 19) in a large, vivid photomontage accompanied by a ten-foot-tall scale model and a selection of drawings, Abraham's design may strike some viewers with the horrifying thought that we are in for another round of Bunshaft's brand of urban brutality. And Abraham has not exactly allayed such fears by comparing his glass facade to a descending guillotine blade. But not to worry. Only twenty-five feet wide and fifteen stories tall, the Austrian Institute is a tiny sliver compared to Bunshaft's block-busting box. Assisted by the structural engineer Guy Nordenson of Ove Arup & Partners, Abra-

ham has skillfully tuned his design to side-street scale with such refinements as the separation of the glass into segments, the exposure of their
exquisitely thin edges, and the slim metal clips that hold them in place.

Still, though it is not a brutal modern box, Abraham's design does make
a strong pitch for rational design, and not everyone will want to hear it.
For the pitch appeals to an ideal of objective truth that is not easily recov-
erable in today's relativistic universe. Isn't everything now a matter of
taste, opinion, point of view? If someone claims that grass is green, doesn't
fairness require equal time for those who insist that it is red or purple?
Isn't substance just another style?

Abraham's truth is not everyone's. But few American buildings today
aspire to honesty on any terms, in part because buildings like Bunshaft's
managed to make reason and objectivity look not only oppressive but dull.
If Abraham's building persuades us that it can still be fruitful to integrate
structure, function, and form, that is partly because he has managed to
make his truth as fascinating as a lie. Some viewers have compared the
building to a metronome. Others see the stone faces of Easter Island. Such
images were not intended, but neither are they unwelcome. This design
renders fact into poetry as imaginative as any fiction, and it invites the
viewer to do the same.

September 26, 1993

WHAT MAKES A BUILDING SHRIVEL UP AND DIE?

Back in the 1960s, Andy Warhol was invited to participate in a group
show, but instead of contributing a painting, Warhol took a broom and
swept the gallery floor. I thought it was one of the smartest works he ever
made—if people could bring themselves to collect soup cans, why not
gather dust?—and I thought of it again recently when the asbestos scare
came crashing down, plunging New York City into panic over the safety of
its public schools. The story highlighted the appalling lack of maintenance in the city's school buildings, but it also illuminated a need to refurbish ways of thinking about architecture itself.

This is not the school story we were supposed to be reading this year.
These were not the pictures we were supposed to see. Instead of the daily
deluge of images of decaying floor tiles, falling-down ceilings, and dis-
traught parents, we were meant to be looking with pride and amazement
at the remarkable new school buildings that have opened their doors this
year throughout the city. The work of the School Construction Authority,
a city agency established in 1988 with an appropriation of $4.3 billion,

these new buildings represent one of the most important public works programs in the country. They ought to be illustrating an uplifting narrative about the city's ability to turn itself around. Instead, the School Construction Authority found itself mired in yet another episode in the continuing saga of urban decrepitude, as the asbestos rained down on its parade.

Earlier this year, some months before the asbestos story broke, I sat with Peter Samton, a New York architect whose firm, Gruzen Samton, has designed three of the new schools that opened this year. We looked at slides and plans of the buildings—one each in Brooklyn (P.S. 6 in Bedford-Stuyvesant), Queens (P.S. 92 in Corona), and Upper Manhattan (P.S. 5 in Washington Heights)—and it was an inspiring, maddening experience.

At a time when many architects have begun to reassert a commitment to the public realm, here is one whose commitment has been unwavering and profound. And his designs for the schools are wonderful: alive with color, light, and thoughtful attention to the students and communities. As the architectural historian Anne Rieselbach wrote in *New Schools for New York*, a book of design proposals initiated by the Architectural League in 1989, "Historically, the school building has been the vessel of hope for the future." Not only the future of children but of the city also: few factors have so hastened the departure of the urban middle class as the erosion of the public school system. Even without the rainbow curriculum, the schools Mr. Samton had designed held out the promise of a brighter New York.

And yet, even while looking at these inspiring images, I found it impossible to ward off darker pictures, images of what the schools might look like a few years down the road: graffiti-scarred, doors hanging from hinges, pigeons roosting in classrooms. We could count on their looking fresh for a year or two, but what would happen when their novelty wore off? And if dilapidation was to be the inevitable fate of these buildings, why bother to build them? Why not use the resources to put the house we have in order? Instead of hiring architects, why not bring out a broom?

Even worse, perhaps, than the likelihood that these new schools would fall into decrepitude is the possibility that building them may even aggravate the problem. Though they have been carefully designed to resist hard wear, and even to look enduring, they nonetheless indulge our appetite for novelty. They perpetuate our indifference to whatever isn't hot off the line. Looking at them, I found myself slipping into a Solzhenitsyn-style mode of wrath about our century's "cult of novelty," though this attitude was somewhat complicated by the suspicion that in a media-driven world, I am part of the cult. Oh, show me the way to the next razzle-dazzle design, and I'll be first in line to write about it.

But the rage for novelty is only part of the problem. The other part is the contradictory expectation that buildings should rise above the moment, impervious to time and its effects, as if they were pyramids or Parthenons, magically immune to the logic of planned obsolescence. When the British critic Adrian Stokes wrote that "architecture is limited to forms without events," he appeared to state the obvious. Things go on inside buildings while buildings stand there passively. But buildings are themselves events. They are configurations in time as well as space; to hold their shape over time, they must be perpetually renewed by the rituals of daily use. Without paintbrushes, brooms, and laughter, buildings shrivel up and die.

Ron Jensen, a former president of the American Public Works Association, thinks there ought to be ribbon-cutting ceremonies not only when bridges or public buildings are dedicated but also when they undergo repairs. Get the mayor out there, invite the press, and strike up the band as the maintenance workers move in to attack the rust. Mr. Jensen's idea is basically the same as Warhol's. It's not just about maintenance; it's about changing point of view. It's about the need to confer dignity and meaning on the dull and familiar as well as the new and splashy. Alas, there aren't enough politicians around to cut the ribbons every time a ceiling crumbles, or enough celebrity artists to sweep up the debris.

The best hope now for architecturally reinforcing the rituals of daily use lies with the practitioners of "green" design. Their buildings foster a sense of connection between ordinary use and the big picture. Buildings like the Audubon Society Headquarters in New York, designed by the Croxton Collaborative, do much more than save energy and prevent exposure to toxic materials like asbestos. They introduce an attitude toward daily routine. They create participatory environments where familiar acts—flipping a light switch, emptying a waste basket, opening a window—acquire heightened importance because they are linked to a larger purpose. They are the bristles, so to speak, of a global broom at which everyone gets a turn.

Of course, we can take the asbestos out of buildings; we can make the air inside them fit to breathe. But what's needed now are designs for buildings with the capacity to affect the atmosphere outside.

October 3, 1993

THE GEHRY HOUSE:
A BRASH LANDMARK GROWS UP

Frank Gehry has remodeled his house, and some people are miserable about it. Young architects in Los Angeles, including several whose careers

Mr. Gehry has helped to nurture, are having a hard time adjusting to the change. They grumble, mostly among themselves, that Mr. Gehry has smoothed away the rough edges that gave the house its character. To hear them talk, you might think that the house belonged to them. And it does. It belongs to everyone who believes that architecture is an art of living.

The house, in Santa Monica, just west of Los Angeles, has been a landmark for fifteen years. The architectural vocabulary it introduced in 1978—a precise balance of fragment and whole, raw and refined, new and old—has inspired a generation of designers. It helped to establish Los Angeles as America's most vibrant city for architectural innovation. And it widened the scope of Mr. Gehry's own practice from a regional to a global sphere.

If it is possible to view in historical terms a building that epitomizes contemporaneity, then this house already stands in the select group of architects' houses that includes Jefferson's Monticello in Virginia, Wright's Taliesin in Wisconsin and Taliesin West in Arizona, and Philip Johnson's Glass House in Connecticut.

And even if it is foolhardy to advance such a claim, those earlier buildings help to clarify what makes the Gehry house important. Jefferson's, Wright's, and Johnson's houses sit isolated in natural landscapes. Refugees from urban congestion, they dramatize their mastery of the environment by extending visual control over nature in vistas as far as the eye can see.

Mr. Gehry's house, too, draws meaning from its context. But the landscape it occupies is the built-up continent of postwar urbanization. Instead of commanding an infinite expanse of fields, forests, desert, or prairie, Mr. Gehry's house sits on a small lot, just a few blocks from the endless commercial strip of Wilshire Boulevard. Its vista is a land filled with millions of dream houses, a decentralized urban America where the desire to escape the city has produced a raucous congestion of its own.

Even Mr. Gehry's own suburban lot was already occupied. A two-story, pink-shingled "dumb little house with charm," as Mr. Gehry famously called it, poked its cute Dutch gambrel roof into the green suburban skyline. Instead of tearing it down, Mr. Gehry turned the old dwelling into the foundation for his own dream. He sliced through walls, extracted ceilings, pared away part of the roof, and wove the partly dismembered remains into a new architectural framework: an industrial shell made of plywood, wire glass, galvanized metal, and chain-link fence.

Though Mr. Gehry denied that he was trying to make a Big Statement, the house was soon widely recognized as a potent expression of contemporary American urbanism. It was as if the old house had begun to break apart under the pressure of proximity to the neighbors, and then began to exert its own pressure outward: pushing back against staid decorum, exposing suburbia's conflicting ideals of community and independence.

Like an eruption of inner-city energy within the tranquil suburb, Mr. Gehry's chain link and rough asphalt suggested that earthquakes aren't the only source of instability in Southern California. The region is also subject to social shocks brought on by its own explosive growth and the competing pressures of its diverse population.

Social pressures also brought on the recent remodeling of the Gehry house, though in this case the pressures were domestic. Mr. Gehry and his wife, Berta, are the parents of two teenage sons. The boys used to share a bedroom on the second floor, just outside the airy, treetop nest of a master bedroom. A few years ago, Alejo, the elder, moved into a spare bedroom downstairs. Then in 1991 Sami, the younger son, decided that he, too, wanted more distance from the nest. His parents were willing, but the house was slightly too cramped to oblige. To give the brothers rooms of equal size, it would be necessary to extend the rear wall of the house a few feet into the backyard.

For Mr. Gehry, this was not destined to be a simple matter of calculating so many square feet. His architecture is an art of relationships. He could not easily change one part of the house without rethinking the whole. Extending the rear wall, for example, would dim the wall's lineup of five wood-framed glass doors, one of the most distinctive features.

Mr. Gehry decided to replace the doors with large picture windows, setting one of them within a sliding frame. But since the doors echoed the wooden framework of an exposed stud wall inside, that wall would also have to come down. And without the wall, the raised floor of the adjacent living room would have to be extended over a sunken "talk pit."

And so on and so on and so on: an aesthetic chain reaction that threatened to pitch the whole house completely out of whack. In 1978, for instance, Mr. Gehry was content to leave walls and ceilings looking raw and unfinished. The visual grit conveyed the exploratory nature of the design. But the remodeling is not a new departure. And Mr. Gehry's design vocabulary has evolved considerably since 1978. Retaining the raw surfaces of the house would have felt contrived, like using artificially weathered wood.

Thus, the main goal of the project was to meet the challenge of growth—his own as well as his family's—while remaining sympathetic to what was already there. As Mr. Gehry put it, "The job was to let the house change without stepping outside its own vernacular."

The basic layout of the house is much the same. The entrance, kitchen, and dining area still occupy the narrow, U-shaped strip of space between the old pink house and the industrial-strength walls that Mr. Gehry wrapped around it in 1978. The kitchen's large, distinctive window and skylight remain intact within their tumbling wooden frames.

But surfaces throughout the house have gone from raw to cooked. Ceilings are fitted with neat wooden battens, covering up formerly exposed beams. The crude asphalt that once lined the kitchen floor has been replaced with square asphalt pavers. In place of plain plywood, there is varnished Douglas fir. These smooth surfaces have brightened the rooms, and now there is air-conditioning.

On the second floor, the boys' old room has become a study for Mrs. Gehry. The master bedroom now features a built-in, glass-topped table that doubles as a skylight for the living room below. Thick glass has also replaced the chain-link floor in an area leading from the bedroom to a balcony that wraps around the side of the house. A steep stair, more like a ship's ladder, ascends from the bedroom to a garret-lookout Mr. Gehry has set aside for reading. Here, plywood bookshelves and walls of exposed wooden slats recall the building's prerenovation roughness, but the slats now frame small windows that are opened and closed by discreet electric motors.

The landscaping around the house is also more formally ordered. An ancient, towering cactus still commands the backyard, but the new paving that surrounds it has replaced the pulverized concrete that once gave the yard the appearance of a vacant city lot. A lap pool, lined with apple green tile, now stretches the width of the yard. On the far side of the pool, the pink-shingled garage has been enlarged by a metal facade. Remodeled for guest quarters, the garage has been requisitioned by the boys as a recreation room.

In front of the house, the landscape designer Nancy Power has arranged a sumptuous oasis of desert flora around a bubbling fountain: water tumbles into a basin from stainless steel faucets, the kind you remember from chemistry class. Overhead, nasturtiums have begun to soften the cantilevered chain-link screens into bucolic trellises. But the real "landscaping" of this house is the fractured panorama of multiple perspectives that unfolds as you look out its windows. As you ascend through the house, your angle of vision pivots downward, directed by openings that frame sky, then treetops, then the motley Santa Monica cityscape in a low-flying bird's-eye view.

Electric windows? A lap pool? A fountain? It is this emphasis on luxury, along with the high level of finish throughout the house, that leaves some people feeling dispossessed. They see the renovation as a reflection of Mr. Gehry's worldly success, with all the risks that success holds for the romantic imagination. Or perhaps they fear that the remodeling marks the passing of their own youth, along with the carefree spontaneity that the house long embodied. "He's given the house a face-lift," said Frank Israel, an admiring Los Angeles architect, whose clients include Hollywood stars.

Mr. Gehry himself is not completely satisfied with the remodeling even after two years' work, and he is still tinkering with designs for the lighting fixtures downstairs. "It was tougher before," he said. "And it was harder to grasp what was going on." Before, he continued, it was harder to tell where the old building stopped and his additions began. There was a tighter mesh between the exposed innards of the old and the rough materials of the new. Now there is a visible sense of separation.

But the remodeling has reaffirmed, not betrayed, the governing idea of this house. It was always a place of growth. Like all of Mr. Gehry's work, the house enlarged the opportunity for individuals and ideas to develop according to their nature, within the social ecology of a city where millions of others are struggling to do the same. Yes, Mr. Gehry concedes, the house is comfortable now. He found it comfortable before the remodeling too. And his sons evidently feel quite at home. They have plastered hockey posters all over his handiwork.

In short, social as well as spatial factors drove this redesign, and its social dimension goes beyond the rearrangement of domestic affairs. While the remodeling of the house was going forward, Mr. Gehry started work on a design for an addition to the Children's Museum in Boston, a project that might inspire some architects with escapist fantasies of Edenic bliss. For Mr. Gehry, the museum project has been an occasion for some fairly grim reflections: What kind of world has his generation created for the next?

His own city has been convulsed by social and racial unrest. What can a building say to children at such a time? How can it allow the possibility of hope but prevent it from becoming yet another burden on the future? How can architecture encourage playfulness as a spur to creativity but discourage it from becoming an evasion of responsibility for the present?

Such far-reaching speculations jostle with the intimacies of daily living. On a Saturday morning, Mr. Gehry will rise at 5:30 to join his sons for a day of ice hockey. The skates now lie in colorful disarray in the backyard. And the collision of these images—urban and domestic; cosmic and mundane—is one way to visualize the mental mechanism at work when Mr. Gehry stands over a table in his office, concentrating on a project, adjusting the elements of a model.

He designs with faith that even small adjustments of form—the placement of a lap pool, the entrance to a museum—can alter the conditions of social reality. They represent a concrete, pragmatic means of bringing disconnected realms into coherent cultural relationship. The Gehry house, for example, is indeed a comfortable nest. It is miles from the harsh conditions of South Central Los Angeles torn by rioting last year. But here, at the long table in the Gehrys' sun-splashed dining area, Mr. Gehry has sat down with the new mayor of Los Angeles, Richard Riordan, to discuss how architects and planners can effectively address the city's agonizing social tensions.

The house itself has much to contribute to that conversation. It says that architecture does not just enclose life but emerges from within it. Buildings need not stand above things, aloof atop a plinth. They can derive their forms from the fray. The tensions of cities, like the tensions of families, can give rise to violence. They also produce moments of joy.

A MAN WHO LIVES IN TWO GLASS HOUSES

Glass, the early German modernists believed, would launch a cultural revolution. Glass walls would not only change the look of buildings. They would transform the lives of those who lived inside them. Stripped of the opaque, protective cover afforded by old-fashioned masonry buildings, civilization would advance toward a light-filled realm of freedom and candor.

Philip Johnson lives in two glass houses. One is the landmark residence in New Canaan, Connecticut, he designed for himself in 1949. The other is the fishbowl of fame that he has inhabited most of his life. And in Johnson's case, at least, it turns out that the early modernists may have had a point. Even those who detest Johnson and his architecture will grant his disarming candor. Always quicker than his critics to concede his faults, Johnson long ago perfected the art of self-deprecation as a shield against attacks by others. When an architect routinely belittles his own work, calls himself a whore, and makes no secret of the fascist sympathies that overtook him in the 1930s, where's the fun in trying to take him down a peg or two?

Whether or not there is any connection between Johnson's frankness and the transparent walls of his country home, the Glass House is widely regarded as his most successful building. His faults may be legion—in fact, Johnson's faults have always been at least as stimulating as his virtues—but the Glass House is not to be classed among them. Inspired by the Farnsworth House, designed by Johnson's mentor, Mies van der Rohe, in 1947, the classically symmetrical pavilion of glass walls set atop a brick base took to an extreme degree the Miesian ideal of "almost nothing."

This fall, the house and the other structures Johnson has added to his Connecticut property over the years are being celebrated with the publication of *The Glass House*, a collection of essays edited by David Whitney and Jeffrey Kipnis. Johnson and his house also figure prominently in another new book, *No Place Like Utopia*, Peter Blake's hugely entertaining memoir of architects and architecture in the postwar decades. Both volumes pay lavish tribute to the design of the house and also to its reputation as a kind of cultural greenhouse where Johnson and his friends sprouted even grander designs for American architecture. "The glass house was a beautiful salon," Blake writes, "and here the worlds of the new architecture and the new arts met on weekends and mapped out the future. Or so it seemed."

Both books reproduce a famous photograph by Arnold Newman of Johnson seated inside the Glass House, an image as eloquent as anything that has been written about either. The picture, which reduces Johnson and the house to a dark shadow veiled by shimmering reflections, recalls a line in a short story by Truman Capote: "Think of nothing things; think of wind." Newman's photograph suggests that transparency can be a form of camouflage, and candor a form of evasion. And indeed, one of Johnson's enduring strengths, for all his public visibility and his legendary power, may well be his ability to impersonate a kind of nothing thing, a fleeting thing, a wisp in the winds of fortune, fashion, and changing times.

Philip Johnson has had a long life and a long career, but the period in which he dominated American architecture was brief. It began in 1974 with the death of Louis Kahn and ended about fifteen years later with the growing recognition that American architecture had been operating for some time without a social contract. It ended, in other words, with the '80s, and all that "the '80s" had come to signify: the breakdown of faith in the democratic ideal of equality and in architecture as a means of attaining it.

Needless to say, Philip Johnson himself did not vanish with the turn of the decade. On the contrary, last year, at the age of eighty-six, he once again demonstrated the extraordinary powers of regeneration that have marked his career for six decades. Squeezed out of the firm he had formed in 1972 with John Burgee, his partner in the boom years, Johnson moved to smaller quarters upstairs in his Lipstick Building on Third Avenue and formed a leaner, meaner firm for recessionary times. But while Burgee slipped into bankruptcy, Johnson forged ahead, not only professionally but aesthetically. Recent projects show him gleefully plundering from the fragmented architecture of Frank Gehry and the folded volumes of Peter Eisenman.

The new firm signified something more than Philip Johnson's legendary resilience, however. It was also a sign that "the '80s" did not end with the '80s. Nor, for that matter, did "the '80s" begin with the '80s. Rather, that decade raised to an excruciating pitch an attitude of extreme subjectivity that long preceded those years, did not die with them, and cannot be willed away by a show of righteous indignation with the decade's fabled excesses.

It is not surprising that Johnson emerged as a figurehead in that time, since his work has long embodied the subjective principle. His designs might be good, or they might be terrible, but who could say? Embracing movements and styles one minute only to drop them with a thud the next, Johnson seems to have made it his mission in life to keep American architecture in a more or less permanent crisis of evaluation. His singular gift has been to undermine the very idea that there can be objective criteria for judging buildings. Taste, willfulness, and what Vincent Scully once called Johnson's "admirably unsentimental wit"—these aspects of the cultivated sensibility have been Johnson's stock-in-trade.

And even if Johnson were to blow away tomorrow, the issues raised by his work would remain to haunt us. Slight though much of the work may be, it nonetheless challenges us to rethink the prospects for architecture as a social art.

Peter Blake's book reminds us how valuable Johnson's subversive mission once appeared. In the 1950s and '60s, when the Modern movement ruled supreme, Johnson's witty, barbed critiques of the movement's "shibboleths" and "crutches" offered a tonic antidote to the status quo. Although the movement claimed to be objective, Johnson exposed the degree to which it was rooted in myths. Unlike Louis Kahn, Johnson did not point Modern architecture in a new direction. Nor, unlike Robert Venturi, did he frame a new set of ideas that other architects could grasp hold of. Johnson's aim was not to revise or rewrite rules but to break them, to assert the claims of artistic freedom in a profession governed by the ideal of norms.

"Free at last," he exclaimed, in a lecture in 1975. It was not the most sensitive phrasing, given that the independence Johnson proclaimed was the architect's freedom to practice without the kind of social conscience that Martin Luther King Jr. symbolized. Still, the comment was a clue to the potent appeal of Johnson's naughtiness. This was the anarchic power of the id, erupting into the sacred precinct of the superego, the tight, responsible world of the stern-faced Modern Fathers, the realm of don't do this, don't do that. Johnson merely gave voice to what others secretly thought when he impishly replied to the fathers, Why not? I want to.

In place of "almost nothing," Johnson evoked an image of practically everything. And in the decades that followed he was able to give form to an endless cavalcade of polymorphous fantasies. Some of these fantasies were capably designed, others were not much more than hastily constructed sketches, but the entire enterprise had the irresistible allure of the

fantastic, an apparition, or a dream. It was as if, instead of creating different designs, Johnson had brought into being a single protean building
that, like a mythological creature, changed shape each time you blinked—
appearing now as a Chippendale highboy, now an old Dutch counting
house, now a lipstick, a mighty Wurlitzer, a turreted castle, the Houses of
Parliament remade in mirrored glass.

And in this copious outpouring of the imagination, it could be said that
Johnson was not the prodigal betrayer of Mies van der Rohe but the perverse fulfillment of his pure architectural reductions, for if you took away
Mies's skin-and-bones architecture you were left with something perhaps
more fundamental still: a mind, a raw psyche, quivering with memories,
images, fears, and desires. The Glass House pushed the Miesian aesthetic
to such an extreme that in effect it turned into its opposite: instead of representing the lucid framework of rationality, Johnson's theatrical, transparent box came oddly to resemble the wiry, cagelike cubes Francis Bacon
painted around his panic-stricken figures of businessmen and popes.

Of course, Johnson's persona of courtly, well-born man about town is
light-years away from Bacon's black, tortured souls. Yet within the world
of large-scale corporate and civic building, Johnson nonetheless injected
the architectural equivalent of what the art critic Donald Kuspit called
Bacon's "hysterical exhibitionism." While each individual building might
be a model of order, each model canceled the order of the design that preceded it. Instead of hysterical painting, Johnson practiced hysterical
designing, raising a skyline of freaks that collectively negated the possibility that any order could embrace the whole. But finally, rolling into the
'90s, Johnson found even the catchall term *postmodernism* too confining,
and discarded it with the remark that "none of us postmodernists were
really any good."

There are limits to Philip Johnson's idea of freedom. He will take architecture in any form so long as it is only a form. His conception of architecture has seldom been sufficiently elastic to accommodate the social and
political content of buildings. From Johnson's perspective, social conscience represents a restraint on creative freedom, the voice of the superego forbidding desire a free reign.

This was not always the case. Johnson has said that his flirtation with
fascism in the 1930s was idealistic. And though the normal course among
American intellectuals in that period was to veer left rather than right, he
was not alone in the belief that individual freedoms would have to be sacrificed to serve the public good. Nor was he the only visual artist who subsequently turned to formalism partly to distance himself from the
discredited political views of his past.

But to profess disbelief in the social and political dimensions of architecture is not, of course, to prevent architecture from being used toward social and political ends. It is merely to deny responsibility for the social and political ends to which buildings are often put. And, in the '80s, that denial also allowed others, like real estate developers, to evade that responsibility by conferring upon them the prestige of architectural patrons.

Such evasions were the hallmark of Johnson's boom years, a time when the voice of the superego was not heard widely in the land, nor were ids much reined in. On the contrary, in the 1980s the id ruled the national psyche. And in that context, the polymorphous projections of Johnson's imagination took on a different aspect. They no longer resisted the status quo. They embodied the status quo. Instead of signifying creative freedom, they began to resemble the traditional claims of privilege.

Only Johnson was not creating charming follies on a gentleman's country estate. He was working for real estate speculators operating in cities where public constraints had eroded. Yet if romantic rebellion was good enough for artists and architects, why couldn't it work for real estate developers? Donald Trump! Free at last!

In theory, the stylistic diversity of postmodernism was socially enlightened because it showed that architects were willing to serve popular taste. But as the '80s wore on, this myth became ever harder to sustain as it became increasingly difficult to locate the citizen in the forest of spectacularly diverse high-rises.

These buildings had indeed solved the problem posed by modern architecture and its dulling of the cityscape with uniform glass boxes. But they raised new questions in turn. If consistent forms could no longer express an architect's adherence to a social ideal, then what idea had taken its place? What principle could prevent architecture from tumbling back into its old status as a plaything of the rich? And without such a principle, how would it be possible to distinguish the idealistic architect from the whore?

The Modern movement, after all, had stood for something more than a style. It stood for a principle: that architecture should satisfy criteria other than the taste of rich patrons. This principle was one of the major clauses in the architect's social contract. And for all the canonical rules of modernism, that canon nonetheless represented a form of freedom: a liberation from the architect's traditional role as servant of the powerful. It is this hard-won freedom that was compromised by the aesthetic credo of "Free at last."

That compromise has turned out to be expensive. The cost is evident not only in such obvious social failures as the collapse of government housing programs and the continuing erosion of urban centers but also in the backlash against aesthetics that these failures have provoked. Many architects and others have come to feel that to practice architecture as an art is at best amoral, at worst a fraud perpetrated on the public at its expense.

But the fallacy of formalism is not in regarding architecture as an art. It is in thinking that art is served by divorcing it from social context. We now know that in the 1980s this divorce served business far more obediently than it did art. Swinging the pendulum away from art would only invert the problem. As much of the most conspicuous art in recent years has shown, art can be as socially engaged as Hillary Rodham Clinton. Art can be an object, and it can be a way of releasing creative energy to flow in new directions.

Even Philip Johnson, for all his devotion to form, has adhered to a social vision, and in 1975 he sketched it out in his "Free at last" speech: "Philosophically, it seems to me that we today are anarchistic, nihilistic, solipsistic, certainly relativist, humorous, cynical, reminiscent of tradition, myth-and-symbol-minded rather than rationalistic or scientifically minded."

These may not be the qualities that leap to mind when we think of social values. They certainly do not seem in step with a time when many would like to see architecture's scattered energies focused on a common purpose. But it may be that Johnson's values are not as alien to that goal as they seem. We are individualistic, competitive, rootless, hungry, exhibitionistic, freakish, and drawn to images and symbols that momentarily relieve the fear of tumbling into the void. We are, in a word, subjective. And architecture is unlikely to sustain a sense of common purpose without a framework that takes our subjectivity into account.

The Glass House is not a bad metaphor for such a framework. For more than forty years the building has been a showcase for qualities of mind that remain exemplary: curiosity, pragmatism, the ability to conceive order and also to question it, receptivity to new ideas along with skepticism that salvation lies with any one of them, and the freedom to imagine forms of architecture even Philip Johnson never dreamed of. But the Glass House also shows that when architects pool their imaginations into a collective dream, they can do great things.

October 17, 1993

FEAR, HOPE, AND THE CHANGING OF THE GUARD

Mayoral elections are referendums of faith in the city. But they are also experiments in terror. Every four years, New Yorkers are bombarded with grotesquely magnified images of urban horror. The challenger tries to persuade us that things have never been worse. The incumbent insists that even greater catastrophes lie ahead if he is turned out of office. Though the contest is local, the contestants act out a national drama. Their alternating appeals to hope and fear reverberate throughout urban America.

Four years ago, New Yorkers united behind David Dinkins with the hope that the election of New York's first black mayor could reinvigorate the city's embattled liberal tradition. Architecture, planning, and urban design have long been part of that tradition, and many New Yorkers who supported Mr. Dinkins hoped that his administration would revive a place for design in urban affairs. After a decade of explosive real estate development (the anarchic cityscape parodied by Anton Furst's set design for the 1989 film *Batman*), people had wearied of the argument that real estate development automatically benefits the city's quality of life. They were looking for a governing intelligence capable of elevating architecture from the bottom line toward loftier ideals.

These hopes went largely unfulfilled. Thanks in large part to the recession, the past four years have not witnessed an acceleration of architectural anarchy. But neither will they be remembered by urbanists as a golden era for the nation's largest city. (Paradoxically, Mr. Dinkins's most idealistic contribution was an economic one: his awarding of city contracts to minority businesses was a major contribution to civic life.) It is far from clear that Rudolph Giuliani harbors any vision of the contribution architects and planners can make toward creating a livable city, though some were encouraged by the endorsement he received from Robert Wagner Jr., a former planning commissioner who will be a leading figure on Mr. Giuliani's transition team. A change in administration by no means guarantees a change in policy. But it is an ideal time to make it clear that change is overdue.

The truth is that architecture faded from the liberal political agenda long before David Dinkins took office. Not since the administration of John Lindsay ended in 1974 has there been a strong coalition between progressive politics and progressive design. What has taken the place of architecture is architectural history: landmarks preservation, connoisseur-ship of period styles, and design guidelines that require new buildings to emulate the appearance of old ones.

Even those with no personal memory of the glorious old Penn Station and its ignominious demise in 1963 can appreciate the logic as well as the benefits of this development. Architecture is an urban intruder: a destroyer of memories, a painful reminder that people have little control over their surroundings. Three decades ago, the preservation movement dramatically increased that control. A movement that had been regarded as an elitist pastime became one of the most powerful tools with which cit-izens could exercise power over the urban landscape. It was a tool directed against real estate development, but inevitably it was turned against archi-tecture. Its particular target was modern architecture, a style whose path had been paved with gestures of contempt for the Beaux Arts and other facets of the city's rich stylistic mix.

The result of these confrontations was a stunning reversal in social and aesthetic values. Where modern architects saw the urban renewal projects of the 1950s and '60s as expressions of social responsibility, others regarded them as an arrogant assaults on the very fabric of their lives. In the years since, the liberal idea has been to resist architecture, not to encourage it, and that resistance remains a valuable force for civic good. But by the end of the 1980s, it had become apparent that this force was insufficient to address the needs of the present. The overarching problem was not change but the pervasive fear of change. A liberal consensus that had staked itself heavily to the past found itself powerless to confront that fear.

The Italian architect Giò Ponti once wrote that the architect's task is "to interpret the life of the inhabitants, transforming it into an expression of civilization and culture." As mayor, David Dinkins performed a similar function. His dignity and compassion—and his ability to grasp how important it was symbolically for New York's first black mayor to project these qualities—offered New York a new portrait of itself. In him, we saw a city that had overcome fear of difference and the unknown. Unfortu-nately, his administration failed to grasp the role that design can play in redrawing an urban portrait. If Mr. Dinkins's record in architecture and urbanism was disappointing, it was not because his performance was any worse than his predecessors' but because he failed to realize that the city was ripe for new ideas in these fields.

When architects rely too much on the past, Lewis Mumford once ob-served, they tend to "think of a new problem in terms of an old solution

for a different problem." Two of the major projects of the Dinkins administration bear Mumford out. The city-sponsored competition to design a
new terminal building in Lower Manhattan for the Staten Island Ferry
was conceived with excellent intentions. By detaching the terminal from
the conventional design procedures of the Department of Transportation,
the city hoped to create something architecturally more distinguished
than the typical engineered shed.

Unfortunately, the competition, held in 1992, coincided with a moment when the criteria for architectural distinction were being thoroughly
reappraised. Architects were in revulsion against the "designer decade" of
the 1980s and its reduction of buildings to islands of style in an ocean of
urban decrepitude. Many of them had begun to look closely at the infrastructure as a way to reconnect individual buildings to the larger forces
that shape urban form.

The ferry terminal project—whose status may be affected by the forthcoming change in administrations—missed a golden opportunity to be on
the cutting edge. What was needed was not a design that separated architecture from engineering but one that integrated architecture into a
regional transportation system. The city's design guidelines, which dwelt
on the historical background of ferries and the New York harbor, evoked
the authority of tradition but ignored the progressive tradition that had
produced such magnificent public works as the George Washington
Bridge. While the winning design, an immense clock face by Venturi,
Scott Brown & Associates with Anderson/Schwartz Architects, played
wittily with historical precedent, the design's stylish irony was a poor substitute for the broad vision that planning once provided.

The most ambitious planning project undertaken by the Dinkins
administration, its "comprehensive plan" for the revitalization of the city's
waterfront, also started with excellent intentions. Seeking to stimulate
economic development along the waterfront and at the same time
enhance public access to it, the plan revolved around a set of zoning regulations designed to balance these competing objectives. Unfortunately, the
new zoning, which was approved by the City Council last month, resembled a formula that has already produced dubious public amenities like the
atriums in Trump Tower, Olympic Tower, and the Sony Building—places
where the public is at best grudgingly accommodated.

Rather than merely balancing the competing interests of the public
and private sectors, the plan could have united the two in the pursuit
of higher goals. The waterfront marks a border between the urban and
natural realms. The plan was an ideal opportunity to introduce ideas
for reconciling these traditionally divided spheres. New design codes

for "sustainable"—environmentally responsible—development. Waste-treatment plants transformed from unwanted projects to desirable public spaces. Incentives for biotechnology and environmental industries to locate on the waterfront, as apparel is concentrated on Seventh Avenue or finance on Wall Street. Recreation areas landscaped by brilliant environmental artists.

Instead of fostering a new relationship between culture and nature, the waterfront plan envisioned nature in nineteenth-century terms, as a scenic backdrop or as a wilderness to be segregated into parklike preserves. With its emphasis on "reclaiming," rather than planning, the waterfront, its use of phrases like *untapped resource* and *last frontier,* even the plan's language was soaked in the thinking of an earlier day: the industrial age that treated nature mainly as raw material to be exploited for human use.

On election night, a Dinkins supporter explained to a television reporter that the mayor had lost because the public had not been sufficiently informed about his achievements. But in architecture and planning, the problem was rather the reverse: it was the administration that seemed to be in the dark about the creative ferment in these fields. Although New York prides itself on being the information capital of the world, somehow it has managed to remain impervious to ideas that have helped other cities move forward: the environmentally based waterfront plan in Toronto; the spectacular array of parks and public spaces in Barcelona; the coordinated, citywide program of public artworks integrated with the infrastructure of Phoenix. The tradition of international competitions that has made contemporary architecture such a vital part of the cultural life of cities throughout Europe and in Japan.

Worse, the city has failed to tap the energy that resides within the city's architecture schools or to enlist the young architects who have amply demonstrated their commitment to public service in projects like the Architectural League's superb studies of urban housing, schools, and parks. There are now two generations of architects who have entered the profession only to encounter a climate of indifference to the imagination. They look around and see a city where it has apparently been decided in advance that every new building should look like the Art Deco apartment buildings of the 1930s. Every street should be lighted by bishop's crook lampposts. Every park should look like an Olmsted park.

No one is arguing that the city should abandon its heritage. The point, rather, is that architecture and architectural history are not the same thing. Though both are fundamental aspects of urbanism, each has a different role to play. While they may be natural antagonists, even the tension between them is a source of strength.

Rudolph Giuliani was elected to hire more cops, not urban visionaries. With a budget deficit of half a billion dollars, it may be unrealistic to hope that he will strengthen the city's woefully understaffed planning department or create an agency similar to the Urban Design Group, which served as a think tank for fresh ideas in the Lindsay years. Still, it is not too much to hope that he will call upon designers as the city musters the energy it needs to face the future.

November 14, 1993

FRANK GEHRY LIFTS CREATIVITY OUT OF THE BOX

The new Frederick R. Weisman Art Museum, designed by Frank Gehry for the University of Minnesota in Minneapolis, may remind you of the first time you saw mercury. You were a child, learning to differentiate between one thing and another, and along came this stuff that threw the whole idea of differentiation into doubt. Is it metal? Water? Magic? An adult version of Silly Putty? How come it neither hardens nor flows? Do you call it a piece or a puddle? Call it a lesson: the mind must make room for a world where things will not always fall neatly into place.

The mercurial quality of the Weisman Museum, which opened three weeks ago, isn't solely due to the quicksilver reflections of light that constantly play over its gleaming stainless steel facade. Nor is it just a matter of the mutable images—a fish, an ice palace, Rapunzel's tower—fleetingly evoked by the facade's flaring, curving facets. It arises, rather, from an idea about art and its place in the contemporary scheme of things. This is Frank Gehry's first art museum. He has designed some brilliant museum installations over the years, and his Temporary Contemporary [renamed The Geffen Contemporary at MOCA], a converted industrial shed, remains one of downtown Los Angeles's enduring joys. But the Weisman is the first art museum Gehry has designed from the ground up, and it invites a closer view of the kinship between art and architecture.

Minneapolis has earned this distinctive addition to its vibrant cultural life. In 1986 an exhibition of Gehry's work, organized at the Walker Art Center here by Mildred and Martin Friedman, brought the architect a national audience. This time the city has given him a dramatic site on a bluff overlooking the Mississippi River, where the museum serves as a gateway to the university's sprawling East Bank Campus.

The building, named for a California entrepreneur, will house the university's collection, which includes notable holdings in early-twentieth-century American art. While scarcely a background building, neither is it an alien presence in a landscape dominated by the changing moods of water and sky and by the industrial vernacular of bridges and mills that the river has given rise to.

The building stretches out to embrace its surroundings, with great steel arcs that join it to the structure of an adjacent river bridge, and with side and rear walls dressed in the masonry uniform of this predominantly redbrick campus. From within, windows (overscaled but with the proportions of residential buildings) afford a visual bridge between the galleries and the Minneapolis skyline. But some will find that the building's closest contextual cousin is the fantastic ice architecture created each year for the Winter Carnival in neighboring St. Paul.

Parking and storage occupy the lower two of the Weisman's four stories, offices the top level. On the third floor are five of the most gorgeous galleries on earth. Gehry set himself a difficult task in creating this radiantly lighted ensemble. He wanted rooms that would be neutral enough to serve art yet not so neutral that the architecture disappears. Expanses of white wall rise from pale wood floors, in the conventional white-cube manner. Higher up, the design increases in formal complexity. The walls break into gently illuminated lighting coves, intersect with white structural trusses, then melt away in the cascade of natural light that pours from skylights down through ceiling recesses carved into graceful, cloudlike curves.

The surprise of this interior is that as the architectural forms grow more assertive, the spaces become more airily abstract. The confined space of the white cube—a form as conventional as a Corinthian colonnade—dissolves into the air. The trusses overhead, while physically massive, are the opposite of visually oppressive. They release the sight from the box into fluid space. The arrangement helps focus the eye as you move toward a painting, then relieves the pressure as you move on. An ingenious mix of natural and artificial light further softens the interior geometry, and so do the vistas of receding, luminous volumes that open up between the galleries. The place breathes.

A similar effect occurs on the building's exterior. At first glance, the facade looks aggressive, recognizably the "exploding silver artichoke" derided by some local jokers. But after a moment, the eye is drawn into the modulated light on the surface, and the hard steel edges soften into silvery reflecting pools of indistinct contour.

To inaugurate the new building, the museum has mounted a small show of contemporary art selected and installed by Gehry himself. Called The Architect's Eye, the show is his tribute to artists whose visions have helped clarify his own. Sculptures by Carl Andre and Donald Judd, for

instance, share Gehry's affinity for tough, industrial forms. Claes Olden-
burg's gigantic soft french fries and ketchup have clearly whetted the
architect's robust appetite for the vernacular of contemporary life.

But Gehry's purpose in showing these works is polemical as well as aesthetic. For years, those who had trouble appreciating Gehry's work described him as more of an artist than an architect. The distinction belittled
architecture more than it did Gehry. It betrayed the state of an art form
hung up on the idea that some inherent antipathy exists between rigor and
creative freedom.

If Gehry has stood apart from conventional practice, it is because he does
not share that hang-up. Rather, like the artists he has chosen for this show,
he grasps that it takes enormous rigor for art to question the boundaries of
its own definition. And, like them, he accepts that testing boundaries is
one of the most vital things art does. But Gehry goes further. His buildings expose the degree to which the licensing of artistic freedom can be a
way to restrain it. When people say, "That's not architecture, it is art,"
they have found a way to put creativity into a box. And they don't see why
Gehry isn't content to design the box. Why won't mercury stay put?

Gehry isn't simply asserting a license to make idiosyncratic shapes.
The Weisman Art Museum is neither oblivious to context nor indifferent
to function. The bathrooms are equipped with unexceptional sinks, the
bookstore with attractive plywood shelves. But these conventional codes
do not impose their order on the experience. Instead, they have been
absorbed, made molten, and recast to make the most of an opportunity to
create a new place. The genius of this place is the idea that a university art
museum shouldn't be designed to keep the lid on everything art stands for.
It should do everything it can to turn the contents loose.

December 12, 1993

THE HOMELESS AND THE NEW COLD WAR

Bang bang. Shiver shiver. Violence and homelessness, homelessness and
violence: this winter, these topics have played over and over in the media,
alternating like the A and B sides of the top-selling disk in the jukebox of
national conscience. Why these depressing tunes? Why now?

Bill Clinton's been in office a year. He campaigned on the theme of
change. He pledged to shift the focus of government from the international arena to the domestic sphere. Yet people are still sleeping in boxes
and still getting shot in the head. Even a society accustomed to instant

pain relievers can't expect these social ills to vanish overnight. But there's no point losing sight of them until they've been addressed.

Global events have heightened our awareness of these domestic issues. With the evil empire gone, there's no one around to feel ideologically superior to. Homelessness and violence are signs that all is not well in the land of free enterprise. Though the Cold War has passed, it has left in its wake a new cold war, a domestic cold war, where women freeze to death on bus-stop benches, bullets assail suburban commuters, and pundits on the left and right skirmish over where to draw the line between rights and responsibilities.

Poverty is not an architectural problem. But homelessness has linked poverty to the home and to private property, social institutions to which architecture is tightly bound. And this linkage reflects, in turn, the fragmenting pressures of the marketplace that intensified during the Cold War years.

If people are out on the street, it is not only because they can't afford to pay for housing. It is also because they've dropped out of cultural history. They have been left behind by the massive dispersal of community life into the suburban, electronically equipped realm of the private home. Prisons, mental hospitals, and welfare hotels make up a big chunk of what's left of public space in an era of shopping malls, theme parks, and corporate campuses. The homeless haunt the streets, parks, and subways like the ghosts of an abandoned civic idea.

Architects did not create the policies that subjected public life to market pressures. Nonetheless, they have helped formulate and perpetuate a series of myths that have made those policies tolerable by concealing the brutal social Darwinism that underlies them. Those myths create the impression that buildings are helping to renew the social contract when in fact they may be shredding it. The mythology is evident not only in the design of buildings but in the rhetoric used to describe them.

Here, for example, is a slide show mounted to promote a new office complex that is scheduled to rise in a downscale part of town. The presentation is packaged in the familiar format of Before and After. Before is a series of archetypal images of urban blight: decaying storefronts; graffiti-sprayed walls; adult-video shops. With After, the blight has disappeared. In its place, smooth granite facades rise from litter-free sidewalks, doors of polished brass open onto inviting lobbies and enclosed shopping arcades. The building skin has been styled to resemble distinguished older buildings in the neighborhood: design will minimize disruption.

Since the city can't afford further erosion of middle-class life, it is hard to resist the logic of this presentation. But there is another logic at work here, which the slides don't show. In the city where every piece of property is valued for its potential profit, every block is vulnerable to redevelopment, and every person inhabits a state of potential eviction. Fewer and fewer people can buy themselves out of that prospect.

In a sense, the architect's Before and After presentation is precisely reversed. The new office towers are not the cure for the run-down street. They are one of its causes. They perpetuate a logic of displacement that can lead to people living in boxes. And this is not a purely local matter of displacing some poor souls to another part of town. Saskia Sassen, a professor of urban planning at Columbia University, believes that globalization is creating an entire culture of eviction the world over.

And here is a report on "edge cities," those lunar outcroppings of tall buildings clustered along the highways, which urges us to interpret these places as spontaneous expressions of popular culture. Since they are not planned by municipal authorities and are evidently successful, they are taken to represent the popular will. In fact, they are built on the elimination of popular will. The whole point of edge cities is that they are placed beyond the reach of municipalities and their tiresome democratic regulations. True, there are no homeless people. There are also no planning agencies, no city councils, and no community boards to impede market pressures. No taxation, no representation.

Here is a prospectus for a "neotraditional" town. It includes some excellent features. The close proximity of houses to one another and to shops uses land far more efficiently than the average suburb, and it decreases dependence on the car. Design regulations seek an agreeable balance between visual unity and diversity. Moreover, the vigor with which these model communities have been promoted in recent years has been constructive. People have been awakened to the degree to which urbanism has spread beyond the political purview of the older central cities.

Nonetheless, the use of the term *urban* to describe these towns is as perilous as it is premature. These communities are primarily residential; two of the most widely touted examples, Seaside and Windsor, are Florida resort communities. Though they may include shops and restaurants, they remain solidly planted on the consuming side of the economic equation. They leave production out of the picture. Only those with the correct consumer credentials are served by them.

But one of the major challenges facing American cities is to integrate consumption with production and thereby generate a broad range of jobs. Otherwise, those outside the consumer loop—mainly young people and members of minorities—stand little chance of gaining access to it. True, many older central cities have not met this challenge, either. But at least they make it harder for people to think that they are grappling with major urban issues when in fact they are escaping them.

Here is a book of beautiful pictures by an architect who has forsaken conventional practice in order to draw imaginary cities. This is an alluring path, and many architects have recently taken it. In a field that has been so roughly battered by market pressures, paper architecture seems to offer idealism a refuge.

But the belief that such refuges still exist may be the most alarming myth of all. The drawing has always been a marketing tool for architects, a means of gaining clients as well as academic positions, lectureships, foundation subsidies, and the precious commodity of renown. But the drawing was once a pledge. It came with the understanding that an architect would use the tools of the profession to change material reality for the better. For the paper architect, the marketing tool has become an end in itself.

Architects are justifiably annoyed by the suggestion that they have a special responsibility to solve the problem of homelessness. For one thing, many of them aren't doing that well themselves these days. No profession has been more affected by the recession. And architects have hardly turned their back on the problem. Many firms have volunteered to design shelters, and the pure dollar value of that service is perhaps not sufficiently appreciated. It involves a good deal more than doodling on a napkin.

Other architects have gone in for guerrilla tactics, setting up huts and lean-tos on public land at night when the police aren't looking. And many of them have simply gone numb. Like everyone else, they're worn down from trying to figure out whether homelessness is a problem or a condition. And they're fatigued that they can't design a private house or a concert hall without inciting someone out there to protest: What about the homeless?

Still, many architects believe that their profession lost its ethical core with the collapse of government housing programs in the 1970s. And even if architecture can't take government's place, it could do more to expose the mythologies that help to keep government officials off the hook. Architectural mythmakers are not cynics. They may be trying simply to mitigate the cruelty of the marketplace, which is hardly an ignoble ambition, or to express an ideal that would be difficult to attain under even the best social circumstances. An architect has the right of any artist to speak of the difference between life as it is and life as it should be.

The problem is that the expression of that difference can become a way of reinforcing it. The fabled pragmatism of the architect can easily become a pernicious form of resignation to the status quo, leading further and further away from the possibility of reform. When the historian Heinrich Klotz says that the defining characteristic of Postmodernism is its capacity for visual fiction, he means it as a compliment. He applauds the rise of the imagination in a profession where banality is often taken as a sign of virtue. But what if postmodern fiction is just the feverish hallucination of the shell-shocked?

Susana Torre, an architect and educator in New York, probably speaks for many these days when she says that the focus of the profession must shift from "representation" to "production." That's a concise if academic way of saying there has been too much emphasis on symbolic form, not enough grappling with the political and economic tools that could enable architects to exchange the symbols for the reality they represent. There's a difference, in other words, between decorating a building with a pineapple, the traditional sign of hospitality, and seeking out a government program to finance housing for deinstitutionalized people, as Ms. Torre has done with her students at Parsons School of Design. You don't have to think that one is superior to the other to recognize the importance of distinguishing between them.

Me, I like pineapples. The juicier the better. For me, the problem isn't representation. It's misrepresentation. It's all the propaganda that has grown up over the years and still lingers in the air like smoke over a battlefield. I hope architects, and others, will pressure Henry Cisneros, secretary of housing and urban development, to fulfill his pledge to revive federal programs for housing. But architects don't have to wait for Mr. Cisneros's permission to clear the air of smoke. If they want to strengthen the profession's ethical core, they could start by sorting out the difference between symbols and lies, art and public relations, myths that pull people into the same picture and those that leave some people out in the cold.

January 9, 1994

RUDE AWAKENING; QUAKE JARS ASSUMPTIONS: A CRITIC'S VIEW

Buildings aren't supposed to murder architecture critics. It's meant to be the other way around. And it is particularly wounding to be menaced by a building you love: the Shangri-La Hotel in Santa Monica, a hostelry beloved by architects and photographers for its sleek Art Deco design and its spectacular views of sea, sky, and palm trees. But these features didn't amount to much when the earthquake struck last Monday.

After the bounce out of bed, the crawl across a heaving floor toward the supposed haven of a doorway, the prayers and curses, the amazement that any building could survive the jolts this one had just been put through, I pulled on clothes and went five flights down to the sidewalk.

The darkness, the cold, the starry sky, the impromptu dress and dazed demeanor of the guests, and even the marine look of the hotel itself inspired thoughts of the *Titanic*, particularly when the word went around that the 6.6 quake might be just the foreshock of a bigger one. The sea that ordinarily looked so idyllic could rise up and swallow us. The whiffs of gas that teased the nostrils could signal an imminent explosion.

For me, the gut issue of survival was suddenly superimposed on professional concerns. I was scheduled to visit two buildings that day, both designed by architects I admire. And for many architecture critics today, the entire city of Los Angeles is Shangri-La—home to some of the most gifted architects now practicing.

But the earthquake made brutally clear that, however remarkable their talents, these architects are operating on a very thin veneer. Indeed, their job is to create that veneer. They design the alluring visual surface that enables people to imagine that they can enjoy a stable life on top of quicksand. After the quake, there was much praise for the maintenance of civility in the face of chaos. Architects translate civility into steel, stone, and glass. But the earthquake showed that architectural civility is not so benign. In a flash, it inverted the usual relationship of the city to its surroundings, revealing that nature is the order, civilization the chaos. At 7:00 a.m., an inspector came by and declared the Shangri-La unsafe.

Eric Owen Moss showed up two hours later, as planned. A luminary of Los Angeles architecture, Mr. Moss drove me to Culver City to look at one of his projects, a commercial building nearing completion. On the way, we took in the sights that those without power couldn't see on their televisions: the cracks in the walls of high-rises; the piles of shattered glass and tumbled-down brick; the ugly fissures in expanses of tile that only a day before had looked pristine. The most unusual sight of all was the people walking on streets where people never walk.

We were also scanning the windshield, on this insultingly sunny day, for some correlation between what we were seeing and the facts coming in over the radio, though the constant adjustment of the numbers gave even facts the unstable quality of the earth under pressure. The death toll that by week's end exceeded fifty people dashed the optimism of early announcements. Not until nightfall would it be estimated that forty-seven thousand people had sought refuge at Red Cross shelters. Since this was a holiday, we saw no sign of the impact that the collapse of three freeway overpasses would make on the traffic circulation that is this city's lifeblood.

What Can't Be Measured

Effects on the quality of people's lives are not easily quantifiable. The estimate of $7 billion in damages, repeated endlessly, began to sound more like superstition than fact: a tribute to an ideal of objectivity that the earthquake itself made mockery of. The news that the quake originated with a previously unknown fault rocked the security that flows from our investment in scientific expertise.

Attempts to explain why some structures are safer than others repeatedly collided against the information that there are different kinds of quakes, that they affect structures differently, and that the greatest hazard may lie in supposing that earthquake-proof design is an absolute proposition. The facts were geared to one dubious idea: that recovery, however expensive, however long it takes, is ultimately possible.

When we finally reached Mr. Moss's building, it turned out to be an anticlimax, even though the design appeared to have much in common with the fractured cityscape we'd just driven through. A large, tilted cube dramatically cantilevered on curved steel trusses, it is a poem of precariousness, a precisely controlled upheaval in space. When completed, the building will deliver a strong aesthetic jolt. On Monday, with the construction scaffolding jiggling around it, the project barely set off a mild perceptual tremor. The building wasn't damaged, only upstaged.

My next stop was a building that expresses even more emphatically the artificiality of California's urban veneer. Designed by the San Francisco firm Holt Hinshaw Pfau Jones, UCLA's nearly completed Chiller Plant is a tour de force of expressionistic technology. With a muscular superstructure of cooling towers, chimneys, and ducts rising boldly from a redbrick base, the plant houses the equipment that air-conditions buildings throughout UCLA's vast Westwood campus. The building's job, in short, is to change the climate. To its credit, the building makes no effort to hide what it's about. On the contrary, Wes Jones, the project's chief designer, is strongly committed to the idea that architecture should reveal the forces that fuel the social engine. "Architecture is supposed to mediate between people and nature," he said. But he acknowledged that buildings can be a means of refusing to reckon with nature. The Chiller Plant enables UCLA's architects to design buildings without full regard for the natural climate. Although it's honest about its function, the function itself is dubious.

Mr. Moss's building puts the critic in a similar quandary. It, too, expresses something pertinent about the built environment. Instead of perpetuating an appearance of ordered normality, the design's skewed forms call attention to the profound lack of order that has led America's second-largest city to be built where perhaps there should be no city at all.

Both buildings deal knowingly with the condition of inhabiting an artificial veneer. But they also extend the veneer. The work of these architects is far superior to countless buildings that do not even acknowledge the veneer. But their excellence will do nothing to remove people from harm's way when the earth rumbles.

And neither will the rumbling. People went out of their way to say they wouldn't think of leaving. The pleasure of living in the warm, golden light; the proximity to ocean, mountains, and desert; the glamour of the California lifestyle, not to mention the schools, museums, industries, agriculture, and everything else that makes civilization worth talking about— these, they say, are worth the risk of earthquakes, fires, and droughts.

Yet is it fair to expect the taxpayers to subsidize that risk? Californians bridle at the question. Elsewhere, Americans live at risk of hurricanes, floods, tornadoes. A fault line runs through Manhattan. Las Vegas is a mirage that thinks it's an oasis. The country is subsidized by cheap oil, cheap labor, the profligate consumption of natural resources. An earthquake should alert people to the folly of disregarding nature. But who wants to wake up from the American Dream.

January 23, 1994

ARCHITECTURE AS SOCIAL ACTION, AND VICE VERSA

Early this month, at a lecture sponsored by New York's Architectural League, Frank Gehry took a shot at those who have been calling on architects to be more socially responsible. It wasn't a cheap shot. It was an honest, spirited defense of values that matter deeply to Gehry and should also matter to anyone who cares about the vitality of the art form he practices. But as a critique of what is going on in architecture today, his comments somewhat missed the mark.

Not long ago, Gehry told the standing-room-only audience, he had turned down an invitation to join a panel discussion on Star Architects and Social Responsibility. He was right to smell a setup: the mere pairing of those two phrases is implicitly judgmental. Stars, after all, aren't meant to be responsible. They just twinkle. Star architects like Gehry, went the unstated message, don't really give a damn about the homeless. They just want to glorify themselves with snazzy artistic statements.

"Just being an architect is an act of social responsibility," Mr. Gehry said. "Even the strangest concoctions of our imaginations have to do with humanist values—with people, society and context. We're all part of the human fabric. And to have this backlash now is strange. I suppose it's human. But I wish people would stop it."

This wasn't the first time Gehry had been put on the defensive. In *City of Quartz*, a 1990 book about Los Angeles, Mike Davis assailed Gehry's "hip portfolio" (the Goldwyn Library in Hollywood, the Loyola Law School building in Los Angeles) as "a nostalgic evocation of revolutionary constructivism and a mercenary celebration of bourgeois-decadent minimalism."

Still, not everyone who has raised the issue of social responsibility is part of an anti-aesthetic backlash. It does not require a great mental stretch to admire Frank Gehry's buildings and to feel compassion for the homeless at the same time. Indeed, his buildings are best appreciated as works that heighten social awareness by formal means. Mike Davis gets the point better than most when he writes that Gehry's work "clarifies the underlying relations of repression, surveillance and exclusion that characterize the fragmented, paranoid spatiality toward which Los Angeles seems to aspire." Not the ideal critical rave, perhaps, but at least Mr. Davis grasps that Mr. Gehry's buildings are not formalist abstractions.

While Mr. Gehry evidently finds his stardom distasteful, he nonetheless believes that the celebrity of architects stands for something good. When he was younger, he told the audience, there were only four or five star architects in the country. Now there are many more whose names are widely known. Isn't this a welcome sign that the public is paying more attention to what architects do? It's not architecture's fault if fame is the index of public interest.

But there's a critical difference between well-known architects of the postwar years and those who came to prominence in the 1970s and '80s. As the sociologist Robert Gutman observes in his book *Architectural Practice*, firms that specialize in the visual packaging of buildings are a recent phenomenon in America. Thirty years ago, a firm assumed responsibility for the technical as well as the aesthetic aspects of building. Today, major projects are often the work of collaborations in which one firm provides the expressive forms while another provides the nuts and bolts.

The reason is not that some architects consider themselves superior to grunt work. Often, clients prefer to have technical work performed by firms that specialize in it. A formalist architect like Peter Eisenman, for example, would not have secured the commission for the Greater Columbus Convention Center had he not joined forces with Richard Trott & Partners, a Columbus firm. An association with the Boston firm Payette Associates has enabled Venturi, Scott Brown & Associates to focus on the facades and main public spaces of science buildings at the University of Pennsylvania, Princeton, and UCLA.

Whether or not this division of labor has advanced the art of architecture, it is not likely to be reversed. The trend throughout the profession has been toward specialization. Yet even die-hard formalists must concede that other areas of specialization are cast into shadow by architecture stars. Not just the nuts and bolts beneath the building skin but the increasingly diverse kinds of practice that lie outside the skin altogether: from educating communities about urban design to drafting public policy on housing, transportation, and public spaces; from documenting historic excavations to imagining potential applications for virtual reality.

These "alternative" practices are changing the shape of architecture. For many architects now entering the profession, creative fulfillment is no longer staked to the design of the individual building. To a degree, this is a realistic response to the dwindling job market for conventional services. But it also reflects the idealistic expectation that the profession should accommodate a broader range of interests. The call for greater social responsibility is one expression of that belief. It's a way of redistributing the stardust, of gaining public recognition for architects whose work affects the environment in unconventional ways.

This expanded field of practice cannot be neatly divided into Art and Social Action. That simplistic division is dissolving within a broader cultural framework. Clearly, there is as much room for vision in the framing of public policy as in the design of a facade. By the same token, a facade doesn't automatically rate the status of art simply because it offers a visual image. If it's important to recognize the social dimension of visual forms like Gehry's, it is also important to discern that architecture comes in forms that don't make striking photographs.

None of this is going to topple the well-designed building from its lofty cultural pedestal. After all, it's not only glossy magazine photography and '80s pizazz that have equated architecture and visual images. It is thousands of years of cultural history. And anyone who serves that tradition as capably as Frank Gehry can twinkle all he likes.

But the fact remains that formal innovation has lost a good deal of the luster it acquired in the 1970s and '80s, when architects were busting loose from the restrictions of the modern canon. Once the principle was established that architects enjoyed virtually unlimited freedom to design in any style, the dazzling diversity of postmodern forms began to lose its creative spark. Diversity of practices, not diversity of forms: that is the news from the edge of architecture today.

February 27, 1994

AN APPRAISAL;
COLUMBUS CIRCLE'S CHANGING FACE:
More than Geometry

There are just three weeks left before the clock runs out on Mortimer Zuckerman's deal to develop the Coliseum site at Columbus Circle. And last week, Donald Trump jumped into this less-than-charmed circle with a proposal to reclad the bleak exterior of the former Gulf & Western Building and convert the interior from offices to condominiums. Meanwhile, one block to the north, the owners of the Mayflower Hotel are studying a plan to build an office tower.

Like the *Niña*, the *Pinta*, and the *Santa Maria*, these three projects could well transport Columbus, or at least his towering, century-old statue, into a whole new world.

It is a troubled site, and its civic prominence only magnifies its architectural incoherence. Stylistically chaotic, unable even to control the flow of traffic that bumps and scrapes around its corroded perimeter, Columbus Circle is a monument to New York's inability to bring distinction or even sanity to its most eminent locations.

Still, it is no wonder that Columbus Circle is a mess, for it is a meeting point of extraordinary urban pressures: a subway hub; a portal not only to Central Park but to the Upper West Side; one of Broadway's periodic interruptions of the Manhattan street grid; a transition between the staid residential boulevard of Central Park West and the commercial corridor that extends down Broadway to Times Square.

It will take more than three big real estate developments to balance these pressures with poise. Indeed, the trio could end up fragmenting the cityscape still further. But this new cycle of building at least offers an occasion to look at the historical context their architects must reckon with.

A Century of Styles

The ticking sound of Mr. Zuckerman's countdown could well be coming from the ground itself, for it is possible to view Columbus Circle as a gigantic clock, an erratic urban timepiece that has been fitfully keeping time for just over a century. Styles mark the hours, starting with the turn-of-the-century City Beautiful movement, represented here by the Columbus Monument at the hub, built in 1892, and by the 1913 *Maine* Monument, the ship of statues that comes sailing in from the park corner.

The ups and downs of modern architecture are registered here, including a good example of Modern design at 240 Central Park South, an apartment and retail complex designed by Mayer & Whittlesey in 1941. With its strongly massed residential blocks rising from a gracefully scalloped retail arcade, this building demonstrates that modern architecture could be highly sympathetic to its surroundings. Even Robert A. M. Stern, an architect not usually enthusiastic about Modern buildings, hails the design, in his book *New York 1930*, as "an exemplar of humane values applied to the problem of high-density city living and as a finely tuned instrument of urbanism."

Does anyone have anything nice to say about the Coliseum? With its facade of dull tan brick, studded with state insignia like a row of grotesquely enlarged souvenir cufflinks, the 1956 building, designed by Leon and Lionel Levy, has long epitomized the fatal proximity of modern minimalism to timeless cheapness. Still, as one approaches the building along Central Park South, the stodgy apparition can nonetheless give rise to a sense of wonder: someone thought this was a good idea.

Two Columbus Circle, now occupied by the city's Department of Cultural Affairs, represented the initial stirrings of dissatisfaction with modernist orthodoxy. The building's architect, Edward Durell Stone, was one of the first to break ranks with his modern contemporaries, and this white marble bauble, originally designed in 1965 for Huntington Hartford's contentiously anti-modern Gallery of Modern Art, threw many architects into an uproar. With its vaguely Venetian loggia and ground-floor colonnade, this cultural campanile violated the modernist taboo against historically derived decoration.

Alas, the taboo was still in place five years later, when Thomas E. Stanley designed the Gulf & Western tower. Urbanistically the weakest building in the circle, the building neither holds the circle's perimeter edge nor respects the lower scale of the Central Park West buildings beyond. Instead of molding itself to Columbus Circle, Gulf & Western simply added new circles of its own: a sunken entrance to the subway station, a raised kiosk for the cinema buried beneath its forlorn plaza. By 1970, however, the Modern movement's ideological foundations had been irremediably weakened: a fact metaphorically confirmed by the Gulf & Western building's legendary sway in high winds.

But Columbus Circle is more than a collection of architectural styles. Its individual buildings represent different urban visions. City Beautiful architects envisioned a city of stately marble vistas, lined with classical colonnades, statues, and fountains. Modern architects imagined a vertical city of soaring towers, rapid movement, and abstract geometric forms.

The context of Columbus Circle, in other words, is not harmony and wholeness; it is conflict and irresolution. It expresses the whim of a city impatient to get on with the next thing. Before we're even halfway around the circle, we have dropped the idea we started out with and begun to look for something else.

Shrinking Towers

Indeed, Mortimer Zuckerman, developer of the Coliseum site, has changed course several times without budging from the same spot. His original design, by Moshe Safdie, called for a pair of towers, one of them seventy-two stories tall, clad in granite and glass. Stodgy the design was not. Perhaps not since the Guggenheim Museum had an architect offered to let loose on the city such an exuberant display of structural acrobatics.

But this was a time when even advocates of modern architecture had conceded that the movement's impact on the urban fabric had been destructive. With its assertive geometric abstraction, its pride in novel forms, its aloof detachment from its surroundings, Safdie's design waved the world's biggest red flag in the face of changing taste.

In 1988 Mr. Zuckerman returned with a new proposal, designed by David Childs of Skidmore, Owings & Merrill. Reduced 20 percent in size, the scheme was radically different in style. Its slim, asymmetrically composed towers were designed to evoke the Art Deco apartment buildings of Central Park West, though by now the term *modern classicism* had been resurrected to describe the style, presumably to purge it of campy associations with white telephones and chrome cocktail shakers.

Unabashedly romantic in its evocation of an earlier New York, the design clothed the profiteering of the 1980s with the glamour of the 1920s, another era of rampant development but one to which distance had lent undeniable enchantment. And this, too, was an urban vision, the product of a time when many postmodern architects believed that history could heal the ugly gashes of modernity. The circular arcade at the building's base, in particular, expressed the postmodern infatuation with the unified urban ensembles of European cities. It was time to turn back the clock.

Scaled Down Again

In the waning days of the Dinkins administration, Mr. Zuckerman announced a new plan, this time sharply reduced in scale. Instead of two mixed-use towers, the plan envisions a single, 600-foot-tall office tower rising on the northern half of the two-block site. It would contain 1.1 million square feet of office and retail space, a reduction of 53 percent from the previous design. The residential portion of the project has been eliminated, and the existing office tower at 10 Columbus Circle would be retained. As in the previous plan, a curving retail arcade would extend along Columbus Circle between Fifty-eighth and Sixtieth streets, though this feature would be redesigned.

The change would not only reduce the bulk of this project, but could also lead to a more thoughtful architectural resolution. Columbus Circle is never going to have the stylistic unity of the Place des Victoires in Paris or the Circus at Bath. Yet for all its stylistic incoherence, the place does possess a latent continuity, an order not of space but of time. And though Columbus Circle is an abysmal example of it, this is nonetheless the order at which New York excels: the layering of visions over time to produce a texture unforeseen by the designers of individual buildings.

Yet, as contemporary architects like Robert Venturi and Frank Gehry have shown, the development of this urban texture need not be left to chance. There is a poetry in heterogeneity that can be heightened by architects who are sensitive to its expressive possibilities. Those who design for an urban space like Columbus Circle confront what Mr. Venturi calls the "difficult whole": messy but also vital; irregular but not dull.

At the moment, Columbus Circle is far from this pleasing democratic condition. It is both irregular and dull, a hodgepodge of the bland. But the new projects in the works could liven things up. Columbus would be at home in a place as vibrant and diverse as the land he sighted.

March 27, 1994

BACK TO THE FUTURE

Modern architecture, it is sometimes said, took a wrong turn in the years after World War II. A movement that had started out in the 1920s with an idealistic agenda for social change had transformed itself into the slick style of American corporate culture. But there was a time when the Modern movement and corporate America were not thought to be opposed in their aims. From the late 1940s to the early 1960s, the industrialist and the designer were commonly viewed as partners, allies in the pursuit of humane goals. General Electric and the disciples of the Bauhaus were of one mind in supposing that progress was the twentieth century's most important product.

And for those who grew up imbibing the atmosphere of those years, modernism's "wrong turn" made for memories that remain extraordinarily potent. Those images of late modernism are now resurfacing, as architects born in the postwar decades ease into the productive phase of their careers. For these architects, a full generation younger than those who formulated the postmodern framework, the Modern movement is not the aesthetic equivalent of a father figure crying out for Oedipal assault. It more nearly resembles a lost paradise, a mechanical Eden from which contemporary society has been rudely expelled.

These younger professionals spent their childhoods in the golden age of the Affluent Society, the optimistic era that adopted the stripped-down, glass-walled International Style as a conspicuous sign of prosperity at home and global influence abroad. In contrast to the socialist utopia envisioned by the Modern movement's European pioneers, this was marketplace modernism, American-made and proud of it. The messianic fervor of the early twentieth century's architectural manifestoes had given way to the visceral thrill of physical realization. "Let us rebuild everything," Le Corbusier declared in the 1920s; by the '50s, that declaration had led to tangible results, with buildings that reshaped the way people looked at the landscape, at art, at city streets, at the workplace, and at the home.

The period was rich in individual buildings of great merit, such as Lever House and the Guggenheim Museum in New York City, and the Case Study houses, a series of modern prototypes designed by a variety of architects and built in and around Los Angeles in the postwar years. These designs carried the ideal of experimentation forward into practical application. Each of them showed how new materials, new methods of construction, and new visual and spatial relationships could produce new perspectives on familiar places and institutions.

But these examples, remarkable as they were, were also episodes in a larger story: the broadening of an avant-garde aesthetic into the cultural mainstream. Modernism at midcentury was still part of the canon of educated taste. Along with abstract painting, atonal music, and New Wave film, it held its place in the curriculum of cultural sophistication. And the commercial victory of modern design pointed toward the possibility that a cherished liberal ideal might soon be attained. An equilibrium could be struck between educated taste and the mass market. After all, executives at The Four Seasons and office workers at Zum Zum lunched in the same design universe. What was to prevent the expansion of the egalitarian spirit to the culture at large? Wouldn't a rising tide lift all art forms?

Though modernism had become the academy, it was still a young academy. And its output was powerfully appealing to young minds. The shiny newness of modern buildings, so like a mechanical birthday toy. The gadget fascination of functionalism. The magic disappearing act performed by walls that dissolved into glass or into the unstructured interior of the open floor plan. Above all, perhaps, there was the narcissistic pleasure that flowed to the young from the prevailing postwar idea that all this was being done for them—for the future. All the glass towers, the superhighways, even the rocket ships so glowingly described by Werner von Braun on *Man in Space*, a late '50s Walt Disney television program: these revolutionary designs had been created for the race of gilded children who would never know the Depression except as a tale told to foster gratitude for the abundant fruits of progress.

To be born into this environment was to be doubly privileged, or perhaps cursed: to mistake the privilege as a birthright, a natural order of things. And, for a brief moment, before the '60s turned into "The Sixties," the young had one foot in the ionosphere of infinite possibility that modernism had spread before it. The future was here, or perhaps just a short flight away on an Eastern Airlines Whisperjet, an icon of the '60s with its crisp white fuselage trimmed with blue stripes and black sans serif type, its flight attendants dressed in Jacqueline Kennedy–style outfits, its image explicitly marketed to youth with the jaunty blue-and-white youth-fare card. Beyond, the whole world beckoned, like the stylized globe on the Pan Am flight bag, another mesmerizing symbol of the blue-and-white life (before metal detectors): the dream of drifting through cloud and sky toward endless happy landings.

And then the dream crashed. A movement that had started out in opposition to the status quo found itself under attack for having become it. Instead of resembling an enlightened coalition between art and industry, modernism came to seem like a mindless juggernaut with designs on everything in sight. The idea that modernism was historically inevitable, a claim often put forward by the movement's advocates, now seemed like the best possible reason to resist it. The idealistic globalism of the International Style had become indistinguishable from the threat of imperial overreach. The blue-and-white life was no longer so pure when bombers began streaking across Southeast Asian skies. The machine in the garden was apparently killing off all the plants.

This about-face in perception demanded something more than simply modifying modern principles. Rather, the principles themselves had to be rejected, as if the entire movement had fallen prey to the market law of planned obsolescence. And, in a sense, it had. The pact with industry turned out to be somewhat Faustian. The pioneer figures of modernism were gone, and with them the movement's creative spark. Consumption, not creation, had become design's dominant force; novelty and change, its governing principles.

To an extent, market forces are also responsible for reviving the aura of modern design. "New Modernism" as a concept fits neatly into the theme of "return" that has been a marketing motif for two decades. At the same time, the modern aura appeals to architects who are looking for fundamentalist principles that can redeem architecture from market tyranny. The expression of structure, the paring away of ornament, the reduction of space to eloquent void: once again, these concepts are seen to deliver design from the superficial whimsies of image, stagecraft, and style. There are also those who concur with the German philosopher Jürgen Habermas that modernity is "an incomplete project," that architects should not abandon modernism's overarching ideal of reason, even if society can do no more than reach fumblingly toward it.

The prospect of a modernist revival is not likely to delight those who believe that architecture has gained from the awareness of history promoted by the Postmodern movement. Actually, today's reappraisal of modernism is partly the result of that movement. For with the deepening of historical awareness has come the understanding that modernism was not a radical break with the past. Rather, it was a flowering of ideas that had been germinating in Western civilization since the Enlightenment. What is driving architects toward modernism today is a fusion of personal and cultural memory: a desire to reconnect with a time in their lives and a moment in architecture that were both suffused with radiant promise.

April 10, 1994

QUEENS WEST: WHY NOT SOMETHING GREAT?

Next month, ground will be broken on Queens West, the seventy-four-acre residential and commercial development on a spectacular waterfront site across the East River from United Nations headquarters. By fall, con-

struction is expected to begin on the project's first building, a thirty-nine-
story apartment building designed by Cesar Pelli. A lot of planning has
gone into this $2.3 billion project, and it has produced some excellent fea-
tures. With the river at its doorstep, the Manhattan skyline for a backdrop, and Grand Central Terminal just one subway stop away, Queens
West is shaping up to be a wonderful place to live.

But for those concerned about the vitality of architecture in New York,
Queens West may turn out to be a disturbing place to visit. Like Battery
Park City, the project provides a framework in which individual buildings
can be joined together in a cohesive urban whole. What it has yet to do is
address one of Battery Park City's most conspicuous shortcomings: its
failure to nurture the architectural creativity that could bring the urban
whole to life. The shortcoming is not limited to Battery Park City. New
York has seen few buildings of genuine distinction arise in recent years.
The issue raised by Queens West is whether the public sector has a responsibility to revive an art form that has languished in historical pastiche.

Queens West, which is sponsored by a triad of government agencies
(the New York State Urban Development Corporation, the New York
City Economic Development Corporation, and the Port Authority of
New York), will be one of the biggest and most visible in a string of recent
real estate development partnerships between the public and private sectors. Conceived ten years ago, at the height of the real estate boom, the
project was originally planned to accommodate back office space, along
with some luxury housing. Subsequently retooled in response to recessionary realities, the final plan envisions a residential development for
people with high, middle, and low incomes. The commercial component
has been reduced to a cluster of three office towers and a hotel.

As at Battery Park City and the redevelopment of Forty-second Street,
an Urban Development Corporation subsidiary has provided a master
plan, infrastructure, public amenities, and overall supervision. Private
firms will develop individual plots in accordance with the master plan. At
Queens West, there are nineteen such parcels, stretching along a mile and
a half of waterfront. These will be developed incrementally, as the economy permits. Overall, the site is about three-quarters the size of Battery
Park City, roughly the size of Riverside South, Donald Trump's planned
development on the Upper West Side of Manhattan. And, like both projects, Queens West aspires to quality in architecture and urban design.

The Queens West master plan, prepared by the New York architecture
firms Beyer Blinder Belle and Gruzen Samton, recalls a number of Battery
Park City's most prominent features. The four commercial towers will be
flanked on the north and south by residential neighborhoods. Streets from
the Queens grid system will be extended onto the site to create continuity

with the adjacent community of Hunters Point and provide "view corridors" toward the river and the skyline beyond. A waterfront esplanade, plaza, and a generous network of community parks, all intelligently designed by Lee Weintraub and Thomas Balsley, will provide the area with twenty-eight acres of beautifully landscaped areas for strolling and recreation. Public artworks will adorn them.

Queens West is by no means a carbon copy of Battery Park City. Perhaps the most conspicuous difference is the seventeen-acre waterfront park, which will preserve the ragged edge, the spatial variety, and even some old industrial relics of the existing waterfront. Two big gantry cranes will grace the plaza with ready-made arches. Shopping will be dispersed along a central avenue that curves to maximize river views. Towers will peak along this spine, descending in height toward the waterfront and the existing community on both sides. At the southern tip of the site, wedge-shaped buildings will form a circular cluster.

But the design guidelines architects must follow are clearly descended from those devised for Battery Park City in 1979. They will encourage the design of buildings that recall the architecture of prewar New York. Towers will sit on bases designed to maintain traditional street walls. Walls are to be of earth-colored stone, masonry, or tile. Metal panels, reflective glass, and dark tinted glass are banned. Air-conditioning and other rooftop equipment must be screened behind distinctive building tops. In Queens West, as at Battery Park City, architecture will reside chiefly in the manipulation of the building skin to create a harmonious urban image.

There is no better building skin manipulator in the business than Cesar Pelli, and his design sets a high standard for what can be achieved within the guidelines. If Queens West's architecture is supposed to look backward, one may as well look back at the best, and Mr. Pelli's design, a bow-front tower clad with a vibrantly patterned red, orange, and light yellow brick facade, is a sophisticated echo of Rockefeller Center. Shallow vertical setbacks, terminating in balconies, evoke the RCA—now GE—Building's sleekly modulated wings, while horizontal bands of contrasting brick, set off by vertical columns of windows, recall unexecuted studies for the building's skin. The result is a more robust, contoured version of the understated (and underrated) apartment tower that Mr. Pelli designed for the Museum of Modern Art in 1985.

But what if you don't think that architecture should resemble a prewar icon? What if you think that architects ought to look to the present for inspiration? And what is the responsibility of the public sector, in these public-private partnerships, to support architecture that breaks the mold?

Battery Park City's 1979 master plan was a superlative idea for its time, even a visionary one. It emerged from a unique convergence of commercial and architectural interests. The Battery Park City Authority had a responsibility to make a financial success of a troubled property. Faced with a history of doomed, aggressively modern designs, the authority determined to create buildings of proven popular appeal.

Its decision to model the design guidelines after places like Gramercy Park and Gracie Square was not based on some abstract idea of beauty or urbanism. Indeed, the abstraction of modern architecture is what they were trying to get away from. The authority modeled the guidelines after places where people wanted to live and were willing to pay a high price for the privilege. If Gramercy Park was a desirable place to live, a place that resembled Gramercy Park would attract paying customers.

At the same time, Battery Park City's aesthetic judgments were driven by something more than hard-line economics. In the 1970s many architects were also looking to popular taste for aesthetic guidance. One of the core ideas of postmodernism was that architects had to get off the *Fountainhead* kick of disregarding public preference. The popularity of places like Gramercy Park was not just an index to commercial values. It was a sign of social values as well. By learning from places with popular appeal, architects hoped to reestablish their connection with a public that had grown intolerant of modern architecture's Promethean stance.

Fifteen years later, however, the defect in this logic has become more apparent. Popularity and social value are not the same thing. Sometimes the socially valuable thing to do is to resist the idea of proven popularity— not for the sake of defiance but to test ideas from which the public might benefit. It is far from clear, moreover, that the way to the public's heart is to cast new parts of the city in the image of old ones. If people choose to live in the older urban centers today, that is partly because they value them as places where new ideas are born, where the atmosphere vibrates around the possibility that some new form of beauty or meaning will emerge in a painting, a book, a song.

Though Battery Park City was valuable as a corrective to modern urbanism, it did not cultivate a creative atmosphere for architecture. Instead, things fell into an arrangement whereby architects were expected to play it safe while public artists got to strut their creative stuff. As an experiment, the arrangement was worth testing. It was beneficial for architects to learn from past examples how to connect buildings to the street and to one another. But amid all this gracious harmony the eye searches in vain for a building that looks connected to the present. There isn't one building with something fresh or stimulating to say about urban life today, the way the United Nations complex embodied the aspirations of the postwar world.

.   .   .

Since the 1970s, as government money for housing and urban development has dwindled, public-private partnerships have become increasingly instrumental in defining the city's future. These partnerships ought to be begging our best architects to reckon with that future. The sympathetic support that the public sector offers artists through its Percent for Art programs should be extended to include the art of building.

One way to accomplish this would be to enlarge the public's role in the selection of architects and the approval of designs. At Battery Park City, a distinguished fine-arts committee oversaw the choice of artists and their proposals. A similar panel, composed of a changing group of first-rate outside advisers, could lift the level of architecture at Queens West. Juried competitions could be organized to select the designers of some buildings, like the United Nations office building that Queens West hopes to attract to the site.

It is true that the sponsors of large developments like Queens West must deal with community boards and public officials who are not invariably receptive to new ideas. They must also deal with developers who resent being told what to do. These forces can be formidable deterrents to creativity, and it's no use pretending that aesthetics will take priority over economics on the agenda of an agency like the Urban Development Corporation. By the same token, it would be foolish to mistake an economic success for an aesthetic triumph. And that is the risk of repeating a formula that is fifteen years old.

May 22, 1994

IN PARIS, A BUILDING THAT MELTS AWAY LIKE ICE

Something seen in a dream, at once invasive and elusive: few buildings capture that unsettling, contradictory power of the subconscious image. Not many even try. No recent building that I can recall reels in the surreal as stylishly as the new Cartier Foundation in Paris designed by Jean Nouvel, the French architect best known for the Arab World Institute. Some buildings go up in flames. This one melts away like ice. Its crystalline, geometrically precise surfaces of glass and steel dissolve in the light into silhouettes, clouds, reflections, the traffic, trees, and skyline of historic Montparnasse.

Talk about Les Must. Those headed to Paris this summer will want to put 261 Boulevard Raspail at the top of their itinerary. For once, the support that the French extend to contemporary architecture inspires not only respect for good intentions but awe at a building it has produced. You can linger here for an hour or longer and not begrudge the time subtracted from a visit to Ste.-Chapelle. In fact, these two very different landmarks have something in common: both join the architect's art to the jeweler's. Medieval craftsmen, legendarily, ground up sapphires to enrich the color of stained glass. At Cartier's chapel to contemporaneity, Nouvel gives industrial glass the restrained opulence of flawlessly cut gems.

The building serves a dual function. With most of the office space dedicated to Cartier's far-flung enterprises in labeled luxury, the building is also headquarters for the Cartier Foundation for Contemporary Art, an outfit that collects the work of living artists and organizes traveling exhibitions. It's the foundation that is reflected in the design of the building and its generous public spaces. Galleries on the ground floor and basement levels will offer changing exhibitions. The gardens surrounding the building will also be used to display art. At the rear of the building, the German-born Conceptualist Lothar Baumgarten is creating a sweeping amphitheater of a garden that will be a living artwork in its own right.

Formally, the building is a vertical sandwich—*non*, Mr. Nouvel interrupts, if you must use this analogy gastronomique, call it a mille-feuille—a club sandwich composed of three immense glass walls that rise parallel to the street. A garden fills the space between the first two layers; an eight-story office building rises between the second and third. The glass street wall is the most dramatic, a crystal billboard advertising itself. Supported from behind by gray steel struts, parted in the center to create an entrance, this weightless, transparent facade resembles a glazed, durable version of the net-hung scaffoldings that screen Parisian buildings undergoing renovation. It declares contemporary art to be something open and changeable, an idea perpetually under construction.

In effect, the street wall creates two screens: one of metal-framed glass, a second of Parisian reflections. Just inside, there is a third screen, this one of trees, most notably a towering cypress said to have been planted by Chateaubriand, who once lived here. The office building that rises behind the trees is not the usual glass box, for its front and rear walls extend a full floor above the top of it and a town-house width on either side.

These extensions are the heart of the design, for they allow the building to retain the transparency that diminishes sharply when glass is tightly wrapped around an enclosed volume. At last, a built work nearly attains the dematerialized state that early Modernists envisioned in their drawings. In warm months, when the glass panels on the ground floor are slid back, the division between inside and outside is further eroded. At night, the city reflected on the front of the glass assumes a density more substantial than the building behind it.

The ground-floor gallery is a good SoHo loft that has died and gone to Paris. Divided in the middle by a reception desk and an elevated bookstore, the three-story space is otherwise unencumbered. Structural columns are confined to the perimeter; stairways of open-mesh steel rise outside the glass enclosure. Light, entering the space from all sides, makes a soft landing on a floor of buff, unpolished concrete. The floor's color, a relief from the building's overall gray palette, extends the grounds indoors. In the foundation's inaugural show, three towering indoor sculptures by Richard Artschwager loomed through the trees like garden follies.

On the upper floors, offices of nearly uniform design continue the Miesian "almost nothing" motif. Stark gray desks sit on panels of gray carpet, set into floors of stainless steel tile. Office doors, made of the same glass as the walls, have been hand-sanded to bring out the material's sea green tint; each door is a translucent Rothko-like panel that fades (like the building) into transparent edges.

But the God in this building's details is called Mattel. Electric roller blinds, affixed to the outside of the glass walls, descend to screen the interior from direct sunlight. Three glass-sided elevator cabs—motorized quartz crystals—glide up and down the rear facade. Desk lamps, fitted with slim metal wands, are activated by the heat of the hand. Their responsiveness to warmth is a welcome reassurance in rooms otherwise so arctically disposed.

Such techno-rococo touches are a Nouvel trademark, close kin to the mechanized sun screen he designed for his Arab World Institute. Alas, that clever device, a casualty of a slashed maintenance budget, no longer whirs. The Cartier building will also need a lot of upkeep; it may well be the most luxurious "almost nothing" since the Seagram Building. Fortunately, with the Cartier label on it, it's not likely to run out of batteries any time soon.

Still, the building may well offend those who deplore the fact that contemporary art has gone so far upscale in recent years. Some may be especially aggrieved to see this glittering showcase arise in Montparnasse, where art once flourished in surroundings of sympathetic shabbiness. The Cartier building is undeniably chic, but it is hospitable to forms of modern glamour that would never pass muster in the Place Vendôme.

Nouvel is not afraid to make poetry out of the zeitgeist, with all its narcissism, its flash, its inability or refusal to maintain a barrier between intellect and style. Contemporaneity, for him, is a funhouse mirror in which artists, models, students, and patrons can admire one another's reflections. You want Bohème? Go play Puccini. Nouvel has designed a faithful portrait of Left Bank life in 1994.

May 29, 1994

FRANK GEHRY'S AMERICAN (CENTER) IN PARIS

Frank Gehry's new building for the American Center in Paris is a love poem on the relationship between freedom and tradition. And what could be more apt for an institution whose purpose is to strengthen the cultural bonds between France and the United States? The venerable civilization that framed the Enlightenment and the modern nation founded on that framework: Gehry's design is at once a warm tribute to their common heritage and a confident demonstration of the creativity required to sustain it.

Americans embarrassed by the desperate martial mirth of Euro Disney can take pride in this building. Witty, urbane, as affable as Gene Kelly, it shows that American architects can do more than exploit the Old World. They can enrich it.

Established in 1931 and formerly allied with the American Cathedral in Paris, the center initially provided a high-minded (and alcohol-free) social hub for virtuous expats. In recent decades a more Dionysian spirit has prevailed—the Living Theater hung out here in the 1960s—and the center has become a lively showcase for contemporary American art, with the accent on music and dance.

Formerly located in Montparnasse (on the site where Jean Nouvel's new building for Cartier opened last month), the center has moved to the neighborhood of Bercy as part of an ambitious plan to stretch the fabric of Paris beyond the historic center. Located to the east of the Bastille district, Bercy was once a center for the wine trade. In the past few years, however, the old warehouses and cobblestoned alleys have given way to modern apartment houses and a brace of public buildings, including the new Ministry of Finance, a sports complex, and a trade center for food and wine.

While the new Bercy does not shriek with the Miami modernism of La Défense, neither does it radiate with Left Bank charm. To humanize it, city planners have carved out an immense new park, parallel to the Seine. The American Center, which opens on Tuesday, is expected to provide a cultural magnet.

Gehry's building is already attracting curious onlookers, though some complain that this California maverick hasn't given them something more in keeping with their image of the Wild West. To a degree, they're right. Though scarcely conventional in appearance, the American Center is not a Hollywood Apache. It is, rather, an American's souvenir of the historic city, transfigured by his understanding of the pressures of urban growth. And it should help people recognize that Gehry's work has long been rooted in a grasp of the complexities of urban context.

What strikes you first is the stone: a mellow, vellum-colored limestone that wrapped around the building immediately establishes it as an anchor of solidity in a sea of glass, concrete, stucco, and steel. This is the stone that steeps historic Paris in the glow of golden ages past, the material from which such ancient landmarks as the Pantheon were fashioned. As you approach this new landmark from the Bercy Metro stop, the glow is all you take in, for the form of the building initially looks unexceptional, a stolid eight-story block with square windows, its northern edge respecting the street wall as if a gendarme were keeping watch.

Then, as you come nearer, the building gradually breaks out of the box: the lower floors jut forward in a two-tier limestone flounce that gives the corner a jagged edge. The projection serves the functional aim of providing a canopy from the weather. But it is also a typical example of Gehry's play with urban forms, for the jutting profile recalls a mansard roof. Instead of lodging it on its customary place on the boulevard skyline, however, Gehry puts his mansard at the building's base, as if to proclaim that the whole place arises from an artist's garret.

On the park side, the building erupts into a more characteristically fragmented Gehry collage, but one that is clearly indebted to French style. A wide apron of zinc curves around the building's southwest corner; above it, a crystallized Parisian cityscape takes shape. In its fractured composition of angles and curves, one can discern the dissected facades of Haussmann boulevards, the zinc of workingmen's bars, the glass canopies of belle epoque hotels, the colliding perspectives of intersecting streets.

This is a frankly Cubist composition, a California cousin of the French Manager's costume Picasso designed in 1917 for the Diaghilev ballet *Parade*. Or, rather, Gehry's design reveals the extent to which the city itself is a Cubist project, a succession of visual slices that add up to a whole.

Inside, Gehry reworks one of the glories of Parisian urbanism: the courtyards that turn the passage between public and private realms into a spatial surprise. Gehry's version, a three-story balconied space enclosed by skylights, is a lobby that also serves as the building's social center. A corridor leads off the lobby toward a cafe and a corner block containing twenty-six apartments, designed for visiting artists. A stairway ascends to a sculptured, free-form balcony that will be used for receptions. From there, visitors proceed to theaters and galleries, including a cinema, two experimental "black box" spaces, and a jewel box of a theater that seats four hundred in sumptuous orange and blue surroundings.

Signs throughout the building are executed in the stencil letters that were a trademark of Le Corbusier, and these graphics do more than identify the rooms. They also help clarify Gehry's place in the lineage of twentieth-century urbanism. For Le Corbusier, the modern industrial city and the historical city were antipathetic. In his utopian vision of Paris, the former has largely replaced the latter. For Gehry, machine-age modernity has joined classical Paris among the city's historical strata.

The American Center is his contribution to the city's quest for an identity in the postindustrial age. Gehry's city remains a center of production, but its main product is culture, a booming enterprise of ideas. Some ideas are rooted in the past: the classical ideal of inquiry and the modernity that arose from it. But the main ingredient in Gehry's urban product is receptivity to the new.

In a building full of implicit symbols, one stands out vividly: a vertical row of cantilevered glass panels, clipped to the park side of the building, that gradually change in angle as they mount in height. The effect is of a window thrown open to let in fresh air, an image that evokes thoughts of California geniality. Actually, the symbolism is neither American nor European. The window looks toward a global culture based on the open mind.

June 5, 1994

"BOSS" DESIGN: A LOS ANGELES SKETCHBOOK

Los Angeles is a work in progress, and the excitement is that the design is still evolving.

Just now, the Getty Center is the Acropolis in reverse, a lofty urban landmark on the rise instead of one in ruin. Brentwood's hilltop city of the arts, a symbol of the surging cultural ambition of Los Angeles, will not be completed for two years. But if construction were halted tomorrow, it would still be worth climbing the hill just to see the sublimely beautiful stone veneer that now clads the Getty's base.

Part of the pleasure of visiting this nascent citadel, which will include the museum and a research center for scholars, is the surprise of seeing Richard Meier work with stone. The purest and palest of all the architects once known as the Whites has gone and got himself a beach-boy tan. Yet the white porcelain panels of Meier's other buildings have often taken on subtle coloration from reflected light, and here the stone resembles a fossilized form of the radiant air around it. A Roman travertine, cleft-cut against the grain, the stone is shot through with yellows, violets, grays, and pinks, an iridescent palette that varies from block to block and from hour to hour as the sun's angle shifts.

But the complex is rising at a moment of skepticism about powerful cultural institutions like the Getty, a time when many people are more inclined to resent their power than respect their culture. Seen from the city below, the Getty hulks against the sky like a fortress; Marcel Breuer's Whitney Museum is a sweet little sand castle by comparison. And while Los Angeles may be ready to exchange the Hollywood sign for a more culturally elevated urban symbol, the Getty's symbolism is double-edged.

Physically remote, the Getty also presents a picture oddly distant from the city whose cultural prestige it is meant to enhance. The cultural vibrancy of Los Angeles today has little to do with either the high-art tradition represented by the Getty or Hollywood's commercial kitsch. It derives partly from the breakdown of that dualism under cataclysmic social and environmental pressures—riots, earthquakes, challenges to the power structure—and from the city's receptivity to ideas that reckon with those pressures.

Power is the theme of one of the newest buildings in town, the UCLA Energy Services Facility, popularly known on campus as the Chiller Plant. Raw power, utility-type power: the plant's chief function is to generate the energy required to light, heat, and cool the entire campus. But the design is also concerned with power on a philosophical level. It invites viewers to ponder the impact of power on those who use it.

Designed by Wes Jones when he was at the San Francisco firm Holt Hinshaw Pfau Jones (he now heads Jones, Partners: Architecture), the plant is indeed a chiller, the air conditioner of the apocalypse. At age thirty-six, Jones is a cold-war child, and a recurring theme of his work, like the Astronauts Memorial he designed for the Kennedy Space Center in 1991, is the interplay of fascination and dread that technology generates in the nuclear age. Jones shares little of the modern architect's belief in technology as a benign social force. He is even less sympathetic toward the postmodern desire to put the machine back in the box and tie it up with bows.

Jones's approach derives from Heidegger's warnings about the spiritual impact of the machine. In Jones's view, the problem in seeking to master nature is not that it jeopardizes the planet but that it threatens humanity. The Lord of the Universe role is a corrosive delusion; masters are corrupted by the subordination of others into a role of servitude. Nature is one of those others. Jones's Chiller Plant is an architectural essay on the need to confront the desire for mastery. It stands not only for the technology to heat or cool a campus, but for the mind-set it takes to build a city in a desert, atop a network of seismic faults.

The plant is a full-service servant. Besides generating power, it houses repair shops and offices for the campus maintenance department. But the main tenants are two gigantic generators, designed by the engineering firm Parsons Main. In effect (and appearance) giant jet engines, their function is not to thrust an aircraft but to transport a campus, lifting it out of its desert habitat into a condition more favorably disposed to scholarly pursuits.

It would be logical to hide the machinery behind normal-looking wraps; this is, after all, a structure whose function is to normalize the environment for human beings. Jones's design partly acknowledges the desire for concealment. Walls of red orange brick, identical in color to those found throughout the campus, clad the building's lower half. Except for some brick panels that tilt down (like overscaled garbage-chute doors), and some segments of contrasting slate blue brick that dance like stylized shadows across its ruddy surface, the bottom part of the building could be a generic campus brick box of the 1960s.

But above the brick, the plant shifts into high expressive gear, first with a tier of immense steel louvers, painted a bland industrial putty tone, then in a barely controlled eruption of mechanical equipment—chimneys, compressors, ducts, pipes—that rise above the louvers, enveloped in an infernal cloud of steam.

This ominous superstructure is an example of what Jones calls "boss" design—mastery in built form. It is the vocabulary of industry, weaponry, engineering, and urban infrastructure. In its poeticized form, boss design was also the grammar of modernism. But while Jones exposes the boss, he suppresses the poetry. His intention is not to celebrate technical prowess but to honor the power of nature. The raw display of industrial strength is a tribute to the mightier natural forces it seeks to control.

The plant is an ecologist's nightmare. It does nothing to decrease the city's disconnection from the natural environment. What it seeks to do is challenge our disconnection from the technology that makes that separation possible. As such, it performs a teaching function. It instructs the university to take responsibility for the environment it has created.

By coincidence, the Chiller Plant sits directly opposite another recent building dedicated to science: the MacDonald Medical Research Laboratory, designed by Venturi, Scott Brown and Associates. The lab was completed two years ago, and even then it looked like a period piece, though a fine one, a decorated shed of patently postmodern vintage.

The MacDonald lab, too, deals in a sophisticated way with issues of screening and exposure. Like Guild House, Venturi's seminal postmodern building of 1963, the lab has a flagrantly false facade, pasted onto the front of the building, and much of the interest resides in the play between the two-dimensionality of the facade and the richness of its ornament. With its bands of patterned red and orange brick interwoven with rows of flush-mounted checkerboard-mullioned windows, the facade is an ornate Victorian pile that has been flattened to a pancake by a century of disbelief. When one of the windows pivots open, at once calling attention to the flatness and breaking out of it into the third dimension, the trompe l'oeil effect is as startling as one of Magritte's.

The MacDonald lab doesn't completely hide the technology within. It also has louvered panels, two little ones that peek out from the roofline on either side of the facade. The effect is a bit like someone making donkey's ears behind someone else's head. It gently mocks the ornament's humanist aspirations and subtly puts into question who's the real boss: the pretty face or the mean machine lurking behind it.

I imagine that from Venturi and Scott Brown's perspective, the Chiller Plant must look like a period piece too. Do all those steaming pipes really add up to a substantial departure from modernism's machines for living? It is true that in the Chiller Plant Jones is dealing with historical themes. He's picking up a strand of history that postmodernists let fall. Implicitly, his design rebukes his postmodern elders for thinking that the machine could be civilized with historical quotations or teased into submission with jokes.

I'm drawn to Jones's side of the street, because he's the challenger in this unplanned contest. He has introduced a polemic as gutsy as the one Venturi mounted thirty years ago, before postmodernism became the boss. Also, as a Cold-War child myself, I'd like to think that architecture can reckon with the complexities of superpowerdom. Yet it's not necessary to reject one of these buildings to appreciate the other. Of course, the architects themselves have taken sides. The strength of both projects reflects the vigor of their designers' convictions. But my overriding response to both is one of gratitude toward a city that has invited architects of conviction to create buildings that matter.

June 12, 1994

RADICAL MODERATION, RIGHT OUT OF THE '60S

Humanism survived the '60s. That's one way to interpret the choice of the fifty-year-old French architect Christian de Portzamparc to receive the

Pritzker Architecture Prize for 1994. Europe's great secular tradition of dignified, classically based building was not blown to bits by the student uprisings of May 1968, when Mr. Portzamparc's generation exploded on to the scene. It is alive and well and giving rise to some of the most noteworthy new buildings in Paris.

Some interpretation of this year's Pritzker selection is definitely called for, because many find Mr. Portzamparc a baffling choice. The prize, which was presented to him on June 14 at a ceremony in Columbus, Indiana, is widely considered architecture's most prestigious honor. Mr. Portzamparc, who was born in Morocco of Breton lineage, is the first French architect to win it, and he is the first Pritzker laureate from the generation that grew up after World War II.

But he remains a mystery man on the architectural scene. Though he has built some of the most important projects in Paris in recent years— ranging from an elliptical concert hall to an imaginative overhaul of aging public housing—coffee tables do not groan beneath lavish monographs of his work; in fact, there are none in print. Mention of his name does not quicken the pulse of the avant-garde. Architecture students, ever alert to new directions in the field, have not been seized by a compulsion to copy Mr. Portzamparc's designs.

Of course, the Pritzker jury did not pluck Mr. Portzamparc (pronounced pore-zahm-PAHRK) from obscurity. With more than twenty projects to his credit, he is an important player in French architecture, and not without admiring fans abroad. In 1984, when his Erik Satie Music Conservatory went up on the Rue de l'Universite, word began to filter out from France that a young architect was forging a middle path between the polemical extremes within Modernism and Postmodernism. With a vocabulary of forms that recalled by turns Le Corbusier and Charles Moore, the Satie held out the tantalizing hope that these antipathetic movements could be imaginatively reconciled.

Still, even the impressive body of work he has completed in the last decade did not launch Mr. Portzamparc into the global orbit of architectural superstardom, and his low profile makes him an anomaly among Pritzker laureates. The list of previous winners, after all, is not a deck of wild cards. It's a Big Time Hall of Fame, a roll call of architects who, for the most part, attained international prominence long before recognition by the Pritzker jury came their way. And the pool from which these winners were drawn hasn't yet dried up. Norman Foster, Arata Isozaki, Peter Eisenman, and Renzo Piano are among those still swimming around out there, celebrated but Pritzkerless, creating some of the most remarkable buildings of this age.

But Mr. Portzamparc has one thing going for him that weighs more in the balance than fame or, perhaps, even talent. He has Paris. He has for his home base a city that in recent years has renewed its sense of cultural mission and invited architects to play a major part in its formation. Fiercely proud of its classical past, ever curious about the new, fully aware of its pivotal location in a newly energized Europe, Paris is pioneering a role for older central cities in the era of global decentralization.

This is a collective undertaking; no one architect can claim credit for it. But Mr. Portzamparc's urbane, stylistically diverse buildings add up to a compelling architectural symbol of a recharged City of Light.

In May, a few days after the announcement of the Pritzker Prize, I spent an afternoon with Mr. Portzamparc, zigzagging around Paris to look at some examples of his work. We met at his office, in a five-story atelier in Montparnasse, designed in the 1930s in the stripped-down Modern style called Esprit Nouveau.

Mr. Portzamparc cites Le Corbusier, the modernist hero who founded the style, as the dominant influence on his work, though some would say that Mr. Portzamparc's sensitivity to urban context is the antithesis of Le Corbusier's aggressive, revolutionary stance. Trained at the École Nationale Supérieure des Beaux-Arts in the 1960s, Mr. Portzamparc is also steeped in the classical tradition that the Beaux-Arts school long exemplified, and he looks toward Le Corbusier much as classical architects once looked toward Rome. He is a Postmodernist for whom early Modernism has become a classic period style.

Mr. Portzamparc met me at his office wearing a gray plaid jacket, a blue shirt, no tie, yellow slacks, and a very grave demeanor. Of medium height, he is possessed of more than medium intensity when talking about his work. Though his buildings can be playful—quite a few of them, metaphorically speaking, wear yellow slacks—they are refreshingly short on irony. But very long on just about everything else. It's no wonder that students don't copy Mr. Portzamparc. How could they? His buildings come in a bewildering assortment of shapes and sizes. They do not add up to a signature style.

At the City of Music, a music conservatory in a complex of buildings in the Parc de la Villette in northeast Paris, construction is nearly completed on the project's second phase, which features an elliptical concert hall encircled by a wonderfully dizzying lobby in the form of a spiral. One day, this part of Paris might be rechristened City of Portzamparc. Across the street from the conservatory, there is a Portzamparc-designed Holiday Inn, a curving green slab with a Miami-modern disposition. A glass office block, just beyond the hotel, shows Mr. Portzamparc hard at work in the buttoned-down mode of corporate culture.

Meanwhile, on the Rue Nationale in southeast Paris, Mr. Portzamparc is rehabilitating several blocks of publicly subsidized housing built in the late 1960s. New balconies and awnings, added while the tenants remained, enliven the facade and enlarge the living spaces within. On the Right Bank, Mr. Portzamparc's Café Beaubourg is the hippest of the hangouts adjoining the Centre Pompidou. With a grand stair floating upward through the two-story space past murals of Mr. Portzamparc's design, the café is a swinging shipboard lounge for a generation born too late for ocean-liner life. In Montparnasse, Mr. Portzamparc's addition to the Bourdelle Museum is a refuge of repose. In this cool shrine to classical sculpture, Mr. Portzamparc carves space with natural light.

In short, Mr. Portzamparc is all over the place, and not just geographically. Aesthetically, his work is a very mixed bag, and not a uniformly successful one. While the citation from the Pritzker jury praises him as a "powerful poet of forms," that appraisal may be premature. For the moment, it seems fair to say that he has more good ideas about architecture than he yet knows how to use.

The City of Music, for example, could be described as a lively but visually dysfunctional marriage between two incompatible modernisms: the rectilinear "German" vernacular of Walter Gropius and the curvaceous "Latin" style of Oscar Niemeyer. The complex is riddled with more curves than a Radio City chorus line, but they don't dance in sync. The windows come in an endless variety of shapes; a collage of decorative surfaces ripples over the walls within and without. Aiming for richness, the design produces an impression of indecision.

There is something oddly Clintonesque about the hybrid, often unresolved quality of this work. Mr. Portzamparc's buildings seem to embody a time frozen by the conflicting desires for change and for a pluralistic inclusiveness that prevents change from unfolding in a clear direction. Still, while Mr. Portzamparc's effort to synthesize conflicting styles may not be an ideal formula for bold aesthetic leadership, it is a good approach to urbanism, because it enables him to respond with great sensitivity to different sites.

Nowhere is the urban dimension of his work more apparent than on the Rue Nationale. A dull parade of medium-rise apartment blocks, the street is an open-air museum of late modern architecture at its anti-urban worst: scaleless, without street life, the bleak face of the bureaucratic state. In the United States, which has no shortage of public housing of this type, calls are often heard to bring in the wrecking ball. In Paris, the goal is to make such buildings work.

If Mr. Portzamparc's retrofit accomplishes this, it is because he respects the social idealism that these buildings originally, if imperfectly, expressed. His metal balconies, fitted with jaunty white and yellow awnings, remain within the modern vernacular. So do a new pair of low-rise structures, surrounded by small parks, that will add a school and a community center to the residential complex. While the additions make up for the shortcomings of modern architecture, they are not pitched in battle against modernism itself. Indeed, Mr. Portzamparc's improvements hark back to Le Corbusier's formula of towers in a park. But their effect is to repair the eroded cityscape this formula often produced.

The result is finely tuned, nuanced urbanism. It is not heroic form making, and its virtues do not translate easily into the striking photographic images on which architects' reputations tend to be built. Photographs of Mr. Portzamparc's Rue des Hautes-Formes, a 1979 housing complex just off the Rue Nationale, are visually underwhelming. They focus the eye on a feeble-looking arch spanning the street leading into the complex.

What the pictures don't capture are the proportions of the street and the buildings flanking it in relation to the traffic artery beyond. These formal relationships are what make the complex work. They give the place the serenity of an enclave without disconnecting it from the city outside. Nor do the photographs show how the tops of the buildings, of buff-colored stucco, bounce the sunlight down into the courtyard below, suffusing with radiance what might otherwise have become a gloomy airshaft.

These thoughtful interventions remind us that the student radicals of the '60s were not the first generation to disrupt Paris. Indeed, their brief rampage was nothing compared to the destruction perpetrated by their modernist elders on the city's historic fabric. The students ripped up some cobblestones. The modernists tore apart whole quarters of Paris and left them desolate for decades.

It is odd to see their vandalism repaired by a one-time "sixty-eighter." But does Mr. Portzamparc fairly represent his generation? Compared to the work of Rem Koolhaas, Jean Nouvel, and Bernard Tschumi, three architects whose edgy outlook was shaped by the upheavals of the 1960s, Mr. Portzamparc's essays in urban harmony may look bland. Indeed, some may feel that by singling out Mr. Portzamparc, the Pritzker jury was not honoring the '60s generation but belatedly exacting revenge upon it, deliberately slighting architects who believe that they have a more radical mission.

Mr. Portzamparc once shared that belief. In the late 1960s, when many architects began to question the impact of the Modern movement, he also came to feel that architecture had become so closely allied with the bureaucratic status quo that it could not serve as an instrument of social change. But by 1970, the year he opened his office, Mr. Portzamparc had recovered his faith in design. Architects might not be able to engineer utopia, he realized, but a good building could still make a difference in people's lives.

Unlike some postmodernists, Mr. Portzamparc never renounced the modern ideal of social progress. But he abandoned the bulldozer approach with which modern architects hoped to achieve it. Instead, he embraced the task of picking up the pieces left behind after the bulldozers went home. His vision is broadly urban but evolutionary, rooted in the conviction that architects can maintain an overview of the city without imposing deadening master plans. Think urbanistically, design architecturally: this could be his credo.

And sometimes Mr. Portzamparc pulls off a space in which his visual and social ambitions come together in a perfect mesh. If there was one moment that crystallized his vision, it occurred as we passed through the organ recital hall at the City of Music. An informal recital was taking place, a quartet of student string players performing for what looked like an audience of their relatives. The hall's design fuses intimacy with grandeur. The ceiling, a soaring yellow cone paneled with wooden acoustical baffles, holds players and listeners within one radiant embrace, conferring a sense of ritual at once familial and urbane. What came forth from the instruments was not just the score of a string quartet. It was the sound of a city that has sheltered civilization for centuries, rehearsing to pass it on.

June 16, 1994

IF YOU SQUINT, THIS IS NOT A FAULTY TOWER

Andy Warhol once said that the reason he started wearing gray wigs when he was still in his thirties is that if he made himself look old, people would be taken aback by his youthful vigor. "When I do something with a normal amount of energy," Warhol explained, "it seems young."

Robert A. M. Stern designs buildings with gray wigs: contemporary projects that are sophisticated pastiches. And the impression of age is sometimes so convincing that we find ourselves startled into feelings of relief and even immense gratitude whenever the buildings show signs of life.

There's much to be grateful for in Mr. Stern's new building for the Brooklyn Law School. Here, an architect celebrated for suburban dream houses and Disney theme-park hotels takes on a task of major civic stature. Located in downtown Brooklyn, across from the historic Borough

Hall, the building occupies part of a plaza bordered by the school's main building (a severe modern block built in 1968), and the Brooklyn Municipal Building, a late Classical Revival edifice of 1924. Wedged tightly into the corner where these two buildings meet, the new addition is an eleven-story tower of white cast stone—Mr. Stern calls it a campanile—designed to remake the law school's image in the dignified style of its classical neighbor.

Straightforward skill substitutes for postmodern irony here, particularly in the exterior elevations, which are governed by a rule of three. Divided vertically into a classical base, shaft, and barrel-vaulted crown, the tower is also organized horizontally in a tripartite arrangement. Three central bays, set with large windows and bordered with pilasters, are flanked by single bays where cast stone predominates over glass. The scaling of these elements is exceptionally fine; so is the cascading fountain effect, formed by columns rising above setbacks, that unites the vertical segments into a whole.

Within are sumptuous rooms, paneled in warm cherrywood and tawny maple: libraries, reading rooms, classrooms, and offices, including some double-height spaces fitted with balconies. On the ceilings, a thousand coffers bloom; chandeliers glow over reading carrels carved into voluptuous volutes. Floors of the new building are joined almost seamlessly to the old—the school's floor space has nearly doubled—and the tower is also deftly spliced into Brooklyn's civic center cityscape. Front windows and an outdoor terrace adjacent to the cafeteria frame views of a recently landscaped park bordering Borough Hall: a pleasing illusion of a campus quadrangle.

And yet, and yet. The building can scarcely breathe. Mr. Stern has stifled the design with an excess of literal period detail. Pediments, medallions, ornamental lanterns, triglyphs, dentils: not even the Parthenon could survive this suffocating blanket of well-bred style. And this is tragic, because beneath the classical dressing, this building has good bones. Squint, and the froufrou fades. What you see looks like architecture. Open your eyes, and you behold a case of talent gone astray. All is correct, all is handsomely laid out, and all has been sacrificed to a misguided equation of history and style. Why has Mr. Stern surrendered the chance to reinvigorate the classicism to which his design pays such elaborate homage?

" 'Can't repeat the past?' he cried incredulously. 'Why, of course you can!' " So insisted the protagonist of *The Great Gatsby*, a book that has long been a touchstone for Mr. Stern's sensibility, and one that holds a key to the problem with the Brooklyn Law School building. It is not a bad model, particularly for an architect whose practice took off in the

1980s, an era that recalled Fitzgerald's in its bleary mix of the cynical and the romantic. "Come back, come back, O glittering and white!" Fitzgerald's sodden lament for his lost New York fairly echoes through Mr. Stern's spectacular books on the city's architectural history, and the architect's ability to reproduce bygone styles holds a strong appeal for those who fear that New York is powerless to buttress its shaky foundations.

But to invoke Fitzgerald is to summon forth a harsh critic. For though he may succeed in emulating Fitzgerald's best-known hero, Mr. Stern has yet to attain the complexity that brought that character into being. Fitzgerald clearly shares his character's infatuation with the trappings of wealth and privilege. But he recognizes that it does not suffice simply to indulge it. He could appreciate the gorgeous yearning behind Gatsby's "unbroken string of successful gestures." But he also recognized the "vast, vulgar, and meretricious beauty" of those gestures. It's that simultaneous articulation of enchantment and disenchantment that brings Fitzgerald's vision to life.

At Mr. Stern's Law School building, no such ambivalence is evident. He offers the eager infatuation but not the critical sense with which Fitzgerald transmuted infatuation into art. Mr. Stern's passion for New York and his knowledge of its history must be counted among the city's major assets. But something more is needed to prevent these strengths from being placed at the service of kitsch.

Kitsch is not, of course, a bad word in every architect's book. As practitioners of a social art, architects are particularly susceptible to the idea that since many people enjoy kitsch, it must be more democratic than architecture that proposes to lead, rather than follow, popular taste. Yet there was a time, some thirty years back, when Mr. Stern's ideas served a critical function. As one of the earliest supporters of Robert Venturi, he helped to challenge the ruling orthodoxies of the International Style. Part of that challenge was to break the Modernist taboo against the historical styles.

But the point of the challenge was not to kick architecture back to the nineteenth century. It was to bring the art up to date. By the mid-1960s, when Venturi published *Complexity and Contradiction in Architecture*, the industrial city was largely a thing of the past. Machine-age imagery no longer sufficed to represent modernity. While Venturi referred to historical forms, he addressed a world that had become far more complex and contradictory than the functionalist aesthetic could plausibly encompass. That aim is hardly served by the law school's literal re-creation of nineteenth-century style.

Clearly Mr. Stern is not employing a period style because he believes that we still live in the nineteenth-century city. Rather, he recognizes that the city has evolved, and believes that architecture can effectively address change by using forms that are impervious to it. Imperviousness to change is not an unattractive prospect, especially to those who can recall the glee with which modern architects wielded the wrecking ball in the name of progress. Even those, like me, who reject the idea that classicism is uniquely equipped to transcend the fluctuations of taste, can identify with the desire to prevent all that is solid from melting into air. Continuity with the past is one of the things cities ought to provide.

But continuity is precisely what an excessively literal periodizing style is unable to supply, for history is not an unbroken string of successful gestures (or landmarks). It is also the dissenting arguments that break up the gestures and alter the course of their development over time. History is the classical facades of the City Beautiful movement, and it is also the opposition to that movement found in the work of Louis Sullivan and Frank Lloyd Wright. It is Daniel Burnham's promotion of the style as suitable for modern democracy and Lewis Mumford's contention that this style served profoundly undemocratic ends.

Naturally, architects are under no obligation to bow to critics of the Classical Revival. But if they choose to ignore them, then what they represent is not history but a gloss over history: a denial of the rich legacy of debate that joins past and present within the framework of ideas about the ways a democracy should build. "Serious art," Iris Murdoch has written, "is a continuous working of meaning in the light of the discovery of some truth." The democratic cityscape records a more or less discontinuous working of meaning in the light of some painful truths indeed. Cities change, much as we might like them to remain the same. The past is not recapturable, however much stone and steel we use to reinforce nostalgia. Architects who turn their backs on these truths not only fail to represent history. They decline to be part of it.

Perhaps Mr. Stern imagines that the Law School is a polemical statement. Perhaps he has seized on the school's poor 1968 building as a chance to demonstrate, once again, the impoverishment of modern forms. Too bad he didn't recognize the opportunity to refresh his own outlook. It has been more than a quarter century since architects gave themselves permission to look toward the past, and the Bauhaus has long been history. With so many good things in this building that owe nothing to period detail, isn't it time to face the possibility that modernists may have had a point when they divorced architecture from style? Surely Mr. Stern has now acquired the confidence necessary to sustain an argument not only with others (dead or living) but with himself?

August 21, 1994

IN CALIFORNIA, AN ART CENTER GROWN FROM FRAGMENTS

A classic Chinese landscape painting does not depict an actual place. It represents an ideal state of harmony between an artist and the universe. The artist has spent a lifetime contemplating mountains, trees, and waterfalls, seeking to merge his life with nature. The painting records a desire for union with the forces that shape the world.

Can artists today derive something of comparable value from the modern American landscape, in all its paved, malled, strip-mined, landfilled, rusted, and Winnebagoed glory? Yes: J. B. Jackson, the distinguished writer on American landscape, has accomplished this with words. In his classic essays, Jackson is neither nostalgic about the pastoral past nor enamored of pop suburban sprawl. He absorbs the natural, he absorbs the man-made, and he extracts from them an infectious confidence that some new order can emerge from the difficult interaction between the two. A contemporary sense of place may yet arise from a vision wide enough to encompass rivers, trailer camps, prairies, freeways, forests, and freedom of movement.

That incipient order animates Frank Israel's new design for the Fine Arts Building at the University of California's Riverside campus. Though it will be a year before construction begins on the $33 million project, the design itself is already a kind of arrival. Riverside's Fine Arts Building is the first major public commission by Mr. Israel, a forty-eight-year-old architect best known for the sophisticated movie production offices he has designed in Los Angeles. With this project, Mr. Israel assumes a leading role among architects who are looking toward landscape to help redefine the ways in which buildings can create a sense of place.

In Mr. Jackson's most recent collection of essays, *A Sense of Place, a Sense of Time*, he writes that "architecture no longer provides the important symbols." Thanks to the car, the highway, and our dependence on them, we no longer experience the landscape as a "composition of well-defined individual spaces" to which buildings once lent well-defined, stable meanings. Instead, urban and rural terrains have dissolved into fluid, loosely differentiated zones, connected by roads that provide access but not a rooted sense of place.

Riverside could be a textbook illustration of this national uprooting. Seventy-five miles east of Los Angeles, the area once blossomed with orange trees; in fact, the Riverside campus originated in 1917 as an agricultural school to support the citrus industry. Over time, however, the groves that lent the region its distinctive character receded, giving way to shapeless urban sprawl. And liberal arts studies eventually displaced agriculture from Riverside's curriculum.

The Fine Arts Building will mark the school's increasing prominence in arts education. Serving the departments of art history, painting, sculpture, photography, dance, and music, the building will also function as an architectural gateway to the 11,000-acre campus and is intended to provide a cultural center for the Riverside community. In addition to studios, classrooms and offices, it will contain indoor and outdoor performance spaces, recital halls, galleries, and a 350-seat auditorium.

Set into a wedge formed by the freeway and an ancient arroyo, the building site is immediately adjacent to a parking lot but commands views of the San Bernardino Mountains to the west. With its slanting walls and projecting, sloping roofs, Mr. Israel's design resembles something between a mall and a mesa: an interpretive formal synthesis of desert terrain and the disjointed urbanism that has grown up there. Dramatically, the design breaks the grid on which the rest of the campus is laid out. Instead of the box shape typical of the buildings designed according to a 1964 campus master plan, the three-story Fine Arts Building is broken up into three interlocking enclosures, shaped like pieces of a jigsaw puzzle, separated by a bent, roughly Y-shaped fissure of paved open space.

In plan, these structures resemble shifting tectonic plates, an effect more geological than architectural; and in fact the design deliberately echoes the arroyo that dips through the campus close to the site's eastern edge—the river (usually dry) from which the city takes its name. The building, like the arroyo, will appear carved by movement not of water but of people moving through an extensive network of courtyards, terraces, bridges, ramps, and staircases that runs over, under, around, and through the design. This is a building not only to be in but to clamber over, a ziggurat for the year 2000.

Fortunately, Mr. Israel's topographical allusions are not as literal as my metaphors. This is twentieth-century-urban building, not eighteenth-century-picturesque. The sloping roofs, covered with zinc panels, may take on cloud (or smog) hues, but they are also assertively sculptural industrial artifacts. Their thrusting, metallic overhangs are a machine-age counterpoint to the bermlike slant of the walls. The walls themselves, of brick and stucco, will tint the building with earth tones, but no one will mistake their crisply folded geometric contours for the slopes of a theme-park Matterhorn.

The design's fragmentation, moreover, refers to more than the natural terrain. Like Frank Gehry, Mr. Israel uses fragmented forms to express the pluralism of the contemporary city. The purpose is not to glorify disorder but to affirm the democratic idea that wholeness, beauty, and coherence do not depend on homogenization.

Mr. Jackson writes that "The road generates its own patterns of movement and settlement and work without so far producing its own kind of landscape beauty or its own sense of place." Mr. Israel confronts that problem not by turning away from the highway's disruptive impact but by using the disruption to create a more fluid vocabulary of forms.

His collaborators in this remarkable design are Annie Chu and Barbara Callas from his own firm, working in association with Boora Architects of Seattle. Faculty and students at Riverside were instrumental in defining the concepts to which the design gives form. Peter Walker, the brilliant San Francisco landscape architect, is Mr. Israel's ideal partner. Mr. Walker's highly formal use of plantings—here and there will be palms, cactus, and orange trees—will complement Mr. Israel's organic design. Together, the pieces of the plan will remind us that those iconic orange groves were not 100 percent natural; they were cultural—horticultural, at least.

Though the Fine Arts Building is a departure from Mr. Israel's Hollywood projects, the emphasis on landscape is not new in his work. Luis Barragán, the Mexican architect and landscape designer, was an early influence on Mr. Israel. Another of his current projects, a library addition at UCLA, is enclosed within a giant earth berm. Like other architects who are working the land—among them Emilio Ambasz, James Cutler, James Wines, Antoine Predock, Henry Smith-Miller, and Laurie Hawkinson— Mr. Israel regards the earth not only as the victim of environmental abuses but as a source of symbolism that can bridge cultural differences. For these architects, the next frontier isn't outer space. It is the planet underfoot.

August 28, 1994

VISIONS OF COMMUNITY WITH ROOTS IN THE '60S

For architects, it's too soon for a Woodstock reunion. In this patient, not to say plodding, art form, the '60s counterculture never had a union in the first place. Architects seldom get to do much building before they're fifty, and beyond that, a movement that defined itself in opposition to

authority was bound to have a rough time claiming an art that is traditionally bound to the status quo. But a countercultural vision of community
has emerged in recent projects by some of the most prominent survivors
of that generation.

Stewart Brand, author of a recent book, *How Buildings Learn*, is not an
architect, but as editor of the *Whole Earth Catalogue*, he was the leading
champion of Buckminster Fuller's geodesic dome, a design that came closest to providing the counterculture with an architectural symbol. Now,
Brand writes that domes "were a massive, total failure." They leaked.
They offered no privacy. They resisted alterations.

Beyond that, Brand has come to feel that innovation in architecture
simply isn't worth the trouble. Though he has kept abreast of changing
times in the field of electronic communications, he condemns architects
and the architectural press for promoting novelty at the user's expense. He
agrees with Peter Calthorpe, the San Francisco architect and planner, that
"many of the follies of his profession would be avoided if architects simply
decided that what they do is craft instead of art." Like Bernard Rudofsky
and Sybil Moholy-Nagy, Brand celebrates the tradition of vernacular
building: barns, bungalows, Cape Cods, and pueblos.

Yet as Brand romantically represents them, all these forms are
domes—forms of sheltered innocence uncorrupted by wily urban ways.
Unlike Plato, Brand wouldn't exile artists from his ideal community. He
would simply forbid them to practice architecture. "Art must be inherently radical," he writes, "but buildings are inherently conservative. Art
must experiment to do its job. Most experiments fail."

Peter Calthorpe designs grown-up, prosperous versions of the hippie
commune. In doing so, he shows that the hippie commune was actually
not that distant from the postwar suburb that its wayward progeny sought
to reject. The suburb promised community but delivered alienation. The
commune held out a hope of realizing the values advertised by the family
room and the white picket fence. Now Calthorpe repackages that hope in
the form of solid real estate.

This seems to me a noble undertaking. And Calthorpe's plans, as outlined in his book *The Next American Metropolis*, probably go as far as
design can toward shaping private suburban development to humane
ends. With their links to mass transit, pedestrian scale, higher density,
and provision for such amenities as open space, scenic vistas, bike paths,
and day care centers, communities like Laguna West, an 800-acre development outside Sacramento, represent an enlightened way to control
suburban growth.

But they are also controlling in less enlightened ways. The fundamental decency of Calthorpe's intentions may obscure the fact that his designs do little to alter what the sociologist M. P. Baumgartner describes as the "moral minimalism" of the American suburb. The image of harmony they present is the result not of social cohesion but of transiency, isolation, and an underlying belief that "conflict is a social contaminant, something to be prevented if at all possible and to be ended quickly once begun."

Weed, Arizona, Michael Sorkin's proposal for a military base conversion, may well epitomize what Stewart Brand thinks is wrong with architecture. Exhibited earlier this year at the Los Angeles Museum of Contemporary Art's Urban Revisions show, it was the only theoretical project on view, and it served as a kind of emblem of the visionary spirit.

Certainly the swirling, organic forms of the large model did not resemble a conventional city or suburb. The catalog described it as a utopian community, combining visionary and agrarian ideals, "where carpenters and artists work alongside engineers and scientists."

Peering closely at the drawings, one could make out forms that might be buildings or gardens or terraced hillsides, composed into flowing patterns possibly interwoven with streets, canals, and bridges. But these elements were not precisely identified, and a viewer might easily mistake them for geological formations, weather satellite photos, or an MRI picture of a hyperactive brain.

I suspect that for Mr. Sorkin this ambiguity holds merit, as does his plan's capacity to evade practical realization. Weed, Arizona, is his sympathetic portrait of an America where a guy could be elected president precisely because he dodged the draft and did inhale.

The antiwar movement also haunts the visionary design of Lebbeus Woods, a New York architect. His projects, presented last spring at Storefront for Art and Architecture in a series of vivid, sinister drawings, propose to make something constructive out of destruction. They are architectural fantasies partly inspired by the exploding buildings that provide such graphic illustration of the turmoil in Sarajevo, South Central Los Angeles, and Beirut.

Resembling at once weapons and a kind of metallic scar tissue formed around the buildings destroyed by them, these designs represent Woods's belief that civilization should retain the memory of the violence inflicted upon it. Architectural reconstruction should do more than smooth over surfaces.

These projects leave Woods vulnerable to the charge that he is exploiting suffering for artistic effects. And even if you grant that he is only trying to expose the brutal reality of our smart and sometimes pretty bombs, his projects have an off-putting macho swagger. Faced with them, I'm inclined to think that Brand has a point about craft. A craftsman toiling to rebuild the Mostar Bridge would score higher on my moral scale than this brilliantly rendered display of anger.

Yet it would be a mistake to take these designs too literally as practical solutions. They are expressions of conscience offered from within a profession that rarely offers its members the chance to exercise an independent voice. Beyond that, Woods's projects function as cultural emissaries. Woods has been visiting Sarajevo regularly since 1992, before the shelling began. He sees architects there to discuss the rebuilding of their city and the international state of their art. This, too, is a form of community building.

Sorkin's polymorphous city serves a similar function; it creates a public space (if only within the museum) out of the perceptions people have of it. Sorkin is one of the most acerbic analysts of our shrinking public realm, and while he has chosen to devote himself primarily to design, projects like this allow him to enhance his critical role.

Sorkin would probably bridle at the suggestion that his plan is not practical. And indeed his quixotic belief that it can be realized may be essential to the one useful service it already performs. It invites us to ask: What do we mean by practical? Aren't we really talking about creating communities that are essentially buying machines? Should architecture be in the business of helping people settle for a market-research idea of life?

As evocative as they are of the counterculture, these projects by Sorkin and Woods remind us that "The Sixties" didn't start in the '60s. That decade brought to a climax romantic impulses that had been coursing through the culture for more than a century before Jimi Hendrix busted up his guitar. The utopian, oppositional stance of Woods and Sorkin extends a tradition that includes A. W. N. Pugin, William Morris, and Frank Lloyd Wright.

Brand's and Calthorpe's ideas spring from the same Romantic roots. Brand's glorification of vernacular building would not have been possible had the Romantic movement not conferred upon modest dwellings the cultural significance once reserved for palaces and cathedrals. That is why Brand's attempts to place architecture beyond the reach of art are unsatisfying and ultimately futile. It is only because buildings are so tightly bound up with ideas that Brand and Calthorpe can do what they do.

And perhaps it is only by putting the 1960s into this larger historical perspective that their generation will be able to draw a coherent idea of community from their own experience. What happens when the Romantic ideal of opposition to social convention becomes a social convention?

What happens when a model once adhered to by an artistic elite pervades an entire culture? And what is the impact of that development on an art form that traditionally articulates a community's shared ideals? The '60s generation doesn't lack the capacity to produce intelligent answers. But perhaps its most valuable service to the community remains its willingness to ask questions.

September 4, 1994

A SHOW BRINGS ON A SEVERE CASE OF PERIOD ENVY

Architecture gets a somewhat desiccated treatment in The Italian Metamorphosis, 1943–68, the Guggenheim Museum's epic survey of postwar Italian culture. Rows of somber little black-and-white photographs, lined up on racks that look like stylized gutters, scarcely throb with the poetry that architects like Carlo Scarpa, Pier Luigi Nervi, Giò Ponti, and Franco Albini brought to modern architecture at midcentury. Still, the show (on view until January 22) can bring on a serious case of period envy. What is most enviable about the presentation is not the quality of individual buildings designed in the postwar decades. It is the extent to which the period produced a sense of itself as a period: an era when architects believed that they were collectively shaping a time and place.

That faith, a cornerstone of the Modern movement, has largely disappeared from architecture today. Where architects once drew meaning from being part of something larger than themselves, many now derive it from the distance they can place between themselves and their contemporaries. Certainly there has been no shortage of architectural movements since 1968; indeed, so many have come and gone that even the tireless chronicler Charles Jencks has grown weary of tracking them. But these movements have tended, on the whole, to splinter architecture rather than unify it.

It's customary to blame the media for this atomized state of affairs. Postmodernism, in particular, has been widely dismissed as a creature of the media's insatiable appetite for novelty. And it is true that much of the movement's intellectual substance seemed to fade in the paparazzi glare that bathed architecture—and everything else—in the 1980s. By the end of the decade, when Deconstruction and then New Modernism rolled around, people were tired of feeling bamboozled into thinking that they had to keep up. They had come to believe that these movements were driven not by ideas but by the marketplace imperative to search out trends, invent them when necessary, and kill them off before boredom set in.

And if the point of the whole game was planned obsolescence, it became logical to ask: Why not beat the system? Why not just refuse to go along with the next thing? Whatever comes along, just say no. Sorry, no more movements. No more shiny new playthings. Folded planes? Sorry, can't use it. Green architecture? Not today, thank you. Infrastructure? Not in my backyard. The New Urbanism? Return to sender. We like the old urbanism just fine.

This knee-jerk resistance to movements may be an understandable antidote to media manipulation. But it has also bred a kind of nihilism, an indifference to architecture's public dimension. A movement doesn't have to be a grand design on the world; it can also be simply one of many stories about the world. And tuning out on what movements have to tell can be as pernicious as the withdrawal of the middle class into gated residential enclaves. And it's not even that effective a form of resistance to market pressures. In the 1980s, with the proliferation of unbuilt "paper" architecture as a form of alternative practice, dropping out became a commodity too.

Compared with the state of exhausted fragmentation in which much of the profession now finds itself, Italian postwar architecture does indeed resemble a model of solidarity. Expressed or exposed structure; volumes reduced to geometric abstraction; unadorned surfaces; flat roofs and the occasional free-form fantasy, like Luciano Baldessari's 1952 pavilion for the Fiera Internazionale in Milan; the buildings represented at the Guggenheim share a common vocabulary of forms. But this picture of unity is partly the illusion of hindsight. As the Guggenheim show makes clear, architects of the period split off into factions without any help from the paparazzi: rationalists, neorealists, inspired by a rural vernacular, and organicists, descended from Frank Lloyd Wright, competed to define the postwar moment. Indeed, in his excellent essay in the show's catalog, the architectural historian Dennis Doordan persuasively argues that this period witnessed the first major challenge to the solidarity of the Modern movement.

Italian architects had political as well as aesthetic reasons for mounting such a challenge. In the 1930s, many of them believed that modernism—clean, muscular, transparent—was the ideal style for a Fascist society. Mussolini gave them a good deal of support. After the war, architects were naturally eager to put the Fascist connection behind them.

One way they did this was to relax the regimentation of orthodox modernism and call for a more diverse vocabulary of forms. By the 1950s, architects like Ernesto Nathan Rogers had begun to advocate an approach that prefigured what Kenneth Frampton calls critical regionalism—the adjustment of modern concepts to local traditions and methods of building. Italian architects, for instance, showed relative restraint in the use of glass, an iconic modern material. Masonry walls, they believed, were effective for integrating modern buildings into the historic context of Italian cities.

Doordan cautions against regarding Italian architects as precursors of Postmodernism. They did not fundamentally reject the ideological framework of modern architecture, nor did they abandon the sense of international solidarity it conferred upon them. They sought merely to adapt modern ideas to regional conditions: in effect, to supervise a collision between a global sense of time and a local sense of place.

Today the situation has completely flipped around. The solidarity of the Modern movement is barely a memory, while the only movement that has come close to replacing it on a global scale is the movement for historic preservation.

If there's an international movement in contemporary architecture, it is found in the travel itineraries of architectural superstars as they jet around the world, inscribing their distinctive signatures on sites in Singapore, Prague, Seoul, and Berlin.

Far from imposing upon the world the kind of universal order envisioned by modernism, today's leading architects now create something closer to what is known in chaos theory as the Butterfly Effect. Consider, for instance, the recent reaction to the news that Zaha Hadid had won a competition to design a new opera house for Cardiff, in Wales. Just as (in James Gleick's words) "a butterfly stirring the air today in Beijing can transform storm systems next month in New York," so Hadid's outrageously beautiful design produced waves of delight and dismay from London to Tokyo. Some may say that's movement enough.

October 30, 1994

REM KOOLHAAS'S NEW YORK STATE OF MIND

New York city's most inspiring architect lives in London, works in Rotterdam, and has yet to build a thing on the North American continent. But for the next three months, Rem Koolhaas has the stage at the Museum of Modern Art, where New Yorkers can see for themselves how their city continues to shape the world even as their own architecture has slipped below world-class standards.

Considering all the fanfare this show has generated, including lavish spreads in the fashion glossies, Threshoedst O.M.A. at MoMA: Rem Koolhaas and the Place of Public Architecture" turns out to be relatively modest in scale. Confined to one top-floor gallery in the Modern's department of architecture and design, the show presents models and drawings for five projects designed in the last five years by Mr. Koolhaas and his Office for Metropolitan Architecture (OMA). Three additional models, depicting urban plans, are displayed on the landing outside. (Models for three private houses are on view in the museum's Education Center on the ground floor.)

But anticipation for this show, which was first scheduled to open more than a year ago, has been mounting for some time. And the hoopla is not incidental to the work on view. This is a show about buildings and cities, but it is also a show about aura: the aura of the city, the role buildings play in creating that aura and the glamour that occasionally surrounds an architect of promise, leading excitable critics to plunge recklessly overboard with extravagant words of praise.

Mr. Koolhaas, who was born in the Netherlands in 1944 and educated at the Architectural Association in London, first achieved public attention with the 1978 publication of his book *Delirious New York*, an ecstatic love poem to Manhattan that challenged conventional thinking in urban design. While planners and urban designers struggled to bring logic, sanity, and order to the built environment, Mr. Koolhaas argued that the glory of the city lies in the exceptional, the excessive, the extreme. A champion of what he called "the culture of congestion," Mr. Koolhaas viewed the Manhattan skyline as a kind of euphoric party, as if architecture had been squeezed vertically not by real estate values but by the eagerness of people to get together on a small island and laugh it up.

Since that colorful debut, Mr. Koolhaas has accumulated an impressive body of built work, including apartment buildings in the Netherlands and Japan, the Netherlands Dance Theater in The Hague, and the Kunsthal, an art exhibition center in Rotterdam. He has also pushed the limits of architecture with provocative designs for projects that so far remain unbuilt, like the Jussieu Library in Paris. But the achievement that has established him most solidly on the international map is Mr. Koolhaas's master plan for Euralille, a commercial project now nearing completion in northern France. Designed to exploit Lille's position as a major hub for Europe's high-speed trains, Euralille includes buildings by the architects Christian de Portzamparc and Jean Nouvel, in addition to a trade and convention center designed by Mr. Koolhaas.

These projects, too, display Mr. Koolhaas's enduring passion for New York: the glass-curtain-wall skyscrapers pioneered by Mies van der Rohe;

the bustling street life of places like Times Square, where peril and pleasure jostle each other in a synergistic mix. But Mr. Koolhaas's most highly burnished New York touchstone is the work of the architect Wallace K. Harrison. Harrison, the subject of a show organized by Mr. Koolhaas in 1980 at the Institute for Architecture and Urban Studies in Manhattan, designed such fabled New York landmarks as the United Nations Headquarters, the Trylon and Perisphere at the 1939 New York World's Fair, and the Hall of Science at the 1964–65 World's Fair. For Mr. Koolhaas, these projects represent the ideal of an architecture at once modern and romantic; they defined an urban mythology for changing times.

Organized by Terence Riley, chief curator of the Modern's architecture and design department, the Koolhaas show was at one point scheduled to run concurrently with last season's mammoth show on Frank Lloyd Wright. The two would have made an illuminating pair, for Mr. Koolhaas's vision of the city is nearly the antithesis of Wright's. Wright, at the threshold of the automobile age, championed the centrifugal city, dispersed into the suburban landscape by the car, the highway, and the romantic ideal of individual autonomy. Mr. Koolhaas stands, by contrast, for the centripetal city: for the urban center that, at the end of the century, continues to act as a cultural magnet and an incubator for ideas. Mr. Koolhaas's designs for archetypal urban institutions—two libraries, a museum, a school, a marketplace—are the core of the Modern's show.

On a certain level, these buildings are about coping. Mr. Riley writes in the exhibition brochure that Mr. Koolhaas and OMA "perceive the city as a survivor." Survivors are not victims. They have earned the right to set their own terms. Cities shouldn't be competing with the suburbs by trying to become more like them. They don't have to turn themselves into theme parks. They have better things to do than indulge the fear that their best days are behind them by encouraging architects to design new buildings that look old.

Mr. Koolhaas is undoubtedly right to question current urban shibboleths. But are the terms he proposes the right ones for the city today? Essentially, Mr. Koolhaas asks us to believe that spectacular public buildings, or spectacular groupings of them, contribute at least as much to the vitality of the city as do the systematic designs of urban planners. Those who crave urban life, he insists, want something more than safe, clean streets, trains that run, and contextual design guidelines for new development. They're looking to be part of a legend in the making. Just as it is the business of music, film, and physics to produce spectacular singers, directors, and theorists, so it is the job of the city to produce wonderful, fabulous places: buildings we'd walk blocks out of our way to see.

This is an odd time to be staking out this position. In the aftermath of the 1980s building boom, a widespread reaction has set in against stand-alone, signature buildings by star architects. The movement today is toward urban systems, social responsibility, and the connective tissue that integrates buildings into community life. If there is any validity to Mr. Koolhaas's position, it must hinge on whether his designs are stronger, architecturally and urbanistically, than the solo performances we've already seen.

I believe that his designs are indeed stronger, and that their strength lies mainly in their forms. After all, any properly run library, school, museum, or convention center should be able to gather crowds. If there's a larger urban dimension in Mr. Koolhaas's designs for these institutions, it is because his forms vibrate on some urban frequency other architects have not yet tuned in to. But how to analyze those vibrations?

Mr. Riley refers to the "marked sense of formlessness" of Mr. Koolhaas's projects, and the visitor to the show is confronted by a dizzying array of forms: ovals, cloud shapes, diagonals, grids, screens of perforated steel and corrugated glass, undulating ramps, elongated triangles, tilted ramps, media projections. These forms are seemingly haphazard in their purpose if not in their skillful composition. And one hesitates to analyze the logic of that composition, not only because it is elusive, but also because Mr. Koolhaas's clear intention is to provide pleasure through the appearance of spontaneity.

Still, one of the major advantages of seeing these projects in a single gallery is that a unifying design concept does emerge. In most of the projects, the defining form arises from Mr. Koolhaas's attempt to loosely reconcile a spiral or pinwheel shape with a square or a rectilinear grid. The spiral harks back to Wright's Guggenheim Museum, the unbuilt "endless museum" project of Le Corbusier, the pinwheel plan of Mies van der Rohe's early villas, the ramp of Harrison's Trylon and Perisphere. But some may feel that Mr. Koolhaas's most pertinent historical precedent is Bruegel's *Tower of Babel*, with its vertiginous terror, its breathtaking hubris, and its iconic image of a polyglot metropolis housed within one monumental coil.

Occasionally, as in his 1989 design for the French National Library in Paris, Mr. Koolhaas places a conventional spiral within a rectangular volume. More often, the spiral is discernible only in the whirling organization of interior spaces. For the Kunsthal in Rotterdam, completed in 1992, the spiral takes the form of a series of squared-off interior ramps. For the Jussieu Library in Paris, entire floors of the high-rise building are sliced and tilted to create a free-form, continuous ramp, dotted with auditoriums, classrooms, and cafés, as if an entire Parisian boulevard had been carefully folded up and placed inside a gleaming crystal box.

At Congrexpo, the oval convention center shortly to open in Lille, visitors will whirl through time and sensibility as well as space. From an auditorium shaped like a Roman amphitheater, they will pass to an erotic fantasy of a theater lined with gold-studded black leatherette. The building's ovoid exterior is clad with a rectilinear collage of flashy finishes: shingled glass, concrete in a tacky black pebble texture, and corrugated glass shot through with metallic filaments, an effect at once gossamer and garish.

For Wright, the spiral was an anti-urban symbol. It signified not only organic growth, but also spatial freedom, particularly the mobility made possible by the car. For Mr. Koolhaas, the spiral also signifies growth but of an urban, artificial kind. Where Wright summoned up images of trees, hills, the highway unrolling across the prairie to escape urban congestion, Mr. Koolhaas ushers us into a tight coil densely packed with shapes, colors, materials, solids, and voids that emulate the city in its complexity, variety, social condensation, and insatiable appetite for spectacle.

But Mr. Koolhaas's designs are not mindless merry-go-rounds. His attempt to merge the grid with the spiral conveys a philosophical message. The square is a symbol of reason, the spiral a sign of romance. In synthesizing these forms, Mr. Koolhaas shows that clarity and reason are not the enemies of romanticism; they are the essential preconditions for it. A clear-eyed view of the contemporary city and a pragmatic grasp of what architects can reasonably achieve within it form the foundation from which a truly lyrical expression can arise.

This idea sets Mr. Koolhaas apart from modernists and postmodernists alike. Orthodox modern architects banished romantic mythmaking in favor of objective truth. Postmodernists hoped to restore a more romantic view of the city, but alas, they saw romance as a restoration, a feeling that could be recaptured only by looking backward to a sepia-tinted past.

Mr. Koolhaas, by contrast, seeks a lyrical mythology for the city as it exists today, with its electronic information circuits gaily humming amid brutal physical decay, its enduring glamour improbably compounded from money, fashion, ambition, fear, destitution, tackiness, and profound hope. He is not the only architect of his generation engaged in that search. But none has carried it further, sustained it with greater inventiveness and poise, or arrived at such rich results. Now that's coping.

In his first-rate design for the show, Mr. Riley had the happy inspiration of using bus-stop poster boxes to organize the gallery space. The boxes are arranged in pinwheel fashion, recalling the free-standing planes of the classic Miesian villa, and each contains a blowup picture of the project displayed beside it. This witty synthesis of the Bauhaus and the Gap elegantly mirrors Mr. Koolhaas's street-smart sensibility as it teases out the logic of his forms.

Don't miss this bus.

November 4, 1994

STAY OF EXECUTION FOR A DAZZLING AIRLINE TERMINAL

Planes should streak in drill formation to salute the New York City Council for voting late last month to uphold the landmark designation of the TWA terminal at Kennedy Airport. And TWA also deserves an aerial loop-the-loop. While the airline contested the designation of parts of Eero Saarinen's 1962 building, described by Robert A. M. Stern as the "Grand Central of the jet age," it had good reason for doing so. In addition to sharing JFK's general state of dilapidation, the TWA terminal is in dire need of design modifications. Airport security regulations and increased air traffic have placed demands on the building unforeseen thirty years ago. Happily, these changes will now be supervised by a preservation architect sensitive to Saarinen's design.

The Grand Central comparison is probably stretching it. While TWA is a powerful piece of expressionistic sculpture, echoing Erich Mendelsohn's dynamic designs of the 1920s, it lacks Grand Central's urban prominence and complexity. Wallace K. Harrison's main terminal for LaGuardia remains the most architecturally distinguished airport building in New York, not least because of the skill with which Harrison knitted the terminal into the context of urban transportation. With its raised roof canopy tilted toward the sky above the terminal's concave facade, the design deftly merges the highway's horizontal curve with an airplane's upward angle of takeoff.

In contrast, TWA sits aloof amid the architectural hodgepodge of JFK's Terminal City, like a bird that has lost its flock. Now partly obscured by a pedestrian sidewalk arcade, TWA's exterior was never its best feature. The two outstretched wings do indeed recall a bird in flight; at the wing tips, the dramatically slanting arched windows convey a powerful image of thrust. But the ungainly contours of the building's massive roof have none of the architectonic poetry that Pier Luigi Nervi coaxed out of reinforced concrete.

TWA, however, is an inside story: the terminal's interior is the most dynamically modeled space of its era. The fluidity of the space is decep-tive, for the design is as tightly controlled as that of a Beaux Arts monu-ment, though here the motif is not the classical one of gravity but rather the modern triumph over it. The curves of the ceiling, joined with clear glass strips, read as cloud cover, while the narrow bridge that bisects the space overhead creates a symbolic horizon. The stairs, with their low ris-ers and wispy metal handrails, ease the body into an illusion of effortless ascent, especially after luggage is shed at check-in. Place head in clouds, breathe lightly: that's the general effect.

But it is only a tease. Travelers discover that they are still earthbound as they proceed into the sealed "umbilical" tubes that lead to the departure satellites. Windowless, spatially compressed, the tubes arc upward in a convex curve that echoes the earth. Gravity tugs uncomfortably at the legs as they proceed through the tubes, until, emerging, they reach the gate, the plane, and beyond. It is a narrative sequence of space: the ancient dream of flight gives birth to the jet-age reality of it.

But the historical significance of TWA lies only partly with what is good about the design. It also lies with what is bad about it, or at least appeared so to Saarinen's contemporaries. As was often the case with Saarinen's designs, critics accused the architect of placing image before function and structural integrity. Modern architecture was not supposed to work that way. A building's appearance was meant to reflect a lucid analysis of its uses and functions and to express the structure that housed them.

While modern architects might fashion a strong image from these ele-ments, they were not supposed to conceive an image first, then figure out how to make it stand up and work. But Saarinen made a career out of doing just that. For the Ingalls ice-skating rink in New Haven, Dulles Air-port in Washington, and the CBS Building in New York, he created build-ings that, in the view of the architectural historian Vincent Scully, gave "the impression of having been designed in the form of models for dra-matic unveiling at board meetings." At TWA, there is so much steel massed within the roof that the building is virtually a steel structure with concrete frosting.

Of course, Saarinen was not alone in sacrificing integrity to image. At the United Nations Secretariat Building, the architects sacrificed func-tional efficiency to a functionalist appearance. The prosthesis was hardly organic, but it did keep the roof from falling down. Mies van der Rohe took some shots for applying nonstructural mullions to the exterior of the Seagram Building. But at least modern architects tried to stay within a rational framework. It was this framework, with its implied rejection of style, that enabled them to feel that they had moved beyond the nine-teenth century and its inability to conceive of architecture except in stylis-tic terms.

Saarinen's dazzling images undermined that framework. Although Saarinen claimed that his designs evolved organically, what appealed to both the public and his corporate clients was the freedom he gave himself to depart from the principles with which modern architects had estab-lished their claims on twentieth-century space. In this sense, TWA sym-bolized more than a flight from an airport. It represented a flight from history—or, at least, into another chapter of it. For in retrospect it is clear that TWA stands at the threshold of an era when increasing numbers of architects would see themselves primarily as image-makers, packagers of corporate identities, generally content to let others cope with such mun-dane chores as space planning and structural engineering.

Whether architecture should have taken this route is another story. Certainly Saarinen was not out of step with the reality of his time: his emphasis on imagery faithfully mirrored the moment when the art of mar-keting and promotion were displacing industrial production as the central fact of corporate life. On the other hand, the transformation of buildings into "building boards" has scarcely insured their longevity. Why should a corporation's attachment to a building outlive its commitment to an ad campaign? Who can remember TWA's slogan from five years ago? Or last week? If it weren't for architectural preservation—a movement that, per-haps not coincidentally, took shape just as architecture entered the image age—what would prevent Saarinen's spectacular vintage logo from vanish-ing into the jet stream?

November 6, 1994

SIGHTING BEAUTY ON THE FAR SIDE OF FEAR

When Hitchcock's *Vertigo* first came out, I was so scared by that silly spiral revolving out of the woman's eye during the movie's opening credits that I wanted to run out of the theater. How could I just sit there in the dark and be willingly engulfed by all the creepiness foretold by that image and by Bernard Herrmann's creepy music? But I stayed, and absorbed what became my earliest memory of art's power to extract pleasure from fear.

Two recent events in architecture brought that memory back to mind. The first was the death last month of John Lautner, the Los Angeles archi-tect whose dramatic hillside houses, designed over the past four decades,

helped define the Southern California lifestyle. The second was the opening of the Rem Koolhaas show at the Museum of Modern Art, an exhibition of public buildings that introduce a rich array of urban images for our
time.

Vertigo plays a conspicuous role in the work of both architects. Lautner's Chemosphere House, built in Hollywood in 1960 (and richly documented in an excellent new monograph on Lautner, published by
Artemis), is an octagonal pod, cantilevered out from a single column set
into the side of a 45-degree slope. What gives the house its drama is the
tension between the sophisticated technology it took to build it and the
primitive sense of fear that wells up as we try to imagine what it would be
like to inhabit such a precarious perch, with its constant menace of the slip
of the foot, the earthquake rumble, the fall into the abyss. Isn't architecture supposed to be about shelter? Psychological as well as physical? But
here, instead of providing a sense of security, the techniques of modern
building have been used to dispel it.

Lautner's Beyer House, a 1983 Malibu residence, evokes even more
eerily Hitchcock's suave blend of glamour and menace. Those taking the
view from the house's seaside terrace might easily imagine themselves taking a staged, Kim Novak–style plunge as the waves, crashing perilously
over a transparent glass partition, threaten to dissolve the place into oblivion. Again, Lautner employs technology—here, plate glass and reinforced
concrete—not only to protect the inhabitants from danger but to expose
them to the sensation of risk. His design suggests that modern life has
gone too far toward isolating people from a primal fear of nature; modern
building techniques can artificially reacquaint them with that primitive
sensation.

Visitors to the Rem Koolhaas show should have spirals coming out of
their eyes; they certainly have enough going into them. In most of Koolhaas's projects, like his designs for the French National Library and the
Jussieu Library in Paris and the Kunsthal in Rotterdam, the Netherlands,
the underlying spatial concept comes from the dynamic interplay between
a spiral or pinwheel shape and a rectilinear square, cube, or grid. The
show is amply stocked with vertiginous images.

In the Center for Art and Media Technology, an unbuilt 1989 design
for Karlsruhe, Germany, an escalator shoots up six stories from an underground train station to an art museum above. In the Espace Piranesien in
Lille, France, a labyrinthine underground cavity is carved out to create a
public space where a highway intersects with the tracks for high-speed
trains. At the Rotterdam Kunsthal, lecture-hall risers are set near the edge
of a ramp, threatening dozing students with the ultimate expulsion.

With Lautner, nature supplies the sense of risk, and it is to be savored privately, at home. With Koolhaas, by contrast, the menace resides in the urban, the artificial. His buildings suggest that the modern city is as traumatic a force as nature, and that the way to deal with the trauma is not to shut our eyes but to fling ourselves into the precarious middle of things and discover the beauty that may await us on the far side of fear.

Koolhaas designs public buildings with important civic functions: libraries, museums, schools. His invitation to make that leap is addressed not to private clients occupying private space but to the crowds that populate the public realm. That is what makes the show at the Modern such an exhilarating occasion. For it arrives at a moment when many people have grown weary of the safe role public architecture has played in recent years, with its emphasis on convention, tradition, accommodation, and taste. These qualities are virtues; but taken to extremes they can seem like an escape from exaggerated fears.

For those who feel that too much ease can suck the life out of things, the Koolhaas show is like a bracing push back to the brink of daring ideas. But it would be missing the point to regard this work as a return to modernism. For the most daring thing about it is the emphatically unmodern subjectivity that pervades all of Koolhaas's designs.

His projects come garbed in modern materials: concrete, plate glass, corrugated metal. They have flat tops and plain geometric lines. But these elements only underscore how decisively Koolhaas has departed from the rational concepts of structure and function used to justify their use. What, for example, is the functional advantage of the sloping ramps at the Rotterdam Kunsthal or the Jussieu Library in Paris? Surely all that floor area didn't have to be tilted just to provide lecture audiences with raked seats? No: the floors are sloped because Koolhaas had the nerve to ask why floors should always be flat, and the aesthetic sense to propose a beautiful alternative.

Koolhaas is not irrational. Those who venture into his buildings aren't risking bodily harm or forswearing delight. And few architects have a more pragmatic grasp of the forces affecting the shape of cities today. But Koolhaas knows that the city itself is not a rational creature. Subjective perception is as much a part of urban reality as the communications technologies that are redefining the urban center.

Indeed, the two are inseparable. The allure of the new; the play of the imagination; the drumbeat of desire: these will continue to drive the city forward no matter what gadgets we place at their service. Rem Koolhaas hatches mind-boggling buildings from the idea that the city's future lies somewhere inside our heads.

November 27, 1994

THE MOMENT WHEN THE WORLD SEEMED NEW

White twilight, modern dusk: a century of utopian optimism is brought to a quiet, lyrical close in the new ground-floor galleries Gae Aulenti has designed for the historic Palazzo della Triennale in Milan. And the show that inaugurated the new space, Expressionism and the New Objectivity, intensified the atmosphere of elegy. Focusing on the pivotal years in the mid-1920s when many European architects embraced the common language of the Modern movement, the show, which runs through today, looked back to the dawn of a radiant idea.

The Palazzo della Triennale, which was designed in 1931 by Giovanni Muzio, is best known as the site of an international design event that once presented the most innovative ideas in the field. In recent years, however, the event, the Milan Triennale, has lost its international luster, just as Milan itself has gone into eclipse as a center for pioneering design. Aulenti's new galleries have been conceived not only to burnish the Triennale's reputation but also to reconfigure its mission.

The palazzo's large ground-floor interiors were designed as flexible spaces, so that exhibitors could overhaul them to suit their needs. But, like their counterparts at the Pompidou Centre in Paris, the Triennale's directors decided that some exhibitions would be better served by a permanent setting. Aulenti, architect of the Pompidou's renovated permanent galleries, was a logical choice to undertake the same job here. As someone who has often felt that Aulenti's work, while always intelligent, shows a weak command of space, I am happy to report that her design for Milan is first-rate.

As with her renovations of the Palazzo Grassi in Venice and the Musée d'Orsay in Paris, Aulenti took on a landmark building. A product of the Fascist era, the Palazzo della Triennale represented an attempt to fuse the two leading movements that competed to become the official Fascist style. Neoclassicism, the style most often identified with the regime, dominates the design, with its imposing, symmetrical entrance, the rows of high Roman arches that surround the lower floors and such features as the grand staircase that jackknifes through the atrium lobby. But the regime also supported Rationalism, Italy's leading modern movement, and its influence is evident in the bare, brick warehouse look of the exterior walls, the exposed concrete structure, and the loftlike interiors of the exhibition floors.

. . .

Gae Aulenti continues this synthesis of modern and classical forms. Her simple, spare design for the 10,000-square-foot ground-floor space is based on an ingenious system of partitions. Each partition is, in effect, an extruded column, topped with a "capital" that flares outward to support small clusters of lamps. Though classically sympathetic, the walls are modern in their geometric clarity as well as in their function, for each partition is also a mechanical device that houses equipment for lighting, security, and air-conditioning. Set parallel to form corridors, or rotated to enclose a gallery, the convex partitions create spaces at once intimate and ample.

The partitions stop short of the twenty-three-foot-high ceiling, exposing the concrete structure. Starkly geometric, yet richly textured by the shadowed recesses between the concrete beams, the roof creates a counterpoint to Aulenti's broad expanses of white wall and the diffuse light that washes over them. Floor-to-ceiling windows look out on to Sempione Park, and at moments Aulenti's design seems to pull the park indoors, as if the partitions had become a terrace colonnade, or, more fancifully, rows of spreading trees. With their dappled light glinting off a floor of dark stained wood, these galleries are a winter garden of shadows.

The show, organized by a team headed by Vittorio Magnago Lampugnani, director of the Frankfurt Architecture Museum (where the show was presented earlier this year), reexamined the roots of modernism in a movement once considered its antithesis. In the years after World War I, Germany's Expressionist architects pushed design to nearly fanatical extremes of the imagination. Bruno Taut proposed vast, flower-shaped temples to be constructed in Alpine valleys, while Hermann Finsterlin produced architectural compositions that resembled genetic mutations.

Little of this work was built, however, and between 1922 and 1925, as if in a mass conversion, most of the Expressionists sobered up. Putting pie-in-the-sky dreams behind them, they embraced the gospel of the New Objectivity—the rational, pragmatic machine-age forms identified with the Bauhaus. Except for a few examples, like Erich Mendelsohn's Einstein Tower in Potsdam, Germany, Expressionism became a lost chapter in architecture history.

What this show tried to demonstrate, however, is that the New Objectivity was not a repudiation of Expressionism but a further development of it. Thus, the glass skyscrapers of Mies van der Rohe, for example, are to be seen not as an embrace of machine-age reality but as a fulfillment of Expressionist fantasy. Instead of looking at modern architects as artists who tried to grapple with the realities of industrial society, in other words, the show presented them as mythmakers at heart, narrators of a particularly compelling form of architectural fiction.

This premise is not entirely new. In his 1973 book, *Expressionist Architecture*, Wolfgang Pehnt pointed out many similarities between the two movements. The modern glass curtain wall, for instance, stemmed from the Expressionist preoccupation with the mystical properties of glass. Walter Gropius and Mies van der Rohe never denied their Expressionist roots.

But there's a huge difference between underscoring what Expressionism and the New Objectivity had in common and smoothing over the significant differences between them. In taking the latter route, the show's curators seemed to fall in with the dubious poststructuralist premise that reality is a cultural construct, not something "out there" that can be objectively known.

There is another, less jaundiced way to interpret this pivotal moment: Expressionism was part of a long and tortuous process through which architects worked their way out of the stylistic mess of the nineteenth century. Strenuous in their determination not to relapse into period revivalism, Expressionist architects groped toward forms that did not mask the reality of their own historical moment. In time, some of them designed buildings, like the glass skyscraper, that helped make that reality a visible part of urban life.

Granted, their truth was partial. Not every aspect of twentieth-century life could be reduced to the naked facts of industrial production. So what? The point is that these architects claimed for themselves the right to look for truth. Looking at their designs today, we don't feel cheated by the fact that the truth they embody is less than all-encompassing. It's enough that they don't lie. In this work, we see architecture transformed into an art of resisting self-deception, a continuous shedding of falsehood.

December 18, 1994

AN ARCHITECT WITH A KNACK FOR SYNTHESIS

Those who try to keep up with contemporary architecture may savor a fling with *On Flirtation*, the title of Adam Phillips's recent collection, subtitled *Psychoanalytic Essays on the Uncommitted Life*. The book (published by Harvard University Press) is a good antidote to the despair that can easily overtake those trying to make coherent sense out of a field that has become increasingly fragmented in recent years. And Mr. Phillips's insights have sharpened my appreciation for one of the field's most gifted practitioners, the Los Angeles architect Franklin D. Israel.

Mr. Phillips, a British therapist, describes how the stories people tell themselves can end up limiting their lives. Habitually, he observes, people try to fit their attachments to others into narratives of commitment and permanence. But what do the prince and princess do with all that happily-ever-after time on their hands? Mr. Phillips asks what it would be like if we stopped measuring the value of things by the standards of fidelity and duration. Flirtation, he proposes, is a way of keeping things in play, of cultivating wishes, of making room for the open-endedness of life.

For all its cheeky contemporary cool, Mr. Phillips's is actually a venerable, deeply Romantic idea, a psychoanalytic reworking of Keats's philosophy of "negative capability." For Keats, "the only means of strengthening one's intellect is to make up one's mind about nothing—to let the mind be a thoroughfare for all thoughts." Such a mind, Keats believed, was "capable of being in uncertainties, mysteries, doubts." For Mr. Phillips, "flirting creates the uncertainty it is also trying to control; and so can make us wonder which ways of knowing, or being known, sustain our interest." The question, Mr. Phillips says, "need not be: should we dispense with our capacity for commitment? But, what does commitment leave out of the picture that we might want?"

Mr. Phillips's critique might seem more applicable to the architecture of thirty years ago, when the field was united by fidelity to a modern future and the architect's responsibility to bring it about. Whatever else it achieved, the Modern movement generated a high degree of consensus about aesthetic principles, social purpose, and the correlation between them.

Since then, the field has been invaded, not to say dominated, by architectural Don Juans. Think of Philip Johnson, with his insatiable appetite for new enthusiasms and his equally powerful compulsion to drop them. Or Stanley Tigerman, the Chicago architect who has skipped over the years from megastructures to pop art to neoclassicism to deconstruction and now holds the cause of social responsibility in his rough embrace. Peter Eisenman has sniffed around for inspiration from Noam Chomsky to Jacques Derrida to chaos theory and will surely go on sniffing. Shouldn't critics now be asking what this lack of commitment has left out of the picture?

Yet if Postmodernist architects have indeed shown an aversion to commitment, for most of them the preferred alternative is not flirtation. It is divorce. As the term *postmodernism* implies, the overarching task for architects of this generation was to place distance between themselves and the Modern movement. Their polymorphous designs have added up to a rite of renunciation, a continuing rejection of Modern orthodoxies. Peter Eisenman, for instance, may flirt with different theories, but somehow his buildings end up surprisingly the same. Those twisted, deformed grids endlessly repeat Mr. Eisenman's argument with the modern cult of reason.

Frank Israel, the subject of a new monograph published by Academy Editions, strikes me as a genuine flirt, as Mr. Phillips describes it. In all of contemporary architecture, there is probably no more restlessly roving eye. Restless but not aimless. For, by immersing himself with considerable verve and passion in the ideas of others, the forty-nine-year-old architect has developed a rich, seductive vision of his own. Best known for his designs for the entertainment industry—offices for Limelight Productions, Propaganda Films, and Virgin Records; private homes for Hollywood luminaries—Mr. Israel has developed an aesthetic of great integrity without restricting himself to a signature style. Too young to be a Postmodernist, Mr. Israel didn't have to divorce himself from modern influence. In a sense, he is a child of modernism's broken home. And he began his career by picking up some of the pieces and turning them back into buildings.

After moving to Los Angeles in the mid-1970s, where he briefly considered abandoning architecture for movie set design, Mr. Israel began to design buildings that resembled sophisticated remakes of Hollywood classics. In his 1988 addition to the Lamy-Newton house in Hancock Park, for example, exposed metal trusses paid explicit homage to the iconic Case Study House designed by Charles and Ray Eames in 1949. In the Weisman Pavilion, a private art gallery in Beverly Hills completed in 1991, corner windows and flowing interior volumes recall California projects by Rudolph Schindler and Frank Lloyd Wright.

If these designs do not appear anachronistic, that is partly because of the way Mr. Israel has altered and combined his modern references. Inspired by the work of a contemporary master, Frank Gehry, Mr. Israel gives his forms a more sculptured, less machine-age treatment than was typical of the early modernists. But there is also something strikingly contemporary about Mr. Israel's flirtation with anachronism itself. "Flirtation puts in disarray our sense of an ending," Mr. Phillips writes, and so does Mr. Israel's use of modern forms. Haven't they outlived their historical moment? If not, what has postmodernism been all about? Mr. Israel's designs defy our impatient desire for closure.

As the new monograph on his work makes clear, Mr. Israel's eye is still roving. In two recent projects—an addition to the Southern Regional Library at the University of California, Los Angeles, and the Fine Arts Building for the University of California's Riverside campus—Mr. Israel incorporates landscape as an architectural feature. In the Drager House, a recent project in Berkeley, he uses folded planes to join walls and roof in a unified composition. Other architects may have pioneered these devices, but none has used them with greater confidence or more sensitivity to context.

Do I hear the word *derivative*? It is true that Mr. Israel is not the world's most original maker of forms. His genius is for synthesis. But his use of this gift should be recognized as an exemplary expression of faith. At a time when the public has splintered into an infinity of "taste cultures" (to use Denise Scott Brown's term), Mr. Israel continues to believe that this most public of all art forms can speak with a collective voice. Derivativeness, in Mr. Israel's case, is a form of dialogue. It's a way of reaching out to connect.

In his essay "On Love," Mr. Phillips quotes a remark of the French psychoanalyst Jacques Lacan: "Love is giving something you haven't got to someone who doesn't exist." Frank Israel practices architecture in the same spirit of glorious folly. He has had the generosity to imagine that architects still have something concrete to offer a time of uncertainties, mysteries, doubts.

January 29, 1995

AN EMPORIUM FOR ART RISES IN THE WEST

Department stores may be a dying breed, but new museums continue to rise, and Mario Botta's new building for the San Francisco Museum of Modern Art, which opened last month, should delight those who lament the passing of the great shopping emporiums. For the $60 million building, the Swiss architect's first American project, could be easily mistaken for the last great Art Deco department store.

I hope that Mr. Botta would not be chagrined by the error. Bonwit Teller, Derry & Toms, May Company: department stores were some of the great creations of the Deco era. And in our era, which has seen mass consumption displace connoisseurship as a top priority for many major museums, the department store is not the worst model a museum's architect might choose. Indeed, in Los Angeles, there are plans afoot to turn May Company's landmark black-and-gold building on Wilshire Boulevard into an annex to the Los Angeles County Museum of Art. In his first museum design, Mr. Botta, working in association with Hellmuth, Obata & Kassabaum, has created a landmark for a time when museums are less punctilious about holding the line between looking at art and window shopping.

I confess that when I first saw the nearly completed structure a year ago, I wished that museum officials would have the wit to inscribe the museum's name outside in gold Lord & Taylorish script. I forgive them for having the good taste not to, however, for the exterior is a richly pleasing urban composition. In a part of town (south of Market Street) where the cityscape runs largely to grays, the museum's ornamentally patterned brown-brick facade (a veneer over structural concrete) throws out a warm Sienese welcome. The stepped profile of the setbacks recalls the monumental form of the ziggurat (a classic Deco motif) without overpowering the street.

Set on an axis with the entrance to Yerba Buena Gardens, the new arts complex and park just across the street, the museum (formerly housed in the classical 1931 War Memorial Veterans Building) eases the transition from the low scale of the gardens to the skyscrapers downtown. And its central turret, with an angled oculus at the top, injects its own distinctive symbolism into the skyline. An eye for an eyeful: What better way to mark a place dedicated to the reciprocal pleasures of looking?

It is wonderful to look at art here. The permanent collection is installed on the second floor, much of it in a stately enfilade of seven galleries that runs along the street side of the building. It's a manageable, even intimate procession, gently punctuated in the center by a window that looks out toward Yerba Buena Gardens. Skylights, made possible by the building's setbacks, filter natural light through deep paraboloid recesses in the ceiling. You swim up to a painting through luminous air.

Ceiling heights change with each floor, and that, along with the natural light and the circular turret, eliminates any trace of monotony or confinement. And there's one thrilling moment at the top of the turret: a thirty-eight-foot-long catwalk, with a nearly transparent grid floor, that you must cross to reach the chapel-like fifth-floor gallery.

The museum's dramatic atrium lobby gives people something to argue about as well as gape at: some find the space architecturally too assertive. I like it a lot. A theatrical space, three stories high, dominated by a central staircase of black granite, the lobby is paved with alternating bands of rough and polished granite that are softly echoed by a ceiling of pale wooden slats. Mr. Botta calls the lobby a piazza, while the staircase—an endless ziggurat that rises toward the turret's circle of light—represents a campanile. It's the sort of space that makes people look up when they enter, and some will be unable to resist extending their arms in the classic Ziegfeld pose as they descend the final flight of steps.

Why, then, do I find myself resisting a building that has so much going for it? Because I am unsettled by the museum's air of flawless composure and by the stilted image of modernity it projects. A new modern art museum, after all, is more than a place to look at modern art. It is also a chance for an architect to say something fresh about the changing nature of modernity. I am not persuaded that Mr. Botta makes the most of the opportunity.

There was a time, in the 1970s, when it seemed that a particular strain of modernism—the Romantic strain that incited modern artists to oppose conventional taste—had run its course. The avant-garde had become institutionalized. The public's taste for provocative art appeared to outstrip artists' capacity to provoke. Modernism had become socially reconciled, if not tamed, and now veered toward the classical model of social accommodation.

That is the idea conveyed by Mr. Botta's design. Its classical symmetry, the perfect balance of Mr. Botta's forms, materials, even his color palette, embody the idea that a state of equilibrium has been struck between art and society and that the task of a modern art museum is to preserve that happy balance.

Today, this classicized view of modernism looks hopelessly naïve. It is now clear that a large, vocal, and politically aggressive segment of the public has little appetite for artistic provocation. And it's questionable whether the harmonious integration of modern art and life is desirable, even as an ideal. In the 1980s, many artists and critics did question it. They asked on what grounds it was still possible to distinguish paintings from other commodities, like cars, fur coats, or high-yield bonds. Perhaps, in fact, the need for art that throws things off balance has never been greater, as the margin outside the marketplace continues to shrink.

This need is not acknowledged by Mr. Botta. What points up the failure is his insistence on presenting himself as a modernist. For years, he has depicted himself as a descendant of Le Corbusier and Louis Kahn. He seems to feel that like these architects, he has found a way, through the use of recognizably modern forms, to reach back toward a rudimentary classicism.

But the legendary modernists Mr. Botta invokes knew where they stood on the timeline. The rawness of invention clings to their work, and with it the conviction that balance in the modern age is attained only with struggle. They understood that to overplay the classical aspect was to risk crossing the line from building into style—into Art Deco, in fact, a style that sometimes went by the name "modern classicism."

Whether by bold design or inadvertence, Mr. Botta has crossed the line into Deco territory. His exactly calibrated symmetry, his stripes, and ornamental brick veneers put all the weight on the classical side of the equation. Yes, the building is full of remembered modernisms—traces of Kahn in the skylights, of Adolph Loos in the granite stripes. And Mr. Botta has contrived to make these references look at home in their Deco setting. That may be because, in his hands, modern ideas have become pedigreed commodities—like the Frank Lloyd Wright candlesticks for sale at Tiffany.

Will this obsessively composed building dampen the museum's ability to put across challenging art? No, to judge from the inaugural presentations of contemporary painting and photography. Clearly, the museum's curatorial staff believes that modern art has not lost its capacity to startle the eye into seeing the world afresh, and Mr. Botta's design will not undermine that belief. Indeed, his galleries should serve the curators well. But the museum has let slip an opportunity to demonstrate its faith in the power of architecture to reckon with the discordance that lurks beneath our masks of composure.

February 12, 1995

PLAYFUL, EVEN GOOFY, BUT WHAT ELSE?
IT'S DISNEY

Completed last November, more than half a century after Snow White bit the apple, the new Disney Feature Animation Building symbolizes a welcome return to the company's roots. And the building's design, by Robert A. M. Stern in association with Morris Architects, is also a return, for it brings back the liberating spirit of play that prevailed in the early years of postmodernism, before the movement congealed into pompous historical poses.

Not that the new building isn't steeped in history. Disney's sprawling global empire of fantasy and real estate was built on animation, and the modest buildings in which Snow White and Bambi were born still stand on the company's lot in Burbank, California. But in the years after Disney's death, in 1966, the company's commitment to animation had faltered. By the time Disney's chairman, Michael Eisner, revived that commitment, with the success of *Beauty and the Beast* in 1991, working quarters for the company's shrunken animation department had been split into eight different off-lot locations. The new building, which brings together most of the department's 1,400 animators beneath one roof, thus signifies a reunion as well as a revival.

Situated just a few yards from the Ventura Freeway, the animation building is actually mouse-shaped in plan, though the trademark "ears" (two ground-floor lobbies) are misshapen and the rodent lacks a tail. In any case, this seems a private joke, evident only in the architect's drawings. The building itself is a cheerful collage, a jolly collision of spaces and symbols dedicated to the serious work of being silly.

You enter beneath a blue, three-story version of the sorcerer's hat Mickey wore in *Fantasia.* Spangled with moon and stars, the hat is a symbol not only of one of the company's best-known productions but of magic, fantasy, the imagination. Set into the pavement beneath the hat is a stylized reel of film that gradually unreels as you proceed toward the reception lobby. It's a reminder that Disney's magic rises from a foundation of technique.

The lobby, a circular, four-story atrium sheathed in glass, is housed at one end of a grand, metallic arc, candy-striped in pink and red, that faces the highway and forms the building's southern edge. Dubbed "the Mohawk" by those possibly too young to remember the streamline era, the arc is partly cosmetic in function: it smoothens out an irregular roofline, a result of zoning height restrictions. And with a shape that echoes a curve in the freeway, the arc turns the building into a conspicuous roadside attraction. This winter, radio traffic reporters have been using it to pinpoint rush-hour delays.

Can you find it in your heart to forgive Robert Stern for taking the mickey out of Peter Behrens? The AEG Turbine Factory in Berlin, designed by Behrens in 1909, is a landmark of the Modern movement; the factory's gigantic slanting glass window is branded on the brain of every architect trained in the years when modernism ruled. At Disney, three of those windows are lined up along the building's northern facade. Mr. Stern is not an architect known for devotion to the modern cause, and he has placed his Behrens windows beneath distinctly unmodern barrel vaults. One begins to smell a mouse. But this building, too, is a factory, an industrial plant for fun. Why shouldn't Mr. Stern have fun with modern icons?

It takes about one and a half million images to create one feature-length animated film, not including the countless drawings involved in preparation. These are done on the building's two upper floors—large, loftlike spaces laid out with partitions to resemble a miniature city.

Corridors—streets and alleys—lead past storyboard-studded walls to the "neighborhoods" where particular films—currently *Pocahontas* and *The Hunchback of Notre Dame*—are being produced. Narrow, skylighted atriums, set beneath the edges of the roof's barrel vaults, help unify the two floors, while a lozenge-shaped grand staircase gives the floors a spatial and social focus.

The top floor is a glory. The barrel vaults, covered with black felt, recede into darkness beyond a lattice of illuminated white trusses. By fortunate accident, the metal fasteners used to attach the felt glimmer like stars, while struts from the trusses thrust upward like klieg lights sweeping the sky at a Hollywood premiere. Mr. Stern has earned the right to use those AEG windows. This is as great a workplace as anything designed by Behrens: a Schinkel night scene reimagined by a high-tech Tinker Bell.

Mr. Stern has limited the visible mouse motif chiefly to his designs for the building's furnishings. Wonderful, podlike seating units, with attached ears for stools (they would also make witty coffee tables) line the atrium within the Mohawk. Behind the reception desk, three clocks, set to the times of the cities (Burbank; Orlando, Florida; and Paris) where the division's animators are at work, are arranged to form a Mickey silhouette. And in the office of Roy Disney, Walt's nephew and the company president, housed inside the sorcerer's hat, Mickeys fashioned of bright steel rings, studded with halogen lamps, ascend like cartoon angels into a cone-shaped void of celestial blue.

It happens that the animation building is right near Forest Lawn Cemetery, and the coincidental juxtaposition of Mr. Stern's building with this legendary landmark of lugubrious kitsch may hold a lesson for postmodern architects. When they try on a grave demeanor, the results are often risible, at least compared with the historical precedents evoked by their designs. It's when they let themselves clown around that they tap something deeper, and invite comparison to Disney himself.

Viewed as an occasion to vent our discontent with modernity, postmodernism has played a constructive role. Who wanted modernity to be so obedient to the machine, or to any authority? The problem began when postmodern architects actually began to believe the "post" bit. They seemed to think that mere discontent sufficed to deliver them from modernity. Instead of enriching the possibilities for reckoning with the modern condition, the movement degenerated into a collective refusal to address it.

Yet there is a truth to postmodern play that is as legitimate as modernism's belief in reason. Play can be as effective as reason in cutting authority down to size. And in retrospect the comic strain of postmodernism can be seen to have evolved out of modernism itself. Not solely because it arose in reaction to modern seriousness but because it continued the modern preoccupation with the weightless, the immaterial, the increasing insubstantiality of form. One could only go so far, after all, in paring down walls, opening up interior spaces, eliminating weight. What was there left to do but lighten up the mood? The Bauhaus instructor Marcel Breuer once predicted that eventually furniture would disappear and people would sit on resilient cushions of air. In Mr. Stern's Disney Feature Animation Building, we're borne aloft on bright balloons of mirth.

March 5, 1995

WHAT OF CITIES IF THE BLUEPRINT IS REPUBLICAN?

Is architecture likely to be affected by the Republican agenda? How can it not be? Architecture is a social art. To a more or less conspicuous degree, every building bears the imprint of the social contract. And last November's elections expressed a national desire to renegotiate the terms of that contract. Sooner or later, that desire will express itself in built form. If things go according to the Contract with America, architects can at least look forward to a brisk trade designing prisons.

A correctional facility may not be every architect's idea of a dream commission, but it could stand as a good symbol for the grim mood in which much of the profession now finds itself. Thus far, the '90s have not been golden years for architecture. Many architects were thrown out of work by the recession and remain underemployed, at least by standards of the 1980s. Some feel cut adrift by the absence of a unifying ideology or style. Others are feeling displaced by the exaggerated claims for cyberspace and virtual reality: Will buildings be reduced to mere pit stops on the information highway? Above all, perhaps, many feel let down by the Clinton administration and its failure to bring architects together behind a compelling urban vision.

Two years ago, there was considerable hope that a new administration would help restore a sense of idealism to a profession that had lost its ethical bearings in the building boom of the 1980s. Clinton was the first baby boom president, the first post–Cold War president, and the first president elected since the population has become predominantly suburban. And he campaigned on the theme of change. It was natural to hope that his administration would help to formulate a new vision of urban America.

Many thrilled to the prospect that the 1990s might conform to Arthur Schlesinger Jr.'s theory about the thirty-year cycle in American liberalism. The 1930s and the 1960s were both recalled as periods of great public works, when architects were able to channel their social idealism into housing, transportation, and parks and in urban design initiatives that raised the level of these projects. Would the 1990s witness a renewal of that tradition?

There were encouraging signs that this hope might be fulfilled. In the past two years, there have been some impressive museum shows dealing with urban issues and countless conferences on the public realm. In trade publications like *Progressive Architecture*, an emphasis on the social dimension of architecture has displaced the aesthetic slant that prevailed in the 1980s. Some architecture schools have revised their curriculums along similar lines.

These efforts, undertaken to boost professional morale, have partly backfired. For one thing, whatever their value in raising the civic consciousness of the profession, the shows, conferences, and publications appeared to make little discernible impact on government decision makers. Indeed, they ran counter to a political trend that was evident long before the November elections. While architects were talking up the virtues of the public realm, politicians were warming to the prospect of privatization. This did not increase the likelihood that the '90s would be a legendary decade of public works.

Then, too, it was disconcerting to see that all the attempts at consciousness-raising did not add up to a coherent picture. For instance, Urban Revisions, an exhibition of recent urban plans at the Museum of Contemporary Art in Los Angeles last year, offered a view of the city as a contemporary Tower of Babel, a metropolis abuzz with the competing voices of modernists, postmodernists, neotraditionalists, deconstructionists, environmentalists, and assorted mavericks. Consensus and solidarity were conspicuously absent.

In Urban Revisions, the colorful display of professional discord presented a strong contrast to the form that idealism took in architecture for much of this century. Coherence, standardization, universal application: these were the hallmarks of the Radiant City proposal drawn up by Le Corbusier in the 1920s. With blocks of nearly identical skyscrapers rising at regular intervals from a lush landscape of green, open space, Le Corbusier's vision of the modern city was taken up as a model by a generation of architects and planners. But to a later generation, the Corbusian model did not look so idealistic. Instead, it came to symbolize the determination by architects to recast the city in their narcissistic self-image. In 1961, following the publication of Jane Jacobs's seminal book *Death and Life of*

Great American Cities, many architects began to reject uniformity and standardization in favor of diversity and complexity.

If Urban Revisions made one thing clear, it was that these values still prevail. Architects remain phobic about master planning. Heterogeneity remains the paramount urban virtue. But what would a government decision maker have made of this well-intentioned, sprawling mess? What kind of vision emerged from all these disparate urban revisions? Or, to put it another way, how can architects come up with a comprehensive vision so long as the idea of comprehensiveness remains in disrepute? While complexity may be an urban virtue, solidarity may have its uses after all.

In other words, the current malaise in the architectural profession stems from something more than disappointment with the Clinton administration. It also arises from the profession's dawning awareness that it is time to rethink some of the assumptions that have guided its thinking on urban issues for the past thirty years. Architecture had "devolved" long before the Republicans proposed scaling down federal programs. But the November elections have thrown the crisis of architecture's devolution into sharp relief. While progressive architects may have grasped the value of complexity, politicians are under no compulsion to follow suit. If voters are willing to spring for easy answers, who are politicians to resist the popular will? Why not build more prisons? Who doesn't want safe streets?

Architects who had their hearts set on the renewal of public works must feel a twinge of envy as they scan the Contract with America, particularly the section on the proposed Taking Back Our Streets Act, with its rousing call to build more jails. Why weren't progressives able to put together an effective agenda for parks, schools, subways, housing, museums, hospitals, recycling plants, and airport transit? But the moment one starts to compile such a list, one begins to see the futility of it, at least compared with the elegant simplicity of the Republican contract. There's nothing wrong with the cities that a few more prisons can't cure is one way to read the contract. It's the ultimate easy answer, as stirring, in its way, as Le Corbusier's Radiant City. But how dispiriting it is to compare these two simplistic visions: the utopian dream city of green, open space and the dystopian nightmare of gates and cells! Has the century of progress been one grand march from hope to fear?

March 12, 1995

ART, SETTING, AND THE ARCHITECTURE
OF THE HEART

Ever since the Guggenheim Museum opened in 1959, critics have said that the building is a terrible place to show paintings. Some have suggested that it would be best to take away the art and leave the museum as a monument to its architect, Frank Lloyd Wright. It's true that Wright's design often doesn't display art to excellent advantage. But occasionally a show comes along in which art and architecture reinforce each other, creating the unified experience Wright envisioned. For me, the Guggenheim's current retrospective of paintings by Ross Bleckner is such a show. I found the whole experience very moving, not least because it prompted me to reflect on how a viewer's personal history and emotions affect the response to visual art.

The show dredged up a memory from my adolescence, when I imagined that I faced a choice. It seemed to me that there were people who let themselves feel things, and others who didn't, and I wanted to belong to the first group. Did I really have a choice? Or was I just discovering who I was? Suffice it to say that I was born in Philadelphia and grew up in a social milieu where inhibition was mistaken for character.

My struggle with that milieu has a lot to do with why I write about art, why I'm drawn to the work of certain artists. If George Balanchine was the artist from whom I learned the most, that is partly because of the tension between the extreme formality of classical ballet and the intense emotion Balanchine brought to it. Some found Balanchine's choreography cold. They missed the fairy-tale plots of Romantic ballet. But who needs a plot when every step has been conceived by an artist who once declared that "everything a man does he does for his ideal woman."

Frank Lloyd Wright's romantic ideal was Frank Lloyd Wright, but at least it can be said that the architect's profound devotion to his love object never wavered. What sucked me into several years of immersion in Wright's work was the extraordinary passion Wright injected into an art form at a time when other twentieth-century architects were trying to turn buildings into machines. You sense Wright's passion most deeply in his houses, with the pinwheeling spaces that prevent one from fully leaving the warmth of the hearth. But the Guggenheim also grips you, some say uncomfortably, in its joyous but tightly coiled embrace.

I first visited the Guggenheim as a teenager, when the building was barely four years old. It is so much a part of my history that I can't claim to have any distance from it. If I later imagined New York as a place where I could feel at home with my feelings, that was partly because this was a city that could build such an exhilarating building.

What impressed me initially was the novelty of Wright's design and the sense of freedom it imparted. Later I came to see it in the context of Wright's ideas. Here, in this urban setting, Wright could not rely on the landscape to express his ideal of organic architecture. Instead he conveyed it with the continuous ramp, which he described as "an unbroken wave," and with the visual unity of interior and exterior that the spiral helped create. Wright also conveyed the organic idea symbolically, with the seed-shaped pool on the ground floor, from which the ramp shoots upward, creating, in effect, the world's largest Art Nouveau tendril. Or one could could see the form as a gigantic sperm. Either way, it stands for life.

The Guggenheim, which is often viewed, not unfairly, as an expression of Wright's ego, also represents the Romantic idea that art should not stand at a discreet distance but rather envelop the viewer, as nature does. Where most museums, even the most modern, embody an ideal of detached contemplation, the Guggenheim pulls you into a vortex, a whirl of space that keeps you off balance, as art itself can.

Walter Pater, the Victorian writer, advised that what a critic needs above all is not an abstract definition of beauty but rather "the power of being deeply moved by the presence of beautiful objects." The key word is *power*. The artist is not the only powerful person in the room. Viewers have power, too: an active, not a passive force. But not everyone welcomes the loss of distance that empathy requires. Frank O'Hara once wrote about a conversation he overheard after the premiere of Balanchine's *Don Quixote*. A man asked the dance critic Edwin Denby what he thought of the ballet. Denby answered that he was very moved by it. The other man demurred: "I was moved right out of the theater." Denby replied, "That's where you belong, then."

People often complain that the Guggenheim's ramp is too narrow to allow adequate distance to view the art. This may be a flaw, but it is also a philosophy. The contraction of distance, the reinforcement of unity between artist and viewer, is what the design seeks to achieve. And whenever I start up the ramp and pass that pool of water, I recall how, long ago, Wright's idea took root in me. Though the building was shaped by the power of Wright's vision, it was my awakened sense of ambition that prompted me to flip a Life Savers candy into the pool and resolve that I'd come back.

I'm glad I'm not an art critic and don't have to appraise Ross Bleckner's paintings, for, like the Guggenheim, Bleckner's work is so bound up with my personal experience that I have no distance from it. I can't say what this work means to art. But I'd feel like a dope if I didn't try to work out what it means to me.

I came late to Bleckner's work, with the 1986 show at the Mary Boone gallery, an exhibition featuring paintings described as the artist's response to AIDS. Some paintings depicted trophies or wreaths honoring the dead. Dots alluded to Kaposi's sarcoma lesions. Lunar light shimmered across black canvases. But I found it hard to accept these paintings as statements about AIDS, because I didn't regard the disease as being only, even mainly, about death. Since only the living would see these pictures, wasn't Bleckner prematurely burying those who were desperate for a ray of hope?

But the work hardly left me cold. I was dazzled by its shrewd synthesis of glamour and morbidity. To me, the blackness stood less for death than for guilt, for the feeling of inadequacy that may overcome us as we reach out to seize happiness, fame, sex, power, and other things that glitter. And Bleckner's frosty, campy images—of chandeliers, banners, flowers, pulsing lights—evoked the way I sometimes viewed gay life in the mid-1980s: death and night life, the kitsch sublime, the erotic Frigidaire.

My response to the work shifted to a more acutely personal plane a few weeks later when my partner was discovered to have AIDS. In the months that followed, I felt immense gratitude toward Bleckner for painting those trophies. When you live with someone who has a fatal illness, it's shocking that the world goes on. Why don't things slow down? Why are they still playing those cheerful tunes on the *Today* show? Why must the culture pound out these incessant promises of infinite self-improvement, while so many of us are looking for ways to reckon with our inevitable decline?

Those affected by AIDS had to award ourselves trophies. Nobody else was handing them out. Yet I also came to appreciate that Bleckner's shamelessly sentimental paintings were more than a protest against the indifference of what was euphemistically called "the general population." They were also a response to his own ostensibly more sophisticated social milieu: the hip worlds of art and fashion boast a virtuosity of inhibition a Philadelphia boy never dreamed of.

By the time Bleckner's next show went up, my partner was dead, and I was too numb to pay attention to the work. Actually, I resented it this time: more AIDS paintings, more shows, no cure in sight. The day I stopped by the gallery, Bleckner was there, standing by a painting of stripes accented with hummingbirds. When I went up to say hello, he shuffled his feet in a little dance, and the squeak of his soles on the polished floor resembled birdcalls. I envied Bleckner his levity, hated him for it.

The show included a painting called *Remember Me*, which I thought I would quickly forget. Red, black, and white stripes on a canvas shaped like a Victorian picture frame, with the title spelled out across the surface in three-dimensional trompe l'oeil. I'd heard that it was inspired by the breakup with a partner and was irked by the juxtaposition of such a casual loss with death. But when I saw the painting again, at the Guggenheim, it was like seeing a familiar face in a crowd of strangers. I stopped to chat. Yes, I do remember you, remember where I was emotionally when I last saw you, several turns of the spiral ago. You're looking fine. Me? I feel great.

The distance of time brought me closer to the painting. Loss is loss, the rejection of love can be more painful than death, and this time the painting did not strike me as an expression of grief over a personal loss. It looked, rather, like a statement about art as a magical means to arrest time.

In a generation Bleckner may be forgotten. His paintings will be banished from places of honor above the sofas of wealthy collectors to their children's dusty attics. But then years later perhaps someone poking around one of those attics will wipe the dust off that funny-shaped object in the corner and notice something red and throbbing beneath the grime. Remember me?

An artist once made a drawing of the Guggenheim in a state of ruin, its concrete cracked and choked with weeds. And in that dilapidated condition, the building appears even more vividly a memorial to Wright. No stranger to rejection, Wright saw New York as a symbol of the architectural establishment that, in his view, had failed to pay adequate tribute to his genius. Here he paid an unforgettable tribute to himself.

Attraction, rejection, fear of longing, fear of exclusion: an intense emotional chemistry bubbled through Wright's building at the show's opening, and only part of it flowed from the paintings. A lot of it came from the glamorous opening-night mob, with its large contingent of scary boys: the young, good-looking men who loiter expectantly on the sidelines of fashion and entertainment, hoping to be plucked from the crowd and offered a modeling job, a condo, a car, or perhaps just a week in the sun.

The cool, predatory frenzy of opening night was distant indeed from the folksy picture ordinarily evoked by Wright: the prairie house, the family hearth, the landscape stretching in all directions. And yet, scary boys and all, the scene couldn't have been truer to the spirit of growth celebrated by Wright's building. The gay subculture, increasingly visible

within the larger culture it has long covertly fertilized, has become a flourishing cultural strain in the decades since the building arose. Bleckner's
show is part of that flowering. So is the hyped-up party atmosphere Bleckner generates.

I can't tell how much of my response is provoked by Bleckner's paintings,
how much by the building, and how much by the experiences they bring
to mind. And I'm not sure that I trust the impulse to sort these things out
just now. If there's an idea embodied in Wright's building, it's that the connection between art and life is at least as important as the separation
between them; that connecting things, in fact, is art's business.

It's a utopian idea. Even Wright couldn't pull it off, and certainly not
here. The Guggenheim, after all, is a museum, not a nightclub, a hospice,
or a Seventh Avenue showroom. The building's walls, its idiosyncratic
shape, define it as a place apart. But to insist on that sense of apartness
once you're inside the building is to overlook what kind of place this is. It's
a place to unlearn the rules of perspective, to give distance a little rest.

Given where I'm coming from, it wasn't a stretch for me to lose perspective on this show. And museumgoers generally, not just critics, need
distance as well as empathy to see art in the round. It's the oscillation
between these positions that gives contemporary art its shimmer. I expect
to go around the spiral myself a few more times before the show comes
down, not because I feel any need to settle the question of its ultimate
meaning or value, but because I want to keep the question in play.

March 26, 1995

A DECLARATION OF THE '60S, BEFORE THE DOUBTS

Bergman movies. Finnish textiles. *Franny and Zooey*. Bertoia chairs. Kind
of takes you back, doesn't it?—to the last liberal moment, before the 1960s
became The Sixties, with all the cultural helter-skelter that decade now
stands for.

The Ford Foundation Building takes you back there too. Designed by
Kevin Roche John Dinkeloo and Associates, this 1967 landmark will
receive the Twenty-five Year Award from the American Institute of Architects at the organization's convention next month. The twelve-story
building is well worth a retrospective look, not only as one of the last first-
rate office buildings to go up in New York but also as the expression of a
time when people were more confident that they knew what first-rate was.

To walk into this building, with its glorious enclosed garden, is to step back into a time of confidence in the power of educated opinion to enforce cultural standards. It is to revisit a time when people knew that European art movies were inherently superior to Hollywood trash, when "good design" did not seem like an attempt to impose elitist taste on mass consumers, when it was possible to believe that progressive social and aesthetic values could march together, hand in hand.

The Ford Foundation Building, at 321 East Forty-second Street, near First Avenue in Manhattan, is a fine example of that belief. Just as the foundation exemplified American philanthropy at its most enlightened, so the building epitomized an ideal of architectural excellence. To begin with, it was plainly a magnificent act of largesse toward the Foundation's employees. The garden, soaring the full twelve stories to the skylight roof, was perhaps the most sumptuous lobby in any Manhattan office building. The placement of the offices along the building's inside perimeter insured that employees enjoyed, in effect, park views. The offices themselves, designed by Warren Platner, were a model of "total design," with features like telephones integrated into desktops.

Still, as distinctive as the building clearly was, it nonetheless remained within the set of values firmly established by the modern movement. The building's unornamented facade manipulated abstract geometric forms and displayed to clear advantage the natural beauty of the warm gray granite. The exposed COR-TEN steel framing showed an innovative use of new materials and building technologies while it also expressed the building's structure. The garden, while imposingly grand, was rationalized on functional grounds as a "thermal buffer" between the offices and the outdoors.

Formalism, functionalism, technical innovation: these were all established modern principles. And when they resulted in a building as gorgeous as this one, it was difficult to dispute their validity. And the validity of modern architecture was the critical subtext of this building's story. The confidence that modernism could continue to evolve within an established framework, that modern architects could innovate without breaking the basic rules: this was as fundamental to the critical success of the building as any of its individual features. It affirmed the authority of those who had embraced modern architecture as a symbol of progressive ideals.

There were those, however, who found visiting the building an unsettling experience. They had heard it described as a great civic contribution. They had heard about the garden. They imagined that the city had been endowed with a spectacular new public space. And this turned out to be grounds for disappointment. True, the public could enter the building, but the garden, while visually inviting, was not a comfortable place to be in. There were no chairs, no benches, no place to sit down. There were steps, but there was also a guard to make sure you didn't recline on them. There was a brick path, but it was more inviting to look at than to walk along. You didn't want to linger even if you were allowed to.

By itself, the discrepancy between the image and the reality may not have seemed like such a big deal. Certainly it did not diminish the building's visual strength, or the amenity afforded its users. But if you had come to suspect that the culture in general was suffering from that kind of discrepancy, then the Ford Foundation was a phenomenon worth pondering. And in fact many people did have precisely that perception about the culture in general. It was called the credibility gap.

Initially applied to the less-than-candid rhetoric about the war in Vietnam of the Lyndon B. Johnson administration, the term also came to stand for a pervasive cultural mismatch between rhetoric and reality, image and substance, word and deed. By 1967, the gap had widened into a chasm. People were eager to look for the sinister substance lurking behind benign cultural images, whether it was the enlightened policies of a foundation financed by a car manufacturer, or the democratic intentions of United States military interventions. Vincent Scully, the architectural historian, gave voice to that impulse when he referred ominously to the "military scale" of the Ford Foundation Building's stark granite facade.

Was this fair? Not if you thought that a building could be detached from its social context. And yet, many of those who wholeheartedly praised the building were relying on the implicit meanings it drew from that context. They just saw the context in different terms. They saw the liberal tradition of modern architecture, its historic commitment to social as well as architectural reform. They regarded modern architecture's acceptance by the establishment as one of that tradition's great triumphs.

Others, however, perceived that the context had been profoundly altered by that victory. It meant that modern forms could be used not only to express progressive social values but also to conceal values that were not at all progressive. So what? Hasn't architecture always been put to such purposes by the rich and powerful? Yes, although it isn't the critic's job to help them get away with it. And modern architecture, after all, had proposed itself as a departure from that precedent. It upheld an ideology of reform. By 1967 the moment had come to recognize the extent to which that ideology had become a mythology, and one alarmingly out of touch with the values it had come to serve.

Yet, on a recent visit to the Ford Foundation, I was struck by how luxurious it was to have this building to criticize. The level of excellence attained by its design is so vastly superior to today's prevailing standards that I felt like jumping into a time machine and defending it from its critics, myself among them.

Nevertheless, the issue raised by the criticism is, if anything, more pertinent now than it was twenty-eight years ago. The difficulty (or futility) of expressing progressive ideas within the visual language of a traditionally conservative art form: this predicament is of particularly acute concern to many younger architects today, who look back to the Modern movement as an idealistic Golden Age of fused social and aesthetic conviction. The Ford Foundation Building can't help them resolve that problem, but it may help them understand it. The building marks the moment when the fusion came unstuck.

April 16, 1995

PRESERVING THE SHRINES OF AN AGE, NOT THE SPIRIT

"Until the first blow fell, no one was convinced that Penn Station really would be demolished or that New York would permit this monumental act of vandalism. . . . We want and deserve tin-can architecture in a tin-horn culture. And we will probably be judged not by the monuments we build but by those we have destroyed."

Those words, first published on the editorial page of this newspaper on October 30, 1963, are among the most important written on architecture in this century. Though Penn Station was destroyed, the words mourning its demise have been chiseled into the record of the art they sought to protect. And the spirit behind the words was written into law less than two years later, in April 1965, when the New York City Landmarks Preservation Commission was created.

Now thirty years old, the legislation approving the landmarks commission is itself a landmark, a monument of architecture and urbanism that has endured legal attacks, public grumblings, and even the occasionally eccentric excesses of its own advocates. Clearly, the commission has meant more to the city than any building of its time. New York Saved: Thirty Years of Landmarks Preservation, a show on view through July 30 at the Museum of the City of New York, documents a sampling of the nearly one thousand buildings and sixty historic districts that have received landmark designation in the past three decades. Grand Central Terminal. The Woolworth Building. The Coney Island Parachute Jump. Ellis Island.

Ladies' Mile. This parade of preservation's greatest hits shows that the movement has been the most influential force toward a civilized urbanism in the past half century.

But the importance of the preservation movement extends beyond the fields of urbanism and architectural history. The movement also deserves recognition in the history of ideas. Preservation emerged as a grassroots movement; it is not usually thought of as a hotbed of sophisticated intellectual discourse. The movement is not, for instance, represented in *Architecture Culture 1943–1968,* Joan Ockman's otherwise comprehensive anthology of developments in postwar architecture. Still, preservation gave rise to one of the era's most influential social critiques. It blew an ear-shattering whistle on the ideology of progress. It helped stop the dogma of newer-is-better dead in its tracks.

Penn Station was in its last years when I began to explore New York, and I confess that the building did not have the effect on me that it apparently had on the architectural historian Vincent Scully: it did not make me feel that I was entering the city like a god. Rather, with the vaults of its concourse soaring into sooty obscurity, the station was the perfect introduction to New York's extraordinary powers of indifference and intimidation. How I loved it! Anything less overpowering would have been a cruel disappointment.

The new station, which began to take shape even before the last remains of the old had been carted off to a New Jersey dump, simply restated the lesson in different terms. As it materialized to New York's blaring sound track of real estate construction, the new station demonstrated the city's chilling power to sweep away everything that couldn't keep up with changing times. For there was a sardonic flip side to the idea of judging the city by the monuments it destroyed: What kind of awesome place was this that used up its greatest buildings like Kleenex?

The old station, built between 1906 and 1910 and modeled after the Roman Baths of Caracalla, was a classical monument. The new station, including the Madison Square Garden complex that arose above it, was an abysmal exercise in modern functionalism. And the stylistic difference between the two buildings tended to obscure the cultural thread that bound them together. Both buildings were symbols of progress. While one referred stylistically to history, and the other appeared to depart from it, both were manifestations of the same cultural tradition. Both were temples to the industrial city and its faith in its endless capacity to remake itself. Over time, the face of progress changed; the religion remained the same.

This, in fact, is a paradox of the preservation movement. In protecting the monuments of the industrial city, preservation has, in a sense, violated their spirit. It has given a sepia, retrospective tint to buildings whose makers looked unflinchingly toward the future. Penn Station, it should be kept in mind, was not only a glorious monument to a civic ideal. It was also a gigantic advertisement for an industry that helped undermine the city by making it possible for people to live elsewhere. The railroad was one of the driving forces that brought the tinhorn culture into explosive being.

Resistant though it was to the cult of progress, preservation has not been a reactionary movement. Rather, as a grassroots phenomenon, it has been "progressive" in the political sense. It has enabled people to gain leverage against market forces, bestowing on private citizens and civic groups the kind of moral and legal authority that once resided with city planning.

But this progressive agenda is a far cry from the monolithic idea of progress that prevailed in the industrial city. And its success in furthering that agenda produced more than a change in law. It produced a change in consciousness. The tradition of New York, after all, was not that of ancient Rome, notwithstanding a train station that looked like the Baths of Caracalla. It was the tradition of the marketplace, the tradition of the new: a custom honored even by the city's name. In this sense, preservation should be celebrated not for affirming tradition but for flouting it.

It happens that the years since the landmarks preservation laws went into effect have not been a golden age for architecture in New York. Is there a connection? Is it Penn Station's revenge that the city should gradually subside into a theme-park version of itself, with retro lampposts lighting the streets where brutal invention once ruled?

Oddly, the retro theme has become disconcertingly similar to the old booster version of progress in providing a simplistic mind-set that architects have followed uncritically. Unlike the old version of progress, however, it has not given rise to buildings of genuine stature. Perhaps this is the natural progression of the industrial city as it tries to adapt itself to the postindustrial age. But the risk today is that we will be judged not by the landmarks we have destroyed but by the ones we have failed to build.

April 30, 1995

A FLARE FOR FANTASY:
Miami Vice MEETS FORTY-SECOND STREET

Ka-boom! Arquitectonica has landed. Landed the job, anyhow. The Miami-based architects, renowned for their colorfully jazzed-up modern designs, have been chosen to create a keystone to the multibuilding complex that represents the rebirth of Times Square—the major new convention hotel planned for Eighth Avenue and Forty-second Street. The legendary mecca of raffish good times and the architectural firm with rhythm, Forty-second Street and Arquitectonica are a match made in honky-tonk heaven.

The fruit of their union will not be mistaken for the Plaza. Don't expect oak paneling, marble columns, or palm trees wafting gently over decorous afternoon teas. Instead, this glitzy Ritz (actually, a Westin) will erupt with vibrant color and flashing lights in a building designed to look like an exploding meteor. Scheduled for completion by January 1, 2000, it's a jazz fanfare for the millennium, an apocalypse with room service.

Selected May 11 over competing designs by two internationally prominent architects, Michael Graves and Zaha Hadid, the hotel will be Arquitectonica's first building in New York. It will also enlarge the Times Square presence of the Disney Corporation, which is affiliated in the project with the designated developer, the Tishman Urban Development Corporation, and also responsible for the renovation of the New Amsterdam Theater just east of the hotel site. As the participation of those corporate Goliaths suggests, this architectural fantasy is big-time business, though money for its completion is yet to be raised. Economic return, not aesthetic merit, is the paramount goal of the project's government sponsors, the New York State Urban Development Corporation and the New York City Economic Development Corporation.

But the best guys won anyhow. While all three designs were good, Arquitectonica's captured the spirit of place: the unsubtle fusion of erotics and economics that is Times Square. Their design embodies the drives, defenses, fantasies, and symbols that animate this legendary crossroads of dollars and desire.

The design is a vertical triptych. Stretching along the north side of Forty-second Street will be an entertainment and retail complex designed by specialists in retail outlets, D'Agostino Izzo Quirk Architects. Housed in a mix of new and renovated structures, the complex will retain the existing scale of the neighboring low-rise buildings while pumping it full of new life. Restaurants, shops, superstores, and an IMAX theater are among the uses currently planned.

A ten-story Disney Vacation Club, containing one hundred time-share apartments, will anchor the corner of Forty-second and Eighth, or possibly blow it away, for the jagged-edged structure is supposed to represent a meteor moments after the crash. Rising above the fallen body is the 680-room hotel, a 47-story tower sheathed with colored glass. A curving streak of light, representing the meteor's trail, splits the skyscraper down the middle. Blue-toned glass clads the west side of the tower in a pattern of vertical stripes, while the east side is glazed with horizontal bands of copper and orange. Some will find the tower's aesthetic unpleasantly reminiscent of the 1964–65 New York World's Fair. I like the flashback to that populuxe extravaganza.

In accordance with the guidelines for the project, the design makes heavy use of lighting and signs. Immense "supersigns" will march across the retail and entertainment complex in a neon Pop Art parade. The tower will erupt periodically in a light show designed by Fisher Marantz, the lighting wizards. High-powered beams within the curving "meteor path" will shoot up into the sky, while clouds of "pixie dust" explode at the base.

New York's leading avant-garde architects, Elizabeth Diller and Ricardo Scofidio, have designed a tower of video monitors for the hotel's Eighth Avenue corner, while a ten-story mural of glass mosaics will cover the vacation club with postcard images of New York landmarks. Why should Arquitectonica resort to these Chamber of Commerce clichés? These architects have already demonstrated an unrivaled talent to create dazzling urban icons of their own.

You may have already seen one. The "sky patio," an outdoor terrace punched into the side of one of Arquitectonica's early high-rises in Miami, was featured in the weekly opening credits of the flashy '80s television series *Miami Vice.* The design epitomized the firm's ability to enliven a spare modern architectural framework with sensuous, surrealistic flair.

A single, iconic palm tree rises in the patio against the blue sky of tropical paradise. But there's a snake in this garden, a red spiral staircase coiling up behind the palm as if to pluck something from its fronds. Who said that the forbidden fruit wasn't a coconut? Or a Coca-Cola? Or coke?

The colors here are primary; so are the implied emotions. A red balcony juts out from a yellow wall, suspended like a diving platform over a blue-tiled Jacuzzi. The red is the color of lipstick on a collar, of passion, perhaps danger. Will we fall or be pushed? Into the whirlpool or into heaven? Pleasure and risk go hand in hand in this vertiginous realm of the senses.

Arquitectonica started building young. That's the first important thing to know about them. Bernardo Fort-Brescia and Laurinda Spear, who founded the firm in 1977, were the first architects of the baby boom generation to build prominent, large-scale projects, like the string of residential high-rises they set along Brickell Avenue in Miami in the early 1980s. At an age when most architects are still in their apprenticeship years, Fort-Brescia and Spear were helping to shape a new image for Miami. That image was youthful, it was sexy, and, above all, it was modern.

That's the second important thing to know about Arquitectonica. As the first voice of its generation to make itself heard in major projects, the firm let it be known that postmodernism had peaked. The younger generation just wasn't picking up on it. Modern architecture, it turned out, hadn't come to an end with I. M. Pei. Indeed, in Arquitectonica's Bauhaus-does-the-rhumba version, modernism never looked livelier.

The firm's vision was evident in their first building, the Spear House, designed in 1977 for Ms. Spear's parents. Much used as a backdrop by fashion photographers in the late 1970s, this was a Bruce Weber photograph of a building: a lean, muscular structure that showed a lot of skin. With a blue swimming pool screened by a wall of glass blocks and pink stucco, the house fused the era's twin obsessions with voyeurism and flesh.

Arquitectonica were hardly the first to bring sensuality to modern design. In the 1930s, Latin American architects forged a sultry tropical version of the International Style. But for those who still equated modern buildings with bleak glass boxes and brutal concrete sheds, Arquitectonica's hedonistic update of Latin modernism came as a jolt, and not always a pleasant one.

I once saw Fort-Brescia drive a student audience crazy with a presentation that dramatized how architecture could be at once aesthetically progressive and socially hard to swallow. One project, a home for a Florida couple, had the students bouncing off the walls. It seemed that the couple enjoyed swimming together, but he liked to swim in fresh water while she liked to swim in sea water. The ingenious solution? A pair of serpentine pools that overlapped each other, I don't remember how, in a kind of acquatic duet. As I recall, there was also a third lane, for exotic fish. And the pool was to be outfitted with a glass bottom, so swimmers, peering down, could behold a temperature-controlled cellar of rare vintage wines.

Then followed the staggeringly beautiful Banco de Credito in Lima, Peru, with boardrooms as glamorous as the sets for a '40s Hollywood musical and an oval entrance atrium that recalled the 1594 anatomical theater at the University of Padua. But those entering the atrium were more likely to be maimed than healed, for its function was to provide sur-veillance for terrorist attacks; the bank was not a beloved institution when the revolutionary group Shining Path was on the rampage. When a jour-nalist friend of mine flew down to write about the building, she was alarmed to find that security guards, toting machine guns, were on hand to accompany her to the bank from her hotel. And she wasn't even making a deposit.

Most architects who build in cities today have to deal with security issues, but somehow Arquitectonica's aesthetic seems to capture this unsettling contemporary mixture of danger and glamour, eros and death. Visitors to Times Square do not generally take bodyguards, despite the area's notoriety as a combat zone. But here a hazard is also likely to come from those who resent the whole Forty-second Street project and detest its sanitized razzmatazz. Those who relish the authentically seedy can hardly be expected to welcome the flag of Disney, the cosponsor, raised over a street corner better known to viewers of the late-night *Robin Byrd Show.*

Some wouldn't want to see Disney putting down roots in any part of town. To them the company stands for theme parks, for fantasylands that are at once irresponsibly escapist and oppressively controlled. Do we want to welcome the arrival of that dubious formula within the city gates? Like it or not, it's here. And its arrival should provoke us to recognize that fan-tasy and control were shaping urban space long before Disney showed up.

It's odd the way we keep compulsively rubbing this spot, Times Square, as if the prurience it signifies had not escaped long ago into the atmosphere and filtered into the culture at large. The French writer Jean Baudrillard once theorized that the function of Disneyland is to keep Americans from seeing that their country is Disney land; the genuine imitations differ only in the accuracy of the simulation. Perhaps one reason we make such a fetish of "cleaning up" Times Square is that it diverts attention from the degree to which the entire culture has become eroticized.

It's hard to take cleaning up Times Square seriously with all those Calvin Klein billboard models bulging voluptuously at skyscraper scale. Still, the billboards help clarify the line between permissible and imper-missible desire. What's taboo is not desire but its satisfaction. Consumer culture thrives on appetite; satisfaction makes the market wither. You can wear Calvin Klein's Escape, but you cannot escape Calvin Klein; cannot avoid the constant bombardment of images designed to keep us in a con-stant state of craving.

If we really wanted to clean up Times Square, we should probably start by banning skyscrapers, not building new ones. Is the city's indefatigable vertical thrust really suitable for viewing by children under seventeen? Arquitectonica's tower is not much naughtier than most. From some angles, the building will appear to be doing a strip, peeling back its glass skin to reveal the reveling of conventioneers. And that orgasmic forty-seven-story light show should be a local landmark like no other. Sometimes a cigar is just a cigar, but an explosion of "pixie dust"? In Times Square?

The architects have described the project as a deliberate evocation of chaos. The eclectic mix of signs, styles, and storefronts in the retail base, especially, is meant to look like a jumbled heap. One could interpret this on a purely cartoon level as the physical upheaval caused by the meteor's impact. Or, on a more sophisticated level of urbanism, one could view the jumble as a metaphor for the havoc unleashed by development in a city from which planning, for the most part, has all but disappeared.

I see this outstandingly smart design as a study in urban psychology. It seeks to visualize the forces that link private emotions and public space. The design's chaotic pileup of signs, stores, and attractions is an invitation not just to consume but to be hungry. I can think of no other recent work of architecture that pictures more accurately the disordered universe that desire brings in its wake.

This is the private universe, the life shaken up by the drives that bring people to the city, to connect with others, with destiny, with themselves. And it's the universe of the city itself, propelled through time by its unflagging willingness to sacrifice order to ambition.

May 21, 1995

WHERE THE READERS ARE INSIDE THE BOOKS

Shutters shut and open; so do minds. I went to Paris expecting to dislike the new Bibliothèque Nationale de France and came away enchanted by it. Like all of the Grands Travaux—the large-scale public works undertaken in the city by President François Mitterrand—the library has sparked considerable animosity. Smart people don't like it. The design by the young French architect Dominique Perrault does indeed defy common sense. What kind of nutty idea is it to put books in high-rise towers and bury readers underground? Why bother to build four glass skyscrapers only to line them inside with rows of wooden shut-

ters? And what can you say about the library's symbolic concept: four
L-shaped towers, grouped around an open square like four immense open
books?

But people go to libraries more for introspection than for panoramic
city views. The library's damp, Seine-side site prohibited carving out sufficient space to store more than two-thirds of the library's 12 million volumes underground. And when you're actually at the library, you may wind
up asking yourself when was the last time you saw a work of architecture
this logical, this clear?

The $1 billion project, which will open in September 1996, is the last
of Mitterrand's Grands Travaux, and the most spectacularly monumental.
The building program as a whole has been criticized for the inflated scale
of the projects—la Grande Arche de la Défense, le Grand Louvre—and
the library's twenty-two-story glass skyscrapers do not exactly keep a low
profile. For some, in fact, the towers may be the salt rubbed in the urban
wound caused by the infamous Tour Montparnasse, the black-glass behe-
moth, built in the late 1960s, that remains a symbol of the overcompensation that can result when a city of distinctive historic character loses
confidence in its own modernity.

Actually, the library casts no shadow over tourist Paris; its towers cannot be seen from the streets of the historic center. Indeed, along with the
Bastille Opera House and the Ministry of Finance, the library is part of an
ambitious scheme to enhance the public amenities of eastern Paris. Situated in the Thirteenth arrondissement, across the Seine from Frank
Gehry's American Center and the new Bercy Park, the library rises from a
ragged cityscape of tall modern buildings, flagrantly devoid of old-world
charm.

Perrault, who was thirty-six when he won the international competition to design the library in 1989, has already accumulated an impressive
body of built work, including schools, housing, and factory buildings
throughout provincial France. His offices are housed in eastern Paris in a
striking glass building, which he designed in 1986, less than a mile from
the library.

The library augments the existing Bibliothèque Nationale, a collection
of buildings near the Palais Royale that is graced with a spectacular main
reading room, a nineteenth-century masterpiece of iron construction by
Henri Labrouste. The new building, which can receive more than three
million visitors a year, will contain 3,600 reading places, about half of
them reserved for research scholars. The rest are set aside for the general
public, which was not accommodated in the old library. An exhibition center, auditorium, conference room, and restaurants will enlarge the public

dimension of the library, which will also serve as the hub of a computer-ized network linking France's regional library system.

Stacking books into the form of a monument: that's the main function of the four towers. But they also state the architectural themes that recur throughout the project. They introduce Perrault's palette: glass, wood, steel, concrete—a quartet that echoes the four towers. They show off, like billboards, the impeccable detailing that Perrault uses to transform his industrial materials into frankly glamorous décor. And they state the design's central concept, the framing of a spatial void.

Offices, behind movable wooden shutters, occupy the first nine floors of the towers. Above, closed shutters screen the caissons where books are stored. The visual effect of wood under glass, which sounds silly, begins to make sense as you approach the library and discover that wood is used extensively throughout the project. The towers anchor the corners of an immense rectangular podium that is made of concrete but is sheathed in unfinished wood, rising one and a half stories above street level. Bor-dered by stairs on all four sides, the podium resembles a stepped pyra-mid. It's an odd collision of architectural codes—a monumental staircase made of a material that brings to mind the creaking floorboards of an old house.

The top of the podium forms an immense deck, or esplanade, some-what nautical in character because of its surface of bare wooden planks. In this wide, open space, the towers contract to a scale more sculptural than architectural. Though too stark and exposed to create a sense of haven, the deck nonetheless possesses the exalting power of the raised urban plat-form (think of the top of the steps at the New York Public Library) to turn a chaotic cityscape into a hypnotically compelling spectacle.

As you cross the deck, an immense well yawns open at the center; drawing nearer, you glimpse the tops of trees. They turn out to be the crowns of tall Roman pines, the tips of a large sunken forest six stories below. Roughly the size of the Palais Royale, the forest exudes a lush calm at the library's heart. Now it may occur to you that Perrault has used wood symbolically as well as visually, to denote paper's raw source. Looking up at the towers, you see that the pale wooden louvers recall the ecru covers of French books. The proximity of nature to culture will remind some vis-itors of French cuisine.

A sloping gangway with a moving tread leads visitors from the deck to the reception hall, three stories below. And here you realize that far from burying readers alive, Perrault has installed them in a stylish modern ver-sion of a medieval cloister. The forest, surrounded by glass walls, is a cloister garden; tall piers of concrete—structural columns—exert a Gothic thrust.

On the two main reading levels, floors and research carrels are made of wood; here the contrasting material is not glass but steel. Perrault sometimes uses steel as if it were a kind of opaque glass, like the steel panels on walls and ceilings that reflect cool light: these eliminate any trace of subterranean gloom. Perrault uses the metal most ingeniously as large panels of steel mesh. First seen on the thin ends of the book towers, where it screens the fire stairs, the steel mesh recurs throughout the library's interior. Perrault loops it like fabric from the ceiling, stretches it taut against windows to soften the light, and hangs it like high-tech blankets from the walls of the four deep escalator lobbies that plunge below the corners of the towers. Rich, red carpeting, along with the wood, takes the chill off the steel.

Looking at these crisp glass towers, some visitors will be tempted to dismiss them as flashbacks to the 1950s and '60s, as pale reprises of the Seagram Building and Lever House in Manhattan. The towers are indeed Miesian in being "almost nothing," but this is a "nothing" that has been brought forward in time by refinements gleaned from the minimalist art of Sol LeWitt, Donald Judd, and Eva Hesse.

And extended backward in time by context. Seen here in Paris, the towers remind you of the deep historical roots from which the International Style arose. Frank Lloyd Wright once criticized Mies for making "nineteenth-century architecture," but a modernist today need not find that description objectionable, especially in Paris, the greatest of all nineteenth-century cities. Wright was probably thinking of that era's great iron and glass sheds: the Crystal Palace, the Grand Palais. Perrault's library is an intelligent descendent of those modern prototypes.

Reading and nothingness. Perrault's design distills moments of French cultural history that we know mainly from books. The thirteenth-century origins of modern intellectual life. The rational grids of Descartes. Boullée's pure geometric forms and the Enlightenment clarity they embodied. The Romantic fling with nature. The Existential void. Words rising from the table in a café, to evaporate into thin air or to be captured in a notebook, a sketch, a book, a building.

June 11, 1995

BROADWAY'S REAL HITS ARE ITS
ANTIQUE THEATERS

Nobody goes to the theater for the theater. It's *Sunset Boulevard*, not the Minskoff, that people are shelling out bucks to see. The theater building is just the frame around the picture, the cover of the book.

But let's look at some frames anyhow. Let's judge some covers. For those frames, those covers, have a drama, a pictorial content, of their own. They affect the total experience of playgoing—and not always for the better. And they can add or detract from the spectacle that is the Theater District itself.

The district is now expanding. In the spring of 1997 the New Amsterdam Theater on West Forty-second Street will open under the auspices of the Disney Corporation. A design by Hardy Holzman Pfeiffer Associates, the New York architectural firm, will restore the theater to its Art Deco splendor. A Canadian company, Livent, has announced plans to renovate two other historic theaters—the Lyric and the Academy—across the street.

The restoration of these landmarks reaffirms a fact of Broadway life: shows come and go, but the theaters remain. They are, in their own way, Broadway's longest-running hits. Actors may become celebrities, but the theaters are royalty, or so some of their names suggest. Palace. Majestic. Royale. Imperial. And their architecture can be as regal as their names.

Alas, the thirty-five playhouses in the Broadway Theater District also suffer from some of the same sense of displacement that afflicts royalty in the modern world. Twenty-five years ago, when I was a student in London, I was shocked one day to hear the Changing of the Guard accompanied by a rousing brass rendition of "Hello, Dolly!" Broadway show tunes? For Her Majesty? What was the world coming to?

Today Broadway has become a New York equivalent to the Changing of the Guard. While movies and television now attract the most energetic forces in popular culture, Broadway has evolved into a stylized cultural ritual. Contemporaneity is the exception on the Great White Way. Here tradition rules, and in this sense we go to Broadway for the frames, or at least for the atmosphere they help conjure up.

The ornate whorls and swags of their sumptuous interiors capture an ethos, a state of mind as distinctive as those that pervade Greenwich Village, Harlem, SoHo, or the Upper East Side. The chandeliers and plaster reliefs are one with the sound of rustling programs, the black-and-white ushers' costumes, the perfume of damp fur on winter Wednesday afternoons. Broadway itself is a frame, an architecture of anticipation.

Red-and-gold disease. That's what Lincoln Kirstein's mother called it when her son, the future ballet impresario, started haunting the theaters of Boston. Named after the colors of the iconic fringed velvet curtain, the contagion typically strikes adolescents between the ages of twelve and fifteen. It hit me around 1960, while I was sitting in the last row of the second balcony of the Erlanger Theater in downtown Philadelphia. I could hardly make out the stage, but for $2.50 I had a magnificent view of the ceiling.

The disease was an itch, the theater a place to scratch it. It wasn't just about show biz. Movies and television couldn't satisfy it. They were industrial products, made for mass distribution. A theater was a place. It was specifically urban. It wouldn't come to you. You went to it. You took a train. Getting there was part of its meaning: the itch was the adolescent one of yearning for a wider world. The stage gave the yearning a focus. The lights went down, the curtain went up, and you got more than a play. You got a two-hour preview of coming attractions: the urban world where you might make a place. The theater, in short, was a place for the care and feeding of dreams.

By the time I got to my dream city in the mid-1960s, I discovered I was part of a generation that had little use for Broadway. Movies were the "relevant" art form. Broadway was for tired businessmen. Theater architecture only confirmed Broadway's obsolescence. All that heavy period décor, that molded plaster and flaking ivory paint were ancient history. Times Square was where you went for movies; you could see a double feature for $2 and dream of being an auteur.

Unfortunately, the '60s generation was not alone in hanging out crepe for the Great White Way. Developers, too, saw Broadway's theaters as so many "underdeveloped" pieces of property that would be better used for skyscrapers. Fortunately, New York had a mayor, John V. Lindsay, who loved the stage and also believed that it was the responsibility of the public sector to protect the city's cultural assets. Alarmed by the prospect of the wrecker's ball, the Lindsay administration created a special zoning district—the city's first—along with legislation that rewarded developers for including new legitimate theaters in their plans for high-rise towers.

Enacted in 1967, the special zoning was enlightened public policy. But it did not protect Broadway from becoming the canyon of tall, cheerless buildings that it is today. And the chilly theaters housed within them—

including the Minskoff, the Gershwin, the Circle in the Square, and the Marriott Marquis—are not likely to precipitate a major outbreak of red-and-gold disease. Hope that the Theater District's historical character could be stabilized did not arrive until the early 1970s, when the Landmarks Commission designated the first of what would eventually total thirty-three theaters as historic landmarks.

The legislation was fought by theater owners on the reasonable grounds that the city had, in effect, landmarked an industry. Without shows to fill the theaters, who cared whether their decorations remained intact? And this was not, moreover, just any industry but an art form that needs the flexibility any art requires if it is to evolve. The theater owners were stuck in a bind; criticized by some for the fossilization of Broadway, they were now compelled by law to freeze their playhouses in time.

By the 1980s, however, some owners had passionately embraced the preservationist cause. Since 1989, for instance, Jujamcyn Theaters has restored three of its five Broadway playhouses, and these brilliant restorations, when contrasted with the newer theaters, help clarify why the older buildings offer a more inviting frame.

One of the best things going for them is their relationship to the street. Few of the older houses have vast, ornate lobbies; often, the ticket vestibule opens directly into the rear of the auditorium. But the streets of the theater district are themselves a lobby, part of an urban procession that begins with Times Square. The bow tie–shaped square is a circus of signs that beckon people toward different destinations, one might even say destinies. Burger King. Colony Records. Howard Johnson. The Hotel Macklowe. Flash Dancers. The David Letterman Show. Die Hard Forever.

But on the side streets, the signs become more specialized. They are theater signs, marquees, and vertical signs, legends spelled out in the white dots of bare electric bulbs. With a ticket in your pocket, you connect the dots. Your destination is special.

The side street is like a filter, dividing more from less privileged crowds. The more privileged gather on the sidewalk, taking in the atmosphere, pausing before handing over the ticket and surrendering to a process of transformation, from a crowd to an audience, with its hierarchical configuration: orchestra or balcony, aisle or rear row side. The transition from exterior to interior is not seamless, but it is fluid, an overture before the overture, a progression of visual and spatial links between the wild, wide-open spectacle of the city and the close focus of the proscenium stage.

At the newer Broadway theaters, the continuity with the street is broken. The Marquis Theater is placed three stories above street level. To reach it, theatergoers have to ride an escalator lined with sad strips of partly burned-out Christmas tree lamps, negotiate a narrow hotel corridor, and weave their way through clumps of the Marriott's guests before entering the hall. It is not a theater environment but that of a hotel, of homogenized "hospitality," better suited to a convention than a chorus line. Like the hotel itself, this theater speaks not of love for the city but of fear of it, fear of its streets, its chaos, its life.

Things aren't much better at the Gershwin, where you enter through a stark square mouth that bears an unmistakable resemblance to the entrance of a parking garage and in fact is one. Instead of honoring pedestrians, treating even casual passersby to a bit of curtain-time glamour, the Gershwin turns them into second-class citizens in a place designed for cars. Overscaled, underdressed, the new theaters themselves are like parking lots for bodies; they give you the unsettling sensation that there's a number stamped on your forehead as well as your ticket.

Part of the bleakness may reflect the fact that they were built by real estate developers, not show biz folk. Their hearts weren't in it. But the modern style of the theaters has never been known for heart in any case. The style has served well for movie houses: movies and modernism were both products of the industrial culture. Moreover, modern architecture's ethic of objective truth suited the realism made possible by movie photography. But a Broadway stage is a platform for artifice. It's a place where even the most realistic situations must be re-created nightly out of smoke and mirrors. And the ornate interiors of Broadway's traditional show houses makes disbelief considerably easier to suspend.

At Jujamcyn's magnificently restored Walter Kerr Theater on West Forty-eighth Street, for example, fantasy engulfs the playgoer before the lights go down. Designed for the Shuberts in 1921 by Herbert J. Krapp, the former Ritz was renovated in 1989 by the architect Francesca Russo, formerly of the Roger Morgan Studio (now with her own firm Campagna & Russo). Working with Howard Rogut of Jujamcyn, Ms. Russo removed a lamentable Art Deco pastiche, created in 1981, and took the theater back to its original design, a free-form interpretation of Italian Renaissance style.

Here, beneath the golden glow of clear glass electric bulbs, griffins prance against rose-colored backdrops, while allegorical depictions of drama and dance cavort in murals surrounding the stage. For viewers plunged into this mythological panorama, it's no great stretch to believe that the human cast of *Love! Valour! Compassion!* is actually frolicking in a pool, or to empathize with the exaggerated characters they play.

Empathy, indeed, is the key to the powerful grip of red-and-gold disease. When Charles Garnier, architect of the Paris Opera, designed the building's interior, he understood that red and gold tonalities heightened the viewer's receptivity to lyric art. Such a palette, he wrote, "penetrates you and stimulates you without you suspecting it."

Ornament, too, had a psychological role to play; it did more than reflect the material excesses of a gilded age. Ornament established a sense of scale. It helped to relieve the sense of confinement, enabling an enclosed space to feel as expansive as the world outside, a globe seen from within. It aided acoustics, reduced tedium, and showed by example that the imagination is generous.

Pioneering for its time, Garnier's deliberate use of color and form to induce a psychological frame of mind became the standard formula for the traditional Broadway stage. The formula was ridiculed by modern dramatists as well as modern designers. What did bogus Italian Renaissance froufrou have to do with the drama of modern life? All that plaster artifice looked like an escape from theater's true essence.

A contemporary audience has a different take on things. We see that the essence of theater is, literally, make-believe, that artifice can be a means of grasping truth, that a piece of silly decoration can lift the curtain on the emotions, other people's and one's own. Then it's on with the show.

July 30, 1995

A "MONSTER" OF A MASTERPIECE IN CONNECTICUT

What is a masterpiece? The Morgan Library in New York periodically asks critics to address this question, but I've been putting off giving it a shot because *masterpiece* is a word I haven't used in years. It's such a big, booming word, the Voice of Posterity speaking; it puts me in mind of the Wizard of Oz, fiddling nervously with his dials behind a curtain. I fear that Toto might come along at any minute and expose the whole creaking mechanism of a critic's apparatus with a rude tug. Isn't it enough for a building to be good? Intelligent? Fun?

A few weeks ago, however, I saw a new building for which the word *masterpiece* seems exactly right: a little pavilion Philip Johnson has built for himself at his home here. Johnson, who turned eighty-nine in July, has announced that he plans to move to Rome when he hits one hundred. In the meantime, he is making arrangements to turn his forty-acre Connecticut estate into a historic site. The new building, situated just inside the entrance to the property, will be the visitors' pavilion. People will gather there to watch a video on Philip Johnson and narrated by him before touring the Glass House, the Sculpture Gallery, and the seven other structures that make up the domain he calls "the diary of an eccentric architect."

The pavilion will certainly give visitors a crash course in Johnson's legendary wit, for what he has designed is an orientation center whose chief function is disorientation—a bending, rippling, twisting structure with an interior that puts computerized morphs to shame.

Johnson calls it the Monster, pronouncing the last syllable with a broad *A*, as in gangsta rap. I'd call the building Love and Death, because of the stark red and black Johnson has painted its two halves. About the size of a largish garage, the pavilion is made of concrete sprayed onto a flexible metal framework. The red side, the building's most prominent, rises out of a green field like a ship's prow—or plunges into the ground like a bloody blade. Its razor-sharp edge reaches a height of twenty feet. The black half ripples around the rear, a slightly sinister shadow, the specter of passion or curiosity spent.

You enter through a glass door, fitted into a gash in the wall, an opening roughly trapezoidal in shape. "Abandon Euclid, all ye who enter here," the doorway might be marked. Inside, only the flat plane of the floor conforms to the conventional grid of Euclidean space. Beyond a small entrance area, the interior twists to the left and widens into a larger space, eventually to be a gift shop. To the right, the pavilion's one window looks out across the field toward the white, freestanding study where Johnson designs. Opposite the window, there's a doorway, shaped like a nose carved into a pumpkin. It leads into a small room where the video will be screened.

Though radically novel, the interior nonetheless recalls Johnson's long-standing preoccupation with "procession"—the modulation of the spaces through which people move. In the 1960s, Johnson articulated that concept in buildings like the New York State Theater, with its spatial sequence from the Lincoln Center Plaza, through the ticket lobby, up the grand marble stairs to the promenade above.

Thirty years later, the concept has borne this strange fruit of a building whose interior may well contain more spatial modulations than in all of Lincoln Center's theaters combined. Every two steps takes you into a different space. The width of the room has changed. The slant of the walls, the ceiling height, the view ahead have changed, and the changes are nearly impossible to predict from the position two steps behind. Without the Euclidean system, with its attendant grids and perspectives, there is no reliable way to mentally connect the space ahead to the one behind. And yet it flows. The effect is a bit like a first swimming lesson. First you sink, then you float.

Johnson asks why it has taken modern architecture to abandon Euclid. He is the right person to be asking the question. The Seagram Building, on which he collaborated with Mies van der Rohe almost forty years ago, was as elegant a farewell to classical geometry as could be imagined. But instead of moving forward, Johnson turned backward—to Boullée, Palladio, Soane; the rest is postmodern "history."

This building looks backward, too, chiefly to German Expressionist architecture designed in the years after World War I: to the workers' monument Walter Gropius designed in 1920, to the organic fantasy designs of Hermann Finsterlin. No doubt Johnson himself will enlighten us about other references in due course. Perhaps he will also be candid enough to admit that he himself had a part in preventing modern architecture from passing beyond Euclid. As an early proponent of the New Objectivity, he helped bury the Expressionist era. That may be why the visitors' pavilion is so strong formally. It has the force of an uncovered repression.

Perhaps it should not be surprising that an avowed formalist has designed a building with such wonderful forms. But the truth is that Johnson's forms have seldom been as strong as his formalist convictions. Frequently, his designs have been not so much forms as gestures—a Chippendale top, a crenellated roof. These gestures made Johnson a leading corporate architect of the 1980s; they served as glorified logos, trademarks in the cityscape. The visitors' pavilion is also strongly gestural, but it doesn't stop there. The building's formal inventiveness is consistent throughout.

What is a masterpiece? It is an object with something important to teach about a maker, a medium, and its time. Johnson's preoccupations with history, form, and procession are all part of the lesson this building could lead a visitor to explore. But the chief lesson here derives from the disorienting space of the building itself, for it distills the most vibrant aspect of Johnson's contribution. Johnson is known as a proselytizer, a champion of new directions. But, in fact, he has been at least as influential in abandoning movements as in advocating them. Mies van der Rohe set a course; Johnson's role has been to change directions. Disorientation, upsetting even apple carts full of perfectly fine apples, has been his area of greatest expertise. The architect's forty-acre "diary" is a record of enthusiasms embraced and dropped: International Style, Neoclassic, Islamic, Constructivist, Gehry contemporary, English picturesque. Johnson has often compressed multiple references into a single design. But the new pavilion captures the giddiness of Johnson's lifelong ride through the twentieth century. In this, the Monster is unique: an ideal introduction to an architect who has found the century's uncertainties ultimately more tantalizing than its beliefs.

September 17, 1995

AMONG THE FOUNTAINS WITH TADAO ANDO: CONCRETE DREAMS IN THE SUN KING'S COURT

Tadao Ando at Versailles? What a silly picture. It's hard to imagine a more howling mismatch between East and West. Mr. Ando, the winner of this year's Pritzker Architecture Prize, is a Japanese architect celebrated for his austere, spiritually ennobling buildings fashioned from smoothly finished raw concrete. Versailles, by contrast so extreme as to seem like a prankster's setup, is the world capital of froufrou, a building synonymous with the ornate excesses of rococo style.

Yet, here is Mr. Ando, placidly strolling in the stately gardens of the Grand Trianon, posing serenely against the gilt-encrusted balustrade of a pink marble staircase. In the distance, fountains play. They will gush for only half an hour or so, for the plumbing that operates them is ancient. Originally, in the mid-1600s, the fountains provided a fleeting visual divertissement only when Louis XIV passed by. Imagine living in a house that erupts with joy at the mere sight of one.

Now it is May, and the waters dance for Mr. Ando, with perhaps a royal splash or two in the direction of the other distinguished guests who have traveled to Versailles to see him accept the Pritzker award, widely considered the most prestigious honor in the field.

Mr. Ando, fifty-three, is the third Japanese architect to receive the Pritzker since 1979, when it was first awarded. It was an unexpected choice. There were rumors that the jury might cause an uproar were they to pass over Arata Isozaki, a Japanese architect several years Mr. Ando's senior who enjoys a much wider reputation internationally. No furor ensued. Instead, the jury's decision was received as an appropriately sober choice for sober times.

Mr. Isozaki, a wildly eclectic architect whose career blossomed in the 1980s, has possibly been tainted by that era's insatiable appetite for riotous formal invention. Mr. Ando's work looks like the morning after. It puts us on a strict aesthetic diet of geometric forms that come in every shade of gray.

Since I haven't been to Japan, I'm familiar with Mr. Ando's work only through photographic images. The cross rising up from the lake outside the Church on the Water in Hokkaido. The crisp glass doorway set into travertine-like concrete in the Azuma House in Sumiyoshi, Osaka. Green garden squares spilling down a hillside on the rooftop of the Rokko housing complex in Hyōgo. Lily pads floating on a concrete disk in Hyōgo's Water Temple.

Marie Antoinette would not have warmed to any of these places.

It is 7:00 on the evening of the ceremony, and about four hundred people have gathered for cocktails on the terrace of the Grand Trianon. An aristocracy of talent, they include previous Pritzker winners, like Hans Hollein of Austria and Fumihiko Maki of Japan, along with the leading lights of French architecture, Christian de Portzamparc (last year's Pritzker laureate), Jean Nouvel, and Dominique Perrault.

A slight mist in the air partly dissolves the palace, the sky, the canal, and the trees into a flat composition in pink, gray, green, and gold. For an instant, one does see a resemblance between the Sun King's realm and Mr. Ando's part of the world: in the elaborate cultivation of nature into attitudes of extreme artifice, in the ritualistic etiquette that once ruled the French court and still surprises visitors to modern Japan.

During the brief presentation ceremony, held inside the palace, the spell of *la vie en rose* is briefly broken. Accepting the award from Jay A. Pritzker, the president of the Hyatt Foundation, which sponsors the award, Mr. Ando announces that he is donating the $100,000 in prize money to a fund to assist victims of the earthquake in Kobe last January. Polite applause. Then the guests climb aboard festive theme-park buses, their loudspeakers softly playing Couperin, for the ten-minute ride to the château. In the fields, sheep strike agreeably pastoral poses. Inside the château, attractive women in pink, Chanel-style suits usher us through the staterooms. The Hall of Mirrors is looking fine. Spotlights are playing on the fountains now. Dinner is served in the Hall of Battles, a windowless, 400-foot-long chamber built by Louis Philippe.

"This place is all about Wow," says Seth Rosenthal, a young New York architect at the banquet. And indeed, the best way to put Versailles in perspective is to realize that you're not supposed to. The palace was made to put you in perspective and to keep you ever mindful that an eye much more powerful than yours is watching to see how obediently you allow your awe to show.

If Mr. Ando is awestruck by all the ceremony surrounding him, he keeps it hidden. On a ride with him out to the château before the ceremony, and later as we walk amid the ordered parterres of André Le

Nôtre's gardens, he emphasizes that while he appreciates the honor very much, he doubts it will have much impact on his life or his work. I resist the temptation to snarl, "Well, give it to someone else, then!"

An intense man of medium height, Mr. Ando is somberly dressed in a dark gray suit and a white shirt. The shirt's round, stand-up collar hints that his is an ecclesiastical rather than aesthetic calling. So does his vaguely priestly air of superiority to worldly things.

This is not Mr. Ando's first visit to Versailles. The architect came here once before, exactly thirty years ago, while on a pilgrimage to see the buildings of Le Corbusier, the French modernist who pioneered the use of concrete as an expressive material. As we walk, I imagine he must be recoiling in horror from this daunting display of visual excess. But no, Mr. Ando replies, "I appreciate the palace as the symbol of a society that has moved on to better things."

It's evident that Mr. Ando believes that his own society has a desperate need now to move on to better things. Since World War II, he explains, Japan has pursued an increasingly materialistic way of life. He does not believe that architecture can flourish in such a culture. The architecture of the 1970s and '80s, he says, is "not for posterity." He continues: "It was just about production. It was not about a graceful way of life. You cannot have both."

Now, he suggests, Japan may be ready for a change in direction. "The bubble has burst," he says.

I tell him that there's something paradoxical about his reception in the West. People are inclined to see his work as "Eastern," meaning mystical, serene. Yet now, as Mr. Ando admits, Japan has surpassed even the United States in its devotion to material things.

How does he see himself? As a representative of his country, or as a person out of step with it?

The architect looks momentarily put out that I don't recognize the depth of his resistance to the prevailing values in contemporary Japan. He considers himself a maverick. He speaks about his unusual education; he has no formal architectural training. Instead, he got a list of the books architecture students were assigned to read in four years, and polished them off in one.

He mentions the antagonism he has generated in Japan's architectural establishment by insisting on living in Osaka, instead of Tokyo. "They say, 'Who does Ando think he is?' "

I find Mr. Ando's candor tonic but out of sync with the occasion. The Pritzker ceremony has the character of an international diplomatic event. Pamela C. Harriman, the American ambassador to France, is here, not a hair out of place or even looking like hair, and the mood of the evening is one of elegantly coiffed conversation. It's a very pleasant atmosphere, and as dusk settles over the gardens, you can easily imagine how Louis XIV used all this splendor to beguile his courtiers into a voluptuous brain death. In this setting, a mind would be a wonderful thing to waste, and much as I admire Mr. Ando for his earnestness, his intensity, I find myself half resenting him for bringing it into this artificial paradise. Who, indeed, does Mr. Ando think he is?

Briefly, Mr. Ando reminds me of the nineteenth-century Chicago architect Louis Sullivan. Like Mr. Ando, Sullivan practiced at a time when his country was entering a period of explosive prosperity. Like Mr. Ando, he felt that his country stood at a crossroads between morality and corruption and that architecture could help his civilization take the higher road.

I'm fascinated by the predicament of the moralist who works in architecture, surely the most material of the arts. Jackson Lears, a distinguished cultural critic, has suggested that a critic's function may be largely to appease the conscience while society drifts ever further into materialist preoccupations.

Le Corbusier was famous for the maxim "Architecture or revolution. Revolution can be avoided." I ask Mr. Ando whether he shares this view of architecture's power to transform a civilization. No, he answers, what inspired him about Le Corbusier was his determination to persevere.

"Le Corbusier came alone to Paris, he encountered resistance to his ideas throughout his life, but he never gave up," he says.

Mr. Ando is less than comfortable talking about the religious overtones of his work. When I question him about the "spiritual" dimension of his buildings, he uses the less-loaded word *psychological* in reply. Perhaps he wants to avoid discussing his own religious beliefs. Perhaps he feels that psychology holds a more universal connotation than religion.

Mr. Ando also looks pained at the suggestion that the spirituality of his work derives from Japanese traditions. No, he replies, he is a modernist. He grew up in a modern country. He was well aware of the work of modern architects from the West, like Le Corbusier and Louis Kahn, and he feels part of their tradition.

We both realize that this conversation is futile. The spiritual message I'm looking for is not to be found in Mr. Ando's words but in his buildings, and these I've yet to see. The photographs strike me as so, well, Lutheran. So Ingmar Bergman. Tortured souls. Flagellations. I prefer a nice Baroque chapel. Loads of angels. Gold sun rays streaming down from plaster clouds. Whipped cream. Still, if Mr. Ando's buildings are as intense as his personality, I'm prepared to be awed.

It's time to dress for dinner. In the lobby of the Grand Trianon Hotel, his wife, Yumiko, appears, wearing a royal blue pleated evening dress designed by Issey Miyake. As a parting present, Mr. Ando hands me his business card, on which he's made a little drawing. It shows a curving grand staircase rising toward an imposing colonnade, a minimalist's quick sketch rendition of Bourbon splendor. Then he tells me there's something particular he'd like to say to American readers. Japan, he says, is boring. He prefers the United States, because Americans are encouraged to have their own dreams and to pursue them. In Japan, he says, people don't let themselves dream.

As he talks, I begin to sense a strong parallel between Versailles and Mr. Ando's architecture: both are social diagrams. One laid out a royal pattern in which all forms, costumes, customs flowed from one person at the center. In Mr. Ando's architecture, every individual is entitled to occupy the center. The concrete voids of his houses are not bleak cells. They are dream chambers, spaces to fill up with as much life as the imagination can encompass. They're about living your own Wow.

As for me, I'm content to have the Hall of Mirrors for my dream palace for one evening. Tomorrow, we head back to work, back to the world of earthquakes, train strikes, dirty streets, and nights spent worrying about such pressing moral issues as how to pay the rent.

Tonight, let us eat cake.

September 21, 1995

REMODELING NEW YORK FOR THE BOURGEOISIE

The restoration of Bryant Park, completed in 1992, is one of the nicest things New York City has done for itself in a long time. And the park's inviting new restaurant, designed by Hardy Holzman Pfeiffer, is a fine place from which to savor the view. With its arcadian, trellised facade, accented by the Mediterranean resort chic of white canvas umbrellas, the restaurant offers a perch from which to enjoy the trees, grass, and fountains, the surrounding cityscape, and, above all, the cheering prospect of people enjoying a public space without fear that something awful is going to happen. No wonder the restaurant, which opened for business last spring, has been hailed as an urban miracle.

The true miracle, perhaps, is that the restoration has recaptured not only a place but also a time, a period before the park fell into disrepair. When the city was prosperous enough to create parks and New Yorkers were not afraid to use them. And yet the sensation is not purely one of nostalgia, for the restoration and the restaurant are also oddly representative of the present era in the city's history. Though Bryant Park resembles an oasis, its revival is not an exception. It is of a piece with many other projects that also seek to reinscribe secure middle-class values within the urban center.

They range in scale from large-scale residential enclaves like Queens West and Riverside South, both loosely modeled after Battery Park City, to the Starbucks-style cafés that have sprouted all over town. Across the city, Business Improvement Districts have been devising design guidelines, as well as providing security and sanitation, once provided by the public sector. In the city's rusting industrial districts, new zoning proposals would encourage the rise of suburban-type "superstores," while chain emporiums like Bed, Bath & Beyond have invaded the city's heart.

The transformation of Forty-second Street into a family entertainment center; the proliferation of theme restaurants on Fifty-seventh Street; the renovation of Penn Station and Grand Central Terminal into upscale shopping malls, with trains attached: there's no sweeping master plan coordinating these projects. If anything, they signify the capitulation of the public planning process to private enterprise. That's one reason it's not easy to grasp what these projects portend. Taken individually—a park here, a chain store there—the projects are of limited significance. Their meaning arises from the aggregation.

And it's a perplexing meaning, because it contradicts the narrative that has ruled the city throughout much of this century: the departure of the middle class and the city's polarization into extremes of rich and poor. These new urban projects fall between those extremes: too accessible and affordable to hold adequate snob appeal for the rich but beyond the reach of the lower economic echelons, they are pitched to those in the middle. Not the lower middle, not even the middle middle, but white-collar professionals. Bed, Bath & Beyond is not, after all, D. Porthault, and Starbucks is not Petrossian. Perhaps, in honor of the increasing influence of Business Improvement Districts, we ought to call this new city Business Class.

It is not a new development, nor is it unique to New York. Many older American cities have sought to reverse their economic decline by fostering a kind of hybrid urban-suburban culture, an ethos that fuses suburban security and standardization with urban congestion and pizazz. Festival marketplaces, like those developed by the Rouse Company in the 1970s, were among the first manifestations of this genre. The gentrification of old brownstone neighborhoods, the conversion of lofts from manufacturing to residential use, the rise of the gay subculture as a stable force in the urban economy: these, too, have contributed to the impression of an urban revival.

If that image has become more conspicuous in the past few years, it is partly because the extremities of the preceding decade—the glitz development of the 1980s, the homelessness of the early 1990s—have receded from the foreground of urban consciousness.

Is that a good thing? Earlier this year, when employees of programs intended to aid homeless people in the Grand Central business district were accused of assaulting them instead, it became apparent that there is something misleading, or at least incomplete, about the Business Class image. Suddenly the difference between a genteel gated suburban community and Business Improvement Districts did not seem so profound. If anything, the Business Improvement District looked more sinister because its gates were invisible. While these districts preserve the city's traditional image as a place of social accessibility, image and reality no longer coincide. Rich and poor are still polarized, but the gap between them is less conspicuous.

It's hard not to be of two minds about this development. On the one hand, those who care about the city's future can only welcome the social and economic stability that a middle class provides. Even if what we're seeing now is in large part image, that isn't necessarily a bad thing. Images can sometimes engender reality: a burnished urban image is far more likely than a tarnished one to attract and maintain businesses, tourism, and other forces pivotal to the city's economic well-being.

Even the most favorable trend, however, has its price, and the cost of the Business Class city needs to be much more talked about. There's a moral authority to the city's openness, for example, a democratic interplay between freedom and equality that has long been central to New York's identity. This stands to be eroded if the urban center is remade into a fortress. Of course, moral authority isn't worth much if there is no city left to embody it. But without that authority, what is the difference between a city and a mall?

Poverty, racial prejudice, environmental abuse: a lot of critical issues are dimly concealed by the veneer of middle-class affluence. Compared to them, it may seem the most trivial of pursuits to talk about the look of the veneer itself: about design, about taste, about art. And yet, it's precisely because the veneer has the potential to deceive that talking about it in visual terms takes on social significance. What lies beneath the veneer is significant, but so is the veneer itself. Does it reflect who we are?

The old Barnes & Noble sale annex on lower Fifth Avenue had orange industrial carpet over floorboards that creaked, and it felt like a firetrap. The new Barnes & Noble store over on Avenue of the Americas has lush green carpet, classical music noodling softly in the background, and a café perched on a balcony. It's so pleasant that you want to linger for hours.

It is pleasant to go into those Starbucks-style coffee bars; the coffee is good and the atmosphere is pleasant. Shopping at the World Financial Center in Battery Park City is pleasant. It is particularly pleasant to see those depressing bunion ads on the subways giving way to bold designs boosting upscale products.

When pleasantness begins to pall, one can go in for excitement. The new Chelsea Piers are exciting! The plunging two-story escalator at Sony's Lincoln Square multiplex is exciting! The interior David Rockwell has designed for the "Official" All Star Cafe, a sports-theme dining and restaurant going up in Times Square, will be very exciting! Pleasant. Exciting! Pleasant. Exciting! Is this architecture? Or an experiment in mass Pavlovian response? Design? Or a drug?

"Middle-class" is often taken as a synonym for the safe, the stodgy, the mediocre. But being middle-class in New York is supposed to mean being culturally aware. Yes, you get some material rewards: a decent place to live, nice clothes, a tasty dinner. But you also keep up with movies, painting, theater. You read a book. If Mark Morris or Laurie Anderson is appearing, you try to get in. You care about what that new curator at the Whitney is going to make of the opportunity. Even if you do not take an active interest in these things, you still have the reassuring knowledge that you're living in a place where almost any cultural appetite can be satisfied.

But if your appetite is for contemporary architecture, you're out of luck. If you go to Paris, London, Barcelona, Los Angeles, Tokyo, and many other cities, there's usually a new building that you have to see, or you will die. You may hate it, but your life depends on it. But when visitors from abroad come here, what do you show them? There's the skyline, of course, and the street gridiron, two of the greatest architectural spectacles of all time. But when it comes to recent buildings of stature, where do you look?

A few weeks ago I was out walking with the fashion designer Isaac Mizrahi, and at one point we strolled past the Millennium, the new luxury high-rise on the Upper West Side. I like the building and was planning to write something favorable about it. But Mizrahi said, "Well, you'll have to tell me what you like about this. Because to me, it's just another eyesore. Maybe a slightly better eyesore."

I wanted to respond, "Well, how would you feel if someone took a look at one of your dresses and said, 'Ugh, another rag on a hook'?" But I had to admit, the man had a point. It's been some time since people could look up and see a building with something fresh or startling to say about the contemporary city and the creativity that drives it.

Thirty years ago, the cityscape found room for works by Mies van der Rohe, Wallace Harrison, Eero Saarinen, Marcel Breuer, Frank Lloyd Wright, Walter Gropius, and Gordon Bunshaft. Not all of their buildings were great; some were terrible. But what they contributed was much more than a handful of potential future landmarks. Even the worst of their projects, like the Pan Am Building, helped create a picture of the city as an open-ended, ongoing project, a place that recognized the power of architecture to symbolize a city's willingness to respond to change with fresh ideas. That symbolism went far toward securing New York's reputation as a global cultural center in the postwar decades.

That's what's missing from this emerging picture of a Business Class New York: some show of public awareness that the city remains a dynamic experiment. Yes, we love to shop, and we deserve a comfortable refuge from urban turmoil. But we're also a city that historically recognizes the difference between creating and consuming. Where are the buildings strong enough to carry that tradition forward?

The irony is that the general level of architectural design in New York is higher than it has been in a generation. The firms that garner many of the most prominent commissions—offices like Polshek Partners Ship Architects, Beyer Blinder Belle, Fox & Fowle, Alexander Cooper & Partners—do superior work. Their sensitive, urbane designs represent an enormous advance over the days when architects approached a building site as an island unto itself. But it is Business Class architecture, not world-class architecture. It seldom risks greatness.

It should be a source of civic pride that some of the world's most celebrated architects live and work in Manhattan and a matter of shame that many of the most gifted seldom build here. And their few New York projects are distant from the center. Richard Meier hasn't built in New York for twenty years—his entire mature career to date—and his last building was in the Bronx. Rafael Viñoly, designer of the most important public building now in construction in Tokyo, built an excellent gymnasium last year in the Bronx. Peter Eisenman built a little fire station ten years ago in Brooklyn. I'm not a great fan of the skyscraper Gwathmey Siegel built on Broadway at West Forty-eighth Street, but I respect it. It's architecture, and it's centrally located.

SITE, the firm that, along with Frank Gehry, won this year's Chrysler Design Awards, has built nothing here except interiors. Ditto Emilio

Ambasz. Michael Graves has designed a shop. John Hejduk has renovated one building. Diana Agrest and Mario Gandelsonas, active in projects from Des Moines to China, have designed, I believe, a town house. Aldo Rossi, who has maintained a New York studio for the past decade, has built nothing here. Arata Isozaki, who also maintains a local office, has designed a discotheque and has collaborated with James Stewart Polshek on the Brooklyn Museum expansion.

Among the younger generation—arguably the most highly educated in history—it's even worse. While their contemporaries in Los Angeles have built enough to be called the Santa Monica school, Steven Holl, Tod Williams and Billie Tsien; Henry Smith-Miller and Laurie Hawkinson; Hariri & Hariri have been confined locally to interior renovations.

Then there is the long list of world-class architects whose work one might expect to see in a city that prides itself on being a cultural capital; to name a few: Tadao Ando, Renzo Piano, Frank Gehry, Rem Koolhaas, Richard Rogers, Rafael Moneo, Toyo Ito, Jean Nouvel, Antoine Predock, Zaha Hadid.

Of course, cities have more important things to do than collect trophy buildings by famous designers. And architecture encompasses important things besides aesthetics. But it's not as if New York were setting new standards in environmentally or socially responsible design, either. And since we are still putting up buildings, and architects are still designing, why can't at least a few of them be alert to the moment we live in?

Some people might prefer architecture to remain confined to consenting adults in the privacy of their converted lofts. The idea has taken hold that architects are to be regarded as rampaging egos, user-unfriendly, contemptuous of the city and its traditions. Though there may be some truth to this, there is also something profoundly anti-urban about making New York endlessly atone for excesses committed by modern architects in Jane Jacobs's day. Most architects have learned their lesson since then. Some have a lot to teach.

September 24, 1995

IN A BYGONE DAY,
THIS WAS THE LOOK OF THE FUTURE

After a bibulous dinner in Fiesole, Gianni Pettena, an architect, historian, and teacher who lives outside Florence, offered to drive my friend and me back to our hotel. "But first," Pettena said, "there's something special I want to show you. The power plant at the Florence train station. Do you know it? No? Strange, but no one knows it. And it's remarkable—the only Futurist building ever built."

We sped down from the hills, fearing collision at every hairpin turn, which is actually the best way to approach a Futurist building. At least in its rhetoric, the Futurist movement was eager to court death in the pursuit of machine-made speed. The movement's ringleader, the poet Filippo Tommaso Marinetti, had said that a car going at full throttle was more beautiful than the *Winged Victory of Samothrace*. And this was before seat belts.

Have a glass or two of wine before you go to see this building. The plant, of russet-colored concrete and brick, is not in the best condition; there are broken windows, and the building looks better through a haze. It's also helpful to be in a frame of mind susceptible to ecstasy. The Futurists preached the ecstasy of movement, the exhilaration of speed, ideas not easily conveyed by a building planted firmly on the ground.

Designed by Angiolo Mazzoni, the power plant was built in 1932, long after Futurism had collapsed. Antonio Sant'Elia, the most prominent architect in a movement that embraced painting, sculpture, music, and, above all, the modern art of media manipulation, died in 1916, without having built any of his visionary projects. By the 1930s, Italy's most progressive architects had embraced Rationalism, the Italian version of the International Style. But Mazzoni had originally been allied with Sant'Elia; in 1914 he signed Sant'Elia's manifesto for Futurist architecture. His design for the Florence power plant is thus a throwback, an oddly successful blend of Futurist, Rationalist, and Art Deco motifs.

Mazzoni, a director of special projects for Italy's state railway system, was known primarily for Rationalist buildings, including many train stations. As Richard Etlin writes in his superb *Modernism in Italian Architecture, 1890–1940*, Mussolini set great store in the design of stations because they were the buildings most seen by foreign tourists: you saw them close-up from the trains that Il Duce made run on time.

The Futurist vision of architecture was not, primarily, one of standalone buildings. It was an urban vision. Sant'Elia's drawings for la Citta Nuova (the New City) in 1914 envisioned a city in which transportation—elevators, bridges, roadways—provided the key architectural elements. Infrastructure became metastructure. Mazzoni's power plant derives much of its impact from the rail viaduct to which it is attached and from its placement just beyond a bend in the tracks. As you look down the street toward the plant, the bend creates the illusion that the building's power has warped the space around it.

The plant's most explicitly Futurist element is the steel superstructure, a colonnade of four chimneys, connected by a catwalk overhead and an open stair to one side. You can see how classical Futurism could be: it's an industrial Parthenon atop its own brick pediment, with belching steam for a frieze. Pettena said the building was much more impressive before the power system was converted to gas. It used to run on coal, which was brought in on trains, then hoisted into the building by crane. At night you could see the coal fires glowing, an infernal spectacle of power, steam, and speed.

It's a dubious distinction to be the only Futurist building, since this was not the most attractive ideology ever associated with an art movement. It celebrated not only speed but violence. Marinetti declared war "the world's own hygiene." He was an early supporter of Mussolini. And he mounted a wicked campaign against pasta.

Sant'Elia, a casualty of that act of global hygiene called World War I, can't be tarred with the Fascist brush; he was dead long before Mussolini marched on Rome. And there's some question as to whether Sant'Elia actually shared the Futurist agenda. Etlin suggests that Sant'Elia might have signed on with the Futurists mainly for the purpose of personal promotion. Even so, one can be appalled by the glorification of phallic energy in Sant'Elia's ideas and in Mazzoni's realization of them.

Looking up at the power plant now, with its row of chimneys that no longer belch smoke, you see, first of all, a proud proclamation of faith in the power of industrial technology. Look again and it's the faith, not the technology, that sticks out, the sense of entitlement implicit in the word *futurism*. The difference is critical. It's the second look that reveals why this building speaks to the present: the plant's confidence, its certainty, its resemblance to a religious edifice have no parallel today.

There's no shortage of architects vending certainties now—classical revivalists, new urbanists, advocates of the new simplicity, deconstructionists. Each of these factions (and others) can articulate its position with apparent poise. I've followed debates among them, and each time I have come away with the feeling that I was seeing a sideshow. No faction has captured the moment as well as our not having to choose among them.

History is a train track, a linear progression from past to future: that's the idea embodied in Mazzoni's station. According to Etlin, Sant'Elia laughed at Marinetti's proposal that the future city would be completely remade by every generation. Sant'Elia was right to laugh. The center of Florence looks substantially intact, even though it had to rebuild itself after a second act of global hygiene. What neither man foresaw was that the future would head off in so many different directions, that before the century was over their notion of history would run out of steam.

October 8, 1995

GETTING GOOFY ON THE SANTA ANA FREEWAY

Let's face it: Americans will never love buildings as much as they love cars. That's just the way it is. We're a mobile society, and buildings don't move. They sit there by the side of the road looking as if they've run out of gas. Few American living rooms can compete with a windshield view of the world whizzing by. Still, a good roadside building can really pep up the scenery.

Frank Gehry is now completing a superb one in Anaheim, home of the archetypical roadside attraction. Situated on the edge of Disneyland, the new Team Disneyland Building stretches nearly nine hundred feet along the Santa Ana Freeway. By the end of the year, the four-story office block will house the nearly 1,100 people who administer the theme park's operations. At the moment, a chain-link fence that runs along the highway partly obscures the lower part of the building; Gehry would like to see the fence removed. But what is the world coming to when Frank Gehry wants to take down a chain-link fence? Welcome to Goofyland.

Like the open-air pavilion Gehry designed for Euro Disney in France, this structure tries to capture the Disney sense of fantasy without surrendering to cuteness. Though this may be a fun factory, it's a factory nonetheless, and the design emphasizes the industrial as well as the playful side of the Disney enterprise.

The building is two-faced: metal-paneled on the freeway side, sculptured stucco on the facade facing the park. On the freeway side, which will be seen mostly from cars, Gehry does little to break down the structure's immense length. In fact, he emphasizes it with a design whose rhythm echoes the hypnotic effect of the broken line down a highway. The wall is covered with steel panels set in a pattern with overlapping edges that recalls fish scales. Scaly, too, is the iridescent finish of the steel, a shade of green that shifts to blue and red-purple, depending on the light and the viewer's angle of vision.

A long wedge of stainless steel with square, toothlike cutouts seems to be propping up the structure at its base. Gehry calls the wedge "a cowcatcher," though it also brings to mind the sharp metal treadles that lend a touch of menace to parking-lot driveways. Or perhaps the wedge is there to emphasize that this wall of scales is just a facade; the design makes the same point by extending the wall a few feet beyond the building's envelope on its southern side. (Gehry and his project designer, Edwin Chan, are in fact responsible only for the exterior and main entrance lobby; the project's executive architect is the Los Angeles firm Langdon Wilson.)

Things get goofier on the park side, where the stucco wall is whipped into free-form Gehry shapes in the middle and on both ends. Painted a color Gehry calls "Dick Tracy yellow," the forms are abstract, not figurative, and their curves, curls, and thrusts project an improvised Play-Doh quality, as if to invite the viewer to help mold them. Canopies of corrugated metal undulate across the yellow surface like twisted versions of the awnings you see over warehouse loading bays.

The heart of the building is the four-story entrance atrium, its walls adorned with broad, curving strokes of black paint against a shocking pink background. It's Goofy's dream of himself as Frank Lloyd Wright: coiling stairways of white plaster rise sinuously through the space; the black designs on the walls are derived from a cut-up Goofy cartoon.

All in fun? Not quite. The Team Disneyland Building exemplifies Gehry's genius for creating quirky forms that allow a range of possible readings. His Dick Tracy yellow, for instance, may make us think of sunshine and happiness, but it is also the industrial shade of yellow that signifies nuclear hazard.

There's a slightly naughty feel to the pink-and-black atrium; its Frederick's of Hollywood color scheme reminds us that Disney now distributes R-rated films as well as family entertainment. The iridescent finish on the steel panels is no less beautiful for looking something like an oil slick.

These hints of the dark underside of play—almost a toxic happiness—are perfectly in keeping with the spirit of Walt Disney, an artist who could imagine birds being threatened by an out-of-control windmill or Mickey Mouse bringing on his own near-death by drowning at the hands of hundreds of pail-toting broomsticks.

Gehry updates that spirit for a culture that has been reshaped in no small part by Disney's values. There's a sign at the entrance to Disneyland that welcomes visitors to THE HAPPIEST PLACE IN THE WORLD. The sign's lack of irony speaks of an earlier time. You try to imagine what "the happiest place" meant in 1955, the year the park opened, when memories of the Depression and World War II were still vivid.

Disneyland was part of the culture of highway hospitality that blossomed in the 1940s: the cloth corsages worn by the hostesses at Howard Johnson's, the Texaco man with his plastic bow tie, the effort to confer urbane courtesy and gentility on the nation's new highways.

Thirty years later, many regard the Disney Company itself as an emblem of the dark side of play. Disney's designs on historic Civil War battlefields; its substitution of the fake for the authentic; the escape it offers from reality into a fairyland—all this has come to symbolize the excesses of a self-indulgent society. Gehry's double-edged design suggests the spooky as well as the sunny side of the Disney legacy. It occupies the increasingly narrow gap between Disneyland and the rest of the world.

November 5, 1995

CHELSEA DAWNING: REAWAKENED AND RESPLENDENT

New York, that eternal narcissist, never tires of having its picture taken, but insists on periodic changes of backdrop. Parts of Manhattan go in and out of favor, just as fashions do. The cast-iron facades of SoHo, the brownstones of the Upper West Side, the crooked alleys of Greenwich Village: different neighborhoods, at various times, have served to represent New York to itself. They stand for some shift in the city's mood, its view of the present or its desire to escape into some fantasy of change.

This year the city wants to pose with Chelsea. It wants to stride along the Avenue of the Americas, where an influx of superstores have brought to life the decaying old department-store buildings north of Seventeenth Street. It wants to firm up its torso at the David Barton Gym and drape itself in a sheet of Egyptian cotton from Bed, Bath & Beyond. It longs to don a pair of designer eye frames from Alain Mikli, assume a studious expression and pluck some Kierkegaard from the shelves at Barnes & Noble. Later, as the sun sinks into the Hudson River, the city will bask in the glowing fluorescent rainbow of Dan Flavin's light sculptures at the Dia Center for the Arts on West Twenty-second Street, try Rollerblading at the Chelsea Piers sports complex on the Hudson, and rush the stage for a curtain call at the Joyce Theater. A late supper at Le Madri or L'Acajou may follow. Then it will dash over to Duggal photo labs on West Twentieth Street and wait breathlessly to see how the pix turned out.

Actually, tapestry might be a more suitable medium for rendering Chelsea's portrait, for the area embodies, more vividly than any other part of town, New York's legendarily eclectic weave. While other neighborhoods have more sharply defined identities, Chelsea retains a sprawling diversity that resists summing up. Here the whole is nearly as great as the sum of the city's other parts.

The place is neither Uptown nor Downtown: this may well be

Chelsea's greatest asset. Stretching between Fourteenth Street and Twenty-ninth Street, from Fifth Avenue west to the river, it's a betwixt-and-between kind of place, a happily muddled middle ground between Manhattan's symbolic polar extremes.

For a long time, this neither-nor nonidentity was considered a defect. Chelsea was where you lived if you couldn't afford to live where you really wanted to live. It was a haven for the marginal, the urbanistically displaced. It still is. But now displacement turns out to be a virtue, even a sign of character and independence.

People are weary of the sudden change of personality and outlook that's supposed to occur when we travel north or south of Fourteenth Street, that legendary line of demarcation between the stuffy and the hip. We know that SoHo has more than its share of stuffy moments, while Sutton Place harbors minds as curious as any on West Broadway. Geography isn't destiny; an address needn't be a rut.

New Superstores

The parade of new superstores along the Avenue of the Americas is probably the most dramatic reason for Chelsea's present moment in the spotlight. The great nineteenth-century "dry goods emporiums"—O'Neill's, an early B. Altman, Siegel-Cooper—had been sitting there in quiet decrepitude for so long that they had become like natural features. It's faintly shocking now to watch these commercial fossils spring back to life as shoppers pour in and out of Filene's Basement, Today's Man, Barnes & Noble, Old Navy, and Bed, Bath & Beyond.

The real shock is that the new stores look wonderfully at home in this period setting. Miraculously, their chain-store homogenization has not given the Avenue of the Americas the feeling of a suburban mall. That is a tribute to the strength of these ornate buildings, and to the sensitivity with which the new retailers have remodeled them. Above all, it's a testament to an urban fabric tough enough to absorb change without coming apart at the seams.

Superstore Chelsea, however, is just one of many vibrant threads woven through the neighborhood tapestry. There's also a Latin Chelsea, a gay Chelsea, an art-gallery Chelsea, a design-studio Chelsea, a publishing Chelsea, and even a cyber Chelsea, in the offices spreading west of Silicon Alley. These subcultures are sufficiently concentrated to make their presence felt, but none is so domineering that it threatens to overwhelm the overall design.

Visual art is newly prominent in Chelsea. Apart from the Chelsea

Hotel, with its famous lobby displaying paintings by former residents, art lovers had little reason to make the trip. But commercial and fashion photographers, served by the labs that stretch across Twentieth Street, have traditionally flocked to the loft buildings of northeast Chelsea. And in the last few years, the far western block of Twenty-second Street has become a SoHo in miniature. The Dia Center for the Arts and the Matthew Marks Gallery have established reputations for major shows. Other prominent galleries are looking for spaces in the blocks just north and south.

Performing arts have been a major Chelsea attraction since 1982, when Hardy Holzman Pfeiffer Associates transformed the Elgin, an Art Deco movie house, into the Joyce, a first-rate theater for dance. The loftlike Dance Theater Workshop, the multimedia Kitchen, and the Sanford Meisner Theater are also stages of citywide stature. Performance art of a lustier sort is put on nightly by oiled "go-go gods" at Chelsea's imaginatively themed gay bars, like Champs, King, Splash, and Rome, a new spot where the bartenders sport leather gladiator garb.

Sea, Sky, and Skyline

Chelsea hasn't much in the way of parks, but it does have a glorious stretch of Hudson River waterfront. The engineers who laid out the Manhattan grid believed the river would satisfy the city's need for open space. They did not foresee ships and cars blocking public access to it. But with the decline of industry, planners have tried to recapture the waterfront for public use. Not everyone is thrilled with the new Chelsea Piers; they question whether a public amenity like the waterfront should be exploited by private developers. And some remain attached to the forlorn sight of rotting industrial sheds. Chelsea Piers is for those who want to enjoy the river without getting tetanus shots.

But Chelsea's most distinctive nature feature is not the Hudson River. It is the sky. Thanks to its unusual local zoning laws, Chelsea enjoys a high degree of exposure to the firmament. Elsewhere, tall buildings are restricted to the avenues; here they are confined to midblock. Sky, natural light, a humanely scaled streetscape are the most obvious benefits, and is it perhaps the case that Chelsea residents enjoy high levels of melanin? In any case, there is a casual San Francisco feel to the street life here, a sense that while it's no doubt admirable to maintain grace under pressure, grace without pressure is even nicer.

Dan Graham's glass pavilion, situated on the roof of the Dia Center for the Arts, offers a gifted artist's interpretation of Chelsea skies. A set of clear glass enclosures, nested within one another, engage curved and flat reflections to dissolve the cityscape into the blue beyond. Augmented by a small espresso bar, the project was conceived by Graham as an urban park: a sky park, where clouds, planes, and rooftop vistas take the place of trees, paths, and lawns. Go on a clear day.

A more traditional route to heaven may be found within the precincts of the General Theological Seminary, one of Chelsea's most distinguished landmarks. With buildings dating from 1836, the seminary is one of the city's oldest examples of Gothic Revival architecture. Unfortunately, the serene courtyard contained within this Gothic quadrangle is now sealed off from the surrounding neighborhood by banal additions made in the 1960s to the seminary's Ninth Avenue side.

From divinity to "divine!" Chelsea's other major campus, the Fashion Institute of Technology, is due for reappraisal; it is actually a decent example of modern urbanism. A two-block-long concrete Brutalist building spans Twenty-seventh Street; it strongly defines the school's Eighth Avenue edge without isolating the campus from the city. Beyond, a collection of midcentury modern buildings shows how architects tried to vary the formula of the functionalist box by manipulating the surface with geometric patterns. This approach, which once seemed dated, is being picked up again by architects who seek to create new forms with folded planes.

London Terrace. The Chelsea Hotel. The Starrett-Lehigh Building. Chelsea's roster of architectural landmarks is as distinguished as that of any other part of town. But it is also notable for its high concentration of public and low-income housing. Stretching north of Twenty-third Street and west of Ninth Avenue, Chelsea's housing projects aren't likely to win landmark status anytime soon. Still, they are conspicuous reminders of the social idealism of an earlier time. Constructed from the 1930s through the '60s, the projects offer a set of variations on the modernist theme of "towers in a park." Alas, the overall effect is more tower than park. The projects break with the street grid but provide little sense of refuge from it.

Provisional, polyglot, hodgepodge, jumble sale: why is this the picture New York wants to snap of itself just now? Perhaps it's because Chelsea's multiple personality mirrors the Postmodern view of the self: faceted, fragmented, fractured, unwilling to play a single role. Or it may be that Chelsea offers an urbane response to today's reactionary political assaults against the city and its culture. More than any other New York City neighborhood, Chelsea embodies our kind of family values: glad of difference, skeptical of sameness, eager to make the streets safe from moralists as well as muggers. Chelsea is New York's lively Right to a Life Party, its empowerment zone for those who want to be themselves.

Say cheese.

November 17, 1995

BUILDINGS BORN OF DREAMS AND DEMONS

This is not a story about a new movement in architecture. It's a story about an old art movement that has resurfaced in contemporary architecture with startling vigor. Surrealism, which flourished between the world wars, was largely driven by Freud's theories. Surrealist painters, writers, and filmmakers hoped to transform culture by injecting it with the powerful energies generated by subconscious mechanisms. The irrational, the erotic, the controlling, devouring, conflicted, and repressed: artists like Breton, Miró, Buñuel, Magritte, and Dalí sought to draw into the daylight the primitive impulses Freud tried to understand through the interpretation of dreams.

Frank Gehry, Rem Koolhaas, Jean Nouvel, Philippe Starck, Raimund Abraham—some of the most highly regarded architects of today—do not describe themselves as Surrealists. Nor will they necessarily welcome being tagged with the name of an art movement that not long ago was thought to have passed irretrievably into history. Their work is emphatically of the present. But, like Surrealism, it reckons with the dark turbulence and contradictions of the inner life. It challenges the conventional view of architecture as the art of putting an ordered public face on things.

Intentionally or not, every building says something about the psyche. But in the century following Freud's earliest research, architects have not made conspicuous use of his ideas. In theory, at least, the Modern movement took its cue from industrial technology. The standardized, the rational, the functional: modern architects embraced values they took to be consistent with scientific objectivity.

Postmodern architecture, as practiced by Robert Venturi and Denise Scott Brown, Robert A. M. Stern, Michael Graves, and Charles Moore, is one line of development leading out of the disillusionment with modern orthodoxy. But in the mid-1970s another path was opened by architects who resisted the postmodern infatuation with period styles. Emilio Ambasz, James Wines, Aldo Rossi, Peter Eisenman, the Miami firm of Arquitectonica, Bernard Tschumi, Mr. Gehry, Mr. Koolhaas: in the work of these architects, subjectivity takes command. Like Surrealists, these architects seem determined to blur the border between waking reality and the dream state. A range of projects, newly completed or under way, has broadened this line of development into a major theme: the playful, the fantastic, the morbid, the mad, the aggressive, the absurd. Introducing such ideas into architecture will strike some as perverse, willful, or contrary. It may be, however, that the perverse and contrary is the most sensible response to a changing public realm.

The Skyscraper as Guillotine

Leave it to a native of Freud's hometown to design a New York skyscraper's nightmare of its own castration. Louis Sullivan, considered the father of the skyscraper, once said its main feature is that it is tall. When the Austrian Cultural Institute, designed by the Vienna-born Raimund Abraham, finally is built on East Fifty-second Street near Fifth Avenue, it may be the first skyscraper to confess the fear engendered by the fantasy of tallness: a building that appears to slice itself down to size even as it rises.

A slim, mid-block tower that tapers as it rises to a height of twenty floors, the building will be clad on the street side by three overlapping planes of glass that jut out sharply, like blades, on their lower edges. Mr. Abraham has compared the facade to a guillotine, a comment that has provoked the displeasure of those who see something uncivil in such a violent image. That's not surprising. Urban life is violent enough as it is. Architecture itself can be violent. Buildings blot out light and views as effectively as blindfolds. They menace cherished landmarks and the memories associated with them. They displace people from their homes. Do we want buildings to dramatize architecture's incessant assault on the city? Wouldn't we prefer architects to mask their aggressiveness behind polite facades? By restricting architects to the safe, the pleasant, the familiar, are we not condemning them to practice their art as a kind of decorative repression?

No design can settle the questions raised by Mr. Abraham's plan. It is enough that he has raised them. Unfortunately, the Austrian government has stalled construction of this project because of political wrangling back home. Austria has given us Sacher torte and crystals, Lipizzaner stallions and the Vienna Boys' Choir, but surely it is Freud who has had the greatest impact on contemporary New York culture. Mr. Abraham has honored that impact with a design of uncommon elegance, honesty, and insight.

Philippe Starck's Labyrinth of Style

There's no name out front, just an imposingly tall, dark green hedge beneath a pristine white Art Deco facade. This is Delano, currently Miami Beach's most fashionable hotel. Designed by Philippe Starck, Delano is the creation of the former nightclub impresario Ian Schrager. Together the pair have collaborated on the Royalton and the Paramount, two of the most imaginatively designed public spaces New York has seen in years. Delano is their most impressive work thus far.

The hedge outside is the box tree that mazes are made of. Pass behind it, and you fall into a labyrinth of style. Billowing white curtains frame the terrace at Delano's entrance, and a huge white lampshade hangs over it. In the breeze, the shade jerks around like a ghostly, demented bell; at night, the swaying cone of light turns the terrace into a stage for shadow dancing. Beyond the front doors, the whole hotel is aligned around a single grand axis, extending from the lobby past sitting areas, breakfast room, bar, and restaurant to the lush pool area in the rear. The elongated perspective is hypnotic; you feel tugged forward, as in a trance, through endless white curtains. It is the scene a Hollywood set designer would envisage for an exquisitely choreographed dream sequence in which a movie star searches for an elusive lover.

Philippe Starck is the most explicitly Surrealist designer in practice. White cast-iron lawn furniture installed in the shallow end of the pool, living room furniture beneath trees outdoors, European-style street lamps suspended between rows of palms: Mr. Starck's indoor-outdoor reversals and juxtapositions call forth a Magritte apparition beneath a Miami moon.

Delano's most surreal element is surely its fabulousness, its unrelenting flow of wit and chic. Fabulousness is intimidating, at least for those who court it. It is selective, yet cannot be considered undemocratic; entrée depends not on birth or money or even achievement but on sensibility, a quality theoretically anyone can acquire. Moreover, fabulousness is most likely to intimidate those who already have entrée, for who can ever be as fabulous as their image?

This is most evident in the hotel's all-white guest rooms. By convention, a hotel room is a place of privacy and security, a home away from home, where you can feel free to be yourself. That freedom is elusive at Delano, however, where the unrelieved whiteness of walls, floors, fabrics, and fixtures reminds you, nanny-like, of how you fall short of perfection. Hair in the sink, socks on the floor, these come popping out of the whiteness like dark stains on your cool reputation. Immense mirrors in gilded frames throw in your face the physical flaws that the hotel's basement gym and its penthouse spa fail to erase. What you need here is not a hairbrush but an airbrush, and perhaps an art director on call at all times.

I loved my stay there last fall precisely because of the self-consciousness the hotel can induce. If Mr. Starck is an artist (I think he is first-rate), his artistry goes way beyond his celebrated visual flair. He grasps the social drama being acted out by the sophisticates his flair appeals to. He sees the powerful connection between advanced sophistication and primal fear. Stylishness does not exist in isolation. It must be displayed. And the desire to display a sense of style is inseparably linked to the fear, even the hope, that one's ordinariness will one day be exposed.

In Paris and Berlin, Nouvel at Play

Advertising, an industry based on dreams, is responsible for some of the most inventive designs in recent years, like the Venice, California, offices of TBWA Chiat/Day, commissioned by Jay Chiat, from Frank Gehry and Gaetano Pesce. Two recent projects by the Parisian architect Jean Nouvel show that he is sharply attuned to the culture of advertising and to the creative challenges it offers architects.

Mr. Nouvel understands the importance of play. He demonstrates this with great wit in the Paris headquarters of CLM/BBDO, which he designed in 1988: the interior resembles a sports arena; in fact, games like basketball and badminton are sometimes played there. Ringed by three tiers of offices, the elliptical atrium has a hardwood floor and is furnished with silly, oversize sofas upholstered in a nubbed rubber fabric that recalls basketballs. The stadium illusion is heightened by hydraulically operated skylights that swing upward, like wings, opening the building's interior to the sky.

His Galeries Lafayette on Friedrichstrasse in Berlin, to be completed next month, transports advertising from sender to receiver, from image-makers to consumers. The design updates the department stores that stretch along Boulevard Haussmann on the Right Bank of the Seine. These now quaint establishments drew on the most advanced art and techology of their time, and so does Mr. Nouvel.

At the building's core are two cones of glass, touching base to base at the ground-floor level. One points down, admitting natural light into the basement office floors; the second, larger cone rises dramatically, punching holes through the seven selling floors. Like a compressed indoor version of Times Square, the cone is a bombardment of light and color. Designer labels and other signs are projected as holographs onto the glass, which serves as a giant store directory. The effect is like being inside the brain of a compulsive shopper, driven into a frenzy by recurring fantasies of Cacharel, Kenzo, and Yves Saint Laurent. Perhaps the mind is that of post–Cold War Berlin, now frantically shopping its way back to the West.

Frank Gehry's Message of the Rose

In recent years, Frank Gehry has been struggling to translate his personal idiom from the small scale of private houses to the epic scale of major public works. Mr. Gehry's design for the new Guggenheim Museum in Bilbao, Spain, scheduled for completion in 1997, may turn out to be the ful-fillment of this profoundly social ambition. The building, part of an immense effort to rejuvenate an aging port city, reflects two of his ruling passions: the industrial cities of the nineteenth century and a romantic belief in the power of art.

Mr. Gehry's design pays homage to Frank Lloyd Wright's Guggen-heim while acknowledging its distance from Wright in time and space. At Bilbao, the central space, like Wright's, is a rotunda, but instead of being tightly wound into a coil the exterior splays emphatically outward. It is as if Mr. Gehry has released the pent-up energy in Wright's spiral by taking a knife to its sides. Strips of metal, marking the scale of the museum's floors, ripple and flare outward into the city in a bold expression of cen-trifugal force.

Mr. Gehry has called this central form a metallic flower. It's typically generous of him to tease us with a figurative reference; we get to tease him back, with free associations of our own. Like Wright's spiral, Mr. Gehry's flower evokes a metaphor of organic growth while it also restates Wright's religious view of art. In New York, Wright conveyed this idea with the zig-gurat, or world mountain, an ancient religious form. In Spain, a predomi-nantly Roman Catholic country, Mr. Gehry delivers the same message with a rose. The central symbol of buildings raised in the Virgin's honor, his flower asserts art's claim to a spiritual dimension. Yet, the industrial material from which he fashions the rose brings the form down to earth, honoring the Surrealist idea that art should perform the Promethean task of injecting creativity into everyday life.

Rem Koolhaas Is Thinking Big

Most architects talk about scale. Rem Koolhaas talks about "Bigness." In his new book *S, M, L, XL,* a collaboration with the graphic designer Bruce Mau, the Dutch architect equates architecture with the primitive desire to dominate. Big muscles, big cars, big bank accounts, big hair.

Architecture does seem to be going the way of bigness, with the prolif-eration of superstores, superstadiums, elephantine convention centers, multi-acre residential developments, and industrial parks. Some regard this with horror; it allows quantity to displace quality. Mr. Koolhaas takes a more analytic approach. Looking at what scares us can tell us who we are.

The architect has had the opportunity not only to think about bigness but also to build it, as the master planner of Euralille, a major office com-plex and convention center in Lille, in northern France. The project was designed to take advantage of Lille's proximity to major trading centers of the European Economic Community and the Chunnel. A highway, a metro, and a high-speed train converge in the center of the complex. Here Mr. Koolhaas has created an artificial cavern called the Piranesian Space, after the eighteenth-century architect best known for his drawings of imaginary, multilevel prisons. By carving away portions of the underground floors, Mr. Koolhaas turns infrastructure into urban spectacle.

Modern architecture could be "surrealist" in this way. The machine imagery of modern buildings exposed the engineering hidden beneath masonry facades, but a modern architect would not deliberately evoke the image of a prison. On the contrary, the machine represented liberation for the modernists, a release from the stifling confinement of outmoded styles. In styling his space after Piranesi, Mr. Koolhaas conveys the image of something infernal. What we see here is not a scene of mechanical efficiency but a spookily Nietzschean display of power.

What do these projects all add up to? That architects can now do weird, scary things? Yes, and also that the public sphere has become weird and scary, at least to those who are made uncomfortable by the degree to which the line between public and private realms has become porous. These are all public buildings. But they project subjective points of view. And they reflect the increasing transformation of the public realm into a stage for the acting out of dreams.

With good reason, people fear that this is a time of withdrawal from the public realm, a time in which objective reality has become an embattled concept. The public realm, it often seems, has been reduced to an arena in which everything is an opinion, all opinions are equal, and truth doesn't stand a chance. These feats of architectural imagination offer no reassurance that such fears are groundless. They do, however, confront those fears, with awareness, sensuousness, and rigor. And they suggest that the public realm, while an indispensable fantasy, is a fantasy nonetheless.

January 7, 1996

THE PRISONER OF BEAUTY

Architecture critics almost never get to live in the buildings they write about, but for ten exceptional days last July I did just that. My friend Seth Rosenthal and I spent our summer vacation at the legendary Casa Malaparte on the isle of Capri.

Some think it is the most beautiful house of the twentieth century. I'll go all the way: the Casa Malaparte is the most beautiful house in the world. My world, anyhow. Completed about half a century ago and now in the midst of a thorough restoration, the house let me live out a fantasy of plunging headlong into a beauty freak's paradise. It gave me a chance not just to live with beauty but also to reflect on what beauty means to me.

Curzio Malaparte, who lived from 1898 to 1957, was a journalist, novelist, playwright, filmmaker, publisher, and political activist. He was a Fascist, a Communist, a dashingly handsome, famously social artist given to glorifying his independence in the grand romantic manner. As a young man (born Kurt Erich Suckert), he gave himself the name Malaparte— "the bad side," because Bonaparte, "the good side," had already been taken.

The house he began to build in the late 1930s is a bad boy's dream palace, a showcase for melodramatic solitude on a fabled island of pleasure. Malaparte called the house his self-portrait. It sits alone on the tip of a rocky promontory overlooking the Bay of Naples. From the edge of the terrace, the cliff drops straight to the sea. The building's restored stucco exterior, freshly repainted Pompeian red, throbs against blue sea and sky. Not far from here is the precipice from which slaves who displeased the Emperor Tiberius were flung to their deaths. Malaparte threw himself into architecture and came up with a work of art.

Each year, scores of architecture students risk their necks dangling from the cliffs above the house to get a better look. But those fortunate enough to be invited to stay at Casa Malaparte usually catch their first glimpse from the water, from the little boat that ferries you there. It is a sight that leaves you spellbound with wonder: How could anyone actually live in such a magnificent setting?

While it's true that the house makes no concession to camouflage, it is acutely responsive to its natural surroundings. Its most famous feature— a wedge-shaped staircase that descends from a broad rooftop terrace— parallels a dip in the rocky terrain. Atop the terrace, a curving white plaster wall tapers to a point as it stretches toward the sea. The wall's jib-like shape mimics the sails of passing boats while accentuating the flat roof, a microcosm in masonry of the horizon it looks out upon.

Malaparte began to plan the house in 1938, after his release from confinement on the islands of Lipari and Ischia. Though an ardent supporter of Mussolini, the writer had been arrested, imprisoned, and confined for statements critical of the Fascist regime. Malaparte's response to the experience was operatic, perhaps sincere. He felt that prison had taught him the meaning of freedom by unchaining his mind. He built the house, in part, as a tribute to his liberation. He wanted to construct a prison from which his imagination could take perpetual flight.

Malaparte wanted a modern house, not a fake rustic villa. After acquiring the land, he hired Adalberto Libera, a prominent Rationalist architect, to prepare a design, and for many years Libera was given sole credit for the completed house. More recent scholarship, like that undertaken by Marida Talamona in her 1992 book *Casa Malaparte* (Princeton Architectural Press), suggests that the client all but abandoned Libera's design soon after receiving his building permit and for the rest of his life worked directly with local contractors to realize his own ideas.

The Plan of the two-story house is shipshape simple. On the ground floor, an entrance hall leads to a wing of five guest bedrooms, trim as cabins on a small yacht. A large tiled kitchen and a small paneled dining room, economically furnished with built-in table and benches, complete the plan.

A narrow stairway leads from the entrance hall to an imposing stone-floored salon on the main floor above. It is an immense but sparsely furnished room with stunning views of the coast. At the far end of the room, a narrow hallway leads to Malaparte's private apartment: two bedrooms, each with its own marble-lined bathroom fitted with a sunken tub. From Malaparte's bedroom, a door opens into a shelf-lined study, still furnished with the writer's books.

The spare, modern geometry of the house is deceptive. Much of what Malaparte conceived has little to do with abstract form, even less to do with function. Many of the design features are symbolic devices, aimed at integrating Malaparte's artistic ideas with his personal history. The exterior staircase, for example, is modeled after the wedge-shaped entrance to the church on Lipari where Malaparte was confined. Grilles on the front door and on ground-floor windows recall the bars of a Roman prison where the writer was also briefly jailed.

But it's not all private imagery, either. There are classical and vernacular elements as well. The exterior staircase, while based on the Lipari church, deliberately resembles the tiered seating of a Greek amphitheater; the sunken marble baths hark back to ancient Rome. Wooden doors, with traditional moldings, are used throughout the house. Tiles with cozy floral patterns cover the bedroom floors.

Malaparte was an admirer of Surrealism, and the prison imagery reflects that movement's preoccupation with the mind's darker recesses. In fact, a surrealist dream logic pervades the entire house. In the neutral white salon, for example, with its stone floor paved like a village piazza and its vistas of sea and sky visible through four large windows, the building appears to have been turned inside out. But then the windows, surrounded not just by moldings but by wide wooden picture frames as well, turn the room outside in—transforming the views into landscape paintings, panoramas for a grand salon.

A small fifth window winks at you from inside the fireplace. As the sun moves lower in the sky, the hearth glows with Promethean fire. In front of the fireplace, there is a naughty Dada touch: a large table has two legs that appear to be classical columns but are in fact factory-made toilets, a Mediterranean remake of Marcel Duchamp.

Restoration of the house, which stood empty for two decades after Malaparte's death in 1957, is now proceeding under the direction of Niccolo Rositani, a Florentine lawyer who is the writer's great-nephew. The facade has been completely restored. Work on the interior is proceeding slowly; each box of tiles, each bag of plaster must be unloaded from small boats and carried by hand up the crooked flight of 114 stairs that lead to the front door. Meanwhile, the house is being used in the summer for conferences on architecture and design.

But this is a writer's house, not an architect's; it is the highly personal essay of a mind untrained in design. The building's eclectic forms and references echo the multiple facets of Malaparte's career, and from the letters Malaparte wrote while building the house, it is evident that he hoped to bring those facets into harmony. W. H. Auden once proposed that civilizations should be measured by "the degree of diversity attained and the degree of unity retained," but at the Casa Malaparte I saw that the individual work of art serves a contrary function. There an artist attained a powerful expression of unity while retaining the complexity of his life and thought.

When prowling around Casa Malaparte, you may not be conscious of all the symbolic references. But even in purely formal terms, the design takes its breathtaking harmony from a highly complex vocabulary: the interplay of interior and exterior, of verticals, horizontals, diagonals, and curves; the melding of Euclidean geometry with the shapes and textures of stone; the balance of colors, materials, and variously shaped windows. The integrity of the composition seems closer to the order of nature than to architecture's typically rational system of organizing space.

The house has an uncommon power to make you part of that order. One afternoon, as we stood on the terrace looking out over the lagoon, we were gripped by the oceanic sensation that the waves, the rocks, the sunlight, the bird cries, and we ourselves were part of a synchronized pattern. The momentary loss of self would have been scary had it not been so ecstatic, so peaceful. Is this how divers feel when they stay underwater too long and succumb to rapture of the deep? Perhaps this was a rapture of the surface.

On another afternoon I discovered the depths from which these beautiful surfaces had emerged. My favorite way to look at the Casa Malaparte was to lie on my back on an inflatable kid-size raft and drift around the small lagoon below the house. The location was hazardous. I had to paddle fast to avoid being run over by the little sightseeing boats that circle the lagoon hourly in summer, loudspeakers in full blare with commentary on the famous Casa Malaparte. My first reaction to this invasion was the typically selfish one of the tourist offended by other tourists. How dare they intrude on Malaparte's solitude! Unlike me, of course, with my Batman raft and magazine assignment and *Sea & Ski*.

Then I realized that gawking tourists were utterly faithful to the spirit of the place. The house was designed for spectacle. With its Greek amphitheater, its indoor piazza, its stagelike roof terrace raised to the sun, the house is a collection of performance spaces. It's a multiplex theater for a one-man show, a house designed by a man who had learned, in prison perhaps, how to be both player and audience.

Jean-Luc Godard captured the building's exhibitionist essence in his movie *Contempt*, which used the house as its main location. One memorable scene finds Brigitte Bardot stretched out on the roof beneath the white concrete sail, wearing only *The Films of Fritz Lang*, spread open on her rear end. It's a classic image of the power of mindless beauty. The Bardot character, a screenwriter's wife, drives the film's plot not by her actions but by her passivity. The men competing for the attention she cannot give are reduced to fools.

The Casa Malaparte, like any beautiful object, exerts a similarly passive power. It's Curzio Malaparte playing Brigitte Bardot, or whoever his Bardot was in 1938. Perhaps that's why, since his death, the house has grown in stature, while Malaparte's writings have faded. The beautiful woman or man who wants to be loved as a whole person is a common enough stereotype. But how often do we hear about the movie maker who longs to be Brigitte Bardot? The writer or politician who wants to be loved as a passive object, adored not for doing but simply for being?

The Casa Malaparte was the home of such a person. It is the portrait of a show-off who ultimately found the perfect way to show off. In his writings, Malaparte remains a man of action. He does, he thinks, therefore he is Curzio Malaparte. Thinking and doing are also present in the house—it took intelligence and sweat to design and build it—but the process of creation remains hidden. It is secondary, minor, of no more immediate consequence than the forces that heaved up the cliffs around it. The Casa

Malaparte need do nothing but lie there. It stretches out, lazily sunning itself on a rock by the sea, serene in the power of beauty to make us want never to leave.

January 28, 1996

A CITY POISED ON GLITTER AND ASHES

The road gets rougher. It's lonelier and tougher. Franklin D. Israel is the man who got away: the native New Yorker who went west and became Frank Israel, Star Architect, Hollywood Architect. Now, at age fifty, Israel is the subject of a vibrant retrospective at the Museum of Contemporary Art in Los Angeles, a show that is also a haunting portrait of Los Angeles at a critical moment in the city's history.

Through the lens of architecture, we are shown an urban drama of extremes: a city precariously balanced between cultural eminence and imminent collapse, between the triviality of the pop culture it pumps out and the civic greatness to which it aspires. Using one architect's work as an example, the Israel retrospective holds out a message of hope that art can help reconcile these extremes, or at least negotiate them with poise.

Architecture, at least from a New Yorker's point of view, is the art that got away, the art that went west because it needed more room to breathe. In the last two decades, Los Angeles has eclipsed New York as the country's leading city for contemporary architecture. The shift west is partly due to technology, perhaps more to mentality. New York is a vertical city, made possible by the steel frame and the elevator. Los Angeles is sprawling, horizontal, as much an extended suburb as a city, with an urban fabric that is simultaneously knitted together and ripped apart by dependence on the car.

Since the mid-1970s, a group of Los Angeles architects has been making architecture out of these challenging urban conditions. Frank Gehry, Thom Mayne, Eric Owen Moss, Frederick Fisher and Craig Hodgetts, and Ming Fung are only some names on this talented roster. Along with the growth of institutions like the Museum of Contemporary Art and the Getty Center, the creativity of these architects is an awesome sign of the city's increasing cultural depth.

These have also been years of painful crisis for Los Angeles, when racial tensions and natural disasters have clouded the city's image as a sun-kissed promised land. Buildings have provided vivid symbols of the city's agony: concrete walls with earthquake cracks, Malibu homes consumed by brush fire, stores ablaze in South Central, violence amid the mansions of Brentwood.

But there's a level on which these extremes are not opposed. Insecurity, sophistication: these are symbiotic forces, joined in the evolution of a great city. They are a cause of discontent as well as a source of fascination for a creative mind. This is the symbiosis that has shaped the work on view in Out of Order, the Israel show at the Museum of Contemporary Art. His buildings epitomize both the deepening of the city's cultural maturity and the agony that has lapped through Los Angeles in recent years. They do not polarize these extremes; nor do they resolve them. They make art out of the tension between them. In doing so, the buildings transcend their purely regional importance as the work of an "L.A. architect" and become more broadly emblematic of the contemporary city in flux.

Israel moved to Los Angeles in 1977. His earliest works are placid. The houses he designed in the 1980s, for clients like Robert Altman, Joel Grey, and Michele Lamy, exude Eastern calm. Trim, spare pavilions, their simple geometric interiors suffused with natural light, the buildings evoke a palmier time in Los Angeles as well as the modern masters who preceded Israel beneath the palms, architects like Rudolph Schindler, Frank Lloyd Wright, Richard Neutra, and Charles and Ray Eames.

In more recent works, the placidity has evaporated. Walls tilt. Rooms twist. Private houses are sheathed with metal panels, as if armoring themselves against assault. Windows have mutated from ordinary rectangles into elongated trapezoids, silent screams of glass. A boat-shaped form appears in many buildings, as if the architect thought it prudent to provide his clients with arks to escape an approaching deluge.

But visitors to the Dan House, a newly completed Israel residence in Malibu, are reminded that fire is a more likely threat than water. Approaching the house, you drive past the chimneys of burned-out show-places, the charred rubble of their foundations drawn into an incongruous composition with spellbinding views of green hills, a sparkling sea. The chimneys register as tombstones to the death of permanence. High-priced real estate gets you a view but no protection from wind and heat. Despite Malibu's cool Pacific vistas, this is desert terrain, where the weather conducts seasonal seminars on the return of dust to dust.

Israel's designs retain great grace. He does not put his clients through ordeals of discomfort. But neither can he grant them refuge from the seismic shift, wildfire, or fickleness of taste that might at any moment sweep through their artfully constructed living spaces, vaporizing them to extinction. He shelters his clients, rather, within structures that evoke the provisional nature of shelter, the elusiveness of that sense of permanence that it was once architecture's mission to secure.

The contours of the Dan House, for instance, echo the lines of the Malibu hills, the sea's blue horizon. But this is not a Frank Lloyd Wright house, comfortably nestling in the landscape. Instead, the house's stretched-out, fragmented forms—its asymmetrical composition, the assortment of shapes, the variety of materials deployed on its facade—convey the sense that an uneasy negotiation is going on between the land and its owners.

That mediatory spirit may well be why Israel was chosen by the Museum of Contemporary Art to represent Los Angeles at this moment. No other architect's work embodies more fully the city's current tension between ephemerality and perpetuity. Then, as the MOCA show's catalog makes painfully clear, earthquakes and fires are not the only natural disasters that have destabilized the city. In an interview with the show's curator, Elizabeth Smith, he talks candidly about his struggle with AIDS and the impact of that struggle on his work.

The disease has also struck Israel's clients. One of his most accomplished buildings, the Goldberg-Bean House, set on a spectacular site in the Hollywood Hills, was sold not long after its completion because one of the two young men who had commissioned the house died. More than most cities, Los Angeles belongs to the living: to youth, promise, radiance. It has fallen to Israel's generation to negotiate a contract between stellar promise and early death.

Visitors enter the show through a piece of architectural sculpture, a giant origami-like pavilion of plaster, whose planes tip to and fro to form canted walls, doorways, a ceiling that dips and thrusts and a dimly illuminated hideaway enclosure, perfect for a rendezvous with Dr. Caligari. From there, they pass into what Israel calls the Blue Room, a somberly lighted, roughly rectangular grotto, where wooden models of his buildings are displayed.

The room is enclosed on three sides by stud walls, affixed with horizontal slats; the models are viewed through openings between the slats. The fourth wall is papered with blueprints for the plaster pavilion. Deep blue light from concealed fluorescent tubes washes the gallery walls behind the slats and spills into the space, an electric version of Chinese ink brushed over watered paper. The stud walls, together with the blueprints, read as metaphors for the process of building. In combining these with the stylized upheaval of the plaster folds, Israel symbolizes this moment in the city's history, or at least his place in it: the "unbuilding" of Los Angeles is integral to the building of a richer, more complex city.

A forty-foot-long light table slices diagonally through the Blue Room's artificial dusk, its surface laminated with Grant Mudford's sparkling color photographs of Israel's built work: private houses, offices for movie production and record companies, a private art museum, and his most recent building, a library for the University of California, Los Angeles. The show's perfect moment comes into focus when you stand at the end of the table and let your eyes glide along its length.

From this sideways vantage point, Israel's individual buildings are unrecognizable, but the scintillating spirit of his work leaps off the table. His angular shapes, his harlequin colors convey the joyousness of confetti tossed in a passing parade. Fragments of intense blue sky in Mudford's pictures pick up the gallery's fluorescent blue. A fold of the plaster origami thrusts over the table like a highway overpass, and suddenly the table is transformed into Frank Israel Boulevard, the architect's grand synthesis of Wilshire, Melrose, Hollywood, and Sunset, compressed into one giant, lit-up toy.

The image of the city street has figured frequently in Israel's work. In a 1992 essay called "Cities Within," he describes how his designs for office interiors, like those for Propaganda Films, bring the scale and variety of the urban streetscape into an enclosed, semi-public realm. This motif can be criticized as a form of introversion, yet another example of society's retreat into private simulations of the public realm. But "Israel Boulevard" sets out another idea: if he has drawn bits of the city inside his buildings, his buildings have also brought life, color, and urbanity to the city outside.

To appreciate the urban dimension of this work, it helps to recall the classic image Los Angeles framed for itself in an earlier chapter of Hollywood history: the lineup of mansions in Beverly Hills and Bel Air, Hollywood's showplace bedroom neighborhoods, with their garishly eclectic period styles that cover the decorative spectrum from the Spanish hacienda to the classical temple, the half-timbered Tudor cottage to the Palladian villa, all lined up in riotous solipsism along curving, palm-lined streets.

Frank Israel knows all about, and loves, that layer of the city's history. Born in 1945, Israel studied architecture at the University of Pennsylvania and Yale in the early days of the Postmodern movement. Robert Venturi and Robert A. M. Stern, who helped shatter the modernist taboo against the use of period styles, were early influences. From Venturi, but also from the appetites of his own generation, Israel absorbed a taste for popular culture. On first moving to Los Angeles, in fact, Israel pursued a career as a movie production designer and worked on sets for *Star Trek*.

Star Trek: The Building. That's the title I would have given the MOCA show, for Israel's view of the world bears a startling resemblance to the twinkling skyscape that the crew of the *Enterprise* gazes out upon while hurtling through deep space. Israel's starry panorama is a filmic montage of history, glamour, and visual delight. It takes in the film-industry luminaries who have hired him, the glittering nighttime vista from the Hollywood Hills, and, not least, the pantheon of great architects like Schindler and Neutra who have influenced his work.

In his introduction to a book on Israel's work, Frank Gehry notes that he has sometimes referred Hollywood clients to Israel because "Frank deals better with 'stars' than anyone else in town." Yet it was thanks to Gehry that at the critical moment, Israel was able to distinguish between Tinseltown hype and the responsibilities of art, and to heed the call of the latter.

The relationship between "the two Franks," as they're often referred to locally, helps explain why Los Angeles has eclipsed New York as the center of American architecture. New York architects like to gesture in the direction of tradition, but they know next to nothing about continuity or the mutual support between generations on which tradition depends. In Los Angeles, architects talk less about tradition; many of them are too busy living it. Despite the city's reputation for freewheeling individualism, it has developed an almost classical order of continuity, due in large part to Gehry's generosity to younger architects.

No one has put this order to more constructive use than Frank Israel and the young architects at work in his office: Steven Shortridge, Annie Chu, and Barbara Callas. Israel's early projects turned the Postmodern revival of period styles on its head. Instead of using history as a weapon against modern architecture, Israel set about to connect his work to modern architecture's history. The connection is expressed most clearly in the Lamy-Newton Pavilion, a 1988 addition to a private house. In this striking example of voluntary apprenticeship, Israel adapted the exposed-wire ceiling trusses from the 1949 Eames House, while the corner windows, divided by horizontal mullions, are borrowed from residential designs by Schindler and Wright.

Like the Lamy-Newton Pavilion, many of Israel's projects are additions to existing structures. Aesthetically, too, they stand for incremental change. But Israel's star trek has also propelled him into new aesthetic worlds, where no modernist had gone before. Like Eric Moss's factory conversions in Culver City, Israel's designs for Propaganda Films, Limelight Productions, and Virgin Records are remodeled buildings originally used for manufacturing. Their design vocabulary expresses the shift from light industry to "the industry."

Israel retains some of the features of these gritty urban sheds. At Limelight Productions, massive roof trusses introduce a sculptural presence. And the remodeling relies on industrial hardware—joints, fasteners, light fixtures—to create visual effects. Gone, however, is any sense of assembly-line regularity. Canted walls, asymmetrical window openings, and a rich collage of materials convey that this workplace thrives on mental play.

Israel's work for the entertainment business makes some people suspicious. Maybe he's having fun. Hollywood has already blurred the line between art and entertainment. Entertainment comes and goes. Isn't art supposed to last?

His work illustrates a paradox. While Los Angeles may have coarsened the culture at large, the city itself has grown more refined. Israel's career is proof. Israel doesn't design what the Disney people call "entertainment architecture." His houses are classics. But their vigor stems partly from Israel's willingness to accept pop culture as an urban force, akin to brush fires and earthquakes, that is constantly loosening the city's grip on permanence. Like everything else there, art has to live in the moment. Israel grasps that this is not a hindrance but a challenge, especially for an art form that has traditionally stood for endurance. Israel's responses to that challenge grow in strength, even as the ground trembles.

March 10, 1996

IN THE PUBLIC INTEREST

In Frankfurt, the American architectect Frank Gehry has just completed the kind of housing project he has long dreamed of building in the United States. Located in a parklike setting outside the city, the project bears no resemblance to the image of bleak vertical barracks for the poor that is usually associated with "public housing." Nor is Gehry's design just a flashy star turn, an artistic tour de force by America's most respected living architect. Rather, it is a modest, deeply humane project in which innovative design has been placed at the service of social responsibility.

In Europe, public housing is called social housing, and the difference is more than semantic: it is philosophic. The public is a political entity that can vote to honor or disregard its moral responsibility to house people decently. Social housing evokes the higher authority of the social contract. That distinction signals a decisive difference in the way contemporary cities are shaped.

The Goldstein Housing Project, as Gehry's complex is called, is located about halfway between the center of the city and the airport. One side of the complex is bordered by the forested greenbelt that encircles Frankfurt. The other side faces onto a park, generously equipped with playing fields and other areas for recreation, built especially for this largely residential part of town. The main concept behind Gehry's design was to create a fluid sense of connection between these two green open spaces.

Gehry's plan is traditional. It reflects the legacy of the "garden city," a concept pioneered by Ebenezer Howard, a social thinker of the late nineteenth century who advocated the creation of green satellite communities outside the polluted industrial center. Widely influential in the early twentieth century, the idea was later abandoned when modern city planners believed that regularly spaced, high-rise buildings more accurately reflected the machine age.

Gehry's eleven-acre site was the last of several housing projects to be developed in this part of town. Earlier projects reflected modernist thinking: long, straight blocks with uniform facades. Gehry's design, by contrast, breaks up the 162-unit complex into a modulated townscape of smaller, low-rise buildings. Ranging from three to five stories, the eight apartment blocks are organized into two U-shaped configurations that allow the landscape to filter in from the parks on either side. Two pedestrian paths pass through the property. One, a straight tree-lined allée, connects the complex to a bus stop (and future tram stop) on the edge of the property. A second curving path winds through the courtyards formed by the two Us, linking the two city parks.

Gehry has designed the apartment blocks to emphasize their individuality. Their flat, stucco surfaces are painted bright red, yellow, and white. Balconies, entrance canopies, and stair towers, rendered in boldly sculptured forms, are clad with zinc. Several smaller zinc-clad structures, housing bicycle garages, community meeting rooms, and a day care center, add to the visual variety.

The apartment layouts are conventional and range in size from studios to four bedrooms. All the units have balconies. Some are trapezoidal enclosures, stacked one on top of another like overlapping shingles. These are the most visually striking feature of the complex. Their sharp, angular thrust may seem harsh, even inhospitable, but less so if one bears in mind that, in Germany, balconies are usually reserved for gardening. Like aerial look-in parks, they create an intermediary green zone between private space and public park.

How natural Gehry makes it seem, traditional urban living within notably unconventional forms. Yet, he has not set out to create a new way of life, merely to build the framework for a better one. And why shouldn't that better life include vigorous architecture? The Goldstein houses go a long way in dispelling the myth that there is something inherently incompatible between architectural innovation and socially responsible design.

America's city planners would do well to emulate the public-private partnership that produced the project and the social attitudes that accompanied it. Typically, Frankfurt accepts bids from private firms to develop and operate new housing on a designated site. This linkage between building and management is crucial; it encourages construction of unusually high quality, to minimize maintenance costs later on. Rents, geared to income, can go as low as 25 percent of market rates. Yet people who move into social housing don't regard it as a way station between the gutter and the suburbs—this is where they expect to live, to raise children, grow old, exchange a large apartment for a smaller one as their needs change. Thoughtful planning reinforces this stability with schools, shopping, and transportation in place before the city accepts bids.

It is a concept worth keeping in mind when contemplating the statistics about the gulf between the rich and poor in America. Yes, we need to refurbish the social contract, but it takes more than money to reinforce the collapsing middle ground. It takes civilization.

July 21, 1996

THE SHORT, SCORNED LIFE OF AN AESTHETIC HERESY:
Designed in Defiance of Modernist Tenets,
2 Columbus Circle Awaits Its Fate

Those *Independence Day* aliens have nothing to teach New Yorkers about the joys of blowing up buildings. We're old pros at this sport. Nobody takes greater pleasure in watching architecture smashed to smithereens.

The newest candidate for this real-life special effect is 2 Columbus Circle, a small marble white elephant of a building on the south side of the circle between Broadway and Eighth Avenue. Occupied by the city's Department of Cultural Affairs, the ten-story building is being sold as part of the city's plan to redevelop the site of the Coliseum.

Along with Donald J. Trump's hotel and condominium tower, on the northern rim of the circle, the redevelopment of both sites announced last week will completely transform this notoriously chaotic civic space. Though it is not certain that 2 Columbus Circle will be demolished, there is little likelihood it will survive. Impractical for commercial use, the building is also unlikely to arouse a campaign to have it designated a landmark.

In fact, from the moment of its opening in 1964, 2 Columbus Circle has always been something of an orphan in the midtown cityscape. "A die-cut Venetian palazzo on lollipops" was the reaction of Ada Louise

Huxtable, the architecture critic for *The New York Times*. Others compared the structure to a "perfume bottle," "a shoe emporium on Main Street," "a marble christening robe."

Why this pileup of critical disfavor? The building's aesthetic merit (or lack of it) was only part of the story. What was also going on here was a crisis in the way aesthetic merit is judged. Who sets standards of taste? Artists or patrons? Critics or the public? Two Columbus Circle opened at a moment when critical judgment was itself being judged.

Originally called the Gallery of Modern Art, the building was designed by Edward Durell Stone, a noted architect whose other works include the General Motors Building on Fifth Avenue, Kennedy Center for the Performing Arts in Washington, and the Pepsico headquarters in Purchase, New York. The Gallery was commissioned by Huntington Hartford, heir to the A&P supermarket chain, a patronage that alone sufficed to prejudice people against the project. Mr. Hartford was a creature of the gossip columns who aspired to be a cultural player.

A sometime backer of Broadway shows, Mr. Hartford was also the publisher of *Show* magazine, one of liveliest glossies of the 1960s. He founded the Gallery of Modern Art with the inflammatory purpose of challenging the canonical view of modernism promoted by established institutions like the Museum of Modern Art, the Guggenheim, and by the era's leading critics.

In 1955 he took out full-page newspaper advertisements attacking Abstract Expressionism. Turning his back on Cubism and other modern movements, Mr. Hartford dedicated his museum to the work of figurative artists like Dalí, Burne-Jones, and Vuillard.

Stone was an ideal architect to design this gallery. Formerly a committed modernist, Stone had codesigned the Museum of Modern Art in 1939. Stone's proscenium arch at Radio City Music Hall and his Mandel House, in Mount Kisco, New York, were also strongly Modernist.

But in the mid-1950s, Stone broke with Modern orthodoxy and began designing buildings decorated with perforated screens, gold columns, and other ornate touches. Projects like the United States Embassy in New Delhi and the United States Pavilion at the 1958 World's Fair in Brussels earned Stone contempt from many architects.

At the Gallery of Modern Art on Columbus Circle, Stone reduced the perforated-screen motif to lacelike borders around the marble facades. The whole design was a flagrant violation of the modernist taboo against historical reference. An arched loggia crowned the top of the building. At the base, colonnades evoked the Doge's Palace in Venice. In effect, the edifice was a remade Venetian bell tower. *Ding-dong!*

As a challenge to the Museum of Modern Art, Mr. Hartford's enterprise was ludicrous. Still, the gallery was a remarkable example of the cultural and material abundance that New York enjoyed in the mid-1960s. And it was a pleasant place to visit. The interior circulation recalled that of the Guggenheim—visitors took an elevator to the top and walked down—though in this case the spiral was square. Main galleries alternated with broad landings where art was also displayed.

One gallery offered a sumptuous group of Vuillards. Another was devoted to Burne-Jones. It was refreshing to see works that, like pre-Raphaelite paintings, lay outside the mainstream. Whether or not they were "modern," they afforded an experience of discovery that was ebbing from the Museum of Modern Art's concentration on the canon.

One of the building's best features was the Gauguin Room, a top-floor restaurant that featured tapestry versions of Gauguin paintings. A kind of tasteful Trader Vic's, the place served cheap and tasty Polynesian cuisine. The columns of the loggia framed extraordinary views of the circle, Broadway and Central Park, a stunning vista that made one feel privileged to be in New York.

But none of the gallery's good features could redeem it from one overarching flaw to critics: Mr. Hartford and Stone had dragged art and architecture back to the bad old days when wealthy patrons were the arbiters of culture. Patrons of modern art were supposed to be like the Rockefellers. They should put up the money and let professionals decide what modern art is supposed to be. This social shift was part of modern art's appeal. In theory, the artist's independence from the patron insured the integrity of art.

Modern architecture stood for a similar idea. The Modern movement had liberated design from the whims of rich clients and empowered architects to dictate terms. These issues were very real in 1964. The city's first glass skyscrapers were not yet ten years old. Modernism was still something to be defended against philistine assaults. In that climate, Stone's aesthetic heresies could scarcely be seen as anything else.

The Gallery of Modern Art had a short life. In 1969, no longer willing to support an expensive venture that had never caught on with the public, Mr. Hartford donated the building to Fairleigh Dickinson University. He sold off his collection two years later. Renamed the New York Cultural Center, and dedicated to temporary shows, the place limped along until 1975, when Gulf and Western Industries bought the building and turned it over to the city. Stone died in 1978. After a series of unsuccessful investments and three seven-figure divorce settlements, Mr. Hartford, now eighty-five, filed for bankruptcy protection in 1992.

Looking back now, one is struck that the negative critical reaction to this building belongs to another era. Today there are few buildings that could arouse such a clear consensus of educated opinion. Indeed, the very concept of informed consensus has fallen into disrepute.

Even before Mr. Hartford quit the museum business, the consensus supporting modernism had begun to crumble. In 1966, Robert Venturi's *Complexity and Contradiction in Architecture* was published. This book suddenly made it respectable for architects to borrow from historical styles. Scholarly books on Victorian art and architecture sparked a reappraisal of an era that the modernists had tried to bury. The belief in a cultural mainstream gave way to the ideal of pluralism.

To an extent, this erosion of consensus has made for a livelier cultural scene. Art movements no longer depend on monolithic support from artists, critics, and museums. There is room for different currents of art to flow simultaneously through the culture.

At the same time, the breakdown of consensus has left art vulnerable to corruption by market pressures. If everything is a matter of opinion, and one person's opinion is as valuable as another's, then the most reliable criterion of value is how much something costs.

In a more enlightened time, a city administration might well commit itself to finding a cultural use for 2 Columbus Circle. But under the circumstances, it seems cruelly apt that the building should end up demolished by the highest bidder.

July 31, 1996

NOSTALGIA TRIPPING IN TIMES SQUARE

We are all of us living in the stars, but some of us are gazing at the gutter. *Nostalgie de la boue*—the sentimental attachment to decrepitude and sleaze—is a venerable urban tradition, and it probably accounts for some of the negative reaction to the retail and entertainment strip now taking shape on Forty-second Street between Seventh and Eighth avenues. Where have they gone, the chicken hawks and stiletto knife displays, the peep-show shills, pickpockets, cokeheads, winos, pimps, and tramps? We had a world-class gutter here. Must we trade it in for a shopping strip of chain retail outlets?

The new stores and restaurants, the beautifully restored New Victory Theater, are all part of the so-called interim plan, the city- and state-sponsored project being implemented pending construction of the four mega-skyscrapers scheduled to straddle the lower end of Times Square.

Thus far, only the eastern end of the block shows the impact; there are also new stores continuing up Seventh Avenue, and two new restaurants around the corner of Forty-third Street.

Meanwhile, work proceeds on the restoration of the New Amsterdam Theater; on the south side of the square, a temporary two-story glass structure houses a sociable pub-in-the-sky, trimmed with bulbs that blink like bubbles in a glass of brew. The first of the four towers, designed by the New York firm Fox & Fowle, will be the new headquarters for Conde Nast, the publishing giant, on Broadway between Forty-second and Forty-third streets.

In its current, partially realized state, the interim plan resembles one of those Before and After ads for plastic surgery. Already it is evident that more than one kind of nostalgia will be available to those who visit the area. For instance, the project makes a powerful appeal to nostalgia for childhood innocence. A lot of the signs, including the banners sporting the development's logo, make heavy use of purple and yellow, a combination that inevitably brings a jolly Easter egg hunt to mind. All they need to do is roll out some bales of green cellophane floss, and we'll all be down on our hands and knees searching for chocolates.

The childhood theme is reinforced by the children's theater productions presented at the New Victory, and it will be further buttressed when the Disney people move into the New Amsterdam and Madame Tussaud's opens down the block. Around the corner, on Seventh Avenue, workers are putting the finishing touches on Cinema Ride, an indoor attraction featuring simulated flight. The transformation of Times Square from a notorious vice zone into a year-round *Babes in Toyland* is shocking, no doubt intentionally so. What better way to signal that the cleanup of the square, pursued in vain for so many years, is finally coming to fruition? But the pre-Freudian view of childhood now on view is less than fully urban.

Nostalgia of another sort, sympathetically related to the childhood theme, is the sentimental view of New York's past as a kinder, more innocent time. The New Victory restoration is wonderful, but that new big brownstone staircase jutting out into the sidewalk, with its ornate lamp fixtures, reads like a claim on turf, a message that the street's future belongs to the past. The same message is extended around the block at the new Stardust Dine-O-Mat, a 1940s theme restaurant at Forty-third Street and Times Square, where the waitresses are uniformed like the Andrews Sisters on canteen duty at the USO. Elsewhere, the idea seems to be to turn back the clock to the 1950s or early '60s, but the result is a bowdlerized version of the era as depicted in *City of Night*, John Rechy's account of the infernal side of Times Square.

I'm actually a sucker for all three forms of nostalgia. I loved the Andrews Sisters even before Susan Sontag coined the term *camp taste*. The other day, looking in through the window of the Dine-O-Mat, I saw a middle-class suburban family enjoying their blue-plate specials. I was delighted to see people like that taking in a part of town that I love. Besides, I found myself thinking, there is always the hope that children might not be fooled by all this innocence stuff, that they'd find a way to be utterly corrupted by city life before nightfall, just as I was when I was their age.

The tableau reminded me of that scene in "The Yellow Bus," Lillian Ross's classic story about the New York visit of a group of high school seniors from Bean Blossom, Kansas, circa 1953. The kids all decide that New York is basically horrible, except for one boy who is swept away by it, and has hatched dreams of returning despite the dismay of his classmates. "You're just not thinking ahead!" one of them says, though clearly what horrifies them (and delights Ross) is precisely that he is thinking ahead, fantasizing about becoming something glorious. A chorus boy, perhaps. He's tasted the Big Apple. He's among the fallen. What Forty-second Street needs now is the kind of intelligence with which Ross turned this sentimental episode into art.

Two components, in particular, could help lift the interim project from the level of commerce to that of genuine urban complexity. The first is signage. Two years before the interim plan got under way, its sponsors invited Creative Time, a group that sponsors innovative art projects in the public realm, to transform the marquees and storefronts of Forty-second Street into a showcase for experimental artworks. The results were mixed, but the spirit was correct, and the project should continue in some form. As a public venture, the interim plan ought to sponsor artworks that do not merely serve the purpose of retail advertising.

The current array of signs, while colorful, shows little imagination, either in their design or in their use of communication technology. Fanciful, technically sophisticated visual displays surely belong here on the street, rather than at the downtown branch of the Guggenheim Museum, where a collection of electronic media projects is on view.

The second component involves the use of the renovated theaters. As the interim plan progresses, responsibility for its success will shift more and more to The New Forty-second Street, the nonprofit group responsible for developing programs for all these performance spaces. The process is similar to that followed by Barcelona in its recent urban revitalization. There architects and planners first created an ambitious citywide network of parks and other public spaces. When these were completed, the focus turned to the task of filling the places with cultural events.

· · ·

After years of inertia, Forty-second Street is at last well on its way to becoming a place. In effect, it's a stage-set Forty-second Street. Nothing wrong with that in a theater district, so long as something culturally valuable is encouraged to take the stage.

New York is the home of artists—Laurie Anderson, Twyla Tharp, Mark Morris, Spike Lee, David Mamet, to name just a few of the most prominent—whose work has raised to the level of art issues like those raised by the redevelopment of Forty-second Street: the place of popular culture; the interaction of public and private trust; the impact of global communications; the displacement of people and neighborhoods; the loss of the past; the poetics of solitude in the social world. The New Forty-second Street should invite artists of their stature to frame a plan for turning this street into a vibrant center for living art that deals with the city itself.

August 25, 1996

IN JAPAN, ART AND A MUSEUM BREATHE AS ONE

Try to visit the Nagi Museum of Contemporary Art in the rain, when the drops form rippling circles within the square enclosure of a shallow pool and the steel wires that rise from the pool in gentle loops make it seem as if the drops have bounced off the surface back into the air, freezing into glistening silver arcs.

Or go when it's sunny, go when it snows. Just go, or try to imagine yourself there. Though Nagi is barely a dot on the map, the museum is more startlingly original than any built by a major city in recent years.

Conceived and designed by Arata Isozaki for a small Japanese town a half day's drive from Tokyo, the Nagi Museum of Contemporary Art exhibits only three works of art. Each is the result of a collaboration between the architect and an artist or artistic team. Each is integral to the architecture. All are described as semipermanent, because the artists are still living. They are free to change their installations. I can't overestimate the power of this strikingly fresh concept to affect the viewer's experience of art.

The museum, completed last year, is one element of a municipal program designed to strengthen the town's cultural life, partly in the hope of encouraging young people to remain in the town instead of migrating to the big city. The budget for the museum was small. When Nagi's mayor approached Isozaki about designing it, the architect asked why money should be used to build a permanent collection, or to shoulder the expense of traveling shows. Why not take the opportunity to create contemporary art? Why not create, as well, a new concept for the contemporary art museum?

Isozaki describes them as three spaces rather than three artworks. The three are represented on the building's exterior by three distinct shapes: a cylinder and a crescent, both sheathed with corrugated metal, and a connecting rectangular solid of cast concrete. Stretched out to define a formal axis for the complex, the concrete block also accommodates the museum's entrance and a coffee shop.

Attached to the block is a three-story cube, covered in red tile, that contains a children's library and a small gallery that exhibits work by local artists, chiefly the calligraphers for which Nagi is noted. The architectural differentiation between these elements supports the idea to which the Nagi museum gives form. The making of a whole—a whole artwork, a whole place, a whole life, a whole city—depends on the capacity to simultaneously separate and join, to connect and detach. The idea is local and global.

Isozaki's names for the three shapes—Sun, Moon, and Earth—refers to imagery from the traditional Japanese garden; the light from many old garden lanterns shines through sun- and moon-shaped perforations in the stone. One of the artworks takes as its point of departure the revered 800-year-old rock garden at the Temple of Ryoan-ji in Kyoto. Created by Shusaku Arakawa and Madeline Gins, who live in New York, the work, Ubiquitous Site, is a comic stroke with cosmic intentions.

The piece is housed within the "sun" cylinder. Visitors enter through a small, winding staircase shrouded in darkness. Inside, one beholds a space that recalls, in miniature, a torus, one of those whirling, round shapes envisioned by NASA scientists for gravity-free space colonies. The barrel slopes upward toward a large, luminous disk: a circle of translucent glass that caps the barrel's southern end. A curving, small-scale replica of Ryoanji's rock garden wraps around either side of the cylinder. A park bench and a seesaw are affixed to the barrel's curved floor. These fixtures are reproduced, upside down, on the curved ceiling above.

This pairing of spatial opposites is matched by the work's psychological effects. The image of the rock garden evokes the sensation of tranquillity associated with Ryoan-ji. But the tilt of the floor, the doubling of images, the elimination of clear distinctions between up and down, left and right, back and front, create the contrary effects of disequilibrium and discomfort. These effects are experienced not just visually but physiologically. One can't easily take one's repose on a park bench when the body's center of gravity has shifted.

Stark white, sun-filled, nearly empty, the crescent-shaped moon space differs radically from the sun but does not send it into eclipse.

Three brass fixtures, attached to one wall, are the room's only overt sign of "art." These are the work of Kazuo Okazaki, the Japanese Surrealist who calls them *hisashi*, the term for the overhanging eaves of traditional Japanese buildings. But these "eaves," created by scraping putty over the edge of a table, are organic, not architectural. They invite viewers to interpret the eave as any form of mediation—trees, umbrellas, religious rituals—between themselves and whatever lies above.

Okazaki's surrealist approach is most evident in the extreme contrast between the relatively small sculptures and the soaring space in which they are shown. One feels that something is missing; one's self, perhaps. The Surrealist dimension is reinforced by the architecture.

Unlike the sun space, the moon is subtly disorienting. Walking through it, visitors may feel that their eyes have been fitted with new lenses: the tapering of the space at either end creates the effect of a panoramic photograph that bends linear perspective toward the direction of peripheral vision.

Earth is the largest and most lyrical of the three projects. Aiko Miyawaki, the artist, is married to Isozaki and has often collaborated with him but never to such stunning effect. This piece is the true contemporary equivalent of the Ryoan-ji garden, a classic for the present.

The work is actually three spaces, arranged in a U shape. A flight of grass terraces and a square concrete cavern, its floor covered with dry pebbles, are joined together by the shallow pool of water. In the cavern and the pool sprout the steel wire sculptures that Miyawaki calls *utsurohi*. The word means "a moment of movement."

Miyawaki's pencil drawings for the project, on view in the museum, suggest that the initial movement is that of a hand moving across a piece of paper. The artist has described the sculptures as an attempt to write in space. One could also call them cursive statues. The drawings convey the sensation of movement. The wires actually move, when stirred by wind or a viewer's hand.

Still or moving, they convey the impression of clouds, fog, the leafy crowns of trees. The movement of people across the land. An ethereal gesture that leads the eye from this miniature representation of the earth to the mountains and sky beyond. A reminder that Earth, too, is a heavenly body, perhaps the most divine.

That's it. And it's enough. For it is peculiar, a century after artists rallied around the cause of art for art's sake, to find oneself in a museum created for art's sake. Strange because for what other sake should art museums exist?

And yet, in large part because of the proliferation of art museums in the last fifteen years, things have got to the point where many people are inclined to say, "Oh, no, not another (groan) art museum!" And the fact is that many contemporary art museums are groans. Even the one Isozaki designed for Los Angeles is not much more than a neutral container for objects.

It's easy, amid all this museum commotion, to forget that these places are not primarily about openings, benefit dinners, blockbuster entertainment, or architectural reviews. They are about the power of art to interpret a civilization to itself. That is their civic role.

In his book *Cracking Up*, the British psychotherapist Christopher Bollas writes: "The self is not the sum of its parts. It is an esthetic intelligence." The Nagi museum says something similar. It has a body (the building) and connected areas of consciousness (the three spaces) in which the facts, feelings, moods, desires, memories, and fears that ordinarily float about freely have been shaped into provisional order.

Of course, curators of permanent collections and changing shows display aesthetic intelligence. So do houses, train stations, zoos, and department stores. And it is unlikely that as Isozaki insists, the Nagi museum will become the norm for contemporary art museums.

But he is correct to distinguish this concept from that of the modern museum. There, a fundamental separation exists between architectural, curatorial, and artistic spheres of intelligence. At Nagi, we cannot separate one from the others. The place takes its meaning from the many possible relationships among these spheres.

The intelligence here is both individual and collaborative. The museum suggests that these two forms of intelligence are not very different. A community may hold contradictory visions of itself. So does one person. The result resembles what Bollas, quoting Wallace Stevens, calls "the poem of the composition of the whole."

October 6, 1996

A PRIMAL PHANTASMAGORIA NOT JUST FOR GAMBLERS

Mohegan Sun, the spectacular, Indian-theme gambling casino that opened on October 12 in this small town in southeastern Connecticut, is a dense, exhilarating forest of symbols. Trees right beside slot machines.

Immense paintings of flowers over card tables. Cryptic Indian signs inter-spersed with flashing neon numbers. Images derived from nature—fish, corn, beans—are set within a context of heightened artificiality created by stage lights, video screens, and the merry abstraction that money becomes here. In the casino's food court, towering foam-rubber pine trees have real pine cones attached to them.

To those unfamiliar with either the customs of the Mohegan Indians or the rites of American gamblers, much of this sign language is incompre-hensible. What compels that woman to choose this slot machine and not that one? What is the meaning of the mandala that has been fashioned into a shade for that sconce? Who was Uncas? Who cares? Shut up and play cards.

It's a pleasure to feel bewildered here. This may present the casino's management with a problem. Mohegan Sun is a place that even the nongambling public can enjoy. On opening night, a spectator immune to the lure of chance could watch a wedding party cavort within the Wolf Den, a soaring enclosure of fake rocks, their peaks surmounted by howl-ing white wolves, while the Everly Brothers—live, in person and looking better than you either hoped or feared—serenaded the happy couple with their '50s hit "All I Have to Do Is Dream." Then the bride kicked off her slippers and everybody broke into the Macarena.

This is a happy place, and an imaginatively realized one. Where else could you find yourself swept into a whirling phantasmagoria of winners and losers, brides and grooms, coins, dice, cards, rocks, wolves, waterfalls, stretched animal skins, forgotten teenage heartthrobs, cloud machines, and attractively decorated restaurants where an international array of one-star food is served with four-star cheerfulness. Don't you hate yourself for lacking the imagination to think up such an outlandish concoction?

The state's second casino, Mohegan Sun is just ten miles from its com-petitor, Foxwoods Resort, operated by the Mashantucket Pequots. Devel-oped by Sun International, a South African company, the new casino is on a site formerly used to manufacture parts for nuclear submarines. The overlay of a Postmodern pleasure palace atop a base of Cold-War build-up will suggest to some the plot for a horror movie Steven Spielberg has yet to make. *Poltergeist 1996*. Ghosts of vanished, noble Indians, angered by the installation of a nuclear power plant on their tribal lands, mutate into a ruthless gang of capitalist entrepreneurs and take Kevin Costner for all he's worth. The casino's design, by the New York architect David Rock-well in association with Brennan Beer Gorman Architects, invites the vis-itor to think in cinematic terms. It is as ambitious a piece of stagecraft as anyone has realized since the days of Cecil B. DeMille.

You enter the casino through corridors that suggest tunnels. The idea is that you've walked into a cave leading to a secret gathering place where the rock melts away to reveal a clearing. The architecture per se is negligible: a corrugated metal ceiling, some exposed ducts, all painted black to create the receding space of a perpetually nighttime sky. The main gambling room below is a big circle, 360 feet in diameter, divided into quadrants. The mandala form recalls a traditional Mohegan symbol; it also echoes the shape of the traditional Roman basilica.

The quadrants are named after the seasons, and decorated accordingly. Large stands of artificial trees are crowned with plastic leaves, their color ranging from winter white to spring green. A corridor running around the room's perimeter leads to restaurants, specialized gaming rooms, bathrooms, and shops. Ceiling decorations and patterns in the carpet lead one through the thirteen moons of the Indian year, while large murals depicting tribal life, local vegetation, and changing skies illustrate the seasonal theme. In the center of the circle is the Wolf Den, the rocky enclosure where entertainers perform around the clock.

The immense space is unified by a series of large, overhead trusses, made of fake wood, designed to evoke the structure used in Mohegan long houses. Clipped to the trusses are stage lights and simulated stretched animal skins that diffuse golden light into the circular space below. The scale and variety of the decorative elements break up the huge space into areas of intimacy. Most of the new American gambling casinos are architecturally ambitious. But usually the architectural images—pyramids, water displays—do not intrude on the casino floor. Mohegan Sun may be the first where the slot machines are actually upstaged by their surroundings.

The effect is by no means as kitschy as it sounds. Clearly the designers have taken great care to learn about the Mohegans. This is not a museum; no attempt has been made to recreate actual Indian buildings or other artifacts. Instead of creating an environment of dubious authenticity, the designers have created an informed and witty collage of stylized Mohegan motifs. The result may be synthetic, but not more so than the current constitution of the Mohegan tribe itself. Several years ago, Sun International assembled the tribe's scattered descendants and financed their application for recognition by the Federal Government. That's why the casino now exists.

The paradox is that whatever its motives for doing so, the casino has actually revived the Mohegans' sense of tribal cohesion. And while the casino's setting is synthetic, it exercises genuine power. The circle of trees evokes memories of cruel children's games, fantasized rituals, tortures, secrets and exclusions. Like the cave, the tree circle recalls architecture's primitive roots. Even if you can't understand the Indian pictograms, you can respond to primal power of place.

The Indian symbols are not the only things that are hard to decipher. The casino itself, as a building type, is a sign that the society at large is trying to interpret.

Is it a sign of prosperity? Communities across the country are looking to casinos to salvage their blighted economies. Is it a sign of decline? The historically aware point to eighteenth-century Venice as a warning that great world powers typically turn to gambling as they fall. A sign of hope? Who enters a gambling casino without expecting to win? Or one of despair? Don't these people have something better to do?

But probably most people are fascinated by the casino for the same reason that they're fascinated by explicit sex scenes in mainstream Hollywood movies, the lyrics of rap songs, the unbuttoned patter on radio talk shows. The casino signifies the shattering of a moral taboo. Anyone old enough to be admitted to a casino grew up in a culture that placed gambling, along with cursing, drinking, and prostitution, on the list of Bad Things. Indeed, in most parts of the country, gambling remains illegal. That is why the Indians have captured this market. Legally, Indians exist outside the borders of this country. They are exempt from the laws in which America's moral prejudices have been inscribed.

Yet tribal law prohibits the Mohegans from playing here. And the people you do see hardly look held in the grip of vice. It's a wholesome, family crowd, happily engaged in a pleasant pastime that, even now, moralists still thunder about. There's even an arcade for children, with no money involved, called Kids Quest. In short, gambling has come into our lives under the sign of Evil. Can we afford to inch it over toward the column called Good? Can we afford not to?

Linguistics is one of the strategies used at Mohegan Sun to engineer this shift. By dropping two letters, gambling becomes gaming, a word with a far more respectable aura. The Indian theme is another strategy, evoking, as it does, the history of oppression by European settlers and the lingering need for restitution. The architecture adds to these factors the dimension of sacred space. This is a basilica here. You're in church!

The larger issues raised by Mohegan Sun may fall outside the purview of an architecture review. But it isn't exactly a work of architecture. Like much, perhaps most of American architecture today, it fits more neatly into the category of anthropology. Mr. Rockwell's design is a habitat for tribal behavior. The tribe conducting its rituals here is not the reconstituted Mohegan people. It is the "nonnative" Americans lining up to enter the Wolf Den. The tableau is handsome, but it doesn't have much to do with art, for the reason that it doesn't have much to do with life. It's rather about escaping life, about checking out of history into a prehistoric year of thirteen lucky moons.

Mohegan Sun is perhaps most fully understood as a symbol of American life in the post–Cold War era. In place of the East-West polarity, we're faced with a vast and growing gulf between winners and losers. Mohegan Sun defends the border between them by denying with great artistry that it exists. It's a big, glamorous wheel of fortune designed to suggest that the difference between winning and losing is just a matter of chance.

October 21, 1996

WHERE A ROOM IS A CALLING CARD

My respect for Japanese etiquette is not everything it should be. On my first trip to Tokyo, in August, I forgot to pack business cards. On the other hand, I did take the precaution of booking myself into the legendary Okura Hotel, so I did not entirely lose face. The Okura gives the face of those who stay there an instant lift. The hotel is in the Toranomon district, just across the street from the United States Embassy, and a privileged ambassadorial aura rubs off on the Okura and its guests. A room here is itself a calling card, a credential that identifies the lodger as a Somebody, or at least as somebody willing to go along with the way the Japanese expect visiting Somebodies to behave. There may be better hotels in Tokyo. Fancier, more expensive, and more modern hotels are numerous throughout the city. Let them all try harder. There is only one Okura.

Opened in 1953, the Okura Hotel is a lovingly maintained period piece. A friend describes the hotel's architecture as Eisenhower Modernism. Cruel but apt. The hotel's main building is a boxy bit of business, a low-rise block of glass and concrete, its facade adorned with ditsy perforated screens. Even the names of the hotel's restaurants evoke the flowery hospitality of the postwar years. Breakfast? Try the Camellia Corner, with lighting fixtures evidently designed to evoke the aurora borealis. For dinner, there's the fabulous Orchid Room, featuring Continental cuisine. Cocktails? The fifties had the right idea. Why bother with martinis if you can't order them straight up in a penthouse bar called the Starlight Lounge?

No one, however, stays at the Okura for the food. At breakfast, the scrambled eggs are a faintly chicken-flavored foam. For lunch, there are sandwiches in several varieties of moistened cardboard. Nonetheless, you may well find yourself ordering frequent rounds of bland dishes simply for the pleasure of watching the spellbinding grace with which they are served. Japan is justifiably famous for elaborate courtesy, but at the Okura, service rises to the level of an art form. Stylized but not stiff, formal but not intimidating, it's like a martial art from which the martial element has been subtracted.

On arrival, you are greeted by a lineup of white gloved bellboys. Even if you're the sort of person who ordinarily insists on carrying your bags from the taxi to the check-in desk, you will refrain from doing that here. The staff does not stand there looking servile, overburdened, or confused. Instead of trying to be helpful, they help. They are your partners in a dance. The choreography with which they relieve you of your bags is so lovely that it would be philistine to protest. If you held on to your luggage, you would feel as if you had stolen it.

The arrival, however, is merely a curtain raiser for the full Kabuki performance that awaits you when it's time to eat. The basic movement goes something like this. The waiter or waitress puts down the plate, stands back, but not straight up. The body remains slightly bent, slightly twisted in a sideways, nearly imperceptible bow, while the arms, acting as a kind of counterbalance to the swiveled hip, gesture toward the dish, the palms of the hands turned outward. It's a real presentation, a grand gesture of offering. The Okura is not a cheap place to stay, but as tipping is virtually unknown in Japan, you may find yourself thinking that a visit here is the bargain of a lifetime. You can't order a peanut without being treated to this amazing floor show, whether you choose the Belle Epoque, the Highlander Bar, the Toh-Ka-Lin, or the Sazanka.

Order breakfast in your room, if only to spare yourself the glare of the Camellia Corner's northern lights. Seven a.m. The doorbell rings. Blurrily, you answer it. A waiter stands framed by the doorway. He does not barge over the threshold crying, "Room service!" He allows a moment for jet-lagged eyes to adjust to the shock. Then: "May I . . . come in?" No one has said "May I?" to you for years, certainly not in such a sincere tone of voice. The pause between the words suggests a reservoir of politesse that, in the West, was drained dry centuries ago. Your overpowering impulse is to throw your arms around this person and say, Where have been all my life? Of course you may come in.

You need things laundered. You have already placed your clothes in the crisp paper bag provided for that purpose. It is embossed with the hotel's logo, a circle of three ginkgo leaves. You regret wrinkling the bag. But it's pleasant to know that your fine washables will on no account touch plastic, even if they are made of it. The laundry is returned a few hours later, in immaculate shape, with a handwritten note from the housekeeper. "Dear . . . , we are so sorry that we could not remove this stain! We did the best we could, but, unfortunately, the stain would not come out." Stain? What stain? Unless, perhaps, it's a tear stain, for the little note sounds so disconsolate you can almost hear the sound of sobbing as you read it.

Young ladies dressed in kimonos stand by the elevators in the main lobby and on the concourse level below. They do nothing but smile, nod, and say good morning. At first you think, How weird to employ a living person to provide an ornamental touch, as if she were a human version of the handsome bowls of flowers that grace the hallways. Later it may occur to you that the service performed by these women is functional as well as decorative. For you must smile back. This accomplishes for your mood what the elevator does for your body.

Few people stay at the Okura because of the décor. The guest rooms are comfortable but unexciting. Though there are some traditionally furnished Japanese accommodations, most of the rooms are like the Orchid Room's cuisine: blandly Continental. Tasteful lamps, pastel fauteuils, somewhat ceremoniously arranged. But there are pluses: a fax in each room, for instance, with idiot-proof instructions for international dialing. Beside the bed there's a convenient console with switches to control the lights and the electrically operated curtains, and buttons that bring in four stations of taped music. Atop the minibar there's a little hot-water heater for brewing tea or coffee. But who would want to forgo the charms of room service for a bag of instant Sanka?

Nonetheless, the hotel's public rooms are wondrous, an immaculately preserved relic of a time when modern architects sought to recast the austerity of modern architecture for the era of postwar prosperity. Golden light, open space: that's the predominant effect of the Okura's famous lobby, perhaps the world's most celebrated meeting place of East and West. Clean, wide, open, flowing spaces, suffused with the radiance of indirect lighting bounced onto golden screens and wall reliefs, are accented by slim, pendant chandeliers, their glass globes molded in the shape of shells. You glide down four low steps—it's the ultimate conversation pit—toward a broad expanse of wheat-colored carpet that rolls on and on, seemingly toward the horizon.

Low modern easy chairs, of relaxed, slightly flying-saucer contour, are arranged in groups around elliptically shaped coffee tables. The chairs, and those sitting in them, are silhouetted against the lobby's rear wall, a translucent surface that recalls shoji screens. This arrangement affords a social strategy as well as an aesthetic effect. People here can recognize arriving guests before they are recognized themselves. This gives them time to rise, step forward, and take the initiative in the ritual exchange of bows.

The design owes more to the "organic" aesthetic of Frank Lloyd Wright than to the machine-age sleekness of the International Style. Indeed, the Okura is more characteristically Wrightian than the Imperial Hotel, the fabled building Wright designed for Tokyo in 1914. But the Okura's grand flow of space signifies something very different from Wright's idea. For Wright, the open floor plan symbolized America, an expansive continent, drawn out in space, wallowing in space, neither wanting nor needing to feel confined within walls. Japan, by contrast, is a tiny, constricted country. Space here is an ultimate luxury, a quantity that is a quality, something to be treated as if it were gold. The expansiveness of the Okura's great interiors must be appreciated as a refuge from deprivation.

So must the hotel as a whole. Today the Okura sits in the capital of a great industrial giant, a global economic superpower, maker of the world's most desirable electronic products. It takes a certain stretch of the imagination to envision the hotel rising in a city, indeed a civilization, that was recently reduced to wartime rubble.

The stretch should nonetheless be made. We've seduced ourselves, in the West, into thinking that we're "postmodern," whatever that may mean. Here one regains an appreciation for modernity as a condition where efficiency and courtesy may coexist, are perhaps even inseparable. In the West we tend to think of service as being old-world, undemocratic, upstairs-downstairs, that sort of thing. Here one gains the sense that there may be a link between Japan's postwar regeneration and the seductive power of a voice that knows how to ask "May I . . . come in?"

November 10, 1996

ARCHITECTURE OF LIGHT AND REMEMBRANCE

Never forget. But there is a great deal more than the Holocaust to remember. There is creativity: the blazing talent of twentieth-century Jews, the inspiration of a people marked for extinction but not destroyed. And there is remembrance itself: the capacity of a culture to bring itself to mind. Memory, creativity: the linkage of these two ideas is the cornerstone of the Skirball Cultural Center, a museum and study center that opened in April in Los Angeles.

Designed by Moshe Safdie, the Skirball Center lies on a stretch of hilly ground beside the San Diego Freeway, halfway between the city's west side and the sprawling San Fernando Valley. Viewed from the road, the Skirball is not an easy building to decipher. It looks new. It looks old. Its walls of concrete, pink stone, and steel send out a contradictory message: the building wants at once to blend into this rugged desert terrain and to attract notice. Gabled roofs echo the line of the hills above. A delicately dirty bloom on the surface of the concrete makes the walls look like old stone. Steel panels reflect the sky, dissolving sections of solid wall into framed pictures of light and space.

It is also apparent, even from a passing car, that the Skirball is a piece of modern architecture. It is assertive. It stands out. It grabs the eye with crisp, geometric forms of concrete and steel that catch the light. In a synthesis of modes at once strong and pliant, the Skirball announces: "Hey, there, I'm a good neighbor! And, by the way, I'm here! Pull in and see me sometime."

If you do pull in, prepare to toss negativity by the roadside. Under the direction of Uri D. Herscher, the Skirball's spirit of optimism is opulent to the point of contagion. Without diminishing the meaning or magnitude of the Holocaust, the place gathers rays of light that have penetrated through a dark century.

Distributed over a fifteen-acre campus, the Skirball includes a library, an auditorium, galleries, and outdoor meeting places. (It was named for Jack and Audrey Skirball, major benefactors of the $90 million project.) But its core is Visions and Values, a lesson on how to connect the eye to heart and mind. The permanent exhibition, organized by Robert Kirschner and Nancy Berman, traces five thousand years of Jewish history but focuses on Jewish life in twentieth-century America. Anchored by a three-quarter scale replica of the Statue of Liberty's torch, the displays include a re-created kitchen from a Lower East Side tenement, a newsstand stocked with Jewish-American publications, and garments by America's greatest clothing designer, Levi Strauss. The show culminates in a kaleidoscopic audiovisual presentation of achievements by writers, scientists, artists, social workers, politicians, media moguls, and financiers. Building on the idea that the power to create is stronger than the will to destroy, the display adds up to the stunning proposition that the twentieth century has been nothing less than a golden age of Jewish achievement.

In architecture, the point is beyond argument. This art has produced an unprecedented flowering of Jewish talent in recent years. A generation ago, Louis I. Kahn stood out not only because of his towering genius but because he worked in a profession largely dominated by the Protestant establishment. Today, Jewish architects lead the field. Besides Safdie, their ranks include Frank Gehry, Richard Meier, Peter Eisenman, Denise Scott Brown, James Ingo Freed, Stanley Tigerman, Robert A. M. Stern, and Eric Owen Moss. Aesthetically and ideologically, this group spans a wide spectrum: from the boldly inventive forms of Gehry to the cartoon classicism of Stern, from the intellectually inquisitive designs of Eisenman and Scott Brown to the evolutionary approach to modern architecture conducted with integrity by Meier and Freed.

Is this worth comment? There is a minefield full of reasons not to. To talk about Jews in the arts—or, for that matter, in the media, finance, psychiatry, and many other fields—is to risk echoing anti-Semitic ravings about Zionist conspiracies. Every salute to Jewish achievement carries with it the danger of buttressing the paranoia of nut cases, as well as the discreet bigotry of polite society. Jewish contributions to the arts have long been subject to nudge-nudge, wink-winking. What was it Nixon said on those tapes? "The arts, you know—they're Jews, they're left-wing. In other words, stay away." Shocking! But the wink-wink goes on.

Then, too, there is the risk that by talking about the particularity of any artist's background, the universality of the art is compromised. This risk has long been faced (or skirted) by critics. Forty years ago, when Abstract Expressionism was at its peak, to examine the potentially Jewish dimension in the work of Barnett Newman or Mark Rothko was to risk courting the kind of philistine reaction that ultimately surfaced in the ridiculing term *Cultureburg*, coined by Tom Wolfe in his 1975 book, *The Painted Word.*

There is also the fatally blasé response: Isn't this old news? Jewish accomplishments have long been acknowledged. Respectful silence is taken as a healthy sign of democracy's capacity to assimilate. So what is the point of making an issue of their impact? Well, why should the Skirball Center exist?

The Skirball exists because the experience of Jews in America has much in common with the experience of most Americans. The particular is the universal; or rather, American cultural vitality stems from the impulse to negotiate between individual and collective experience. Culture here, to borrow Peter Gay's description of Weimar Germany, reflects the paradox that the outsider is an insider. Art is not dispensed from high to low in a fixed hierarchy. It erupts from self-invention as individuals and groups make a place for themselves on democracy's common and constantly shifting ground.

How could the story not have major implications for architecture, historically the art most directly engaged with distinguishing inside from outside? Land, shelter, stability, the impulse to find a place to stand, the envisioning of relationships between public and private realms: these are among architecture's essentials. So, to flip the coin, is the impulse to exclude, to be superior: the gated community, the restricted club. Architecture has been the gentleman's art, the vaguely creative WASP profession, the classical column raised as the barricade against undesirables. The emergence of Jewish-American architects pertains to both sides of the coin. To the extent that architecture has been an establishment art, the experience of Jewish architects differs from that of Jewish painters, writers, and composers. They are insiders, blessed with the opportunity to describe outsider experience in the medium of the consummate insider art.

Louis Kahn was revered not just for his architecture but also for the reverence in which he held architecture—and his fearlessness in saying so in words that often sounded biblical. "The beginning of any work must start from Belief," he wrote. "I distrust competitions because the design is unlikely to stem from Belief, which is of religious essence out of a commonness sensed from other men."

There is nothing specifically Jewish about his references to religion and belief; his inspirations included Christian monasteries and pagan temples. The architectural historian David G. De Long wrote, for Kahn, "places of meeting shared essential qualities that rendered differences between secular and religious use secondary in importance." This is not to say that Kahn promoted secular ideas at the expense of religious ones. His designs, whether for a synagogue, a church, a government assembly, or a laboratory, came from a negotiation between secular and religious spheres. He conducted that negotiation in the context of an increasingly secular society. Indeed, his power lay in the vigor with which he resisted that context while flourishing within it. Jews are not the only people who have struggled with this problem. But Jewish identity has often hinged on the capacity to negotiate: for a place to stand, the right to dignity, the freedom to be.

On a tour of the Skirball last spring, I asked Safdie whether there was anything explicitly Jewish about its design. He answered that there was no historical "Jewish" style comparable to Classical, Gothic, or Moorish styles. Jewish architects, rather, worked within building traditions indigenous to the places where they settled. Nonetheless, in designing the Skirball, he said, he had in mind the image of a garden. Jews, Safdie said, were the first people to imagine a paradise on earth. His verdant image will become clearer as foliage covers the trellises over walkways connecting parts of the campus. Already the cluster of buildings resembles an encampment around an oasis.

Though Sepulveda Pass lies in the middle of Los Angeles, it is not a developed urban place. Coyotes are out there somewhere. Sagebrush barely holds the hills together. Even if the Skirball had not been designed by an Israeli, its surroundings would recall the terrain of Israel. In Los Angeles terms, of course, the pass is brilliantly urban: the freeway represents urbanity here more than buildings do. As the cars stream by they seem more deeply rooted than the Skirball. Not in space but in meaning: the city's mobile sense of place.

A generation ago, Jews were American architecture's most enlightened patrons. Now they are its most gifted practitioners, too. The Roman Catholic Church recently confirmed this view. In honor of the forthcoming Jubilee Year, the Vatican organized a competition to design a Church for the Year 2000. The six finalists (the projects go on view on Friday at the Urban Center in New York, 457 Madison Avenue at Fifty-first Street) included three Americans: Peter Eisenman, Frank Gehry, and Richard Meier, who won the commission.

Richard Meier
Wrestling with the Symbolic

"I do not think that anyone realizes the novelty of this," the architectural historian Bruno Zevi wrote about Meier's commission in the Italian journal *l'Architettura:*

> You must remember that for centuries and millenniums the Jews were defined, at best, as faithless. They were accused of murder, of procuring the death of the symbol of humanity, of the Son of the Father, of the Son of God.
>
> Until the day upon which a Pope, motivated by a universal vision without precedents, decided to accomplish an unforeseeable, unheard-of, epochal act. He decided to call the head rabbi of the Jewish people and asked permission to be received at the synagogue, in order to resume contact with his, he said, "higher brothers." The rabbi responded, "Welcome."

A reconciliation is under way in Meier's design, too: an agreeable encounter between the formalist aesthetic for which he is known and the symbolic language that modernists like Meier once so sternly rejected. The church is to be built in a working-class district near Rome, amid high-rise housing blocks. It will rise in an open space between two blocks, a passage that leads from fields to the main shopping street. Philosophically, the idea descends from Bernini's grand colonnade at St. Peter's, the arms of mother church reaching out to embrace the world.

The building's major formal gesture consists of three curving walls that rise to enfold the chapel. Skylights catch the light and diffuse it into the sanctuary below. Curves like these are unprecedented in Meier's work. So is the symbolism the walls represent. Clearly they stand for the Christian Trinity, but Meier is not likely to spell out that meaning. He is a formalist, committed to abstraction. For him to acknowledge a symbolic meaning is to commit an aesthetic taboo, akin to uttering the unmentionable name of God. He would rather acknowledge his indebtedness to Alvar Aalto than confess: These walls stand for Father, Son, and Holy Spirit.

This taboo is worth pausing over. In "Iconophobia," published in a 1981 collection of essays, Kenneth Clark drew a parallel between abstract painting and the Hebraic prohibition against representation. The comparison was insightful but undeveloped: Clark does not acknowledge that the impulse to shroud or blur meanings may be universal. Aesthetic formalism, it should be recalled, emerged in part in an ecumenical spirit, in the belief that pure forms could transcend differences implicit in content.

In 1963, Meier organized a show on synagogue architecture at the Jewish Museum in New York. It was remarkable not just because of the caliber and variety of the designs but because it represented a rare instance in this century when an intelligent effort was made to link architectural and religious values. A Kahn drawing of his design for the unbuilt Mikveh Israel appeared on the catalog cover, and the show itself can be seen as a tribute to the spiritual aura Kahn brought to his field. Reading the catalog today, you can see that the architects were struggling with something momentous: the desire to free themselves from nineteenth-century forms and attitudes while retaining the historical idea that architecture is a sacred calling.

It's extraordinary that Meier is wrestling, perhaps for the first time in his career, with issues raised by his show thirty-three years ago. The church is his first explicitly religious building. Admirers of Meier's work are aware that his passions for whiteness, light, clarity, and openness are in themselves spiritually symbolic. Those qualities are in full evidence here but informed by his awareness of iconography and its historical value. The result is a knowing negotiation between modern formalism and the metaphoric approach that historically preceded it. It reflects a desire for something more than aesthetics to fill the void left by religion's withdrawal from a secular society.

Peter Eisenman
Raising a Question for Every Answer

In his 1966 book, *Frank Lloyd Wright: A Study in Architectural Content,* Norris Kelly Smith characterized Jewish thought as dynamic, vigorous, passionate; classical thought, by contrast, was static, moderate, and harmonious. The distinction is worth recalling: you don't have to be Jewish to engage in what Smith regarded as "Jewish thought." Wright, raised as a Unitarian, expressed it with the open floor plan, the pinwheeling interiors of prairie houses, the impulse to flee the city for new horizons.

At least in his contempt for classicism, Peter Eisenman is a match for Wright. Earlier this year, he was commissioned to design a Jewish Museum for San Francisco. Housed in an old power plant opposite Yerba Buena Gardens, the museum will take its place among the complex of museums and performance spaces that have sprung up around the Moscone Convention Center south of Market Street. As a renovation, the Jewish museum may not offer the creative scope he enjoyed in projects like the Wexner Center for the Arts in Columbus, Ohio, and the Aronoff Center for the Arts in Cincinnati, yet he has approached the project with the same inquisitive vigor.

In a proposal that helped him gain the commission, he wrote: "It has been said of the Talmud that rather than having an answer for every question, Jewish culture and identity has a question for every answer. The question is asked, Is God good? Instead of providing the answer, the book gives no answer. Rather, it is a catalogue of the debate. The answer is the debate, the argument itself."

Eisenman's design, still in development, uses two strategies to turn the museum into a visual and spatial equivalent of this Talmudic tradition. The first visualizes the project not as a building but as an urban passage linking Market Street to Yerba Buena Gardens. This, in effect will stretch the architecture outside the building envelope. Pedestrians will be drawn through a warped Eisenman environment whether or not they intend to enter the building.

The second device is an electronic facade, an enormous screen at the rear of the power plant, that will physically upstage it. The screen can be programmed as curators see fit: coverage of chess tournaments, news from the Middle East, sacred objects from the collection, a visitor's search through cyberspace for events in Jewish history.

Layers of meaning overlap here. One is the juxtaposition of two kinds of power: the industrial model, represented by the power station, and its displacement by the information economy. Another reflects San Francisco's leadership in communications technology. Finally, the screen reflects the degree to which members of the information society have become electronic nomads, not unlike "wandering Jews," surfing the net for fragments of meaning and place.

Frank Gehry
A Bump and a Bow into History

The liberation of Czechoslovakia from a totalitarian regime called for symbols. The most potent of these was the election of a dissident artist, Vaclav Havel, as political leader. Another was the choice of Frank Gehry to design a new building for a prominent riverfront location in the center of Prague. Though commissioned by a private firm, a Dutch insurance company, the building nonetheless held civic importance. Havel, as it happened, lived in the building next to the site. His support was instrumental in gaining approval for a new and somewhat rambunctious addition to one of the world's most beautiful cities.

The building, completed in May, has come to be known as Fred and Ginger—Gehry's nickname, derived from the building's two towers, one of masonry, the other of glass with a pinch in its side. To me, though, it recalls a number Astaire performed with Rita Hayworth to the tune of "I'm Old-Fashioned" in the 1942 film *You Were Never Lovelier.* The couple bumps into each other while trying to pass through a doorway, then bow with exaggerated courtesy. A lot of bumping and bowing is occurring as this startlingly contemporary building tries to enter into the city's history.

The basic elements of Gehry's design—corner towers with ornamental crown, window proportions, decorative moldings on the plaster facade—derive from local traditions, but they are nudged into the contemporary poise of controlled disarray. Windows are staggered; moldings wave across the facade, as if of independent mind from the structure they animate; the dome atop Fred is woven of steel mesh strips.

The Czechs loathed the figuration implied by the name Fred and Ginger—they'd had their fill of representational art in the years of Soviet domination—so it is worth noting that Gehry had no intention of creating an oversize kitschy Hollywood figurine. The pinch was made to frame the view of Prague Castle. Still, the spirit of dance conjured by Gehry's nickname is apt: formal but breezy, deferential to the occasion but fancy-free. Gehry would be the last to deny that figuration plays a part in his architecture. The fish form that often occurs in his designs is derived in part from a childhood nickname. But it also represents something elusive: the right to assert an identity, the right to wriggle free from the identity imposed by others.

In these projects, the negotiation is not between a particular and a universal but between two universals—one social, the other religious—that coexist. One is what Kahn called "the commonness between men." The other is the relationship between people and the idea of transcendence. The social being has good reason to be wary of the religious; that wariness is called tolerance. The religious being is right to be wary of the social; that wariness is part of faith. Contemporary architecture is one of many forms in which people of different faiths reckon with the line between them.

December 15, 1996

DARLING: HAVING A SURREAL TIME. ARE YOU HERE, TOO?

The Mondrian hotel, Hollywood's newest hot spot, is a magnificent design for dubious living: a smart place for a time when smart people are finding it very hard to merge.

One corner of the Mondrian's lobby is furnished with wooden schoolroom chairs, the kind that come with little desks attached to them. The desk tops are laminated with game boards. You can push the chairs together to form a couple or a group, but however you maneuver them, the gathering will be one of soloists, protected by the rules of their own games. The chairs are a perfect metaphor for a time of short-stay relationships: check in, check out, rearrange the chairs.

The Mondrian is the newest collaboration between the designer Philippe Starck and Ian Schrager, hotelier extraordinaire, the gifted pair responsible for the Royalton and Paramount hotels in New York and the instantly legendary Delano in Miami Beach.

The hotel is ideally sited on the Sunset Strip, right across from the House of Blues. The Mondrian is the House of Whites: freshly painted inside and out in the white-on-white, would-be-virgin motif that Mr. Starck employed at the Delano with such blinding success.

The Los Angeles project is a remodeling of an older building originally designed for apartments and later converted into a hotel. The exterior has been whitewashed, and under Mr. Starck's supervision the twelve-story high-rise has become an aptly neutral container for the sensual dreamscape inside. The frigid and the sensual, the intimate and the remote: Mr. Starck's interweaving of these opposites produces subtly unsettling designs. This quality is evident not only in the Mondrian but also in many of the objects in *Starck*, a new monograph on the designer's work.

You drive up to the hotel entrance through two wooden "doors," fifty-foot-tall mahogany monoliths, fitted with curving steel handles. It is a theatrical gesture but also an intelligent one: the doors divert attention from the banality of the facade and even render it into a tastefully discreet background. They also announce the playfully overbearing surrealist logic that reigns beyond.

The lobby is low-ceilinged but grand. An elevator bank, opposite the entrance, is wrapped with pleated transparent curtains, suspended behind glass, and bathed with golden light. The device creates the illusion of an atrium, brightening an interior that would otherwise feel gloomy and confined. And the curtains have a saucy, silky glamour, as if Frederick's of Hollywood had introduced a lingerie line for lobbies.

Three large freestanding frames of maple surround the elevator doors, turning them into full-scale portraits of themselves. The seating is eccentrically mismatched, like rocks in a Buddhist garden. Here a white plastic chair from the 1960s, there a raw, sawed-off section of log; here a chaise strikingly extended as if to accommodate stilt dancers, there an Art Nouveau classic. Mr. Starck has selected, mixed, and placed these objects with a wit and freedom that do not quite mask the mood of gilded detachment.

Reception to the right, refreshments to the left. Let's turn left. As at the Delano, an extravagantly long table juts at an angle across the lobby. Mornings, breakfast is served here, coffee and croissants at a kicky fashion commune. At night, the doors of an oversize armoire are flung open to disclose a rolling bar, but the fixture is mainly symbolic. The martinis are mixed elsewhere. Count on the cocktails to convert the dizzy image of communal living into something like the real thing.

The Mondrian's best feature is its large terrace, just beyond the lobby. With teak flooring, glass windbreaks, and a border of deck chairs, it feels like the sun deck on an ocean liner or, better yet, a movie set version of one. Because the ground slopes steeply down from Sunset, the deck creates a sensation of hovering in space.

On one side of the terrace is a swimming pool, on the other a grand allée formed by gigantic flowerpots, topped with a trellis arch wound round with hanging pink blooms. Here come the brides, all dressed in complimentary white bathrobes.

Going up? An ethereal artwork by James Turrell, duplicated on each floor, greets guests as they step off the elevator on the way to their rooms. A rectangle of light, its sides bowed in the shape of a television screen, floats in the space ahead. The light changes in color and intensity. You will want to peer into the square to figure out how. To accommodate the Turrell, the overhead hallway lights are dimmed nearly to furtive tunnel-of-love levels. Some guests may find themselves clutching their Prada bags even tighter.

The dimness intensifies the brightness of the rooms. Most are one-bedroom suites, agreeably priced at less than $200. The rooms are generous in size, less stylized, and more subtly handsome than the accommodations at Mr. Starck's other hotels.

Beautifully proportioned panels of gray and tan soften the white walls. Gray green wooden tables with gray marble tops offer relief from the white sofas, chairs, and bed.

Surrealism pokes through the walls with faint inscriptions on the tan panels: THINK behind the desk, DREAM over the bed. ME is frosted on the shaving mirror.

Decal eyes stare spookily from walls, chairs, bathroom doors. Along with the mirror doors on the bedside closets, the eyes reflect another of the obsessions Mr. Starck shares with Mr. Schrager's fashionable clientele: exhibitionism and voyeurism, gazing and posing, the symbiosis between objects and subjects and especially between those who cannot decide which is which.

The best looking of all, though, is through the large ribbon windows, especially from the rooms facing east: Impressionist sunrises, the fresh smog rising like morning mist; Dada dusks, as the billboards on Sunset Boulevard light up. The steady movement of traffic along the strip's curves is as mesmerizing as any river flow.

In the distance, the downtown skyline gleams, a remarkable apparition, particularly when you are looking at it from a place that defines itself as the new center of things.

Mr. Starck's lavishly illustrated new book, *Starck*, published by Taschen, provides an encyclopedia of virtually everything the man has designed to date. The book provides a useful context in which to place his newest work. It also offers a good opportunity to consider some of the issues Mr. Starck's detractors raise: His work is too trendy. He is indifferent to the user's comfort. He is a publicity hound, obsessed with fame and glamour.

In his book, Mr. Starck's exhibitionism is on full display. The cover, for instance, shows the designer topless, tattooed with images of his designs, and the pages within treat us to images of him sailing on his boat, standing on his head, cavorting with pals. There is even a mug shot of his stitched-up face after a brawl. "Pax now," reads the caption.

But Mr. Starck is introspective about his compulsion to show off. He writes that as an adolescent he felt invisible. He identified with the character Claude Rains played in the *Invisible Man* movies, the guy who can be seen only when wrapped up in bandages. Now, he says, "I create things with which I surround myself, and which allow me to exist. What you see around me are gum labels, which I make, prostheses, Christmas decorations. When I stop producing, I will disappear."

The statement brings to mind Freud's famous explanation of the artist's capacity to gain fame, wealth, and love by diving into the neuroses that usually obstruct a neurotic's ambitions.

But of course, not everyone may enjoy spending the night inside Mr. Starck's psychotherapy. It is easier to deal with such explorations in art, where we are protected by the distance that artistic conventions place between object and viewer. But in the room where we go to sleep, wake up, dress and undress, make phone calls, such sensations can be much more unsettling. One can appreciate them as challenges, but not everyone wants to be challenged by what is, after all, just a room in a hotel.

In an interview published in the book, Mr. Starck speaks dismissively of design. "The urgent thing today is not to create a car or a chair which is more beautiful than another," he says. "What is urgent is for us all to fight with every means at our disposal against the fact that something is becoming extinct: love."

Make love, not design? Sounds more than a little sappy, not to mention disingenuous, coming from someone who spends his time creating beautiful cars and chairs. But in fact, eroticism is the basis of Mr. Starck's aesthetic. The archetypal Philippe Starck shape is a combination phallic and fertility symbol, a horn of plenty, so to speak.

The book shows countless variations on this theme, from toothbrushes to lighting fixtures, even an Olympic torch. None of the designs are indecent, but many are more than subliminally sexualized.

Mr. Starck's visual merging of the sexes is disturbing, just as contemporary relationships are. Men are not from Mars, women are not from Venus; we're all aliens from planet Earth, and never before have the distinctions between us held less cultural meaning.

There are greater differences between the chairs in the Mondrian's lobby than between the genders of the people sitting in them. The contraction of distance has become as frightening as the gulf we were brought up to regard as nature. The impulse now may be to widen the gulf, to push the other away.

You feel that impulse often in Mr. Starck's interiors; at times it seems that you enjoy a more intimate connection with the furniture than with other people.

I once spent a miserable weekend at the Delano because the intimacy imposed by the design forced me to realize I was getting more attention from the chairs than from a companion whose gaze seldom strayed from

Mr. Starck's striking full-length mirror. And what reflection was I interested in?

Though the critics may well be right about his vanity, his tenuous grip on practicality, none of this changes the fact that Mr. Starck is the most gifted and fertile designer living. Comfort is subjective, and many designers have outstanding marketing skills. None has taken a marriage of visual talent and psychological insight to such a high pitch of invention.

And it is precisely this blend that makes people uncomfortable. What is truly disturbing about Mr. Starck is that he can make something beautiful and entertaining out of social and psychological conditions that people are deeply troubled by.

The ability to create beauty out of fear was always the power of Surrealism, though in the movement's heyday, artists generally kept things at a safe remove: in a picture frame, on a pedestal, on a movie screen. Occasionally, there were Surrealist events, but seldom Surrealist environments.

But it is not surprising that, nearly a century after the publication of Freud's *The Interpretation of Dreams,* Surrealist ideas should be filtering more directly into everyday life. Socially speaking, of course, Mr. Starck's environments are still rarefied. Even at $170 a suite, the Mondrian is not accessible to those who stay at Motel 6. But then, as one character sighs to another in James Baldwin's novel *Another Country:* "Love is expensive. One must put furniture around it, or it goes."

December 19, 1996

A CRYSTAL PALACE OF CULTURE AND COMMERCE

Japan's new Tokyo International Forum is such a perfectly realized building that you may actually find yourself hoping that a flaw will turn up. Everything about this complex of theaters and convention halls has been thought through with precision. The only thing it can be faulted for is a pursuit of excellence so unyielding that it seems not quite to deserve a place in our world of scintillating compromise.

Designed by the New York architect Rafael Viñoly, the $1.5 billion Forum opened on Friday. His design was selected in 1989 from among 395 entries in Japan's first international competition. The architect may be best known in the United States for the sports center at Lehman College in the Bronx (his most important New York project to date). A current project is the design for a new sports stadium for Princeton University to replace Palmer Stadium.

Viñoly's design for the monumental Forum flies in the face of architectural history, or at least runs against the current preoccupations of many leading contemporary architects. It is lucid, whole, and completely straightforward, qualities that have not enjoyed wide favor in architecture for some time. A text is not needed to comprehend it. It does not speak in codes. Some will call it Modern, but it is a tribute to this building's strength that one wants to protect it from standard appellations of style and taste. In a lecture, Viñoly once said that architecture is "an art of dealing with heaviness," and that is what you get here: a feat of creativity in which floors, ceilings, and walls have been made to soar.

The Forum occupies a privileged site in the heart of Tokyo, steps away from the city's main train station and a five-minute walk from the Imperial Palace Gardens. Though built with private money, the Forum is a civic, indeed a national, symbol, a monument to Japan's global economic power.

It is a hybrid building: a place where concerts and other performing arts events will take place amid trade fairs and conventions: Lincoln Center crossed with the Javits Center, in effect. Americans can be discomforted by the mixing of culture and commerce, but in Japan, the most progressive art is typically displayed in department stores. There's nothing contrary about a building that brings Kabuki, Beethoven, and cars together under the same roof.

And what a roof! Hagia Sophia, the Guggenheim Museum, and Grand Central Terminal have a new cousin. By day a glittering crystal, at night a glowing lantern, the Forum's Glass Hall joins the ranks of the world's great spaces. Like some lighter-than-air vessel, the hall's ship-shaped roofing slices through the Tokyo cityscape. The atrium roof of metal and glass was designed in collaboration with the structural engineer Kunio Watanabe. It is wonderful to see that even in a built-up contemporary city, a strong horizontal arc can become a landmark as emphatically as a skyscraper.

As you approach, the Forum divides itself into two structures joined by a public plaza. The Glass Hall rises on one side, tapering to a blade-sharp corner at both ends. On the other side, the Forum's four main meeting halls occupy a graduated row of gray concrete cubes. The plaza is actually more like a two-block-long pedestrian promenade. Beautifully landscaped and furnished with seating, the plaza is meant to be an oasis for office workers in the financial district nearby. The visual effect of this outdoor space is of a man-made ravine, a portage between rippling glass reflections and a cliff of faceted gray stone.

You will want to go into the Glass Hall immediately, but first you ought to look at the fire stairs set between the concrete cubes. These are the Rolex of fire stairs, immaculately engineered cascades of open-mesh steel that rise without a crude or wasted motion. If you climb a flight or two of them, you will get the key to the whole building.

It's almost unheard of for architects today to devote themselves to this level of detail. We pretend not to mind, because if we did we'd go crazy. We accept that architects develop concepts, sketches, drawings, and models, and then hand the project over to an "associated" firm to create the physical object in space. Here we're dealing with a radically different economy of mind. The bolt beneath our feet emerged from the same aesthetic intelligence that conceived the space around it. An architect is making architecture, and we almost can't stand it. It is dizzying to realize that excellence is a polite term for obsession.

And these are just the back stairs. Officially, people arriving to attend functions at the Forum will enter from the opposite side, facing the street. Once inside, you grasp that Viñoly has chosen to celebrate Japan's power with a lavish display of the country's scarcest commodity: space. There hasn't been a spatial sweep like this since the Paris Opera House: wide lobbies with floors of white glass illuminated from below lead to escalator banks of such glamour that you may have to squelch the impulse to ride them twice. Or give in to it. At the top of the escalators are mezzanines with glass walls that look out to the plaza and back down to the entrance lobbies. The play of reflections infinitely expands the interior's already sizable three dimensions.

The Forum's four meeting halls are misnamed. They go by letters of the alphabet and ought to start out small, but Hall D is the smallest. This is a screening room intended mostly for showing movies about Tokyo and Japan to foreign visitors. Black leather seats, luxurious darkness. Hall C is the gem of the lot, startlingly warm in the midst of so much glass, steel, and concrete, a resonant interior of wood, related to the rest of the building by the rectilinear geometry of the sculptured walls. The impression is of being inside a Cubist violin.

Hall B is a banquet hall, a showplace for the wedding reception that went to heaven but still in the end a banquet hall, its impressively high ceilings functionally justified by the hot air destined to rise nightly from the rostrum. Hall A: unimaginably huge, said to be Japan's largest theater. Kabuki time. Ice-skating spectaculars. Madonna. Michael Jackson. The walls here, too, are of illuminated glass, set at mind-bending angles that make you feel giddy but somehow bring the last row closer to the stage. The point is, it all works.

Now go into the Glass Hall. The moment of entrance recalls a visitor's first sight of the upper chapel of Ste.-Chapelle. The Glass Hall is not a church, and this is twentieth-century Japan, not thirteenth-century

France. But this is as good as space gets without age and religion to mold its character. And the sense of it is Gothic: just two slim columns support the skeletal frame from which the structure is hung. The impression is of watching trapeze artists at work within the world's largest marquise diamond.

The awesome impression isn't solely due to the hall's height and transparency. It also comes from the discovery that a transparent object can hold so much surprise.

Just inside the entrance, the floor drops away from ground level to reveal the third major component of the Forum: an underground exposition hall that runs nearly the full length of the site. The plaza is this hall's roof. In a master stroke of space craft, what appeared to be solid ground is flattened into a thin horizontal plane. Conference rooms for the conventioneers are ranged in rows along the wall opposite the plaza. Like the entire hall these spaces muffle the noise from the curving train tracks from which the hall takes it shape.

The Forum has been criticized by Japanese architects. They are careful to point out that what bothers them is not the building's design but its commercial function in the center of the city. The Tokyo International Forum went up around the same time as a new museum of contemporary art, a building on Tokyo's outskirts. Arata Isozaki, Japan's leading architect, among others, thinks that the locations should have been reversed. He regards the Forum as the symbol of Japan's bloated bubble economy.

Isozaki's view is part of the soul-searching going on throughout Japan today following the bubble's collapse. But the Tokyo International Forum is a very bad symbol of the excesses of the bubble economy. Not even Tadao Ando has produced a building with greater moral and aesthetic integrity. And it's that rigor, I suspect, that disturbs some architects.

This is an absolutist building. The scrupulousness of Viñoly's detailing and the clarity of his aesthetic are of a piece. It has the authority of a True Faith. And we're not supposed to believe in that concept anymore. We're supposed to be allergic to the sort of canons laid down by the Modern movement.

And yet this building possesses none of the shortcomings for which modernist buildings were faulted. It is not visually impoverished. It does not lack delight. No major public building designed by a postmodern architect is as elegant or as full of surprise. Walking through it, you don't even think "modernism," "functionalism," or "machines for living." You think about George Balanchine. Or a Thoroughbred racehorse. Or ancient Greece. You think about physical poise.

Perhaps this building's disturbing power is that it challenges the True

Faith of relativism, pluralism, and the mediocrities that those beliefs have sent spinning in the world. It upholds a belief in reason that predates the Modern movement. It is eighteenth century, not twentieth, in its outlook, and the outlook is fine. The enduring value of European Enlightenment: that is what's right about Viñoly's contribution to modern Japan.

January 12, 1997

WORTHY OF A WORLD CAPITAL

Good news. The wildly imperfect process of creating civic architecture in New York has produced a first-rate piece of design. It's time to rub our eyes. Wake up and see the architecture. Step up to one big question.

Will New Yorkers recognize the chance to make a marriage between a major civic site and a design worthy of its stature? Or will we derail a process that richly deserves our contempt and in doing so kill off an excellent project and set architecture in New York back another twenty-five years?

The project is Murphy/Jahn's design for Tishman Speyer Properties' proposed redevelopment of the Coliseum site on Columbus Circle, one of the most important locations in the world's greatest city, and Helmut Jahn has come up with a plan that is more than worthy of this site. It is on a par with the best architecture in the world today.

Many of us will be strongly tempted to disbelieve this. New Yorkers are more than entitled to be cynical about the schemes our public agencies come up with. And Helmut Jahn is probably not the first name you would think of in connection with a solid work of design. For many New Yorkers, Jahn brings to mind unpleasant images of glitzy skyscrapers from the go-go '80s.

But times and architects change. Don't trust my word for it. Judge for yourself. Nine competing designs for the Coliseum project will be on view through the end of the month in the Coliseum's lobby. A more ambitious show, sponsored by the Municipal Art Society, will open on Tuesday at the Urban Center, 457 Madison Avenue. Debate on the merits of all nine projects will take place on February 19 and 20 at 2 Columbus Circle. These events, also presented by the Municipal Art Society, could prove invaluable to restoring the well-being of architecture in New York. Or they could just reinforce the denial that contemporary architecture in New York is far less creative than this vibrant city deserves.

The issue transcends the respective merits of the designs. It even overarches the dismal political process that produced them. How do you make discriminations in a relativistic universe? How do you distinguish architecture from the kind of architectural impersonations proposed by a majority of the developers for the Coliseum site? How do you persuade public officials that the values of art, while subjective, are no less real than the hard facts of the bottom line?

Probably many New Yorkers don't even want to hear about the Coliseum project. Talk about déjà vu all over again. Twelve years ago, an earlier round of proposals subjected the city to an urban psychodrama that dragged on for four years. Aesthetically, the choices lay between Moshe Safdie's strident piece of glass origami and David Childs's nostalgic Art Deco reprise.

No building resulted from that contest. First lawsuits, then the collapse of the real estate market, prevented the realization of either project. But the exercise was not fruitless. At least New Yorkers got to see the intellectual bankruptcy of the public agencies responsible for building in the public realm. The redevelopment of this major civic site was conducted as if it were a fire sale. Art counted for nothing. The bottom line ruled.

Public officials even seemed to take it as a point of pride that they were not "imposing" their aesthetic judgments—as if anyone in their right mind were expecting them to do that, as if the only two choices available to civic building were the aesthetic dictatorship of politicians or the tyranny of the bottom line. What was expected then, and what is expected now, is that public agencies adopt the mechanism of the design competition, an arrangement accepted as a matter of course by every other major city in the civilized world.

Sadly, New York seems no closer to recognizing the value of this device today than it was twelve years ago. Once again, economic factors alone are likely to determine the outcome of this process. At a news conference on the nine proposals, officials of the Metropolitan Transportation Authority and the Empire State Development Corporation declined to say what role, if any, designers would play in the selection of the developer, which is expected to take place in the spring.

The MTA's indifference to architecture was not a surprise. It could have been gleaned from the request for proposals that the agency sent out last July. Apart from a vague reference to the desire for a "world-class" plan and a requirement that the new building define a circular street wall, the document offered little guidance to the meaning or cultural value of this site.

Let's write our own.

Columbus Circle is a child of the City Beautiful movement, born just over a century ago. The Columbian Exposition, held in Chicago in 1893, with its famous White City, set out the movement's guiding ideas: classical, academic, monumental, homogeneous, dedicated to sweeping urban vistas of Beaux Arts buildings adorned with fountains and heroic statues. The movement produced some noble cityscapes and buildings, like the New York Public Library and Bryant Park, as well as comically unrealized visions like Columbus Circle.

No point trying to exhume the movement's precepts today. They represent an outmoded style of art and an objectionable political philosophy. As Lewis Mumford observed decades ago, the City Beautiful movement was the perfect style for America's imperial phase, of trusts and monopolies, of the exploitation of regions by industrial urban centers. But there's no reason architects couldn't ask themselves to visualize the beauty of the contemporary city.

Indeed, New York's most important buildings of this century have done precisely that. The United Nations headquarters, the Seagram Building, the TWA terminal at Kennedy Airport: each of these, in different ways, channeled urban energy into built form. More recent projects, outside New York, have also crystallized the beauty of particular cities. Arquitectonica's Atlantis condominium tower in Miami; Jean Nouvel's Cartier Foundation in Paris; Arata Isozaki's Convention Hall for Nara, Japan; Frank Gehry's plan for the Walt Disney Concert Hall in downtown Los Angeles: these projects, too, show that the beauty of cities changes.

Like most of the other plans, Jahn's reuses the existing Coliseum and adjacent office building at 10 Columbus Circle. The tan brick facades are stripped away; the office tower is enlarged with structural additions that transform the floor plan from a rectangle to a trapezoid. This then becomes the base for two triangular towers, each forty stories high, rising at the east and west ends of the site. The whole composition is then wrapped in a taut glass skin.

This is no plain glass box. Like Nouvel in his design for the Cartier Foundation in Paris, Jahn pushes glass beyond its standard curtain-wall application. On both towers and base, Jahn cantilevers the glass skin beyond the building envelope, so that one sees the glass as pure transparency, as well as the semiopaque curtain wall.

The design's tripartite division is forthrightly classical. Public areas—stores, restaurants, exhibition space, a museum—are housed in the curving base that defines the site's circular street wall. The glass trapezoid contains offices. Twin towers, two precisely placed prisms, will house condominium apartments. Classical, too, and classically modern are the exposure of structure and the deference of its forms to light and void. Who wouldn't make a detour to watch the towers reach up, grab a square of sky and rotate the space gently between them?

The Polshek Partnership's plan for Millennium Partners is the only other proposal that one could reasonably call architecture. Like Jahn, Polshek defines the street wall with a cinematically grand curving glass screen, though Polshek contains his screen within a metal frame and projects it toward the sidewalk. Two glass towers, soberly expressionist, rise from the curving base. But Polshek's is cautious compared with Jahn's design.

Evaluating a project like the Coliseum involves two kinds of truth. One kind is objective; it can be quantified. The MTA has not provided any financial data, such as how much each developer proposes to pay for the site, but the difference between, say, a $250 million bid from one developer and a $300 million bid from another developer is a coolly factual $50 million. The other kind is subjective—no one can prove that Jahn's and Polshek's designs are superior to the other seven—but it is a truth nonetheless. Indeed, it's one of the highest truths that art and architecture can lay claim to.

The purpose of a design competition is to honor that claim. The decision of a jury is, of course, the result of opinions. But the jury process is grounded in the belief that informed opinions of art are more likely than uninformed opinions to distinguish good from bad. It may not always work out that way—look at last year's overbearing winning design to expand the Victoria and Albert Museum in London. But even in a case like that, the design competition still stands for an important principle: subjectivity is a serious matter. It is not the same as chance, whim, or public relations. Any architect can hire a publicist to write words like *bold, visionary, dramatic, inventive*. The architect may believe them; a public official, unveiling a design at a news conference, may repeat them with something like stirring conviction. Occasionally they may even be true.

In 1987, New Yorkers justly fought the Coliseum proposal because of the shadows it threatened to cast over Central Park. Will they rally to support this building because it would actually improve the play of light and shadow on the West Side skyline?

A sentence from F. Scott Fitzgerald's "The Crack-Up" comes to mind: "New York had all the iridescence of the beginning of the world." Fitzgerald was talking about 1920s, and the great giddy skyscrapers that were redefining the Jazz Age skyline. Like no other New York building in the last twenty-five years, Jahn's design recaptures the romantic promise of

Fitzgerald's great lost city. A scaffold, cloaked in light, the project conveys with minimal means the enduring idea of New York as the great world capital of permanent becoming. You could imagine Christopher Columbus making port in this radiant image of the New World.

January 19, 1997

RETHINKING THE MEANING OF THE MODERN

And the winner is—modern architecture! That's the announcement the Museum of Modern Art would like to make when it finally selects an architect to design its expanded Manhattan campus. No big names. No razzle-dazzle designs in instantly recognizable signature style. No prizes for best song, most congenial contestant, wizard special effects. Rather, museum officials hope that the process of redesigning one of the world's most vital cultural institutions will itself be the lead performer.

Last week, the museum announced an international list of ten architects invited to compete for the commission, a project that is not simply an addition or expansion but of another order of magnitude. The architects have been encouraged to rethink the configuration of the entire campus, which now includes the Dorset Hotel on West Fifty-fourth Street, bordering the rear of the sculpture garden, which was acquired last February.

The architects are Wiel Arets and Rem Koolhaas of the Netherlands; Toyo Ito and Yoshio Taniguchi of Japan; the French architect Dominique Perrault; the Swiss team of Jacques Herzog and Pierre de Meuron; and four New York firms: Steven Holl, Bernard Tschumi, Rafael Viñoly, and the office of Tod Williams and Billie Tsien. By May, three finalists will be chosen. The commission will be awarded by the end of the year.

Speaking on behalf of the Museum of Modern Art's trustees, Glenn D. Lowry, the director, said the selection process itself would help to "conceptualize a modern museum in the context of the future."

The museum convened a three-day conference last October at the Rockefeller estate in Westchester County, to discuss the expansion on a conceptual level. Discussions were held between curators, critics, and architects, including several, like Peter Eisenman and Arata Isozaki, who were not included on the final list. Last fall, the museum also sponsored a series of public lectures and symposiums on the expansion project. Another series will take place when the ten designs are put on view.

The architects on the list are relatively youthful. Most are in their fifties. Some architects who were not invited to compete have expressed surprise, bafflement, even anger, at this emphasis on younger architects— as if the museum had deliberately chosen to take a slap at more established architects like Norman Foster, Richard Meier, and Charles Gwathmey. These architects, a generation older than those on the Modern's list, are the names one expects to find on short lists for prestigious projects.

Actually, the Modern's tilt toward youth makes perfect sense. The architects on the list represent a generation that has felt compelled to reinvent the idea of modernism for itself. The generation preceding theirs includes a number of distinguished architects, like Foster, Meier, and Gwathmey, whose work is strongly rooted in the values of the Modern movement. Still, at a pivotal moment, the work of these designers was less influential than that of Robert Venturi, Charles Moore, Michael Graves, and others of their contemporaries who chose to promote the Postmodern cause.

Younger architects, especially in the United States, grew up having to reckon with the repudiation by their elders of twentieth-century history. They were educated in a climate that subjected modernism to constant criticism and ridicule. The sterility of modern architecture. The anti-urbanism of modern architecture. The indifference of modern architects to popular needs and tastes.

The Museum of Modern Art, meanwhile, was undergoing its own crisis of identity. In the 1970s and '80s, the museum stood at a crossroads. How could a modern museum survive in what was widely labeled a postmodern world? Had modernism become a closed historical chapter? Should the museum simply devote itself to filling out the record in a story that had reached the end? Or did modernism represent a set of values that could feed into the future?

The Modern itself had helped to precipitate this crisis. In 1966, the museum published Robert Venturi's *Complexity and Contradiction in Architecture*, a book that instantly became the bible of postmodernism, the text that encouraged architects to repudiate the aesthetic values on which the museum had been founded. Later, Philip Johnson, who was a founding director of the museum's architecture and design department as well as a prominent museum trustee, further complicated matters when he began crusading against the Modern movement he had once championed.

Arthur Drexler, the museum's longtime architecture curator, didn't help matters much by basically sitting on his hands throughout this period, committing his department to what seemed like an endless recycling of shows on the great Modern masters. In 1984, Drexler commented to me that the only contemporary designed objects he judged adequate to the museum's aesthetic standards were pieces of military hardware, like the Stealth bomber. As one contemplated the Bell helicopter that still hovers at the entrance to the design galleries, one imagined Drexler as an embattled figure sitting atop a stockpile of weapons, manning the barricades against Postmodern incursions.

The 1985 expansion by Cesar Pelli is an enduring symbol of that crisis. Here the museum entrusted its redesign to an architect whose adherence to Modern principle, never particularly firm, soon lapsed into a purely commercial practice dedicated to producing decorative building skins. Pelli was the perfect architect for a moment when the museum hoped to ensure its future not by aesthetic but economic means, erecting a profit-making condominium tower on its property and refashioning the museum itself in the image of a suburban mall.

Since then there has been a changing of the guard: a new president, a new director, new curators, a rejuvenated department of architecture and design. This new group, mostly under age fifty, is of a generation that regards the modern, and the Modern, from quite a different perspective. Born well after the pioneering days of the Modern movement, this generation accepts as a matter of course that the "modern movement" and the polemical struggles of that movement are a matter of history. But they also perceive modernism as an ongoing way of relating to the present.

John Summerson, the British critic and historian, was referring to the Modern movement when he wrote in 1947 of the need to "sort out those aging ideas that get encrusted round past creative achievement and clog the proper working of the imagination in changing times." For Summerson, in other words, modernism had already grown stale fifty years ago, a decade before the Seagram Building went up. But for many architects today, especially the generation represented by the list, the sorting out of aging ideas could serve as an excellent definition of modernism itself. The definition evokes no particular style or philosophy. It merely proposes that time moves on, that the imagination can be stifled, that creativity is, in part, an act of mental hygiene.

The museum's trustees are wise to view the process of selecting an architect as a creative venture in its own right. It's an opportunity for the museum to sort out some aging ideas that got encrusted round the institution itself. Like the idea that there is some inherent conflict between the traditional and the modern: the second grew organically out of the first. Or that historically there was only one correct, canonical "modernism" rather than Futurism, Constructivism, Bauhaus, de Stijl, Expressionism, and many other modernisms.

We value the Modern as a place where this sorting-out goes on, where modernism is presented within a framework of changing awareness. Many of the architects on the museum's list have embraced that framework as the essence of contemporary architecture. Pioneer modernists spoke of transforming entire cities, of remaking the world. Modern architects today are more likely to speak of heightening our consciousness of the modern world. The function they see for architecture is much like the museum's own historical goal.

I hope they won't forget that it's also one of the world's great spots for dating.

January 26, 1997

FORM FOLLOWS FUNCTION INTO IDEAL CIRCLES

Tibetans have their mandalas, and we've got ours. Rotary phones. Thermostats. Camera lenses. Steering wheels. Clocks. Henry Dreyfuss, the industrial designer, was the master mandala maker of the American century. Dreyfuss was an industrial designer at a time when industry was a state religion, a faith as yet unsullied by evidence of cultural and environmental degradation. Henry Dreyfuss Directing Design, a major show now at Cooper-Hewitt, National Design Museum, recalls a time when dialing the phone or setting the thermostat had the aura of ritual acts, tantamount to turning the prayer wheels of progress.

Organized by Russell Flinchum, the author of a new book on Dreyfuss's life and work, this is the most solidly realized design show to appear in New York City in years. Clearly organized, with no ideological axes to grind, the show is perfectly pitched to a contemporary audience. The wall texts do not preach. They inform. Mr. Flinchum presents Dreyfuss's values, trusting that visitors will bring their own critical equipment to bear on the designer's achievement. Handsomely designed by Adam Yarinsky and Josh Pulver with graphics by Jen Roos, the show would have satisfied Dreyfuss's demand for organic wholeness.

Dreyfuss lived from 1904 to 1972, and his career spanned several periods in taste, from Art Deco to Pop. But he was esteemed for his ability to transcend style. Unlike the work of Raymond Loewy, Donald Deskey, and Norman Bel Geddes, his designs were seldom flashy. Early on, Dreyfuss vowed that he would never confine himself to packaging. He wouldn't accept a job unless he worked on a product's innards as well.

In professional circles, he was known as the pioneer of "human factors." Put simply, this meant that a design should fit the user, not the other way around. Dreyfuss represented the idea graphically with "Joe" and "Josephine," idealized male and female silhouettes bristling with measurements from head to toe: Vitruvian Man remade for the Machine Age. In the show, the concept is illustrated by a clever please-touch display of telephones, before and after Dreyfuss went to work for Bell Telephone Laboratories. The Dreyfuss phone lets the user cradle the receiver between neck and shoulder, leaving the hands free to take notes.

Yet it would misconstrue Dreyfuss to regard him as a functionalist, as another phone, the Princess model of 1959, amply demonstrates. As a working appliance, the Princess left a lot to be desired. The receiver was constantly falling off the lozenge-shaped base. The base itself tended to topple when a number was dialed. Still, the Princess was certainly a lovely new shape, a tribute in pink or aqua plastic to the sex kitten allure of Ann-Margret, Shelley Fabares, and Sandra Dee.

Henry Dreyfuss was an artist; the tools of his art were the techniques of modern industry. This ideal had been promoted by the Bauhaus in the 1920s, but none of the designers associated with that school truly attained it. Dreyfuss, and the many gifted designers employed by him, fully embodied Walter Gropius's view of the modern artist as an "Apollo in the Marketplace."

The show conveys this by dividing Dreyfuss's career into segments, each associated with one of the industrial giants who retained his services. His Big Ben clock designs, first produced for Westclox in 1932, remain classics. With their plain round faces and no-nonsense numerals (and an alarm that increased in volume as the morning seconds ticked by), Big Bens were designed to complement any décor, but their visual neutrality was deceptive. Westclox was not simply mass-producing clocks. It was mass-producing time, synchronizing the American home with assembly-line precision.

Dreyfuss's design for the New York Central Railroad's *20th Century Limited*, introduced in 1938, epitomizes his crisp, businesslike style. Instead of a hodgepodge of mismatched cars, Dreyfuss created an integrated design that coordinated every detail, from the cowcatcher on the front of the locomotive to the matchbooks in the dining car. The renderings of the train's suave, understated interiors show that the cartoonist Bruce MacCall's parodies of this era scarcely exaggerate: after dinner, the lights in the dining car turned from white to red, rust-colored china appeared on the tables, and "Café Century" rolled on through the night.

After the sleek urbanity of the twentieth century, the farm equipment Dreyfuss designed for John Deere & Company in the 1940s jolts the eye. But there they are, two big tractors, corn yellow and green, high as an elephant's eye. Just looking at them may leave you feeling in need of a hernia truss. But you've got to be impressed by a designer who could seat tractor drivers in comfortable, executive style while at the same time over-hauling the glamorous Persian Room supper club at the Plaza Hotel in Manhattan.

Dreyfuss's work for Polaroid was perhaps the most explicitly con-sumerist of his career; none of the models he designed remained in pro-duction for long. Indeed, the Swinger, a cheap camera of molded white plastic that perfectly captured the 1960s in blurry black-and-white pic-tures, looked instantly disposable. More memorable was the SX-70, intro-duced in 1972. With a luxurious case of brushed metal and brown leather, this camera almost imparted a feeling of quality to the images it produced.

The show concludes with a corridor devoted to the iconic golden man-dala, the Honeywell Round Thermostat, the device that kept the house warm during the Cold War. Mr. Flinchum recounts that one of Dreyfuss's favorite pastimes was to draw perfect circles freehand. With the Round, Dreyfuss was able to inscribe his circles in millions of American homes.

The design was deceptively simple. First conceived in 1942, the ther-mostat was in development for more than a decade before it finally went on the market. For part of that time, Dreyfuss worked on the project inde-pendently, without a contract. The design's functional justification was that home owners wouldn't have to worry about having a crooked upright thermostat hanging on the wall. And later, with the introduction of the Honeywell Tap-Lite in 1957, they could push a round button to summon light as well as heat.

If Americans did respond to Dreyfuss's hypnotic symbols of wholeness, the reason may be that the Cold War was an era when the American envi-ronment split in two. On the surface, many middle-class Americans sought an image of genteel traditionalism: the Country Squire station wagon; the Georgian-style house filled with reproduced Chippendale or French Provincial antiques. Even on the road, they pulled into Howard Johnson's cupola-topped, orange-roof version of a Colonial home.

But beneath this veneer of gracious living seethed the subterranean, Dr. Strangelove world of nuclear tests, fallout shelters, and the burgeon-ing military-industrial complex that President Dwight D. Eisenhower at once supported and criticized. It was an environment of dissociation, but each needed the other. The consumer society and the military buildup were both imperative to the country's new place in the world.

One can see Dreyfuss's designs as links between these two cultures. The concept of human factors, in fact, originated with the military, in research on the use of cockpit controls by fighter pilots. As Mr. Flinchum points out in his book, *Henry Dreyfuss, Industrial Designer: The Man in the Brown Suit*, the concept had more to do with psychology than physiology.

Later, psychology would be used to figure out what motivates consumers to buy.

Looking back on Dreyfuss's work, from the perspective of post–Cold War disarray, the mandala takes on a somewhat baleful, Cyclopean aspect, the eye of a global superpower on the make. But the great virtue of Dreyfuss's designs is that they didn't lie about the world Americans were creating for themselves. They were frankly industrial objects, domesticated by design for American homes. Few American artists have attained such dynamic poise between imagination and power.

March 28, 1997

MAKING A RUSH-HOUR BATTLEGROUND HIGH ART

New York, the great vertical city, must get back to thinking horizontally. There are other boroughs out there besides Manhattan—four big ones—and the city cannot afford to regard them as depositories for superstores, landfills, juvenile detention centers, and such. Nor will the city happily survive the great sucking force that would, for instance, leave Yankee Stadium hanging on the edge of Manhattan.

In Paris and in Barcelona, to cite two prominent examples, planners understand that new buildings can play a critical role in stretching the urban horizon beyond the dense central core. In New York, urban stretching has historically been the task of transportation—bridges, tunnels, subways—monumental works in their own fashion.

Staten Island is now embarking on a project in which infrastructure and architecture are imaginatively joined. As designed by Peter Eisenman, the project will expand the site of the existing St. George Ferry Terminal and create a new home for the Staten Island Institute of Art and Sciences. The $100 million plan is to be financed by government and private money, with construction to begin in 1998. Combining ferry operations with a museum, this is the most innovative civic project to go forward in New York in more than a generation.

The focus is on relationships: between transportation and destination, movement and repose, energy and place. The building is also the most buoyant Eisenman has yet designed. Its most spectacular feature is a large, translucent roof of faceted, whirling contour. Viewed from the water, the roof recalls the weatherman's pinwheel sign for a hurricane. Formally, it recalls the sinuous metal roof of the convention center Eisenman designed for Columbus, Ohio, a serpentine construction that brings to mind the flow of goods and information over highways and fiber-optic cables.

Though Eisenman's buildings may look expressionistic, their plan is usually grounded in an "objective" method. To calculate the roof design for the ferry project, he used a computer program that generates laminar flows, a technique typically used in the design of planes, ships, and cars, to register the disturbance of air or water by an obstruction. In this case the site was treated as the obstruction to the flow of ferries and commuter buses. Essentially, it locates a scale of order within turbulent chaos.

The existing terminal building will be renovated, its exterior clad in Kevlar, the translucent steel material from which the museum's roof will be fashioned. On the east side, a broad public plaza will be set atop a parking garage. These two strongly horizontal elements will emphasize the assertively non-Euclidean geometry of the roof. The interiors should be a marvel, comparable in sculptural strength to the great vaulted spaces of Eero Saarinen's TWA Terminal at Kennedy International Airport.

The institute, which now uses the slogan From Cicadas to Chagall, is, in effect, a science museum, though its permanent collection, housed in a small Georgian Revival building a short walk from the terminal, is a potpourri of oddments: butterflies, a Monet, antique silver, fossil fish. In its new home, the emphasis will be on temporary exhibitions, beefed up with interactive video technology and other Wow devices. One might expect, for instance, an exhibit that shows how a butterfly sees. The emphasis on perception, indeed, could help bring art and science into coherent relationship.

This is Peter Eisenman's second New York building. The first, a fire station in the Bedford-Stuyvesant section of Brooklyn, attracted little notice on its completion ten years ago. The station dates from a period when Eisenman, in association with Jaquelin Robertson, was trying to make the transition from paper architect to builder. In the process, his ideas were often watered down into decorative surface effects. The fire station's most distinctive feature, in fact, is an arrangement of red neon tubes, conceived in collaboration with Robert Slutsky, that flash when the firefighters are on call.

Eisenman has had better luck since branching out on his own. His designs have grown progressively larger in scale and aesthetic ambition. And the ferry project should encourage people to see that this legendarily radical designer is more than accessible. He is an ace entertainer as well. I confess that when I first saw this design, the image that sprang to mind was of Tommy Velour, Lily Tomlin's impersonation of a Las Vegas lounge singer. Eisenman's act—the performance of an avant-garde architect—is also sort of corny in this day and age. But he imbues the role with an affection that is almost sexual.

That's more apparent here than in earlier projects, like the Wexner

Center for the Arts, another Columbus project, completed in 1989. There, Eisenman's obsession with rotated grids often grated on the senses, like the screech of chalk on a blackboard. But creating actual buildings has sensitized Eisenman to architecture's sensuality, evident here in the curves of the light, translucent skin. *Ka-chunk-chunk-chunk.*

And what about the Other Terminal, the famous clock-adorned Whitehall Ferry Terminal, designed by Venturi, Scott Brown and Associates and Anderson/Schwartz Architects in 1992? Opposed by Staten Island residents, the design was later modified considerably. Indeed, Venturi, Scott Brown resigned the commission late last year, feeling that their concept had been compromised. Less than three weeks ago, city officials announced a plan to turn the project over to the New York firm of Anderson/Schwartz Architects. Frederic Schwartz, a partner in the firm, has been associated with Venturi, Scott Brown on a number of projects, including Whitehall.

The loss of Venturi, Scott Brown's original design is not a major catastrophe. Yet, together, the Whitehall and Staten Island projects do make a highly memorable pair, an unmatched set we might call History and Theory. Eisenman, of course, is commonly thought of as a theorist, an architect inspired by linguistic and literary speculation. Venturi is the man whose 1966 book, *Complexity and Contradiction in Architecture*, gave architects license to draw once again on the historical styles.

But haven't these two leading architects been stuck with the wrong tags? Surely Venturi is the more compelling theorist. His philosophy was established early on, in terms that are easily grasped. Even the title of Venturi's "gentle manifesto" offered readers a lucid idea of its content. Still, his implicit view of history as eternal and unchanging is less than profound. It's amusing, no doubt, to note the resemblance between, say, JumboTron signboards and Ravenna's Byzantine mosaics. Yet at a certain point one needs to think about differences as well as similarities. How did civilization get from mosaics to JumboTrons? What does the change portend?

Eisenman's theories, in contrast, are generally imported from other disciplines. And he prefers enlisting academics to interpret his buildings rather than shouldering the burden himself. No American architect of his generation has probed deeper into the philosophical roots of historical change. He seeks to challenge not the Modern movement but the Enlightenment concepts that ground it.

Despite their considerable differences, both architects have responded creatively to the major crisis that confronted their generation: the collapse of historicism, the erosion of the nineteenth-century idea that every era should produce its own distinctive style. Trained at a time when modernists believed they had left the nineteenth century behind, they came to see that modernism only extended that century's belief in the concept of a historical mainstream.

Some people are dismayed by History and Theory. They're alarmed that especially in today's architecture schools, these fields of study threaten to supplant traditional practice. Why can't architects content themselves with the task of manipulating the physical environment for the well-being of contemporary users?

The fact is that architecture has traditionally reckoned with the task of creating a culture's connective tissue. Above and beyond the user-friendliness of individual buildings, architecture operates on the level of metaphor. For more than a century, historicism defined that metaphoric level. As recently as the International Style, the mainstream idea gave individual architects the sense of common purpose. Today, History and Theory together—the speculative connection of ideas and events—provide a comparable common ground. Together, they are the metaphoric infrastructure for a time when the mainstream has broken up into many turbulent flows.

April 6, 1997

A CHANCE FOR AN ARCHITECT TO LET HIS IMAGINATION RUN FREE

Times Square, once called "the crossroads of the world," is itself at a crossroads of creativity. In the last two years, the area has been revitalized by colorful signs, retail stores, and renovated theaters. Much of this vitality, however, is temporary. It stems from an interim plan put in place by city and state officials pending more ambitious redevelopment projects.

These efforts are now getting nearer. At least four more major sites are coming up for redevelopment, three of them at the intersection of Broadway and Forty-second Street. With all the public and private money to be pumped into this historic district, there is the potential to give a powerful boost to creative architecture in New York. And there is the danger that creativity will be stifled by boosterish imitations of it.

Frank O. Gehry, whose buildings have changed the shape of American architecture, has proposed a redesigning of the tower at 1 Times Square.

Yes, the place where the ball drops at midnight on New Year's Eve. Designed by Cyrus L. W. Eidlitz and Andrew C. McKenzie, the Times Tower was completed in 1903. Even without exterior signs, apart from a modest logo just beneath the cornice, the twenty-five-story campanile was a stunningly conspicuous advertisement for the newspaper that built it. The first New Year's Eve extravaganza, coinciding with the renaming of Longacre Square in the paper's honor, took place at the end of 1904.

This year, Warner Bros hired Mr. Gehry to do something dreamy with the site. The company has leased the building and intends to open a Warner Bros Studio Store there. Mr. Gehry was invited to let his imagination range freely, without regard to cost. He was not interested, he told Warner executives, in making graphic design but would welcome the chance to create something architectural. The result is an elaborate twenty-five-story clock tower with movable walls of billowing metal mesh. An exhibition devoted to the project, including drawings and five scale models, will open on April 16 at the Ace Gallery, 275 Hudson Street, in the West Village.

But the strong likelihood is that Mr. Gehry's design won't be built, certainly not in this form. The cost, an estimated $60 million to $85 million, is prohibitive. And Mr. Gehry's major projects typically evolve considerably in the course of design development. So this isn't a "New Design Unveiled!" article. Nor is it an East Coast version of the "Gehry Project Imperiled!" articles that have swirled around his design for the Walt Disney Concert Hall in Los Angeles. This is about an idea: the creative response of one of the world's most inventive architects to the role and future of this historic corner of New York. And it offers a welcome opportunity to sort out the differences between architecture and real estate, art and entertainment, creativity and simulated consumer versions of it.

Design as Process, Without Explanation

Those fortunate enough to visit Mr. Gehry's Santa Monica office can see how much emphasis he places on process. A few years ago, when he was commissioned by Knoll to design some lightweight wooden chairs, he set himself the task of designing a new chair every day for several months. One long wall was hung floor to ceiling with these prototypes. Another room is lined with models that trace the evolution of his design for Disney Hall.

But seekers after explanations for Mr. Gehry's unusual forms may be frustrated. While the architect can be highly articulate, he does not fully trust words. Mr. Gehry would rather err on the side of taciturnity than of garrulousness.

A few years ago, Mr. Gehry incurred the displeasure of some Czech intellectuals when he nicknamed an office building he designed for Prague Fred and Ginger. For some Czechs, figurative art holds an unpleasant association with Socialist Realism. Mr. Gehry didn't start out with a figurative idea. But when he indented one edge of the building to frame a vista of Prague Castle, the silhouette recalled the flaring gown of a ballroom dancer.

Mr. Gehry does admit, however, that his design for Warner Bros was inspired by another famous show biz couple, from television's golden age: Sid Caesar and Imogene Coca. In a famous skit on *Your Show of Shows*, the two comedians played human cuckoos in a clock that goes berserk.

Why not? This is, after all, Times Square. *The New York Times* built the tower. (The newspaper moved its headquarters out of the building in 1913 and sold it in 1961.) Time Warner will be its next tenant. What is time without a clock? And this is where, at the stroke of midnight, throngs are convulsed with public madness: kiss strangers, toot horns, put on funny hats, lose their minds. Even at its most squalid moments, Times Square has remained the symbolic epicenter of American popular culture.

Time, the media, popular culture, public lunacy, commerce: if all this adds up to the spirit of Times Square, Mr. Gehry has clearly wrapped it all up and tapped into the history of the building as well. First, he has stripped the tower down to its steel skeleton, the building's most enduring feature. Allied Chemical, which acquired the building in 1962, sheared away the Italianate masonry facades and reclad the building in a clinical coat of white marble, mercifully obscured by signs. Mr. Gehry's plan removes the marble and preserves the signs.

A layer of metal mesh is then draped over the skeleton. At last! A genuine curtain wall: a building skin that goes up and down, billows and gathers in folds. The mesh is manipulated by a giant clockwork mechanism, visible through the skin, programmed to provide a continuous animated spectacle day and night. Comic book personalities from the Warner Bros stable—Superman, say, or Tweety Bird—would periodically pop out from behind the mesh, occasionally accompanied by a burst of smoke. At intervals steam clouds could filter through the mesh, enveloping the entire building like a live-in Camel sign. At night, the mesh would turn nearly transparent, revealing mechanical tableaux inside the building's frame.

A Warner Bros store in the basement would be visible through a street-level glass structure enclosing the entrance. A public plaza open to a height of four stories would take up the rest of the ground floor. Looking up, pedestrians could watch the clockwork mechanism in action. Three more public areas—a restaurant, a bar (both glass enclosed), and a mesh-wrapped outdoor terrace—would be lodged higher in the tower. Signboards on the tower would help stabilize the building's shifting contours, like buttons on a flowing coat.

Rules May Be Out, but Patterns Exist

It used to be said that Mr. Gehry created an "architecture of no rules." It's true that he relies on intuition more than most architects. Yet his intuition has led him, if not to rules, than at least to recurring patterns. His initial drawings for a project often suggest a burst of energy, and as his models evolve, they express a desire for what William Blake called energy's "pure delight." That goal reaches a climax with the changing, flexible walls of the Times Square design.

Wrapping is another pattern. Mr. Gehry first used it in the 1976 remodeling of his Santa Monica home, where he enclosed parts of the existing house with panels of chain-link fence. The device reappears in his design for Disney Hall, with a wrapping of French limestone. The mesh skin of the tower design descends from the chain-link fence, though the model does not accurately present the delicacy of his treatment. At his Edgemar shopping arcade in Santa Monica, he suspended chain link around the top of an outdoor fire stair; the moiré effect and the metallic glint created the stunning effect of cascading light. That effect should be even more pronounced in the tower, where the mesh would be finer, more fully dimensional, and subject to movement from wind as well as grinding gears.

Then there is the "rule" that the art critic Arthur C. Danto calls "the transfiguration of the commonplace," the artistic elevation of humble materials and forms. In the past, Mr. Gehry made architecture out of ply-wood, zinc, and corrugated metal. Here the "commonplace" element is the structural frame, construction scaffolding and netting used to shroud buildings during renovation. Probably many New Yorkers have been impressed by the visual power of this hardware, an effect few completed buildings can match. The architect heightens the effect with aesthetic intent.

Symbol of Freedom, This Time in Art

Mr. Gehry's sensitivity to context may be the most difficult pattern to trace in his work, especially when looking only at a model, which excludes not only a site's physical surroundings but also its history and meaning. Perhaps this pattern is best described as interactive. Mr. Gehry takes in scale, materials, memories, and circulation as if they were brilliant lines of dialogue urging him toward a similarly sharp repartee. Public response extends the exchange into the social realm.

His forms, while novel, are not unprecedented. The rich contours of the tower's skin, for instance, will not shock anyone familiar with the voluptuous contortions of the High Baroque. The rippling folds will not look strange to fans of Casa Milà, Gaudí's Art Nouveau masterpiece in Barcelona. Nor would this be the first local landmark to put on a metal dress: the Statue of Liberty is virtually an official symbol of America.

Mr. Gehry's exposure of the structure should remind us that Liberty's engineering armature was created by Gustave Eiffel. That's one way to see this project: a Statue of Liberty for an era when Times Square has become the city's Ellis Island, a symbolic port of entry for many of the city's newest arrivals. At least it's a terrific symbol of the creative freedom for which the city stands.

Prominent Parisians initially detested Eiffel's tower, and Mr. Gehry's design may also provoke hostility. When an artist confronts our sense of propriety, propriety is supposed to bark back. Vital cities don't shrink from the art of being disturbed. What's disturbing about this design is that it pushes the current ethos of the "new Times Square" to reveal its underlying logic. Mr. Gehry grasps the spirit of infantilism at large in this area today: the happy-face regressiveness, the laid-on-thick veneer of innocence and play, an ethos conceived in reaction to the area's lingering reputation for vice and crime.

Forty-second Street now is a cleaned-up id, an adult fantasy of youthful desire. Mr. Gehry's design is adult fantasy; it even strips. That's what distinguishes it from, say, the Disney Store across the street. It's the difference between children's theater and theater: art that can enthrall even children.

April 7, 1997

A FLOWER REOPENS IN THE BRONX

The Victorians were the first to hate Victorian architecture. With one major exception, they detested their own buildings. The exception was the great glass greenhouse. The conservatory, the winter garden, the Crystal Palace: this type of building Victorians passionately admired.

So do we. On Saturday, the magnificent Enid A. Haupt Conservatory, the glittering glass centerpiece of the New York Botanical Garden, reopens after a restoration that took four years and cost $25 million, of which probably not one penny was spent on Windex. This beautiful glass bubble, completed in 1902, is the largest building of its type in America, and one of the finest in the world.

Many today can appreciate Victorian architecture's full range. Its contorted madness mirrors our own with a fidelity that few living architects even want to aim for. The greenhouse, however, appeals to us, as it did to the Victorians, as a place of rare sanity. It is calm, reasoned, elegant, and scientific. It is the seed crystal from which modern architecture eventually took shape.

Restored by the New York architectural firm of Beyer Blinder Belle, the Haupt Conservatory can once again hold its sparkling glass head up high amid the great architectural symbols of New York. The building has long been one of the few landmarks outside Manhattan routinely depicted in stylized renderings of the city's skyline. The Yankees may be unhappy in the Bronx, but palm trees like it just fine.

The Victorians put curtains on their curtains and in polite company refrained from referring to the pieces of wood that support a piano as "legs." So you can imagine the breathless ecstasy with which they embraced any excuse for beholding a building of pure transparency and its proudly nude light metal structure. This was almost as intoxicating as glimpsing an ankle.

The restoration should enable us to see this building type afresh. Beyer Blinder Belle has recovered its light, airy beauty. Visitors must peer deeper to see the conservatory's historical roots. In no way is this building an example of quaint Victoriana—a sort of Palm Court without tea. It is, rather, a cornerstone of modernity. As Georg Kohlmaier and Barna von Sartory observe in their encyclopedic 1986 book, *Houses of Glass* (MIT Press), the greenhouse was integral to the culture of the machine. "The prerequisite for the development of technology and science in the industrial age," they write, "was the practical exploitation of nature in such a way that natural processes could be understood and controlled and could be called upon whenever needed."

The greenhouse expressed that need practically and symbolically. Here plants could be studied scientifically, while the conservatory as a whole represented the mastery of modern science over nature. It fed the nineteenth-century rage for classification, widening the gulf between nature and culture even as it brought the two together under one roof.

The conservatory was also a response to the social tensions of the industrial city. Like the public park, the winter garden was an instrument of social reform. At a time when agricultural workers were flocking to the city in search of freedom, the city provided freedom in the form of an artificial version of the countryside they had left behind. The greenhouse was a wholesome, alternative form of escapism, designed for people who otherwise sought relief in taverns, dance halls, and other depraved urban delights.

Gregory Long, the botanical garden's president, suggested on a recent tour that the Victorian conservatory was also nurtured by England's imperial expansion. Plants were collected from parts of the world colonized by the British. Just as Japanese gardens were often laid out as miniature versions of Japan, so the conservatory enclosed a microcosm of the British Empire. The display of tropical plants expressed something far more serious than a taste for the exotic. It also denoted pride in ownership, or, to put it more politely, in the long, committed reach of England's civilizing mission.

If the Victorians exempted greenhouses from their low architectural esteem, that is partly because they did not regard them as architecture at all. Rather, they were structures produced by the extension of gardening into the scientific realm of engineering. Their emphasis was on function. As John Summerson noted, the designs of greenhouse designers like Joseph Paxton were "unstigmatized by style." Like railway sheds and iron bridges, they stood apart from the stylistic debates between classicists and gothicists, ancients and moderns.

As such, the greenhouse came to exert great influence over architects who sought a proper style of building for the industrial age. The immense popularity of the Crystal Palace, designed by Paxton for the first World's Fair, held in London's Hyde Park in 1851, offered the hope that glass architecture could serve people as well as it did plants.

In due course, it did. The glass office tower, the canonical expression of twentieth-century modernism, is a vertical form of the greenhouse made possible by steel and the elevator. The skyscraper's prefabricated modular construction, glass walls, and open interior all descend directly from greenhouse design.

And in its own oblique way, the glass tower was also an imperial gesture. As the paradigm of the "International Style," it was the premier architectural symbol of global corporate culture, an emblem of power that continues to transform skylines around the world. It, too, represents mastery over nature, and culture as well. Total air-conditioning. Total homogenization. Total twenty-four-hour club sandwich, with stale chips and tepid coffee.

Our notion of mastery differs from that of the Victorians. It is emotional, not scientific, a fluctuation between pity and fear. Isn't it a shame that we're destroying the rain forest! Look out for that virus!

Much as we depend on that mastery, we don't quite want to take responsibility for it. The restoration has given us back a historic landmark, but in the years separating us from the Victorians, our relationship to nature has profoundly changed. What we seek to conserve now is not individual plants, transplanted from their native habitats, but rather nature itself.

We don't take great pride in global ownership. We are rather embarrassed about it, in fact. We know that our mastery has attained such extremes that Australian children must now wear hats on their way to school because the depleted ozone layer makes their skin vulnerable to cancer. We bow down less eagerly to science, even though our physical and intellectual survival remains dependent on it, because our well-being has been brutally assaulted by so many scientific breakthroughs.

One is reminded of this, if any reminder were necessary, by the broadcasting antenna being erected by Fordham University outside the Botanical Garden's walls. It has been argued that, if one counts oneself a defender of the modern, one is not entitled to criticize this conspicuously mechanical sign of progress.

Wrong. The modern idea is that society should channel technology toward human ends in the light of increasing awareness. Modernity rests on the multiple perspective. Your neighbor's point of view counts for something important, that is to say. In this sense, Fordham's tower is not only unmodern. It is prehistorically territorial. Law of the jungle. Me big major university. You weak little green plant. Uga uga uga.

Horticulture, in other words, is a major part of culture, never more so than today, when life itself is contingent on cultural values. The conservatory has come to represent an ideal very nearly the opposite of its original intention. It now stands as a symbol not of triumph but of impending catastrophe, brought about by the same forces that coaxed the greenhouse into being. And we cannot be certain, as we walk along its immensely inspiring paths, whether our steps are taking us closer to the apocalypse or helping us to resist it.

May 1, 1997

ARCHITECTS' VISIONS OF HOW THE MODERN MAY ONE DAY APPEAR

The Museum of Modern Art has set itself the task of trying to figure out what modernism is, was, or will become. The occasion for this exercise is the museum's plan to expand its midtown campus. Toward a New Museum of Modern Art, a show that opens today, presents ideas by ten architectural firms invited to compete for the commission.

The show does not present finished designs for buildings. Instead, the ten architects were given one month last winter to develop concepts in the form of sketchbooks. Based on those, the trustees narrowed the list last month to three finalists: Jacques Herzog and Pierre de Meuron of Switzerland; Bernard Tschumi of New York; and Yoshio Taniguchi of Tokyo.

Also on view are projects by Steven Holl, Rafael Viñoly, and Tod Williams and Billie Tsien, all of New York; Rem Koolhaas and Wiel Arets of the Netherlands; Toyo Ito of Japan; and Dominique Perrault of France. Organized mainly so the public could compare and evaluate these ten designs, the show also offers an opportunity to examine the museum's selection process.

More than most architectural competitions, this one has been conducted as a kind of learning experience for the building committee. Members of the museum's board of trustees have traveled around the world to look at recent work. A weekend conference with architects was held last summer at Pocantico, the Rockefellers' Westchester estate, with a follow-up meeting at the museum in February. The winning design will be chosen by the end of this year.

This approach seems distinctly Clinton era, like those meetings the president-elect held in Little Rock, Arkansas, before taking office. Thorough, broad-minded, and idealistic, the process has succeeded in raising expectations to a very high level. That level is not sustained by the work on view in this show.

The show was organized by Terence Riley, chief curator of the museum's department of architecture and design, and by an associate curator, Matilda McQuaid. Mr. Riley also served as architectural adviser to the building committee of the museum's board of trustees. Each firm was presented with a green cardboard shirt box with the instruction that the presentation had to fit inside it. These have now been unpacked, their contents laid out on ten wooden tables designed by Mr. Riley to resemble drafting boards.

The clarity of the display does not, however, make the ten projects easy to understand. Even professionals may find it difficult to locate the playing field on which these architects were invited to compete. The architects took their ideas to different stages of development. Some remained within the rough sketchbook format. Others developed their ideas more fully into schematic designs. One even published a weighty, bound, limited-edition book. This diversity makes it hard to distinguish design from presentation.

The constraints faced by the architects are not easily grasped. Zoning restrictions, air rights, the recommendations of a function analysis prepared by the New York firm Cooper, Robertson & Partners, the question of what to preserve from the museum's existing buildings, the addition of a new site occupied by the Dorset Hotel: without being versed in these interwoven conditions, it's nearly impossible to assess the forms these architects came up with.

It may be helpful here to visualize the lady inside the magician's box that gets stuck through with swords. Her contortions are minor compared to the maneuvers these architects had to make. This is an interstitial building, a design that will have to fit into the spaces between the museum's existing parts, knitting them into some kind of a coherent whole. Or at least a seductively incoherent one.

This project, in short, doesn't easily lend itself to big-statement architecture. It does, however, enable architects to respond creatively to the addition as a building type. This, in fact, is what could be most progressive about the winning design. The "commission of the decade" could turn out to be a low-profile reckoning with the dense urban condition. All the concepts deserve fuller consideration than space permits. But in this show, the three finalists are bound to be the focus of attention.

Clearly, the museum's trustees did not warm to schemes that seemed too personal, poetic, or startling. The finalists have submitted rational, pragmatic schemes that will not subject the existing campus to major shock therapy.

Taniguchi's is the most classically modern of the schemes and so understated that one can easily overlook the skill with which it incorporates the museum's existing buildings into a harmonious whole. This is basically the same Modern, only bigger and better. Even the original 1939 building did not attain so serene a design.

The design is conservative but impeccably proportioned, and it comes along at a time when changing taste is bringing the International Style back into public favor. In this sense Mr. Taniguchi's design would be as faithful to this moment as the original building was to its time.

It says a lot about the competition that the design by Herzog and de Meuron, architects known for tight, even inhibited, buildings, is the most bumptious of the three finalists. They have presented a mosaic of ideas, from materials and wall treatments to historical examples of museum design. Gathered into a portfolio, the mosaic builds up into two different concepts: an "agglomerate" design, which would allow the museum's component buildings to retain their distinct identities, as in a small village. A triangular glass tower on the Dorset site would become the village's campanile.

In their "conglomerate" plan, galleries, offices, auditoriums, shops, and restaurant would all be wrapped within a glass building envelope of nearly uniform height and appearance. Aesthetically, the project harks back to the museum's own midtown guest house, a Philip Johnson gem of 1950.

Bernard Tschumi has used the competition as an opportunity to clean up his woolly act. To be sure, his presentation comes adorned with some pretentious pedigrees. It is dedicated to Italo Calvino, for example, and includes some arcane talk about a sponge, a ready-to-wear version of Gilles Deleuze's rhizome theory. But Mr. Tschumi's plan is so simple and clear you might almost mistake it for the work of Richard Gluckman, the minimalist designer of the Whitney's expansion.

In orthodox Modern fashion, Tschumi designed from the inside out, a procedure he emphasizes by including no renderings of what the museum would look like from the street. Instead, the focus is on the floor plan for the galleries. Two floors feature a large square doughnut, called the core. Its hole is called the satellite. The museum's permanent collection would be displayed in the core, in a chronological narrative of modern art. The satellite could display works that suggest alternatives to the traditional history.

Then, in a variation on the Corbusian concept of the plan as the generator of space, Mr. Tschumi has turned the design restrictions into a logical set of interlocking spatial sequences. The concept here is as much curatorial as architectural. Still, of all the designs, Mr. Tschumi's is the only one that tries to spatialize the museum's present historical situation. It is both the custodian of a modern tradition and a living institution that must periodically rethink that tradition as time moves on.

The show gives one the feeling that the competitors were misled. At this stage of the process they were encouraged to pursue ideas as far as their imaginations could carry them, without regard to budget and other practical factors. They worked with the understanding that they would deal with the pragmatics of architecture at the next stage, even if that meant starting their designs over again from scratch. Considering the relative conservatism of the three finalists' designs, it would seem that the rules were later changed. The museum cast its net wide, only to conclude that on second thought it preferred narrowness.

This is not a minor disappointment. The museum and the city have both been through hard times. Postmodernism, a movement that started out as farce but soon turned into tragedy, caused the museum to lose confidence in its mission.

Until Mr. Riley's arrival in 1992, the architecture and design department had been in retreat for years. The department's default is one reason why New York's architecture now lags behind that of other world cities.

The announcement of the first list of candidates raised the hope that the expansion's design could go far toward closing that gap. The show will leave many with the impression that this hope was unrealistic. Has the selection process enabled these architects to do their best work? Did it create a context in which the value of their work could be best appreciated? These are the pertinent questions raised by this show. My answer to both is to quote something Janet Flanner once said in a different context: "I wonder. And I disbelieve."

May 3, 1997

A PALACE FOR A NEW MAGIC KINGDOM, FORTY-SECOND STREET

The Age of Discovery may be past, but the Age of Rediscovery is still young. One of the most important treasures unearthed by today's intrepid explorers is the Great American Street. The opening next Sunday of the New Amsterdam Theater, the magnificently restored 1903 show palace on West Forty-second Street, is above all an occasion to celebrate one of the most spectacular of these treasures.

Renovated with breathtaking skill by Hugh Hardy of the New York firm Hardy Holzman Pfeiffer, the New Amsterdam instantly becomes the keystone of a street that is also a major feat of urban reclamation. Forty-second Street itself has become a piece of theater, a metropolitan melodrama one might call the Boulevard of Broken Nightmares. After decades of futile cleanup campaigns, the place is no longer gripped by crime, vice, and decay. Instead, there are shops, theme restaurants, two restored theaters, mammoth flashing signs, amusement arcades. Above all, there are people, milling around, gazing in amazement at other people milling around, as if it were the first warm day of spring.

And there is much more to come. A multiplex movie house holding as many as twenty-five auditoriums. The Roundabout Theater, which is scheduled to relocate to the Selwyn Theater. The Ford Center for the Performing Arts rising on the site of the Lyric and the Apollo theaters. A new ten-story building that will house rehearsal studios for theater and dance companies. And that's not even to mention the four office towers that will eventually rise on all four corners of this legendary Crossroads of the World.

But what will it all add up to? That is the question to ask, now that this renewal project has reached a state of critical mass. How will the plot turn out?

This street has the potential to become one of the most culturally important in urban America. It could do much more than revitalize one street. It could also redefine the relationship between the center city and American popular culture. Or it could simply be a bright but chuckle-headed exercise in consumerism.

The New Amsterdam's opening adds to the suspense. A triumph of the art and ideology of preservation, the renovation shows how far urbanism has progressed since the days of postwar urban renewal, when few planners would think twice about consigning architectural gems to the junk heap. The project is also a measure of what can be accomplished by partnerships between the public and private sectors—in this case, between the Walt Disney Company and the city and state agencies that sponsored the renovation.

At the same time, the project raises questions about the impact of these partnerships on the cultural vitality of New York. The New Amsterdam is a glorious container, but as yet no more than that. It is the most recent chapter in the phenomenon the French theorist Guy Debord once termed "the society of the spectacle," a society eager to drug itself with endless images of desire.

It is hard to imagine that hard-bitten, gold-digging Ziegfeld girls and oily Adolphe Menjou types ever felt at home at the New Amsterdam Theater, for the place is an architectural version of an American Eden, the unsullied natural paradise in which European explorers cast the New World.

Laurel leaves, branches, vines, wreaths, bouquets, roses, heliotrope, grapes, apples, figs, berries, nuts, parrots, peacocks, mice, squirrels: there is scarcely an inch in the theater's interior not encrusted by some plaster specimen of flora or fauna, tumbling out in profusion. In this arcadian setting, you would expect to see Isadora Duncan in a Greek tunic rather than a chorus girl in ostrich plumes.

Henry Beaumont Herts and Hugh Tallant, the architects, also designed the Opera House at the Brooklyn Academy of Music, and the New Amsterdam's auditorium is quite similar to it in its curved, egg-shaped interior, with a domed ceiling and oval boxes. But the New Amsterdam goes well beyond the Opera House in terms of ornament. A late-blooming American version of Art Nouveau, somewhere between Louis Sullivan and Victor Horta, the design tames the style's sinuous, hothouse eroticism but magnifies its opulence.

Instead of the red-and-gold theme of the European opera house, the colors here are green, rose, and sand. The proscenium arcs overhead like a spreading crown of trees. The boxes and balconies ascend toward the ceiling like the slope of a hill. At the top of the dome, four classically draped women hang rigidly from the treetops: angels on swings.

Too much is not enough here. In the basement's New Amsterdam Room, formerly the men's smoking lounge, wings sprout from an angel's torso as well as his shoulders. Clouds, stars, electric bulbs, and a golden halo wreathe his head. In short, this is a theater where people are not likely to start stamping their feet over a late curtain.

Rather than re-create the New Amsterdam as it appeared when new, the architects have attempted what they call an "interpretive restoration," retaining later additions like the Art Deco marquee. They have reconstructed the boxes, which were torn from the walls when the theater was converted to a movie house in 1947, and have virtually re-created from scratch the interior architectural ornament, which was almost obliterated by water damage in the 1980s.

It is hard to imagine a better patron than the Walt Disney Company for this Cinderella transformation. But Disney's arrival in New York has evoked powerfully ambivalent responses. As the brand name of family entertainment, Disney offers assurance not only to parents but to others who grasp that New York's future depends in no small measure on its capacity to accommodate the middle class. At the same time, those mouse ears terrify some people who see the aspirations of the urban middle class swiftly sinking beneath the values that govern suburban malls.

In the last four years, as the project has taken shape, Times Square has been the focus of complaints about the replacement of raunchy authenticity by a synthetic theme-park atmosphere. Some critics believe that in the name of saving the city, the government agencies sponsoring this venture may actually be killing it. They envision the emergence of a city where the only culture is corporate culture, where entertainment has stifled art and demands for security have muffled the claims of difference and dissent.

As Michael Sorkin put it in his 1992 book, *Variations on a Theme Park*, "The struggle to reclaim the city is the struggle for democracy itself."

I count myself a watchful supporter of the redevelopment of Times Square. The expulsion of porn doesn't strike me as a major threat to free speech. Maybe I'm a 1950s person. I smoke, eat steak, drink martinis, and if people want to look at dirty pictures, I think they ought to go to Paris, ooh-la-la.

Besides that, as someone who has been following this story for more than thirty years, I regard in wonder that things have turned out so well. It may be natural to view this state- and city-sponsored project as the work of some monolithic political-commercial complex. This opinion could not be further from the truth. Forty-second Street now reflects the determination of some energetic and enlightened public servants who fought hard to prevent the street from turning into a granite corporate canyon.

If this street had stars in the sidewalk, some of them should be inscribed with the names of Rebecca Robertson, Cora Cahan, Gretchen Dykstra, Robert A. M. Stern, Tibor Kalman, and Hugh Hardy—the group of public officials and design professionals responsible for guiding the street's redevelopment. The public response to their efforts has ensured that, at the very least, the development of this street will be incremental. It will evolve over time.

Already the street has become the infrastructure for the nation's media central, a public space that brings together the producers and consumers of popular culture. The Condé Nast building, now going up on Forty-second Street and Broadway, will reinforce a concentration already represented by the Bertelsmann Building at Forty-fifth Street, site of the Virgin Megastore, and the Forty-third Street headquarters of this newspaper. One block east along Forty-second Street is HBO headquarters and, across the street in Bryant Park, the seasonal tents for the Seventh on Sixth fashion shows.

But something is missing from this picture, an ingredient that could lift the whole enterprise into the cultural stratosphere: art. What is needed here, specifically, in this project sponsored by the public, is a forum for artists whose work is animated by the tensions between high culture and popular entertainment.

Those tensions have been driving the culture throughout the last half century, sparking an entire literature and inspiring several generations of artists. Writers like John Kouwenhoven, Marshall McLuhan, Guy

Debord, Susan Sontag, Umberto Eco, Jean Beaudrillard, and George W. S. Trow. Artists like Andy Warhol, Twyla Tharp, Barbara Kruger, Laurie Anderson, Cindy Sherman. What is glaringly absent from the new Times Square is the awareness and creativity that these artists represent.

It is not a minor omission. Mass media, popular entertainment—these phenomena represent the most powerful economic forces at work in the modern world. The Forty-second Street project is the most important opportunity we now have to connect these forces to the contemporary urban condition. Artists are the most qualified people to make that connection.

Twyla Tharp is entirely correct when she insists that her dances deal with "major community problems"—questions of leadership, hierarchy, cooperation, estrangement, and courage. Laurie Anderson's multimedia performances explore the coercive influence of the homogenized global monoculture and the capacity of Americans to resist or even transform its overpowering advance.

These artists, and many others, have chosen to work in established forms of popular entertainment: pop music, movies, television, Broadway musicals. They have used these media to reflect critically on the media themselves, exploiting their power not simply to seduce and entertain but to enlighten and inspire.

Pop culture is alienating as well as binding. We all love Lucy. But it's not just gangsta rap and daytime talk shows that are socially corrosive. Popular culture is inherently a major force for estrangement. Think about Joe Camel. Cigarettes, once representative of urban sophistication, now have people in a most unsophisticated uproar.

Think about cars: how this national emblem of personal autonomy later became a cage on wheels, a rolling threat not only to the environment it sought to conquer but to the conquerers, the drivers who became the driven, charioteers in a race against the obsolescence of the industrial age.

The whole point of a city is to work these things out in public. That's the meaning of Sorkin's observation. Strike, scream at people, light up in public, make a fool of yourself, fall in the gutter, pick yourself up, move on.

I doubt that anyone seriously denies the importance of family entertainment in the contemporary city. On the contrary, those who care about the city's future should applaud efforts to accommodate the urban middle class. What raises skepticism is the use of culture to mask a latent hostility toward culture in all its messy, anxious vitality.

The point is this: the street is itself a form of popular culture, a medium as powerful as television, newsprint, or the World Wide Web. No form of "interactivity" yet devised is more potently democratic. The

American street is sacred space, for all its saturation in secular, materialistic values. Any great street turns each step into a stride toward freedom.

In 1903, the New Amsterdam was shamelessly escapist: in the industrial city, a theater might well want to resemble a park; it performed a similar function. The context of the New Amsterdam has changed. New York is no longer an industrial city. It is an informational city, driven largely by images. It is folly to think that the meaning of the restoration is the same as the meaning of the original design. The New Amsterdam was, essentially, an escape from business. The restored New Amsterdam is business itself, a building integral to the economy of tourism and mass media on which New York's economy now largely depends.

Some of us can remember seeing movies in the New Amsterdam as recently as the early 1970s. Cheap double bills. The lights were so dark that we didn't notice that the boxes had been torn from the walls. We were movie-generation people who could take in four films in one evening and didn't care if the surroundings were grungy. If anything, the battered surrounding added to the experience. Run-down places ripen the imagination. That is a basic New York story.

Decay, estrangement: these are not concepts with which civic boosters are ordinarily comfortable. Yet they are major aspects of urban beauty. Edward Hopper captured this beauty. So have James Baldwin, Joan Didion, George Tooker, Paul Cadmus, Jerome Robbins, Savion Glover, David Byrne. There are artists waiting now in the wings to interpret not only the community of the street but also the solitude of the street. Their vision is imperative to New York's enduring capacity to strengthen modernity's connective tissue.

The Glorification of the American Girl: Wasn't that a Ziegfeld slogan, when the New Amsterdam was young? How about the Glorification of the American Misfit? That's one of the things a great city strives for. It offers an Arcadia of opportunity where misfits get to make something creative from the experience of not fitting in. It sometimes happens that the weird niches misfits carve out for themselves turn out to be shape of things to come.

May 11, 1997

MAKE THE MODERN MODERN? HOW VERY RASH!

Modern art is better than ever! At least, it's just as scary. This is the awful truth disclosed by Rem Koolhaas's proposal for the expansion of the

Museum of Modern Art's midtown campus. Youthful, even bratty, shimmering with bright new ways to frighten the horses, Koolhaas's design would literally burst the old Modern apart at the seams.

The design could destroy the place, and possibly save it. Koolhaas's proposal can be glimpsed, but barely, in an exhibition now in the museum's top-floor galleries of architecture and design. Toward the New Museum of Modern Art: Sketchbooks by 10 Architects presents the results of the first round in the competition to design the expansion. Koolhaas, at one time regarded as a leading contender for the commission, did not place among the three finalists.

The three proposals, all as tasteful as table water biscuits, are by Jacques Herzog and Pierrre de Meuron of Switzerland, Yoshio Taniguchi of Japan, and Bernard Tschumi of New York. A winner will be chosen by the end of the year. As the show's title suggests, these are not fully worked out designs but concepts, some quite rough in form.

Koolhaas presented his proposal in the form of a nearly 400-page hardbound book. Like *S, M, L, XL*, the massive tome Koolhaas brought out in 1995, this volume is a stylish production that reproduces the texture of an architect's thought. Sketches, hard-line drawings, photomontages, images of models, renderings, philosophical musings, jokes visual and verbal are organized with a cinematic sense of pace.

At the museum, unfortunately, Koolhaas's book is displayed behind glass; visitors can't peruse its contents. As much a philosophical critique of the museum as a plan for its physical enlargement, the book deserves wider circulation. In years to come, many will look back on it as the Modern that could have been.

Koolhaas begins by reviewing the museum's history and analyzing its present situation. This makes for a sweet-and-sour show-and-tell. With deftly chosen images and quotations from the museum's founders, Koolhaas evokes the days when the Modern was new and its novelty stood in sharp contrast—philosophically and architecturally—to the world around it.

The contrast has grown fuzzy. Instead of a crisp frame enclosing intimate galleries, the museum is now an unfocused blur. As Koolhaas puts it: "The old part of MoMA is shabby. The new part of MoMA is tacky." He supports these views with color pictures that coolly capture the museum's physical shortcomings.

Koolhaas's design does not propose to restore the museum to its original purity. Nor does he rail against the museum's fall from artistic purity. He takes as a given that the Modern has many functions other than aesthetic contemplation. It sells watches. It throws parties. It courts the media. It makes deals. These functions, Koolhaas believes, could be architecturally expressed.

A garden surrounds Koolhaas's museum. To create it, he takes a can opener to the existing buildings on West Fifty-third Street and slices off the ground floor, turning them into a floating slab. On the West Fifty-fourth Street side, Koolhaas sinks Philip Johnson's much-loved sculpture garden, intact, to basement level, allowing visual contact between the garden and the street. At the eastern end of the garden, now occupied by the museum restaurant, Koolhaas places what he calls the Forum. This he envisions as a Miesian "universal space" enclosed by glass, to be used for lectures, concerts, conferences, temporary shows, and social events.

The museum's six curatorial departments—offices for curators, support staff, preparers—would be based, one department per floor, in the original museum building, designed by Edward Durell Stone and Philip L. Goodwin, and completed in 1939. A new seven-story tower for administrative offices would be built atop Johnson's 1964 addition, the site of the present bookstore. Koolhaas calls this tower MoMA Inc., as if the museum were an industry whose chief product is cultural prestige.

The museum's main galleries would be contained within a new six-story building, to the west of Cesar Pelli's 1985 residential Museum Tower. It would run the full block, from Fifty-third to Fifty-fourth Street. Atop this generic box, Koolhaas proposes to plant a slim sixteen-story triangular spire, its shape and dimensions conforming to the zoning envelope of allowable development the museum would acquire by tearing down the Dorset Hotel. A multiuse structure, the triangle would contain study centers, private viewing rooms, restaurants.

Koolhaas conceives these structures as episodes in an architectural narrative. Or call it a flowchart, a diagram of circulation. Money and power, accumulated by MoMA Inc., are converted into energy that is channeled into the curatorial departments. Here, artifacts are selected, then hauled out of storage and put on public display.

Just as the 1939 building derived its aesthetic from industrial architecture, so Koolhaas proposes, in effect, a factory for the postindustrial city, an urban center geared for the manufacture of culture. Inside the building, Koolhaas proposes to make visible other museum operations that are ordinarily screened from view. Circulation—of artworks and people—gets big play here.

In place of the shopping mall escalators in Pelli's garden hall, Koolhaas proposes a grand moving staircase. He includes, as well, provisions for a new mode of transport. Developed by Otis, the Odyssey transport system is a cross between an elevator and a funicular tram. The same car can move vertically, horizontally, and diagonally.

Some design elements extend familiar Koolhaas preoccupations. His aesthetic has been described as a synthesis of Miesian classicism and the romantic imagery of Wallace K. Harrison; both sources are in evidence here. The architect's renderings of the museum's interiors echo the photomontages Mies himself devised for several museum projects. The triangle and square tower recall Harrison's pairings of different forms, like the Trylon and Perisphere, or the General Assembly and Secretariat buildings at the United Nations Headquarters. Like Koolhaas's Piranesian Space at the Chunnel station in the French city of Lille, the Odyssey system expresses Koolhaas's weakness for technologically assisted disorientation.

Koolhaas's vertical forms hark back to the "culture of congestion," theme of his legendary book, *Delirious New York*. Unlike the other proposals, Koolhaas's design for the Modern actually embraces the Museum Tower instead of ignoring it. You get the sense that he'd want to put a residential high-rise on the site even if one weren't already there, and that, just like Pelli, Koolhaas would also clad it with a glass skin inspired by Mondrian.

This plan is not easy to love. It doesn't begin to be elegant. It lacks the grace of formal simplicity. With or without Harrison as precedent, Koolhaas's vertical forms don't rhyme in the mind. His cutaway ground floor brings to mind the gloomy space beneath the floating garden slab of Lever House. His sunken garden will elicit shudders of recognition from those who've suffered the damp sculpture moat at the Whitney. The whiffs of technology, like the automated painting retrieval system, summon forth memories of French rinky-dink modernism from the 1960s.

And then Koolhaas has such a cheeky attitude. MoMA Inc., indeed. Trustees support art museums to bestow gentility upon money, power, and social ambition, not to have the mask ripped away. Koolhaas rubs in his social commentary with images of stuffy Gilded Age dinner parties, complete with crystal chandeliers. In one collage, a seated woman turns a cold shoulder to a Matisse. The woman is Jessica Mitford, as depicted on the jacket of her book *The American Way of Death*.

Because of these and other digs, some people have interpreted Koolhaas's submission as a send-up of the competition rather than a serious bid to win it. As those who've heard the architect lecture will recognize, however, this is just the way Koolhaas thinks. Here, in what is, after all, a sketchbook, prepared in less than a month, Koolhaas is simply thinking out loud.

His jokes are serious, and on target. The chandeliers and the Stanford White dinner party are visual shorthand for the overbred curatorial intelligence that has often haunted the halls of the Museum of Modern Art—including this competition. Isn't this, more or less, what the finalists propose to give us: polite Gilded Age dinner spaces, reclad in the International Style?

Why invite Koolhaas to the party and expect him to be anything less than Koolhaas? Nothing in his proposal should surprise anyone who has leafed through *S, M, L, XL*. Isn't anyone at the Modern curious to see where Koolhaas might take his ideas? Yet the truth is that to make something successful from this proposal would take a client with more strength of will than the Modern is presently able to muster. It would take a client with the capacity to think yes and no simultaneously: Yes, your mind is working. No, you may not sink our garden into the basement. No, you can't cut away the ground floor. You may not use robots. Cut the cute stuff about MoMA Inc. Nix the chandeliers. Can the Odyssey. Got any more ideas?

If Koolhaas ever was a favored contender for this project, it was not because he was best known of the ten architects, or because he was hot, or because he had put out an 800-pound book, all of which happen to be true. He was favored because no architect had a more focused view of the postindustrial city and of architecture's role in its cultural development.

As his attempts to wed Mies and Harrison suggest, Koolhaas collapses dualistic ways of thinking. His aesthetic probes the lines that allegedly separate reason and folly, subjectivity and objectivity, world and dream. It seeks relationships more complex, in other words, than the simple old-versus-new opposition embodied in the Museum of Modern Art's original design.

Even the old Modern, however, challenged one of Western culture's most vexing dualisms, the one between art and life. That's why the architecture and design department was created. It's easy to overlook how successful the department's mission turned out to be: not in remaking the world according to the tenets of Good Design, but rather (like Duchamp or Warhol) in calling into question the difference between art and other things.

The culture has taken that idea and run with it, leaving the Modern behind in the dust of a concept it pioneered. The Koolhaas proposal, even in unbuilt form, clears away the dust. Rude, brash, aiming a deflationary arrow at our willingness to puff milquetoast as risky, his proposal slaps the museum awake from a deep postmodern slumber.

June 15, 1997

THE DESIGNS OF A GENIUS REDESIGNING HIMSELF

When America's westward expansion finally reached the Pacific coast, the artist's imagination became the country's new frontier. Or so one might conclude from a show of uncommon beauty on view at the Whitney Museum of American Art, Frank Lloyd Wright: Designs for an American Landscape, 1922–32. The show, first presented at the Canadian Center for Architecture, offers five projects, all unbuilt, in which Wright developed a range of innovative forms for buildings far removed from the urban center. Not coincidentally, the show also depicts an artist in the painful process of re-creating himself.

This exhibition is a result of a recently forged alliance between the Canadian Center and the Whitney Museum. Since its founding in 1989, the Center has presented some of the most intelligent architecture shows to be seen anywhere today. Now, thanks to the Whitney, New Yorkers won't have to journey to Montreal to view them.

Good news for us. But the work on view at the Whitney occupies such a peak of genius, and it has been assembled with such sensitivity, scholarship, and skill, that those who care about architecture may feel more than a little ashamed for not having leaped onto a plane and rushed to see it earlier. There are drawings here as ravishing as any that Wright produced: as beautiful, that is to say, as any architectural drawings that exist on earth. There are times when understatement is useful. This is not one of those times.

The show, organized by David G. De Long of the University of Pennsylvania and beautifully designed by the New York architect George Ranalli, includes roughly one hundred drawings, architectural models, and computer renderings. One might call it A Man and His Pencils. Wright used to talk about the joy it gave him to spread a selection of colored pencils in his hand and see the colors sparkling in the sun. The architect could be grandiose when talking about himself, and the image of him contemplating the tools of his trade may seem off-puttingly divine. That's the way Wright was. And when you see what he accomplished with these tools, Wright's high opinion of himself begins to look like objective fact.

Wright designed these five projects in the decade following his completion of the Imperial Hotel in Tokyo. These were not Wright's happiest years. He had little work. His personal life was a shambles. Eventually, with the completion of the Fallingwater residence outside Pittsburgh and the Johnson's Wax Headquarters in Racine, Wisconsin, in 1936, his career burst into a second flowering. But meanwhile, Wright was widely perceived as a burned-out case.

We should all burn out so vibrantly. Even though these five projects were not built, this is a show of rebirth, of new beginnings. Here the American landscape becomes a metaphor for the eternal American belief in fresh starts. The car becomes a symbol for moving on.

Go west, middle-aged man. In his earlier years in Chicago, Wright developed a predominantly horizontal vocabulary of forms for the midwestern prairie. In these projects, he devised a formal vocabulary for three different terrains: mountain, desert, and lake. All but one of the projects were designed for the American West. All five utilized the concrete-block construction he employed in the Mayan-inspired houses he built in Los Angeles in the 1920s. All typify the anti-urban strain that would dominate Wright's thought in later years. Now the car enjoys the pride of place Wright had once granted the hearth.

The Doheny Ranch Development, planned in 1923, is the only true suburban project among the five. Conceived for a stretch of the Santa Monica Mountains subsequently known as Beverly Hills, the scheme boasts genuine Hollywood glamour; it could be a set for a vanished sequence from the film *Lost Horizon.* A community of homes spread over 411 acres would have been linked by roads and viaducts. To a degree, this is an early version of what architects in the 1960s called the megastructure, but one that draws hill and valley into its lush, sprawling mass.

In 1923, Wright prepared an even more arcadian dreamscape, a vacation colony for Lake Tahoe. Like Wright's residential designs for Los Angeles, the Tahoe project also drew on pre-Columbian forms. Here the Mayan influence is evident in the battered concrete bases of the cabins, while their tall wooden roofs evoke wigwams.

Wright's integration of these structures with nature is as impressive as the forms themselves. Rocks and boulders cluster around the cabins' bases. The wooden roofs echo the surrounding forest, Adirondack-style. Wright also designed a series of floating barges that would have dissolved the borders between building, land, and water. An offshore lodge to be erected on piles in the lake features "water courts," aquatic atriums enclosed within the building's long, low-slung wings.

The drawings convey an image of baptismal purity. And yet, looking at them in the light of Wright's turbulent life at the time, one is inclined to see this as a place of infidelities and indiscretions, unsolved murders, mysterious drownings, untold Prohibition-era delights.

The American desert provided Wright with almost too poetically apt a setting for the hardships of his middle years. In 1934, with the construction of Taliesin West, the architect made Arizona his winter home. Ten years earlier, however, he prepared a desert oasis for the insurance tycoon A. M. Johnson.

Johnson had already built a small compound of Spanish-style houses on the edge of Death Valley. He invited Wright to join him there on one trip and asked the architect for recommendations on improving the property. Wright responded in typical fashion by drawing up an ambitious proposal that would have enclosed the existing structures within a long, linear building sited to take advantage of the views, the terrain and the approach by car. The plan included terraced farming, fountains, and a chapel.

In 1928, Wright was commissioned to design a new hotel outside Phoenix, San Marcos in the Desert. Not long before, he had helped a former apprentice with the design for the fabulous Arizona Biltmore. (That hotel's magnificent lobby, never officially credited to Wright, produces an impact on the body that is felt nowhere except in Wright's buildings.)

For San Marcos, he produced a long, three-story block with setbacks and balconies, a form adopted by many other architects almost forty years later. The folded planes of the ceiling in the hotel's dining room anticipated the geometric experiments of avant-garde architects today. Again, as in Death Valley, the flat desert plane enables Wright to orient the building around the roadway approaching it.

The most delirious design in the show is the Gordon Strong Automobile Objective, which Wright designed in 1925 for the top of Sugarloaf Mountain in Maryland. Here the spiral makes its first appearance in Wright's work. Later he would use this form for projects as various as a jewelry store, a car showroom, a parking garage, and the great Guggenheim Museum in Manhattan.

The Automobile Objective, as its name implies, was a tourist destination, designed to lure people out for a drive. And the design makes clear the cosmic terms in which Wright regarded cars. Its ziggurat shape recalls the sacred "world mountain" temples of ancient Sumeria. Inside the temple, Wright proposed to build a planetarium.

What's striking about all these projects is that Wright proceeded as if he, personally, had discovered America. He is starting over from scratch, as if the nation had not already been invaded by neoclassical, Gothic Revival, and other European styles of building. Sybil Maholy-Nagy was not exaggerating when she observed that Wright was the first architect in history who felt obliged to design an entire continent.

And Wright was hardly the only American for whom the car and the highway symbolized the freedom to seek the future, to speed away from past mistakes: failed marriages, botched careers, the wretched confines of tradition. In hindsight, of course, this optimism seems painfully naïve. No force has done more to despoil the American environment than the car culture and its insatiable gobbling of the American land.

Wright cannot be wholly absolved from responsibility for the megalopolitan sprawl of the postwar years. "When people ask me where they should build," the architect wrote in the early 1950s, "I tell them to go far from the city, at least as twice as far as think they should go. And when others follow, as they will, move on!"

Yet in those same years, Wright found himself railing against the electric power lines stretching across his beloved Arizona desert, their metal stanchions disfiguring his glorious mountain views. Soon, tract houses, cars, and asphalt would be dumped upon the landscape in overpowering abundance. The nation's economy would become critically dependent on this mass production, never mind that the pileup of industrial production would be hazardous to mental and physical health.

In short, this show will leave the alert visitor hungering for a sequel, in which today's most informed thinkers would be asked to work through the history and prospects of the desert we have built in the wake of Wright's ideas.

July 18, 1997

FOR THE BODY, A CURVY HOME THAT CALLS TO THE SOUL

This very pleasant, small, modern city on the northwest coast of Spain is the site of a recent building designed by Arata Isozaki. La Coruña has a working waterfront, with rows of cranes and gantries. Above the harbor, scores of modern apartment blocks should mar the horizon but somehow don't, perhaps because they are scaled to the low, hilly terrain. Marine light drenches the town.

La Coruña has one famous landmark, called the Tower of Hercules. It is a lighthouse, a square structure made of stone. Courses of masonry on the building's exterior spiral upward around the tower, traces of a ramp once used to climb to the summit. The form evokes fantasies of the Pharos, and even Babel. In the center of town, older buildings show off a fine example of vernacular design: enclosed balconies, housed within a slim vertical glass box, with a grid of white mullions dividing the panes. The effect is airy and hypnotic, like the metal balconies in Barcelona.

This year, La Coruña opened a waterfront esplanade that winds from the harbor to a large inlet. Even on hot days, sportif types are running around. You may prefer to stroll, breathing the sea air, admiring the light, perhaps stopping for lunch at Manda Truco, a family-run restaurant that became famous a few years ago when the owner's daughter married a local soccer star. On no account should you pass up the lightly fried sardines.

From there it's a short walk to what may be the most beautiful piece of architecture Arata Isozaki has yet built. Completed in 1995, the building houses a science museum called Domus, Museum of Mankind. The museum is small and highly focused. Its subject is the human being and the body, our mobile home.

Just inside the museum's entrance, there is a replica of a small, paleolithic frieze depicting a female figure, as full-figured as the Venus of Willendorf. In her upheld arm she holds a horn: a symbol of fecundity, at once phallus and shell. The figure symbolizes the idea of "domus" as seen by Ramón A. Núñez, the museum's director: the home is not just a shelter but a state of desire.

In form and sensuousness, the museum's architecture echoes the horn shape. The building sits at the edge of a cliff overlooking an inlet and the sea beyond. The side facing inland is jagged, a form the architect adapted from the folding Japanese screen. But the folds also resemble a granite synthesis of the rugged stone cliffs and the craggy nearby townscape.

The wall facing the sea is smooth, concave, and nearly windowless. Its curvature is both horizontal and vertical. (Isozaki employs a similar shape in his convention hall for the Japanese city of Nara.) Made of concrete panels, the wall is clad with rows of slate, its gray flecked with gold. Isozaki has compared the wall to a billowing sail. It also brings to mind a ship's hull and swelling water.

From sidelong angles, which is how the building is ordinarily glimpsed, perspective creates the illusion that the wall is horn-shaped, tapering to a peak as it curves out of sight. The rows of slate also give the wall an animal aspect, the hide of a beast too big to pet with the hand but not with the eye. From one end of the wall's granite base, a grand stair ripples down to the esplanade.

Inside, the exhibitions are displayed on three levels: a main floor and, above, two deep balconies shaped like irregular terraces. The floors are of concrete, surfaced with large panels of dark green slate, its surface rough but polished to a high sheen. The inner side of the building's curved wall is fully exposed, the concrete panels rising from floor to ceiling in a gentle concave arc. If a whale gave birth to an atrium, it would look like this.

The museum's permanent exhibition covers every corner of the human house, from the organs to the senses, from DNA to muscular movement. There are breathing tubes full of revolting smells, and an interactive *Mona Lisa*. There are video presentations of conception, pregnancy, birth. Most of the exhibits suggest links between nature and culture.

In the heart section, for instance, you get not only the usual spooky walk through room-size ventricles—*lub-dub, lub-dub*—but also a vitrine full of heart-related signs. Valentine candies. Heart-shaped Lolita sunglasses. The Virgin's Sacred Heart, pierced with swords. Blood circulates; so do symbols.

The building itself suggests symbolic images. Besides the ship, the sail, the horn, the sea, Isozaki draws an analogy between the facade and the body's largest organ, the skin. I also see a form that seeks to reconcile speed and stillness: the curved wall streaks past the eye like a comet, while nonetheless conveying stability. Like Erich Mendelsohn's work in the 1920s, this building belongs to what the social historian Stephen Kern called "the culture of time and space." It offers an image of shelter for the world of rapid movement that science and technology have helped create.

Of course, these are at best literary associations. It is pleasant to let them flow into the mind, and then flow out again, leaving just the spectacle of a curve, some slate, some golden flecks and the light playing off them. One could look at this shape for hours without getting bored. And, since this is a science museum, and one that isn't too sophisticated to raise unanswerable questions, a visitor may find it natural to ask: What's going on in the eye of the beholder? Why is this shape so compelling?

A "science of beauty" is probably best left to the people at Estée Lauder. There's probably no way to objectively explain the work Isozaki's brain performs when he takes into account the specifics of site, climate, program, materials, construction techniques, history, client desires, and other variables. But perhaps science could shed light on the relationship between this space and its time.

For instance, the neuroscientist Gerald Edelman believes that people create the architecture of their brains in the process of learning. Everyone's wiring differs. What if it could be shown that patterns in the wiring change over generations? Monticello's design, one assumes, drew on Jefferson's left- and right-brain faculties.

But should we expect a different kind of architecture to emerge in a time that knows about the difference between these faculties? Knows that each of us has the capacity for reason and intuition, that these faculties emanate from within different sections of the same skull? That art and science, while distinct disciplines, are symbiotically intertwined?

Such an architecture has emerged in La Coruña. In this building, art and science are neither separated nor merged. But their desire for union has proved fertile.

July 20, 1997

SEARCHING FOR YOURSELF IN VERSACE'S MIRROR

Two years ago, a single pair of black vinyl Versace jeans hung on the rack at Century 21, the discount store in lower Manhattan. They were black, lightweight, and shiny, and they'd been marked down from $400 to something like $110. But someone else's hand reached out to grab the hanger before I did, and then the pants were gone. He who hesitates will never wear Versace, at least not at a bargain price.

Darn! I wanted those pants. They were just what every sensitive man wants to wear to his own midlife crisis.

You need not call the Psychic Friends Network to be convinced that there is such a thing as reincarnation. All you have to do is shop. I had come to feel that my life in recent years had turned into an out-of-body experience. (Middle-aged writers are highly susceptible to this feeling, I am told.) I thought, Well, I'll just shop my way back into physicality. I will join the David Barton Gym (went once). Drink MET-Rx (one sip and down the drain). And those Versace jeans looked like a good incarnation, but then they were gone: not just the pants but the fantasy of looking like a stud.

And then—the miracle of Century 21—the hand reappeared and put the hanger back on the rack. The pants were mine, but the fantasy proved more elusive. When I got home and tried them on, I looked as if I had tied two black plastic garbage bags around my legs. I stood up straight and sucked in my gut. Garbage bags. What a letdown. Still, I didn't feel as if I'd thrown away my $110. That's not much to pay for the kick of briefly envisioning yourself as trashy.

Sexy pants. Garbage bags. What's the difference, anyway? In his excellent book *The Fashion Conspiracy*, Nicholas Coleridge tells a story about dining on a stormy winter night at a fashionable but nearly empty restaurant in Milan, Italy. A striking couple is seated a few tables away. He's older; she's wearing a dress made of tight leather straps. The writer sends a note to the table: "Who designed the dress?" A note comes back: "Gianni Versace." Would Mr. Coleridge like to join them for coffee?

It turns out that the man selects the woman's clothes. He pays for them, and he looks at them. This is what these two people do. They travel, they shop, and they have dinner. He is her mirror. Or probably it's the other way around. Mr. Coleridge doesn't delve deeply into the woman's emotional predicament. From his account, you'd think that a sizable chunk of her psyche is happy to have this treatment. WWW, as folks used to say. What Woman Wouldn't?

Perhaps the call signals should have been SOS: "Help, help. I am being held captive inside a dress of black leather straps at a restaurant in Milan. I am trapped within the fantasy of the man at my table who is eating a plate of linguini served in squid-ink sauce, and we are both trapped inside the dream world of Gianni Versace. We are twenty thousand leagues under the sea. Bring us the check, and get us out of here."

Suppose the person sitting across the table had been a man. Or don't merely suppose. Pick up any one of the luxuriously produced coffee-table books put out by Mr. Versace in recent years. These books are desolate, packed with pictures recycled from other coffee-table books and magazines, images religiously known to the culturally informed audience that a talented Italian designer should not have tried to court. Cecil Beaton, Cocteau, all that. Forget about secondhand smoke. It's the secondhand sensibility that gets you every time.

Some people do read *Playboy*. Really. And some say they feel privileged to look at pictures of Gianni Versace's houses. Others will take one glance and say, "How gauche."

Mr. Versace's books offered a high gloss version of a low-camp view of male nudes. These pictures come off just as adolescent boasting.

In Italy, people loved Mr. Versace as an anachronism, a man caught up in a thoroughly medieval spectacle. Here were two rivals, Mr. Versace and Giorgio Armani, dueling with each other over who would rule Milan. Instead of sending out armies to spill each other's blood in the streets, these rivals dispatched images. Their weapons were pieces of paper, sniff inserts in fashion magazines. In the warfare state of contemporary culture, these images are as lethally competitive as the troops sent forth by the Sforzas.

In recent years, Miami Beach became a distant battlefield of these images, a Hanoi for rival designers. But the place has been working itself up to this embattled state for some time. Long ago, Miami Beach became the capital of a phenomenon that goes by the long and sterile name *objectification*. Translation: the impulse to regard other people not as human beings but as objects of lust or scorn.

Jews were targeted in the 1950s, when the words *Miami Beach* became a punch line for anti-Semitic jokes. Old people came after. Then Cubans. Then gay men. Each group was subjected to riotous put-downs. Only gradually has the psychopathology of such jokes sunk in. Those who look down on other people still find it surprising to be looked down upon in turn.

How else are we supposed to cope with the unfairness of things? There is both humor and risk in our fascination with extremes. Yes, it's perfect beach weather, and yes, the culture is playing with dynamite. Women have openly begun to explore the realm of the acting subject, men the life of the passive object.

Fashion has coaxed the culture into a new game. Some love to play by the new rules. Many resent that the rules are changing, faster than fashion itself.

July 20, 1997

IN FORM AND FUNCTION, IT'S A TALE OF TWO TERMINALS

But where is the soup? The onion soup? Where are the pig's trotters? *Sacré bleu!* If you're going to remake Washington's National Airport in the image of Les Halles, the legendary food market of Paris, shouldn't you at least offer the weary traveler some tempting French dish?

Forget it. If you want to buy a watch, a pair of khakis, or a tennis bracelet like the ones you've seen on QVC, you've come to the right place. The new National Airport is a department store halfheartedly disguised as a transportation terminal. But if you're hungry, be forewarned: pack a sandwich, or take your place in the long lines at California Pizza.

Designed by Cesar Pelli, and built at a cost of $450 million, the new terminal building expands to near-extinction one of the nation's most beloved airports. National is about as door-to-door as an airport can be. You land, you get off the plane, and you are right across the Potomac River from that life-size revolving rack of postcards known as Washington, D.C. The entrance into the city is at once convenient and grand.

The design of the old airport, now retitled Terminal A, lent itself to a sense of governmental occasion. It is Post Office architecture, WPA architecture, New Deal architecture: concrete Art Deco toned down into brusquely efficient curves. Even a tobacco company lobbyist could feel proud hailing a cab from the building's streamlined porte cochere.

The new North Terminal makes no noticeable attempt to relate to the old in terms of style. From the outside, the building is unexceptional and unobjectionable. It's a glass shed with some yellow loops traced across the facade. The building's architectural moments, such as they are, are offered within. The terminal's big gesture is the vista along a 1,600-foot-long central concourse, a steel construction painted Easter Bunny colors: happy-face yellow and robin's-egg blue.

Columns, a whole petrified forest of them, rise airily into a roof of fifty-four egg-shaped domes, each dome framing a circular skylight. The natural light is abundant and wonderful, even though it calls attention to the terminal's ugly terrazzo floor, a dull tartan of pink, gray, and buff.

Artists, many of them famous, have been commissioned to design large mosaic disks set into the floor beneath the domes. The building's treatment of art will leave you crying out for less. Three piers extend the design motif out to a total of thirty-one new departure gates. With all that glass, all that metal, all that terrazzo, you can imagine what the acoustics are like. The sound of even a softly screaming child suffices to make eardrums throb up and down the concourse.

As a piece of urban infrastructure, the terminal cannot be faulted. Up to now, if you wanted to take Washington's excellent subway out to the airport, you could easily find yourself slithering down grass slopes and dodging highway traffic to make your flight. The new terminal incorporates pedestrian bridges that connect to the subway stop and to two parking garages.

But the soul of this new structure has nothing to do with transportation. It lies, rather, with the crescent-shaped display counters set up in front of the glass walls that might otherwise offer unobstructed views of the city across the river. Perfumes, jewelry, stuffed animals, sunglasses: this is not just a new National Airport. It's a new Washington Mall. And some may well prefer it to the old Washington Mall. The old one is dusty and dirty. It lacks summertime shade.

The new Washington Mall is air-conditioned and spiffy. And there is even wit involved in the idea of styling an airport after the iron and glass sheds Victor Baltard designed in 1857 for Les Halles. Airports today are beyond air travel. They are not simply places for getting on and off planes. They are marketplaces where shops and restaurants outnumber the waiting areas for planes. Buckle your seat belts! Lingerie!

Airports are also hubs in the international marketing of ideas, the public spaces that figure most largely in the imagination of those properly outfitted with laptops and cell phones, the leaders of a society driven by the exchange of information. There is logic to fashioning an airport after one of the world's greatest markets.

It is logical, too, to conceive a major new building in Washington as an homage to Paris, the city that has long been Washington's guiding architectural ideal. A Frenchman planned the American capital. The city's government buildings adhere to the classical principles of the French Beaux-Arts school.

In this era of deregulation, perhaps people don't want to arrive at an airport that recalls the New Deal. If hospitals, prisons, and schools are going to be privatized, why shouldn't an airport strive to be Macy's?

We're living in an era of deregulated architecture, too. And what is ultimately most dismaying about the new National Airport isn't the commercialization of public space. It's that the building fails to go all the way on its own terms. The new National Airport could be glorious if they would fit it out with tables spread with blue-checked tablecloths, strolling accordion players, can-can girls, black-turtlenecked existentialists wreathed with smoke from unfiltered Gitane cigarettes, a weekly Juliette Greco look-alike contest, and baggage carts equipped with klaxons from expired Citroën 2CVs. The metal detectors should be redesigned to resemble guillotines, and the government inspectors ought to dress up as Madame Defarge.

July 28, 1997

THE MIRACLE IN BILBAO

If you want to look into the heart of American art today, you are going to need a passport. You will have to pack your bags, leave the U.S.A., and find your way to Bilbao, a small, rusty city in the northeast corner of Spain. The trip is not convenient, and you should not expect to have much fun while you're there. This is Basque country. A region proudly, if not officially, independent from the rest of Spain, it is also bleakly free from Spanish sophistication. Oh, and by the way, you might get blown up. Basque country is not Bosnia. But it's not Disney World, either. History here has not been sanitized into a colorful spectacle for your viewing enjoyment. People are actually living history here, punctuated by periodic violence. Those who visit Bilbao, however, may come away thinking that art is not entirely remote from matters of life and death.

Bilbao has lately become a pilgrimage town. The word is out that miracles still occur, and that a major one has happened here. The city's new Guggenheim Museum, a satellite of the Solomon R. Guggenheim Foundation in New York, opens on October 19. But people have been flocking to Bilbao for nearly two years, just to watch the building's skeleton take shape. "Have you been to Bilbao?" In architectural circles, that question has acquired the status of a shibboleth. Have you seen the light? Have you seen the future? Does it work? Does it play?

Designed by Frank Gehry, the Bilbao Guggenheim is the most important building yet completed by the California architect. The miracle taking place here, however, is not Gehry's building, wondrous as it is. The miraculous occurrence is the extravagant optimism that enters into the outlook of those who have made the pilgrimage. What if American art has not, after all, played itself out to its last entropic wheeze? What if standards of cultural achievement have not irretrievably dissolved in the vast, tepid bath of relativity, telemarketing, and manipulated public opinion? Has it even become possible, once again, to think about beauty as a form of truth?

Ring-a-ding-ding.

Frank Gehry, who is sixty-eight, has been an important figure in architecture since 1978, the year he completed the remodeling of his home in Santa Monica, California. An extensively overhauled version of a generic Dutch-roofed suburban house, the building employed an original vocabulary of crude industrial materials: chain-link fence, plywood, galvanized zinc, cinder block, exposed wood framing. These he arranged into a composition of lopsided cubes, exposed-stud walls, and other unruly shapes. In the past five years, Gehry has completed such major buildings as the University of Toledo Center for the Visual Arts, the Weisman Art Museum in Minneapolis, the American Center in Paris, an office building in Prague. These projects not only represent an enlargement in architectural scale. They have also extended what seemed a purely private, idiosyncratic language into the larger dimension of public meaning.

Gehry's own house was a tour de force, but it was, after all, an architect's home. And a California architect's home, at that. Even ten years ago, it wasn't uncommon to hear him described as "an artist"—a maker of sculptures rather than buildings—or "Looney Tunes." People still say such things, in fact. Yet the scale of the new buildings and their high-profile reception in the news media suggest that the architectural climate has changed. People now recognize not only that Gehry is an architect—one who can bring in a major project like the Guggenheim on time and on budget—but that his work is able to arouse a broad range of meanings, associations, and projections, not least in those who actively dislike it. The idea has gained wider acceptance that art and Looney-Tuneville actually speak to broad contemporary social and cultural norms. The real fruitcakes today may be those who persist in denying this.

Question for a Sunday afternoon: What is a masterpiece?

(a) Giò Ponti said that the architect's task is to interpret a community to itself. (b) Iris Murdoch wrote, "Serious art is a continuous working of meaning in the light of the discovery of some truth." (c) Diana Vreeland once described *Vogue* magazine as "the myth of the next reality." (d) All of the above. Answer: (d) All of the above. Add up these ideas, and you won't be far from a working definition of the ideal America's greatest architects have long aspired to.

Another question: What is a community at the end of the twentieth century? A focus group, a concentration camp, a chat room on the Internet, an address book, a dance club, all those afflicted with a particular incurable disease, a gender, an age bracket, a waiting room, owners of silver BMWs, organized crime, everyone who swears by a particular brand of painkiller, and a two-block stretch of Manhattan on any weekday at lunch hour.

Social fragmentation is one of the truths Frank Gehry has sought to explore in his work, not because he loves to see things fall apart but, on the contrary, because he seeks meaning in a culture that would otherwise dissolve all intelligence in a deluge of demographics. Truth No. 2: These differences are superficial. People need love and they need work. These are the places meaning comes from. Everything else is superfluous. Truth No. 3: Superfluous things are a hoot and a holler. Superficiality can be wonderful. The Myth of the Next Reality, aka Utopia, is that there is a place where differences and commonalities, unity and diversity, can be seen as the poles around which beauty revolves. The axis between these poles is called empathy.

That most divine of all human qualities—empathy—is the source of meaning in Frank Gehry's designs. His aim is not to found a school, not to create a style. Rather, he is possessed by the gaga nineteenth-century notion that by exercising their imaginations, artists can inspire others to use their own.

From the airport, you approach Bilbao through a hilly landscape that grows gradually more civilized with the brutal mess of urban industry. The road cuts through a valley: Bilbao and its river, the Nervión, suddenly appear, spread out like a dreamscape, far beneath what you took to be a low point of the land. Gehry's building, too, flashes briefly into view, its curving walls of titanium steel glinting an unmistakable welcome. Then the taxi plunges into the city and the river disappears, the museum vanishes and you are swallowed up by the streets of an unremarkable town.

This entrance should be considered part of Gehry's design. Consider, by contrast, the approach to the Metropolitan Museum in New York, where the ceremonial way is paved via Fifth Avenue, a blocklong Beaux Arts facade, a grand staircase. In Bilbao, the procession includes slag heaps, a decayed industrial riverfront, bridges, highway overpasses. The scene is neither sylvan nor classically urbane. But it strongly projects an image of the industrial power that drove the nineteenth-century city into being. That city is the wellspring of Frank Gehry's architecture. Often he wears the costume of a working-class hero: blue shirts, windbreakers, baggy slacks. Some have taken this for affectation. It isn't. Gehry is a man deeply ingrained with appreciation for the industrial city as the place where eighteenth-century theories of modern democracy were put into messy practice, the place where wits, nerve, work, education, and dreaming displaced ownership of land as the basis of the good life.

Gehry was born too late to be a builder of that city. His career, rather, has corresponded to—indeed epitomizes—the transformation of the industrial metropolis into the postindustrial urban center, the place where tourism and cultural enterprise are now expected to fill the void left by the exportation of factory production to the Third World. The standard remedy is: Send in the artists. Build a museum, a performing arts center; change the zoning regulations so that industrial buildings can be converted to artists' lofts. The theory is that, in a postindustrial society, factory production will be supplanted by more creative work—that instead of blue-collar workers, the city will become home to "symbolic analysts," to use Robert Reich's phrase. In practice, production has given way to consumption: franchise outlets for cookies, ice cream, T-shirts; the invasion of the urban center by the ethos of the suburban mall. There are worse alternatives. Also better ones.

Bilbao, Spain's fourth-largest city, was once a shipbuilding town. The Bilbao Guggenheim is part of an ambitious plan to retool the city as an international center of culture and finance. Other projects, in addition to the $100 million museum, include a new subway system with stations designed by Norman Foster and a new airport designed by Santiago Calatrava. The Guggenheim, which has been expanding its international operations since the appointment of Thomas Krens as director in 1988, reached an agreement to open the Bilbao branch six years ago. Two regional governments have underwritten the costs of constructing and operating it for at least twenty years. In exchange, the Guggenheim will provide use of its collection of modern and contemporary art, curatorial expertise, and prestige.

Krens, who worked closely with Gehry on the museum's design, has been frequently maligned by those who resent his global aspirations, his wheeler-dealer ways. But let the bean counters count beans, the gum chewers chew gum. As the patron of projects by Gehry, Arata Isozaki, Gae Aulenti, Zaha Hadid, and Hans Hollein, Krens has given architecture stronger support than any other American museum director in the past half century.

In July, I go to meet Gehry in Bilbao for a preview of the museum. "Do you want to see the building?" he asks, when we meet at my hotel. What a card. We walk along the Calle de Iparraguirre, which frames a vista of the building's central rotunda. It strikes me that that street's visual clutter— parked cars, traffic signs, lampposts—magnifies rather than distracts from the building's impression. The museum looks like nothing else, but nonetheless looks at home. Even the dotted line painted down the middle of the street and the stripes of the pedestrian crosswalk at the corner look somehow Gehry-fied, an accidental version of the lines Renaissance artists used with such precision in architectural drawings to highlight the new laws of visual perspective.

The rotunda, rising 138 feet above street level, is wrapped with voluptuous curves of steel clad in titanium panels. The eye takes in this vista more as a mass of gathered light than as a proper building. The darkness of the narrow street turns the metal's brightness into a retinal explosion. But the light is soft. The metal seems to absorb light as well as reflect it, like the dull side of a piece of tinfoil. The expanses of titanium, partly discolored by weathering, are changed in appearance by clouds and the location of the sun. The metal folds mount higher toward the rotunda's center, like the leaves of an artichoke with clipped tips.

A pillbox of metal and glass protrudes at a slight tilt from the top of this steel blossom. As we walk toward the building, Gehry says that he now regrets this feature: "It looks like a pimple. But I guess it's OK for a face to have a pimple." On closer approach, a wing of more conventional dimensions slips into a view. It is boxy, as modern buildings were once supposed to be, and contains suites of classical galleries. The wing's rectangular contour serves as a foil, so to speak, for the foil. It is clad in honey-colored limestone. Light bounces back and forth between stone and metal as if within the facets of crystal embedded in rock.

A reverse grand staircase—funnel-shaped, it descends instead of rising—pours you into the building, leading you into the great spatial surprise of the museum's atrium. Even if you entered at ground level, the atrium would be a marvel. Contained spaces can seem immensely more vast than their containers—think of Frank Lloyd Wright's Guggenheim or New York's Grand Central Terminal. But because the staircase Gehry has designed draws you down a full story below ground level, the atrium pitches you into an enclosed version of the state of surreality that overtakes you on entering Bilbao. Pinch yourself, but don't wake up. It's better just to dream this.

The atrium offers a distilled concentration of the building's material vocabulary. Stone, glass, titanium, curves, straight lines, opacity, transparency, openness, and enclosure are brought into sensuous conjunction.

You may think, as you stand within this space, that the Tower of Babel story was a myth concocted by people who were afraid of diversity. Here you see that many languages can not only coexist but also babble around within a broad and vibrant vista of the world.

Galleries stretch out from the atrium in a variety of shapes and sizes. Two wings contain classically rectangular, if overscaled, galleries that open off one another in the traditional linear enfilade. Rubens's gigantic allegorical paintings of Marie de' Medici, one of the Louvre's finest treasures, would look fabulous here. The symmetrical form of the galleries is partly masked by the exterior's metal whorls and also by the petal shapes of the galleries clustered round them. By now you get the point that something is being said here on behalf of irregularity. Hurtling off in a third direction, parallel to the riverfront, is the most dramatic of the galleries, a 433-foot-long tube of space: a tunnel or internal boulevard. Gehry calls it "the boat." As you proceed along it, there are shifts in scale and contour, as there might be on a city street. The ceiling, supported by giant, white trusses, drops in a swift decline from an outlandishly high eighty-five feet to less than half that. The walls contract; the acoustics change.

The show doesn't end here. It continues outside, where the exit to the riverfront is even more ceremonially grand than the building's entrance. A metal canopy, held aloft by a single slender column, seems to billow in the breeze ninety-two feet above the ground, and the entire riverfront facade looks windswept. Toward the right, a city bridge slips over a corner of the building, the roadway forking into two overpasses as it makes contact. Then, on the bridge's far side, the building flares up into a pair of steel towers, their arcs echoing, in vertical form, the fork in the road.

The towers are clad on three sides only, revealing the metal framework within. Though containing no usable spaces, they are not functionless. They enable the museum to be seen along the river and from the city's downtown. Like the Twin Towers in New York, they are symbols of themselves. And they are also emblematic of Gehry's intention to merge with urban infrastructure. In the past, Gehry has often used building skins as wrappers, surfaces that part to reveal the volume within. Here he has used three-dimensional forms to wrap his arms around a city.

At the time of my visit, only one artwork had been installed, Richard Serra's *Snake*. Perhaps it is not possible to evaluate the building without considering the question of how well it functions as a showcase for art. It may be, however, that one of this building's major functions is to live that question through. Over time, people will judge how well or how badly the museum displays individual works of art. But these judgments may well be shaped by the increasing awareness that art resides only partly within individual artworks. It also lives in the spirit of risk and experimentation that works of art help sustain. This awareness is a central characteristic of the postindustrial city, as well as a theme of contemporary art. Art has spilled out of its classical containers into performance, the media, fashion, and other ephemeral forms of expression. By the same token, at least since the advent of conceptual art, the task for many artists has been not only to create objects but also to escape their confining dimensions.

The Bilbao Guggenheim is an object, of course, however skillfully Gehry has intertwined the museum with the city around it. Still, inside and out, it's a spectacular embodiment of the tension between objects and the world beyond them. Within these far-from-neutral galleries, artworks will inevitably be drawn into complex relationships with the architecture and with one another. Outside, the design overflows any ordinary conception of what a museum, or any building, should resemble. Like the Basque region, this building is a place of contested borders.

Gehry says that, like many young architects, he started out wanting to change the world. He was concerned with city planning, social justice, a more equitable environment. Yet he has managed to effect change on a scale few architects achieve.

In Los Angeles in 1983, Gehry took a service station for municipal vehicles and converted it into the Temporary Contemporary museum [now The Geffen Contemporary at MOCA], a building that declared an end to the city's sense of cultural inferiority far more effectively than Arata Isozaki's permanent Museum of Contemporary Art. The Temporary's shrewd and gritty informality told Los Angelenos that an architectural intelligence of unequaled stature was one of their own.

Gehry's impact has been on consciousness, that is to say, not just particular parcels of land. And in the postindustrial city, it may no longer be possible to divorce consciousness from material reality. What was once the radical outlook of Surrealism has become part of the logic of everyday life. Ideas, images, and illusions now occupy the places once held by sweaters, ball bearings, and vacuum tubes.

Several weeks ago, when I was visiting Los Angeles, Gehry said, "You know, I wasn't supposed to be this." Meaning, I suppose, this big honcho. Or this big Looney Tune. I didn't press him to say how he used to think his life would turn out. I didn't want to force him to be falsely modest, or even genuinely so. But it must be scary to find people looking at you and writing about you as a person who has changed an art form and in the process is changing a culture. I imagine that sometimes Gehry must feel like the movie director Marcello Mastroianni plays in Fellini's *8 ½*, when, during the news conference scene, he tries to crawl under the table to get away as one of the reporters cackles with glee: "He has nothing to say! Nothing to say!"

In one sense, in fact, Gehry does have nothing to say. His language is architecture, not words. Though Gehry actually writes with beautiful clarity and his lectures have become extraordinary pieces of stand-up humor, he distrusts words. He lives on the opposite side of the world from architects like Peter Eisenman who feel that they cannot proceed safely into the world unless armored with academic jargon.

The first time I visited Gehry's Santa Monica office, I had to fight off a feeling of awkwardness because he was so taciturn. Basically, he just guided me around, pausing here and there to point out and just barely identify a model for a new project or a sample of materials. Since I was there to learn, I took Gehry's silence as part of the lesson. I sensed he felt that words have the power to limit, and therefore to exclude. People can make their own pictures.

Gehry sometimes does put labels on buildings, but usually these are like jokes or pet names. (In Prague, there's Fred and Ginger.) Rarely, he will include a form that's explicitly metaphoric: in Paris, there's a series of glass panels, jutting out at different angles, that are meant to be a symbol of the openness of American culture and of France's receptivity to the United States. More typically, a figurative element will turn up transformed into an abstraction. Once I mentioned to Gehry that part of his design for the Walt Disney Concert Hall in Los Angeles reminded me of the scalloped side of a bass viol. He wasn't dismayed that the source of an abstract shape had been recognized. He said, "You know, I have been looking at that!"

Fools give you reasons. Wise men never try. An architecture critic has no choice but to be foolish on this occasion, however. If a critic wants to say that the Bilbao Guggenheim is, in effect, a Lourdes for a crippled culture, then some kind of case must be made.

The Bilbao Guggenheim is approached through time as well as space: to get there, the visitor passes through history and geography both. This building's design and construction have coincided with the waning of a period when American architecture spectacularly lost its way.

Postmodernism, "with its sad air of the parade's gone by," in Arlene Croce's choice phrase, started out as a constructive movement. In the mid-1960s, a few architects set out to educate themselves about the history of an art form that a Bauhaus-influenced education had plowed under. Gifted architects like Robert Venturi, Aldo Rossi, and Charles Moore used these ideas to free themselves from the strangulating orthodoxies of the modern movement. This period lasted for ten years. By the mid-1980s, the movement had deteriorated into a career strategy for reactionaries, opportunists, and their deeply uncultivated promoters. These people had spent, maybe, a summer vacation in Europe and somehow arrived at the belief that this experience entitled them to be spokesmodels for the Great Western Tradition. Even without the help of the Disney company, architecture plummeted into the realm of the packaged tour.

Postmodernism gained architects aesthetic freedom. Few made good use of it. Despite intermittent creative flashes, the movement overall resembled a shelf of Harlequin romance novels pretentiously mislabeled as literature. I think of the past twenty years as the Franziska Schanz-kowska period of American architecture, in honor of the Polish factory worker who jumped into a Berlin canal and resurfaced moments later as the Grand Duchess Anastasia.

Like Schanzkowska, many Postmodernists were inspired dreamers and schemers, but their movement bore no more relation to history than Schanzkowska did to the Romanovs. Instead, it pandered to people's fear of history, holding out the delusion that they could step out of their own life and times.

One reason people have descended on Bilbao with such hope is that with this building, American architecture has jumped back into the present with a splash. This antique art form has made it. It has come through. And so has the consensus of informed opinion that once made it possible to say, This is better than that.

It can take a while for an event to work its way into consciousness. After my first visit to the building, I went back to the hotel to write notes. It was early evening and starting to rain. I took a break to look out the window and saw a woman standing alone outside a bar across the street. She was wearing a long, white dress with matching white pumps, and she carried a pearlescent handbag. Was her date late? Had she been stood up?

When I looked back a bit later, she was gone. And I asked myself, Why can't a building capture a moment like that? Then I realized that the reason I'd had that thought was that I'd just come from such a building. And that the building I'd just come from was the reincarnation of Marilyn Monroe.

There's a scene in *The Misfits* in which she goes out to Eli Wallach's unfinished house in the Nevada desert, to try the house, the desert, and her future on for size. "I can go in and I can come out—I can go in and I can come out," Monroe cries with delight, after some cinder blocks were put down where the front step is supposed to be. Wallach points to the unadorned balloon frame: "This was gonna be another bedroom." Monroe says wistfully, "It's even nice this way."

What twins the actress and the building in my memory is that both of them stand for an American style of freedom. That style is voluptuous, emotional, intuitive, and exhibitionist. It is mobile, fluid, material, mercurial, fearless, radiant, and as fragile as a newborn child. It can't resist doing a dance with all the voices that say "No." It wants to take up a lot of space. And when the impulse strikes, it likes to let its dress fly up in the air.

What was Monroe's secret for looking sexy on film? Maybe she took her acting teacher's advice and thought about Frank Sinatra and a Coke. What does Frank Gehry think about when he is coaxing these mercurial images out of his mind? He could be thinking about a fish. In interviews, the architect has said that as a child his schoolmates called him Fish. It seems that his grandmother used to prepare gefilte fish in the bathtub of the apartment where he grew up and that the scent clung to his skin. True or not, the fish has been a recurring image in Gehry's work for many years. He has designed lamps, restaurants, even bus stops in the form of fish. The panels of metal and stone applied to the surface of the Guggenheim adhere to the overlapping pattern of scales.

Gehry and Monroe never met. But for a period of time they reclined on the same couch; consulted the same analyst, anyhow. Even without knowing that, you recognize that Bilbao is a sanctuary of free association. It's a bird, it's a plane, it's Superman. It's a ship, an artichoke, the miracle of the rose. A first glimpse of the building tells you that the second glimpse is going to be different from the first. A second glimpse tells you that a third is going to be different still. If there is an order to this architecture, it is not one that can be predicted from one or two visual slices of its precisely calculated free-form geometry. But the building's spirit of freedom is hard to miss.

You can go in, and you can come out. The interplay between in and out has been a recurring theme of architecture for the past century. The open floor plan of Frank Lloyd Wright. The primary colors and forms of Theo van Doesburg. The glass curtain walls of Ludwig Mies van der Rohe. Twentieth-century architecture has unfolded as a series of variations on the relationship between the interior and exterior of buildings, bodies, minds—between public and private realms. Gehry extends this tradition into an era when communications technology is further shifting the boundaries between public and private space, and when an awareness of psychology has permeated and transformed the dynamics of public and private life. But his means of extending that tradition are not the same as those of the classical modernists. Instead of trying to further reduce architectural form to the bare minimum, he has gone deeper into the psychological space where images are formed and farther out into the city that helps to shape them.

I realized on that first visit to Gehry's office that his designs offer few clues to the inner recesses of the architect's mind. Rather, they are an invitation for viewers to explore their own. His main preoccupation is with subtly adjusting the relationships among the forms he employs. Mine is to learn why, upon leaving his Guggenheim, a forty-nine-year-old architecture critic might suddenly find himself speaking in the voice of Marilyn Monroe. Her presence in Bilbao is totally my projection. Gehry's delight in arousing such responses, however, is genuine.

Titanium is tough. But it's a piece of Kleenex compared with the mind of an introvert who has learned to function in extroverted ways. Isn't this the great lesson of all art museums? Even if you only think of them as excellent places to cruise, you get the basic idea. For an hour or so, you get to share the same space with a group of strangers. As you can see for yourself from the stuff on the walls, the possibilities are endless.

That is not the kind of contact that architecture ordinarily encourages. This is not a field in which introverts easily flourish. But occasionally power and imagination join hands; the Guggenheim Museum effected such a union half a century ago when it hired Frank Lloyd Wright to design its building on Fifth Avenue. It has done so once again with its new building in Bilbao.

It's not so tough for painters or sculptors to project empathy into the world. That's what the public expects from artists, after all. Ah, yes, artists, such sensitive souls, so creative and tragic. And now it's Sunday. We will go to a museum and peer into their troubled souls. And then have brunch. Bloody Mary or mimosa? But when empathy enters into architecture, a milestone has been reached. An art form that has long depended upon appeals to external authority—history, science, context, tradition, religion, philosophy, or style—has at last come to the realization that nobody cares about that sort of thing anymore. Architecture has stepped off her pedestal. She's waiting for her date outside a bar on a rainy early evening in Bilbao, Spain.

The Bilbao Guggenheim is cause for collective pride. If one lesson can be salvaged from the painted desert in which American architecture has been stranded in recent years, it is this: When a culture lets itself settle for anything less than great, there's no telling how low it will sink. Nor is it easy to recognize the moment when the rot sets in. Architecture, no less than politics, is an art of the possible. The field has almost infinite tolerance for those who want to rob space of decency and meaning.

Here's the saving grace. We know what it's like to feel fully alive. The feeling may not happen often, but when it does, we're there. It can happen at the movies, watching baseball, while dancing, in love, at the beach, on a street, in the company of others, or in perfect solitude. However long it lasts, it's an undeniable fact. It's not a theory, not a yearning for the unattainable. It's a real reason to scream. Lose composure. Throw hats into the air. It's a victory for all when any one of us finds a path into freedom, as Frank Gehry has this year in Bilbao, and beyond.

September 7, 1997

IT'S DARK. IT'S SCARY. IT'S YOUR GARAGE.

There are no second stories in American houses. Not, at least, in the classic postwar suburban ranch house, the prototype of modern living that millions have called home. For who among us is willing to place ourselves above our cars? As the French critic Roland Barthes observed, cars today are the exact equivalent of great Gothic cathedrals: "I mean the supreme creation of an era, conceived with passion by unknown artists, and consumed in image if not in usage by a whole population, which appropriates them as purely magical objects." It would be sacrilegious, in other words, to tower over the antenna.

Garages are not cathedrals, but they are undeniably Gothic. The garage is a spooky place, all dark shadows, dampness, and danger. As a building type, it is the antithesis of everything the car represents. It is windowless and motionless. The top doesn't come down. The radio does not blare. If the car drives our dreams of freedom, the garage fuels claustrophobic nightmares.

Filmmakers have long used the garage as a suitably gloomy setting for gothic goings-on. Consider the opening scene in Blake Edwards's 1962 movie, *Experiment in Terror,* when Lee Remick finds herself trapped in her own Marin County garage with the silhouette of an asthmatic extortionist played by Ross Martin. Martin's labored breathing is like the voice of the garage itself: suffocating; airless; the hoarse, vocal version of exhaust fumes. Or, in an urban twist, think of the dark and threatening Washington garage where Robert Redford meets the shadowy Deep Throat in *All the President's Men.*

The generic, archetypal garage, however, is suburban. I don't drive, so I have a certain amount of sympathy for this poor, arrested structure, stopped forever at a red light while the traffic of life passes it by. And I am acutely conscious of the great suburban deception that the garage is an appendage to the house.

The truth is that it's the other way around. The single-family, four-bedroom house is essentially a chauffeur's quarters, cut happily adrift from any mansion.

Residential architecture goes to some lengths to conceal this dependent relationship. If a side of the garage faces the street, there might be a false window, complete with shutters. House and garage will be clad in the same siding, as if the car's quarters were a bedroom wing. The front lawn, a driveway beautification program, softens the machine-age forces that created the suburb and keep it humming along.

It would be wonderful, I think, if residential architecture conveyed its dependence on car culture more truthfully. Instead of the false window, why not a wall of glass and atmospheric lighting to display the car's lines to full advantage?

In fact, throughout this century, several notable architects have tried to bring the house and the car into congruent relationship. Frank Lloyd Wright, the progenitor of the American ranch house, said the carport was his invention. True or not, he had the right idea. Wright wanted the individual American home to be seen as part of something collective: the decentralized metropolis he called Broadacre City.

The carport made that connection explicit: it displayed the car in a state of readiness, sheltered from sun and rain but not screened from public view. It offered the symbolic message that in the decentered city the car is the maker of context. It supplied the physical linkages once provided by the matching cornice lines, similarities of scale, and facade treatments of the traditional city street.

In 1981, SITE, a New York design firm, unveiled a project that could be easily adapted to express the codependence of domestic architecture and the car. Highrise of Homes was conceived as a ten-story structure of steel and concrete, with a central elevator and service core. Each floor was divided into parcels to be sold independently and developed by each owner. In effect, each floor is a suburban street, the entire complex a suburban subdivision, with a shopping mall at ground floor.

A parking garage occupies the tower's three-story base, but visually the entire high-rise reads as a parking garage, a set of platforms in which houses are displayed as if they occupied long-term spaces. SITE conceived the project for an urban center, but one could envision it as a suburban development—like Seaside, a planned community—for those reluctant to choose between center-city density and suburban sprawl.

In 1990, the New York firm Diller and Scofidio designed another visionary project in which the garage was reconceived. The Slow House, a vacation home in the Hamptons commissioned by an art collector, was an exploration of vision and the cultural devices that frame our view of the world: the car windshield, the television screen, the picture window. Foundations for the building were laid, but the design, which won a Progressive Architecture award in 1991, was never completed.

. . .

The horn-shaped house would have overlooked a classic ocean vista. The architects themselves described the project as a door leading to a window. Indeed, the picture-window view, though outside the owner's property lines, was treated as the building's most valuable asset. For the architects, the design did not begin at the front door. It began, rather, in the city, where the owner climbed into his car and sat before the windshield, a device through which images of the decentered city would unfold.

The garage was conceived as an automotive docking station, a place for the car to roll in and gain its first glimpse of the water, the windshield aligned with a miniature version of the picture window inside the house itself. The sides of the garage were to be made of glass, another form of framing, to display the vehicle of weekend escape.

The point is that architects have seen in the garage, this lowly building type, the potential to reckon imaginatively with a force that in many ways has been so destructive of traditional urban values. James Wines, the chief designer at SITE, once wrote about the need for architecture to deliver its message to people traveling sixty miles an hour. The garage awaits new interpretations of a mobile society that, now and then, stops.

October 16, 1997

A MIDAS OF THE GOLD
(YES, I DO MEAN GOLD) CUDGEL

Bad timing? Or tasteless publicity stunt? Over the weekend, copies of Donald Trump's irresistibly scrappy new book, *The Art of the Comeback*, arrived in bookstores, while city officials slapped a stop-work order on Riverside South, the residential complex Mr. Trump is developing on the Upper West Side of Manhattan. A coincidence, surely, that the project contained defective concrete. Still, it's a measure of Mr. Trump's power to inspire lurid fantasies that one might fleetingly imagine otherwise. Did he order up a batch of bad concrete just to sell a book?

For Mr. Trump, in any case, there can be no comeback without controversy. In fact, of all the civic arts, contention is the one he has most brilliantly mastered. With it, this unusual man has given New York more delirious pleasure than any public figure of his generation.

Real estate and architecture are two different things, but even the most uninspired real estate is a powerful shaper of urban form. There are those who say that Mr. Trump is not a real real estate developer—that he is not in a class with the Tishmans, the Rudins, and the other New York families who have been in the business forever without claiming more than their share of limelight. But he is top dog in the wave-making business, and wave making is, if anything, more vital than real estate in the shaping of urban life. That's why I count myself a fan.

Periodically, Mr. Trump phones up and urges me, in the most charming way, to revisit his Trump International Hotel and Tower on Columbus Circle. I wrote a story on the building when it was under construction. He considered the story negative, though I didn't intend it that way. I compared the building to Andy Warhol's *Gold Marilyn Monroe*, a wonderful painting in the collection of the Museum of Modern Art. As it happens, the painting was donated to the museum by Mr. Trump's architect, Philip Johnson.

I suspect that the issue here may have more to do with power than architectural aesthetics. Can an architecture critic be cajoled into eating his words? Will I at least admit that the building's glass skin is not gold, as I had written, but bronze?

No problem. John Ruskin felt that he had never covered a subject completely until he had contradicted himself at least six times, so I don't mind saying that, whatever the color is called, the finished building does do magical things with changing light. But a critic would be doing the man an injustice if all he did was haul out superlatives. Mr. Trump grasps as well as anyone that conflict is a great city's most important cultural product. "With what pleasure one would applaud Stravinsky on the cheeks of one's neighbors," as Jean Cocteau described controversy at the premiere of *The Rite of Spring*.

The building will always look gold to me, just as the glass at the Seagram Building will always look bronze, even though Philip Johnson, who helped design that building, too, insists that the Seagram's glass is actually pink. I picked it out myself, the architect says. A pink Seagram? Sounds like a cocktail. And the Columbus Circle building will always stand as a symbol of the man who plays the role of Midas in the popular imagination. People have said that Mr. Trump has no inner life, that he does everything for show. On the contrary, the man is nothing but inner life. But he wears his deepest impulses as if they were business attire, which in his case they probably are. Biggest. Tallest. Richest. Best. Greatest. Top. I look forward to the day when those primal instincts find full expression in the design of his buildings, not just in the pride he takes in owning and constructing them.

As the architect Diana Agrest has said, the city is the subconscious of architecture. More buildings should let the fantasy pop through. Stanford White let classicism rip. Frank Lloyd Wright, Wallace K. Harrison, Eero Saarinen, and, yes, Philip Johnson often fed their designs on dreams. In Mr. Trump's case, the lion's share of the fantasy gets eaten up by the man himself.

But Trump Taj Mahal, the opulent casino on the Atlantic City boardwalk, does tap into something infernal and divine. The domes, the arches, the crystal chandeliers, the electronic whistles, the golden moldings, the change carts, the one-way mirrored ceilings, the surveillance cameras, the cards, the money: this is a rationally orchestrated form of madness, as are the fights that take place in the adjacent arena.

Ding! Out comes Hector (Macho) Camacho, dressed in an animal-skin loincloth, and, from the other corner, an older boxer who takes a pounding. Blood spurts. The crowd screams, "Stop the fight!" The odd mix of bloodlust and compassion evokes a pagan religion. Showgirls in bathing suits sashay around the ring, holding up cards with the number of each round. Someone says, "Joe DiMaggio is here."

But what are we doing inside this darkened room, when there is the Atlantic Ocean outside, and the boardwalk, and what's left of Steel Pier? All this spoiled innocence. Mr. Trump tried to revive the Diving Horse, Steel Pier's star attraction, but animal-rights activists stopped him, and he's the first to admit that the poor beast never voluntarily took the plunge. So we will go and eat saltwater taffy, and maybe get up a game of miniature golf. If it's raining, we will sit by the window and play Monopoly, gaze at the horizon, and remember the days when any child could buy sparklers in red, green, silver, and gold.

November 5, 1997

A MOUNTAINTOP TEMPLE WHERE ART'S FUTURE WORSHIPS ITS PAST

It is ribbon-cutting time at the Getty Center, Los Angeles's stupendous new castle of classical beauty. At the end of this week, the Getty Center will lower the drawbridge, raise the portcullis, and throw open the gates, figuratively speaking. At last the public will get to see what fifteen years, a billion dollars, and the imagination of Richard Meier, the architect, have wrought in the name of J. Paul Getty and in the name of art.

A work of this size and complexity is not easy to grasp, much less grade. Even a critic who has paid regular visits to the site since bulldozers began pushing the dirt around in 1987 can agreeably lose his way among the buildings, gardens, and terraces that adorn the Getty Center's 110-acre mountaintop. Still, the basic ingredients of this complex can be summarized briefly: nineteenth-century concept, twentieth-century design, twenty-first-century city. The Getty Center is distilled from these three slices of time. It is an old-fashioned museum, housed within a scrupulously modern set of buildings, pitched high above a city that has seldom shown a strong inclination to shoulder the weight of cultural memory.

The distillation is not smooth. Should it be? Los Angeles is not a smooth city. It is tied together by a network of monumental fissures called freeways. Its citizens contend with quakes. They seldom venture into public unless armored by cars against contact with others.

In the last decade, the Getty Center has opened up a new set of fissures in the city's cultural life. It has divided public opinion about its mission, site, and design and its meaning for the future of the city it overlooks.

Critics say that the place is overbearing. That it's too detached from the city and its cultural needs. That it would have been better to build it downtown or to apportion its various units among different neighborhoods. That the center's advance reservations policy and limited parking will restrict public access. That even the crisp abstract geometry of its architecture indicates an arrogant refusal to engage.

These issues will not be settled anytime soon. Meanwhile, the Getty should take pride in arousing discontent. By doing so, it has already changed the culture of Los Angeles. It has given this culturally laid-back city something to fight about.

The Getty Center is the creation of the Getty Trust, a foundation created in 1982 with a $700 million bequest from the oil billionaire J. Paul Getty. The center brings together on one campus the major divisions operated by the trust. Of these the best known is the J. Paul Getty Museum, whose power of acquisition has caused curators and museum directors worldwide to turn green. The original Getty Museum, housed in a Roman villa in Malibu, California, will continue as a showcase for the museum's collection of classical antiquities.

A Marble Mountain as the Pieces Come Together

In 1984, after an international search, the trust hired Richard Meier to design what was widely called the commission of the century. But when dreams like this come true, who needs nightmares?

In his new book, *Building the Getty*, Mr. Meier recounts his contretemps with vigilant groups in the Brentwood neighborhood, overbearing trustees, stubborn landscape designers, and other tribulations. Beyond these, the architect had to cope with the pressures that go with such a monumental project: demands on his time, the envy of colleagues, performance anxiety, the isolation inevitably thrust on those who undertake any work of unprecedented scale and public responsibility.

Above all, Mr. Meier and Michael J. Palladino, the project's architect, had to deal with a fabulous sore thumb of a site. The Getty sits atop a western slope of the Sepulveda Pass, where the San Diego Freeway plunges through the Santa Monica mountains. When you're up there, the site is glorious but, from beneath, the complex casts a medieval shadow. We're above criticism, the Getty seems to announce; we're up too high to hear it. And, anyhow, whoever likes the people who live in the fancy house on the hill?

Let's climb it. Or, rather, board the tram for the five-minute ride that conveys visitors from the Getty garage to the Center itself. How shocking it is to be riding in Los Angeles in a vehicle that almost resembles public transportation. This collective vehicular experience is perhaps even more amazing than the views of the hills. Despite the trappings of modern convenience, we're on our way to see something ancient: the treasure chest, the civic storehouse with which a city dramatizes its superiority over other cities by amassing artworks created by other cities.

This game has been going on since our ancestors lived in caves. Yet it wasn't until the nineteenth century that this archaic sign of power was transformed into the enlightened form of the encyclopedic museum with its classical architecture, exalted location, imposing enfilades.

The Getty may well be the last of a genre typified by the Louvre, the Metropolitan, the Kunsthistorisches Museum in Vienna. Although it seems as if we're riding the subway, actually we're ascending the world's longest flight of marble steps, an electric version of the grand staircases that in classical museums symbolize the ascent to Parnassus.

When we reach the top and leave the tram, metaphor becomes material. In place of hillside chaparral, we behold a mountain of marble: enough travertine to clad a chain of Campidoglios. You never saw a more beautifully cut stone, nor a stone that proclaims so frankly that it has been installed strictly for your viewing pleasure. Mounted over concrete, the travertine panels perform no structural function, as you can clearly grasp from the gaps between them. Set off by contrasting walls of ivory metal panels and broad expanses of glass, the rough-surfaced stone takes the light like jewelry.

To the right ascends a marble staircase of such monumental splendor that it would be uncivil to call it anything but *un grand escalier*. It rises to the museum's front door. We will resist the temptation to go inside, however. Instead, we will walk around the grounds, then visit the museum, then stroll around outside for a second look. It takes more than one viewing before the Getty's pieces begin to add up.

We now find ourselves in a garden of Euclidean delights, a plot of land dedicated to the cultivation of squares, cubes, arcs, cylinders, and grids, relieved by the occasional biomorphic curve. These shapes have been gathered together in the form of six buildings, of which the Getty Museum is by far the largest. There are also two administration buildings, the Research Institute for the History of Art and the Humanities, an auditorium, and a restaurant. Ranging from two to three stories (to limit the height, additional floors have been placed below ground level), the structures are surrounded by gardens, plazas, and fountains.

In theory, if not in fact, the division of the complex into six buildings mitigates the center's monumental effect. Each of the six structures is further fragmented formally by balconies, windows, cuts through the walls, canopies, subscreens, elevator shafts, and stairs. These strongly sculptured forms convey structure and function, while capturing and modulating space and light. The result resembles three-dimensional collage, recalling pioneering modernist experiments by El Lissitzky and Theo van Doesburg.

Other whiffs of architectural history filter through. The 1930s villas of Le Corbusier. Fallingwater. Wright's textile block houses of the 1920s. Walter Gropius's Palace of Soviets. The strong geometry of the buildings and the overall grid on which they sit may also put us in mind of the plans for ideal cities conceived in the climate of Renaissance humanism.

A Modern Classic: An Entryway to the Mind

This lineage is apt. Mr. Meier wants to remind visitors that Southern California architecture is not limited to the pop vernacular of Egyptian movie palaces, streamlined apartment buildings, and Googie coffee shops. Wright, Richard Neutra, Rudolph Schindler, and Charles and Ray Eames also worked there, producing buildings whose aesthetic rigor sets them well apart from pop stereotypes. Mr. Meier wants to extend that tradition into the present.

In fact, what Mr. Meier has created here is a symphonic set of variations on the classical elements of twentieth-century structure. Rotation. Rhythm. The interplay between solid and void, transparency and opacity, curved and orthogonal forms. The cantilever. The module. The grid. The Getty Center is a summation, and a masterly one. Conventional modern forms join more traditional architectural devices stripped down to their naked modern skins.

The critic Michael Sorkin once wrote a story to the effect that modern architecture has been a staging ground for Earth's venture into outer space. But at the Getty you gain the sense that modernism has also been a preparation for the voyage into inner space. This may be one reason the art museum has become the paradigmatic building type of our time.

It's not so easy to enter into the life of the mind, but the Getty offers a thoughtful preparation. Even before you go into the galleries, the abstract quality of the architecture has inducted you into the world of ideas. And the ethereal light of the mountaintop helps clear the brain. From the terraces, you see a long ribbon of skyscrapers unrolling from east to west. This is Wilshire Boulevard. But when the day is hazy, as it usually is, you may find yourself imagining that the boulevard is the final stretch of some grand transcontinental avenue, a North American axis extending from coast to coast.

Then the Getty may strike you as the embodiment of an idea that has been dragged cross-country, becoming more and more abstract as it proceeds west. There is enough Roman stone to remind you that this is a European idea, a privileged, aristocratic idea. But the stone has been carved into panels of such thinness that it looks like a memory of all the old marble left behind.

By the time you're ready to enter the museum lobby, you may be too spoiled to appreciate it. This glass rotunda is one of the world's greatest spaces, ho-hum. But you're entitled to a moment to catch your breath.

The scale of the galleries is intimate. The upper portion of their walls slopes inward to form a square funnel shape, like the interior of a mansard roof. Natural light radiates softly downward. You have the impression that you are not simply stepping up to a painting but preparing to walk inside it.

There are ridiculous moments. A society decorator, Thierry Despont, was hired to install a series of period rooms. This stuff might have been better left by the roadside somewhere east of Wichita, Kansas. But the period rooms do have the virtue of reminding us why modern architecture had to be invented and has not gone out of style. Who has time to dust? But Mr. Despont has chosen good colors for the walls of the painting galleries.

The collection stops at 1900, at the threshold of the century in which abstract art flourished. But in the final painting, James Ensor's *Christ's Entry into Brussels in 1889*, figuration is already dissolving and faces have become masks. It's an ideal image to contemplate before stepping outside to confront the twentieth century and the impending twenty-first.

Los Angeles has long had a problem balancing nature and culture. Historically, nature has been the city's main attraction: the sun, the sea, the palms, the tans, the option to live out of doors. About culture the city has been more ambivalent. It's not even certain that it wants to be a city. "Ignorance," as Oscar Wilde's Lady Bracknell says, "is like a delicate exotic fruit. Touch it, and the bloom is gone." How will all this art and high culture affect the lifeguards on *Baywatch*?

A Role for Nature: Problems of Logic and of Fauna

The Getty hasn't done too well with nature. Landscaping, which includes contributions by Dan Kiley, Laurie Olin, and Robert Irwin, is by far the Center's weakest element. Some of it, like the cactus garden designed by Mr. Olin, just looks silly. The truncated cone atop which the cactuses are set looks like a cast-off from the Albany Mall. The sloping hillside, planted with three thousand California live oaks in a rigid grid formation, carries us back to the tortured topiary gardens of the ancien régime. The logic behind the landscaping is clear: the design extends the architecture's abstraction out onto the earth. But the logic is wrong. This should be a place for nature's patterns to express themselves.

There are some good features in the landscape, especially the pools set into the stone. But the overall effect falls far short of Mr. Meier's aim to integrate architecture and nature. Domination, not integration, is the impression here.

A few months ago, Mr. Meier invited a few people to join him at the Getty Center to watch the sunset. In the late afternoon, the place is a miracle. The great California light spills down on your body, into your eyes. It gets more and more golden, and by twilight you're having a pure Apollo moment. The rough surface of the travertine picks up and intensifies the light, until it seems that energy is turning into matter.

As he was leaving, Mr. Meier noticed that his group had been joined by four deer. They were feeding on one of the Getty's small but verdant gardens. When the group approached, the deer gamboled away. But at some point in the evening, the animals must have returned. By morning, the garden had been gobbled up. This struck me as an allegory for where the Getty now stands.

Park designers use the term *desire lines* to describe tracks carved into the grass by those who don't follow the paths. The Getty is going to have to acquire some desire lines. Not only in its gardens but in its sense of identity. It shouldn't be satisfied with allowing the city to come to it. It should also discover the city.

Of course, the Getty can afford to roll out new gardens every time the deer come to dinner. And it is serenely well placed to keep the rest of the city at bay for as long as it likes. Perhaps it is best to keep in mind that its opening is the beginning of a process as well as the conclusion of one. Construction is over; a new phase of interaction begins.

Hungry fauna and carping critics are both part of this process. In time, criticism of the Getty will be appreciated as one of the its major contributions to the city's cultural life. The debate may alter the city's cultural ecology even more extensively than the Getty itself. It has taken almost a generation to build this place. It may take another generation before the place settles into its own cracks. This elongated sense of time is another of the Getty's gifts. In the city of rapid change and cultural acceleration, here's a clear statement of the idea that art is worth slowing down for.

December 1, 1997

LEADING LIGHTS, WHOSE DESTINY WAS TO BE DIMMED

Paul Rudolph and Aldo Rossi, two giants of twentieth-century architecture, died in 1997. Rudolph and Rossi belonged to different generations. They were of different nationalities. Aesthetically, their work was poles apart.

But the careers of these two men traced a similar arc through time. Both endured a blazing moment of commanding influence. Then, the moment passed. For a time, in the 1960s, it was Rudolph, Rudolph, Rudolph. Ten years later, it was Rossi, Rossi, Rossi. After that, the void.

The ebbing of these two architects' public stature is a part of the legacy each left behind. The trajectories of their careers illuminate the ongoing crisis in evaluation that has enlivened and deformed architecture for the last half century. Was their later work really so bad? Was their early work overvalued? Why do we sacrifice artists who reach for transcendence from within a material world? Or do they immolate themselves?

In the mid-1960s, Rudolph was the man to watch. Of all American architects living at that time, only Louis I. Kahn was held in higher esteem. Born in 1918, Rudolph established his reputation with a series of small houses in Florida. The best of these, never built, he called the Open and Shut House. A variation on California's seminal Case Study dwellings of the postwar years, the Open and Shut house was one of the first designs to inject psychology into modern architecture's rigorously rational and objective state of mind. A three-dimensional frame fitted with shades, the house was a study in the relationship between voyeurism and exhibitionism. Who's looking? Who's showing off? It depends on your point of view.

In 1957 Rudolph became dean of Yale University's School of Art and Architecture, a position he held until 1965. In those years, Yale was the most advanced patron of architecture in the United States. The campus was studded with buildings by Kahn, Eero Saarinen, Gordon Bunshaft, and Kevin Roche. Two of Rudolph's buildings enhanced the school's reputation. His Temple Street parking garage, a dynamic horizontal composition of concrete, was the first design since Frank Lloyd Wright's that sought to create a place of dignity for the car. Rudolph's Art and Architecture Building, also of concrete, was esteemed for the striking contrast between its aggressive, Brutalist exterior and the deftly modulated flow of its interiors.

Now, if you happened to be the best and brightest architect in the United States in the mid-1960s, then it went without saying that you were the greatest in the world. It was taken for granted in the postwar decades that the torch of creativity had passed from Europe to the United States. Progressive American architects illustrated this passage by freely cribbing from European precedent. Hence, Rudolph's parking garage owed a clear debt to the German Expressionist Erich Mendelsohn. His Art and Architecture Building was an almighty hallelujah to Le Corbusier.

But Rudolph borrowed something much weightier than European forms. He borrowed historicism, the nineteenth-century idea that each era should forge its own style of design. Then, while still a young man, he watched his reputation crumble beneath the collapse of that idea. Who says that a period has to have a style? Why must there be these rules? About function, about structure, about whatever. By 1968 the Modern movement's statements had grown stale. The future belonged to those who were asking those questions.

As the Postmodern movement gathered momentum—Yale was one of the movement's engines—Rudolph gradually withdrew from the scene. He continued to build major projects, mostly in Southeast Asia, that attracted dwindling attention in the press. Yet a few years ago, at a lecture at the Cooper-Hewitt Museum, he drew a large audience of quite young architects who clearly esteemed his work as a principled way of building.

Rossi, born in Milan in 1931, was modernism's most thoughtful questioner. His first book, *The Architecture of the City*, was published in 1966, the year Robert Venturi's *Complexity and Contradiction in Architecture* also appeared. Rossi's book had less immediate impact. But it was by far the more poetic performance. In place of historicism, he proposed memory as architecture's guiding idea. Brilliant. Why hadn't anyone thought of that before? Forget about Rome, Paris, Athens, and Luxor. What matters, instead, are the images of these hallowed places that we hold within our minds.

Rossi personalized the past. He liked to say that he never invented forms. Rather, he remembered them. The city, in his view, was a theater, a playhouse for collective memory. One of Rossi's first major projects, the Cemetery of San Cataldo in Modena, Italy (1971–84), translated this deeply emotional idea into stark physical reality. As much a work of landscape and city planning as of architectural design, the cemetery's low perimeter buildings enclose a courtyard; near the entrance there rises the ossuary, a stark red cube studded with a grid of square, windowless openings that stare out like empty sockets, proclaiming that architecture's meaning lay not with the future but with the past. It treated dead people and dead forms as sentient beings. They did not take history to their graves but rather commanded time from their graves. It mocked progress, historicism's vulgar offshoot, with the grinning skull of death.

Then came the floating Teatro del Mondo, a feature of the 1980 Venice Biennale. A wooden octagon mounted on a barge, the theater became Rossi's signature work, an essay in severity and evanescence. The base of the tower was of natural wood, which appeared golden in the Venetian light. The top was painted sky blue and capped with a jaunty little finial. The theater was moored in the lagoon, a site described by Rossi as "a place where architecture ended and the world of the imagination or even the irrational began."

These early projects were visually austere, but not in the functionalist manner of modernism. Rather, he used a limited vocabulary of iconic forms—the gable, the square Roman window, the staircase, the colonnade—to create symbolically primitive shelters. The Marxist critics who dominated Italy's architectural discourse adored Rossi's aesthetic asceticism. And he won the respect of others, like myself, who believed that classicism had not played itself out.

In the mid-1980s, Rossi's work became increasingly ornate. His buildings adorned themselves with alarming polychromy. Their rooflines sprouted exaggerated cornices. Columns turned into kitsch colonnades. Rossi created some wonderful projects in this time: Centro Torri, his shopping center outside Milan, is one of the century's great works. Like Rudolph's parking garage, it embodies the belief that even stridently anti-urban ways of life are entitled to urban forms of dignity.

And then Rossi went deeper into his obsession with blue. Volare. *Nel blu, dipinto di blu*. In renderings of his later work, buildings often came to seem like simple excuses for backgrounds of sky blue. It was as if, after dragging us down to the ashen underworld, Rossi wished to give us a taste of resurrection.

But Rossi also pumped out many cloddish designs. The UNY shopping center in Nagoya, Japan. The Disney office complex in Orlando, Florida. These and many other late projects got very cutesy-wutesy: primary colors, kindergarten-block shapes. It seemed like a case of deliberate regression, to use the author Robert Harbison's phrase. Instead of the haunting quality of memory, Rossi's architecture now came coated in saccharine layers of nostalgia.

The Yale architectural historian Vincent Scully once wrote that Rudolph represented that side of the American consciousness that is always trying to find and to identify the self. Rossi represented something similar. Both men were basically introverts who managed to flourish in an extrovert's profession. Probably what counted most to both was constructing their own worlds, not occupying the center stage in ours. And they worked at a time when architecture was withdrawing from the modern goal of redesigning the world.

In the epigraph to his *Scientific Autobiography*, published in 1981, Rossi writes appreciatively of "the disorder of things, if limited and somehow honest." But what then, he asks, could an architect, a maker of order, aspire to? "Certainly to small things, having seen that the possibility of great ones was historically precluded."

December 25, 1997

AALTO, A MODERNIST AHEAD OF HIS TIME

The Museum of Modern Art's new Alvar Aalto show is a sleeping beauty. Impeccable scholarship, lucid presentation, an admirable refusal to impose on Aalto an alien point of view: these are the exhibition's considerable strengths. But they aren't enough to bring Aalto to life. The show makes loving him feel morbidly perverse.

Alvar Aalto: Between Humanism and Materialism, organized by Peter Reed, an associate curator in the Modern's department of architecture and design, is a large, comprehensive exhibition, honoring the centennial of the great Finnish architect's birth. The show, which runs through May 19, features many drawings from the Aalto Archive in Helsinki that have never before been shown outside Finland. In all, forty-five buildings and unbuilt projects are represented, with archival and new photographs, drawings, and scale models, including some specially constructed for this event. There is even a small viewing room that presents video walk-throughs of five principal buildings.

Some visitors are likely to approach this show defensively. Aalto, who died in 1976, has long stood as a paragon of aesthetic and mental hygiene. It can be painful to contemplate his work from the vantage point of our environmentally and ideologically degraded end of the century. The work is also hard to pin down. A regionalist but not a reactionary, an ally of industry who declined to worship the machine, Aalto deflates common preconceptions about the Modern movement. In place of rigid grids, exposed concrete, and hard glass facades, Aalto created free-form curves, warm, wooden interiors, facades of irregularly laid red brick.

During his life, Aalto's nationality gave him an aura of otherness; people regarded him as a special case whose work derived from exotic conditions: those lakes, that birch, that Finland, a country where even the factory smokestacks look to be pumping out fresh air. The young nation was not yet independent when Aalto was born. Its people spoke a peculiar language, seemingly related to no other.

In retrospect, it should be clearer that nationality was only part of what set him apart. His true distinction is that his architecture was ahead of its time. His work was an assault on binary thinking, the tendency to see things as either-or. This objective was similar to that undertaken in recent years by Robert Venturi, Frank Gehry, Peter Eisenman, and Rem Kool-haas. Regrettably, this show fails to clarify the critical importance of this ambition, to Aalto and to ourselves.

Like Louis Kahn and other architects of his generation, Aalto began his career by designing in an eclectic classical style. His early work is presented at the opening of the show, as a kind of prelude. In 1924 Aalto acquired the habit of summering in Italy. He returned to his native town of Jyväskylä with the ambition to turn it into a Florence of the north. Piazzas and fish balls, a filling combination. In 1925 Aalto designed the handsome Worker's Club, which brings to mind a miniature Doge's Palace.

Traces of classicism linger in Aalto's later designs. The Roman house reappears in his recurring use of courtyard and atrium. In the 1940s he developed a curved tile that, when wrapped around a column, resembled classical fluting. Chairs with seats and backs of scrolled wood recall Ionic volutes.

Aalto embraced the modern movement in 1928, with the hope that this fresh style could steer his young nation into the future. His enthusiasm for Modern orthodoxy soon faded, but the period produced two major projects. The first was an office building and printing plant for the *Turun Sanomat*, a newspaper in the seaport of Turku. By the late 1920s, this city had established itself as the progressive alternative to stodgy Helsinki. Aalto housed the news within the new, a crisply functionalist building in the Walter Gropius mold. A blowup of the day's front page in a display case on the front of the building provided the sole form of decoration.

In 1929 Aalto won the competition to design the Paimio Tuberculosis Sanatorium, a commission of national importance. He used a Le Corbusian idiom this time, creating a machine for getting well in, with balconies, roof terraces, and rooms equipped with standardized basins, lighting, and other fixtures. A tribute to Le Corbusier's Esprit Nouveau preoccupation with health and fitness, the design placed architecture at the service of light, fresh air, and the liberation of body and mind from the weight of tradition and stuffy décor.

At Paimio, Aalto introduced the first of his beautiful furniture pieces, one of the highlights of the show. The chairs are cantilevered abstractions in the Bauhaus manner but with frames fashioned from unpainted wood instead of steel; they recall the roots of the German design school in the British Arts and Crafts movement. The famous Savoy vase, contoured like the shores of a lake, is nearly impossible to arrange flowers in, but Aalto's sketches for the vase are among the loveliest pieces in the show.

By the mid-1930s, Aalto's aesthetic had evolved beyond rationalism, just in time to take its place on the international stage. He designed the Finnish Pavilion for the Paris International Exhibition of 1936–37. It was just steps from the pavilions of Germany and the Soviet Union, two overblown neoclassical structures that faced each other across the fairground's central axis like the enemies they would become.

The Blossoming of a New Talent

Aalto's design, by contrast, offered what W. H. Auden called the vision of Dame Kind, nature in its benevolent aspect. A box with rounded corners, clad in wood, was set within a low U-shaped structure of jagged, irregular contour. Trees surrounded the pavilion, and one entered it via courtyards. There were columns made from birch trunks, and pillars formed of handwrapped bamboo stalks. In atmosphere, the work evoked a park or small forest whose trees have generously composed themselves into human habitation. Americans and Europeans recognized the blossoming of a new talent.

Three years later, for the 1939 New York World's Fair, Aalto designed another Finnish Pavilion with a stunning theatrical interior. Three undulating tiers of wooden battens hovered over the main space. These were inset with large photographs depicting scenes from Finnish industry and agriculture, while a projection booth cast moving images on a side wall.

Aalto said the form was inspired by the northern lights. They brought to mind Finland's lakes and forests.

Symbolism aside, what many visitors responded to most strongly was the free-flowing space, an organic enclosure that surpassed anything even Frank Lloyd Wright had achieved at that time. Though the building stood for only two years, like Mies van der Rohe's Barcelona Pavilion, it lived on in memory and in pictures, fixing the iconic image of Aalto's aesthetic.

The building's appeal was partly erotic. This was true of the New York World's Fair as a whole, with its gleaming, mechanized appeals to consumer desires. But Aalto's design redirected the erotic focus from cars to bodies. Like a gigantic sauna, the Finnish Pavilion offered a glimpse of a natural, not to say naturist, Eden where people felt comfortable in their bodies and enjoyed them without guilt.

There was another, more specialized source of the building's power, rooted in the unfolding history of the Modern movement. In the late 1920s, many European architects rejected Expressionism, the utopian, sculpturally voluptuous style that had preoccupied many of them since World War I. Instead they embraced the objective, rational aesthetic associated with the Bauhaus. Mr. Reed, the show's curator, suggests that Aalto's work represented the return of the repressed: the psychological dimension of dream and fantasy to which Expressionism had given form.

As the show moves into Aalto's postwar work, a visitor's mind starts to wander. This is partly because of the usual architecture show problem. We're looking at representations of buildings, not walking through space. It is clear from the drawings and photographs that the work itself is not dull.

Aalto did not like tall buildings, but a high-rise apartment block he designed in 1958 for Bremen, Germany, looks extraordinary: a fan-shaped floor plan spreading out from a linear service core. And his 1959 Opera House for Essen, Germany, must be a place where a listener can easily feel transported. The auditorium's curved white balconies project against ultramarine walls like gull wings soaring toward dusk. But the continuity between Aalto's very different forms is not brought into focus.

In her excellent catalog essay, Marja-Riitta Norri, director of the Museum of Finnish Architecture, writes this: "Aalto believed that 'the simultaneous solution of opposites was the first necessary condition for a building or any human achievement to attain the level of culture.' " That quotation defines the point of view that is missing from this show. I don't know whether the Finnish language is as permeated by dualisms as English is, or to what extent Finnish civilization absorbed the Enlightenment and its rage to dichotomize. Using the language of architecture, however, Aalto carried out an exemplary alternative to binary thought.

A horizontal line invites a diagonal. A straight line complements a curve. An interior opens into a courtyard. Convexity and concavity cavort. Function and form are inseparable but distinct, like the head and tail of one coin. So are architecture and landscape, the building and the city. A person should be able to walk through a forest, Aalto said, on the way from home to work.

Though the holding together of opposites is a classical Western ideal, the ideal was badly eroded by rationalist eighteenth-century thought. Today, however, science itself is steering thought away from rationalism's rigid compartments. Indeterminacy, contingency, fuzzy thinking—concepts like these have emerged as fundamental to a contemporary sense of order.

It is encouraging to know that an architect was struggling with such ideas early on, and disappointing that this show did not use that struggle to create a strong conceptual spine. Many viewers may leave the museum thinking that the show is just one more tribute to another dead white modernist. This is too bad. Architecture shows may not be able to give us space, but, by bringing the past to life in the present, they can warp time. Aalto's work still has the power to feed into the future. This show has not awakened it.

February 26, 1998

A RETURN TO THE GLAMOUR OF FLYING: KENNEDY'S NEW TERMINAL OFFERS STYLE AND COMFORT FOR JADED TRAVELERS

No one goes to Kennedy International Airport expecting other than a deeply grim hour or two before boarding time. At best, the hour might be thought of as an anthropological field trip. This is the best place in New York to verify the news reports: Americans are indeed obese. We probably got that way in airports, gobbling french fries in an effort to dispel the anxiety produced by ugly surroundings, no smoking, irrational fears of crashing, and the reasonable expectation that our luggage is on its way to the moon.

The new Terminal One, which was formally dedicated yesterday and is scheduled to open to the public at the end of the month, could go a long way toward changing that view. It is an excellent building, at once muscular and calm and, above all, lucid. If you fly out of Kennedy on an airline other than the four that occupy the new edifice—Air France, Lufthansa, Korean Air, and Japan Airlines—talk this over with your therapist. You've now got a chance to spend that preboarding time in a pleasant place. Take it.

Architecturally, the building aspires to potency. It is packed with a breathtaking amount of thrust. Giant steel trusses. Dramatically cantilevered canopies. Soaring ceilings. Spotlighted columns. Jetways that not only extend and retract, in the usual fashion, but also rise and fall between two concourse levels at the press of a button.

All this dazzling engineering is meant to invoke the spirit of flight. It is possible that most travelers today are too sophisticated, or jaded, for such concepts—we just want to arrive at Point B in one piece, thank you. But Terminal One does offer an incredible flight through time. It's a trip back to an era before Kennedy became a theme park of life in modern Albania, to a time when jet travel still felt new and glamorous. Put on your Ray-Bans, and don't forget your tote bag!

The building stands on the site of the old Eastern Airlines terminal. In its last years, after Eastern went bust, the terminal sat there half gutted, with white curtains flapping in the abandoned Ionosphere Lounge and a snack bar where a portable TV set sat on a counter next to hot dogs revolving inside an electric grill. Perhaps the place should have been preserved as an example of what happens when private industry fails to take care of a public amenity.

Terminal One is also a private venture, built and operated by the four airlines that have relocated there. Designed by William Nicholas Bodouva & Associates of Manhattan, which also designed the US Airways terminal at LaGuardia Airport, it is the first completely new terminal building to go up at Kennedy since British Airways constructed its slant-sided pavilion twenty-five years ago.

The building is not a megastructure. With only eleven parking gates for aircraft, it's a small oasis in Kennedy's desert of decrepitude. But with a new International Arrivals Building now in the works, Terminal One is also a preview of things to come.

The new building is not a monument in the manner of Eero Saarinen's pavilion for TWA. Rather, the architects have recognized that the airport setting is monumental enough. Its roadways, runways, jetways, and hangars define an architectural language as epic as anything in ancient Rome. With lines that echo the ramps, Terminal One seems to grow organically from this infrastructure.

This is the first passenger building you come to as you pull off the Van Wyck Expressway. The paved ramps frame the terminal like a Russian

Constructionist vision. As you pull up to the drop-off, you pass the berth for Air France's Concorde. The sight of this sleek vehicle can go far toward overcoming jaded feelings about the culture of space and time.

An aerodynamically styled metal and glass canopy protrudes thirty-five feet out over the ramp for departing passengers, gesturing toward the trim metal cage of a parking garage directly opposite. It's a neat composition that will be even finer when, as planned, a monorail starts operating parallel to the road. Like the main building at LaGuardia, Terminal One fans out radially from the car ramp. In plan, the main hall and the concourse beyond resemble two thick pie crusts nestled together.

The main hall, six hundred feet in length, is a shed of steel and glass. A curved glass lip runs along the roof's curbside edge, the first of many skylights that saturate Terminal One with natural light. Sunlight is the big thing in airports these days. This one has more light than your pineal gland can use. Because of the hall's gentle convex curve, the trusses overhead create the impression of a loosely coiled spring.

Instead of continuous counters, check-in and ticketing desks are organized into four rectangular islands with generous open space around them. Beyond, escalators rise to a mezzanine floor with a central rotunda containing a food court and shops. The moving stairs are set beside walls of water streaming over black granite, a display sponsored by Perrier. An atrium on the mezzanine level lets you peer down to the floor below, where passengers proceed to the jetways after clearing security. Unfortunately, the view is obstructed by an artwork designed to foil the tossing of contraband. Can't they make lasers for that kind of thing? Or at least install some public art–type thing made out of oxygen masks, airplane dinner trays, and inflatable emergency chutes?

Clarity is the new terminal's great virtue. You always know where you are and where you're going. You even know you're on planet Earth. In addition to the skylights, there are big picture windows looking out over the airport and, on a clear day, the Manhattan skyline. The glass is tinted a light, warm gray. Miraculously, it even makes the Delta terminal look as though it's posing for an architectural photographer.

Even the passport-control room has loads of natural light. It is deeply shocking to enter an area like this without feeling that you should sink to your knees and apologize for being alive. But this space actually communicates the thought you want to hear: Welcome home.

Of course, a place this spiffy raises two obvious questions. Why was Kennedy ever allowed to deteriorate to such a scandalously decrepit state? And what's to prevent it from happening again? Even before the airlines were deregulated, the place was at the mercy of private industry. And we've seen what a joyous occasion industry made of entering this major gateway to the home of free enterprise.

So what happens if Korean Air goes belly-up, or Perrier stops sponsoring the water wall? If people lose their taste for duty-free Dunhill, Courvoisier, and Sonia Rykiel, and Chuck E. Cheese takes over the upscale French bistro on the mezzanine floor? We've all seen malls past their prime.

Terminal One, in other words, isn't a building. It's a service operation. Do avail yourself of it now. The service couldn't get any better. Unless the world changes, it will certainly get worse.

May 15, 1998

OF SCULPTURE AND THE PAST REVIVIFIED

The announcement read simply, *Ellsworth Kelly: Sculpture for a Large Wall, 1957*, a title that didn't prepare me for a reunion with an old friend. But there it was, alarmingly visible through the window of the Matthew Marks Gallery at 522 West Twenty-second Street in Chelsea: the portal to the city of my youth. The piece, an immense aluminum construction created by Mr. Kelly for the Transportation Building in downtown Philadelphia, which remains on view through Saturday, has been a joy of the spring season.

At the opening, Mr. Marks, who rescued the sculpture from demolition, mentioned that I was the first person he'd met who had seen the piece at its original site when it was relatively new. My memory of it is vivid indeed. Everyone has an age of discovery, and mine began at the age of ten when I figured out how to catch the suburban commuter train to downtown Philadelphia.

Now, Philadelphia was a place where a woman once sued Josephine Baker because during her act Baker used to throw fruit out into the audience, and this woman claimed she'd been hit on the head by a flying pineapple, I think it was. Philadelphia, in other words, was a town where Josephine Baker could throw fruit out into the audience and people would just sit on their hands. If things were that grim downtown, imagine what the suburbs were like.

It was a thirty-minute ride from the suburb where my parents lived to Suburban Station, an underground terminal tucked beneath the city's asphalt skin. There was more than one route to the surface. Mine detoured through an inconspicuous stairway up to the lobby of the new

Sheraton Hotel. The lobby had that mildly sweet, peach Melba smell of well-tended hotels, as well as racy carpets streaked with green, orange, and pink. A bookstore in the lobby always seemed to be displaying the latest best seller by Jack Paar. Then, from the Sheraton, you could pass into the lobby of the Transportation Building next door.

These two buildings were parts of Penn Center, a massive redevelopment of Philadelphia's downtown core. Planned by Edmund Bacon, the nation's leading city planner in the postwar decades, the complex of offices and hotels was the largest development the city had seen since the 1920s. Penn Center was not a critical success.

Louis Kahn, whose design for the area had been rejected, commented that if the plan had been submitted by a first-year architecture student, the grade would be zero. Later, Penn Center was reviled as a prime example of disastrous modern city planning: lamentable in the spare geometry of its buildings, its disregard for the vitality of the traditional street.

All true, no doubt, but it was great nonetheless to have such a fine group of modern lobbies. People passing through lobbies like these must certainly be on their way to doing modern things. I guessed they must be doing advertising, this being the most modern occupation I could imagine. They were creating ads for Campbell's soup or Smirnoff vodka. And when they arrived in the morning, they wore Martin Balsam hats of trim charcoal gray with narrow brims, wide bands, and a little feather stuck in them.

One corner of the building contained a Greyhound bus terminal. In those days, the place didn't give the impression that buses were for poor people. These buses, remember, had Scenicruiser service. And airports then were still just landing fields. The aura of transportation was both democratic and transcendent.

Mr. Kelly's wall sculpture was installed over the elevators and, opposite these, framed by glass, were the doors to the city. As you walked through the lobby, you selected yourself to be part of the city, to be a lover of modern art, and to see modern art and the city as two aspects of the present. The desire to join that present was the impulse that drove you through the door.

Mr. Kelly was thirty-three when he received this commission. It came his way in 1956 through Richard Kelly (no relation), a lighting designer he met one night in a New York City bar. Mr. Kelly was first hired to design a group of seven brass window screens for the Transportation Building's Post House Restaurant. The lobby project followed. Mr. Kelly was paid $200 for his work and gained the antagonism of his client, the building's developer, who disliked the sculpture so much that he refused to illuminate it at night. The client might have thought he'd been hit by a flying pineapple, too.

In the catalog essay, James Meyer writes about Mr. Kelly's youthful desire to collaborate with architects. While living in Paris in the early 1950s, he sought out Le Corbusier to discuss such collaborations, and there are discernably Corbusian aspects to the Philadelphia sculpture: the machine fabrication, the primary colors, the elemental geometric shapes. Mr. Kelly understood that he risked having his work interpreted as design rather than art. In fact, he was dismayed one day to find that the management of the Post House had taped its menu to one of his brass screens. A few years later, the screens were thrown out with no more ceremony than if they'd been a set of venetian blinds.

I was too uneducated to wonder whether the lobby sculpture was art or design or to know that the distinction mattered. For me, the piece mainly represented novelty. At the Franklin Institute, the science museum a few blocks away, novelty came in the form of a room-size UNIVAC computer. At Penn Center, it arrived as 104 pieces of anodized aluminum, stretched out on parallel metal bars to a length of 65 feet. Yet on some inarticulate level I sensed that the sculpture, while novel, corresponded to familiar patterns.

In 1957 George Balanchine choreographed his great masterpiece *Agon.* Lincoln Kirstein, writing about the ballet some years later, described Balanchine's work as a process of uncovering: "Creativity, on the human level, is simply what might be called an uncovering of commentary on innumerable facts of measure and order (parts of which may include disorder: chaos, hazard, cruelty, injustice, and death)."

Kirstein's viewpoint, while mystical, is nonetheless a useful one for examining art in an urban context. In choreographing *Agon,* Balanchine used a seventeenth-century manual of French court dances to reveal what the classically trained body could do in movement, and he also revealed something essential about twentieth-century New York: the city's harmonies and distortions, the playfulness and anxiety of relationships in the modern world.

Penn Center, whatever its defects, was also an uncovering—it disclosed a city gripped at once by hope for change and fear of it—and so was Mr. Kelly's wall sculpture. In the abstraction of their forms, both projects revealed the city's transition from industrial production to "symbolic analysis," to use Robert Reich's phrase.

Mr. Kelly's piece showed what some aluminum scraps could become when arranged and painted like so. Beyond that, the sculpture revealed distinctly urban kinds of movement, as different as the walking styles of pedestrians in the streets outside. Like Mondrian's New York paintings, it revealed how a color, a shape, or a gesture—of buildings, people, cars, shopwindows—can catch the eye, hold it for a second, then lose it to other shapes and colors, or combine with them in changing rhythms.

Above all, the piece revealed the movement of the eye itself—restless, curious, delighted, or dissatisfied—and the power of retinal movement to trigger ideas. Like a Rorschach blot, then, it ultimately revealed the self. And suggested, in its context, that revelation of self is not a small part of a city's business. The collisions, surprises, the Walk/Don't Walk (dis)connections—flying pineapples—arouse aspects of the psyche that might otherwise remain submerged.

June 17, 1998

LOOKING AT THE LAWN, AND BELOW THE SURFACE

Something awful is happening to the planet Earth. It has been invaded by the Earth-snatchers. It is being turned into a pod planet, one lawn at a time. Thirty-two million acres have been snatched thus far on the North American continent alone. More land is now occupied by lawns than is given over to the cultivation of wheat, corn, or tobacco. It costs $750 million annually to seed this turf. Another $25 billion is invested each year in mowers, clippers, gardening gloves, hoses, and other do-it-yourself tools.

Life on the pod planet can be delightful, especially in the month of July. You can lie on your back on the lawn and stare at the sky. Make a grass kazoo. Cut open a maple seed and stick it on your nose. Season your jeans with grass stains. Become a Cheever character and run out sobbing into the night.

The American Lawn: Surface of Everyday Life, a corker of a show at the Canadian Center for Architecture in Montreal, begins with a ride on a lawn sprinkler. Or at least the video depiction of one. Back and forth the camera swings, scanning the archetypal patch of grass, oscillating between peripheral glimpses of equally iconic neighbors on either side: the no-nonsense lady trimming her hedge to clipped perfection, the cool kids hanging out by the garage. In the background, water hisses.

The video is projected onto the floor, and you hesitate to step on it. Your shadow might block the projection. Thus the show stylishly connects two kinds of transgression: one associated with land, the other with museums. Keep Off. Don't Touch. That kind of elegant connection occurs throughout this show.

It's probably best seen as one large piece of multimedia design, in which ideas ricochet among artworks, aerial satellite photographs, squares of sod, television news footage, solar-powered robot lawn mowers, even a pink flamingo or two.

The lawn is a natural subject for a summer show, if also a highly perverse one. Even those who don't own a lawn might wish to preserve that small plot of green as a symbolic escape from civilization. This show plunges us into history, economics, sociology, psychology, and other cold-weather pursuits. The lawn is our last little shred of Eden. Trees of Knowledge are no more wanted here than weeds. Can't we please keep thinking off the grass?

The American Lawn gives little quarter to innocence. There are no pictures of kids leaping through sprinklers. No shots of lovers discovering splendor in the grass. But the show does confer innocence upon the visitor, for we are left feeling that there is everything yet to learn about the everyday world we live in.

In 1976 Elizabeth Drew wrote a beautiful article for *The New Yorker* about the mood of the country on the Fourth of July in the bicentennial year. She describes how the news media, the politicians, and the salesmen have done everything within their power to appropriate the event, and in the process nearly killed it off. But they didn't kill it off. People found ways to act spontaneously. They ate burgers, drank beer, paraded in small-town marching bands, cheered displays of fireworks as if the spectacle expressed a set of values to which they still subscribed.

Ignoring authority may be one way to resist it, but this show rests on the democratic principle that it's better to be informed.

The curators start with the premise that the lawn represents the fusion of two traditions: the "cultivated" model of great European estates and private parks, and the "vernacular" example of the small colonial garden. This distinction, first analyzed by the historian John Kouwenhoven, held firm until the late nineteenth century. With the emergence of suburban communities, this distinction began to collapse into the continental green tapestry of today.

"Cultivated" takes on a literal meaning here. In the forthcoming catalog, Georges Teyssot writes that "certain horticulturalists like Sara Stein have come to consider the lawn a surface that while vegetal is artificial in that it attains its emerald splendor only when subjected to perpetual torture. 'Continual amputation is a critical aspect of lawn care,' Stein has observed. 'Cutting grass regularly—preventing it from reaching up and flowering—forces it to sprout still more blades, more rhizomes, more roots, to become an ever more impenetrable mat, until it becomes the perfect lawn, the perfect sealant through which nothing else can grow.'"

Lawn care, in other words, is much like road care and serves a similar purpose. "Like the interstate highway system," the author Michael Pollan has observed, "the lawn has served to unify the American landscape." But differences, conflicts, and nature itself are not as easily mowed down as grass.

The architectural historian Reyner Banham used to horrify professional audiences by declaring that architecture is that which changes land use. But the truth of that statement becomes ever more apparent with the daily expansion of urban sprawl. The American Lawn is about land use. There are ideas behind the cultivation of wheat, corn, and tobacco, and tension lurks beneath the two-inch layer of green stuff on which Americans have staged their placid dreams for more than a century.

The American Lawn is the last in an ambitious cycle of shows on The American Century organized by Phyllis Lambert, the Canadian Center's dynamic director. The whole series has been a triumph, but the inaugural show, Scenes from the Life to Come, and the present exhibition are examples of curatorial brilliance.

It was organized by a stellar team: Mr. Teyssot, Alessandra Ponte, Mark Wigley, Beatriz Colomina, Elizabeth Diller, and Ricardo Scofidio. Mark Wasiuta and Gwynne Keathley assisted the team. Diller & Scofidio Architects, of New York, designed the installation.

Since cultural values tend to coax up their opposites, a space dedicated to harmony and independence can easily become a battlefield. Is an overgrown lawn a protected form of speech? How about Christmas ornaments on the lawn? Or a cross-burning? Does the postal service have right-of-way when delivering the mail?

Excerpts from court cases in which lawns figured as contested terrain are featured in one gallery, along with a row of stereopticons. Each of these contains a 3-D image of the border between two neighboring lawns. In one shot, it is clear that one neighbor is a fastidious raker while the other has allowed a half-dozen picturesque leaves to gather, the slob. In another, a well-watered plot abuts a parched one. The groomed and the neglected strike a recurring theme, played out across the continent in contrapuntal variations. Sometimes the grass is less green. Often it is brown.

In a section on the competitive lawn, the contest at first looks more sporting. The focus here is on the intricate patterns mowed into the grass in sports stadiums. But there is greater competition here than meets the eye. What's at stake is not just victory in a game but lucrative broadcasting contracts. To make sports events more telegenic, stadium managements have commissioned increasingly elaborate designs for animating the playing surface, including plaids, swirls, and sunburst motifs. These video lawns are vying for ratings.

Another kind of contest is documented by photographs of golf courses in desert climates like Arizona. The contest here is between nature and our visual image of it. These artificially created terrains have already altered local weather patterns, and, if chaos theory is correct, their impact could well be global. But aren't they beautiful, these emerald islands adrift in what looks like a giant sand trap of planetary proportions? Is this a preview of coming attractions?

The Power Lawn is represented in two formats, corporate and governmental. In the 1960s, as corporate headquarters relocated to the suburbs, their International Style headquarters were typically surrounded by grandiose grass plinths. These served as moats, visual statements of intimidation. This retro-feudal form is handsomely represented by professional black-and-white architectural photographs of the period. These lawns are so stark, so flat, so blatantly designed to hold the world at bay that it would be shocking to pollute them with anything as capricious as color.

The North Lawn of the White House, by contrast, is a backdrop for chaos: the unruly spectacle of political protest. Not that it was designed for that, but here democracy has happily appropriated one of its major symbols. Rallies are presented in television news footage, screened on small monitors suspended from sleek metal arms down the center of the gallery. Another monitor displays scenes of presidential arrivals and departures by helicopter on the South Lawn.

By now our eyes are so primed to notice sheared surfaces that we may detect a resemblance between a neglected lawn and the autumn-haze mink coat Pat Nixon wore when she and her husband took off for China. On the other hand, in a contrast that recalls one of those stereopticon views, Mrs. Nixon's hairstyle is luscious and as beautifully tended as a French garden, while the president's hair is patchy.

Hand-painted glass slides line the perimeter of a gallery on Idyll and Anxiety. Drawn from a collection assembled in the 1920s and '30s by the Garden Club of America, they depict scenes as ravishing as pastorals by Boucher and Fragonard. Ah, the poplars, the willows, the urns bulging with moss atop balustrades wrapped around terraces on which visions of loveliness, graceful ladies and their escorts, will momentarily appear!

It is unnerving to think that many of them were painted during the Dust Bowl years.

The flip side of this reverie is projected on a screen that slices into the gallery's center: clips from movies in which the dark subconscious of pastoral bliss punches through the thin green crust.

Blue Velvet, naturally, but also a great comic sequence from the 1956 version of *Invasion of the Body Snatchers*, in which Kevin McCarthy tries to persuade a reluctant neighbor that she should consult a psychiatrist about her wild suspicion that something awful has happened to Uncle Ira (shown obsessively mowing the lawn next door).

Pod person or mental patient, what's it going to be?

Lawns have their pathology, too: fungi, viruses, nematodes, insects, air pollution, dog urine. Color photographs of these and other afflictions are mounted on one wall, the particular strain identified below in a Latinate script of old botany prints.

These are clearly offered for our viewing pleasure with a degree of gleeful relish: they convey a city dweller's delight over trouble in suburban paradise. But these pastoral sores are also easy on the eyes. Even if the artist Mel Chin (not represented in the show) had not called attention to the aesthetic dimension of ecological imbalance, the resemblance of these images to abstract painting would be impossible to miss.

This is a visual and philosophical show, not a scientific or ecological one. While it observes the environmental impact of the suburban way of life, it does not preach the virtues of recycling or condemn our failure to adopt methods for sustainable urban growth. The show documents and analyzes. It fertilizes the cultural terrain from which even environmental issues draw meaning.

Across from the disease wall there's a vitrine displaying square samples of grass, natural and artificial. Both types have been engineered to enhance desirable qualities, like springiness, color, or resistance to weather. The point of the display is to suggest not that there is no difference between nature and artifice but that modern life has rendered the contrast less extreme. Once, cultural meaning revolved around the polarity dividing the two. Now it has moved deeper into the space between.

Diller and Scofidio's work occupies a middle space, too: between theory and conventional practice. Though they have published several books, and a housing project of theirs is nearing completion in Gifu, Japan, the team is best known for temporary installations, like those created for the Museum of Modern Art, the Walker Art Center, and the Creative Times public-art program on Forty-second Street. The two are not paper architects. They enjoy making things too much, and their pleasure shows.

The American Lawn is not as chillingly analytic as it may sound. It's true that the curators come out of the academy, and their thinking owes much to poststructuralist philosophy. But the show pulsates with such intelligence, wit, and even glamour that it can't be taken as a lecture-room performance.

The Garden Club slides, for example, are not set up to be mocked. They are gorgeous fantasies, to be cherished as such. The notion that suburban normalcy represses difference might seem obvious if the exchange with Uncle Ira were less enjoyably hilarious. One can admire the stark beauty of Ezra Stoller's architectural photos while recoiling from the meaning of the lawns he depicts.

Diller and Scofidio know how to entertain as well as edify. Though they rely extensively on dialectic, the technique seldom becomes oppressively schematic. And the team always creates seductive hardware.

Little magnifying glasses to highlight passages of text in a row of old gardening books. The thinnest metal vermicelli cable to hold the stereopticons. A glass table, supported atop the soles of athletic footgear, to demonstrate the changing shape of grip. A red zipper LED sign flickers mysteriously behind the reflection of grass in a two-way mirror.

There's a bright shimmer to this exhibition, an aura of energy and delight that you may associate more with walks in the country than with trips to museums. If I had to account for this shimmering effect, I would say that Diller and Scofidio's main concern is the differentiation of meaning and that for them, this process is inseparable from image, space, and form.

Diller and Scofidio's work is now much imitated. You can't lead unless you're willing to tolerate followers, and a critic should not cringe each time he encounters a superficial emulation of this pair's visual and intellectual effects. Still, leaders and followers are not of the same cultural order of being, and seeing the real thing is a pleasure. I came away from The American Lawn convinced that intelligence is as generous, merciless, and playful as nature, and no less increasingly rare.

July 5, 1998

CHOOSING PROSE OVER POETRY TO SPAN A BAY

When it comes to bridge designers practicing in the world today, there's the Spanish architect and engineer Santiago Calatrava and there's everyone else. Isn't that awful? This fact has certainly lent an air of independence, if not futility, to San Francisco's search for a new design for the Bay Bridge. Why should Bay Area residents settle for genius and deprive themselves of the freedom to choose something second-rate?

In June the Metropolitan Transportation Commission approved a new design for the bridge's eastern span, the 2.1-mile stretch from Yerba Buena Island to Oakland. Heavily damaged in the 1989 earthquake, this segment was judged unlikely to withstand an even stronger quake that seismologists predict will occur within the next century. The Bay Area regards the new $1.3 billion bridge as its major millennial project, a public work intended to carry the region into the next century and proclaim its culturally progressive spirit. Unfortunately, the winning design is not yet up to that ambition.

If I had $1.3 billion lying around, I'd hire Mr. Calatrava and put him to work. But public involvement in public works is one of the Bay Area's glories. In recent years, San Francisco has built a new main public library, a new museum of art, a performing arts complex, and an innovative water treatment plant, among other major projects, all of them objects of lively public debate. But none aroused as much passion as the new Bay Bridge: newspaper columns and editorials, letters to the editor, civic group newsletters, weird unsolicited proposals, grassroots campaigns to include provisions for bicycles and rail transit. All this should be regarded as a form of civic bridge building. It has helped reinforce the connections between people and place that make this such a great place to live.

Needless to say, it's not San Francisco's fault that Mr. Calatrava did not respond to the commission's open call for proposals. But it is not too late to bump it up a few notches. This scheme represents only 15 percent of the eastern span. Its longest stretch, the other 85 percent, is a causeway that descends into Oakland. The design for this major section of the bridge is still in development. And with Jerry Brown returned to active politics as Oakland's mayor, there is even greater incentive to urge the commission to insist on an innovative design.

The western span, which extends from Yerba Buena Island to San Francisco, will be structurally reinforced but retain its current appearance. Though this section may lack the travel-poster panache of the Golden Gate, it is a vibrant expression of the engineer's art. Its dull gray color is perfectly suited to a city often shrouded in fog. The tall towers, accented with cross-bracing, recede single file into mist, beckoning the eye to follow. It is industrial, even martial poetry, a reminder of the area's proud heritage.

By contrast, the old eastern span would make a fine runner-up in an amateur matchstick contest. With its roadway partly enclosed in a hulking structural framework, it can't seem to decide whether it's a bridge or a tunnel. Not much poetry there.

The winning design, by the firm T. Y. Lin International/Moffatt & Nichol Engineers of San Francisco, is a suspension bridge, featuring a single, tapering tower of four trapezoidal steel columns connected by transverse beams. The tower is asymmetrically placed, with the long part of the span reaching across the water. In technical terms, the tower is "self-anchored"; the road deck serves as a compression member. One large cable is draped from the tower's peak; slender suspender cables attach the main cable to girders beneath the road deck. The effect is delicate, even lacy.

Funds have been allocated for a bicycle lane, and there are provisions for future inclusion of rail. Construction could begin in two years, and take three years to complete.

There were three runner-ups in the competition. The first, another single-tower design, was a cable-stayed structure, with fan-shaped planes of cables splayed out from a concrete tower to the road deck's edges. (The effect is similar to a bridge Mr. Calatrava designed for Bordeaux in 1991, but this was a swing bridge, and the revolving motion of its central section gave functional meaning to the tower's spindle-like form.) The other runner-ups were twin-towered designs, with slim portals framing each roadway. Imagine the Brooklyn Bridge after a hunger strike and you've got the picture.

The weakest element in both schemes, however, is a clunky causeway descending into Oakland. In each case, it would come clomping through the water on stiff concrete columns like an elephant wading in the ocean. One version has flaring supports at the tops of columns—Dumbo with harlequin shades. Either causeway would be exhilarating to drive along, but neither would enhance the landscape. Few would fault the earth if it tried to shake them off.

This century has seen the flowering of two master bridge builders: Robert Maillart and Mr. Calatrava. Maillart, born in 1872, was Swiss, and his sturdy designs of reinforced concrete have a solidly Protestant appeal. Mr. Calatrava, born in Valencia in 1951, is said to spend two months a year in a convent retreat, and his work is discernibly Catholic in spirit. His plan for a science museum in Valencia has the fundamental elements of a great Gothic cathedral: light, ribbed construction; nave, narthex, and spire. Like Louis Kahn, Mr. Calatrava brings to design the devotion of prayer.

He was trained as an engineer as well as an architect. This is not to suggest a hierarchical relationship between the two fields. If anything, Mr. Calatrava's engineering background has given him a far deeper grasp of the poetics of structure than most architects can claim. "Building a bridge is, in my opinion, a symbolic gesture," he has written, "linked with the needs of the people crossing and the surmounting of an obstacle. Thus, the history of bridges is very important, with their origin in that single stepping stone to cross a quietly running stream."

A city seeking a new civic symbol should look deeply into the subject of symbolism itself. "We project our soul onto a landscape," the Jungian psychoanalyst Marie-Louise von Franz wrote in her book *The Way of the Dream*, written with Fraser Boa. The most poetic element in the winning design for the Bay Bridge is that the central tower embodies the symbolic form Dr. von Franz called the Ladder to Heaven. Her interpretation springs from Jacob's dream of angels climbing up and down a stair from the sky to the place where he slept. On awakening, Jacob realized this was a holy place. Or, in Dr. von Franz's terms, the ladder is the place of "communication with the upper deities."

It's no illusion that crossing a bridge can induce an exalted state. It's a mythical archetype that comes most vividly to life on days when hazy light obliterates the border between sea and sky, suspending the traveler in a state of blurred distinctions.

Santiago Calatrava himself recalls another Jungian symbol: the star, the person able to attract and hold the projections of others. Mr. Calatrava holds the hopes of those who know how transcendent the beauty of engineering can be. Many people resent the idea of architecture stars. They equate stardom with monster egos. But in Jungian terms the reverse is true: stars serve something larger than their selves.

Actually, San Francisco shouldn't have such a hard time with the idea that talent is not evenly distributed. Look at the city itself. For most Americans, San Francisco is Top Burg, the most perfectly realized urban setting on the North American continent. Here, little cable cars climb halfway to the stars. The new bridge should strive to lift the traveler even higher.

August 23, 1998

RESTORATION LIBERATES GRAND VISTAS, AND IDEAS

Lasers, acrobats, a symphony for orchestra and train whistle, flamenco dancers, a mariachi band, a 1½-ton cast-iron bald eagle, vintage trains, and even politicians: these were among the attractions yesterday and today in New York's celebration of the rededication of Grand Central Terminal.

Such a grand and gaudy civic vaudeville show is entirely in keeping with the spirit of this, the palace of all train stations. Designed by Warren and Wetmore with Reed and Stem, Grand Central is the mecca of preservationists, commuters, and city-lovers alike.

And the restoration of the 1913 landmark, by the New York firm of Beyer Blinder Belle, is a triumphant piece of work.

With the possible exception of Central Park's renovation, started in the 1980s under the direction of Elizabeth Barlow Rogers of the Central Park

Conservancy, this is the greatest feat of historical preservation in the city's history. The restoration of the main concourse's ceiling alone, the perfect sky for city dwellers who seldom get to see much of the real one, easily deserves aerial somersaults by the Big Apple Circus trapeze artists scheduled to soar this evening beneath its twinkling stellar constellation.

But this year also is the twentieth anniversary of the Supreme Court decision that affirmed the city's right to protect Grand Central and, by extension, other landmark buildings, from destruction. That is reason for the whole town to burst into flamenco. The Metropolitan Transportation Authority, the terminal's owner, should be serenaded by mariachi players for investing $200 million in a project that conforms so enthusiastically to the spirit of the court's decision.

This week's festivities focus on the completion of work on the main concourse, the station's architectural heart. The restored Waiting Room, now used for exhibitions, parties, and other events, opened two years ago, and the food court taking shape on the lower concourse will not be completed until next year. Impressive as the building's major public spaces are, however, Beyer Blinder Belle's greatest accomplishment has been to reveal that Grand Central is above all a monument to movement. The Mercury figure in the sculpture group facing Park Avenue South is not an idle idol. The entire building is governed by ideas of freedom of access and circulation.

Who doesn't love taking a taxi on the viaduct that wraps around Grand Central before plunging through the arches in the Helmsley Building? The ride offers an exhilarating liberation from the urban grid. The restoration has clarified the degree to which that sense of freedom permeates the building itself.

The architects have contributed two main architectural features to the main concourse. The new eastern staircase, which threatened to diminish the room's amplitude, has the opposite effect of magnifying it. By increasing access to the concourse balconies, it adds an observation deck that renders the scene below an epic urban spectacle.

Even more impressive is the uncovering of the ramps, located just behind the ticket windows, that lead down to the lower level and its fabled Oyster Bar. Instead of acting as a barrier, the ticket booths now serve as a screen, enlarging the space and the vista of possibilities. Along with the escalators leading to the lobby of the MetLife Building, the ramps enhance the terminal's identity as a place of vertical as well as horizontal circulation, a hub where trains, subways, elevators, taxis, and pedestrians briefly converge before setting off in different directions.

Beyer Blinder Belle has labored to make the station a destination, a place for shopping and dining, like Union Station in Washington. Rents from these operations will help finance the renovations. Fortunately, unlike Union Station's designers, Beyer Blinder Belle has accomplished this without destroying the building's architectural grandeur. (Most shops will be located along corridors leading from the concourse to Lexington Avenue.)

More important, the architects have retained the idea that the station is primarily a place of transition. Like Ellis Island, whose restoration in 1991 was also designed by Beyer Blinder Belle, Grand Central is one of the most thrilling symbols of the city's receptivity, its openness to people and to ideas. Metaphorically, it stands not just for the movement of people but also for the freedom of thought that occurs during movement—the ideas, the shifts in perspective that arise from the refusal to remain stuck in a fixed place or time.

Much as I like all those trapeze artists, light shows, and bald eagles, I chose a more perverse way to celebrate Grand Central's rededication. I rented a video of John Frankenheimer's 1966 thriller, *Seconds*. For those too young to have seen it, the plot goes like this: a beaten-down, middle-aged banker is about to board the train home to Scarsdale when a stranger hands him a note with an address scribbled on it. This encounter leads the banker into the clutches of The Company, a sinister outfit that stages fake deaths for life's disappointed, overhauls their bodies, gives them new identities and a fresh start in life. After much plastic surgery and months of physical training, the banker emerges as—Rock Hudson!

Rock moves to Malibu and becomes a swinger, but eventually it transpires that his new world is something like the town in *The Truman Show*—artificial and controlled. His neighbors are also "reborns," or security officers from The Company. And when Rock tries to escape, he finds that there's no getting out alive.

Now the building where the banker met his fate has had a face-lift of its own. The results are stunning, better than Rock's. But this transformation, too, has a noirish aspect. It has to do with what the building itself is about: that literal and metaphorical freedom of circulation. This freedom is one of New York's most important traditions, but in recent decades it has become severely circumscribed. Nowhere is this more evident than in New York's failure to encourage architecture that is either artistically first-rate or socially progressive.

The anniversary of the Supreme Court's decision is indeed cause for celebration, with lasers, symphonies, the works. But only the wildest wishful thinking could imagine that a single building of landmark quality has been constructed in Manhattan in the intervening decades. This may or may not be coincidence. But it is certainly true that landmarks preservation—architectural history—has been asked to do the work of architecture. The result has not, as yet, turned the city into a stage set like *The Truman Show*. But it reflects a city that has turned in on itself, and in doing so has lost its receptivity to change.

I'm not drawing this parallel with a horror movie because I want to rain on Grand Central's parade. On the contrary, I would like the building's underlying message to be as clear as its beautifully restored architecture.

October 2, 1998

AN ISLAMIC REMINDER OF THE SACRED IN DESIGN

Aga Khan: the name shimmers with glamour. Fabulous wealth. Palatial houses. Racehorses. Yachts. Jewels. Royal prerogative. As if that weren't enough, the Aga Khan is also the most important figure in the world of architecture today. In a ceremony at the Alhambra in Spain last Friday, Prince Karim Aga Khan honored seven buildings and urban plans, winners of the 1998 Aga Khan Awards for Architecture.

Founded in 1977 with the relatively modest aim of raising the standards of modern building in the Islamic world, the awards program has since become far more significant. By focusing the attention of Western architects, planners, historians, critics, and the public on new building in the developing Islamic world, he has created a dynamic forum for defining architecture's place in the global culture emerging in the wake of the Cold War.

Though less well known than the Pritzker Architecture Prize—often described as architecture's Nobel—the Aga Khan's awards program has embraced a far broader cultural mission. Unlike the Pritzker Prize, the Aga Khan awards go to projects, not architects. In addition to appraising aesthetic merit, jurors assess social needs, economic growth, environmental impact, and the relationship between local traditions and innovations in contemporary architecture worldwide.

This year, for example, the winners include the restoration of Hebron Old Town on the West Bank, the design of a leper hospital in Chopda Taluka, India, a new arts center in Lahore, Pakistan, and Tuwaiq Palace, a recreation center for the diplomatic quarter in Riyadh, Saudi Arabia. The range of projects is typical of those awarded in previous years. They adhere to no aesthetic school, historical style, or theoretical doctrine. But they do expand ideas on architecture beyond Western frames of reference. And they alter the context in which even Western buildings should be appraised. Above all, the awards program has created an opportunity for

Westerners to reckon with the withdrawal of architecture's spiritural dimension from the public realm.

In his commencement address at Brown University in 1996, the Aga Khan observed, "For all Muslims, the concepts of Din and Dunya, Faith and World, are inextricably linked." At sixty-one, the Aga Khan is imam, or leader, of the Ismaili sect of Shia Muslims, an affluent group of about 13 million members who reside mainly in India, Pakistan, Bangladesh, Kenya, Egypt, the former Soviet Republics, and other communities worldwide. He traces his descent from Mohammed through Fatima, the Prophet's daughter. A man of independent wealth, he also receives tithes from his followers and uses the money to support public works in Ismaili communities.

As imam, the Aga Khan is responsible for the material as well as the spiritual well-being of his followers. Based at his Secretariat in Chantilly, less than an hour from Paris, the prince exercises his authority through the Aga Khan Development Network, a group of organizations that relies extensively on volunteers in Ismaili communities. The prince's interest in architecture began with his experience as a dissatisfied client, frustrated with the poor quality of the schools, hospitals, housing, and other projects he had commissioned to serve Ismaili communities. Since then, he has also established a program to restore historic cities, including buildings in Cairo, Zanzibar, and Samarkand, and funded the study of Islamic architecture at Harvard and the University of Pennsylvania.

I first learned of the awards in the late 1980s in *Mimar,* the prince's sumptuously produced magazine dedicated to new buildings and restoration projects in the Islamic world (alas, it has since ceased publication). Another royal, the prince of Wales, was then making waves with attacks on modern architecture that were little more than dim appeals to reactionary taste.

Like the British prince, the Aga Khan sought to build upon architectural traditions But his approach was dramatically different. Instead of villainizing modernity as the enemy of history, he grasped that modernization is a part of history. He perceived that nothing historically significant could be achieved by merely hating the present.

The British and the Ismaili prince share one overarching concern: the withdrawal of architecture's sacred dimension from the public realm. Architecture is traditionally an art form of the rich, but it is also a medium that since prehistoric times has been used to stake a place for spiritual values in everyday life. As recently as the late nineteenth century, the design of ecclesiastical buildings played a central role in British architectural discourse. Today that focus has all but vanished. The extent to which its disappearance has made ours a time of mourning is perhaps not fully realized.

I went to Turkey to look at a small group of projects that have received the Aga Khan Award for architecture over the years. My itinerary included a mosque in Ankara, a reforestation program outside the Turkish capital, a park in Istanbul, and a group of vacation houses in the Aegean resort town of Bodrum, under the guidance of Suha Ozkan, an architect who directs the program from the Geneva offices of the Aga Khan Trust for Culture. Turkey is not, as a matter of fact, a center of Ismaili life. Since 1922 it has been ruled, if at times tenuously, by a secular government. But, as a country that has long symbolized the threshold between East and West, it is steeped in the cross-cultural spirit that guides the awards program.

I wanted to look at buildings outside the superpower frame of reference, to step outside the membrane that has come to enclose much of American architecture within the environment of consumer fantasy. What drew me to the awards program initially was the belief that the end of the Cold War had precipitated a crisis for American architecture, urbanism, and those who write about these fields. After World War II, architects enjoyed substantial moral authority, a reflection of their simultaneous commitment to creative discipline and social responsibility. Much of that authority has evaporated. Today American architecture often resembles an infernal bubble machine run by evil clowns.

Amusement parks with swan hotels, Egyptian gambling casinos, pseudo-urban shopping malls, gated communities, pasteboard versions of history with comic-book historians to endorse them. It is as if all the energy once exerted to contain Soviet aggression has imploded, enclosing the world's superpower within the bubbular fantasy that a changing world can be understood by dominating it, monitoring it, contacting it through cyberspace.

Mosque of the Grand National Assembly, Ankara

I'm finding it hard to focus on the architecture because I can't figure out why Can is still wearing his tan loafers. We're in a mosque, for heaven's sake. I've left my shoes outside, and I'm not even Muslim. Is Can trying to make a statement? Or perhaps the gaffe is mine. Maybe you're supposed to wear shoes in a mosque attached to the Turkish equivalent of our Capitol building: the legislative heart of a modern secular state. Both are reasonable conjectures. The building itself makes a political statement. It was deliberately designed to reinforce the secular government against those who would see Turkey ruled by clerical law.

Designed by Behruz Çinici, in association with his son, the stubbornly shod Can, the concrete building is situated on the secular equivalent of sacred soil. The Assembly's 1930s buildings, in modern classical style, embody the political legacy of Ataturk, modern Turkey's founder. Cinici, a student of the Assembly's architect, declared he would not design a conventional mosque on Ataturk's land.

Critics of Mies van der Rohe's design for the Illinois Institution of Technology campus once complained that you can't distinguish the chapel from the boiler plant. The Assembly's mosque distances itself even further from the conventions of sacred architecture. It deliberately inverts the elements of traditional mosque design.

In many mosques, the entrance is approached through an open arcade that partly screens the main facade. Here there is nothing but a long row of concrete pedestals—symbolic bases of the columns that the architects have declined to provide. Instead of a dome, the roof mounts in low steps to form an elongated ziggurat. Clerestories between the levels admit light into the prayer hall below. On the right side of the building, where a minaret would typically rise, a set of steps leads up to two platforms, both open to the sky.

The mosque's most unconventional element is visible from within the prayer hall. Instead of facing a solid wall, kneeling worshippers face a large glass window and, beyond it, a sumptuous, multilevel sunken garden with pools, fountains, trees, a waterfall, and a profusion of water plants. It is a representation of paradise, an image of the afterlife to which devout Muslims aspire. Can Çinici tells me that for Muslims, life is a threshold at which we stand, preparing ourselves throughout life, through faith and devotion, for entrance into heaven. The Çinicis designed an architectural interpretation of that threshhold. Beyond the garden, one beholds the earth berm, an intimation of death and burial.

I like the threshold image, not only as a key to this building's meaning but as a metaphor for the awards program itself, as a doorway into realms of deeper understanding of the post–Cold War world. The awards are presented every three years, after a selection process that is elaborate, well financed, and rigorous. Several hundred nominations are proposed by a network of architects and critics throughout the Islamic world. An international master jury meets in Geneva to review the nominees and make an initial cut. Experts conduct extensive field research on the finalists. The jury picks the winners at a second review in Geneva six months later.

The composition of the master jury changes with each cycle. Over the years, non-Muslims on the panel have included Charles Correa, Peter Eisenman, Frank Gehry, Hans Hollein, Fumihiko Maki, Charles Moore, Álvaro Siza, James Stirling, Kenzo Tange, and Robert Venturi. Excerpts from the jury's deliberations are published in book form. These are adding up to a permanent record of the impact of global change on the art of creating place.

But why is Can still wearing his shoes? (Because, I later learned, he was flustered by showing a Western journalist around his building.) Or, why does this building continue to cause anxiety? Just months before my trip, last year, the Turkish military intervened to prevent the ruling party from mandating religious education in the nation's public schools. The ground occupied by the mosque, in other words, is contested as well as sacred space. Here formal invention serves architecture's unparalleled power to open the pores to history and meaning.

Reforestation Program, Middle East Technical University, Ankara

Since 1961, 1 million trees have been planted annually on the hills outside Ankara: pine, cedar, oak, poplar, almond, and plum. The 11,000-acre-plus project of the Middle East Technical Institute has altered the city's climate, creating milder winters and summers and helping to decrease air pollution. The forest has also become a haven for abundant life and an oasis for the eyes.

But perhaps the major impact of the forest has been to limit urban sprawl. Turkish law forbids the development of forest land. Like the mosque's sunken garden, the forest offers a vision of paradise, but the delights here are earthly as well. The forest offers greenery in a desert, a parched terrain of banal housing that spreads outward from Ankara's urban core.

At the Technical University, classes are conducted in English, campus buildings are designed in the Brutalist style, and architectural instruction is derived from the Bauhaus model. It strikes me that the reforestation program lies partly within the tradition of British Arts and Crafts. Like that movement, the program is grounded in the values of simplicity, social reform, and truth to materials; in rejection of the shoddy and the ornate. Arts and Crafts was more than a style. No other movement declared more emphatically the withdrawal of the religious dimension from the public sphere. With it, belief withdrew into the sanctity of the home, the privacy of what we now call lifestyle. It is heartening to see that tradition revived on the urban scale of collective expression.

Vacation Houses, Bodrum

The Mausoleum at Halicarnassus, one of the Seven Wonders of the World, is now a big pit in the back streets of Bodrum, a hip resort town on the Aegean coast. In the early fifteenth century, Crusaders pillaged the Mausoleum, quarrying it for stone to build the Castle of St. John, a fortress that still stands on a mole in the harbor. But enough rubble was left lying around in the nineteenth century to construct two small stone houses built on the waterfront. These are now the property of the record producer Ahmet Ertegun and his wife, Mica, who remodeled the buildings in 1973 with the architect Turgut Cansever.

On the ground floor, the rooms are cool and white, with high ceilings and floors strewn with blue- and white-striped cushions. The bedrooms, lodged in a newer annex, are more richly decorated. The old buildings and the new enclose a garden of enchantment. It covers a small area, but tall trees are mingled with short ones and the foliage bursts out at eye level, creating an effect at once infinite and intimate. Mausolus was a tyrant, and the Crusaders were terrorists. It's a joy to see these ancient stones recycled into a house rebuilt by jazz.

After an afternoon in this garden, it comes as a letdown to visit another award-winning project, the Demir Holiday Village, also designed by Turgut Cansever. Like Seaside in Florida, this resort offers itself as a model for urban development. And, like the reforestation program, it was designed to limit sprawl. In two decades, Bodrum has gone through a San Tropez–style transformation, from fishing village and hippie colony to a booming resort that makes South Beach look sleepy. The hills surrounding the harbor bristle with stumpy white apartment buildings of no distinction.

By contrast, the holiday village is compact, its houses unified by stone walls, terraces, and stairs that organize the dwellings in a staggered arrangement on the hillside site. It's a rustic Habitat, Acapulco on Alka-Seltzer. If you care about architecture, this is the sort of project you're supposed to admire. But the rooms in the houses are minuscule, the sun is gone from the water in the afternoon, and the entire complex is so tight and repressed that you want to blare a transistor radio and race back to the sprawl. Why bother with Bodrum if you want to be square? I'm glad to see that Turkey has bubbles too.

Dolmabahçe Palace Gardens, Istanbul

Completed in 1856, Dolmabahçe Palace is the superbubble of a burnt-out superpower, the last seat of the Ottoman rulers before the sultanate was dissolved in 1922. An imperial palace can feel like a desert too. The grandiosity of this European-style palace is more oppressive than Death Valley. It is one gigantic package of everything that Arts and Crafts designers rebelled against: twenty-five-ton crystal chandeliers, bearskin rugs (gifts from the czar), diamond-encrusted demitasse cups, gilded moldings, red brocade. Just climbing the Crystal Staircase, with its Baccarat balustrade, can induce reverse vertigo: you fear you won't make it to the top. This is the center of an empire rapidly devolving into the so-called Sick Man of Europe, a nation whose assets and interests were dominated by businessmen and politicians of the major European powers.

But the Aga Khan Award wasn't presented to this project for interior decoration. Rather, the award honored the restoration of the palace gardens and the decision to open them to the public. Istanbul is not rich in parks, and this is a fine one. The palace stands at the mouth of the Bosphorus. An esplanade, with five water gates, is one of world's great river walks. Among Istanbul's public spaces, I prefer the square between the Hagia Sophia and the Blue Mosque, where people come to sit on benches and contemplate great buildings. But, for a native of the eastern United States, it is a thrilling reversal to gaze westward across water toward the European shore.

Arab World Institute, Paris

"One can't write directly about the soul," Virginia Woolf states in her diary. "Looked at, it vanishes. But look at the ceiling, at the cheaper beasts in the Zoo which are exposed to walkers in Regents Park, and the soul slips in."

On the way back to New York, I stop off in Paris to pay my respects to the Aga Khan in Chantilly. It also happens that the one Western building to receive an Aga Khan award is in a Left Bank riverside location at the foot of the Boulevard Saint-Germain. Jean Nouvel is an architect I greatly admire, but I've never been a fan of his Arab World Institute. Each time I enter this visually cool, gunmetal gray building, the body temperature drops.

But the Institute's lozenge shape makes good use of its site, and the views from its rooftop restaurant outclass those from the Tour d'Argent. And the building makes a historical point. Its most noted feature is a south-facing sunscreen wall made up of hundreds of light-sensitive irises, which was designed to control the light entering the building. Arranged in blocks fitted into a grid, the irises form patterns resembling arabesques: a reminder that Western technology arose from the genius of Islamic mathematicians. We've taken that inspiration in more than one direction. The irises stopped working within weeks of the building's opening, but we still love the image of science even when appliances break down. And, to me, Nouvel's arctic architecture is a fine thermal symbol of the chilly rationalist philosophy for which Paris was long the supreme urban center.

. . .

I feel as if I've been traveling around inside one of architecture's most interesting minds, but the Aga Khan's Chantilly compound feels oddly bland. The road winds through a lovely, leafy park. Stables to the right; the prince's house to the right; the Secretariat just ahead, the latter blond in effect. Tawny limestone walls; floors of honey-colored marble; ecru carpeting; brass accents. Only the small foyer to the prince's office, encrusted with a collection of mineral crystals, gives an Oriental impression. Inside, chairs and sofas are upholstered in blue and white.

I came here to run two ideas by the prince. Can he confirm my impression that his interest in architecture stems from that art's capacity to unite spirit and matter in the landscape of everyday life? Yes, he answered, his eyes lighting up, as if to suggest that no point is more fundamental to his thinking.

And what about using the threshold as a metaphor for this story? This idea he rejected. It evoked for him images of conquest, of crossing a border with the intention of colonizing the territory on the other side. The threshold also implies terrain left behind—epochs, values, roots. Neither image fits the prince's mission. His aim, rather, has been to create a meeting ground for cultural exchange.

Some critics have said that the buildings commissioned by the Aga Khan are still not up the level of the projects honored by his awards. Others have wondered whether the money it takes to run the program might not be better spent on actual buildings. Both criticisms miss the point. The aim of the awards program is to construct a worldview, and this is priceless.

With a morning plane to catch, I had no time to pretend that I was actually visiting Paris. But before turning in I decided to walk down to the Seine and see its banks bathed in the harsh glare of the *bateaux mouches*. There I encountered something unexpected: an impromptu memorial to Princess Diana, sculptured from thousands of letters, cards, flowers, and photographs. These were massed around the base of the replica of Liberty's torch that stands on the quai at the bottom of the Avenue George V. Visitors replenish offerings there to this day.

The princess had died the night before I left New York for Turkey, and since I'd been out of touch with the news, I hadn't heard about the cascades of grief generated by her death. Surprising, too, was the volume of cards and letters written in Arabic script. *Pour Diana, Reine d'Islam*, one large placard read.

Like the princess's death, the site of the memorial was an accident of fate; the torch stands at the entrance to the Alma Tunnel, where the car in which Diana was riding spun out of control and crashed. But I thought it paradoxically apt that this public expression of grief was clustered around this golden symbol of liberty, of French Enlightenment values and their passage to the United States.

Those values included religious freedom, and even the right to be free of religion in the public sphere. This is a cherished principle of modern democracy, an idea to be defended with vigor. Yet it seemed to me that more than a princess was being mourned here. Our separation of Faith from World has also left a void, fleetingly filled by this collective floral tribute.

October 11, 1998

LIVING BOLDLY ON THE EVENT HORIZON

No matter how many rooms or closets you have in the house, there is seldom enough space for time. That's one reason why architecture continues to evolve. Architects have but a brief interval to greet the present before time slips away.

In the outskirts of Bordeaux, Rem Koolhaas has designed a house for the millennium. It is a space for facing the unknown: for risk, mystery, surprise, and suspense, a house where floors and walls disappear, and inside merges with outside in a sparkling play of reflections.

The place is haunted by flickering memories of Edgar Allan Poe and his fearless, youthful descendants, the Hardy Boys, Frank and Joe. At any minute Nancy Drew will pull up in her roadster, looking for her boyfriend, Ned, or to ask directions back to River Heights, the town she left behind. But the place has already become a prime destination for architecture fans who look toward Mr. Koolhaas to find a way to the here and now.

To get into the spirit of this building, it helps to go back to the Symbolists, the poets and artists who, at the end of nineteenth century, reacted against realism and began exploring moods, atmospheres, perversities, fears, and other subjective realms. The movement as such did not penetrate far into architecture. The swirls and tendrils of Art Nouveau designers evoked some symbolist motifs: Munch's and Redon's graphic splashes in the waves of the subconscious. Later work by Le Corbusier (the chapel of Notre Dame du Haut at Ronchamp) and a few landscaped buildings by Luis Barragán are arguably symbolist in use of color, shadow, and form to evoke emotional depth.

It is surprising, however, to see such qualities surfacing in a contemporary house. But this house was conceived under unusual circumstances. The owner, a newspaper publisher, had already decided to build his family a new home when he was injured in an automobile accident that caused internal injuries and cost him the use of his legs.

At the time, the client had already decided to move from a town house in the center of Bordeaux and had asked several architects to compete for the design of a new home in the city's lush suburbs. After the accident, he decided it would be easier to work with one architect, and awarded the commission to Mr. Koolhaas, who is based in Rotterdam, the Netherlands. The result, though not yet fully furnished, has already become a mecca, one of those rare buildings people feel they must visit to see what the present looks like.

You approach the house through a forecourt enclosed on three sides by Barragán-like walls, thin, horizontal slabs of concrete pierced by wide rectangular arches. A moon gate is on one wall. In front of the house, the driveway spirals in on itself and tapers to a sharp point. The shape brings to mind the Saul Bass title sequence for a Hitchcock thriller, and if James Stewart got out of the wrong side of the car, he might well swoon, since the ground drops off abruptly along one edge of the drive.

The house is three stories tall, a glass sandwich served between two slices of concrete, garnished lightly with furniture and art. There are two entrances on the ground floor. One leads through a cavelike hallway of molded concrete to an outdoor terrace on the second floor, the second into a large, open-plan space with a kitchen and dining area at one end. The floor is lined with a polished, cool green resin. Here one also encounters the building's most exceptional feature: a large platform the size of a small room, designed to move at the touch of a button between the three floors.

This elevator is the core of the house. Furnished with the owner's desk, the 10½ x 11 foot platform is mounted atop a column of polished steel and driven by machinery buried beneath the ground floor. In addition to providing the disabled owner with mobility, it keeps the house in a state of visual flux. The platform occupies just enough of the building's floor area so that, when it moves from one level to another, it changes the house's spatial composition. The movement alters the dimensions of each floor and enlarges or impedes the flow of space between them.

The platform is open on three sides, with the fourth enclosed by glass bookshelves that rise through all three floors. Guard panels slide into place as it ascends from the ground-floor kitchen to the living area on the second floor and a bedroom on the third. On whatever level, the desk assumes the symbolic presence of a control panel for the entire house. The backdrop of books, illuminated by a skylight and accented by a

Gilbert and George painting mounted between the second and third floors, imply that control will be brilliantly exercised.

Stairs, partly screening an office, ascend from the kitchen to the main floor, a living area unlike any other: a piano nobile with a piano mobile. Aluminum panels, buffed to a matte finish, cover the floor and intensify the light pouring in from three glass walls. The furniture, a mix of modern classics (Breuer, Bertoia) and French Provincial comfort pieces, was carefully chosen and just as carefully disarranged. Along one wall there is seating on a cushioned stone bench that also contains a fireplace.

About a third of this floor is an outdoor terrace, paved with travertine. An earth berm, banked against the rear of the ground floor, rises to meet the terrace in a gentle grass slope. The glass wall facing the slope and the view is mechanized and slides open to unite the living area with the outdoors. The terrace is sheltered beneath the concrete slab of the building's top story. A large cylinder, of concrete wrapped in polished steel, houses a spiral staircase leading from the floor below to the children's quarters above while providing structural support. Reflections in its convex surface dematerialize the column, and a low stack of firewood stretches along one side of the terrace. The counterpoint between these materials—the raw and rustic against the polished industrial—gives the terrace the serene simplicity of a Japanese garden.

On the top floor, concrete walls, stained brown and punctured only by porthole windows, project the privacy of a harem, so I will let the floor keep its secrets except to say that the bedrooms are cozy, that the portholes are not arbitrarily placed but correspond to the height of the owner, his wife, and their three children in seated, standing, and reclining positions. Besides providing views and light, the windows inject effervescence into what might otherwise recall a 1960s Brutalist housing block.

I would call this house a shelter from shelter, a concept I've earned the right to defend. I bumped my head in one spot and scratched my thumb on another, leaving a bloody smear on the light blue taffeta curtain being fitted for a living-room glass wall. The thought crossed my mind that Mr. Koolhaas had designed a house in which only the disabled could safely live. But the place brought back memories of *The Disappearing Floor*, a Hardy Boys mystery that features a nutty inventor who lives in an old house equipped with such grotesqueries as a mechanical ghost and a bedroom whose floor drops away, leaving the furniture suspended in midair.

In the Bordeaux house, you can't completely escape the tension between the concrete slabs and the light open space between them. If the platform can descend, why not the roof? Yet the atmosphere throughout is breezy, the building's connection to land and sky arcadian. On the second floor, the general effect is of life lived as a picnic, and you don't have to run for shelter if it rains.

But there's scant refuge here for normalcy. The building—which cost $1.5 million to construct—does much more than accommodate the owner's physical disabilities. It uses them as a springboard to imagine ways of being in the world.

While Mr. Koolhaas uses the industrial materials and uncluttered spaces favored by architects of the Modern movement, he employs them toward radically different ends. Modernists favored standardization, the use of structural components and visual forms that conveyed the rational ethos of industrial mass production.

Mr. Koolhaas subverts this entirely. It is the ghost in the machine, to use the novelist Arthur Koestler's phrase, that haunts him, the dimensions of human experience that cannot be standardized, rationalized, or predicted. The concrete top floor is supported at one end by a large black truss, supported on columns, and stabilized at the other end by a counterweight suspended from a steel girder mounted atop the roof. This structural arrangement, while securing the building, also expresses its inherent instability. It assumes the metaphoric values of conflict and balance, of stresses met with equipoise and imaginatively resolved.

The Russian formalists analyzed narrative structure as a process in which a state of equilibrium is disturbed by a series of events until a heightened sense of balance is finally attained. Anyone who has visited the Eiffel Tower knows that buildings can create this kind of narrative. On each stage to the top, you catch your breath and pass through fear until gaining the summit. (For some of us, the new state of equilibrium isn't felt until our feet again touch ground).

In *The Disappearing Floor*, the plot is resolved when Joe and Frank realize that the crazy inventor isn't a villain but rather the victim of a group of thieves. What they don't fully grasp is that they themselves are not the pair of normal lads they present to the reader. They're the Hardy Boys. They're freaks. They're never going to grow up and have full lives. They're condemned to forever trying to please their father, Fenton, even though they're already master crime-busters, while Dad is just a stick that smokes a pipe.

Mr. Koolhaas has embraced the challenge of designing a house for a disabled man and his family as an opportunity to say something about this millennial moment. We don't know where we'll be tomorrow, much less two years hence. Life does throw curves. Floors do disappear; planes and stock markets go up and down; tycoons and terrorists conspire; life does not go on as before.

At fifty-four, Rem Koolhaas is also a freak. No architect of his generation is more extravagantly talented. None has found more eloquent ways to embody his generation's perplexities and ambivalences about its own changing times. His career has been a suspense story that has kept admirers enthralled. The opening of his retrospective at the Museum of Modern Art three years ago drew a pop star's turnout. Two of his books, *Delirious New York* and *S, M, L, XL* (Monicelli Press, 1995), have been critical hits.

But he has also alienated potential clients, written rude letters to editors, lost out in competitions to architects of lesser talent, and borne the animosity of those with less-blazing gifts. He retains his generation's distrust of authority but knows that architecture is not something you go off and do by yourself in the woods.

Every realized building has come to seem like a triumph against great odds: the train station at Euralille, a 469-acre communications, financial, and entertainment hub in northern France, for which Mr. Koolhaas designed the master plan; the Villa dall'Ava in Paris; the Netherlands Dance Theater in The Hague; the Kunsthal in Rotterdam. All of them are courageous, for architect and clients alike, but the new Bordeaux project conveys particular urgency of Mr. Koolhaas's determination to step into the unknown.

November 19, 1998

THE VILLAGE AS A SATIRIST'S MILIEU AND MUSE

Time for holiday shopping. Why not first stop at a bookstore and give yourself a treat? This is a good season to catch up on reading. It's also good for rambling around the neighborhood of a writer many readers are only now beginning to catch up with: the brilliant social satirist Dawn Powell. Her glittering novels, especially those set in New York, offer a rare opportunity to reflect on the dependence of cities and books for mutual survival. Take home a stack. You'll thank me.

Powell, who died in 1965, would have been 102 years old last Saturday. This is a shocking milestone, for Powell's voice is among the freshest in contemporary letters. Her writing flourished in the 1940s and '50s, but only recently has she begun to receive her full due. The campaign to rescue her from oblivion was begun by Gore Vidal and led by Tim Page, the chief music critic for *The Washington Post*, author of a new biography on Powell and a former music critic for *The New York Times*. It has been a miracle of modern literary life.

Eleven of Powell's fifteen novels are in print, more than at any point in her stressed-out lifetime. Published by Steerforth Press, the handsome paperback editions feature atmospheric New York cityscapes bordered with dusky, metallic colors. The voice that emerges from those covers is as sharp as their design. Powell's tone is comic, but her themes are profound. Collectively, her books paint a panorama of the energies a great city marshals to corrode as well as nurture people's dreams. They also attest to one woman's triumph over dragons.

Where She Lived

"I don't know why anyone in New York worries about good neighborhoods," she said. "They never see their neighbors anyway so it might as well be a bad neighborhood."

—From Dawn Powell's *Time to Be Born* (1942)

A native of Ohio, Powell spent most of her life in Greenwich Village. In a letter to a friend in the late 1950s, she writes about a niece who came to New York but declined her aunt's invitation to visit because it would have conflicted with a scheduled tour of the Village. "I was so startled to think I almost prevented them from seeing mysterious Greenwich Village that I didn't think to say," as an acquaintance suggested, " 'But dearie, your Auntie Dawn *is* Greenwich Village.' "

Powell may exaggerate, but her unspoken retort was not an overstatement. Late in her life, *The New York Times Magazine* published a picture of Powell in a local antiques store. *Life* magazine posed her in some Village coffeehouses for an article that never ran. And her books offer the most luminous portrayal of life downtown in the era between Edna St. Vincent Millay and the Stonewall uprising.

The Village has changed dramatically since Powell's death. Rents have skyrocketed. The Loews movie theater on Greenwich Avenue, the Women's House of Detention, the Brevoort Hotel, and other landmarks are barely memories. Bohemia dispersed long ago to the East Village, SoHo, TriBeCa, and beyond. Most catastrophically, the bookstores that once lined Eighth Street and Fourth Avenue have dwindled to a small fraction of their former number.

Still, thanks to preservation laws that did not exist in Powell's day, much of the neighborhood's physical character remains intact. Blocks of low-rise buildings let in lots of sky. West of Avenue of the Americas, the Manhattan grid remains happily scrambled. West Fourth Street still crosses West Tenth Street. Most of the buildings Powell lived in still stand. And the place retains its image as a refuge from social conventions and constraints. Her novels and the city illuminate each other: the desire for refuge is a pivotal idea in her writing.

"There must be some place along the route, a halfway house in time where the runners may pause and ask themselves why they run, what is the prize and is it the prize they really want," Powell reflects in her novel *The Wicked Pavilion*. "What became of Beauty? Where went Love? There must be havens where they may at least be remembered."

Greenwich Village offered Powell refuge but not security. Perhaps she didn't want that. She wasn't a stranger to comfort. From the early 1940s through the mid-'50s, she occupied a duplex in a doorman building on a good block of Tenth Street, complete with a top-floor maid's room that she used as a writing studio. But she was not one for putting down roots. Her diary is peppered with periodic descriptions of moves from one apartment to the next, and this nomadism corresponded to something in her temperament.

In 1937 she wrote in her diary: "Homes are bad places. Either they are so comfortable that no other place else could offer as much sheer convenience, yet psychic and family connections are such that you can never enjoy these comforts—this cozy study filled with invisible foes, interruptions, responsibilities, worry, hatred. Or else you have no comfortable place in your home to work and in spite of privacy and other ideal personal relations are unable to enjoy it."

She thought of herself as "a permanent visitor" in New York. *My Home Is Far Away*, the title of one of her most autobiographical novels, conveyed a perpetual desire for displacement. To write, she would sometimes hole up at seaside hotels, like the Traymore in Atlantic City or the Half Moon in Coney Island. Summers were often spent in a tumbledown cottage on Long Island's North Shore.

Powell could be romantic about squalor. In *The Wicked Pavilion*, she tracks one of her characters as he makes a nocturnal visit to a dilapidated house way out in Queens (she had College Point in mind) that he had shared years before with two pals who were seeking their private Bohemia, a simulation of Left Bank Paris. Here, isolated from worldly distractions, the trio devoted themselves to art.

Powell never lived in College Point, but a few years after the publication of this book she found herself virtually homeless. In 1958, when her building went co-op, Powell and her husband, Joseph Gousha, had to give up their apartment. Powell was in her early sixties. Her husband, an advertising executive, had recently retired. For two years the couple lived in sublets and cheap hotels. Possessions went into King Arthur Express Storage. Mostly books, plus: "One hall desk, oak. Doll head in carton and dolls. Secretary desk. Three straight chairs. One large dirty rug. Three small dirty rugs."

When her husband became mortally ill, Powell found an airless flat with a deceptively impressive Fifth Avenue address. Later, with financial help from a friend, Powell moved into a penthouse apartment in a prewar high-rise on the corner of Christopher and Bleecker streets. (I briefly sublet this place in the late 1970s, long before I'd heard of Dawn Powell.) The elegant reprise was short-lived. Two years after she moved in, Powell was interred in a mass grave on Hart Island, New York's Potter's Field.

Where She Dined

"Why does anybody come here?" countered Ricky.

Philippe gave this question some judicious thought. "They come because they have always come here," he said.

Why did they come here the first time, then?

Nobody ever comes to the Julien for the first time.

—From *The Wicked Pavilion* (1954)

Powell hardly lived as a hermit. She and Gousha spent much of their time and income dining out, and it showed. Powell was plump. But she relished the social spectacle far more than the food. In her diary she seldom raves about dishes. Instead there are snippets like this:

"Nov. 3, 1952. Ethel regarded her first drink politely, allowing it to simmer before her for several minutes, as if it was merely a formality like a service plate to be taken away untouched when something she really wished would be served. However, just as the other ladies were ordering a second round she suddenly dashed off her potion in one gulp and by dinner time was quite as tight as anyone else."

In *The Wicked Pavilion*, Powell wrote a whole book about a restaurant. The Café Julien, a kind of Grand Central for the book's characters, is based on Powell's favorite hangout, the Café Lafayette, on the ground floor of a hotel that was on University Place between Eighth and Ninth streets. Reginald Marsh painted a picture of the place to illustrate the jacket of the book's first edition. Remember café curtains?

The Lafayette was the haven's haven, a mixture of new and familiar faces where Powell found provisional stability amid urban flux. The café turned out to be nearly as impermanent as a dust jacket. The hotel was torn down in the 1950s to make way for a concrete apartment block, the ugly Brevoort East.

To read about the other restaurants Powell frequented is to return to a time before American cooking became inventive. For culinary adventure, you ate Italian, Chinese, Spanish, and so on. You can taste the period's flavor at Powell's surviving Village haunts, places like El Faro, at Horatio and

Greenwich streets, and Grand Ticino on Thompson Street. At the Ticino, writers used to stow their manuscripts in shelves that still hang above the tables.

For fancy nights out, Powell and Gousha headed uptown, to the Rainbow Room, the 21 Club, Tavern on the Green, or the St. Regis Hotel. But if I were giving a dinner in Powell's honor, I might hold it at Grange Hall. The restaurant wasn't around in her day, but it has an archetypal Village location. The heartland cuisine recalls Powell's Ohio childhood.

But maybe the best way to revisit Powell's New York would be to drop by Chumley's, a former speakeasy with a still unmarked door, guzzle two or three gin martinis in quick succession, and rush out into the streets before the buzz wears off. Any city can look magical when you're bombed, as Powell, Gousha, and their friends often were. Considering how much alcohol they consumed, it's amazing that Powell was so productive. It's also fair to say that the city looks after drunks. If she'd moved to the country, like Jackson Pollock, she might well have run into a tree.

Powell was not a secret drinker, nor did she condemn the usual vices. In her diary she deplores "the hypocrisy of blaming X's downfall on alcohol, women, and social climbing, when these were precisely the things that enabled him to become a success in the first place." Viewed from our present puritanical perspective, she and her pals seem enviably free from guilt or shame.

But some reviewers were put off by Powell's reluctance to be a moral judge. What Mr. Vidal termed her Petronian neutrality was often taken as cynicism. Powell professed surprise at this reaction. She believed she was defending love and beauty from the forces arrayed against them: arrogance, betrayal, and competitiveness, to name a few.

Where She Lives On

Sept. 29, 1959. The Coney Island Sunday Crowd around Washington Square . . . Girls carrying on fight. One walking ahead. Other shouts "I tell you I'm sick—I don't feel good—I'm sick." The other one pushes on. "Okay, you're sick. Eat a hamburger."
—From *The Diaries of Dawn Powell: 1931–1965*

If there's to be a commemorative plaque, Mr. Page suggests it should be placed at 106 Perry Street. Powell wrote or began several of her best novels there. But I propose that they rename the Washington Arch in her honor. The Dawn Powell Arch. She was very fond of this City Beautiful souvenir. On walks, she would stroll down to the arch, take in the light, and eavesdrop on conversations. Then she might walk back along Eighth

Street, perhaps stopping for a milk shake before she returned home and poured the day's first drink.

For many, the Dawn Powell revival is driven by something more than the pleasure of discovering a forgotten first-rate writer. There is also the fear that the city she wrote about won't be around much longer in a form Powell would recognize, i.e., a New York that can't sustain writers capable of chronicling it. In the essay that sparked the revival, published in 1987 in *The New York Review of Books*, Mr. Vidal already delivers last rites.

It's easy to agree with Mr. Vidal when you walk around the Village today and note the scarcity of bookstores. Of the few that remain, only Three Lives & Company (another spot that opened well after Powell's death) projects a proper bibliophilic fervor. It's fabulous that we'll soon be able to download books into palm-sized computers, but the experience won't be the same as letting your eyes graze over the covers of books that a literate manager has arranged in a shopwindow.

The physicality of Powell's books is as eloquent as a skyscraper. A shelf of them is a skyline. They are palpable tributes to the towering city of work. The diaries document this repeatedly: Powell goes out into the streets, into bars, theaters, and other people's houses, returns home with images, chunks of dialogue, fashions them into a city on the page, sends her portrayal back into the world, awaits reviews, musters her spirits against disappointing sales, meditates on her unpopularity, sallies forth and begins again. The process was itself a magic wheel turning, each spin animating city and author alike.

Powell's diaries offer written proof that the city was never comfortable for writers, and perhaps shouldn't be. A self-created observer, Powell did not oppose change. In her last novel, *The Golden Spur*, a young man, savoring his first day in New York, stands on a sidewalk and watches wreckers pull down an old department store. He asks the gentleman beside him why the event has drawn such a big crowd. The man replies:

> "In the first place this was a splendid old landmark and people like to see the old order blown up. Then there is the glorious dirt and uproar which are the vitamins of New York, and of course the secret hope that the street will cave in and swallow us all up."
>
> Jonathan looked down uneasily at the boards underfoot.
>
> "Dear old Wanamaker's." His companion sighed. "If I had paid their nasty little bill, perhaps they would never have come to this. Well, mustn't get sentimental."

December 4, 1998

BLUEPRINT: THE SHOCK OF THE FAMILIAR

In Greek mythology, Morpheus is the god of dreams. But I also like to think of him as the deity who presides over design. *Morph* means "form." Morphology is the study of shapes. Metamorphosis is the transformation of appearance. And these are dreamy times for design.

There has never been more stuff, and stuff must have a shape, an appearance, a boundary in two or three dimensions to distinguish it from other stuff. Even water, and perhaps eventually air, must arrive in distinctive bottles. The shapes are no longer content simply to arise. They explode, mutate, and multiply. Design is now subject to the whimsical laws and seasonal revisions of fashion, the quick impulses of journalism.

There is no dominant style, no prevailing trend. There's just more and more stuff that has been styled, molded, carved, folded, patterned, cut-and-pasted, prototyped, mocked up, punched up, laid out, recycled, and shrink-wrapped. Modernity has rendered the material world into some kind of plasma that is perpetually prodded and massaged into an endless variety of contours. Look around. Our designed world has the polymorphousness of clouds, the rapid, shifting, irrational play of dreams. Let's call it morphomania.

Is it a good dream or a nightmare? Design today is certainly a challenge for a critic who wants to make sense of, much less evaluate, the things designers shape. In the eighteenth century, it was believed that design could be evaluated according to universal laws. The purpose of cultivating taste was to educate the senses to their essence.

Today the most powerful laws governing design are dictated by the marketplace. Catch the eye. Stimulate desire. Move the merchandise. Yet even in the market-driven world of contemporary design there adheres a mythological dimension.

Design, that is, reaches into the psyche as well as the pocketbook. Like dreams, forms can hold momentous meaning, never more so than today, when images have gone far toward displacing words as a medium of communication. This issue of the *New York Times Magazine* tries to interpret the shapes that are bombarding our psyches.

We are all morphomaniacs now. Exhibit A: My medicine cabinet. Here's a partial inventory:

• Colognes: Chanel pour Monsieur—classic square bottle designed by Coco herself. CK One—frosted hip flask; Chanel updated. Issey Miyake's cologne for men—a morphomaniac's delight; the bottle morphs from a curved base to a flat top. • Braun electric toothbrush—something the Bauhaus might have created if Hitler hadn't shut it down. • Band-Aid Sheer strips—relics of Oleg Cassini's "Sheer Look" of the 1950s. • Moisturizers: St. Ives dry-skin lotion—banal plastic bottle, but I like it better than Oil of Olay, Erno Laszlo, Clinique M, or other more attractively packaged brands that cost five times as much. No-brand moisturizer from bathroom at the Montalembert—plain white tube; souvenir of the best-designed Left Bank hotel. • Bayer aspirin—less effective for my headaches than Excedrin, but bottle bears quintessential label. • Effexor sample box—best packaging for a designer drug; shield-shaped tablets undistinguished compared with Prozac's two-toned pastel bullet-head capsule. • Mach 3 razor—cute guy performs supersonic striptease in the commercials; body clearly enhanced by electronic surgery. • Right Guard Sport Clear Stick—nice concept but sticky and horrible to use. Et cetera.

The cabinet is a morphomaniac microcosm. Somebody thought of these shapes. Or maybe not. Perhaps they're just emanations of what the physiologist Rupert Sheldrake calls morphogenetic fields—resonant, invisible forces that shape living beings and their patterns of behavior. Perhaps something Darwinian is going on here, and the design of perfume bottles, vacuum cleaners, cars, and hairstyles has taken on a life of its own, a struggle for survival in the sleek jungles of advanced capitalist culture.

To me, design is an art of transition: a method of building bridges between our inner and outer worlds. I derive this concept from D. W. Winnicott, the great British psychoanalyst who specialized in child development. Winnicott believed that in the process of separating from their mothers, children use what he called transitional objects: a toy, a spoon, a blanket or pillow. Such objects, Winnicott thought, play a pivotal role in our gradual apprehension that we have been born into a world over which we do not exercise omnipotent control. As much as parents or other human beings, transitional objects teach us the difference between objective and subjective states. They also help us comprehend that our inner and outer realms are seldom sharply divided.

Design is a sort of cultural transitional object. The things a designer produces, a consumer buys, and an advertising agency garnishes with seductive graphic flourishes extend into adult life the process of simultaneously merging with, and differentiating ourselves from, the world of others. Plates, chairs, curtains, computer-graphic interfaces—these artifacts and images are currency in the dynamic exchange between the worlds we've absorbed and the larger cultural universe. We create our buildings, and our buildings create us, it has been said. Design carries this process a step further. With design, we assert moods, tastes, whims, and aspirations for change.

In the late 1960s I worked in the display department of Design Research, a store on Fifty-seventh Street long famous as the only retail establishment in New York where you could buy the objects on view in the design collection of the Museum of Modern Art. Founded by Benjamin Thompson, the Cambridge, Massachusetts, architect who would later pioneer the concept of the festival marketplace in Boston, San Francisco, New York, and other American cities, the store stocked classics of modern furniture by Thonet, Aalto, Mies van der Rohe, Breuer, Magistretti, Hoffmann, and Eames. It also introduced innovative work by young Italian designers like Joe Colombo.

This was the only time in my life I ever got to fool around with visual forms in a public setting, and it was the best fun a boy ever had. I loved arranging the furniture, playing with spotlights and gels, fiddling with table arrangements, changing fabrics, deciding what to display in the store's great two-story arched window. These were my toys, my playthings, objects that eased my transition into the realms of architecture and design, the fields that I wanted to write about.

The store's aesthetic embodied principles that began with Arts and Crafts and continued with the Bauhaus and the Good Design shows of the 1950s: functionality, truth to materials, simplicity of geometric form, the use of new materials and methods. But the fact is that by the time I made the store my playground, the movement it stood for had largely run its course.

Around 1970, a speaker at the International Design Conference in Aspen, Colorado, an annual convocation of Good Design's true believers, is said to have lamented the recent appearance of kitsch objects like telephones shaped in the image of Mickey Mouse. Then a student stood up and asked, But why shouldn't a telephone look like Mickey Mouse? Posed in this context, the question was shattering. If someone could say such a thing at the Chautauqua of Good Design, then the entire Arts and Crafts/Bauhaus project had already passed into history.

In the three decades since, a good deal of design has been shaped in the image of Mickey Mouse. Design has become a form of entertainment, fashion, or play. Ettore Sottsass, Gaetano Pesce, Tibor Kalman, Philippe Starck, Shiro Kuramata: the most celebrated and influential designers of the past two decades have not sought to establish a set of rules for good design. Drawing on sources as diverse as Surrealism, pop culture, fairy tales, and agitprop, they have developed highly personal vocabularies that resist being categorized.

Initially, the work of these designers may have seemed only a perverse reaction to the previous generation's idealization of cold, objective truth. In fact, designers like Sottsass and Starck have expressed a reality no less gripping than that embraced by the Bauhaus. The Good Design aesthetic was based on industrial production and its rational, standardized methods of operation. Today design responds to the reality of the distribution system: marketing, reception, stimulation, novelty, and change. And in the culture of advanced capitalism, distribution has largely displaced production as the dominant economic force. An awareness of this shift, intellectual or intuitive, distinguishes the work of today's best designers.

I am in no position to disparage this development. At Design Research, I was part of it. Fun, change, surprise, a desire to move the merchandise: these were precisely the impulses that kept me working late those Friday nights. Much as I respected the Good Design aesthetic, I had no wish to surrender to the superego mentality with which it laid down rules of taste. ("Taste is the only morality!" John Ruskin, the nut, once thundered from his secular pulpit.)

Objects produced by the Bauhaus were fruits of the imagination. They were transitional objects that had served previous generations of designers in negotiating the social contract of an earlier day. For that negotiation process to continue, the imagination had to move in new directions.

Design today may be amorphous, but it is not impervious to historical perspective. It operates on a spectrum between two extremes that have developed over time. One is reduction: the movement toward objects ever more abstract, increasingly compact, fleeting, and ephemeral. At this extreme lie holography, virtual reality, and the image of a computer graphic zipping across the screen of an ultrathin laptop on the fold-down tray of an airliner in flight. This extreme is governed by the notion that all design aspires to the condition of light, or pure energy, articulated into form.

At the opposite extreme is the millennial phenomenon Jean Baudrillard has called the Dance of the Fossils—the impulse to unearth, uproot, and uncover every artifact produced throughout cultural history and assign it a cultural value: personal, historical, and financial. No pot, no teaspoon, no funerary urn can be allowed to rest in peace. You can see this dance performed regularly on *Antiques Roadshow*, the hilarious PBS program on which appraisers assess the merits and value of often repulsive heirlooms. These are transitional objects for their owners, seeking a place in the larger scheme of things.

Since it is the nature of extremes to meet, it should not be surprising that this has happened in the field of design. *Antiques Roadshow* is a good example. It's an electronic Dance of the Fossils, a moving archaeological dig in which antique artifacts parade before our eyes in ephemeral pictures of light. Though the show is compulsively watchable, the best thing about it is that you can switch the channel or turn it off. You can have an ugly soup tureen one minute and a blank screen the next.

The blank screen—the tabula rasa—is the design many of us dream of these days: a clean, well-lighted, sparsely furnished space. John Pawson, Richard Gluckman, Deborah Berke, and other architects have specialized in creating such environments, primarily for members of the baby boom generation. Paradoxically, many of them are renovated lofts, situated in light-industrial buildings that once churned out stuff. Now their function is to keep the world of stuff at bay, to prevent their tenants from drowning in the waves of cascading images flooding the world.

"Elegance is refusal," said the legendary fashion editor Diana Vreeland, and the minimalist loft is supremely elegant in this sense. Its owners will not take part in the orgy of choices that the consumer society urges everybody to attend. They do more than refuse stuff. They reject exposing the subjectivity that is revealed when one piece of stuff is preferred to another. This, too, is paradoxical. In the minimalist loft, the Winnicottian relationship between inner and outer worlds has been reversed. The private living space has taken on the guise of objectivity: neutral, value-free, as if this were a found space, not an impeccably designed one.

The world outside, meanwhile, has become subjectified, rendered into a changing collage of personal whims and fancies. This is to be expected in a culture dominated by the distribution system. That system exists, after all, not to make things but to sell them, to appeal to individual impulses, tastes, desires. As a result, the public realm has become a collective repository of dreams and designs from which the self requires refuge.

Toward the end of his life, Arthur Drexler, the longtime head of the architecture and design department at the Museum of Modern Art, told me that the only objects he hadn't acquired for the department's permanent collection but wished he had were examples of military hardware. I suspect Drexler was indulging in a bit of projective identification. Nothing would have pleased him more than to dispatch a Stealth bomber to wipe out the entire Postmodern movement. But it is true that only military technicians seemed at that time willing to follow principles of good design.

I regret that Drexler didn't live another ten years. I suspect he would have found much to admire in the designs made possible by the communications revolution: cell phones, laptops, fax machines, digital camcorders, even the fluid new architectural forms that computer software has only begun to make possible. These, too, are weapons in the competition to acquire power, status, and money in a peacetime world.

Choice can be tyrannical. Still, somebody out there must like chocolate-mint powdered coffee. And life hasn't been the same since Pepperidge Farm dropped the Brown Sugar cookie from its Old Fashioned line. Maybe it was too old-fashioned. Or perhaps we should take a hint from Martha Stewart and bake our own. Fat chance. In any case, the triumph of free enterprise guarantees that morphomania will spread to parts of the world once undisturbed by the sorrows of shopping.

Whitman famously said that the cure for the ills of democracy is more democracy. And perhaps the cure for monomania is more design. More morphs. More makeovers, logos, gadgets, and miracle fabrics, along with more trash compactors and recycling centers, until the day arrives when dreams and things can no longer be told apart.

December 13, 1998

A TWELVE-BLOCK GLIMMER OF HOPE
FOR NEW YORK

Architecture or real estate, what's it going to be? Does New York have room for both? These are the basic questions raised by the Canadian Center for Architecture's competition to redesign an important piece of land on the west side of midtown Manhattan.

And these questions open up other questions in turn. Why must New York invest so much money, time, and energy in the vain pretense that architecture and real estate are the same thing? Wouldn't it be cheaper, not to mention more culturally invigorating, just to put New York back on the map as a center of architectural thought?

Conceived by Phyllis Lambert, founding director of the Canadian Center, a powerhouse of architectural culture in Montreal, the West Side project is the first in a series of competitions to be held every three years. Each of these, officially called the IFCCA Prize Competition for the Design of Cities, will address the modern needs of a different city around the world. The winner will receive $100,000.

The overall aim of the program is to stimulate new ways of thinking about the design and planning of cities for the twenty-first century. In New York the goal is to set a high architectural standard for an area that seems destined for major commercial development in the near future.

The last three decades have been a golden age for architectural preservation in New York, and the importance of this should not be underestimated. It's pleasing that the city is approaching the millennium with an extraordinary appreciation for the history it has passed through to get there. But this has not been an era of opportunity for architects, in Giò Ponti's words, "to interpret the life of the inhabitants, transforming it into an expression of civilization and culture." This competition offers an opportunity to interpret life on the threshold the city is now crossing.

The site is a twelve-block corridor that stretches from Eighth Avenue to the Hudson River. It is bounded on its southern edge by Thirtieth Street, on the north by Thirty-fourth. It's the sort of area that is often described as urban wasteland: a tangle of railyards, storage depots, tunnel entrances, and highway overpasses.

But in fact the finalists will have a hard time matching the robust appeal of this infrastructural display. Ringed along its western edges by parking lots, car repair shops, and brick industrial lofts, the area is a frayed remnant of industrial New York, part of the city's vibrant cultural mix that now seems all the more precious as working-class Manhattan fades ever further into memory. There is a glamour to the unglamorous that the bright stars of contemporary architecture have mostly failed to reckon with, though anyone seeking the key to Frank Gehry's success will find it in his fascination with this paradox.

Until recently, developers have shunned the area as commercially unviable. But city officials, including Joseph B. Rose, chairman of the City Planning Commission and a member of the competition jury, regard this as a major development corridor. In January, Mayor Giuliani affirmed Mr. Rose's vision when he introduced a proposal to build a sports stadium in this corridor, along with a relocated Madison Square Garden.

The site also includes the James A. Farley Building, now home of the General Post Office but soon to house a new Penn Station, designed by Skidmore, Owings & Merrill, along with the Manhattan terminal for a new rail link to Kennedy International Airport. This design, in turn, will clear the present Garden site for eventual redevelopment. With projects like these in the works, along with the strip's proximity to the existing Javits convention center, it is hard to imagine a better site for demonstrating that despite their considerable differences, architects and real estate developers share a common stake in the future of New York.

The competition finalists were chosen from more than 150 submissions from around the world. Cedric Price of Great Britain is the elder statesman of the group. In fact, Mr. Price has exuded a statesmanly aura since the outset of his career, in the early '60s, when he functioned as a guru to the British megastructure movement and mentored that movement's pop offshoot, Archigram. Best known for the Fun Palace, an unbuilt project of 1962, Mr. Price remains a keeper of the '60s flames of change, merriment, social engagement, and provocation. A few years ago he distinguished himself at a hearing before a British preservation group that was considering granting landmark status to one of his few built works. Mr. Price showed up and vigorously opposed the honor.

Peter Eisenman of New York is the Gertrude Stein of contemporary architecture. That's not meant as a put-down. It simply implies that (unlike, say, Stein's contemporary, Virginia Woolf) Mr. Eisenman shrinks from fully inhabiting his medium. Possibly he would not take this as a criticism. He spent a large chunk of his career steeping himself in the theories of Jacques Derrida and other poststructuralist philosophers, theorists who promulgated such antihumanist concepts as the "death of the author."

Perhaps as a result of their influence, Mr. Eisenman has often claimed that his architecture is produced without design. The conceit is that his forms are shaped by topography, historical memory, and other forces latent in the urban landscape. This approach could result in a design sensitively attuned to the site's existing infrastructural tangle. Or it could produce a plan as monotonous, in its geometrically assertive way, as the barren concrete plazas that commercial developers typically use to hide the city's untidy innards.

Bear in mind that Mr. Eisenman's experimental work—like the Aronoff Center for the Arts at the University of Cincinnati—has opened the door for some of the most talented architects in the emerging generation. Thom Mayne belongs to the tradition of Richard Neutra, Charles and Ray Eames, and Rudolph Schindler—architects who resisted the image of Southern California as the promised land of kitsch and established it as a testing ground for rigorous experimentation. But Mr. Mayne's elegantly aggressive designs have little in common with the open, spare spaces of his predecessors. Instead his angular, fragmented designs represent the anxiety lurking in the shadows of the bright California sunshine.

Mr. Mayne, whose public projects already include the Comprehensive Cancer Treatment Center and Cedars-Sinai Medical Center in Los Angeles, is at a moment of professional transition from residential and commercial work to a series of public schools in Southern California.

Ben van Berkel, based in Amsterdam, belongs to a generation younger than Rem Koolhaas, and it is salutary to see an architect absorbing information from his seniors instead of trying to bump them off. Mr. van Berkel is not a '60s person. Yet he has inherited Mr. Koolhaas's ambivalence toward architecture as an expression of corporate power. His theoretical approach is drier than that of Mr. Koolhaas, but his forms, like the Erasmus Bridge in Rotterdam, are just as juicy: fluid, fragmented, enraptured with urban surprise.

Jesse Reiser and Nanako Umemoto are two of a group of young architects who have come to be known as the blobmeisters. They have grown up with the development of advanced computer programs that enable them to model infinitely varied, three-dimensional geometries, like their design for the Yokohama Port Terminal. Though virtually all architectural firms now rely heavily on the computer, blobsters like Greg Lynn and Kevi Sottma of the Ocean Group, and Mr. Reiser and Ms. Umemoto make designs that create the impression of an endless tumble through cyberspace. These designers are intoxicated by the freedom the computer allows them, much as the early modernists were thrilled by the open spaces allowed by industrial construction techniques. Those looking to ride today's wave of tomorrow could do worse than check out this beach.

The finalists span three generations but have much in common. All have wrestled with the tension between the design of individual buildings and the planning of the larger city. All have designed buildings during a period when city planning, particularly in the United States, has fallen into general collapse. All have dealt in intelligent ways with architecture as a medium for focusing relationships outside the building, not just creating stand-alone, free-floating objects in space. Not least, the designs of all five finalists have trendy sex appeal. If architects have learned one thing in this century, it is that creating a sense of place is contingent on creating a sense of time. If they have learned a second thing, it is that this construction can take multiple forms.

The finalists met last week to tour the site and have until June to produce their plans. The winner will be chosen in mid-June, and an exhibition of all five proposals will be held in the Waiting Room at Grand Central Terminal toward the end of the summer. This is a fine choice of venue, not only because it guarantees wide public exposure but also because the great Beaux Arts terminal is our supreme example of rendering transportation infrastructure into architecture on the grand scale.

The composition of the jury is as important as the list of finalists. In addition to Ms. Lambert, it includes four distinguished architects: Mr. Gehry, Arata Isozaki, Elizabeth Diller, and Rafael Moneo. Gary Hack, a city planner and dean of the Graduate School of Fine Arts, University of Pennyslvania, and Ralph Lerner, dean of the Graduate School of Architecture at Princeton University, come to the jury bearing weighty academic credentials.

But if this project stands a chance of making an impact on New York, that is because the jury also includes the two public officials who rule over this site.

Charles A. Gargano, chairman of the Empire State Development Cor-

poration, wields thumbs-up/thumbs-down power over the ultimate disposition of the site. It is controlled by the Metropolitan Transportation
Authority, a state agency. Any plans for building there are ultimately subject to Mr. Gargano's approval. Mr. Rose is part of an administration that
has covered itself with glory in reversing New York's fortunes as a negative
magnet but has yet to attract enough innovative projects to make the city
an architectural center.

Mr. Rose may be the competition's key juror. He is a public official
who cares about architecture but is also a pragmatist. He holds office in a
city that has all but eliminated architecture from the public realm and
compelled the city's architects to work in foreign cities or on paper. His
presence on the jury does not guarantee that the winning plan will be realized. But he has indicated that he would like the competition to result in
something more than another flurry of paper fantasies.

New York is a developers' town. That's not going to change, nor
should we want it to. Development is part of the fuel that keeps this city
on the move. What we expect, however, is some correlation between
quantity and quality, between booms and busts in the real estate market
and the quality of the city's architecture. There has been no such correlation for more than thirty years, when architects of the caliber of Frank
Lloyd Wright, Mies van der Rohe, Marcel Breuer, Eero Saarinen, Gordon Bunshaft, and Kevin Roche were creating some of their best work
here.

Phyllis Lambert became part of that cycle when she persuaded her
father, Samuel Bronfman, to hire Mies and Philip Johnson to design the
Seagram Building. She has stepped back into the picture as a kind of Cultural Improvement District. She is challenging the tyranny of the misdi-
rected relativism that has allowed New York's architecture to devolve
toward new lows of mediocrity.

Since architecture is a public art, it might seem vital that the public
weigh in on major public projects. But this does not negate the difference
between opinions and informed opinions. Harold Bloom, in his *Western
Canon*, calls upon Hazlitt to remind us that "the principle of universal suf-
frage is by no means applicable to matters of taste." Taste is subjective, and
informed opinion can be wrong. Still, the juried competition, when
organized with intelligence and integrity, is the best system we have for
insuring that commercial values are not confused with cultural ones.

In an ideal city, there would be a consensus of taste among public,
developers, architects, and critics. Or better yet, conflicts would be aired
at a high level of debate. But compared with Paris, Barcelona, Dublin, and
other cities, New York has failed to stimulate consensus or debate. Of

course, it is possible for architecture and real estate to coexist. But the best way to increase the likelihood of that is to remain aware of the difference between them.

March 14, 1999

THE PREMIERE OF A KOOLHAAS FANTASY

New York has served itself a little slice of architecture: the new Second Stage Theater on Eighth Avenue and Forty-third Street. Designed by Rem Koolhaas, the awesomely talented Dutch architect, in association with Richard Gluckman of New York, the 296-seat playhouse is an architectural hors d'oeuvre, really just a piece or two of sushi on a plate.

But it's fresh and tangy, a morsel of the sophisticated design many New Yorkers have been craving. To paraphrase Oscar Wilde, this latest addition to the Theater District is exquisite and leaves one unsatisfied.

Founded twenty years ago by Robyn Goodman and by Carole Rothman, who remains the group's artistic director, the Second Stage, previously on the Upper West Side, specializes in American plays. Its new season officially opens next week with performances of *That Championship Season* by Jason Miller.

The group's new home is an oasis in our newly upgraded Times Square neighborhood. There is no themeing, no nostalgia, plaster nymphs, or gilt rosettes. It's a light, modest arena for smart, modern playgoers.

This is Mr. Koolhaas's second project for New York; his design for the Lehmann Maupin Gallery in SoHo was completed in 1996. The theater, at 307 West Forty-third Street in Clinton, occupies a four-story former bank building that had stood empty for eight years. Built in 1927, the building has trim Art Deco lines, ornamented with stylized polychrome foliage. The Koolhaas-Gluckman design leaves the exterior nearly intact. It incorporates many features of the original building, a necessity dictated by the restricted budget and one that contributes to its aesthetic effect.

The entrance is through a plain glass door on Forty-third Street. An outer lobby, painted light gray, leads to a box office within the bank's safe, its thick steel door plainly visible.

The theater proper is on the second floor, a tall space, once the main banking hall. In the upstairs lobby, walls and floor are painted screeching orange, a vibrant color at once tropical citrus grove and toxic defoliant. We are not in Mickey Mouse land anymore.

There is no fixed division between the upstairs lobby and the auditorium. Rather, a large, bleacher-like wedge of seats in the middle of the second floor defines it into different areas in one continuous flow: lobby, stage, backstage, seating, and aisles.

The wedge, about twelve feet tall at the rear, is asymmetrically placed and finished with epoxy resin in a deep shade of green gray. An aisle leads along one side of the wedge to the front of the house. Twelve-foot-tall windows, fitted with acoustical glass, punctuate the wall across the aisle, framing views of Forty-third Street. The wall is draped with gold velour curtains studded with steel grommets. At performance time, the curtains can be drawn. When left open, the city itself is onstage here.

So is backstage, in part. Performers reach the stage via a second aisle, enclosed behind a side wall of translucent corrugated plastic on the far side of the wedge. With the house lights on behind it, this wall glows with a cheap, industrial glamour. When the lights are off, the plastic panels take on the glint of satin-finish steel.

The seats are of black wood, fitted with resilient pads made from a gel originally developed for bicycle seats. The pads are the color of parchment and partly translucent; the shade darkens at the edges, like gold velvet, an effect that echoes the plush of the curtains. A rectangular cut in the plastic wall reveals a shallow mezzanine furnished with a dozen or so movable chairs.

There is no permanent stage or proscenium. Right now the theater has both; these are part of the set. Directors and designers are free to construct a different staging and scenic arrangement for each production. There is generous space from which to suspend lights, backdrops, and other items from above the stage. Tracks for theatrical lighting extend the full length and width of the auditorium.

The Koolhaas flair for naughtiness is restricted to two bathrooms, set into the rear of the seating wedge and entered through the lobby. These, too, are painted orange, with naked fluorescent tubes glaring out from above the mirrors at eye level. The reflection is perversely consoling: this is the worst you are going to look all day.

Straightforwardness filtered through a wayward imagination: this is a Koolhaas design, all right. A theater with windows? No wall between lobby and auditorium? These ideas may be odd to contemplate, but they fit. They animate the intersection between those two Vitruvian virtues, commodity and delight. So do simple features like the gel seat pads, the strip of galvanized steel grating used as a guardrail on one side of the wedge, the off-center placement of a center aisle between the seats, and a quirky curve at the top of the aisle.

As readers of Mr. Koolhaas's book *S, M, L, XL* may recall, the architect has periodically flirted with the idea of writing screenplays. But he has largely sublimated this ambition into design. City views, saturated color, translucent surfaces, the sculptural treatment of function, and the mix of cheap, costly, space-age, and traditional materials, custom-made and off-the-peg hardware: these disparate elements are harmoniously composed in a serpentine flow of space, as a cinematic montage is organized in time.

It is a performance space for spectators as well as actors, in the sense that clothes by Prada and Jil Sander are costumes for the urban stage. These designers dress people for a mythology of the present. Koolhaas and Gluckman extend that mythical element into the architectural dimension. You can show up in Gap clothes and absorb the full effect.

New York is poor in such spaces. Philippe Starck's interiors for the Royalton and Paramount hotels are holding up well for a couple of zeitgeist zones. John Pawson's Madison Avenue shop for Calvin Klein and Adam Tihany's design for Jean-Georges, a restaurant on Columbus Circle, are potential classics. The new Comme des Garçons shop in Chelsea tries too hard, but who can blame the store's designers for overcompensation? Perhaps they're just trying to make up for the dullness of most retail interiors.

Among cultural institutions, we've got the galleries Mr. Gluckman designed last year for the Whitney Museum of American Art, Frederick Fisher's renovations at the P.S. 1 Contemporary Art Center, and that's about it. There's been no aesthetically alert theatrical space since Raimund Abraham's design for the Anthology Film Archives in the 1980s.

The Second Stage is a work in progress, its completion contingent on additional fund-raising. A small marquee has been designed for the entrance, and there are plans to uncover and soundproof five more of those grand windows in the auditorium, including three behind the stage. This would make it possible to turn the theater into a floating urban platform, hovering above the street at dream's-eye level.

A pity that the company's productions are limited to American plays. Don't you want to see Beckett, Orton, Pinter, Genet, and Shakespeare staged in a house with orange bathrooms? Sure you do. And what a gem of a showcase this theater would be for art films. If design were a draw, the new Second Stage would become the most sought after screening room in town.

April 8, 1999

THE NEW BERLIN—
BUILDING ON THE RUBBLE OF HISTORY:
ONCE AGAIN, A CITY REWARDS THE WALKER

It's safe to go walking again in Berlin. In fact, the time has come for city-lovers to reclaim Germany's once and future capital as a spiritual home. For it was here, in the early decades of the century, that *flanerie*—the practice of strolling leisurely around a big city just to take in the sights—came into its own as a modern art form. After twelve years of Nazi brutality and forty-four years of cold war, this gentle art has once again become a possibility.

There are many new sights to take in. Buildings by Rafael Moneo, Dominique Perrault, Richard Rogers, Jean Nouvel, Josef Kleihues, and other luminaries of contemporary architecture. Scores of office buildings in a crisp modern idiom. Vibrantly restored landmarks in the former Eastern sector, like the Hackescher Hof, a complex of galleries, design studios, cafés, and courtyards that has become the center of Berlin's architectural life. The former showcase of the West is now a gateway to the East, a part of the globe caught up in writing a new chapter of world history. Berlin is suffused with the promise and anxiety of that enterprise.

The flaneur, initially a French type, entered literature in the nineteenth century in the writing of Charles Baudelaire. But, as Anke Gleber recounts in her fine new book, *The Art of Taking a Walk*, it was in Weimar Berlin that the literature of city walking blossomed into an intellectual movement. Walter Benjamin's *One-Way Street*, Siegfried Kracauer's *Streets in Berlin, and Elsewhere*, and Franz Hessel's *Sightseeing Trip* celebrate flanerie as an essential education in modern sensibility.

These writers viewed Berlin through lenses cut and polished by the young century's art movements: Futurism, Cubism, Expressionism, Surrealism. For them the modern industrial city might not be a work of art, but walking through it could be. Bustling crowds, shopwindows, arc lights, neon signs, cinemas, hotel lobbies, grand cafés, posters, handbills, advertising kiosks, the rustle of newspapers, the movement of trams and cars, the accelerating pace of urban change: all this added up to something more than idle spectacle. It was the leading university for training minds to comprehend the modern world.

Benjamin's 1928 essay *One-Way Street* is perhaps the crucial text of flaneur writing. In it, Benjamin records the impressions of a walker forever seeking the next vista, the next streetscape, the next corner at which to turn. For the book's first edition, the cover shows a trio of one-way street signs: arrows pointing to the left, the word *Einbahnstrasse* emblazoned within them.

The sign evokes the arrow of time. Like the flaneur, the city is moving ever forward. After World War I, Wilhelmine Berlin, the imperial city, is breaking up like an ice floe. Its fragments recede into the past, along with the social stability that the imperial monuments were designed to reinforce.

Last February I went to Berlin to follow in the footsteps of the Weimar flaneurs. A paradoxical task to assign oneself: even if much of the flaneurs' Berlin had not been physically obliterated by hot and cold war and urban redevelopment, retrospection runs counter to the flaneurial spirit. But Berlin is now a city of two-way streets. All those building cranes swiveling confidently on the skyline proclaim, City on the Move! Advance! This Way Forward! But this has also become a city where much of the traffic is headed backward: toward history, memory, and their traces.

And the post–Cold War years have revealed a Berlin that is a museum of itself. The city's International Style buildings have become period pieces that one passes on the way to other period pieces: the Reichstag. The Victory Column. The Schinkel buildings. The New Synagogue. Brandenburg Gate. Monuments of the Soviet era. In today's Berlin, a cup and saucer from the legendary Café Josty, retrieved from the rubble around the wall, have acquired an aura nearly as precious as Schliemann's gold. Chunks of the wall itself, like the Elgin Marbles, have entered museums. The limestone facade and gilded public rooms of the fabled Hotel Esplanade are enshrined within a new apartment block of steel and glass.

Walking eastward along the southern edge of the Tiergarten, we come upon the Culture Forum, a trio of modern buildings that are especially poignant: Mies van der Rohe's New National Gallery, Hans Scharoun's Berlin Philharmonic Hall, and the same architect's State Library. Though built after the war, they were designed by architects who attained prominence in the Weimar years. Disconnected from one another by roads, traffic, parking, and their own monumentality, the three buildings float in an urban vacuum: an art museum, a library, a concert hall in the center of a city where books were burned, paintings banned, music silenced, culture extinguished.

Metal Forest of Cranes

Beyond these modern landmarks lies the onetime heart of the flaneur universe: Potsdamer Platz. For the last five years, this has been the largest construction site in Europe: the densest part of the city's metal forest of cranes. Here Germany has concentrated its hopes for Berlin: capital city, city of tomorrow, millennial metropolis.

But the three major commercial developments rising in and around Potsdamer Platz face daunting competition from ghosts. This was the hub of Weimar flanerie: site of Europe's first electric traffic sign (1924), installed to orchestrate the movement of cars, buses, trams, and crowds of people on their way to work. Roughly equivalent, as a social magnet, to Times Square or Piccadilly Circus, this is where full-time flaneurs lolled in the lobbies of the Palast, Bellevue, and Fürstenhof hotels, browsed in the Wertheim department store, or passed the time at Josty, Haus Vater-land, the Pschorr Haus, and other cafés and beer halls. And here, in 1932, rose Columbus Haus, a commercial building designed by Erich Mendel-sohn, the city's finest example of the New Architecture pioneered by the Bauhaus.

Then, in the Cold War, this was the epicenter of the Death Zone, the flattened strip of rubble, weeds, wild rabbits, and searchlight beams patrolled by East German border guards. Some think this blood-soaked wasteland had as much right to landmark status as the Brandenburg Gate. Many regard the corporate district of the new Potsdamer Platz as a classier kind of wasteland.

You are now entering the Sony Sector. The Daimler-Benz Sector. The A&T Sector. Like postwar Berlin, Potsdamer Platz and the adjacent Leipziger Platz are divided into zones of occupation, in this case three. Each is controlled by a different corporate giant and has been planned under the supervision of a different architect. The Sony and Daimler-Benz areas are now substantially built. The third, for the real estate devel-opment company A&T, is scheduled for completion next year. Plans for all the schemes are on view inside Info-Box, the red, rectangular high-tech structure that has become the symbol of a city in progress.

In the nineteenth century, architects sought to fix equations between period styles and architectural functions: Gothic for churches, Roman for government buildings, and so on. Something like that has been attempted at Potsdamer Platz. The three architects have adopted different approaches, keyed to the ratio between masonry and glass and their con-notations of tradition and modernity.

Sony's European headquarters, designed by Helmut Jahn, is the most compact of the three developments and the most assertively modernistic. It is a triangle of seven buildings, all with sleek glass curtain walls, set on a podium raised above street level. Runway lights blink from the corner of the most prominent tower, suggesting messages beamed upward toward communications satellites. Enclosed within the triangle is the Sony

Forum, a circular, tent-roofed mall, ringed with theaters for IMAX presentations and other amusements.

At the opposite end of the glass spectrum is Park Kolonnaden, a mixed-use project planned and partly designed by Giorgio Grassi for A&T. The most traditional of the three areas, the park is intended to knit the new Potsdamer Platz into the city's historical fabric. Its five large buildings face a landscaped strip that extends south from Potsdamer Platz to the Landwehrkanal. Their U- and H-shaped plans are modeled after classical town palace designs. The buildings are clad in light red brick, with entrance pavilions of light stone that protrude into the courtyards. Rectangular windows are punched through otherwise unadorned facades.

With nineteen new buildings, the Daimler-Benz section is by far the largest of the new developments. In addition to those designed by Renzo Piano himself, there are projects by Arata Isozaki, Richard Rogers, and others. In his own buildings, Piano contrasts crisp glass and steel with thin panels of warm terra-cotta brick. This is the static Piano of the IRCAM annex in Paris, not the dynamic Piano of the Pompidou Center across the way. The buildings are fiercely elegant, especially at the corners where streets meet at acute angles. Until you actually walk around them, the facades look like freestanding screens.

Rogers's glass office building on Linkstrasse is an hommage to two industrial-age icons. The central portion is shaped as a half ziggurat, recalling Joseph Paxton's original Crystal Palace, while a corner turret brings to mind the famous stair tower of the model factory designed by Werkbund Gropius for the Cologne Werkbund Exhibition in 1914. Isozaki's office building for the Berliner Volksbank looks like an hommage to American motel wallpaper: a lackluster holiday for café au lait tiles. Are these feeble, patterned facades intended to mock the triumph of mass consumption?

Edge City, Capitalist Wall

So the new Potsdamer Platz conjugates space. Its three parts evoke three phases in the history of Berlin: the imperial city of Baroque palaces, the industrial city of mechanical production, and the informational city of advanced electronic communications. If this were a theme park, one might call these three sections Main Street (A&T), Factory Town (Daimler-Benz), and Cyber Land (Sony).

What Potsdamer Platz truly resembles, however, is an edge city: one of those private, development-driven urbanoid clusters that have sprouted up across the American landscape in recent years. It is reassuring that the new Potsdamer Platz is notably without nationalist expressions. The downside of this is that the place could be anywhere. Like other edge cities, it occupies a kind of nebulous international airport space.

Still, as edge cities go, Potsdamer Platz is going to be pretty fantastic. Not every edge city has a Hyatt Hotel designed by Rafael Moneo or a theater designed by Renzo Piano on a plaza named after Marlene Dietrich. Not every edge city is surrounded by the Reichstag, Brandenburg Gate, and the Altes Museum or sits in the heart of one of Europe's most historically charged cities.

Despite the three aesthetic approaches governing Potsdamer Platz, the effect is surprisingly homogeneous. This is partly the result of design guidelines devised by Hans Stimmann, Berlin's director of planning. Of course, anything this large put up this fast is bound to seem artificial. The result is bound to disappoint those who were hoping for the lively heterogeneity that prevailed here in the 1920s.

But the new version cannot be counted an insult to the memory of the old. In the Weimar years, the area offered a picture postcard version of the developed industrial city. Now it is a perfected portrait of the informational city. Its hallmark is abstraction. This is true even of Grassi's buildings for A&T. Aldo Rossi in his early years was not this severe. The buildings' derivation from eighteenth-century precedent only highlights the extent to which these buildings have been rendered as geometrically abstract diagrams—X rays of the Baroque.

But people can be forgiven for regarding Potsdamer Platz as a continuation of the wall by capitalist means. All edge cities are, in effect, walls. Detached from older urban centers, they are visual and psychological screens between members of the global consumer society and those who, willingly or unwillingly, have not signed up.

The Info-Box, which was conceived as a temporary structure, looks more substantial than the buildings showcased in it. Designed by Schneider and Schumacher in 1995, the structure reckons with its immediate urban condition. Made of red enameled steel panels, inset with big picture windows, the box is held aloft on scaffold-like prongs; it resembles an enlarged version of a construction crane cabin. Its provisional quality, simple geometry, and airy defiance of gravity embrace with perfect poise the area's prevailing mode of abstraction. Here is a renewed version of Piano and Rogers's work from the 1960s, when these architects, inspired by Archigram's vision of Instant City, designed the Pompidou Center.

The Info-Box is a walk-in video screen. Visitors take a simulated helicopter flight over Potsdamer Platz. We learn that virtual streets will be among the Sony Forum's featured attractions. But won't they be redundant? How will we distinguish the virtual streets from the real? Simply by stepping into Potsdamer Platz, we've agreed to become virtual people—

or at least to behave like them. We're a featured attraction ourselves: the people in a would-be people place.

This is preferable to being gunned down in a Death Zone. It is also alienating, but no less valuable for that. The Weimar flaneurs were at home with alienation. They understood it to be one of the modern city's most poetic products.

Checkpoint Charlie Revisited

"Perhaps the cold war ended therefore as a result of a simple administrative error," Mark Mazower writes in his recent book *Dark Continent.* "More than one Western journalist claims the credit for having posed the vital question at the November 9 press conference in East Berlin: from when did the newly liberalized travel regulations for East Germans—just announced by Günter Schabowski, the exhausted Communist Party chief in East Berlin—come into effect? Without instructions on this point, Schabowski replied off the cuff: From this moment.

"Later he admitted the authorities had not anticipated the rush, the emotional drive that drove thousands within hours to Checkpoint Charlie. Bewildered border guards had no idea what to do with them; by the time the politicians ordered them to let people through, they had started to do so anyway."

Philip Johnson Haus, an office building that now sits on the spot occupied a decade ago by Checkpoint Charlie, is strangely oblivious to the history of its site. It could be an emergency airlift from the Beverly Hills stretch of Wilshire Boulevard. But Johnson is a celebrity in Berlin, a fact exploited during construction by the building's developer, when a huge black-and-white billboard of the architect adorned the fence surrounding the site. One night some students stole the billboard. Eventually, a ransom note turned up: "We've kidnapped Philip Johnson." Later a package arrived containing the billboard's severed ear.

You know you've reached East Berlin when you come upon a little garden enclosed by chain-link fence that contains chunks of the wall. It's called the East Side gallery. The wall fragments are covered with graffiti. One of them depicts an R. Crumb–style bimbo, her hourglass figure bulging out of a devil red dress. It's a sin to tear down history, the sexpot pouts to passersby.

Over the last few years, West and East Berlin have evolved into a kind of uptown-downtown division of urban lifestyle. Kurfürstendamm remains the major spine for department stores, smart shops, elegant hotels, restaurants, and movie palaces. The eastern edge of Mitte is where artists want to live. You could imagine you were in the Marais or the SoHo of an earlier day. It is the same paradox that cultural workers dedicated to the new are drawn to live amid the old. Buildings have been fixed up. Narrow streets are full of galleries, shops specializing in art books, trendy cafés. There is also a residual glamour from the Communist years, the sense that traces of political radicalism still linger from obsolete underground movements.

The Meaning of Glass

Berlin's flaneurs were not architecture critics. They were mainly concerned with states of mind. They used the stimuli of urban spectacle to heighten awareness of contradictions, ambivalence, conflicts between repulsion and desire, the splits, loose ends, and discontinuities of the nervous system. Their writings prefigure what would later be called urban semiotics, a field explored by Françoise Choay, Roland Barthes, Umberto Eco, and other writers, most of them French.

Jean Nouvel's design for Galeries Lafayette emerges from this school of thought. Situated on Friedrichstrasse, in the former Eastern sector, the building reflects a semiotic sense of the relationship between inner and outer worlds. Before World War II, Friedrichstrasse was Berlin's Fifth Avenue, the town's smartest shopping street. After the war, that role shifted to Kurfürstendamm in the West. Nouvel's design is part of a larger plan to restore Friedrichstrasse as a corridor of luxury shopping.

Nouvel does not attempt to avoid the task of disguising profit-taking by exciting desire. Rather, he embraces the task with a frenzy that pushes the design into the realm of surreal comedy. Typically, a shopping mall will adopt a unifying architectural motif: Swiss village, high-tech, or southwestern pueblo. At Galeries Layette, the motif is optical illusion.

Like a mall, this building is focused on the interior. Its main feature is a central glass atrium formed by two cones, their bases back to back. At once transparent and reflective, the cones resemble giant nineteenth-century optical devices. They fracture the interior into a kaleidoscope of luxury, status, and fashion. Shoppers and sales counters appear to hover in the air: a trick effect, like the images in anamorphic mirrors.

In *Techniques of the Observer*, Jonathan Crary argues that optical instruments were more than toys. These devices precipitated new ways of seeing. Breaking with classical ideas of perception established in the Renaissance, nineteenth-century scientists explored the idea that perceptions are shaped more decisively by neural apparatus than by the external reality the eyes behold. By the 1920s, this fragmented, disjointed way of seeing had worked itself into the writings of the Berlin flaneurs.

Galeries Lafayette's location in the East gives Nouvel's optical tricks an added historical dimension. For decades West Berlin was sustained as a show window, a display of the material well-being afforded by free enterprise. One can imagine the atrium as the mental landscape of East Berliners peering over the wall into the Western showcase, visions of cashmere, blue jeans, and credit cards dancing in their heads.

Norman Foster's dome for the Reichstag is a powerful civic symbol, precisely because it resembles a ghost—an ectoplasmic cupola for a haunted building in a town of many specters. Beehive-shaped, the glass dome harks back to the teens, when architects like Bruno Taut believed that the replacement of masonry by glass would help usher in a democratic utopia of transparency, freedom, and social responsibility. Colored glass destroys hatred. Glass opens up a new age. So went two of the mottos inscribed at the base of the dome of the Glass Pavilion that Taut designed for the 1914 Werkbund Exhibition in Cologne.

If only. But the glass facades of Mendelsohn's Columbus Haus did not prevent the SS from converting the building's top six floors into a central "protective custody" prison. This was in March 1933, barely a month after Hindenburg signed into law the emergency measures following the Reichstag burning. Mendelsohn's ribbon windows were easily blocked off. His large, open floor plans could be converted as easily to penal use or to retail, as in the Woolworth store that occupied the ground floor. Loading bays at the rear of Columbus Haus permitted the inconspicuous transport of prisoners.

Between 1933 and 1936, an estimated six hundred Communists, Jews, homosexuals, and other political undesirables were detained at what was, in effect, the first Nazi concentration camp. By then, flanerie had given way to goose steps. On the night of November 9, 1938—Kristallnacht—the Nazis unleashed a new symbolism for glass.

So one sees Foster's transparent dome as, in part, a monument to doomed utopias. It has already begun to function as a kind of Duomo to Berlin. Visible from many distant vantage points, it gives the city an emotional and a physical scale as well as a suitably fractured scale of time. A spiral ramp winds within the dome. Accessible to the public, the ramp conveys the idea that citizens can keep an eye on government proceedings. Viewed from outside, the spiral suggests another meaning, perhaps more apt: history does not unfold in linear fashion. And where is the point of orientation that would let a person or a people judge whether a turn is for better or worse?

Postwar Zigzag

Given Berlin's pivotal place in the cold war, people are naturally looking to this city for signs of the contours a post–Cold War world might assume. We look for cultural indicators as well as political and economic ones, and we expect their significance to be global. The Cold War was, among other things, a clash of ideas, and for half a century it held the world within its nuclear, binary embrace. By rights, the city that embodied that clash should be bubbling over with cultural ferment.

Daniel Libeskind's Jewish Museum is as vital a cultural expression of this time as an architecture critic can hope to find. I approached this building with apprehension. It doesn't photograph well. In plans it looks fragmented, which the building itself is not. The museum is not explicitly concerned with cold-war issues; it is dedicated to the cultural history of Berlin's Jews. A corner of it is consecrated to the Holocaust, but the museum draws meaning from deep historical strata that were frozen during the Cold War. A zigzag of concrete, steel, and zinc, the building appears to reel through time from the Enlightenment to Prussian militarism, German Romanticism, Marxism, Fascism, and on into the future.

Libeskind's building stands adjacent to the Berlin Museum in the Kreuzberg district. The museum is in an eighteenth-century classical edifice that was built as the city's high courthouse and is now being restored under Libeskind's supervision. The Jewish Museum is a five-story, rectangular-bar building that has been bent and folded into a zigzag shape, with ten sharply angled turns. The segments veer now left, now right, now double back. They are clad in panels of unweathered zinc that reflect the changing light of hour, weather, and season.

The segments gradually increase in length. In height and width they are scaled to the eighteenth-century building, which emphasizes the difference in form between the two. This contrast invites the idea that Libeskind is unfolding the irregular history that transpired in and around Berlin's classically ordered structures. The angled form is abstract but invites multiple meanings: a lightning bolt (from a cloud, or an SS uniform); a jagged tear at the fabric of a city and a civilization as well as a crude attempt to stitch the fabric back together; a river of time; a labyrinth; the unforeseen turns of history; a serpent, symbol of evil and wisdom both; a Star of David sliced apart and reassembled.

Not least, the shape evokes the flaneurs' rambling path through the city. A wall plaque in the lobby identifies Benjamin's *One-Way Street* as one of Libeskind's inspirations. But, like contemporary Berlin, his building is in fact a two-way street, steeped in memory but able to press on. The design pays its debt to the past by resembling nothing ever before built.

The museum's irregular plan is echoed by its windows. Slashed into the zinc surface as if by a laser can opener, these openings range in size and shape from small, triangular gashes to conventional ribbon fenestration on the top floor, where the offices are. Most of the windows take the form of long, thin strips, sliced diagonally across the zinc, occasionally overlapping, suggesting a series of crossroads. Though seemingly abstract, this imagery is in fact cartographic. Libeskind has mapped the addresses of prominent figures in Berlin's intellectual history, Jews and non-Jews. The diagonal windows connect these points on the city's cultural map. They evoke the city's creatively fertile past.

The building entrance is not visible from outside. One gains access by descending a long staircase from inside the Berlin Museum. The stair suggests the site of an archaeological dig. It prepares you to encounter layers of history and emotion. And it parallels the experience that with age we feel less and less distant from earlier times.

From the bottom of the stair extends a corridor, its floor slightly raked; to the eye, it looks convexly curved, like a roadbed. Eye and foot both relay the message that you are not entering a place dedicated to normalcy. The lobby expands upon the flaneur motif. Corridors lead off in several directions, past walls resembling street blocks or triangular corners. Strips of overhead lighting, recessed into black ceilings, suggest that in this underground city day and night are one. Overall, these crisp but slightly deformed spaces update Expressionist architecture and film design: a look back at Caligari from the end of the century that witnessed modernism's rise and fall.

Inside the museum, you are scarcely conscious of the building's zigzag envelope. Rather, the interior is dominated by what Libeskind calls the Void, a series of five spaces that form a kind of interrupted atrium. Disconnected but arranged along a single axis, these cavities of poured concrete rise the full height of the building and provide its organizing spine. Visitors cross through them on bridges that connect the galleries. The void spaces are unheated and will not be used to display art. For Libeskind they represent the culture that was wiped out by the Holocaust.

Art will be installed in the galleries later this year. Installation will be a curatorial challenge, but this should not be a case in which architecture overwhelms art. In this context of geometric aberration, the galleries look almost conventional. They are irregularly sized and shaped, and the diagonal windows periodically interrupt the walls. But these features should counter museum fatigue and thus assist rather than hinder viewing.

Two parts of the museum stand outside the zinc enclosure. A garden, named for the writer E. T. A. Hoffmann, encloses a mazelike grid of tall, square columns that rise at a disorienting tilt from a bed of cobblestones that is itself slightly raked. The columns are in fact planters: a single tree sprouts from the top of each. Hoffmann was employed as a lawyer in the courthouse, and the garden could well be a setting for a tale of transformation. In its perverse way it is a classical composition, one of the most poetic expressions yet devised for the idea that columns originated as trees fabricated in stone. In this context religious connotations inevitably arise: an Eden and a cemetery, a paradise out of reach. All but one of the columns contains dirt from Berlin; the other has dirt from Jerusalem.

The garden's most impressive effect, however, is the optical distortion it imposes on the surrounding cityscape. Viewed through the lens created by the columns and ground, nearby buildings (housing blocks from the 1960s) appear to reel back from the street, as if buffeted by wind or taken by surprise.

Echoes and a Soul

Libeskind was born in Lodz, not far from Chelmno, where the first Nazi extermination center began operating in 1941. Most of the Jews killed there came from Lodz. In his documentary film *Shoah*, Claude Lanzmann asks a Mrs. Michelson, the wife of a Nazi schoolteacher in Chelmno, whether she had ever seen the gas vans that were used there.

"No—yes, from the outside," she says. "They shuttled back and forth. I never looked inside; I didn't see the Jews inside them. I only saw things from the outside."

Like James Ingo Freed in his design for the United States Holocaust Memorial Museum in Washington, Libeskind extracts psychological meaning from the relationship between interior and exterior space. In one corner of the museum, he has attempted to evoke the experience of being inside with all possibility of escaping to the outside foreclosed. Through a metal door, you enter a tall chamber of gray concrete. The space is unheated and looks like something between a chimney and an abandoned, burned-out chapel. It is dimly lighted by a single spotlight and the diffused glow from a concealed window at the top. There is no sound. This is what it feels like to be incinerated by numbness, to be a living being imprisoned within cold gray ashes.

If Germany's new capital has a soul, it exists within this concrete corner. The space is dedicated to the Holocaust, yet it reverberates with other historical echoes. For example, it is a place to reflect on the moral condition of the Weimar flaneurs. Was there not, perhaps, something irresponsible in their attitude of detachment, their willingness to be be dazzled by spectacle in the pursuit of modernity? Did their passivity invite their fate? Did their preoccupation with subjective vision render them powerless in the face of objective political reality?

"I am a camera with its shutter open, quite passive, recording, not thinking," Christopher Isherwood writes in *Berlin Diary*, a British flâneur's record of the city in 1930. This is a chilling attitude to profess three years before Hitler came to power. But Isherwood intended his words to be chilling. He was, of course, more than a camera. He wrote to convey the truth beneath the surface of things, including his own desire for detachment.

Benjamin, Hessel, and Kracauer were more than critically engaged with the culture of their time. They belonged to its living fiber. In the Weimar years, work like theirs gave modernity its meaning. They gained authority thereby. Under Hitler, they paid for that gain with exile and death. They were eliminated, that is to say, not because they were passive observers of their times, but because they were active participants in shaping them. They were despised by people who, when they heard the word *culture*, reached for their guns.

The recollection of that savagery has become the starting point for culture in the post–Cold War world. This is where the walk resumes.

April 11, 1999

CULTURE'S POWER HOUSES: THE MUSEUM BECOMES AN ENGINE OF URBAN REDESIGN

I want to hold on to the moment after I checked into my hotel in Bilbao, Spain, dropped off my bags in the room, and rushed out to walk around the city's new Guggenheim Museum. By chance I ran into the museum's architect, Frank Gehry, outside the hotel, and he asked if I wanted to go look at the building with him.

That was not what I'd had in mind. I love to arrive in a new town and just walk around, letting impressions sink in, before heading off to inspect a new building. But this was an occasion to let the unexpected happen: the designer of this museum, a building already celebrated months before it opened, also walking around by himself, checking the impressions his work made from different parts of the city—streets, angles, distances.

Anyway, how do you answer a question like that? Look at the building? What building? Oh, no, I came to Bilbao because somebody recommended the local variety of blood sausage, or because I'm interested in Basque separatism.

Seventy-five years ago, the subject of this article might have been the opening of a shipyard, but it is the late '90s, so I was there for the opening of a museum. Bilbao was once a shipbuilding town, but that industry has dried up locally, leaving the city high and dry. The solution has been to fill the void with culture: a museum, a concert hall, a sports arena, and, of course, the architecture in which these enterprises are housed.

This pattern has been repeated in Paris, Barcelona, Helsinki, San Francisco, Cleveland, and countless smaller cities, like North Adams, Massachussets, where the sprawling Massachussets Museum of Contemporary Art will open next month in the onetime factory buildings of the Sprague Electric Company. These cities have ceased to be centers for industry and have become domains of culture. Along with financial management and tourism, culture is now a leading urban industry.

No longer merely the ornament of power, culture is a power in its own right. Of course, museums are not the only engines of this transformation—theaters, commercial galleries, jazz clubs, and other varieties of nightlife, book fairs, music festivals, loft conversions, architectural walking tours, and, not least, computer software firms are also driving the industrialization of culture. But the museum occupies a privileged place in the hierarchical scheme of things. It symbolizes the civilized idea that cultural and material values are not the same.

Frank Gehry led me over to a street a block or two away that runs perpendicular to the Nervión River and leads straight to the museum's entrance. Photographs of the building framed by the view down this street have been widely published but are misleading, for they emphasize the difference between Mr. Gehry's titanium-clad structure and the masonry vernacular of Bilbao's streets. But when seeing the museum firsthand, you are struck by how uncommonly sympathetic it is to the tough riverside surroundings of this decayed town.

"I see all the mistakes," Mr. Gehry said, and he pointed out what he considered to be one of them, a skylight that pokes through the metal skin of the roof. It didn't look like a mistake to me, but then I wondered, Should I be looking for mistakes? Later on, as we rounded the side of the museum, I thought, Well, maybe I don't like the convex curves that frame the window of that big rectilinear piece that shoots up in the air. They're so refined.

But who cares? This was magic time, an adventure in goose bumps. My hair would have been standing on end if it hadn't been plastered down with so much mousse. Architecture will never be the same. Cities will never be the same. And it all came out of the brains of two people, Frank

Gehry and his patron, Thomas Krens, the Guggenheim's director. People will like the building, or they won't; they'll come to see it, or they won't. The point is that an idea has been expressed here about the function of the museum in the contemporary city, and the idea, to give it a name, is Subjective Truth.

No one can prove that something is or is not good architecture. There are no scientific tests to determine the quality of art, no rules for declaring such-and-such work to be a masterpiece. These are matters of judgment. But that does not mean that the concept of truth has no relevance to these questions; it is possible to discriminate in a relativistic universe—that is what museums are about, and cities, and critics, too. The lack of objective standards is what makes culture so dynamic.

Museums, industrial cities, and newspapers are fundamentally nineteenth-century institutions. The present century has been largely one of transition, a bridge that extends from the great industrial cities of the past to the global information network to which the older urban centers must now adjust.

The announcement, earlier this year, that Levi Strauss was shutting down eleven factories in the United States is a good illustration of this transition. It was unsettling to learn that Levi's jeans, a venerable American icon, would henceforth be produced on foreign soil. But the news was not surprising. In the last three decades, manufacturing has been overwhelmingly exported to countries that offer cheap labor.

Still, if the United States would no longer produce Levi's, it would nonetheless continue to produce images of Levi's. In advertising campaigns, movies, television programs, music videos, and fashion magazines, Levi's would figure as signs of youthfulness, sexuality, informality, the great American style. The archetypal American uniform had shifted categories, in other words. It had left the field of industrial manufacturing and entered the sphere of culture.

This development has changed more than the physical landscape of the city, or its social demographics. The proliferation of museums partly reflects the uncertainty many people feel about the future of the city. And a museum is, among other things, a school that trains us to live with uncertainty in creative ways.

In the subatomic realm, the distinction between objectivity and subjectivity begins to break down. Depending on the method used to perceive it, light will register as either particles or waves. Some argue that since such phenomena are not experienced outside sophisticated laboratory settings, they have no bearing on ordinary life, that the laws of classical (Newtonian) physics remain valid. The point is, however, that since Heisenberg formulated the Uncertainty Principle, it has no longer been possible to equate science exclusively with objectivity. Science itself has placed limits on that equation.

I think that the modern museum, and the contemporary city as a whole, extend a similar message throughout everyday life: Truth cannot be equated exclusively with objectivity. Museums stand for the idea that some things are culturally more valuable than others; hierarchies do exist.

This idea cannot be proved, nor can aesthetic judgments be verified by time or popular referendum. Tastes change, and intelligent people disagree. This complexity is a truth of the urban condition.

Further adventures in the goose-bumps trade, three shows whose intelligence still inspires me:

1. Willem de Kooning in East Hampton, Guggenheim Museum, New York City, 1977. Few people will come out and say that Frank Lloyd Wright's rotunda is the ideal place to display paintings. Also, this period of de Kooning's work—semi-abstractions suggesting summer days at the beach, with sea, sky, sunlight, gulls, women, waves—is not considered the artist's best. (One critic said the canvases looked painted in mayonnaise.) But there can be a chemistry between building and painting that makes the entire experience soar.

Wright compared the ramp to an unbroken ocean wave; and sometimes the sound of murmuring visitors, percolating upward through the tall space, creates an aquatic or marine effect, like bubbles effervescing through surf. The show was like a collaboration between two old men splashing around together in the Fountain of Youth.

2. Wonderblock, Museum of Contemporary Art, Vienna, 1989. In honor of some anniversary or other having to do with Freud, Vienna staged several shows on psychological themes. Wonderblock, the German term for those self-erasing sketch pads children use, featured eighteenth- and nineteenth-century mechanical contraptions designed to diagnose and treat mental disorders. These were exhibited with paintings that plumbed dream states, by artists like Fuseli and Goya.

The labels were in German, and there was no English catalog, but not knowing precisely what I was looking at made these medical machines seem all the more hilarious: chairs equipped with gears, pullies, and elaborate gauges of copper and brass; padded booths with helmets and arm clamps; pneumatic couches. These Rube Goldberg devices were stunningly handsome, and each reverberated with the authority of science. But they looked far more psychotic than any of the maladies they were intended to cure—vapors, hysterias, unbalanced humors, moral degenerations.

3. La Ville, the Pompidou Center, Paris, 1992. A blockbuster show of twentieth-century urban visions, half of them by painters, the others by architects: paintings, renderings, photographs, and, in the final segment, a battery of video monitors showing architects and artists commenting on the city's future.

This epic display, mounted on the museum's top floor, was accompanied by three smaller shows that explored different facets of urban culture. A ground-floor gallery draped in black velvet presented a heartbreaking array of black-and-white photographs of libraries, mosques, office towers, and other buildings in Sarajevo that had been reduced to ruins in the outbreak of Balkan hostilities in the early '90s.

In the basement galleries, a retrospective of the work of Ettore Sottsass clearly demonstrated this designer's cosmopolitan aesthetic, with objects that synthesized a broad range of Mediterranean, Indian, Japanese, American, and other global influences. A fourth gallery honored the work of Walter Benjamin, the German philosopher, literary critic, and student of city life. Street signs, stereopticons, photographs of shopping arcades and amusement parks, and other visual artifacts helped to evoke the mind of one of this century's most gifted urban thinkers.

There was a fifth exhibition: the city of Paris, laid out like a panorama as visitors went up or down the Pompidou's glass-enclosed escalator, a city that, after viewing these shows, could never look the same.

Like Frank Gehry's design for Bilbao, exhibitions like these collapse the psychological wall between subjective perception and objective reality, allowing the two to momentarily fuse. The effect can be powerfully visceral.

In his book *Understanding the Present: Science and the Soul of Modern Man* (Doubleday), the British science writer Bryan Appleyard attacks the cultural impact of scientific rationalism. "Science works, but is it the truth?" Mr. Appleyard rhetorically asks. Though not explicitly written as such, his book can be read as a manifesto for the twenty-first-century urban project. With its functionalist architecture, rational planning, synchronized workforce, and sociological models, the industrial city was governed by scientifically ordered measurements, quantities, statistics. The challenge of the postindustrial city is to realize that subjectivity and objectivity are not opposites, but two sides of one coin in the inherently unstable currency of culture. One looks to the museum for leadership in that direction.

April 21, 1999

NEW ZONING LEAVES ROOM FOR
SKYLINE OF THE FUTURE

Joseph B. Rose wants to make New York safe for architecture once again.

That is one clear point that emerged in a wide-ranging speech on the reform of zoning policy that Mr. Rose, the Giuliani administration's Planning Commission chairman, delivered yesterday at City Hall. Speaking to an audience that included planners, urban designers, and community activists, Mr. Rose declared, "We are not Colonial Williamsburg, and the world's greatest and most dynamic city should be a hospitable environment for bold new structures."

But how is this estimable goal to be attained? Not everyone will be pleased with the answer.

In part, Mr. Rose hopes to discourage remakes of past mistakes by restricting the height of buildings outside of the midtown and downtown business districts. At the same time, he wants to encourage excellence by exempting some buildings from those same limits on height.

"The public process should be able to grant waivers from some regulations on the basis of exceptional design," he stated. "To that end, I am convening an advisory body to help us figure out how we can prudently introduce such values into our zoning."

In a city as economically dependent on real estate development as New York, Mr. Rose's call for height restrictions may be the splashiest of his proposals. In a sense it may also be the easiest to accomplish. For the city's architectural community, however, his most significant goal was that city government recognize that it has a legitimate role to play in raising the standards of architectural quality in New York. Referring to the stringent laws on landmark preservation now in place, Mr. Rose said, "If we can bend over backward on behalf of great old buildings, I am confident we can figure out how to do so for great new ones, too."

That's the really hard part. Mr. Rose's plan is a welcome opportunity. But, given the slim chance of a sudden civic rage for innovative design, can New York seize it?

For it is not a simple matter for any government agency to venture into the murky and subjective realm of aesthetic evaluation. Mr. Rose can anticipate challenges to this initiative from the City Council, whose approval is required, and, most likely, from the legal system, in which the debate over landmarks legislation was fought all the way to the United

States Supreme Court. He surely will arouse the ire of community boards that have enjoyed considerable power over the design of new buildings.

Not least, Mr. Rose can expect opposition from residents who will undoubtedly question his willingness to override the new zoning regulations on the basis of outstanding design. Who will make the determination that a design is outstanding? What values will be represented by the advisory panel Mr. Rose proposes to create? How can this group gain the trust and respect of communities affected by its decisions?

In addition to proposing an advisory panel on architectural design, Mr. Rose declared his intention to abolish the urban planning model that has governed high-rise development since the adoption in 1961 of the Zoning Resolution.

"The 1961 zoning imposed an aesthetic regime of a tower in the park, which has proven to be a fundamentally flawed, anti-urban, and anti–New York concept," he said. "We are going to drive a stake through the heart of tower-in-the-park zoning and its trail of exceptions, caveats, and interpretive gymnastics."

In practice, the revised zoning would limit the transfer of air rights and permission to build "bonus" floors in exchange for the creation of public plazas. Instead, the Department of City Planning will propose a unified set of bulk regulations for middle- to high-density development.

Mr. Rose is not proposing a new architectural aesthetic. Rather, he seeks to liquidate two old ones that have persisted past their prime.

The first, the tower-in-the-park concept, originated in the 1920s with the French architect Le Corbusier. At the time it was a visionary idea for introducing light and open space into congested urban areas, and for preparing the city to cope with the age of the automobile. The concept was taken up after World War II by idealistic American architects, with results that often fell far short of the ideal.

The taste for historical pastiche began in the 1960s in a similarly idealistic spirit. It represented a reaction against the sterility of streets like Avenue of the Americas after they became lined with relatively uniform glass towers in the modernist mode. It was not until the 1980s that this aesthetic began to harden into a retrograde and profoundly suburban approach to architecture and urban design. Then, we began to see these tragic remakes of cast-iron lampposts, these ersatz 1920s facades pasted over contemporary residential buildings.

The Postmodern movement has become an aesthetic tyranny: a fear of change. As a result, New York has been deprived of projects like the Guggenheim Museum in Bilbao, Spain; the new Jewish Museum in Berlin; and the Congrexpo conventional hall in Lille, France. These buildings have helped their cities face the future with aplomb.

From an architecture critic's perspective, the big picture is this: Mr. Rose is chief planner of a city where architecture in recent years has become a world-class joke. He spoke for many when he urged, "Instead of cloaking ourselves only in the architectural garb of the 19th and early 20th centuries, we must be able to add to our built environment the best of the early 21st century as well."

Still, if this sentiment is widespread, it has not yet attained the political and social clout that the preservation movement eventually acquired. Many people feel comfortable with buildings that recall the past, not only because of their reassuring familiarity but because they give communities a sense of control over their surroundings. Others recoil from the new as if it were a form of aesthetic terrorism.

New York's civic groups and cultural institutions have done little to whet the public's appetite for architectural innovation. For example, the Municipal Art Society, a group that should have been keeping the city on its architectural toes, has instead contributed to the city's creative torpor. While the city's architecture schools, like those at Columbia University and Cooper Union, have fostered creativity among their students, the schools have shown little initiative in transmitting this spirit outside the classroom, even when it comes to the design of new buildings on their own campuses.

Community groups, and others, may be alarmed by Mr. Rose's linkage between quality and quantity. They are right to be on guard. No one wants to see design used as a rationale for overdevelopment, particularly in a town that has lost its architectural bearings. Still, as Donald Trump's design for a 900-foot skyscraper just north of the United Nations demonstrates, loopholes in the existing regulations already allow developers to pile on bulk. Quantity with quality is a better deal than quantity without.

Mr. Rose has yet to spell out the steps he will take to implement the concept of a design advisory board, or the other proposals outlined in his speech. It's going to be a bumpy ride, but this idea deserves a chance to succeed, and even to fail. It will not be easy to convince people that, even in the subjective realm of taste, it is possible to sort out good ideas from bad ones, or to persuade them that, even when a public agency makes an aesthetic fumble, the effort to discriminate is itself worthwhile.

As Alfred North Whitehead put it, "It is the business of the future to be dangerous." Buildings that reflect cultural change can be shocking, but providing such shocks, and provoking public debate over their value, are tasks a vital city should perform.

April 21, 1999

IF THE CITYSCAPE IS ONLY A DREAM

Despite fortune cookie dialogue and a dubious Nietzschean subtext, *The Matrix* is a film that deserves to be a classic. It will certainly become one for those who value the power of sci-fi movies to crystallize moments of urban sensibility. *Metropolis, Alphaville, The Tenth Victim,* and *Blade Runner* are also classics of this genre. Like them, *The Matrix* is basically an adventure in stylish mise-en-scène. The special effects offer more than eye-popping trappings. They're the heart of the plot.

Without giving too much of the story away to the six people in the world who haven't yet seen the movie: the action is set in a postapocalyptic world ruled by artificial intelligence. People's brains have been programmed to think that they're living ordinary lives in conventional cities circa 1999—a sort of *Truman Show* stage set for everybody. In fact, humans inhabit a kind of postatomic-blast Hiroshima on a global scale. The aim of the Good Guys and Gals (Morpheus, Neo, Trinity) is to liberate everyone from delusion so that they can perceive the world as it is.

This crypto-Buddhist parable reverses the usual sci-fi setup. Here special effects are used to depict the "real world" (a burned-out Chicago), while still and action photography of a real city (Sydney, Australia) is used to represent the Matrix—an elaborate system of neurologically induced special effects.

This is the second major urban adventure movie produced by Joel Silver. *Streets of Fire,* coproduced by Mr. Silver and Lawrence Gordon and directed by Walter Hill in 1984, was not a commercial success but was admired by many in the art world. Like the East Village gallery scene, then at its peak, this film sought a glamorous mythology in the rubble of the abandoned inner city. It was a vibrant allegory of the malign neglect endured by American cities during the Cold War.

An elevated subway track was the movie's main scenic feature. The crumbling track explicitly evoked the policy of "deferred maintenance" adopted by the New York City transit system, contributing to its gradual decay. Implicitly, the track stood for the extension of such policies to the city as a whole. We were all living in the gutter, but some artists saw rough poetry in the harsh light of neon signs, streetlights, headlamps, and trashcan fires filtered through the noxious mists rising from the streets. As the painter John Button once put it, "New York's manhole covers gush with steam because the city is so close to hell."

Mr. Silver's new film, by contrast, allegorizes anxieties that have emerged in the post–Cold War years. In the era of the one remaining superpower, a single dominant ideology and the spreading advance of the Internet, the Matrix can easily stand for what some have called "the monoculture": the network of shopping malls, theme parks, edge cities, suburban subdivisions, convention centers, and hotels built around the consumer culture of advanced capitalism and its market research standards of normalcy.

Without an ideological adversary, it's easy to fall into an only-the-paranoid-survive mentality. How can you tell whether you're being manipulated? Or, what form of manipulation do you prefer? Watching *The Matrix*, you're never entirely certain what is real photography, what is computer-generated imagery, what is a location, what is a set, what actions are performed by actors, what by stand-ins.

A similarly ambient quality permeates the film on the level of ideas. The Wachowski brothers have been presented as naïfs, a couple of comic book–bingeing carpenters from the Windy City. But the idea of diffused power/intelligence seems to come straight from Michel Foucault, and many viewers will undoubtedly see references to Lacanian psychology, Kabbalism, Mahayana Buddhism, Christian eschatology, Romantic rebellion, Surrealist painting, and other sources amid the rapid whirl of kickboxing, morphing, scrolling digits, and bang-bang firepower. The viewer bobs through religions, philosophies, arts, and sciences like a cork on a sea of liquefied civilizations. But squint, and the drama is reduced to colored light projected in space.

Mr. Silver is best known for action movies like the *Lethal Weapon* series, but he has also become a figure in architecture circles, mainly because of his passion for the work of Frank Lloyd Wright. In 1984 he bought and now lives in the Storer House, one of the four concrete "textile block" houses that Wright built in Los Angeles in the 1920s. It's not a stretch to see parallels between the producer's house and ideas that flicker through his movie. In both, the message is freedom from repression, symbolized by the ability to move fluidly through space.

Wright expressed this Romantic ideal by rejecting historical European styles, eliminating the confinement of enclosed rooms, and developing new building technologies that (in theory) expressed the inherent qualities of his materials. In the Storer House, built on a hillside, he extended the concept of the open floor plan vertically: when you ascend the stair from the lower to the upper living room, you become conscious of being in two different spaces at the same time. The effect is not dissimilar from that experienced by the movie heroes when their digitized selves sally forth into the Matrix, leaving their bodies behind at home base.

I happened to see *The Matrix* at the new United Artists multiplex on Union Square South, an appalling spot with all the charm of a high-security prison. The poor moviegoer rises through a bleakly Piranesian escalator core, past Sheetrock walls painted a sullen gray. On the landings, the walls are adorned with what look like tubes of spangled gift wrap. The twinkling tubes, hung from hooks, swing limply in the air-conditioned breeze.

The place would be less offensive if it weren't for a recorded message, repeatedly piped through tinny speakers, that welcomes moviegoers to this abysmal place and touts its state-of-the-art virtues as if we were witnessing the second coming of Radio City Music Hall. The Matrix has got our ears, in other words, and you halfway wish it could control our vision as well. I found myself in the position of Cypher, the movie's Judas figure, who knows that the steak he's eating is just an illusion, but he really loves the illusion. I would gladly have turned in my popcorn if I could have been fooled into thinking I was at the Roxy. Even the real Roxy was a fantasy.

The truth is that architecture has always functioned as a matrix, an enveloping environment that embodies a worldview. In *The Architect of Desire*, Suzannah Lessard writes about the fear that overtook her on a visit to the Bowery Savings Bank, an ornate Beaux Arts building designed by her great-grandfather Stanford White in 1895. "The source of the fear was the very geniality of the architecture," Lessard observes, "its delicacy, its glow, its enspelling seductiveness." One could diagnose similar impulses in London's Regency terraces, Versailles, Baroque cathedrals, and virtually any form of urban organization back to the time when our ancestors painted on the walls of caves.

Today, architecture has fragmented into a grid of overlapping matrices, spheres of influence each with a distinctive worldview and a set of architectural projections.

THE TERRORIST MATRIX — As much the creation of the monoculture as of those who violently oppose it, this is the shadow world of mad bombers, chemical warriors, militia fanatics, fringe cults, street gangs. (High-security architecture; gated communities; video surveillance of public spaces; black helicopters; prisons.)

THE ECOMATRIX — The dystopian realm of shrinking rain forests, diminished biodiversity, depleted ozone, drug-resistant viruses. (Green architecture; Biosphere 2; Mexico City).

THE CYBERMATRIX — The informational utopia of mass literacy, transnational affiliations, instant gratifications, spaces and objects with continuously morphing shapes. (Smart buildings; Sim City; blob designs created with software programs developed for animated films.)

THE OLD-BOY MATRIX — White male architects sitting around not saying what they really think about other white male architects at the table.

THE PR MATRIX — Architects spinning freely within the suspension of disbelief in their own mediocrity, sustained by the control their profession exercises over the architecture and design press.

THE THEORY MATRIX — Aka Critical Architecture: officially opposed to the monoculture, unofficially (and understandably) eager for whatever commissions it might cough up.

THE MATRIX MATRIX — With its own Web site (www.whatisthe matrix.com), probable sequels and prequels, and forthcoming product tie-ins, like groovy Matrix sunglasses. I can't wait to get a pair. Then I'll be just as good-looking as Keanu.

"There is absolutely no inevitability so long as there is a willingness to contemplate what is happening," wrote Marshall McLuhan at the end of his 1966 book *The Medium Is the Message*. I take that to be the moral of this media-mad movie. It's the point of this column as well.

May 2, 1999

AN APPRECIATION: STYLE AND SYMBOLISM
MEET IN DESIGN FOR PENN STATION

Beaux Arts on the rebound? No. A great act of civic vandalism undone? That was never in the cards. But if you can set such golden platitudes aside, you may begin to appreciate the intrinsic merits of the superb new plan to remodel the historic James A. Farley Building, the old General Post Office on Eighth Avenue between Thirty-first and Thirty-third streets, into a future home for Pennsylvania Station.

It would be folly to see this plan as an attempt to resurrect the original Penn Station, the legendary McKim, Mead & White edifice that was torn down in the mid-1960s and has haunted the city's conscience ever since.

On the contrary, the best news about this plan is that it should finally lay Penn Station's tired old ghost to rest.

Designed by David M. Childs of the New York office of Skidmore, Owings & Merrill, the new plan offers a lean, sinewy architecture that is held together, both visually and structurally, by metal trusses. Within the Farley Building's stone wrapper of classical columns and pilasters there are bright, airy interiors, consistently logical patterns for passenger circulation, and a spectacular flow of space that cascades from street level down to the train platforms four stories below.

The design is to be unveiled by President Clinton on Wednesday in a ceremony at the Farley Building. Governor George E. Pataki, Senator Daniel Patrick Moynihan, and Transportation Secretary Rodney Slater are expected to attend, as well as Charles A. Gargano, president of the Empire State Development Corporation, and other public officials.

The project faces several obstacles before work can proceed. About $134 million of its estimated $484 million cost is not yet in place. (About $350 million has already been committed from federal, state, and city sources; officials involved in the project say they hope Mr. Clinton's appearance will spur approval of the rest.) The design might also face challenges from the state's historic preservation officer, Bernadette Castro, whose approval is required before alterations can be made on the landmark structure.

Mr. Childs's plan deserves swift approval. But the design's aesthetic and functional virtues may well be secondary to its symbolic value. In an era better known for the decrepitude of its infrastructure than for inspiring new visions of the city's future, the plan comes as proof that New York can still undertake major public works. This is the most important transportation project undertaken in New York City in several generations.

Penn Station is already the nation's most heavily trafficked transportation center. When completed in 2003, it will serve more passengers a year than the three regional airports combined. It will provide a hub for major transportation systems, including Amtrak, the New Jersey Transit System, the Long Island Rail Road, the city's subway system, and new rail links to Kennedy and Newark International Airports.

The Farley Building, which covers more than eight acres, was constructed in two stages, each part roughly the same size. Mr. Childs's design takes advantage of this two-part configuration.

The postal service will continue to occupy most of the building's 1935 annex—the western half of the site—mainly for trucking in the tons of unsolicited mail-order catalogs that daily clog the nation's mailboxes. The new station will be housed in the original part of the building, completed in 1913. But the postal service will continue to operate its retail office at the top of the grand staircase that extends the full length of the Eighth Avenue facade. New Yorkers will still have the horrible pleasure of bounding up the stairs as midnight approaches each April 15.

When the annex was constructed, a ninety-foot roadway was installed between it and the original building as a docking station for trucks. Mr. Childs's plan converts this space into the station's main entrance and ticketing hall. The hall is sheltered beneath a soaring roof that is braced on the west side by a huge metal truss. Despite its scale, the truss makes an ethereal impression. Its struts are thin, and Mr. Childs would like to fashion them from nickel, perhaps in memory of the nickel silver that graced the tables in the dining cars of yore. This metal takes the light like a star. You want to send it a rose.

The truss is shaped in a curve that recalls a radio antenna, an apt piece of symbolism for an era in which the satellite has gone far toward replacing the mail train as a communications relay. On the east side, the truss is draped with a glass skin that tapers down toward the edges, making a series of graceful, geometric folds that eventually splay out to form wedge-shaped canopies. These project out over the sidewalks at either end.

Rising seventy-five feet above the Farley Building's roofline, the curving space frame is the design's most conspicuous exterior feature. Slicing the building neatly in two, it indicates from afar that the station's entrances are at midblock, halfway between Eighth and Ninth avenues. It also allows natural light to flood the ticketing hall. This will be a great public space.

Once inside, air travelers will be able to check in and deposit their bags at counters, located on the west side of the hall, before boarding the train to the plane. First-class passengers will have the option of waiting for the train in lounges on the level below. Rail passengers will be ticketed at counters lining the east side of the hall. They can then proceed into the station's most spectacular space. Now called the train concourse, it is housed within the enclosed courtyard that was once the main sorting room for the city's mail.

Overhead, double trusses of steel have been retained from the original design. In renderings the trusses look heavy, even oppressive. This should not be surprising, for they once contained catwalks patrolled by inspectors whose job was to see that the sorters below were not pocketing the mail. In the station, the catwalks will be gone, the trusses will support clear skylights, and their ponderousness will be considerably mitigated by the space cascading beneath them.

This cascade is the interior's most dramatic feature. The descent from the ticketing hall to the trains will be made by escalator, broken in stages by two platforms, each almost two blocks wide. On their way to the trains, departing passengers will command clear vistas from street level to the tracks.

The platforms, which Mr. Childs calls "trays," will hold seated waiting areas and will be ringed by shops and restaurants. The station will include about fifty thousand square feet of retail space in all. A media wall, surrounding the departure board, can be programmed to announce weather conditions, cultural events, and other information about travel destinations. The best place to get short ribs in St. Louis. Land prices in the Rockies. Elvis sightings in Memphis. Crime rates on Capitol Hill.

In short, the train concourse is the reverse of the fluorescent-soaked, bargain-basement ambience of the present Penn Station. It should create the monumental sense of occasion for which the old Penn Station was justly celebrated.

Some preservationists would like the metal truss to be scaled back in size, so that it would be barely visible from the street. There have also been calls for a small "classical" waiting room to be placed on the station's street floor level. Such ideas expose an extremely shallow view of history. What the plan offers now is a huge classical waiting room. And the truss, in its present scale, is not merely a flashy modern flourish. It is the key to the whole design. It's a sign of recognition that structural expression is the classicism of our time.

This idea was implied in the platform concourse of the original Penn Station, where columns and arches of steel echoed the Beaux Arts design of the general waiting room but were left uncovered by masonry cladding. Until the concourse's glass roof was blacked out by wartime requirements, it could be seen that this was essentially Crystal Palace architecture. Like Joseph Paxton's 1851 London exhibition hall, this was a precursor of the metal-and-glass structures later built in what would come to be called the International Style.

Penn Station as a whole, however, perpetuated the problem that had perplexed architects in the nineteenth century and prevented that style from coming to fruition. Throughout Europe, in fact, no building type better embodied that problem than the metropolitan train station. With its metal shed concealed behind a masonry facade, the station epitomized the dichotomy between architecture and structural engineering. And it dramatized the extent to which engineering often exceeded architecture in expressive power.

Victorian architects were haunted by this discrepancy. It would take another generation before modern architects like Mies van der Rohe, Le Corbusier, and Walter Gropius resolved the dichotomy. They accomplished this by stripping away the historical styles and allowing structural engineering to shape architectural form.

This act of synthesis proved a mixed blessing. On the one hand, it contributed to a discrediting of period revival architecture. It made it possible for owners to contemplate tearing down such glorious buildings as Penn Station, the Produce Exchange Building, and the Astor Hotel. At the same time, the fusion of architecture and engineering gave birth to a classical style for the machine age, as epitomized by the Seagram Building on Park Avenue.

No firm did more to propagate this style than Skidmore, Owings & Merrill. New York is replete with examples, including the Manufacturers Hanover Trust Building (now Chase Bank) on Fifth Avenue and Forty-fourth Street. The Pepsi-Cola Building on Park Avenue at Sixtieth Street. The First National City Bank (now Citibank) branch at Kennedy Airport.

These exquisite buildings are machine-age temples, serene pavilions for the era of steel construction, elevators, and plate glass. With such designs, Skidmore, Owings & Merrill asserted its claim to represent the center of gravity in American architecture, the position occupied by McKim, Mead & White a half-century before.

Mr. Childs's Penn Station design restates his firm's commitment to the clear architectonic principles that guided it during its greatest years. If nothing can bring back the old station, at least this rigorous new design can sharpen our appreciation for the golden age of classical modern architecture that flowered fifty years after the heyday of McKim, Mead & White.

This recognition of our strengths is a foundation New York can build on. Mr. Childs's design does so. The urban story here may be the birth of a great station. But the architectural angle is the creative resurgence of Skidmore, Owings & Merrill.

May 16, 1999

A STUNNING PIER HOTEL DESIGN STANDS OUT AMID A FLAWED PLAN

Sensationally great new building. First-rate park design. Half-baked master plan.

These are the main ingredients of an uneven proposal for DUMBO (Down Under the Manhattan Bridge Overpass), the sixty-one-acre site on the Brooklyn waterfront between the Manhattan and Brooklyn bridges.

The chances are slim that the project will ever be executed in its present form. Some local community groups are determined to stop it altogether.

Still, even though the master plan needs a lot more work, the proposal deserves a serious look. Let's pretend that the plan is a serving suggestion, as they say on a box of Triscuits.

Start with the River Hotel, envisioned as the anchor for the entire project. It has been designed by the French architect Jean Nouvel, the most original architect of his generation. And this design is one of Mr. Nouvel's most impressive works. New York has not seen a new building of its caliber in decades. This is architecture—the real thing. It is not a simulation, not corporate schlock, not yet another retro sigh. *Vive la différence.*

And *vive l'amour.* Mr. Nouvel has clearly fallen in love with his site: the two monumental bridges that enclose it; the water traffic; the raw, industrial milieu; and above all, the views—of the harbor, the East River piers, the Manhattan skyline, and the subways whooshing across the Manhattan Bridge. His design literally and figuratively reflects this wildly romantic context. And it plays on the narcissism of a city in thrall to its self-image as the center of the world.

The hotel takes the form of a nine-story pier. Indeed, it projects out over the water where a pier once stood, cantilevered from a lower, rectangular structure that contains a sixteen-screen multiplex and a ground floor of shops. The pier rises to one hundred feet, stopping just short of the Manhattan Bridge roadway.

In keeping with the site's industrial ambience, Mr. Nouvel has employed what he calls a sober aesthetic. The building, of steel and concrete construction, is clad with gray metal panels and so-called white glass, a material of unusual transparency without the green tint typical of plate glass. The facade is a grid that derives its proportions from the hotel rooms within. To take advantage of the views, Mr. Nouvel has rotated these rooms 90 degrees from the standard hotel design, so that their long sides face outward. This gives the grid facade a strongly horizontal emphasis and also enlarges the views from the rooms to wide-screen scale.

Since the hotel will be seen by bridge and water traffic, Mr. Nouvel has treated the building's underside and its roof as if they, too, are facades. Two floors of public rooms, enclosed within glass walls uninterrupted by window mullions, are suspended beneath the building in an inverted ziggurat configuration. An expanse of glass is set into the floor of the lower of these levels, allowing views of the water rippling below.

Since heating and air-conditioning will be supplied by off-site energy centers, the roof is clear of mechanical equipment. Instead the view from the bridge will be a geometric pattern of skylights and outdoor, landscaped patios that admit light into the hotel's top-floor rooms.

Those who have visited Mr. Nouvel's Cartier Foundation for Contemporary Art in Paris know that the architect is a genius with reflections. He deploys that talent here with the strategic placement of mirrors in the hotel's public and private rooms, and by crowning the roof with a long, slanted mirror that casts skyline reflections into the rooms below.

A new Empire–Fulton Ferry State Park has been conceived by M. Paul Friedberg, a master of landscape design. His plan enlarges the existing park and improves access to it by removing an abandoned government building beneath the Brooklyn Bridge. In its place would be a visitors' center and a formal entrance to the park, now entered through a narrow alley to the east.

Mr. Friedberg has split the park in two. The first section is an upgraded version of the existing park and would be dedicated largely to sports, with an outdoor ice-skating rink and an elaborate antique carousel.

On the far side of the hotel, Mr. Friedberg has proposed an ecological park that would emulate the condition of the shoreline before Colonial times. Between these two parks would be a small marina, enclosed within public walkways that should offer a spectacular place to watch the sun set behind the Manhattan skyline.

The park has a potential weakness. Its eastern edge is bordered by Empire Stores, a stretch of historic brick warehouses between parkland and Water Street. The plan designates the lower two floors of these publicly owned landmark structures for retail use. That would be fine if the shops were restricted to refreshments or merchandise related to sports, horticulture, and maritime history. But what is to prevent the park from becoming the front lawn for a chain-store commercial strip?

In fact, it is with the treatment of Empire Stores that the master plan, by the preservation architects Beyer Blinder Belle, falls apart. In addition to the retail uses proposed for the first two floors, the plan sets aside the upper floors of these buildings for a museum. But what kind of museum? A Museum of Dust Bunnies? No institution has yet been named.

As for the retail component, the plan's renderings feature every cliché in the festival marketplace book: glass canopies that deface the historic buildings they purport to preserve. Banners. Repainted versions of faded signs. On the rooftop, a giant, amazingly corny neon sign. A rooftop sculpture garden, as shown on a site model, looks like the miniature golf course from hell. It saps the roof's industrial strength.

There are two things wrong with the plan. The first concerns urban design. The creators of these markets make a big fuss about the distinctive character of the old buildings they recycle. Then they dress them up with trimmings that obliterate that character and produce a homogenized Festival Marketplace Look.

Glass canopies and banners may seem like minor details in a project of this scale. Yet they have the power to destroy precisely the sense of place that the designers intend to create. It is disheartening that a client with the smarts to hire one of the world's most inventive architects would then surround his work with outmoded ideas.

The second problem concerns urban land-use policy and lies partly beyond the scope of the DUMBO plan. Thirty years ago it made sense to recycle older buildings as shopping centers. Surely this was preferable to the prevailing urban renewal strategy of ripping the cityscape to pieces. But, over the years, a basic flaw in the festival marketplace concept became evident. Wholly dedicated to consumption, such centers make no quarter for production. Thus they ignore one-half of the urban equation on which a city's vitality depends.

Two Trees, the project's developer, is promoting DUMBO as an artists' district. In this sense the area could be productive. Even so, when a developer proposes a festival marketplace, especially one in former industrial buildings, the question needs to be asked: How will this project support urban productivity? How can it reinforce the city's eroding industrial base?

One answer would be to link DUMBO, physically and perhaps even economically, to the film production studios that are planned for the Brooklyn Navy Yard, just east of the site. In Times Square, developers have seized the opportunity to bring together the producers and consumers of entertainment and information in a part of town long dedicated to popular culture. Something similar could occur on the Brooklyn waterfront.

Mr. Nouvel's multiplex would acquire a deeper level of urban meaning if it were located in coherent relationship to a place where films are made. His proposal to place movie screens on the hotel's exterior could extend the cinematic dimension into the northern edge of the park. Hollywood on the Brooklyn waterfront? You bet.

But it would require government initiative to bring such a synergistic concept to fruition. The lack of a plan to link the two projects is not something for which the developers alone can be held accountable. Nonetheless, the DUMBO plan will probably be opposed by many whose real grievance is with the city's failure to create a comprehensive waterfront plan.

This is an era of public-private partnerships in which the public sector has too often confined its role to issuing permits to the private sector. Many citizens are justified in concluding that it would be better to halt all private development until the city has put forward a comprehensive vision.

That would be a shame in this case. While the master plan must be rethought, the project has much to recommend it. Those who care about the state of architecture in New York will have reason to grieve if Mr. Nouvel's beautiful design falls victim to a failure of the political imagination.

May 24, 1999

A HUMBLE MANHOLE COVER CONVEYS THE GLOBAL GRID

At last, a piece of New York City street furniture that doesn't look as if it was unearthed from an archaeological dig. The winning design for Con Edison's Millennial Manhole Cover, selected on September 15 from seven proposals, is a freshly minted metropolitan coin: graphically crisp, emphatically abstract, but with an abstraction's subliminal power to evoke a multitude of images.

Titled Global Energy, the manhole cover was designed by Karim Rashid, an international hotshot whose work is in the collections of the Museum of Modern Art and others. Mr. Rashid's manhole cover is intended to represent New York as the center of an international data network. It morphs the Manhattan street grid into a stylized, globe-shaped pattern that recalls the arcs of longitude and latitude on a Mercator map. The design will be executed in cast iron and will weigh 314 pounds.

If the manhole were a commemorative coin, the flip side would be emblazoned with the profile of Manuel Castells, the urban theorist who has gone further than any other thinker in exploring the impact of data technology on traditional urban centers. In his book *The Informational City*, Mr. Castells introduced the concept of the space of flows, the network of transnational finance through which capital is constantly on the move. Mr. Rashid's grid could be said to represent this space in graphic form.

For some of us, Mr. Rashid's design will bring back pleasant memories of a more physical kind of flow, the jet stream of international travel that swelled in the postwar decades. The design resembles an inverted version of the Pan Am logo, a motif that once symbolized the freedom to roam the world, American hegemony, blue-and-white skies, jet contrails. It signified American global hegemony, even more than did an American passport, as a benign force for peace: not all-conquering, not polluting, but uniting the world in a dream of harmonious modernity.

The overlay of grid and globe sugggests another image, the reverse of Pan Am's logo, for this could be a map of our inner world, the network of memories and associations that Italo Calvino describes as a model of the modern self. In his book *Six Memos for the Next Millennium*, Mr. Calvino lauds the Italian writer Carlo Emilio Gadda for composing fiction in which the least thing is seen as the center of a network of relationships that the writer cannot restrain himself from following.

Mr. Rashid has employed a manhole cover, surely a least thing in the cosmic scheme of things, to convey a similar pattern of global interconnection. The designer's nomadic sensibility may be partly derived from his own background. Born in Egypt, educated in England and Canada, Mr. Rashid, thirty-eight, now lives in New York. While less well known than Philippe Starck, Michael Graves, and other superstars of mass-produced style, Mr. Rashid is gaining wide recognition as a major talent of his generation.

A show of all seven designs will open October 27 at the Municipal Art Society, 457 Madison Avenue at Fifty-first Street in Manhattan. Con Ed hopes to install about 150 of the covers by the end of December. With steam wafting up around their edges, they should make hot spots for dancing in the New Year.

September 26, 1999

A TOWER THAT FLAUNTS ITS CONTRADICTIONS

I hope that the completion of the new Condé Nast headquarters last month will make people think twice before complaining about the Disneyfication of Times Square. Things are better than that, and worse.

Disney is but one in a group of media giants that have chosen to settle here. Besides Condé Nast, publishers of *The New Yorker, Vogue, Vanity Fair,* and other glamorous titles, the group includes Reuters, Bertelsmann, Billboard Publications, and MTV. Ornamenting this mediacratic convergence are the new television studios that have begun to blossom along the sidewalks of Broadway and Seventh Avenue like exotic hothouse fruits. Times Square has always stood for popular culture and entertainment, but never has such a concentration of pop producers and consumers been gathered together in one place.

This development is surely preferable to the hulking quartet of nearly identical corporate towers originally planned to rise here. Unless it's not. For, despite the great differences in architecture, signage, and market niche, the new Times Square is now suffused with a sense of sameness, of homogenized spectacle. But perhaps even this is useful. It's a striking demonstration of the protean nature of the monoculture: the system of promotion, distribution, and consumption on which advanced capitalism relies.

The Condé Nast Building at 4 Times Square shows how capably commercial architecture has adapted to this system. The building's design offers a picture of commercial architecture at its most inventive. If that seems like a contradiction in terms, so is 4 Times Square. A house divided against itself, it wants to be at once a background building and a foreground building, both star and chorus. Robert Fox and Bruce Fowle, the two principals in Fox & Fowle Architects, are attentive students of urban context. They invariably try to do the right thing. Sometimes, too many right things.

Fox & Fowle has described its approach to the design of the fifty-one-story tower as one of layering. The layers begin at the ground-floor level with commercial signs and the armatures that support them. They continue up the shaft of the building with a series of shallow setbacks in glass and stone. The composition of the setbacks varies in each of the building's four elevations, with the proportion of glass increasing as the tower rises. I call this building a Phoebe because, like the unctuous Broadway wannabe who shows up at Anne Baxter's apartment at the end of *All About Eve*, 4 Times Square seems to be bowing to itself in a three-sided mirror. This Phoebe bows in four directions, one per side.

The Forty-second Street facade gives us Phoebe by Day: this is Career Phoebe. She bows not to the naughty, gaudy Deuce but toward the classical composition of the New York Public Library and Bryant Park nearby. She gets to wear lots of well-tailored gray flannel granite here, along with some striking acccessories: a trim glass canopy above the entrance and some understated, brushed aluminum trim.

Phoebe by Night. On the town, with starlight in her eyes, she reflects all the glitter and tinsel of the Great White Way. Here is where you find the electrical signage, the NASDAQ studio, and the big round cylinder on the corner, seven stories tall, with punch-through windows. There's also a door partway up, and I regret that this will be covered with the NASDAQ sign, because I was having fantasies that this could be turned into a dummy Special Projects office for expired Condé Nast editors. Inside the cylinder, there would be a *Potemkin* reception area, with nice leather sofas and a secretary on hand to show the editor around his or her new office. This would turn out to be a gangplank cantilevered over Seventh Avenue.

Phoebe in Paris. The top of the tower is our Eiffel Tower moment: the square steel structure pops out of the building envelope and rises an additional seventy feet to form a crown of exposed girders. From these will be suspended four gigantic billboards, two of them tilted slightly to catch the gaze of tourists in the street. But the building may be too tall for that gesture. It will be impossible to judge the effect until the billboards are in operation, but it's not too soon to note that the signs will also be clearly visible from many other parts of town and probably from New Jersey, too, and that this is likely to cause an outcry.

With good reason. New York's illuminated skyscraper crowns, brilliantly orchestrated by the lighting designer Douglas Leigh in the 1970s, have been one of the major civic achievements of recent years. Part of what makes them great is that they are uncommercial. For once, the city has transcended individual self-interest and gained at least the illusion of a collective expression. The signs at 4 Times Square could detract from this accomplishment.

A microwave radio antenna pokes up in the center of the steel supercube. This is the building's steeple, the electronic obelisk of an information age. Figuratively, if not literally, it feeds Times Square out into the atmosphere. The whole crown will one day become an antenna farm for cell phone service providers. Even now, however, it looks like a bunch of hardware someone left out on the roof to rust.

The architects chose to disregard my grooming suggestions. Too bad! As I suggested in a review of the design, the building could do without the cornices and finials that articulate the top edges of the planes. Presumably, these are intended to emphasize scale. But scale in a glass curtain wall building comes from the rhythm of window mullions and from glimpses of the spaces, partitions, and ceiling fixtures inside. These hints of depth make a good impression on 4 Times Square's western elevation. They would look even better without the metal bangs.

So would the structural crown. That's one tough piece of engineering up there. It's not just a show-off thing. It expresses the fact that the building turns the usual order of skyscraper construction upside down. Here, mechanical equipment ordinarily found in the basement has been relocated to the tower's top floors. The weight of the equipment serves as a damper, which enabled the architects to lighten the building's structural frame.

It would be difficult to read the text of the crown under any circumstances, but the attempts at refinement on the lower stories create an effect of incoherence. We have two very different sensibilities at work, without an effective transition or contrast between them. I admire Fox & Fowle for attempting a new kind of crown; we're all weary of the paperweight building tops that architects like Cesar Pelli have made their stock-in-trade. But at 4 Times Square an opportunity was lost to rethink how the cultivated tradition of modern architecture grew out of the vernacular tradition of engineering, and how this, in turn, is giving way to forms derived from information technologies.

The building's strongest feature is the curved edge on the southwest side. Glare from the sun melts the edge; this helps reduce the impression of bulk. Looking up at it, you can see that the building envelope wanted to be a much simpler composition of volumes and planes. In her mind's eye, Phoebe sees herself as a casual girl—Weekend Phoebe—dressed down in the Gap, Calvin Klein, and other classic American labels prominently featured on the billboards of Times Square and on the sides of buses jolting by them.

People who work in the area are having a hard time adjusting to all this commotion, the crowds, the construction, the lines of people waiting just to cross the street, the hordes of television and music fans gawking at their idols. But Times Square has become a baroque exercise in crowd manipulation. The Baroque period gave us spectacular urban ensembles, like St. Peter's Square, all designed for gathering the faithful into the fold lest they be tempted by the forces of the Reformation. At Times Square, people are brought back into the streets lest they remain utterly captive to their television sets.

In the Baroque Age, the faithful paid a price for allowing themselves to be seduced by spectacle. That is no less true in Times Square. The price for the Baroque population was to accept the absolute authority of the Roman Catholic Church. For the MTV faithful, the price is to fall in line with the monoculture. Baroque architects produced a dazzling array of forms, but they all glorified one central authority. Similarly, in Times Square the monoculture comes in every size, shape, color, and taste, but all is sliced from the same Styrofoam slab.

It is great to see people on the streets. But the cost of drawing them there could be substantial. In media terms, Times Square represents the blurring of the boundary between advertising and editorial, and the resulting distortions of truth. In architectural terms, it represents a blurring of the boundary between art and commerce, and a sacrifice of the idea that architecture is also a medium for conveying truths about the urban condition. Truth in architecture is not the same as accuracy in news reporting. It is not an objective truth. But the idea that architecture and real estate are the same thing is one of the grander deceptions New York practices upon itself. Just ask Phoebe. Phoebe knows all about it.

September 26, 1999

ART DECO AUTHENTICITY

Radio City Music Hall, which reopens tonight after a seven-month, $70 million restoration, is Manhattan's version of a natural wonder. It's our Rainbow Arch, our Old Faithful, our Niagara Falls. The great hall's awesome beauty can be seen once again in the genius of its original conception. New York will see no finer way to celebrate this millennial year.

Supervised by Hugh Hardy of the New York firm Hardy Holzman Pfeiffer Associates, the restoration does more than scour away the tarnish that had built up in the sixty-seven years since the music hall opened. Mr. Hardy has also given the city a matchless lesson in the difference between historic preservation and theme-park simulation. He has offered this lesson twice before, at the New Amsterdam and New Victory theaters on Forty-second Street. But the distinction cannot be restated too often. Today many preservationists are content to watch New York subside into a Disneyfied version of itself. Mr. Hardy's faithful restoration of the music hall restores the importance of authenticity in a city flooded with fakes.

Completed in 1932, the music hall is a tribute to the Rockefeller family's spirit of culturally progressive enterprise. Like Rockefeller Center, which surrounds it in Midtown, the theater countered the Great Depression with a great infusion of hope in the city's future. Radio City! Live from Radio City! The name of the place encapsulated New York's post–World War I identity as an imperial city that governed its far-flung empire with jazz and radio waves, not Roman roads and legionnaires.

You didn't have to be a New Yorker to live in Radio City. You had only to tune in live music, comedy, soap operas, and news. But for those out there in radio land who wanted a physical mecca, the music hall was just the ticket. Like Times Square today, with its publishing headquarters, storefront broadcasting studios, and news zippers, the music hall enticed consumers into a fantasy world of ethereal entertainment. With walls and ceiling collapsed into seamless, receding echoes of the proscenium arch, with stairs and balconies that waft the eye ever upward toward colored light and reflective gold leaf, the hall looks fashioned from radio beams momentarily frozen in space.

Three New York architectural firms are credited with the design of the theater (originally called the International Music Hall). These firms brought to harmonious realization the unlikely alliance between the patrician Rockefellers and the plebeian Samuel L. Rothafel, known as Roxy, an impresario of movie palaces for the masses. What brought these bands of the social spectrum together, apart from the profit motive, was the belief in modernity and a mythology of speed, change, novelty, and movement sufficiently compelling to excite a majority of citizens in the world's oldest modern democracy.

The music hall was originally envisioned as part of a grander cultural scheme that would have gone even further in this democratic direction. The 1928 plan for Rockefeller Center called for an opera house on the Fifth Avenue side of the site. In addition the Rockefeller family hoped to cut through the two blocks between Fifty-first and Fifty-third streets, thus linking the center to the Museum of Modern Art. These plans were never realized.

Always seen as a place for families, the music hall opened at a time when family entertainment might include ballet, symphony, and opera, along with comedy, popular song, acrobatics, and the Rockettes. The vaudeville mix was recognizably of the radio age, when folks gathered round the Bakelite console to hear their favorite shows. The music hall gave them tunes and great visuals besides.

The building is a triumph of processional design. Its most dramatic aspect is an expanded version of an effect common in theater architecture: the disarming contrast between a small-scale exterior and an interior of epic proportions. A reverse of the magic trick in which an elephant is made to disappear, the colossal theater materializes within a container of finite dimensions. The entrance and ticket lobby are lodged on the ground floor of an office tower that gives little sign of the grandiose space inside. Though the building is tall, it takes its scale from the regulation-size windows punched through its stone facades.

The magic continues inside in a three-part sequence of spatial decompression. The ticket lobby is in keeping with the scale of the building's exterior, but the box offices anticipate the amplitude within. There are so many of them, and all for one theater: a soloplex. The box offices may remind some of passport-control counters. The comparison is apt, for from here we proceed to a grand ocean liner of a space, the Grand Foyer. If the *Normandie* had a sister ship, this would be its grandest public room. Moderne rather than modern, the foyer is one of the world's great Art Deco interiors, its length and height amplified by mirrors of gold-backed glass.

Quest for the Fountain of Eternal Youth, a mural by Ezra Winter opposite the entrance, dominates the space. Malcolm Cowley, the literary critic, used a picture of the mural on the dust jacket of his memoir of the 1930s, *The Dream of the Golden Mountains*. To Cowley the image epitomized the Depression sensibility, the vision of a new cultural order struggling to be born. For us the mural might signify the hall itself: eternally young, eternally new, a landmark in the history of the future. Now the music hall has taken a deep drink from its own fountain.

Entering the auditorium, we find ourselves on the deck of the ocean liner, gazing out to sea. Roxy is standing beside us, watching the sun rising from the horizon, or maybe sinking beneath it—accounts differ—though rising sounds more American. Suddenly it occurs to Roxy that this is precisely the image he wants his architects to capture for his new 6,000-seat show palace. In time the showman's wish is conveyed to the young Edward Durell Stone, a draftsman in one of the three architectural firms responsible for the design. In later life Stone will make his mark with Manhattan buildings like the Museum of Modern Art, the General Motors Building, and the marble Venetian confection at 2 Columbus Circle. At age thirty Stone finds himself designing the most stupendous arch this side of Rome.

That is the legend, anyhow. No anecdotes are required, however, to understand the auditorium's formal power. This derives from the plain, unadorned half circle of the proscenium, and from the projection of that shape from the front to the rear of the house. Like a dome, the design eliminates both walls and ceiling. We could be seated within a half dome or one quadrant of a sphere or egg. This is why the auditorium is psychologically so overwhelming. We're sitting inside a segment of an imaginary globe that continues behind the rear wall and doubles back underneath the feet. The stage stands at the equator.

A dome is achieved by rotating an arch 180 degrees. At Radio City the (approximate) quadrant dome is fashioned by telescoping the proscenium in arcs of ever-increasing spans. Intimacy is not this hall's strong suit. No matter where you sit, you have the sensation of tumbling through the sky. This feeling is heightened by the broad strips of air-conditioning grilles, also used for lighting, that radiate longitudinally from the proscenium. These bands further diminish the orientation that walls and ceiling usually provide. It's a cinematic effect, the architectural equivalent of the simultaneous reverse track and forward zoom in Hitchcock's *Vertigo*.

For design historians the music hall is forever linked to Donald Deskey, responsible for the theater's iconic Art Deco interiors. Deskey was a favorite of the Rockefeller family. In 1930 he designed a picture gallery on the top floor of John D. Rockefeller's town house on West Fifty-fourth Street. The gallery, one of the seeds of the Museum of Modern Art, was demolished, along with the town house, to make way for the new museum. (The gallery's print room of Bakelite and aluminum was partly re-created and displayed at the museum recently.)

Plate-glass vanity tables, metal tube chairs, mohair sofas, round mirrors, balustrades, light fixtures, theater seats: these are some of the classic pieces Deskey created for the hall. He also orchestrated the work of artists (Stuart Davis Winter) and designers to ornament the lounges, bathrooms, smoking room, and staircases. These have been faithfully restored to mint condition. Mr. Hardy's client, James L. Dolan of Cablevision Systems Corporation, the music hall's owner, instructed the architect to re-create a place that his mother would like.

Mr. Hardy refrained from contemporary interpolations. Instead of reproducing Deskey's pieces, he has reupholstered them. He has researched and re-created the original colors and patterns for floor and wall coverings, retrieving the hall's interiors from decades of accumulated grime. Rooms that had dissolved into a murky brown soup have reemerged in gleaming gold, silver, red, and blue. Paul Marantz and Jules Fisher, the lighting designers, deserve equal credit for rejuvenating spaces that could not exist without incandescence.

Tonight's opening puts a happy ending on a story that began in 1978, when city and state officials intervened to prevent the Rockefellers from tearing down their showplace. Kent L. Barwick, newly appointed chairman of the New York City Landmarks Preservation Commission, led the campaign to designate the music hall's interior a landmark. Richard A. Kahan, president of the New York State Urban Development Corporation, committed emergency funds to keep the hall open and created a company to operate it.

After restoring two theaters on Forty-second Street and with the completion of the music hall, Mr. Hardy fears being typecast as a preservation architect for theaters. He shouldn't worry about it. The significance of these projects extends beyond their walls. At this moment of preservation run amok, the line between true and bogus history should be sharply drawn. At the music hall, Mr. Hardy and Mr. Dolan resisted suggestions that to attract a modern audience the place should be tarted up with Las Vegas glitz. This would have obscured the fact that the music hall is one of the places where the fabulous Vegas-style showroom was born.

It is brilliant that a television executive like Mr. Dolan didn't buy into the television mentality that holds many architects and even preservationists in its grip. There is a difference between a radio and a hall—between the social spaces created by architecture and those shaped by broadcasting. At the reborn Radio City Music Hall, architecture has the last word.

October 4, 1999

TRUMP, HIS GILDED TASTE, AND ME

Antiquity Now

"Mr. President!" "Mr. President!" It has come to this. At Madison Square Garden, people are rising from their seats and calling out "Mr. President!" to Donald J. Trump, the real estate tycoon. This year, the nation of Washington, Jefferson, Lincoln, and Eleanor Roosevelt reached the point at which magazine editors, talk show hosts, and screaming crowds have lunged at the entertaining possibility that Donald Trump might run for the highest office in the land.

I've come to the Garden hoping something like this will happen. A Ricky Martin concert is the pretext for being here. But the real draw on this October night is the chance to witness firsthand the most recent example of the merger of politics and entertainment. Presidential candidates have been nominated in the Garden's several incarnations. Millions have been entertained by musicians, athletes, and clowns. Tonight, the hall's political and theatrical functions have collapsed into each other in a blaze of limelight. Off stage as well as on, it's *"viva la vida loca"* time.

Mr. Trump and his companion, Melania Knauss, are sitting some distance away on the Garden floor. I'm chatting with my friend when we notice a rise in the volume of preconcert racket, a murmur of voices: "Who is it?" From where we're sitting, we can't see the cause of the commotion at first, but then Mr. Trump and Ms. Knauss are standing up, waving to the crowd. Ricky Martin fans start packing into the aisles. Bodyguards materialize. Mr. Trump and Ms. Knauss head up the aisle, working the crowd along the way. We've paid for our own seats, but Mr. Trump can't not be a host, and here he is, holding a fistful of Ben & Jerry's Totally Nuts ice cream bars as he stirs up our side of the house.

Mr. Trump builds buildings. I write about them. So far he hasn't given me an occasion to write glowingly about his architecture projects. It would be great if this changed. I'm not hopeful. But I love the color, contentiousness, and comedy Mr. Trump brings to the contemporary urban scene. Adrian Stokes, the British art critic, once wrote, "Architecture is limited to forms without events." I disagree. As a social, public, and urban art form, architecture can't be separated from the events that buildings contain, shape, and provoke.

Trump's persona is one of these events. So is architecture criticism, whether in written appraisals or in the comments of sidewalk superintendents. Even when criticism is negative, it is part of the fabric that holds a great city together. I don't hate Mr. Trump's buildings, but even if that were the case, I would still see them as a challenge to examine my preferences in relation to his.

For some years now, I've been playing Ascyltos to his Trimalchio, two characters in Petronius's *Satyricon*, the most celebrated fictional depiction of life in Nero's Rome. According to Tacitus, Petronius was called *arbiter elegantiae* because the emperor consulted him on all matters of taste. In my version of the novel, set in present-day New York, Mr. Trump is the fabulously rich promoter who basks in public attention. I'm the student of Epicureanism trying to make some sense of contemporary taste. He's an important figure in my continuing education. While his buildings may not fulfill the ancient Epicurean ideal of moderation in all things, they clearly hold great appeal for those who have made his real estate enterprise a huge success.

In any case, Ascyltos was not the ideal Epicurean but rather a satirical version of one. The poor scholar worried more about his next meal than about the refinements of beauty. His picaresque odyssey took him through a cross section of Roman "taste cultures" (to borrow a term from the sociologist Herbert Gans). Federico Fellini captured some of these in his 1969 movie version of the novel. The classical villa of the dignified patrician and his wife. The ancient museum festooned with fragments of Greek and Egyptian art. The smoky lair of the priestess. The garish night world of theaters and bordellos.

But the diversity of contemporary New York makes Nero's Rome seem like a Shaker village by comparison. Here a daily drama emerges from the constant border-crossing from one environment to the next. French bistro. Bauhaus. Roman bathhouse. Petit Trianon. Latin marqueta. Gothic cathedral. Japanese teahouse. Hospital hygienic. The eclectic mix of the city's public and private spaces is more stimulating than any one of its components. That stimulation is why we live in New york.

But some, confused by this stunning mosaic of aesthetic disarray, have singled out Donald Trump as a supreme example of Bad Taste, whatever that might be. The shiny marble, bronze and brass, the gilded building crowns, the gaudy Atlantic City casinos, the spangled showgirls: it all adds up in their eyes to vulgar excess, an unsophisticate's delight in meretricious baubles. He has become a point of orientation in an environment where cultural bearings are easily lost. Faced with the claims of competing taste cultures, it is scarcely possible to talk about Good Taste and keep a straight face. The subject is pure *Saturday Night Live*. Bad Taste is more useful. In a pluralistic world, lightning rods are more reliable than compasses. And the wrinkled nose is a universal symbol of the desire to feel superior to whatever seems threatening.

Two thousand years after Petronius wrote his novel, Trimalchio remains its most familiar character, his feast its central event, the most colorful contemporary description we have of the excesses of the ancient classical world. And what will be remembered of New York, I wonder, two millenniums from now? Today we are in the waning hours of the century New York has ruled. Two thousand years hence, there may be nothing here but rubble disturbing the surface of a swamp. A tropical breeze blows around reeds, insects, reptiles, heating up twisted clumps of metal.

A forbidden zone, this place has long beckoned adolescents to explore its fetid shallows. One day, a group of them stumbles upon a submerged, rusted object that when polished up is identified by experts in interstellar life as the letter *T* in a language once used on an abandoned planet. Gradually, secrets of yet another lost civilization are revealed. There are rumors of an ancient city of gold.

In 1995 I wrote a column about Trump International Tower and Hotel, the fifty-two-story residential high-rise then in construction on Columbus Circle. The column wasn't a rave, and Mr. Trump was irate about it, because the building was not yet complete. There was a charade over firing his architect, Philip Johnson, who called to tell me about it. I suggested that the three of us meet to talk and proposed a location: in front of Andy Warhol's *Gold Marilyn* painting at the Museum of Modern Art.

I'd mentioned the painting in my article. There's an obvious parallel between it and Mr. Trump himself. The man has attained the status of a popular icon, set against the gold of celebrity. Mr. Johnson, not a stranger to celebrity culture, once owned the painting, which he later gave to the museum. I had a personal reason for choosing this meeting place. Warhol was the first close friend I made in New York (and also the first one I lost). In 1965, when I was a freshman at the University of Pennsylvania, the artist had his first museum retrospective, at Penn's Institute of Contemporary Art. We met soon after the show's opening. I started going up to New York on weekends to hang out. One time, I mentioned my interest in architecture. "Oh, architecture is really the only thing left," Warhol said in that breathy voice of his. "We can help. We know Philip Johnson. We can get you into Yale."

Mr. Trump can't know the meaning this painting holds for me. I suspect that he cares nothing about its art-historical value, either. He doesn't strike me as a museumgoing kind of guy. To my eyes, however, his public persona is itself a cultural artifact of museum quality. I want to study his condition in this context. I also hope that the context can help persuade him that my story was not malicious. I don't share Mr. Trump's taste, but I love his style. I far prefer it to the style of those who buy their ideas off the peg at Ralph Lauren. And I'm curious to know how he will deal with that.

A Wednesday morning before the museum is open. Winter, very cold. Mr. Johnson and I are waiting in the lobby. He's wearing his famous astrakhan fur hat. Limousine pulls up, very black. Mr. Trump gets out with three associates. Gray and blond. Great color combination. But a terrible expression on his face: pursed mouth, no smile, I'm going to get this guy.

We head upstairs and clip through the galleries. When we reach the room where the *Marilyn* is hanging, I point it out. "Philip gave that. Isn't it great?" There's a large sculpture in the middle of the room, a brass floor piece by Donald Judd. Evidently Mr. Trump mistakes it for a coffee table, for he uses it as one, tossing his overcoat and some binders full of pictures on top of it as we walk over to the painting. Mr. Trump barely glances at the *Marilyn*, but this doesn't matter. My goal is to capture them together in the same frame. He's a work of art himself, as well as a piece of work, a living self-portrait with a trademark signature sought by foreign banks, condo dwellers, autograph hounds, advertisers, and publishers. Warhol's dream was to live off putting his signature on soup cans. Mr. Trump has more or less fulfilled it.

I'm the one who should be baring teeth here. I'm a big Art Deco lover and Mr. Trump once tore down a fine example of it: the old Bonwit Teller building that stood on the site of Trump Tower. Mr. Trump had agreed to preserve the Deco reliefs from the Bonwit Teller facade, but one day the pieces tumbled to the sidewalk and smashed to bits. Have you seen the television ad where Mr. Trump, playing himself, accidentally drops a piece of pottery on the floor? I wonder if the breakage at Bonwit's was similarly scripted. Oops!

Mr. Trump did not apologize for his carelessness. Instead he invited a *New York Times* reporter to inspect an example of his taste in decorative art. As I recall, the specimen turned out to be a lion's-head bathroom fixture selected by his first wife, Ivana, for the Grand Hyatt Hotel on Forty-second Street, the developer's first Manhattan project. Wise men have said there's no arguing with taste. Was a reporter about to rush in?

In 1986 I saw Mr. Trump in person for the first time. I'd gone uptown to see my friend Encolpius, who was marching in the Columbus Day Parade. I happened to hit Fifth Avenue just as Mayor Koch's car drove by Trump Tower. The developer was standing in front of the building, with his eight-year-old son at his side, both of them dressed in Sunday suits. Mr. Koch gave them a big smile and a vigorous wave, the Trumps waved back, and suddenly Fifth Avenue was Main Street in a small town on the

Fourth of July, with Mr. Trump the town's main shopkeeper standing on the porch of his emporium as the parade passed by.

It's quite possible that these two men despised each other. And I'm certain that Mr. Trump's appearance was motivated more by hunger for recognition than by selfless civic spirit. But who thinks that Main Street is innocent of calculation and intrigue? Who cares that Jacqueline Kennedy stage-managed her son's salute?

Mr. Trump wants to show me some prize additions to his own real estate collection: Mar-A-Lago, the Post estate in Palm Beach; the Meyers estate in Bedford Hills, New York; 40 Wall Street. These are presented as evidence that Mr. Trump's taste deserves the respect of any honest critic. To me, these buildings don't quite register as architecture. They look to me like signs of money, status, power. These signs are fascinating in their own right, as are diamonds, furs, yachts, and other tokens of the deluxe life enjoyed in Marbella, St. Bart's, and other playgrounds of the rich. To Mr. Trump, quality means luxury details—fine marble, imported wood, sparkling fixtures—and fast-track construction. To me, it means risk-taking ideas, original perceptions, spirit of place and time, and self-construction—the same qualities Mr. Trump projects in his public persona, in fact.

I'd prefer to talk about the new buildings Mr. Trump might be contemplating. But I keep my mouth shut. Since I'm here to educate myself in a taste culture, I'm pleased to look at these trophies through Mr. Trump's eyes. His comments are easily summarized: Everything is the best. With this zest for self-appraisal, why should he care what critics think?

By the end of the meeting, he senses that I've come to learn, not to judge. I'm exercising what Keats called negative capability: suspending judgment is the best way to strengthen the critical faculty. But I can sense Mr. Trump's disappointment that I'm not more adversarial. In a panel discussion a few years earlier, Mr. Trump winked at me from the far end of the table as he told the audience that he wanted to build the kind of buildings that would earn good reviews from the *Times*. The wink was as telling as the words: Maybe Mr. Trump would like a good review. But he also relishes a dust-up.

"How dare he!" "How dare he!" This is Mr. Trump on a later occasion, shaking his fist at the sky, as he acts out his impression of the Palm Beach neighbors who oppose Mr. Trump's plan to subdivide Mar-A-Lago into smaller parcels of land. Watching him, you might think he enjoys taking the part of his opponents as much as he likes playing himself. Unfortunately, on this occasion, I won't be one. But at least Mr. Trump has found in me a connoisseur of the combative style. I believe that conflict is the most valuable cultural product a great city puts out. This is why I organized this momentary convergence of Warhol, Mr. Johnson, and Mr. Trump. All three gentlemen have put out more than their share. The city has fed itself on the friction they have caused.

Nature Is Greater than Art

Donald Trump has to be the center of attention. I have to turn everything into a story. These are character defects, symptoms of extreme narcissism, perhaps even borderline personality disorders. But they make for a nice bond between writer and subject. The bond has survived visits to a boxing match, two gambling casinos, a condominium sales office, and Palm Beach—all ordeals, as far as I am concerned.

The Ricky Martin concert is another matter. Thanks to Mr. Martin, I've been meditating on the concept of *duende,* a Spanish word for which there is no exact English equivalent. Literally *duende* means imp or dwarf, but it is perhaps closer to what we call soul. It's often used to describe dancers or musicians. Santiago Calatrava, the Spanish architect and engineer, says it can also refer to the spirit of a place. He says that if you're walking along one day and suddenly feel like singing, that's the duende. He mentions the time of the year in Seville when orange trees blossom and scent the air.

Generally, the duendes don't feel welcome in our part of the world. We're all too repressed. Being imps, however, they like to make a surprise appearance from time to time and drive us out of our minds, as Ricky Martin has been doing in our part of the world for the past year. Mr. Martin has a project: making people feel glad to be alive. The songs, the voice, the movement, and the elaborate packaging have all contributed to the success of this project. So have his extraordinary good looks, as attested by countless magazine covers.

For the vast majority of his fans, Mr. Martin's dreamboat looks are a fact, a piece of good news to appreciate and to fantasize about. From a critical perspective, the singer's beauty is more complicated. Criticism is partly an art of complicating simple things (it's a luxury item in this sense). And beauty, historically, has topped the list of things critics like to worry about. It is the pivotal issue in addressing the question of Mr. Trump's taste.

This is something most people won't want to think about: Mr. Trump is a beauty freak. We all like to tee-hee him about the arm candy, the models, the showgirls. This is easy and fun. It's harder to accept that the behavior some call womanizing is not a radical departure from what we call art. The Greeks understood this. Their concept of beauty derived from nature. The human body is nature's perfect creation. The gymnasium is where this perfection is realized. An art studio, so to speak. The old men go to the gym to admire the young male form.

As a universal point of reference, the body isn't bad. Everybody has one. The classical temple takes this a step further, merging anatomical analogies with landscape. The temple adorns a sacred site of earth. Columns are stylized trees. Figurative sculpture articulates the connection between architectural form and human physique. Caryatids, a fusion of animal, vegetable, and mineral, hold up the roof. The erotic origins of art and architecture are thereby advertised. Duendes welcome here.

Modern Americans seldom experience union with nature outside erotic relationships and childbearing. Parks, zoos, wildlife sanctuaries, adventure tours, wide-screen movies, and other virtual environments have rendered much of the rest of nature into picturesque attractions. Corporations are working to close off the sexual option as well. Sex remains dangerous, not just because of infectious disease. Beauty is always killing the beast. This is the idea of the sublime developed by art theorists in the nineteenth century. Beauty and terror are inseparable. They come from the same place.

This is one reason people like to describe some women as bimbos. It takes the terror out of beauty to treat it as a joke. Bimbos are in the eye of the beholder, in other words. Melania Knauss is indeed beautiful, in the style of Jacqueline Bisset, but with a less faraway look in her eyes. She and Ricky Martin make a sublime pair. Mr. Trump has organized a trip backstage to see the star before the concert starts. Barbara Walters can't get in. Bette Midler can't get in. But Mr. Trump gets in, with lots of "Mr. President!" "Mr. President!" along the way.

Encolpius and I tag along and wait outside the dressing room. Mr. Trump calls out, "Get in here and see this guy! He's better looking than his pictures!" Mr. Trump does have an eye for male beauty. Once, striding through the lobby on a tour of 40 Wall Street, he spies an Adonis working on an elevator cab. Mr. Trump points to him: "What are you doing fixing elevators? You should be a top movie star." Sounds like a pickup line. But in front of twenty working hard-hats?

Walter Pater, the guru of the nineteenth-century Aesthetic movement, said art critics don't need a fixed definition of beauty. They need only the power to be moved by it. A repressed Romantic, Pater evidently couldn't distinguish aesthetic response from an erection. The Greeks would be with him on that. And they understood that not all bodies are created equal. The Greeks never took democracy that far. We're counting on technology to level the playing field in the beauty competition. And on politics to ensure that looks don't count. But Pascal was right: had Cleopatra's nose been shorter, the face of the world would have changed.

Rich people can afford more nature than the rest of us. Then they usually muck it up. There's no better example of this than Palm Beach. The climate is extraordinary; the palm trees, flowers, and sunsets are magnificent, and so are many of the houses. But the way of life is impossible. The jewelry, clothes, and hairdos. The scary gift-shop bibelots. The liquor store that's as prominent as a city hall. And the bodies, most of them, are far beyond the reach of any technology we'll live to see. An anthropologist like Margaret Mead might make sense of this, but I want to hire a sound truck and go through the streets exclaiming, "People, you don't want to live this way!"

I'm disappointed that Mr. Trump wants to spend his weekends here. He's youthful, not stuffy, and doesn't crave isolation. Shirley Bassey belongs on his sound track, not Rudy Vallee. An essential part of his taste was formed watching James Bond movies, and I regret that he hasn't carried this over into his architecture. Those fantastic Ken Adam sets. The great Fontainebleau Hotel. The tan young man in white trunks plunging off the high diving board into the modern blue yonder.

Mar-A-Lago is a Citizen Kane's Museum-by-the-Sea. The place is an encyclopedia of taste cultures, with more period rooms than the Met. You could spend two months here and pick up a good education in the history of decorative art, moving from perpendicular Gothic to American Federal to a child's bedroom with fairy-tale scenes hand-painted by Disney himself. Our time is scarcely represented, except by the plutocratic desire for pedigree.

What must appeal to Mr. Trump is the estate's theatricality. One of its architects was Joseph Urban, a Vienna-born talent who achieved his greatest success as Florenz Ziegfeld's favorite stage designer. This national landmark is a permanent set, where the cereal heiress Marjorie Merriweather Post could count her profits from Post Toasties. She, too, had a thing for gold. The fixtures in her bathroom are made of it.

This domain of high artifice is a good place to see the peculiar weave of fact and illusion that holds Mr. Trump's world together. A black Lamborghini Diablo sits near the entrance to the house. The car is real. Encolpius took it out for a spin. But it's not Mr. Trump's car. He says the car company gives him a new one each year, provided he parks it out front. Is he saying it's much classier to be lent a fresh Lamborghini than to own one? Of course. He's also saying rich men's toys are to be played with. Not owning them is part of the game.

Later, we explore the famous tower suite where Michael Jackson and Lisa Marie Presley spent their honeymoon. The bedroom is small, but the ceiling must be twelve feet high. A clerestory festooned with potted plants runs around the room's octagonal circumference. I assume the plants are fake, and why not? They're too far away to make any difference to the eye. Encolpius puts a chair on a table and goes up to check. They're real. Someone must bring a ladder in to water them, then worry about drips. Did Michael get splashed? Did his mascara start to run?

The best space at Trump Taj Mahal is one the public doesn't get to see: the crawl area above the dropped ceiling over the slot machine rooms. This area is accessible only from the white, fluorescent-lighted high-security chambers where video monitors flicker and money is counted and packed for transport by trucks.

The dropped ceiling is made of see-through mirror panels framed by ornate Mogul filigree. Gamblers know they're being watched. Little effort has been made to conceal the clusters of (real) surveillance cameras overhead. These are so effective that the casino's security staff seldom ventures into the crawl space, but it is designed for use. The area is tall enough that you don't have to crawl. Catwalks lead off in all directions. It's like a computer space, a virtual environment sandwiched between two planes. Through the lower plane, you glimpse the gambling floor, though the flashing lights and electronic burblings of the one-armed bandits seem distant. One wants Pierce Brosnan to materialize on the catwalk and struggle with an archfiend, who plunges through the mirrored ceiling as lady snipers in catsuits open fire with corks popped from chilled bottles of foaming pink Champagne.

The high-roller suites, decorated in Egyptian, Roman, and other motifs, are more fabulous but less interesting. Mr. Trump sells fantasies, and these rooms are free, if you don't mind dropping several thou at the table. Behind the *Arabian Nights* dreams is an elaborate and completely rational machine designed to harvest cash. My fantasy is to see how the rational and the irrational are joined. Above the mirrors, in the crawl space, this dream comes true.

Life in the Ruins

Beauty flows from universal and eternal principles. The purpose of the art academy is to identify these principles and encourage conformity to them: if taste were properly cultivated, everyone would like the same things. In the eighteenth century, many Enlightenment thinkers subscribed to these beliefs. They live on today in debased form: advertising copy ("The timeless beauty of the Ding-Dong Watch"). Art writing conducted on the level of advertising copy ("The universal language of abstract form"). Social climbing ("Classic, impeccable, but warm—that was Jackie!").

More ominously, the universalist ideal persists in convention hotels, airport lounges, fast-food outlets, and other homogenized environments of the global monoculture. Everyone's taste has been cultivated and everyone likes small-figure maroon wall-to-wall carpeting with borders of contrasting cream. You can love it but you can't leave it.

This was Pop Art's message. "Pop Art is liking things," Warhol said. Give us the serenity to accept what we cannot change. Acquiesce to the inevitable. This idea was culturally therapeutic for the generation that came of age in the postwar consumer society. But Warhol was also terrified by many of the things he professed to like. Painting Coca-Cola bottles was a way of mastering a standard of normalcy that this completely weird person could never measure up to.

Pop Art helped overeducated neurasthenics to enjoy common pleasures. When Ricky Martin arrives onstage, standing on the hood of a white 1964 Mustang, I'm happy to overlook the dark side of pop culture: the deadening conformity, the media brainwashing, the indifference to difference, the philistinism. Blue jeans, Coca-Cola, white T-shirts, Marilyn Monroe are cultural achievements Americans can be proud of. Uniformity can be a blissful escape from the torture of having a discriminating mind.

Pater advised critics: "The first step towards seeing one's object as it really is, is to know one's impression as it really is, to discriminate it, to realize it distinctly." And if one's impression is ambivalent? This is the question Pop Art raised regarding modern American taste. Mr. Trump poses the same question. I can give myself over to enjoying the spectacle of the man and his accouterments. His pleasure in them is infectious. But when I go looking for architecture, I keep coming up short.

Quantity is a pop culture quality. The most records. The most tickets. The most magazine covers, newspaper stories, Web site hits. The most votes in a presidential campaign. Since the Pyramids, quantity has been a quality in architecture, too. That's why it was worth going to court to protect Grand Central Terminal. Rem Koolhaas talks about Bigness as a necessary response to the fragmented urban center. The twentieth century has seen no greater architectural wonder than the Manhattan skyline. Donald Trump will not be the last person who wants to be part of it. The sky's supposed to be the limit here.

But his most recent project, Trump World Tower on First Avenue, has aroused the wrath of many New Yorkers on account of its height. Billed as the world's tallest residential building, this bronze, glass-sheathed lightning rod will rise seventy stories to a height of 861 feet. "Aesthetic outrage," "monstrosity" are some of the milder epithets it has attracted. Opponents have also gone to court to stop it, unsuccessfully thus far.

I wish I could agree with the opposition. If it were going to block my views, no doubt I'd be hell on a keyboard. I also wish I could defend the project against its detractors. But the truth is that New York forfeited its right to complain about aesthetic outrage some time ago. In terms of contemporary architecture, the entire city is an aesthetic outrage. The city has achieved a fine record in architectural preservation, and the value of this should not be underestimated. But our support for contemporary work, for buildings that interpret changing relationships in urban life, has all but evaporated.

A builder with Mr. Trump's ambition, and his public presence, could make a difference here, of course. If he wants to be the hip swinger, the 007 dude, why won't he connect with contemporary architects with proven talent to transform such desires into art? Arquitectonica, Rem Koolhaas, Zaha Hadid, Jean Nouvel, Thom Mayne . . . One can rattle off names, but the point is this: What's objectionable about Mr. Trump's taste is not the desire for attention, for the best, the most, the tallest, the most eye-catching. It is his failure to realize these desires creatively in the architectural medium. The persona is a force of nature. The buildings don't rise to the occasion.

Mr. Trump would say they're selling like hotcakes, they're the most expensive square footage in New York, they're full of rich, rich people, the marble is the finest in the land, I'm a businessman, the guys you like are kooks and crazies.

I would say: Yes, they're just like you. Do you want other developers to get the glory for buildings that embody the daring, kid-with-a-dream image you project?

The problem is not Mr. Trump's alone. How can he be blamed for not knowing what New York hasn't taught him? On Central Park South, the developer had to cope with a city official's suggestion that he build a 1930s skyscraper on the site of the St. Moritz Hotel. At Riverside South, his residential development on the West Side, he was compelled by five civic groups to work with a set of design guidelines that essentially guaranteed that the architecture would be dead on arrival. How can he be criticized for narcissism if the city doesn't even recognize how pathological it is to go on gazing in the rearview mirror? No architecture please. We're too tasteful.

In the final scene of *Fellini Satyricon*, we see Nero's Rome suddenly transformed into a crumbling fresco on the wall of a ruined seaside villa. Encolpius has been murdered. Ascyltos has fallen in with a group of sailors who are about to depart on a voyage to unknown islands. The camera freezes on a picture of him on the shore, walking toward the sea. Two thousand years pass and we see the two companions as well as Trimalchio and the film's other characters reunited as flecks of paint.

The conclusion is moving for many reasons, one of them being the gentleness with which the director restates the cautionary theme: our passions, rages, successes, and failures are all vanity. Life itself, he has shown, is not. The duendes matter. If it's vanity to want buildings that express ideas like this, let's be vain.

December 19, 1999

CRYSTAL CORRIDOR IN THE CITY OF GLASS

Season's greetings! Time to tickle another sacred cow.

The MetLife (formerly Pan Am) Building at the foot of Park Avenue is one of the worst disasters ever to befall the New York cityscape. All New Yorkers acknowledge the universal truth of this belief. None would dare challenge it, unless they are stupid, desperate for attention, or completely out of their minds.

But Kivi Sotamaa, a young Finnish architect who is not mad, dumb, or sensationalistic, likes the MetLife Building very much. Mr. Sotamaa may hesitate before saying so. He is twenty-eight, polite, and lives in Helsinki. He understands that the dreadfulness of the building is an article of local faith. But on a recent evening, as we were walking down Park Avenue, we looked up the gray cliff of MetLife's concrete northern facade, and I found myself looking at the architecture through his eyes. Att-r-r-ractive brute!

Mr. Sotamaa, a finalist in the competition held earlier this year to design a time capsule for *The New York Times*, admires the proportions of the three-dimensional facade and the rhythm of its windows. He likes the procession through the lobby to the escalators that descend to the main concourse at Grand Central Terminal. Most startling of all, Mr. Sotamaa appreciates the closure that the building brings to the southern end of Park Avenue, and to the grand boulevard of International Style office towers leading toward it.

Mr. Sotamaa's view will not be applauded by those who have long considered this stretch of Park Avenue a sorry display of the skinny glass boxes that began to take over the skyline in the postwar decades. But to him, and to a surprising number of other architects and city-lovers, the so-called Park Avenue Corridor is the architectural heart of the twentieth century. The corridor is the crystallization of the New York myth, the soaring city of work and ambition, where the sky is the limit and dreams are fulfilled. It symbolizes New York's displacement of Paris as the century's most vibrant City of Light.

The corridor contains several individual buildings of distinction from the 1950s to '60s, including the Seagram Building, Lever House, 500 Park

Avenue (originally the Pepsi-Cola Building), and the Chase Building (originally the Union Carbide Building), the last three designed by the New York firm Skidmore, Owings & Merrill, and Philip Johnson's Russell Sage Foundation (originally Asia House). James Ingo Freed's Park Tower, completed in 1981, is a somber late addition to the group, while Frank Lloyd Wright's 1958 Mercedes-Benz (originally Jaguar) showroom offers a quirky footnote to the ramp of the Guggenheim Museum's rotunda.

But much of the corridor's power lies in the aggregate, in the mix of lesser buildings with well-known landmarks. At the century's outset, long before the first curtain wall was actually hung, architects used to dream about the gleaming cities that glass would enable them to build. Here, the dream was realized. It looks particularly misty at this time of year, when the sun sets early and the street shimmers with holiday sparkle. Like towering ice palaces, the buildings glint with silver, white, and gold.

The term *International Style* was coined by Philip Johnson and Henry Russell Hitchcock for an exhibition in 1932 at the Museum of Modern Art. Though the show included a few United States buildings and established Mr. Johnson as an arbiter of American architectural taste, the term became mainly linked to the work of European modernists like J. J. P. Oud, Mies van der Rohe, Le Corbusier, and Alvar Aalto. In the postwar decades, the International Style became shorthand for the steel-and-glass towers like the Seagram Building, the supreme example of the genre, designed by Mies and Johnson in 1957–58.

Mies described his own aesthetic as one of "almost nothing," a paring down of form to the discreet articulation of construction and enclosure. Walls were reduced to the transparent membrane of the glass curtain wall. Structure was expressed on the exterior by the application of nonstructural I-beams. This approach exemplified the architect's belief that less is more. It enlarged the artistic significance of proportion, scale, quality of materials, and refinement of detail.

Not long ago, it was said that these buildings represented a rejection of history. In fact, modern architects merely declined to use historical period styles. No movement has ever set down roots into deeper historical soil. Mies himself was strongly influenced by Karl Friedrich Schinkel, the exemplar of neoclassicism in nineteenth-century Berlin. The rationalism associated with the style harked back to the ideal of scientific objectivity promoted by the eighteenth-century Enlightenment. From the nineteenth-century realist movement came such modernist beliefs as truth to materials and the rejection of showy display. Above all, the International Style was grounded in nineteenth-century historicism: the view that each epoch should produce a distinctive architectural style.

The Will of an Epoch

According to this linear view (restated by plaster casts in countless turn-of-the-century museums), Egyptians, Romans, and the medieval French had each produced a style. Therefore, the modern, industrial age should have its own manner of building. As Mies famously said, architecture is the will of an epoch translated into space. As an embodiment of this belief, the International Style can be seen as the nineteenth century's last gasp. Though it became a symbol of the twentieth-century metropolis, in fact it represented an aestheticized version of the train sheds, factories, bridges, and other engineering marvels of the nineteenth-century industrial city. Far from rejecting history, in other words, the architects of the Park Avenue Corridor were actually behind the times. They developed the perfect vernacular for an era in urban history that had already begun to wane by the time their buildings arose.

Interest in the International Style has been building in the last decade. In 1992 Terence Riley, now chief curator of the Modern's architecture and design department, remounted the museum's 1932 show at Columbia University. The same year, Hani Rashid, a professor at Columbia's architecture school, chose the Park Avenue Corridor as one of three Manhattan sites for a design project in his studio. This past term, Michael Maltzan, an architect based in Los Angeles, led a group of students at Harvard's Graduate School of Design in a similar project based on Craig Ellwood's classic Art Center College of Design in Pasadena.

Most of the Park Avenue Corridor's buildings have reached the age when they qualify for landmark designation, which would afford them the protection of the city's preservation laws. This is a moment of irony: those laws were enacted partly to curtail the proliferation of modernist buildings and the loss of the fine old masonry edifices that they replaced. Like them or not, however, the historic and aesthetic value of these buildings must now be reckoned with. Interpretations of their meaning must be rethought.

Is it really true, for example, that the International Style contradicted public taste? This has been one of the hoary myths on which preservationists and postmodernists have relied since the 1970s. But in the early 1960s, the International Style was a symbol of urban sophistication in many Hollywood movies, as accurate a barometer as we have of popular desires. In *Breakfast at Tiffany's, The Best of Everything,* and even several Doris Day comedies, the glass tower epitomized worldly aspiration and success.

Nowhere is the collision between preservation and the International

Style more apparent than in the space that once served as the lobby for 500 Park Avenue. Originally designed for Pepsi-Cola, now PepsiCo, which subsequently sold it to Olivetti, it is a paragon of excellence in corporate design. Furnished simply with a reception desk, the lobby was a rectangular bubble of space on which the entire building seemed to float. Two years ago the gorgeous space was chopped in two to house a pair of retail establishments. (Lever House is more fortunate. The building's owners have hired David Childs of Skidmore, Owings, & Merrill to restore the exterior and to design new office interiors in keeping with Gordon Bunshaft's original design.)

The desecration of 500 Park raises the issue of how effectively landmark laws can protect glass buildings. Since the main effect of the glass is to dissolve the boundary between inside and outside, it makes little sense to preserve only exteriors. But interiors, which are usually bland as well as subject to the changing needs of owners and tenants, scarcely seem worth designation. At the same time, when office lighting fixtures are replaced without sensitivity, the effect on the facade can be ruinous.

Landmark experts face the same question that the Museum of Modern Art has had to tackle. Does *modernism* refer to a finite historical period or to an ongoing tradition of innovation? In its plans for expanding the museum, the Modern has more or less dodged the issue by hiring an architect (Yoshio Taniguchi) whose work, while contemporary, is rooted in Miesian ideas. This approach makes sense for an institution that wishes to show that it is both receptive to the present moment and respectful of its past. But it won't be of much use to preservationists who hope that the period could be historically bracketed, any more than terms like *Late Modern* or *Neomodern* accurately describe architects like Mr. Freed, Richard Meier, Charles Gwathmey, or Rafael Viñoly, whose work extends what they themselves regard as an unbroken line of historical development.

Essence over Style

In fact, if the Modern movement was historicism's last gasp, then the whole concept of identifying works by period and period styles has become fairly pointless. A curatorial conceit, the term *International Style* never meant much to the architects who were chosen for the Modern's 1932 show. To most of them, for that matter, modernism was not to be seen as a style but rather the rejection of style in favor of essence. Mies, in fact, described his work as building art *(Baukunst)*; to him, the word *architecture* was overly freighted with superfluous connotations.

My view of this work is partly nostalgic, partly polemical. At fifty-two,

I'm old enough to recall New York as the city where, in the 1960s, the most creatively ambitious work in the world was happening. Today I'd like to see the city rescued from the suburban rage for safety that postmodernism ushered in.

I can't see the MetLife Building with any pretense of impartiality. Much of the meaning it held for me evaporated when they banned helicopter flights from the roof and later, when Pan Am itself shriveled away. The airline conferred on the building a unique set of relationships between it, the city, and the rest of the world. To many young baby boomers, Pan Am signified the idea that United States hegemony in the postwar world was essentially benign. The airline's blue-and-white globe logo represented freedom—the power to go anywhere, be anyone, lose oneself in the clouds.

You could arrive at the building by subway, train, taxi, or on foot, take the escalator from Grand Central's concourse up to the lobby, ride the elevator to the roof, grab a helicopter to Kennedy Airport, and board a jet clipper overseas. This sequence was the closest the city ever came to realizing the 1920s dream of airships moored to the tops of skyscrapers. The connection to Grand Central was critical: a pylon to the glory of twentieth-century travel soared above a triumphal monument to the earthbound transport of an earlier day. The building implicitly enlarged the meaning of Grand Central to include the place of New York in the nation and the place of the nation in the world.

Today air travel is not something to look forward to: flight attendants have lost their glamour, the depleted ozone layer has been identified as carcinogenic, and United States global dominance sometimes calls forth images of exploited third-world workers. Yet the MetLife Building nonetheless retains intrinsic merits. For a start, it bears the signature straightforwardness of the Bauhaus founder Walter Gropius, one of three architects who collaborated on the design. Gropius preferred collaboration to individual artistic statement. Even Miesian elegance was superfluous to him. Japanese vernacular architecture was his aesthetic ideal. It is expressed here in the uniform prefabricated spandrels, the ribbon windows, and the exposed concrete.

Like Giò Ponti's Pirelli Tower in Milan (another transportation landmark), the lozenge form of the floor plan expresses the service core at the center, containing the elevators that make tall buildings possible. The plan also created a faceted facade that diminished the impression of bulk. Compared to the Pirelli Tower, the MetLife Building lacks finesse. In compensation, the building offered public access: to its generous lobby spaces, the rooftop heliport, and the Sky Club restaurant on the penthouse floor.

The lobbies were destroyed in 1987 by Warren Platner's remodeling: a parade of golden headdresses, earrings, ferns, and limp hankies evidently conceived to evoke a floor-show version of an Aztec wedding festival at a fifth-rate Las Vegas casino. The building's true core, however, is ethical and remains intact. It is the surrender of the individual voice to a collective cultural expression.

A Different Angle

Architects younger than I am—like Mr. Sotamaa, Lindy Roy, Mr. Rashid, Lise-Anne Couture, Jesse Reiser, and Nanako Umemoto, who were joined by the critic Jeffrey Kipnis at a recent meeting with Philip Johnson at the Seagram Building—see the slice of architecture along Park Avenue from a slightly different angle. They weren't around when buildings like the Ford Foundation, the Guggenheim Museum, the CBS Building, and Lever House were new. They can't recall a time before the distinction had broken down between art and art history, and the city was more inclined to accept Whitehead's idea that the business of the future is to be dangerous.

At the same time, they've managed to remain insulated from the hostility that International Style buildings still arouse. Most of them teach in schools where the work of Eero Saarinen, Mies, and Mr. Bunshaft is studied and venerated. They are able to see well beyond the glass box surface into deeper levels of meaning and value. None of these architects is reworking the International Style. If they're united by any aesthetic, it is the polymorphous one still being forged with the aid of computer software. But they appreciate the intellectual rigor that animates this work and the solidarity among the architects who produced it.

Many young designers have learned to look at Manhattan through the lens ground and polished by the Dutch architect Rem Koolhaas. In his book *Delirious New York* and other writings, Mr. Koolhaas resisted the standard, simplistic pro or con: rational on the one hand, sterile on the other. Instead he showed that in pursuit of a rational city, modern architects had brought forth a highly surrealistic one. In the reflections of the crystal canyon, the world of external reality merges with the subjective realm of ambition, fantasy, and desire.

No design in recent years has given firmer shape to this idea than Christian de Portzamparc's LVMH Tower at 19-21 East Fifty-seventh Street. Described by Mr. Portzamparc as an homage to the city of glass, the twenty-three-story tower features a faceted glass skin that unfolds like a crystal flower. While the tower can't possibly be mistaken for an International Style skyscraper, LVMH responds to the context of the mythical New York where modernity took root. And it is the first blossom that this root has sent forth in many years.

So here's my holiday toast to our great city. Architecture is back. May it stick around a while.

December 24, 1999

THE PASSAGES OF PARIS AND OF BENJAMIN'S MIND

Some of us don't read fiction. We live on history, biography, criticism, reporting, and what used to be called belles-lettres. We will be feasting on Walter Benjamin's Arcades Project for years to come. Just published in its first full English-language edition, *The Arcades Project* should also win readers with broader tastes. By any standard, the appearance of this long-awaited work is a towering literary event.

A sprawling, fragmented meditation on the ethos of nineteenth-century Paris, *The Arcades Project* was left incomplete on Benjamin's death in 1940. In recent decades, as portions of the book have appeared in English, the unfinished opus has acquired legendary status. *The Arcades Project* (Belknap Press/Harvard University Press) surpasses its legend. It captures the relationship between a writer and a city in a form as richly developed as those presented in the great cosmopolitan novels of Proust, Joyce, Musil, and Isherwood. Those who fall under Benjamin's spell may find themselves less willing to suspend their disbelief in fiction. The city will offer sufficient fantasy to meet most needs.

Who was Walter Benjamin? For highbrow city-lovers, he was the Man of the Twentieth Century. His essays on Berlin and Paris have long been required reading in art and architecture schools around the world. They are among the seminal texts in the field of cultural studies and the ethnographic approach it has fostered toward art. People read Benjamin not only (or even mainly) to learn about the particular topics he took on— Belle Epoque fashions, Art Nouveau interiors, iron construction—but also to absorb his methods of urban analysis and extravagantly cultivated sensibility. For architecture critics, he stands as the supreme master at subjecting buildings to the rigor of dialectical thinking. His informed negations, his techniques for stripping away the lies a society tells about itself, are among the sharpest tools we have for unmasking the deceptions perpetrated by architects in the present day.

Benjamin was born in Berlin in 1892 to a family of upper-middle-class Jews. His father was a successful art dealer. His formal education, which began in Berlin and continued in Switzerland during World War I, included philosophy, literature, and aesthetics. In his early student days, Benjamin was active in the Zionist movement. On his return to Berlin in 1920, he contributed book reviews and essays to the Feuilleton, or Culture section, of the *Frankfurter Zeitung* and other newspapers. His voice joined the raucous chorus of the Weimar years.

What became *The Arcades Project* started out as a newspaper article. Benjamin worked on the project, with periodic interruptions, from 1927 until his death thirteen years later. In 1940, fearing capture by the Nazis while he waited to cross the border from France to Spain, Benjamin killed himself with an overdose of morphine. He was forty-eight. After his death, the manuscript was recovered by the essayist Georges Batailles, who delivered it to the Bibliothèque National in Paris, where Benjamin had conducted much of his research.

The bulk of the published edition is divided into thirty-six sections, labeled A–R. The translators call these sections *convolutes,* from the Latin word for bundle, file, or sheaf, a reference to the folders Benjamin used to organize the loose, handwritten pages of his manuscript. The titles suggest the range of his subject matter. The Flaneur. Baudelaire. Haussmannization. Fashion. Photography. Prostitution. Gambling.

Along with his own reflections, which range in length from one sentence to several pages, the convolutes are stuffed with undigested research material: passages from historical sources and Benjamin's contemporaries in literature and philosophy. The book includes two sections containing early drafts and sketches, and two essays called "exposés." Written in 1935 and 1939, and intended as outlines, the essays are Benjamin's attempt to boil down his fragments into extended expository form. As published, the book gives readers the chance to digest this material for themselves.

The book is 960 pages long. Where to begin? The theoretical heart of the book is Convolute N, "On the Theory of Knowledge, Theory of Progress." In fact, a reader could start anywhere. Like a strand of intellectual DNA, every page contains the code to Benjamin's sensibility. Forensics, anyone?

The arcade itself is a building type that proliferated in early nineteenth-century Paris before Haussmann's grand boulevards ripped through the city's ancient fabric. Typically sheltered beneath an iron-and-glass roof, the arcade was a blocklong pedestrian passage nestled between two masonry structures. It was lined on either side with small shops, tea-rooms, amusements, and other commercial attractions. At one time, more than three hundred arcades punctuated the Paris cityscape. About thirty now remain, most of them clustered on the Right Bank in the First and Second arrondisements.

Travelers to Europe may be more familiar with the still-fashionable British counterparts like London's Burlington and Piccadilly arcades. Milan's Galleria, near the Duomo, is the cathedral of this commercial genre. More recently, the type has reappeared in the minimalls that dot the sprawling map of Los Angeles. Some regard it as the embryo of the suburban shopping mall. The arcade's most immediate progeny, however, was the grand magasin, the imposing turn-of-the-century department store, exemplified by Au Printemps and Galeries Lafayettes. The magasin was, in effect, a vertical arcade, a stack of interior streets lined with hand-bags, hats, cosmetics, and other consumer goods and fantasies.

For Benjamin, the Paris arcade was the most important building type of the nineteenth century. The arcade may have lacked the heroic muscularity of train stations, bridges, and other feats of Victorian engineering. It had none of the classical gravitas sought by the Beaux Arts–trained architects of monumental public buildings. But the arcade represented a pivotal moment in modern history. With it, society began its transition from a culture of production to one of consumption. Beneath the arcade's greenhouse roof, the technical apparatus of the industrial society was used to furnish people's minds with images of desire. Benjamin will now take the apparatus apart.

His analytic approach could be summarized as a fusion of Marxist and Freudian schools of thought. Benjamin did not read Marx until late in life, however, and he rejected the scientific claims of orthodox psychoanalysis. Perhaps on account of what Harold Bloom calls the anxiety of influence, perhaps because he wished to avoid the objective detachment these two ideologies claimed to represent, Benjamin chose to absorb his ideas from indirect sources.

From the philosopher Theodor Adorno he acquired the skills of "negative dialectic," a rejection of the classical idea that the process of negation should lead to positive conclusions. From Brecht he learned that a popular art form could advance the cause of a Communist utopia. (Benjamin's Jewish heritage, meanwhile, was intensified by his long friendship with Gershom Scholem, a scholar of the Kabbala and its tradition of mystical literature.)

But the most important direct influence on *The Arcades Project* came from Surrealism. From Surrealists Benjamin acquired the belief that social revolution and psychological analysis went hand in hand. The liberation of society from ancient hierarchies; the liberation of minds from self-imposed repression: Surrealists like Breton considered these complementary pursuits. Viewed in historical context, *The Arcades Project* can be seen as the great nonfiction epic of Surrealist literature. Interweaving dreams and their analysis in a single text, the book evokes the demented rationality that we associate with Borges.

"Dada was the mother of Surrealism. Its father was the arcade." Benjamin is referring to the Passage de l'Opéra, an arcade where the Surrealists had often gathered to discuss their ideas. It would be more accurate to say that Surrealism and *The Arcades Project* were both rooted in Haussmann's boulevards. Their construction exposed the decrepit parts of Paris that had long been hidden within the maze of medieval streets. Chaos spilled out into plain view like secrets of the urban unconscious.

Haussmann lined the new boulevards with endless dream factories (theaters, cafés, department stores), adorning avenues that had been designed to facilitate cannon fire and troop movement in case of civil unrest. The results were a jarring mixture of pleasure and fear, euphoria, and paranoia, a Surrealist composition similar to the one we see today in Rudolph Giuliani's New York.

The arcades had grown shabby long before Benjamin came to Paris. Haussmann's boulevards had reduced them to haunted ballrooms populated by the ghosts of yesterday's fashions. Places dedicated to the pursuit of novelty, the arcades were doomed by the desire they inspired. But under Benjamin's eye, the faded arcade became something new again: an intellectual reflection. Like the ruins of the Roman forum in Goethe's day, the decaying arcade was a springboard for his imagination.

For Benjamin, the twentieth century is trapped inside the previous century's dream. By interpreting the dream, he hopes to rouse his contemporaries from their collective slumber. The arcade is where the dream was manufactured. Like the factories that produced the wares sold there, the arcade was an industrial machine. It relied on display, advertising, newspapers, and the other new technologies of consumer manipulation.

The Passage des Panoramas (extant, though the three cylindrical viewing chambers that gave the arcade its name are gone) represents another kind of technology, which the critic Jonathan Crary has called the "techniques of the observer." Zoetropes, kaleidoscopes, stereopticons: these optical devices performed a function similar to that of contemporary painting and fiction. They taught modern city dwellers how to perceive the larger panorama that was taking shape around them. Through them, the urban environment was transformed into a dazzling pattern of subjective spaces.

The arcade itself was a visual device: a spatial frame around the shopwindows that inspired passersby with the desire to purchase *la vie en rose*.

Behind the windows, novelties continuously appear. Parisians regard themselves in the reflective glass. Benjamin uses the word *phantasmagoria* to describe the dream state in which the social contract is rewritten. The Arcades Project is an Enlightenment project. By bringing awareness to its readers, the book will release them from the hold of manufactured states of mind.

Sixty years after his death, the phantasmagoria has become even more gripping. Industrial production has been shipped overseas. The manipulation industries—advertising, fashion, mass media, spin—have extended their influence to global dimensions. The nineteenth-century dream has been carried over to the twenty-first. All of Paris is an arcade, and many American cities have remade themselves as shopping malls in order to survive. Cities are fun! Cities R Us! And the streets are safer than ever!

Why wake up? And how effective a wake-up call can a choppy, overweight, sixty-year-old book possibly be?

In their introduction, the translators address a mystery that has long been part of the book's appeal. Is *The Arcades Project* unfinished, or simply unwritten? In 1936 Benjamin professed to Scholem that not a syllable of the text had yet been written. How could it have been? The book had its genesis as a feuilleton story. This grew into plans for an essay, for a book, for another book. By 1930 it had expanded to what he described as "the theater of all my struggles and all my ideas." Over time, the project mutated into the literary equivalent of its subject: a discontinuous maze, composed of brief insights and digressions, along with quotations that glitter from the pages like wares in a shopwindow.

One enters a maze to get lost, as Benjamin observed. Did he want to find a way out? He's trying to hold all of nineteenth-century Paris in his head—its ideas, plastic art forms, merchandise, as well as its buildings and streets. At the same time he's trying to fashion a new lens for bringing this bygone city into sharp, contemporary focus. Given more time, he might well have rendered his encyclopedic insights into seamless, panoramic prose. But the question of what might have been has a power of its own. That mystery is congruent with the enigmatic urban spectacle he set out to analyze. Of necessity, the reader is transformed into an intellectual flaneur, a stroller through an imagination so overcharged that Benjamin can barely sort out his own thoughts.

The Arcades Project, itself a ruin, has served a similar function for writers today. In a convolute on demolition sites, Benjamin writes that such places make ideal "sources for teaching the theory of construction." With *The Arcades Project*, he provided a model for succeeding generations of writers who have transformed the city into a major chapter in the history of ideas. If the urban center no longer holds, it can at least remain an enduring focus for awareness.

More ruins: Marx, Freud, Surrealism. We look back at *The Arcades Project* through the wreckage of many ideological and artistic movements, including the three that influenced Benjamin's thought. The Communist experiment has failed. Freud's assertions of scientific method have been discredited. Surrealism is regarded as a closed historical chapter. "Away with these old ideas!"

But the issues addressed by these movements have not disappeared. Social inequity and warped personalities are no less glaring in public life today. What has visibly diminished is the will to increase public awareness of these problems and the cultural forces that veil them. Our promised liberation from old ideas, like the New Deal, is seldom more than a smoke screen to cover the return of even older, less appetizing ideas. Oligarchy, for example. Social Darwinism. Or the relegation of art to the painting of curlicues on an unsavory status quo.

Art was a stumbling block for Benjamin. Trapped within his negative dialectic, beauty was a suspect concept. This skepticism was shared by the Surrealists, who believed that they were making anti-art. (The published form of his convolutes may be the ultimate anti-book.) For Marxists, art was a fetish commodity. For Freudians, it was an abnormality to be diagnosed.

But where, in this bleak pathological landscape, was Benjamin to place the beauty of his own mind? Where, for that matter, was he to place the beauty of the city that clearly intoxicated him? He may have wished to awaken people from the dream of the nineteenth century. He brutally exposed the social and psychological forces that had shaped it. But could he honestly claim to be immune to the charms of the dream city created by those forces?

Are only writers allowed to be aware? Are painters, photographers, fashion and interior designers forbidden to enlarge the public's consciousness of its time and place? Are architects doomed to constructing mazes for mice? Why spend all that time in Paris? Why write a book? Could Benjamin ask himself such questions without short-circuiting his brain? Could these contradictions be the rocks on which *The Arcades Project* crashed?

And yet, even if Benjamin found scant quarter for his own artistic genius, his book casts a penetrating light into the art of our time. Some of today's most creatively ambitious designs—projects by Frank Gehry, Rem Koolhaas, Jean Nouvel, Diller and Scofidio, Philippe Starck—can be seen as late flowerings of Surrealism, a movement seldom expressed in architecture up to now. In them, we see reflections of the changes that have transpired in the city since the waning of the Modern movement.

Benjamin's writings are even more useful in interpreting less flamboyant contemporary work. The depth of meaning he saw in common architectural forms—thresholds, mirrors, lighting fixtures—can now be seen in the work of architects like Steven Holl, Henry Smith-Miller and Laurie Hawkinson, Tod Williams, and Billie Tsien. In a building by Williams and Tsien, for example, a door is seldom just a door, nor merely an abstract geometrical form. It is also a social and psychological device that pivots us between our outer and inner worlds. A threshold is a metaphoric as well as literal boundary.

Architecture critics poking around in Benjamin's ruin will encounter a challenge of minotaurian proportions. Can we prove that buildings amount to more than walls in a maze? That they are not just instruments of public manipulation? Ordinarily, we don't even try. We accept that most buildings are lies. We even embrace the fantasies when they are told in entertaining style. In the few moments that Postmodernism was clicking, some of us went along with its grand charade of a return to classical tradition.

But if we claim that some buildings more than others deserve to be regarded as art, then the question of hierarchy arises. And with it the issue of truth. Otherwise, how can hierarchical rankings be sustained? Benjamin's negative dialectic provides the tools for subjecting buildings to closer interrogation.

In their own time, buildings by Sullivan, Wright, Mies van der Rohe, Le Corbusier were esteemed because they bore at least a contingent relationship to truth. Like Benjamin, they conducted a negative dialectic, stripping away the fakery of revivalist styles. We value work by Gehry and Koolhaas for similar reasons. In it we see a negation of modern architecture's claim to hard, objective truth, and an enlargement of the subjective dimension that modern architects kept under wraps.

Would Benjamin have banned the light from Paris skies? The Jicky perfume that gave the woman walking ahead of him on the boulevard her indefinable allure? I doubt it. For a critic, this is the ultimate negation. We take the dialectic as far as we can, then surrender to beauty with relief.

January 16, 2000

EXPLORING SPACE AND TIME, HERE AND NOW

Others may care about parallel universes, black holes, or the possibility of punching through our local space-time configuration into past or future states. What matters to me is the challenge of punching into the present. This trick is harder to pull off than one might think. But Elizabeth Diller and Ricardo Scofidio, the New York architects, have been performing it, with increasing success, for nearly twenty years. Two recent projects, both realized in ephemeral forms, have expanded the New York audience for the work of these gifted space-timers.

One of them, a play called *Jet Lag*, has already vanished into memory, after a recent limited run at the Kitchen, the performance space in Chelsea. The Brasserie, a restaurant in the basement of the Seagram Building, has settled in for a longer run, though management has already begun to fiddle with the Diller and Scofidio design. Duration, as it happens, is a theme of both projects. They are both space-times in which it becomes fleetingly possible to project ourselves outside the grip of past and future, into the immediate moment.

Jet Lag was a collaboration between Diller and Scofidio and the Builders Association, a performance group directed by Marianne Weems. The work was originally commissioned by MASS MoCA, a sprawling arts complex in North Adams, Massachusetts, where it was staged as one of the center's inaugural events. The play starts out with a line that some will recall as the opening sentence from *The Medium Is the Message*, Marshall McLuhan's 1966 cult classic: "Good Morning!" In the performance that follows, video, radio (broadcast and short-wave), in-flight movies, telephone, and other media are the major characters. The human actors speak a language that derives almost entirely from media clichés. As in the recent film *The Matrix*, they are playthings of the artificial intelligence that has evolved beyond human control.

Unlike *The Matrix*, *Jet Lag* is not set in some future dystopia. The action takes place in the present time, and it reveals the extent to which the world, thanks to the media, has already fallen into what McLuhan called the "narcosis of Narcissus," an insentient, dreamlike state induced by our infatuation with the images of ourselves that the media pump out. The character who speaks the opening line appears to be a sailor setting out on a solo voyage around the world. Or his voyage might be a hoax: he could be staging the event from a media center in a basement or a garage.

Or the play's entire action might be unfolding within his head. The production suggests an overlapping of all three possibilities.

In part 2 of the play, we watch an older woman and her grandson as they fly endlessly back and forth across the Atlantic. Perhaps the two are searching for the lost sailor (the woman's son, the boy's father), or trying to escape from him. In reality, the two are spellbound by the jet-age ethos of travel, the ethereal anonymity of airports, the routine of flight protocols, the pseudodrama of in-flight movies. The grandmother spouts platitudes of correct passenger behavior, as if she were a walking handbook for human cattle in a jet-age stockyard. The grandson's rebelliousness, equally programmed, could be piped in from the channels on his complimentary headphones.

The multimedia setting, which shifts from passenger compartments to airport waiting lounges to escalators to people movers to video surveillance images of them, puts a twist on the familiar period-dating question, "What time is this place?" In airports, we're more likely to wonder, what place is this time?

Diller and Scofidio conceived the idea for the play, which was inspired by two real but incredible stories, and also designed the elaborate mediatheque that produces its mise-en-scène. The script, by Jessica Chalmers, and the set could not exist without each other. The set is rigorously architectural in the relationship of its parts to the whole. But without the actors and the theatrical format, the production would lack the immediacy of real-life time and real-time life. And without the sets, the script would be annoyingly schematic.

Arthur Miller initially thought the set of *Death of a Salesman* should resemble a man's head because he envisioned the action taking place in the mind of Willy Loman. I could see *Jet Lag* rechristened *Death of a Sailsman:* its central figure is a man who may or may not be a sailor who perishes at sea. In *Jet Lag* the sea becomes a metaphor for what Manuel Castells, the urban theorist, calls the electronic "space of flows," the communications network that keeps capital constantly on the move. We're supposed to be in the age of cybernetics, a term adopted from the Greek word for helmsman. The hope was that computers and other electronic media would enable us to be captains of our own ships. *Jet Lag* sends the dystopian message that we are all captive passengers on a ship drifting rudderless across the techno-environment we have made.

New York has cultural bipolar disorder. Things are either very lethargic and inert, or so speeded up that we cannot relax with them for more than five minutes. But a good piece of architecture can create a space between these extremes. One can linger there a while without fear of being embalmed. The Seagram Building is such a place. For more than forty years, it has provided a seat of grace in midtown Manhattan. The Four Seasons restaurant, on the second floor, has offered an ideal perch from which to savor the essential qualities of Mies van der Rohe's architecture: transparency, void space, refined structural expression. Without creating a theme restaurant on the motif of the International Style, the new Brasserie restaurant, two floors below, offers a set of contemporary variations on these Miesian ideas.

As might have been predicted, the big news about the Brasserie is not the restaurant's design, superior as it is, but the public reception of it. This is a moment when journalists get to call Diller and Scofidio trendy and downtown. That's journalese for "I'm afraid of being made a fool of." Or, "There may be more going on here, or less, than I have time to figure out." As it happens, reception is a major theme in the Brasserie and other Diller and Scofidio projects. All architects operate in a kind of time lag between the conception of an idea and its realization in social space. Think of it as similar to the six-second taped delay sometimes used on radio call-in shows. Diller and Scofidio translate this gap into visual and spatial terms.

The site is a basement, but not just any cellar. It is pierced by the steel structure of a building that may well be the world's foremost example of modern structural expression. As Diller and Scofidio see it, the basement represents the Miesian subconscious. Here the Seagram Building's engineers concealed the subterranean structural contortions it took to support the rationalist structure that rises from the street. The building's physical structure is not visually expressed within the new Brasserie. Rather, the design plays with the conceptual framework of the Miesian aesthetic.

In contrast to rationality, Diller and Scofidio give Mies a Surreal twist. Transparency, for instance, has given way to translucency. Tabletops of molded pale green resin allow glimpses of the legs and the cantilevered braces that support them. They are structural ghosts, dimly visible through hazy planes. Above the bar, rows of wine bottles float behind a translucent white resin wall. The treads of an incomparably elegant staircase, also fashioned from green plastic, create the sensation of wading into water one short step at a time.

Video technology extends the Miesian concept of the wall as a membrane between inside and outside. A surveillance camera photographs patrons as they come through the revolving door. The halting time-lapse images are projected from monitors behind the bar. Another monitor, focused on the street, feeds live coverage to a large monitor by the front desk.

These elements are a scaled-down version of the original concept, which called for projecting surveillance images of the street onto large screens on either side of the entrance stair. This idea played upon the notion that the Seagram Building presents a mediated view of the world. The tinted glass and the cagelike structure filtered the city through the Miesian aesthetic. Glass, in other words, was a medium, not just a material. Diller and Scofidio substitute video for plate glass.

Unfortunately, the scaled-down version dilutes the concept's impact. But it remains strong enough to create the atmosphere of life in a mediated world. At the reception desk, nice young women greet guests. On the video monitors, reception is rendered into perception: the cold eye of the surveillance camera jostles against the hostess's accommodating smile. There's clear glass in the new Brasserie, too, but, in another flip on Mies, here it is used structurally. In the smaller of the restaurant's two dining rooms, tilted glass panels support a long banquette.

Though it has none of the luxurious amplitude of the Four Seasons, the Brasserie is spatially richer. This is mainly because of the visibility of the entrance stair from most of the tables. The architects also enlarge the sense of open space by playing with enclosure. This is most evident in the treatment of the semienclosed booths, with tilted dividers that extend from floor to ceiling, and in the counterpoint between the large and small dining rooms. But it also extends to the restrooms. A single sink, of red molded resin, runs through a slot in the wall dividing the men's and women's rooms. Besides creating surprise aural effects, the arrangement highlights the permeability of the membrane between public and private space.

Arthur Danto coined the term *transformation of the commonplace* to describe how artists like Duchamp and Warhol gave ordinary objects the aura of art. William Burroughs coined the phrase "the naked lunch" to describe a Zen-like moment of heightened awareness when a morsel of food on the end of a fork comes into sharp mental focus. It holds oceanic meaning and no meaning. The moment is one of possibility. We're not on autopilot. We're not held in the grip of memory or of fantasy about the future, not trapped between loss and desire.

Diller and Scofidio's Brasserie is a place of heightened awareness and social possibility. Can one transform lunch or dinner into meaningful exchange? Is there space for listening as well as talking, or just the polite drone of people assassinating each other across tables set for two?

Jet Lag and the Brasserie hark back to legendary ephemeral projects from the early twentieth century. I am thinking of *Triadic Ballet*, staged at the Bauhaus by the painter Oskar Schlemmer in 1922. And Café l'Aubette, a Strasbourg brasserie designed in 1925 by the de Stijl architect Theo van Doesburg. Many of us have tried to imagine what it was like to witness these epochal works. But would we have recognized their importance if we had been around at the time? Do we recognize their equivalents today? Are we willing to show up for our own time?

Being present is a moral as well as an artistic issue. We are responsible for knowing our place in history. Schlemmer, van Doesburg, and Mies were not merely creating formal abstractions. Their projects were manifestos. They invited the public, and themselves, to sample the naked lunch of the early twentieth century. Diller and Scofidio are extending that invitation today. The food is divine.

February 6, 2000

IT'S SOMETHING NEW UNDER THE STARS (AND LOOKING UP)

The new Rose Center for Earth and Space at the American Museum of Natural History brings us face-to-face with something commensurate to our capacity for wonder. Night and day, astronomers, astrophysicists, and weekend stargazers behold awesome images of the unknown. Even reading about their exploits can give a person goose bumps.

For New Yorkers who care about architecture, the wonder won't be limited to the star show. Even before the building opened, many of us were rubbing our eyes in disbelief that it exists at all. Designed by the New York firm Polshek Partnership, the planetarium is an aesthetic apparition as well as a major civic event. Is it possible that a public building of such prominence could arrive unburdened by the trappings of historical pastiche that have suffocated New York architecture in recent decades? Is it possible that an august institution like this, in a part of town notoriously hostile to change, has produced a work of architecture?

Hard to believe. Even harder to understand. Like a quasar, a black hole, or a subatomic particle, the planetarium defies easy comprehension. But there it is, nonetheless: architecture, not the theme-park simulation of it that has distorted the cityscape for so long like the convex lens on a rearview mirror. Here is that rare instance where a time, a place, a function, an architect, and a client (the heroic Ellen V. Futter, president of the museum) have come into perfect alignment to produce an intelligent design that will also appeal to broad public taste. It's like finding another world.

The Rose Center, on West Eighty-first Street between Central Park West and Columbus Avenue, replaces the Aztec Art Deco movie palace that housed the Hayden Planetarium. The demolition of that delightfully campy structure is one of this project's most welcome side effects. It has dealt a blow to the preservationist mentality that has gripped New York for thirty years to increasingly morbid effect.

Whatever your feelings about the old planetarium, you cannot accuse the new one of lacking long-term historical memory. The design is saturated with it. This is a mature Modern building, a structure unafraid of revealing the deep roots from which modern architecture arose. The design's historical awareness far exceeds that of buildings that merely ape period styles.

The science museum is an Enlightenment concept. It derives from Newton's revolutionary ideas about the physical laws of the universe. In 1780–90, the French architect Étienne-Louis Boullée designed a celebrated (but unbuilt) monument to Newton that remains perhaps the greatest example of the desire to translate Enlightenment values into architectural form. "O Newton," wrote Boullée, "as by the extent of your wisdom and the sublimity of your genius you determined the shape of the earth; I have conceived the idea of enveloping you in your own discovery."

The design was an immense sphere, supported by a tiered cylindrical base. Huge cuts in the base, inverted arches, allowed views of the sphere's lower half. A planetarium occupied the interior of the sphere. Stars were illuminated by sunlight shining through small holes in the dome. Visitors would enter through subterranean passages and emerge at a memorial to Newton built at the base. Trees were to be planted along the perimeter of the cylinder, a visual reminder that these abstract geometrical forms derive their meaning from nature, or at least the eighteenth century's understanding of it.

The Museum of Natural History has essentially brought Boullée's design to realization more than two hundred years after it was conceived. The basics are all here—the sphere (eighty-seven feet in diameter, contained within a seven-story, ninety-five-foot-tall glass cube), the planetarium, the structural base, and the counterpoint between abstract geometry and organic form. In place of Newton's cenotaph, we have an extraordinary Zeiss star projector rising from the center of the planetarium. Instead of rings of trees, we have planted terraces and the nearby landscape of Central Park. Nonetheless, the design transports us to an era when physicists called themselves natural philosophers and the United States was new.

And it propels us into the architecture that emerged in the twentieth century as the built version of Enlightenment thought. Boullée did not have glass, steel, electric light, air-conditioning, or prefabricated construction. The aesthetic treatment of these modern materials and methods did not become commonplace until 1919, with the appearance of the New Objectivity in Germany. The pragmatic industrial vocabulary of that movement is the basic language of the planetarium and other projects designed by the Polshek office. Here Modern form is given the inflection of Wallace K. Harrison, architect of the Trylon and Perisphere at the 1939 New York World's Fair.

Time to look at the building designed by James Stewart Polshek and Todd H. Schliemann, the principal architects. What we see on approaching the Rose Center may well be the finest example of glass curtain wall construction ever realized in the United States. Cheap glass, poor craftsmanship, and the compression of individual panes by mullions and spandrels have done much to distort the image of glass architecture. Here we see glass as the transcendent material envisioned by architects who pioneered its use in the early twentieth century.

The glass is of the water white variety, so called because it is purified of the iron that gives most glass a greenish tint. It is expensive glass, and looks it. Resilient gaskets join the panels; thus there is little buckling or distortion in the reflections. The transparent skin vividly reveals the structure that supports it. Made of vertical trusses as thin as Gothic tracery, the structure evokes comparisons once drawn between glass architecture and medieval cathedrals. The soaring trusses counteract the cube's tendency to look squat.

The architects must have been looking at recent glass architecture in Europe. The glazed edges of the cube's roofline show the influence of Jean Nouvel's dazzling Cartier Foundation in Paris. Along with the glass's uncommon purity, the transparent edges prevent the structure from hardening into the stonelike solid that diminishes the lightness of the typical glass tower. Somewhere Truman Capote writes about the dusk in Central Park falling like blue flakes. No New York building has ever taken better advantage of the blue hour. Picking up reflections from the sky, the trees, the buildings along Eighty-first Street and the yellow light framed by their windows, the glass turns into a boxful of mood indigo.

One must keep that ball-in-a-box picture in mind on entering the building. The scale of the interior does allow the entire sphere to register on close inspection. This is initially deflating. We're used to buildings whose interiors expand dramatically beyond the expectations created by their exterior scale. Older Broadway theaters commonly create this effect. At the Rose Center, the sequence is reversed. The nearly scaleless geometric grandeur of the exterior shrinks to a series of smaller spatial vignettes. The white sphere still dominates, but we behold it up close, an astronaut's view of the moon in the minutes before landing.

To get inside the cube, visitors pass through a lobby and onto a balcony that looks out onto the structural base of the globe and the open exhibition space beneath it. The floor is paved with black terrazzo sprinkled with twinkling crystal chips. Pale blue light glows from circular lighting coves in the ceiling, a Morris Lapidus effect. It is traditional to place a compression chamber between a building's exterior and a tall room within—a kind of air lock for the eyes. Even the Guggenheim Museum has one. But the Rose Center interior never opens up to full-throttle, opera-house dimensions. Instead of gazing at infinite space, we find ourselves staring at the nether regions of a finite object.

A sweeping staircase descends from the balcony to the floor of Cullman Hall of the Universe. It goes far toward regaining the exterior's spatial grandeur. Some visitors may be put off by the stair's Ziegfeld Follies theatricality. It screams Party Space! But this place ought to have swank parties, preferably with Yma Sumac warbling Incan high-priestess arias on the building's roaring sound system.

Two elements vie for attention in the lower part of the cube. One is a spiral ramp that corkscrews one and a half turns around the sphere, starting at the equator line. A mind-expanding walk through space-time, the ramp presents a captioned history of the universe, from the Big Bang to the appearance of *Homo sapiens*, which occurred less than a second ago on the cosmic scale of things. Concealed neon lighting keys this time line to the spectrum shifts astronomers use to measure time and distance. The building's most dynamic moment arrives as you approach one full turn of the ramp. Gazing back at the spiral's curving edge, you become a heavenly body streaking through space that is warped by the gravity of the globe.

Juxtaposed to the ramp's sinuous curve is the muscular steel tripod that holds the sphere aloft. Each leg is three-pronged. Six struts support the globe, three hold up the ramp. Tough-guy stuff, big and brawny. Charles Atlas. Or Atlas himself, for the exhibition space is a temple for the modern mythology of science, appointed with video monitors, projection discs, touch-screens, and other techno-fetishes of the information age.

Floor mosaics and low dividers give this area the appearance of a free-form, organic space, to use Frank Lloyd Wright's terminology. The effect is magnified by the ramp and the softly swelling underbelly of the globe. Stretch your fingers skyward and you can feel like a mythical hero too, especially if the weight of the globe overhead puts you in mind of crashing asteroids. (A cartoon image of a meteor striking Manhattan is a design source for Polshek.)

Three glass-enclosed elevators (another Nouvel touch) rise six stories to a penthouse that deserves to be a café or other public space. From there, a glass-enclosed bridge pierces the building's cosmic heart: the

Hayden Planetarium, which is nestled in the sphere's top half. Function-ally, formally and symbolically, this sequence is first-rate. From the street, we have seen the world from the perspective of a Newtonian God: we're outside the universe and outside the building, too. Inside the globe, our perspective shifts. We're sitting on a small stone, circling a modest star, in a universe whose size is calculated according to scientific laws that may turn out to be relative.

Does it serve any purpose to peg the Rose Center stylistically? Clearly, many New Yorkers have reacted to it as if they'd never seen a Modern building before. Others see it as a reprise of a period style they evidently believe died some years back, around the time Philip Johnson and John Burgee's AT&T building opened. The museum, for its part, has charac-terized the Rose Center as an example of progressive design.

In a parochial sense, this is true. Until Christian de Portzamparc's LVMH Tower opened last year on East Fifty-seventh Street, Manhattan had not seen a serious piece of modern architecture in years. In fact, since 1966, the year the Ford Foundation building was completed, the city has scarcely seen serious architecture of any kind. This is no coincidence. The collapse of New York architecture is a direct result of the postmodern reaction against the International Style. But it turns out that modern architecture cannot be equated with a particular style. Around the world, architecture has continued to evolve, despite New York's rage to leave itself out of the loop.

Like many contemporary buildings, the Rose Center is eclectic. It absorbs historical elements and contemporary influences into an organic whole. Neoclassicism. Bauhaus. Populuxe. Euro Millennial. At moments—the sunrise entrance arch on Eighty-first Street; the grand staircase; the pastel planets dangling above; the stardust paving—the entire edifice teeters on the verge of camp.

If New York hadn't lost confidence in its creative energies, the Rose Center would look less startling. It would be seen as part of a continuum that includes Richard Meier's Canal Plus headquarters (Paris), James Ingo Freed's United States Holocaust Memorial Museum (Washington), Rafael Viñoly's Tokyo International Forum, and other recent works by distin-guished New York architects. But architecture in New York is an inter-rupted art. The Rose Center interrupts the interruption.

February 13, 2000

TRAY CHIC

A piece of architecture has landed in Times Square. Only a select few will get to see it. But for employees of Condé Nast—publishers of *Vogue, The New Yorker, Architectural Digest,* and other guides to civilized living—lunch will be garnished with genius. The Condé Nast cafeteria designed by Frank Gehry for the company's new building, at 4 Times Square, is now at their service.

The cafeteria seats 260, with an additional 70 places provided in a suite of private dining rooms. This promises to be a tight squeeze for an organization with 1,900 employees. James Truman, editorial director of Condé Nast and the man who masterminded this project, says that separate seatings will be arranged to accommodate demand. Still, even with staggered lunch hours, the cafeteria could easily resemble the crowded sidewalks of the newly overhauled Times Square.

There the resemblance stops. At New York's bright new crossroads of information and entertainment, most of the visual excitement is provided by fancy electronic machines. At the Condé Nast cafeteria, the interest is rooted in the traditional elements of architectural form: space, shape, scale, materials, color, light, and the relationships among them.

The room continues the experiments in fluidity that Gehry has been conducting for the past decade. These include the Guggenheim Museum in Bilbao, the Walt Disney Concert Hall in downtown Los Angeles, the Experience Music Project in Seattle, and an unbuilt design for the Samsung Museum in Seoul. As these projects have appeared, Gehry has revealed a striking affinity for Art Nouveau architecture. In contrast to the angular geometries of his earlier work, his latest buildings undulate, ripple, and swell like a maiden's tresses. Devotees of turn-of-the-century Parisian brasseries will feel the shock experienced by patrons who visited these establishments when they were new. But Gehry's whorls are not confined to the two dimensions of applied ornament. They oscillate through space.

In the past, as in his use of shapes derived from fish, squid, and, recently, horses, Gehry has occasionally looked to the natural world for inspiration. To my knowledge, however, this is the first time he has used landscape as a point of departure. From the curving counters of the servery to the reflections in the glass partitions that arc through the room beyond, the café creates the impression of a small city park that has become unexpectedly lodged on the fourth floor of a midtown skyscraper. Tornadoes have caused weirder things to happen.

Panels of blue titanium are affixed to the room's walls and ceiling. The ceiling is coffered with white cloudlike shapes that project downward from the blue surface. The floor below is made from plain ash plywood. Thirty-nine booths, providing most of the seating, are upholstered with imitation leather the color of warm stone. The wooden tables are egg-shaped and finished with yolk yellow tops. An earth palette beneath a lustrous sky.

The glass partitions dominate the middle zone between firmament and ground. Buckled, torqued, as if by the pressure of the stainless steel bolts used to mount them, the panels overlap at the edges, and this, along with the light green tint of the glass, creates an effect of reeds bending in a breeze. The blue titanium walls are also visible through the glass and glimpsed in reflections across its surface. The sparkle of light mirrored in the rippled surface amplifies the aqueous impression. The result is an underwater hypostyle hall.

For all the novelty of Gehry's forms, the ideas percolating through them were sketched out more than a century ago by the British architect William Lethaby. In his 1891 book, *Architecture, Mysticism and Myth*, Lethaby predicted the rise of new architectural forms that would recast the labyrinth, the painted sky, the rippling floor, and other symbolic devices employed by ancient theocratic civilizations. "Old architecture lived because it had a purpose," Lethaby wrote. "Modern architecture, to be real, must not be a mere envelope without contents. . . . The message will still be of nature and man, of order and beauty, but all will be sweetness, simplicity, freedom, confidence, and light. . . . The new, the future, is to aid life and train it, so that beauty may flow into the soul like a breeze."

To aid life and train it: Condé Nast is a major provider of symbolic content, a dream factory of periodic excursions into narcissism's most exquisitely tended gardens. The company's fashion and beauty magazines offer monthly reflections on the human form as a universal intersection between nature and culture. Gehry has provided an ideal background for those who put out these primers in cultivation. He even puts them into the picture. Exiting the café through a side corridor, gazelles and other svelte creatures pass along a wall of rippling mirrors. Their figures merge, contort, morph, and liquefy. The panoramic image changes constantly, forming and reforming in the eye of the beholder. Why shouldn't beauty flow into the soul like a fresh scent strip?

April 23, 2000

OUR ANXIETIES TO THE LIONS

The excavation of Rome continues. Not the physical Rome—imperial city of marble monuments, stone quarry for later Romes built atop the early ones. Rather, work has resumed on the symbolic Rome, the Christian emblem of cruelty and intrigue, vanity and lust, corruption and damnation. Real digs are supervised by archaelogists. The symbolic one has long been directed by Hollywood and its corps of experts in the uncovering of desires and fears.

On Friday, *Gladiator*, directed by Ridley Scott, resumes the dig for sunken metaphors on a scale not seen since the late 1950s and early 1960s, when audiences lined up for two-part spectaculars like William Wyler's *Ben-Hur*, Joseph L. Mankiewicz's *Cleopatra*, and Stanley Kubrick's *Spartacus*. In the spirit of these legendary epics, *Gladiator* is an allegory of its own time. The first Roman cinema spectacular to be made by Hollywood since the end of the Cold War, it is a meditation on the perplexity of the world's sole surviving superpower.

Quo vadis? Where does America go from here? After expansion, implosion—this is the diagnosis set forth by *Gladiator* in period costume. After all the world has been conquered, Rome splits apart under mounting pressure from the forces of Good and Evil—republican heroes and tyrannical knaves. The populace, meanwhile, is regaled by Hollywood spectaculars staged in the grand new Colosseum. The special effects grow ever more dazzling and surreal. Christians are thrown to lions. The arena is flooded for naval battles. Caesar puts on a Yankee cap. The crowd screams for more.

Why revive this genre of movie now? DreamWorks, the movie's producer, boasts of special effects made possible by computer-imaging techniques. Rome can be built in a day. Just run some paintings by Cole, David, and Alma-Tadema through the scanner, *et* voilà! Better yet, feed *Ben-Hur* and *Spartacus* through the computer, in their entirety. Morph well, reheat, and serve. Ours is an era of remakes and postmodern simulations. The technology makes it easier to recycle familiar images. The Colosseum, the White House, the intergalactic spaceship, the skyline, the ghetto, the corporate headquarters: whether computer- or carpenter-generated, these settings are features in a symbolic landscape in which a fragmented society can participate in the myth of a common culture.

Some have found it difficult to identify with this myth as rendered by the Roman spectaculars of the postwar years. *Ben-Hur*, for example, was not a reassuring experience for many American Jews, who had to reckon with anti-Semitism in that era. Shifting the anti-Semitism from American WASPs to ancient Romans did not dull the pain of living in the world of *Gentlemen's Agreement*, the restricted neighborhood, the whispered slur, the secret quota. Nor was it reassuring that Ben-Hur was Jewish, given that his redemption was contingent on his becoming a follower of Christ.

Wyler's *Tale of the Christ*, as *Ben-Hur* was subtitled, is worth keeping in mind as we witness the construction of another hero myth: the legend of *The Greatest Generation*, to borrow the title of Tom Brokaw's recent best-selling book. There's no reason to doubt the courage and sacrifice shown by the Americans who struggled through the Depression and World War II. The story of these gladiators holds a powerfully inspiring message for our vastly more self-indulgent times.

But to complete the record, another story must be told: the story of what it was like to grow up as a child of the greatest generation. What was it like to grow up in the early years of the Cold War, beneath the shadow of the bomb? What was it like for the children who went to the Roman spectacles of those years, before television brought images of warfare into the nuclear family home?

Dad has a high-paying job in the military-industrial complex. By day he works to develop the hardware for guided missiles. At night he comes to an authentic Colonial home with flame-shaped light bulbs. This setting helps soothe the trauma caused by atrocities overseas. Mom is back in the kitchen, doing her best to follow a cheerful script about marriage and family life. Her chipper moods are periodically interrupted by hushed-up stays at rest homes. Dad sighs a lot and loses his temper. Princess is already exhibiting the first signs of bulimia. Young Butch, meanwhile, is growing up queer and has taken to spending afternoons at blood-soaked Steve Reeves movies in preparation for the day when he starts a career as a serial killer.

Everybody, it turns out, is following a script of normalcy. In situations not covered by the script, nobody knows what to say. And with early adolescence comes a need to break out of the script. Hormones raging, Butch begins to sense that there's something not normal about his angle on the world. It is at this point, age twelve, that Butch discovers Downtown. He makes the discovery when the entire family dresses up one Saturday and goes to a reserved-seat first-run showing of *Ben-Hur*. But the movie turned out to be a sideshow compared with the city itself. Streets, crowds, theater marquees, shopwindows—all composed themselves into a place where any kind of script could be written. *Ben-Hur* was a childhood event. The city beckoned toward adulthood.

The release of *Gladiator* happens to coincide with another Roman spectacular. For Holy Year, celebrated by Roman Catholics every quarter century, the Eternal City has put on its finest clothes. For the rest of 2000, Rome will be a destination for faithful pilgrims and tourists alike. Even less than ordinarily a place for daily living, the city is transformed into a symbol of itself. It is a Christian epic, an architectural drama. Ancient Roman monuments, like the Colosseum and the recently reopened remains of Nero's Golden House, portray the pagan era at its most wanton. The pilgrimage route, seven churches visited by the pious, forms an avenue of redemption. Baroque Rome, the creation of Sixtus V, is the Church Triumphant, the victory of virtue over sin.

If you must choose only one spectacle this year, go to Rome. There you'll have the opportunity to see the ingredient that the cinematic versions tend to overlook. Rome is an Italian city, populated by Italian people living rich, Italian lives. Romans, like others, have been living with lust and guilt for thousands of years, and they learned long ago the wisdom of turning hypocrisy into art. At the Sistine Chapel, you behold a ceiling full of coiling erotic figures. The pleasures and sins of the flesh are two parts of one organic system. They coil round and round like the columns in the baldachino Bernini fashioned for St. Peter's (with bronze stripped from the ancient Pantheon).

If you go, please pay special attention to the confessionals. Non-Catholics have an image, reinforced by movies and television, of the confessional as a hidden place shrouded in deep shadow, where people sneak in when no one is looking. In Italian churches, confessionals are as conspicuous as video arcades. Made of dark wood, with ornate pediments, they stand out against white walls. Even their interiors offer no place to hide. There's lighting, and the occupants may not even bother to pull the little voting-booth-style curtain. If you read lips and speak Italian, there's a good chance you'll know all. But the design alone tells you that these are major fixtures of liturgical technology. Machines for converting vice into virtue, they relieve the conscience of guilt.

The postwar Roman epics were sprawling adventures in hypocrisy: moral tales that allowed audiences to indulge vicariously in pull-out-the-stops orgies. Lavish sets and wardrobes, bloodshed, dissolution, stars, money, nastiness, and flesh. Still, despite the Roman settings and violent plots, the epics actually depict the moral climate in the Age of Eisenhower, when the tyranny of normalcy ruled the cultural landscape. You can imagine how displaced Butch felt.

The DreamWorks revival of this campy entertainment genre reflects, in part, the New Normalcy of our time. The glorification of the Greatest Generation is part of this phenomenon. So is the oxymoronically named New Urbanism movement, with its compact suburban subdivisions and houses fabricated from Cheez Whiz. Unfortunately, we have yet to perfect a way of managing hypocrisy with the Italian flair. In fact, we are now dismantling the system that went far toward accommodating diversity and complexity in the postwar years: the symbiotic relationship between squeaky-clean suburbs and torrid Cities of the Plain.

All grown up, Butch drifts downward into the arena of his mind, through the broken pieces of his private archaeology. He dreams back to a time before *Playgirl* centerfolds, Chippendale dancers, Calvin Klein underwear ads, and RuPaul, back, back before Richard Nixon lost an election because his face was a national eyesore, back to a time when the American moral fiber was held together by the strict segregation of men and women into acting subjects and passive objects.

In this divided landscape of rigid role assignment, the postwar he-man was a transgressive figure. The plot required him to be admired for the virtues of his actions. Casting and costume design, meanwhile, ensured that action took a distant second place to his role as an object of desire. The discreetly placed towel, the concealing shadow, or the loincloth professionally distressed to be peekaboo threadbare—fittings, fittings—were the only concessions to virtue that actually created a stir. They exploded the modesty that they were supposed to represent. Thus clad, the male action figure insinuated himself into the mind as the embodiment of a conflict between violence and sex.

By 1960, Butch is spending so much time downtown he might as well buy a commuter ticket. His parents don't approve of this, suspecting that sex is somehow involved. This is true only in a voyeuristic sense. Butch is actually pursuing what Auden called the Vision of Eros. By this, the poet referred not to physical pleasure as such but to a world in which intolerance does not inhibit the natural desire to give love and receive it. Butch has this vision in the hypnotic rhythm of the streets.

But by age eight, without understanding what they are, Butch has developed erotic feelings for sailing instructors, lifeguards, and other athletic types. He also knows that it's not safe to act out these emotions. Even the wrong kind of look could land him in a hospital bed. Downtown, however, the male physique presents itself to be admired by anyone who buys a ticket, along with biblical trappings or the aura of classical myth. Downtown represents freedom to be aroused without even the need to acknowledge what's really going on. These pictures are, after all, family entertainment, or, in the case of Steve Reeves vehicles, kiddie matinees.

It is also a place where theater and movies present stories nearly as twisted as Butch's mind. What was *The Roman Spring of Mrs. Stone* actually about? A passive gladiator who wins the fight without moving a muscle. Gore Vidal has told the story about persuading Stephen Boyd, in the role of Ben-Hur's boyhood friend, to play a pivotal scene with Charlton Heston as if the two had once been lovers. Heston is not to be let in on the joke. In *Spartacus*, Tony Curtis and Laurence Olivier discuss sexual preferences in culinary terms. Oysters or eels. Even downtown, some loves don't want to speak their names.

Butch ought to know that the regime of normalcy is itself a historical abnormality. He's read two novels by Mary Renault. He knows that Catullus, not Charlton Heston, is the representative figure of ancient Rome. Even in the Roman spectaculars of the '20s and '30s, images of men were more explicitly erotic.

Nonetheless, postwar normalcy is the abnormality Butch must learn to live with. Somewhere in the background, a presidential aide is arrested at a Washington YMCA. In *Advise and Consent*, a senator commits suicide when a political adversary threatens to expose a youthful fling. A radio host is saying, "I wouldn't want the plane I'm flying on to be piloted by someone who had those kind of thoughts on his mind!" By now Butch is at war within himself. If there is any possibility of escaping normalcy, it lies downtown. But the child wouldn't have a roof over his head if Dad weren't busy designing gyroscopes to guide weapons of mass destruction. The Urban and Suburban conditions are a duality that won't let Butch go. His drives take a turn toward Thanatos. He begins to have fantasies about what Charlton Heston would look like without a head.

Parents will want to know if *Gladiator* is too violent for children. No and yes. The movie's special effects are so prominent, and the action so highly aestheticized by art direction, that the bloodshed registers mainly as operatic mise-en-scène. Some veil of snow is always falling, some gossamer drapery is always rippling, the wind is always rustling in octoplasmic sound. But there's a horrible scene in which the Gladiator, played by Russell Crowe, cuts an insignia from his flesh. And the hero does make a living decapitating people. We are not spared the graphic details.

The gore, however, is used to illustrate that the character is a true-blue postwar suburbanite at heart. The dying Caesar, played by Richard Harris, begs him to go to Rome to become the city's protector, but the Gladiator dreads going to that cesspool. He has thoughts only of his farm in the hills, where the wife and kid wait to greet him at the gates. You've never seen such dreamy rows of poplars. Welcome home, Joe. The lawn needs mowing. But when Caesar expires, decadent Romans intervene, and blow the American dream to smithereens.

In actuality, the post–Cold War implosion has produced the opposite effect: a revival of normalcy on a scale not seen since Ike and Mamie's day. In contrast to Ike and Mamie's day, however, the regime of normalcy now focuses its energies on the urban centers as well as the American Dreamland outside them.

This is evident not only in the actions of the city's Caesarian protectors—police crackdowns, curbs on First Amendment rights, the notion that pasties are required for reasons of public health—but also in the increasing saturation of urban life with suburban values: chain stores, theme restaurants, festival marketplaces, ersatz period architecture, and even cultural events that purport to challenge norms. Last year's Sensation show at the Brooklyn Museum of Art, for instance, offered a Disneyfied idea of provocation—a Shock Mall. No wonder it received a PTA-style response.

Quo vadis, indeed. *The Matrix*, last year's Oscar winner for special effects, proposed one answer that lingers in the mind. In this futurist gladiatorial spectacle, we all live in a maximum-security prison. We are held there by the illusion that the year is 1999 and all is normal. Implosion is permanently implanted in our brains. The erotic is harnessed in the service of machines. Neo, the movie's high-tech hero, wants to make the world safe for that cosmic abnormality called life. Thumbs up.

Butch dozes off again. He dreams of the ideal city: no street crime, no homeless people, no squeegie men. The trains run on time. Great special effects. Triumphal arches and surveillance cameras stretch as far as the eye can see. A decadent democracy has been reformed. Libido has been suppressed.

Thumbs down.

April 30, 2000

REACHING FOR POWER OVER STREETS AND SKY

Is architecture an art? What restrictions can government place on architects without violating constitutional principles?

A new proposal to overhaul the city's zoning laws is now forcing New Yorkers to confront these fundamental questions. Titled the Unified Bulk Program, the proposal amounts to the architectural manifesto of the Giuliani administration—a major statement on the most famous skyline in the universe. The statement goes something like this: "New York to Architecture: Drop Dead!" At the precise moment when things are looking up for the continuous art of building our great city, here comes the cultural equivalent of the street crimes unit. Back in line! Back in line! We got architecture off the streets forty years ago, and we're not going to let it back now!

Proposed by the Department of City Planning, the Unified Bulk Program is now wending its way through the public review process required before it can become law. The plan has already been endorsed by community boards. The City Council is expected to vote on it sometime this summer.

But what is it? And why is it here? What's the point? It's hard to get straight answers to such questions. At a public hearing in late April, it was obvious that even members of the city's Planning Commission were in the dark. In a series of exchanges with representatives from civic and real estate groups, the commissioners seemed as eager as anyone to figure out just what their own staff had cooked up. With only a few weeks left to make revisions, the plan headed for the City Council vote has many people asking, "Say what?"

But there is no apparent strategy to deceive the public. The issue is much more complicated. Real estate development and municipal government are two relics of the nineteenth-century industrial city. In the information age, the power of both groups has vastly diminished. They are both in major denial about this. Both sense that the center of power has shifted to the cultural plane. But neither of them knows how to climb up there. The Unified Bulk Program is supposed to give them a boost. It's designed to give a cultural aura to what are fundamentally economic and political transactions. Unfortunately, it does so at the expense of architecture that has a genuine cultural contribution to make.

Some features are discernible within the program's nebula of charts, graphs, codes, and bureaucratic jargon. Three of these would have a substantial impact on architecture in New York. The first two we might call the Tops and Bottoms of the new urban silhouette.

- The plan would set height limits on new skyscrapers throughout the city. Depending on location, the height would vary from 360 feet to 495 feet to 720 feet. Large swaths of midtown and lower Manhattan would be exempt, along with downtown Brooklyn and Long Island City, Queens.
- The plan would abolish current zoning regulations that encourage developers to create small public parks and plazas in exchange for added height. Instead, new towers would sit on low-rise bases that extend to the street wall. These would typically be used for retail. The planning department describes this so-called contextual format

as a rejection of the towers-in-a-park concept encouraged by the 1961 zoning resolution, which is still in effect.

• The third provision, by far the most ominous of the three, calls for the creation of a design review panel within the city planning department. Chosen by the department's chairman, a political appointee, the panel would consist of "architects and others concerned with design issues." Assuming a function now held by the city's Board of Standards and Appeals, it would review applications from developers seeking special permits that would exempt them from the new contextual zoning.

Since the Unified Bulk Program is a political as well as a cultural document, it's worth speculating about the political motives behind it, even though, with such a secretive and rigid city administration, it is natural to suspect the worst. Here are some suspicions.

The Law of the Instrument states: the instrument must be used. With so many planning functions now performed by other city, state, and federal agencies, as well as private business improvement districts, something must be found for City Planning to do. Here it is.

With only two years remaining in his term as planning chairman, Joseph B. Rose wants to be remembered for doing Something. The Something could just as easily be Something Else. It happens to be this.

The program is an elaborate operation intended primarily to give Mr. Rose control over the special permit procedure now supervised by the Board of Standards and Appeals. Mr. Rose, who comes from one of New York's most illustrious real estate families, has the makings of a frustrated architect. The special permit process would enable him and his successors to fiddle with forms and shapes without being subject to public scrutiny or accountability.

Hence, the ultimate goal of the Unified Bulk Program is to turn the city planning chairman—whoever it may be—into the design czar of New York, with sweeping powers to define the cityscape for years to come.

Like architecture, the Unified Bulk Program can be analyzed on two planes: the material and the metaphoric. Real estate developers will find the program's material implications of greater interest. What must they do to comply? How much will compliance cost them, in time and square feet? Will there be a grace period for projects in the works? Will the new zoning simplify permits? How will it affect the market?

Those interested primarily in architectural values must reckon with the program's symbolic as well as its material value. The two realms are interlocked. In architecture, quantity can be a quality. To some developers, tall buildings may signify little more than tall profits. But they are also elements in a skyline that rivals the Gothic cathedral in symbolic power.

By the same token, developers may regard a bonus plaza simply as a device that enables them to add more rentable floors. But it is also a void in a city that has little tolerance for undeveloped land. In this case, lack of quantity is a quality, at least if you like voids.

The sky and the street are in themselves symbolic. They are contested spaces where the rights of private ownership and public use come into frequent conflict. Contestation, in fact, is what these spaces symbolize. We can quantify them in terms of shadow, sky exposure, required seating, and trees, but their symbolic value lies in the tension between freedom and equality in a democratic society.

Contextualism, the overarching ideology of the Unified Bulk Program, offers to resolve this tension in symbolic form. By limiting the visual impact of new buildings, contextual architecture is supposed to give people the sense that they are in control of their surroundings. This, at least, is the underlying theory. The abolition of plazas, the requirement that buildings extend to street walls, is intended to preserve the existing character of neighborhoods. The adoption of height limits, similarly, is meant to preserve the existing skyline as a picture postcard. The competitive urges of developers like Donald Trump will not be permitted to disturb its Art Deco ziggurat contour.

In practice things are far less ideal. It is easy to find examples of bonus plazas to illustrate the argument that these public spaces should be abolished. What such examples actually show, of course, is that they were poorly designed, that their developers have no stake in maintaining them, and that city officials lack the will to demand improvements. But there are other examples—I happen to live in a building blessed with one—in which the bonus park beautifully fulfills its original concept. In real as well as symbolic terms, the park helps bridge the chasm between private luxury and public amenity. This was a worthy experiment for the capital of modern democracy to undertake.

It scares me to imagine the mentality that wants to preserve the skyline in its present form. It is painful, of course, to make that skyward stretch each time a new skyscraper takes shape and towers over its neighbors. But that stretch is the context of New York. Changes in scale, evolutions in form: these are traditional training exercises for a city that prides itself on its ability to adapt to change. If you don't stop before the miracle happens, a building that once seemed objectionably out of scale may eventually look custom-made to your perception. It is hard to believe that New Yorkers will take to squat, stubby towers with quite the same pride they take in the Woolworth Building, the Chrysler Building, and Rockefeller Center.

At one time, it may have made sense to equate the term *context* with a new building's immediate physical surroundings. But the context has changed. The informational city is global. New buildings in New York are inevitably seen in the context of new buildings going up in London, Tokyo, Paris, Sydney, and other cosmopolitan centers. And as New York has demonstrated all too glaringly in recent years, abject obedience to the conventional idea of context may violate the expanded context of contemporary urban life.

History is repeating itself. This is the first thing about the Unified Bulk Program that will strike those whose memories stretch back as far as the 1960s. Once again, the New York planning department is laying down a set of zoning regulations based on ideas that have been around for forty years.

The 1961 zoning resolution, which the Unified Bulk Program is intended to counteract, was based on ideas first proposed by the French architect Le Corbusier in the 1920s. A critique of picturesque city planning principles then in effect, Le Corbusier's 1923 plan for the Contemporary City was a hybrid of the English garden city and the Futurist utopia of mechanized transportation. By replacing traditional streets with highways and elevators, the plan would clear congested ground area for green, open space.

The model was taken up by American planners and architects in the postwar years, with mixed results. In New York, Stuyvesant Town, Silver Towers, Waterside remain fine examples of the towers-in-a-park genre. Used as a formula for low-income housing, however, the concept became synonymous with the projects, high-rise ghettos for blacks. By the time of the 1961 zoning, in other words, what began as a critique of the status quo had hardened into a new version of it. It had become the dogma of its time.

Contextualism began as a critique of that dogma, in fact. In 1961 Jane Jacobs's *The Death and Life of Great American Cities* was an explicit attack on the towers-in-a-park model. Not long after, preservationists widened their scope from individual buildings to entire so-called historic districts. By the late 1960s, it was customary to regard developers and architects as enemies of the city. The animosity was intensified by the postmodern movement, which promised to create buildings more attuned to popular taste.

Now this critique, too, has congealed into dogma, and is about to be codified into law in turn. And we have already seen the current dogma's dubious architectural consequences. Historic neighborhoods, like South Street Seaport, converted into shopping malls. New neighborhoods, like Battery Park City, designed like prewar theme parks. And stumpy towers on low-rise bases, like 1 Union Square South.

But the most toxic effect of the contextualist dogma is invisible. It is the virtual disappearance of architecture from New York in recent decades. The theme park stuff would be almost tolerable if the city had encouraged the development of architecture as an art of reckoning creatively with the changing urban condition. But it has not. Instead, it has continued to regard architecture as an alien presence, an immanent invasion from Mars.

One positive thing must be said about the Unified Bulk Program. It represents a long-overdue challenge to the excessive power wielded by the city's Landmarks Preservation Commission in recent years. With the creation of historic districts, the Landmarks Commission has usurped the role of city planning and led the way in the conversion of Manhattan into a theme park. Unfortunately, city planning's effort to check this development does not go far enough. The program's uncritical acceptance of contextualism in fact portends more Disneyfication.

Too tall, too short, or just right for Goldilocks. Here's the weird thing: everything proposed by the Unified Bulk Program is entirely a matter of taste. Height, context, and quality are all areas where subjectivity reigns. They are matters of personal opinion. I like tall buildings and voids. Others don't. We may all disagree about what distinguishes architecture from real estate. This is as it should be. But how did we get to the point where the legislation of taste could be considered an acceptable function of city planning?

Zoning began in 1916 as an instrument for protecting public health. People shouldn't live in airless tenements or work in office or industrial buildings that lack adequate light and ventilation. Housing shouldn't be built next to factories or slaughterhouses. The Corbusian Ville Radieuse ("radiant city") was promoted as a public health mission. Open space would bring in light and fresh air, eliminating the congestion that bred disease. This was a reasonable, even a scientific, approach to designing cities before penicillin had been introduced.

In the postwar decades, urban renewal in the United States also came packaged with the rhetoric of hygiene. Slums were cancer. Planners were surgeons. Slum clearance was an operation to remove tumors from the urban body. The goal of planning for public health had shifted from the realm of physical reality to that of metaphor. A tuberculosis pathogen is a physical entity. But a tenement is not a tumor. To view it as such required a certain way of seeing. It reflected culturally constructed ideas about good and bad ways to live.

Mercifully, the Unified Bulk Program doesn't even bother with public health metaphors. But contextualism comes with a mythology of its own—the veneer of Junior League politesse often wielded by philistines on a rampage. "Practical," "attractive," "innovative," "within the city's enduring traditions"—or: sensible pumps, a string of pearls, and a splash of naughty French perfume.

With this program, city planning has crossed a decisive line. Without even a nod to the quantifiable goals that brought zoning into being, it has set up shop in the sphere of aesthetic preference. By embracing contextualism—or any other aesthetic concept—city planning enters an area where constitutional protections could apply. While the First Amendment does not protect all forms of communication, the Unified Bulk Program compels us to ask to what extent architecture is a protected form of speech.

In the field of urban semiotics, taste is defined as ideology codified in space. The Unified Bulk Program is a highly ideological document in this sense. It aims to impose an aesthetic standard on buildings throughout New York. But it also offers a golden opportunity to crack the contextual code.

We inhabit the hub of the advanced capitalist world. We love it here, and even if we wanted to leave, there's no other world to go to. But many of the ills associated with cities—economic inequality, social fragmentation, disregard for the economically unproductive, the gap between public and private amenity—are by-products of our way of life. Saskia Sassen, a professor of urban planning at Columbia University, has described ours as the Eviction Society. We exist in a perpetual state of displacement and dislocation created by the economic cycles that drive the fluctuating value of land.

Architecture has traditionally been used to compensate for these unsavory effects. A century ago, the robber barons of the Gilded Age commissioned architects to design such beloved landmarks as the New York Public Library and the Metropolitan Museum of Art. Later, the magnificent spectacle of the Manhattan skyline went far toward mitigating the violence its construction inflicted on the urban landscape. The bonus plaza was conceived as a benefit for those who do not profit from the real estate industry.

Another compensation—some might even say redemption—is the freedom to respond creatively to our way of life. This is no less true in architecture than it is in literature, painting, photography, song, or dance. From the Brooklyn Bridge to Frank Gehry's design for a new Guggenheim museum proposed for a site close by, New York's greatest buildings have provided signposts to change. They are forms of communication in which the imagination is placed at the service of truth about its time.

Up to a point, contextualism offers a useful compensation for the eviction economy. It is in the public interest to protect the environment from being incessantly blown to smithereens. Beyond that point, contextualism becomes a form of brainwashing. Like the private shopping mall designed to look like a public town square, the contextual veneer sends out a false message about the city we actually inhabit.

The single most powerful deterrent to architecture in New York is the blurring of the distinction between architecture and real estate. Cities may be able to survive without architecture. They can't survive without discrimination in taste. What would be the point? Cities are places where people are supposed to give their best. Without discrimination, who's to know what *best* means? Few would claim that Harlequin Romances are literature, yet we now have a skyline packed with Harlequin Romance buildings, clamoring to be recognized as architecture. How to deny them this status in a city where the real thing hardly ever comes along?

It's easy to overlook one crucial fact about the urban shift from industrial to cultural production: one major industry has not been left behind. Real estate development is an industry of the old economy that remains active in the city of the new. Other forms of manufacturing have been squeezed out of town or shipped overseas. But real estate development still cranks out material product in a city where all else has dematerialized into pixels. When we peer up and watch the cranes swiveling on the skyline, we should keep in mind that we are looking at relics of the old industrial city towering—if unsteadily—over the rise of the new.

And we should keep in mind that municipal government, too, is a relic of the old industrial city—a dinosaur from the era of *Meet John Doe*. Smoke-pumping factories, cigar-chomping tycoons, duplicitous union bosses, agitating longshoremen—all gone now. Alas, our pols seem to think they're still governing this vanished burg. Except when it comes to hiring campaign strategists, our pols know little about the city of symbolic analysis they govern.

Real estate developers and politicians, in other words, need each other more than ever. In addition to their traditional economic codependence—donations made by developers in exchange for a climate favorable to them—there is the need for moral support as the pair of them venture into a city that they do not understand or particularly care for. And why should they like a city that is fast accelerating beyond their nineteenth-century reach?

The Unified Bulk Program represents a strategic alliance between these two aging powers trying to survive in a rapidly changing urban environment. Because of its proposed height restrictions, some regard the program as anti-development. The real estate community has responded as if this were in fact the case. But this is just a bit of roughhouse between the dinosaurs. The truth is that both City Hall and developers stand to gain from this transaction. There are those who still believe that contextualism is a positive architectural idea, rather than the anti-architectural refuge it has become. By embracing contextualism as an aesthetic, developers and politicians acquire the aura of cultural value. In their own minds, at least, this qualifies them for citizenship in the cultural city.

The design review process proposed by the Unified Bulk Program will provide a more hazardous route to cultural distinction. Imagine that you are a developer. Your architect has proposed a design that does not conform to the contextual zoning. You have two options. You can apply to the Department of City Planning for a special permit. The approval process could take up to a year, with no guarantee that a permit would be granted. Or you can fire your architect and hire a hack.

But let's suppose that you really want to do the right thing. You apply for the permit. The design review panel is convened. The architect walks into the room to present his project, and the entire table is seated with hacks. The worst kind of hacks. Hacks with opinions. One hack wants a stepped silhouette; another wants an Art Deco crown; a third wants an avant-garde fold; a fourth wants glass instead of stone. If your architect will agree to these modifications, the panel will recommend granting the permit. Otherwise—hack, hack, hack.

You will still end up with hackery, just as if you hadn't bothered to go through the process. And the hackery will be much more expensive. But for the extra dough you'll get to put a little golden sticker on your hack job: the City Hall Mark of Excellence. People can go on mistaking real estate for architecture, and rejecting genuine architecture for being weird, far-out, and alien.

Government does have a role to play in raising architectural standards. Paris, Barcelona, Helsinki, Berlin, Tokyo, and many other cities use the independent jury system for that purpose. The function of the jury system is to protect architecture from political and economic pressures. As framed by the Unified Bulk Program, the design review panel could well have the opposite effect.

This appraisal could not have been written in 1961, even if the Unified Bulk Program had existed then. Forty years ago, planners and architects operated in a city where the concept of culture had little significance outside the sphere of anthropology. This has changed. The term now extends far beyond the compass of any particular field and has become a common tool for making connections between art, economics, psychology, philosophy, and many other fields.

Architects today are operating in this expanded cultural framework. This is the context of architecture today. It is emerging in the work of designers as various as Renzo Piano, Peter Eisenman, Frank Gehry, Rem Koolhaas, Steven Holl, Eric Owen Moss, Thom Mayne, and Zaha Hadid.

The Unified Bulk Program has stumbled into this context but is in no way part of it. That is what makes its cultural pretensions so ludicrous. Here was an opportunity for city planning to enlarge the conceptual framework for architecture in New York, to bring architecture into line with the transformations now overtaking urban life everywhere. That opportunity has been lost. Instead, city planning has reheated stale ideas and proposes to pass them into law. It's difficult to accept the inevitability of this.

May 14, 2000

FUSING BEAUTY AND TERROR, REVERENCE AND DESECRATION

It may seem heartless to think about beauty in the wake of human tragedy. But the aftershock from news of the Concorde disaster was linked to the emotions beauty can stir up. One hundred and fourteen people died as a result of last week's crash. Compared with a single life, the plane itself is nothing, just metal, rubber, and oil. These were nonetheless combined into one of the most important cultural artifacts of the twentieth century. In the thirty-one years since the first Concorde was rolled out, only a select few have flown on it. But this swan of a craft has winged through the imaginations of millions more. It's not just the French or the British who look up admiringly when the Concorde flies overhead. Anyone with an eye looks up.

To see: A masterpiece of contrapuntal aesthetics. The contrast between thin, elongated fuselage and wide, swept-back wings. Between the curve of the wings and the rectangular engines beneath them. The proportions of windows in relation to fuselage. The triangular configuration formed by the needle-point nose and the wingtips (or, when on the ground, the bird-like landing gear). The ugly duckling-into-swan metamorphosis when the drooped nose swings back into place. The Concorde's elegance arises from these formal relationships.

The plane's beauty is existential. Profit taking doesn't keep it aloft. A round-trip ticket costs in the neighborhood of $10,000. Even when full, however, the Concorde has lost money. National pride is one reason it has stayed in service. The pain of writing off what it cost to develop the plane may be another. But an ineffable factor is also at work: a reverential feeling akin to the impulse to admire an oak, contemplate a painting, or gaze up at a Gothic spire.

The Concorde is French (or half French) in the sense that the Chartres Cathedral is French, but the plane's appeal is global to the extent that French civilization is available to others. In 1955 Roland Barthes wrote that cars were the precise modern equivalent of the great Gothic cathedrals: "I mean the supreme creation of an era, conceived with passion by unknown artists, and consumed in image if not in usage by a whole population which appropriates them as purely magical objects." In the mid-'50s new cars could even satisfy the pangs of aspiration. But by the 1960s the United States space program had raised the stakes. Aspiration now came in the form of altitude and the skyward thrust of jet propulsion. The Concorde was Europe's answer to our Apollo mission. Let the Americans catapult their tin cans, play golf, and plant metal flags on the moon. We Europeans will turn space into a secular idea of heaven: Champagne, caviar, and freshly laundered linen napkins on the headrests.

No doubt many brave young souls do dream of becoming astronauts when they grow up. But a trip to Paris on the Concorde does not involve settling for less. A rich person I know says that the one thing she truly enjoys about having money is that it makes traveling easier. Mass travel, in other words, is what gravity used to be in the early days of flight: an oppressive condition from which only the privileged manage to escape.

Yet the Concorde has long been trailed by a whiff of morbidity. Until last week the plane's safety record had been impeccable. But its status as a cultural icon was always fragile. When the United States canceled its program to develop supersonic transport for civilians, the British-French endeavor was left without competition and the benefits that accrue from it. It is not always so great to be the only game in town. Without competition, there was no incentive to update the aircraft and none of the improvements that succeeding generations of supersonic craft might have developed.

As a result, Concorde pilots must use their brains to operate controls that on newer subsonic jets are run by computer. Who knows whether more advanced controls would have alerted the pilots last Monday to the flames shooting out of the engines? Or whether advanced technology could have reduced noise, increased headroom, extended the range of flights, or eventually brought down fares? The craft's obsolescence was thus virtually guaranteed before the first flight took off.

In this, the Concorde resembles the *Queen Elizabeth* 2, which began transatlantic service in the summer of 1969. Like the Concorde, the new Cunard liner was launched as a fusion of luxury and modernity. Unlike the stodgy Art Deco interiors of the *Queen Mary* and earlier *Queen Elizabeth*, the *QE2* was fitted with dramatic jet black carpets and molded plastic fix-tures. But who cared? Design did not suffice to conquer time. No luxury could compete with speed.

In the 1970s ads promoting a package deal started to appear in glossy magazines. Sail first-class to Europe on the *QE2*, fly home on the Con-corde. The package, presented as a cutting-edge experience, was actually an invitation to indulge yourself in not one but two obsolete forms of travel. Five days' worth of shuffleboard and midnight buffets. Three and a half hours on an plane whose days became numbered when carriers cast their lot with the 747. To gain a few hours over regular jets, you had to travel on a plane that was swiftly becoming a museum piece of aeronautics.

For some, the Concorde disaster evoked the memory of the destruc-tion of an earlier legendary transatlantic vessel. On February 9, 1942, while being refitted for wartime use, the French liner *Normandie* caught fire at its Hudson River berth. Attempts to put out the flames filled the ship with so much water that it capsized. The *Normandie* lay on its side for the remainder of the war and never sailed again.

As smoke from the fire drifted over Manhattan, it was understood that this was not an ordinary military mishap. For many, the *Normandie* was the most beautiful object created in the twentieth century. It epitomized the style and sophistication for which the French were celebrated. Some com-pared it to the Parthenon. And its destruction was an occasion to look for meanings deeper than the tragedy's immediate cause. The welder's torch was an instrument in a ritual enactment of the ancient idea that beauty itself may be condemned to play a tragic, sacrificial role in human affairs.

Our relationship to beauty is not entirely positive. The power to be moved by it can flow in more than one direction. For Socrates, erotic attraction was to be directed toward a higher, moral craving. From there it is but a step toward thinking that physical beauty is a bad thing. The next step is to regard beauty as an opportunity to relieve intense rage. Destroy the idol! Crush Salome!

Three days after the Concorde crash I found myself in the middle of an exchange between Peter Eisenman, the architect, and his wife, Cynthia Davidson, editor of *ANY* magazine. Mr. Eisenman said, "Hey, the Stealth bomber is beautiful, too." To which Ms. Davidson objected: "No! The Concorde is beautiful. The Stealth bomber is terrifying." My position is that beauty is terrifying. Like Homer's Helen or Michelangelo's *David*, beauty throws everything into an uproar.

There is pleasure as well as horror to be found in the desecration of beautiful things. After the French Revolution, the Ste.-Chapelle was used for storing flour. The Ottomans stockpiled gunpowder in the Parthenon. The Normandie, appropriated by the United States from France's Vichy government, was being converted into a troop ship when it burned. Something there is that doesn't like art.

There's a risk in dwelling too much on the Concorde's obsolescence. The risk is that we blind ourselves even further to the outmoded ways of thinking coursing through culture today. The Concorde's beauty emerged from the context of the 1960s, a period interior decorators now call retro. We've given ourselves the luxury of periodizing progress. At Disney World, the Futureland attractions have been redesigned as Jetson-style, nostalgic attractions.

This luxury is turning out to be expensive, and not just because an original Eames chair can cost thousands. The fundamentals of the '60s context have not disappeared. As Ms. Davidson reminded me, the demand for speed is greater, not less, in today's world. As Mr. Eisenman suggested, the military faces few obstacles in meeting that demand. Technically there's nothing to prevent development of a supersonic passenger craft capable of altitudes from which the sonic boom would not reach Earth. The Concorde crash, in other words, ought to shock people out of retro ways of thinking in all spheres of culture. It could easily be used as an opportunity to affirm them.

July 31, 2000

HOW MODERN DESIGN REMAINS FAITHFUL
TO ITS CONTEXT

In the absence of alternatives, there may be no more important project under way in New York right now than David Childs's restoration of Lever House, the International Style skyscraper on Park Avenue at Fifty-fourth Street. Designed by Gordon Bunshaft and completed in 1952, Lever House was the first glass curtain wall tower to rise in New York. It remains among the twentieth century's major landmarks.

Lever House established Skidmore, Owings & Merrill as the most progressive firm in the postwar United States. Along with the Seagram Building, the Guggenheim Museum, the CBS Building, and the United Nations headquarters, it helped make New York the leading city for architectural innovation in those years. Mr. Childs became chairman of SOM in 1990. His homage to Bunshaft is no mere sentimental journey. The restoration, due for completion this fall, is uncovering qualities that are becoming valued in architecture once again.

Uncommon Ground, a book by Thomas Leatherbarrow, should help admirers of modern architecture to form a more precisely analytic appreciation of those qualities. Mr. Leatherbarrow, a professor of architecture at the University of Pennsylvania, also provides a key for interpreting contemporary work, including recent projects by Mr. Childs, Rafael Viñoly, and Peter Eisenman.

The book, due in October from MIT Press, is a revisionist work. It corrects the distorted view that modern architects were insensitive to the physical context of their buildings. Focusing on projects by Richard Neutra and two less well known figures, Antonin Raymond and Aris Konstantinidis, Mr. Leatherbarrow shows that modernists did not regard building sites simply as blank slates for inscribing their fantasies of a uniform, technological society.

Further, he contests the notion that modern architects were latter-day Vandals, intent on shattering the cultural continuity of regional and urban life. Rather, the best of them adapted industrial building techniques to the lay of the land. Modern design mediated between prefabricated construction and local topography. It reconciled the homogenizing nature of modernity with regional differences. Its aim was to prevent the shattering of continuity in the industrialized world, not to accelerate it.

In other words, Frank Lloyd Wright and Luis Barragán were not the only architects who took landscape into account. Architects like Neutra regarded the city as an evolving topography in which landscape and successive layers of built form intersected over time.

But why use past tense? The International Research Institute for Climate Prediction at Columbia University's Lamont-Doherty Earth Observatory, completed earlier this year, perfectly illustrates Mr. Leatherbarrow's ideas. Designed by Viñoly, the Institute is the most sensitively sited building I've visited since Tod Williams and Billie Tsien's Neurosciences Institute in La Jolla, California. Both are science buildings. Both command impressive natural, partially urbanized sites. Both embody a conception of science as the culture of nature.

Viñoly's project is in Palisades, New York, on a cliff-top site on the west side of the Hudson. The Institute's design is as serenely elegant as its name is clunky. Almost Wrightian in its relationship to the landscape, the Institute is composed of two arc-shaped wings that overlap at the center, forming a double-width lobby area at the building's entrance. The roof is also designed as two pairs of overlapping arcs. A clerestory between the arcs illuminates the corridor that bisects the full length of the building's interior.

Mr. Leatherbarrow writes that the modern relationship between construction and topography is best seen in section (a cutaway drawing), rather than in plan (from above) or elevation (from outside). The Institute's central corridor offers a walk through this idea. The ground on which the building sits slopes gradually down toward the north. The land has not been leveled off. This is translated into the interior by flights of steps that break the corridor into segments.

Materials and exposed structure further integrate construction and site. The corridor runs beneath an arcade of wood bow trusses that support the roof and create an outside-in impression of trees. Internal office windows, facing into the corridor, pull light and views into the core. Bearing walls are made from the same local stone that erupts in boulders from the ground outside. The arcs of the wings and the metal roof echo contours of land and water.

According to Mr. Leatherbarrow, the conflict between technological progress and cultural continuity exists only in theory, not in the real world of architecture. Viñoly's building proves the point. The Palisades were formed 200 million years ago. One of the functions of the climate research institute is to monitor the global warming that could result in their submersion. Try that on for continuity.

Earlier this year, in a review of Peter Eisenman's design for the Staten Island Institute of Arts and Sciences, I wrote that Eisenman's buildings should be seen as links between the history of places and the history of ideas. At the site of a recent design for a hotel on the Friedrichstrasse in Berlin, these two histories already run closely parallel. The Hotel am Spreedreieck is an homage to two unbuilt Berlin projects designed by Mies van der Rohe in 1921 and 1922. The two projects were Mies's first explorations of the glass tower, a type that culminated in the completion of the Seagram Building thirty-seven years later. Eisenman's plan, situated on the exact spot of Mies's 1921 project (no site was designated for the 1922 project), takes the International Style tower back to its Expressionist roots.

In 1921 Mies had yet to rationally integrate steel construction into his skyscraper aesthetic. His Berlin towers were as much Expressionist as they were modern. Eisenman has essentially reversed the course of Mies's later development. His design uses a scientific technique to arrive at an Expressionist result. The design was generated by computer. Mies's two Berlin designs were loaded into the software and morphed into a single, composite structure.

The hotel combines the three-pointed star configuration of Mies's 1921 ground plan with the biomorphic contours of his 1922 scheme. The result is indescribably sexy. As with Mies's projects, the hotel's most prominent feature is the floor planes, stacked one above the other like a theatrical multiplex of urban stages. It's peekaboo time, not only for the hotel guests but also for Berlin and for Mies, its greatest twentieth-century architect. The irrational within the rationalist stands exposed. Eisenman's site is the history of modern architecture and of the role Berlin played in it before Hitler came to power.

The most conspicuous feature of the Lever House restoration is the repair of the glass curtain wall. The spandrel glass, originally a uniform green, had become a random two-tone mix. But the restoration should also open our eyes to the fact that Bunshaft's design involved more than wrapping a pretty skin around some steel and concrete. The building's importance lies with the integral relationship between skin, structure, and site. At Lever House, skin and section are one.

The stretch of International Style towers along Park Avenue south of Fifty-ninth Street has been criticized for destroying Park Avenue's sense of place. Precisely the opposite is true. The towers revealed a deeper sense of place than the masonry buildings that preceded them. Park Avenue is a feat of engineering: a viaduct for cars suspended over the train tracks that run beneath. The machine aesthetic of the towers raises this infrastructural dimension above the ground.

The exposed columns of Lever House punch through the thin crust of sidewalk and convey the impression of stilts straddling the subterranean tracks. The window mullions extend that vertical thrust to the skyline. The tower's floating base and stacked floor planes reveal that New York is a horizontal as well as a vertical city. Each floor replicates the slice of ground beneath it.

Apart from the advantage it takes of sunlight, Lever House does not reflect the natural topography of Manhattan. Rather, the design adapts construction to the artificial topography of a city that has evolved over time. Lever House itself is part of the city's accretive nature. So is its restoration. Half a century after its completion, we see the building with fresh eyes.

When new, Lever House was received as a sign of progress, socially and aesthetically. Office workers benefited from the natural light and the clear, open spaces. The city gained from being among the first to realize the utopian ideal visualized by Mies and other modernists. These qualities are still evident. But they are enriched by our awareness of a psychological dimension underlying the modern forms. Park Avenue is a CAT scan of New York's collective brain: our ambition, our exhibitionism, our compulsion to build platforms for our ideas. The city is more up-front about these urges than it was fifty years ago. In that sense, Lever House can stand for progress still.

August 6, 2000

TIBOR KALMAN: SEEING, DISBELIEVING

Since Tibor Kalman was a friend of mine, I'm not able to write an objective review of Tiborocity: Design and Undesign by Tibor Kalman, the New Museum of Contemporary Art's lively retrospective of the late graphic designer's work. But I'd feel idiotic if I didn't write a personal story before the show comes down this weekend.

Tiborocity had me shadowboxing with my friend, who died last year, over some of the issues we used to argue about. What is sensibility? What is visual culture? How do you maintain, or even measure, integrity in the consumer society? Those are a few of the issues we didn't exhaust in Tibor's lifetime. Continuing the conversation is my way of remembering him.

Tibor was an artist of the distribution system—the economic framework that bridges the gap between production and consumption. His métier encompassed art direction, graphic and product design, corporate branding, and exhibition display. M&Co, his New York studio, achieved high visibility with designs for *Artforum* and *Interview* magazines; CD covers for Talking Heads and Laurie Anderson; brochures for Red Square, an East Village apartment building; and perhaps most memorably, a line of surrealistic watches and clocks. The tone throughout was satirical, a lightly mocking wit deployed against design, against the consumer, against the trendiness embodied by M&Co and its clients.

Since we live in an era dominated by distribution, Tibor's work was intrinsically provocative, for how can art exist within it? Art, even Andy Warhol's, deals with truth, with the difference between life as it is and as we would like it to be. Distribution techniques—advertising, graphic design, commercial photography, public relations, store display—traffic in distortion and the exploitation of hope. That pill is not going to help you lose weight. You know this perfectly well. So does the manufacturer. The principal function of the distribution system is to loosen our mutual grip on reality.

Tibor and I both started out as window dressers. His windows (for the company that evolved into Barnes & Noble) featured books. Mine (for a shop called Design Research) showcased classic modern design. Our later paths led us toward the reverse of our respective displays. But the opposites remained conjoined. I write about the world of visual appearances. Tibor's designs often featured words.

A conflict between word and image initially brought us together. In 1985 Tibor was hired as the art director for *Artforum* magazine. I wrote the magazine's architecture column. The magazine already had a reputation for creating great layouts at the expense of writing. Tibor pushed this to an extreme. For his first issue, he had the notion of isolating random letters throughout the text and printing them in light blue instead of black. In my column, the letter *e* was chosen for this transformation. Since it made the text nearly unreadable, I naturally saw his fiddling as a sign of disrespect.

In hindsight, I can see that he was giving tit for tat. Oscar Wilde said, "The primary aim of the critic is to see the object as in itself it really is not." Why shouldn't design return the favor? Why not art-direct a poor critic's column out of recognition?

Like others who started out in the late 1960s, Tibor had a complicated relationship to authority. The counterculture, which many baby boomers saw as a bright beginning, came to a messy end. The last gasp of nineteenth-century Romanticism, it marked the dissipation of Romantic attitudes from a cultural elite to every adolescent's natural rite of passage. Rebellion became generic.

For some, the new media and information industries represented the rebirth of countercultural thinking in mainstream form. You really do have to Think Different to navigate the Web. You can create an entire worldview from a laptop. Point of view, sensibility, radiance can be transmitted worldwide. Tibor mainly worked in traditional media. As he was essentially a graphic designer, most of his output consisted of magazines, record and CD covers, and print and TV ads, with the occasional foray into product design and even urban design. Still, he was a McLuhan child, a global villager who regarded media as a consciousness-raising device and advocated liberation from the linear authority of print culture.

The show suggests that Tibor's medium was as much tactile as visual. He traded in textures of thought: shapes, colors, stylistic periods, atmospheres rubbing one another like subway riders. Think of his umbrella lined with a blue sky, a Magritte prêt-à-porter, the Surrealist icon made democratic and practical.

The closest I ever came to having a maiden auntie to send me a Christmas fruitcake each year was the holiday gift that arrived annually from Tibor's company. These tended to have socially uplifting themes. One year it would be a medicine cabinet in the shape of a red cross. Another year it would be a secondhand book stuffed with paper money. Included were envelopes, preaddressed to charities. (I spent the dough on myself.)

I took professional interest in Tibor's work for the Forty-second Street

Redevelopment Authority. Along with Robert A. M. Stern, Tibor was instrumental in creating the so-called interim plan, a set of guidelines governing the look of storefronts, signage, and other elements in the rebuilding of Times Square. Besides contributing ideas, Tibor designed an immense sidewalk installation for the south side of Forty-second Street on the short block between Broadway and Seventh Avenue.

Titled *Everybody*, the project, designed with Scott Stowell, crystallized Tibor's aspirations for the revamped Crossroads of the World: socially inclusive, focused on the street, Surrealist in spirit. The major element was a large billboard, mounted just above sidewalk level. The word *Everybody* was spelled out in black letters against a background of school-bus yellow. Attached to the billboard was a small assortment of funky chairs. These could be reached by climbing a set of ziggurat-shaped bleachers. When seated, you gazed out on the midtown circus with your feet dangling in air.

The project revolved, if just intuitively, around Surrealism's two intellectual poles: Freudian dream space (the slight elevation above street level evokes the loss of gravity, the low-altitude flight of dreaming hysterics), and Marxian social justice (the place serves the people, not the other way around). The school-bus yellow was itself a major component of the sign: Tibor's was largely an educational sensibility. He loved to absorb and to share.

All these things come across very clearly throughout the New Museum exhibition. It displays the range of artifacts Tibor collected, and his designs expressed the fusion of his references. Generosity and humility, more than political consciousness, were the transforming agents in his creative process. Perhaps the capacity to learn in public is the active ingredient in the creative sensibility.

The worst betrayal anyone can commit in my eyes is to move to Italy and leave me behind. So I was not disposed to forgive Tibor for accepting an offer to go to Rome as the editor of *Colors*, an advertorial magazine put out by Benetton, the clothing manufacturer. Nor was I inclined to like the magazine. I've never liked Benetton's clothes.

But I could see how frustrating it was for Tibor to design a magazine without exercising creative control over it. And I could also see the appeal of this particular magazine. There aren't many publications out there that draw a firm line between advertising and editorial. So it was disarming to come upon a magazine that was entirely up-front about being an ad. Still, *Colors* was an ad. It skewed the contract between the editor and the audience.

I confess that in my memory the magazine is largely a blur. Only a few images stand out from it, like those depicting Queen Elizabeth II as a dark-skinned, tropical monarch and Spike Lee as white-skinned suburban hip-hop devotee.

Tibor's magazine led him deeper and deeper into his own contradictions. That is what was so great about it. Unfortunately, it didn't give him space or time to work them out. These conflicts stemmed from the same problem: visual culture is a contradiction in terms.

Visual literacy once seemed like a liberating concept—a release from the musty weight of history, books, linear thinking, and the print tradition that McLuhan had consigned to history's dustbin. Images, and the prospect of communicating through images alone, offered the hope of changing consciousness. It was a logical repository for the counterculture's universalist ideals.

By the mid-1980s, however, it had become clear that these ambitions could not be attained by instinct alone. A more analytic, historically informed approach was needed to prevent visual culture from degenerating into a cult of ignorance and commercial manipulation. One afternoon, when Tibor and I were wandering through the splendors of Baroque Rome, I wondered whether he and I were seeing the same thing. Here was the most extravagant display of visual culture staged by Western civilization. Did Tibor get the Baroque message? All was possible, all could be questioned, provided that you accepted the absolute authority of the church. Sculptures, fountains, urban vistas, murals, buildings—the most sumptuous entertainments would be provided for those who surrendered their souls to the Father.

In Tibor's magazine, every social injustice could be exposed, every authority mocked—provided you flew the United Colors of Benetton. Every image was permissible, every pictorial juxtaposition would be laid out, provided you saluted the flag of visual culture. Which I did not. It had become the banner of the consumer society, a system as authoritarian as that of seventeenth-century Rome.

A few days after seeing the show, I was talking with Tod Williams, thirty-one, director of the critically acclaimed movie *The Adventures of Sebastian Cole*. He told me, "For my generation, images are garbage."

I had to laugh. What made the comment so devastating is that proponents of visual culture were always playing the generation card. They exploited adolescent illiteracy for self-serving ends. The notion of visual culture justified their own lack of cultivation (why read?) while giving them a sense of moral purpose (as teachers of visual literacy). In one breath, they announced: "The future belongs to the imagists, and . . . let's do it for the kids."

These two dubious messages provided the slim intellectual content of

Colors No. 13, the last issue Tibor edited before returning to New York. This provocative number contained pages of pictures and one page of text. These were agreeably laid out. A nice album of pix. A style book of personal adornment (tattoos, makeup, eyeglass frames); of erotic and violent encounters (mating carrots, a car crash). Rows of toes next to rows of noses. Blood. Variety meats. Surgery. At the end, a confused editorial argued that the editors didn't really think that pictures were more truthful, but somehow they were. Words to that effect. Then a suggestion that if you've wasted time reading the editorial you owe it to yourself to go back and stare at a picture for the same length of time, et cetera.

After my conversation with Tod Williams, I thought, yes, issue No. 13 was basically a load of garbage. The editorial was trashy too. It said: "Look at my garbage. Don't like what you see? Look again. Harder." And it was generational garbage. A baby boomer was saying to his younger audience: "Here, take our priceless garbage. We give it to you—the leaders of the twenty-first century. Yours to cherish. Yours to adore."

Actually, I don't think that images are garbage. I doubt very much that a filmmaker like Tod Williams does, either. People like us must be scopophiliacs to do what we do. But visual culture per se is not a visual phenomenon. It has barely a glancing relationship to aesthetics in any form. Rather, it is a social, psychological, political, and, above all, an economic manifestation. To be visually literate, in any but the most superficial consumerist fashion, you have to tear aside the screen of images and locate the nonvisual factors that are running the show.

My hunch is that, if Tibor's life hadn't been cut short, he would have done just that. He would have had a commercially successful way to educate people about the many facets of visuality. We would all be hooked on Tibor.com, where we would find combined access to the most extraordinary array of images and the most dazzling written insights into the visual apparatus. We would have Avedon's "Dovima with Elephants" along with commentaries on it by Arthur Danto and Janet Malcolm. We could download entire libraries of the greats illustrated with before-and-after pictures of cosmetic makeovers. Tibor would return to showcasing books, in other words, much as the window of this page is dressed with his designs.

August 17, 2000

PUBLIC SPACE OR PRIVATE,
A COMPULSION TO FILL IT

Horror vacui—fear of emptiness—is the driving force in contemporary American taste. Along with the commercial interests that exploit this fear, it is the major factor now shaping attitudes toward public spaces, urban centers, and even suburban sprawl.

Every public space must be packed with distractions. Food and flower vendors, musicians, banners, fountains, benches, and plants must fill every midblock plaza. They must be packed with young urban professionals, picturesquely enjoying wrap sandwiches and bottles of Evian water. Otherwise, it is a failure. Periodically, photographs of empty spaces will be published. Captions will say: These are failures.

Streets are too empty. They must have more billboards, public art, or distinctive street furniture. Trees are too empty. They must be hung with Christmas lights or signs identifying their species. Train stations and airports are too empty. They must become so-called destination places or be, in professional parlance, packed with program—specialty shops for chocolates, sunglasses, lingerie, and watches, along with eating spots featuring Mexican, New England, Deli, and Healthy cuisine.

Suburban lawns are too empty. Houses must be built on smaller lots. They must be filled up with the latest weed killers and lined with free-form planting beds that are themselves filled with bags of redwood chips. Iced tea is too empty. It must be lightly laced with mango juice or it cannot be enjoyed. Water is too empty. It must come flavored with orange, lime, or wild cherry. This whole package is called the New Urbanism.

Perhaps the time has come to change the criteria for measuring success. Emptiness may not be a quality to be feared. Perhaps the Japanese are not the only people with the capacity to appreciate the quality of a void. After all, there is often little difference between a failed American public space and a Zen garden. Why shouldn't we, too, learn to recognize the value of hollowness?

Recently I have been revisiting Michelangelo Antonioni's classic movies of the early 1960s—*L'Avventura*, *La Notte*, *L'eclisse*, and *Red Desert*. As much portraits of places as they are essays in plot and character, they have lost none of their power to convey fragmented social relationships and the oblique urban environments in which human affairs unfold. Existential films noir, these movies portray a kind of space that remains useful in the present moment of urban transformation: space noir. Emptiness is its essential quality.

I find *L'eclisse* the most haunting. Monica Vitti and Alain Delon hold the screen by virtue of their physical beauty, but the entire movie seems like one big buildup to the final scene, in which the two actors pointedly fail to appear. They have made desultory plans to meet at "the usual place," a highway intersection on the outskirts of Rome. Vitti lives nearby, in a modern flat.

Throughout the movie, the director contrasts this antiseptic, postwar environment with the medieval streets of the historic center. But he betrays no sentimental attachment to the ancient city. Frank Lloyd Wright once condemned cities as places for "mutual assignations and assassinations." That is roughly what Antonioni shows us too. Stock-brokers slaughtering each other on the floor of the Borsa. Lovers seducing and rejecting one another all over town.

In town, these passions are softened by the cafés, newsstands, dim palazzo interiors, narrow streets, the weathered masonry of the buildings lining them and other furniture from the attic of old-world charm. In the modern outskirts, we still get the assignations and assassinations, but we get them pure, without the comforting distractations. Instead, the passive-aggression of phone calls and traffic transpires amid the abstract geometry of the postwar utopia.

When new, Antonioni's movies were received in fairly one-dimensional terms. They were thought to depict the malaise of the modern world. The fragmented cityscapes and industrial wastelands were even seen as causes of the sickness. In retrospect, the disaffection of Antonioni's characters looks like a human condition, not merely a modern one. There is no malaise, no need for a cure. There is only an emotional reality to be confronted. And with what elegance, what style, Antonioni's characters face it! Such exquisite doubt, such refined anxiety. What an artistic gesture of refusal the pair make by not showing up—not venturing to disturb the noir composition of streetlights and headlamps blinking on at dusk.

Antonioni's cinematography was once criticized for being too beautiful for his existential subject matter. Today, the beauty holds the meaning. From an urban point of view, his movies are premonitory fables. They anticipate the conversion of the rusting, postindustrial metropolis into the increasingly aestheticized city of art.

The desire to see these movies again, after nearly forty years, was aroused by a group of projects that represent the most recent phase of this conversion. I refer to the art parks or culture districts now taking shape in Pittsburgh, downtown Los Angeles, Philadelphia, Newark, Charleston, and other cities nationwide. In New York, two such projects are under way. In Brooklyn, an art zone is now being planned for the area surrounding the Brooklyn Academy of Music. In Manhattan, architects are now submitting bids for the redevelopment of the buildings and open spaces at Lincoln Center, the grandparent of all performing arts centers. These projects offer an opportunity to rethink the criteria by which the success of public spaces is to be judged.

Many enlightened people helped shape the standards currently in use. They include Jane Jacobs, William H. Whyte, Benjamin J. Thompson, Kevin Lynch, Edward Logue, and James Rouse. Thompson is the unsung figure of the group, though he was the visionary who first conceived what would later be called the festival marketplace. Thompson was a young partner in the Architects Collaborative, a Cambridge, Massachusetts, firm established by Walter Gropius. Later, he succeeded Gropius as dean of Harvard's Graduate School of Design. Despite his modernist pedigree, Thompson recognized that the modern vision of the city was flawed. In the era of suburban exodus, the urban core was not sufficiently alluring to attract people after work hours.

Like Rem Koolhaas decades later, Thompson recognized the potential of shopping to animate inert urban space. In the 1960s, Thompson created the first of a chain of retail establishments, called Design Research, that specialized in modern furniture and accessories for the home. He also owned a restaurant in Harvard Square. Faneuil Hall, the first of the Rouse-Thompson collaborations, opened in 1976. With it, the new retail-populist paradigm was launched.

When creative responses become formulaic, they can stifle creativity later on. Thompson's vision has suffered this fate. The festival marketplace remains a useful concept for orchestrating certain kinds of urban space. But its very success created new problems in turn. For one thing, it displaced urban diversity with a homogenized atmosphere of chain stores, coordinated street furniture, banners, and signs. As a controlled, commercial environment, it eroded the distinction between the open urban environment and such suburban places as the shopping mall, the theme park, and the residential enclave. Consumerism, when working properly, should increase access to the public realm. When applied to public urban space, it raises invisible, exclusionary barriers.

That's one reason why modern architecture's failed public spaces are looking quite good these days. There's no pressure to spend $2 for a cookie. A stroll across Chase Manhattan Plaza, in Lower Manhattan, offers a refreshing vacation from distractions. You're in the heart of a huge bank, but there are no commercial interruptions. The emptiness is ideal for sorting out inner and outer worlds. It's a democratic space, too. Democratic and popular are not, after all, synonyms. There are moments, in fact, when the two concepts are at odds. A city that offers the alternative of unpopular spaces is more accessible than a city that only tolerates popular success.

And I wonder if failed space isn't more conducive to creativity. This may be a Romantic notion, but it's also a Classical idea. Think of Goethe pondering Roman ruins. Postindustrial cities that are seeking to remake themselves as cultural centers might also benefit from pondering the success of failure: the glamour of their own collapse.

The aura of failure: this is what I find appealing about the outdoor lighting system designed by Richard Gluckman and Robert Wilson for the Pittsburgh Cultural Trust, a sixteen-block performing arts district now being realized in downtown Pittsburgh. Using theatrical scrims, natural light, and artificial illumination, Gluckman and Wilson have woven a discontinuous maze through the districts back alleys. The lighting effects, a changing blend of blue, green, and white, have the phosphorescence of decay.

The project serves a practical function. It's supposed to reassure culture consumers that muggers and junkies aren't lurking in the alleys. But instead of going merry and festive, the lighting has a consumptive pallor. Gluckman designed Pittsburgh's Andy Warhol Museum, and the noir spaces he designed with Wilson are strikingly Warholian. Particularly as presented serially in renderings (as it appears in a new monograph on Gluckman's work), the design evokes Warhol's Shadow paintings of the late 1970s. The lighting seems to shimmer between the pop extremes of obscurity and fame. The light will make your skin look as bad as Andy's.

Emptiness, obscurity, failure, bleakness, pallor—such noir terms are not found in the vocabulary of civic success with which urban revitalization programs are typically promoted. But these terms should be permissible wherever culture comes up. Even an artist like Warhol, with all that diamond dust in his eyes, knew that too much glitter is unhealthy for art.

August 27, 2000

THE AIR-CONDITIONED REVERIE
OF A FUNDAMENTALIST

Summertime in Houston. This is what it's like to be a martyr to city love. Heat and mugginess drive the body into underground streets and climate-controlled rooms, behind sealed windows and closed doors. The mind

The New York Times 1992–2007

feels trapped too. Intellectually, you know that you're in a great American city. Physically, you feel absent.

The sensation of absence must be acute for Rafael Moneo, architect of the new Audrey Jones Beck Building at Houston's Museum of Fine Arts. In Moneo's native Spain, builders have been coping with heat for eons. Here in Texas, a onetime Spanish colony, architecture is for all practical purposes a network of sealed membranes, constructed around air-conditioning systems and linked together by cars chilled to bone-rattling discomfort.

The week I went to Houston, a photograph appeared on the front page of this newspaper depicting the apparent melting of the polar ice cap. Yes, Virginia, Santa's workshop is underwater. Compared to this alarming piece of news, the Beck Building is scarcely worth mentioning. Nonetheless, the building is a good one. It deserves a positive story. But so does the link, however remote, between the Beck and our watery top of the world.

Usually, when I arrive in a city to look at a building, I spend some hours prowling the vicinity to orient myself to the site. In Houston, it was too hot to prowl, or even to inspect the Beck Building's exterior, except from the window of my hotel room across the street. From this perspective, the building's context was the window, the newspaper, and a bowl of complimentary fruit. Still life with art museum. *Nature morte.*

Still, even a discouraged city-lover would risk dehydration to visit a building by Ludwig Mies van der Rohe. Two previous additions to the Museum of Fine Arts were designed by the great master, in 1958 and 1974. These have now been renovated, to coincide with the Beck Building's opening last May, when the weather may have been more conducive to architectural appreciation.

Moneo was an excellent choice to build on Miesian precedent. Like Mies, Moneo is a fundamentalist. He believes in essences, architectural values that endure. "I am committed," he said, "to an architecture that maintains faith in the principles and the mechanisms architecture has always had."

Like Mies, who preferred the term *building art* to *architecture*, Moneo embraces material construction as architecture's basic fact. He is not a structural expressionist. The stone surfaces of the Beck Building conceal load-bearing steel and concrete construction. But Moneo's forms and volumes do not violate the logic of the materials and methods used to fabricate them.

The Beck is a square, two-story box. It occupies an entire block in the museum district a few miles from downtown, across the street from the Mies expansion and the museum's original home, a 1924 Beaux Arts temple. All four sides of the Beck are covered with a light pink stone that shimmers with a lustrous, Mediterranean bloom. Only spare geometric cuts are made in the facades: some large windows framed in bronze; a wedge-shaped trough that allows the sun to reach a skylight; air grilles. On the west side, a deep reveal shelters the main entrance.

The Beck's roof can be counted a fifth facade. It supports the building's most conspicuous urbanistic device: a grid of louvered light boxes that illuminate the galleries below. Night photographs taken from above suggest that the lanterns were intended to echo the downtown skyline some miles away. This effect is not apparent from the street. Nonetheless, the roofline makes an elegant nighttime apparition.

Two entrances to the Beck cause anxious indecision, particularly since the main one is concealed in deep shadow beneath an overhang and separated from the street by a driveway. The driveway is partly screened by a thick cement wall that has been molded into scored letters forming the museum's name. The lettering, designed by Massimo Vignelli, is astonishingly unattractive. If the intention was to recall the thick walls of adobe construction, the gesture is hollow here.

Blast of conditioned air. Ticket lobby. Then, as the body adjusts, a vision of space-on-space: an atrium of an amplitude that you wouldn't believe possible in a two-story building, even with the little penthouse that enables the atrium to punch through the roofline. You are instantly relieved on entering, and not just by the coolness. The atrium's compressed, almost intimate monumentality states that Moneo knows everything there is to know about museum fatigue, including how to spare you from it.

Classically composed yet dynamic, the atrium is animated by two diagonals that slice asymmetrically through it. A staircase to the left, an escalator to the right form two triangles that face each other in reverse—two flipped halves of a divided square. The length and thinness of the two banks magnify the room's scale. The space is further enlivened by the eclectic array of antique sculptures that face you like a committee welcoming you to the history of art.

Take the escalator to the permanent collection. You may be halfway through it before your eye is drawn to the Beck's signal detail: a cubic convergence of planes and textures. A narrow strip of stone is set into the floor around the perimeter of each gallery. Playing against the stained, dark oak floor, the strips are light-catchers, horizontal frames that extend the wall's surface into the space of the room. Just above the stone, thin, louvered aluminum air-conditioning grilles are mounted at the base of the wall. The doorways between the classically proportioned galleries are framed with brushed bronze panels.

It may strike you that the entire building was designed to create a sympathetic environment for this device for framing space and light. While the skylights, with their louvered light boxes, are formally more assertive, the detailing in the galleries themselves defines the visitor's experience. They helped persuade me that the Museum of Fine Arts has the richest collection I've seen in many years.

On leaving the Beck, you get another slap in the face. The blast of heat is only part of the shock. There is also the abrupt transition from the visual to the physical, from the sphere of retinal experience to a world where eye and brain are but two organs in a wholly constituted body.

This is what an art museum is supposed to do, you might say: create a space ruled by the sense of sight. But to become aware of this specialized function is to see that Moneo's building is part of the general fragmentation of culture after all. And this awareness extends to the urban context. Like the Beck, the great majority of our buildings are dedicated to the creation of visual effects. In this sense, the Beck symbolizes architecture's role in the detachment of the eye from the rest of nature.

The interesting thing about fundamentalists is the many fundamentals that their thinking does not take into account. Architecture's obedience to the eye is a relatively recent phenomenon in the history of building. The ancient Mediterranean sculptures that greet visitors to the Beck Building served a religious function. Greek sculpture, for example, was attached to the temple, which itself derived its meaning and value from the sacred earth site on which it stood. Differentiation—into bodies, selves, disciplines, sites, and cities—was seen by the Greeks as a dreadful if necessary part of life. From it grew tragic theater.

The differentiation of space into the modern art museum is also wonderful and terrible. For the Greeks, art as well as religion supplied the connective tissue that prevents differentiation from pulling human life to pieces. For us, art is a thing apart. In a modern democracy, it is neither possible nor desirable to return to the Greek model. But it is possible to imagine how, working within the logic of art, the Beck Building might have articulated the tragic as well as the triumphal dimension of the modern art museum.

The museum's collection is traditionally organized by region, chronology, and school. Overall, it traces a narrative of progressive abstraction, from funerary sculpture, created for the body and the earth, to the thin, gorgeous lines of an Agnes Martin painting and spare geometric shapes of the museum's sculpture garden, created in 1986 by Isamu Noguchi. Along the way, we pass through the Italian Renaissance and the modern transition from the sacred to the secular, from the content-laden form of the religious icon to the illusionary device of single-point perspective.

The museum's architecture tells a similar story. The Beaux Arts building is an abstraction of classical architecture. The Mies expansion pushes neoclassicism to the extreme reduction of glass and steel. The Moneo building, while clad in stone, recapitulates the Miesian ethic of formal reduction and spatial clarity. Even the stone—a real material that provides the Beck's formal decoration—represents the earth in abstract form. The story reaches a climax with *The Inner Light,* an installation of artificial light created expressly for the Beck by James Turrell. Progressing from earth to sky, physical to ethereal, the story is fundamentally religious in nature, a ritual procession in the temple of art.

The story is still unfolding. The contemporary informational city is an ethereal zone, held aloft by streams of os and 1s generated by rapid electronic impulses. For now, however, its citizens still dwell in bodies, sealed buildings, and cars, and these continue to create an invisible but highly unethereal substance: greenhouse gases.

Houston is the capital of the oil economy. That economy built the city, defined its shape, and makes it habitable. Even the Museum of Fine Arts reminds us of the city's dependence on energy. Across the street from the Beck stands a second new building—a shadow Beck—which houses the museum's air-conditioning system and a parking garage. Unfortunately, the shadow Beck has been designed to conceal this infrastructure. It would have been better had Moneo chosen to aestheticize it.

The Museum of Fine Arts has a nice trove of sculptures by Jean Tinguely, including *Bascule VII,* a work from 1967. It is pictured in the museum's guidebook, along with a boldface quotation from the artist: "All machines are art." This is a fundamental modern tenet, one of the founding beliefs of New York's Museum of Modern Art. If Moneo's thinking were sufficiently elastic to incorporate this idea, the shadow Beck might have gained equal standing with its twin. This could have been achieved in four easy steps: eliminate the walls; install solar panels on the roof (an inverse of the Beck's lanterns); light up the interior (Turrell could have been turned loose on this); and declare the shadow Beck a new museum acquisition—*Air-Conditioning, with Cars.*

Peter Eisenman once said the function of architecture is to "problematize" things. That is partly true in the case of the Beck. It is possible to give the building high marks and still come away thinking that something is wrong. Has one toured the wrong building? Perhaps it is a mistake to think of the Beck's concrete walls as its structure. Its deeper structure may lie in the shadow building across the street. Without cars, the museum would be inaccessible. Without air-conditioning, it would be uninhabitable. Compared with this infrastructure, the Beck's structure is almost incidental.

· · ·

Art museums traditionally put a fine gloss over the dark side of baron robbery. I see no reason to disparage this civilized practice. But the context of culture has changed dramatically in the quarter century since the Mies expansion was completed. Clients didn't habitually conduct global searches for architects. Before moon landings and satellite photography, the North Pole seemed far, far away. It required a stretch to see any connection between an air-conditioning system in Houston and an ecological catastrophe on the polar extremities. Now it takes a stretch to overlook one.

The ice caps were once purely natural phenomena. Now they are cultural phenomena as well, the product of an evolving global operating system that has drawn together the producers and consumers of buildings and cars to create what an art historian might reasonably describe as the most ambitious earthwork of historical time. Perhaps the time has come to uncreate this masterpiece. This will require a global effort too. Cultural institutions have a pivotal role to play in it. We look to them for self-awareness and for traction—for signs that the operating system can receive sufficient feedback to avoid the self-destructive explosive fate Tinguely sometimes planned for his exploding mechanical sculptures.

Our shadow Beck would not reduce oil consumption by one drop. But it could work powerfully on the level of metaphor, the plane on which art museums and their contents communicate. Like Tinguely's sculptures, the Beck Building might have spoken metaphorically about its own civilization. I think it would say: "Houston, we have a problem."

September 17, 2000

INTERIOR CITY: HOTEL AS THE NEW COSMOPOLIS

Design euphoria finally has a New York home. Ian Schrager's new hotel, the Hudson, contains a thousand guest rooms, a suite of public rooms, and an outdoor garden, but the main attraction is the imagination with which Mr. Schrager and Philippe Starck have redesigned the face of the cosmopolitan idea. For the city of strangers, they have proposed an aesthetic of strangeness. It's a match.

The Hudson, which opened Tuesday on Fifty-eighth Street between Eighth and Ninth avenues, pumps up New York's legendary status as a noble social experiment. It also brings Mr. Schrager into focus as one of the outstanding social scientists of our time. How much rejection will people risk for the sake of feeling accepted? How much unfamiliarity can they tolerate? Sociologists routinely address questions along these lines. In Mr. Schrager's environments, people get to live the questions.

How much design can people tolerate? How many people are willing to pay for a room in which all but a few inches of floor space is covered by the mattress? How do you create a raving, Dionysian bar scene without repelling the Apollonian creative types you would also like to attract? These are a few of the experiments that will be conducted on paying volunteers inside the Hudson hotel.

But this project also raises questions about the city outside its doors. Why has New York architecture been driven inside? What does it mean that talented architects of Mr. Starck's generation are lucky if they get to work on loft, restaurant, and store interiors? What does this portend for a city that takes civic pride in its cosmopolitan composition?

I have always loved hotels, and I never tire of Philippe Starck. I could live serenely in one of the Hudson's small $95-a-night bedrooms. Each is a perfect pillbox, your daily vitamin of space. The minimum requirements include a queen-size bed, little reading lamps with shades that reproduce watercolors by Francesco Clemente, and an emaciated desk. Perfect for writing spare prose. Only the slimmest laptops need apply.

You enter the room through a tiny hall: for a room this size, any hall feels extravagant. Shower/bath on the left. Storage on the right. A mini-stereo set and a mini-minibar. A mini-window above the headboard, and that's it. Suites are available, starting at $150, but why bother. Sleep small. Dream big. That's the Hudson idea. It's an Eloise concept. The grown-up world as seen through children's eyes.

At the Hudson, everything is a play on scale, from the stretch-version *Vertigo* escalators at the entrance to the bento box rooms upstairs. Just the thought of a 1,000-room Schrager hotel is a wild exaggeration. This boutique hotel is designed for Gulliver's travels.

Is design the new lingua franca for global travelers? Thomas Fisher, dean of the college of architecture and landscape architecture at the University of Minnesota, is dedicating a new division of his school to that idea. And why not? Design has functioned throughout history as a system of signs. Check out Chartres. Now it serves as a communications medium for the new economy. Checkout and check-in.

Postliterate people will feel most welcome at the Hudson. At the entrance, no name, no letters, no typography disturb the design. Instead there is a torch with an eternal flame, suspended beside a doorway sheathed with chartreuse glass. In Colonial days, hospitality was symbolized by carved wooden pineapples placed by the door. At the Hudson, citron twists are evidently the fruit of choice.

Just inside the entrance there will be gift shops specializing in the well-designed traveler's needs. But if you're checking in, you will want to step aboard the escalator that carries you up two floors through a narrow tunnel bathed with yellow green light. You will feel like a sip of margarita rising through a straw. (Carry your own paper umbrella.)

The main lobbies of all grand hotels are stage sets. At the Hudson, the play appears to take place in a lively town square. There ought to be gesticulating extras milling about in a crowd scene, saying things like "Cheese and crackers, cheese and crackers," while pretending to converse among themselves. The centerpiece of this square, in effect its statue or fountain, is a long wooden desk carved with a mock Bavarian motif, and an enormous Baccarat chandelier with hologram candles designed by Ingo Maurer.

The lobby is ringed with the sort of refreshment spots you would expect to find in a well-appointed piazza. Only a Surrealist sense of surprise unites the different styles in which the public rooms are designed. Collegiate Gothic is the motif in the restaurant, or Cafeteria, as it is called here. Heavy brown curtains. Heavy oak chairs. Refectory tables with heavy oak benches. The effect is *The Belles of St. Trinian's:* a gang of louche students running amok in the seedy boarding school that now occupies a former stately home.

The bar is Kubrick territory. The translucent floor, illuminated from beneath, sets off tables and chairs like game pieces on a board. Make your move toward a Regency side chair with silicone cushions. Or pull up a log, equipped with backrests, designed by the Dutch firm Droog. Overhead, a fresco by Mr. Clemente brings back memories of similar work executed by the artist for the Palladium, an earlier Schrager experiment. To my eye, the ceiling creates a stronger impact than the installation conceived for the Guggenheim Museum's Clemente retrospective last year.

More postliteracy awaits in the Library, a room of clublike ambience with bookshelves that wrap around the walls. But the shelves are too high to reach. They are pitched at balcony height, but there is no balcony, and no rolling ladder.

Lower down, however, are slanting, lectern-like shelves displaying art books. And desks with computer screens set into the surface. The room is dominated, however, by a pool table of British imperial aspirations, and the immense metallic shade of the Ingo Maurer lamp suspended above.

Eloise will take over the park. She will not want for attention here. Installed in the courtyard between the building's two wings, the so-called

Private Park has been conceived as a theater: the play within the play. Readings and recitals will be offered, along with drinks and snacks, while the guest rooms looking on to the garden will form tier upon tier of private boxes.

A glass roof partly encloses the park, which is furnished with huge topiary pots, an immense rake, and other grossly inflated garden tools. But some may find that the most gracious touch is the existing balustrade overlooking West Fifty-seventh Street. Classic Georgian in style, it is an icon for gracious prewar city life, as well as a fine place to perch and pose.

The dream logic of Mr. Starck's design invites the possibility that things could turn nightmarish. At any moment, the brick walls of the park might dissolve and we would behold a scene out of Genet. From the courtyard of a vast panopticon, we would see road warriors in their terry-cloth robes, isolated in $95 cells, grimly wishing away the confinement with flicks of the speed dial. Let's wander over to the Library, where Alba Clemente is reading aloud selected passages from Cocteau's *La Voix Humaine* to an audience of crows and pigeons.

It strikes me that Mr. Starck may be feeling at home with himself. What is notable about the Hudson is that few pieces of furniture bear the designer's tradmark. Instead he has curated environments that include furnishings by other well-known designers (Charles and Ray Eames, Ingo Maurer, Droog), along with generic examples of period styles. Executed with precision and spirit by Anda Andrei and Michael Overington, long-time players on Mr. Schrager's team, the result is more relaxed, more diverse, less insistent on controlling the atmosphere.

If I had the means, I would furnish each room with a copy of Bonnie Menes Kahn's wonderful book *Cosmopolitan Culture: The Gilt-Edged Dream of a Tolerant City* (Atheneum, 1988). The book is not quite Eloise. It is a grown-up valentine to a certain ideal of city life. The cosmopolitan cities are the cities of great architecture, great art, great music, the cities of great renown, Ms. Kahn writes. It is no accident that where the stranger is welcome, there is both tolerance and genius.

She has many provocative things to say about the social forces that make and break a great cosmopolis, but the key to it all is the spirit of tolerance for strangers. I'd go further and say that what makes the difference is a ravenous appetite for strangers, even an inexhaustible desire to be a stranger. Nightlife flourishes on this principle. The great Peter Gay, writing on Weimar Berlin, termed this phenomenon the outsider as insider. This idea is dramatized at the Hudson. It is a *Mahagonny, I Am a Camera, Street Song* world.

Which isn't to say that everyone will feel comfortable here. New York is the most judgmental city in the world, and the Hudson can't help keeping up that tradition, too. It helps to be a certain kind of narcissist, the type who never throws a fit to get attention because he always assumes he's getting it, even when he's being ignored. It also helps to be a creative type with more dash than cash, as *Vogue* used to call it.

The Hudson is a refuge for such people, and for all those who crave what is lacking in the city outside: the realization of contemporaneity in public, urban space. Think about what happens in the street: you make a split-second decision whether to marry, kill, or stare right through everybody who comes walking toward you on the sidewalk. This complex of reactions is primal, uncivilized, self-centered, basic, romantic, and normal. They are tolerant and intolerant at the same time. They wouldn't work with people you know. They depend on your tolerance for strangers. Variations on this experience can be found in music, publishing, theater, dance, and any other quarter of the city where cultural values hold sway.

The Hudson transposes the street dynamic into a compact indoor version. Like it, hate it, like it, hate it. A man with a bad toupee walks through. Oh, the humanity! Oh, the unstylishness! This is the worst thing that ever happened in the world! But if you feel at home here, it's because you enjoy being a stranger among strangers, and the sense of freedom that arises from it.

Mr. Starck has codified that sensation in color, scale, light, and space. It can, he shows, be done. And that's not a minor lesson in New York at a time when the city's builders have become addicted to an architecture that merely reassures us with signs of the all too familiar. In this sense the Hudson is a ghetto for architecture, an art form for which New York has developed almost zero tolerance over the years, an art that must now be practiced in privacy between consenting adults.

The Hudson has an unmarked entrance, elevators for mass transit, a brick air shaft for a park, and a public library with a pool table. Community boards can't shut it down, the Landmarks Commission can't declare it inappropriate, and city planners can't subject it to the approval of so-called design advisers. Imagine the possibilities if the city at large were to be liberated from the intolerance coded within such restraints.

October 5, 2000

WHERE EGO SASHAYS IN STYLE

The Guggenheim Museum has served up another plateau of urban history: a retrospective of the Milanese fashion designer Giorgio Armani.

This show may lack the depth of the Guggenheim's other urban excavations, like The Great Utopia, The Italian Metamorphosis: 1943–1968, and the recent 1900: Art at the Crossroads. But what it lacks in depth it makes up for with sparkle. Organized by Germano Celant and Harold Koda, Giorgio Armani: Retrospective polishes up a familiar facet of urban life: the grand promenade through flattering reflections of ourselves (superimposed on fantasies of how much better we would look if we could afford nice clothes) that we take through the great shopping streets of Paris, Milan, and New York. The show's pretext may be Mr. Armani, but its real subject is autoerotica, and the perverse generosity of which extreme narcissists are capable. And the show does it without mirrors.

Frank Lloyd Wright, the Guggenheim's architect, would have loved this show. Wright cared a lot about clothes. He even designed some—for himself, naturally (those dashing tweed capes!), but also for some of the women who inhabited his Prairie houses. Picture it: Arts and Crafts furniture, a matinee musicale, and a hostess in a Wright-designed tea gown to complete the cultivated composition. The last Mrs. Wright, the tigerish Olgivanna, was a vision in white and Cherokee red.

The commercial aspect of the Armani show wouldn't trouble Wright much, either. Visitors to the Mercedes-Benz (originally Jaguar) showroom on Park Avenue, or the jewelery boutique shop off Union Square in San Francisco, can see that the spiral was entirely compatible with fashion and cash. This year, Mr. Armani pledged a major chunk of dough (perhaps as much as $15 million) to the Guggenheim as part of a global partner sponsorship (gifts that can go to Guggenheim projects anywhere in the world). And it has been speculated that this show was contingent on the designer's financial support, which the museum has denied. (*InStyle* magazine, a Time Warner enterprise, is the show's official sponsor.) The arrangement raises serious questions of institutional ethics, which I'll get to further on. But what a bore it is to think about such matters when you're looking at pretty things.

The major affinity between Wright and Mr. Armani is that the Guggenheim's spiral and fashion are both signs of life. I can recall no other Guggenheim exhibition devoted entirely to the human form, or at least its mannequin simulacrum. The Armani retrospective, in fact, presents an inverted version of a life class. Instead of the undraped body, the show offers just the drapes. The mannequins have been pared down to the edges of the costumes, creating the special effect of Invisible Women. These cluster in groups, arrayed in the building's structural bays, spatial modules with the proportions of shopwindows. The presentation recalls the close relationship between fashion and Surrealism that flourished in New York in the 1940s.

So, to a degree, does Robert Wilson's installation, at least when you consider that Isamu Noguchi was partly inspired by Surrealism's preoccupation with Freud. Architectural transformations of the Guggenheim rotunda have been a hallmark of the museum under the direction of Thomas Krens. Mr. Wilson's may be the best yet. On entering, you find yourself within a hugely magnified version of a Noguchi paper lantern turned inside out. A ribbon of white theatrical scrim winds almost continuously from the lowest coil of the spiral nearly to the top. Lighting, designed by A. J. Weissbard, glows from within. The dome's skylight has been dimmed; Wright's built-in ramp lighting is blocked by temporary walls.

The walls are painted a dark taupe, the color of volcanic mud. Floors have been fitted with gray carpet except on the top level, which is carpeted in black. The monotony is relieved by the clothes, of course, and also by visual vignettes that occur along the ramp: cracks in the mud, illuminated from behind; stands of fiberoptic reeds; light panels in the floor.

Mr. Wilson's aesthetic is a Zen version of midwestern blandness: slow, flat, dull. Here he gives us a regional department store in the state of satori, le Salon de Paris with one hand clapping. The carpeted floors account for much of the calm. A collage of religious and exotic sounds, created by Michael Galasso, amplifies the Eastern mood. Chanter?

Sashay. Don't bother with that walk-down-from-the-top routine. This retrospective is designed for ascension, and it's good for the calf muscles besides. In the High Gallery, the double-height space near the bottom of the ramp, Mr. Wilson has installed a yin-yang, topsy-turvy runway. Visitors walk down the center of the space, on illuminated panels of white glass, while evening costumes are mounted on bleachers that rise on either side. How cruel to subject us poor slobs to the inspection of these peerless (and headless) women of style!

But the tableaux are awesome, the outfits all black and white. En masse, they display a power of invention not seen since Cecil Beaton's famous Ascot scene in *My Fair Lady*. Plaids, stripes, florals, herringbones, chevrons, and other patterns, rendered in sequins, tweed, silk, linen, beads, and feathers, these dresses introduce the motif of unity and multiplicity that runs the entire length of the ramp.

If, like me, you don't follow fashion closely, you may well have a stereotypical image of Armani fashion. The image is androgynous, monochrome, uniform, and fluid. Isn't this the guy who, in the 1980s, put men and women into the power suit? I came here half expecting to see an *Arrangement in Slate and Mushroom*, with museumgoers providing the only variety in sight.

The fluid part we got right. Otherwise, this show, which includes more than four hundred costumes, explodes that preconception into as many smithereens. Along stretches of the ramp, we pass through monochromatic interludes, but these only heighten the designer's fecund talent for formal differentiation. And Mr. Armani uses color, particularly in floral fabrics, with the exuberance of an English gardener.

The show is organized by themes, not chronology, which makes it tempting to use the word *timeless,* as if fashion, of all things, could stand outside time. The stuck-clock effect, I would say, derives from the poise Mr. Armani maintains between theme and variation. The theme is Mr. Armani's concept of ideal body proportions. The concept is Vitruvian as updated by Leonardo. This body image is fixed, eternal, and universal, like the Hitchcock character Miss Torso. Once it is accepted, there is no reason to give the theme another thought. The designer is free to play with variations: palette, pattern, fabric, texture, collage, degree of transparency or opacity, brilliance or subtlety of ornamental detail.

The thematic approach allows the curators to display Mr. Armani's own sense of historical awareness. Thus we come to a set of black dress variations, elaborate gowns said to be inspired by the mourning dress of the late Victorians. All this bombazine, just because the beloved Albert died? Get over it, Queenie.

The German philosopher Walter Benjamin wrote that the architecture of the city is experienced through peripheral vision and should be analyzed and discussed as a fleeting, mercurial art. You could say as much about fashion, particularly as it is encountered on the runway or the street. When I heard about Mr. Wilson's plan for the scrims, I was afraid he would sacrifice one of the Guggenheim's glories: the opportunity to experience art on the periphery, across the atrium space, on several levels at once.

In fact, Mr. Wilson's design enhances this wonderful effect. You can't see the costumes in any detail, of course, but you can discern their colors and shapes, and these glimpses are as tantalizing as a model's runway turn, or a stranger admiring her reflection in a window. And when you arrive at the shapes, peripheral vision may not be enough. I am thinking, for example, of a group of costumes on the third level, with beaded floral and arabesque motifs on see-through netting. Plan to be there when Mr. Galasso's sound track segues into sitar music. You do not need spiritual austerities to enter into a contemplative state: here every possible organic and geometric shape seems to rise up from a cosmic soup, then dissolve back into it.

Another rhythm plays counterpoint to the shift between close-up and periphery: a continuous alteration between art and commodity. Some of Mr. Armani's fabrics made me want to burst into tears, like Daisy

Buchanan. They have an emotional power similar to art. The next minute I'd be thinking, "But I could own one of these pieces!" They're within human range. So it goes; admire, covet, admire, covet, round and round the room.

The men's sportswear, a quilted leather jacket in particular, brought back memories of when I first became aware of fashion and would fantasize over pictures in *l'Uomo Vogue*. Now, at fifty-two, I could dress in mourning for a fantasy that I never pursued. I've lived my whole life the wrong way!

On the androgyny question: I am not young. And I did live in London in the days of Ossie Clark and the Chelsea Cobbler. But I must say that no one at my end of the world ever made much fuss over gender differences in dressing. For those of us who buy dress shirts from Brooks Brothers, jeans from Levi Strauss, and T-shirts from wherever, gender is a nonstarter. So the surprise, for me, is that Mr. Armani's clothes are remarkably gender-specific. Can anyone living recall a time when suits for women looked weird? And the guy clothes are for guys: leathers, rich wools, the suits we once called Continental.

Gender differentiation takes its toll on the visitor's concentration. Toward the top of the spiral, the men thin out and disappear. One misses them: the contrast between girls and guys below helps to keep one's attention focused. And a guy doesn't feel quite welcome at this gathering of ball-gowned sorority sisters unless he's carrying a corsage.

Into the two side galleries. One gallery on celebrity. Strangely dowdy after the Rotunda's grand promenade. Half the Oscar nominees look as if they want to play Amanda Wingfield. All of them could get a lift from a commentary by Joan Rivers. The gallery's shoe-box proportions are unsympathetic to Mr. Armani's Vitruvian ideal. It's weird to see a Ricky Martin outfit without the navel showing, like a temple sculpture without the ruby in its third eye.

Second side gallery: the spring-summer 2000 collection. It is best left to fashion critics. The atmosphere here is too much like a boutique for my comfort. The great thing about fashion shows in museums is that you get to examine the merchandise without salespeople making you feel like dirt. In this gallery, the museum guards come off as maximum-strength floorwalkers.

Now I get to have my Savanarola moment. I'm not going to beat up on the Guggenheim for doing what all museums have been doing since the dawn of time. There never has been a fixed border between cultural institutions and private enterprise. The boundary has always been fluid. For more than a decade, it has been under intense renegotiation, in part to compensate for diminished public financing for the arts. Narcissism should be part of this discussion, too.

As I hope I've made clear, I respect fashion, I respect Mr. Armani's artistry, and I think the show looks great. I think it's grand to display fashion in an art museum. But showing fashion in a museum is one thing. Importing fashion-world values into a museum's decision-making process is something else. The transferral of those trade values is not grand at all.

Historical amnesia, intellectual pretension, cronyism, promotion, delusion, sycophancy, bribery, betrayal, all wrapped up in press releases passed off as journalism: these are some of the lubricants that make the wheels of fashion turn. If you enjoy the fashion spectacle, you wouldn't want to miss one treacherous moment. In the Eastern spirit of the Armani show, you could even say that such ugliness makes the beauty possible. In any case, it's not against the law.

Museums, however, are not commercial institutions, even if they sometimes behave otherwise. Museums may, of course, be swayed by intellectual fashions. This is not in itself objectionable, or even avoidable. The British Museum has reconsidered its display of the Elgin Marbles several times over the years, and the evolution of taste illustrated by these alterations is itself of cultural interest. Intellectual fashion may be healthy for a living cultural institution. The values of commercial fashion, however, are not. Commercial fashion, like any business, depends on smoothness: on greasing the wheels of designers, their investors, the fashion press, celebrity clients, and retail advertisers. The credibility of museums depends on traction: on their ability to resist the smoothness of the market system.

Museums don't need that traction to get publicity, attract crowds, and even put on worthwhile shows. Without it, however, there's nothing particularly special about them apart from the cachet of their names. I could live without the cachet. If traction isn't available, I'll settle for candor. I would prefer it if the Guggenheim came out and said: "We need the money! We want to fix up the Dogana in Venice and we need $15 million! You got a problem with that?" This would at least be an ethical stance, if not a noble one.

This is where the Armani show's theme of self-absorption becomes a metaphor for the predicament of many cultural institutions today. Those who want to import fashion values into the art world don't get up in the morning and ask themselves, "What can I do today to sabotage civilization?" In the overlapping worlds of fashion and contemporary art, there is no shortage of pret-à-porter rationalizations for conflicts of interest. Many of them are rooted in the Romantic myth that formal training and conventional morality are the enemies of creativity and truth. We're free! Down with the old walls! We're breaking through! (Never mind that today's free spirits are aching to get into the institutions that the Romantics were trying to get out of.)

Then there's the Specialness factor. What some may see as intellectual corruption is in fact to be seen as enlightened obedience to a higher calling of profound cultural value, which critics, benighted fools, are unable to discern. Don't worry. Trust us. In the future, the truth will be revealed. Postmodern thinking is very Special in this sense. It is a fancy way of applying commercial values to art.

The truth is that we'll never know whether, without his eight-figure pledge, the Guggenheim would have mounted a retrospective on the work of Giorgio Armani. Just as we'll never know whether the Metropolitan Museum would have presented a show of Cartier jewels without financial support from the House of Cartier. Or whether the Museum of Modern Art would have devoted a show to a Ferrari without support from Ferrari. Or whether the Brooklyn Museum of Art would have presented Sensation without a check from Charles Saatchi.

The artists will never know, either, and neither will the institutions, for that matter. That's the way narcissism works. I doubt this will ruin Mr. Armani's day. Unlike Mr. Wilson's mannequins, the designer appears to have a head on his shoulders. Narcissism is his business. Enlightenment is a cultural institution's stock-in-trade. The light fades where delusion rules.

October 20, 2000

A RARE OPPORTUNITY FOR REAL ARCHITECTURE
WHERE IT'S NEEDED

We were getting a lot of mail from readers complaining that I never write about New York buildings, so my employers decided to build one. Not just any building but a work of architecture, a project with the potential to raise the quality of building in New York. Last week, when I learned that Renzo Piano had been chosen to design the new headquarters for *The New York Times*, I knew that we had such a project.

The intended site is the east side of Eighth Avenue, between Fortieth and Forty-first streets, across from the Port Authority Bus Terminal. The plan depends on the approval of the board of directors of The New York Times Company, as well as city and state permits to lease the site. Piano was chosen from among three finalists. The others were the British architect Sir Norman Foster and Cesar Pelli of New Haven. The architects of a fourth proposal, Frank O. Gehry and David Childs of Skidmore, Owings & Merrill, withdrew from the competition several weeks before the final choice was made.

The images of all four plans presented in these pages, including Piano's, are studies. The goal of the selection process was to choose an architect rather than a design. In a process like this, it is common for a proposal to undergo substantial revision after the architect is chosen. Architect and client may even decide to start again from scratch. The client is looking for a set of intangibles: a texture of thought, a feeling of compatibility, the sense that something historical has been set in motion by the first encounter.

It is too soon to evaluate Piano's design, and it will never be possible to assess what the other finalists might have done. But it is not premature to talk about some of the issues raised by the proposals, and by the selection process itself. Nor is it too soon to state that Piano has been given the chance, and unquestionably possesses the skills, to design the most important corporate skyscraper to be built in New York since Eero Saarinen's CBS Building in 1965.

I am a part of this story, a footnote who gets to tell the tale. At the invitation of Michael Golden, the vice chairman of The New York Times Company, and with the approval of my editors, I met periodically, over a six-month stretch, with the group responsible for choosing an architect for the new Times Building.

I had serious reservations about crossing the line from the News Department to the corporate side of the paper. The *Times* does not permit its critics to serve on arts juries. This policy is wise, not only because it constrains us from abusing the authority of the newspaper and from potential conflicts of interest. More important, sitting on a jury removes us from our natural habitat—the realm of ideas and values and their artistic expression—where we go in search of stories. That realm is our reality.

I am not a disengaged critic. The cultural dimension of building stirs me emotionally. I have minimal interest in personalities or politics, except as these play out on a symbolic or allegorical plane. Architecture's practical dimension is one of the things that make it exciting to write about, but the practicalities do not lack outspoken advocates. The metaphoric dimension is less easily grasped, particularly in a city like New York, which has seen so little thoughtful architecture in recent years.

This is where a critic can be useful. The symbolic level is where architecture itself kicks in. When it does, land use rises above the level of real estate speculation. Buildings earn the space they occupy on other than economic terms. Defining those terms is what a critic does. More important, his job is to insist that those terms, while not quantifiable, are as substantial as the materials from which buildings are made and the money it costs to build them. My job is to say: Architecture is real. Over the months, I had ample opportunity to do my job. I also learned about factors that have eroded New York's status as a city where serious architecture is possible.

The selection of an architect for the Times Building was conducted as a fifty-fifty partnership between The New York Times Company and Forest City Ratner, a real estate development firm whose projects include Metrotech, the office complex in downtown Brooklyn. The Times Building will be slightly under seven hundred feet, or forty-five stories, tall. The lower half of the tower will be occupied by the paper's newsroom, its business division, and corporate offices. Space in the top half will be leased to outside tenants. A six-story base will include an atrium for shops and restaurants and an auditorium for lectures, forums, and other public events. Forest City plans to occupy one floor of office space. The *Times* assumed primary responsibility for selecting an architect.

I attended meetings of the Design Advisory Group, composed of staff members of the *Times* and Forest City Ratner, occasionally joined by representatives of the Forty-second Street Redevelopment Authority, a subsidiary of the Empire State Development Corporation, and of the Economic Development Corporation, a city agency. A smaller group was designated to arrive at a consensus on the final choice.

I'm not going to report on what transpired behind closed doors. Here I want to sort out some thoughts that occurred to me in the course of looking at the four finalists' designs. At the last meeting I attended, when there was movement to revive a proposal that had been previously passed over, someone present observed aloud that we seemed to be on shifting ground. I felt I had been on shifting ground the entire six months.

In fact, architecture itself is always on shifting ground. Architects try to pin down ideas that are floating in the cultural atmosphere, chief among them, perhaps, the evolving relationship of self to community in a modern democracy. There's nothing inherently stable in that relationship, or in the processes architects and clients use to articulate it in urban space.

The guidelines for the selection process were prepared by the client partners and presented in impressively large, handsome books. The guidelines struck me as a road map to mediocrity. In the criteria for evaluating previous work of the firms being considered, "architecture" was folded in with objective standards, like whether a firm produces works within budget and has extensive experience with skyscraper design. The truth is that architecture can't be quantified. And to judge from recent additions to the New York cityscape, prior experience with skyscraper design struck me as possible grounds for disqualification.

Architecture, meanwhile, was defined as "compatible/compelling design vocabulary." If compatible meant contextual, this standard was an open invitation to all kinds of mischief. Architecture should contribute to, rather than fit in with, its surroundings. Compelling, besides being generally incompatible with compatible, suggested to me a standard of formal values more suitable for architectural photography and rendering than for architecture itself. The concept is oblivious of the relational values from which architecture is made: of outside to inside; top to bottom; structure to expression; content to form.

Somehow, however, we got from that unpromising start to a stunning outcome. Renzo Piano's design embodies those relational values, and others, in radiant form.

Piano, who has offices in Genoa and Paris, is the world's greatest living practitioner of what I call "normative" architecture. Others call it "the classical humanist tradition," which sounds more dignified. But why not just come out and say it? He's Italian.

Piano's aesthetic is as much urban as it is architectural. All Italians know that when you get a bit of money, you do something to ornament the city. You put up a church, create a nice civic square, commission a statue. Then, when the money goes away, the church is still standing. The statue remains. As Piano mentioned to me, "Even when people are poor, they don't have to live in a poor way." They still have the richness of their surroundings. He has brought that philosophy to projects in Berlin, Paris, Sydney, and other centers of cosmopolitan life.

We're at the crest of a building boom in New York. The city is feeling very rich. But with a few exceptions—Columbus Center, the Rose Earth and Space Center at the American Museum of Natural History, LVMH Tower—I see few buildings that will be worth preserving for the future. In fact, if it were possible to cancel most of the current construction, the world would be a better place. The 1980s, too, were a time of vast mediocrity. What Piano brings to the job, apart from his talent, is a deeply ingrained sense of civic responsibility, a conviction that the *Times* must give back, through architecture, the good fortune it has enjoyed.

I don't want to make too much about Piano's Renaissance humanist lineage. He lives in different times. Nonetheless, he shares with Michelangelo, da Vinci, and Brunelleschi the belief that art and science exist within the same cultural continuum. This idea has been evident from the first building that brought Piano wide recognition: the Pompidou Center in Paris, designed in collaboration with Richard Rogers and completed in

1977. Controversial when new, the exoskeletal structure set off a debate that helped make it the most visited tourist attraction in Paris. For the Times project, Piano will employ new techniques in structural engineering, vertical circulation, and curtain wall construction, in association with Fox & Fowle, the architects of the Condé Nast and Reuters buildings in Times Square.

I see the Times project, in its present form, as a work of urban landscape. The building's base, which Piano describes as Baroque, is made of concrete slabs that float, at eleven different levels, around three sides of a central atrium. The programming of this space needs work. The Baroque idea (to draw people in) is valid. Once there, people should experience something beautiful. Current renderings, however, show something like a media mall, in a Fun Palace configuration that recalls the work of the British architect Cedric Price from the 1960s. There is too little contrast with the city outside.

Anyone who has gone for a ride on the Pompidou's escalator knows that Piano is a great poet of circulation. Now he is playing with ways to organize the tower's elevators. Instead of a central elevator core, he prefers a side arrangement that would give office floors the spaciousness of a piazza. What I'm waiting for, however, is to see how he plans to connect the building to the Eighth Avenue subway and Port Authority station. The connection could turn the tower into an infrastructural midtown gateway.

Piano has planned additional landscape features for two upstairs levels. He envisions the roof of the base as the site for a water park, a shallow pool that would reflect the tower on its surface and bounce sunlight back up onto the tower's skin. This poetic device could become a setting for instant squalor, not to mention a source of leaks. There will be a garden on the roof, protected by extensions of the glass curtain wall above the building envelope.

What is New York's cityscape about? Escaping gravity and heaviness without losing touch with the ground. The Brooklyn Bridge, Central Park, the Seagram Building, and other New York landmarks embody this idea. For the Times tower, Piano has designed a triple-skin wall that lifts the material city's grid into a metaphysical realm. A thermal wall of double-pane panel is shielded on the exterior by a sunscreen of white ceramic rods. These last are interrupted at eye-level by bands of fixed, slender blinds. Inside the offices, movable blinds or shades will increase the layers to four.

Piano has used this system before, usually in combination with orange masonry panels. Here, the metal, glass, and ceramic surface will shimmer without interruption across the entire expanse of wall. Indentations at the corners will allow the expression of the walls as independent planes. This effect will be heightened by the extension of the glass high above the roof line.

Piano uses terms like *vibration, breathing,* and *magic* to describe what he calls the "immaterials" of architecture. It is with these qualities that the reality of his architecture resides. But he comes from a family of builders. And he works within a tradition of close collaboration between architects and those who fabricate their work. He reminds us that the term *design* originated in the Renaissance with the Italian word for "drawing." The concept signified the architect's emergence as a specialist apart from building. From it, we derive the conception of architecture as the meeting ground for matter and mind. Piano will invite New York to revisit that ground.

Cesar Pelli designed a perfect bull's-eye for those who can't help enlisting the *Times* as a target for resentment. Pelli is the house architect of the monoculture, a designer of iconic corporate towers that bear less relationship to their surroundings than to other corporate icons around the world. To create these, he often borrows forms from the iconography of ancient authoritarian regimes. At the World Financial Center in Battery Park City, for example, the four towers are variously crowned with a pyramid, a ziggurat, a dome, and a mastaba.

Pelli's use of these symbols reflects the formalist idea that they have been cleansed of their original meanings by subsequent usage and can now be appreciated as abstract geometric shapes. I never bought this idea, and Pelli's design for Petronas Towers in Kuala Lumpur, based as it is on regional motifs, suggests that Pelli himself is prepared to abandon it when he chooses. In any case, the triumph of formalism was never so complete that viewers aren't free to locate meanings even where the architect chooses to deny them.

For the Times proposal, Pelli selected the obelisk, that most ancient authoritarian symbol. Since its appearance in ancient Egypt, the obelisk has been recontextualized many times over. Its meaning has changed in each context. In Baroque Rome, it represents the triumph of the Christian church over pagan superstition. In Washington, it is a tribute to the symbolic founder of the first modern democracy. In New York, it is the archetypal skyscraper, a sign of material aspiration.

But we are living in a time when our liveliest minds are engaged in challenging forms of authority and the codes that represent it. Hierarchy, paternalism, control: visual symbols cannot, after all, be detached from the power relationships that govern social behavior. Indeed, globalization, and its monocultural effects, have made it ever more urgent to reject the idea that symbols can be used as purely abstract forms. It is an assertion of social and artistic responsibility to insist that forms have meanings.

One of the things we know about the monoculture is that it is protean. Its appearance constantly morphs. This mutability diverts attention from the fact that the underlying economic power relationships remain the same. Pelli's design, for example, draws from a recent avant-garde preoccupation with folded planes. This motif has appeared in the work of Peter Eisenman and others. A high-style French version of it materialized in New York last year in Christian de Portzamparc's glass facade for the LVMH Tower on Fifty-seventh Street.

Pelli has regularized the folded plane motif, and in doing so turned its meaning into the opposite of that intended by architects associated with this motif. Others have used the folded plane to challenge classical notions of hierachy. Pelli's obelisk affirms them. It is symmetrical. It is without scale. The pattern of its window mullions is nearly identical throughout. From top almost to bottom, it is an authoritarian object.

On the ground floor, the motif changes. The obelisk rests on a "happy face" base of retail shops. This, too, is part of the monocultural structure. Buy a pair of khakis. Consume the festival atmosphere. Literally support what some might call your oppressors, the folks who peer down from the structure's upper floors.

I was disheartened by the inclusion of Pelli among the finalists. Evidently, my message about the reality of architecture wasn't getting through. I could accept that this slick corporate object might represent a developer's view of the *Times*. I could not accept that it represented the paper's view of itself. Yes, the *Times* is a powerful institution, but of a particular kind. It is not part of so-called black car culture. We take subways. The newsroom reaches daily toward the Enlightenment ideals of free speech and independent inquiry, however imperfectly. The newsroom itself, as well as its coverage of news, has been powerfully affected by debates over authority that have unfolded in architecture and throughout the culture. The paper has the responsibility to challenge and correct, not blindly affirm, the corporate world's view of itself.

Pelli's obelisk stood as aloof from these issues as it did from the site's physical context. Aloofness, in fact, is what clients hire Pelli to provide. This arm's-length attitude extends to Pelli's relationship to his own buildings. The architect, an agreeable man, likes to tell potential clients that, in his native Spanish, *pelli* means "skin," and thus he naturally came to think of the building skin as the essence of architecture. He leaves most of the rest to specialists in other fields.

It is true that there are many historical precedents for emphasizing facade design over space and structure. It is also true that Mr. Pelli has designed some attractive building skins. But the thing to bear in mind is that the equation of architecture with building skins is what most developers want to believe. They want the image of architecture without the expense and inconvenience of the real thing. Pelli provides that image for people whose interest lies in denying architecture's reality. This denial goes far toward explaining why New York architecture is in such bad shape. Why go through this process to end up with more of the same?

Norman Foster also creates power fetishes, but they are unquestionably works of architecture. Their elegance is mathematical as well as aesthetic. Sir Norman Foster thinks holistically. He gets his mind around structure, space, program, and image, making of them an integrated system. He turns problem solving into art. And he is acutely responsible to the well-being of those who inhabit his buildings.

His proposal for the Times Building didn't work for the clients, who saw it as not sufficiently flexible to accommodate the building's lease tenants. The design is a space frame in the shape of a right triangle. Along the hypotenuse, winter gardens were planned at intervals of seven stories. Each seven-story segment was conceived as a village in a vertical urban stack. The effect was an apotheosis of the New York setback.

The combination of three (sides) and seven (floor intervals) illustrates the mystical-mathematical fascination of Foster's work. What I liked best about this plan was the implied shapes that would result if the triangle were multiplied. Double, turn upside down, and you get a rectangular solid. Double this, and you arrive at a square. Viewers may well have perceived these ghost shapes in the midtown context.

Anyone who is less than 100 percent enthusiastic for a Foster building in New York must feel like the ingrate of all time. I prize few qualities higher than rational thought. But I don't fully trust its architectural expression. My generation was strongly influenced by Robert Venturi's 1966 book, *Complexity and Contradiction in Architecture*. We came to appreciate the nonstraightforward, the hybrid, the slightly deranged. Some of also us came to suspect that pure rationality too often serves to mask a highly irrational will to power.

At my last meeting with the group, someone asked which of the four proposals I preferred. I replied that if I were in their shoes, I would find it painful to choose between Piano and Gehry/Childs. The two teams had not designed equally good versions of the same thing. They had designed two different things. Two entirely different beasts. One rational and classic, the other Romantic and Gothic. Unlike the nineteenth-century critics who debated which style was best, we know that classical and Gothic represent more than different tastes. They correspond to different mental faculties, the right and left sides of the brain. Yet Piano's design is clearly sensuous, and Gehry/Childs's design incorporates the classicism of the International Style.

The truth is, I was madly in love with the Gehry/Childs proposal. Gehry's work will do that to you. It doesn't want you to keep your distance. From the outset, Gehry had told the clients he intended to design them "an object of desire." He and Childs made good on the promise. As I sit here, I'm looking at a six-inch-tall glass model of their design. Am I a masochist, or what?

I will have the opportunity to write about the Gehry/Childs proposal next May, when models and sketches of it will be part of the Gehry retrospective at the Solomon R. Guggenheim Foundation. I need the distance, after all. For now, my attraction to it is based on my preoccupation with dualisms, on the cultural as well as the psychological plane. I believe collaboration between "name" architects is the wave of the future. The Gehry/Childs plan was a true collaboration, by two outstanding architects of different cities, skills and outlooks, who between them produced a major miracle.

There has been speculation about why the Gehry/Childs team withdrew. Mine is that the proposal was defeated by the very factors that made it great: the attempt to create a shared reality from four different points of view. However much they may have agreed on economic and practical matters, the *Times* and the developers represented two cultures. This made for unusual discussions with all the teams but Pelli's, who alone among the four finalists has embraced with something like passion the pragmatics of commercial real estate development. With the Gehry/Childs proposal, the structure changed shape. What was, in effect, a three-way conversion was enlarged to four. The lines of communication increased exponentially.

Partnerships between two firms are common in architecturally ambitious projects. Usually, however, tasks are divided between a signature, so-called design architect and an executive architect, reponsible for more detailed drawings and other construction documents. This will be the arrangement between Renzo Piano Building Workshop and Fox & Fowle. The Gehry/Childs team, however, was not usual. The two firms had to devise novel ways to implement a pioneering arrangement. They, too, represented two cultures. The clients had to believe that the arrangement between them could work in practical terms.

Could four cultures intertwine? Where would the design work be done? Would the architects' two staffs get along? Would David Childs feel overshadowed by Frank Gehry? Would there be overlap between tasks? Would this affect fees? The share value of *Times* stockholders? Who would be in charge? Would the curtain wall work? Could the clients accept that, under any circumstances, architecture cannot be achieved by relying on standard real estate procedures? Given the ambition of this proposal, and the city's virtual innocence of all things architectural for many years, such obstacles to realization were inevitable.

Another factor must be confronted. Its name is love. In a 1959 essay on "The Sublime and the Good," Iris Murdoch writes: "Art and morality are, with certain provisos, one. Their essence is the same. Love is the perception of individuals. Love is the extremely difficult realization that something other than oneself is real."

Frank Gehry has always insisted that to do his best work, he needs a close relationship with a strong client. What he is really saying is that he needs a client's love. This is not a diva thing that suddenly came over him when he became the It Architect. To judge by a 1969 interview about the client-architect relationship, published in *Designers West*, Gehry has been saying the same thing all along. His job is to empathize with the client's reality. He expects the same.

It has always been clear that Gehry packs emotion into his work. What is less apparent is that much of this emotion emanates from his relationship to the client. In the case of the Times project, Gehry believed that he had demonstrated his affection for the paper by entering a competition in the first place (something he no longer does), by devoting much time, money, and energy to the design (the Gehry/Childs design was the most highly developed of the four), and by producing a work that differs substantially from the Bilbao Museum and is in no sense inferior to it.

Gehry felt that his feelings were not reciprocated. This I understand completely. I once offered my resignation here for the simple reason that I felt I wasn't appreciated in proportion to the energy I was putting in. I was wrong, and so was Gehry. From the day he and Childs presented the project at 229 West Forty-third Street, the tide of opinion began to shift in their direction.

For me, this shift was the most extraordinary part of the process. Just a week before, the clients had regarded Gehry with suspicion, as someone who might produce something unacceptably funny, weird, or arbitrary. By the time the presentation was over, roughly half the people present had psychologically moved into the building. (Or so indicated a poll that was taken shortly thenafter.) In fact, there is a great deal of passion circulating through 229 West Forty-third Street. But the *Times* does not typically wear its heart on its sleeve. And I suspect that any developer's "due dili-

gence" procedures are about as tender and heartwarming as a visit from
the IRS.

This episode brings to mind a poem of Auden's:

> *If you see a fair form, chase it*
> *And if possible embrace it,*
> *Be it a girl or boy.*
> *Don't be bashful: be brash, be fresh.*
> *Life is short, so enjoy*
> *Whatever contact your flesh*
> *May at the moment crave:*
> *There's no sex life in the grave.*

But is this lusty philosophy suitable for what is still widely thought of
as the newspaper of record?

Great buildings break rules. Piano will give us something subtler, more
refined—more normative—than the design conceived by Gehry and
Childs. Yet I'm confident that Piano's will be great. Since the 1970s, the
reigning law in New York building has been: thou shalt not commit architecture here. That rule will now be shattered by Piano—with luck, beyond
repair.

October 22, 2000

A RATIONAL VISION THAT LETS
YOU KNOW WHO'S BOSS

The new United States Courthouse and Federal Building in Central Islip,
New York, designed by Richard Meier & Partners, brings to mind those
guided visualizations in which we are instructed to imagine our parents
growing infinitesimally small. The objective of this mental exercise is not
to bump off the parents but to render them within the emotional scale of
the child's empathic power. Richard Meier's courthouse has a similar
effect. Topping off at twelve stories, the building is not small; in recent
summers, Fire Island vacationers have watched it nearing completion
across the water. But compared with Meier's Olympian Getty Center, the
courthouse is a bagatelle. We have to readjust the scale of our mental landscape to take it in. In doing so, we restore Meier to the human scale of his
contemporaries.

The building is white, the ground it sits upon is flat. Whiteness and flatness, along with scale, are the critical factors for which adjustments must be made. You will recall that the Getty is only intermittently white. Meier's signature color cannot be seen from beneath its hilltop site. Much of the complex is clad in split-faced travertine. Metal panels, long stretches of them, are finished with dull tan enamel, ostensibly to protect the center's Brentwood neighbors from glare. Thus one greets the Islip courthouse with a welcome-home salute.

It is good to have Richard Meier back on terra firma. But the world has changed since he ascended to Getty heaven. In 1986 it was barely possible for American architects to think in nineteenth-century terms of a grand historical mainstream, late modern or postmodern, as the case might be. By the time the '90s rolled around, the evaporation of the historicist mainstream had become too obvious to deny. One time line does not fit all. The individual architect's capacity to embrace an entire cultural moment was diminished by this realization. Instead, to paraphrase Apollinaire, even (or especially) buildings designed by parent figures had come to resemble gestures in the solitudes.

The suburban setting of the courthouse amplifies the contemporary architect's isolation. The building, designed in association with the Spector Group of North Hills, New York, rises near the middle of a three-zone, linear landscape strip: one outer edge is the Great South Bay, facing Fire Island. The other is suburban development. Down the middle runs the classic black and green sandwich of the American parkway: the Long Island Expressway, bordered on either side by shallow foliage screens. To see the courthouse at its best, organize a summer day with a clear blue sky and keep your eyes peeled as you approach the Central Islip exit. Rising above the leaves, with the sky outlining its crisp silhouette, the building is a car culture apparition, a fulfillment of Frank Lloyd Wright's seventy-year-old prophecy of the decentralized metropolis that we now call urban sprawl.

With a Richard Meier building there is always a subtle tension between functional expression and sculptural articulation. Once you know how the building works programmatically, you can read its interior organization from without. But on first approach, the eye is enticed by the play of abstract forms. We see walls, of course, along with windows, an entrance, and a roof, all clearly denoted. But the functional clarity is upstaged by Meier's formal vocabulary, a fusion of Le Corbusier and de Stijl. Cone, curve, slab, fin, grid, and other strong geometric shapes are arranged with heroic confidence. The scale of the Islip courthouse compels us to acknowledge afresh Meier's genius for composition. That is the building's greatest gift.

Here the abstract dimension is heightened by the broad plaza from which the courthouse rises. Slightly elevated, admirably bare, this podium is a void space that precedes the formal and functional differentiation into plaintiffs and defendants, judges and judged. And what a great performance space for high school marching bands, baton twirlers, beauty contests, and marathon country bake-offs.

The main facade has the look of the most elegant appliance manufactured this side of the Rhine valley. Projecting forward from the building envelope, the facade frames the stacked upper floors on which twenty-four courtrooms are lodged. Glazed, and finely tuned with window mullions and shallow sunscreens, it is a light, airy version of Le Corbusier's concrete sunscreens. A structural wall, clad with flat gray stone, sets off the slight bow curve and the transparency of the facade.

The courthouse is cross-axial in plan. The major axis, which runs perpendicular to the main facade, contains three ceremonial spaces of imposing gravity. The first of these, which projects into the plaza, is held within an immense white cone of cooling-tower contour that recalls Le Corbusier's truncated dome for the General Assembly Building in Chandigarh, India, the capital of Punjab. Within is a soaring rotunda, a luxury of space seldom seen in government buildings since the '40s. This assault on the tyranny of low ceilings rises 190 feet from floor to skylight. Its function is metaphysical: to capture and dramatize the changing light of day.

The abstract immensity of the space invites multiple readings. It is an offering to the idea of Justice as a concept without which modern democracy could not function. Its abstraction is a reminder that we are governed by laws, not men. (This last principle extends, alas, to the putty-colored smoke detectors that mar the rotunda's otherwise flawless white volume; they have apparently been installed to prevent architecture as well as smoking.) On a less reassuring level, the baroque amplitude of the space overwhelms the visitor with the power of the state and its bureaucracy. In this enveloping whiteness, Long Island melancholics will undoubtedly feel guilty until proven innocent.

The sinister dimension thickens in the second of the ceremonial spaces, a tall box of an atrium that also reaches the full height of the building and gives visual access to the floors above. This is the courthouse's main space, the center of its cross-axial composition. The space is rationalized Piranesi: a cell block without cells. This impression derives from the balconies that connect the two wings of the cross-axis, where the courtrooms are located. Gray stone augments the shadows in the white arrangement. Neutral rather than abstract, it is a place of echoes, footfalls, and discreet surveillance.

From here we ascend one level to the last stop on the ceremonial axis: a large courtroom to be used primarily for civic events. Here the industrial aesthetic of the public areas gives way to wood-paneled walls and plush green carpeting. The room is awesome but not scary. Personally, I would like to see Judge Judy glaring down from the bench, but in fact the hall will be used for high-profile court cases and swearing-in ceremonies for new American citizens.

If they don't behave, they could end up back in the atrium. This is the dispatch center for the courtrooms upstairs. Television monitors announce case, time, and court part: now boarding for personal bankruptcy. Upstairs, the courtrooms are placed between two circulation corridors, one of them for lawyers, plaintiffs, and witnesses; the other, glass-enclosed, for judges and administrative staff. From the balconies, we can recognize the tripartite organization of the building's entire plan—three ceremonial spaces; three zones of functional space—and comprehend the expression of both function and ceremony on the three-part, asymmetrical facade.

White building. Black robes. Philosophically and aesthetically, it's a match. If someone has to play the daddy in American architecture today, I'm glad it's Richard Meier. He sits in judgment on himself. Too harshly, in fact. This much is evident in the strict separation Meier enforces between his buildings and his sculptures, cast-metal compositions fashioned from the wood cuttings he retrieves from the floor of his model shop. Architecture is rational; art is intuitive. This is the implicit message of that separation.

The validity of the message is in dispute. This was the issue raised by the nearly simultaneous completion of the Getty Center and Frank Gehry's Guggenheim Museum in Bilbao, Spain. Faced with the contrast between these two extraordinary structures, people were tempted to ask, Why should architecture restrict itself to rationality? Why can't buildings benefit from the intuitive faculty associated with art?

I have long wanted to see Meier turn one of his sculptures into a megastructure or a vertical city. The result could be glorious, and in fact I think with the Getty it very nearly happened. The great thing about the Getty is it takes reason to such an extreme of scale that it becomes a form of folly. When the model for the project was unveiled some years back, what we beheld was something out of Borges: an obsession with logic had turned into its opposite, a labyrinth that defied logical comprehension. The completed project has the same effect.

The courthouse invites similarly perverse interpretations. A few weeks before the courthouse opened, I had a conversation with Leonard D. Wexler, senior judge of the United States District Court for the Eastern District, who is, in effect, the building's client. He mentioned that some of his constituents would have preferred a more conservative building. Risking contempt of court, I replied that Meier is a very conservative architect. Both of us were right. Without the spine of the historicist mainstream, architects can no longer enforce a particular interpretation of their forms. And if this building can be called progressive, that is because it projects into the present the deep space of historical memory: the space of Piranesi, and of the neoclassical architects directly influenced by him— like the designers of the Capitol building in Washington, for example, the place where laws are made and bent.

I doubt very much that Meier has sought to evoke the darker recesses of Piranesian space, the dim corners explored by Freud, Kafka, Borges, Foucault, Rem Koolhaas, Tim Burton, Ridley Scott, and others. Still, Meier can't remove himself from a history that has repeatedly plunged modern civilization into the Enlightenment's deepest shadows. No highway, no plaza, no white veneer can insulate any building from the connotations evoked by its forms.

We can't not know that some expressions of order are motivated by thoroughly irrational desires for control. What's so rational about cars, highways, or suburbs? The courthouse invites the ambiguous, Surrealist reading of Goya's famous etching *The Sleep of Reason Produces Monsters.* Reason can be a form of sleep in which monsters are commanded to appear.

November 19, 2000

LINCOLN CENTER'S NEXT BIG PRODUCTION: ITSELF

Fewer and fewer things are not television. The dwindling list includes music, dance, theater, opera, movies, and architecture. All six of these holdouts against post-civilization can be seen struggling for their lives at Lincoln Center for the Performing Arts. The arts complex itself is a grand artistic synthesis—an opera, or *Gesamtkunstwerk*, in Wagner's term—of pre-electronic communications. Nightly, it stages a meta-performance by artists, audiences, and the physical settings that allow contact between them in public space.

In the interest of survival, the settings are about to be remade. Lincoln Center is in the planning stage of a project that will result in the overhaul of its theaters and public spaces and perhaps even the replacement of some of them. The project could cost up to $1.5 billion and take a decade to complete. Lincoln Center officials hope to present a plan by early summer.

Bigger lobbies. More rehearsal space. Comfortable dressing rooms and offices. These are on the reasonable wish lists of Lincoln Center's constituent companies. There is also talk of building a second opera house on the site of Damrosch Park, perhaps with a revenue-producing office tower rising above it. They can build up, down, front and sideways, but space is limited in all directions. There is no excuse, however, to set limits on architectural imagination. Not in a place dedicated to art.

Much has changed in the decades since Lincoln Center was built: the needs of the resident companies; the city's scale; its relationship to the world; the sources of its native cultural vitality; its economic shift from an industrial to a cultural base; and the impact of mass media on traditional forms. The reconstruction is an opportunity to reckon with these changes, not just forms and functions but the ideas behind them. Even if the visible changes amount to minor alterations (and this is not likely), these should be informed by full awareness of the transformations in urban life.

Above all, the project should be seen as a civic exercise in self-evaluation. Like the plans now being developed for the Con Edison site on the East River edge of midtown Manhattan and the proposal to host the Olympic Games in 2012, the Lincoln Center project is an opportunity to refocus the city's image by architectural means. I have neither prescriptions nor proscriptions to offer Lincoln Center's decision makers on the aesthetic direction their plans should take. I suggest only that they follow the advice of the architectural historian John Summerson and "sort out those aging ideas that get encrusted around past creative achievement and clog the proper workings of the imagination in changing times."

Recently a friend sent me a photograph of Lincoln Center under construction. If you squint, the site looks like an ancient ruin: a Dionysian festival district, perhaps, dug up on Mediterranean shores. What I want to do here is conduct a kind of archaeological expedition: to dig up other fragments from the ethos that produced Lincoln Center, in the belief that its officials will want to build on an awareness of what they have.

I will hunt around, especially, for shards from the imagination of Philip Johnson, the second-youngest of the architects who led the Lincoln Center project and, with Max Abramovitz, one of the two living members of the group. His role exceeded those of the others. He was architect of the New York State Theater, the most successful of the theaters; he designed the main plaza, and he prepared the site plan for the buildings that surround it. His work reveals the shifting values of the period that produced Lincoln Center.

When the complex was built, architects of major civic projects typically took a blank-slate approach. Under the aegis of urban renewal, they swept away vast tracts of cityscape to create a clean surface for their designs. Lincoln Center is a monument to the tabula rasa way of doing

things. Those days are long gone. Instead there are landmarks laws to protect entire districts from demolition, and community boards who demand
that new buildings emulate the appearance of old ones. Architects themselves think in terms of physical context, incremental change, and historical continuity. It's possible that these are now among the aging ideas to be
sorted out.

No part of Lincoln Center has been landmarked. Nonetheless, it is a
historic site. For better or worse, it is the mother of all performing arts
centers. It echoes with memories of great performances. And it represents
a pivotal moment in the history of architectural taste, a time when the
orthodoxies of modern architecture were beginning to crumble. In this
sense Lincoln Center stands at the threshhold of the present state of the
art. It ushered in an era of confusion that has since gone by many names:
eclecticism, pluralism, postmodernism, or the relativity of taste.

It should not be surprising, then, if even the most enlightened of Lincoln Center's officials find themselves without a fixed set of preconceptions for the redesign. They are, in effect, reaping the uncertainty sown
at Lincoln Center four decades ago. An excavation of the Lincoln Center era can uncover much about the unfolding of architecture in the
years ahead. It can also help clarify directions the designers may wish to
pursue.

Planning for Lincoln Center began in 1955. The main theaters opened
from 1962 (Philharmonic, now Avery Fisher, Hall) to 1966 (the Metropolitan Opera), with the Juilliard School arriving in 1969. Public and critical
reception of the houses and the overall complex was mixed. Lincoln Center had novelty going for it, and optimism, and these qualities were more
highly prized in architecture in the 1960s than they are today. But the
positive response they generated was offset by negative reactions to the
plan.

Many of these had to do with the basic concept of concentrating so
many groups in one place. Why should art be set apart from the city,
detached in an art zone instead of integrated into the urban fabric? This
seemed like a nineteenth-century view of art. The concept also jeopard-
ized the future of some well-known buildings and the neighborhoods they
anchored. The old Met was demolished, and Philharmonic officials hoped
that Carnegie Hall would vaporize too.

Disappointment with the design revolved largely around the idea that
the architects had retreated from the prevailing tenets of modernism—
relation of form to function and interior space; expression of structure and
materials—and instead had indulged a preoccupation with style, ornamentation, theatrical effects, and historical reference. This, too, betrayed
what many considered a nineteenth-century cast of mind, a throwback to

the days when Victorian architects concerned themselves with "the styles."

"Monumental Temporary" was one epithet applied to the result, meaning: such confused intentions could only produce an architectural muddle. This was a reasonable criticism to make according to the standards of the day. In hindsight, however, it seems more likely that the problem lay at least as much with the standards as with the buildings to which they were applied. What seemed then to be an isolated instance of confusion—a momentary lapse—turned out to be a crisis in evaluation that has persisted to the present day.

The crisis involved the relationship of form and meaning. Modern architecture initially held strongly democratic, not to say socialist, connotations. Anti-elitist, nonhierarchical, socially as well as aesthetically progressive, it signified, and was intended to foster, solidarity among artists, intellectuals, workers, builders, and patrons.

By the 1960s, however, this chain of connotations had broken. So-called Good Design had become a hallmark of elite good taste. The modern office tower was the new emblem of corporate power. And the masses did not universally take to the progressive dispensation initiated on their behalf. Many refused to accept the connection between aesthetic and social reform. Others looked toward buildings precisely as a refuge from the accelerating pace of social and technological change.

Moreover, there was a dawning awareness of the extent to which modern architecture was itself saturated with nineteenth-century thinking. It was an extension of the historicist idea that each age produced a distinctive style. Modern forms might speak of technology, but this too was rapidly becoming a dated concept, a belated reference to the industrial city of the Victorians.

For all these reasons, it was no longer possible for modern architects to maintain control over the public's interpretation of their forms. Nor was it possible to sustain the ideal of a common vocabulary for the era. The era itself was changing. What was to be signified, and by what forms?

Nowhere is the midcentury crisis more evident than in the work of Philip Johnson. In the late 1950s Johnson had yet to establish an identity as a major builder. He was best known for his Glass House in New Canaan, Connecticut, and the Museum of Modern Art sculpture garden, and as Mies van der Rohe's associate on the Seagram Building.

Because of such projects, people had pegged Johnson as a house architect for the rich and as a tastemaker for those who aspired to live like them. As such he came to represent the conflict between modernism's egalitarian ideology and its later status as an idiom for the privileged. In the 1930s, as founding director-curator of the design department at the

Museum of Modern Art, Johnson became the most energetic and influential promoter of modern architecture in the United States. After the war, he used that influence to establish modernism as the preferred image for the country's enlightened ruling class.

But by the '50s, Johnson had wearied of the Miesian aesthetic. He wrote against what he called the shibboleths and crutches of modern architecture. He argued that references to historical precedent could not be purged. He designed projects with deliberate quotations from classical architects like Ledoux. Given Johnson's tastemaker credentials, these heresies could not be dismissed as the waywardness of a single architect. They signified an erosion of the standards by which architecture had been judged and of the solidarity that had sustained them.

The New York State Theater was one of two New York projects designed by Johnson and completed in 1964. The second was the New York State Pavilion at the New York World's Fair in Flushing Meadows, Queens. (The building's rusting skeleton can still be seen en route to the airport.) Both projects were sponsored by the Rockefeller family, which had supported the Modern movement with its unparalleled fusion of social, economic, political, and cultural authority. And both departed from modernist norms.

The fair was a watershed event in the redefinition of postwar values. Critically it was a fiasco. Sophisticated people attacked it for lacking a coherent point of view, a governing aesthetic, or any larger sense of purpose apart from Robert Moses's desire to create what would later become the world's most hideous park. But if you look at old photos of the fairgrounds, you may well wonder what the carping was about.

No governing aesthetic? In fact, the whole place looks to have been planned down to the last detail just yesterday by a dream team consisting of Rem Koolhaas, Robert Venturi, and Denise Scott Brown. The clash of forms, the automated transportation systems, even the bubbular roofs of the Brass Rail restaurants: this was a preview of *Learning from Las Vegas* crossed with *Delirious New York*. In fact, the 1964–65 fair predicted the future with far greater accuracy than the 1939 World of Tomorrow had done.

But in 1964, few could have named the defining quality generated by the fair: irony. This quality was not on conspicuous display in the fair's environment. It was created in the mind of the beholder. Only an ironist would have realized that you didn't have to choose between the austere Spanish Pavilion and its kitschy Belgian cousin. Only an ironist could appreciate the installation that Jean Rosenthal designed for Michelangelo's *Pietà* in the Vatican Pavilion. The great marble sculpture looked like a novelty ice cube floating in a Trader Vic's cocktail made with blue curaçao. And why not? When else would the *Pietà* get to take a vacation from St. Peter's? Why shouldn't it want to dive into a big blue daiquiri?

The irony didn't come out of nowhere. It was an effect of the Cold War, a strategy for coping with the culture of mass consumption on which American prosperity depended. While industry was pumping out the furniture of suburban life—cars, appliances, situation comedies—modern architects were trying to keep kitsch at bay. How ironic was that for an aesthetic originally designed to represent the masses?

Perhaps alone among the fair's attractions, the New York State Pavilion captured the ironic stance. A double agent of a building, it carried dual credentials from the realms of high and low art. Technically it was a mature modern building, one that visibly expressed such structural innovations as its perimeter columns of slip-formed concrete. But these were combined with elements of pure *Populuxe* (to use Thomas Hine's nifty term): the roof of orange and blue plastic (state colors); the flying saucer observation platforms; and the rocket-pod elevators that ascended to them.

The Pavilion was a people place. Beneath the garish roof, on a plaza inscribed with a giant map of the state, there were continuous performances by youth orchestras, high school glee clubs and marching bands, pop and jazz combos, and other musical groups of less than stellar profile. The Pavilion's exterior was encrusted with works by Lichtenstein, Rosenquist, Warhol.

Warhol's *Most Wanted Men* was an American *Pietà*. The mural depicted mug shots from a 1962 FBI poster, blown up to the scale of May Day in Red Square. Painted over soon after the fair opened, it was a martyr to puritan sensitivities. The authorities feared lawsuits by families of the wanted, and there were other reasons to feel squeamish. Subliminal homoeroticism; anti-heroism; glorification of the outlaw; recognition that portraiture was alive and well in popular art.

Warhol said Pop Art was about "liking things." This idea marked a turning point in Cold War attitudes. Pop Art offered an allegory of redemption. Guilty pleasures were purified. You could like Disneyland without despising yourself. The popularity of the Belgian Pavilion was nothing to be feared. Pop culture just wanted to play with us.

Only an ironist could appreciate that Monumental Temporary was exactly what Lincoln Center wanted to be. If you had put the site on a couch and asked it to tell you its dreams, it would have said: "All my life I have secretly longed to be Monumental Temporary.

"I want glass facades and travertine walls. No diamonds, please. Give me rhinestones. Arches that look paper-thin. An opera house with Sputnik

chandeliers that rise heavenward at curtain time. A massive grand staircase
that goes nowhere. Just a place to pose on yards of red carpet. The biggest
bad Chagalls in this poor diva's world.

"And an orchestra hall with movable kite-shaped acoustical panels.
We'll call them clouds and put little lights in them. Frame the stage with
spindly gold room dividers. And if we don't like it, we can tear it down and
start all over again!"

Done!

Wallace K. Harrison, architect of the Metropolitan Opera house, knew
all about Monumental Temporary. Another beneficiary of Rockefeller
largesse, Harrison had designed the Trylon and Perisphere for the 1939
World's Fair. And his various schemes for the Met, especially those rendered by the incomparable Hugh Ferriss, could have furnished a fair
entirely on their own.

The completed building, however, is the most disappointing of Lincoln Center's theaters. The great staircase has Saarinen's fluidity of plastic
composition, but the rest of the house is dim. My sense of irony has never
sufficed to take in the Chagalls. At the Paris Opera House, Chagall's ceiling had the benefit of contrast. At the Met, the painter's murals set the
tone, and it's a bad one. Got gilt?

Johnson has described the work of those years as his ballet school period.
The term evokes Picasso's neoclassical work in the interwar years—lightly
draped maidens gamboling amid columns on Mediterranean beaches—
and Stravinsky's ballet *Pulcinella*, for which Picasso designed the sets.
There is, too, a hint of the British cult of the beautiful young man, the
Pierrot or *puer eternus* figure, and of his American devotees, including
Pavel Tchelitchew, Paul Cadmus, and, not least, Lincoln Kirstein,
founder, with George Balanchine, of the New York City Ballet, and Johnson's closest friend.

There is an erotic undercurrent at the State Theater, where the New
York City Ballet performs, that you don't find at the other houses. It flows
partly from the overt eroticism of the spectacle on stage, and also from the
amorous state of anticipation emanating from the other side of the footlights. But it is also in the architecture: the deep red and gold of the auditorium; the tactility of the bronze railings and the quilted pattern stenciled
on the balcony fronts; the awesome carnality of the Nadelman sculptures;
and the mellow, seductive lighting bounced from the promenade's gold
leaf ceiling to the room's creamy marble floor.

Johnson's abiding preoccupation at the time was the idea of procession,
the differentiation of spaces through which people pass. This was a departure from the structurally organized spaces of Mies. Procession in archi-

tecture is akin to narrative in literature. It describes the passage from an initial state of equilibrium through one or more unbalancing episodes to a heightened state of equipoise. At the State Theater, the narrative unfolds from the outdoor room of the plaza, through the spatial comprehension of the outer and inner lobbies, up the grand travertine staircases and their landings to the promenade: the outdoor plaza's dream of itself.

Auxiliary spaces—the outdoor loggia, the perimeter balconies—allow different degrees of distance from the story. Then the performance part of the narrative kicks in: stairs and corridors leading to the auditorium; the membrane of the theater walls; the Baroque organization of the seating; at last, the big gold curtain, brightly lit. The technique is strip-tease. Cultivated citizens are transformed into voyeurs by the progressive shedding of envelopes and wraps.

Beneath the wraps lay the invisible man: Balanchine. The State Theater was designed expressly for him. In the years between its opening and Balanchine's death in 1983, the theater was the brutal city's closest approximation to a temple of art. In the State Theater years, Balanchine was the last heroic figure of modern art—a bridge from Diaghilev's day to Warhol's. Since no one could predict how long he would go on choreographing, it was urgent to make oneself available to every step his company took.

The 1970s were a good time to drop out of architecture and go to dance. Architecture was being rapidly consumed by a false and corrosive polarity between history and modernity, as if one could exist without the other. It was like oxygen to observe the ease with which Balanchine circulated through time, music, styles, and sources, remaining firmly within the tradition of classical ballet while extending it toward the most advanced expressions of theatrical art to be seen on any American stage.

Formal and conceptual analogies to architecture were abundantly evident on Balanchine's stage: cantilevered construction; command of gravity; off-balance compression; music as platform; transitions from private to shared to social space. But what kept me coming back was his relationship to time, starting with the staggering amount of historical integration Balanchine poured into the training of his dancers.

Agon, choreographed in 1958 to a score by Stravinsky, is the supreme example of this. The Seagram Building was completed the following year, and the ballet's resemblance to it was evident in the absence of sets, costumes, and plot; in the positive use of subtraction (Stravinsky's silences, Balanchine's pauses); and in the illusory exposure of bodies that are in fact heavily clothed by classical technique.

The score was loosely inspired by a manual of seventeenth-century French court dances: sarabandes, galliards, and branles. This source material is scarcely discernible in the choreography, though the classical ballet vocabulary was also codified at the French court. The title *Agon* links the ballet to *Apollo* and *Orpheus*, two previous Greek-themed works, story ballets also set to Stravinsky scores.

The plot in *Agon* is abstract: it is the struggle between the music and the choreography and between the two lead dancers. Their duet, a study in the active and passive aggression in romantic pairings, illustrated Balanchine's idea that conflict is fundamental to relationships. Every New Yorker can identify with that idea. We more or less patented it as a form of social conduct.

It was difficult to leave the State Theater and face a world where architects were arguing over Classicism versus Modernism. Ballet and architecture are different art forms with different historical traditions, but artists in both fields have faced the same issue: how to look at the relationship between past and present. Balanchine and Stravinsky defined one approach to this relationship. *Classicism* and *Modernism* are just names, words, terms for some of the many strands of information that contemporary artists can feed into the future if they have the talent to use them.

Nor was it useful to hear architects debating the relative value of appealing to elite or popular taste, as if it were possible for talented architects to choose one, the other, or both. You came away from the State Theater convinced that art finds its own audience (or fails to) when artists say whatever they have to say as well as they can in the course of practice. Regarding the equal devotion Balanchine gave to crowd-pleasing spectacles and more ascetic works, Arlene Croce wrote, "If Balanchine does not discriminate among his poetic resources, why should we?" But perhaps only an artist of Balanchine's gifts can use that degree of freedom.

Architecture, too, is a performing art. Like procession, it unfolds in time as well as space. There is now an opportunity to mount a new $1.5 billion production of an act that has grown stale with age. The pivotal issue confronting the architects is the relationship between Lincoln Center and the city around it.

Forty years ago, the spatial isolation of the complex was a separation from chaos. That meaning has been lost. The cityscape has been substantially drained of its chaotic character. If anything, it is now too orderly, too homogenized, too contextual, too—suburban. For Lincoln Center to stand out now, it will have to be slightly insane. Not everyone knows how to do this.

And the relationship of forms to meanings has shifted once again. No one seriously equates classicism with popularity, or aesthetic innovation with the elite; not since Bilbao, anyhow. No one goes to cities in search of suburban values. People expect to be wowed. They know that cities have an obligation to produce culture, not just to consume it, and that architecture, our most public art even in the TV age, is the most powerful form in which that obligation can be renewed.

January 21, 2001

DEFINING BEAUTY IN SWANKY AMERICAN TERMS

The password is . . . swanky. The music to remember it by is sung by Shirley Bassey. The fleeting image is a tan young man in a white bathing suit plunging off the high board, somersaulting out of the deep blue sky into the water of a sky blue pool. Cut to shot of Sean Connery wearing a light blue terry-cloth playsuit. Anyone else would look ridiculous in such a getup, but not James Bond. He looks . . . swanky.

Any piece of architecture would look stupid if it were wearing staircases that went nowhere, ceilings with swiss cheese holes in them, and an allegorical statue salvaged from the first-class dining saloon of the S.S. *Normandie*. But somehow Morris Lapidus pulled it off. At the Fontainebleau Hotel scene of the Miami shots in *Goldfinger*, Lapidus made swiss cheese holes look . . . swanky. Maybe not Elsa Maxwell, Duke of Windsor, or lunch at the Colony swanky, but swanky as in a Madison Avenue, early-1960s view of sophisticated city life.

Swank-brand cufflinks. Swank tie clips and tie tacks. Tuxedos by After Six. There really was Something About That Aqua Velva Man. And the Fontainebleau was not to be laughed at, even if the hotel's white concave shape resembled the rim of a toilet seat. The password was swanky and swanky meant sex.

Lapidus, who died last month in Miami Beach at the age of ninety-eight, left behind a legacy of imaginative midcentury buildings and the critical controversy they swirled up. He is best known as the leading designer of Florida resort architecture in the 1950s. The Fontainebleau and Eden Roc are considered his masterpieces. He designed three hotels for Manhattan: the Summit, the Americana, and the Sheraton Motor Inn. None of them was warmly received by the city's architecture critics. The Summit, in particular, was a target for major ridicule. As such, it is a landmark in the history of taste, a monument to nomadism as a way of life.

Completed in 1961, the Summit was the first major hotel built in New York since the 1930s. The twenty-one-story slab building, curved in an S shape to squeeze more rooms onto its site, stretched halfway from Lexington to Third. The exteriors were clad in dark blue brick covered with a pattern of turquoise tile rectangles. In a city with few color buildings, the Summit's palette splashed midtown with an image of Caribbean surf.

The public rooms offered a set of theatrical variations on Latin American motifs. A Gaucho Room featured steer-head light fixtures on gold plastic walls. Curtains of wood beads greeted patrons at the entrance to the Carioca Lounge. The walls of Casa de Café were encrusted with cast stone versions of pre-Columbian sculpture. In the main lobby, transparent plastic armchairs were arrayed beneath a ceiling of golden swirls.

Lapidus was not the only modern architect to incorporate Latin motifs in postwar building. Wallace K. Harrison, for example, borrowed from the sidewalks of Ipanema in his pavement design for the extension of Rockefeller Center across the Avenue of the Americas. Alexander Girard's La Fonda del Sol, a restaurant in the Time-Life Building, was a critical as well as a popular success. But at the Summit, an entire building was infected by tropical sensuality, or at least a cartoon version of it. Critics responded as if to a threat.

"Too far from the beach." Walter McQuade's dismissal of the hotel in *The Nation* was the barb that stuck. But what if the problem was that New York itself was too close to the beach? What if New York, in fact, were itself nothing but a beach? This was the startling possibility that the Summit Hotel proposed. The city may have built up a few layers of history since the Dutch settlers landed, like the early Venetians in the Lagoon, but it was still a beach, with shifting Gold Coasts, crumbling sand castles, and gulls circling over garbage barges. What was there but puritan censure to keep the whole city from subsiding into a primitive state? Or from recognizing that we had never left it?

The conflict over Lapidus was only partly between high- and lowbrow taste. There was also a generational divide. In the 1960s everyone I knew loved Lapidus, for the same reason we loved *Goldfinger*. Both carried the seal of parental disapproval. Like Miami Beach, Lapidus stood for a certain idea of the exotic. Eroticism was part of it. Jewishness was part of it. Difference in itself is swanky. So is power. Lapidus gave us the power to see beauty where others saw trash, humor where others saw bad taste, feeling where others saw a breach in decorum. The freedom to see what you like can be potent. The young are experts at it. It is often the only power they have. Lapidus was a spring break all year round.

"Under the sidewalk, the beach." So went the famous graffito scrawled on a Paris sidewalk during the 1968 student-worker uprisings. Pleasure beckons beneath so-called civilization, in other words. If you add the word *alas* to the end of the sentence, it could serve as an epigraph for *The American Scene*, Henry James's chronicle of his travels through the eastern United States in 1904, after twenty years of living as an American abroad.

Here James depicts United States civilization as a kind of shipwreck cast up on a foreign beach, flotsam from which a culture has yet to develop.

James sets his last chapter in Florida. At the Royal Poinciana and the Breakers, two tony Palm Beach hotels, James finds the ultimate expression of what he calls "the hotel spirit," or "the hotel civilization." These are his terms for the mobile, transient, fly-by-night ethos of salesmen, tourists, and other Americans on the move. Which to James meant nearly all Americans.

But in Florida, the geographical extremity of the East Coast, James summarizes his views on beauty and why the United States has yet to produce anything worthy of the name.

Art, for James, is contingent on urbanity, and urbanity is the product of generation after generation of individuals in conflict, rubbing shoulders, squabbling, differing, and thus acquiring over time the polish of cultivated taste. Urbanity cannot flourish in a vacuum, even if the vacuum is as beautifully fashioned as the Breakers and Royal Poinciana. These palaces of consumption—and, by extension, the entire country—are no more than a clearing between ocean and jungle. At any moment, the jungle may grow back. Perhaps it has never receded.

It's astonishing to see how accurately James forecast our new turn-of-the-century condition: atomized, vacuum-packed into malls, theme parks, multiplexes, and gated communities. Yet clearly our relationship to beauty has changed. We no longer wait for beauty to appear on old-world terms. It appears, even in Europe, on American terms. On hotel terms. On the terms of transatlantic modernity that James himself helped to formulate. We love our road movies, car chases, paintings by Ed Ruscha, even our urban sprawl. We love our nomadism, in short, our ambient point of view.

The Summit Hotel was part of this change in perception. The building's critics helped make it so. Their attacks were essential for the airing of conflict on which urbanity depends. More important, they revealed sources of anxiety that are still aroused by certain forms of architecture today.

Have you been wondering, perhaps, why Frank Gehry, Rem Koolhaas, and Peter Eisenman have been criticized for maintenance problems with their buildings, while Richard Meier, Charles Gwathmey, and Norman Foster have gone relatively unscathed? I have. Buildings that are not normative, that appeal to the emotions, that find beauty in the commonplace, transgress rules of decorum that are even more rigid now than in Lapidus's time. They are all too close to the beach; too far from the rational, sensible, and orderly; too nomadic in their aesthetic sensibility. As for Philippe Starck, he's too . . . swanky.

"Great creations of taste and faith never express themselves primarily in terms of mere convenience and zeal," James wrote, "and all the waiting money and the general fury have, at the most, the sole value of being destined to be good for beauty when it shall appear." Lapidus helped us to see it.

February 4, 2001

IMAGINATIVE LEAPS INTO THE REAL WORLD

In architecture, it is always the '30s. Buildings can never be entirely divorced from social reality, since they make up a good chunk of it. Nor can they be isolated from the world of ideas. They make up a hefty slice of the intellectual sphere as well. With luck, there will always be openings for those who wish to debate whether architecture is best seen as a form of art or one of social service.

Edmund Wilson's idea of the triple thinker, a '30s concept imported from literature, offers a useful way to look at the debate. First published in 1938, *The Triple Thinkers* set forth Wilson's ideal of the writer's relationship to society. The book, a collection of essays, reflected Wilson's disenchantment with Marxism as a way of reforming society or even adequately describing it.

Wilson's triple thinkers (they include Pushkin, James, Shaw, and Flaubert, from whom Wilson borrowed the phrase) are unwilling to renounce responsibility either to themselves or to their society. They reject confinement in a private garden of self-cultivation and the frustration of political action. Instead, they seek meaning in the tensions between their inner and outer worlds. These tensions stimulate imaginative leaps into the triple thought: the work of art that functions as a moral guide.

Art for art's sake. Its antithesis (the double thought) is the dedication of art to social reform. The triple thought is the realization that beauty is not some transcendant, eternal abstraction but something that arises from historical circumstances and that can enlarge the historical awareness of an audience.

What brought Wilson's idea up again for me is the recent announcement that the Whitney Museum of American Art has hired Rem Koolhaas to work on a vision plan for the museum's future development. This is the second important commission Koolhaas has received in New York in recent months. He is already working on a plan, which will include a new building, for the cultural district now being developed in Brooklyn by Harvey Lichtenstein, chairman of the Brooklyn Academy of Music Local Development Corporation. Along with Frank Gehry's design for the

Solomon R. Guggenheim Foundation in Lower Manhattan, these projects will raise New York architecture to a level that hasn't been seen since the '60s.

No one has done more to draw architecture back to the cultural arena than Gehry and Koolhaas. The concept of the triple thinker helps explain why. The forthcoming projects by these architects will be artworks for the public exhibition of artworks. They will not help house the homeless. They may even drive up rents. But as practitioners of triple thinking, these two architects have demonstrated how the art of building can be a morally illuminating act.

Koolhaas and Gehry are both poets. The sources of their lyric gifts are unknowable. Still, when their work is set against the field of architecture today, some qualities stand out. Both, for example, have powerfully ambivalent attitudes toward authority. With Gehry, it comes from the tradition of the modern artist, with Koolhaas from the counterculture of the '60s, but the two have ended up with the same confidence in the architect's expertise.

In an interview more than thirty years ago, Gehry said: "Our architectural vocabulary is better than our clients'; our visual intellect is more highly evolved; we are the experts, and that is why we are hired. I want to provide services at the highest possible level, and to do so I have to deal with the real issues, the clearest statement of the problem uncluttered by 'How was it done before?' or 'Give them what they want' hang-ups."

These hang-ups signify social as well as architectural norms. Gehry's great gift is to present aesthetic disobedience and urban disturbance as pure exercises in social responsibility. His irregular forms evoke the heated discussion between self and society. Often, his imaginative process resembles an exchange between a piece of modern sculpture (de Kooning's *Clamdigger*, say, or Brancusi's *The Kiss*) and the rusted remains of the nineteenth-century industrial city as it morphs into the global cultural marketplace of the twenty-first.

The sculpture is a sign of subjective perception. The city stands for objective fact. Gehry's expertise is to mediate between these two conditions. Robert Rauschenberg's famous description of himself as someone who works in the space between art and life helps explain the importance this American artist has long held for Gehry. Both negotiate deals for space between imperfect selves and flawed social worlds. These spaces are dedicated to the idea of transforming both self and society.

All great modern building—from the individual monument to the vernacular urban ensemble—is the product of triple thinking. If that's an overstatement, it's still as reliable a criterion as any I can think of.

Our time is rich in triple architecture. James Ingo Freed's United

States Holocaust Memorial Museum in Washington is a masterpiece of the genre. So is Maya Lin's Vietnam Veterans Memorial. Robert Venturi and Denise Scott Brown have been triple thinking for forty years. Projects by Jean Nouvel, Philippe Starck, Elizabeth Diller and Ricardo Scofidio, Daniel Libeskind, Peter Eisenman, Thom Mayne, Ben van Berkel, and Caroline Bos, and other members of the so-called avant-garde, should also be seen as expressive interactions between the architect's creative process and his or her social contract.

As these examples indicate, triple thinking does not produce a particular set of forms or a recognizable style. What it produces is a way of thinking about relationships, on the social and the artistic plane. What it produces is disturbance.

Rem Koolhaas is the most verbally articulate triple thinker in architecture today. A book, not a building, established his reputation, the so-called retroactive manifesto *Delirious New York* reissued in 1994. The book's title fused the two halves of his dialectic. New York is the capital of advanced capitalism. In the absence of a superior analytic tool, the city demands a Marxian interpretation. Delirium, a mental disorder, invites a Freudian reading. These two schools of thought place Koolhaas on a Surrealist playing field. Most architectural games are played on this field today, in fact, even those acted out in ignorance of the boundaries. And, like some Surrealist painters, Koolhaas has the genius to make us forget where we are and know where we are at the same time. We're at once inside our minds and in a post–Cold War world, and both of these places have been damaged by history.

The Freudian history is personal, the Marxian history is social, but in both instances a diagnosis is called for. It often seems to me that the architect's task today is to shape spaces that don't make the world more diseased than it is. Koolhaas is a diagnostician who presents his findings in architectural relationships. His rendering of analysis into sensuous form gives these buildings their startlingly immediate sense of life.

Koolhaas's work has long revolved around a dialogue between Europe and the United States. In the early years, it resembled a midatlantic exchange between Mies van der Rohe and Wallace K. Harrison. Mies made light, precise, rational, reductive envelopes of space. Harrison embodied grand, iconic, theatrical gestures, like the United Nations Headquarters and the Trylon and Perisphere at the 1939 New York World's Fair. From these two figures, Koolhaas fashioned a vocabulary of spirals and grids that still informs his designs.

His house for a family in Bordeaux, for instance, is approached by a concrete driveway in the shape of a spiral. The house itself is a rethought, three-story version of Mies's Farnsworth House. The rear wall is punctured with round port-hole windows that recall Harrison's control tower at LaGuardia Airport.

New York is no longer the standard bearer of liberal conscience that it was for most of the twentieth century. No single artwork is going to change this. But imperfect social relationships are the content of the triple thinker's art.

In his study project for the Museum of Modern Art's 1997 competition to redesign its midtown campus, Koolhaas took circulation as his organizing idea. Using the new Odyssey escalator technology developed by Otis, he proposed a system for moving stairs, platforms, and rooms vertically and diagonally through interior space.

He also excised the ground floor from the existing museum, creating a slab that floated over an outdoor space extending from Fifty-second to Fifty-third streets, allowing the city to penetrate the museum envelope. Thus, the design linked the mechanized vertical transport to New York's great horizontal public space, the street.

Koolhaas's notes for the project, which have been privately published, show that he began working out these spatial relationships before arriving at the visual forms of buildings. His goal was to weaken the existing boundaries between private (the museum) and public space (the street). His design resumed the modern task of relaxing the conventions of social and psychological encounter.

You will not need *Das Kapital* or *The Interpretation of Dreams* to find your way around Koolhaas's vision plan for the Whitney. Koolhaas excels in conveying the idea that architecture is an art of organizing urban relationships, not the styling of discrete objects in space. Whether as journalist, screenwriter, teacher, or architect, he has done nothing all his life but study the differences between cities, the extent to which it is in their nature to grow and the role architects play in its unfolding. That is his area of expertise.

Yours, too, perhaps. You are invited to assign your own voices to the spatial and formal sequences Koolhaas devises. In fact, as in a classical course of psychoanalysis, you are expected to do so.

But Americans get spooked when people refer to Marx and Freud in a positive light. This is one of the joys of mentioning them. Freud and Marx! Marx and Freud! Trick or Treat! In our public discourse, one stands for the gulag and nuclear warfare, the other for quackery and the insanity defense. They're unwelcome reminders of imperfection on the golden field of success.

I see no cultural advantage in dismissing the schools of thought initiated by these thinkers. As scientific systems, political parties, substitute religions, and sources of illustrational art, they're silly or worse. But they continue to provide useful techniques for describing certain features of historical continuity. Along with the continuing debates over their ideas, Marx and Freud still figure in the cultural landscape where European architects build.

Our dismissal of them, in fact, supports the view, advanced by the London School of Economics professor John Gray, that the United States can no longer be regarded as a Western country. We've rejected the modern tradition of self-examination that holds Western societies together. It is as if freedom, equality, accountability, and other strands of social tissue have frayed beyond repair. Or, as some have put it, the United States didn't win the Cold War. We were just the second to lose it. Instead of mass famine, we've got reality TV.

February 25, 2001

A MESSAGE FROM A POET OF PUBLIC AND PRIVATE MEMORY

It should be possible to talk about an architect's state of mind without implying that his work can be reduced to a set of psychological symptoms. In the case of the new Scholastic Building, in New York's SoHo district, such a discussion may be unavoidable. The architect, Aldo Rossi, who died in 1997 at the age of sixty-six, put psychology back on the architectural map. He was also a major artist who incorporated his own temperament into his design aesthetic.

Memory, empathy, intersubjectivity—the idea that buildings can reshape the boundaries between public and private space: these ideas began with Rossi and the two books that established his reputation, *The Architecture of the City* (1966) and *A Scientific Autobiography* (1981). The Surrealist current in contemporary architecture also stems from Rossi and his attempts to render the enigmatic atmosphere of de Chirico's paintings in urban space. The Scholastic Building, one of several American projects left unfinished at his death, is the enigmatic product of a career cut short.

The children's publishing and media company building at 557 Broadway, between Prince and Spring streets, has been completed with sensitivity and devotion by Rossi's New York office, Studio di Architettura, under Morris Adjmi, who has developed many Rossi projects into buildable designs. Without question, the building is Rossi's. Its main facade resembles the brick surface of Il Palazzo, the hotel he designed in 1987 for

Fukuoka, Japan. The bright polychromy—metal painted red, white, and green, the colors of the Italian flag—is characteristic of later projects he designed for the United States, including the recently completed ABC headquarters in Burbank, California. The fusion of industrial and classical forms is a recurring motif in his work.

The facade is a grid of half-columns, beams, and spandrels, capped with a cornice. Rendered in metal, the columns and beams suggest structural elements but are in fact applied decoration. Concrete structural columns are concealed within the white half-columns, abstract versions of the classical Tuscan order. The Mercer Street facade is even more industrial in appearance. The splayed columns and beams, again painted red, could easily pass for an expressed structural frame.

Fake classical fronts are common in SoHo. The Cast Iron District takes its name from the industrially produced ornamental facades bolted onto manufacturing lofts. Rossi gives this precedent a surreal inversion with facades that resemble structure. In his original concept, the industrial appearance would have been magnified: instead of red-painted metal, he planned to use COR-TEN steel, a once fashionable material that oxidizes to a plummy brown rust.

The change, approved by Rossi, was radical nonetheless. It is the Scholastic Building's most enigmatic aspect. I can speculate that, in an effort to be more "contextual," he borrowed the red from the terra-cotta facade of the Singer Building next door. But I find this degree of compliance hard to accept in light of his earlier work. To accept the building's Pop Art palette, I have to see it as Rossi's response to our hypomanic culture and its mounting intolerance for melancholy like that embodied in his work.

Recently I bought one of the handsome macchinettas, the stove-top espresso makers, that Rossi designed for Alessi. There was an instruction booklet inside the box, with a text in which he asserts that the macchinetta was the last invention for making coffee. This is so Rossi. Everything had to be the last of its kind. Every summer the last summer, every shadow cast by the last light of the day. I bought my macchinetta at the last duty-free store at the last gate at Malpensa Airport in Milan before boarding the last transatlantic flight of the day. It had to be that way. Otherwise, the pot would surely forget how to make the last cup of coffee.

Rossi's vision was always melancholic. For years his best-known work was the San Cataldo cemetery in Modena, designed between 1971 and 1984. It was a major pilgrimage site for architects. Later, the emblematic Rossi building was the Teatro del Mondo, a floating theater designed in 1979. The steel-and-wood structure was moored adjacent to the Dogana in Venice, at the mouth of the Grand Canal, which he described as "a place where architecture ended and the world of the imagination or even the irrational began." The theater attained an afterlife in photographs that capture its voyage out to sea.

Counterbalancing these memento mori were designs in which he tried to recapture memories of childhood innocence. Red- and white-striped beach cabanas, a holiday version of the primitive hut once taught to students as architecture's point of anthropological origin. Red- and white-striped lighthouses, another seaside attraction. Rossi combined motifs of innocence and mortality in some projects. His designs for elementary and secondary schools, for example, included forms derived from the cabanas and from the chimney at Modena cemetery. Clocks appeared, totems of passing time.

He built his architecture on faith that a harmonious relationship existed between his personal memory and the collective history embedded in the city. His efforts to reconcile the extremes of childhood and death may be the most characteristically Italian aspect of his work. A civilization that exalts the *Pietà* is one that grasps a fundamental oneness of the womb and the grave. Rossi's city is a stage on which the rituals that carry us from birth to death are acted out. His buildings are acts of procreation.

New York, however, is the capital of secular distractions. We accept worldly substitutes for ideas that once possessed sacred value. In architecture, concepts like innovation, progress, demolition, preservation, context, and historical precedent have the aura of sacraments. Yet they lack the stability once assured by religious authority. Instead, they are pegged to market value.

Rossi's American buildings resemble the Ginger and Fred characters in Fellini's 1986 film of that name. They are old theater pros made to look more than slightly ridiculous and out of place in the world of television. What good was surrealism in the nation that gave us airline pasta primavera, the Bellagio Hotel, and the reduced-scale Doge's Palace at Epcot Center? Or, for that matter, the reactionary school of postmodern architecture, an escape from history committed in history's name? Tibor Kalman, the graphic designer, used to say that once you accepted that tray of airline food on the flight from Italy to the United States, it was all over. You had approved the abstract, compartmentalized version of experiences once woven into the fabric of everyday life.

But what choice do you have? If you buy the plane ticket, you might as well accept the tray. You've endorsed modernity long before boarding time. You've endorsed uprootedness, displacement, eviction, violence, and the sense of imminent loss suggested by the plume of smoke in a de Chirico painting. Technology, industry are upon us. History, time, and America are coming to smash everything to bits. And we should be happy about it! No long faces. No crepe, no mourning. We're a nation of optimists, yessiree. Accept that tray, in other words, and you reject everything Rossi knew and believed in. You leave behind a world where emotions are knitted into the physical structure of the city and enter a space where they are afflictions requiring medical attention.

I would have preferred the Scholastic Building to be clad in the same matte metallic finish Rossi used for the coffeepot. It has the metallic sheen of modernity but the industrial gleam is instantly compromised by stains. The metal displays use and time. It is urbane. He featured enormous, architecturally scaled coffeepots in drawings of imaginary cities. It was a surrealistic gesture: the ingestion of caffeine is as necessary as the street in the urban experience. But how useful is it in a decaffeinated civilization that prefers driving to walking?

When Rossi put memory back on the architectural table, it was in the nature of a discovery. Modern architects had always sought to point up affinities between industrial buildings and classical architecture. Sant'Elia, Terragni, Ponti, Le Corbusier, Mies van der Rohe, Kahn, and countless others did this. For Rossi, this affinity could be more clearly expressed and understood in terms of urban relationships. He voided the void, erased the blank slate, and filled it with images that blurred the line between personal and cultural memory. He helped establish incremental building as a constructive approach to modernization.

In the United States, he encountered a place where memory is mostly occupied by void. Here, even memories have become "memories." Retro fashions. Golden oldies. Comfort food. Bishop's crook lampposts. Historic districts, like SoHo, for example, which, in his drawings of the Scholastic Building, looks a lot like Venice. Walls and windows are out of plumb, as if Broadway were the Grand Canal, the cars and buses were vaporetti, and the loft buildings had settled erratically as their 600-year-old pilings sank into the mud of the lagoon.

It's an interesting metaphor for a city whose architects have worked overtime in recent years to turn the place into a theme-park version of itself. And a charming reminder that the Haughaut Building, a few blocks south, was modeled after Sansavino's library opposite the Doge's Palace.

But the metaphor loses something in translation to built form. SoHo is not Venice. The area's gentrification, of which the Scholastic Building is part, illustrates the kind of violence to which cities are subjected by market values. Light manufacturing and artists have been tossed out to make room for the delights of downtown living. These memories are not comfortably glossed over by coats of bright paint.

For the intersubjectivity idea to work, Rossi's memory can provide no more than half the equation. The other half must come from us. And "us" is not just what the market demands. It refers to those of us with a powerful memory of Rossi. Our view of architecture was formed, in part, by his ideas. Our memories of his early work explain why people like me, who regarded Postmodern architecture as one more instance of American social insecurity gone awry, exempted him. We followed his work even when it took what seemed a wrong direction. He didn't use history as an authority to hide behind. He put himself out there.

April 1, 2001

CAMELOT'S ONCE AND FUTURE GLAMOUR

The Metropolitan Museum of Art has expanded its armor collection to include the Costume Institute. Jacqueline Kennedy: The White House Years—Selections From the John F. Kennedy Presidential Library and Museum presents the wardrobe of a woman who became embattled by the very forces she helped set in motion. Like Joan of Arc, in fact.

In Mrs. Kennedy's case, martyrdom arrived in the form of iconography: the world of images, celebrities, logos, and sound bites. In the conflict between privacy and publicity, the line between them was battered, we now know, beyond repair. But the clothes held up beautifully.

Organized with intelligence and flair by Hamish Bowles, an editor at *Vogue*, the show represents a triumph of substance over style. With surprisingly little variety in the clothes themselves, Mr. Bowles has drawn upon news photos and other materials that set the clothes in historical context.

With magazine covers, film and video clips, music, and other mixed-media ephemera, the installation weaves together an astonishingly vivid tapestry of the cultural forces that coursed through the Kennedy years. I would go so far as to call this a first-rate show of political art, perhaps the most startling example of the genre since the Met presented the exhibition Harlem on My Mind in 1968. It is also the strongest show I've seen on the role played by the media in the transformation of modern American life.

When her husband introduced himself as "the man who accompanied Jacqueline Kennedy to Paris," he was prophetic. There probably won't be a better occasion than this show to examine why this First Lady feared that her glamour might outshine her husband's political achievements.

This woman wrote her own script. President Kennedy needed his family, and battalions of advisers, courtiers, historians, medical experts, and other technicians to put his identity together. Jackie created herself. Oh, yes, there was Sister Parish to help with chintzes, and Oleg Cassini to sketch the frocks. But these were just props. The author of the play was the lady herself.

The show, presented by the Costume Institute on the museum's second floor, starts off chronologically, with clothes Mrs. Kennedy wore during the 1960 presidential campaign, and continues thematically, with sections devoted to travel clothes, riding outfits, formal regalia for state dinners, and everyday wear.

The campaign clothes are remarkably self-effacing. Except for some red and blue uniforms—their intensity recalls the early days of color television—the nearly monochromatic shades tend toward the (gasp) mousy. Mrs. Kennedy appears to be saying that her outfits can be as modest as Pat Nixon's Good Republican Cloth Coats.

This has the outrageous effect of magnifying Mrs. Kennedy's youth, beauty, and personal style. And when you zoom in closer, the shapes are unmistakably Givenchy 1959: wide cut, with wide-welt borders (like the orange model Audrey Hepburn wore when shoplifting a Halloween mask at the 5-and-10-cent store). Photographed from the back as a campaign limousine heads up Fifth Avenue, she waves her gloved hand, unfurling the broad sleeve of her coat like the wing of some gorgeous descendant of a prehistoric bird of prey.

There was a Darwinian aspect to the 1960 election: the survival of the most attractive. Since Mrs. Kennedy outranked her husband on that evolutionary scale, her contribution to the Democratic victory should not be minimized. We were now well into the Cold War. And we had learned that this war would be fought not with weapons but with images. The missile gap was more a matter of perceptions than facts. Nuclear deterrence was propaganda. If a Soviet leader was crass enough to bang his shoe on the table at the United Nations, what other savagery might he be capable of? If Nikita S. Khrushchev could threaten, "We will bury you," what could prevent the escalation of psychological warfare into mutually assured destruction?

And who is to say that the psychological damage wasn't as real, in its way, as physical injury? Or that it didn't require a healing power, too? Mrs. Kennedy projected the counterperception of the ancient civilizing impulse. The handsome face was antique, Greek, classical; the clothes were classic modern French. They adhered in all essentials to the design philosophy enunciated in the 1920s by Gabrielle Chanel. "With these scissors I cut away all that was inessential in the creations of others": that was Chanel's basic message. Or, as her fellow modernist Mies van der Rohe expressed it, "Less is more."

Mrs. Kennedy's riding clothes were British. But British riding gear, sportswear, and sailing attire were a major influence on Chanel in the 1920s, acquired during the designer's liaison with the duke of Westminster. Jazz Age flappers, an American import, inspired the *garçonne* look Chanel introduced in 1923.

The appeal of reductive modernism was international, never more so than in the 1950s and early '60s, when the Miesian aesthetic was embraced in architecture as the public face of the so-called Affluent Society. Simple shapes, sumptuous materials: the same rules applied to the Seagram Building and Mrs. Kennedy's image. Also, both had good posture. And vigor. Different typologies allowed minimal variations. A German cut worked for a building, a British cut for a horse. For a dress, the cut must be French.

The iconic shape is the beige wool crepe dress Mrs. Kennedy wore for the Inauguration ceremony on January 20, 1961. Designed by Oleg Cassini, the overblouse dress featured three-quarter-length sleeves, a scoop neck, and a hem at the knee. The cut was a form-fitting, crisp silhouette; two deep folds at the waist allowed the skirt to fall from the hips like a column. Mrs. Kennedy added a fur collar, a ruby-and-diamond clip from Tiffany, and one of Halston's famous pillbox hats. You don't expect variety in uniforms, and there is little here. But in other variations the sleeves were longer or shorter; fabrics and colors changed; the waist could be fitted or gathered, the severity softened by a bow, a flower, a ruffle, a cockade. The skirt usually flares.

Givenchy, Cassini, Bergdorf Goodman, Herbert Sondheim, Chez Ninon: others could do Chanel better than Chanel herself now, and back then it might have made a difference whose name was on the label. Cassini has been reported to be dissatisfied that the show gives him insufficient credit as major author of Mrs. Kennedy's image. Anyone who designed the shimmering apricot silk dress she wore on a boat ride during her trip to India in 1962 should indeed have his name in lights.

But Cassini was born in France, fashion was French, and the entire image, orchestrated by Mrs. Kennedy herself, was intended to project the aura of France as a cultural beacon enlightening the world. The diplomatic language. Les beaux arts. La vie de bohème. Le paradis artificiel: gardens, fountains, coiffeur, cuisine, son et lumière. Cassini, who designed for Hollywood, knew how to sustain that aura under lights.

If the campaign costumes are autumnally drab, in the First Lady's wardrobe it is perennially spring. The day dresses tend toward pastel: green, blue, yellow, pink. Easter, in fact, the ascension after sacrifice: a subliminal association in the house of the nation's first Roman Catholic president. Then, for stark theatrical contrast, there is the black-on-black outfit designed by Cassini for Mrs. Kennedy's meeting with Pope John XXIII. His Holiness wears white.

At the White House the First Lady does, for she considers white the most suitable for grand occasions. The seating charts resemble large, radiant stars, with names, in formal script, for rays. Music from *Camelot*, the Broadway musical, plays in the background. Eliza Doolittle, Cinderella, Black Jack Bouvier's daughter come to the ball.

Each head of state lights up in Mrs. Kennedy's presence. No head of state lights up in Nina Khrushchev's presence. This is not the reason the 1961 Vienna summit meeting was such a flop. But looking at pictures of the First Lady and the Soviet leader sharing a joke, you can easily imagine that the two of them could have ended the Cold War in a few minutes. Perhaps she comments on that shoe. At least he made a fashion statement. So much more stylish than that irate finger jabbing of Jack's.

Near the beginning of the show there is the famous portrait of Jacqueline Bouvier, the inquiring photographer, holding her camera up to face the viewer. (She is wearing a uniform even then: garçonne at large.) It is hard not to see the exhibition that follows as the projection of her mind's eye. Her camera establishes a relationship to the world while the unseen photographer's camera reverses it. She could have taken the picture herself while gazing into a mirror. And then walked through the mirror. Into the show itself. Into the life of an icon.

And into a life of black and white. The show's installation dramatizes the extent to which the public in those days saw its public figures in black, white, and gray, like a page of newsprint. They were personified headlines. Arrangements in Ben-day dots. The pastel day dresses recall the colors of tinted postcards. The video monitors emphasize that the clothes were content for the media that were becoming the new form of public space, altering its relationship to private life in the process.

Mrs. Kennedy was a major agent of this change. Part of the show's fascination comes from speculating on the question of nature and nurture. How much of her persona was the product of family breeding? How much was due to iron will, the ambition to act on a global stage? Certainly the patrician image was both true and stylized, a cross between the real Anastasia and the fake one. The affinity for art, even in its wilder forms, was real, and only partly sublimated into the conventions of "good taste." The diction was deliberately pitched at a level below her awareness. A notch or two lower, and Mrs. Kennedy might have let loose with Jayne Mansfield squeals.

There's a Brothers Grimm story called "The Boy Who Went Out to Learn Fear." The final image in the show brought that title to mind. A black-and-white photograph, greatly enlarged, depicts the president and

Mrs. Kennedy sitting in the back of a limousine. The two are smiling at each other. It freezes a classic public-private moment: a scene of intimacy between two people at the center of a nation that had yet to discover that everyone wants to be a star.

The scene is not Dallas, the year not 1963, though I think we're meant to be jolted by the possibility that these two stunning creatures are headed for an appointment in Samara. We're relieved to discover that the picture was taken the year before, but the discovery precipitates an even worse letdown because the picture was made in an America that had yet to be blown apart, first by one assassin, then by an army of them, until we had exhausted faith in our destiny and the entire world's supply of goodwill that the Kennedys had helped to inspire.

Wallowing in our poison now seems to be the national pastime. Art may not be the highest form of redemption from toxicity, but it's a good one. In the show's last gallery we see fashion transformed into something more enduring: the preservation of architectural landmarks, a field that continued to hold Mrs. Kennedy's interest beyond the White House years. But throughout the show we see glimpses of her contributions to the arts: gala performances at the White House, speeches she gave on visits overseas.

It was possible, back in the early 1960s, to discount this work as the purely ornamental pastime of a young First Lady. It seemed of a piece with seating a dinner, arranging flowers, redecorating the premises. It is not possible to make that mistake today, when culture has assumed such a major role politically and economically in the conduct of world affairs. It does not seem a small thing now to have made art a matter of national policy. In an age still racked by fear—missile shield, anyone?—it is vivifying to be reminded that the desire for beauty can survive the rage to destroy.

May 4, 2001

POSTCARDS FROM THE OLD WORLD GONE GLOBAL

The hottest tourist attraction today is tourism itself. Some people travel to foreign cities for the art, architecture, shopping, music, and food, or to send back postcards from the road. Others go for the road. They're fascinated by the culture of airports, business-class hotels, laptops, and convention centers. And they're concerned about the impact of tourism on urban life everywhere.

I've got one foot in each group. I'm paid to report on buildings. But buildings are pieces of the city, and potent instruments for urban change. They have become integral to the continuing transformation of nineteenth-century industrial cities into centers of cultural production. As this process unfolds, it becomes harder to differentiate between traditional Baedecker attractions—landmarks that cosmopolites have long traveled to see—and those explicitly designed to lure tourist dollars. From my perspective, many contemporary buildings now derive value from the parts they play in an emerging global civilization. That is the story that gets this tourist on the plane.

Of all cities today, Vienna may offer the best vantage point for observing the impact of cultural tourism on the older urban centers. The city is now barely a husk of the world capital it was a century ago, when its artists and intellectuals and its polyglot population made Vienna the supreme embodiment of cosmopolitanism in modern times. But that historic backdrop makes a perfect contrast to the tourist culture of today. Vienna's golden age was a triumph of difference, produced by the clash of ethnic groups, classes, artistic movements, and ideas. As an integral part of the global monoculture, tourism promotes sameness—the homogeneity of business hotels, packaged tours, and international retail chains.

Like most cultural tourists, I want it both ways: tomorrow's standardized convenience and yesterday's haphazard charm. My redeeming grace is an interest in architectural languages. The look of buildings. The ideologies they embody. The social complexities and contradictions they reveal and cover up. And it happens that architectural languages are proliferating even as spoken tongues and dialects are withering away. A few architects are dealing creatively with the phenomenon of globalization. Others are content to recast older cities into theme-park extensions of nearby international airports. I like the first kind. When I get off the plane, I want a big sign to greet me: ARCHITECTURE SPOKEN HERE.

The Architect

"Yoo-hoo! Mr. Architecture Fan! Over here!"

Dong! Less than five minutes out of Vienna's airport, tourists approaching the city by car get a glimpse of something great. Quick. Look. Behold the Gasometer, a quartet of old municipal gas tanks that have been transformed into new apartment buildings. One tank is partly wrapped by a thin curving slab, indented in the middle, like the waist of a long apron. The gas tanks are dark red brick. The curving slab is bright metal and glass. This roadside apparition resembles the torso of a stout, giant waitress. Standing with invisible hands on hips, she thunders at passing traffic, "What's your pleasure, *bitte schön!*" She could be the masterpiece of parabuilding we've been waiting for, but . . .

. . . Now the taxi speeds ahead, through a silvery gray industrial zone on Vienna's outskirts. We'll come back to the Gasometer tomorrow, put on hard hats, explore the place on foot, wreck our shoes, get hot and dusty. But now we have appointments to keep with the Ringstrasse, the inner city, and the inner city's inner city: the ghost town of Schnitzler, Klimt, Berg, Mach, Loos, Wittgenstein, and Freud. And with Wolf Prix, architect of one of the four Gasometer tanks. I'm meeting Prix for lunch at tourist Vienna's ground zero, the Sacher Hotel.

Fate has selected Prix, of the Vienna firm Coop Himmel(b)lau, to represent those architects who are recasting the old cosmopolitan ideal within the new monocultural framework. His buildings are deeply rooted in Viennese intellectual and artistic history. That is to say, they are profoundly anti-Viennese. Like Freud, Loos, and Wittgenstein, Prix opposes the Vienna of old-world charm, cozy domesticity, and imposing imperial facades. Or perhaps "radical ambivalence" is a better term to describe Prix's attitude toward his native town. Like his artistic antecedents, Prix exists in symbiotic antagonism with comfort.

This is why I have chosen to stay at the Sacher and why I insist that Prix join me for lunch at the hotel's outdoor café. He shows up wearing dark glasses. It's true that the day is sunny. It's also true that Prix appears genuinely embarrassed to be seen at the Sacher. He says he has never been here before. ("It is everything I most hate about Vienna." "Excellent. You love to hate it. Make yourself more uncomfortable. Have a torte.")

But mainly the dark glasses seem to offer Prix protection from the world outside his head. Many architects live inside their domes. The look of befuddlement on their faces when they are not in sight of a building they admire can be painful to behold. Yet Prix's introversion is also distinctly Viennese. It betrays the distrust of external reality that was essential for intelligent people who wished to keep their sanity during the Biedermeier Age.

Vienna's public image is synthetic. It was constructed to give a semblance of unity to the multicultural Hapsburg Empire. Constructing the unified identity was as important a Viennese industry as administering the empire. Deconstructing it was the task of artists, intellectuals, and others whose minds groped toward the social complexities beneath surfaces of whipped cream. Loos's attacks on architectural ornament, Freud's theory of repression, Klimt's depiction of women as tubercular wraiths—these are a few of the strategies with which turn-of-the-century Viennese resisted the claims of public imagery on private reality.

Prix is now in the business of projecting his private reality into the public sphere. In the last few years he has crossed the threshold from visionary to a designer of major projects in Austria, Germany, France, and

Mexico. Coop Himmel(b)lau was founded in 1968 by Prix and his partner, Helmut Swiczinsky. In those days, if you were young and wanted to start an architectural studio, you didn't call it Prix and Swiczinsky. Particularly if you were on a plane home from Paris and it was 1968, the year of the student uprising. You wanted your name to sound like a terrorist organization or at least a rock group.

Coop Himmel(b)lau means Blue Sky Collaborative, suggesting a pop utopian fusion of Pan Am and the Beach Boys, with contrails of Danny the Red and his student revolutionaries. The name was meant to evoke not just a young person's view of azure from a jet window, but also the mutability of clouds. Why can't buildings form, gather, storm, thunder, flare, and disperse, as cities do?

Until recently, Coop Himmel(b)lau had only one built work to its credit: a reptilian-looking parabuilding attached to the top floor of an old building in the inner city. Essentially a skylight that added some extra space to a law firm's penthouse library, the parasitical design updates the Hapsburg tradition of draping the skyline with big, scary eagles.

Prix has enjoyed a cult following in the United States since the 1970s, when a monograph of his conceptual work began circulating here. One project, entitled Hot Flats, was an urban residential tower with a large glass flame on the top. The lamp flashed red when apartments came on the market; another sign tracked fluctuating prices in the housing market. More useful sociologically than our airplane warning lights, the fixture was an early signal of the extent to which the '60s generation would resurrect the Freudian and Marxian roots of Surrealist art.

In 1988 Prix was one of six architects featured in Philip Johnson's Deconstructivist Architecture show at the Museum of Modern Art. He is probably the sole member of the group to give the term *deconstruction* substantial meaning. In his designs, structure and function are subordinate to the building program. The program's components are treated as spatial episodes in an overall narrative structure, much like the meeting halls in Vladimir Tatlin's 1920 proposed Monument to the Third Communist International. The sense of affinity with others internationally, while alas not emphasized by the show, was the most valuable piece of information it offered.

A few weeks ago, Prix produced a piece of pocket philosophy that playfully illuminates his current aesthetic approach: "Architecture today is a dog. And architects are the dog breeders." I find this a useful metaphor for much of what is happening in the world of architecture today. Urban and intellectual history; regionalism; technology; global finance; media spectacle; consumerism; access to experience and information; shifting attitudes toward public and private space: each of these is a genetic strain. As globalization continues, the codes can be studied, altered, or recombined. There will be strange breeds ahead.

The Tower

Today, Prix tells a small group of American guests, he will show us three projects that will transform the shape of Vienna: the Block, the Tower, and the Dome. He gestures toward three compass points on the urban horizon, like a Robert Moses conjuring up a vast metropolitan vision of massive public works: highways, bridges, tunnels, airports, shipping piers, and parks. How could anything less extensive transform a city's shape?

It takes a moment to realize that the three buildings Prix is talking about are his own, and that the Vienna we'll be touring is the city inside his head. Why not? Architecture deals with the organization of fantasy as well as space. And the three projects, all apartment buildings, are essays on the psychological boundaries between public and private realms.

The SEG Tower, completed in 1998, is in Donau City, a new development created when plans for a World's Fair collapsed with the Berlin Wall in 1989. Donau City, across the Danube Canal from the old inner city, is a kind of edge city, similar to La Défense in Paris. Though well served by public transportation, its aesthetic character is driven by a car-culture ethos. Jacques Tati could have a holiday here.

The SEG tower is the most elegant work of social housing I have seen. Twenty-five stories tall, the tower contains seventy apartments, along with offices and several eating places. The ninth floor is occupied by a sky lobby—a communal space that includes a playground, a cyber café, and a sundeck.

The tower stands out in the cityscape because of its shape and the fine proportions of its metal and glass facades. The building tapers as it rises, thanks to a sloping skin that creates a wedge or modified obelisk silhouette. The walls are glass and metal grids, detailed with a precision we seldom see in the United States, even in luxury housing.

The design is dominated by one elevation, a double-layer glass curtain wall, with winter gardens sandwiched between the glass. The concept was developed primarily for climate control and energy savings, as well as for access to enclosed green space. Though the loftlike units are large, many residents use the gardens for storage. One result is that the tower's principal facade is ornamented with stuff. Private belongings as public art: Why didn't you think of that?

I don't know whether Prix intended this effect. Perhaps the humor was subconscious. Either way, the tower is a remarkable new landmark for the city of Freud. A century after *The Interpretation of Dreams*, we should be getting on with The Analysis of Stuff: why we want it, why we keep it, why we can't stop producing more and more of it. Private property raises public questions. Prix has given them a strong and stylish public face.

The Block

Prix's residential buildings are political as well as architectural achievements. They depend upon inspired leadership within the city's agencies for planning and housing, drawing on a tradition of innovative social housing that goes back to the Red Vienna period after World War I, when the city was administered by a socialist government. Though outside the inner city, and well off the beaten tourist track, social housing is the spine on which Vienna's architectural history has rested for the past eighty years.

The SEG Block, where Prix himself lives, was completed last year. The building has yet to find itself. Formally and socially, it is immensely more ambitious than the SEG Tower, but thus far its complex architectural forms have failed to generate a comparable degree of social interaction.

The Block, which is fourteen stories tall, is in the nondescript East Station area of Vienna's Second District. It contains 142 apartments, mostly duplexes, in addition to 25 office units. Prix designed the project as a prototype suitable for replication, in the manner of Le Corbusier's Unité d'Habitation. The Block is the antithesis of a machine-age artifact, however. Variety, not standardization, guided the design of the apartments. Fragmentation, more than unity, is evidently the aesthetic goal.

This block is hollow. U-shaped in plan, the design is introverted. Terraces, bridges, balconies, and staircases bisect the large, open courtyard, sometimes intersecting with one another in overlapping vertical layers of space. Sunlight suffuses the courtyard; lawns, trees, and flowers soften the sharp geometry of the architectural forms. But the building's monochrome palette exacerbates the lack of critical mass. The open spaces will need more program to make them as lively as the design.

The walls facing the street are also sculpturally articulated. The facades evoke Frank Gehry's, in fact, in their collage-like composition. The materials are stuccoed concrete, relieved by portions of glass. But, again, the image of community evoked by the forms tends to emphasize that a community has yet to materialize. I wanted to hang laundry lines, I confess, or find some other means of bringing the inner life of the inhabitants into public space.

At the Karl Marx Haus, the great granddaddy of Viennese social housing, the courtyards are formally spartan, but the personalities of individual tenants read more easily in contrast. Curtains, a flowerpot, a woman leaning out the window, reassert Red Vienna's Utopian aspirations. The Block is not a failure, just a project yet to be fulfilled. There are places in its courtyard where the energy of the architecture almost compensates for the absence of screaming children. And the project shows once again that a city famed for its resistance to change has long shown surprising support for innovation in housing.

The Dome

By the time we reach the Gasometer, Prix's ambition to reshape the face of Vienna no longer seems far-fetched. Great cities are states of mind. This tour is changing mine. Prix has drawn a triangle—a wedge—whose points lie outside the inner city. The wedge plunges through the center as we imagine it. Prix's goal, I am beginning to realize, is not to revitalize the Vienna of a hundred years ago. Rather, he seeks to reimagine historic Vienna within a global context.

No city today is the center of things. It is the interaction between cities, at once competitive and sympathetic, that is driving urban culture in new directions. Literally and culturally, Prix's buildings emerge from the overlap of the global monoculture and the traditional cosmopolitan ideal.

Paolo Costa, the mayor of Venice, told me recently that he objects to the term *centro storico*, or historic center, because the implication is that a city's outskirts have no history. Of course, thinking that the outskirts have no history—particularly if the outskirts are industrial—is what makes them so attractive. Ah, an industrial wasteland! The void of it all! But this becomes harder and harder to do as former manufacturing zones are converted to office and residential use.

The Gasometer project is one of the most impressive such conversions any city has undertaken. Since public access to the buildings' interiors is limited, the Gasometer may not become an urban "detonator" of the magnitude of the Guggenheim Museum in Bilbao. But it will detonate an explosion of possibilities in your mind, I assure you, if you're lucky enough to go there. (The Gasometer subway stop is a short ride from the prehistoric city center.) Architectural history is happening here.

There are four Gasometer tanks in all, two designed by Wilhelm Holzbauer and Manfred Wehdorn, and one each by Coop Himmel(b)lau and Jean Nouvel. They are linked in pairs by underground and aerial connectors. 2 + 2 = 1: this variation on binary structure is the first of many plays on duality that underscore the Gasometer's allure.

Round things are infinite. This is why Vienna's Ringstrasse is so hypnotic. As you proceed around it, you lose the sense of orientation. Your relationship to east-west and north-south polarities is not fixed. The Gasometer tanks are similarly disorienting. Though the lineup of tanks gives them a linear orientation, each compels individual attention. The tanks are huge: the Prater Ferris wheel could fit comfortably in the open space within each one. Now that they've become "architecture," the effect is of four industrial-age Pantheons lined up by the side of the road.

Actually, what's left of the original tanks was always intended as architecture. The four brick cylinders were designed in 1896 by Franz Kapaum to mask the gasworks' actual plumbing. He gave them the somewhat jolly look of Alpine Gothic castle keeps. One could imagine hundreds of Rapunzels letting down their hair from the upper stories.

But there were no upper stories. The Rapunzels would have had to stand on tall ladders. The cylinders were mere shells, like stage sets. Like the facades of Victorian railway stations, they are classic illustrations of the nineteenth-century dichotomy between architecture and engineering. Theoretically, the dichotomy was resolved by Modernism's functionalist aesthetic. The remodeled Gasometer revisits the dilemma. Only now, the industrial building has been placed outside the brick "architectural" shell.

This reversal is expressed not only in Prix's metal-and-glass shield but also in the design for other new buildings in the Gasometer complex: an office block, a shopping center, a multiplex. (Other office and residential buildings are planned.) These are also executed in a discreet high-tech vocabulary, formally in keeping with the industrial ethos of this highway zone. The Gasometer retroactively places this "ahistoric" district within a historical frame.

As it is well documented that I am only interested in stars, I didn't bother with the two tanks designed by local firms. (Actually, both have been inaccessible during my visits.) And I've only caught a glimpse of the Nouvel. It is sleeker than Prix's tank, a high-tech classical design, with large vertical windows that open the interior to the outdoors. And it seems far closer to the airport—any airport, especially Charles de Gaulle—than to Vienna's historic center. Mesdames et messieurs, you have all been upgraded from coach to Concorde. . . .

Prix's tank is spatially more complex. Of the four tanks, it is the only one with a major public component: a large underground amphitheater, to be used for pop concerts and such. The shield serves as the arena's urban marker. It is also a fine piece of generational heraldry. The age group that invented the modern pop concert at last asserts a distinctive place in the skyline. Blue skies.

Just above the amphitheater, but still underground, there is a round plaza surrounded by a circular mini-mall for restaurants and shops. An adjacent underground vault, two stories high, serves as an entrance lobby for the apartments. Illuminated by clerestories, it is dramatic, Piranesian, but not overdesigned. These are signally great spaces.

Piranesian, too, are the passages that connect the new, inner drum of apartments with the shield outside. Vertical segments of the brick cylinder have been removed, but the remaining brick is left exposed, creating an archaeological impression, like old Roman walls. As you pass through them, you're reminded that Rome is full of parabuildings, later structures built over, in, and around ancient markets, temples, and circuses. You half expect to see weeds growing out of the brick. Most Roman of all is the dome of sky above the open atrium space in the heart of the tank. It resembles a Pantheon oculus rethought by the artist James Turrell, who designed the Roden Crater. The sky does appear to curve, as if the building were encased within a *Truman Show* enclosure. Jet contrails wanted.

Overall, the design projects an uncanny sense of in-betweenness. We seem to be moving within an intermediary zone between city and airport, ground and sky, inside and outside, openness and enclosure, public and private. Let's call it the zone between Here and Elsewhere. We've been here before. Sidewalk cafés occupy this zone. So do those places in Manhattan where the cityscape is momentarily interrupted by bridge or tunnel approaches that highway engineers try to weave into the street grid. River piers; top-floor restaurants in skyscrapers; tenement rooftops; the Brooklyn Bridge. The zone is not so esoteric or avant-garde.

Quite a few architects today are engaged in aestheticizing transitional space. Zaha Hadid's museums for Cincinnati and Rome; the International Port Terminal designed by Farshid Mussavi and Alejandro Zaero-Polo of Foreign Office Architects in London; Peter Eisenman's Staten Island Institute for Arts and Sciences; the Milwaukee Art Museum in Wisconsin by Santiago Calatrava; and Rem Koolhaas's master plan for Lille are recent examples. Rather than projecting that theme-park urbanism idea, "sense of place," these designs reveal a sense of displacement, of a freely elected mobility or an involuntary state of eviction. They accurately reflect the instabilities of urban life today.

There actually is a new urbanism today, and it has nothing to do with so-called New Urbanism. Like Prix's concept of the New Architecture, the real new urbanism is a dog. Here and Elsewhere are its major genetic strains.

August 12, 2001

AUSTRO TURF

Some people think that architecture critics are in the business of promoting their personal taste. In my case, the opposite is true. I write to get as far away from my taste as possible. This story is an exception, up to a point. There is one architect whose work reflects my taste and incites me to escape it at the same time: Adolf Loos. His designs embody the idea that, in the modern city, taste should be constantly challenged.

Loos, who lived from 1870 to 1933, was a forerunner of what some now call minimalism. Today he may be best known for his 1908 essay, "Ornament and Crime." Even before Mies van der Rohe introduced himself to the world with the Barcelona Pavilion, Loos championed an architecture of severe reduction. At a time when designers across Europe were enmeshed in the flowing tendrils of Art Nouveau, Loos hacked away the vines. Instead of inventing new decorative systems, Loos proposed eliminating decoration altogether. Architecture was, for him, a process of mental and cultural hygiene.

> Please be stronger than your past.
> The future may still give you a chance.
> —George Michael, "Cowboys and Angels"

Sing that song again, mister! So what if there's no absolute progress in art? Some art helps us cope better as life rolls along. We don't have to keep rushing and rushing around, chasing one another in a fog, bumping into the same dumb furniture. Clarity is character. Even if architecture cannot reform society, it can clarify our vision of the status quo. Loos stands for this idea: a lucid view of self and others requires perpetual polishing of the lens.

Loos was a pivotal figure in the community of artists and intellectuals that flourished in Vienna's fin de siècle. He not only frequented the city's famous coffeehouses, but also designed one. You can visit Café Museum today, though little remains of Loos's design. Never mind. What matters are the echoes of the conversations that once transpired there. In those years, the city's best minds were often engaged by a pivotal set of issues. What is the proper relationship between private and public life? Between politics and the imagination? Between our inner and outer worlds? Freud,

Schnitzler, Wittgenstein, Klimt, Hofmannsthal, Mach, and others were stirring these deep thoughts around in their coffee.

Architecture reckons with the relationship between public and private on the material plane as well as the conceptual one. Buildings are hinges between interiors and the street. Loos clarified the function of the hinge in formal and spatial terms. It was, for him, a site of moral action, a place where self and society negotiate the boundaries between private rights and public responsibilities.

The American Bar, designed by Loos in 1907, is a most relaxing place to enjoy your private rights in public. A key landmark in the history of modern architecture, the tiny cocktail spot is also known as the Kärntner Bar and is just off Kärntnerstrasse in Vienna's inner city. When was a landmark ever this minute? As your eyes adjust to interiors darkened by deep mahogany walls, you realize that the place is even smaller than it appears at first: a band of mirrors at clerestory height multiplies its dimensions. Then when you take your seat at the far banquette facing the door, your eye is drawn up to a large panel of backlighted alabaster that dissolves the front wall into a shaft of sunlight caught by thinning clouds.

Overhead, the ceiling is coffered with marble. That's ornament up there, no doubt about it. Police! Police! But Loos was not opposed to ornament per se. His argument was with those of his contemporaries who sought to invent new decorative systems. Loos himself was not averse to employing ornamental devices that had passed into vernacular use. In this sense, his approach anticipated Robert Venturi's use of classical motifs. Venturian, too, is the stylized stained-glass American flag on the bar's entrance facade. Salute Jasper Johns.

The American Bar was an institution that flourished across Europe in the 1920s, along with flappers, jazz, and beach resorts. The counter with stools in front, and bottles of booze behind the patron, imbibed the New World spirit as much as cocktails. Loos himself was indebted to the American idea. His approach to architecture was partly formulated during a three-year sojourn to the States after his student days. Like other Europeans, Loos was impressed by the scale and vigor of our industrial culture. Factories, grain silos, bridges: to European observers, such feats of engineering possessed the primitive vitality of archaic Greek architecture. His own designs aspire toward spartan simplicity.

Nowhere was this aspiration more fully realized than at Loos Haus, the largest of his built works. Now home to the Raiffeisen-Landesbank, the building was originally designed for Goldman and Salatsch, a swell gentlemen's tailor. It occupies a prominent site on Michaelerplatz, directly opposite the entrance gate to the Hapsburg imperial apartments. Reportedly, Franz Joseph was so disgusted by the view of the building from his windows that he permanently pulled the curtains. Loos Haus also offended the young Adolf Hitler. In his watercolor paintings of Michael-erplatz, rendered when he was living in a homeless shelter, Hitler replaced Loos's building with an imaginary faux Baroque edifice of his own design.

A period cartoon of the building shows Loos in a moment of inspira-tion as he gazes down at a storm-drain cover while walking down the street. But what a drain cover! Looshaus defines luxury as the twentieth century later came to perceive it: fine materials, polished surfaces, sump-tuous spaces, refined details. Even now, these elements are clearly legible as metaphors for the spiritual rewards of spartan living.

Access to Looshaus is limited today. And the present banking floor atmosphere is a far cry from that of Goldman and Salatsch, where Loos established a clear continuity between architectural and sartorial values. But you can still experience that continuity at the legendary Knize shop, built by Loos in 1913. Today Knize sells sportswear made by other design-ers, as well as its own bespoke attire. The clothing is of refined, Loosian taste (I peeked inside last April and came away with three jackets), and the shop itself enjoys landmark protection.

From the small entrance facade and ground floor, to the sizable main floor upstairs, the impression is one of good grooming rather than design. The two shopwindows flanking the entrance are discreet. Inside, a narrow aisle divides the sales counter from ceiling-high cabinets for shirts. Ascending the small spiral stair at the rear of the shop, you may imagine that you are trying on the world's first modern space for size.

Display cabinets, fitting rooms, dressing rooms, open storage areas for fabrics, seating areas with round tables and club chairs: though the spaces are devoid of overt machine-age references, they have a distinct nautical feel. With none of the ponderousness or medievalism of the Arts and Crafts movement, Knize is an essay on the aesthetic of craft. A new vocab-ulary takes shape amid the bolts of cloth. Economy of means, easy access to tools, openness to the eye, scale shaped to human form: It fits. It's me!

The store's atmosphere is British, but not stuffy. It is the Britain of navy uniforms, country wear, sports attire: the same sources that inspired Coco Chanel, in fact. With her scissors, Chanel once said, she had cut away all that was inessential in the creations of others. Loos might have made the same claim for his pencil. In fact, he was keenly interested in fashion. He wrote about clothes. British gentlemen's attire, Loos maintained, was the only suitable form of dress. Haberdashers were among his most important clients. Their advertising also supported publication of *Das Andere* (The Other), a polemical broadsheet that Loos put out in his early years. Loos's interest in fashion was in large part polemical. For him, architecture was not an art. Rather, it was analogous to fashion: an enlightened response to the material need for shelter, as fashion is a cultivated solution to the body's need for clothes. Architecture and fashion were not culturally inferior to art in Loos's eyes. Rather, both were tantamount to philosophy, or should at least take their cue from the world of ideas.

Loos developed his ideas in tandem with Ludwig Wittgenstein, the brilliant philosopher who sought to refute all philosophical systems. In fact, it has been argued that Loos provided the basis of Wittgenstein's most influential theories. For Wittgenstein, philosophy was a little trick that the Greeks had played on us. All philosophical problems are essentially semantic problems. Clear away the rhetoric, and the problems disappear. "What can be said at all, can be said clearly," Wittgenstein insisted. "Whereof one cannot speak, thereof one must remain silent."

For Loos, the nineteenth-century debates over architectural style were so much rhetoric. Strip away the styles and a building will appear. Organize interior spaces and circulation; add walls, a roof, windows, doors, and plumbing; decorate to taste; and move in. If you build it, architecture will come: this was the general idea. It was one of the main roots of what would later be called functionalism. In 1926 Wittgenstein codesigned a house in Vienna for his sister. (Thanks to the historian Bernhard Leitner, the house was spared demolition and has been restored to mint condition.) Wittgenstein's collaborator on the project was Paul Engelmann, a pupil of Loos's. Their design carries the master's spartan approach to nearly sadistic extremes. Glass doors and windows with thin metal frames, even floors of iron; the whole place feels like one big clang—closer in spirit to Peter Eisenman than to Adolf Loos.

A Loos interior, by contrast, is warm. Lots of mahogany. Oak. Pear wood. Walls and wood trim painted bright colors. Leather. Fur. Amusing lighting fixtures with lampshades of gathered silk—intimations of Philippe Starck. Loos did not believe that architects should retain control over interior decoration, at least in private houses. He wasn't a Frank Lloyd Wright. You bought it, it's yours. Enjoy. The private and public realms, while overlapping, remain distinct.

Loos's approach is no longer Other. It is normative. It's Wallpaper, as sophisticated people, with some disdain, now describe the minimalist aesthetic promoted by that magazine. It's background. A snore. Black jeans, white T-shirts. "Real simple." Uniforms. I've decorated my version of it with splashy views of the Manhattan skyline, more books than I have room for, unkempt piles of writing and research material that litter every available surface. Housecleaning is a Loosian homage. Picking up the room excavates a neutral space that is ideal for an architecture critic who distrusts norms. It reminds me that norms do have a place. My place, in fact.

September 23, 2001

FORGET THE SHOES,
PRADA'S NEW STORE STOCKS IDEAS

This is a year for opening presents early. Last week, Tod Williams and Billie Tsien's beautiful new home for the American Folk Art Museum opened its doors on West Fifty-third Street, next door to the Museum of Modern Art. Yesterday, Prada's SoHo store, designed by Rem Koolhaas, opened on Broadway and Prince. Someone has been making a list of architecture fans, and checking it twice.

For a place whose opening has been delayed almost as long as Chanel's postwar comeback, the Prada store delivers a surprising jolt. Just a few weeks ago, the store was shaping up to be a landmark of unbeatably bad timing. With all around us counseling restraint on luxury, with Prada itself the target of cackling over its troubled finances, the launching of an estimated $40 million flagship emporium—in traumatized Lower Manhattan, no less—looked headed toward a calamitous capsize.

Then you walk through the door to discover that time and space have revolved into miraculous alignment. Architecture, at least, has come through. Even if Prada were to tumble into Chapter 11 by New Year's Eve, New Yorkers would still have had a blessed two weeks to walk through a model block of intelligent optimism about urban life. Think of this as a museum show on indefinite display. However precarious Prada's assets, its grip on the imagination is firm. If we must shop to save America, some of us won't mind shopping for architecture. If you're in the market for ideas, here's the place to stock up. Try Contemporaneity—your free gift.

Entered on the ground floor of the building where a diminished version of the Guggenheim Museum's SoHo branch holds down what is left of the fort, the store shoots through a full block from Broadway to Mercer Street. It is not a narrow space, but the extreme length creates the quality of a vortex. On a clear day, you can see Milan.

To the left, just past an oversized pair of Statue of Liberty–green mannequins that guard the door, the eye is caught by a clear glass cylinder: the shaft for a round elevator that descends to the basement level, where much of Prada's merchandise is located.

The cylindrical elevator is the first of many technological flourishes with which the store is garnished. Used for displaying merchandise as well as transporting shoppers, it signals the design's extreme flexibility. Set off by a wall and ceiling of corrugated plastic, the sparkling glass shaft epitomizes the game between luxury and rawness that is everywhere played out.

The north wall is covered with wallpaper, designed by the local firm 2x4. The design will change as new collections are introduced. At the moment, the pattern evokes images of large carnivorous plants. Why don't you . . . paper your little boy's room with Venus flytraps? Alas, the wall of horrors is not for sale.

Space itself is the ultimate luxury at Prada; space, and the dedication of so little room to stuff you can buy. Much of the two-story interior is taken up by what Mr. Koolhaas calls the Wave. A Big Kahuna version of a visual motif that is by now virtually the logo of progressive design, this concave shape extends the full length of the store. The Wave's trough, which dips down to the store's basement level, is Mr. Koolhaas's most conspicuous architectural move.

Mr. Koolhaas and Miuccia Prada are kindred spirits. Both of them have exploited the potential of their respective art forms to engage in social criticism. The irony of this ambition, particularly in the sphere of fashion, does not escape them, but is accepted as a broad condition of modern life. No arts are inherently more capable of exploring the fantasy structure of the contemporary city than architecture and fashion.

The Prada people showed up one day two years ago at Mr. Koolhaas's Rotterdam office, "out of the blue," the architect says. The conversation led to commissions for stores in Los Angeles and San Francisco in addition to SoHo. (According to Mr. Koolhaas, plans for the West Coast stores are proceeding.) Along the way, the architect has ventured far beyond the boundaries of conventional store design. Technical innovations, marketing strategies, imaging concepts, and social analysis have been incorporated into the program.

The opening of the Prada store is accompanied by a catalog of telephone-book size. It chronicles all three American projects commissioned from Mr. Koolhaas by Prada. Gaga Napoléonism permeates the pages. Charts map the coincidence between future stores and centers of globalized capital in Europe, Asia, and the United States. OMA, Mr. Koolhaas's Rotterdam-based Office for Metropolitan Architecture, is photographed in conference with the staff of AMO, the architect's recently formed think tank. Drawings, maquettes, computer renderings, and pictures of new synthetic materials are tumbled together with polemical slogans.

On the book's cover, red flags part to form a curtain framing a perplexed road warrior: the worker-slash-model for globalized times. Suits of the World, Get Wired! Laid out on the diagonal, the Prada logo evokes the Cyrillic typeface for Pravda: the Truth, or whatever passes for it under totalitarian rule. All this is cause for mirth. But those familiar with contemporary European styles of thought will recognize something more: an effort to reckon with the collapse of extremities in the post–Cold War period.

Several streams of cultural history feed into the Prada store, creating a context with greater depth than its immediate SoHo environs. Prada is rooted in the aesthetic of Arte Povera, an Italian art variant on minimalist art popular in the 1970s. The term was coined by Germano Celant, the curator who now directs the Prada Foundation, which sponsors various cultural projects. (Mr. Celant is also an associate curator of contemporary art at the Guggenheim Museum.) Arte Povera was perverse. Its artists wanted to get away from the privileged aura of the museum and expensive materials. They made work from old bedding and tar-stained rope and displayed it in barren, out-of-the-way locations. But somehow you always needed a private jet to get there. You couldn't afford to be povera at all.

This aesthetic was rooted, in turn, in the social and ethical complexities of Italian Communism, for years the preferred political affiliation of fashion designers, editors, and other comrades in the upper echelons of style. Miuccia Prada is described in the company's press material as a former Communist. Fans of Antonioni and Bertolucci will see no insurmountable conflict here. Last year there were rumors that Prada hoped to acquire *L'unità*, the Italian Communist Party's defunct newspaper. Many of us who are not communists would still consider subscribing, if not defecting, to gain an aesthetic perspective on the news as well as Continental comic relief from it.

There was also a rumor that Prada might back Mr. Koolhaas as a candidate for a seat in the Italian Parliament. One notes this not as an incidental aside, but as an insight into the personality structure of the most important architect of his generation. Mr. Koolhaas is architecture's most advanced triple thinker, in Flaubert's phrase—for him, art arises from a continuous negotiation between objective reality and the subjective perception of it.

This dialectic skill is handsomely illustrated in *The Harvard Design School Guide to Shopping*, whose publication coincides with the opening of the Prada store. Prepared under Mr. Koolhaas's supervision by students at Harvard's Graduate School of Design, the book offers a critical reckoning with the mutation of public space in advanced capitalist society. As startlingly factual as they are ideological, the studies collected here portray a stoic acceptance of realities (advertising, shopping malls) that critics often harangue against.

Call Mr. Koolhaas perverse, or counterintuitive. In the 1970s, when architects and planners were fighting against urban congestion, he celebrated it in his book *Delirious New York*. Today, when convention encourages architects to oppose the privatization of public space, Mr. Koolhaas again takes the contrary point of view. If fashion historically represents a trivial pursuit in comparison to architecture, Mr. Koolhaas will inevitably be drawn to it.

He has been influenced not only by fashion's emphasis on image but by the technical production of fashion and even customer service. It is evident throughout the Prada store, which was designed in association with the New York firm ARO [Architecture Research Office]. The precise layering of materials; the integration of advanced technology with craft; the interplay between seamed and seamless spaces, finished and unfinished surfaces: these have assumed a new prominence in Mr. Koolhaas's approach.

The sloping contours of the Wave, lined with polished zebrawood, form an arena for flexible presentations. One slope is ranked with stadium steps. By day the steps are used to display merchandise like handbags and shoes. At night they become seating for art events. On the slope opposite, a small platform folds down to create a cantilevered stage. A row of cast-iron columns, sheathed in white at their bases, forms one side of the jewel-box theater's porous walls. Like the rest of the store, the space is activated by the interplay between the open and the bounded, the seamless and the seamed.

In contrast to the Wave, a set of metal boxes, in sizes small, medium, and extra-large, hang from tracks mounted on the ceiling. A Surrealist inversion, they define the upended skyline of a city that has moved indoors and flipped its head. The track system enables the density of the cityscape to be variously configured. Partly enclosed by metal screens, the boxes can be used as showcases for clothes or cages for intrepid go-go dancers.

Too bad you can't rent Prada's dressing rooms for the night. They are as extra-large as the Hudson Hotel's guest rooms are compact. You could move in here with the city version of the nuclear family: you and three or four of your newest best friends. Here's where Mr. Koolhaas's so-called in-store technology gets the fullest play, starting with the glass that encloses each room. Touch the button, and the electrified material peekaboos you, toggling from transparent to opaque.

Large video panels replace the traditional three-sided mirror with live cam shots of your back and sides. ATM-style screens give you access to data on size, style, and availability. Other techno-features require less customer participation. Scanning antennas, copper ribbons embedded like industrial jewelry in the glass, keep track of what you take in and out of the rooms. Prada is considering using the scanners for customers to charge their purchases automatically just by carrying them out the door.

The lower level of the store is reached by a staircase, surfaced with a sandwich of wood and steel, that descends alongside the stadium seating, to a U-shaped maze of shopping departments. The walls of the maze are lined with particleboard, finished in green or pink. Spackling of the seams and rivets is left deliberately exposed, and even the rough edges of the white substance appear meticulously designed. Sweaters and shirts are displayed, on shelves of open stock, housed in rolling banks adapted from library stacks.

On the west side of the lower level is a pharmacy for cosmetic products. Beyond that is a warren of specialness alcoves, a VIP maze within a maze, where everyone will want to be seen trying to enter or leave without being noticed.

You will want to pay attention to flat video monitors, placed throughout the store, on which is shown a continuous montage of images chosen to project the Prada sensibility. Scenes from Antonioni's *Red Desert* are a typically revealing motif. An aestheticized depiction of Marxism, featuring factories whose chimneys belch tinted yellow and pink smoke, the film typifies the particular blend of high style and social consciousness that the Italians have made their own.

At the Prada store, Antonioni is recast as a shopping experience. Consumption takes the place of production in the postindustrial landscape. Miuccia Prada plays Monica Vitti to Rem Koolhaas's Richard Harris. Anomie, anyone?

We could learn a lot now from European efforts to weave art, philosophy, and politics into a more supple social fabric. These days, it takes triple thinking just to cope with life. Shop! But don't flaunt it. Be scared! But act normal. Big Brother is lurking inside your vanity. Smile! We're turning into Singapore. At last, a practical use for those tar-stained ropes.

December 16, 2001

WITH VIEWING PLATFORMS,
A DIGNIFIED APPROACH TO GROUND ZERO

Transparency—unobstructed vision—is the solid virtue that will hold aloft a set of public viewing platforms on the perimeter of Ground Zero. Construction has begun on the first of four nearly identical platforms now proposed. The temporary structure is on Fulton Street, between Church Street and Broadway, just south of St. Paul Chapel, and it is to be completed by Friday.

Designed by an independent group of architects with support from a diverse group of city officials, union leaders, and private donors, the viewing platforms are also notable for the disarming ease with which they have glided through unusually dense thickets of red tape. A city still in shock from September's terrorist attack has managed to create a quiet, dignified approach to what is now historic ground.

The platforms, a grassroots initiative, were designed by four of the city's most highly respected architects: David Rockwell (Rockwell Group), Kevin Kennon, Elizabeth Diller and Ricardo Scofidio (Diller & Scofidio). Major support for the project was extended by Mayor Rudolph W. Giuliani and the heads of two city agencies, Christyne Lategano-Nicholas, of NYC & Company, the tourist and convention bureau; and Richard Sheirer of the Office of Emergency Management.

Built of exposed metal scaffolding and plywood planks, the platforms are visually neutral. They are not intended to be a memorial. Nonetheless, the design recalls an inverted version of Maya Lin's understated Vietnam Veterans Memorial in Washington. U-shaped in plan, the platforms will be inserted like plugs into streets running perpendicular to the sixteen-acre site.

Two long, shallow plywood ramps, one for entering, the other for leaving, are attached to the platforms, which are thirteen feet aboveground. The ramps are fifteen feet wide and three hundred feet long, and visitors climbing them will gain a heightened awareness of their body weight, a physical metaphor for the gravity of the occasion. The narrow incline should also evoke a ceremonial procession. A plain birchwood wall, set between the ramps, is for posting photographs, writings, and other expressions of memory, tribute, and grief from visitors.

The station under construction will be entered from the Broadway end of the ramp on Fulton Street. The platform is to be thirty by fifty feet. An estimated three hundred to four hundred people can gather on the platform at a time. The entire structure will support more than one thousand visitors at a time.

This project is unaffiliated with the professional groups already organized to prepare a coordinated response by New York architects to the terrorist attack. Materials, labor, design, and engineering services were donated. Focus Lighting and the Atlantic-Heydt Corporation, a Queens hoisting and scaffolding concern, led the project's realization, which also relied on assistance from the many city departments overseeing the site.

The Alliance for Downtown New York, a business improvement district, will maintain the structures. Larry A. Silverstein, who acquired the lease on the World Trade Center last summer, has donated $100,000 to defray additional expenses for building the first platform. The architects have established a nonprofit organization, the WTC Platform Foundation, to raise the money to complete all four.

If feelings could be weighed, even rows of solid steel columns would not suffice to hold them up. The project is as emotionally charged as its design is simple. Though television has familiarized the world with Ground Zero, an unmediated encounter with the site is still overwhelming. The experience includes more than the sight of wreckage. No less moving are the placards, signatures, snapshots, writings, flags, and other signs of personal loss.

For three months no property in the world has been subject to greater pressure from public attention. It has even become a contested site. Surviving spouses, children, other family members, friends, uniformed officers, coworkers, public officials, downtown neighbors, ordinary citizens, journalists, real estate developers, architects: all have a right to be here, though their motives sometimes conflict.

Since September 11, many architects and artists have put forth unsolicited proposals for Ground Zero. Some of them have organized to develop coherent plans for the future of the financial district. With a new mayor about to take office and a redevelopment agency now in place, the city has moved closer to that future. There is now a clearer sense that decisions will be made.

New buildings will or won't rise at Ground Zero. The financial center will or will not be induced to hold. Architecture and public spaces will be modeled after Battery Park City or after a more progressive vision of the contemporary city. Suspense will dissipate.

Given all these pressures, the appearance of the platforms could stir controversy. A decision has been made: one project is proceeding, others will not. The matter was not put to a referendum. No design competition was held. Issues of process and accountability were suspended. But this project emerged from a process of its own. Initiative, thoughtfulness, pragmatism, and stealth were among its key components.

Most of the visions proposed by architects fell into one of two extremes. The bulk of them were personal fantasies projected onto the site with scant thought of realization. At the other extreme were ideas developed by the professional groups, like the American Institute of Architects, the Real Estate Board of New York, and the New York City Partnership. At one extreme, designers transmitted into a void. The other extreme is the void.

The professional groups were unable to grasp the basic priorities. The most prominent of these groups, the Rebuild Infrastructure Task Force, had its eyes set on the hyperinflated agenda suggested by its title. The terrorist attack, while earth-shattering, produced no need to rebuild New York or its infrastructure.

Within weeks of the attack this group had created a privatized bureaucracy of its own. Its agenda was often mystifying, contradictory, and self-serving. Immediate needs for public access and transportation became linked to sugarplum visions of new office towers and rail lines. Too much effort went into supporting the idea that a memorial and an office park could be agreeably accommodated on one site. Not enough effort was directed at examining that premise and others.

The viewing platform project emerged from dissatisfaction with this professionalized status quo. Weekend crowds had established the need to provide public access to the site. A design was needed to serve the need. It had to be easy and cheap, sturdy, and flexible. It had to come in without arousing opposition and with the mayor's blessing. It didn't have to deal with complexities of meaning.

But the design does hold meaning. It embodies stoic principles. It treats the need for design as a reduction to essentials. The result has substance. Stop the mystification, the grandiosity, the use of architecture to disconnect our history from ourselves. Give the city back. These ideas deserve to outlive the limited duration of the platforms themselves.

In fact, a potential parallel exists between this design and the so-called interim plan that was adopted for Forty-second Street in 1992 after the collapse of a plan to build four nearly identical office towers on Times Square. Emphasizing diversity, communications, and media spectacle instead of uniform corporate gigantism, the interim plan guided Times Square toward its current identity as a meeting ground for the producers and consumers of popular culture.

The temporary viewing platforms could perform a similarly pivotal role in reconceptualizing the identity of Lower Manhattan. Other choices will eventually be made, decisions that will affect the cityscape for generations. Our builders could choose the no-risk option represented by Battery Park City: Ye Olde New York retrofitted with pseudo-progressive public art. Or just when the value of risk-taking itself is in jeopardy, they could look for new ways to interpret the city to itself.

There is no need to rush. What we're looking at is a process of taking stock that has barely commenced. Renzo Piano, architect of the future headquarters of *The New York Times*, told a reporter recently that the architects who could design well for Ground Zero are now only four or five years old. It takes time to achieve transparency where meaning is concerned.

December 22, 2001

LEAPING FROM ONE VOID INTO OTHERS

We are looking for substance or, failing that, for traction against the natural desire to seize on the meaning of things too soon. New York is far from absorbing the piece of world history that crashed into it in September. But the pressures to make sense of Ground Zero are great. Some of the pressure arises from the desire to help survivors of the terrorist attacks deal with the burden of grief. Some of it also arises from the tendency of bureaucracies to take on momentum with a logic all their own. This pressure can easily result in the burial of meaning rather than the discovery of it.

A bureaucracy is now in place for the rebuilding of New York's financial district. The Lower Manhattan Redevelopment Authority, as the organization is called, is a division of the Empire State Development Corporation, the state agency led by Charles A. Gargano, an appointee of Governor George E. Pataki. With one exception, the authority's board of directors is a lineup of captains of industry, including top executives from financial services and communications companies and from public agencies for construction and economic development. Madelyn Wils, the authority's sole female director, represents Community Board 1, the local planning unit for Lower Manhattan.

John C. Whitehead, a former Goldman Sachs president who heads the new Redevelopment Authority, has said that the group's top priority is the design and construction of a memorial to the terrorists' victims. Ideas for this project have been taking shape since September. Pressure to proceed swiftly toward a design have been escalating, with the rationale that the design process is also a healing process. This thinking is sound.

There is a serious danger, however, that the scope of the design process will be too narrowly defined. The wounds in need of healing go deeper than Ground Zero and spread wider than the suffering of victims and survivors. The attack was an assault on a great city and its relationship to the rest of the world. It was an assault on history and on the American withdrawal from history in the post–Cold War era. We should be skeptical of the desire for closure, one of our nation's pet chimeras, until we have faced its opposite: opening the civic imagination to the accelerating globalization of the urban realm. This opening, too, should be part of the design development.

The formation of the redevelopment authority signified the end of a process as well as the beginning of one. Actions taken and not taken between mid-September and late November are now part of the permanent record of twenty-first-century New York architecture. Historians will be analyzing them for decades. Meanwhile, this phase of recovery clarified some useful information for planners now working toward short-term and medium-range goals.

There are immediate needs to repair the transportation system into and out of Lower Manhattan. These should be linked to long-range planning for regional transportation. Such plans are contingent on the effectiveness of our congressional delegation in securing federal support.

There are plans to construct public viewing platforms around the perimeter of the World Trade Center site. Two towers of high-beam light, depicted on the cover of *The New York Times Magazine* on September 23, should be piercing the night sky by the end of the month. Many of us who live downtown never knew or admitted how attached we had become to the retail infrastructure, including stores like Century 21, Borders, Staples, Lenscrafters, Brooks Brothers, and the Gap.

There is, however, no current need for office space, and hence no rationale for granting developers emergency concessions, like the suspension of zoning and environmental regulations. Questions that initially seemed pressing—taller towers versus lower ones; modernist plazas versus Ye Olde Towne Squares—are moot. Even if Larry Silverstein, the leaseholder on the twin towers, feels compelled to produce designs to satisfy his insurers, no one else need think about new buildings yet.

In general, however, this phase was notable for the lack of substantial ideas it produced. Efforts to rally the city's architects resulted in rounds of meetings, organizational strategies, motivational pep talks, and general scurrying. Eventually, those efforts could be pivotal in reframing architectural discourse in this country around issues of cultural weight. If so, it will be because of the monumental vacuum that this hyperactivity exposed.

What we face now, in fact, are twin voids: one local, the other global. The first arises from the abdication of the public sector in the area of city planning. The second comes from New York's isolation from the rest of the urbanizing globe. Both stem from the collapse of historical perspective under the pressures of privatization.

The aggressive response of corporate architecture firms and their developer clients to the terrorist attacks was not New York architecture's finest hour. Nonetheless, much of this behavior can be diagnosed as a symptom of the privatization of city planning over the last two decades. Never has this surrender of civic responsibility been more starkly illustrated than in recent weeks.

"We should think like capitalists, not like Communists," Mayor Rudolph W. Giuliani said in his budget address earlier this year. The implied equation of the commonweal with the Cominterm sums up a role reversal that began during the Koch administration and is now nearly complete. City officials scurry about like Mickey Mouse entrepreneurs, plotting their next career moves. Corporate architects, despite clear conflicts of interest, try to act like public servants, with evident sincerity in a few cases. Nobody, meanwhile, bothers to look to the City Planning Commission for leadership. That demoralized, dysfunctional agency represents the power void in which all were operating before the state's redevelopment agency was set up.

Will the public sector reclaim it? For an extended period or for emergency use only? These questions deserve protracted debate. There will be efforts to neutralize the discussion, however. Municipal politics and real estate development have become, in effect, two divisions of the same industry: the City Hall–Development Complex, we might call it.

Politicians depend on real estate developers to finance their campaigns. Developers need politicians to help keep things all in the family when private contracts are awarded or special permits are sought. Architects may or may not like this status quo, but few of them are suicidal enough or courageous enough to demand reform. Our mayor-elect, Michael R. Bloomberg, is less beholden to the Complex. He is better placed to encourage developers to aim higher. But he is also taking office at a time when budgets for public services must be drastically curtailed. Privatization is likely to accelerate.

If faith in the City Planning Commission can't be restored, why bother keeping this agency around? We already have the city's Economic Development Corporation to expedite private development. In my scheme of things, City Planning would be retained, but recast within a more cultural, less legalistic framework. The agency should operate as a cosmopolitan think tank. Its primary mission should be to coordinate local growth with broader developments in global urbanization. Mayor Bloomberg can run it from his private jet.

A planning agency for contemporary New York should be guided by an overarching set of ideas that looks beyond municipal boundaries: great cities always have more in common with one another than with the nations in which they are located. Technology has drawn into close proximity great cities from the past as well as today's urban centers. Urban policy is now inseparable from foreign policy, at least on the cultural plane. The city is global.

Such an agency could create something substantial out of Void 2. In the last fourteen weeks, we have witnessed the shocking culmination of a crisis that has been building for more than a decade. The war on terrorism illuminates, among other things, the widening gap between our advanced technology and the world that technology has enabled us to dominate.

This "culture gap" began with the dismantling of the Berlin Wall in 1989. For twenty-eight years, that structure symbolized the polarization of history into a global binary structure reinforced by nuclear arms. A new phase of world history began with the wall's collapse. The United States has yet to work itself free from the wreckage. It hasn't calculated the degree to which its place in the postwar era depends on historical awareness.

In October I was persuaded to cancel a trip to Syria. I had thought of the trip as an act of personal healing. My perspective on the contemporary city was shattered by the attack on the Twin Towers, and I didn't feel I could regain it without making a pilgrimage to the part of the world where cities were first imagined.

Aleppo, my destination, has been a cosmopolitan center for more than four thousand years. Over the millennia, Aleppo has been destroyed and rebuilt often. They have a saying there: "Every civilized person has two homes, his own and Syria." New York could benefit now from the knowledge that civilization includes the destruction as well as the creation and re-creation of great things. Aleppo was in the news again recently. Mohamed Atta, the Egyptian who studied engineering and city planning and is believed to have led the September 11 attack, wrote his thesis on the destruction of Aleppo's historic fabric by modern design.

On its Web site, the Aleppo hotel I was booked into appears to be a plain modern slab, floating in the usual modern void. It has a trio of penthouse restaurants, serving Chinese, Italian, and American cuisine. There are good mountain views from the upper floors, along with the attraction of not being able to see the hotel when you are inside it. But Aleppo has survived Hittites, Mongols, Persians, Greeks, Romans, Crusaders, Venetians, and Ottomans. It may even survive modern technology, and tourists like me.

But could our technology survive without Aleppo? Possibly not. Our machines are too dependent on the fragile network of relationships within the Near and Middle East that protects our access to oil. Those machines include the planes that enable us to fly around the world for peaceful or military purposes. They have been underused for peaceful purposes, if by that we mean not only activities undertaken without arms, but also actions that explicitly promote peace by enlarging our cultural awareness of the world that our machines control.

George Bush Sr. described the Persian Gulf War of 1991 as a defense of the American way of life. His son has defined the current conflict as a defense of civilization itself. We would like to think that those two objectives are compatible. But the increasing divergence between them has been the overarching story of the post–Cold War period.

This gap has expanded even further since September 11. Hot war is not the ideal way to build bridges. The appearance on best-seller lists of books on Islam is one sign that the gap may eventually be narrowed. It may take more than a generation before this cultural perspective penetrates foreign policy. But the work we do now at Ground Zero could help move the process forward.

Television. Skyscrapers. Jet planes. Mr. Atta took three examples of modern technology and combined them into a single weapon of mass destruction and terror. The result was a cultural statement as well as an act of murderous aggression. One can't unpack the meaning of Ground Zero without understanding its historical dimensions. We might start by recognizing that one-third of the world's population embraces Islam. We could also recall the number of nations convinced of their destiny to lead.

Anyone can create his or her own authority for the redevelopment of Lower Manhattan. Mine includes two thinkers who have expanded my framework for historical awareness: the neuroscientist Gerald Edelman and the historian Fernand Braudel. Braudel, author of the recent posthumously published *Memory and the Mediterranean* (Alfred A. Knopf), used *la longue durée* to describe the framework I am looking for. The term is imperfectly translated as "the long perspective."

Perspective involves more than placing ourselves in illuminating relationships with historical artifacts. It also requires the process of illumination itself: perspectival adjustments in our interior landscapes, our private worlds of memories, learning, and concepts. Mr. Edelman has described this process as "building a bridge toward consciousness."

The first task of my redevelopment authority would be to build a bridge toward a more complex consciousness of the urbanizing world. If you enjoy traveling—around the globe and within the mind—you have much to contribute to this work. You're carrying around a superior technology, a bunch of neurons in your head ideally suited to mapping modernity and your place within it.

My postponed Syrian trip was motivated by impulse. I wanted to touch some old stones, and memorize the experience in relationship to other stones I have stroked on the road. For example, I was looking forward to visiting one building, completed in 1325, that originally housed the Venetian Embassy. The word *embassy* is euphemistic: in those days the Near Eastern region lay within the Venetian maritime empire. I've spent many hours looking at contemporary art in the Arsenale, the shipyard from which the Venetian fleet set forth, and not enough time walking around the navy's far-flung destinations.

Stones are dots. Minds connect them. It is hard to understand Venice if you approach it from the West. But when you look back at Europe from the Asian side of the Bosporus, the pieces start falling into place. By pieces I mean stones: the actual materials from which Venice is made. In 1023 a law was passed compelling Venetian merchants to return from their Eastern voyages with treasures suitable for adorning the basilica of St. Mark. More than five hundred of these precious objects, including marble columns from Syria, now decorate the church's facade.

Venetians saw themselves as "the third Rome," after Constantinople. That is one reason that Venetian Gothic, with its heavy reliance on perforated screens, resembles an Oriental style. For Ruskin, the Doge's Palace was "the central building of the world" because its design fused Romanesque, Byzantine, and northern Gothic motifs. Through Ruskin and the nineteenth-century Venetian Gothic Revival, the stone trail leads to Great Britain and the United States. Its most recent incarnation is the Venetian Hotel in Las Vegas.

Touch enough stones, and you are on your way to developing your own longue durée. Think of it as a cultural radar system. Its antennas must be periodically readjusted, not only in response to current events, but also to receive memories of past adjustments. When the system is down, the causes and effects of events cannot be detected. Those linkages go the way of old radio waves, out into the ether.

The system is down. There is little coherent relationship between foreign policy and historical awareness. Our foreign policy is for machines. We have not found ways to integrate into policy the global civilization that technology is creating. This task should be performed by cities, starting with New York.

One feature great cities have in common is the capacity to re-create themselves after an assault. Under traumatic circumstances, New York has joined an ancient and illustrious roster. The dialogue about cities is synonymous with history. This discussion is now global. Young as we are, history is calling on New York to lead it.

December 23, 2001

THE DEADLY IMPORTANCE OF MAKING DISTINCTIONS

Architecture is a protagonist in the public realm. Often, it is called upon to enact the primal drama of loss and compensation. When the loss is great, compensation is often visualized in terms of civic grandeur. The losses this year were incalculable.

The attacks on the World Trade Center were felt across many dimensions of space and time: from the neighborhood to the globe; from the televised real-time moment to history's multiple points of view. The attacks' target was modern civilization. Civilization fought back, not just with weapons and slogans but with the capacity to contemplate its highly complex self. The attack drove home the importance of discriminating between modern, progressive outlooks and oppressive, feudal ones.

Discrimination was the big story in architecture this year. This matters; that doesn't. This is useful; that's a waste of time. This feeds into the future; that is stuck in a dead end. Clarity itself came into sharper focus. This is an idea; that is a box of orange Jell-O. This is architecture; that is et cetera, et cetera, et cetera. Such distinctions are not easily made, but they are worth the time and effort it takes to form cultivated opinions.

The need for more penetrating analytic tools became urgent before September 11. In March a team of real estate developers organized a competition to select the architects to plan an office and residential complex for the so-called Con Ed site, a nine-acre property on the East River waterfront just south of the United Nations headquarters. Announced with great fanfare as an international search for architects of major talent, the competition invited submissions from three winners of the Pritzker Architecture Prize and other noted figures on the world stage. It ended with the choice of two local firms of lesser distinction.

During the selection process, Richard Meier and Peter Eisenman withdrew after they were asked to play a subordinate role as consulting architects. Rodolfo Machado and Jorge Silvetti, Boston architects who had agreed to participate as consultants, later resigned as well.

In the past, episodes like this tended to fall beneath a critic's radar. On the premise that all architects are created equal, it is often assumed that only fully realized designs should be subject to critical appraisal. Actually, all phases of the building art—including zoning, economics, politics, context, history, aesthetics, and ideology—fall within the traditional scope of critical interpretation.

To these factors must be added the inflated and inflationary pressures of professional marketing. Architects operate in an increasingly competitive market and in an aesthetically eclectic period that is not guided by educated consensus on matters of taste or style. The profession benefits from the myth that its members cannot be qualitatively ranked.

The Con Ed competition illustrated H. H. Richardson's belief that the first law of American architecture was to "get the job." The developers didn't want to pay for architecture. But Richardson never suggested that marketing should be the only law. Concepts other than social Darwinism should make an appearance from time to time. Architects can't buck the market system and shouldn't try. They should use the system as an intellectual as well as an economic framework. They should make vivid architecture from the system's inherent contradictions.

"How can you criticize people for doing what they think is right?" I was asked that question, in one form or another, many times this past year. My routine answer: "I read a lot of history."

In the weeks following the attacks, the Con Ed competition came to seem like a warm-up for the full-dress performance of an anxious status quo. The city's leading corporate architecture firms linked arms with their developer-clients to devise strategies for turning a catastrophe into a business opportunity. An ad hoc group, the Rebuild Infrastructure Task Force, convinced its members that they had earned the moral stature of firefighters, medical personnel, emergency volunteers. Onlookers were less persuaded.

The attacks required the entire city to draw on its deepest resources of historical awareness and imaginative reflection. But it did not entitle architects to assume that they had been awarded a special franchise to answer the call. Survivors, philosophers, firefighters, shopkeepers, musicians, window dressers, and dentists have at least as much right to the public's attention. All of us have had to fight feelings of helplessness.

Quite a few projects did deserve the limelight this year. In New York they included the American Museum of Folk Art, designed by Tod Williams and Billie Tsien; the Prada store in SoHo, by Rem Koolhaas; the Neue Galerie New York, by Annabelle Selldorf; and the Melrose Community Center in the Bronx, by Diana Agrest and Mario Gandelsonas. There were also promising designs for future projects by Norman Foster, Jean Nouvel, Gwathmey-Siegel, and Diller & Ricardo Scofidio. Preservationists rallied to prevent the disfigurement of Eero Saarinen's TWA terminal at Kennedy Airport.

Out of town, there were openings of new buildings by Mr. Koolhaas,

Tadao Ando, Santiago Calatrava, and Rafael Viñoly. I wasn't able to cover most of those works. The unfolding of events in the politics of New York architecture was a story I couldn't overlook. This story was not, in any case, so divorced from the aesthetics of architecture as you might think. The political story went far toward explaining why the city's architecture so seldom registers on the artistic scale.

From my window at home, I have a good view of the Secretariat Building of the United Nations. It was completed just half a century ago. It was my beacon on the skyline throughout 2001.

This was a year in which many, including those of us who are not pacifists, decided that world peace wasn't too corny a topic to think about. The architects of the United Nations headquarters were among the heroic figures of a great generation. Like the members of the United Nations, they were not afraid to face the contradictions of their time, particularly those that emerged from conflicts between global and regional perspectives.

Nor were they afraid to be criticized for doing what they believed was right. As they understood it, generating conflict was essential to the development of discrimination. Looking back at contemporary commentary on the United Nations, much of it hostile, you will realize that great architecture seldom reinforces preconceived ideas of normalcy. It parts company with them, and, in the process, reveals conflicts that have long been lurking underground. Such revelations provide the fuel that drives public life forward.

December 30, 2001

A COURTYARD AT THE HEART OF THE STORY

Architecture tells a story, Renzo Piano says. This is a classical idea. But the genre of storytelling was literary before it was visual, oral before it was literary. The story was always spatial, however. In its antique origins, the story was about the land. With the Greeks, architecture narrates the history of the sacred site it occupies. With the Romans, the building becomes the sacred site. It is autobiographical, self-reflexive, postmodern. It narrates itself.

Renzo Piano's new design for additions to the Morgan Library is two stories, recounted simultaneously. One is about burial, the other about excavation. Or, put together, death and reincarnation, a sequence as fundamental to paganism as it is to Christianity. The Morgan Library's collection of rare books and illuminated manuscripts is unsurpassed in the United States. Metaphorically, at least, it is a sacred site, certainly for those who believe in the transcendent value of words. Piano's design excavates the cultural history of narrative even as it inters the Morgan's collection—the library's spiritual heart—within the ground.

Piano's design completes the consolidation of the Morgan's Murray Hill campus, situated on the western half of the block between Thirty-sixth and Thirty-seventh streets along Madison Avenue. It will replace three structures completed between 1962 and 1991. Roughly half the $75 million project is to be underground. This will allow the design's visible portions to be lower than the rooflines of the library's existing buildings.

Beneath grade, Piano proposes to cut into the bedrock of Manhattan schist on which the library sits. Into this cavity he will insert a four-story subterranean vault, containing stacks. These lead off from an atrium lined with metal stairs. A 250-seat auditorium, site of the spoken word, is also located here. The space is Piranesian, Borgesian, even Pythian. If the stacks could speak, the tone would be that of oracular utterance. Here are all the answers to all but one of the riddles ever asked.

The arrangement reverses Dominique Perrault's design for the Bibliothèque Nationale in Paris, whose damp riverbank location mitigated against underground storage. There, books are conspicuously housed in a quartet of book-shaped towers. Piano's vault, though invisible, nonetheless exerts symbolic presence. All unread books are buried treasure. Knowledge is to be found not only in data from the world but also in the connections between images and ideas that occur in the mind, with and without our conscious awareness. Access is democratic and self-selecting. The inner compulsion to learn is the opposite of an elitist proposition.

The design above ground is "infill" architecture: a set of three new pavilions, facing into a glass-roofed courtyard, that will be inserted between three of the existing buildings: the J. P. Morgan house, the original library building, and its subsequent annex. Since these structures differ in style, materials, and relationship to the street, their context is one of contrast, scale, and sequence. It is a context of time as well as space, in other words, one of adding to rather than fitting in with.

Piano's design responds straightforwardly to this context. It adheres to the scale of the existing structures but departs from them in form, materials, and proportions. The palette is glass and painted steel, the color as yet undecided. The forms are stark but not brutal. For example, the steel panels of the main facades sit flat on the ground—"Toc!" Piano interjects, as his arms describe how the panels set down—but the panels are recessed within frames and grooved at the edges, to evoke the image of moldings. Stair towers are faced with glass, and the airy spring of the metal stairs again reveals Piano as architecture's great poet of circulation.

The courtyard, however, is the focal point of the design's circulation system. It replaces the inelegant Garden Court designed by Voorsanger and Mills and completed in 1990. But the architects of that addition were constrained by its relatively unambitious scope. With an overall plan that radiates from the center of the site to the three streets bordering it, the new courtyard will be integrated more organically into the new complex. The courtyard's glass roof is a refined version of the nineteenth-century engineering projects that inspired many architects in the early years of the twentieth.

It is the heart of the story as well as the Morgan campus. Morgan, of course, was an industrialist as well as a financier. He and his fellow tycoons made fortunes in steel, railroads, shipping, and oil. Piano's design transforms the steel-and-glass industrial vernacular into a classical idiom. More properly, it reveals the formal affinities that modern architects saw between the architecture of antiquity and industrial engineering. Like the old Pennsylvania Station, the design achieves its most eloquent effects in the interplay between revealing and concealing its steel-age structure. *La storia:* in Italian, history and a story are the same word.

The design doesn't fit the rancid image of modern architecture still held by many New Yorkers who should know better. Nowhere is Piano's departure from the image more evident than in his design for a new gallery that will be inserted between the Morgan house and library facing Thirty-sixth Street. A windowless steel cube, twenty feet on each side, the room is intended for displaying individual books of exceptional rarity. But its real function is to show off the beauty of classically proportioned space.

If you are classically inclined, you are always on the lookout for the Good, the True, and the Beautiful. As I see it, the Good means service to others; the True means truth to self; and the Beautiful articulates the continuous union and separation of selves and others over time. Piano's design is as complete a rendition of these virtues as New York has seen since the Seagram Building. Its most classical aspect is that it is a work of connective tissue, not an independent object free-floating in space.

Service to others is the critical issue raised by this project. Which is to say that the city's reception of this work is no small part of the adventure its architect has undertaken. A humanist architect like Piano naturally hopes for a positive response from the community he serves. The good news is that the New York City Landmarks Preservation Commission, under the solid leadership of Sherida Paulsen, has so far responded positively to Piano's design. A decision is expected on February 26.

Others, with a variety of motives, are likely to be less favorably disposed. Piano is an outsider, and therefore vulnerable to attack by local architects who shy away from criticizing one another. Robert A. M. Stern, objecting to elements of the design in a letter to the Landmarks Commission, adopted the tone of a great Beaux-Arts master admonishing a callow apprentice. This was predictable. Stern represents a brand of theme-park design that has misrepresented itself as classicism—as architecture, for that matter—for three decades.

The brand was built on a false polarity between Classicism and Modernism, the latter taken to be a "style" developed in the 1920s and '30s. The brand's stock, which has been tumbling in recent years, stands to fall still further as work like Piano's alerts people to the flimsiness of its underlying premise.

This is not the first time a New York project by Piano has been targeted by a local architect. In 2000, at a symposium organized by the Museum of Modern Art on the subject of pragmatism, Peter Eisenman caused a slight commotion by showing a slide of Piano's design for a fifty-two-story headquarters for *The New York Times* on Eighth Avenue opposite the Port Authority Terminal. The tower is expected to be completed by 2005. Eisenman offered the crudely rendered image as self-evident proof that the design, and therefore the philosophy, were objectionable. Piano has also aroused xenophobic reactions from local firms whose fortunes are staked on their presumed identity as beleaguered modernists, valiantly keeping the old Bauhaus flame burning while all around them have lost their heads.

None of this matters one iota. All the ideological posturing simply reinforces the creative stalemate that has gripped New York architecture in recent decades. What may have once resembled intellectual positions are now just sales positions: marketing tricks. These architects are only serving their own brands. Because of them, the public has come to regard most architects as preening egos. Piano's design may cause some of them to reconsider. It should also remind people that truth to oneself and service to others are not incompatible.

In his appraisal of the Guggenheim Museum, Lewis Mumford took Frank Lloyd Wright to task for unleashing his titanic ego on the world. "It seems not to have occurred to him that he could surrender a portion of his individuality to the community, in order to have it returned to him, enriched, at a higher level." In recent decades, the city has been excessively vigilant in rooting out architectural individuality as if it were a crime against the people.

Piano's design for the Morgan Library shows us that the street runs both ways. There are times when the public should surrender a portion of its collectivity in order to have the sense of community restored to it, at a higher level, by an architect of exceptional talent.

Piano, of course, has an ideological outlook, but his perspective hasn't been bent out of shape by the need to carve out positions on matters so monumentally inconsequential to architecture as pragmatism, avant-gardism, appropriateness, or style. He's serving something larger—a vision of urban life in which selves and others can meet in approximate serenity.

February 10, 2002

A LESSON ABROAD:
GET COMFORTABLE WITH CONTINUITY

New York architecture is beginning to remind me of art-movie houses in the early 1960s: the best stuff now is coming from overseas. For better or worse, this is a phenomenon.

Christian de Portzamparc, Renzo Piano, Aldo Rossi, Jean Nouvel, Sir Norman Foster, Yoshio Taniguchi, Rem Koolhaas, Philippe Starck, and David Chipperfield have all designed projects for New York in recent years. Since I've given much of this work favorable notice, I'm happy to explain my reasons. This is also a good time to explore some of the reasons New York architects are disturbed to see a few high-profile jobs going to their colleagues from abroad.

American architects operate with a major disadvantage. They practice in a country that has been more than willing to abandon its cities and, with them, the cultural continuity that cities provide. Architects abroad have not faced this problem, at least not on such a scale. Among the many forms of devastation wreaked on cities globally during the twentieth century, suburban development may seem slight. However, the complex of industries and public agencies that made suburbanization possible, did so at the city's expense.

Elsewhere, architects are likely to develop a more complex understanding of the city's role as an instrument of continuity in the modern world. Their cities have educated them in the dynamic relationship between stability and change. They need not fear that, at any moment, the urban ground will drop away beneath their feet. And they are less subject to the warped perspective that such fears induce.

As a result, foreign architects have a clearer view of the global context in which the contemporary city now operates. Their contribution to cities around the world, including their own, is rooted in this perspective. They grasp that the architect's responsibility is to displace the familiar with a sense of otherness.

Flashback. Venice, 1980. The Architecture Biennale. Organized by the

Roman architect Paolo Portoghesi, the Biennale sought to establish Post-modernism as an international movement. The effort failed. The movement had a few European proponents, but most of them withdrew after a brief flirtation with period styles. Others accepted their status as reactionaries, and a few are still down there in the trenches, hissing and giggling, as if unaware that the battle is over.

Otherwise, Postmodernism was an American (and literary) proposition. Here the movement appealed not to our reverence for history but to our profound revulsion against it. Invent as you go is the style here, and it's often a wonderful thing. No one is more impressed than Europeans by the energy that is freed up when people don't feel bound to their past. An invented past can be a form of freedom.

It can also result in wanton waste. Such was the case here, when post-modern architects started spinning the weird fiction that the Modern movement had broken with history. This fable was doubly wasteful. It not only trashed that movement's creative achievements. It took an axe to the 500-year-old intellectual roots from which that movement sprang. What we had here was not just the usual Oedipal repudiation of the immediate past but the trivialization of history by its transformation into a marketing gimmick.

Sometimes I think that continuity is all my generation is good for. We learned it the hard way. As guinea pigs for suburbanization, we grew up in the increasingly atomized atmosphere of the car culture. We understood that our parents (the Greatest Generation) had moved away from the city for our benefit. This added guilt to the terror of social fragmentation. The guinea pigs were expected to feel grateful for gifts that were driving us out of our minds.

The "counterculture" of the '60s and early '70s was at once an expression of this madness and an attempt to find a way out of it. Suburban architecture advertised the idea of community even as social mobility (up, down, and sideways) undermined it. The youth culture did attain solidarity among its members, but at the cost of aggravating discontinuity between generations. Its ideology did not favor alliances with the economic and institutional powers that bring architecture into being.

The American Museum of Folk Art, which opened late last year on West Fifty-third Street, is some kind of miracle. Quite apart from its intrinsic architectural merits, the building is evidence that all is not lost for those of the '60s generation who have committed themselves to practicing in New York. Tod Williams and Billie Tsien, the architects, are no longer young, but the maturity of their work is no small part of its appeal. It reflects a triumph over two generations of cultural disruption.

This city has been a nightmare for architects of Williams and Tsien's generation. Ambivalence toward authority has been partly responsible for it. You could hardly blame postmodernists for rushing in where architects of more substantial ambition feared to go.

Christian de Portzamparc was the first architect of this generation to win the Pritzker Architecture Prize. To date, no Americans born since World War II have received this honor. This omission is not because the Americans lack talent, or because the Pritzker jurors are anti-American. It is because American cities do not possess a sufficient degree of historical awareness for contemporary architecture to flourish.

Postmodernists are not the only amnesiacs among us. Two years ago, when Portzamparc's LVMH Tower opened on East Fifty-seventh Street, a New York critic complained that Portzamparc had adopted the formal motif of folded planes without embracing the ideological intent of other architects who had used similar motifs. The remark illustrated the lamentable provinciality of what passes for architectural commentary here.

Portzamparc is a conservative architect. Continuity is his métier. He was awarded the Pritzker in part because of his efforts to work past the bankrupt polarity between the Modern movement and the Beaux Arts toward a contemporary vocabulary. Portzamparc has absorbed the disruptions of the 1960s as a natural consequence of his urbanity. Paris, his hometown, has absorbed them too. It's not his fault if New York chose to bury, rather than digest, the turmoil of those years.

Plans to expand the LVMH Tower were halted last year, a casualty of the economic downturn. The expansion would have made Portzamparc's allegiance to continuity even clearer. In its present form, the tower stands as a foil to the black granite IBM building across the street. In the expanded version, Portzamparc incorporates an obelisk-shaped slice that mirrors IBM. This is then sandwiched between a new slab of fritted glass that wraps around the corner of Madison Avenue. The design remains an homage to the International Style skyscrapers of Park Avenue, but as reconsidered by eyes trained in the beauty of incremental change.

Continuity is not synonymous with stasis. As the Greeks taught, it is contingent on our willingness to let the old die. The Postmodernists had it exactly backward. Somehow they got it into their heads that culture survives by killing off the new. Their apologists twisted themselves into all kinds of rhetorical knots to suggest, for example, that Postmodernism was the new (uh-huh), that modernity was a closed historical chapter (tell me another), or that the public craves only the familiar (false, but in any case, who cares?).

Anyone who bothered to get on a plane could see that this rhetoric was rubbish. Indeed, in recent years, one has had to get on a plane to see architecture, not some bent simulation of it. Postmodernism had much of the city tied up in knots, and its loopiness persists.

The River Hotel, a project designed three years ago by Jean Nouvel for a site on Brooklyn's East River waterfront, was a political as well as an economic casualty. The project's developer, David C. Walentas, was initially backed by City Hall, which later withdrew its support. It's a project worth remembering nonetheless. The design was outstanding. The hotel's program, which included a multiplex cinema, was ideally matched to the redevelopment of the waterfront for movie studios. (And I suspect that the concept of the cineplex-hotel has a great future. Check in and catch up on pop culture.)

What it possessed above all was confidence. There's no point calling it a "modern" building. What else would a building be? And Nouvel didn't have to go through an Oedipal drama to design it. For him, there was no postmodern father to kill off. The same is true for Foster, Piano, Taniguchi, Koolhaas, Starck, Chipperfield, and Williams and Tsien. These architects have found less cataclysmic ways to work out their problems in buildings.

The Magician. L'eclisse. La Dolce Vita. Alphaville. Contempt. By the 1970s, American directors had absorbed a good deal from their foreign colleagues, and soon surpassed them in artistic ambition. This is what I hope foreign architects will do for New York: reacquaint us with confidence in the city's future so that we will be ready to greet it.

February 24, 2002

WHEN ART PUTS DOWN A BET
IN A HOUSE OF GAMES

The two Las Vegas satellites launched last year by the Guggenheim Museum will disappoint those who have been hoping to have their faith in the mother institution restored. Lodged in the base of the Venetian Hotel, an architectural collage of vapid scenographic effects, the two pavilions are not disgraceful. Rem Koolhaas, who designed them, has brought some architecture into the picture. More, in fact, than was strictly necessary.

Probably no design could redeem the vanity behind this venture. Far from "bringing art to the masses," the Guggenheim has brought corporate branding to an anticipated public that has thus far failed to show up.

But the enterprise has delivered a crisis for the museum itself. The Guggenheim's efforts to remake itself in the image of a multinational corporation—with outposts for culture consumers in Spain, Germany, Austria, Japan, Brazil, and elsewhere around the world—have reached the point of philosophical collapse.

The two pavilions form a bifurcated parabuilding within the Venetian's nightmarish trompe l'oeil. The Guggenheim Hermitage, jointly sponsored with the Russian state museum in St. Petersburg, draws its opening show from the collections of both institutions. The Art of the Motorcycle, originally presented in New York, inaugurates the Guggenheim Las Vegas.

A vast circular gaming floor separates the two parts. But we are tempted to see this wheel of light and noise as integral to the museum's undertaking, both as a contrast to the art and as an extension of it. Art is a crapshoot, you may imagine: artists risk their lives on the pursuit of visions, without knowing how their fellow creatures or posterity will judge the results.

The Hermitage branch is a brown rectangular box fashioned from oxidized COR-TEN steel. Three fat, freestanding partitions, also of COR-TEN, divide the space into four galleries. Mounted on pivots, the partitions can be swiveled to create different gallery configurations. COR-TEN, a material widely used by architects in the '6os and by Richard Serra in large-scale sculptures, has been rendered nearly unrecognizable here. Its surface has been waxed, and this treatment eliminates the rough, plummy bloom that the material presents in its raw state. The impression is of leather, or an expensive grade of simulated hide. Each partition, composed of several panels, thus brings to mind a wall of Samsonite Rothkos.

The panels themselves are problematic. Steel contracts and expands according to temperature. The panels require expansion joints, or seams. These create rectilinear patterns of shadow, an awkward background for displaying paintings. Deeper shadows gather at the bases and tops of the partitions, which stop short of floor and ceiling. Above, light emanates without confidence from a folded baffle of pale maple wood. The twilight effect is aggravated by a long strip of glass, set into the pavilion's outer wall, and a vertical window in one corner. The natural light admitted by these apertures is distracting, like glare penetrating a darkened room from a partly cracked-open door.

The group of paintings now on view is small but magnificent, focusing on Postimpressionism at the masterpiece level. The paintings are protected by glass. It's a fine glass, imperceptible from most angles, benignly unreflective, but in combination with the shadowy room, it creates an added challenge to viewing. Here is work by artists who were throwing light and color on squares of canvas as no other artists had ever thrown them before, presented inside a container that sucks the light right out of the room.

Guggenheim Las Vegas, the second pavilion, is bigger, better, and brighter. A well-proportioned version of the space-frame sheds that proliferated in the 1970s, the structure is heavy on hardware but airy with light and space. The roof is supported with large metal trusses, and a wide escalator descends to the lower level; but these machine maneuvers are offset by panels of translucent and transparent glass that help break up the large-span space and give it a shimmery depth.

Like that of the Pompidou Center in Paris, Koolhaas's design descends from Cedric Price's Fun Palace, an unbuilt but highly influential project of 1962. A sort of pinball learning center, with mechanized, movable floors and walls, the Fun Palace was a pivot between the grim modernist megastructure and the comic-strip fantasies of the British group Archigram. Price was less concerned with form—the building was just a kit of prefab industrial parts—than with the mix of uses. Juxtaposition, density, and flexibility were values it promoted.

Koolhaas's design would lend itself beautifully to a more varied program. As it stands, the space relies for animation on an installation design by Edwin Chan, from the office of Frank Gehry. Made of sheets of stainless steel that have been sculptured into towering whorls, waves, and curving walls, the setting goes far toward capturing the spirit of the Global Guggenheim. Motorcycles, paintings, sculptures, altarpieces, designer gowns, performance events, architectural models—whirling, circling in space, as if they were streams of digital code, os and 1s, just waiting to be downloaded into a walk-in terminal equipped with bathrooms and a bookshop, and then back up there again, whirling and swirling, dipping and diving.

Except that art doesn't really work that way. Neither does looking at art. Movement can be a great subject for art, as the Futurists and others since them have shown. And it's been a central subject for architecture all along: we experience buildings by proceeding through them and by walking or riding past them, sometimes even on motorcycles.

But museums are social spaces. They contain material objects. To travel, the objects must be insured, packed, shipped, unpacked, and properly lighted. All this is very cumbersome. People don't travel through the cyber-ether, either. They get brutalized by cash-short airlines and worse. None of these things are abstractions. But the Las Vegas Guggenheims leave you with the nagging feeling that you're a statistic on someone else's itinerary. They would have sent you via e-mail if that were possible.

In theory, the Guggenheim and Koolhaas should have made an ideal match. The two have been key players in the cultural politics of the post–Cold War era. Koolhaas has emerged as a first-rate satirist of free enterprise run amok. He aestheticizes our ambivalence to the mixed blessings of life after "the end of history." He has been criticized for wanting it both ways—to be part of the global monoculture while remaining independent from its culturally leveling effects. But this is precisely why so much is riding on him now. In this country, none of us have a choice but to have it both ways. Everyone is in everyone else's pockets. It has become ethically impossible to create architecture in this country without taking the reality of economic anarchy into artistic account.

It misreads Koolhaas to think that he wants to transform society. But some of us think that the creative path of art offers a means of transforming the self, in socially constructive ways, and that those who follow this path thus provide useful and inspiring models for living. Our period happens to be rich in such examples. Koolhaas and many other architects of his generation have been furnishing our global cities with essays in what the sociologist Ulrich Beck has called "reflexive modernism"—work that addresses the shortcomings of modernity as they reveal themselves over time.

But a reflexive modernist can't do much to redeem an institution that declines to be reflexive about itself. That is the problem that has overtaken the Guggenheim in recent years. A decade ago, Thomas Krens foresaw that museums could be instrumental in shaping the cultural contours of globalization. What he eventually called the Global Guggenheim seemed a worthwhile experiment in channeling the flow of international capital toward new visions of cosmopolitan life.

Some Guggenheim shows from the last decade—The Great Utopia and The Italian Metamorphosis, for example—were broad, probing surveys that equaled in intellectual scope the director's transnational goals. Increasingly, however, the museum's programs have become pale adjuncts to those goals.

Exhibitions are almost invariably linked to ulterior motives: a donation, a future museum site, the director's personal history, or some primitive desire for notoriety. The temporary installations in Frank Lloyd Wright's rotunda, culminating in Jean Nouvel's obnoxious all-black void, have become indistinguishable from changing disco décor. The Virtual Guggenheim, a cyber museum announced with great fanfare, has turned out to be little more than a sophomoric screen saver. Whatever you thought of the motorcycle show when it was first displayed in New York, seeing it again in Las Vegas is like reliving a hangover.

Krens is not alone in the post–Cold War boat, and I prefer his ostentation to the demure connoisseurial posturings of his colleagues at other museums. But flamboyance is no substitute for self-reflection, and without that quality Krens has come to resemble a modern version of Wagner's Bavarian patron, mad King Ludwig, putting up palace after palace until his wits gave out.

Krens has been a great architectural patron. But the Global Guggenheim has created an atmosphere in which art and architecture have become secondary to institutional promotion. The art of the deal is what the museum is practicing now, and one does not care to see the ideas of artists presented in such surroundings or to feel that the public's attendance serves mainly as a form of credit for leveraging the next deal. We end up feeling used, and to no purpose of overarching cultural value.

The Guggenheim could not have foreseen the economic and tourist slump that followed last year's terrorist attacks. But it should see the slump as a blessing. The global merry-go-round has stopped spinning. The moment is here to reflect on the possibility that the Guggenheim brand is no longer an asset, but has become a cultural liability in the eyes of many who once thought of themselves as fans.

April 14, 2002

A GIFT OF VIENNA THAT SKIPS THE *Schlag*

In architecture, the history of ideas is more reliable than the history of forms. It was almost worth suffering through Postmodernism to absorb this simple lesson. Visually similar forms can convey appreciably different meanings. Not all glass elevations deliver the same message as that presented by the landmarks of the International Style. In the case of the new Austrian Cultural Forum, at 11 East Fifty-second Street in Manhattan, the message is quite contrary. In contrast to the lucid rationality of the modern glass tower, the Forum projects the idea that serious disturbances may lie beneath a relatively smooth appearance. Call this a psycho building: every skyline goes a little crazy sometimes.

Designed by the Austrian-born New York architect Raimund Abraham, the Forum has been a long time in gestation. Mr. Abraham's design was chosen in 1992 from 226 entries in a blind competition. (The jurors included Richard Meier, Charles Gwathmey, Kenneth Frampton, and Hermann Czech.) His design was presented in New York the following year at the Museum of Modern Art. Thereafter, the building became the subject of prolonged debate among Austrian government officials in what amounted to a referendum on national identity. For a cultural showcase abroad, should Austria project an image of reassurance, an architectural equivalent of old-world charm, or ally itself with the astringent side of the Viennese soul?

Perhaps the delay was beneficial. New York is hungrier than it was ten years ago for architecture of this caliber, and better primed to appreciate its urbanity and depth. More important, this city has become aware of its stake in the living tradition of modern architecture. There may be many out there who still believe that New York would be happier if all traces of modernity could be removed from the cityscape, but I suspect that such people are in retreat. As citizens of the Enlightenment, our deepest cultural roots are still planted in modern soil.

Mr. Abraham's design is a gateway into the tradition of modernity associated with Vienna at the turn of the last century. It is a complicated tradition, filled with contradiction, rage, and high anxiety about the modern city and the forms it should take. Those who find the Abraham design too aggressive should keep in mind that antagonism toward the city is heartily Viennese.

Today we can visit Vienna and eat pastries in the coffee shops frequented by Freud, Loos, Kokoschka. But what did those guys talk about? They spent much of their time ranting about how much they hated Vienna. Their hatred was genuine. But that was also the manner in which they expressed their love. The Austrian Cultural Forum arrives at a moment when many New Yorkers can easily identify with that old Viennese ambivalence. We sincerely hate a great deal about New York right now. We feel alienated by the city's conversion from a place of production to one increasingly geared to the economy of mass consumption. We despise the great leveling of cultural ambition created by catering to the mass audience with empty spectacles.

In architecture, we go bananas when asked to accept that "appropriateness" and "contextualism" are somehow less aggressive or tyrannical than the rigid application of early-twentieth-century Modernist dogma. We wonder if recovery from the Giuliani era's suppression of civil discourse will ever be possible.

Yet, of course, we wouldn't dream of living anywhere else because, first of all, it's our town. Also because New York remains the world's great beacon of opportunity. And finally, because it's our job to pass on an even more open and energetic city than the one that took us in.

The Forum is a twenty-four-story sliver tower, a mere twenty-five feet wide. Viewed head-on, the building appears compressed between the wider structures that flank its mid-block site. Diagonal steel braces, visible behind the glass skin, stabilize the structure against wind. But the braces also appear to exert pressure outside, as if the tower were using its neighbors for resistance in an isometric exercise. The building's structure is concrete. Mr. Abraham has divided it, front to back, into three vertical parts. The parts bear names. The glass facade is "the mask." Beyond that is "the core," containing the main structural elements and enclosed spaces. To the rear of the building are "the vertebrae," an exterior circulation spine formed by a double fire stair of poured concrete.

The mask is the most visible segment. Cantilevered from the structural core, it features four sloping louvers of bladelike glass framed with dull gray zinc. A zinc-sheathed concrete box containing the director's office projects beyond the louvers; a glass-enclosed library is positioned just beneath. The glass does not convey lightness or transparency. A heavy glass, heavily tinted, it presents a materiality akin to masonry. It is not made for shattering into photogenic smithereens but for breaking the bones of anyone stupid enough to try to smash it.

Mr. Abraham himself has likened the facade to the blade of a guillotine: the glass louvers slice slivers of sky. Others have seen a resemblance to a metronome or to an Easter Island monolith. We mustn't be afraid of such metaphors. Mr. Abraham considers himself a symbolist. The wonder is that he is able to coax symbolism out of functional necessities, like the need for external egress and conformance to the legal zoning envelope.

Public spaces are on the ground and lower levels. Forms and materials are tough, but the circulation flow is graceful. From beneath the sidewalk canopy, one progresses through lobby and galleries in a seamless loop. A skylight at the rear of the base draws the eye forward and allows a worm's-eye view of the vertebrae stairs, switchbacking skyward.

A mezzanine level leads to a small auditorium with a miniature balcony and a teeny-tiny café just outside. Upstairs are a duplex library, meeting rooms, offices, and the director's private residence. These interiors enable visitors to appreciate the organic quality of the entire building. Like the American Folk Art Museum, completed last year, the design integrates structure, form, space, and circulation into a united whole.

There is thus a Viennese perversity in Mr. Abraham's calling his facade "the mask." Compared with many postmodern skyscrapers, snappy building skins held together by who knows what kind of thingummy inside, the Forum is the soul of integrity. Yet it does not represent itself publicly as Truth. It is a disguise, beneath which we may uncover the mechanisms with which our own multiple disguises are manufactured.

The Forum is the second major venue for Austrian art to open in New York in the last five months. Farther uptown, the Neue Galerie has rekindled interest in the Viennese Modern tradition. Is something going on? Well, yes. Since the end of the Cold War, it has become increasingly clear that Vienna, past and present, has a pivotal role to play in developing a new cosmopolitan outlook.

The Forum's programs, which will focus on contemporary work in literature, fine art, music, architecture, and film, are part of this development. And the building itself should encourage visitors to dig deeper into the historical terrain of Viennese Modernism. Many will find themselves on oddly familiar ground. The building's capacity to operate on a deeply symbolic level, for example, draws on Viennese sources that have become part of the air we breathe.

For example, it happens that the Forum's director, Christoph Thun-Hohenstein, bears the family name of an Austrian count who turned up one night in Freud's dreams, where he inadvertently helped induce the birth of psychoanalysis. Every student of psychoanalysis knows the so-called Revolutionary Dream. It is integral to the history of twentieth-century thought. (Freud recounts the dream in chapter 5 of *The Interpretation of Dreams*.)

But the circumstances preceding the dream are worth noting here. In August 1893, Freud was waiting on a railway platform for a train bound for Aussee, his summer vacation spot. As he looked on, Count Franz Anton Thun arrived at the station, swept onto the platform, brushed the ticket taker aside, and commandeered a compartment as if it were his private carriage. Count Thun, a high government official, was on his way to see the emperor.

After his train pulled out, Freud found himself humming an aria from Mozart's *The Marriage of Figaro*. "If the count wishes to dance a step, I will call the tune," the libretto reads in one translation. Figaro's mocking of the aristocracy, Freud knew, was what caused the original Beaumarchais play to be banned by Louis XVI in 1778. And Freud's recounting of the affair invites us to see him as Figaro, a figure who toppled the established social order and ultimately "called the tune" for the modern intelligentsia.

And so, by a coincidence of fate, a Thun is living within a beautiful building designed by an architect who has shown equal disobedience to the elaborate rigmaroles of the status quo. "It seems to project beyond the street wall," an official of a local civic group sniffed when the Forum was on the rise, as if all right-minded people would naturally condemn such churlish behavior.

In fact, Mr. Abraham has reconnected New York to a tradition that once played a greater role in our architecture than it does today. Here we encounter the idea that patrons should serve culture, not the other way around. Power should serve imagination. Society should hold artists responsible for revealing their authentic selves, not for conforming to its own conventions.

An architect has reasserted the right to make architecture, and this turns out to be completely OK. It has been a long time since a New York building served this idea with such confidence and distinction. The building's lessons are philosophical rather than formal. I think of it as "the wedge," because it invites New York to reacquaint itself with the distinction between people-pleasing fluff and the kind of architecture that gets inside your head.

April 19, 2002

A HANDSOME HUNK OF A GLASS TOWER

Although Donald Trump prefers to publicize the aggressive side of his nature—it's the manly thing to do—he is also the only beauty freak at large in New York City real estate development. Aggression and desire, violence and sex: put them together and they add up to Trump World Tower, undeniably the most primal building New York has seen in quite a while.

I wasn't brought up to count floors in skyscrapers, so I don't know whether the seventy-two-story Trump World Tower across from the United Nations, on First Avenue between Forty-seventh and Forty-eighth streets, is the world's tallest residential building, as Mr. Trump has claimed. And it is aggressive even to advertise the idea that something is an extremity of its type: tallest, biggest, speediest, richest, or whatever. How you feel about Trump World Tower is likely to reflect how you respond to the presence of competition in your space.

Designed by the New York architect Costas Kondylis to Trump's specifications, the tower has found a surprising number of admirers among New York's younger architects. Terence Riley, chief curator of architecture and design at the Museum of Modern Art, says it's his favorite new building. Riley has a picture-postcard view of the tower from his new office at the Modern's temporary location in Long Island City. "It's a Trump building, so you're not supposed to like it," Riley says. "But it works urbanistically, and the glass curtain wall is the best New York has seen in a long time."

From downtown, the tower also makes a good impression. Its visual appeal derives, first of all, from the contrast between its amplitude of scale and its simplicity of shape. Then, like the Empire State Building, there is an unbalanced ratio of width to depth. Depending on your perspective, the tower shifts from sliveresque to monolithic. After all the froufrou launched into the skyline for the past generation—the fussy attempts at three-dimensional collage; the ersatz Art Deco confections weighed down by stepped silhouettes and ornate crowns—it is pleasing to see a flat roof raised to the top of the skyline by four flush glass walls.

All of us go tut-tut over the building's lobby, not because it's glitzy but because no effort has been made to coordinate the glitz with the Miesian vocabulary of the somber exterior. The lobby cries out for Barcelona chairs, preferably upholstered in gold lamé. And glass-topped Barcelona tables could be encrusted with cubic zirconiums to outrageous effect.

The tower's appeal is as much polemical as it is aesthetic. It punches through the morbid notion that the midtown skyline should be forever dominated by two Art Deco skyscrapers, the Empire State and Chrysler buildings, as if these cherished icons couldn't stand the competition. Philadelphia got over the taboo against building higher than the statue of William Penn that crowns its City Hall. Eventually, New York will conquer a phobia about tall buildings that had set in well before 9/11.

Le Corbusier's observation that New York's skyscrapers aren't tall enough makes even more sense today than when he made it in the 1930s. The observation had as much to do with the aggressive temperament of New Yorkers as with the physical appearance of their city, and I sense no general abatement of the city's Darwinian drives. For better and worse, we're more in touch with our instincts than we used to be.

Architecture, we forget at our peril, is inherently violent. It invariably subtracts from the range of available possibilities, especially the perennially attractive option of building nothing at all. In this sense construction sites are crime scenes. Memories, landscapes, slices of sky, beloved vistas, and old neighborhoods are violated even when buildings of distinction take their place. Perhaps the most architecture can do is convert aggression into desire, its primitive twin. Beauty is an effect of this emotional transmutation.

On a human level, I prefer most developers to most architects, because (to borrow Truman Capote's terms) developers tend to be Unspoiled Monsters, whereas architects are often very Spoiled Monsters indeed. Possessed by the desire to control, they are also convinced that their aggression is redeemed by a high artistic calling, proof of which is usually lacking. Monsters don't come more Unspoiled than Donald Trump, and the World Tower is the fullest expression of his purity to date.

It's not surprising that unofficial approval of Trump's building should come by way of the Museum of Modern Art. The tower embodies the Miesian aesthetic through which the Modern's design department's taste was initially formulated. Though Philip Johnson, the department's founding curator, later turned away from that aesthetic, the Modern itself has seldom strayed far from its roots, and indeed has survived the "postmodern" assault on the historical chapter it represents.

It has become commonplace to suggest that only Mies van der Rohe could pull off a Miesian building, as if only dumb glass boxes lay within the range of everyone else. But now it's becoming more evident that a dumb glass box is preferable to a dumb masonry box, or a dumb collage box, and that, in any case, technology has greatly expanded the expressive potential of glass.

I regret that Trump World Tower did not take greater advantage of this. I would have liked to see a more conspicuous articulation of the floor plates than dark glass allows. A vertical is nothing more than stacked horizontals: chunks of land abstracted and repeated skyward. Supertransparent "white" glass and other technical innovations enable architects to convey this idea clearly.

I hope Trump sticks with this material. The World Tower is not innovative architecture. But neither is it reactionary, unlike Trump Place, the developer's other recent venture into the skyline, under way on the Upper West Side between Fifty-ninth and Seventy-second streets. Clearly, Trump does better when he ignores his critics than when he pays attention to them. This is the lesson one gains by comparing these two projects.

The Municipal Art Society, a leading New York height-phobia spreader, campaigned against the World Tower's height and eventually brought suit to halt the project. The group lost.

At Trump Place (which started out as Riverside South), meanwhile, the Society and a coalition of civic organizations succeeded in imposing a master plan and design guidelines prepared by Skidmore, Owings & Merrill. (Disclosure: in 1991 I was invited to sit in on two meetings held to discuss ideas for the project's public space and outdoor sculpture programs.) The result, Trump reports, is a roaring commercial success.

But does anyone think it's architecture? I would call it a perfected portrait of late-twentieth-century hypocrisy. The idea, I recall, was to emulate the residential buildings of Central Park West. Why? Had the architects of the 1920s and '30s possessed large-span plate glass, they would have been among the first to spring for it. Glass, in any case, is far more "contextual" than masonry for waterfront locations: its reflective surface mirrors that of water; it yields a more radiant light. Context, moreover, is a matter of time as well as place. At Trump Place, ahistorical mutants masquerade as historical landmarks.

Of course, Trump's responsibility for these Spoiled Monsters is limited. He didn't want to work with the guidelines in the first place. Going along with them merely revealed the Municipal Art Society's blindness to contemporary architecture and to beauty in any form.

Trump Place reflects the values of an organization that routinely tries to mask its territorial aggressions behind facades of politesse. In a perverse way, Trump Place is a landmark. It signifies a time when tastefulness was mistaken for beauty.

June 2, 2002

LESSONS OF A HUMANIST
WHO CAN DISTURB THE PEACE

Renzo Piano wants to turn me into a project. "We have to teach you to appreciate serenity more," he says. Piano is preaching to the converted. I dream of spending my days staring at ocean waves. This is not a sign of personal strength but reflects my dissolute appetite for vacation values. Life is struggle, without conflict organisms die, and one of the greatest virtues of the city is its capacity to tolerate the cultural tensions that generate art.

But, for a day, I'm willing to play along with Piano's plan. It's tough to write about serenity head-on without sounding like a jerk. And the opportunity to learn from great architects is the keenest pleasure of my job. For the past year, since Piano was awarded the commission to design the future headquarters of *The New York Times*, it's been an honor to spend time with him. I've been discovering how much struggle it takes to create even a fleeting sense of peace.

Today I'm meeting him at San Giovanni Rotondo, in southern Italy on the Adriatic coast. Piano will be spending the afternoon with the construction crew now working on the Church of Thanksgiving, a vast sacred building he designed to hold a maximum capacity of eight thousand souls. He's invited me to trail him around the site.

For Americans, San Giovanni Rotondo has two big draws. First, we get to see for ourselves that Italians are actually capable of building ugly towns. Not every human habitation in this lovely land is San Gimignano. Then, San Giovanni is one of the best places to witness the persistence of unreason in the modern world. Like Lourdes, it is a pilgrimage site for those in search of divine intervention in flawed or damaged human affairs. People come here out of veneration for Padre Pio, a charismatic Capuchin friar who lived in the local monastery from 1916 until his death in 1968.

Last month he was declared a saint, though he had been a cause of controversy within Vatican circles for many years because he had displayed stig-
mata and his followers had claimed he could predict the future and heal
the sick.

The construction of the church, like the growth of the town, has paralleled the friar's progress toward canonization. To see the building now is
to gain some insight into the medieval mentality that caused great works
of architecture to rise above twisted streets lined with mud, wattle, and
dung.

San Giovanni is nestled on the side of hills spilling down toward a plain
that stretches to the sea. Taking advantage of the change in levels, the
church is approached from beneath, through a long arcade bordered by
cypresses. The arcade rises gently, but at an incline steeper than that of its
roof. The forced perspective amplifies a sense of distance. Past the arcade,
the path turns right, bringing you within sight of the church's roofline.
Another right turn leads to the entrance of an immense, fan-shaped plaza.
The southern sunlight, reflected off the stone paving, is nearly blinding.

Like a natural amphitheater, the plaza slopes down toward the
entrance to the church, which rises at the base of the fan shape. The
entrance is broad, with a soaring glass facade rising from a long row of
glass doors. On passing through the doors, you find that the fan of the
plaza is actually the outermost segment of a nautilus shape that forms the
ground plan of the church itself. We are spiraling inward—that is to say,
from a wide gathering place in the outdoors toward the vortex at the heart
of the interior, where the altar stands. This sequence of assembly is an
asymmetrical equivalent of the approach to St. Peter's in Rome.

The plan's nautilus shape is reflected overhead in the design of the
roof. Made of wood with lead covering, the roof is divided into overlapping, horn-shaped segments. Clerestories articulate the separation
between them.

Twenty-seven stone arches hold the roof aloft. The stone, quarried
locally, is smooth cut into blocks that are held together only by the force
of compression. The spans are anchored to the ground by concrete bases.
Knuckle-shaped joints punctuate the arches, giving the structure a skeletal
appearance. Some visitors will be reminded of the crypt of Santa Maria
della Concezione in Rome. One of the city's grislier tourist attractions, the
underground site is decorated with the skulls and bones of unearthed
Capuchins. In fact, the spiritual center of Piano's church also lies underground, in the crypt where Padre Pio will eventually be interred. Part of a
vast subterranean labyrinth, the crypt lies directly beneath the altar,
another concept that recalls St. Peter's.

The arches are arranged in two curving rows that radiate outward from the altar. The rows overlap, so the arches spring forward into space like two teams of synchronized divers. This arrangement also breaks down the scale of the room so that the overall effect combines the grandeur of a Baroque nave with the intimacy of ambulatory chapels.

"Architecture says serious things to thoughtful people," Pier Luigi Nervi once told a colleague. It also makes nice places for dancing nymphs. Back in Rome, I watched several teams of coltishly graceful young gymnasts go through choreographed routines in a competition held at the Palazzo del Sport. The building itself, a marvel of athletic engineering, was designed by Nervi, the great master of reinforced concrete structure, for the 1960 Rome Olympics. The young women seemed to draw energy from the building's youthful spring.

A larger, outdoor stadium designed by Nervi is just yards away. Both are to be renovated after completion of the Auditorium, a three-hall performing arts complex designed by Piano for an area adjacent to the Olympic buildings. The National Center for Contemporary Art, designed by Zaha Hadid, is to rise on a site just across the main boulevard that runs through the Flaminia district.

If you can't make it to San Giovanni Rotondo, I strongly encourage a visit to the Auditorium. One of the three halls, of medium size, is already in use. I'll be back to review the entire project when it is completed. But it is a rare experience to observe both projects take shape.

Piano is a humanist, perhaps the leading exemplar of that tradition in our time. Yet he has attained that place by reversing one of the fundamental developments from which humanism emerged. The Renaissance was contingent on the separation of architecture from building. It relied on the development of techniques for drawing *(il disegno)*, which in turn propelled a shift from construction toward theory. Henceforth, architectural practice would consist largely of manipulating abstract symbols.

Piano, by contrast, has collapsed the divide between metaphor and material. Born into a family of builders, he approaches design as a technique for "making architecture out of building" (to borrow a phrase from the historian Neil Levine). This is the most fully modern aspect of Piano's work. It has nothing to do with style but much to do with elegance, in the mathematical as well as the corporeal sense of that term. Seen in the context of his ideas, Piano can give lightness of being even to solid brick walls.

Despite his enduring focus on technological innovation, Piano is sometimes belittled as overly conservative. Though his workshop in Genoa uses computer programs as design tools, Piano's mind is not trained on the grand horizons of the digital age. Structure and function engage him. His attitude toward materials recalls that of the Arts and Crafts movement of more than a century ago. Today this attitude seldom

generates critical excitement unless it is focused on the development and
application of new materials of patently space-age genesis.

Novelty is useful in its own right. So is the revision of history that
comes with the passage of time. For me, Piano's work is squarely contemporary because it compels us to face the extent to which tradition is the
source of many things traditionalists most deplore. The treatment of
architecture as two-dimensional images. Blob-making computer programs. Virtual environments. Transparency. The dematerialization of
architecture is a more elemental consequence of the classical rebirth than
the reduction of history to an encyclopedia of period styles.

Thanks to that consequence, the public has become familiar with the
idea that architecture exists as much in the inner world of the observer as
in the sphere of material reality. And it could be that serenity resides in the
precision with which an architect can hold these two realms in a state of
equipoise. If you let your eyes trace one of the long spans in Piano's
church, you will notice that only one end of the arc is anchored in concrete. The other is deeply rooted in memory.

July 14, 2002

PEACE LOBBY

Effective immediately, the State, Justice, Treasury, and Interior departments will be superceded by the Super Agency for All-American Style. As
we all know, President Bush's restructuring of federal agencies is largely
cosmetic. Therefore, we may as well let makeup artists and other professional image consultants take over the job. (See policy memos: "Domestic
Security—It's About the Eyes," "Dull Lips Sink Ships," et al.)

Given that the major conflicts threatening the world today are cultural,
it is time to concede that politicians will never understand them. Designers, however, know what it takes to get along under trying circumstances.
They know how to talk to people: clients, consumers, and the press. Do
not underestimate their skills in conflict resolution. They have saved
many rocky marriages. They will not fail the community of nations.

Architects will not only design embassies but also occupy them. Interior, industrial, fashion, and graphic designers will be our new consular
corps. And all of us will look to the fountainhead (or is it the Fontainebleau?) of stylish international relations: the legendary Hilton International hotels.

Constructed in the 1950s and '60s, Conrad Hilton's global empire was
the world's first major architectural statement on the subject of jet-age

mobility—a transition from the International style of the '30s to today's monoculture, with its power to flatten cultural differences into global sameness. But the hotels made a good-faith effort to strike a reasonable balance between the homogenizing forces of modernity and the particulars of regional identity. Today this effort may strike us as naïve. It consisted in many cases of upholstering harsh modern buildings with deluxe versions of ethnic ornamentation.

Still, Hilton's ideological objectives were not sinister. When he began to build internationally, the United States had recently helped to win a just war. Our citizens and their leaders had lived through the Depression. Amid the postwar optimism and prosperity, few could imagine that the appetite for modernity's fruit might not be universally shared.

I feel fortunate to be old enough to remember when modernity still felt clean, if not entirely new. Glad to have been young enough, also; too short in years to distinguish what was genuinely idealistic about the Cold War years from what was substantially a form of propaganda. When I was growing up in the '50s and early '60s, everything modern seemed worth running after. And when I look back at some of that era's architectural artifacts, I still find the distinction hard to discern. For a time, the ideals of democracy and of material prosperity were so tightly woven together that both could be easily transmitted in the same architectural code.

Freedom, success, and modernity were also embodied by Hilton himself. A native New Mexican, son of a small-town businessman, Hilton gained his first glimpse of the wide world while stationed in France during World War I, and on one level the International hotels were a boy's dream of a suitcase covered with exotic travel stickers: Athens, Rome, Istanbul. From this yearning was born the diffusion of the jet-set dream.

And then along came Zsa Zsa. Hilton's marriage to the most glittering of the Gabor sisters symbolized his public embodiment of that dream. Zsa Zsa was an icon for the masses, and so was the self-styled "Mr. Hotel." And for the price of a room, anyone could ascend to the stratosphere, at least for a night.

From 1953 to 1966, Hilton constructed sixteen luxury hotels in foreign cities. These are the subject of a brilliant study by Annabel Jane Wharton, published last year by the University of Chicago Press. Titled *Building the Cold War*, the book precisely decodes the ideology embodied by midcentury modern design.

It is remarkable how much effort and intelligence went into the planning of these hotels. None, bear in mind, has joined the canon of great twentieth-century masterworks. Some of them, however, should be included—on aesthetic as well as sociological grounds, and also for the high degree of awareness with which they sought to coax architecture out of agonizing cultural conflicts. In light of the turmoil in the Middle East, Wharton's account of the design of the hotels in Cairo (1959), Tel Aviv (1965), and Jerusalem (1974) is particularly fascinating.

The Nile Hilton in Cairo was a kind of West Berlin in miniature, an effort to showcase the advantages of capitalism in a country that had attained independence only seven years before. The hotel was designed by Welton Becket, a California architect best known for the fabulous Dorothy Chandler Pavilion in downtown Los Angeles, but who also produced buildings in styles as various as those that line the streets of Beverly Hills.

Becket's talent for pastiche was extremely useful in creating a hotel that was essentially a high-rise billboard for the Western way of life. The Egyptian president Gamal Abdel Nasser, who sponsored the project, was eager to project a modern image for his young nation. His geopolitical loyalties, however, were divided. His young nation needed money. He was happy to accept Soviet support for the Aswan Dam, but he was also eager for investment from capitalists. Hilton saw his hotel not just as a profitable investment, but also as a form of propaganda. "In our current expansion," the hotelier wrote, "Hilton Hotels International views itself as a medium for bettering the understanding of peoples by extending the best we have to offer in the American enterprise system to other countries."

As Wharton writes, the Hilton was sited to turn its back on Cairo, a medieval city of crowds and poverty. Instead the windows and balconies of the best rooms framed postcard views of the pyramids, essentially erasing four thousand years of Egyptian history from the tourist's experience (and obstructing Cairo's view of Egypt's own past in the process).

The interior, which featured ersatz tomb reliefs and hieroglyphs, echoed this contraction of space and time between ancient Egypt and the modern West. From within and without, the views affirmed notions of a cultural mainstream flowing from the pharaohs to ourselves. The unsubtle message was that a common bond of tradition joined Egypt and the United States to a degree unmatched by the Soviet "East."

The Tel Aviv and Jerusalem Hiltons embodied a different political agenda. Both were explicitly Zionist in ambition. Designed by Ya'acov Rechter, they were rooted in the intention to build a European country in an Eastern region. Nice work if you can get it, and Israel's architects had been getting it well before the country's creation in 1948.

Tel Aviv, in particular, was an experimental ground for the first generation of architects to emigrate from Europe to Palestine. In the 1930s, it became the world's most complete urban realization of ideas developed at the Bauhaus under the direction of Walter Gropius.

In hindsight, it is clear that the European origins of modern architecture would be grounds for conflict with local customs. But the architects of the time believed that modern architecture was inherently capable of transcending, if not precisely bridging, the gulfs that separated cultures.

The ambition may have been utopian, but European architects had already succeeded in transforming utopian dreams into realized buildings. After World War II, they had produced the templates for social housing in the Netherlands, Germany, Italy, France, Britain, and other nations. That aesthetic, conventionally associated with the Bauhaus, had also been embraced by wealthy patrons. Modern architecture had bridged the social classes, in other words. Why couldn't it narrow the gaps between cultural traditions?

With structures of rough exposed concrete and sharply geometric balconies and windows, Rechter's Brutalist Hilton hotels reflected the influence of Le Corbusier and Louis Kahn. Glass was less conspicuous. Intended to attain greater harmony with the landscape and ancient building traditions, the concrete also conveyed the impression of fortresses under siege. Those who have actually stayed in a Hilton discover soon enough that the fortress appearance is deceptive. The function of the design is not to keep people out but to prevent those who are in from leaving. Good guests should stay within the grounds and spend their dollars there. I first encountered this strategy thirty years ago during a stay at what was then the Kahala Hilton [now the Kahala Mandarin Oriental] in Honolulu. Situated in a compound outside Honolulu, the Kahala was surrounded by a golf course, gardens, and artificial lagoons in which porpoises leapt and plunged in synchronized routines. There was a Polynesian floor show.

Chandeliers made of beach glass hung in the huge lobby, which also came furnished with a hostess, an attractive woman dressed in a long flowered gown, a variation on the muumuu. Since this was my first visit to Hawaii, I wanted to see something besides the hotel—something of Hawaii, in fact.

"But this is Hawaii," the hostess said. "This is the best of Hawaii."

"I mean, the real Hawaii."

"But this is the real Hawaii. We have everything here. Would you like to go to our luau? There is no other Hawaii."

I retreated, so confused that I would have believed the hostess had she continued further in this surreal vein: "There is no real Hawaii. There is no Hawaii." What idiot went to the Kahala Hilton for reality, anyhow? Or to Hawaii, for that matter? You want authenticity? Go home!

Hawaii, the lady tried to tell me, is a state of mind. So are Istanbul, Athens, Cairo, and the other cities that came to be dominated by Hilton's out-of-scale dream palaces. The emotional interior, the inner world, is the true foreign land. But this, of course, more nearly resembles the psychology of the prison than of the traditional traveler. Alcatraz would make a fine resort, too, if they let Philippe Starck do it over with billowing white curtains.

And is it not true that boutique hotels are Hilton's Postmodern equivalent? Hotels like the ones Starck has designed have become icons in the era of globalization. This era has intensified a struggle that has been going on since the end of World War II: a culture war between the creative classes clustered in older urban centers and the consumer-based lifestyle of the suburbs. Boutique hotels have become our embassies of urbanity. Forget the United Nations. What we need now is a League of Cities: a Secretariat of Cosmopolitan Style.

August 18, 2002

A LATIN JOLT TO THE SKYLINE

The redevelopment of Times Square has finally produced a building worth talking about: the new Westin Hotel on Eighth Avenue between Forty-second and Forty-third streets. And people are talking about it for a welcome reason. The Westin has raised a flag over the issue of taste. Translation: Many people find it ugly. Hideous. The very embodiment of beauty's evil twin.

Look up, people. This is New York. We live in one great ugly town. Not being too hung up on beauty is what makes life here possible, even thrilling. In exchange for surrendering refinement, we get a kind of urban poetry that is the envy of the world. Sometimes it takes outsiders to see it. Often, outsiders introduce new rhymes. The beauty resides, in some sense, in staying an outsider. The Westin is the consummate outsider's hotel.

Developed and owned by Tishman Realty and Construction Company, the 800-room Westin is the first major New York hotel to open since The Four Seasons in 1993. The building is a sign—a bill-ding-board, in Robert Venturi's phrase—and the sign says: WELCOME TO NUEVA YORK. Latin American architecture is here! It is the first completed New York project by Arquitectonica, the Miami-based firm led by Bernardo Fort-Brescia and Laurinda Spear.

Mr. Fort-Brescia, who was born in Lima, Peru, and Ms. Spear were the first architects of the baby boom generation to win large-scale commissions. The Spear House in Miami, designed in 1977 with Rem Koolhaas, was one of the most photographed houses of the late twentieth century.

Influenced by the Mexican architect Luis Barragán, the design introduced the firm's carnivalesque vocabulary of crisp, brightly colored, geometric forms.

Among the first of their large-scale commissions were three residential high-rises on Miami's Brickell Avenue that were instrumental in defining a new identity for the city. By then, Miami had largely ceased to be a city of the south. It had become a metropolis of the north, a magnet for people and capital from throughout Latin America. The influx of Cuban refugees had been superseded by waves of vibrant cosmopolitanism to which the Brickell Avenue buildings gave a strong public face.

The Latin strain is moving farther north again. North Americans are long accustomed to it in music, theater, film, literature, and dance. It has been a presence in New York architecture too, but is seldom grasped as such. We have work by Latin American architects here but not, thus far, an easily discernible Latin American architecture. This is changing.

The city's shifting demographic is one reason our architecture seems destined to become increasingly Latinized in the years ahead. A more important reason stems from the exhaustion of the northern European version of the Western tradition. That linear, nineteenth-century view of history has fallen apart as a measure of urban architecture. Postmodernism, a movement that tried to extend that line beyond its natural span, had the opposite effect of running it into the ground.

One tradition does not fit all. There are other routes back to the Mediterranean, paths that do not take us through London, Paris, and Berlin. And the future of New York architecture may well represent the further unfolding of southern routes from the Old World to the New. If so, the Westin Hotel is a pivotal building. Like it or not, the building signifies an important shift in the history of taste.

Arquitectonica has acquired two additional New York commissions since work on the hotel began: a large residential project in Long Island City, Queens, and, with the New York office of Cooper, Robertson & Partners, an urban design plan for the Penn yards site on the west side of midtown Manhattan.

The hotel's forty-five-story tower rises behind a ten-story base. The base, which itself appears to float above the four-story E Walk entertainment complex, is the weakest part of the design. The base's corset silhouette is comely. Its painted surface goes flat.

The base is an improvement on the original design, which envisioned a vast and redundant mural of New York City tourist attractions. That has been replaced by an abstract domino of punched-up masonry colors. But the colors don't hold their own with the design-controlled signage that wraps the base along Forty-second Street. And the abstract patterns unhappily recall the two-dimensional public art projects of thirty years ago.

If the owners take my advice, they will redo the base with a stylized version of Calvin Klein billboards. A folded photomural. Black-and-white pictures of pouty young people. Some slashes of color for accent, perhaps. An homage to the street's unsanitized, John Rechy, Russ Meyer past. (The graphic designer Tibor Kalman would have known how to do it.)

The tower is erotic enough. You might take it for a New York twenty-first-century version of the Victorian Cupid around which Picadilly Circus revolves. The tower is, in any case, the first of the area's new buildings to project a clear sense of place into the midtown skyline. It is as if the libidinous energies driven underground by "the New 42" have found momentary release. The glass skin of the tower is postmodernized Mondrian: *Broadway Samba.* A shallow arc, extending the full height of the tower, splits the southern facade in two. Blue glass predominates on the western half, pink orange on the east. The skin is accented with stripes of contrasting colors that evoke the movement of traffic on uptown and crosstown streets. *Beep-beep. Toot-toot.* Joris-Karl Huysmans, author of the fin de siècle classic *À Rebours (Against Nature),* considered blue and orange the most decadent of all color combinations. The tones here fit that description. They remind me of the strange pink patina acquired by mid-century navy blue American sedans after too many harsh scourings and hours in the sun. The tower's lopsided crown is one of the larkiest on the skyline. Instead of one more Art Deco retread, it forgoes symmetry for syncopation. At regular intervals, lights recessed within the vertical arc perform a blast-off number, shooting up the facade of the building and far into the night sky.

Inside, the colors fade to quieter pastels, combined with wood and metallic finishes. Two atrium spaces, both of irregular contour, are housed within the base, which also contains a business-class section that can be used for small conventions and private events. Arquitectonica custom-designed the interiors. Elegant and efficient, the 863 rooms are executed in a nearly monochrome palette in pleasing contrast to the exterior's carnival skin.

That skin is the main target of the sidewalk superintendents' wrath. It is indeed garish. None of that Vuitton Tower subtle-veil surface treatment here! Last summer I saw the tower from Richard Meier's window. I felt his pain. Yet a more refined facade would not have drawn so much attention to the pressing issue of taste. The truth is that beauty and ugliness have been up for grabs for some time, and not just on Forty-second Street. There's a crisis in evaluation going on all over town. It's one of the reasons discussions of the future of the World Trade Center site have been going around in circles. People can't agree on directions, movements, or styles. It is daunting to contemplate the strong possibility that we may have to judge buildings without recourse to such familiar frameworks. Yet that likelihood must now be faced. If the ruckus over the Westin is loud, that is partly because such a reckoning is overdue.

It has been a decade since state officials relaunched the Times Square redevelopment project. The youngsters for whom the place was initially conceived are now old enough to rent X-rated movies. There have been other changes. Ten years ago, New York architecture was still tyrannized by a protectionist retro ethos. That tyranny has lost its grip. The city has worked up a healthier appetite for change.

Still, change isn't supposed to be comfortable, and even at the best of times architecture is a conservative art. Those with long memories will recall a similar controversy that erupted in 1961 with the completion of the Summit Hotel (renovated by Loews and renamed the Metropolitan) on Lexington Avenue and Fifty-first Street. The hotel was designed by Morris Lapidus, also of Miami, a big-time architectural outsider of his day.

The hotel's theme was Latin America. The curvilinear building, clad in green and turquoise tile, recalled Brazilian housing blocks of the 1950s. Palm fronds waved at the door. Inside, guests seeking refreshment could choose from the Gaucho Room, the Carioca Lounge, and the Casa de Café. Beneath skull-shaped light sconces, they sat surrounded by fake pre-Columbian ornaments.

The critics hated it. One of them, Russell Lynes, at least had the wit to turn his revulsion into confessional social comedy. "We are snobbishly intolerant in New York of the subculture of Florida," Lynes wrote, "and we wish they would keep everything but their pompano and oranges down there where it belongs and not foul our nest with their taste. Ours is bad enough already; we need no help from the provinces."

But there was a note of bigotry beneath some of the rumblings over taste. "Too far from the beach," wrote one critic, a remark that, in 1961, could be read as code for "too Jewish." And I suspect that for many who liked the Summit, including myself, the Jewishness, not the ersatz South Americana, helped account for the appeal. Why shouldn't the Fontainebleau have an East Side pied-à-terre?

The Westin is too Latin. It's Almodóvar. A building on the edge of a nervous breakdown. Over the edge, even. One might see that arc of light as a gauge of urban anxiety level. Here comes another crackdown on something: sex, smoking, loud noise, loud colors, whatever. Anything that sticks out.

The Summit's negative reception shows that New York's intolerance of outsiders is nothing new. But I envy the confidence with which Lynes could describe Lapidus as a provincial. In 1961 that was a simple statement of fact. Thirty years later, the tables had turned. Only now are we beginning to emerge from a period in which New York's architecture became the most inbred, the least cosmopolitan of all world-class cities.

I leave to intrepid future historians the task of sorting out the sordid details of the process by which a deeply provincial protectionism tightened its grip in the 1970s and '80s. Suffice it to say that the city of Russell Lynes found room for work by Frank Lloyd Wright, Mies van der Rohe, Eero Saarinen, Walter Gropius, Pier Luigi Nervi, Marcel Breuer, and other outsiders. Even Lapidus made return engagements. Though the work of these architects sometimes fell short of expectations, their creative ambition boosted the city to the level of architectural history.

No comparable record of receptivity exists for the 1970s and '80s. And the local firms who flourished in those years were gazing into rearview mirrors. They were as out of touch with architectural developments internationally as they were with social and cultural currents here at home.

It's catch-up time. New York has never truly known what it's like to build outside a northern European framework. And the city has ceased to be a northern European province. There is, in other words, a gap between who we are and how we build. New York is a Western city, but there is more than one way to be Western. New York has many. But we are just starting to trace alternative architectural paths.

Enrique Norten's planned addition to the Brooklyn Public Library, for example, will do more than enlarge the architectural prospects for New York's future. It will also help to uncover a different Western past. Arquitectonica's residential project for Long Island City, which is still in design development, could expand the New World beyond the cheerless vision of lost New York.

Yet it may well require more "ugly" buildings before the city's builders begin to recognize the magnitude of the shift taking place beneath our noses. The change is more momentous than the cosmetic swings we have lately seen between modernism and tradition. It involves the understanding that there are many modernisms, each with its own set of traditions, all of them with deep historical roots. The difficulty of adjusting to this idea is only part of the crisis in evaluation facing those uncertain about how to build. But the most promising and accessible way out of the impasse may lie with outsiders.

A revised critical framework will be needed to interpret their contributions. It will not exclude such values as beauty or ugliness, good taste or bad. But such terms will be recast within an outline of difference and sameness, of fusion and separation, bridges and boundaries, proximity and distance. Such frameworks already exist. They have enabled us to appreciate the dynamic interaction between the creative process and the social contract. Until one is assimilated by New York architecture, aesthetic evaluation will amount to little more than glorified police profiling.

October 20, 2002

CASTLES IN THE AIR ADORN CITIES ON PAPER

First there was God, then came history, now there is the survival of the fittest. I'm not prepared to argue that this sequence represents the Ascent of Man. I am simply trying to tell you how architecture became the inspired mess it is today. It isn't all Philip Johnson's fault. He had helpers. Major historical influences were at work. And you should know something about these unseen forces if you want to get the most out of The Changing of the Avant-Garde, an important show of architectural drawings now on view at the Museum of Modern Art's temporary headquarters in Long Island City, Queens.

Organized by Terence Riley, chief curator of the Modern's department of architecture and design, the show focuses on conceptual projects from the 1960s and '70s, a period when architects were rapidly shedding the aesthetic restraints of the Modern movement. Much more was going on here than the challenge to an architectural aesthetic, however. Western architects were gradually waking up to a momentous possibility. Never before, it seemed, had they been less constrained by authority, by an ideological scaffolding strong enough to stabilize the meaning and value of their forms.

It's no wonder that the period is memorable more for paper fantasies than for buildings. An architecture without authority risks becoming one without clients. And we are only just now learning how hard it is to rebuild public support for architecture that takes risks.

The Changing of the Avant-Garde honors the gift of the Howard Gilman Collection of Visionary Architectural Drawings, which was donated to the Modern two years ago. Pierre Apraxine, the collection's curator, has helped select work for the show, which is supplemented by drawings from the same period drawn from the Modern's archives.

Inevitably, this arrangement has produced a distorted view of the time. The show is far from encyclopedic. And it does not reckon with the Modern's own role during a period that witnessed the decline of the values the museum was partly founded to promote. Nonetheless, it hits enough high spots to establish the period's importance. What we see here are the roots of architecture's revival as an art of ideas.

Chronologically organized, the show begins with a selection of drawings of the Dymaxion House by Buckminster Fuller, the famed designer of the geodesic dome. Conceived in 1927, the house predates the period in question, but Fuller's influence did not become widespread until the emergence of the counterculture in the late 1960s and early '70s. In 1969, with the publication of the first *Whole Earth Catalog*, "Bucky's dome" became the counterculture's chief tribal totem.

Fuller's technologically attuned work came to represent an impersonal vernacular, an idealized solution to every need for human shelter. To a degree, his designs were an escape from architecture, and this urge to flee was one of the period's defining characteristics. "How much does your building weigh?" Fuller would ask, as if the whole idea of architecture had become too weighty and cumbersome for Spaceship Earth.

Yona Friedman's Spatial City, a project of 1958–59, was even lighter than Fuller's domes. At least it promised to release entire cities from gravitational force. A kind of horizontal Eiffel Tower, suspended over existing urban development, the project was both superstructure and infrastructure. It resembled a jungle gym on which temporary structures could disport themselves like gangly children. Power, water, and other services would be contained inside the structural elements of the metal three-dimensional grid, with housing and other buildings inserted into the open spaces between them.

A ludic dimension had taken hold; the city came to be seen as a gigantic fun fair (a vision coming to frightening fruition in the theme-park styling that would grip urban planning decades later). Play and eroticism figured in many conceptual projects of the period, but none exercised greater influence than Cedric Price's Fun Palace, a project of 1959–61. The concept would find form eventually in 1977, with the completion of the Pompidou Center in Paris.

The idea for the Fun Palace was supposedly first hatched (on Forty-second Street) by Mr. Price and the theater director Joan Littlewood on a visit the two made to America that year. The design reflected the increasing whimsy of postimperial Britain. Architecture? Fun? This was a clear philosophical departure from the Brutalist style associated with Britain's welfare state.

Part open university, part indoor amusement park, it was meant to be housed within an immense structure recognizably descended from Paxton's Crystal Palace. Permanently affixed building cranes enabled walls and floors to be constantly rearranged, like Tinkertoys. One sees this as a metaphor for the situation in which architects then found themselves, with no sturdy ideological scaffold on which to build.

In contrast to the material dimension of structure and function, fun implied a psychic state. The emotional content of buildings is one of several themes traced by the Modern's exhibition. Images of solitude, pleasure, fear, and aggression haunt the designers' imaginations, much as reason and objectivity had preoccupied their elders.

Perhaps the show's overarching theme is architecture's changing relationship to the city. Instead of regarding the nineteenth-century industrial city as a technologically obsolescent problem, architects began to embrace it as a source of inspiration. The large-scale, comprehensive master plan gave way to the concept of the individual building as an urban intervention.

The megastructure—a single building housing a variety of uses—was the pivotal building type in this transition. In place of catastrophic urban renewal, the megastructure was, in effect, a city within a building. The Fun Palace is one example of this type. Another is Paul Rudolph's plan for the Lower Manhattan Expressway. (The World Trade Center, in fact, was a variation of it, containing offices, transportation, shops, a hotel, and public spaces within an organically conceived complex.) Paradoxically, by enlarging the scale of the individual building, architects were taking a step toward contracting the scale of their ambition over entire cities.

Aldo Rossi took the decisive step with the publication of his 1966 book, *The Architecture of the City*, and with his designs for the Cemetery of San Cataldo in Modena, Italy (with Gianni Braghieri), which he began in 1971. The book's appeal was manifold. Rossi was an architect. Unlike Jane Jacobs, whose widely influential 1961 book, *The Death and Life of Great American Cities*, also argued in favor of the microscale, Rossi wasn't handicapped by contempt for the Modern movement. It is a melancholic book, one that views the city through de Chirico's Surrealist eye.

With Rossi, we reach the point at which the distinction between the modern and the traditional is no longer tenable. In his later work, Rossi conducted a somewhat Disneyfied flirtation with period styles. Initially, his sympathy for the past was quite different. It was a meditation on personal memory, a reflection on the ominously mute symbolism with which buildings are invested by children and other innocent observers. We give buildings theatrical meanings quite independent of the historical circumstances that produced them.

Memory is not the same as history. It is an internal, not an external authority. As such, it cannot support the transcendent ideological framework that history had been providing architecture for four hundred years.

Modernism itself was part of that framework. Modern architects simply took nineteenth-century historicism—the view that every epoch produces a distinctive architectural style—and projected it onto the twentieth century. The death of Modernism, then, was the death of history, and the death of authority also, at least for the purposes of a democratic secular society. Until the Renaissance, after all, architecture had known no other authority but God.

In his design for the Modena cemetery, Rossi invokes religion to conduct a last rite for architecture itself. Derelict, imperfect, the city now becomes an authority by default. And we plunge deeply into the Surrealist terrain occupied by architecture today: the area of overlap between metaphor and material, between politics and the psyche.

A Surrealist would describe this terrain as the space between Freud and Marx. But particularly in American cities, it would be more accurate to call it the space of Darwin. For we are not used to dealing with buildings here on their intrinsic aesthetic or conceptual merits. We are used to dealing with power, and with the use of politics to confer prestige on work that may be entirely lacking in cultural value. This is the point at which the Museum of Modern Art's own role since the 1960s becomes germane to the show's subject.

As the leading arbiter of early- to mid-twentieth-century architectural taste, the Modern inherited the École des Beaux-Arts's authority to confer historical stature. For the last forty years, the museum's role has become fuzzier. In 1966 it courageously published Robert Venturi's *Complexity and Contradiction in Architecture*, the book that set American Postmodernism in motion. Conscientiously, the museum declined to support the reactionary work to which that movement ultimately led.

Yet the Modern has offered only intermittent support for contemporary work of substance. In the past decade, we have had major shows on Kahn, Wright, Aalto, and Mies, while an entire generation of living architects (Richard Meier, Peter Eisenman, Frank Gehry, Álvaro Siza, Sir Richard Rogers) has been overlooked for full-scale retrospectives. We get power-brokering group shows of work by younger architects, while blazing talents like Zaha Hadid, Jean Nouvel, and Thom Mayne fail to receive their full due. Developments in Asia and Latin America go largely untracked. No show has come close to this year's Venice Architecture Biennale in bringing the international architecture scene into panoramic focus. New York needs it more than Venice does.

I hope that the Modern gives up these Greatest Hits of Modernism, already. They've become the curatorial equivalent of Postmodernism's period recyclings. Contemporary architecture has regained public interest but still needs sustained institutional support to maintain momentum.

That became clear earlier this year, when the Lower Manhattan Development Corporation tried to imprint Ground Zero with the hokey New Urbanist real estate formulas favored by Alexander Garvin, the agency's head of planning and design. The Changing of the Avant-Garde is a welcome undertaking, but it should also come as a cautionary tale about what happens when visionary architects start taking the future for granted.

I recognize that the Modern is now on hiatus. I've come to think of MoMA/Queens as MoMA/Spa. Perhaps they should hand out blue terrycloth robes, bottles of spring water, and little bento boxes with low-calorie cuisine. We could all get really relaxed and comfortable.

Unfortunately, architecture is not on hiatus. Architecture is on a roll right now, but it is also feeling somewhat anxious, particularly in New York, a city where architecture is only beginning to reassert its own authority after years of displacement by retrograde real estate development. I hope it won't be too long before the Modern reestablishes its leadership in these changing times.

October 25, 2002

FASHION'S HIGH PRIESTESS OF GNOSTICISM

Why don't you . . . give all your ideas away to other people, so that you'll fill up again with new ones? Diana Vreeland, the great fashion editor, understood that this is how creative minds work. It's fatal to be a hoarder. When you have an idea, get it out there. Pretend you're Josephine Baker, tossing fruit into the audience. Hit someone on the head with a pineapple. Circulate the energy. Distribute the wealth. Rinse your child's hair with dead Champagne.

This is a gnostic way of thinking. Now relax. It's Sunday. You won't mind a bit of gnosticism with your Styles. Glamour and knowledge both share the same root in gnosis (secret learning), so why shouldn't gnosticism be fashion's true faith?

The Gnostics were a religious order, circa the year 0, but in modern times it makes better sense to view them as a personality type. Vreeland was one of them.

"If you do not bring bring forth what is within you," the Gnostics believed, "what you do not bring forth will destroy you." And I suspect Vreeland truly believed that if she had an idea and didn't get it out there, it would kill her. Killer-diller. If she couldn't come out with observations like "Pink is the navy blue of India," she would die.

Thanks in part to those observations, she hasn't. Or, rather, the point of view defined by Vreeland's insights remains indispensable. It is the viewpoint of fearlessness, the stance of "Why not?" And if Vreeland's legend looms larger today than it did during her lifetime, that may be because this particular stance has become harder to sustain.

Vreeland is the subject of a new biography by Eleanor Dwight, and it is the first to explore the personality behind the histrionic public persona. The book rides a wave of printed material by and about Vreeland that did not begin until years after her retirement from *Vogue*. *Allure*, a coffee-table book, written with Christopher Hemphill, of black-and-white photographs punctuated with Vreeland's taped recollections of them, was published in 1980 and has been reissued this year.

The first book was followed in 1984 by the editor's memoir, *DV.* Two additional volumes of Vreeland's musings have appeared in the last year: *Why Don't You?* a collection of her columns for *Harper's Bazaar*, and *Vreeland Memos*, an issue of the fashion periodical *Visionaire*.

Why don't you . . . buy Dwight's biography and read it, so that I don't have to try your patience with one of those supercompressed summaries that nobody reads anyhow? "Elegance is refusal," Vreeland once pronounced. I don't know whether this is a gnostic idea precisely. But it appears to be an essential antidote to excessive gnostic fecundity. If what you have to bring forth is tedious, just leave it alone.

Vogue in the 1960s was as much the creature of its time as it was the creation of an editor. At the beginning of the decade, fashion magazines reflected a relatively rarefied realm of elegance, style, and social poise. Ten years later, they had become a mass medium. Vreeland's *Vogue* occupied the pivotal place in this transformation. Herself a latter-day Edwardian Woman of Style, she hit her manic professional stride in the postwar years, when people were just beginning to grasp the full extent of changes brought about by mass communications.

These circumstances are unrepeatable. That's why it is pointless to complain that no magazine quite like Vreeland's exists today. No world like hers exists today. When she started out, celebrity was tantamount to notoriety. Now the news media are glamorous in their own right. Today everybody knows who Diana Vreeland was. In her own time, she communicated to audiences who never gave much thought to who an editor was.

I know, because I was part of it. When I started reading *Vogue* in my early teenage years, I had little interest in fashion and knew even less about it. Rather, like *The New Yorker*, and Ada Louise Huxtable's architecture columns, *Vogue* represented what I recognized as an urban point of view. I found my suburban life confining. It was a relief to project myself into the escapist fantasies offered by those texts. I wouldn't know of the existence of Diana Vreeland or William Shawn, the editor of *The New*

Yorker, until many years later. Now the situation has changed. We're all regaled by the antics of editors without magazines.

Vreeland, I later read in a biography of Alexander Liberman by Calvin Tomkins and Dodie Kazanjian, once described *Vogue* as "the myth of the next reality." The myth was accurate in my case. The next reality was relatively exempt from the pleasures of cold-war normalcy.

People were onto something when they called Vreeland the high priestess of fashion. She was a Gnostic priestess. In the gnostic system, there was an outer mystery for the many and an inner mystery for the few. So it was with Vreeland's *Vogue*. Many readers may have regarded it as the leading fashion magazine. Others, too few to constitute a mass readership, understood that glamour has to do only incidentally with clothes. It has mainly to do with personality structure, with the places we choose to dwell or avoid within the architecture of our subconscious fantasies.

Now, the point of gnosticism is to be reborn to the divine within oneself. If "the divine" is not acceptable, you can substitute the truth within oneself. Or, as the psychotherapist D. W. Winnicott called it, the authentic self. But Vreeland probably would be comfortable with the divine.

Why don't you bring out that divine thing that is within you? If you don't, that divine thing will slay you.

In any case, you have to kill off the inauthentic, or at least not let it take over the executive committee of the self. Vreeland was vigilant in this regard. Of course, she was also a fabulist. She made up or grossly exaggerated her accounts of her past and the world around her. But if she had stuck to the facts, she would have falsified her self. She had "the wound" of the creative artist: an unshakeable disbelief in her potential to be loved, coupled with an iron determination to conceal this disbelief from herself. From this stemmed her power as an architect of other people's desires.

Ms. Dwight's biography is, among many other marvels, a brilliant study in the relationship between love and work. The book is a treatise of changing mores too, of course, but at heart it is a report from the front lines in the struggle to craft new identities for men and women in the modern world of work. The evidence suggests that Vreeland was not a feminist. She was, however, a strong woman and a breadwinner who reformed the decorous world of fashion magazines within her muscular grip.

Vreeland's is the flip side of the "Lady in the Dark" story. This extraordinary woman blossomed when circumstances forced her to create a world outside her marriage to a man of limited emotional and financial resources. Reed Vreeland looked the part of leisured money. The leisure part was real. He was a Ralph Lauren ad campaign before a Ralph Lauren was even dreamed of, but evidently possessed neither the earning power nor the work ethic of an average male model. A woman who considered herself unattractive might see him as a catch.

But what a lot of hard work it must have taken for Vreeland to believe that he was worthy of her devotion! The fantasies it must have taken to fill up the vacuum between herself and a human version of the spotted-elk-hide trunks she advised her readers at *Harper's Bazaar* to strap on the backs of their touring cars! She was herself the driver. And although it is pleasing in life to travel with attractive luggage, greater rewards await those who travel light. A higher quality of attention will be paid to the active partner in the wider world.

"I know what they're going to wear before they wear it, eat before they eat it, say before they say it, think before they think it, and go before they go there!" This astonishing outburst, once overheard by Richard Avedon, could be taken as evidence of a fashion dictator's disrespect for her readers. But perhaps the woman was simply reassuring herself that she could trust her instincts.

What else did she have to go on? It's not as if she was dealing with anything rational. In *DV,* Vreeland recounts the possibly apocryphal story of assigning a photographer to shoot a picture against a green background. The photographer strikes out after three attempts. " 'I asked for billiard table green!' I am supposed to have said. 'But this is a billiard table, Mrs. Vreeland,' the photographer said. 'My dear,' I apparently said, 'I meant the idea of billiard table green, not a billiard table.' "

In other words, it did not pay to follow this dictator literally. Far better to respond with instincts of one's own. This, I think, was the core clause in Vreeland's contract with her readers. We expected her to know where we were going before we went there. We were traveling to places deeper within ourselves.

November 17, 2002

THE MEMORIAL WOULD LIVE IN THE ARCHITECTURE

First, you die. What happens next is a matter of faith, decomposition, conjecture, or surprise. Even happenstance cries out for some kind of organizing principle, however, and the Greeks were on to something when they declared Memory (Mnemosyne) to be the mother of civilization. The dead have done their work. Now the onus is on us. Pass it on and pass on. From the chain of memory, cities are built.

On Wednesday, the Lower Manhattan Development Corporation was scheduled to present the results of a design study for the rebuilding of the

World Trade Center site. The work is to be shown at the Winter Garden of the World Financial Center in Battery Park City through February 3. In theory, the designs do not include specific plans for a memorial to those who died when the Twin Towers were destroyed. A separate competition has been scheduled for that part of the redevelopment project. But how could you reasonably expect architects to keep their minds off the project's architectural heart?

Perhaps another competition won't be needed; on the basis of the newest architectural designs, it could be redundant. Several of the architects used the same phrase to describe their projects: "The whole thing is a memorial." I expect their work will be seen that way by many visitors to the exhibition.

An international group called United Architects, for example, has situated the memorial site partly under the footprints where the two towers once stood. Looking upward—toward a vista of sky framed by skyscrapers like a clearing in a forest—would be part of the memorial experience.

Another group, Think Architects, has lodged a memorial within the upper reaches of an open-frame tower. But the frame itself deliberately evokes the helical structure of DNA, as if to suggest that the life of the World Trade Center continues in altered form. The Egyptian scale of the colossal gateways designed by Richard Meier, Charles Gwathmey, Peter Eisenman, and Steven Holl reminds us that tombs gave birth to the monumental tradition.

If the architects have exceeded the design study's requirements, we should be grateful. They've helped to expose a major defect of the entire design process thus far: the attempt to contain architecture within such restrictive boundaries that it cannot perform its legitimate poetic function.

The design process got off on the wrong foot when the development corporation tried to separate planning from architecture, thereby relegating the latter discipline to the status of an afterthought. The study project, which followed one organized by the *New York Times Magazine* last summer, was undertaken to rectify this problem. This time around, architects have been given the opportunity to drive the planning process. They haven't done such a bad job of it.

But it is no less inorganic to divorce the design of a project from its architectural heart. This is a bureaucratic approach, not an urbanistic one. And it fails to grasp a fundamental aspect of 9/11 that has haunted the city's dreams for more than a year. September 11 was a dismemberment: a violent separation. The poetic function is needed to create new connective tissue. That is a just function for architecture in the public sphere.

We need to examine the phenomenon of contemporary memorials

before this function can be adequately performed. By this I don't mean simply reviewing recent examples of memorials and trying to decide which of them are more or less well or badly done. I mean asking why it is that this building type has come to such prominence in our national life in the last twenty years.

On a certain level, it's all Maya Lin's fault. If Lin hadn't acquitted herself with such genius in her design for the Vietnam Veterans Memorial in Washington, none of this would have happened. Since that project's completion in 1982, it has sometimes seemed as if every instance of mortality must be publicly commemorated in durable form. Memorials like the field of 168 chairs in Oklahoma City—Act III of *Our Town* in an open-air production—have not dulled the power of Lin's design, but neither have they equaled it. They have contributed, rather, to a growing sense of memorial fatigue, a semipermanent state of mourning.

I wonder whether our memorials are not in themselves, collectively, an expression of chronic fatigue on a national scale. It's apt that the cycle began with Vietnam. The exhaustion precipitated by that protracted struggle endures. Even when they commemorate tragedies like the Great Irish Famine, memorials could be our way of grieving over the "perpetual war for perpetual peace" that still shadows us at home.

I've been thinking of our memorial culture as a symbol of national metamorphosis, a transformation not only in how we Americans see ourselves but in who we actually are. Twelve years ago, some people said we hadn't won the Cold War; we were just the second to lose. I found myself recalling that thought often in the last fifteen months. It is certainly reassuring to possess the military strength to defend ourselves from attack. But can't we just get on to whatever the next thing is after being a superpower?

So the metamorphosis, if that's what it is, is still in progress. We're no longer the radiant, benign, optimistic hero of the postwar years, our white Pan Am jets streaking through peaceful blue skies over gleaming glass skyscrapers. Nor are we yet the self-sufficient, self-respecting citizen of the world we would like to become. Meanwhile, we can retreat into our memories and pray for better times.

New York has been going through a metamorphosis of its own. Consciously or not—and life would be unbearable if we were conscious of it too much of the time—our great city has been in an intermittent state of grief since the fiscal crisis of the mid-1970s. We're no longer the uncontested center of the cultural or financial universe. Nor have we yet mutated into a leading star of the emerging global culture.

There's so much to mourn, starting with the winnowing of the city's creative ranks by AIDS. Then it will take a long time to recover from the chilling of civil discourse that occurred during the Giuliani years. Sure, the streets got safer, but what happened to the public realm? The new Times Square is wonderful, unless it's not, but it is painful to contemplate the prospect of a city recast in the sanitized image promoted by Times Square's redevelopers.

Maybe we should get used to it. September 11 has accelerated the transformation of buildings into high-security bunkers, protected behind what architects now call "sacrificial facades" (air pockets designed to resist car-bomb blasts). Such defensive techniques reinforce pressures of social fragmentation that have been at work for decades.

"The whole thing is a memorial." One might expand the scale of reference to include most of contemporary New York. I'm thinking of Jean Baudrillard's caustic observation about Disney World. Americans rely on it to prevent themselves from seeing that the rest of the country is Disney Land too. An analogy could be drawn with the memorial contemplated for Ground Zero. As a community event, this project distracts us from the extent to which the contemporary city has become a memorial of itself in 1928, the apogee of Art Deco Manhattan.

All cities are memorials. Civilization is mostly a history of rebuilding them after catastrophes, not planning them from scratch. But the modern cosmopolitan city differs from the old royal palace compound. It is host to different memories, traditions, and expectations. The cityscape records their interplay over time.

This dynamic escaped the notice of our architects and planners for more than a generation. Vincent Scully, an architectural historian, was speaking for this faction when he wrote, in 1999, "We tend to hope that New York and Chicago will stay pretty much as they are."

We do? Are we dead yet?

Not quite. Actually, contemporary architecture was starting to push through the retro crust in the years before 9/11, and it is heartening to see this growth continue with the projects unveiled last week. They include ideas on a level of ambition not seen locally for a half century. This is all the more remarkable given that officials of the development project have not displayed a notably progressive cast of mind. On the contrary, the agency's own in-house planners, Peterson Littenberg, are followers of the reactionary architect Léon Krier, Prince Charles's architectural adviser. With this firm on retainer, we risk seeing all of Manhattan below Canal Street morphing into a cenotaph, a cityscape frozen like Pompeii at the hour the Twin Towers collapsed.

Many people are naturally offended by the perception of Ground Zero as a potential site for great contemporary architecture. Wouldn't that be tantamount to dancing on a mass grave? Wouldn't it be more dignified to imagine retaining the open space as a void, a park, a lake? Does anyone really think we've reached the point where such questions can be satisfactorily resolved? Should we be getting there faster or slower?

That's what we're finding out. The whole thing is the memorial: the designs; the debates they provoke; the self-awareness that emerges in the course of the debate; and the shifting shape of the city in the light of that awareness.

December 22, 2002

A HERITAGE REDISCOVERED, THEN REMADE

Inside many a thin building is a fat one straining to get out. Frank Gehry lets it out. Like many of his other projects, Mr. Gehry's new concert hall for Bard College is a Balanchine dancer with the build of a Victorian banker.

The two-theater complex, the Richard B. Fisher Center for the Performing Arts, ripples across a sylvan setting here, about an hour north of New York. Girded with curving panels of stainless steel, the building gives a new twist to Walter Pater's old adage that all art constantly aspires to the condition of music. Here music might well morph into a hippo in a tutu, whirling *en pointe.*

In this setting nature and culture are indivisible. The Hudson River school painters were pivotal figures in the forging of American identity in the nineteenth century. Respect for that heritage has thus far protected the Hudson valley from overdevelopment. It is now a cultural landscape, an art park in which the stately mansions of Dutchess County figure as sculptural expressions of an urbanizing society.

Bard's president, Leon Botstein, who also conducts symphonies, has emerged as a great patron of architecture. In 1989 he commissioned Robert Venturi and Denise Scott Brown to design an addition to the college library, housed in an old Greek Revival temple on a hillside. Cathy Simon and James Stewart Polshek have also designed substantial additions to the campus. An interpretive portrait of those projects could lay the ground for a good general survey of American contemporary architecture.

The budget for the Fisher Center was a relatively modest $62 million. Mr. Gehry has responded by concentrating his resources on the building's principal facade and the public spaces just behind it. He encloses back-of-the-house functions within a plain box. He used the same Main Street false-front device in his 1993 design for the Weisman Art Museum at the

University of Minnesota at Minneapolis. In that project a shiny, wavy gravy of steel faces the Mississippi River; the plain box, to the rear, is clad in red brick. At Bard the metal facade looks toward the campus across a landscape of fields and wooded lanes. The box, of plaster over concrete, contains a smaller, black box theater, along with offices, rehearsal studios, and a scenery shop.

But front and rear are integrated more effectively here. The Weisman, seen in the round, gives the impression of a tooth with a crown on it. At Bard the box is sheltered by a steel roof that sweeps backward from the facade, like a silver ribbon wrapped around both halves.

Also, unlike the Weisman, the Bard center is a horizontal composition. Surrounded by trees, just a short walk from the Hudson, Fisher Center is as much a piece of American landscape as anything by Wright. Given Mr. Gehry's affinity with Oscar Niemeyer, there is no reason not to think that the contour of the roof suggests the silhouette of a female form. Maybe it's the limbs and torso of a June Taylor dancer, viewed through a kaleidoscope.

Those reared on Mr. Venturi's aesthetic of complexity and contradiction (or on Main Street, for that matter) will find the division between front and rear a natural, even functionalist, means of organizing space.

The facade and lobbies honor the sense of public occasion. The plain box serves culture workers. The two groups meet on the common ground of performance space.

Showtime. As you approach the hall's main entrance, a portion of the roof appears to rise up like a curtain, allowing you to enter through the transparent membrane of a tall glass wall. Shoulders back. Head high. Soaring to a height of four stories, the lobby is a stage for social spectacle. Scene: a small opera house of eighteenth-century scale, in modern industrial dress. Balconies to peer down from. Lofty metal stairs to reach them.

Mr. Gehry will tell you that the low budget forced him to choose narrow prefab panes for the glass wall. To my eye the panes are as characteristic of Mr. Gehry as the rippling steel. He has been using them at least since the Goldwyn Library, a high-security fortress in Hollywood. The library's perimeter walls are brutally frank about their protective function, but the tall casement windows are of Palladian proportions, fit for an ideal villa in a high-crime zone.

There's no brutality at Bard, just lots of exposed hardware: athletically poised metal trusses, struts, and braces that are themselves performers in a ballet méchanique.

Piranesi, not Palladio, though, is the figure who presides over the lobby, not the first great, ennobling American public space to have been inspired by a great architect of imaginary prisons. Bulfinch was there first.

Orpheus calls. The main hall is lyre-shaped, gently classical in symmetry, scale, and proportions. It's an airy but intimate room, with seating for up to 950 people. An orchestra shell, made of eight movable towers, is rolled into place for concerts. The shell, faced with panels of pale Douglas fir, is removed for opera and other theatrical events.

The wooden stage floor is stained a deep mauve, a lush contrast to the light wood shell. Chevron-shaped pine baffles adorn the fronts of the room's three balconies; the walls are concrete.

When the accoustician told Mr. Gehry that he needed some detailing to help splinter the sound, the architect took a sheet of paper and made some doodles on it. Those arabesques now decorate the walls.

Did I mention that you are walking into history here? A new building by Mr. Gehry is an opportunity to discover why Michael Kammen used the phrase *mystic chords of memory* for the title of his 1991 book on American tradition. To focus exclusively on the novelty of Mr. Gehry's formal vocabulary is to misrepresent him. The power of his architecture lies more in the echoes of the past that are evoked by his transformation of common historical sources.

Piranesi, Orpheus, the Hudson River school: Mr. Gehry himself avoids acknowledging such highfalutin references and may not even be aware of them. If he were too aware, he most likely would not go there. He is too interested in the unexpected. The last thing he wants is status by pedigreed association.

Nor do visitors need to be conscious of the social and cultural heritage Mr. Gehry's work transforms. The pleasure derives from losing sight of the familiar as well as from recovering it from the deep well of modern amnesia. That intuitive, alternating process explains why the Fisher Center seems to vibrate like a well-tempered mind.

April 23, 2003

FROM OLYMPUS, DIVINE DRESSES

Now, this is the kind of looting we admire: old looting; remote, half-forgotten, lost-in-the-mists-of-time looting. As if the priceless rubble had been spirited away not by base temple robbers but by beauteous beings attuned to the highest spiritual calling.

Or, if we must have new loot, let it be in the form of purloined ideas: inspiration, as it used to be called. Echoes are more ethereal than stones. And concepts are nearly as gossamer as the gowns in Goddess, the new show at the Metropolitan Museum of Art's Costume Institute. As feather-light, in fact, as the show itself. Blow gently, ye Aeolian winds, or the entire exhibition may float up and away into the trees of Central Park.

Organized by the Costume Institute's curator, Harold Koda, Goddess presents a couture version of Arcadia, late-eighteenth-century Europe's sanitized re-creation of a Greece that never was. Gamboling Graces. Primavera. One hundred and forty variations on the theme of nymphs wrapped in gauze. That's the harmonious and sisterly conceit.

This may not be the ideal moment for arcadian idylls, however. Not when large chunks of our Mediterranean heritage have just been blown to smithereens. It is peculiar, moreover, to see such an important art museum standing history on its head. The presentation mingles fragments of ancient Greek statuary with twentieth-century fashions that resemble them. This combination is intended to illustrate what Philippe de Montebello, the Met's director, describes in the show's catalog as "the unbroken line of classical influence."

Actually, the twentieth-century fashions on view depict precisely the reverse process: how modern Europeans created a purely ahistorical myth of Greek ancestry to compensate for the collapse of unifying social traditions in their own times. Goddess echoes but does not illuminate this neoclassical impulse. It withholds from viewers the cultural history of the myth the clothes act out.

It is delightful when fashion makes light of history, less so when museums make a shambles of it. But begone, dull conscience. Let's be fancy and carefree. Fashion is fashion. Primavera is the right idea for the season. And Goddess is one of the most beautiful shows the Costume Institute has ever put on.

Three red-robed Nikes greet the viewer on the way to the Met's own intimate Hades, the basement galleries where the Costume Institute is infernally lodged. Identically garbed in gowns of layered scarlet chiffon designed by Issey Miyake, the trio bring to mind the scene in *Funny Face* in which Audrey Hepburn holds aloft a red silk wrap to mimic the Victory of Samothrace looming behind her. Take the picture!

These rippling "waterfall" dresses make the perfect introduction to a show that should leave many visitors with the feeling that modern civilization is vastly superior to that of the Greeks. They did have superb profiles. But our cosmetic surgery is improving every day. Greek plays aren't as good as Shakespeare's; their sculpture is less virtuosic than Bernini's. Even our dresses are superior to their statues, particularly when Jennifer Lopez wears them.

And we live longer. The average Greek life span was thirty-two years. No wonder the Greeks went in for total simplicity. Who had time to waste on shopping? If you spent your free hours at the gym, you stood a good chance of leaving a pretty corpse. Like Chanel, the Greeks devised a way of dressing that worked for them and stuck with it. They practically invented cloning, at least in matters of art.

Actually, as a text on the wall informs, Greek women had three basic outfits to choose from: the chiton, a plain chemise, worn floor-length; the peplos, a chemise with a deep overhang of cloth to the waist; and the himation, a large cloak, similar to the Roman toga, that could be draped in many ways. The show's modern dresses offer variations on these proto-types, which are sometimes used in combination.

With few exceptions, the modern examples are drawn from the world of high fashion. There is an etymological justification for this focus: the word *classical* initially referred to languages associated with upper-class society, as opposed to vernacular forms of expression. The haute couture approach, however, has some major disadvantages. By excluding athletic attire, for example, it fails to connect contemporary values to the pivotal place the Greeks granted to the human body.

The omission of that specialized form of sportswear, the ballet costume, is especially glaring. Balanchine's use of practice clothes in Stra-vinsky ballets like *Agon* was the supreme expression of classical tempera-ment in the twentieth century. Isamu Noguchi's designs for *Orpheus* and Barbara Karinska's costumes for *Chaconne* would have made handsome additions.

The omission of modern folk or tribal dress is also an unfortunate lapse. You would never guess from looking at this show that there are still parts of the world—Turkey, for one—where people commonly wear tunics of beautifully pleated muslin. (I used to wear those shirts many years ago, when I was a student and had hair as long as a Cretan bull dancer, and believe me, they opened doors.) Universality is often held to be a leading characteristic of classical art. True or not, that notion is ren-dered more convincing by an inclusive approach.

The show's sensibility is rooted in 1930s Hollywood. Lighting for black-and-white movies conferred on Hollywood stars a monochromatic allure similar to that attained by Greek buildings and sculptures after cen-turies of weathering had stripped away their original polychrome finishes. It is a Depression-era mood that we encounter here—in other words, an atmosphere oddly parallel to that of present-day America, where most consumers are compelled by economic necessity to live their dreams vic-ariously on Oscar night.

The show's black-and-white poster presents the archetypal image: evening pajamas designed by Madeleine Vionnet in 1931. As pho-tographed by George Hoyningen-Huene, the outfit is black and white and silver all over, as if cut from the screen implanted in many a young 1930s shopgirl's head. Miuccia Prada updates the siren image in a pleated silk jersey dress designed in 2002.

Fluidity is a leading motif: a metaphor for women's freedom. Madame Grès, Pierre Balmain, and Edward Molyneux define the Venus genre with long gowns possibly conceived in a marriage between a column and the sea.

The galleries are packed with showstoppers. May I present Venus and Juno? Designed by Christian Dior in 1949, evening gowns named for those two Olympians typify a strain of Surrealist Baroque. The Venus dress, named after Botticelli's depiction of Aphrodite, is festooned with immense oyster shells made from opalescent sequins and rhinestones. The wide skirt of Dior's Junon dress is encrusted with overlapping, wavelike scales made of blue, green, and rust sequins. Thank you, ladies.

The show's peak is a white wedding dress designed by Yohji Yamamoto in 1998. Evidently conceived for a bride who wanted to have her cake and be it, too, this is a wild froth of a dress, again a baroque manifestation, barely held together by coils of silk braid. Slice?

Alexander McQueen's "shipwreck dress" of 2003 is a study in beige silk crepe tatters. As if urban life were analogous to rough weather, the dress ends in torn and shredded hems. This could be the winding shroud for Isadora Duncan, made from remnants of the scarf that broke her neck when one trailing end got caught in the wheel of the roadster she was riding in.

These four very different dresses highlight the show's most authentically classical theme: the Greeks' passion for discovering unifying patterns in the world around them. Greek physicians practiced a method called the doctrine of signatures: since the form of walnuts resembled that of brains, the nut was commonly prescribed for mental disorders.

Waves pass through hair, fabric, and water. Greek art emphasized the similarity between them. In the Dior gowns, seashells, scales, and wavelets morph into one another, as if by design or surrealist transformation. This is what poetry meant to the Greeks: the art of weaving connective tissue.

Goddess can be seen as one big showcase of fashion signatures. Mariano Fortuny's early-twentieth-century pleated dresses wear the strongest personal sign. As familiar as they have become in recent decades, these gem-colored sheaths still powerfully evoke the mythical world of Marcel Proust.

You'd think it would become tiresome to review the repetition of pleats, harness bodices, columnar sheaths, and other standard devices. But discovering the infinite variations on these motifs is as untiring as watching waves break on the sand.

In a famous essay, "The Greeks and Us," Auden urges his readers to judge civilization by "the degree of diversity attained and unity retained." Yet in modern civilization something like the reverse standard must be applied. Diversity is a given. Unity must be fought for. Unification is what Greece signified to modern Europeans, who did not lay eyes on the Acropolis until 1751.

To the modern mind, ancient Greece was first of all a symbol of nationalism. During the Greek war of independence from the Turks (and Islam), the need arose for a unifying myth of Western origins. The myth of our descent from the Greeks satisfied that need. (Until then, Rome was our official ancestor.)

The same myth was invoked to gloss over the social upheaval caused by the industrial revolution. Parallels could be drawn between the rationality of machine production and the refined economy of Greek art. Modern science, as Peter Gay has argued, is a kind of paganism, a form of nature worship. The neoclassical notion of timeless, universal aesthetic values derived from the view that cultural experience was subject to scientific law.

History and timelessness may be intellectually irreconcilable, but who cares if you're wearing Halston? Perhaps the last major designer to dedicate his career to fashioning a contemporary classical image, Halston is represented here by a trio of simple chiffon evening gowns that command the elegance of polychrome columns. Unpleated, the chiffon would gather into supple, flutelike folds when worn by bodies in motion, subtly transforming the Doric into the Ionic order.

Halston is my idea of a myth of origins. Norma Kamali is a strong contender, too. No one makes filminess look more desirable. Seen here, Ms. Kamali's diaphanous outfits lack the benefit of contrast with the stark gray concrete walls of her flagship store in New York. But they capture the odd fusion of innocence and eroticism on which the appeal of Arcadia is substantially based.

Tom Ford's do, too. At least the context of this show helps to clarify Mr. Ford's intentions as a designer, such as they are. Gucci, his fashion house, paid for this show, with additional support from Condé Nast Publications, and Mr. Ford's essays in goddess style put in cameo appearances here and there among groupings of dresses by other designers. Peekaboo, we see you, Tom!

Thus far, Mr. Ford's brilliance as a projector of images has outdazzled his talent for design. That isn't meant as criticism. What else does anyone want today besides an image? A new car? The Ford designs, represented by the clothes on view, may not bring on fainting spells. But they signal the most fertile of the directions the designer has set for himself.

Savagery and violence, the dark underside of classical restraint, are more than hinted at by Mr. Ford's deconstructed evening gown of brown silk chiffon designed in 2002 for Yves Saint Laurent Rive Gauche. A true classic, the dress appears tailored less for a nymph than for a maenad, an intoxicated celebrant of Dionysian rites.

We prettify spring, but for the ancients it was a time of violence, when new vegetation cracks the surface of the earth. It is difficult, now, for novelty to break through fashion's upper crust.

May 2, 2003

THE WAY WE LIVE NOW: 5-18-03; WHO GETS IT?

Richard Florida calls them "the creative class," and there is no point denying that the audience for architecture is an elite. But it is different from most elite groups because almost anyone can join it. It's not based on money or breeding. On the contrary, it's based on feelings of displacement that those with wealth or inherited privilege are usually in a position to ignore.

Many of them, or should I say us, are displaced suburbanites: children of the postwar suburban exodus who discovered by the onset of adolescence the unlikelihood that we would ever be able to afford houses as nice as the ones we grew up in. We could, however, afford plane tickets. And so, in the 1960s and '70s, there commenced the restless globe-trotting of baby boomers, hungry for the sense of otherness largely absent from suburban life. We went in search of places to excite us, buildings to show us new ways of seeing and modes of living.

Exchange students, backpackers, self-romanticized gypsies, we grew up taking for granted that modernity was synonymous with the ability to change the scene. But in fact we were pioneering a mobile way of life that did not become widely shared until our adolescence had passed. Pan Am, Braniff, TWA, Eastern, National: most of the airlines that enabled us to spread our young wings no longer exist.

Florida's book, *The Rise of the Creative Class*, outlines the demographics of a group that has been variously called yuppies or bourgeois bohemians. I prefer cosmopolites, a privatized city-state department, with stronger allegiances to cities than to the nations in which they are located.

While architecture provides symbolic destinations for this group, design gives individuals the tools to construct their own identities— through the clothes they wear, the gadgets they use, the furniture they choose for their apartments and houses. To a degree, the search for identity through design echoes the Good Design movement promoted half a century ago by the Museum of Modern Art, the Aspen Design Conference, and the Illinois Institute of Technology. Today, as in the earlier era, designers are seeking to work within the modern system of mass production and distribution.

The new design aesthetic, however, is far more varied. In the 1950s, Good Design represented a Platonic fusion of function and abstract form. Braun appliances, Breuer furniture, and Marimekko fabrics epitomized this ideal. In those days, expressing your aptitude for design was easy. There weren't a lot of choices.

Now there is nothing but choices. At Target discount stores, for example, consumers can mix and match the diametrically opposed design visions of Philippe Starck and Michael Graves. Technology is also a big part of it. People have become knowledgeable critics about the look, feel, and capabilities of cell phones, portable computers, and flat-screen television sets, pushing manufacturers to engage in a kind of arms race in which design is the crucial element.

The contemporary design vocabulary includes the biomorphic surrealism of Starck, the minimalism of John Pawson and Richard Gluckman, "blob" designs by Greg Lynn and the Scandinavian collaborate OCEAN North, classic modern pieces by Charles Eames and George Nelson, and expressionist work by Ron Arad, Karim Rashid, Ettore Sottsass, and Marc Newson.

All of this feeds into a culture that makes new demands on buildings. In the postwar decades, global architecture still adhered to the prewar tenets of the International Style. It was thought that a limited vocabulary of forms would confer modern, machine-age unity upon the heterogeneous cultures of the world.

Today cities value difference. Gehry's design for a new Guggenheim branch in Lower Manhattan, for example, was resisted by many who felt it looked too much like Bilbao. This represents a considerable shift from forty years ago. Few then would have discounted a glass tower by Mies van der Rohe on the grounds that his towers all looked alike. Close resemblance to a Mies tower was what every downtown skyline craved.

Barcelona remains the model for cities looking to recast themselves in a cosmopolitan image. After the death of Franco, the city was gripped by a design fever that culminated with the summer Olympics in 1992. Oriol Bohigas oversaw a citywide campaign of public works, awarding projects to younger firms as well as to international stars like Gehry, Richard Meier, Arata Isozaki, and Santiago Calatrava. Civic monuments were restored, and a series of so-called social spaces—parks, plazas, promenades, and bridges—was put in place. There was also the phenomenon of designer bars, clubs, and other stylish environments whose chief draw was the drama of the space itself.

Sadly, no other city has undertaken a campaign as organized, focused, and ambitious as Barcelona's. Still, urban centers around the world have become design hothouses, offering a constantly changing tableau of smaller-scale work. The ever-growing cosmopolitan class is what subsidizes this process, drives the competition, raises the stakes.

It's easy to ridicule cosmopolites as captives to trend, as mindless addicts of cheap luxury labels. But their growing influence—marked by a receptivity to newness, as well as an insistence on quality—is having important effects on the life of cities. Nowhere has this been clearer than in the design process still unfolding in Lower Manhattan over the future of Ground Zero. The process was by no means as open as some public officials would have us believe. Nonetheless, the adoption of a design competition in response to public pressure was a major turning point. No longer could politicians and developers ignore the audience for new architecture that had emerged in the previous decade.

Design competitions are perhaps the most useful tool we have for sustaining public interest in architecture. They bring credibility to a process that is necessarily subjective. And there is no more effective instrument for disseminating ideas to a broad public audience. A design competition engages people to contemplate change, including changes in their own points of view.

Architecture is not just sculpture blown up to urban scale. It is a social art and, for many, it will always operate as a symbol of unwanted change. But this is not a bad thing. Arousing conflict is one of the social functions architecture performs. In this way it differs from theme parks, shopping malls, and gated residential enclaves, where reassurance is the primary function. The architect's job, as Giò Ponti once observed, is to "interpret the life of the inhabitants." The results can be as disturbing and as rewarding as the interpretation of dreams.

May 18, 2003

ZAHA HADID'S URBAN MOTHERSHIP

Architectural and urban history were made here recently with the opening of Zaha Hadid's first American building, the Lois and Richard Rosenthal Center for Contemporary Art, in Cincinnati. It is an amazing building, a work of international stature that confidently meets the high expectations aroused by this prodigiously gifted architect for nearly two decades. Might as well blurt it out: the Rosenthal Center is the most important American building to be completed since the end of the Cold War.

Coincidentally, a comprehensive retrospective of Hadid's work opened last month at the Austrian Museum of Applied Arts in Vienna. Easily the most visually sumptuous architecture show to be seen anywhere in years, the exhibition puts the spotlight on a cluster of Hadid's recently completed buildings and other projects now moving toward construction. These include a train station in Strasbourg, France; a monumental ski jump, with lodge, in Innsbruck, Austria; a BMW plant in Leipzig, Germany; and a contemporary art museum in Rome.

The Iraqi-born Hadid, at fifty-two, is crossing a threshold, in other words. Up to now she has been known mainly for her lushly seductive paintings and drawings of unrealized projects, like the Peak Club in Hong Kong (1982) and the Cardiff Opera House (1994). Encountering a finished Hadid building—in the round, at full scale, within a pulsing downtown setting—is like meeting a new architect for the first time.

Hadid's renderings and models have already trained two generations to look at the city through different eyes. The Rosenthal Center performs a similar function for the body. It can be experienced as an exercise in heightening the mind-body connection, in fact. The design does not stint on visual spectacle. Inside and out, it presents vantage points of sufficient variety to keep photographers snapping happily for many years to come.

But the building's power is fully disclosed only to those who engage it with their feet as well as their eyes. Hadid's renderings have long conveyed the impression of movement. The building gives this impression concrete form. Not even Saarinen's TWA terminal draws richer spatial textures out of architecture's circulatory systems. Wandering through the building is like exploring the varied and unpredictable terrain of present time. Staring right into the present is immensely more shocking than gazing at some corny crystal ball.

The Contemporary Arts Center (originally the Modern Art Society), founded in 1939, sponsors a program of changing exhibitions but lacks a permanent collection. It made national headlines in 1990, when it was prosecuted for including sexually charged images in a retrospective of photographs by Robert Mapplethorpe. The cause célèbre helped widen the museum's base of support.

Its new building is located directly across the street from the Aronoff Center for the Performing Arts, a weak example of contextual design by Cesar Pelli. Pelli's dull arrangement of orange brick boxes at least helps set off Hadid's more penetrating approach to framing urban relationships.

The Rosenthal Center is a vertical museum, contained within a stack of concrete and metal cubic and rectangular enclosures that articulate the gallery spaces inside. The stack is as tall as an average ten-story building. Variations in ceiling height, the use of mezzanine levels, and an irregularly shaped atrium reduce the actual number of floors. I gave up trying to count them. Instead I gave myself over to the finely tempered rhythm of spatial compression and expansion that draws a visitor through the building.

The exterior strikes my eye as an architectural application of the push-pull technique associated with Hans Hoffmann's abstract paintings. The cubic enclosures recede and project, creating a sculptural surface of animation and depth. The forms are made mostly of raw concrete, punctuated by a large trapezoid finished with blackened aluminum and by windows of clear and blue-tinted glass. These shapes are not purely orthogonal but are slightly angled and tapered as they slip by one another across the facades.

The building occupies a rectangular corner site and rises from an imposing, two-story lobby framed with glass. Entered from the broad side, the lobby extends the sidewalk surface indoors, forming a wide, concrete ribbon that stretches the full width of the site. At the far end, the surface curls up vertically to suggest a seamless and gravity-free continuity between floor and wall.

Too bad the slope doesn't start on the sidewalk. It would be bliss for skateboarders. Still, the device introduces visitors to a building that Hadid has conceived as a vertical city street. For mass transit, take the elevator. Otherwise, proceed by foot, up a freestanding, switchback staircase enclosed in black steel. Again this is a sculptural presence, not just in the aggressive angularity of the stairs but in their counterpoint with the lobby's expansive volume and its nearly monochrome surfaces of gray, white, and buff.

Up the stairs, you gain the dream sensation of breaking through a solid membrane into an alternative world: the steps lead you up into a soaring atrium space suffused from above with natural light. The atrium's compressed verticality plays against the lobby's broad horizontal volume. It's a Baroque effect, as if a secret portal had opened up in the ceiling of a Piranesian prison, letting the sun shine in and confined imaginations float out.

The building's prevailing mood is Baroque, in its play of geometric variations and, especially, in its artful arrangement of processional spaces. Like Balanchine condensing an evening's worth of choreography into a twenty-minute ballet, Hadid compresses Blenheim Palace into spaces that occupy a fraction of the area Vanborough had to work with.

Or call it Baroque as reconceived by Duchamp in his early cubist phase. Staircase descending nude concrete. Like Duchamp, Hadid presents a rhythm of multiple perspectives, roughly synchronized with the movements of bodies propelled by curious minds. Hadid's large painted renderings have accustomed us to this approach, but it's spectacular to see it fully realized. Walter Benjamin maintained that architecture is fully experienced peripherally, through slightly unfocused perceptions. That is the concept operating here.

Hadid has described the museum as a "catalog of spaces." The galleries are not neutral white boxes. Their walls are slightly angled. Rooms of assorted sizes, pitched on different levels, are joined by ramps. But the proportions throughout are graceful. And the galleries are designed to be reconfigured by temporary partitions for different shows. The fourth-story level contains the building's heart. A kind of sky lobby, surrounding the staircase atrium, functions like an aerial piazza: a resting place for visitors moving through galleries, ramps, stairs. It sounds more complicated than it is. The balance between form and open space is impeccable. Call it a contemporary version of Tiepolo, with voluptuous voids in place of clouds.

Hadid's preoccupation with movement has a precedent in the Futurist designs of Sant'Elia and the streamlined contours of Erich Mendelsohn. Her most notable departure from these precedents is the subtle complexity of the building's relationship to the city around it. The cubical facade thrusts the street grid skyward. The lobby floor does the same for the ground plane. Upstairs, windows and a small outdoor terrace frame views as fragmented as the city itself. We survey a metropolis that has concluded one phase of urban development and is witnessing the dawn of another, a place where people live not of necessity but because they want to be part of a future that invites surprise. Markus Dochantschi of New York was the project architect for the building. KZF Design of Cincinnati is the architect of record.

More than two thousand people showed up for the opening of Hadid's retrospective in Vienna. (Zaha Hadid: Architecture remains on view through August 17.) At the door, attendants gave out T-shirts emblazoned with a Hadid quote: "Would they call me a diva if I were a guy?" I would. Or I would call her a star, which is scarcely an improvement. Fame is a gender-blind, equal-opportunity stigma in architecture these days.

Those who don't follow the field closely are sometimes surprised by the degree of rancor that the mention of stardom stirs up. The reasons for this resentment are not obscure. One is that architecture still defines itself as a licensed profession, not an art. As in law or medicine, architecture clings to the notion that its practitioners are equals. They attend the same schools, pass the same tests, pay the same dues to the same professional organizations.

When architects like Hadid become stars—when their work becomes an event worthy of press coverage—it is often assumed that they must be good at working the media. Better, perhaps, than they are at designing buildings. Actually, the press is interested in stars chiefly in a Jungian sense: stars are individuals capable of attracting and holding the projections of others. They communicate, often in ways that neither they nor their audiences fully comprehend, much less control.

It would take too much euphemism and psychological speculation to analyze Hadid's communicative apparatus in depth. But those who want insight into the phenomenon of stardom have no business disregarding the subconscious fantasy structures that enable some architects to send messages and audiences to receive them. Indeed, in a field that now admits limitless aesthetic approaches, psychology has largely displaced style as the source of architectural form. Audiences for movies, fiction, and even sports have taken this kind of shift in stride.

Those who can't make it to the Vienna show this summer are advised to get hold of its catalog. The book doesn't provide the same depth of insight that visitors get from moving through the show's labyrinthine spaces. But it offers enough visual evidence to speculate on the architecture of Hadid's fantasies. By turns curved and spiked, voluptuous and menacing, Hadid's formal vocabulary recalls that of Arshile Gorky. The tension in the work derives from the precarious balance Hadid maintains between these emotional poles. This helps explain the ambivalence her work has aroused. Admirers like myself are passionate about it. Potential clients, however, have evidently been fearful: the ratio between raw talent and built work is wildly out of whack.

A student of D. W. Winnicott, the British child psychologist, might say that Gorky's vocabulary signifies a young personality's attempt to reckon with the difference between a mother's "good" (nurturing) and "bad" (withholding) breasts. I venture to say the same about Hadid's vocabulary. Its appeal is exquisitely primal. That is what makes it so urban.

In Beaux Arts days, architecture was called "the mother art." Today, we might call it "the good enough mother art," after Winnicott's phrase for supportive maternal care. For many of Hadid's generation, for whom uprootedness is the social norm, the city has become a surrogate in later life for the good enough mother, architecture the medium through which we ourselves enact the nurturing role.

This emotional dynamic goes far toward explaining the expansion in the audience for contemporary architecture over the last decade. Baroque processional architecture was shaped by court protocol. Ambassadors could proceed just so far into a suite of rooms before the prince's attendants would come forward to greet them. In contemporary architecture, the protocol derives from subconscious interactions between individuals in shared social space. This is the thread that connects work by architects as aesthetically various as Thom Mayne, Frank Gehry, Steven Holl, and Rem Koolhaas.

Let me refine (but not deflate) that opening burst of hyperbole. The Rosenthal Center defines the architectural context of the post–Cold War era. Like Hadid herself, the building links traditional cosmopolitan values with the phenomenon of globalization. Hadid's experiences as a woman and a native of the Middle East have sharpened her insights into that phenomenon. She grasps that contemporary urbanism, like current architectural practice, unfolds within a global framework. The Rosenthal Center embodies her historical awareness.

Like any artist, Hadid is reluctant to have the semantics of her supple forms pinned down. Depending on her mood, she will or won't acknowledge Arabic calligraphy as a formal source. Her family, she points out, is well off, educated, and modern. (Now based in London, she hasn't visited Iraq in thirty years.) When Hadid speaks of her university training in mathematics, she does not press the point that her field of study is of Islamic origin.

Yet she will describe her student years in Beirut, Lebanon, as the happiest of her life. This was toward the end of the period depicted by Fouad Ajami in his 1998 book, *The Dream Palace of the Arabs*, when Islamic intellectuals were building cultural bridges to the modern West. Urban life was and remains a common cause between the two worlds. As Americans have recently been reminded, cities, cosmopolitanism, civilization itself, and, in that sense, we ourselves descend from Middle Eastern origins. Half the world hails from Club Med. The central marketplace where people could set aside tribal differences and coexist in peace—that's the idea Baghdad was invented for.

In the West, mobility typically holds connotations of advanced technology and social displacement. In the Middle East, it is associated with nomadism and other ancient tribal traditions. Hadid can draw on both sources as easily as she can converse in different tongues. She recasts the ancient story of cities in service to her time.

June 8, 2003

BLOND AMBITION ON RED BRICK

Lately Richard Meier has been reclaiming the rare quality that he started out with. I mean the quality of radiance: the Apollonian virtues of clarity, order, simplicity, and light.

Since 1997, when he finally finished work on the Getty Center in Los Angeles, Mr. Meier has been brightening up his repertory with exquisite structures on a smaller scale. The architect's aesthetic approach has not changed. The times have. So has the historical context. A formal vocabulary that once seemed constrained by the dogmas of the International Style now stands for freedom from the woolier rhetoric of the Postmodern 1980s.

Nowhere does this shift come into clearer focus than at 173 and 176 Perry Street, two residential buildings Mr. Meier recently completed on the far west side of Greenwich Village. The glass towers, which face each other across the narrow village street, are as handsome to look at as the Hudson River views they overlook from their floor-to-ceiling windows. They catch the light reflected from the water like a pair of frozen fountains.

Early this year, even on cold winter days, sidewalk superintendents could be seen stomping about outside the buildings, as if there were something thrillingly novel about construction in New York. Perhaps some of them were scouting out vantage points for peeping at the boldface names who have signed up to move into the glamorous cages. Most, I suspect, were feasting their eyes on architecture, a genuine novelty to behold rising at any construction site in a town where the art of building still counts in some circles as delinquent behavior.

We like architects more than architecture here. In the last few years, several residential high-rises by star designers have gone up in Manhattan. There is little to say about them apart from reciting their names. On Perry Street, by contrast, Mr. Meier has fashioned work for the historical imagination to feed on. Apart from their intrinsic formal qualities, the buildings reveal how a city goes about constructing a context of time.

From the West Side Highway, the towers create a neoclassical impression. A modern glass version of an eighteenth-century European gateway: that's the initial effect. But the symmetrical image is deceptive. In plan, the south tower is more than double the size of its uptown twin. This imbalance recalls the two pairs of asymmetrically sited residential high-rises designed by Mies van der Rohe for Lake Shore Drive in Chicago. So does the waterfront location.

The Perry Street towers are fifteen stories tall, with one apartment per floor. Mr. Meier's spare geometric forms knit these perpendiculars into a harmonious composition. The result is two sets of stacked urban stages, each with excellent sightlines: a multiplex for exhibitionists and the voyeurs who adore them.

The structure is concrete, with curtain walls of glass and painted metal. The division is expressed on the exterior by fire stairs enclosed within gray concrete cores. In glass buildings, floor slabs perform the expressive function formerly taken by walls. Viewed through the glass curtain wall, the empty volumes between floors and ceilings become formal elements. So do the curtains, blinds, and lighting, installed by tenants.

The lightness of the floor slabs and structural columns is further refined by the pristine delicacy of the exterior's white metal frames. Shadow boxes, mullions, and railings appear to stretch the glass skin taut against the envelope formed by the slabs. Balconies with tinted blue glass side panels extend the platforms beyond the skin. The south facades mirror each other across Perry Street, uniting the double block.

It strikes me that the towers are a pair of Hitchcock blondes. The white metal framework of their facades is so crisp and pure that the towers could be two twins dressed for First Communion. But inside, fireworks: two towers full of racy Rear Windows. I do believe that's Miss Torso up there, practicing jazz dance right now. Soon to be joined by Nicole Kidman, Calvin Klein, Jean-Georges Vongerichten, and I forget the rest. How will they handle window treatments? The world anxiously awaits.

Or, to state the matter more clinically, the subtext of these buildings is the friction between what Beatriz Colomina, a senior professor at Princeton's School of Architecture, has called privacy and publicity: the conflicting desires for refuge and exposure. This is a dominant theme throughout contemporary architecture today. Mr. Meier's buildings may lack the emotional risk-taking we encounter in work by Frank Gehry or Wolf Prix. But their formal understatement heightens the underlying tension between a viewer's inner and outer worlds.

Glass, metal, natural light, white surfaces, orthogonal geometry, solid, and void: this basic vocabulary can be found in any number of twentieth-century machine-age buildings. Mr. Meier's formal vocabulary does not, in itself, account for the bold impression the buildings make. Nor can it be explained by some imaginary pendulum shift in public taste from "history" back to "modernity." No one with any taste ever fell for that ahistorical piece of Postmodern spin.

On Perry Street we witness the complex display of actual history at work. We witness conflict, that is to say: the formation of urban context through the contest of ideas. One of those contests got under way not far from here more than forty years ago with the 1961 publication of Jane Jacobs's *The Death and Life of Great American Cities.* The book was one of twentieth-century architecture's most traumatic events. Its impact is still felt in cities across the land. Greenwich Village was the crucible for some the book's most influential ideas. Ms. Jacobs's vision of the ideal city was inspired by her own block of nearby Hudson Street. West Village Houses, a low-rise complex a few blocks south designed by Perkins & Will in the 1970s, was New York City's first attempt to apply her ideas to planning.

Ms. Jacobs's book was an attack on modern city planning, not on modern architecture per se. Its impact on architecture was devastating nonetheless. One of the Modern movement's central tenets was that architecture and planning were indivisible. This fusion allowed modernists to regard their cause as progressive in social as well as artistic terms. It fell to Ms. Jacobs to expose the limits of this claim.

The Radiant City (Ville Radieuse), Le Corbusier's 1925 vision of a city of high-rise towers separated from one another by open parkland, was the central target of her critique. After World War II, this plan became a standard template for urban renewal projects around the country. Its application enabled American architects to perpetuate the self-image of social conscience.

As Ms. Jacobs saw it, modern city plans were not true social undertakings. They were works of art writ large. The Radiant City was a piece of graphic design or sculpture, an aesthetic exercise with little basis in the practical realities of urban life. "A city cannot be a work of art," Ms. Jacobs insisted: this was her book's single italicized idea. In hindsight, it's clear that the crisis provoked by Ms. Jacobs went far deeper than a conflict over the merits and defects of modern architecture. It involved the crumbling of historicism: the nineteenth-century belief that each epoch should produce its own distinctive style. Modern architects may have rejected the use of period styles, but they clung to the basic historicist creed. An industrial society should have buildings to match.

By the early 1960s, this idea was in retreat. The historical inevitability of modernism, if not modern architecture per se, was no longer credible. A modern society could live happily without being herded into towers in a park. Ms. Jacobs had a sound point to make: society and art represent different systems of meaning and value. Still, one of architecture's major functions is to negotiate changing relationships between the two. If the concept of "place" has any meaning, it lies in the vigor with which social and artistic values confront one another in urban space.

Art, moreover, is one of the best techniques we have for apprehending urban complexity. De Kooning, Tinguely, Rauschenberg, Warhol, Twyla Tharp, and Spike Lee have variously shown us what kind of artworks the modern city wants to be, or already is. For more than three decades, contemporary artists have held up mirrors to the pluralism of urban life. Yet if we look back at New York's architectural record during the same period, it is fair to conclude that the skyline has suffered more from the absence of art than from the presence of it.

Ms. Jacobs can't be faulted for this. Like Le Corbusier, she was a polemicist who knew how to score points that needed to be made at a particular time. Forty years ago, when she was scoring points against art, she can't have been hoping for the tyranny of petit bourgeois taste that holds New York building and planning in its philistine grip. But look what we ended up with: a city where architecture is routinely denigrated as weird, elitist, or avant-garde.

Some may dismiss the Perry Street buildings for not being weird or cutting-edge enough. Compared with Mr. Gehry, Rem Koolhaas, or Zaha Hadid, Mr. Meier is indeed a conservative architect. One of the most valuable functions performed by the Perry Street buildings, in fact, is to reinforce the conservative edge of contemporary architecture's range. Beyond that line lie Postmodernism, contextualism, and New Urbanism. Since these movements presented themselves as anti-architecture, what was the point in conferring architectural status upon them?

By now it should be obvious that these "isms" have been anti-urban, too. They have obstructed efforts in New York and other American cities to face the challenges of globalization and its impact on urban centers. Last year, for example, New Urbanists almost succeeded in foisting a retro theme park on Ground Zero. The process of planning the future of the World Trade Center site was irreparably damaged by the energy wasted in that preposterous effort.

A Hegelian might say that Mr. Meier's new buildings are the synthesis of Le Corbusier and Ms. Jacobs. The Radiant City has been scaled down to two towers facing each other across a traditional city street. This assessment would not, however, account for the unique quality of radiance Mr. Meier has achieved in this design. For that we have to look at the architect's unique relationship to urban history.

What distinguishes Mr. Meier from previous generations of modernists is a shift in ideology. Le Corbusier and Mies van der Rohe were historicists. They believed that the machine age demanded expression in a particular formal vocabulary. So did second-generation modernists like Gordon Bunshaft, the architect of the Lever House on Park Avenue.

Richard Meier is a formalist. His work reflects the ideology that prevailed in the 1950s and '60s, when the Museum of Modern Art was the supreme arbiter of urbane taste. Mr. Meier may harbor historicist sympathies, for all I know. Many architects couldn't get up in the morning if they weren't convinced that their way is the best way for their time. As a formalist, however, Mr. Meier seeks less to express history than to transcend it: to attain a level of geometric abstraction high above the fray.

Mr. Meier makes sculptures in addition to buildings. A group of them will be on display this fall at the High Museum of Art in Atlanta, designed by Mr. Meier, as part of an anniversary observation. I would like to see it, to test a theory: the primary function of these artworks is to deceive Mr. Meier into thinking that his buildings are not artworks too.

Earlier generations of modernists rarely gave themselves permission to reach for the degree of abstraction Mr. Meier has maintained throughout his career. Mr. Meier's trademark white metal panels, for instance, are a far cry from Le Corbusier's raw concrete walls. Le Corbusier developed the potential of new materials and methods. Mr. Meier exploits the capacity of glass to dissolve materiality altogether. On Perry Street, the Corbusian *brise-soleil,* a concrete sunscreen device for use in tropical climes, has been etherealized into flat metal filigree on the western facades.

Formalism led to a bizarre blurring of the categories of art and architecture. With artists like Frank Stella, Donald Judd, Tony Smith, Sol LeWitt, and Dan Flavin, painting and sculpture became almost indistinguishable from design. With architects like Mr. Meier, Peter Eisenman, Mr. Gehry, and Harry Cobb, buildings took on the identity of abstract sculpture. Increasingly, the distinctions between the fields came to depend on context: the environments in which objects are presented for our contemplation.

We know that the Perry Street buildings are architecture because they are located on a street and are scaled accordingly. But if we look through the glass walls into the spaces behind them, a very different kind of environment is revealed. It is industrial loft space, the neutral but aesthetically charged environment that became standard for art galleries by the early 1970s. Rather than modernist hymns to machine technology, the towers represent the apotheosis of what the art critic Brian Doherty called "the white cube." That is where their radiance comes from. As Mr. Doherty pointed out in a seminal *Artforum* essay in 1976, the aestheticized void of the gallery was a major part of the artistic experience. Surely that's one of the major reasons for the success of the Dia Art Foundation's new installations in Beacon, New York. Warhol's "shadow" paintings, for example, are a function of the industrial space required to show them.

Loft spaces are platforms. They take the place of traditional pedestals. Artworks add to the atmosphere, but a pile of old tires would do nearly as well. Without the platform, the white walls, the track lighting and the volume enclosed within them, the atmosphere can't move in.

In the contemporary city, loft space has acquired a new set of meanings. The reuse of old factories by artists, galleries, and the industries that support them epitomizes the current conversion of entire cities from manufacturing to cultural production. Mr. Meier's buildings are monuments to this transformation. The space has become the art. The people inside it, too. Call this workers' housing for a city of culture workers. A place where an overabundance of energy goes into the construction of the self.

June 19, 2003

A BUILDING WITH A SONG IN ITS HEART

Some great buildings allow you silence. Others give you song. The new McCormick Tribune Campus Center in Chicago got my fingers snapping. On my visit this weekend before Tuesday's dedication, the Goo Goo Dolls were playing on the building's sound system. But another track was playing inside my head: a bouncy 2002 lounge tune by Joseph Malik with a silly lyric that goes, "You oughta take it all in and check it all out."

Shall we? We'll let McCormick Center show us how. Designed by Rem Koolhaas and the Office for Metropolitan Architecture, the $48.2 million project is a bazaar of a building, a souk of sensations that stands in vibrant contrast to the immaculately modern desert around it. Situated on the main campus of the Illinois Institute of Technology, this is the Dutch architect's first completed building in the United States. If you want to know what all the fuss over Mr. Koolhaas has been about, this student center is an exemplary place to start. It's Koolhaas à go-go, a masterwork for the young and curious.

A train runs through it. The center's most striking feature is the oval tube of corrugated stainless steel that slices through the building overhead. Designed to muffle the noise from elevated trains that cross through the 120-acre South Side campus, the 530-foot-long tube establishes a spatial and conceptual axis for the architectural composition. It's a metaphor for absorption, for a receptive frame of mind. Stuff comes in. Stuff goes out. In between there's a process called education, also known as checking things out.

The students have already adopted The Tube as their school's unofficial logo. A campus newspaper of that title is apparently in the works. But the big steel cylinder isn't the only logo Koolhaas and his team have incorporated into the design. The structure beneath the tracks creates one too.

The tube is held aloft by seven concrete V-shaped prongs. Five thrust upward from within the building, punching through the concrete roof. A shallow pitched roof flipped on its head, it echoes the shape of the prongs. If you're much older than you pretend to be, you will recognize the similarity of these overlaid contours as the swanky double boomerang Chrysler adopted in 1955 as the logo for its new corporate face. The Forward Look, it was called. What better symbol could there be for a school with deep roots in the golden age of industrial design?

But look wider, look deeper. Another V is rushing toward us on the big memory screen, an image as vast as Jefferson's nostril on Mount Rushmore. It's VistaVision! This spectacular horizontal film format was used by Hitchcock for *North by Northwest*, *Vertigo*, and *To Catch a Thief*. Are you getting the picture? This Is . . . Rem-o-Rama!

I associate freely because the McCormick Center was made for precisely that. It is a place where our private memory screens are brought together in a public setting, the better to check them out. In fact, this building goes far toward explaining the excitement contemporary architecture has been generating in the United States for a decade.

The most significant buildings produced in this period are not unified by style. Designed by individual architects or collaborative teams, they differ greatly in appearance. If some of the best are linked by a common theme, the link is conceptual rather than visual. It is the idea that we live perpetually on the threshold between our inner and outer worlds. This is a psychological bond, not a visual one, but the link is no less cultural for that. It reflects the view that architecture is a philosophy of urban life.

Designed in partnership with Holabird & Root, Studio Gang Architects, and Ove Arup & Partners, McCormick Center is custom-made for examining this premise. The campus was designed by Ludwig Mies van der Rohe in 1941, a few years after he arrived from Germany. It is the great architect's most ambitious effort in modern city planning. Many would consider this effort a contradiction in terms. Even admirers of modern architecture concede that the movement's blank-slate approach to urbanism was catastrophic for urban centers.

Mies's philosophy differed from the conventional model of postwar urban renewal, a sweeping approach on the concepts of Le Corbusier. Mies did not propose to rebuild cities from scratch. Instead he saw individual building projects as islands of order and stability surrounded by the chaos of a culture in decline. Skepticism rather than any impulse to reform was Mies's urban attitude.

His philosophy took on personal meaning at the Illinois Institute of Technology. From 1938 to 1958, Mies reigned as dean of its architecture school. Crown Hall, designed by Mies to house what is now the College of

Architecture, is the jewel of the campus, a classical temple remade for modern times. This is where students came to imbibe the master's principles. These included the belief that every architect must discover his own creative path.

No contemporary architect has embodied this belief better than Rem Koolhaas. If the new student radiates with the Vitruvian quality of fitness, that is partly because Mr. Koolhaas long ago adopted Mies as his father figure. Predictably, the relationship is fraught with ambivalence.

Nowhere is this more evident than in the V shape of the roof. For Mies, famously, pitched roofs were anathema. Were Mr. Koolhaas's instincts purely Oedipal, he might have used one. But the inverted pitch of the student center goes Mies one better. Instead of flattening the roof, in the manner of the master, Mr. Koolhaas turns it upside down.

Koolhaas fans will recognize this ambivalence as characteristic. From the start of his career, the architect has opposed the tendency toward Oedipal overthrow that is rampant in his profession. This helps explain the midcentury modernist decorative details he often uses, whether portholes, boomerangs, or spirals. He celebrates the era of a father who took in much more than Less is More.

Ready for More? The building's exterior scarcely hints at the cascade of images, spaces, and perspectives that gush within. Were it not for the tube penetrating the ceiling and the ceiling's angled flair, the McCormick's interior would be a labyrinth nearly without orientation. It comes close to that anyhow. But the overhead train has enabled Mr. Koolhaas to treat the building as a cross-axial composition.

Inside, the cross-axis is spatially exploded, rather like a Cubist painting. Instead of organizing the interior along straight lines, Mr. Koolhaas has arranged the spaces on a diagonal grid. Some spaces are enclosed: an auditorium, ballroom, private offices, and meeting rooms. Over all, however, the interior is wide open and unfolds on changing levels. A result is a Miesian "universal space" densely packed with a universe of contrasting images.

Wood-patterned wallpaper. Shimmering op-art lenticular surfaces. Patterned fabrics by Petra Blaisse. A grand stair, painted green, that masterfully incorporates a ramp for wheelchairs into the treads and risers. Courtyards, handsomely planted, suffused with natural light: these again are nods to Miesian precedent and to similar devices by Wallace K. Harrison. At 110,000 square feet, the open space is a wide enough screen to let these multiple devices breath. As if for the first time, we see that architecture is actually 3-D.

More logos, on the micro scale: little humanoid icons, designed by Michael Rock of the New York firm 2 x 4, recur throughout the premises.

These are signs for signs' sake, graphics that convey the idea of information more vividly than they do the functions that they ostensibly identify. Where's the student bulletin board? Get lost!

And found. Snap! Near the center of the center, the building pulls away to reveal the fourth dimension, time. Through a plate-glass window, we see a corner of the Commons building next door, designed by Mies a half century ago. The exposed corner, of steel and glass, is all the orientation we really need. The seed crystal from which the McCormick Center has sprung, it shows that Mies, too, was a maker of icons. He called them I-beams, glass curtain walls, flat roofs.

We can appreciate these features here, in the crisp purity of Mies's intentions. Daddy is still in the details. Thanks to a living master, we can also see how the spirit of our age has transformed Mies's ideas.

October 2, 2003

A MOON PALACE FOR THE HOLLYWOOD DREAM

Walt Disney Concert Hall, the new home of the Los Angeles Philharmonic, is a French curve in a city of T-squares. The T-squares are loving it madly. Why shouldn't they? Disney Hall was designed for them. It's a home for everyone who's ever felt like a French curve in a T-square world.

Designed by Frank Gehry, the $274 million hall opens on October 23. Esa-Pekka Salonen, the Philharmonic's charismatic young music director, will conduct *The Rite of Spring*. Wrong season, right rite: Disney Hall is a riotous rebirth. Not just for downtown Los Angeles, where the building is situated, and not just for the whole sprawling mixed-up La-La. What is being reborn is the idea of the urban center as a democratic institution: a place where voices can be heard.

Disney Hall has at least a dual personality and moods enough to spare. On the outside it is a moon palace, a buoyant composition of silvery reflected light. Inside the light shifts to gold. Sitting atop the downtown Bunker Hill district, Disney Hall is the most gallant building you are ever likely to see. And it will be opening its doors to everyone who has fought for the chance to be generous, to others and to themselves. From some approaches Disney Hall first appears as a luminous crescent hovering between skyscrapers. The light playing off its surface is uncanny, though we have often been in its presence. It is the light of the silver screen and of the round reflectors used on photo and video locations: the light of the Hollywood dream.

Now imagine a moon apple: a hollow sphere of lunar light. Somebody hands you a knife and says, "Cut!" How many shapes can you make? Peel a ribbon. Carve out squares of curving surfaces, concave and convex. Change the dimensions. Turn some slices inside out. Tweak. Stretch. When you're done, compose the pieces into a flowering cabbage. Then into a cabbage rose. Rearrange. Magnify. Reproduce the contours with large panels of stainless steel etched to a soft matte finish. Jump in and soar.

The technique is cubist. No seamless image reveals the whole. Disney Hall must be assembled within the mind piece by piece as you approach and walk around it. A Surrealist ethos also suffuses the design: the imagineering impulse of Disney as well as of Magritte. Pumpkin into carriage, cabbage into concert hall, bippidi-bobbidi-boo. Though the forms are abstract, fleeting images can be glimpsed in them. Drive-in movie screens. The curving edge of a bass cello. A ship's prow. Sails. The Rust Belt before the rust. If you're unwilling to mix your metaphors, you've come to the wrong place. These elusive, mutable images heighten the perception that a metamorphosis is in process. And they convey the idea that change is as much the product of the viewer's imagination as it is of a designer's.

A wall of glass is recessed beneath the steel flower on the Grand Avenue side of the building. The hall is entered here, through doors that can be lifted to create a nearly seamless continuity between inside and out. Even from outside, you can see that the interior design shifts to a different key. Stylized trees, recalling Gothic buttresses, can be glimpsed through the glass. The squared-off trunks and branches are clad with naturally finished Douglas fir, as are most of the interior surfaces. The warm wood reads as a modern version of gold.

Serpentine lobbies surround the auditorium, which is set diagonally to the building site. The adjustment is initially disorienting, but you won't get lost if you let your intuition lead the way. That is the way to go anyhow inside Disney Hall. Ahead lies a gathering of hunches: Let's try it this way. No, maybe this way. Make up your mind! I don't want to. The design of the auditorium started out Hans Scharoun's way. Scharoun's Berlin Philharmonic Hall (1963) gave Mr. Gehry and Mr. Salonen the idea of presenting the orchestra in the round. The elimination of the proscenium arch fuses musicians and listeners into a single spatial event. But the stage has not been lost. The entire room has become a stage. This impression is due in large part to the billowing wood of the hall's ceiling. The billows evoke the swags of an opera house curtain, perpetually going up.

There are 2,265 seats. These are arranged on steeply raked terraces around the semicircular stage. Natural light filters into the hall through skylights concealed at the four corners. This celestial effect is Baroque, as is the barely contained commotion of a pipe organ that faces the conductor's podium on the far side of the orchestra. The splayed pipes of this focal point bring to mind the bursting gilded rays of an altarpiece by Bernini.

Yasuhisa Toyota and Minoru Nagata are the hall's acoustical engineers. Custom dictates that the architectural design of a new concert hall be reviewed separately from its acoustical performance. Yet after listening to music in the golden hall, I am unable to oblige. A recent rehearsal of Mozart's Symphony No. 32 nearly brought on an attack of Stendhal's syndrome, the notoriously romantic state of panic induced by aesthetic ecstasy. Audience, music, architecture were infused by a sensation of unity so profound that time stopped. Those immune to the power of metaphor sometimes scoff at the idea that Mr. Gehry's architecture is democratic. That idea is affirmed here by the materials, the multiple perspectives the design encourages, and above all by the organization of the seats.

When I saw the models of the final design, I remember thinking that the seats on the top row of the house looked a bit sad. There are only a few, widely spaced: they appear exposed. But when I finally got to sit in one, I felt downright special. Seeing those seats from a distance is also a pleasure, because the people sitting in them register as individuals, just as the musicians do. The audience feels less like a mass, more like a diverse assembly. The hall is full of such reminders that architecture is a philosophy of urban life.

Metamorphosis happens, and not only in Walt Disney's classic films. Cities do it all the time. Los Angeles has done it now. The building pulls together the strands of many individual stories and creates an extraordinarily gallant setting in which they can be screened. An urban metamorphosis is a victory for the inner life. Charles Garnier understood this when designing the Paris Opera, completed in 1874. The building itself was not the star attraction. The main event was the relationship between the stage and Baron Georges-Eugène Haussmann's Paris. Figurative paintings and sculptures, the choice of colors, the progression of theatrical spaces from the boulevard to the proscenium arch: by means of such devices, Garnier translated the vernacular of the streets into an inner, psychological space. The result (to borrow Christopher Curtis Mead's term from his 1991 book on Garnier) was an "architecture of empathy." Artists and audiences were brought together.

Radically different forms can produce startlingly similar effects. Mr. Gehry's design also embodies an empathic approach. Los Angeles has its own vernacular traditions. Above all the city has an ethos, to which Mr. Gehry's buildings have been giving shape for many years. If you want to make unity out of the city's architecture, you must get in the car and zigzag around town, turning the windshield this way and that, as if it were a lens, piling image next to image like a David Hockney photomontage. En route you will learn everything it takes to apprehend a cubist building, perhaps even to design one.

You don't need an architecture critic to tell you how beautifully this desert garden is ruled by surreal juxtaposition. But let me point you toward a fine example of it as an ideal approach to Disney Hall: the fabulous Bunker Hill Steps. Designed by Lawrence Halprin and completed in 1990, this local landmark ascends 103 steps from the street opposite the downtown Central Library to the top of Bunker Hill. Flanking the grand flight is a set of up and down escalators; down the center, water cascades over rocks.

Because of its height and the baroque curves of its treads, it is often compared to the Spanish Steps in Rome. Usually the comparison is accompanied by snickers. In truth, the stairs are a comic piece of infrastructure: the baroque and the mechanized side by side; cold canyon corporate architecture with Mediterranean splash. But thanks to Disney Hall, Halprin's staircase has surpassed the Spanish Steps in cultural substance. The ascent now moves toward an emotional climax. Each skyscraper, plaza, and skywalk is a step on the way to one civilizing thought: To speak is human, but to listen is divine.

October 23, 2003

DESIGN GUIDELINES FOR GROUND ZERO
POINT MORE TO SPACE CITY, U.S.A.

How did we end up in Houston? That is the burning question raised by a new set of design guidelines for the office towers at Ground Zero. True, we've got a hole the size of Texas sitting down there in Lower Manhattan. But how did Ground Zero come to inherit a vision of glitzy, structurally inept towers that would look more at home in an office park for energy companies in Space City, U.S.A.?

Students of architecture and urbanism will be pondering such questions for years. Many of the answers lie beyond an architecture critic's grasp. They will be found within the realms of politics and economics. But no building can be properly analyzed without taking the social and ideological structures of power into account. The guidelines, which were prepared by Studio Daniel Libeskind, reveal the extent to which such structures have dishonored the Ground Zero design process, which was supposed to be open and democratic.

Thus far the guidelines, which are dated October 23 and 27, exist only in draft form. But they have already been circulated among the group of architects retained by the developer Larry A. Silverstein to design office towers for Ground Zero. The Lower Manhattan Development Corporation, of course, says that these guidelines are already outdated, that the process is still very fluid.

Even so, they do provide a glimpse into Mr. Libeskind's inflated ambitions for the World Trade Center site. Contradicting his earlier assurances that different architects would design the towers, the drawings establish that Mr. Libeskind's intention all along has been to become their sole architect. What he calls design guidelines are just short of schematic designs for actual buildings. Mr. Silverstein's architects, not to mention the Lower Manhattan Development Corporation, would be fools to accept them.

So would we. In fact, the time has come to examine in some detail the Ground Zero design process as it has unfolded in the last two years. The process began as a political story and has again become one. What's needed now is a cultural framework for interpreting it. Until such a scaffold is in place, it will be impossible to make artistic sense of this or that scrap of design as it comes floating along.

More balloons are due shortly. On November 17 the development corporation will present designs by finalists in the competition for a memorial to the victims of 9/11. Next month Mr. Silverstein is expected to present a preliminary design by David M. Childs of Skidmore, Owings & Merrill and Mr. Libeskind for Freedom Tower, the first office tower on the construction schedule.

Mr. Libeskind's design guidelines build on material presented in September as the Refined Master Site Plan. The title was odd: the public had yet to see a master plan. What they saw was a patched-together collage of an obsolete site plan, new plans for below-grade uses (chiefly transportation), and architectural renderings submitted by Mr. Libeskind in February.

Unless you've been living on Mars, you've already seen those illustrations and the familiar features depicted in them: the wedge of light, the exposed slurry wall, the spiral of skyscrapers culminating in the 1,776-foot-tall Freedom Tower, and so on. Mr. Libeskind's plan partly transforms those images into architectural designs. Though less impressionistic than the earlier images, the drawings present a set of highly articulated building envelopes. These are shaped entirely by formal concerns and do not reflect a serious analysis of structure, circulation, and interior organization. Those, presumedly, would be left to the individual architects on Mr. Silverstein's team. Not a lot else would be. If these guidelines—or ones anywhere near as rigid—are adopted, Mr. Childs, Jean Nouvel, Fumihiko Maki, and Norman Foster, architects whose experience, talent, and professional experience vastly exceed Mr. Libeskind's, would be reduced to the level of executive architects, producing working drawings for designs they had virtually no hand in shaping.

Forget Freedom Tower. It should be renamed Straitjacket Tower. The guidelines for it are so rigid as to virtually exclude Mr. Childs from shaping the building he was hired to design. As a formal composition, the design is feeble. Conceptually, it is kitsch, with its broadcasting spire intended to echo the Statue of Liberty's upraised arm more nearly resembling a skyward salute. The design is not worth the increased expense that its complex and illogical structure would incur.

When first appraising this proposal last December, I noted its resemblance to unbuilt designs for the Stadtkrone, or city crown, developed by German Expressionist architects in the early twentieth century. Those with a sense of history have found this resemblance highly disturbing. For historians of the Expressionist period, the Stadtkrone has long been a controversial concept. The architecture critic Wolfgang Pehnt, among others, has seen it as a forerunner of National Socialist ideology. As developed by Expressionists like Bruno Taut, the city crown's imposing scale, its subordination of individuals to the mass, its homogenous formal vocabulary, and its aura of religious spectacle offered a glimpse of a totalizing aesthetic that came to fruition in the cathedral of light, Albert Speer's design for the 1936 Nuremberg rallies.

Similar forms, of course, can convey different meanings. Expressionism has inspired many architects of Mr. Libeskind's generation to design projects that are antifascistic. But the Libeskind design flirts perilously with the ideology of its source. It is, for one thing, a creation of the state, and its rhetorical themes conform obediently to prevailing political views. The "assault on freedom"—Mr. Libeskind's phrase for his plan's underlying theme—is a propagandistic notion, not a historical fact.

Any design guidelines that insist on restrictiveness and homogeneity should be rejected. There is not just one way to respond to 9/11. The exclusion of other architectural visions is an assault on the idea of the city as a place where every voice counts. Design guidelines in general are problematic for Ground Zero. Commonly used in suburban residential neighborhoods, they are now most often associated with the followers of the New Urbanism, developers of suburban communities known for their "traditional" period pastiche styles. Plans originally prepared for the Lower Manhattan Development Corporation by the New York firms Peterson Littenberg and Beyer Blinder Belle adhered to this retro design philosophy. That is one reason for which these plans were rejected by the public at town hall meetings held at the Javits Center in July of last year. The development corporation's "innovative design study," organized after that meeting, was intended to bring contemporary architecture into consideration. The selection of Daniel Libeskind was the end result of that process.

Yet as David W. Dunlap noted in *The New York Times* in March, Mr. Libeskind's proposal was strikingly similar to the earlier plans. It differed chiefly in the angular and fragmented forms of the buildings depicted in Mr. Libeskind's renderings. The problem is that those illustrations were not intended as designs for buildings, a task that in any case fell outside the scope of the planning tasks that the architect was hired to perform. Rather, they were stand-ins for the buildings that would be designed by the "other architects" that Mr. Libeskind himself had specified. That inclusiveness was possibly the best feature that his proposal had to recommend it.

I don't doubt that Mr. Libeskind and his supporters believe that artistic principles are at stake in the formulation of his guidelines. Even, or perhaps especially, considering the doubt that has already been raised about the wedge of light, the slurry wall, and other features, I wouldn't expect them to think any other way.

But there are other ways to think, build, and remember. Isn't this the point of freedom? The point of cities? The point of art? We need not recast our urban centers according to suburban styles of taste, or in the image of cities where rigid conformity is the rule.

"Art," Marshall McLuhan wrote, "is anything you can get away with." In that sense, at least, the guidelines are of the highest artistic order.

November 8, 2003

LUNCH BOX FOR ART: A NEW MUSEUM

The New Museum of Contemporary Art wants to build a seven-story bento box for art on the Bowery. Plans and models for this deftly composed lunch break of a building are now on view in the museum's mezzanine gallery, at 583 Broadway, between Houston and Prince streets in SoHo. Produced by SANAA, a Tokyo firm, the design should please those who believe that art museums should be neutral containers. If executed with proper attention to detail, the building will also delight the Victorians among us who incline toward tender passion.

It may seem odd to describe so minimalist a design as Victorian. It may be doubly odd to portray as tender a building that will be encased within tough galvanized zinc. Yet it was the Victorians who recognized the elo-quence of the Crystal Palace, one of Minimalism's primary sources. And Minimalism's master, Mies van der Rohe, showed the world that industrial materials can be sweet.

This legacy should be kept in mind when the issue of context comes up. Like every substantial building that has gone up in Manhattan in the past decade, SANAA's design demonstrates the fecundity that occurs when the idea of context is distinguished from mere adjacency. Add to, rather than fit in with: this is the crux of the distinction. When a building is dedicated to contemporaneity, as the New Museum will be, the design should add to the present.

SANAA was chosen in April from a short list of younger, relatively unsung firms. These global talent hunts have become artworks in them-selves, a genre of Arte Povera, perhaps, in which small struggling offices perform the function once played by hemp, rocks, and other humble materials. "Feed me! Feed me!" The spectacle can be as heartbreaking as the death of Little Nell. Kazuyo Sejima, one of SANAA's two principal partners, is not an unknown. A former associate of Toyo Ito and a pro-tégée of Arata Isozaki, she has been much talked about on the interna-tional circuit in recent years. Mr. Isozaki launched her on the global stage in 2000, when he commissioned her to design an installation at the Japan-ese Pavilion for the Venice Architecture Biennale.

Entitled "City of Girls," the project featured rows of plastic daisies planted in beds of white gravel and was intended to capture the flair of the Japanese techno-virgins who made the world safe for shopping magazines like *Lucky*. Knowingly or not, Ms. Sejima stepped into one of the privi-leged roles in architecture today: the foreigner who simultaneously affirms and deflates local notions of difference. The project's title and location invited visitors to project images of the feminine and the Asian onto its pure white surfaces. The plastic flowers allowed us to detect the universal in our omnipotent modernity and its discontents.

In parts of Asia, it is said, the desirable is modern, the undesirable is Western. We in the West have often found our own modernity to be highly undesirable, however, and SANAA's design can be seen as an expression of a continuing project to transform the aggressive energies of modern life into states of desire. Whatever Eastern qualities SANAA has brought to the design, it is strongly rooted in the broad historical main-stream of contemporary New York.

Designed by Ms. Sejima and Ryue Nishizawa, the firm's other princi-pal partner, the new New Museum will be on the Bowery, just opposite the intersection with Prince Street, which terminates there. This site will give the museum visual access to and from deepest SoHo, where the museum's cultural roots are planted. Though first situated on the Greenwich Village campus of The New School, which gave the institution its name, the New Museum has been integral to the transformation of the old industrial city into the culture factory that it is today.

SANAA's design encodes that history in urban space. Little lofts. Little SoHo lofts that died and went to heaven. That is one entrancing image that the museum's exterior brings to mind. The contemporary city is a search for the philosopher's stone capable of transforming rust into the life of the mind. Frankly, I was expecting the firm to produce a more transparent building envelope. SANAA is noted for delicate, veil-like facades, and the museum has spoken of its desire to appear open to the neighboring community. So it is surprising to see that the museum's elevations use less glass than those of the Whitney. The opaque zinc-finished steel may take some getting used to.

I'm prepared to like it immediately, however. There is more than one way to be open. We don't often see metal used as a light, reflective skin. With the moiré patterns that will glimmer across its galvanized surface, I expect that the skin will be nearly as veil-like as glass. This zinc plating really is that familiar, cheap silvery gray stuff air ducts are made of, a reminder that modern architecture is a form of industrial alchemy.

The idea of openness is conveyed more emphatically by the shape of the building envelope, perhaps, than by its materials. Each of the building's seven floors is represented as a distinct rectangular box. These are stacked atop one another, in an off-axis composition, like a chest of partly open drawers. This arrangement allows variety in the size and proportions of each floor. It also creates setbacks that are used for open-air terraces and for skylights to naturally illuminate the galleries below. At night, the building's metallic exterior will be washed with artificial lighting from within.

There are three main gallery floors, on the third, fourth, and fifth levels. At least two of these will be connected by internal stairs. A vertical circulation core, of elevators and fire stairs, provides access throughout the building. The galleries are simple enclosures of space, treated as the luxury object that we in New York know space to be. As they do in Japan, only more so. This is perhaps where the Eastern quality of the design can be sensed. In Japan the cost of a building is only a fraction of that of the space on which it stands. Remember how, in SoHo, lofts used to be described as "raw" space? At the New Museum, the loftlike galleries are cool, fresh, immaculately sliced sashimi.

One floor of offices, on the second level. A ground-floor café and bookshop. In the basement, a 200-seat auditorium and a media lounge. In the penthouse, party time! A square box of a space, including something called the Empire Bar, with wraparound terraces and views in all directions. Smaller galleries are tucked away throughout the museum. Happenstance encouraged.

More than half the funds have been raised for a $35 million capital project that includes the cost of building the 60,000-square-foot structure. The museum hopes to begin construction next October, with an opening projected for the spring of 2006. Guggenheimer Architects of New York is SANAA's associated local architect. The project architect is Florian Idenburg. Structural engineering is by the dashing and talented Guy Nordenson, without whose services few contemporary buildings would dare to rise.

November 14, 2003

A BUILDING'S BOLD SPIRIT, CLAD IN MARBLE AND CONTROVERSY

Let us now celebrate the aristocratic satisfaction of not pleasing. Huntington Hartford gave himself that pleasure when he commissioned Edward Durell Stone to design the Gallery of Modern Art (1964), the legendarily exotic building at 2 Columbus Circle.

A campaign is under way to have the building declared a city landmark before it undergoes a major renovation. I would regret the loss of the building. Whether the campaign succeeds, I hope that New Yorkers will take the opportunity to renew the independent spirit the building embodies.

The Preservation League of New York State has put 2 Columbus Circle on its Seven to Save list, an annual selection of the state's most endangered landmarks. Along with Landmark West! and other civic groups, the Preservation League is seeking a hearing before the New York City Landmarks Preservation Commission. The groups want to prevent the building from being remodeled by its soon-to-be owner, the Museum of Arts & Design, formerly the American Craft Museum. (More information is available on the Preservation League's Web site, www.preservenys.org.)

Designed by Brad Cloepfil of Allied Works Architecture in Portland, Oregon, the remodeling plans propose to reclad the building with terra cotta and glass, creating a scrimlike effect. The building's marble skin, porthole windows, and Venetian Gothic–inspired details would be eliminated. The proposed facades appear intentionally underwhelming. The small, invited competition organized by the museum included more impressive efforts. Perhaps the museum hoped to forestall opposition by choosing the least aggressive design.

If so, the strategy backfired. The problem is not Mr. Cloepfil's plan. It is his client's choice of a design that stood little chance of rallying supporters. You can forgive the museum for making what it probably took to be a highly civic gesture. But what's so civic about fearfulness? Or so historically minded? The distinction of 2 Columbus Circle is that Stone was out of step. You do not necessarily improve on such a building by replacing it with something recessive. If anything, you punch up the idea of difference, as Zaha Hadid did in her proposal for the project. You go with a design that stands a chance of kicking up a storm.

I support the League's position. But I regret that its interpretation of the building is so badly skewed; 2 Columbus Circle is hardly the "icon of the Modern movement" described by the group's literature. Modern architects and critics reviled Stone for what they called aesthetic apostasy. Those who esteem the building as a precursor of Postmodernism are on historically firmer ground, but is this anything to be proud of?

That depends on which Postmodernism you have in mind. If by that we mean explicit references to historical styles, 2 Columbus Circle can be blamed for pointing the way toward the decline of New York architecture. If we mean drawing inspiration from the past, then there was no need to have a Postmodernism at all. Le Corbusier, Mies van der Rohe, Frank Lloyd Wright, and Louis Kahn are just a few of the modern architects who acknowledged their indebtedness to historical precedent.

The truth is that Stone's use of a style like Venetian Gothic is barely incidental to the importance of 2 Columbus Circle. The style was merely the means by which Stone broke ranks. Breaking ranks is what mattered, and I suspect that the attachment many of us feel for the building is due in large part to nostalgia for the period when New York was more hospitable than it is now to the kind of controversy breaking ranks can create.

The ideal of "not pleasing" is fundamental to modern art and modern criticism. The primary job of the critic who takes after Baudelaire is to cast off fear, the fear of saying the wrong thing, forming the wrong judgment, thinking the wrong thought. Criticism, like research science, is based on the absolute right to be wrong.

Like the museum it was designed for, Stone's building was intended as critique. Up to a point it was autocritique. A designer, with Philip Goodwin, of the Museum of Modern Art in 1939, Stone was initially a disciple of the International Style. In the 1950s he had some kind of conversion experience, which I believe involved being seated on a plane next to Aline Saarinen, an art critic for *The New York Times*. Thereafter he began designing ornamental screens.

The late '50s and early '60s, then, became the great era of ornamental screens. They were to that period what fritted and translucent glass facades like that designed by Allied Works are to ours: veils. The reference was not to the past but to the East, and to a sanitized version of the erotic energies associated with it. Rita Hayworth as Salome. The Forbidden. In this sense Stone was part of America's great libidinous awakening in the postwar decades, architecture's Peppermint Lounge.

Hartford was part of it, too. His crusade against the formalist orthodoxies of the Museum of Modern Art was largely a liberation of the repressed, with Salvador Dalí standing in for Freud. At the top of Stone's building, behind the screen of the loggia, was the two-story Gauguin Room (the museum's restaurant), and also its crowning impulse: the escape from civilization and its constraints on the senses.

Ms. Hadid's design picked up on the confidence of Stone's design and the era that produced it. Taking the porthole windows as her point of departure, she enlarged their size by several orders of magnitude, producing facades that evoked classic Pucci fabric designs. Now these were some scary veils. And I think the city was ready for it. At least the audience for contemporary architecture would have had something worth fighting for.

The fight itself is worth fighting for. Only a decade after Hartford's museum opened, New York architecture began to be overtaken by a tyranny of politeness, a fear of breaking ranks that has yet to loosen its grip. The battle cry for architectural consensus that followed the attacks on September 11 shows how deeply entrenched is the city's resistance to facing the unknown.

Historically, preservationists have been part of this resistance, not just, or even mainly, because some of them may oppose change, but because their criteria for conferring value are obsolete. This is becoming increasingly clear as more postwar buildings come eligible for landmark status. "Typical of its period," "an important example of its style": criteria like these betray a nineteenth-century historicist approach to the past. They do not account for the dynamic, dialectic role that buildings play over time.

Peter Eisenman is right to suggest that buildings create problems: this is what 2 Columbus Circle has in common with Lever House, the Solomon R. Guggenheim Museum, the MetLife (originally Pan Am) Building, the TWA. Flight Center at Kennedy Airport, and other works of the period. All of them were great problems. All of them deserve to be valued as such, if their history is not to be falsified, and if we are to regain a healthy appetite for more of the same.

November 24, 2003

UNCERTAIN FUTURE FOR THE PAST'S TREASURES

Stranded! That's how I feel each time the World Monuments Fund releases its list of 100 most endangered sites. As if the present were a beach onto which every artifact of humankind will eventually wash up. A vast inventory already lies there, waterlogged on the sand, with flies buzzing around: mosques, palaces, little mud-baked villages, tombs to die for, temples, rock paintings: much of this in advanced states of disintegration.

And here we go stumbling around, pressed into service as the dutiful custodians of all this stuff when we barely have time to pick up the apartment and schlep our shirts to the laundry. And just when we think we're close to getting the last lot tagged, numbered, debarnacled, and cataloged, another wave hits the sand bringing more stuff.

Another wave came crashing down a few weeks ago, with the arrival of the 2004 list. The list is compiled every two years from sites nominated by individuals, preservation groups, and government agencies. Sites can be relisted, and those reappearing this year include some in Lower Manhattan and ancient palaces at Nimrud and Nineveh in Iraq. The connection illuminates a cultural framework that transcends discord, a scaffolding also in need of constant repair.

The 2004 list has some surprises. Antarctica appears for the first time. The polar caps may be melting, but surely protection can be found for Ernest Shackleton's expedition hut. The hut is infested with microbes. I can testify that the ruins of Ephesus, the ancient pilgrimage city with the Temple of Artemis, now in Turkey, are infested with tourists. I felt like a total pest when I visited that site six years ago. The place was crawling with us.

The list also features sites that straddle national boundaries, like the Jesuit missions built to indoctrinate the Guaraní Indians in Argentina, Brazil, and Paraguay. Perhaps the most haunting addition is Perm 36, the only intact gulag in Russia. Built of timber by prisoners in 1946, its camp buildings are near collapse.

The Ghazni minarets in Afghanistan. Strawberry Hill, Horace Walpole's pioneering venture in Gothic Revival near London. The Ennis Brown House in Los Angeles, one of Frank Lloyd Wright's landmark textile-block houses from the 1920s. And my poor Battersea Power Station, designed by Giles Gilbert Scott and completed in 1932: the puffing stacks of this abandoned monument to industrial power in London greeted me with great yellow Art Deco clouds each morning when I left the house for school.

You see what I mean. The salvage is overwhelming, the size of it a painful reminder of our inadequacy as cultural stewards. One is strongly tempted to withdraw into comic fantasy: the grand heritage of civilization with laugh track as an *I Love Lucy* episode. Architecture is a luxury. Preserving it is a double luxury. And if the World Monuments Fund were restricted to advocating architectural preservation, its mission would be one luxury among many. But the fund stands for something much greater than that. It represents the cosmopolitan virtues of tolerance and aesthetic discrimination. This set of mental attitudes is not a luxury at all. It is a precondition for peace, and has been so for at least four thousand years, first with individual cities, now with the entire globe. More than a scrapbook of monuments, the 2004 list is a workout for global consciousness: a cultural equivalent of the Kyoto Protocol on climate change. My holiday wish is that a copy of the list be placed beneath each sparkling tree.

It will take more than superior military intelligence to prevent future catastrophes like September 11. Cultural and psychological intelligence will be required as well. The responsibility for negotiating boundaries does not lie exclusively with nation-states. It also rests with cultural structures that support transnational goals. The World Monuments Fund is a model of this type. At the same time, though, preservation groups are overdue for a major leap of consciousness. Preservation was not born forty years ago, the day after Pennsylvania Station was demolished. Nor, except in localized conflicts, has this movement been the strategic opponent of modern architecture it is often taken to be.

The preservation movement has a history as important as any monument, dating at least to the eighteenth century. It is sometimes said to begin with the unearthing of Herculaneum in 1709 and of Pompeii 1748. As a philosophy, preservation served the needs of Enlightenment thinkers to cast doubt on religious faith and provide aesthetic alternatives to Rococo style. The obsolescence of pagan beliefs was used to undermine the idea of religion and thereby serve the cause of reason. The simplicity of classical forms served that period's new taste for geometry. Preservation grew out of archaeology and the notion that history can be practiced as a form of science. In the nineteenth century this notion morphed into the linear view of the past known as historicism. Flipped around by the century that followed, historicism produced the idea of progress. When the new Pennsylvania Station replaced the old, one form of modernity devoured the other.

The meal left a bad taste in the mouth, the taste of crisis. By the mid-

1960s historicism was finally breaking down. The Modern movement, whose pioneers believed themselves to be progressing beyond the nineteenth century, were actually perpetuating it. The idea that each epoch should produce its own distinctive style of art was one of historicism's fundamental tenets. The collapse of modern architecture signaled that this idea had run out of steam. The rest has been a comedy of trend stories and unveilings of the next big thing.

The World Monuments Fund list strikes me as an inadvertent parody of these journalistic genres: a cover story on the next hot neighborhoods, or a list of the Top 100 getaways, or a special advertising section sponsored by American Express. I do not mean this as a put-down. The fund's list holds a libidinous appeal that is oddly lacking from most preservationist appeals. Where does it come from?

Partly it is the venture's global scale, which is sexy in the way Alexander the Great was sexy (at least as portrayed by Richard Burton), potent with the aphrodisiac of power. This appeal is combined with the maternal instinct to protect vulnerable offspring from attack. The exoticism of travel is another element. The fund's list is sponsored by American Express, perhaps partly as an expression of corporate conscience. Tourism does potentially jeopardize the attractions off which it feeds.

But the core of the list's appeal, I believe, is the power of narrative. We miss historicism, even if we have never heard of it. We miss the coherence that the linear view of culture conferred on seemingly random events. We miss the March of Progress, even if we hate the destruction it has wreaked. The craving for new buildings that look old, the ludic delight in Jules Verne techno-future tales projected by publications like *Wired* magazine: these apparent extremes satisfy nostalgic longings for an unrecoverable nineteenth-century view of ourselves in relation to time.

The watch list by itself has not resolved the crisis precipitated by historicism's collapse. But it points the way toward a resolution: it provides an interpretive framework suitable for the era of globalization. The list speaks not of history but of histories, a multitude of stories now available for our edification. There is no end to them, it seems. We like Babel, it turns out. We enjoy the many shapes of language, in words and images, especially when the storytellers are ancient and perhaps even wise. Listeners wanted.

And from within the multiplicity of shapes there does emerge a narrative thread. It leads episodically from ancient times to the present. It is the story of cosmopolitan life, the tale of the cultural marketplace, a saga that has driven urban development from Damascus to New York.

Tolerance of others, discrimination between cultural authority and other forms of social power: these are the leading concepts of the cosmopolitan story.

How are they holding up in your part of the world?

THIS YEAR'S TIDE OF HISTORY'S DECAYING SITES

Africa

EGYPT
Khasekhemwy at Hierakonpolis
Mortuary Temple of Amenhotep III
Sabil Ruqayya Dudu

KENYA
Mtwapa Heritage Site

MALI
Bandiagara Escarpment Cultural
    Landscape

MOROCCO
Sahrij and Sbaiyin Madrassa
    Complex

NIGERIA
Benin City Earthworks

SOUTH AFRICA
Richtersveld Cultural Landscape

UGANDA
Kampala Historic Buildings

The Americas

ARGENTINA, BRAZIL, AND PARAGUAY
Jesuit Guaraní Missions

BOLIVIA
Vallegrande Area Rock Art Sites

BRAZIL
San Francisco Convent

CANADA
St. John's Anglican Church

CHILE
Humberstone and Santa Laura
    Industrial Complex

CUBA
Calzada del Cerro

ECUADOR
Las Peñas
Bolivar Theater

EL SALVADOR
San Miguel Arcangel and Santa Cruz
    de Roma Churches

GUATEMALA
Usumacinta River Cultural Landscape

JAMAICA
Falmouth Historic Town

MEXICO
San Francisco de Tzintzuntzan
    Convent
Quetzalcoatl Temple
La Tercena
Oxtotitlán Paintings
Pimería Alta Missions

PANAMA
Panama Canal area

PARAGUAY
Paraguay Railway System

PERU
Our Lady of Guadalupe Monastery
Angasmarca Temple
Kuelap Fortress
Túcume Archaeological Complex

TRINIDAD AND TOBAGO
Banwarie Trace Archaeological Site

UNITED STATES
Church of St. Ann and the Holy
    Trinity, Brooklyn Heights, New
    York.
Historic Lower Manhattan
Ennis Brown House, Los Angeles
North Family Shaker Site, New
    Lebanon, New York
Iglesia San José, San Juan, Puerto
    Rico
Plum Orchard Historic District,
    Cumberland Island, Georgia

VENEZUELA
Real Fuerza de Santiago de Arroyo
La Guaira Historic City

Antarctica
Ernest Shackleton's Expedition Hut

Asia
CHINA
Ohel Rachel Synagogue
Great Wall of China Cultural
    Landscape (Beijing)
Cockcrow Postal Town
Puning Temple Statues
Tianshui Traditional Houses

INDIA
Osmania University College for
    Women
Quila Mubarak
Dalhousie Square
Bhuj Darbargadh

INDONESIA
Omo Hada
Tamansari Water Castle

JAPAN
Tomo Port Town

MONGOLIA
Geser Sum Monastery

TAIWAN
Jungshe Village

Europe
ALBANIA
Voskopoji Churches

BRITAIN
Stowe House
Battersea Power Station
Strawberry Hill
St. Vincent's Street Church

BULGARIA
Vidin Synagogue

CZECH REPUBLIC
Chotesov Monastery
St. Anne's Church

FINLAND
Helsinki-Malmi Airport

GEORGIA
Timotesubani Virgin Church

GREECE
Palaikastro Archaeological Site
Helike Archaeological Site

HUNGARY
Turony Church

IRELAND
Headfort House
Athassel Abbey

ITALY
Port of Trajan Archaeological Park
Tuff-Towns and Vie Cave

POLAND
Old Lublin Theater

PORTUGAL
Roman Villa of Rabaçal

RUSSIA
The Chinese Palace at Oranienbaum
Narcomfin Building
Perm 36

SLOVAKIA
Three Greek Catholic churches

SLOVENIA
Lanthieri Manor

SPAIN
Pazo de San Miguel das Peñcas

TURKEY
Temple of Augustus
Little Hagia Sophia Mosque
Central Izmir Synagogues
Ephesus Archaeological Site
Kariye Museum

UKRAINE
Tyras-Belgorod Fortress
Panticapaeum Ancient City

YUGOSLAVIA
Prizren Historic Center

Australia
Dampier Rock Art Complex

Middle East
AFGHANISTAN
Ghazni Minarets

IRAQ
Nineveh and Nimrud Palaces
Erbil Citadel

ISRAEL
Apollonia-Arsuf

JORDAN
Ain Ghazal

LEBANON
Iskandarouna a Naqoura cultural
    landscape

PALESTINIAN TERRITORIES
Tell Balatah (Shechem, or Ancient
    Nablus)
Al Qasem Palace

SYRIA
Bosra Ancient City
Amrit Archaeological Site

TURKMENISTAN
Old Nisa

December 16, 2003

PATH STATION BECOMES A PROCESSION OF FLIGHT

An exorcism was held yesterday at the World Financial Center Winter Garden at Battery Park City. The spirit of diminished expectations that produced the Winter Garden and buildings like it was severed from the soul of New York. In place of suburban shopping-mall atrium design, there emerged civic architecture of the highest order.

Santiago Calatrava's design for the World Trade Center PATH station should satisfy those who believe that buildings planned for Ground Zero must aspire to a spiritual dimension. Over the years, many people have discerned a metaphysical element in Mr. Calatrava's work. I hope New Yorkers will detect its presence too. With deep appreciation, I congratulate the Port Authority for commissioning Mr. Calatrava, the great Spanish architect and engineer, to design a building with the power to shape the future of New York. It is a pleasure to report, for once, that public officials are not overstating the case when they describe a design as breathtaking.

Mr. Calatrava has the creative magnetism that the Spanish know as *duende*. The envious call this quality star power. I call it soul. Derived from *duen de casa* (lord of the house), duende descends on great poets, musicians, and dancers at peak moments of inspiration. It has alighted on Mr. Calatrava once again. The PATH station will be more than a building. It will cast out the defeatist attitude that has clogged New York's architectural arteries since the destruction of the old Pennsylvania Station.

The PATH station has been designed in collaboration with the Downtown Design Partnership, a joint venture between two local firms, DMJM Harris and the STV Group. It is aligned on an east-west axis, occupying a portion of the site designated as the Wedge of Light in Daniel Libeskind's Ground Zero plan. In place of a wedge (in reality an inglorious traffic intersection), there will arise what Mr. Calatrava envisions as a bird, most likely a dove, released from the hands of a child. No more secondhand Statues of Liberty here, in other words. Rather, a prayer for peace.

The outspread wings of this elusive bird are the design's most dramatic feature. Composed of steel and glass, the wings form two gigantic canopies that will shelter an open plaza surrounding the station. Some may see the shadow of an angel in this architectural image: a descendant of those great winged sculptures that descended on the skylines of great European cities in the mid-nineteenth century. Bethesda Fountain in

Central Park is their worthy American cousin. Mr. Calatrava has revived the genre in the form of an entire building.

The bird's torso reminds this viewer of Eero Saarinen's magnificent ice-hockey rink at Yale. Like other Saarinen projects, such as the former TWA terminal at Kennedy Airport, the rink was criticized for making a showy display of structure that lacked structural justification. This criticism has been aimed at Mr. Calatrava, also. Though trained in engineering as well as architecture, Mr. Calatrava is a highly expressive, not to say an expressionistic, architect. Yet he differs from Saarinen in one crucial respect. His expressive gestures do not rely on concealed structural support; they have the integrity of their own physical being.

Mr. Calatrava needs no hints from the solar system to make architecture out of light. He has been doing it for years. The genius of his design unfolds underground, where light from the roof cascades down three levels from the street to the train platforms. The intermediary levels of the mezzanine and concourse are sleek, dynamic spaces, open to the sky. At night, lighting from within the building will illuminate the plaza and the office towers surrounding it.

It is easy to mistake Mr. Calatrava as an architect of sweetness and light. Risk and mortality are seldom absent from his designs. In the time capsule he designed four years ago for the *New York Times Magazine*, for example, a steel thorn appears to project forward from a pair of full-bodied lips. Like Henry Moore, Mr. Calatrava is often inspired by the skeletal remains of living forms. This formal source acquires greater depth of meaning at Ground Zero. The spreading canopies portend the afterlife.

"The duende will not approach if he does not see the possibility of death," wrote García Lorca, the poet who introduced the creative imp to many non-Hispanic readers. Mr. Calatrava's reading of the concept is lighter. He once compared it to whiff of orange blossoms on the hills around Valencia. But in both cases the image derives from the land.

This is the gentle paradox of Mr. Calatrava's transportation designs. They bring a sense of rootedness to the experience of movement. This quality may derive from Mr. Calatrava's affinity for Gothic religious architecture. The great cathedrals, too, are epic processionals, walks through lightness of structure, enclosure, and space.

It helps to visualize the station's design in conjunction with Reflecting Absence, the memorial designed by Michael Arad and Peter Walker. Both projects emphasize procession into the ground. The memorial procession will be darker. In the station, circulation will be radiant. The penetration of depth will be common to both.

Mr. Calatrava is a poet of movement. Bridges and rail stations are among his finest lyrics. They connect the traveler not only to points in space, but also to the cosmopolitan idea. It has been a long time since New York has forged this strong a link to the rest of the world. It is poetry in the ancient sense of connective tissue: the beliefs and aspirations that hold a society together.

In Europe, the winged statue was a totem of an earlier cosmopolitan age, an era when the continent was linked by trains. Infrastructure gave us modern cosmopolitanism, that is to say. May the art of making connections help bring peace.

January 23, 2004

GLAMOROUS GLASS GIVES 10 COLUMBUS CIRCLE A LOOK OF CRYSTALLIZED NOIR

It is good to see Skidmore, Owings & Merrill back in the business of piling up big chunks of quartz. Stone was never this firm's strength. Ten Columbus Circle does ample penance for the opaque minerals Skidmore deployed so extravagantly during its neo–Art Deco phase. There's some flame-pattern gray granite at the building's base, but it's there mainly for contrast with the giant cluster of glass crystals, which appears to have been quarried from the sky.

Designed by David Childs, with Mustafa K. Abadan as lead partner, the building has great glamour. It is far more romantic than the Jazz Age tributes conceived by Mr. Childs in his wanton postmodern youth. With 10 Columbus, the mood is modern noir. The two towers are worthy descendants of Radio City. The building draws us into the city of long shadows, relieved here and there by silver glints.

If you're of a certain antiquity, you may recall a protest that was held in the 1980s against the shadows that an earlier version of this building would have cast on Central Park. (In a gesture that Christo might have dreamed up in collaboration with Gene Kelly, the protesters carried open umbrellas.) Mr. Childs's response to the demonstration is somewhat perverse. As realized, the two towers of 10 Columbus Circle have taken the form of shadows themselves: they resemble the oblique, cinematic oblong forms cast over the cityscape in black-and-white movies of the 1940s and '50s. Now we've got four shadows for the price of two.

There are sound contextual reasons for it. The parallelogram shape of the towers derives from the angle of Broadway's intersection with the orthogonal street grid of Manhattan. The towers thus appear to be extruded out of irregularities in the existing urban fabric. This reverses the figure-ground relationship of the 1980s design, which imposed the hulking towers symmetrically on axis with Central Park West. In that form, the composition resembled the Colossi of Memnon at Luxor. The design's Art Deco trim heightened the anachronistic Egyptian Revival effect.

The realized building remains Egyptian in scale (the towers could have gone higher), while the plain geometric forms hark back to the architect Amenhotep. You will notice an echo in the pyramid-shaped pilasters used by Philip Johnson for the Trump International Hotel and Condominiums across the street. You will also notice Mr. Trump's signs advising prospective tenants at 10 Columbus that his own building will ruin their views. What apprentice thought up that self-defeating campaign? ("You're fired!") Mr. Johnson's design isn't that bad.

Ten Columbus is a balancing act. Besides negotiating the angles introduced by Broadway, the design squares the circle, with street grid around it. The base is composed of overlapping grids, which create an impression of an arcade in two dimensions. The overlap technique derives from the temple fronts Palladio superimposed on the facades of his sixteenth-century churches. At the roofline of the base, a curving course of angled glass panels serves the function of pediment and frieze.

The classical elements and proportions reach back to Columbus Circle's roots in the City Beautiful movement of the turn of the last century, a legacy marked by the statue of Columbus atop his column and by the *Maine* Memorial at the southwest entrance to Central Park. Mr. Childs had this background in mind when designing the first version. One of the follies of that period was the notion that architects should resume the City Beautiful project, effectively wiping out the modernist "rejection of history" that had aborted it.

What was lost sight of then was the degree to which the beauty of New York City derives from heterogeneity. Diversity is its history, too, a saga of which the City Beautiful vision is one chapter among many. Ten Columbus folds that chapter into its forms, along with Art Deco and International Style. In formal terms, the result may not be an architectural breakthrough. But the building adds its own synthetic DNA to the circle's rich, eclectic mix.

Jazz at Lincoln Center, a performance and rehearsal space designed by Rafael Viñoly, will occupy the top portion of the grand portal that occupies the center of the base, on axis with Central Park South. I'm inclined to see the architecture above the base as crystallized jazz. This is where the design fully expresses its urban ambitions, particularly in the flaring gem-cut setbacks that mediate between the base and the towers.

This is scenographic, not architectonic design. Gordon Bunshaft, the glass master of Skidmore's International Style phase, might well have disapproved. It is the ghost of another architect, Wallace K. Harrison, that hovers benignly over this design.

The architect of the Trylon and Perisphere at the 1939 World's Fair, a collaborator on Rockefeller Center, the United Nations headquarters and Lincoln Center, and not least the designer of Time Inc.'s previous headquarters on Avenue of the Americas, Harrison was perhaps the most gifted iconographer in mid-twentieth-century New York.

Instead of mimicking a tradition, 10 Columbus perpetuates one. Mr. Childs had hoped to use a brighter shade of glass, one that was pale white in effect. This would have produced a different aesthetic but not necessarily a better one. The darkness of mood will remind some spectators of Black Rock, the CBS headquarters on Fifty-second Street designed by Eero Saarinen. That building, too, was criticized for emphasizing iconography over structural expression.

Opinion will be divided over the mall of shops and restaurants that occupies the base of 10 Columbus. To appreciate this place, it probably helps to be a surrealist like Walter Benjamin. Chronicler of the shopping arcades that preceded department stores, most notably in Paris, Benjamin saw such places as the dream labyrinths of the industrial age. Some atmospheres require a haze: if it weren't for New York's smoking laws, the restaurant arcade at 10 Columbus would be an apparition. So, wear shades or squint.

No one has done more than Rem Koolhaas to quicken our appreciation for the surreal density of Manhattan. The multiple uses of 10 Columbus—corporate headquarters, performing arts complex, condos, a hotel, restaurants, and shops—are very much in the spirit of Mr. Koolhaas, as is the semblance of Harrison. But invoking Mr. Koolhaas here is double-edged. If the reference helps to reveal the contemporaneity of 10 Columbus, it also reminds us of the distance that still separates New York from the most inspired architecture of our day.

I see no reason why Mr. Childs shouldn't step into Harrison's shoes. Though over sixty, he is still the most promising young architect in New York. For years he handicapped himself with the doctrine of appropriateness, a dogma in place of a conviction. There may be no such thing as progress in the history of architecture, but in the development of individual architects and cities the concept still holds. That is what 10 Columbus proves.

Harrison himself was less appreciated in his own time than he has come to be in ours. His theatricality was held against him. In the case of Mr. Childs, the reverse appears to be true. When he turns up the footlights and lets drama come to the fore, as he has here, an imagination lights up.

February 4, 2004

FOR LOWER MANHATTAN, TOWER OFFERS A RESIDENTIAL STAIRWAY TO THE SKY

Santiago Calatrava has designed a skyscraper with the buoyancy of a child's balloon. The design takes me back to 1966 and the helium-filled Mylar *Silver Cloud* sculptures that Andy Warhol presented that year at Leo Castelli's gallery. The tower is effervescent, lighter than air. Yet its impact on the skyline is likely to be profound, not merely as an individual work of genius but as an example of what can be achieved when a city rediscovers the quality of delight.

This is the first residential building Mr. Calatrava has designed in the United States, but 80 South Street Tower, at Fletcher and South streets in Lower Manhattan, is based on a series of sculptures that he began in the 1980s. For these studies in rhythm, Mr. Calatrava used a modular vocabulary of identically sized marble cubes. Wires hold them in suspension in various vertical and diagonal configurations. The basic concept is flexible. Though the South Street Tower is strictly vertical, the same technique could be used to cantilever a structure out over the water, say, at a 45-degree angle.

On South Street, twelve modular cubes, clad in glass, would be stacked into a tower of alternating solids and voids, cantilevered from either side of a central service core in a series of contrapuntal steps. Each cube measures forty-five feet to a side and contains four floors of living space, at slightly more than two thousand square feet per floor. The concrete core, a slender rectangle in plan, contains elevators, fire stairs, and risers for plumbing and power. A metal armature attached to the outer sides of the cubes provides additional support.

This arrangement leaves the interiors of the cubes unencumbered by columns and plumbing. The modules can be configured to contain one to four apartments each, and are served by separate elevators. Each cube, except the highest, provides an outdoor terrace for the one above. It would be a stairway-to-penthouse paradise, rising from a base of eight or nine stories. Frank J. Sciame Jr., the building's developer, said he hoped that he could attract a cultural institution to occupy the base, as if Mr. Calatrava's design were not enough of a cultural attraction on its own. Eighty South Street Tower would be the most original skyscraper to go up in the United States in many years. It would restore New York to a place where innovative architecture is generated, not merely acquired. And as the vision of a private developer, the tower rebukes all the hollow claims of boldness and excitement our builders habitually assert.

I mention Warhol because of the atmosphere of freedom those ridiculous silver pillows created around them. They were a child's garden of existentialism—bits of nothingness, faintly stirring in the breeze of gallerygoer conversation. Still, there was a precision to them: Warhol would go in and adjust the little lead weights attached to the corners so that they would float in midair. And they were balanced, in the rear gallery, by the wallpaper with those silly pink cows.

How did it happen that 1966 suddenly appeared to be encapsulated by the fleeting whimsy of silver clouds and pink cows? It seems that Mr. Calatrava has captured the imagination of New York. Hooray for us. As the warm reception that greeted his design for the World Trade Center transportation hub suggests, the city trusts him, to a degree it has seldom believed in any single architect in many years. This response may have as much to do with Mr. Calatrava's character as with the formal properties of his designs. In a field overpopulated with blowhards, his evident humility stands out. So does the apparent lack of irony. Though the work is eminently sophisticated in formal terms, the optimism it projects is disarmingly naïve. How dare an architect conjure these transcendent illusions for our disillusioned times! Does he believe this to be an age of faith, capable of building cathedrals?

Recently Mr. Calatrava has been reading Spinoza. You don't have to do likewise to make sense of his work. But for those seeking insight into its qualities, I strongly recommend Antonio Damasio's excellent book *Looking for Spinoza: Joy, Sorrow, and the Feeling Brain*. Dr. Damasio, a neurologist, has achieved renown by challenging our lingering tendency to regard reason and emotion as polar opposites. Science suggests otherwise. Dr. Damasio, like Freud and Nietzsche, regards these faculties as necessary partners in a dialectic intent on freedom from debilitating habit.

The book will not sit well with those who think that architecture is an art of people-pleasing. Spinoza's scheme of things was undeniably elitist. Only those with disciplined and educated intellects, Dr. Damasio writes, could accumulate sufficient knowledge and reason to put their intuitions to constructive use. But this path toward freedom is accessible to all who would make the sacrifices it entails.

Eighty South Street Tower conveys the idea that an entire city can embark on such a path. That is the design's great gift. This idea is transmitted in the design's perfect balance between the familiar and the unexpected. We recognize the similarity of the individual glass cubes to International Style office towers of the mid-twentieth century. But we have never seen one of those towers dance. From certain angles, this building is all hips. *Chicka-boom!*

We cherish the skyscrapers of prewar New York partly because of their articulated tops and stepped silhouettes. Eighty South Street can be seen as a building made almost entirely out of tops. Or, because the design uses an industrial aesthetic, we can see the cubes as echoes of Manhattan's water towers, those great building tops that are not made for aesthetic contemplation. Thus Mr. Calatrava recaptures that once vigorous exchange between our cultivated and vernacular traditions.

Every sports fan knows that it takes discipline as well as talent to play with the rules of the game. Architecture is no different. A city is never more fully human than when expertise—our own or someone else's—allows us access to ebullience, lightness, and delight.

March 3, 2004

PLANET PRADA

Miuccia Prada has stamped her name on an era by alleviating the isolation of creative people. For such sensitive types, the ultimate luxury is to feel that they are part of a community. This is the service Prada provides. She has made the world safe for people with overdeveloped inner lives. Fashion is one of the techniques she has used to accomplish this. Her outspoken ambivalence about fashion is another. Some designers struggle to make a statement. Prada evidently struggles not to. She is an artist: she would rather hide than speak.

Sometimes, Prada hides behind the art of others. The Prada Foundation, established in 1995 by Prada and her husband, Patrizio Bertelli, is a shopwindow filled with masks. Directed by the legendary critic and curator Germano Celant, the foundation sponsors exhibitions and other worthy cultural causes. (The foundation has a Web site: www.fondazione prada.org.) In the past decade, it has presented exhibitions by Tom Friedman, Anish Kapoor, Michael Heizer, Sam Taylor-Wood, and Louise Bourgeois, among others. Beautifully produced catalogs accompany the shows.

Last year the foundation branched out into philosophy. In November it financed a new chair in aesthetics at the University of Vita-Salute San Raffaele in Milan. The position will be held by Massimo Cacciari, a former mayor of Venice who is perhaps Italy's most celebrated theorist of art. In the United States, Cacciari is best known for his scholarship on the art and architecture of Vienna at the turn of the last century.

Most recently, Prada sponsored the production of an hourlong film by the Milanese artist Francesco Vezzoli. A dual tribute to Italian art-house cinema and American kitsch, the film features appearances by Catherine Deneuve, Jeanne Moreau, and Marianne Faithfull. It had its premiere in Milan last month, along with Vezzoli's ghost theater: an installation of 120 embroidered Charles Rennie Mackintosh chairs.

All this is Prada. Prada, Prada, Prada. As are the Prada shops designed by Rem Koolhaas and Herzog & de Meuron; the church in suburban Milan transformed by Dan Flavin into a radiant grotto; and the 2002 conference on contemporary social challenges organized in collaboration with a Milanese prison.

That's a lot for a company that started out as a maker of tastefully understated luggage. Or for a woman who started out as a political activist for left-wing causes. But I confess I will not be satisfied until Prada has personally designed an airport. And perhaps even an airline to go with it. Global transportation infrastructure: this seems to me the direction in which Prada is headed. From baggage to baggage claim, Prada, Prada, Prada. With some shopping, art, and philosophy along the way.

Prada's cultural projects interest me chiefly because they help to clarify the personality and intentions of a fashion genius. No one needs Prada to gain access to the work of Louise Bourgeois or Anish Kapoor. We admire her for the same reason we have always admired Italians. No one can match their talent for engineering mythologies of daily life. Since the 1960s, the Italians have exercised that talent only sporadically on the world stage. Yet those with memories of the postwar decades will not find it difficult to regard design as a serious form of communication.

Nor should we see any inherent contradiction between Prada's political sympathies and her success in business. Poets hold things tgether. Italian poets—in design, film, and fine art—have been working the contradictions between politics and art for a century and more. The work of Giò Ponti, Joe Colombo, the Castiglione brothers still activate living memory, even if Milan is no longer the design center it once was. The world is not what it was. What good are home furnishings for a time when people are living out of suitcases and scarcely have time to unpack?

Prada is on to something. People want experiences now more than they want things. They want something other than TV. They want excuses to be together in social space so they can figure out how the contemporary city is supposed to work. Things provide the excuses. They are pretexts for the authentic errand of being outside.

The Prada store that opened in New York's SoHo district in December 2001 is a prime example of this. For weeks before the opening, those of us who live downtown found ourselves at the mercy of two equally unwelcome fantasies. Pundits wanted Lower Manhattan to remain a dead zone, a backdrop for their moralistic pronouncements. City planners wanted the place to be a shopping mall thronged with happy-go-lucky but somber tourists.

We kept hearing that the community wanted this, that the community didn't want that, and after all that irrelevant chatter it was startling to come face-to-face with the community itself at the opening of the Prada store. What the community wanted was to be here. If there was luxury in the air, it wasn't coming from the clothes, the fancy in-store technology, or even the fabulous blocklong space. The luxury was making contact with people you hadn't seen together in one place since 9/11. It was the experience of being with the most solipsistic people on earth and loving them more than ever.

Georges Bataille argued that all culture is luxury. It's what we do with the energy that is left over after our material needs are met. Luxury, in the modern sense, means the transformation of the commonplace, in Arthur Danto's phrase. It means the creation of value from unpromising situations. Frank Lloyd Wright created luxury from empty space, Chanel from jersey sportswear, Louis Kahn from poured concrete. Prada creates it out of the desire to be rescued from the isolation that a creative life demands.

Francesco Vezzoli creates it from old '60s movies, television game shows, and the desire for continuity with a period he is too young to have known. Vezzoli's film is inspired by *Comizi d'Amore*, a 1964 documentary by Pier Paolo Pasolini. The movie consists of brief interviews, conducted with people across a broad spectrum of Italian society, on the subjects of love and sexual mores. Vezzoli recasts Pasolini for the age of Berlusconi.

Why are so many young artists fascinated by the 1960s? Because the romantic concept of an avant-garde bohemia breathed its last gasp then, I suppose. Thereafter, artists and thinkers would have to share their space with pop musicians, fashion photographers, advertisers, and tourists. The space is getting crowded. But in the labyrinth where ideas take shape, there is still only room for one.

April 11, 2004

THE LIBRARY THAT PUTS ON FISHNETS
AND HITS THE DISCO

At a dark hour, Seattle's new Central Library is a blazing chandelier to swing your dreams upon. If an American city can erect a civic project as brave as this one, the sun hasn't set on the West. In more than thirty years of writing about architecture, this is the most exciting new building it has been my honor to review. I could go on piling up superlatives like cars in a multiple collision, but take my word: there's going to be a whole lot of rubbernecking going on.

The new library, which opens next Sunday, was designed by Rem Koolhaas/OMA of the Netherlands in collaboration with the Seattle firm LMN Architects. Joshua Ramus of OMA was the partner in charge. It is the centerpiece of an ambitious initiative to revamp and expand Seattle's library system citywide. This is Seattle, don't forget: a city where fortunes have been made on the premise that books, and even cities, may be rendered obsolete by digital technology. Yet this new library sets an example for cities nationwide.

What cities need most of all are strong clients, like Deborah L. Jacobs, Seattle's city librarian. This is a client who knows exactly what she wants. Terrifying. But there's never been a great building without a strong client in the history of the world, and Ms. Jacobs is now up there with popes and princes as an instigator of fabulous cities.

Her achievement is all the more remarkable in light of Seattle's nasty encounters with architecture in recent years. The Seattle Art Museum, designed by Robert Venturi and Denise Scott Brown, is a rancid piece of work. Frank Gehry's Experience Music Project looks like something that crawled out of the sea, rolled over, and died. With a record like that, it is understandable that the proposal for the library aroused fierce local opposition.

It shows strength of character that Ms. Jacobs and her supporters persisted with their vision: a spiraling space for a growing number of books; a centralized area for the librarians to help patrons. The $196.4 million capital plan, known as Libraries for All, was approved by voters in 1998. In addition to the new Central Library, the measure provided for the construction of five branch libraries and the overhauling of an additional twenty-two.

Client fortitude is expressed by the Central Library's design. Quite apart from its strengths in structure, form, and space, the building exemplifies Rem Koolhaas's reliance on the architectural program: the organization of space according to use and function. Because of the clarity of this example, the Central Library's impact on architecture could be profound. It makes art out of the relationship between architect and client.

The first impression is pure bling-bling: an urban montage of starburst images without a special lens. With a faceted exterior of glass and steel, this is a big rock-candy mountain of a building, twinkling in the middle of office buildings. The library occupies a full city block, bounded by Fourth and Fifth avenues and Spring and Madison streets. Seattle's federal courthouse is across the street. A striking Miesian office tower rises on the opposite side. It's a fantastic location.

The library's exterior is an angular composition of folded planes. Walls are of glass, supported by a diagonal grid of light blue metal that covers almost the entire surface. At first glance, the irregular angles, folds, and shapes seem arbitrary. The building's structure is hard to discern, and the overall grid pattern looks like a perverse exaggeration of the abstract geometries used by mid-twentieth-century architects for decorative relief.

Ages ago, Mr. Koolhaas used to stay at the UN Plaza Hotel in Manhattan, Kevin Roche's crisp variation on the International Style, and on approaching the library for the first time it occurred to me that Mr. Koolhaas had turned the hotel inside out. The exterior resembles an inverted, Expressionist version of the Ambassador Grill, the hotel's ground-floor restaurant. The Zagat Survey describes the restaurant's design as a "mirrored-disco look" that "needs updating." Exactly. Who knew that dated disco bling-bling makes an ideal motif for a twenty-first-century library?

More to the point, who but Mr. Koolhaas knows how to embrace such campy themes and transform them into serious urbanism? This has been a constant in his work for thirty years. Pop Art is one of his roots. Fortunately, there are others. Anybody can put a pair of mouse ears on a building and proclaim his or her love for the people. Not everyone can pump up disco décor toward a new plateau in the art of making cities.

Nor can just anyone make the plateau seem like a natural progression from what has gone before. Beyond that, Mr. Koolhaas has long been motivated by the desire to counter the Oedipal impulse that pervades his profession, tending to emphasize continuity over rupture. This is evident not only in his frequent allusions to modern architects like Mies van der Rohe and Wallace K. Harrison, but in his affinity with the work of Venturi and Scott Brown. Ancient Greek temples, you'll recall, were originally painted with loud colors. Athens was altogether bling-bling.

A Koolhaas building is always engrossed in conversation with its place in history as well as urban space. You'll want to walk around the library a few times before plunging in. The site is steeply raked. This plays tricks with the eyes, making it nearly impossible to register the building's scale accurately. Its four elevations are different; the profile changes constantly. Tapered facets create the effect of forced perspective, altering the apparent dimensions of the building envelope. Planes that initially look rectangular are seen on closer inspection to be trapezoidal. Why? There are, in fact, logical reasons for these seemingly capricious moves, but they do not disclose themselves until you are inside the building, and then only gradually.

Enter at the top of the slope, on the library's Fifth Avenue side, for the building to make the grandest possible entrance into your mind. There's another entrance at the bottom, on the Fourth Avenue side, but it appears scaled for schoolchildren. (Though what kind of adult would deprive a child of the memory of a spectacular encounter with space?)

Eat your heart out, I. M. Pei. Compared to the Central Library's soaring atrium lobby, the entrance pyramid at the Louvre looks like a gadget from the Sharper Image catalog. The atrium extends along the southern half of the building. Walking through is like walking a gangplank, or stepping out onto a high diving board. At the far end, you find yourself gazing down to the sidewalk through the glass underside of an overhang.

Aesthetics have entered into the design of the building at the earliest stages of planning, in other words, before the purely visual decisions have been made. It is pointless, with this project, to separate formal and social organization. How people use a space is no less a matter of form than the most abstract visual composition. As such, a building program can be subject to aesthetic articulation. This is the meaning of the Central Library. It thinks its way beyond our dualistic tendency to polarize social and aesthetic values. Who says we need to take sides? The interplay between them can be beautiful.

One of the platforms, called the Books Spiral, epitomizes the Koolhaas approach. Designed to place roughly 75 percent of the library's collection in accessible, open space, this is the largest of the five platforms. It is a continuous, square ramp, four levels in height, that provides ease and clarity of circulation as well as storage for books. Koolhaas fans will recognize this feature from an unbuilt library he designed in the early 1990s for the Jussieu Campus of the University of Paris on the Left Bank. Some critics thought the spiral concept defied gravity, common sense, and safety. As realized, it is an entirely pragmatic solution to a common institutional problem: how to accommodate an expanding collection of books without having to divide particular fields of information over more than one floor. The concrete ramp looks expensive but wasn't. The form was fabricated using parking lot construction technology. You'll love it if you're in a wheelchair.

I'm not suggesting that the spiral design was driven purely by pragmatics, only that it serves pragmatic needs. Spirals and pinwheels have long figured in Mr. Koolhaas's architecture, for reasons that have as much to do with historical memory and psychology as with practical dictates. The point is elegance of mind. Social, technical, and psychological goals are fused into comprehensible form. The fusion is where the art takes shape.

Another example: the Mixing Chamber. This is the heart of the library, the platform where librarians greet readers and help them locate books. It feels like the deck of a big ship. In a conventional library, you would expect to find this service on a lower floor. But we know from other projects that Mr. Koolhaas likes to "displace the positions," as he puts it. His proposed expansion of the Whitney Museum of American Art would have situated the entrance lobby halfway between the street and the top-floor levels. The Mixing Chamber flaunts a similar distaste for convention. In actuality, its unusual placement ensures a far more efficient use of staff time, since they will be in a centralized location.

Stairs and escalators—vertical circulation—are painted bright chartreuse, except for a grand staircase that leads, through a mouthlike opening, to the public meeting rooms. These stairs are painted a yummy lipstick red, as are the cavernous corridors off which the meeting rooms open. We have, it seems, entered the body politic with a good deal of passion.

Other vignettes: carpeted flooring by Petra Blaisse. Vegetation motifs, leaves, and grasses, a glimpse of paradise, but slightly toxic. A corner of the Mixing Chamber, with a view so vertiginous that you want to scream. But it's a library, so you can't. Views upward toward the black undersides of the platforms, as if you're gazing up into a building from where a basement used to be before it was washed out to sea.

Mr. Koolhaas's attitude toward the architectural program recalls Louis Kahn's relationship to a building's plumbing, the ducts and pipes that he sometimes refused to conceal. Kahn professed to hate the plumbing, but claimed that the pipes would ruin his building if he didn't allow them visible expression. Likewise, by making the building out of the organizational requirements, Mr. Koolhaas prevents them from interfering with his architecture. By making his clients' needs fundamental to his aesthetic, he neutralizes their capacity to ruin his effects.

Mr. Koolhaas's attitude toward structure is similarly ambivalent. You will see several structural systems at work in the library. They are brought into coherent visual harmony only intermittently. Oh, look, some crossbracing. Over there, fat columns thrust up and inward at an assortment of splayed angles, like the trunks of some exotic tree.

Lovers of Venetian Gothic architecture may suspect that Mr. Koolhaas has revived the quality that John Ruskin called savageness or rudeness. If they needed to illuminate a council chamber in the Doge's Palace, they punched a window in the wall. Never mind if it didn't line up with other windows, or shattered the symmetry of the facade. Contingency had its own aesthetic charms.

Such buildings are narratives. We did this, and then we did that. And it may be useful to see the Central Library as a series of episodes in urban space. There are crowd scenes and moments of intense solitary absorption. Intense vertigo gives way to erotic stimulation. Over here, you're an actor, over there a spectator. Don't look now, but the library could be reading you.

Ruskin, a romantic, was deeply engaged with the emotional content of buildings as well as with their place in the social scheme of things. He's a useful figure to think back upon from the perspective of today, when much of our most vital architecture is parked at the intersection of psychoanalysis and political science.

The Central Library will appeal to those who suspect that the subconscious may be more exact—more rational, in fact—than the faculty of conscious reasoning. If you've ever waked up with the solution to a problem that defeated you the night before, you will feel at home in this building. So will anyone who wants to know where architecture is going.

These programmatic zones have been rendered as slablike structures, of different sizes and shapes, stacked atop one another like buildings along a vertical street. Mr. Koolhaas calls these structures "platforms." In ascending order, they are designed for parking; entrance and orientation; community meeting rooms; book stacks and circulation desks; and administration offices. The platforms are staggered to create overhangs on the street, as stipulated by city planners, and to take advantage of magnificent views. The top level of each platform, akin to a roof, is an open, public space. The overall effect is of hanging terraces suspended beneath earth and sky.

The interior's overhanging platforms have been draped with a metal-and-glass building skin, as if it were a piece of cloth. Hence the exterior folds. So what looks from the outside like a willful exercise in complex geometry is actually a simple envelope to enclose mass. The interior becomes a greenhouse; the exterior a compressed, five-sided, Rubik's Cube of a skyline. Bling!

May 16, 2004

FOR THE CLASSY AND THE CLIMBERS,
THE HIGH PRIEST OF ART DECO

A fantastic ocean liner has pulled up alongside Fifth Avenue. All aboard the S.S. *Ruhlmann*! Not even the *Normandie* had such posh. This ship of a show is first-class all the way.

Ruhlmann: Genius of Art Deco, moored at the Metropolitan Museum of Art, surveys the work of France's leading furniture designer of the 1920s. It is the first full Ruhlmann retrospective in seventy years. That means a lot of luxury. Not to mention a lot of ebony. And gilt. All of it polished to a high Parisian gloss.

The show has been organized by J. Stewart Johnson and Jared Goss of the Metropolitan, along with Rosalind Pepall of the Montreal Museum of Fine Arts, where the show will later travel. It is displayed in the Met's special exhibitions gallery on the ground floor, and to get there, you must pass through classical sculptures by the yard. This is a fortunate circumstance. Émile-Jacques Ruhlmann (1879–1933) epitomized the neoclassical wave that crashed upon French art in the years after World War I.

Like other designers of the period, Ruhlmann opposed his work to the Art Nouveau style that had enveloped Europe at the turn of the century. Life had changed. There was a widespread revulsion against nineteenth-century Romanticism and everything it stood for: preening emotion, heroic bombast, loss of control. Progressive artists like Stravinsky and Picasso deployed classical motifs, as if to sever modernism from its Romantic roots. Le Corbusier and Mies van der Rohe designed residential pavilions with the chaste solemnity of Doric temples. After 1925, elite taste coalesced around a style launched at that year's Exposition Internationale des Arts Décoratifs et Industriels Modernes in Paris. The style was subsequently christened Art Deco in honor of this event.

Since the revival of interest in Art Deco in the 1960s, the style has acquired connotations of mass consumption: Hollywood movie sets, New York skyscrapers, ziggurats for everybody. The Ruhlmann show recalls that the term classical originally denoted class, not mass. It described the language of elites. Seldom can such a tongue have been enunciated more precisely than it is by Ruhlmann. Every stick of his furniture sniffs: drop dead.

The show presents upward of one hundred pieces of furniture and decorative accessories, most of them drawn from the Metropolitan's extensive

Ruhlmann collection. These are augmented by renderings for interiors and other drawings, photographs, and documents. A companion show, Art Deco Paris, showcases additional objects, designed by Puiforcat, Lalique, and other contemporaries of Ruhlmann.

The Ruhlmann show is installed in a swanky setting, designed by Daniel Kershaw, that somewhat recalls a department store. You almost expect to see a Lalique crystal fountain in the center, spraying Shalimar into the air. In its place there is a gigantic urn-shaped porcelain lamp, one of a quartet that Ruhlmann designed in 1927 for the great French liner the *Île de France*. It is an object to be worshipped, an idol of style.

Ruhlmann practiced an art of making wood look wealthy. No pine need apply. Instead, we move in the exclusive company of amarynth, amboina, palissander, rosewood, and kingwood. The wood veneers are burnished to such a high degree of polish that they almost pass for rare minerals. In fact, when we come to a large panel of onyx, set into the front of a 1930 metal-and-glass sideboard, this ordinarily sumptuous material manages to look cheap. Ruhlmann designed for the class of new rich created by modern industry, families like the Renaults, the Voisins, and the Rodiers. He considered them equivalent to the titled aristocracy of the past. He had no affinity for the factory aesthetic espoused by the Bauhaus. His clients sought differentiation from workers, not stylized kinship to them.

His furniture defined the possibilities of breeding in the machine age. The edges of his rectangular surfaces are often subtly curved, as if to reproach the obvious. Slender, tapered, the fluted legs tiptoe delicately across the floor like a ballerina *en pointe*. Late in his career, in deference to the new Bauhaus aesthetic, Ruhlmann designed some pieces in steel. But he plated the metal with nickel. It might as well be sterling silver.

Some of Ruhlmann's finest pieces resulted from collaboration. A ravishing case in point: the black lacquer dressing table he designed in 1927 for a Miss Redhead. The surface is decorated with white cubist patterns, designed by Jean Dunand, which appear to warp the table's volume. Though the patterns look sprayed on, they were in fact created by embedding tiny pieces of cracked egg shell into the wet lacqeur.

Here's a surprise: Ruhlmann's head was full of bubbles. Cheerful circular, spiral, and vermiform motifs occur everywhere in his designs: set with marquetry into table tops; woven into textiles and carpets; sketched freehand in renderings of ornamented ceilings and walls. These motifs illustrate a Parisian take on cultural change. A decade we call the Roaring Twenties is known to the French as les Années Folles, the Crazy Years. That's what these effervescent forms seem to be about: Champagne, esprit, and the Folies-Bergère.

Dunand, in fact, designed scenery for the Folies-Bergère; this was before the libidinous spectacle evolved into a purely tourist attraction. And Ruhlmann himself seemed incapable of designing anything that lacked theatricality. Two marble bathrooms, designed for gentlemen in 1925, have the classical severity of stage sets by Adolphe Appia or Edward Gordon Craig. Ruhlmann was, after all, designing a mythology as well as suites of rooms. In the period between the wars, the newly rich of France wanted the security of classicism to guard themselves against a changing world that they themselves had set in motion. Weren't Renaults actually chariots, bearing nymphs and deities across the skyline of Paris?

As Bruno Foucart notes in the show's catalog, "Perhaps it is more appropriate to speak of a Ruhlmann 'atmosphere' rather than a Ruhlmann style." It's an atmosphere that in retrospect has come to denote the glamour of travel: great liners, luxury trains, the daring flights of Charles Lindbergh and Antoine de Saint-Exupéry. Cinema was new.

The adaptation of style to change: this is probably what most recommends Ruhlmann to viewers of the present day. But what strange new world are we adapting to? Before 9/11, designers were well on their way to devising visual mythologies for the contemporary city. Figures like Phillippe Starck, Rem Koolhaas, Jean Nouvel, and Thom Mayne were among the leading innovators of early-twenty-first-century style. I trust they still are.

But the mood now also favors less flamboyant responses to contemporaneity. SANAA, the firm established by the Japanese architects Kazuyo Sejima and Ryue Nishizawa, is a name often cited these days for designs that embody stoic charms. Chad Oppenheim, based in Miami, is another of these vastly talented minimalists-come-lately.

But I confess that Ruhlmann's bubbly motifs strike me as uncannily prophetic. Whether we're looking at Mr. Koolhaas's porthole windows, Greg Lynn's blob shapes, or the patterns Frank Gehry designed for the accoustics of Fisher Center at Bard College, we see echoes of Ruhlmann's polymorphic foam.

Some viewers will be reminded of screen savers. Or even computer software. Imagine some kind of electronic plasma flowing around the globe, occasionally "snapping to grid" to create virtual offices, auditoriums, gymnasiums, and other public spaces. Let the S.S. *Ruhlmann* transport us into postperspectival space.

June 18, 2004

PEEP SHOW

Things could be so much worse. I might have turned into one of those people who disapproves of trends. Can you imagine a gloomier fate? To be the kind of person who, when anything really great comes along, feels that they're supposed to say, "Well, it may look great now, but how do you think it's going to look five years from now?"

Hotel QT—André Balazs's new, no-frills hotel, at 125 West Forty-fifth Street in Times Square—looks terrific now, and in five years it will look even better. While a trendy hotel rules, an obsolete one is absolute. If a spot isn't hot, it can't cool down, and the heat can't come back to haunt us.

QT is Winchell-esque irony: in the land of the loudmouth gossipmonger, "quiet" meant "shhhout!" There was also a hotshot tip sheet back then called *On the QT.* Styling itself "the Class Magazine in its Field," *On the QT* published such tony twists on the genre as "Lesbian Suitcase Girls of Greenwich Village" and "Buddy Hackett: New 'Rat' for the Ratpack?" A spicy collage of its pages papers QT's walls. We'll pretend we haven't read them.

Besides, there's too much else to look at. Looking—peeping, actually—is QT's design motif. Designed by the immensely talented New York architect Lindy Roy, the hotel does include one fabulous frill: a pool the size of a postage stamp, which graces the ground floor. Just big enough for making a splash, the pool area can be glimpsed through windows set into the walls that enclose it. For the seriously enthralled, one side of the pool is flanked by a rank of bleachers. Fashionable flesh as floor show: that's no-frills entertainment in the new Times Square.

Check-in at QT also appears to be inspired by the performing arts. The counter, just inside the front door, resembles an art-house ticket booth. A floor of concrete sidewalk paving amplifies the box-office effect. A long corridor to the rear serves as an elevator lobby. It leads past the pool area to a small bar. Upstairs, the rooms, of which there are 140, range in size from broom closet to ship's cabin. All are outfitted with nautical efficiency. Good Evening, Mr. and Mrs. America and everyone else who feels completely at sea in these trendy times.

It's pleasing to see a hotel design that builds on Times Square's present strength as a magnet for media companies. With all the complaining that goes on about the area's Disney-fication, people tend to lose sight of the positive side of its redevelopment. Producers and consumers of popular culture and information have been brought together in an unprecedented concentration. In addition to Disney, the cast of media producers includes Condé Nast, Reuters, and MTV, as well as the paper for which Times Square was named.

There's something for every sense around here—and now a place to sleep off sensory bombardment. In fact, QT would make an ideal weekend getaway for New Yorkers who want to escape the distractions of home and catch up on the distraction of movies. And if you're a person after my heart, you will duck across Forty-fifth Street and pay homage to one of the holiest sites in hot-spot heaven: the Peppermint Lounge, the place where the Twist got its start, and perhaps the 1960s along with it. It was located directly opposite the hotel. And though the lounge is gone, the spirit of Joey Dee lives on.

The Twist socialized the body. Suddenly, personal familiarity with the sacroiliac was no longer restricted to doctors, athletes, and ecdysiasts like Virginia "Ding-Dong" Bell. Everybody had a spinal cord. City life descended to the lumbar region, and has more or less stayed there ever since. This is the physical genealogy from which QT's aesthetic descends.

Roy's design is body conscious. The lines are sinewy, the palette fleshy. In the bar, there are banquettes of pink leather and mohair, with additional seating on cork stools. The room is wrapped in panels of buff cedar. In the hallways upstairs, the ceilings are imprinted with patterns of wavy hair. Will they change the wave, the color, the cut as fashion demands? Vitruvian Man and Woman will feel right at home in the diminutive rooms. Everything is within reach of a well-toned arm. Except for a smart little table and a chair, the furniture is built-in. The table swivels. So will you.

But all this hotness is getting to me. Time to cool down. Fancy a dip? Let's swim tonight, like we did last summer forty-four years ago.

April 3, 2005

EDEN ROCKS

A Miami Beach native is a freak of culture, a mutant strain of generativity that has somehow managed to persist and even thrive in a place where human endurance is typically measured in weekends. Two of these charmed Miami mutants—a native son and daughter—have spliced their genes together and come up with a book. Mitchell Wolfson Jr. (known as Micky) is the son, Michele Oka Doner the daughter, and the splice is called *Miami Beach: Blueprint of an Eden*, published this month by Feierabend Unique Books. What will they try breeding next? Flamingos and towel boys?

Perhaps you did not realize that Miami Beach is a city. It has a city hall and everything. Michele and Micky—it would be unfriendly to refer to the authors of so personal an album by anything other than their first names—are each the child of a former Miami Beach mayor (Mitchell Wolfson in 1943, and Kenneth Oka from 1957 to 1959, and again from 1961 to 1963). They've got Coppertone in their blood and a long, leisured lineage of vivid Caribbean skies.

The two have also made substantial contributions in their own right. Micky is the founder of the Wolfsonian, one of America's most remarkable museums. Located in a renovated storage building on Miami Beach's Washington Avenue, the Wolfsonian is largely dedicated to the dark art of political propaganda. There exists no institution similarly equipped to teach us about the ritual washing of brains. Michele is an artist who deploys plant forms in sculptural constructions of astonishing delicacy and strength. She also makes art you can walk on. *A Walk on the Beach*, a 22,000-square-foot work created in 1995, adorns the floor of Miami International Airport. They love their city, not as an escape from somewhere else, but as home.

Blueprint of an Eden presents history as scrapbook, a social chronicle by collage. In this volume, recipes, sheet music, snapshots, newspaper clippings, and personal correspondence are more telling than the book's written narrative. The visual jumble is well suited to a city evidently concocted from the gleanings of beachcomers. They've come in waves, the makers of this culturally fluid strand—farmers, land speculators, show-biz impresarios, Jews, Cubans, old folks, gays, European fashionistas. Each swell of the communal tide has laid down its own layer of signs, code of etiquette, architecture, cooking, fashion, and popular pastimes. The layers may be thin, but like coral they have built up to form pieces of a great American city, perhaps the only one whose fortunes can still be charted on a rising curve.

Miami Beach is no longer a southern city of North America but a northern city of the Latin South. That helps to account for the rise. But the city's present allure is also a consequence of its relationship to the changing world around it. The ephemerality of its population, the allegiance to amusement, the fundamentalist reverence for all matters of style and image: these qualities no longer suffice to set Miami Beach apart from the rest of the United States. They are existential earmarks, rather, of the national psyche. In this altered state of mind, the Eden Roc becomes equivalent to Plymouth Rock: the cornerstone of an identity that has become a new social norm.

Leafing through the book, then, is like sifting through the results of an archaeological dig of contemporary imagination. Here are the fabled mink stoles, worn in the pastel salons of air-conditioned hotels. Here the ladies of the Miami Beach Garden Club pose with shovels as the ground is ceremoniously broken for their new garden center. Orchids line up for a snapshot before their transformation into last night's wilted corsages. An entire chapter is devoted to the design of the Carib, a tropical-modern movie palace that was built by Micky's father in 1950. And here are tons of ornamental ironwork, decorations stripped from Spanish-style buildings and later melted down and recast to make munitions for World War II.

A chapter on wartime Miami Beach reminds us that Micky is the founder of a periodical called *The Journal of Decorative and Propaganda Arts*. The title alone won my heart when I saw my first copy many years ago. To slam ornament together with mass psychology was such a superior act of Surrealist engineering that it changed the way I've looked at design ever since. The book gives me a new slant on alligator belts.

What do all the keepsakes add up to? Simply this: Miami Beach is a great city of audiences, perhaps the greatest metropolis to arise, like Tinker Bell, on the strength of applause. Hollywood may be the greatest producer of spectacles, but Miami Beach has no equal as a generator of spectators. Electing an owner of movie theaters to city hall reflected a native logic. Mayor Wolfson practiced the art of gathering people together in space for the pursuit of laughter and suspense. He was an industrialist of the ephemeral occasions from which Miami Beach was built.

"Smile for the camera." That's the chief skill required for those who'd like to follow this colorful blueprint. Beauty queens, movie stars, heads of state and lesser dignitaries, nightclub habituées, odd recipients of keys to the city (I cherish mine as another person might esteem the key to an exotic roadster). The overall tone is set not by the well-known faces, however, but by the unfamiliar grins of the nameless, the expressions of those who will be remembered as the living embodiment of good cheer. As in Japan, the local genius expresses itself in presentation, but it is the audience that is being presented, not a rare object, an awesome view, or an artful arrangement of food or flowers. It is as members of the audience that these individuals are able to see themselves as a community, rather than the scattered fragments of an atomized society. I'll spray my copy lavishly with orange blossom, kiss my key, and dive in.

October 9, 2005

THE SECRET HISTORY OF 2 COLUMBUS CIRCLE

The Audience 1

1.

What is the sound of New York with one hand clapping? New York without a gay audience. Take away that highly strung social instrument, and many glorious rafters would never ring again.

This bleak subtraction from urban sonority is not likely to happen. Another hundred homosexuals just got off the train. They didn't come here to sit on their hands. The art of the ovation will not be lost so long as one of us is still standing.

But the seasoned gay audience—that is another matter. The audience with memory; the crowd of people who can recall the echoes of ovations, hoots, and silences, reverberating down over the years, season after season, decade after decade; the audience that can remember a time before innocent perversity calcified into brittle postmodern irony: this audience has fallen prematurely silent.

A quarter century has passed since the first cases of AIDS were reported in the United States. The duration of the epidemic now spans more than a generation. Officially, it has claimed the lives of almost 140,000 New Yorkers. That figure represents more memory than even the greatest cities can stand to lose.

The cultural consequences of this loss were recognized early on. The impact is usually described in terms of the artists who have died from the disease. The depletion of the gay audience is more insidious, however. An audience retains the memory of a vanished performer. But who retains the memories of a disappearing audience?

Imagine the World Series without veteran sports fans. You could still fill the stadium. The crowd would still roar. But a quality of reverberation wouldn't be there any more. A network of shared information that once existed for the purpose of lighting up in the presence of excellence would have shut down, as if someone had taken the concept of discrimination off life support.

Now instead of a stadium imagine the city. Imagine urban culture instead of the game. Think about what happens to the level of performance when the seasoned audience in this arena disappears. This you don't have to imagine, actually. All it takes is an ear for picking up silence.

People say that the quality of life in New York has improved. I am confident that they have the statistics to prove it. There are no bad neighborhoods left in New York. Isn't that great? But this change in the city's fortunes, if that's what it is, didn't start with Rudolph Giuliani's campaign against the squeegee men. The history is far longer than that. The change began in the 1960s with the introduction of a new set of attitudes about the meaning of the city and its future prospects. The gay audience that came of age in the 1960s played a leading role in this chapter of urban history. But much of that history remains to be told.

The controversy over 2 Columbus Circle has made me painfully conscious of the gaps, or should I say chasms, that have yet be filled in. In my mind, in fact, this battered white marble bonbon of a building has come to symbolize the absence of a generation that is no longer here to speak for itself. I cannot speak for all of those who want to preserve 2 Columbus Circle. But I can say what the building signified to a group of people who helped to reinvent the idea of the city when the concept of the urban center was widely thought to be running out of time.

I am not saying that any of these people liked the building. I am not saying they found it beautiful. It makes me smile to imagine some of the cracks my pals might have made at the building's expense. And some of them probably didn't live long enough to make up their minds. Ambivalence is a kind of meaning, particularly when remembering those whose lives were over before they reached the age when people start thinking about what mattered to them when they were younger. Their silence is unbearable to think about. Not thinking about it is worse.

One day there will be a miniseries. They'll call it something snappy, like *The Greatest Gay Generation.* It would be immodest of me to call it that, since I'm a member of it, and also because my role was mostly limited to that of enthusiastic bystander. Then, as now, the glory goes to the activists.

Nonetheless, in the city of forty years ago, it was a kind of activism simply to be yourself. Hundreds of us were active in this aggressively passive sense. Bystanders—members of the audience—also had a transforming role in the New York of the 1960s. It is we who picked up on the new attitudes about the city, usually in ways we could not have put into words. Instead we put them into the practice of living. Others followed our example.

Some of the ideas we picked up on were embodied by 2 Columbus Circle, by the architecture and by what went on inside it. It stood for the concepts of alternative vision, of resistence to accepted wisdom, of dissent from a framework of values that had lost touch the complexities of cosmopolitan life. The gay audience stood for those things, too. Even if we didn't like it, we could identify with it. After all, how many other buildings of the period can you think of that have been routinely described as unusual, bizarre, strange, and other synonyms for queer?

The Gallery of Modern Art, as 2 Columbus Circle was originally known, was designed by Edward Durell Stone and completed in 1965. The building was commissioned by Huntington Hartford as a showcase for his collection of figurative painting. In 2000, when it turned thirty-five, the building reached the eligible age to be considered for designation by the New York City Landmarks Preservation Commission.

You might say they've had this date from the beginning. The building and the Landmarks Commission both turn forty this year. The pair are suited in temperament also. The Commission was established in large part to deter the relentless assault of modernity on the city's past. Stone's design was among the first to break the modern taboo against the use of period styles.

But the Landmarks Commission is playing hard to get. Twice, it has rejected requests to hold public hearings on the eligibility of 2 Columbus Circle. Meanwhile, the city acquired the property and has sold it to the Museum of Arts and Design, an institution formerly known as the American Craft Museum. MAD, as the museum is identified on its Web site, has commissioned a design to remodel the building from the Seattle firm Brad Cloepfil/Allied Works.

The City's Position Has Been Challenged in the Courts. Status of Challenges

As the controversy developed, questions have been raised about the commission's handling of cases other than 2 Columbus Circle. Last November the Women's City Club of New York released a report entitled *Problems Experienced by Community Groups Working with the Landmarks Preservation Commission.* Sponsored by more than a dozen civic groups, the report concludes that the commission's performance has been chronically deficient in nine areas. These include lack of transparency in the designation process; inadequate protection for city-owned property; and failure to set clear guidelines for public input.

Procedural reform will not suffice to solve all of the problems revealed by the 2 Columbus Circle controversy, however. It has also become necessary to clarify the concept of landmarks in light of changing times. At forty, the commission is also due for reappraisal. It is our only public agency with an explicit mandate to represent historical awareness of evolving urban form. In the case of 2 Columbus Circle, however, the commission has shown itself more willing to erase history than to raise public awareness of it.

An important point has been lost sight of in this debate. A building does not have to be an important work of architecture in order to become a first-rate landmark. The intrinsic qualities of a building's design, while of interest in themselves, are essentially irrelevent to its value as a potential landmark. What matters about a landmark is not how a building is made, but how it is remembered.

I hate to be the one to tell you this, but the old Pennsylvania Station was actually a fairly dreary piece of architecture. Walking into its cold, cavernous spaces was like arriving in Philadelphia two hours before you had to. A latecomer to the City Beautiful movement in monumental design, the station lacked the conviction and the complexity of Grand Central Terminal and the New York Public Library.

But Penn Station was a magnetic civic symbol. It was a crime to tear a building that had become so deeply impregnated with New York's emotional life. The stony gray spaces had their own distinctive atmosphere. Like a gigantic sponge for intense expectations, they soaked up the psychic energy of arrival, departure, separation, reunion, and boredom that had accumulated over the years along with the soot, water damage, and flimsy commercial intrusions.

The station's architectural infelicities enhanced the drama of arrival. You wanted to fight back, defy the granite indifference of those vast chilly rooms. Here she is, boys! Here she is, world! Here's . . . well, it was up to you to fill in the blank.

This is how landmarks are made. Landmarks begin where buildings stop, after the architects and clients have done their work. They exist on the reception, not the production side of the urban system. A landmark is the creation of an audience, the sum of qualities projected onto a building by those who live with it and build on the impressions they have formed.

That is what the people who marched to prevent the demolition of Penn station rallied to protect. It wasn't about the building. It was about an idea of the city as a social space that exists within the minds of those who love it and who, by virtue of that attachment, can claim a stake that transcends the rights of property owners.

2.

We were the children of white flight, the first generation to grow up in the postwar American suburbs. As adolescents, we turned around and flew the other way, like pigeons released to find their way home. We were living a theory before we were old enough to know what a theory is: children often act out the subconscious fantasies of their parents. Our parents had defined the city as a source of fear. On some level we understood that the fear disguised a desire. And so, against their objections, and against the way society was going, we went downtown to fulfill it.

We must have seemed a bit like those scary blond children in *Village of the Damned.* In 1961, at the sight of Audrey Hepburn getting out of the cab behind the opening credits of *Breakfast at Tiffany's*, a weird glow came into our eyes. There was a place where misfits could be movie stars, or just be themselves and breathe. It was only a matter of time before we converged on the vicinity of Fifth Avenue and Fifty-seventh Street.

The fortunate among us—the ones with a knack for finding teachers—put this waiting time to good use. We spent it living another theory of which we had no conscious conception. We learned how to become members of what Herbert Gans would call a "taste culture," a social group bound together by its aesthetic preferences. It's not possible to understand the significance 2 Columbus Circle without grasping how this concept applied to us.

Nor is it possible to understand New York in the second half of the twentieth century without recalling how gay taste culture, in that period, ceased to be a subculture and became, in effect, a top culture, an audience whose outlook shaped the attitudes of the city at large. By now, these attitudes are commonplace. They are woven so deeply into the urban vernacular that some may find it difficult, boring, or inconvenient to imagine that the outlook can be credited to a particular social group. But if preservation isn't up to such imaginative feats, we can kiss history good-bye. We can even kiss off the history of the history of preservation.

Would there have been a preservation movement without the gay audience? After reading a recent book by Will Fellows, a social historian based in Wisconsin, I'm inclined to doubt it. Titled *A Passion to Preserve: Gay Men as Keepers of Culture* (University of Wisconsin Press), the book profiles thirty preservationists in communities across the United States. It is a remarkable chronicle of one of the most influential grassroots movements in urban America.

As Fellows is careful to emphasize, women have been as prominent as men in the preservation movement. He credits a coalition between gay men and straight women for providing the movement's backbone, and this should should come as no surprise. In modern times, few fields of cultural endeavor have not relied on this cross-gender alliance for critical support. Its history remains to be written.

Fellows may be the first, however, to trace the historical links between the mocking stereotype of "nice young men who sell antiques" and the city dwellers who have revitalized downtown neighborhoods all over the nation. A taste culture once popularly associated with retrieving Art Deco desk clocks from Auntie's attic soon came to embrace the Manhattan skyline. This was a retrieval operation, too, quite possibly the most important urban renewal project since the rebuilding of San Francisco after the earthquake and fire of 1906.

White flight was a tsunami. We were the Red Cross, or a substantial part of it. And it is useful to know that we started small. The value of what came later is easier to appreciate if you see that preservation started with a knack for pulling stuff out of the trash. Paraphrasing no less an authority than Liberace, Fellows refers to "the thrill of redemption," the kick that comes from polishing up a discarded kazoo and displaying it proudly, as if it were the golden lyre of Orpheus himself.

Another theory after the fact: in the act of redeeming the discarded object we redeem an undervalued self. We restore dignity to a part of our being that is reviled by society and even by we ourselves. Some compensate for a sense of shame by projecting badness onto others. We turned the other cookie jar. Somebody must have loved it once. It could be loved again, even worshipped and adored. By restoring pieces of junk to a place of affection, we transform an inner conflict into a source of creative energy.

Until the 1960s, this process took place covertly. Identification with unidentified decorative objects was socially permissible in places where homosexuality was banned. But the thrill of self-redemption became much more public as the 1960s unfolded. Political activism, particularly after the Stonewall riots of 1969, went far toward revoking the ban. But the riots were the culmination of a decade when increasing numbers of gay people found it impossible to live covertly. We came to New York because we didn't think we'd have to. If you'd survived ostracism as a teenage suburban fairy in the Age of Eisenhower, you didn't move to New York to learn how to act butch.

We were like immigrants, in a sense, but with a critical difference: our place of origin wasn't some faraway locale. We'd been displaced from the heartland. Consequently, our aesthetic preferences were not exotic imports. They were drawn from the mainstream—plucked from the majority's wastebasket, rather: the vast inventory of objects, styles, and ideas that had been subject to displacement themselves, cast by the wayside as the twentieth century hurtled along its one-way route of progress.

You could say that our taste was perverse. You could also say that it served, as a form of crooked wisdom, to correct the far more profligate perversities of the age. What kind of normality was it that lived by the laws of planned obsolescence, that conferred an aura of intense desirability on objects one minute and withdrew it five minutes later?

What kind of normality would wake up one morning and decide that the city's time was up, that the moment had come to pile into the station wagon and leave civilization behind? Good-bye, civilization! Adios, museums, concert halls, libraries! So long, streets. Eros, ta-ta! Our love was great while it lasted, but onward and outward we must go, into the arms of major appliances.

3.

If you design your neighborhood to look like Eden, don't be surprised if snakes show up. In 1964 the name Huntington Hartford slithered into our suburban garden on the masthead of *Show* magazine, a glossy monthly on the visual and performing arts that Hartford published in the early 1960s. Somebody must have goofed. *Show* did not belong in the company of respectable periodicals my high school subscribed to. After two issues, the subscription was canceled. Its content had been judged unsuitable for the future leaders of suburban America then in training at a place that styled itself "a country day school for boys."

The covers were problematic. One issue featured a picture of Baby Jane Holtzer, the Warhol superstar, photographed in a Pop blonde bombshell impersonation. A pair of blue and orange plastic New York World's Fair sunglasses covered her eyes. Between her teeth she clenched a miniature U.S. flag. A prescient glimpse at the pornography of fame that was only beginning to engulf the American psyche, the irreverent image looked like a hooker in library racks accustomed to displaying copies of *Saturday Review*, *The Atlantic*, and the Episcopalian dust that gathered on them.

But the cover story inside the issue gave far graver offense. A feature on the new "underground" movie movement then in full good-and-evil flower, the story was illustrated with stills from several independent films, including *The Iliac Passion*, directed by Gregory Markopolous. A location shot from this movie showed the ruins of an ancient Greek temple. Two nude men stood in for classical statues.

The figures were discreetly posed. The image was not obscene. But a Latin instructor objected to it. It's not so easy to leave eros behind: this was the sort of school where rumors of food seasoned with saltpeter was once a common rite of adolescent passage. Even if you recognized that the iliac passion is an archaic term for appenticitis, the name of the movie still sounded slightly off-color, and once these things got started, you never knew where they might lead. Today it's a "Greek" photo in an art magazine. Tomorrow an entire Latin class could be stricken with the iliac passion.

Kinsey was in the air. Why, anyone could be susceptible, and the temptations were everywhere in the early 1960s. Two boys had been spotted in the hallway having a conversation about John Rechy's *City of Night*, a bestselling novel of 1964 with a male prostitute protagonist. Another child had been seen with a copy of *Another Country*. At lunch, a sophomore brought up *Naked Lunch*. What next, Sartre's *Saint Genet*?

Even *Time* magazine, in those days a weekly newsletter from the world of the fathers, could not be counted on to hold in the line. In 1964 *Time* published a story about Susan Sontag's "Notes on Camp" that attracted a far larger audience than the readership of the *Partisan Review*, where the essay had first appeared. Would *Time* be canceled next? Would the children of America be transformed into pillars of salt?

Cue *Bolero*. Though the formation of the gay audience was partly crystallized by art, it was driven by the same adolescent hormones that pulsed throughout the late 1950s and early '60s to the sounds of Elvis, the Shirelles, the Beach Boys, and the Dave Clark Five. But imagine an *American Bandstand* where the kids had to sign false names at the door, as we would be asked to at the Stonewall, because at any moment, while you were out there on the dance floor, the place might be raided by vice cops.

Now imagine that all this hormonal buildup was occurring before you even knew about the existence of places like the Stonewall. All that iliac passion was mounting toward its high adolescent peaks, yet it might be a crime to look at the wrong picture, or to respond to it the wrong way, and the vice cop might be working undercover, as a Latin teacher, perhaps, or even more deeply disguised, as guilt, denial, or some other emotion that had yet to be named or understood.

And eventually, when the moment came to transform this libidinous energy into political action, was it any wonder that the event took place in the street outside a dance bar? The libido must go somewhere. And it is famously adhesive, Freud observed. Once it becomes attached to an object, it doesn't want to let go. And we had attached ourselves to the city surrounding the Stonewall many light-years before we signed our fake names at the door and found the courage to ask a stranger to dance.

4.

1965 was the year you couldn't go anywhere without running into a Belgian waffle. This nauseating concoction of sugar and grease had been introduced the year before at the Belgian Pavilion at the New York World's Fair. By the following summer, Belgian waffle stands were sprouting all over town.

The Belgian Pavilion was a big hit, too, and its popularity was a source of consideration to our local custodians of good taste. A full-scale replica of a Flemish village, complete with winding streets, medieval facades, and a town square, the pavilion embodied the idea of kitsch so authentically that it reached the level of satire. How could the capital of the twentieth century have produced such a spectacle? Why had the public embraced it?

It's not easy to be a custodian of taste in the midst of a cultural watershed. But this is precisely what was happening. In 1965 New York was in the midst of a transition between two frames of cultural reference. As the decade began, the city had attained the pinnacle of High Modern New York. The New York school of abstract painting and the new International Style glass skyscrapers were among this period's most conspicuous symbols, and it must have seemed like it could go on forever. A world of platonic essences had been revealed, a realm of abstract shapes, of forms distilled to minimal articulation of their functions. Was this not perfection?

And it was not hard to evaluate. Why, it was almost like science! A critic could go tick, tick, tick down a list. True to the nature of the materials used? Check. A factual basis for aesthetic form in structure and function? Check. If a design scored four out of five or so of these requirements, it could be safely declared to be "of its time."

Times pass. The 1960s ushered in a different set of ideas about the evaluation of cultural artifacts. Pop Art was perhaps the most important influence in this framework. The significance of this movement extended far beyond the sphere of painting. In a sense, Pop was not primarily about art works at all. Rather, like preservation, Pop stood for the reality of audiences. As Warhol said, "Pop Art is liking things." That applied particularly to things that you were not supposed to like. It did not mean liking things because they were bad. It meant questioning the categories. It meant disregarding the blind spots of received opinion. The goal was not to abandon standards but to reform them in the light of evolving urban conditions.

The message, again, was redemption. Objects banished to the margins of cultural value were given the pedestal treatment, a tactic designed to challenge the hierarchical basis on which such discriminations are made. Why don't more architects design buildings with lollipops? Most of those glass towers would look better if they were retrofitted with curtains of Murano lace!

Yet even a newly arrived New Yorker could sympathize with the dismay of the taste custodians. High Modern New York was the uncontested center of the postwar world. The city had invested much of its identity in that framework. It was hard to accept that its moment was already passing. Why, the paint had barely had time to dry at Lever House! People were still squawking about that gosh-dang newfangled abstract art! Was High Modernism already set to join Victorian Revivalism in history's junk heap?

No and yes. No, to the extent that New York wished to remain a modern city, and to the extent that the achievements of the postwar decades could become a platform for further creative development. Yes, because by end of the 1960s it had become evident that High Modern framework had indeed become as obsolete as a piece of Victorian bricabrac; that this frame of reference actually was a piece of Victorian bricabrac, in fact, for all the radiant inventiveness of the work it produced.

The plot thickens. The interpretation grows denser, too, I regret to say, but we have reached a point in the saga where people will either quicken to the play of ideas on the skyline or choose to cross the street. There's a lovely sale going on over there. Don't let me stop you. The ideas will be waiting for those who want to plunge deeper into the recesses of history where the full meaning of 2 Columbus Circle is revealed in all its Gothic horror.

Not everyone can take it. In some still spinning circles of opinion, it is as if the 1960s never happened. The decade amounted to little more than a flirtation with ideas that alternated between frivolity and nihilism, assuming it was even worth bothering to tell them apart. Those who hold this view have been longing for the day when architecture would return to its senses and give us that old time modern religion one more time. They welcome Brad Cloepfil's design for remodeling 2 Columbus Circle as a sign that this prayer for a return to order is being answered at long last.

We are indeed in the midst of a modernoid revival that promises to remodel Manhattan in the image of an office park for Swiss pharmaceutical companies. Perhaps this represents an effort to solve the national health crisis by symbolic means. But there can be no return to the kind of order modern architecture once represented. The ideological framework that supported a unifying aesthetic order was crumbling even as the first International Style skyscrapers began to march up and down Park Avenue. It won't be coming back except as farce.

5.

New York, too, was living a theory before it figured out what the theory was. It was acting out the theory of historicism, the linear, nineteenth-century view of history as a grand succession of epochs, each with its distinctive style of art and architecture. Victorian period revival architecture was based on this premise. So was the Bauhaus. This founding academy of modernism simply flipped historicism around. In place of tradition, the Bauhaus preached the idea of progress. But the premise was precisely the same. Since the Egyptians, the Greeks, and the Florentines had each produced a distinctive style, well, by gosh and by golly, we ought to have one too!

Useful as a technique for organizing information about the past, particularly when the science of archaeology was new, historicism became much more than that: an ideological framework to which important questions about the present could be referred. How had the Romans handled law, the Florentines money? Let's invent something called aesthetics, and name it after the Greeks! We'll decorate the cemeteries with pyramids and sphinxes. Didn't the Egyptians have a thing about death?

As the philosopher Allan Megill has argued, historicism soon became a secular religion for the Victorians, a source of authority for stable meanings and values at a time of socially disorienting change. Unfortunately, as is sometimes the case with religion, followers of historicism fell into the habit of mistaking meanings for facts. Nowhere did this problem become more glaring than in High Modern New York.

"Architecture is the will of an epoch translated into space," Mies van der Rohe had once declared. The custodians of High Modern New York appeared to believe that this pronouncement was to be taken literally. And so there began an inquisition to root out heretical views, to insure that the designs for all New York buildings conformed to the will of the epoch as Mies van der Rohe, and a few others, had defined it. Those who disobeyed the epochal will—the almighty zeitgeist—would be shown the instruments of torture.

Two Columbus Circle never stood a chance with that unwelcoming committee. Although Edward Durell Stone, the building's architect, had been an early convert to the modern cause—in 1939, with Philip Godwin, he had codesigned the Museum of Modern Art—he was also among the movement's first defectors. By the mid-1950s, with projects like the U.S. embassy in Delhi, Stone had begun to ornament the facades of his buildings with lacy screens of vaguely Moorish derivation. The result might be described as First Lady architecture, an aesthetic of soft power to complement the harsh realities of cold-war geopolitics.

The role of First Lady, however, was very far from the Will of the Epoch modern architects thought that they represented. They had styled themselves, rather, as realists, tough guys; butch crew cuts were much in vogue among them. Aestheticized versions of structural engineers, and social engineers as well, they were theoretically creatures of reason, uncompromising adherents to the law of cold, objective truth. For them, the cardinal sin was to be "arbitrary," to include any element that could not be rationalized on the basis of structure or function. Any architect who strayed into subjectivity or caprice could expect to be hauled before the inquisition.

At 2 Columbus Circle, the screen motif was confined to the borders of the building envelope: a colonnade at the base; arches for the penthouse loggia; and vertical bands of perforated windows at the corners. These screening devices were arranged in a composition derived from Venetian Gothic architecture, a stylistic reference certain to create an uproar. There was no greater taboo in the inquisitors' handbook than the stricture against the period styles. That was probably because, by the 1960s, modernism was well on its way to becoming a period style itself.

And, when you thought about it, what was innately rational or realistic about concrete, steel, or glass? What was so objective about styling architecture after engineering? Alternatively, what was so terrible about fantasy? From a certain angle, the International Style office tower could be admired as a product of the purest fantasy. (The iconic glass tower had partly originated as such, in fact, in the visionary projects of German Expressionists like Bruno Taut, a chapter that had been airbrushed out of the standard histories of the Modern movement.)

And what was so modern about this tower, or so inherently architectural? The values promulgated by the Bauhaus had all been codified in the mid-nineteenth century by Manet and other French Realist painters. The industrialism they celebrated had been displaced long ago by the ethos of consumerism. All this might have been read into the popularity of the Belgian Pavilion at the New York World's Fair. If you were locked into historicism, however, and especially if you didn't even know how historicism worked, that was not a reading you were willing or able to decipher.

What you wanted, rather, was to prop up your dwindling authority by any means possible: to pass off opinions as facts, substitute assertions for arguments, make scary accusations of "revisionism" against those whose grasp of history was often much firmer and more complex than your own, and grow indignant when the amorous energy of other people attaches itself to other things. Along the way there will be breathtaking displays of the genetic fallacy (I was there, therefore *I know*, therefore shut up).

And if you want to know why New York architecture went so far south in the 1970s and after, the short answer is that the city was willing to settle for prescriptions when it should have been looking for diagnoses. Academic responses to the collapse of the historicist framework instead of reckoning with the collapse creatively by showing that even without that framework it was nonetheless possible to make artistic discriminations. New York settled for what it already knew, and fell into the habit of tuning out or rejecting information that didn't conform to the familiar.

That pattern was set by savage critical responses to the Gallery of Modern Art, the Belgian Pavilion, the Summit Hotel, and other projects that offered audiences aesthetic alternatives. Fortunately, there was preservation. Audiences seeking alternatives to the modern academy found a wealth of empathic architecture in the stockpile of buildings from the past. Hence it is less ironic than it may seem that preservationists have now rallied around buildings like the Summit and 2 Columbus Circle. The imaginative possibilities suggested by these projects had been more richly realized by older buildings than they were by critically sanctioned new ones.

Forty years after the fact, it has become clear that 2 Columbus Circle functioned as a screen for projecting academic anxieties about a crumbling status quo. Such screens can be very useful. By identifying what is excluded, they reveal dimensions of experience that have yet to be integrated into the image a city holds of itself. And now it is time to look behind the screen.

The Audience 2

6.

Huntington Hartford probably never wore a tie tack. But he gave the impression that he would have been happier had he been born into a world where swanky guys wore tie tacks all the time. Sadly, Hartford was born on the right side of the tracks at a time when the wrong and right sides were trading places. So he was reduced to building a swanky museum.

Only the Capitol Hilton was swankier, especially when the Rat Pack was in residence in the years of Camelot. But the Gallery of Modern Art served better drinks. Its Singapore Sling, served in the duplex penthouse Gauguin Room restaurant, was the essence of lounge culture served straight up. The rest of the joint was classy, too. The walls were paneled with rare woods. Dark brass railings and lighting fixtures glinted against them. The galleries were intimately scaled, and arranged around the central elevator core in a square spiral. Large galleries alternated with small as you proceeded through the museum.

Even the light looked bronzed. Natural light, diffused through the round perforated windows, enhanced the mood of contemplative reverie, as did the geometric pattern of the perforations and the glimpses of Columbus Circle through them. Most days, pipe organ recitals were presented in a small basement auditorium.

The Gauguin Room was one of the decade's most handsomely appointed interiors. You expected no less from a place built with a fortune made on groceries. Lodged in the double-height penthouse, the room gazed out over Central Park and the Upper West Side through a row of slender arches. There was low banquet seating, white cloths on the table, and a refined version of Trader Vic's Polynesian cuisine, served up for an era when a white plate adorned with a ruby ring of spiced apple sufficed to denote refinement. On the walls, tapestry versions of Gauguin paintings sounded kitschier than they looked. The real paintings would have looked out of place.

Hartford's generosity was startling, particularly if you knew that the entire project had grown out of his petulant antagonism toward the Museum of Modern Art and its support for abstract painting. The Modern's version of history was among the major targets Hartford's book, *Art or Anarchy*, a polemic published the same year the Gallery opened. At the museum, Hartford exchanged petulance for seduction. It worked for George Hamilton too.

And talk about the thrill of redemption! Two Columbus Circle was a veritable Lourdes for handicapped artwork, a storehouse of paintings disabled by critical disfavor and neglect. Burne-Jones can walk!

I remember three highlights. Since my acquaintance with Pre-Raphaelite painting had been largely confined to illustrations in books, it was a treat to see one of Edward Burne-Jones's picture cycles first hand. Burne-Jones's detractors were right. His paintings were illustrations. They did look better in books. But it's nice to see big illustrations. And the story they illustrated was secondary. What stood out was the pattern, the painter's gift for ornament, and his transparently obsessive conviction that these were beauty's basic truth. Burne-Jones and Pollock did not, perhaps, live on separate planets. They were exploring different corners of the same inner world.

Pattern was also the outstanding value in a group of paintings by Édouard Vuillard. A few years later, in fact, when Vuillard was discovered by the counterculture, his incessant pattern making with color, light, and shade was said to evoke the effect of psychedelic drugs. Though held in considerably less regard in those days than now, Vuillard was hardly Hartford's discovery. But he gave the work prominence, and presented enough examples that the intensity of the painter's dappled vision could be savored as if for the first time.

The centerpiece: ardently theatrical, it was epitomized by the immense canvas he commissioned Salvador Dalí to paint especially for the Gallery of Modern Art. Entitled *The Discovery of America by Christopher Columbus*, the picture (now on view at the Dalí Museum in St. Petersburg, Florida) represents the Spanish Surrealist at the pinnacle of the royalism and religiosity that overtook him in later years. Resembling the cadaver of an altarpiece by Rubens or Velázquez, the painting stands nearly fourteen feet tall. Dalí's wife, Gala, its central figure, is depicted as a Baroque saint. Her hands folded in prayer, her eyes gaze heavenward while Columbus and a band of cohorts from a local YMCA pool prepare to assault the New World.

Rudolph Giuliani, had he been mayor at the time, might have tripled the museum's budget on the basis of that painting alone. Yet the appearance of piety was as deceptive as the impression of impiety some viewers formed years later of Chris Ofili's DUMBO dung-encrusted *Madonna and Child. The Discovery of America* was in fact a Rosetta Stone of Dalí's voyeuristic fixations. In those days one did still not speak publically of such proclivities. Even Dalí's own exhibitionistic provocations concealed as much as they revealed. But how much needed to be spelled out?

Dalí was beyond redemption. But a superb collection of work by other Surrealist artists was the lyrical core of Hartford's museum. For those already familiar with this movement, the Gallery held few surprises. Pavel Tchelitchew, Eugene Berman, Man Ray, and other Surrealists were already represented at the Museum of Modern Art, the Philadelphia Art Museum, the Wadsworth Atheneum, and elsewhere. But the concentration here, in so small a venue, cast a Surrealist spell over the whole. Indeed, your responses to the Gallery were likely to depend in large part on your attitudes toward Surrealism at that moment in time.

How much needed to be spelled out? The question is not entirely rhetorical. Ambiguity holds a different value in art than it does in politics or social relations. D. W. Winnicott observed that artists are driven by a conflict between the desire to communicate and an even stronger desire to hide. The art audience is prone to a complementary conflict. We're often torn between the need to overlook and the compulsion to expose.

Social conditions can strongly influence the balance between these competing drives. In 1965 the social conditions of art were changing dramatically. The emergence of the gay audience was, among other things, a search for identity. This reinforced the desire to expose dimensions of art

7.

But Burne-Jones? Who'd have thought that the Pre-Raphaelites would be part of this future? Show me your hands. In fact, everything Victorian would be part of a future in which people started to become acquainted with the old industrial cities as if for the first time. If the future of progress was an issue, then one naturally wanted to learn everything there was to know about its past. The gay audience had a head start here. The Victorian city was our spiritual home, Morticia Addams our Martha Stewart.

This is the world that Edward Gorey illustrated and (along with railroad aficionado Lucius Beebe) helped to invent in the macabre picture books that he began publishing privately in 1953. An affinity with "decadence" was part of the appeal. This was the world of heightened artificiality created by Wilde, Beardsley, Pater, and Huysmans, the atmosphere of the Yellow Book, green carnation, incense burners, peacock feathers, blue and white china, Liberty textiles, and the color mauve.

But the appeal went deeper than decorative frills. The Victorian age was the age of unconsciously self-satirizing paternalistic authority. It was the age of hysteria, a malady typically associated with women, yet the Victorian city revealed that the male version could be far more severe. The fantastic entries in architectural competitions. The peculiar revivals of medieval chivalry. The invented heraldry of Empire. The gigantic history paintings and even more gigantic versions Victorian architects tried to make of them. This was lunacy at its lavish, pre-Freudian best, when no one knew the difference between the superego and the id and often mistook one for the other. Pre–income tax, too, which meant that few fantasies were automatically precluded from attaining built form.

We're accustomed to thinking of architecture as an expression of power. It's easy to overlook that it is more often an expression of powerlessness. Once the authority that decreed the building of a splendid palace has ebbed, we are left with a gorgeous meditation on vanity. We are then better placed to perceive the vanity exercised by the authorities of our own time. That doesn't mean we can't admire them. Vanities can be fabulous. Even the delusion that they are more than vanities can be fabulous, so long as they do not acquire the authority of natural law to which all must conform.

Minorities tend to be more receptive than others in the use of history as a critique. We have less invested in the authority being criticized. For American gay men of my generation, the relationship to paternal authority could be particularly complex, fear-ridden, and beyond resolution. The Victorian city and its hysterical artifacts offered a surrogate parenthood for the articulation of conflicts not easily expressed between fathers and sons. And it has lost none of its relevance for those at a loss to understand why 1960s still inspire hysterical calls for a return to paternalistic ways.

John Ruskin, the Victorian art critic, haunts the crumbling halls of 2 Columbus Circle, as he did when the building was new. Venetian Gothic, the style of architecture from which the building's design is derived, was Ruskin's obsession. His best-selling book, *The Stones of Venice*, persuaded many of his contemporaries to share it. The book was a polemic against the classical revival and the rationalist frame of mind embodied by it. The issues raised by the polemic engage people still, even if they've never heard of Ruskin, much less read him. Indeed, their endurance goes far toward explaining the reactions Stone's design has aroused for the past forty years.

Ruskin was a Romantic. As such, he considered reason and emotion to be essentially opposed. Like Dickens, Ruskin distrusted bean counters. In his view, the nineteenth-century cult of business was to be resisted as a dehumanizing system of values. He saw the great Victorian works of iron engineering as an expression of the same system. Hence he doubted that iron construction could ever give rise to architecture.

For this, of course, twentieth-century modernists could not forgive him. Turning engineering into architecture is precisely what they were determined to do. Only in Chicago, perhaps, was that intention fulfilled with greater brilliance than it was in High Modern New York. No wonder the ideologues of that era had no use for Ruskin. Wasn't he that humbug who bankrupted Whistler, went around proclaiming that architecture is a matter of decoration, and ended up in a madhouse preaching in Latin to the birds?

Yet it was hard to hold Ruskin's madness against him. His world was madder still. A. W. N. Pugin, the Gothic Revival designer, waited until after he'd designed the furniture for the Houses of Parliament before he went into the nuthouse. Thomas Jekyll was carted off in restraints after Whistler painted over his decorations for the famous Peacock Room. When they picked him up, Jekyll was on hands and knees, pounding the floor, and screaming. "Peacocks! Peacocks!"

Jekyll's case came to mind when critics of 2 Columbus Circle were overheard raving about "Lollipops! Lollipops!" A lollipop building fell into the same category as a Victorian gingerbread house. This was a very tasty category indeed. All of New York fell into it, actually. Manhattan was a gingerbread house with a grid running through it, a Gothic film noir romance, where steam came out of the streets because (as the painter John Button may have been the first to say) the city was so close to hell.

So maybe Ruskin wasn't so mad after all to urge Venetian Gothic on the Victorians as a style worth emulating. He perceived that, on a certain level, the modern city was a Romantic artifact. It was a big mess of a place, an unwieldy conglomeration whose emotional life could be neither contained nor expressed by rational logic.

The Gallery of Modern Art was a perfect illustration of this idea. Just when the rationalists thought they had everything under control, out popped this piece of architectural libido with a picture inside that recast Christopher Columbus as a Midnight Cowboy. Venetian Gothic was back, but this time it was Swanky. Ruskin with a tie tack. Fenway Court *avec* Polynesian cuisine. The design didn't fit into the rationalist grids, but why should it have tried? It was designed for a Circle, not for squares.

A Nietzschean might describe this libidinous urban outburst as an example of the Eternal Return. Nietzsche never ruled out lollipops as a form this phenomenon might take. But it would take many other shapes before long. A year after the Gallery opened, the Museum of Modern Art published Robert Venturi's *Complexity and Contradiction in Architecture.* It does not detract from the originality of this highly influential book to note that some its most compelling ideas echo principles outlined by Ruskin in *The Stones of Venice.* The same echoes are heard throughout architecture today in the emphasis on the subjective dimension that has emerged in work by Rem Koolhaas, Frank Gehry, Philippe Starck, Christian de Portzamparc, and other leading designers.

In 1965 this future had yet to unfold, and our comprehension of its historical roots is still not fully formed. Forty years ago our awareness of history possibly drifted back no further than the famous party scene in *Breakfast at Tiffany's.* Decorative room dividers were swanky. Jumbo bird cages with cut-out ogee arches were swanky, especially with stuffed parrots in them. Both totems were present in Holly Golightly's skimpily furnished apartment in the East Sixties, where the party scene took place.

Stone's screens evolved out of modern functionalism. The fixed concrete sunscreen, termed by Le Corbusier the *brise-soleil,* was designed to restrict direct sunlight from entering hermetically sealed, air-conditioned modern buildings. That was the theory, anyhow. In actuality, function provided the rationale for reintroducing pattern and texture to the surface of modern buildings. It was not uncommon to see skyscrapers with concrete sunscreens facing north.

Stone took this motif to the next logical step: a frankly ornamental screen that might be used to screen light but could be valued for its formal properties. This step led to others in turn: the use of the screen to evoke past or exotic styles of architecture without imitating them, for example, and the recognition that such uses were acceptably functional in their own way. Their function was to connote transient meaning, create ambience, evoke memory, and enlarge the expressive possibilities for architecture in cities that had already left behind the industrial society from which modernism's mechanistic concept of function had been derived. We would not have to rely exclusively on the preservation of older buildings to stir up subjective associations. The design of new ones could also animate the boundaries between public and private realms.

This poetic function has proved remarkably enduring. We see it displayed today in the pages of *Cargo, Wallpaper,* and other trendy magazines, where the ornamental screen of 1960s architecture is now a preferred backdrop for fashion spreads. It's back, along with lounge music, lounges, cocktails, and everything swanky. Yesterday's First Lady architecture is just what today's Metrosexual craves. The Pre-Raphaelites would have understood this and even claimed credit for it on behalf of First Ladies everywhere.

8.

In the movie version, we will call it Metro New York: the urban frame of reference that began to take shape in the 1960s as the children of postwar white flight rediscovered downtown. Its function was to uncover a new set of meanings for the aging industrial city in the postindustrial age. It crystallized around the power of the audience as a learning instrument, a technique for acquiring information that cannot be obtained solo. The undertaking began with adolescent rebellion but before long turned into a very different kind of pursuit: the rebuilding of continuity with past forms that were still viable, above all the form of the urban center itself.

Nobody was following a deliberate program. For that matter, no such program exists today, and the process is still unfolding. Back then, the intentions were even more obscure. People were going on pictures, songs, heartache, and other adolescent instincts, doing the things people have been doing in cities for four thousand years. It is only in hindsight that the instincts added up to meanings. Performing the addition—synthesizing the total—is one of the critical tasks preservationists perform.

An audience is more than a group of passive consumers. It can be a productive unit as well. An audience produces demand, a stage, giggles, an erotic charge *(limbic resonance)*, a texture of thought or climate of opinion that ripples outward into the larger social milieu. It produces a baseline of expectations, the pressure to maintain or raise it, and the memory to recognize when and how far it has slipped.

In recent years the audience has produced an audience for itself. Indeed, to judge from American reading habits, the sociology of audiences is rapidly emerging as a highly promising frame of reference for interpreting contemporary urban affairs. Books like Malcolm Gladwell's *The Tipping Point*, James Surowiecki's *The Wisdom of Crowds*, Philip Ball's *Critical Mass*, and John Seely Brown and Paul Duguid's *The Social Life of Information* have given more complex pictures of the audience than the familiar negative stereotypes of destructive mobs, totalitarian masses, and mindless consumers.

Wittingly or not, these writers are building on a considerable body of literature on the social diffusion of ideas that has been in formation since the late 1960s. Some of this work, like the "reception theory" that took root in German literary circles in the early 1970s, is still little known in the United States (for reasons that reception theory helps to illuminate). Ideas subsequently initiated by Pierre Bourdieu, Michel de Certeau, and others have partly filtered into public consciousness through academic channels.

Network theory, popularized by certain books, has further enlarged a field of information formerly confined to media studies. So have works on the sociology of globalization by thinkers like Saskia Sassen, Manuel Castells, and Ulrich Beck. Taken as a whole, this body of work has recast the framework of cosmopolitan life for the age of globalization.

New York, like every cosmopolitan city, was living these theories before the theories were framed. But it was in the 1960s that the authority of the audience began to displace the top-down management of cultural value. This should not be confused with majority rule. Those who rediscovered city life in the 1960s were scarcely in the majority, nor are city-lovers today. Otherwise, recent presidential candidates of both parties would not have made such a conspicuous spectacle of not campaigning in cities.

Even during the ballet boom of the 1970s, those of us who felt we couldn't afford to miss a performance of the New York City Ballet never thought we were a majority, even among the audiences that actually showed up. And thank heaven they did. There would have been no Balanchine without them. But they did need a little help in the applause department. Thanks to us, the cast of *Stravinsky Violin Concerto* never took fewer than two extra bows.

The audience is the public transformed into infinitely complex patterns. The study of those patterns is a legacy of the 1960s. In the modern years, the public was often reduced to a standardized set of minimum requirements. An audience demands maximum possibilities. That was the ethos of Metro New York.

9.

Two Columbus Circle had a second life, and then a third one, after Hartford closed his museum in 1969. The role of the audience expanded during each of these phases. First, Fairleigh Dickinson University acquired the property and decided to operate it as a *Kunsthalle* for changing exhibitions. The place was renamed the New York Cultural Center. The Center's second director was Mario Amaya, a gifted young curator who had attained brief notoriety when he was wounded during the 1968 assault on Andy Warhol.

The Kunsthalle was a novel concept for New York. Younger New Yorkers sensed that the concept might translate into a reflection of ourselves. The idea of an art museum without an art collection even seemed vaguely Warholian. Without a permanent collection and an established board of trustees with the capacity to bestow social prestige on potential members, the Center would have to create an audience from people not already served by the existing institutions.

Even in a time of idealism, this venture was too utopian to survive. The potential audience was obsessed with movies and the experience of movie-going. The immediacy of mass media fed into the prevailing pop mythology more reliably than museums. In an effort to tap into it, the Center inaugurated Cabaret in the Sky, a makeshift nightclub that materialized at fitful intervals in the former premises of the Gauguin Room. A descendent of 1960s happenings, the room proposed the social gathering as a genre of performance art. Female impersonators like Jackie Curtis and Holly Woodlawn were among the featured attractions. At least these perfect voids of talent did not distract the audience from admiring itself.

Drag queens played an important role in that period. Their job was to neutralize fears of inadequacy on the part of their audience. They turned performance anxiety into moments of comic triumph. The effect wasn't too dissimilar from the double take Johnny Carson would do to suggest that a joke in the monologue hadn't gone over. And it took a kind of talent to convey the idea of self-acceptance while wearing glitter eye shadow and a bad wig.

The Center was poorly funded. Amaya had energy and imagination but the place suffered from an unsettling contrast between the luxury of Hartford's interiors, which remained intact, and the poverty of Amaya's installations. The ethos of downtown-goes-uptown wasn't enough to sustain the venture at a time when what was left of the zeitgeist was gravitating in the opposite direction. Location, location, location. This venture, too, had a life of four years.

·   ·   ·

In 1978, 2 Columbus Circle was purchased by Gulf & Western, whose headquarters were located in the tower opposite, a building later remodeled by Philip Johnson for Donald Trump. Gulf & Western then presented the property to the city, which used it to house the Department of Cultural Affairs. Henry Geldzahler, curator of twentieth-century art at the Metropolitan Museum, was appointed commissioner of the department, a position he held until 1982. He was the first city commissioner to refer publically to his identity as a gay man.

Received wisdom has it that 2 Columbus Circle never found itself. My recollection is different. When the Cultural Affairs Department was installed there, it struck me that the building had found a function very much in keeping with the presence it projected. Geldzahler had cracked that his appointment was like being made wheat commissioner of Kansas. The building could handle that kind of humor, as it could also handle the large Warhol portrait of Geldzahler that was hung over the commissioner's desk.

Friends who worked there complained terribly. The building could handle that also. Those were great years for complaining. And if the building struck some as a misfit, well, that was better than having a culture that tried to fit in. New York was not Kansas, after all. The pop grandeur of the curving white marble facade was both stately and absurd: an embassy building on lollipops, sovereign turf for the kids with scary light shining out of their eyes. Out front, the official flags snapping in the wind might have been raised as a salute to Jasper Johns.

Peter Gay coined the phrase *the outsider as insider* to describe the creative ferment of Weimar Germany. Perhaps this was the thread of continuity the gay audience came here to pick up. In 1969 a group of irate transvestites sparked a social movement when they refused to be intimidated by New York City policemen during a raid on a dance bar run by the Mob. A decade later, a city commissioner found the courage to see the social value in being open about his private life.

An insider came out. And the personal was cultural as well as political. Think of all the energy that was tied up in the denial of identity. Then imagine the consequences of releasing it. That was a big part of the energy that drove New York in the 1970s, and it involved much more than openness about sexual orientation. Energy had been tied up in all kinds of facades for a very long time.

The illusions of High Modern New York were magnificent. They embodied the creative energy of artists who had once been outsiders themselves. You had to genuinely love that work in order to let it go. But then the day comes when you realize that you've been trying to please people that don't want to be pleased and probably aren't worth pleasing anyhow. Isn't that how modernism started out? The Bauhaus wasn't built by people pleasers.

The Audience 3

10.

Now Stone's building is in the midst of Life Number Four. This incarnation began eight years ago, when the Landmarks Preservation Commission first declined to consider the eligibility of 2 Columbus Circle for official designation. It has already been highly productive. In fact, I can't imagine a more fitting way to celebrate the commission's fortieth anniversary than the conflict this building has generated thus far. Whatever fate has in store for Stone's design, it already deserves a serious plaque for the bizarre picture the controversy has revealed of our great city's present state of mind.

If it weren't for this conflict, I might not have recognized the need to reckon with the impact of the absent audience apart from the scale of personal loss. When I look at the building now, that fantastic Cabaret in the Sky is still playing up in heaven. They're putting on a show called Crooked Wisdom. The performers may not be conventionally talented, but they do know how to connect, even from a place beyond the clouds. Encore!

And because there's nothing like a negative for revealing a positive, the absent audience has heightened my awareness of the productive capacities of audiences, living or dead. The pivotal role Geldzahler performed during his tenure as commissioner of cultural affairs, for example, has become clarified in hindsight. Those years are remembered by many as a low point for New York. Ladies and gentlemen, the Bronx was burning. But this was also the period when the city awoke to the significance that the audience for urban culture would play in reversing its fortunes.

The audience was Geldzahler's wheat. His job was to cultivate this human grain. His agency did not produce paintings, books, or ballets. Building on the achievements of his predecessor Thomas Hoving, he supported institutions that were developing audiences for these artifacts and for the city that showcased them.

This support structure would become inceasingly important in shoring up the city's dwindling economic base. Culture itself would move from the outside to the inside, from the political and economic points of view. Factories might go abroad, corporate headquarters relocate to suburban office parks, the financial industry to networks of computer terminals, but culture would stick around. It would be the goose with an unlimited sup-ply of golden eggs.

Perhaps predictably, the passage from out to in has turned out to be an extremely mixed blessing. It has generated a need for reform in all areas of cultural enterprise, preservation not least among them. We would be fool-ish to expect reform to come from within our cultural institutions. It's safe to assume that many of them like things just the way they are. In the case of preservation, reform will be driven by the same pressure that brought our landmarks laws into existence in the first place: a willingness to see things as they are.

Marketers and politicians have little use for crooked wisdom. Or for straight wisdom, either, it is often whispered. Profit taking and political advantage make their worlds go round. Audience manipulation is a peren-nial *spécialité* of their *maison*. They do it very well. Failure is not an option, as the saying goes. Neither is risk. Which is why all but a fraction of cul-tural enterprises sponsored by them are artistically null.

This is a problem. Cities now depend more than ever on their cultural products. But the same dependency breeds an increasing desire to play it safe. And safety seldom gives rise to value where creativity is concerned. The result is a death spiral of meaning, in which the imperative to avoid risk chases in increasingly desperate fashion after the diminishing aura of cultural prestige. In the process, assertions of public value are inflated to the point of meaningless, and beyond, so that they attain almost allegori-cal stature.

You could not invent a better example of this inflationary process than the plans New York City has hatched for 2 Columbus Circle. The Museum of Arts and Design, the bidder selected to acquire the property, used to be known as the American Crafts Museum. It was a laudable insti-tution. Its origami classes were second to none. Any Appalachian holler would have been proud to give it a home, including a new porch. In the days when Joan Mondale was shaping national arts policy, that would have been enough.

Not anymore. By today's inflated standards of cultural prestige, craft won't pay the rent. Now, Art can pay the rent. And Design is big right now. Hey! Let's put 'em together and double the fun!

Why didn't *you* think of that?

Those not versed in the ways of image consultants can be forgiven for thinking that with the name change came a loss of focus, perhaps even a failure of mission. But such worries mistake the nature of the enterprise at hand. The fuzziness of purpose is actually beneficial, in precisely the same way that it was beneficial for the General Water Company to change its name to Vivendi when it wished to shed its image as an enterprise in water and waste management. A craft museum will always evoke images of pots, quilts, baskets, flea markets, and arthritic hands covered with liver spots. But a Vivendi can be anything so long as it's totally overblown and offers a wide range of exciting activities the whole family can enjoy.

Next, hold a design competition. People love that! Pick the blandest entry and proclaim that it is bold. The design might strike knowledgable observers as wanly derivative of early work by Steven Holl. But Holl has a reputation for being an artist—in fact, he is one—and artists can be awfully difficult to work with. And, really, will anyone be able to tell the difference between the original and the copy? Is there really such a thing as originality these days? Didn't Holl get his ideas from the Golden Section? Who cares?

Only one person, actually. That is often the case when cultural controversies play themselves out on political terrain. Whoever the players, whatever the script, the play is invariably orchestrated for an Audience of One. At Ground Zero, George Pataki is the One. In the case of 2 Columbus Circle, Michael Bloomberg is the One. The One is whoever happens to be sitting in the chair, the One with the power to determine a different outcome of events.

Now, because issues like the future of 2 Columbus Circle are the public's business, and because the controversy is partly played out in media, you might think that the public is the intended audience for this production. You are supposed to think that, in fact. The truth is that for all intents and purposes the public has been reduced to the level of spear-carriers, extras in crowd scenes, and special effects: stooges, in short.

And so, from the perspective of audience theory, the most fascinating part of the spectacle is a part the public does not usually get to see: the orchestration of the production, the succession of images, sounds, and arranged behind the scenes for the benefit of the Audience of One. Political analysts call it the spin, and it is hardly surprising to find political techniques deployed in the frenzied hustling after cultural prestige that has gone so far to displace more substantial forms of artistic experience. The surprise is that cultural spin has been so poorly documented. Some future social scientist may well conclude that the chief function of 2 Columbus, in its fourth phase of existence, is to create a golden opportunity to rectify this remarkable oversight.

Keeping in mind that we are living at a time when yelling power at truth has come to be seen as morally equivalent to speaking truth to power, and perhaps even superior to it (more practical, less elitist, less confusing to the kids); keeping in mind, also, that such situations are sometimes reversible, our interest now passes to the lively sphere of paraculture: the political apparatus designed to orchestrate events of dubious cultural value the performance for the Audience of One.

I'm sure Thorstein Veblen had a better name for them, but I call them the rushers: members of the elite squad of image consultants, unregistered lobbyists, independent promoters, and serial base-touchers that has emerged to service the market for cultural aura. They are the well-connected orchestrators for the performance commanded by the Audience of One. In a more spiritual age, rushers might have peddled papal indulgences. Today, the indulgence is art.

Step right up, step right up, this way to Parnassus! There's rusher script for every occasion. Are you worried about community resistence to another ugly office tower? Try placing a cheesy sculpture outside, and call it Public Art. What public would be ungrateful enough to refuse the gift of art that has their name on it? Certainly not the fantasy of the public projected by rushers for the Audience of One.

It is often within the power of the One to grant financial relief to developers who can demonstrate their dedication to high artistic values. Design competitions can be presented as evidence of this worthy civic spirit. Of course, it has all been decided in advance that the project will be designed by a local bottom-feeder. But who's to know?

Pritzker Prize–winning architects will be invited to submit proposals. Their names will appear in press releases announcing the commencement of a global search for a dream team of the most brilliant talents of the day. Elaborate presentations will be prepared. The suspense has been scored by Bernard Herrmann. But you don't need to peek inside the envelope. You already know the outcome. "The Winner is . . . Bottom Feeder!" But the One has been royally entertained, the developer has received his entitlements, and the rushers who organized this delirious divertissement have already moved on to the next.

Touching base here, touching base there, manufacturing false consensus all over the place wearing more hats than a sombrero salesman on the Tijuana border (they are legendary committee joiners), switching them as often as each e-mail, phone call, and breakfast demands, rushers are driven by the compulsion to vaporize the principle of artistic discrimination that they pretend to represent.

The rusher script for protecting endangered landmarks from the threat of designation is particularly satisfying. Special rusher tours and presentations are arranged for prominent opinion makers. Their attention is drawn to the dilapidated interiors of the potential landmark. (Never mind that interiors are seldom designated.) Before and After, that hoary developer's trick, gets a full-court workout: snap shots of decay are juxtaposed with artist's renderings of the great heavenly glory that will come our way when the obstructionists stand aside.

Then, with the topsy-turvy logic that obtains when politics is mistaken for art, preservationists will be reviled as elitists driven by contempt for We the People. Accusations of bad faith will be hurled by purveyors of false consciousness. Damage control will turn bad publicity toward solidifying of advantage. The whirlwind cannot afford to stop whirling. Were that to happen, first one, then two, and then ultimately every board-certified rusher in town might start to wonder why it is that such lavish expenditures of energy are required to maintain such an inert status quo. It would never pay to start asking such questions.

You have to love the rushers. They approach the sublime in their effort to fuse art's ancient transcendent associations with blatantly aggressive Darwinism. If the trading of cultural aura were a regulated industry, they would have been carted off to the pokey long ago. But if that were to happen, New York would fall apart at the seams. No serious student of audience theory should resist the impulse to give them a big hand. They reveal too much about the apparatus that they work so hard to conceal.

The key to the paraculture system is this. While the entire production has been constructed for the Audience of One, it would be performed even if no One were sitting in the chair. In fact, the underlying purpose of the spectacle is to transform the One into a chair, a piece of furniture without the eyes to see or the ears to hear any information that might tend to disrupt the One's plans and perhaps ruin his day.

In this sense we might say that the Audience of One is essentially an audience in negative, an absent audience, in fact. And by the same logic we might even say that the spectacle is a nonperformance, a pageant of disconnection, black-lit by negative energy, staged to protect the One from having to pay attention to what is actually going on. Not holding a public hearing about 2 Columbus Circle is a perfect example of the nonperformance for the absent Audience of One.

But there is so much else One must not pay attention to also. One must avoid picking up a copy of *Cargo*, *Wallpaper*, or any other trendy magazine out there. One of the criteria used to identify potential landmarks is that it be characteristic of its period. Two Columbus Circle's alleged failure to meet this criterion has been cited as a reason to disqualify it. It would be deeply embarrassing if news about the ubiquitous perforated masonry screen were to travel beyond the few hundred million fashionistas who've seen examples of it depicted in the pages of glossy magazines.

One's behavior is contagious. Just as, in olden days, the king's laughter could reduce the entire court to puddles of helpless mirth, so One's avoidance of contradiction ripples outward to create a larger audience in negative for the nonperformance. For there are entire networks of Ones and would-be Ones out there, empty chairs floating in their own Baroque spheres of Oneness, ready to align themselves whenever their nonattendance is required. Before long, the nonattending audience begins to assume the character of a taste culture, a community united by a strong preference for nada, nothing, *rien du tout*.

11.

I have few tears to shed for buildings that die without loss of life. My quarrel is with a state of affairs whereby an agency established to enlarge the city's awareness of history has been drawn into the business of erasing history. The New York City Landmarks Preservation Commission did not create this state of affairs. And it would be unrealistic to expect the commission to lead the way out of it. As the controversy over 2 Columbus Circle has shown, the agency has become one more in an inky cluster of rubber stamps. Its independence and integrity somehow got lost in the bureaucratic shuffle.

But can you imagine what could be accomplished if just tiny fraction of the power required to stir the wind could be diverted toward matters of substance? Think about what the Landmarks Preservation Commission could achieve, for example, if its members stopped acting like would-be connoisseurs and strove to realize the agency's potential as a school of thought.

Fat chance. But the prospects for reform will be increased if the private sector continues to demand it. Groups like Landmark West and Docomomo will have to articulate where the bar of expectations should be set. To reach that goal, it could be useful to keep in mind the circumstances that gave rise to the landmarks agency in the first place, particularly as they contrast with conditions today.

Forty years ago reverence for heritage was not a celebrated New York trait. If you owned a few books by Nikolaus Pevsner, had crossed the Atlantic once or twice, and signed up with the Book of the Month Club just to get your hands on a dollar edition of Will and Ariel Durant's *The Age of Enlightenment*, you were practically a bona fide historian. Against a backdrop of general indifference, the new Landmarks Commission stood out like a beacon of historical awareness.

The picture has changed considerably since then. There has been an astonishing reversal of figure and ground. Coffee tables all over town groan beneath the weight of books about the city's buildings. Entire bookstores are devoted to them. You can Google your way into archives all over the globe. Cultural tourism has given New Yorkers a base for comparing our management of urban affairs to that of other cities.

Ours is a golden age of historical awareness, not just in architecture but in global history. Many institutions have understandably found it difficult to keep pace. Yet it is only by keeping pace that they earn the authority they are supposed to exercise. The Landmarks Commission was never a blazing tower of scholarly rigor. But its heart was in the right place, it benefited from the underdog status that had long been the preservationist's lot in life, and it was motivated by genuine curiosity about buildings that needed to be redeemed from scorn and neglect. These qualities evaporated long ago.

Yet it is hard to sustain indignation toward an agency that lacks the proper resources to do its job. The Landmarks Commission has a staff of four to serve all five boroughs. Surveying the city for potential landmarks is out of the question. The agency can barely keep up with requests for hearings from the private sector. Necessarily, it has come to rely on independent promoters whose interests may run contrary to the agency's goals.

Lack of resources has also made it easy for the Landmarks Commission to misconstrue what those goals are. The Commission appears to believe that it is in the posterity business. But posterity is not a historical concept. It is a political concept. It has less to do with history than flags have to do with art. Yet politicians love it. They appear to believe that posterity lifts them to a plateau above politics, though from other seats in the house it is obvious that politicians seldom look more political than when they go out in public with the artificial glow of eternity radiating from their heads. But for an Audience of One a posterity machine is a handy device to have at One's disposal. Excelsior!

But since posterity exists outside of history, those manning the machine may come to imagine that they are immune from history also, that they, too, are operating from a place beyond the clouds, where the mysteries of eternal life are accessible only to the chosen. Of course, what we're really dealing with here is small group of political appointees sitting behind closed doors, attempting to perform irrelevant tasks for which they are in any case unqualified. Preservation is not connoisseurship, nor is it architectural criticism on thirty-five-year tape delay. It is a socialized form of curiosity: the research and management of urban memory for a society driven by powerful impulses to forget.

The history of preservation is a history not of objects, but of perceptions, and we are inventing it as we go along. The field has not been around long enough to produce experts. Television has been around much longer. The modern custodianship of older buildings evolved out of new ways of seeing them and the cities that produced them. And our perceptions are still evolving. There's no reason why preservation should be locked into the approaches of one or two generations. Succeeding generations will have their own thoughts about how the past should be fed into the future.

Techniques that were once serviceable—the correlation of landmarks of periods or styles; the criterion of "appropriateness" to existing context—have become conceptual period pieces in themselves. They might once have been necessary props in devising a legal framework for preservation, but their effect has been to distort history and to create a misleading picture of preservation as well. A new conceptual framework is needed for buildings that are now reaching eligible age.

No generation can claim to be greatly experienced in appraising the merit of potential landmarks built during its adult lifetime. The city has not become accustomed to thinking that way about them. We are used to thinking that what matters is whether or not a building is *supposed* to be important to us. In fact, what matters are the reasons why a building actually was or is important, whether it deserves to be or not.

After all, what difference does it make if you try to tell another person that the Parachute Jump at Coney Island deserves to be important? No difference at all. Nothing you can say could make the Parachute Jump worse than it already is. The old ride is a wreck, the parachutes disappeared long ago, but the relic is worth keeping around anyhow as a sign of the people who came here and bought a ticket to experience fear as a summertime pleasure.

Then those people moved away to find a better life. They're living in Florida now, the ones remaining. We'll all meet up there one day, if we're lucky. We'll be standing in line to get our prescriptions filled at the Rite Aid drugstore. I'll invite you over to my place. We'll listen to scratchy CDs of Bernard Herrmann movie scores and watch my books rot in the damp.

But not quite yet. There's still unfinished business here. Mnemosyne is calling. She hates to be disobeyed. This is a time for telling stories. Not some other time. This time: the present. Forget about the Audience of One. That audience isn't even listening. How could it? It's a chair, a magical piece of furniture equipped with earphones that are permanently tuned to canned applause.

These stories are for the audience of several. They're about people who got their vertigo from reading Ferlinghetti's "A Coney Island of the Mind" at a precocious age. Some of us were prepared to jump without a parachute into a city of kindred souls. For us, the new Guggenheim

Museum was more roller coaster than a boy could ever wish for, even if Lewis Mumford hated it, even though the abstract expressionist painters got up a petition to protest it. This other group was discovering that it was possible to drown out large, belligerent choruses of loud, brilliantly orchestrated no's with a brief round of wild applause for maybe's. Nobody comes to the city to be merely the effects of other people's causes. We have fresh causes to make.

Note: The above essay is the uncut version of "The Secret History of 2 Columbus Circle," an edited version of which appeared in the *Times* on January 8, 2006.

THE GRASSI IS GREENER

For days, perfume flacons rattled all over Paris. Seamstresses dropped stitches. Up in the sky, Air France flight attendants abandoned their duty-free carts and strapped themselves in for a bumpy ride. These were just a few of the rumored afterquakes following last year's shock deluxe: François Pinault, the richest art collector in France, had abandoned his plans to build a museum on an island in the Seine. Instead, Pinault would install his collection of modern and contemporary masterpieces at the Palazzo Grassi in Venice.

The Paris project had been in the works for five years. Tadao Ando had prepared a design. The site had been cleared for construction. Then the French government, under assault at the time for the lavish lives supposedly enjoyed by a few prominent officials, got cold feet about proceeding with a project that required public support. Pinault gave the government a deadline to make up its mind. The date passed. Within hours, it seemed, the billionaire had reached an agreement with Paolo Costa, then the mayor of Venice, to move the entire project to the great city on the lagoon. For the prestige of Paris, a city whose embrace of contemporary art had been somewhat halfhearted until the 1990s, the cancellation of the Pinault project delivered a major black eye.

A second shock: barely one year has passed between Pinault's decision and the imminent opening, on April 30, of his inaugural show at the Palazzo Grassi. This accelerated timetable is unheard of in Venice, where it ordinarily takes an eternity to arrive at decisions of even minor civic consequence.

In this astonishingly short span of time, the interior of the palace has been sensitively remodeled, again to a design by Tadao Ando. Alison Gingeras, a brilliant young curator on the staff of the Guggenheim Museum in New York, has put together a breathtaking array of works from Pinault's collection, a selection that ranges chronologically from Mark Rothko to Jeff Koons. The result is likely to upstage the Peggy Guggenheim Collection, a museum that has long dominated the field of modern art in Venice. And the focused vision on view may even jolt some of the trustees at the Museum of Modern Art in New York out of the complacency that has enervated their own institution in recent years.

Shock No. 3: the Palazzo Grassi is only one part of the program Pinault has envisioned for Venice. With the sponsorship of the present mayor, the distinguished philosopher Massimo Caccari, Pinault will also be presenting exhibitions at the Punta della Dogana, the site of the venerable customhouse of Venice. Located at the mouth of the Grand Canal, the Dogana is crowned by the world's most hypnotic weather vane: a bronze figure of Fortune revolving atop a gilded globe. Other museum directors have dreamed for years of leasing this historic property. What has Pinault got that they don't?

Artémis, Pinault's investment firm, occupies a large town house on Place François I on the Right Bank of Paris, not far from Avenue Montaigne. The entrance, from a courtyard, is out of proportion to the building's facade. A flight of dark gray stone steps leads up to a glass door of exaggerated height and into a lobby on the second floor. On arrival, a visitor is likely to feel like Alice. Where, oh, where is that potion that will make me feel tall enough to reach the doorknob?

Maybe Gucci makes a spray version. Or Yves Saint Laurent. Or Bottega Veneta, Alexander McQueen, Balenciaga, Roger & Gallet, or any one of the other confidence-building labels owned by the Gucci Group, one of Pinault's many commercial enterprises. Fnac, the department-store chain, is another profitable asset, but it is the luxury brands, combined with a reticent personality, that have conferred on Pinault a mystique enjoyed by few European businessmen.

Yet this image is an apt one for Venice. It brings to mind the fusion of secrecy, determination, and opulence for which the Venetian Republic was celebrated in the years when it dominated trade in Europe and the eastern Mediterranean. Silks, precious stones, and cast metals, fragrant spices and unguents, carpets, lacework, and mirrors manufactured by methods that were a state secret—Venice presided over an empire of the senses, a global territory governed as much by the powers of seduction and stimulation as by the insistent Venetian navy. Ships transporting these luxuries all passed through the Dogana, enriching the city's sumptuous image throughout the centuries when Fortune's winds blew in its favor.

French restraint, rather than Venetian opulence, rules the interior design of Pinault's Paris office. Though not designed by Ando, the spaces are in harmony with his cool precision. Paintings and sculptures add color to the monochrome enclosures of white walls and gray floors. The art is impeccably installed, yet the effect of calm can nonetheless evoke disquiet for one who grew up with the Romantic notion that art should keep its distance from decoration. If it weren't for the lack of moldings, we could be back in a Classical age, before paintings detached themselves from walls.

When the door to Pinault's office opens, a visitor's eye first lights upon a painting by Lucio Fontana. It is an uncommon Fontana: the canvas is white; the single slash in the fabric is vertical. In this strictly regulated environment, where not even a reporter's questions are left to chance, it would be ungracious to dismiss the thought that this prominently placed work is a de facto self-portrait of its owner. It is the picture of an elusive I, a shadowy number 1. An *éminence blanche*, more absence than presence, the figure in the portrait is nonetheless determined to make his mark. The veiled aggression may even leave scars.

An art collection is inevitably a self-portrait. It offers insight into areas of subjectivity that a collector might have trouble expressing in other ways. It becomes clear, in the course of a conversation with Pinault, that I would learn more about him by staring at the pictures on the walls than by listening to the words that come out of his mouth. In the hall outside his office, my eye was caught by what looked like a display of butterflies under glass. On closer inspection, the colorful species turned out to be made out of pencil shavings, so I wasn't far wrong. The idea was still metamorphosis, or what Arthur Danto calls the transformation of the commonplace: an ordinary operation has transformed paper-thin slices of wood and colored lead into creatures with rainbow wings.

That's *progress*, a word Pinault uses to signify development or evolution. An artist, a collection, a business—all should progress naturally. A native of Brittany, Pinault began his collection thirty years ago with paintings by Paul Sérusier and other Postimpressionist artists of that region. The full extent of his progress since then is not publicly known. A French curator approached about working for the Paris museum project met with Pinault every month for a year before learning about the works it might display. The Palazzo Grassi presentation is the first time his collection will be shown.

Pinault affirms with a quick smile that only a very determined person could cause a project in Venice to be realized with such speed: "You have to be, in business. I am not getting any younger, and we wasted five years in Paris." In the short time allotted for our interview, I find it difficult to draw him out on his philosophy of collecting. This is frustrating: a friend of mine who has spent time with Pinault says that he loves talking to young artists. But why should he allow a reporter to edit his thoughts when his artists will say it all for him?

Architecture is autobiography, also. A client's choice of designer portrays a particular balance between a desire to communicate and an instinct to hide. At the Palazzo Grassi, Ando has accomplished the exceptional feat of turning receptivity into visual action. Like those of the Fontana, Ando's interiors are recessive but not neutral. In the newly remodeled galleries, the white plaster walls glow with reflected light, as if delighted to be paying attention to others.

As a fan of Gae Aulenti, I confess to being dismayed when I heard that her previous remodeling of the Palazzo Grassi was going to be substantially dismantled. So I must also confess to feeling disloyal in finding Ando's design a substantial improvement. The interiors have been simplified. Aulenti's signature squared-off quatrefoils and tent-shaped white lighting fixtures are gone. Doorways in the upstairs galleries have been aligned to create classical enfilades. Colors in the enclosed central courtyard have been retained, along with the palace's ornately carved wood ornament, but the atrium is now suffused with light filtered by a large vellum panel suspended beneath the skylights.

I once spent an hour wandering with Ando around the gardens of Versailles. We were there to attend a ceremony at which he was presented with the Pritzker Architecture Prize. The choice of location seemed to me hilarious, and I couldn't resist asking Ando how he felt about it. He replied that he was pleased to be honored in a country that had worked its way so far beyond the values embodied by the palace.

At the Palazzo Grassi, Ando has had the opportunity to make a similar statement in visual terms. The last great palace to be built on the Grand Canal, the Palazzo Grassi is a product of Venetian decadence. Carnivals and gambling had replaced shipping and conquest. Ando's minimalist interior conveys the modern transcendence of the inner life. As such, it is an ideal partner for much of the art displayed in the inaugural show. Individual galleries are devoted to work by Rothko, Twombly, and Judd. It is a conservative showing: Koons and Hirst, also represented, are by now old masters of the new. Its strength lies in its vision of continuity between postwar and contemporary art.

Subsequent exhibitions at the Palazzo Grassi will not be limited to works from Pinault's collection. As in previous years, when it was under the patronage of Fiat, the museum will present historical surveys and shows devoted to the work of single artists. The Dogana, which will also be remodeled by Ando, will be reserved for works owned by Pinault. Future plans also include the restoration of a small theater at the rear of the Palazzo Grassi. It will be used for movie and video programs and as an auditorium for conferences. A program for scholarly publications is also taking shape.

Nationalist sentiments notwithstanding, Pinault's Venetian venture should be seen as part of the continuing process of Europe's self-definition. Geography and history are critical factors here. While Italy is a southern country, the position of Venice on the northern Adriatic coast places it close to the center of Western Europe. That's partly why the city was able to dominate European trade for so many centuries.

For much of that time, moreover, Venice regarded itself as a city of the East, the heir to Byzantine glory. Constantinople and Alexandria were major influences on its architecture. The eastern Mediterranean was integral to its identity. These traditions, which once seemed to be exotic relics from the distant past, have assumed new importance at a time when Europe has begun to imagine itself as the "west coast" of Eurasia, a single continent united in its pursuit of self-sufficiency for an emerging post-American age. Luxury trade and cultural tourism have become integral parts of this cosmopolitan reconfiguration. Contemporary art is one of the lenses that bring it into focus.

April 30, 2006

SCHADENFREUDE.COM

You know it as TripAdvisor.com, the Web site devoted to user opinions of hotels, restaurants, and other variables of the mobile life. But I call it TheDivineComedyHitsTheRoad.com. Initially we go to the site for practical advice on future travels. But what prolongs the visit are the stories—the tales that invite us to judge, condemn, or identify with our fellow travelers.

As with Dante, the reports from the circles of hell are especially mesmerizing. Who wants to read about somebody else's paradise, after all? What we all really want to know is that somebody else is paying dearly to have a far worse time than us. On this point, at least, TripAdvisor is thoroughly reliable. The cries of those condemned to luxury can break your heart.

When a review starts off with the reassurance that "My husband and I have stayed at some of the best hotels in the world," brace yourself for a recitative of blighted fantasy. "The room was a box," "the bed was a rock," and the staff was "utterly rude." "The shower was horrible," "the room stunk," "our tub would back up, yuck!" Or "room décor was tired, restaurants were tired, lobby was tired." I could use a little nap myself.

Such sour memories of five-star hotels suggest that TripAdvisor is a hotbed of reverse snobbery. The grand hotels of historical legend very seldom make it to the site's top ranks. Instead the site specializes in a genre of literary retribution called Puttin' Down the Ritz. The chief pleasure in these stories is imagining how their disgruntled authors looked to the targets of their vengeance.

A frequent motif is that unless you're a Somebody, you'll be treated like dirt. These tales often sound like songs of inexperience.

If you want to stay at the Gritti, the Ritz, or the Eden, the least you can do is be on your guard against intimidation by imaginary slights. Otherwise, you could find yourself converting the imaginary into the painfully real. When in doubt, tip lavishly. Never fear that overtipping will reveal your insecurity. Instead, think of palm greasing as the cheapest form of security available to a nomadic humankind. That club sandwich will taste more than twice as good if you double the gratuity.

Yet we cannot assume that security is what these reviewers actually crave. We all know people who seek out opportunities to protest their mistreatment by others. Thanks to TripAdvisor, we now have an electronic trail of the great, globe-spanning distances such folks are willing to travel in search of the perfect snub.

I used to value this kind of review as a deterrent to the sort of malcontents you wouldn't want to find sitting next to you at your favorite hotel bar. Then I realized that the principle of self-selection cuts both ways. There must be people out there on whom a certain kind of bad review exercises an irresistibly magnetic attraction: "I'll show them who's Nobody around here!"

There is another class of guest, to which I belong, for whom staying in a great hotel is not enough. What we want is to return to a great hotel. Short of death and certain fleeting romantic encounters, being welcomed back is the nearest possible approximation of returning to the womb. This sensation is seldom available on a first visit to any establishment. The point of returning to the womb isn't the womb. It's the idea of returning to it. That way lies paradise.

Some hoteliers grasp this intuitively. The truth is they wouldn't know you from Adam or Eve.

Some computer code has tipped them off that you're a returning guest. Nonetheless, the really good ones can fake an embrace that would fool the prodigal son. The place hasn't been the same since you left. Now it can live again. The room you liked so much the last time is ready. Not a fold in the curtains has changed.

Alas, this deluxe regression is not without risk. The place could close down, change owners, decide to modernize, and then where would you be? Stuck with a four-star version of birth trauma in a big city of heartless strangers. This happened to me last Christmas at an *hôtel de charme* in Central Europe. After just two visits I had formed a deeply neurotic attachment to this wonderfully atmospheric spot. Then the owners decided to embark on an expansion program that will most likely assassinate the hotel's character. Ouch!

I haven't mustered the courage to share this experience with my fellow TripAdvisors.

The site has no ratings for separation anxiety.

But I can reliably say that checkout was truly terrible. The manager gave me a CD of music to remember it all by: Baroque concertos commissioned by the owner's ancestors in the eighteenth century. When I listen to it, I hear heartbeats. Then, a slap.

September 24, 2006

FREUDIAN SLIPCOVERS

The name Sigmund Freud does not figure on the honor rolls of the world's eminent furniture designers. Why should it? All Freud did was throw some old carpets and pillows on a couch designed by somebody else. And yet, some designers have attained enduring fame by doing less. An engineer upended a suspension bridge, and behold! The Eiffel Tower. An obscure Hungarian draftsman added a few twists to a chrome bicycle bar, and people have been perching on Breuer chairs ever since.

I'm sure that Freud selected his carpets with no less care. And I need hardly tell you that the result has had a greater impact on history than possibly any piece of furniture since the invention of the royal throne. Perhaps that's because one of the functions of the Freudian couch is to undo the damage inflicted by thrones over the millenniums: I mean the damage inflicted by external authority, by the coercive belief that the meaning and value of events require certification by those who place themselves above the law of cause and effect.

I can't think of a better way to celebrate the 150th anniversary of Freud's birth than by emphasizing that those external authorities include

Freud himself. Though many of Freud's theories have turned out to be unsound, he would have been the first to chuck the ones that didn't pan out. The man was an empiricist. He recognized not only the limits of psychoanalysis but also that neuroscience would be waiting to pick up his research on the far side. That's one reason he is revered today by leading neuroscientists like Antonio Damasio and Gerald Edelman. Far from disproving Freud, these researchers are reinforcing his insistence on the biological basis of mental drives, in the process retrieving analysis from the sexually sanitized versions of it, like Jung's, that Freud fought against in his lifetime.

Decorating tip for analysts: Why don't you embroider a little pillow for the couch that says, HERE LIES TROY? Archaeology, which was evolving into a systematic science at the same time Freud was developing his theories, only rarely turns up treasures. It mainly studies trash. So does psychoanalysis: whole mountains of detritus, layer after layer of broken pots and promises. The patient is often scarcely more aware of this garbage than a mound of Turkish soil was aware that beneath it lay Ilium's toppled towers.

Those who idealize scientific objectivity may be disheartened to learn that archaeology does not rest on a stable platform of pure fact. Scientific methods are employed: geological stratification, carbon dating, linguistics. But to interpret the mute objects that come out of the earth—to make history from them—archaeologists must, to a greater or lesser degree, descend into the subterranean realm of their own subconscious fantasies.

Which, of course, can result in misinterpretation: the "lustral baths" that Sir Arthur Evans unearthed at Knossos were more likely to have been latrines. The history of archaeology is thus a chronicle of compromises: ongoing negotiations between what we can objectively measure and our zeal to comprehend more than we know how to prove.

Freud completed his home-office decorating scheme with dozens of archaeological artifacts, statuettes of ancient deities unearthed from Mediterranean shores. "My old and filthy gods," he called them, an epithet that might have referred to the dirty residue from their excavation sites, the erotic drives many of them symbolized, the image of impurity projected onto paganism by the Judeo-Christian ethos, or Freud's own identification of artistic achievement with excrement. Like an archaeologist, as Freud saw it, the analyst brought such buried associations to the surface of consciousness.

Even if the Freudian couch is not headed for the attic, as many believe, it is nonetheless an archaeological relic in its own right, an artifact of the era that dethroned the worldview of classical science, which previously had been taken for common sense. If only those cushions could talk! The history they would tell is also a record of compromises, efforts to minimize pain that continue to influence behavior even though they have ceased to be effective and have probably been forgotten. Chances are that the authority figures with whom we've compromised—Ozzie and Harriet; Marcus Welby, M.D.; and the bully down the block—disappeared long ago, though they left echoes of their voices behind to repeat and repeat commands. "Kneel and beg my pardon!" The filthy gods are never satisfied.

Freud's couch looked like something out of *Arabian Nights*, but its function was very Bauhaus. Though we remember the Bauhaus school today chiefly through the chairs it produced, its primary function was to incubate a process of thinking. A spartan Bauhaus interior represented something more than the elimination of old clutter. Its function was also to ask why it is that we want to hold on to old clutter. Where does the desire come from to surround ourselves with overstuffed armchairs, heavy curtains, historical paintings with complicated frames?

On the couch, we lease some space to ask similar questions about the mind's interior decoration. If the voices of authority are so oppressive, what makes us want to go on mimicking them inside our heads? If the compromises are so disadvantageous, why do we cling to them? "When you feel your song is orchestrated wrong," Noël Coward used to sing, "why should you prolong your stay?" Why, indeed? Why can't you sail away? What's holding you back?

The analyst's couch does have this much in common with the classic Bauhaus designs: it must be the most uncomfortable piece of furniture ever designed for relaxation. The Bauhaus designers weren't aiming for comfort, either. They were looking to see what might happen when the familiar props of comfort were taken away, when the conventional array of domestic defenses and distractions were eliminated from the idea of home. What fantasies, emotions, and fears would come springing out of the void they left behind? What compromises would clients feel compelled to make to endure the freedom of the open floor plan, the transparency and exposure of floor-to-ceiling glass? Could a willingness to tolerate discomfort lead toward the resilient self that the modern world seemed to demand? The unpredictable range of responses to such questions was integral to the process that the Bauhaus set in motion. There might be a place for that old Poussin after all.

After a century of Freudian analysis, we know we've got room for that old neurosis, and perhaps even a minor personality disorder or two. Shades of obsession and hysteria do spice up a dull room. They might not look so great over the couch, but there's tons of space to hide them underneath it. They'll be our filthy little secrets. Dressed in Freud costumes, we'll take them out on Halloween, knock on doors, and scare the neighbors.

October 8, 2006

THE HEIR BAG

"My government will introduce legislation bequeathing all my titles, dominions, realms, chattels, corgis, et cetera, and so on, in perpetuity, to my loyal collection of handbags. . . ."

Tell me, now. Would it have surprised you had Queen Elizabeth II included this item in her annual recital of actions to be taken by Her Majesty's government in the coming year? Would it have surprised Her Majesty? How would we know? Her annual speech at Westminster is noted for the immaculate sangfroid of its delivery. Even when announcing policies she must surely find distastefully republican, she does not hesitate, wince, sigh, roll her eyes, or grumble under her breath.

I hope Her Majesty lives forever. When she goes, It goes, It being "the Firm," as the Windsors are said to call the business of being the royal family. And I will miss It, despite the evident determination of the queen's heirs to trash the entire concept of royalty. Indeed, I see only one possible way around this: that upon the queen's death, the throne will pass to an object or objects as reliably imperturbable as the throne itself: her handbags.

Things were going well for the royals so long as they upheld the unwritten commitment to imitate inanimate objects. Confidence in the Firm did not begin to crumble until the late 1960s, when the queen's advisers came to think that British subjects wanted the Windsors to impersonate human beings. Big mistake! But there seemed no pulling back. From there it was a logical progression toward the delusion that being human means being yourself.

The consequences might have been less catastrophic had the younger members of the Firm been in possession of more attractive selves. Alas, when the facades came down, what a bunch of undesirables they turned out to be. Of all the queen's dependents, only the handbags seem able to uphold their dignity. I understand her hats are admired by many. I prefer her in a smart scarf, preferably worn in a light drizzle with sensible gumboots. The hats make her look old. And while some may regard them as a perverse form of stoicism, the queen doing her bit to prepare the nation for the moment when she follows her beloved Queen Mother, the hats make me yearn for when she was dressed by Norman Hartnell.

They called it the new Elizabethan age. 1951: Festival of Britain. 1953: Coronation. Radiant young queen. Gallant Greek consort. Clouds of In Love, Hartnell's glorious perfume, now sadly discontinued. Elizabeth had a lovely, open smile, in contrast to her solemn look on state occasions. Her figure took equally well to official robes, military garb, and girlish frocks. She could look stern, but haughtiness was beneath her.

Elizabeth's head was perfectly proportioned to her height, and what a weight it had to carry! Not just those skull-numbing crowns but also the burden of exchanging the Empire (once nearly a quarter of the world's landmass, often pink on classroom maps) for a diminished "imperial commonwealth." And she carried on as if the diminishment were merely the result of smart, modern tailoring, a custom-made global outfit for the ingénue figure she cut.

It strikes me now that the queen's handbag is a symbol of this contraction. The bag—often made by Launer London, holder of the Royal Warrant for handbags—is invariably smallish. Its contents are said to be limited to a handkerchief, comb, lipstick, and compact. The symbolism of this minimal kit-on-a-strap is not difficult to unpack. The lipstick represents the pink that once colored the maps. The mirror is the sea o'er which Britannia's navies once ruled. The handkerchief represents the Industrial Revolution, specifically the spinning jenny, and the process by which raw materials from the colonies were transformed into the fine stuffs for which the British are still esteemed. The comb signifies the personal maintenance required when crowns come off. The loss of imperial India, on August 15, 1947, was a particularly Bad Hair Day. And then Suez.

An empire in a bag: Isn't that what we all crave? Along with some handy tools for repairing the damage empires inflict upon the rulers as well as the ruled? Add it all up, and the message of the handbag is clear: This woman has traveled far, she has traveled light, and she has traveled alone. Even when she had the royal yacht at her disposal and was surrounded by sailors, she was cloaked in solitude, with no one to turn to but horses, dogs, and doltish freaks of human nature.

Again, this is stoicism transformed into fashion, a lesson in the endurance of hardship turned into a fashion accessory. If your husband walked two paces behind you, wouldn't you look for a prosthetic device to take your arm on stressful state occasions? Such resourcefulness should be rewarded with highest honors.

There is ample precedent for deriving titles from inanimate objects. Think of the Order of the Garter. The present heir has even harbored a fantasy of being reincarnated as a tampon. But wouldn't a handbag be more suitable for public receptions? The honorific initials, H.R.H., could remain. And in the spirit of republicanism, referendums would determine which handbag ascends in majesty to rule the dwindling waves.

February 25, 2007

HEARTS OF THE CITY

A Dozen Years

Metroscope

Atomic Secrets

2006

A DOZEN YEARS

A crescent moon rose up in the sky on the evening of 9/11. For a brief time you could see Venus, the evening star, not far away. From my window in Lower Manhattan, I could look at the midtown Manhattan skyline sparkling beneath them. The sky, at that hour a deepening blue, was otherwise empty. The vast indigo field heightened the proximity of the two lights, mating them into an accidental pair. Given the events of that disastrous day, the configuration brought to my suggestible mind the Islamic symbol, but with a significant difference. Instead of cupping Venus within the crescent's hollow, the moon turned its convex back on her.

The reversal looked martial. The crescent shape evoked the curve of a bow. The star was the tip of an arrow. I thought of the Japanese flag, and of the rays that would shoot out from the flag's red sun disk sun in times of war, and wondered if there was some equivalent version in Islam when armies sally forth to battle infidels. Or maybe, if I were looking at the sky from, say, Mecca, instead of Lower Manhattan, the symbol would not appear turned inside out.

But this is crazy! Stars, crescents, moons, Japanese war flags, Mars, Venus, Mecca . . . Just forget about it, Herbert. Only what if . . . Isn't it just possible that a group of people who would fly airplanes into skyscrapers might well be the sort of people who would consult star maps? . . . Don't fundamentalists set great store by omens? Signs from the heavens? And not fundamentalists only, but people who read horoscopes, or close their eyes, put their hands together, and pray, "Oh, please, send me a sign. Just some kind of sign . . ."

Perhaps I was hallucinating: what I saw in the sky was merely a sign that I was in shock. Since my phone wasn't working, I couldn't call anyone and say, "Have you looked up in the sky? Would you go to the window? What do you make of that? Isn't it weird?" The word *weird* will settle many questions, at least temporarily, especially if two people agree that it applies. When one of the two is on television, the question can be permanently settled, at least for today. But, with the power out, I had no way of knowing whether some enterprising newscaster had looked out the window and spotted their weird sighting. I imagine most of them were looking in the opposite direction.

I live on the forty-fourth floor of a high-rise six blocks north of what was the World Trade Center. The apartment has spectacular views to the north and east, but most of the downtown skyline is outside my range of vision. I watched the towers collapse on television and might have missed even that in real time if a friend hadn't called from Helsinki. I'd been out late the night before and was just putting one leg out of bed when the phone rang. It was Kivi Sotamaa, a young Finnish architect I'd met a few years earlier. My mind was too bleary to comprehend what he was saying.

"Are you OK?"

What?

"There's a riot at the World Monetary Fund in Helsinki."

Huh?

"Herbert, just go to the window. Can you see the World Trade Center?"

The window in my office has a partial southern exposure. My mind was waking up as I made my way to it. What I saw at first was a beautiful day with clear blue skies. Then, craning my neck to look south, I saw that much of the sky was obliterated by billows of smoke. Erupting from a source I couldn't see, the gray, black, and white clouds mounted higher as they billowed outward, their colors intermingling, layering atop one another, as the smoke spread further to the east. I looked down at ground and saw hundreds of people, maybe more, dashing north through Foley Square.

I got off the phone and turned on the TV. At that point both towers were still standing. Cameras were trained on them from a distance. Telephoto shots of them were intercut with live reports from the streets in the tower's vicinity. At one point one of street cameras caught up with Mayor Rudolph Giuliani, who was shown sprinting up Church Street. "Head north, head north," the mayor advised the viewers between gulps for air. I decided to stay put.

The power to my building cut out about twenty minutes later, taking the television down with it, but not before it had shown what we all feared and on some inaccessible level wanted to see, as the first and then the second tower fell. When the picture went dark, I took stock. I suspected that I was in a partial state of shock, and that if I wanted to avoid panic it was best to stay home. The order was: *Move slowly.*

I'd been shaken up by the Northridge earthquake on a trip to Los Angeles in 1994. The most disorienting part of the experience was being tossed out of my hotel before the sun had come up. But on that occasion, I'd had my day planned—I was scheduled to visit two buildings—and I had a hunch that if I kept to plan I might nail down a good story. The result, "Rude Awakenings," came out that Sunday in the Week in Review section of *The New York Times*. My disorientation that morning was part of the story, as I moved through a big city that nature hadn't provided for, talking to architects whose job was to build it.

I had no such hunches on 9/11. All I had was this strange diptych framed by my windows. The left panel depicted a sunny day; the right, smoke pouring from massive destruction. If this were a diptych, the sequence would be read in time rather than the space, a Before and an After. City goes about its business. City is struck down. Pompeii before and after Vesuvius erupts. The panels might illustrate a moral lesson. Adam and Eve before and after the Fall. Paradise, desert. Original Sin.

What else did the vista remind me of? Auden's poem about Breugel's painting of *The Fall of Icarus*. In the great expanse of the city, nothing appeared to have changed, while over there in the corner (if you really craned your neck) you could almost make out the architect's son plunging to the ground. . . .

Cut it out! Oh, honey, turn that page. Evocations, connotations, wonders, and signs. Relax that reflex! This story does not have your name on it. But when you work for a newspaper the impulse to get the story is hard to resist. Following through on that impulse is what you're being paid for. If you're not actively engaged in that process, you have no reason to be there. Which, at a certain primitive level, translates into having no reason for being. A newsroom operates on that primitive level. It has to. And you have to function on that plane also if you want to survive. But this was a day for accepting the truth that I had nothing useful to say apart from *"Move slowly."*

Everything did not change on 9/11. A thread of continuity connects the period that began that day to the years leading up to it. We are all experts in this thread. We have learned it from novels, movies, sports events, and the performances of dancers; the uncertainties of love, politics, careers, sickness, and child rearing. The thread is called suspense.

Since 9/11, this thread has tightened its hold on the American imagination. Will we catch Suddam Hussein, Bin Laden, or Karl Rove? What next, after New Orleans? Will our plane go down? Are we destined for World War III? When will our creditors decide to collect? Will the heating of the global atmosphere leave any dry land?

It is unsettling to live in a time when the question mark has displaced other forms of punctuation. Under controlled circumstances, however, many people will pay to experience this form of discomfort. Will the roller coaster fly off the tracks? The murderer get away with it? The Yankees lose the pennant? In such conditions, suspense become a privilege. Pain is transformed into pleasure. The impulse to look away is overridden by curiosity about the outcome and the thrill that accompanies it.

In real life the situation is different, not just because our lives, fortunes, or happiness may hang in the balance, but because we feel that our actions can often affect the outcome. We can vote, find a cure, file for divorce. We don't want to watch and wait. We want to figure out where our area of responsibility lies. What can we do?

This book is about the thread of suspense that became woven into the fabric of American cultural life from the period that began with the dismantling of the Berlin Wall in November 1989 and concluded with the destruction of the World Trade Center twelve years later. For the sake of economy, I call this period the '90s. It started with a sense of optimism about the direction the world might take now that it was released from the tensions between the United States and the Soviet Union that had gripped the globe for decades. In the aftermath of 9/11, that initial mood of hope flipped into its opposite. Before long, the prospect of an open cosmopolitan society also seemed to have gone up in smoke.

To a degree, therefore, this book resembles an archaeological expedition through the recent past. It surveys the 1990s from the ruins of a dream. But its outlook on the future is by no means pessimistic. The cosmopolitan frame of reference that began to take shape in the 1990s was not a fantasy. It was based on more than hopes and dreams. It arose from research conducted by dedicated scholars in social science, economics, cultural and media studies, urban planning, and other fields. It also arose from the astonishing flowering of historical writing that emerged in the post–Cold War years.

The information produced in the course of that decade, and the technology that opened up public access to it, has not gone up in smoke. The research continues. So does innovation in communications technology. The pre-9/11 world will not be restored. Recovery from the damage inflicted by the political leadership of the United States will take more than a generation, and the United States will be in some respects a weaker nation even so. We are now learning that this is not necessarily a prospect to be feared. It will encourage us to rethink the concept of strength. And to build upon the substantial foundations laid down in the 1990s by acts of intellect and imagination.

In that decade, architecture became a medium for transmitting some of the features of the cosmopolitan framework to a broader sector of the public than had previously enjoyed access to scholarly work. For this sector, the function of buildings was not limited to the adornment of real estate parcels. Buildings also became catchment areas for those who wished to learn about the changing relationship of the traditional urban center to a world in flux.

For the preceeding two decades and more, American architects and planners had operated on the premise that the challenges facing them could be effectively addressed by remodeling the cityscape in the image of better days gone by. This ethos persists, in the form of the reactionary New Urbanist organization, a group that has specialized in the design of suburban residential enclaves for the rich. By the end of the 1980s, however, the connection between this movement and radical right-wing politics had become harder to overlook.

For example, Léon Krier, the founding theorist of the movement, had initially made his name by attacking buildings commissioned by "foreign bankers" in his native Belgium. Krier's American followers were generally successful in sanitizing his record. But for those who'd grown up in the era of the "restricted" (gentiles-only) suburbs, the odor of bigotry was unmistakable. That such a mentality should be driving the design of cities like New York was more than a little obscene, particularly when you take into account the opportunities that were missed to respond creatively to changing times. At the precise moment when American cities needed to redefine their relationship to an emerging global culture, they turned their back on an art form that has traditionally been used to register and project the evolution of urban identity.

Until 1994, when Raimund Abraham's design for the Austrian Cultural Forum was completed, no serious architecture had been built in Manhattan for more than a quarter of a century. Two generations of architects had come of age doubting that such a thing was even possible. People who wanted to see contemporaneity represented in the cityscape had no choice but to get on a plane.

I started practicing journalism in 1984, when Ingrid Sischy invited me to contribute a monthly column on architecture to *Artforum* magazine. I think of those columns as fumbling attempts at short form writing. Even so, they registered with readers. The magazine had acquired a kind of glamour under Ingrid's editorship, which corresponded to (and helped to fuel) the explosive growth of the art market in those years. My column benefited from this allure.

I wasn't the only critic out there writing in opposition to the prevailing postmodern credo. Douglas Davis, a kindred spirit, had a much broader readership at *Newsweek*. But a new voice coming from the margins can often cause a bigger stir than a familiar figure in the mass media. Invitations to write for other publications followed. In 1992 I joined the staff of *The New York Times* as the paper's architecture critic, an assignment that lasted twelve years.

A staff lunch was held at a hotel in Times Square a few weeks after I started at the *Times*. Max Frankel, the paper's executive editor, stood up to

the ship all looked so neat, and the power was so clean. It was almost better than going to Belgium to see the Atomium, the Theme Pavilion of the
1958 Brussels World's Fair. And if the Belgians, of all people, could put up
an eight-story metallic emblem of the atomic age, who was I to worry
about the religion it appeared to symbolize?

Yet today, whenever I see John Frankenheimer's movie *The Manchurian
Candidate,* I feel a horrifying sense of identification with the Korean War
veterans in the movie who suffer recurring nightmares from which they
wake up screaming. Those soldiers had been brainwashed, and so had we
all. A sense of horror lurked beneath the surface of cold-war normalcy. It
was the horror of secrets. Life looked great on the surface—*Ding!* There
goes the paperboy on his bike!—but privately everyone knew that at any
moment something awful might pop through. And nobody knew just what
it was.

My family had been well rewarded for subscribing to the cold-war
ethos. My father's contribution to that set of values put good food on the
table and paid the bills for my very expensive education. But the ethos
required enormous and ever-thickening defenses against the unease
inflicted on its subscribers. What did we really know about the paperboy,
after all? Wasn't his voice a little strange?

Everything was a secret, not just the classified information obtained by
people like Julius and Ethel Rosenberg. Anything that might be viewed as
abnormal was a secret. Unhappiness was a secret. It was a secret that wives
cannot, in fact, be lovers, too. It was a secret that labor-saving devices created slaves out of those who craved, operated, and worked to purchase
them. It was a secret that upward mobility was an emotional roller coaster,
that it consisted mostly of always having to say good-bye to one thing after
another without really knowing how to deal with a life of continuous
farewells.

The living room was a secret. A forbidden zone. The new slipcovers
were not, in fact, the reason why sitting down there was taboo. That was
just the cover story. It was used to conceal the inability of family members
to hold a conversation. Who knew what other secrets might come tumbling out if they actually sat down and talked? The cause of Mother's
headaches might come up. Loose lips might sink the house, the furniture,
and all the people inside into a hole in the ground. Then a truck would
pull into the driveway, workmen would fill up the hole with topsoil, and
then cover the site with rolls of sod and grass all ready to mow.

By the mid-1950s, television was rapidly helping to reduce conscious
awareness of this problem, however. The Box transformed this handicap
into a form of civility. If you invited Jack Benny into your house, it would
be rude to interrupt him, *n'est-ce pas?*

Not all of the era's secrets were psychological. The infrastructure for developing and maintaining the cold-war way of life were also camouflaged. But the camouflage relied heavily on psychological devices. Friendly men at the service station put a tiger in your tank, as if obtaining (and burning) gasoline were child's play. Chiquita Banana endowed dubious economic and political arrangements with Latin American countries with the sassy rhythms of a nightclub act.

It was not always possible to suppress awareness of the subterranean passages where advantageous deals ensured fresh supplies of bananas and oil. Best-selling books by Barbara Ward, Rachel Carson, and other writers warned of the violence that such deals often inflicted on the planet and its peoples. Yet this awareness served chiefly to intensify the anxiety of cold-war life. It did not lead to the planning of viable alternatives. On the contrary, the majority of white middle-class Americans felt they had no alternative to the map laid out by the highway builders, asphalt suppliers, car and tire makers, oil companies, and suburban residential developers. Even today, that map has the image of historical inevitability. Without it, could the United States have paved its way into the prosperous postwar years?

In World War II and the American Dream, an exhibition held at the National Building Museum in Washington in 1994, the distinguished curator Donald Albrecht documented the conversion of America's wartime industries into engines for producing the postwar American suburb. If the war industries had helped to lift the United States out of the Depression, then suburbia was the continuation of war by other means. Its development helped to ensure that the country would not tumble back into economic collapse.

In this crypto-battle, the enemy was the old industrial city. Downtowns were now stigmatized as historically obsolete zones, fated to descend ever further into the chaos of poverty, crime, and sexual impropriety. Victory over this nemesis would be measured by the distance obtained between it and us, as progress conveyed us outward toward a place in General Electric's magic garden. It is shocking to recall how quickly and smoothly this campaign was carried out, with little thought given to the trauma it might inflict on those who waged it. Of course, little enough attention was paid in those days to the traumas experienced in actual warfare. Why should people have been traumatized by lawns? Mowing grass was hardly Iwo Jima.

And so an entirely new invention, the suburban Nuclear Family, was willingly accepted in the guise of an ancient rural tradition. The dissociation between substance and appearance made for nightmares from which some Americans woke up screaming. Meanwhile, the Cold War helped to keep the disguise in place. The conflict was economic as well as military. The material well-being of the middle class offered incontestable proof of our superiority. Even Nikita Khrushchev would confess that the sight of all those sparkling blue swimming pools, glimpsed from an airplane circling over Los Angeles, caused him to doubt that the Communist system could prevail.

Superiority has its costs, however, in domestic as well as military affairs, and in the 1960s the toll exacted by postwar life became increasingly difficult to contain. The first generation to grow up in the postwar suburb had now entered its majority. In all this landscape of tradition that had been rolled out in the preceeding two decades, few members of this generation were able to locate a spot where they could carry tradition forward. And why should they, since the tradition was scarcely older than they were? How could they, since they could not begin to afford houses as nice as the ones they'd grown up in? And so, in a perverse version of England's eighteenth-century Laws of Enclosure, baby boomers bred amid symbols of stability found themselves without the prospect of gaining any for themselves or for the children they might want to bring into the world.

Decades later, faced with the privatization of civic services once provided by government agencies, people could be heard lamenting the loss of the public realm. But the search for that vanishing entity should begin by examining the loss of the private realm during the cold-war period. Those who moved to the suburbs found more than the peace and quiet they had bargained for. They also found themselves burdened with responsibilities once borne by urban centers. The reinforcement of social norms, for example, now passed from municipal institutions to the Nuclear Family, isolated by mobility and new patterns of land use.

This transfer left even less room for private life than families had known in the midst of urban congestion. The private sphere is not synonymous with solitude or isolation. It's not limited to what goes on behind closed doors. On the contrary, it is contingent on a web of social relationships—with aunts, cousins, friends, coworkers, shopkeepers, acquaintanceships formed in the street—that have evolved over millennia of city life. In the cold-war period, this web was swept away. The Nuclear Family stumbled around in the crabgrass like a social amputee, trying on new models of cars, hobbies, communication, and household appliances as if they were prosthetic devices.

You could take the family out of the city, but you could not eliminate from the family what the city represented, at least not if the city stood for the subconscious, as it often has for Americans since prerevolutionary times. In the Cold War, the prospect of abandoning the subconscious became technologically feasible for the majority of Americans. The mind, of course, had other ideas. But how would it execute them without messing up the slipcovers?

We're still living that question. One answer presented itself in the 1960s: mutant forms of social behavior would be necessary for adapting to the Nuclear environment. An atomized society would breed atomic creatures with the skills needed to survive in it. This breeding process continues. Despite (and to an extent because of) the reactionary techniques that have been deployed to return to the rigid authority of the postwar years, Americans are still respondingly creatively to the social upheaval of the cold-war years. Their ideas are integral to the identity that the contemporary city began to forge for itself when those years ended.

Suppose that life had imitated art. Let's delete all cold-war references from the history of the 1950s and '60s. In that case, my father would not have been trying to educate the young generation about the peaceful use of atomic energy. He would have been a sociopath who took pleasure in exposing children to the destructive power that had incinerated two Japanese cities in the previous decade. How's that as a substitute for blindman's bluff?

In a manner of speaking, life caught up with Bodega Bay in 1989. At least references to the Cold War would now be cast in the past tense. But what about patterns of social behavior formed during that period? The big external threat has been removed. What would happen to the penchant for secrecy and other forms of discontent? Would restraints on the pleasure principle be relaxed?

The generation that had grown up in the Cold War now occupied positions of leadership in American society. How prepared was that generation to lead? Of what did our preparation consist? Did we know where we came from, even? That we had been raised on a raft? Whether we were privy to this information or not, was any behavior other than sociopathy a realistic option?

INDEX

Aalto, Alvar, 369, 448–52, 489, 718
  Bremen apartments and, 451
  Essen Opera House and, 451
  Finnish Pavilions and, 450–1
  Modernism and, 449, 451–2, 551
  MoMA show on, 448–9, 451–2
  Paimio Tuberculosis Sanatorium and, 450
  and *Turun Sanomat* office building and
    printing plant, 449–50
A&T, 502–4
ABC's Burbank, Calif., headquarters, 649
Abraham, Raimund, 331–2
  Anthology Film Archives and, 499
  Austrian Cultural Forum and, 332,
    696–9, 839
  Austrian Cultural Institute and, 200–2
Abstract Expressionism, abstract
  expressionism, 349, 366, 805, 821
Adams, Henry, 136, 148
Adjmi, Morris, 648
AEG Turbine Factory, 283–4
Aga Khan Awards for Architecture, 469–71,
  475–6
Agon, 457, 639–40, 730
Agrest, Diana, 110–11, 118, 322, 438–9,
  684
AIDS, xiii, 19–21, 139, 290–1, 343, 725,
  789
Albert, Edouard, 157–9
Aleppo, 680
Allied Chemical, 395
Allied Works Architecture, 758, 760, 791
All the President's Men, 435
Aloff, Mindy, 197
Amaya, Mario, 811
Ambasz, Emilio, 34–9, 258, 321–2, 331
American Bar (Vienna), 666
American Center (Paris), 242–4, 303, 425,
  431
American Craft Museum, *see* Museum of
  Arts and Design
American Express, 763
American Folk Art Museum, 669, 684, 690,
  698
American Institute of Architects (AIA), 153,
  292, 675
  Art in Architecture conference of, 22–3
  Salk Institute and, 83

American Museum of Natural History, 120
  Rose Center at, 567–8, 621
Amtrak, 186–9, 523
Anderson/Schwartz Architects, 141, 215,
  392
Ando, Tadao, 313–17, 322, 379, 685, 823–5
  Azuma House and, 314
  and Church on the Water, 314
  Palazzo Grassi and, 821, 824
  Pritzker Prize and, 313–16, 824
  Rokko housing complex and, 314
Andrei, Anda, 611
Andy Warhol Museum, 603
Ankara
  Middle East Technical Institute in, 473
  Mosque of the Grand National Assembly
    in, 471–3
Anthology Film Archives, 499
Antiques Roadshow, 490–1
Antonioni, Michelangelo, 600–1, 671, 673
Appleton, Jay, 161
Appleyard, Bryan, 515
Apraxine, Pierre, 715
Arab World Institute, 239, 241, 475
Arakawa, Shusaku, 355
Archigram, 493, 504, 694
architects, architecture
  advocacy, 13, 17–18
  aesthetic freedom of, xiv–xv
  autobiographical nature of, 824
  of brain, 419
  celebrity of, 5, 227–8, 264, 267, 322, 341,
    466, 481, 500, 636, 738–9, 741, 767
  democratization of, 133–5
  designer, 5–6
  diversity of practices in, 229
  division of labor in, 227–8
  elitism associated with, 21, 211–12, 733,
    744
  endangered, 761–7
  First Lady, 799, 809
  foreign, 689–92
  green, 263, 521
  image problems of, 15
  liberal political agenda and, 213–14
  lived-in, 13
  masterpieces in, 425–6
  matrix function of, 521–2

Chase (Union Carbide) Building, 92–3,
    551, 602
Château de Rambouillet, 133–4
Chaux, 81
Chelsea, 116, 327–30, 499, 563
Chelsea Hotel, 328–30
Chelsea Piers, 320, 327, 329
Chemosphere House, 272
Chiat, Jay, 334
Chicago, Ill., 3, 65, 81–2, 129, 195–7, 277,
    316, 415, 519–20, 725, 746, 807
    860–880 Lake Shore Drive and, 195–6,
    742
    World's Fair in, 82, 136–7, 382
Chicago Architecture and Design show,
    196–7
Children's Museum (Boston), 206
Childs, David, 591–2
    Columbus Circle and, 231, 380, 769–72
    Freedom Tower and, 753–4
    Lever House and, 553, 591
    The New York Times Building and, 619,
    625–8
    Penn Station and, 523–6
Chiller Plant, 225–6, 243–5
Chin, Mel, 462
Chopda Taluka leper hospital, 469
Christo, 25
Chrysler Building, 110, 582, 701
Chu, Annie, 258, 345
Chumley's, 485
Church of Thanksgiving, 703–4, 706
Church on the Water, 314
Cincinnati, Ohio, 664
    Aronoff Center for the Arts in, 370, 494
    Lois and Richard Rosenthal Center in,
    735, 738
Cinema Ride, 352
Çinici, Behruz, 471–2
Çinici, Can, 471–3
Cisneros, Henry G., 152, 162, 223
Citibank (First National City Bank), 526
Citrohan House, 7, 62
City Beautiful movement, 24–5, 129,
    136–7, 230, 255, 382, 485, 770, 792
City Edge, 32
City of Music, 249–50, 252
Clark, Eleanor, 107
Clark, Kenneth, 369
Classicism, classicism, xiv, 76, 80–1, 107,
    136, 192, 201, 208, 247–50, 253, 255,
    281, 288, 324, 366–7, 399, 412, 428,
    449, 471–2, 506, 532, 545, 562, 603,
    605, 636, 640, 687–8, 748, 795, 823
    Casa Malaparte and, 338–9
    Columbus Circle and, 231, 382–3, 770

Great Britain and, 55, 57, 61
Met Goddess show and, 730–3
The New York Times Building and,
    625–6
Penn Station and, 187, 525
Rossi and, 447, 649
Ruhlmann and, 782, 784
Ruskin and, 73–4, 81, 807
Salk Institute and, 84–5
Venturi and, 73, 666
Clemente, Francesco, 609–10
Clinton, Bill, 219–20, 401, 523
    disappointment with, 285, 287
    urban planning and, 150–4
CLM/BBDO headquarters, 334
Cloepfil, Brad, 758–9, 791, 798
Cloisters, 110
Coates, Nigel, 55
Cocteau, Jean, 438, 611
Coleridge, Nicholas, 420–1
Coliseum, Coliseum site (New York),
    229–31, 348, 380–4
Cologne, Werkbund Exhibition in, 503,
    507
Colomina, Beatriz, 460, 742
Colors, 597–9
Colosseum (Rome), 574, 576
Columbia University, 221, 518, 552, 585
    International Research Institute for
    Climate Prediction of, 592–3
Columbus, Ohio
    Greater Columbus Convention Center
    in, 176–9, 200, 228, 390
    Wexner Center in, 178, 370, 392
Columbus Circle, 121, 229–32, 438, 499
    Coliseum site redevelopment and,
    229–31, 348, 380–4
    10, 232, 382, 769–72
    Trump and, 229, 541, 770
    2, *see* 2 Columbus Circle
Columbus Haus, 41–2, 502, 507
Comizi d'Amore, 776
Comme des Garçons, 499
community, visions of, 258–62
Comprehensive Cancer Treatment Center,
    494
Concorde crash, 588–91
Condé Nast building, 352, 407, 531–4, 622
    cafeteria of, 572–3
Condé Nast Publications, 732, 786
Con Edison, Con Edison site
    Millennial Manhole Cover and, 530–1
    proposals for, 633, 683–4
Coney Island, N.Y., 483, 485
    Parachute Jump in, 295, 820
Congrexpo convention hall, 268, 517

Contemporary City for Three Million, 8, 583

Contempt, 340

Contract with America, 285, 287

Cooper, Alexander, 155

Cooper, Robertson & Partners, 402, 711

Cooper-Hewitt, National Design Museum, 387–9, 446

Coop Himmelb(l)au, 28, 658–9, 662

cosmopolites, 733–5

Costa, Paolo, 662, 821

counterculture, 596, 598, 645, 690, 716, 802

and visions of community, 258–61

Coward, Noël, 829

Cowley, Malcolm, 536–7

Cram, Ralph Adams, 147–9

Crary, Jonathan, 506, 559

Creative Time, 353, 462

Croce, Arlene, 431, 640

Croton Water System, 120

Crown Hall, 197, 747–8

Croxton Collaborative, 200

Crystal Night, 42, 46–7, 507

Crystal Palace, 3, 54, 68, 195, 305, 397, 399, 503, 525, 716, 756

Cubitt, Lewis, 54

Dachau, 42, 166–7

D'Agostino Izzo Quirk Architects, 298

Daimler-Benz, 502–4

Dalí, Salvador, 331, 349, 760

The Discovery of America by Christopher Columbus by, 803, 808

Damasio, Antonio, 773, 828

Damrosch Park, 633

Dan House, 342–3

Danto, Arthur C., 396, 566, 599, 776, 823

Darwin, Charles, 718

Davidson, Cynthia, 590–1

Davis, Douglas, 839

Davis, Mike, 227

Debord, Guy, 405, 408

de Chirico, Giorgio, 84, 648, 650, 717

Deconstruction, deconstruction, 60, 82, 262, 277, 286, 324, 658–9

MoMA show on, 28–34, 50, 659

de Kooning, Willem, 514, 645, 744

Delano, 332–3, 372–3, 375–6

De Long, David G., 84, 367, 414

de Meuron, Pierre, 384, 401, 403, 410

Demir Holiday Village, 474

de Montebello, Philippe, 729

Denari, Neil, 135

Denby, Edwin, 289

Derrida, Jacques, 31, 178, 277, 494

design, designers, 66–8, 487–92

Dreyfuss and, 387–9

Good Design and, 29, 62, 67–8, 72, 489–90, 635, 734

Hudson and, 609–11

Kalman and, 595–9, 650, 712

morphology and, 487–8, 492

total, 66, 70, 293

see also fashion

Designers West, 627

Design Research, 489–90, 595, 602

Deskey, Donald, 387, 537–8

Despont, Thierry, 443

de Stijl, 566, 629

Detroit, Mich., 41, 92, 128

Dia Center for the Arts, 327, 329, 745

Diana, Princess of Wales, 476–7

Dickens, Charles, 130, 132–3, 807

Diller, Elizabeth, 495, 561–7, 646, 674, 684, 840

Brasserie and, 563, 565–7

Canadian Center lawn show and, 460, 462–3

Jet Lag and, 563–4

Slow House and, 436

Westin Hotel and, 299

Dinkeloo, John, 66, 292

Dinkins, David, 171, 213–16, 232

Dior, Christian, 731

disabled, 478–80

Discontinuous Spaces show, 181–2

Disneyland, 301, 325–7

Disney Vacation Club, 299

Disney World, 725

Dixon, Anne, 194

DMJM Harris, 767

Dochantschi, Markus, 738

Doge's Palace, 349, 449, 650–1, 781

Ruskin on, 73–4, 682

Doheny Ranch Development, 415

Doherty, Brian, 745

Dolan, James L., 538

Dolmabahçe Palace Gardens, 474–5

Domus, Museum of Mankind, 418–19

Doner, Michele Oka, 786–8

Doordan, Dennis, 263–4

Dorfsman, Lou, 64

Dorothy Chandler Pavilion, 708

Dorset Hotel, 384, 402–3, 411

Down Under the Manhattan Bridge Overpass (DUMBO), 526–30, 803

Drager House, 279

DreamWorks, 574, 577

Drew, Elizabeth, 459

Drexler, Arthur, 29, 385–6, 491

Dreyfuss, Henry, 387–90
Droog, 610–11
Duany, Andrés, 190
Dubus, Jean, 162–4
Duchamp, Marcel, 145, 339, 413, 566,
　737–8
duendes, 544–5, 550, 767–8
Dulles Airport, 270
Dunand, Jean, 783–4
Dunlap, David W., 755
Dwight, Eleanor, 720–1
Dymaxion House, 716

Eames, Charles, 68, 278, 342, 442, 489,
　494, 611, 734
Eames, Ray, 278, 342, 442, 489, 494, 611
Eames House, 345
earthquakes, 224–6, 317, 463
　Japan and, 194, 314
　Los Angeles and, 224, 226, 242–3, 272,
　　341–3, 346, 440, 836
Eastern Airlines terminal (Kennedy
　International Airport), 453
Eastern State Penitentiary, 130–3
East River, 121, 527, 692
　Con Edison site and, 633, 683
　Queens West and, 235–7
East Village, 24, 482, 519, 595
Eckstut, Stan, 154–6
eclisse, L', 600–1
Edelman, Gerald, 419, 681, 828
Eden Roc, 641, 787
Edgemar shopping arcade, 396
Edison Terrace, 190–2
Edwardian architecture, Edwardians, 51,
　56, 128, 720
Edwards, Blake, 435
Eidlitz, Cyrus L. W., 394
Eiffel Tower, 163, 397, 480, 532–3, 716,
　827
860–880 Lake Shore Drive, 195–7, 742
80 South Street Tower, 772–4
Einstein Tower, 275
Eisenhower, Dwight D., 389
Eisenman, Peter, 209, 248, 321, 331, 366,
　368, 384, 390–3, 431, 449, 472, 588,
　590–4, 607, 624, 643, 646, 668, 683,
　688, 718, 723, 745, 760
　Aronoff Center and, 370, 494
　Bedford-Stuyvesant fire station and, 391
　Concorde and, 590–1
　flirting of, 277–8
　Frankfurt University Biocenter and, 33
　Greater Columbus Convention Center
　　and, 176–9, 200, 228, 390

and Hotel am Spreedreieck, 593–4
　Jewish Museum and, 370–1
　MoMA Deconstructivist Architecture
　　show and, 28, 31, 33
　St. George Ferry Terminal expansion
　　and, 390–2
　and Staten Island Institute of Arts and
　　Sciences, 390–1, 593, 664
　West Side project and, 494
　Wexner Center and, 178, 370, 391–2
Eisner, Michael, 282–3
Elias, Norbert, 24
Elizabeth II, Queen of Great Britain, 598,
　830–2
Ellerbe Becket, 171–3
Ellis, Bret Easton, 107
Ellis Island, 295, 397, 468
Ellwood, Craig, 552
Empire–Fulton Ferry State Park, 528
Empire State Building, 110, 700–1
Empire Stores, 528
Engelmann, Paul, 668
Enid A. Haupt Conservatory, 397–400
Enlightenment, 4, 10, 30, 33, 50, 60, 80–1,
　130, 133, 170, 245, 305, 380, 451, 477,
　508, 547, 551, 560, 568, 618, 624, 697,
　762
　Modernism and, 235, 392
　U.S. Holocaust Museum and, 47–8, 50
Ennis Brown House, 761, 765
Ensor, James, 443
Ephesus archaeological site, 761, 766
Epicureanism, 540
Equitable Center, 23
Erasmus Bridge, 494
Erik Satie Music Conservatory, 248
Erlanger Theater, 307
Ertegun, Ahmet and Mica, 474
Espace Piranesien, 272, 336, 412
Essen Opera House, 451
Etlin, Richard, 323–4
Euralille, 265, 335–6, 481
Euro Disney, 245, 325
Evans, Sir Arthur, 828
Everybody, 597
E Walk entertainment complex, 711
Experience Music Project, 572, 777
Experiment in Terror, 435
Exposition Internationale des Arts
　Décoratifs et Industriels Modernes,
　782
Expressionism, expressionism, 46, 70, 178,
　201, 269, 274–6, 312, 383, 386, 391,
　446, 451, 500, 509, 604, 734, 754, 778,
　800
　Modernism and, 64–5

Expressionism and the New Objectivity
show, 274–6

Fallet House, 8
Fallingwater, 161, 415, 442
Faneuil Hall, 602
Farnsworth House, 208, 646
fashion, 774–6
    Armani and, 421, 612–18
    Kennedy and, 652–6
    Met Goddess show and, 728–33
    Prada and, 774–5
    Versace and, 420–1
Fashion Institute of Technology, 330
Federal Plaza (Lower Manhattan), 25
Federal Triangle Building (Washington,
    D.C.), 149
Fellini, Federico, 650
Fellini Satyricon, 540, 549–50
Fellows, Will, 793–4
Ferlinghetti, Lawrence, 820
Ferrer, Fernando, 173
Ferriss, Hugh, 109, 638
festival marketplace, 528–9, 602
Festival of Britain style, 51–2
Fieldman, Michael, 171–3
Fifth Avenue, 108, 319–20, 349, 484, 536,
    542–3, 653
    Guggenheim on, xv, 135, 233, 289, 291,
        335, 416, 424, 426–7, 433–4, 514, 585,
        693, 695, 822
    Manufacturers Hanover Trust on, 82, 93,
        526
film, films, 62, 124, 137, 180, 233, 306, 340,
    432–3, 435, 468–9, 519–22, 529,
    574–9, 598–601, 641–3, 692, 699,
    775–6, 788, 795–6, 825, 848
    of Antonioni, 600–1, 671, 673
    of Fellini, 540, 549–50
    of Hitchcock, 271–2, 478, 537, 747
    Holocaust and, 40, 42–3, 51, 166, 169,
        510
    lawns and, 461–3
    on Roman Empire, 574–6, 578–9
Fine Arts Building (Riverside), 256–8, 279
Finland, 448–51
Finsterlin, Hermann, 275, 312
First National City Bank (Citibank), 526
Fisher, Frederick, 341, 499
Fisher, Jules, 538
Fisher, Thomas, 609
Fisher Marantz, 299
Fitzgerald, F. Scott, 253–4, 383–4
500 Park Avenue (Pepsi-Cola Building), 62,
    526, 550–1, 553

Flanner, Janet, 107–8, 404
Flavin, Dan, 745, 775
Flinchum, Russell, 387, 389
Florence, 322–4, 339, 449
    power plant in, 323–4
Florida, Richard, 733
Folies-Bergère, 783–4
Fonda del Sol, La, 642
Fontainebleau Hotel, 641, 713
Fontana, Lucio, 823–4
Football Hall of Fame, 142
Ford, Tom, 732–3
Ford Center for the Performing Arts, 405
Ford Foundation Building, 66–7, 201,
    292–5, 555, 571
Forest City Ratner, 620
Fort-Brescia, Bernardo, 300, 710
    Edison Terrace and, 190, 192
Fortuny, Mariano, 731
Forty-second Street, 462, 535, 538, 542
    Condé Nast Building and, 352, 532
    Kalman and, 596–7
    New Amsterdam Theater and, 298,
        404–5
    redevelopment of, 124–5, 127, 236,
        298–9, 301, 318, 351–4, 393, 397,
        407–8, 596–7, 620, 676
    Westin Hotel and, 298, 710–12
40 Wall Street, 543, 545
Foster, Sir Norman, 6, 248, 385, 427, 507,
    643, 689, 692, 754, 841
    The New York Times Building and, 619,
        625
Foucart, Bruno, 784
Foucault, Michel, 31, 132, 159, 520, 632
Four Seasons, The, 68, 234, 565–6, 710
Fox & Fowle Architects, 321
    and Condé Nast Building, 352, 532–4,
        622
    and The New York Times Building, 622,
        626
    and 101 Avenue of the Americas, 115–16
Foxwoods Resort, 358
Frampton, Kenneth, 17, 19, 139, 264, 696
France, French, 10, 30, 33, 54, 68, 130,
    193, 314–16, 325, 379, 405, 412, 457,
    477, 500, 517, 527, 540, 583, 588–91,
    707, 709, 800
    American Center and, 245–7
    and Cathedral Church of St. John the
        Divine, 147–8
    Concorde and, 588–9
    Kennedy and, 653–4
    Normandie and, 590–1
    Pinault and, 821–3
    Portzamparc and, 247–8

Gothic (*cont'd*)
  The New York Times Building and,
    625–6
  2 Columbus Circle and, 798, 800, 807
  see also Venetian Gothic
Gousha, Joseph, 483–5
Graham, Dan, 329–30
Grand Central Terminal, 94, 118–19, 136,
    142, 149, 187, 236, 269, 295, 318, 377,
    428, 495, 548, 792
  MetLife Building and, 550, 554
  restoration and rededication of, 466–9
Grande Bibliothèque, 163
Grand Hyatt Hotel, 542
Grand Palais, 305
Grand Ticino, 485
Grange Hall, 485
Grassi, Giorgio, 503–4
Graves, Michael, 9, 18, 34, 298, 322, 331,
    385, 531, 734
Gray, John, 648
Great Britain, 51–61, 73, 75, 85, 110, 131,
    199, 277, 357, 386, 399, 450, 470, 473,
    488, 493–4, 515, 531, 539, 573, 583,
    610, 615, 622, 638, 654, 667, 694, 709,
    716, 739, 830–1, 842, 850
  Concorde and, 588–9
  endangered sites in, 761–2, 765
  Modernism and, 53–7, 59–61
  and *A Vision of Britain*, 52–4, 56–7, 59–60
Great Depression, 108–9, 120, 234, 326,
    535–7, 575, 707, 730, 843, 849
Greater Columbus Convention Center,
    176–9, 200, 228, 390
Greece, Greeks, 56, 134, 606, 666, 668,
    685, 691, 722, 729–33, 778, 795–6,
    799
  Met Goddess show and, 729–32
Greenwich Village, 110, 115, 155, 306–7,
    327, 741, 743, 757
  Powell and, 482–6
Gropius, Walter, 72, 81, 91, 134, 321, 442,
    450, 525–6, 602, 708, 714
  Expressionism and, 276, 312
  Modernism and, 175, 250, 388
  Pan Am Building and, 66, 554
Ground Zero, *see* World Trade Center,
    World Trade Center site
Gruzen Samton, 198, 236
Gucci Group, 732, 822
Guggenheimer Architects, 758
Guggenheim Museum, 62, 201, 231,
    288–92, 353, 377, 555, 570, 591, 671,
    692–6, 760, 821–2
  Armani retrospective at, 612–18
  Art of the Motorcycle show at, 693–5

  in Bilbao, xv, 334–5, 424–35, 511–13,
    515, 517, 572, 627, 631, 640, 662, 734
  Bleckner retrospective at, 288, 290–2
  Clemente retrospective at, 610
  de Kooning show at, 514
  on Fifth Avenue, xv, 135, 233, 289, 291,
    335, 416, 424, 426–7, 433–4, 514, 585,
    693, 695, 822
  Gehry retrospective at, xv, 626
  Global, 695–6
  Hermitage Branch of, 692–5
  The Italian Metamorphosis show at,
    262–3, 695
  Lower Manhattan branch of, 645, 734
  SoHo branch of, 669
  2 Columbus Circle and, 349–50
  virtual, 695
  Wright and, 158, 267, 288–9, 291–2,
    335, 416, 428, 433–4, 514, 551,
    613–14, 688, 695
Guild House, 72, 75, 244
Guimard, Hector, 134
Gulf & Western, 229–31, 350, 812
Gutman, Robert, 227
Gwathmey, Charles, 385, 553, 643, 696,
    723
Gwathmey Siegel, 321, 684

Habermas, Jurgen, 235
Hack, Gary, 495
Hackescher Hof, 500
Hadid, Zaha, xiv–xv, 55, 172, 298, 322, 427,
    549, 588, 664, 705, 718, 735–40, 744
  Austrian Museum retrospective on, 736,
    738–9
  Cardiff Opera House and, 264, 736
  and Lois and Richard Rosenthal Center,
    735–8, 740
  MoMA Deconstructivist Architecture
    show and, 28–9, 31–4
  2 Columbus Circle and, 759–60
Hagia Sophia, 377, 475
Hague, The, 265, 481
Halles, Les, 422–3
Halprin, Lawrence, 752
Halston, 654, 732
Hardy, Hugh, 404, 407, 535, 538
Hardy Holzman Pfeiffer Associates, 306,
    317, 329, 404, 535
Harriman, Pamela C., 315–16
Harrison, Wallace K., 321, 439, 748,
    771–2, 778
  LaGuardia projects and, 269, 647
  Metropolitan Opera House and, 158,
    638

MoMA expansions and, 412–13
Rockefeller Center and, 642
and Trylon and Perisphere, 266–7, 412, 569, 638, 646, 771
United Nations and, 266, 412, 646
Hart Plaza, 92
Harvard Design School Guide to Shopping, The, 671
Harvard University, 470, 552, 602, 671
Haughaut Building, 651
Haussmann, Baron Georges-Eugène, 184, 557, 559, 751
Havel, Vaclav, 371
Haviland, John, 130–1, 133
Hawkinson, Laurie, 26–8, 181–2, 258, 322, 562
Hayden Planetarium, 568, 571
Hazucha, Claire S., 179
Hebron Old Town, 469
Hejduk, John, 322
Hellmuth, Obata & Kassabaum, 186, 280
Hemphill, Christopher, 720
Hennepin Avenue Entertainment Centrum, 77–9
Herscher, Uri D., 365
Herts, Henry Beaumont, 406
Herzog, Jacques, 384, 401, 403, 410
Herzog & de Meuron, 775
Hessel, Franz, 111, 500, 511
High Museum of Art, 745
Highrise of Homes, 436–7
Hildebrand, Grant, 160–1
Hill, Walter, 519
Hilton International hotels, 706–10
Hitchcock, Alfred, 271–2, 478, 537, 747
Hitchcock, Henry-Russell, 17, 62, 551
Hitler, Adolf, 488, 594, 667
  Holocaust and, 50, 167, 169
  Modernism and, 41–2
Hoffmann, E. T. A., 510
Hoffmann, Hans, 737
Holabird & Root, 747
Holiday Inn (Paris), 249
Holl, Steven, 322, 562, 588, 740, 815
  MoMA expansions and, 384, 401
  World Trade Center site and, 723
Hollein, Hans, 314, 427, 472
Holocaust, 40, 42–5, 47–51, 165–71, 507–10
  Berlin and, 508–9
  Skirball Cultural Center and, 364–5
  Wiesel on, 165
  see also United States Holocaust Memorial Museum
Holt Hinshaw Pfau Jones, 225, 243
Holzbauer, Wilhelm, 662

Holzer, Baby Jane, 795
homelessness, 164, 220–3, 319
  social idealism and, 19–21
  and social responsibility of architects, 222–3, 227
  urbanism and, 80, 152, 154
Honeywell Round Thermostats, 389
Hotel am Spreedreieck, 593–4
Hotel Esplanade, 501
Hotel QT, 785–6
Hot Flats, 659
Houses of Parliament, British, 55–6, 210, 807
Houston, Tex., 603–8, 752
  Museum of Fine Arts in, 604–8
Hoving, Thomas, 813
  Making the Mummies Dance by, 94–9
Howard, Ebenezer, 54, 110, 347
Howard Gilman Collection of Visionary Architectural Drawings, 715
Hoyningen-Huene, George, 730–1
Hudson (hotel), 608–12, 672
Hudson River, 109, 590
  Chelsea and, 327, 329
  Morton Street Park and, 154–5
Hudson Square, 115–16
Huntington Hartford, George, 230, 349–51, 758, 760, 791, 795, 801–4, 811
Huxtable, Ada Louise, 60, 103, 720, 846–7
  Ford Foundation Building and, 67
  on Le Corbusier's Pessac houses, 13–14
  2 Columbus Circle and, 348–9
Huysmans, Joris-Karl, 712, 806
Hyatt Foundation, 314
Hyatt Hotel (Berlin), 504
Hyatt Regency Hotel (Atlanta), 127–8

IBM building, 691
IBM Pavilion, 68–9
Idenburg, Florian, 758
IFCCA Prize Competition for the Design of Cities, 492
Iliac Passion, The, 795–6
Illinois Institute of Technology, 5, 46, 472, 734, 746–9
  Crown Hall at, 747–8
  McCormick Tribune Campus Center at, 746, 749
Immeubles Villas, 163–5
I. M. Pei & Partners, 162
Imperfect Utopia, 26–8
Imperial Hotel, 364, 414
impure form, doctrine of, 30–1
Info-Box, 502, 504

Ingalls Hockey Rink, 64, 270, 768
Instant City, 504
Institute for Architecture and Urban
    Studies, 266
Institute for Contemporary Art, 94, 97
Intermodal Surface Transportation
    Efficiency Act (ISTEA), 153
International Arrivals Building (Kennedy
    International Airport), 453
International Design Conference, 489
International Port Terminal, 664
International Research Institute for
    Climate Prediction, 592–3
International Style, 8, 47, 55, 67–8, 141,
    192, 254, 305, 312, 323, 364, 393, 399,
    413, 461, 501, 525, 565, 571, 591, 593,
    626, 696, 707, 734, 759, 774, 778,
    800
    LVMH Tower and, 555–6
    Modernism and, 233–4, 300, 551, 553
    MoMA expansions and, 402–3
    MoMA show on, 17, 33, 62, 551–3
    New York and, 797–8
    Park Avenue Corridor and, 550–3, 691
    10 Columbus Circle and, 770–1
Invasion of the Body Snatchers, 461–2
Iraq, 736, 740, 761, 766
IRCAM annex, 503
Isamu Noguchi Garden Museum, 93–4
Isherwood, Christopher, 511, 556
Islam, 57, 312, 469–73, 475–6, 681, 732,
    740, 835
    Aga Khan Awards and, 469–70, 472
    and Mosque of the Grand National
        Assembly, 471–3
Isozaki, Arata, 248, 313, 322, 384, 427, 495,
    734, 756, 841
    Berliner Volksbank and, 503
    La Coruña building of, 417–20
    Nagi Museum and, 354–7, 379, 430
    Nara Convention Hall and, 382, 418
Israel, Franklin D., xiv, 197, 277–9, 341–6
    Dan House and, 342–3
    Drager House and, 279
    flirting of, 277–8
    Gehry's Santa Monica house and, 205
    Goldberg-Bean House and, 343
    Lamy-Newton house and, 278, 345
    MOCA retrospective on, 341–4
    Postmodernism and, 344–5
    Propaganda Films and, 278, 344–6
    Riverside's Fine Arts Building and,
        256–8, 279
    Weisman Pavilion and, 278
Istanbul, 471, 474–5, 707, 709
Italy, 71, 107–8, 214, 274, 309–10, 323,

368, 449, 531, 576–7, 597, 606, 671,
    673, 687, 703, 709, 717, 775–6, 825
    Piano and, 621, 623
    postwar architecture in, 262–4, 695
    Rossi and, 446–7, 649–50
    Versace in, 420–1
Ito, Toyo, 322, 384, 401, 756

Jackson, J. B., 256, 258
Jackson Park, 137
Jacob K. Javits Convention Center, 46, 170,
    177, 377, 493, 755
Jacobs, Deborah L., 777
Jacobs, Jane, 79–80, 129, 184–5, 322, 602
    *The Death and Life of Great American
    Cities* by, 17, 110, 184, 286–7, 583,
    717, 743–4
Jacquenet House, 8
Jaguar (Mercedes-Benz) showroom, 551,
    613
Jahn, Helmut, 5–7, 70
    Coliseum site and, 380, 382–4
    Sony's European Headquarters and, 502
    United Airlines terminal and, 3, 6–7
James, Henry, 115, 642–4
James A. Farley Building, 186–7, 493,
    522–4
Japan, 65, 216, 265, 382, 399, 554, 600,
    693, 757, 784, 788, 835, 851
    Ando and, 313–17
    earthquakes and, 194, 314
    Nagi Museum and, 354–6
    Noguchi and, 89–93
    Okura Hotel and, 361–4
    Tokyo International Forum and, 192–4,
        376–80
Japanese Pavilion, 756
Jazz at Lincoln Center, 770–1
Jean-Georges, 499
Jeanneret, Charles-Édouard, *see* Le
    Corbusier
Jefferson, Thomas, 134, 203, 419, 747
Jefferson Memorial, 46, 170
Jekyll, Thomas, 807
Jencks, Charles, 10, 174, 262
Jensen, Ron, 199
Jerusalem, 92, 708
Jet Lag, 563–4, 566
Jewish Museum (Berlin), 508–10, 517
Jewish Museum (New York), 149, 369
Jewish Museum (San Francisco), 370–1
Jews, Judaism, 40–3, 96, 364–72, 421, 575,
    642, 713, 787, 844–6
    architects among, 365–72
    Benjamin and, 557–8

Berlin and, 507–9, 557
Holocaust and, 40, 43, 45, 49–50, 169,
   364, 508–9
Skirball Cultural Center and, 364–7
John Deere & Company, 388–9
John F. Kennedy International Airport, *see*
   Kennedy International Airport
Johns, Jasper, 666, 812
Johnson, A. M., 416
Johnson, J. Stewart, 782
Johnson, Lyndon B., 69, 294
Johnson, Philip, 64, 70–1, 109, 174,
   207–13, 277, 385, 438–9, 505, 555,
   715, 812
   AT&T Headquarters and, 3, 571
   fascist sympathies of, 207, 211
   Glass House and, 203, 207–8, 210,
      212–13, 310–13, 635
   idea of freedom of, 209–12
   Lincoln Center and, 633, 636, 638
   Modernism and, 209–10, 635–6
   MoMA and, 17, 28–9, 33–4, 62, 403,
      411, 635–6, 659, 701–2
   and Museum of Broadcasting, 70
   New York State Pavilion and, 636
   New York State Theater and, 311, 636
   Seagram Building and, 312, 438, 496,
      551, 635
   subversive mission of, 209–10
   Times Square and, 124–5, 127
   and Trump International Hotel and
      Condominiums, 770
   and Trump's meeting with Muschamp,
      541–4
Johnson's Wax Headquarters, 415
John XXIII, Pope, 655
Jones, Wes, 225, 243–5
Joyce Theater, 327, 329
J. Paul Getty Museum, 440
Judd, Donald, 219, 305, 542, 745, 824
Jujamcyn Theaters, 308–9
Jung, Carl, 88, 465–6, 739, 828
Jussieu Library, xiv, 157–9, 265, 267–8,
   272–3, 779

Kael, Pauline, 109
Kahala Hilton, 709
Kahan, Richard A., 173, 538
Kahn, Bonnie Menes, 611
Kahn, Louis I., 49, 208–9, 316, 365, 445–6,
   449, 456, 709, 718, 776, 780
   death of, 208
   Kimbell Art Museum and, 87, 139–40
   Mikveh Israel and, 369
   Modernism and, 281–2, 651, 759

Salk Institute and, 83–8, 138–41
   spirituality of, 367, 369, 372, 465
Kalman, Tibor, 407, 489, 595–9, 650, 712
   Colors and, 597–9
   Forty-second Street and, 596–7
   New Museum of Contemporary Art
      retrospective on, 595, 597–8
Kamali, Norma, 732
Kammen, Michael, 728
Kapaum, Franz, 663
Kapoor, Anish, 774–5
Kaprow, Alan, 95
Karinska, Barbara, 730
Karl Marx Haus, 661–2
Kazanjian, Dodie, 721
Keats, John, 277, 543
Kelly, Ellsworth, 455–8
Kelly, Richard, 456
Kendell, William, 186–7
Kennedy, Jacqueline, 234, 543, 652–6
Kennedy, John F., 69, 151, 652–6
Kennedy Center for the Performing Arts,
   349
Kennedy International Airport, 493, 523,
   526, 554
   Eastern Airlines terminal at, 453
   International Arrivals Building at, 453
   Terminal City of, 4–5
   Terminal One at, 452–5
   TWA terminal at, 64, 269–71, 382, 391,
      453, 684, 736, 760, 768
Kennedy Space Center, 243
Kern, Stephen, 419
Kershaw, Daniel, 783
Khrushchev, Nikita S., 653, 655, 850
Kiefer, Anselm, 43–4
Kimbell Art Museum, 87, 139–40
King, Rodney, 172
King's Cross train station, 54
Kipnis, Jeffrey, 208, 555
Kirschner, Robert, 365
Kirstein, Lincoln, 307, 457, 638, 805
Klotz, Heinrich, 223
Knauss, Melania, 539, 545
Knize shop, 667
Koch, Edward, 61, 542–3, 679
Koda, Harold, 613, 729
Koestler, Arthur, 480
Kohlmaier, Georg, 398
Kohn Pedersen Fox, 124
Kolbowski, Silvia, 181
Kondylis, Costas, 700
Koolhaas, Rem, xiv–xv, 55, 110–11, 156–9,
   251, 322, 331, 449, 494, 548–9, 561–2,
   588, 602, 632, 636, 643–7, 664, 684–5,
   689, 740, 744, 771, 784, 808, 840

Koolhaas, Rem (*cont'd*)
  and Bibliothèque Nationale de France,
    267, 272
  Bordeaux house design of, 477–81, 646–7
  Brooklyn cultural district and, 644–5
  and Center for Art and Media
    Technology, 272
  comparisons between Lautner and, 272
  Congrexpo and, 268
  Delirious New York by, 110, 265, 412, 481,
    555, 646, 672
  Espace Piranesien and, 272, 336, 412
  Euralille and, 265, 335–6, 481
  Guggenheim Hermitage and, 692, 694–5
  Jussieu Library and, xiv, 157–9, 265,
    267–8, 272–3, 779
  Kunsthal and, 265, 267, 272–3, 481
  Lehmann Maupin Gallery and, 497
  McCormick Tribune Campus Center
    and, 746, 748
  Mies van der Rohe and, 265, 646, 748–9
  MoMA Deconstructivist Architecture
    show and, 28–9
  MoMA expansions and, 384, 401,
    409–13, 647
  MoMA shows on, 264–9, 272–3, 481
  Prada shops and, 669–72, 684, 775
  Seattle's Central Library and, 777–81
  Second Stage Theater and, 497–9
  S, M, L, XL by, 335, 410, 413, 481,
    498–9
  Spear House and, 710
  triple thinking of, 645–6, 671
  Whitney and, 644–5, 647, 780
Koons, Jeff, 822, 824
Kouwenhoven, John, 407–8, 459
Kracauer, Siegfried, 111, 500, 511
Krapp, Herbert J., 309
Krauss, Rosalind, 89
Krens, Thomas, 614, 695–6
  Bilbao Guggenheim and, 427, 513
Krier, Léon, 725, 839
Kruger, Barbara, 26–8, 181
Kunsthal (Rotterdam), 265, 267, 272–3,
    481
Kushner, Robert, 74
Kuspit, Donald, 210
Kyoto, 90–1, 355
KZF Design, 738

Labrouste, Henri, 303
Lacan, Jacques, 279
La Coruña, 417–20
LaGuardia Airport, 120, 453–4
  control tower at, 647

  main terminal of, 269
  USAir terminal at, 182, 453
Laguna West, 259
Lahore arts center, 469
La Jolla, Calif.
  Neurosciences Institute in, 592
  Salk Institute in, 83, 138
Lake Shore Drive high-rises, 195–7, 742
Lake Tahoe, 415
Lambert, Phyllis, 460, 492, 496
Lampugnani, Vittorio Magnago, 275
Lamy-Newton house, 278, 342, 345
Landmark West, 818
Land of the Pharaohs, 180
landscape, landscaping, 92, 155, 181–2,
    194, 233, 237, 253, 279, 286, 289, 447,
    452, 473–4, 476–7, 528, 545, 568, 622,
    629, 701
  and art in architecture, 24, 26–7
  Gehry's Santa Monica house and, 203,
    205
  Getty Center and, 440, 444–5
  and International Research Institute for
    Climate Prediction, 592–3
  Lucille Halsell Conservatory and, 34–6,
    39
  Riverside's Fine Arts Building and, 256–8
  Salk Institute and, 86, 140
  Skirball Cultural Center and, 365, 368
  Wright and, xv, 343, 414–17, 592, 727
Lang, Fritz, 62
Langdon Wilson, 326
Lanzmann, Claude, 40, 510
Lapidus, Morris, 178, 570, 641–4
  Summit Hotel and, 641–2, 713–14
Las Vegas, Nev., 72, 226, 682
  Guggenheim Hermitage and, 692–5
Lategano-Nicholas, Christyne, 674
la Tourette, monastery of, 8
Latrobe, Benjamin, 131, 133
Launer London, 831
Lauren, Ralph, 721–2
Lautner, John, 271–3
lawns, 600, 849
  Canadian Center show on, 458–63
Lears, Jackson, 148, 316
Leatherbarrow, Thomas, 591–3
Le Corbusier (Charles-Édouard Jeanneret),
    17, 35, 67, 72, 247–9, 267, 403, 446,
    450, 457, 525–6, 562, 629–30, 661,
    701, 709, 743–5
  Ando influenced by, 315–16
  Bordeaux houses of, 12
  centennial of, 8–10, 12, 14
  Chandigarh General Assembly Building
    and, 8, 630

Citrohan House and, 7, 62
comparisons between Gehry and,
    14–15
Contemporary City plan of, 8, 583
death of, 9
Immeubles Villas and, 163–5
Modernism and, 4, 7–15, 62, 65, 175,
    191, 233, 247, 249, 281, 315, 551, 651,
    744–5, 759, 808
and Notre Dame du Haut, 8, 477
Portzamparc influenced by, 249, 251
Radiant City of, 286–7, 584, 743–4
residential housing and, 7–8, 12–14, 38,
    62, 134, 162–5, 251, 442, 782
urban design and, 8–9, 13, 163, 286–7,
    517, 743–4, 747
zoning policy and, 583–4
Ledbetter, Lee, 19–21
Ledoux, Claude-Nicolas, 81, 636
Lège, Le Corbusier's houses for, 12–13
Lehman College, Viñoly's gymnasium for,
    193, 321, 376
Lehmann Maupin Gallery, 497
Leigh, Douglas, 533
Leitner, Bernhard, 668
Le Nôtre, André, 314–15
Lerner, Ralph, 495
Leroy, Yann Andre, 19
Lessard, Suzannah, 521
Lethaby, William, 54, 573
Lever House, 62–3, 65, 82, 233, 305, 412,
    550–1, 553, 555, 744, 760, 798
restoration of, 591, 594
Levine, Neal, 75, 705
Levi Strauss, 365, 513, 616
Levy, Leon and Lionel, 230
Lewis Thomas Laboratory, 74–6, 82
LeWitt, Sol, 31, 305, 745
Libera, Adalberto, 338
Liberace, 794
Liberman, Alexander, 721
Liberty City, Fla., 190–2
Libeskind, Daniel, 646, 767
    City Edge and, 32
    Ground Zero design guidelines and,
        752–5
    Jewish Museum and, 508–10
    MoMA Deconstructivist Architecture
        show and, 28, 31
Lichtenstein, Harvey, 644
Life, 28, 65, 482
Limelight Productions, 278, 345
Lin, Maya, 25, 44, 51, 646, 674, 724
Lincoln Center for the Performing Arts,
    311, 377, 632–40, 771
Metropolitan Opera in, 634, 638

New York State Theater in, 633, 636,
    638–40
redevelopment of, 602, 632–3
Lincoln Memorial, 44, 46, 169–70
Lindbergh, Charles, 51, 109
Lindsay, John V., 151, 214, 217, 307
Linkstrasse office building, 503
Lipstick Building, 209
Lissitzky, El, 442
Littlewood, Joan, 716
Livent, 306
LMN Architects, 777
Local 32B-32J, 115
Lois and Richard Rosenthal Center for
    Contemporary Art, 735–8, 740
London, 9, 55–7, 150, 264–5, 320, 383,
    521, 558, 583, 616, 664, 711, 740
    Architectural Association in, xiv, 55
    Charles and, 56–7
    Crystal Palace in, 399, 525
    endangered sites in, 761–2
    World's Fair in, 68, 195, 399
Long, Gregory, 399
Long Beach Island, 179–80
Longchamps, 108
Long Island City, N.Y., 93, 580
    Arquitectonica's residential project in,
        711, 714
    MoMA in, 499, 700, 715, 719
Loos, Adolf, 282, 658
    American Bar and, 666
    Knize shop and, 667
    Vienna and, 201, 665–8, 697
Loos Haus, 666–7
Los Angeles, Calif., 89, 107, 128, 135, 197,
    224–7, 233, 242–5, 260, 278–80, 286,
    320, 322, 326, 341–6, 357, 415, 494,
    520, 552, 558, 601, 670, 708, 727, 850
    Chiller Plant and, 243–4
    earthquakes and, 224, 226, 242–3, 272,
        341–3, 346, 440, 836
    Ennis Brown House in, 761, 765
    Geffen Contemporary at MOCA in, 217,
        430
    Gehry's Santa Monica house and, 202–3,
        205–7
    Getty Center in, 242, 341, 439–41,
        443–5, 741
    Israel's MOCA retrospective and, 341–3
    Lautner and, 271–2
    May Company in, 279–80
    Mondrian in, 372–4
    New York architecturally eclipsed by,
        341, 345
    Riverside's Fine Arts Building and, 256–7
    Skirball Cultural Center in, 364, 368

Modernism, modernism (*cont'd*)
  Columbus Circle and, 230–1, 349–51,
    382–3, 759, 769–70, 791, 798, 800,
    808–9
  demise of, 10, 13, 61–2, 66–7, 175,
    232–5, 351, 446, 562, 718, 763, 801,
    842
  Edison Terrace and, 191–2
  and Expressionism and the New
    Objectivity show, 274–6
  Ford Foundation Building and, 293–5
  foreign architects and, 689, 691–2
  Freed and, 46, 553
  Getty Center and, 440, 442–3
  glass and, 3–4, 41, 48, 63, 65, 82, 233–4,
    283, 300, 350, 399, 449, 517
  Hilton hotels, 707–9
  historical rupture caused by, 10–12, 14
  history of, 54–5
  Holocaust and, 40, 48–51
  Italian postwar architecture and, 263–4
  of Jahn, 3, 5–6
  Johnson and, 209–10, 635–6
  Kennedy and, 652–4
  Koolhaas and, 268, 273, 480, 695, 748
  Leatherbarrow on, 592–3
  Le Corbusier and, 4, 7–15, 62, 65, 175,
    191, 233, 247, 249, 281, 315, 551, 651,
    744–5, 759, 808
  Lincoln Center and, 634–5, 640
  Loos and, 666–7
  Lucille Halsell Conservatory and, 35, 38
  Meier and, 6, 368, 553, 744–5
  MoMA Deconstructivist Architecture
    show and, 30, 33
  MoMA expansions and, 385–7, 401–3,
    412, 553
  New York and, 61–3, 68, 797–800, 807,
    810, 812–13
  Noguchi and, 89–92
  Okura Hotel and, 361, 363–4
  and 101 Avenue of the Americas, 115–16
  Park Avenue Corridor and, 551–2
  Penn Station and, 186–8, 296, 525–6
  popularity of, 82, 233–4
  Portzamparc and, 248–52, 691
  Rose Center and, 568–9, 571
  Rossi and, 447, 651, 717
  Ruhlmann and, 782–3
  Ruskin and, 74–5, 807
  Salk Institute and, 84–5
  and San Francisco Museum of Modern
    Art, 281–2
  social idealism and, 16–19, 21
  South Bronx Police Academy and, 172–5
  technology and, 4–5, 10

  Tokyo International Forum and, 193,
    195, 377, 379
  urban design and, 41, 58, 60, 184, 233,
    385, 592, 635, 681
  Venturi and, 72–3, 75–6, 79–80, 175,
    392–3
  war between Postmodernism and, xiv,
    9–11, 30, 173–5, 235, 278, 284–5, 331,
    385–6, 431, 491, 517, 690–2, 702, 742
Mohegan Sun, 357–61
Moholy-Nagy, Sybil, 106, 259, 416
Molinari, Guy V., 142
Mondale, Joan, 814
Mondrian, Piet, 412, 458, 712
Mondrian (hotel), 372–6
Moneo, Rafael, 322, 495, 500, 504
  Audrey Jones Beck Building and, 604–7
Monroe, Marilyn, xv, 432–4, 548
Monticello, 203, 419
Montparnasse, 303
  Cartier Foundation and, 239, 241, 245
  Portzamparc and, 249–50
Montreal Museum of Fine Arts, 782
Monument to the Third Communist
    International, 659
Moore, Charles, 82, 248, 331, 385, 431,
    472
Moore, Henry, 22, 768
Morgan Library, 310, 685–9
morphology, 487–8, 492
Morris, William, 54, 134, 261
Morris Architects, 282
Morton, James Parks, 149
Morton Street Park, 154–6
Moses, Robert, 110, 636, 660
Mosque of the Grand National Assembly,
    471–3
Moss, Eric Owen, xiv, 197, 224–6, 341,
    345, 366, 588
Mozart, Wolfgang Amadeus, 699, 751
Mudford, Grant, 84, 343–4
Mumford, Lewis, 60, 79, 188, 215, 255, 382
  Chicago World's Fair and, 136–7
  Guggenheim Museum and, 688, 821
  on New York, 108–11
Municipal Art Society, 380, 531
  Steel, Stone, and Backbone show of,
    119–21
  Trump World Tower and, 702–3
Murdoch, Iris, 255, 426, 627
Murray, Natalia Denesi, 107–8
Musée d'Orsay, 274
Museum of Arts and Design (American
    Craft Museum), 23, 758–9
  2 Columbus Circle acquired by, 791,
    814–15

Museum of Broadcasting, 70
Museum of Contemporary Art (MOCA), 144
  Geffen Contemporary at, 217, 430
  Israel retrospective at, 341–4
  Urban Revisions show at, 260, 286–7
Museum of Contemporary Art (Vienna), 514–15
  Wonderblock show at, 514
Museum of Fine Arts (Houston), Audrey Jones Beck Building at, 604–8
Museum of Modern Art (MoMA), 67, 110, 151, 181, 438, 462, 530, 536–7, 585, 607, 635–6, 745, 759–60, 799, 803, 805, 808, 822
  Aalto show at, 448–9, 451–2
  and Ambasz, 35–7
  Austrian Cultural Forum and, 696
  and Austrian Cultural Institute, 200, 202
  Beaux Arts architecture show at, 81
  The Changing of the Avant-Garde show at, 715–19
  condominium tower above, 237, 386, 411–12
  Deconstructivist Architecture show at, 28–34, 50, 659
  and design, 62, 489, 491
  expansions of, 384–7, 401–4, 409–13, 553, 647
  Good Design shows at, 62
  identity crisis of, 385–6, 404
  International Style show at, 17, 33, 62, 551–3
  Kennedy's wardrobe at, 652–6
  Koolhaas shows at, 264–9, 272–3, 481
  in Long Island City, 499, 700, 715, 719
  and Tokyo International Forum, 192, 194
  Toward a New Museum of Modern Art show at, 401–4, 410
  Trump's meeting with Muschamp at, 541–4
  and Trump World Tower, 700–2
  and 2 Columbus Circle, 349–50
Museum of the City of New York, 295
Mussavi, Farshid, 664
Mussolini, Benito, 263, 323–4, 337
Muzio, Giovanni, 274
Myers, John Bernard, 804

Nagata, Minoru, 145, 751
Nagi Museum of Contemporary Art, 354–7, 379, 430
Nara Convention Hall, 382, 418
Nasser, Gamal Abdel, 708

National Air and Space Museum, 51
National Airport (Washington, D.C.), 422–4
National Building Museum, 849
National Center for Contemporary Art (Rome), 705
National Football Hall of Fame, 75
Nazis, 40–2, 557
  Berlin and, 500, 507
  Holocaust and, 40, 49, 51, 167, 507, 510
Neoclassicism, neoclassicism, 80–1, 133–4, 274, 277, 312, 416, 450, 551, 571, 607, 632, 638, 729, 732, 741
Nervi, Pier Luigi, 262, 269, 705, 714
Netherlands Dance Theater, 265, 481
Neue Galerie, 684, 698
Neurosciences Institute (La Jolla), 592
Neutra, Richard, 342, 345, 442, 494, 592
New Amsterdam Theater, 298, 306, 352, 404–6, 409, 535, 538
Newark, N.J., 182, 601
New Delhi, U.S. Embassy in, 349, 799
New Jersey Institute of Architecture, 182
Newman, Arnold, 208
Newman, Barnett, 94, 366
New Modernism, 235, 262
New Museum of Contemporary Art, 595, 597–8, 755–8
New National Gallery, 501
New Objectivity, 46, 81, 107, 274–6, 312, 569
New Republic, The, xiii–xiv, 109
New Schools for New York, 198
Newton, Isaac, 568, 571
New Urbanism, 263, 577, 600, 664, 754, 839
  Ground Zero and, 719, 744
New Victory Theater, 351–2, 535, 538
New York, New Yorkers, xiii, 3, 45, 89–94, 106–11, 115, 117–20, 139, 151, 154–8, 170–5, 177–81, 185–7, 192–3, 198–201, 209, 223, 226, 260, 269–70, 314, 332–3, 355, 358, 368–9, 372, 376, 389–90, 396, 398, 420, 426–9, 436–8, 456–8, 460, 516–19, 533, 554–6, 559, 563–5, 590–1, 599, 601–2, 607–9, 611–13, 644–50, 686–93, 710–15, 723–5, 732, 744, 748, 754, 763, 778, 782, 786, 792–801, 809–14, 817–22, 847
  American Folk Art Museum in, 684, 690
  architectually eclipsed by Los Angeles, 341, 345
  and art in architecture, 22–5
  Austrian Cultural Forum and, 332, 696–700, 839

New York, New Yorkers (*cont'd*)
Austrian Cultural Institute and, 200–1
Broadway Theater District and, 306–9
and Cathedral Church of St. John the
  Divine, 147, 149
CBS Building in, 61–3, 65, 67, 69, 270,
  619
Chelsea and, 327–30
Columbus Circle and, 229, 231–2, 350,
  380–4, 758–60, 770–1, 801, 804,
  811–14
Condé Nast cafeteria and, 572–3
design and, 387, 489
DUMBO and, 527–30
80 South Street Tower and, 772–4
Ford Foundation Building and, 66,
  292–3
foreign architects and, 689–92
gays and, 789–90, 793–6, 805, 811–12
Grand Central Terminal and, 136, 428,
  466–9
Ground Zero and, 674–8
Guggenheim Museum in, xv, 135, 233,
  289, 291, 335, 416, 424, 427, 433–4,
  514, 585, 645, 669, 693, 695, 734, 822
Hudson in, 608–9, 611–12
Jewish Museum in, 149, 369
Koolhaas and, 156–7, 264–6
Lever House in, 233, 305, 591, 594
Lincoln Center and, 633–4, 636, 640
LVMH Tower in, 571, 621, 624, 691
mayoral politics in, 213–17
Met and, 96, 98–9, 426
middle-class remodeling of, 317–22
Millennial Manhole Cover and, 530–1
Modernism and, 61–3, 68, 797–800, 807,
  810, 812–13
MoMA expansions and, 384, 402, 647
Morgan Library and, 310, 686–8
Morton Street Park and, 154–6
Mumford's writings on, 108–11
and Municipal Art Society Steel, Stone,
  and Backbone show, 119–20
Muschamp's *New York Times* employment
  and, 104, 106
new Kennedy Airport terminal and,
  452–4
The New York Times Building and,
  618–25, 627–8
Noguchi and, 89–92
and opening of New Amsterdam
  Theater, 405–6, 409
Park Avenue Corridor and, 550
Penn Station and, 123, 186–7, 295–6,
  523, 792
Powell and, 482–6

Prada's SoHo store and, 669, 672, 684,
  776
preservationism and, 295–7, 516–17, 549
Queens West and, 236–7, 239
Radio City and, 535–6, 538
revitalizing waterfront of, 215–16
Rose Center in, 567–71, 621
Rossi and, 648–50
school buildings and, 198–9
Seagram Building in, 305, 382, 687
Second Stage Theater in, 497–9
September 11 terrorist attacks on, 674–9,
  682, 684, 701, 723, 725, 760, 837
skyscraper boom in, 109–10
social idealism and, 15–20
South Bronx Police Academy and, 171–5
Staten Island Ferry terminal and, 141–3,
  175, 215, 392
Stern and, 254–5
Summit Hotel in, 641–2, 713–14
Surrealism in, 804–5
Times Square and, 125–6, 298–9, 302,
  352–3, 393–4, 406–7
Trump and, 437–8, 540–1, 544, 548–9,
  700
Trump World Tower and, 700–2
unconventional architecture and, 180–1
Westin Hotel in, 710–12
West Side project in, 492–7
Whitney in, 414, 644
Woolworth Building in, 178–9, 582
World's Fairs in, 68–9, 111, 158, 266,
  299, 450–1, 569, 636–8, 646, 771, 795,
  797, 800–1
World Trade Center in, 429, 767, 769
Wright and, 266, 414
zoning policy in, 516–18, 579–88
New York Botanical Garden, 397–400
New York Central Railroad, 388
New York City Ballet, 638, 810
New York Cultural Center, *see* 2 Columbus
  Circle
New Yorker, The, 108–9, 459, 531, 572,
  720–1
New York Public Library, 120, 136, 304,
  382, 532, 585, 792
New York State Pavilion, 636–7
New York State Theater, 311, 633, 636,
  638–40
New York Times, The, xiii, xvi, 15, 349, 395,
  481, 755, 759, 786, 836, 846–7
Muschamp's employment with, 103–6,
  839–40
time capsule of, 550, 768
Trump and, 542–3
New York Times Building, The, 618–28

Foster's design for, 619, 625
Gehry/Childs's design for, 619, 625–8
Pelli's design for, 619, 623–6
Piano's design for, 618–19, 621–3, 625–6, 628, 676, 688, 703
selecting architect for, 619–21, 627
New York Times Magazine, The, 482, 487, 678, 723, 768
New York University, 162
Niemeyer, Oscar, 250, 727
Nietzsche, Friedrich, 110, 336, 519, 773, 808
Nile Hilton, 708–9
Ninevah and Nimrud Palaces, 761, 766
9 West Fifty-seventh Street, 201–2
Nishizawa, Ryue, 756, 784
Nixon, Richard, 76, 366, 461
Noguchi, Isamu, 614, 730
    architectural collaborations of, 92–3
    Ashton's book on, 88–94
    Chase Building and, 92–3
    and Houston's Museum of Fine Arts, 606
    Marine Midland Bank Headquarters and, 93
Nordenson, Guy, 182, 202, 758
Normandie, S.S., 590–1, 641
Norri, Marja-Riitta, 451
North Carolina Museum of Art, 26–8, 181
Notre Dame du Haut, 8, 477
Nouvel, Jean, 111, 251, 265, 314, 322, 331, 549, 561–2, 569–70, 646, 662, 684, 689, 695, 718, 754, 784, 840
    Arab World Institute and, 239, 241, 475
    Berlin and, 500, 506
    Cartier Foundation and, xiv, 239–42, 245, 382, 528, 569
    CLM/BBDO headquarters and, 334
    Galeries Lafayette and, 334, 506–7
    River Hotel and, 527–30, 692
Nuclear Family, 849–50
Núñez, Ramón A., 418

Oberlin College, 76
Ocean Group, 495, 734
Ockman, Joan, 296
Odyssey transport system, 411–13, 647
Office for Metropolitan Architecture (OMA), 157, 265–6, 670, 746, 777
Official All Star Cafe, 320
Ofili, Chris, 803
O'Hara, Frank, 289
O'Hare International Airport, 3, 6–7, 129
Okazaki, Kazuo, 356

Okura Hotel, 361–4
Olmsted, Frederick Law, 27, 120–1, 216
Olympic Games, 122, 633, 705, 734
Olympic Tower, 215
101 Avenue of the Americas, 115–16
173 and 176 Perry Street, 741–6
1 Times Square, 393–7
Open and Shut House, 445–6
Opera House (Brooklyn Academy of Music), 406
Oppenheim, Chad, 784
Orchard Beach, 120
Ouroussoff, Nicolai, xiii–xvi
Ove Arup & Partners, 182, 199, 747
Overington, Michael, 611
Ozkan, Suha, 471

Page, Tim, 481, 485
Paimio Tuberculosis Sanatorium, 450
painting, painters, 22, 38, 53–6, 59, 74, 81, 121, 124, 434, 561, 589, 745, 751, 797, 805–7, 823
    Charles on, 53–4
    Guggenheim Hermitage and, 693–4
    Holocaust and, 42–4
    2 Columbus Circle and, 791, 802–3
    Victorianism and, 55–6
Palais Royale, 303–4
Palazzo, Il, 648–9
Palazzo della Triennale, 274–5
Palazzo del Sport, 705
Palazzo Grassi, 274, 821–5
Paley, William S., 69–71
Palladino, Michael J., 441
Palladium hotel, 610
Palm Beach, Fla., 543–4, 546, 643
Pan Am (MetLife) Building, 66, 321, 467, 550, 554–5, 760
Pan Am logo, 530–1
Paramount hotel, 332–3, 372, 499
Parc de la Villette, 28–9
Paris, 29, 31, 107, 134, 184, 232, 272–4, 316, 320, 334, 390, 397, 457, 475, 481, 483, 496, 503, 512, 532, 550, 556–62, 571–2, 583, 587, 589, 613, 642, 652, 659–60, 711, 782–4, 805
    American Center in, 245–7, 303, 425, 431
    arcades in, 557–60, 771
    Benjamin and, 556, 558–62, 771
    Bibliothèque Nationale de France in, 267, 302–5, 557, 686
    Canal Plus headquarters in, 200, 571
    Cartier Foundation in, xiv, 239–42, 245, 382, 528, 569

Paris (*cont'd*)
  Jussieu Library in, xiv, 157–8, 265,
    267–8, 272–3, 779
  Le Corbusier and, 8–9, 163
  Noguchi and, 89–90, 92
  Pinault and, 821–3
  Pompidou Center in, 193, 274, 515,
    621–2, 694, 716
  Portzamparc and, 248–52, 691
  public housing in, 162–5
  Washington National Airport and, 422–4
Paris International Exhibition, 450
Paris Opera, 310, 378, 638, 751
Park Avenue, 17, 66, 555, 798
  500 Park Avenue, 62, 526, 550–1, 553
  Lever House on, 591, 594, 744
Park Avenue Corridor, 550–3, 691
Park Kolonnaden, 503
Park Tower, 551
Park Tower Realty, 125
Parsons Main, 243
Parsons School of Design, xiv, 162, 184–5,
  223
Parthenon, 590
Pasolini, Pier Paolo, 776
Pataki, George E., 523, 677, 815
Pater, Walter, 289, 545, 548, 726, 806
PATH station (World Trade Center),
  767–9
Patkin, Izhar, 31
Paulsen, Sherida, 687
Pavillon, Le (France), 68
Pawson, John, 491, 499, 734
Paxton, Joseph, 3, 54, 68, 195, 399, 503,
  525, 716
Payette Associates, 74, 228
Peachtree Center Plaza, 128
Peck, Robert, 153
Peggy Guggenheim Collection, 822
Pehnt, Wolfgang, 276, 754
Pei, I. M., 46–7, 51, 71, 162, 779
  Modernism and, 5, 300
Pei Cobb Freed & Partners, 149, 166,
  169–70
Pelli, Cesar, 533–4, 736
  MoMA and, 237, 386, 411–12
  National Airport and, 422
  The New York Times Building and, 619,
    623–6
  Queens West and, 236–7
  World Financial Center and, 623
Penn, William, 72
Penn Center, 456–7
Pennsylvania, University of, xiv, 49, 228,
  344, 414, 470, 495, 541, 592
Pennsylvania Plan, 131–2

Pennsylvania Station, 123, 142, 295–7, 493,
  687
  demolition of, 66, 186, 188, 214, 295,
    522, 762, 767, 792
  resurrection of, 186–9, 296, 318, 522–6,
    762
  retail operations at, 187–9, 318, 525
Penn yards site, 711
Pepall, Rosalind, 782
Peppermint Lounge, 786
Pepsico headquarters, 349
Pepsi-Cola Building (500 Park Avenue), 62,
  526, 550–1, 553
Percent for Art programs, 239
Perkins & Will, 743
Perrault, Dominique, 314, 500
  and Bibliothèque Nationale de France,
    302–5, 686
  MoMA expansions and, 384, 401
Perry Street buildings, 741–6
Pesce, Gaetano, 334, 489
Pessac, Le Corbusier's houses for, 12–14
Peterson Littenberg, 725, 754
Petronas Towers, 623
Petronius, *Satyricon* by, 540–1
Pettena, Gianni, 322–4
Pettison, Harriet, 86–7
Pevsner, Nikolaus, 54, 64, 191, 818
Pew Charitable Trusts, 130
Philadelphia, Pa., xiii–xiv, 72, 106, 141,
  288, 290, 307, 601, 701, 792, 843, 847
  Eastern State Penitentiary and, 130–3
  Thirtieth Street Station in, 189
  Transportation Building in, 455–7
  Warhol's show in, 94, 97
Philadelphia Museum of Art, 130, 803
Philadelphia Navy Yard, 847
Philip Johnson Haus, 505
Phillips, Adam, 276–9
Phoenix, Ariz., 216
Piano, Renzo, 151, 248, 322, 588, 692,
  703–6, 841
  Berlin and, 503–4
  and Church of Thanksgiving, 703–4, 706
  Ground Zero and, 676
  IRCAM annex and, 503
  Morgan Library and, 685–9
  The New York Times Building and,
    618–19, 621–3, 625–6, 628, 676, 688,
    703
  Pompidou Center and, 503–4, 621–2
Picasso, Pablo, 86, 247, 638, 782
Pinault, François, 821–5
Piñon, Helio, 123
Pio, Padre, 703–4
Piranesi, Giovanni Battista, 131, 133, 182

Pirelli Tower, 554
Pittsburgh Cultural Trust, 603
Plaça dels Països Catalans, La, 122–4
Plater-Zyberk, Elizabeth, 190
Platner, Warren, 293, 555
Plaza Hotel, 389
Poe, Edgar Allan, 21, 31, 477
Police Academy building (South Bronx),
    171–5
Pollan, Michael, 460
Pollock, Jackson, 485, 802
Polshek, James Stewart, 322, 569–70, 726
Polshek Partnership Architects, 321, 383,
    567
Pompidou Center, 193, 274, 503–4, 621–2,
    694, 716
    La Ville show at, 515
Ponti, Giò, 214, 262, 425–6, 493, 554, 651,
    735, 775, 840
Pop Art, 94, 97–8, 299, 387, 548, 637, 649,
    797, 805
Port Authority Bus Terminal, 618, 622, 688
Portman, John, 128–30
Portoghesi, Paolo, 690
Portzamparc, Christian de, 247–52, 265,
    314, 689, 808
    Bourdelle Museum and, 250
    Café Beaubourg and, 250
    and City of Music, 249–50, 252
    LVMH Tower and, 555, 571, 624, 691
    Pritzker Prize and, 248–51, 691
    and Rue des Hautes-Formes housing
        complex, 251
    Rue Nationale apartments and, 250–1
Post estate, 543, 546
Postmodernism, postmodernism, xiii–xiv, 6,
    9–12, 60, 70, 79, 82, 107, 116, 125,
    147, 173–6, 180, 182, 196, 210–11,
    223, 229, 238, 243, 252–3, 262, 264,
    268, 282, 284–6, 300, 330–1, 358, 364,
    379, 431–2, 446, 552, 554, 562, 571,
    618, 629, 634, 650, 652, 690–3,
    710–12, 741–2, 744, 769, 789, 839
    Austrian Cultural Forum and, 696, 698
    Austrian Cultural Institute and, 201
    Charles and, 52, 57
    Columbus Circle and, 231–2, 759
    foreign architects and, 690, 692
    historical rupture caused by, 11–12
    Israel and, 344–5
    Johnson and, 210, 312
    Lucille Halsell Conservatory and, 34–5
    MoMA Deconstructivist Architecture
        show and, 29–30
    MoMA expansions and, 385–6, 404, 413
    Portzamparc and, 248–9, 252

task of, 277–8
U.S. Holocaust Museum and, 47–8
Venturi and, xiv, 72, 171, 244–5, 331,
    344, 385, 431, 718
war between Modernism and, xiv, 9–11,
    30, 173–5, 235, 278, 284–5, 331,
    385–6, 431, 491, 517, 690–2, 702,
    742
Potsdam, Einstein Tower in, 275
Powell, Dawn, 481–6
Power, Nancy, 205
Prada, Miuccia, 670–1, 673, 731
    Prada Foundation and, 774–5
Prada's SoHo store, 669–73, 684, 776
Prague, Gehry's tower for, 371, 395, 425,
    431
Pran, Peter, 172–4
preservationism, preservation movement,
    18, 60–1, 88, 149, 200, 214, 264, 494,
    528, 568, 656, 797, 809, 813–14,
    816–20
    Broadway Theater District and, 308–9
    Eastern State Penitentiary and, 130–1
    endangered sites and, 761–3
    gays in, 793–5
    Grand Central Terminal and, 467–9
    Modernism and, 66, 553, 801
    New York and, 295–7, 516–17, 549
    Park Avenue Corridor and, 552–3
    Penn Station and, 186, 188, 296–7, 523,
        525
    Radio City and, 535, 538
    TWA terminal and, 269, 271, 684
    2 Columbus Circle and, 758, 760, 790–2,
        801, 813, 817–18
    zoning policy and, 583–4
Price, Cedric
    Fun Palace and, 493, 622, 694, 716
    West Side project and, 493–4
Princeton University, 74–6, 95, 228, 376,
    495, 742
    Gordon Wu Hall at, 75–6
    Lewis Thomas Lab at, 74–6, 82
Pritzker, Jay A., 314
Pritzker Architecture Prize, 469, 683, 816
    Ando and, 313–16, 824
    Portzamparc and, 248–51, 691
Prix, Wolf, xiv, 658–64, 742
    Block and, 660–2
    Gasometer and, 662–3
    Hot Flats and, 659
    SEG Tower and, 660–1
Propaganda Films, 278, 344–6
Proust, Marcel, 556, 731
P.S. 1 Contemporary Art Center, 499, 700,
    715, 719

public art, 92–4, 176, 237, 600, 660, 676, 816
   and art in architecture, 22–8
   Noguchi and, 89, 92–3
Pugin, A. W. N., 56, 261, 807
Pulver, Josh, 387
Punta della Dogana, 822, 824–5

Queen Elizabeth 2 (QE2), 589–90
Queens-Midtown Tunnel, 120
Queens West, 235–7, 239, 318
Quennell, Nicholas, 26–8, 181

Radiant City (Ville Radieuse), 286–7, 584, 743–4
Radio City Music Hall, 349, 521, 769
   restoration of, 535–8
railway stations, 123, 169, 189, 600
   Modernism and, 3–4
   in Victorian era, 3–6, 525, 663
Raleigh, N.C., 26–8, 181
Ralph Applebaum Associates, 169
Ramada Renaissance Hotel (2 Times Square), 127
Ramus, Joshua, 777
Ranalli, George, 414
Rashid, Hani, 552
Rashid, Karim, 530–1, 555, 734
Rationalism, 274, 323, 338
Rauch, John, 71
Rauschenberg, Robert, 645, 744
Reagan, Ronald, 11–12, 76
Realism, realism, 10, 90, 395, 551, 800
Rechter, Ya'acov, 708–9
Rechy, John, 352, 796
Red Desert, 600, 673
Red House, 134
Reed, Henry Hope, 66
Reed, Peter, 448, 451
Reed and Stem, 466
Reflecting Absence, 768–9
Reich, Robert, 150, 427, 457
Reichstag, 501, 504, 507
Reiser, Jesse, 494–5, 555
Renaissance, 73, 309–10, 428, 506, 606, 621, 623, 705, 718
Renaissance Center, 41, 128
residential housing, residential towers, xiii, 17–23, 32, 36, 53, 74–7, 116–19, 130, 138, 141, 181, 213, 220–1, 299–300, 303, 330, 342–8, 474, 575, 600, 623, 657–61, 683, 709, 716, 741–3, 754, 772
   Aalto and, 449, 451

Ando and, 314, 317
Arquitectonica and, 190–2, 300, 382, 711, 714
and art in architecture, 22–3, 26
Columbus Circle and, 230–2
and democratization of architecture, 134–5
Edison Terrace and, 190–2
860–880 Lake Shore Drive and, 195–7
garages and, 435–7
Gehry and, 14, 28–9, 145, 202–7, 334, 346–7, 396, 425
Israel and, 278–9, 342–6
Johnson and, 310–11, 635
Koolhaas and, 29, 265, 477–81, 646–7
Lautner and, 271–3
Le Corbusier and, 7–8, 12–14, 38, 62, 134, 162–5, 251, 442, 782
Meier and, 741–2
middle class and, 318, 320
Mies van der Rohe and, 134, 195–7, 208, 267–9, 742, 782
MoMA Deconstructivist Architecture show and, 28–9, 31
Portzamparc and, 248, 250–1
Prix and, 659–61
public housing and, 162–5, 346–8
Queens West and, 235–7
Rudolph and, 445–6
social idealism and, 18–22
Trump and, 541–3, 546–9, 700
Trump Palace and, 117–19
Trump World Tower and, 700, 702
Venturi and, 72, 74–5
Wright and, 159–61, 288, 291, 343, 345, 370, 415–16, 436, 442, 520, 613, 761
Richard B. Fisher Center for the Performing Arts, 726–8, 784
Richards Medical Building, 49
Richardson, H. H., 684
Richard Trott & Partners, 228
Richmond Prison, 131
Rieselbach, Anne, 198
Riley, Terence, 194, 404, 552, 700, 715
   MoMA expansions and, 401–2
   MoMA Koolhaas show and, 266–8
Riordan, Richard, 207
River Hotel, 527–30, 692
Riverside South (Trump Place), 236, 318, 437, 549, 702–3
Robertson, Jaquelin, 391
Roche, Kevin, 149, 446, 496
   Ford Foundation Building and, 66, 292
   Met's continuity problem and, 96–7, 99
   UN Plaza Hotel and, 778
Rock, Michael, 748

Rockefeller, John D., 537
Rockefeller Apartments, 110
Rockefeller Center, 109–11, 149, 192, 237,
    535–6, 582, 642, 771
Rockefeller family, 62, 110, 350, 384, 401
    Lincoln Center and, 636, 638
    Radio City and, 535–8
Rockwell, David, 320, 358, 360, 674
Rogers, Elizabeth Barlow, 466–7
Rogers, Ernesto Nathan, 263–4
Rogers, Sir Richard, 322, 718
    Berlin and, 500, 503–4
    Linkstrasse office building and, 503
    Pompidou Center and, 504, 621–2
Rogut, Howard, 309
Rokko housing complex, 314
Roman Baths of Caracalla, 296–7
Romanesque, 75, 148, 682
Romans, Roman Empire, 502, 559, 685, 732
    films on, 574–6, 578–9
Romanticism, romanticism, 11, 24, 46, 58,
    145, 205, 211, 231, 261, 268, 277, 281,
    288–9, 305, 412, 508, 520, 545, 596,
    603, 617–18, 625, 776, 781–2, 823
    Ruskin and, 781, 807–8
Rome, 597–8, 601, 603, 623, 664, 704–5,
    707, 736, 752
    Colosseum in, 574, 576
    National Center for Contemporary Art
    in, 705
Roos, Jen, 387
Rose, Joseph B.
    West Side project, 493, 496
    zoning policy and, 516–18, 581
Rose Center for Earth and Space, 567–71,
    621
Rosen, Laura, 120–1
Rosenquist, James, 637
    F-111 by, 95, 97
Rosenthal, Jean, 636
Rosenthal, Seth, 314, 336, 339
Rosenthal, Tony, 94
Rositani, Niccolo, 339
Ross, Lillian, 353
Rossi, Aldo, xiv, 57, 322, 331, 431, 445–8,
    504, 648–52, 689
    The Architecture of the City by, 446, 648,
    717
    Centro Torri and, 447
    Il Palazzo and, 648–9
    San Cataldo cemetery and, 447, 649–50,
    717–18
    Scholastic Building and, 648–9, 651
    A Scientific Autobiography by, 448, 648
    and Teatro del Mondo, 447, 649–50
Rothafel, Samuel L. "Roxy," 535–7

Rothko, Mark, 241, 366, 693, 822, 824
Rothman, Carole, 497
Rotterdam
    Erasmus Bridge in, 494
    Koolhaas's apartment building and
    observation tower for, 29
    Kunsthal in, 265, 267, 272–3, 481
Roundabout Theater, 405
Rouse, James, 129, 602
Rouse Company, 318
Roy, Lindy, 555, 785–6
Royal Poinciana, 643
Royalton, 332–3, 372, 499
Rudofsky, Bernard, 259
Rudolph, Paul, 445–8, 717
    and Open and Shut House, 445–6
    Temple Street parking garage and, 446–7
    and Yale's Art and Architecture Building,
    67, 446
Rue des Hautes-Formes housing complex,
    251
Rue Nationale apartments, 250–1
Ruhlmann, Émile-Jacques, 782–4
Ruscha, Ed, 643
Ruskin, John, 53–4, 73–5, 78, 80–2, 109,
    148, 438, 490
    Classicism and, 73–4, 81, 807
    on Venetian Gothic, 73–4, 682, 781,
    807–8
Russia, Russians, 19, 172, 185, 371, 450,
    470–1, 480, 501, 653, 655, 693, 708,
    838, 841
    endangered sites in, 761, 766
    MoMA Deconstructivist Architecture
    show and, 28–31
Russo, Francesca, 309

Saarinen, Aline, 759
Saarinen, Eero, 321, 439, 446, 448, 496,
    555, 638, 714
    CBS Building and, 61, 63–6, 69–71, 270,
    619, 771
    death of, 66, 69
    Dulles Airport and, 270
    IBM Pavilion and, 68
    Ingalls Hockey Rink and, 64, 270, 768
    Modernism and, 5, 63–4
    TWA terminal and, 64, 269–71, 391,
    453, 684, 736, 768
Saatchi, Charles, 618
Saatchi & Saatchi headquarters, 116
Sabowsky, Daniel, 191
Safdie, Moshe, 365–8
    Columbus Circle and, 231, 381
    Skirball Cultural Center and, 365, 367–8

Storer House, 520
Storey, G. A., 59
Stotzer House, 8
Stowell, Scott, 597
Stravinsky, Igor, 438, 638–40, 730, 782
Studio di Architettura, 648
Studio Gang Architects, 747
Stuttgart, Weissenhof housing exhibition
    in, 134
Stuyvesant High School, 141
Stuyvesant Town, 583
STV Group, 767
suburbs, suburbia, xiii–xv, 26, 51, 77, 106,
    135, 150, 179, 196, 220–1, 252, 285,
    328, 353, 386, 427, 455, 478, 517, 554,
    558, 577–8, 598, 602, 637, 640–1,
    689–90, 720, 733, 754–5, 767, 794–5,
    813–14, 839, 841–50
    garages and, 435–6
    Gehry and, 145, 203–4, 207, 425
    lawns in, 459, 462–3, 600
    middle class and, 318–19
    Mumford and, 108, 110
    Portman's atrium hotels and, 128–30
    U.S. Courthouse and Federal Building
      in, 629, 632
    Venturi and, 72, 75
    and visions of community, 259–60
    white flight and, 792, 794
    Wright and, 159–60, 266, 415
Sullivan, Louis, 65, 196, 255, 316, 332, 406,
    562
Summerson, John, 58–60, 386, 399, 633
Summit (Metropolitan) Hotel, 641–3,
    713–14, 801
Sun International, 358–9
Sunnyside Gardens, N.Y., 110
Supreme Court, U.S., 467–8, 517
Surrealism, surrealism, 338, 356, 376, 430,
    489, 500, 520, 565, 613–14, 632, 659,
    672, 717–18, 731, 788, 803–5
    Benjamin and, 558–9, 561–2, 771
    Cartier Foundation and, xiv, 239
    gays and, 804–5
    Gehry and, 111, 331, 335
    Kalman and, 595–7
    Koolhaas and, 111, 555, 646, 771
    Mondrian and, 373–4
    Rossi and, 648–51, 717
    Starck and, 331, 333, 734
    2 Columbus Circle and, 803–4, 808
    Walt Disney Concert Hall and, 750,
      752
Swiczinsky, Helmut, 659
Sydney, 519, 583, 621
Syria, 680–2

Taking Back Our Streets Act, 287
Talamona, Marida, 338
Taliesin, 203
Taliesin West, 203, 416
Tallant, Hugh, 406
Taniguchi, Yoshio, 384, 401–3, 410, 553,
    689, 692
Tatlin, Vladimir, 34, 659
Taut, Bruno, 42, 275, 507, 754, 800
TBWA Chiat/Day offices, 334
Team Disneyland Building, 325–7
Teatro del Mondo, 447, 649–50
Teitelbaum, David, 149
Tel Aviv, Hilton hotel in, 708
Television City, 5
Temple of Ryoan-ji, 355–6
Temple Street parking garage, 446–7
10 Columbus Circle, 232, 382, 769–72
Terminal City (Kennedy International
    Airport), 4–5
Terminal One (Kennedy International
    Airport), 452–5
Textualized Landscape, 181
Teyssot, Georges, 459–60
Think Architects, 723
Thirtieth Street Station, 189
Thompson, Benjamin J., 489, 602
Thun, Count Franz Anton, 699
Thun-Hohenstein, Christoph, 699
Tiffany, 134, 282, 654
Tigerman, Stanley, 277, 366
    and Art Institute of Chicago's
    architecture and design show, 196–7
Tihany, Adam, 499
Time-Life Building, 642, 771
Times Square, 124–9, 141, 229, 266, 307–8,
    320, 334, 497, 502, 529, 531–5, 839
    Condé Nast Building in, 531–4, 572, 622
    Hotel QT and, 785–6
    Marriott Marquis Hotel in, 128–9
    nostalgia in, 351–2
    1 Times Square, 393–7
    redevelopment of, 124–7, 298–9, 301–2,
      351–4, 393–7, 406–9, 597, 676, 710,
      713, 725, 785
    2 Times Square, 127
    Westin Hotel in, 298–9, 302, 710–13
Time Warner, 395
Tinguely, Jean, 607–8, 744
Tisch, Laurence, 70
Tishman Realty and Construction
    Company, 710
Tishman Speyer Properties, 380
Tishman Urban Development
    Corporation, 298
TKTS booth, 127

T Magazine, xvi
Tokyo, 264, 315, 320–1, 583, 587, 755
    Imperial Hotel in, 364, 414
    Nagi Museum and, 354, 379
    Okura Hotel in, 361, 364
Tokyo International Forum, 192–5, 376–80, 571
Tomkins, Calvin, 721
Torre, Susana, 139, 223
Total Design, total design, 66, 70, 293
tourism, 656–8, 680, 761, 763, 784
Tour Montparnasse, 303
tower-in-the-park concept, 517, 581, 583
Tower of Hercules, 417
Toyota, Yasuhisa, 751
Transportation Building, 455–7
Treblinka, 47
Triadic Ballet, 566
TriBeCa, 115, 482
Trinity Church, 115
TripAdvisor.com, 825–7
triple thinking, 644–7, 671
Truman, James, 572
Trump, Donald J., 211, 236, 348, 437–9, 518, 539–49, 582, 812
    beauty appreciated by, 544–5, 547, 700
    Columbus Circle and, 229, 541, 770
    40 Wall Street and, 543, 545
    Muschamp's relationship with, 539–44
    Palm Beach and, 543–4, 546
    Trump World Tower and, 700–3
Trump International Hotel and Tower, 438, 541–2, 770
Trump Palace, 117–19
Trump Place (Riverside South), 236, 318, 437, 549, 702–3
Trump Taj Mahal, 439, 547
Trump Tower, 215, 542–3, 546–7
Trump World Tower, 518, 548–9, 700–3
Trylon and Perisphere, 266–7, 412, 569, 638, 646, 771
Tschumi, Bernard, 55, 251, 331, 840
    MoMA Deconstructivist Architecture show and, 28–9, 31
    MoMA expansions and, 384, 401, 403, 410
    and Parc de la Villette, 28–9
Tsien, Billie, 135, 200, 322, 562, 592, 690–2, 840
    American Folk Art Museum and, 669, 684, 690
    MoMA expansions and, 384, 401
Turkey, 471–6, 730, 732
    endangered sites in, 761, 766
    Mosque of the Grand National Assembly in, 471–3

Turner, Ted, 70
Turrell, James, 154, 373–4, 607, 664
Turun Sanomat office building and printing plant, 449–50
Tuwaiq Palace, 469
TWA terminal (Kennedy International Airport), 64, 269–71, 382, 391, 453, 684, 736, 760, 768
20th Century Limited, 388
2 Columbus Circle, 230, 348–51, 380, 537, 789–804, 807–9, 811–15
    acquired by Museum of Arts and Design, 791, 814–15
    controversy over, 790–1, 813, 815, 817–18
    preservation of, 758, 760, 790–2, 801, 813, 817–18
    remodeling of, 758–60, 791, 798, 815
    screen motif of, 800, 808–9, 817
240 Central Park South, 230
2 Times Square (Ramada Renaissance Hotel), 127
Two Trees, 529
T. Y. Lin International/Moffatt & Nichol Engineers, 464
Tyng, Anne Griswold, 88, 139–40

Umemoto, Nanako, 494–5, 555
Unified Bulk Program, 579–88
Union Carbide (Chase) Building, 92–3, 551, 602
Union Station (Washington, D.C.), 189, 467–8
unità, L', 671
United Airlines Terminal (O'Hare International Airport), 3, 6–7
United Architects, 723
Unité d'Habitation, 661
United Nations, 62, 82, 92, 238–9, 266, 270, 382, 412, 518, 591, 646, 653, 683, 685, 700, 710, 771
    Queens West and, 235, 239
United States Courthouse and Federal Building (Central Islip), 628–32
United States Embassies, 361
    in New Delhi, 349, 799
United States Holocaust Memorial Museum, 44–51, 165–71, 510, 571, 645–6
    entrances of, 47–9, 168
    Hall of Remembrance of, 45–9, 170
    Hall of Witness of, 45, 48, 50, 168–9
    hexagonal feature of, 49–50, 170
    opening of, 165–6
    representationalism of, 47–50

A NOTE ABOUT THE AUTHOR

Herbert Muschamp is the author of *File Under Architecture* and *Man About Town: Frank Lloyd Wright in New York City*. He died in 2007.

A NOTE ON THE TYPE

This book was set in Janson, a typeface made by Nicholas Kis (1650–1702).

Composed by Creative Graphics, Allentown, Pennsylvania
Printed and bound by Berryville Graphics, Berryville, Virginia
Book design by Robert C. Olsson